The **Shelly Cashman** Series®

Microsoft® 365® & Office®

First Edition

Advanced

Victoria Kaye
Susan L. Sebok
Mark Shellman
Misty E. Vermaat
Jill West

Australia • Brazil • Canada • Mexico • Singapore • United Kingdom • United States

***The Shelly Cashman Series® Microsoft® 365® & Office® Advanced*, First Edition**

Victoria Kaye, Susan L. Sebok, Mark Shellman, Misty E. Vermaat, Jill West

SVP, Product Management: Cheryl Costantini

VP, Product Management & Marketing: Thais Alencar

Senior Product Director, Portfolio Product Management: Mark Santee

Portfolio Product Director: Rita Lombard

Senior Portfolio Product Manager: Amy Savino

Senior Product Assistant: Ciara Boynton

Learning Designer: Zenya Molnar

Senior Content Manager: Anne Orgren

Digital Project Manager: Jim Vaughey

Developmental Editors: Mary-Terese Cozzola, Deb Kaufmann, Lyn Markowicz

Senior Director, Product Marketing: Danae April

Senior Marketing Manager: Mackenzie Paine

Portfolio Specialist: Matt Schiesl

Content Acquisition Analyst: Callum Panno

Production Service: Lumina Datamatics Ltd.

Senior Designer: Erin Griffin

Cover Image Source: Milos Plazacic/ Shutterstock.com

Mac Users: If you're working through this product using a Mac, some of the steps may vary. Additional information for Mac users is included with the Data files for this product.

Disclaimer: This text is intended for instructional purposes only; data is fictional and does not belong to any real persons or companies.

Disclaimer: The material in this text was written using Microsoft Windows 11 and Office 365 Professional Plus and was Quality Assurance tested before the publication date. As Microsoft continually updates the Windows operating system and Office 365, your software experience may vary slightly from what is presented in the printed text.

Previous edition(s): © 2023, © 2020, © 2017

For product information and technology assistance, contact us at **Cengage Customer & Sales Support, 1-800-354-9706 or support.cengage.com.**

For permission to use material from this text or product, submit all requests online at **www.copyright.com.**

Library of Congress Control Number: 2025901228

Student Edition ISBN: 978-0-357-88410-2

Loose-Leaf Edition ISBN: 978-0-357-88148-4

Cengage
5191 Natorp Boulevard
Mason, OH 45040
USA

Cengage is a leading provider of customized learning solutions. Our employees reside in nearly 40 different countries and serve digital learners in 165 countries around the world. Find your local representative at **www.cengage.com.**

To learn more about Cengage platforms and services, register or access your online learning solution, or purchase materials for your course, visit **www.cengage.com.**

Notice to the Reader

Publisher does not warrant or guarantee any of the products described herein or perform any independent analysis in connection with any of the product information contained herein. Publisher does not assume, and expressly disclaims, any obligation to obtain and include information other than that provided to it by the manufacturer. The reader is expressly warned to consider and adopt all safety precautions that might be indicated by the activities described herein and to avoid all potential hazards. By following the instructions contained herein, the reader willingly assumes all risks in connection with such instructions. The publisher makes no representations or warranties of any kind, including but not limited to, the warranties of fitness for particular purpose or merchantability, nor are any such representations implied with respect to the material set forth herein, and the publisher takes no responsibility with respect to such material. The publisher shall not be liable for any special, consequential, or exemplary damages resulting, in whole or part, from the readers' use of, or reliance upon, this material.

Printed at CLDPC, USA, 01-25

Brief Contents

Contents

Module 9: Creating a Reference Document ... WD 9-1

Module 10: Creating an Online Form ... WD 10-1

PowerPoint

Excel

Module 9: Formula Auditing, Data Validation, and Complex Problem Solving .... EX 9-1

Module 10: Data Analysis with Power Tools and Creating Macros .... EX 10-1

Access

Preface: The Shelly Cashman Series®: Microsoft® 365® & Office®

The Shelly Cashman Series® offers application-specific comprehensive print titles for Word®, Excel®, PowerPoint®, Access®, Publisher®, Outlook®, and Windows®. The modules (chapters) of the four main Microsoft® applications (Word®, Excel®, PowerPoint®, and Access®) are also offered together in each of three print titles organized by level: introductory, intermediate, and advanced. The MindTap Collection includes all of the preceding content, plus additional digital-only content for Teams®, the Mac operating system, and more.

About the Authors

Word: Misty E. Vermaat has more than 30 years of experience in the field of computer and information technology. In addition to consulting in the field, she was an Associate Professor at Purdue University Calumet, teaching or developing courses in Microsoft® Office, computer concepts, database management, systems analysis and design, and programming. Since 1990, she has led the development of the Shelly Cashman Series and has authored and co-authored numerous series textbooks, including many editions of Discovering Computers, Discovering Computers Fundamentals, Microsoft® Publisher®, and Microsoft® Word® books.

PowerPoint: Susan L. Sebok is a retired professor at South Suburban College in South Holland, Illinois, and is also a licensed attorney. Working with the leading Shelly Cashman Series® since 1993, she has co-authored several successful textbooks, including multiple versions of Discovering Computers and Microsoft® PowerPoint®. She holds both Master of Arts and Juris Doctor degrees.

Excel: Victoria Kaye brings her industry knowledge and instructor experience to Cengage Group for the Shelly Cashman Series. As an avid Excel user with Microsoft teaching experience ranging from secondary to undergraduate levels, she is thrilled to be part of the esteemed Shelly Cashman Excel Series legacy.

Dr. Mark Shellman is an instructor and Chair of the Information Technology Department at Gaston College in Dallas, North Carolina. Dr. Mark, as his students call him, prides himself on being student-centered and loves learning himself. His favorite subjects in the information technology realm include databases and programming languages. Dr. Mark has been teaching for more than 30 years and has co-authored several texts in the New Perspective series on Microsoft® Office 365 & Access®, along with a textbook on Structured Query Language.

Access: Jill West authors Cengage courses for CompTIA Cloud+, CompTIA Network+, Data Communications, Technology for Success, and the popular Shelly Cashman Series. She has taught kindergarten through college and currently teaches computer technology courses at Georgia Northwestern Technical College. Jill specializes in designing innovative, critical-thinking activities and building courses that teach popular IT certifications. She regularly presents at conferences and webinars on preparing for CompTIA certifications, teaching cloud computing and computer networking, and mentoring lifelong student learners in IT. She's a member of the 2019 inaugural cohort of Faculty Ambassadors for AWS Educate and is currently an AWS Academy Accredited Educator. Jill and her husband, Mike, live in northwest Georgia with two children at home and two off to college.

Windows 11: Steven M. Freund serves as a lead instructor of various Microsoft® Office, computer concepts, programming, and Internet technology courses throughout central Florida. An integral author for the successful Shelly Cashman Series since 2001, he has presented at the annual customer conference, the Shelly Cashman Series Institute, and other customer events. Freund has co-authored multiple editions of Discovering Computers, Mozilla Firefox, Windows® Internet Explorer, Windows® Office, and Dreamweaver books. In addition, he has written numerous successful instructor supplements. He attended the University of Central Florida.

Preface for the Instructor

Shelly Cashman's trademark step-by-step, screen-by-screen, project-based approach encourages students to expand their understanding of Office applications through hands-on experimentation and critical thinking. Module learning objectives are mapped to Microsoft Office Specialist certification objectives, reinforcing the critical skills needed for success in college and career. Other Ways boxes help users identify alternate click paths to achieve a step, while BTW sidebars offer helpful hints as readers work through projects, enabling them to make the most of Microsoft Office tools. MindTap and updated SAM (Skills Assessment Manager) online resources are also available to guide additional study to maximize results.

Shelly Cashman prepares students for success in the real world by using current and relevant scenarios that apply to everyday life and careers. It also prepares students to take the Microsoft Office Specialist (MOS) exam, which they can leverage in their careers.

Shelly Cashman is designed for students at two- and four-year schools as well as in continuing education programs. Skill levels can range from experienced — for those with a foundational understanding from prior exposure to technology — to introductory — for those using a computer or technology device for the first time.

The Shelly Cashman Series® offers application-specific comprehensive print titles for Word®, Excel®, PowerPoint®, Access®, Publisher®, Outlook®, and Windows®. The modules (chapters) of the four main Microsoft® applications (Word®, Excel®, PowerPoint®, and Access®) are also offered together in each of three print titles organized by level: introductory, intermediate, and advanced. The MindTap Collection includes all of the preceding content, plus additional digital-only content for Teams®, the Mac operating system, and more.

Market research is conducted semi-annually with both current Cengage users and those who use other learning materials. The focus of the market research is to gain insights into the user experience and overall learner needs so we can continuously evolve our content to exceed user expectations. We survey hundreds of instructors to ensure we gather information from a large and varied demographic.

New to This Edition

Shelly Cashman provides thoroughly updated coverage that reflects current Microsoft® 365® features. Narrative content has been authored using Microsoft® 365 Business Standard. Module projects incorporate career topics that apply diversity, equity, and inclusion principles and ensure accessibility. All projects, assignments, and lessons have been refreshed with authentic case scenarios that focus on practical skills and employability.

Word: New features in the Word content include the enhanced Accessibility Checker, which identifies potential accessibility issues and presents suggestions to make documents more inclusive. The Word coverage also introduces Focus mode, the updated collaboration experience, Microsoft's expanded search tool, and voice options. The Immersive Reader is covered, as is the ability to create a private document copy and use Word's screen reader.

PowerPoint: The PowerPoint content introduces the new commenting experience, which lets users display comments in contextual view or the Comments pane. The comment anchor helps reviewers identify specific slide elements with comments and place the comment bubble anywhere on the slide. With the revised search feature, users can enter a word or phrase in the Search box to find the definition. Microsoft Search also provides support articles to help perform tasks. Users can record and save a presentation that includes digital inking to capture text, drawings, and annotations, and then play back animated drawings. The Speaker Coach uses artificial intelligence (AI) to improve presentation skills by giving feedback on body language, the use of sensitive and filler words, and perceived mispronounced words.

Excel: With the Excel modules, students learn both long-standing Excel functions and tools as well as the most recent innovations. Updates to the Excel content include the new XLOOKUP and LET functions, dynamic arrays, and the Analyze Data feature. Also covered is the Accessibility Checker, which identifies issues and offers solutions to produce an accessible workbook.

Access: New features in the Access coverage include updated, real-world scenarios from a variety of industries that illustrate the relevance of Access databases in today's businesses. Completely updated projects use gapped Start and Solution files to ensure students use new, authentic files for each project from one module to the next. Module projects alternate between two sets of scenarios for expanded relevance and practicality. Further, an off-module scenario database receives updates comparable to the on-module scenario so students see similar progression in all databases. A Solutions to Critical Thinking Questions document for each module guides instructors on what to look for in student work. Critical Thinking Questions invite students to engage with the module's skills and information at a conceptual level, and to reflect on their learning, thinking processes, and the relevance of learned skills to their chosen careers.

Windows: The updates to the Windows modules reflect the changes from Windows 10 to Windows 11. New end-of-module exercises incorporate current terminology and features. Module projects have been updated with the latest Windows 11 features, including widgets, the revised Start and Search menus, and the Immersive Reader.

Organization of the Text

The *Shelly Cashman Series: Microsoft 365 & Office, First Edition* is a comprehensive introduction to Microsoft applications and is intended for students in introductory computing courses. Each application is divided into modules within the three levels — introductory, intermediate, and advanced. Each module introduces a topic through a real-world project and presents content that aligns directly with the learning objectives listed at the beginning of the module. To enable students to practice and apply skills learned, each module ends with a summary and a Consider This: Plan Ahead master planning guide that students use as they complete assignments and create projects on their own. Lastly, the end-of-module assignments are related to the top 25 industries for each application and include critical thinking questions. To increase students' confidence in their abilities, the assignments build from applying skills to experimenting beyond the module content to implementing a solution using creative thinking and problem-solving approaches.

Features of the Text

The features of the text, which are found consistently throughout all modules, are designed to aid the student in a specific way.

The projects are focused on employability based on current research and data. They use authentic case scenarios and a step-by-step approach to be as engaging, comprehensive, and easy to use as possible.

Heading levels organize topics within a module. Unique to the Shelly Cashman Series are "To-Do" heading levels for step-by-step task sequences. A To-Do head lead-in paragraph may include a **Why?** element to clarify why students are performing the steps.

To Display a Different Tab on the Ribbon

When you start Word, the ribbon displays 11 main tabs: File, Home, Insert, Draw, Design, Layout, References, Mailings, Review, View, and Help. (Note that depending on the type of computer or device you are using, the Draw tab may not appear.) The tab currently displayed is called the active tab. To display a different tab on the ribbon, you click the tab. The following step displays the View tab, that is, makes it the active tab. **Why?** When working with Word, you may need to switch tabs to access other options for working with a document or to verify settings.

Step-by-step sequences include the following features:

Q&A boxes provide troubleshooting information, equivalent touch instructions, or an additional explanation for a step.

Experiment steps encourage students to explore a feature such as the Themes gallery.

- If necessary, scroll to and then point to Facet in the Themes gallery to display a Live Preview of that theme applied to the document (Figure 1–37).
- **Experiment:** Point to various themes in the Themes gallery to display a Live Preview of the various themes applied to the document in the document window.

Q&A What is Live Preview?
Recall from the discussion earlier in this module that Live Preview is a feature that allows you to point to a gallery choice and see its effect in the document — without actually selecting the choice.

Can I use Live Preview on a touch screen?
Live Preview may not be available on all touch screens.

Other Ways provide additional methods to accomplish the tasks covered in specific To-Do steps.

Other Ways

1. Right-click paragraph (or if using touch, tap 'Show Context Menu' button on Mini toolbar), click Paragraph on shortcut menu, click Indents and Spacing tab (Paragraph dialog box), click Alignment arrow, click Centered, click OK
2. Click Paragraph Dialog Box Launcher (Home tab or Layout tab | Paragraph group), click Indents and Spacing tab (Paragraph dialog box), click Alignment arrow, click Centered, click OK
3. Press CTRL+E

By the Way (BTW) boxes are short marginal elements that add value for students by expanding on information in the module.

BTW
Printing Document Properties
To print document properties, click File on the ribbon to open Backstage view, click Print in Backstage view to display the Print screen, click the first button in the Settings area to display a list of options specifying what you can print, click Document Info in the list to specify you want to print the document properties instead of the actual document, and then click the Print button in the Print screen to print the document properties on the currently selected printer.

Other in-text pedagogical elements include the following:

Key terms are bold and blue in the running text. In the MindTap, each bolded key term is linked to its definition in the Master Glossary.

> Calibri and Calibri Light are **sans serif fonts**, which are fonts that do not ends of their characters. Other fonts such as Calisto MT are **serif fonts**,

Consider This is a pedagogical sidebar in the form of a question and answer that appears within the module and in the end-of-module student assignments. The question addresses conceptual or critical thinking topics, general information about the app, or other important information students should know.

> **Consider This**
>
> **How do you use the touch keyboard with a touch screen?**
>
> To display the on-screen touch keyboard, tap the Touch Keyboard button on the Windows taskbar. When finished using the touch keyboard, tap the X button on the touch keyboard to close the keyboard.

Break Point is a note to students that indicates a good place to take a break. Every module includes at least one break point.

> **Break Point:** If you want to take a break, this is a good place to do so. You can exit Word now. To resume later, start Word and continue following the steps from this location forward.

SAM Upload and Download icons are for SAM users. A SAM download icon appears next to any step where students download a data file to begin a SAM Project.

> **1**
>
> • sam ↓ Click the Start button on the Windows taskbar to display the Start

A SAM upload icon appears next to any step where students submit a file to SAM for a completed SAM Project.

> **3**
>
> • Click the 'Clear Search String' button to remove the search string and redisplay all objects.
>
> **Q&A** Did I have to click the button to redisplay all objects? Could I simply have erased the current string to achieve the same result?
>
> You did not have to click the button. You could have used DEL or BACKSPACE to erase the current search string.
>
> • If desired, sign out of your Microsoft account.
>
> •  sam ↑ Exit Access.

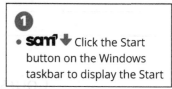

Figure callouts point to important parts of a screen and include two types:

Action/navigation callouts point to commands or buttons used in the step. Action/navigation callout boxes are a different color from explanatory callouts to help students easily locate screen elements referenced in step instructions.

Explanatory callouts direct students to other significant screen elements in the figure.

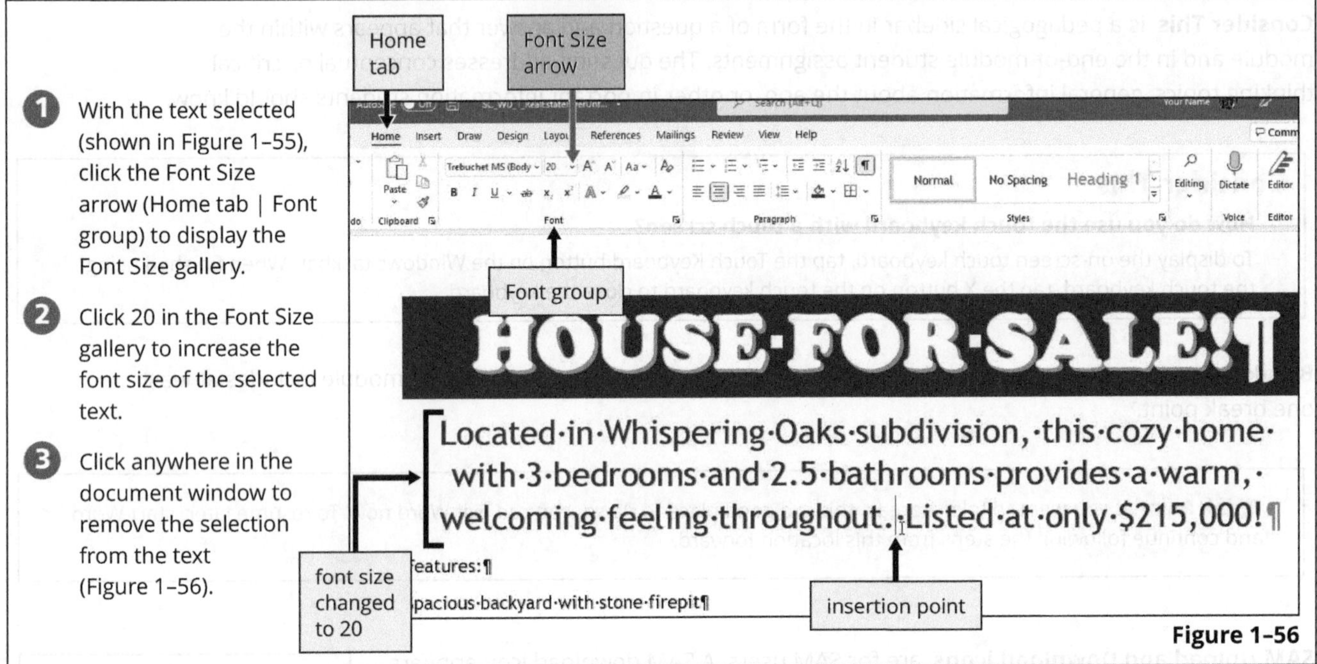

Figure 1–56

Course Solutions

Online Learning Platform: MindTap with SAM

The Shelly Cashman Series MindTap Collection, powered by SAM (Skills Assessment Manager), enables proficiency in Microsoft Office and computing concepts for your Introductory Computing courses. With a library of renowned course materials, including ready-to-assign, auto-graded learning modules, you can easily adapt your course to best prepare students for the evolving job market. In addition to an eReader that includes the full content of the printed book, The Shelly Cashman Series, First Edition MindTap course includes the following:

- SAM Textbook Projects: Follow the steps and scenarios outlined in the textbook readings; enable students to complete projects based on a real-world scenario live in Microsoft Office applications and submit them in SAM for automatic grading and feedback.
- SAM Training and Exam: Trainings teach students to complete specific skills in a simulated Microsoft application environment while exams allow students to demonstrate their proficiency (also in a simulated environment).
- SAM Projects: Students complete projects based on real-world scenarios live in Microsoft applications and submit the projects in SAM for automatic grading and feedback. SAM offers several types of projects, each with a unique purpose: 1A and 1B, critical thinking, end of module, capstone, and integration.

- Microsoft Office Specialist (MOS) resources: Training and exams are based on the Microsoft Office 365 Objective Domains for the MOS Exam and exam simulation that replicates the test-taking environment of the MOS exam for Word, Excel, Access, PowerPoint, and Outlook.

To learn more, go to: https://www.cengage.com/mindtap-collections/

Ancillary Package

Additional instructor and student resources for this product are available online. Instructor assets include an Instructor Manual, an Educator Guide, PowerPoint® slides, a Guide to Teaching Online, Solution Files, a test bank powered by Cognero®, and a Transition Guide. Student assets include data files and a glossary. Sign up or sign in at www.cengage.com to search for and access this product and its online resources. The instructor and student companion sites contain ancillary material for the full Shelly Cashman Series Collection, along with instructions on how to find specific content within the companion site.

- Instructor Manual: This guide provides additional instructional material to assist in class preparation, including module objectives, module outlines, discussion questions, and additional activities and assignments. Each outline corresponds directly with the content in the module, and additional discussion questions and activities are aligned to headings in the book.
- Educator Guide: The MindTap Educator Guide contains a detailed outline of the corresponding MindTap course, including activity types and time on task. The SAM Educator Guide explains how to use SAM functionality to maximize your course.
- PowerPoint slides: The slides may be used to guide classroom presentations, to provide to students for module review, or to print as classroom handouts. The slides align closely with the book while activities and the self-assessment align with module learning objectives and supplement the content in the book.
- Guide to Teaching Online: This guide presents technological and pedagogical considerations and suggestions for teaching the Introductory Computing course when you can't be in the same room with students.
- Solution and Answer Guide: The answers to the critical thinking questions are written by the author and correspond to critical thinking questions in the end-of-module activities.
- Solution files: These files provide solutions to all textbook projects for instructors to use to grade student work.
    - Instructors using SAM do not need solution files since projects are auto-graded within SAM.
    - Solution files are provided on the instructor companion site for instructors *not* using SAM.
- Data files: These files are provided for students to complete the projects in each module.
    - Students using SAM to complete the projects download the required data files directly from SAM.
    - Students who are *not* using SAM to complete the projects can find data files on the student companion site and within MindTap.
- Test banks: A comprehensive test bank, offered in Cognero, Word, Blackboard, Moodle, Desire2Learn, Canvas, and SAM formats, contains questions aligned with each module's learning objectives and is written by subject matter experts. Powered by Cognero, Cengage Testing is a flexible, online system that allows you to author, edit, and manage test bank content from multiple Cengage solutions and to create multiple test versions that you can deliver from your LMS, your classroom, or wherever you want.
- Transition Guide: This guide highlights all of the changes in the text and in the digital offerings from the previous edition to the current one so that instructors know what to expect.

Acknowledgments

Jill West: It's always a privilege to work with the incredible teams Cengage puts together, and this course is no exception. I've worked on many projects under the energetic and resourceful leadership of Amy Savino, whom I greatly admire and will forever be thankful for her vote of confidence in me when I needed it most. I've thoroughly enjoyed getting to know Anne Orgren, who has been our attentive and supportive content manager, providing just enough guidance exactly when needed. I can't say enough good things about MT Cozzola, developmental editor for this project. With her diversity of talents and skills, she has been a learner advocate, bringing the student's perspective to every conversation and providing synergistic insight. And I'm grateful for another opportunity to work with learning designer Zenya Molnar, who brings creative solutions to design challenges. Many other folks worked diligently behind the scenes to ensure consistency of quality, design, and innovation — their efforts are enthusiastically noted and greatly appreciated.

I owe a special thanks to my husband, Mike, for his tireless support and encouragement. And thanks to my kiddos: Winn, Sarah, Daniel, and Zack.

Victoria Kaye: Thank you for the many individuals who have made this edition possible. A text like this is not done without great effort, teamwork, and planning. Thank you to those individuals who contributed their expertise to this text, and an extra special thank you to developmental editors Barbara Clemens and MT Cozzola. Without your vast knowledge and careful consideration, this edition would not be possible. Thank you to the editorial team and their staff: Amy Savino, Senior Portfolio Product Manager; Anne Orgren, Senior Content Manager; and Zenya Molnar, Learning Designer. It is simply not possible to sum up the value of your contributions.

Getting to Know Microsoft Office Versions

Cengage is proud to bring you the next edition of Microsoft Office. This edition was designed to provide a robust learning experience that is not dependent upon a specific version of Office.

Microsoft supports several versions and editions of Office: (Refer to Table 1 below for more information)

- **Microsoft 365 (formerly known as Office 365):** A service that delivers the most up-to-date, feature-rich, modern Microsoft productivity applications direct to your device. There are several combinations of Microsoft 365 programs for business, educational, and personal use. Microsoft 365 is cloud-based, meaning it is stored, managed, and processed on a network of remote servers hosted on the Internet, rather than on local servers or personal computers. Microsoft 365 offers extra online storage and cloud-connected features, as well as updates with the latest features, fixes, and security updates. Microsoft 365 is purchased for a monthly subscription fee that keeps your software up to date with the latest features.
- **Office 2021:** The Microsoft "on-premises" version of the Office apps, available for both PCs and Macintosh computers, offered as a static, one-time purchase and outside of the subscription model. Unlike Microsoft 365, Office 2021 does not include online product updates with new features.
- **Microsoft 365 Online (formerly known as Office Online):** A free, simplified version of Microsoft web applications (Teams, Access, Word, Excel, PowerPoint, and OneNote) that lets users create and edit files collaboratively.
- **Office 365 Education:** A free subscription including Word, Excel, PowerPoint, OneNote, and now Microsoft Teams, plus additional classroom tools. Only available for students and educators at select institutions.

Table 1 Microsoft Office applications — uses and availability

Application	Use	Availability/Editions
Word	Create documents and improve your writing with intelligent assistance features.	Microsoft 365 Family, Home, Business, Office 2021, Office 365 Education
Excel	Simplify complex data into easy-to-read spreadsheets.	Microsoft 365 Personal, Home, Business, Office 2021, Office 365 Education
PowerPoint	Create presentations that stand out.	Home, Business, Office 2021, Office 365 Education
OneNote	A digital notebook for all your note-taking needs.	Home, Office 365 Education
OneDrive	Save and share your files and photos wherever you are.	Home, Business
Outlook	Manage your email, calendar, tasks, and contacts all in one place.	Home, Business
SharePoint	Create team sites to share information, files, and resources.	Business
Publisher	Create polished, professional layouts without the hassle.	Home, Business, Office 2021 (PC only)
Access	Create your own database apps easily in formats that serve your business best.	Home, Business, Office 2021 (PC only)
Teams	Bring everyone together in one place to meet, chat, call, and collaborate.	Business, Office 365 Education
Exchange	Business-class email and calendaring.	Business

Over time, the Microsoft 365 cloud interface will continuously update using its web connection, offering new application features and functions, while Office 2021 will remain static.

Because Microsoft 365 releases updates continuously, your onscreen experience may differ from what you see in this product. For example, the more advanced features and functionalities covered in this product may not be available in Microsoft 365 Online, may have updated from what you see in Office 2021, or may be from a post-publication update of Microsoft 365.

For up-to-date information on the differences between Microsoft 365, Office 2021, and Microsoft 365 Online, please visit the Microsoft Support website.

Cengage is committed to providing high-quality learning solutions for you to gain the knowledge and skills that will empower you throughout your educational and professional careers.

Thank you for using our product, and we look forward to exploring the future of Microsoft Office with you!

Using SAM Projects and Textbook Projects

SAM (Skills Assessment Manager) **Projects** allow you to actively apply the skills you learned in Microsoft Word, Excel, PowerPoint, or Access. You can also submit your work to SAM for online grading. You can use SAM Projects to become a more productive student and use these skills throughout your career.

To complete SAM Textbook Projects, please follow these steps:

SAM Textbook Projects allow you to complete a project as you follow along with the steps in the textbook. As you read the module, look for icons that indicate when you should download **sam**↓ your SAM Start file(s) and when to upload **sam**↑ your solution file to SAM for grading.

Everything you need to complete this project is provided within SAM. You can launch the eBook directly from SAM, which will allow you to take notes, highlight, and create a custom study guide, or you can use a print textbook or your mobile app. Download IOS or Download Android.

To get started, launch your SAM Project assignment from SAM, MindTap, or a link within your learning management system.

1. Step 1:
   Download Files
   - Click the "Download All" button or the individual links to download your **Start File** and **Support File(s)** (when available). You must use the SAM Start file.
   - Click the Instructions link to launch the eBook (or use the print textbook or mobile app).
   - Disregard any steps in the textbook that ask you to create a new file or to use a file from a location outside of SAM.
   - Look for the SAM Download icon **sam**↓ to begin working with your start file.
   - Follow the module's step-by-step instructions until you reach the SAM Upload icon **sam**↑.
   - Save and close the file.

2. Step 2:
   Save Work to SAM
   - Ensure you rename your project file to match the Expected File Name.
   - Upload your in-progress or completed file to SAM. You can download the file to continue working or submit it for grading in the next step.
3. Step 3:
   Submit for Grading
   - Upload your completed solution file to SAM for immediate feedback and to view the available Reports.
     - The **Graded Summary Report** provides a detailed list of project steps, your score, and feedback to aid you in revising and resubmitting the project.
     - The **Study Guide** provides your score for each project step and links to the associated training and textbook pages.
   - If additional attempts are allowed, use your reports to assist with revising and resubmitting your project.
   - To re-submit your project, download the file you saved in step 2.
   - Edit, save, and close the file, then re-upload and submit it again.

For all other SAM Projects, please follow these steps:

To get started, launch your SAM Project assignment from SAM, MindTap, or a link within your learning management system.

1. Step 1:
   Download Files
   - Click the "Download All" button or the individual links to download your **Instruction File**, **Start File**, and **Support File(s)** (when available). You must use the SAM Start file.
   - Open the Instruction file and follow the step-by-step instructions. Ensure you rename your project file to match the Expected File Name (change _1 to _2 at the end of the file name).

2. Step 2:
   Save Work to SAM
   - Upload your in-progress or completed file to SAM. You can download the file to continue working or submit it for grading in the next step.
3. Step 3:
   Submit for Grading
   - Upload the completed file to SAM for immediate feedback and to view available Reports.
     - The **Graded Summary Report** provides a detailed list of project steps, your score, and feedback to aid you in revising and resubmitting the project.
     - The **Study Guide** provides your score for each project step and links to the associated training and textbook pages.
   - If additional attempts are allowed, use your reports to assist with revising and resubmitting your project.
   - To re-submit the project, download the file saved in step 2.
   - Edit, save, and close the file, then re-upload and submit it again.

For additional tips to successfully complete your SAM Projects, please view our SAM Video Tutorials.

Using Collaboration, Integration, and Charts

Objectives

After completing this module, you will be able to:

- Customize the status bar
- Enable tracked changes, track changes, and disable tracked changes
- Change how tracked changes and document markup appear in the Word window
- Accept and reject tracked changes
- Compare Word documents
- Combine Word documents
- Link an Excel worksheet to a Word document
- Break a link
- Insert, edit, and format a Word chart
- View and scroll through side-by-side documents
- Create a document for a blog post
- Insert a quick table
- Publish a blog post
- Use the Immersive Reader tab

Introduction

Word provides the capability for users to work with other users, or **collaborate**, on a document. For example, you can show edits made to a document so that others can review the edits. You also can merge edits from multiple users or compare two documents to determine the differences between them.

From Word, you can interact with other programs and incorporate the data and objects from those programs in a Word document. For example, you can link an Excel worksheet in a Word document or publish a blog post from Word. You also can use the charting features of Microsoft 365 in Word.

Project: Memo with Chart

A memo is an informal document that businesses may use to correspond with others. Memos often are internal to an organization, for example, to employees or coworkers.

The project in this module uses Word to produce the memo shown in Figure 8–1. First, you open an existing document that contains the memo and the Word table. Next, you edit the document, showing the changes so that other users can review the changes. The changes appear on the screen with options that allow the author of the document to accept or reject the changes. Then, you chart the Word table using charting features available in several Microsoft 365 apps. In this module, you also learn how to link an Excel worksheet to a Word document, create a document for a blog post, and use the Immersive Reader tab.

MEMO

Flora Vista College

To: All Faculty and Staff

From: Bandile Engberg, Vice President, Enrollment Management and Student Success

Date: August 8, 2029

Subject: Job Placement Findings

As we embark on a new semester, I would like to highlight the findings from our recent graduate job placement study. The table and chart below summarize the results by department. In the upcoming days, a post on our department blog will announce that the average job placement rate of our graduates exceeds 90 percent in all areas! Please be sure to share this exciting news with all our incoming and returning students.

Job Placement Study: Five-Year Analysis

Department	Total Graduates	Total Placements
Business	4,975	4,577
Education	2,476	2,328
Health Sciences	1,054	959
Humanities	1,268	1,147
Physical Sciences	5,990	5,421
Social Sciences	6,372	5,962

Word table

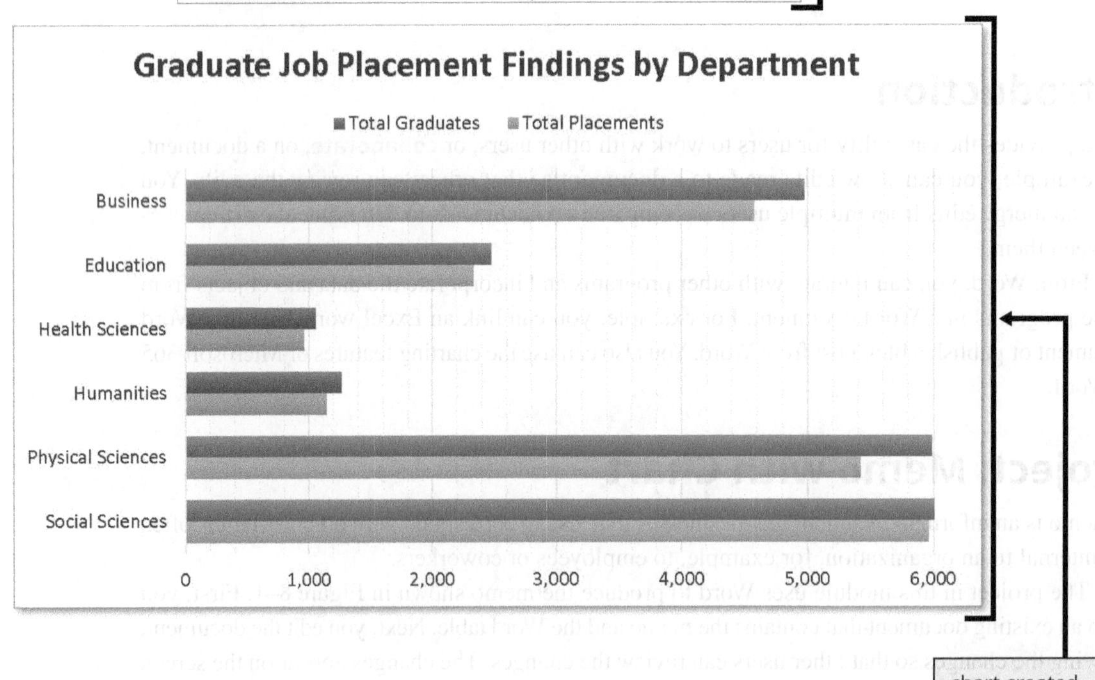

chart created from Word table

Figure 8–1

You will perform the following general tasks as you progress through this module:

1. Track changes in the memo with the table.
2. Review the tracked changes.
3. Link an Excel worksheet to a Word document.
4. Chart a Word table using Word's contextual chart tabs.
5. Create and publish a blog post.
6. Use the Immersive Reader tab.

To Start Word and Specify Settings

If you are using a computer to step through the project in this module and you want your screens to match the figures in this book, you should change your screen's resolution to 1366 × 768. The following steps start Word, display formatting marks, and verify ruler and Mouse mode settings.

1. Start Word and create a blank document in the Word window. If necessary, maximize the Word window.
2. If the Print Layout button on the status bar is not selected, click it so that your screen is in Print Layout view (as shown in Figure 8–2).
3. If the 'Show/Hide ¶' button (Home tab | Paragraph group) is not selected already, click it to display formatting marks on the screen.
4. Verify that the Ruler check box (View tab | Show group) is not selected. (If it is selected, click it to remove the check mark because you do not want the rulers to appear on the screen.)
5. If you are using a mouse and you want your screens to match the figures in the book, verify that you are using Mouse mode by doing the following: display the Quick Access Toolbar, if necessary, by clicking the 'Ribbon Display Options' button at the right edge of the ribbon and then clicking 'Show Quick Access Toolbar' on the menu; clicking the 'Touch/Mouse Mode' button on the Quick Access Toolbar and then, if necessary, clicking Mouse on the menu (if your Quick Access Toolbar does not display the 'Touch/Mouse Mode' button, click the 'Customize Quick Access Toolbar' button on the Quick Access Toolbar and then click Touch/Mouse Mode on the menu to add the button to the Quick Access Toolbar); then hide the Quick Access Toolbar by clicking the 'Ribbon Display Options' button at the right edge of the ribbon and then clicking 'Hide Quick Access Toolbar' on the menu.

Reviewing a Document

Word provides many tools that allow users to collaborate on a document. One set of collaboration tools within Word allows you to track changes in a document and review the changes. That is, one computer user can create a document and another user(s) can make changes in the same document. Those changes then appear on the screen with options that allow the originator (author) to accept or reject the changes. With another collaboration tool, you can compare and/or merge two or more documents to determine the differences between them.

To illustrate Word's collaboration tools, this section follows these general steps:

1. Open a document to be reviewed.
2. Track changes in the document.
3. Accept and reject the tracked changes. For illustration purposes, you assume the role of originator (author) of the document in this step.
4. Compare the reviewed document to the original to view the differences.
5. Combine the original document with the reviewed document and with another reviewer's suggestions.

BTW

The Ribbon and Screen Resolution

Word may change how the groups and buttons within the groups appear on the ribbon, depending on the screen resolution of your computer. Thus, your ribbon may look different from the ones in this book if you are using a screen resolution other than 1366 × 768.

BTW
Document Inspector
If you wanted to ensure that all revisions were removed from a document, you could use the document inspector. Open Backstage view, display the Info screen, click the 'Check for Issues' button, and then click Inspect Document. Place a check mark in the 'Comments, Revisions, and Versions' check box and then click the Inspect button (Document Inspector dialog box). If any revisions are located, click the Remove All button.

To Open a Document and Save It with a New File Name

Assume your coworker has created a draft of a memo and is sending it to you for review. The file, called SC_WD_8-1.docx, is located in the Data Files. Please contact your instructor for information about accessing the Data Files. To preserve the original memo, you save the open document with a new file name. The following steps save an open document with a new file name.

If your instructor wants you to submit your work as a SAM Project for automatic grading, you must download the Data Files from the assignment launch page.

1. Navigate to the location of the Data Files on your hard drive, OneDrive, or other storage location.
2. sam ↓ Open the file named SC_WD_8-1.docx.
3. Navigate to the desired save location on your hard drive, OneDrive, or other storage location.
4. Save the file just opened on your hard drive, OneDrive, or other storage location using SC_WD_8_FloraVistaCollegeMemo_withTrackedChanges as the file name.
5. Display the View tab and then click the One Page button (View tab | Zoom group) to display the entire page in the document window (Figure 8–2).
6. Click the Page Width button (View tab | Zoom group) to display the page the same width as the document window.

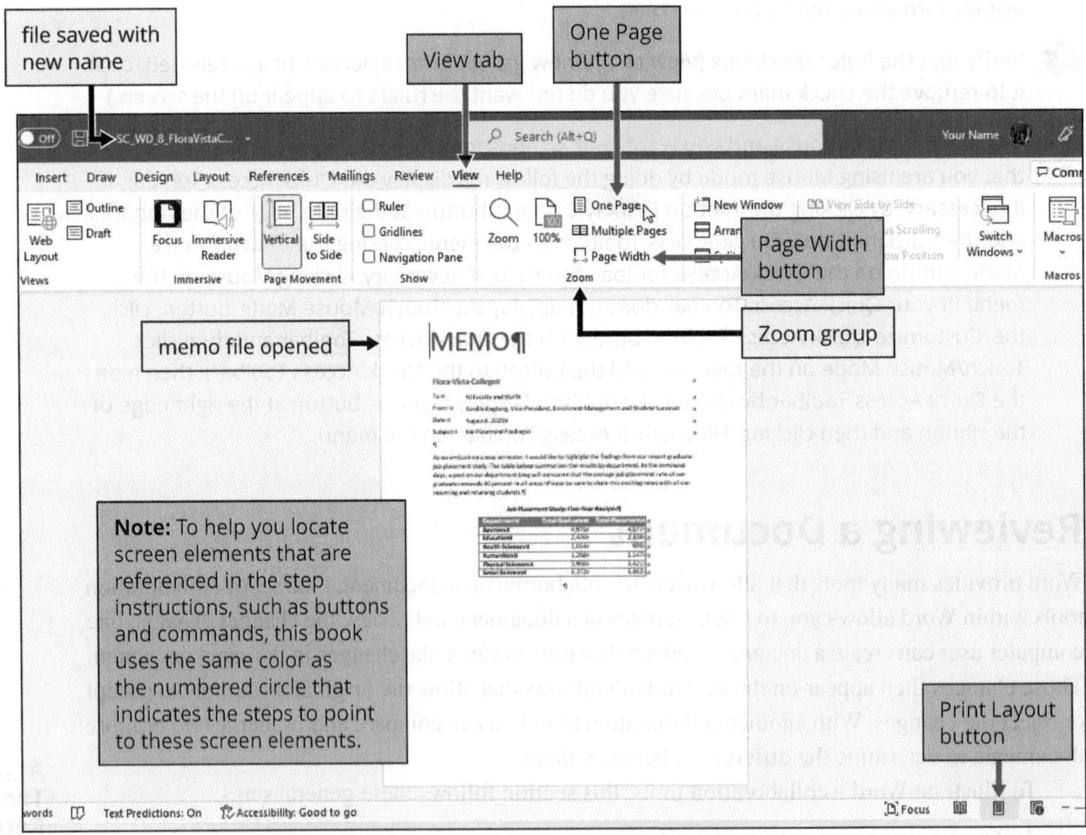

Figure 8–2

To Customize the Status Bar

You can customize the items that appear on the status bar. The status bar presents information about a document, the progress of current tasks, the status of certain commands and keys, and controls for viewing. Some indicators and buttons appear and disappear as you type text or perform certain commands. Others remain on the status bar at all times.

The following steps customize the status bar to show the Track Changes indicator. **Why?** The Track Changes indicator does not appear by default on the status bar.

- If the status bar does not show a desired item (in this case, the Track Changes indicator), right-click anywhere on the status bar to display the Customize Status Bar menu.

- Click the item on the Customize Status Bar menu that you want to show (in this case, Track Changes) to place a check mark beside the item, which also immediately may show as an indicator on the status bar (Figure 8–3).

Q&A Why do the Customize Status Bar menu and status bar on my screen display the word, On, instead of the word, Off?
Tracked changes already have been enabled in your document. To disable them, you would click the Track Changes indicator on the status bar. Each time you click the indicator on the status bar, the tracked changes toggle on or off.

Can I show or hide any of the items listed on the Customize Status Bar menu?
Yes, click the item to display or remove its check mark.

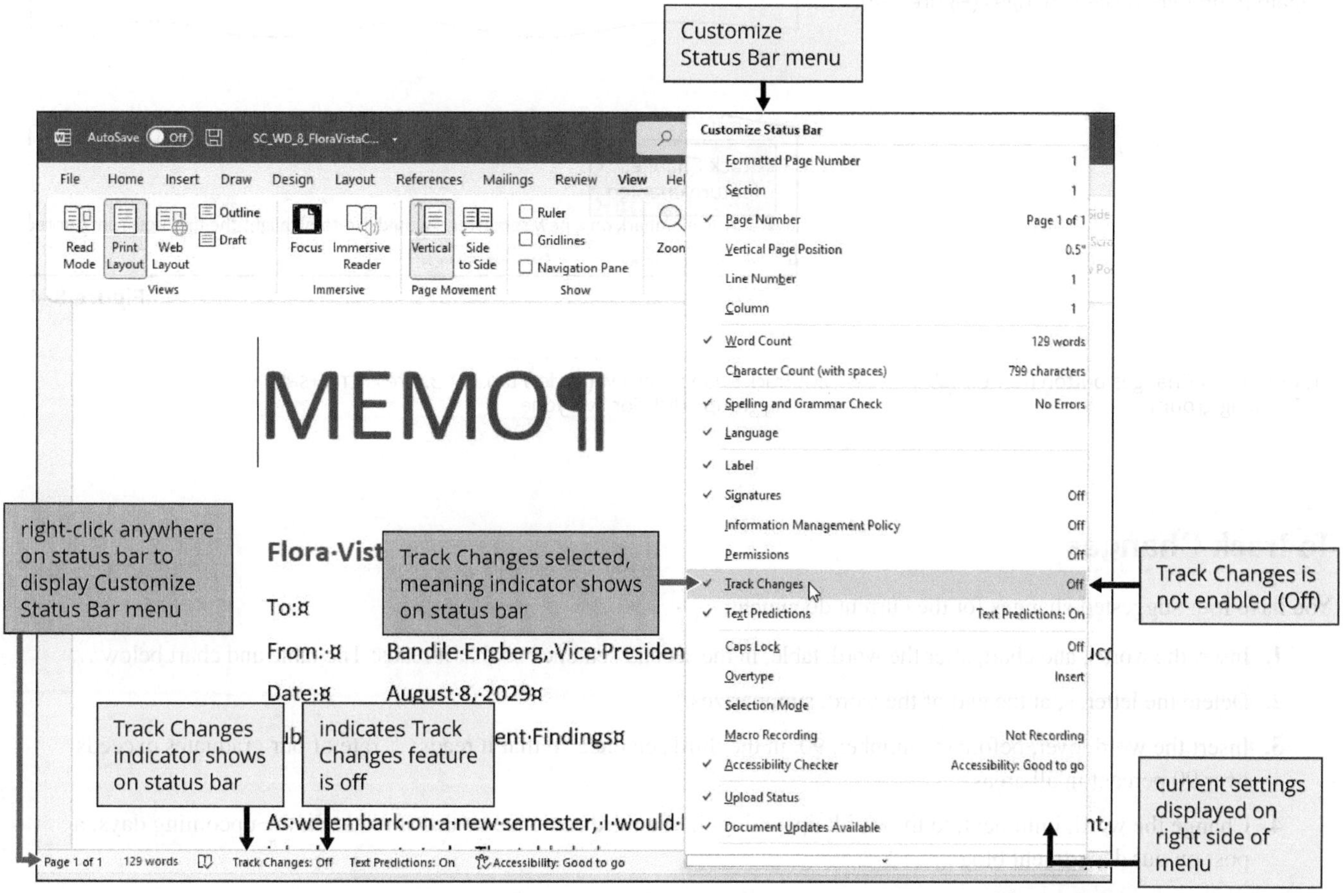

Customize Status Bar menu

right-click anywhere on status bar to display Customize Status Bar menu

Track Changes selected, meaning indicator shows on status bar

Track Changes is not enabled (Off)

Track Changes indicator shows on status bar

indicates Track Changes feature is off

current settings displayed on right side of menu

Figure 8–3

- Click anywhere outside of the Customize Status Bar menu or press ESC to remove the menu from the screen.

To Enable Tracked Changes

When you edit a document that has the track changes feature enabled, Word uses annotations to mark all text or graphics that you insert, delete, or modify and refers to the revisions as **markups**, **revision marks**, or **annotations**. An author can identify the changes a reviewer (user) has made by reviewing the markups in a document. The author also can accept or reject any change that a reviewer has made to a document.

The following step enables tracked changes. **Why?** To track changes in a document, you must enable (turn on) the track changes feature.

1

- If the Track Changes indicator on the status bar shows that the track changes feature is off, click the Track Changes indicator on the status bar to enable the track changes feature.
- **Experiment:** Display the Review tab. Click the Track Changes button (Review tab | Tracking group) to disable tracked changes. Click the Track Changes button again to enable tracked changes. Click the Track Changes indicator on the status bar to disable tracked changes. Click the Track Changes indicator on the status bar again to enable tracked changes (Figure 8–4).

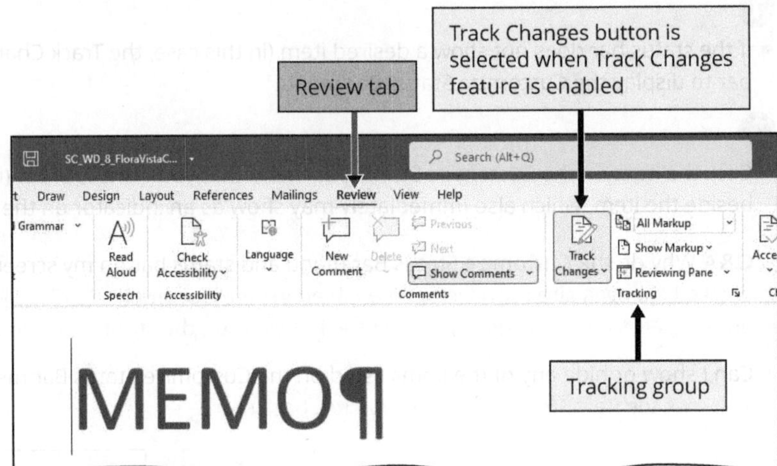

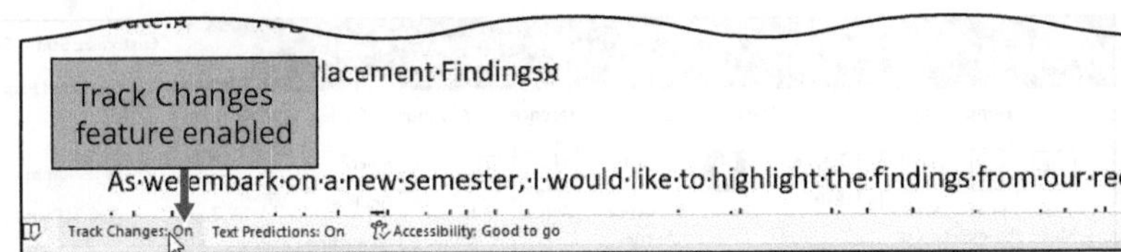

Figure 8–4

Other Ways

1. Click Track Changes button (Review tab | Tracking group)
2. Click Track Changes arrow (Review tab | Tracking group), click For Everyone
3. Press CTRL+SHIFT+E

To Track Changes

You have four suggested changes for the current document:

1. Insert the words, and chart, after the word, table, in the second sentence so that it reads: The table and chart below …
2. Delete the letter, s, at the end of the word, summarizes.
3. Insert the word, over, before the number, 90, in the third sentence so that it reads: ... rate of our graduates exceeds over 90 percent in all areas!
4. Change the word, imminent, to the word, upcoming, in the third sentence so that it reads: In the upcoming days, a post on our department blog ....

The following steps track these changes as you enter them in the document. **Why?** You want edits you make to the document to show so that others can review the edits.

- Scroll to display the first paragraph of text in the document window and then position the insertion point immediately to the left of the word, below, in the second sentence of the memo to position the insertion point at the location for the tracked change (Figure 8–5).

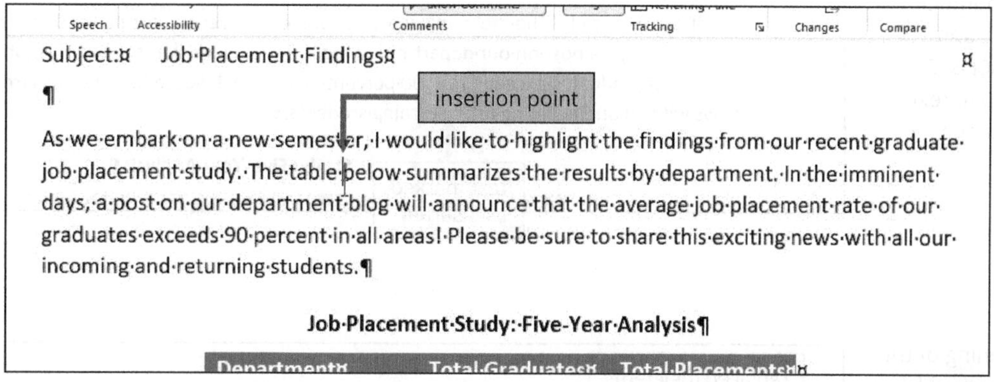

Figure 8–5

- Type **and chart** and then press SPACEBAR to insert the typed text as a tracked change (Figure 8–6).

Q&A Why is the inserted text in color and underlined?
When the track changes feature is enabled, Word marks (signals) all text inserts by underlining them and changing their color and marks all deletions by striking through them and changing their color.

What is the vertical bar in the margin?
The bar is called a changed line, which indicates a tracked change is on the line to the right of the bar. You can click the changed line to toggle between showing or hiding tracked changes.

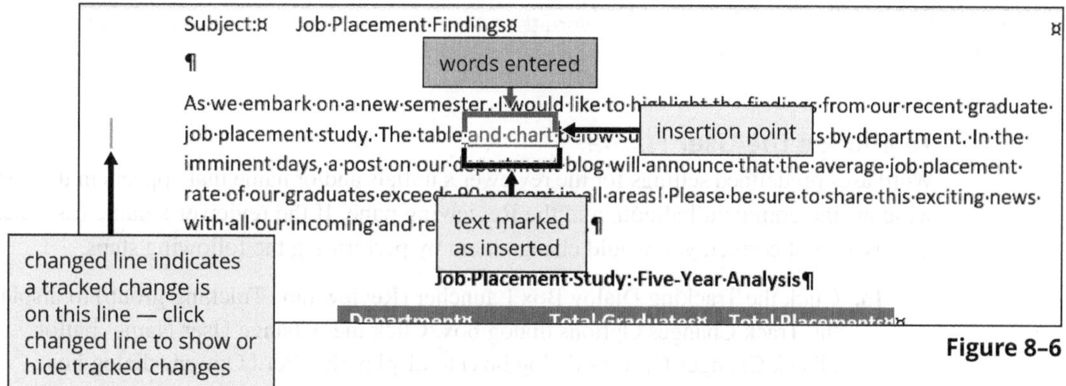

Figure 8–6

- In the same sentence, delete the s at the end of the word, summarizes (so that it reads, summarize), to mark the letter for deletion (Figure 8–7).

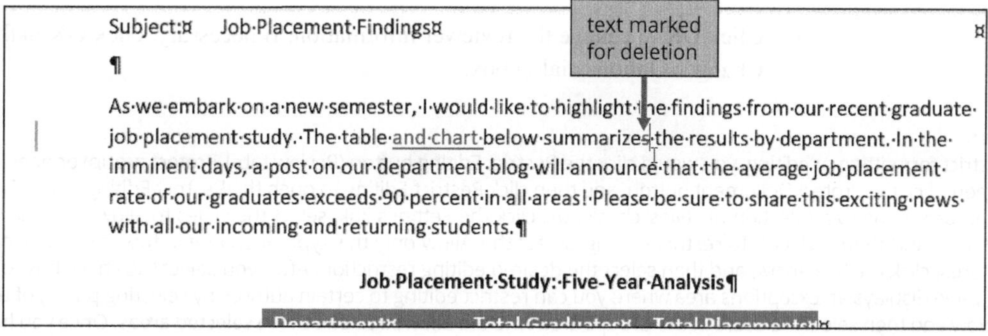

Figure 8–7

- In the next sentence, position the insertion point immediately to the left of the number, 90. Type **over** and then press SPACEBAR to insert the typed text as a tracked change (Figure 8–8).

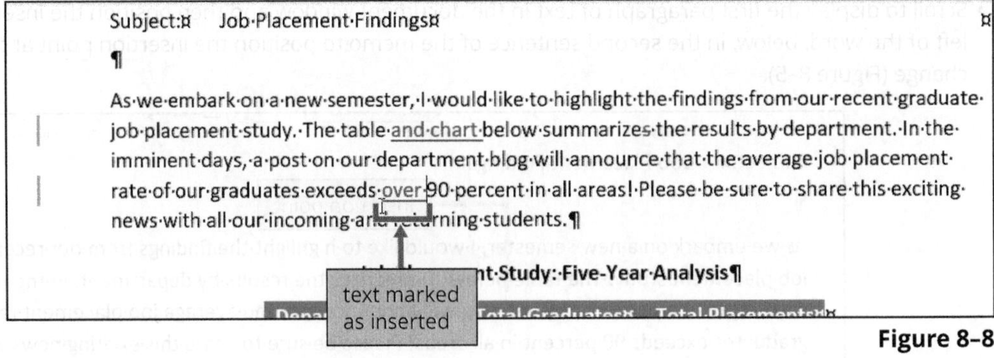

Figure 8–8

- Near the beginning of the same sentence, double-click the word, imminent, to select it.
- Type **upcoming** as the replacement text, which tracks the changes of a deletion and an insertion (Figure 8–9).

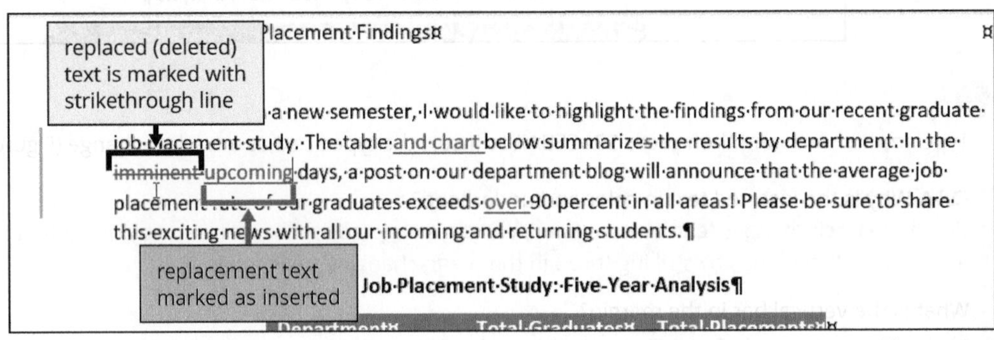

Figure 8–9

Q&A Can I view the name of the person who tracked a change?

You can point to a tracked change in the document window; Word then will display a ScreenTip that identifies the reviewer's name and the type of change made by that reviewer.

To Change the User Name

Word uses predefined settings for the reviewer's initials and/or name that appears in the document window, the comment balloon, and the Reviewing pane. If the reviewer's name (user name) or initials are not correct, you would change them by performing the following steps.

1a. Click the Tracking Dialog Box Launcher (Review tab | Tracking group) to display the Track Changes Options dialog box. Click the 'Change User Name' button (Track Changes Options dialog box) to display the Word Options dialog box.

or

1b. Open Backstage view and then click Options to display the Word Options dialog box. If necessary, click General in the left pane.

2. Enter the correct name in the User name text box (Word Options dialog box), and enter the correct initials in the Initials text box.

3. Click OK to change the reviewer information. If necessary, click OK in the Track Changes Options dialog box.

BTW
Limiting Authors
If you wanted to restrict formatting or editing, you would click the Restrict Editing button (Review tab | Protect group) or open Backstage view, display the Info screen, click the Protect Document button, and then click Restrict Editing to open the Restrict Editing pane. To restrict formatting, select the 'Limit formatting to a selection of styles' check box, click the Settings link, select the styles to allow and disallow (Formatting Restrictions dialog box), and then click OK. To restrict editing, select the 'Allow only this type of editing in the document' check box in the Editing restrictions area, click the box arrow, and then select the desired editing restriction. After you select the check box to restrict editing, the Restrict Editing pane displays an Exceptions area where you can restrict editing to certain authors by selecting part(s) of the document in the document window and then select the users in the Groups area who are allowed to edit those selected areas. Once you have specified all formatting and editing restrictions, click the 'Yes, Start Enforcing Protection' button. To block authors from making changes to selected text, click the Block Authors button (Review tab | Protect group) and then select the authors to block in the list. (Note that this button is disabled (dim) unless you are sharing the document with other users.)

To Change How Markups Are Displayed

The tracked changes entered in the previous steps appeared inline, which means that the insertions are underlined and the deletions are shown as strikethroughs. The default Word setting displays comments and formatting changes in balloons in a markup area to the right of the document and all other changes inline. If you wanted to change how markups (and comments) are displayed, you would perform the following steps.

1. Click the Show Markup button (Review tab | Tracking group) to display the Show Markup menu and then point to Balloons on the Show Markup menu.
2. If you want all revisions to appear in balloons, click 'Show Revisions in Balloons' on the Balloons submenu. If you want to use the default Word setting, click 'Show Only Formatting in Balloons' on the Balloons submenu.

BTW
Lock Tracking
If you wanted to require a password to turn off tracked changes (lock tracking), you would click the Track Changes arrow (Review tab | Tracking group), click Lock Tracking on the Track Changes menu, enter the password in each text box, and then click OK (Lock Tracking dialog box). If you do not enter a password, Word will turn off tracked changes but will not require a password to unlock tracking. To turn off tracked changes (unlock tracking), follow the same procedure, entering the password when prompted, if necessary.

To Disable Tracked Changes

When you have finished tracking changes, you should disable (turn off) the track changes feature so that Word stops marking your revisions. You follow the same steps to disable tracked changes as you did to enable them; that is, the indicator or button or keyboard shortcut functions as a toggle, turning the track changes feature on or off each time the command is issued. The following step disables tracked changes.

BTW
Tracking Only Your Changes
If you wanted to track only the changes you make to a document and not force others to track their changes in the document, you would click the Track Changes arrow (Review tab | Tracking group) and then click Just Mine on the Track Changes menu. To track changes made by all users of the document, you would click the Track Changes arrow (Review tab | Tracking group) and then click For Everyone on the Track Changes menu.

1 To turn the track changes feature off, click the Track Changes indicator on the status bar, or click the Track Changes button (Review tab | Tracking group), or press CTRL+SHIFT+E (Figure 8–10).

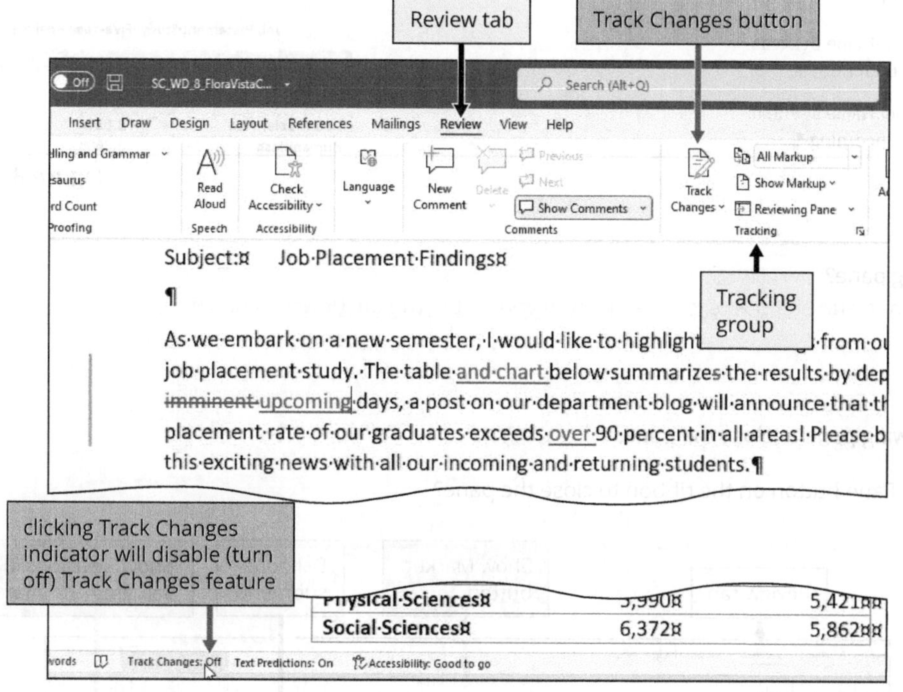

Figure 8–10

To Use the Reviewing Pane or the Markup Area

Word provides a Reviewing pane that can be opened and then displayed either at the left edge (vertically) or the bottom (horizontally) of the screen. **Why?** As an alternative to reading through tracked changes in the document window or in balloons in the markup area, some users prefer to view tracked changes in the Reviewing pane. The following steps open the Reviewing pane.

- If necessary, display the Review tab. Click the Reviewing Pane arrow (Review tab | Tracking group) to display the Reviewing Pane menu (Figure 8–11).

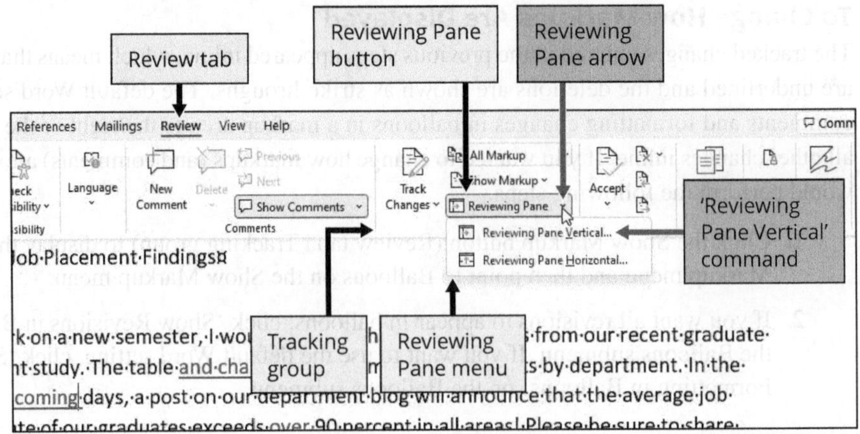

Figure 8–11

2

- Click 'Reviewing Pane Vertical' on the Reviewing Pane menu to open the Reviewing pane on the left side of the Word window (Figure 8–12).

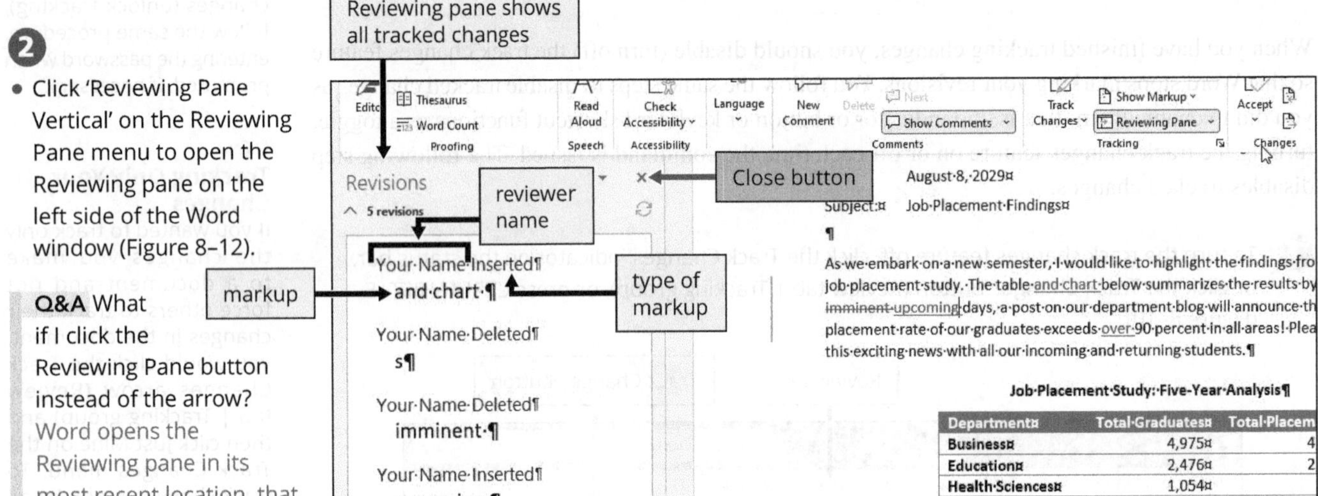

Figure 8–12

Q&A What if I click the Reviewing Pane button instead of the arrow? Word opens the Reviewing pane in its most recent location, that is, either vertically on the left side of the screen or horizontally on the bottom of the screen.

Can I edit revisions in the Reviewing pane?
Yes. Simply click in the Reviewing pane and edit the text the same way you edit in the document window.

- Click the Close button in the Reviewing pane to close the pane.

Q&A Can I also click the Reviewing Pane button on the ribbon to close the pane?
Yes.

- Click the Show Markup button (Review tab | Tracking group) to display the Show Markup menu.
- Point to Balloons on the Show Markup menu to display the Balloons submenu (Figure 8–13).

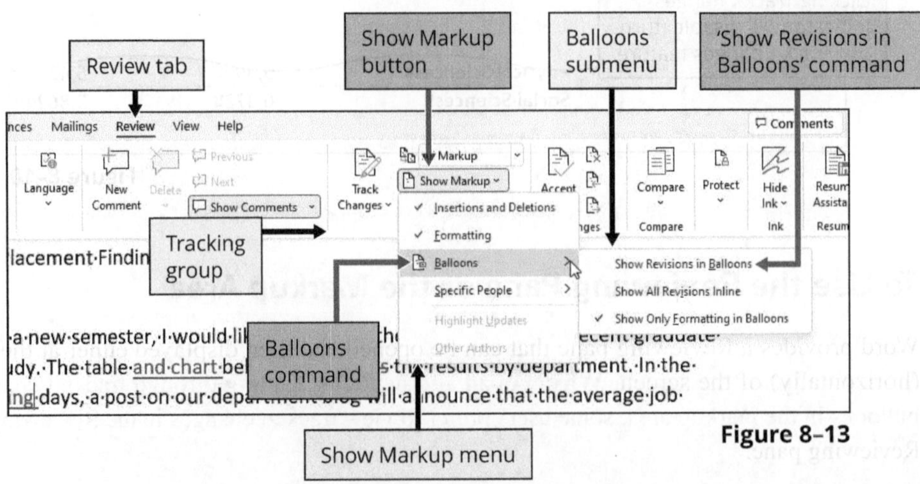

Figure 8–13

5

- Click 'Show Revisions in Balloons' on the Balloons submenu to show the markup area in the Word window (Figure 8–14). If necessary, change the zoom so that the markup area is displayed in the Word window.

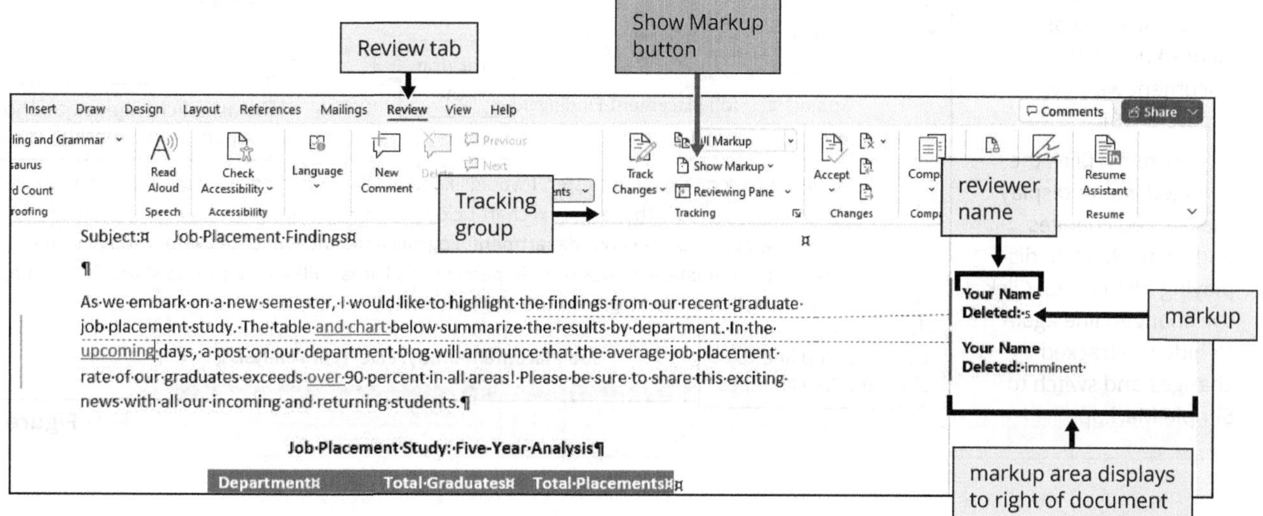

Figure 8–14

6

- Click the Show Markup button (Review tab | Tracking group) to display the Show Markup menu.
- Point to Balloons on the Show Markup menu to display the Balloons submenu and then click 'Show Only Formatting in Balloons' on the Balloons submenu to remove the markup area from the Word window and place all markups except formatting inline.
- If necessary, change the zoom to page width.

To Display Tracked Changes as Simple Markup

Word provides a Simple Markup option instead of the All Markup option for viewing tracked changes and comments. **Why?** Some users feel the All Markup option clutters the screen and prefer the cleaner appearance of the Simple Markup option. The following steps display tracked changes using the Simple Markup option.

1

- Click the 'Display for Review' arrow (Review tab | Tracking group) to display the Display for Review menu (Figure 8–15).

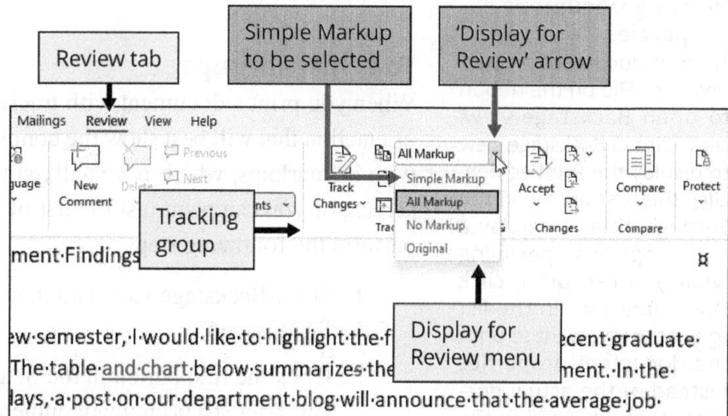

Figure 8–15

- Click Simple Markup on the Display for Review menu to show a simple markup instead of all markups in the document window (Figure 8–16).
  - **Experiment:** Click the changed line to display the tracked changes and switch back to displaying All Markup. Click the changed line again to hide the tracked changes and switch to Simple Markup.

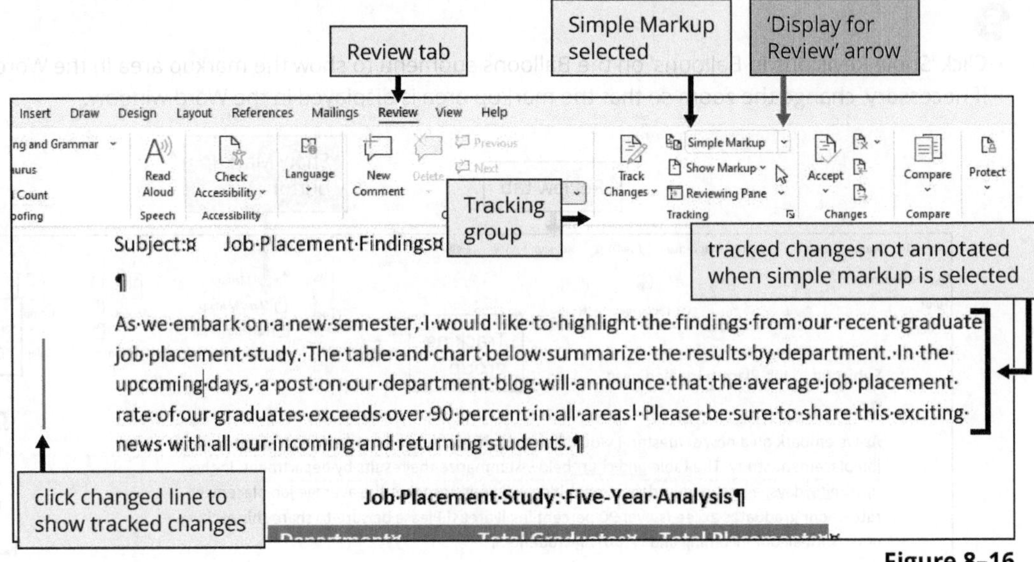

Figure 8–16

To Show All Markup

You prefer to show all markup where tracked changes are annotated in the document window. The following steps show all markup.

Click the 'Display for Review' arrow (Review tab | Tracking group) (shown in Figure 8–16) and then click All Markup on the Display for Review menu to instruct Word to display the document with all proposed edits shown as markup (shown in Figure 8–17).

Q&A What are the other Display for Review options?
If you click the 'Display for Review' arrow, several options appear. Simple Markup means Word incorporates proposed changes in the document and places a changed line near the margin of the line containing the proposed change. All Markup means that all proposed changes are annotated in the document. No Markup shows the proposed edits as part of the final document, instead of as markup. Original shows the document before changes.

Save the memo again on the same storage location with the same file name.

BTW
Printing Document Properties
To print document properties, click File on the ribbon to open Backstage view, click Print in Backstage view to display the Print screen, click the first button in the Settings area to display a list of options specifying what you can print, click Document Info in the list to specify you want to print the document properties instead of the actual document, and then click the Print button in the Print screen to print the document properties on the currently selected printer.

To Print Markups

When you print a document with tracked changes, Word chooses the zoom percentage and page orientation that will best show the comments on the printed document. You can print the document with its markups, which is visually similar to how the Word window shows the markups on the screen, or you can print just the list of the markups. If you wanted to print markups, you would perform the following steps.

1. Open Backstage view and then click Print in Backstage view to display the Print screen.
2. Click the first button in the Settings area to display a list of options specifying what you can print. To print the document with the markups, if necessary, place a check mark to the left of Print Markup. To print just the markups (without printing the document), click 'List of Markup' in the Document Info area.
3. Click the Print button in the Print area in Backstage view.

Reviewing Tracked Changes

After tracking changes in a document, you send the document to the originator for his or her review. For demonstration purposes in this module, you assume the role of originator and review the tracked changes in the document.

To do this, be sure the markups are displayed on the screen. Click the Show Markup button (Review tab | Tracking group) and verify that the 'Insertions and Deletions' and Formatting commands each contain a check mark. Ensure the 'Display for Review' box (Review tab | Tracking group) shows All Markup; if it does not, click the 'Display for Review' arrow (Review tab | Tracking group) and then click All Markup on the Display for Review menu. This option shows the final document with tracked changes.

If you wanted to observe how a document would appear if you accepted all the changes, without actually accepting them, click the 'Display for Review' arrow (Review tab | Tracking group) and then click No Markup on the Display for Review menu. If you print this view of the document, it will print how the document will appear if you accept all the changes. If you wanted to observe how the document appeared before any changes were made, click the 'Display for Review' arrow (Review tab | Tracking group) and then click Original on the Display for Review menu. When you have finished reviewing the various options, if necessary, click the 'Display for Review' arrow (Review tab | Tracking group) and then click All Markup on the Display for Review menu.

BTW

Inserting Document Properties

If you wanted to insert document properties into a document, you would click the Explore Quick Parts button (Insert tab | Text group) to display the Explore Quick Parts menu, point to Document Property on the Explore Quick Parts menu, and then click the property you want to insert on the Document Property menu. If you wanted to insert document properties into a header or footer, you would display the Header & Footer tab, click the Document Info button (Header & Footer tab | Insert group), click the document property to insert or point to Document Property on the Document Info menu, and then click the document property to insert.

To Review Tracked Changes

The next step is to review the tracked changes in the marked-up document using the Review tab. **Why?** You could scroll through the document and point to each markup to read it, but you might overlook one or more changes using this technique. A more efficient method is to use the Review tab to review the changes one at a time, deciding whether to accept, modify, or delete each change. The following steps review the changes in the document.

- Position the insertion point at the beginning of the document, so that Word begins the review of tracked changes from the top of the document.
- Click the Next Change button (Review tab | Changes group), which causes Word to locate and select the first markup in the document (in this case, the inserted words, and chart) (Figure 8–17).

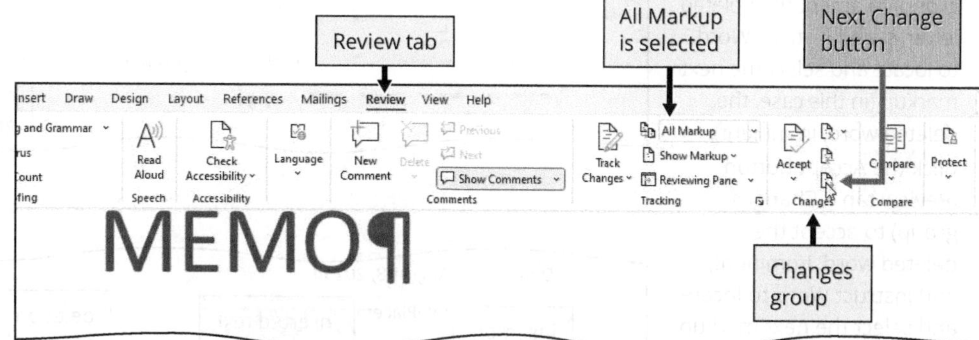

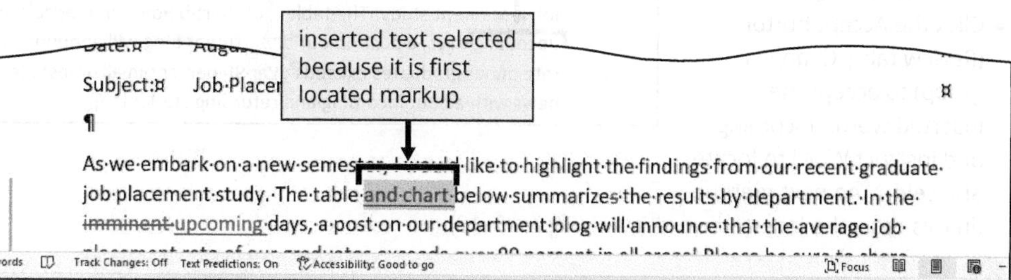

Figure 8–17

Q&A What if my document also had contained comments?

When you click the Next Change button (Review tab | Changes group), Word locates only the next tracked change. To display the next comment, you would click the Next Comment button in the Comments group.

2

- Because you agree with this change, click the Accept button (Review tab | Changes group) to accept the insertion of the words, and chart, and instruct Word to locate and select the next markup (in this case, the deleted letter, s) (Figure 8–18).

Q&A What if I accidentally click the Accept arrow (Review tab | Changes group)?
Click 'Accept and Move to Next' on the Accept menu.

What if I wanted to accept the change but not search for the next tracked change?
You would click the Accept arrow and then click 'Accept This Change' on the Accept menu.

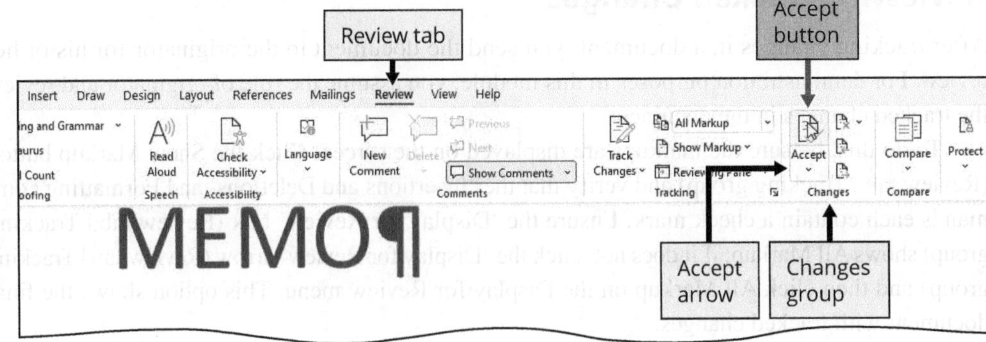

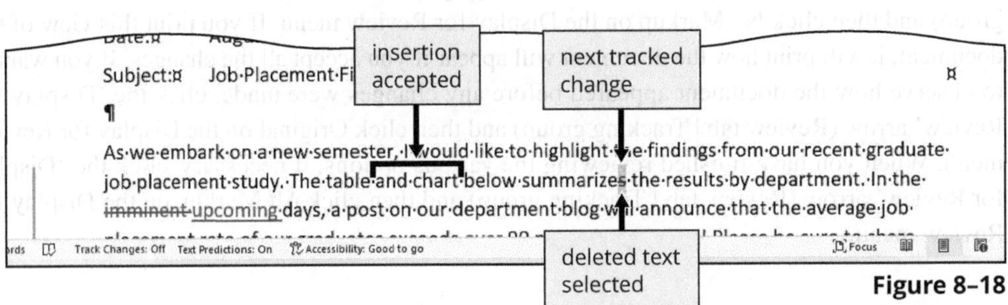

Figure 8–18

3

- Click the Accept button (Review tab | Changes group) to accept the deleted letter, s, and instruct Word to locate and select the next markup (in this case, the deleted word, imminent).
- Click the Accept button (Review tab | Changes group) to accept the deleted word, imminent, and instruct Word to locate and select the next markup (in this case, the inserted word, upcoming).
- Click the Accept button (Review tab | Changes group) to accept the inserted word, upcoming, and instruct Word to locate and select the next markup (in this case, the inserted word, over) (Figure 8–19).

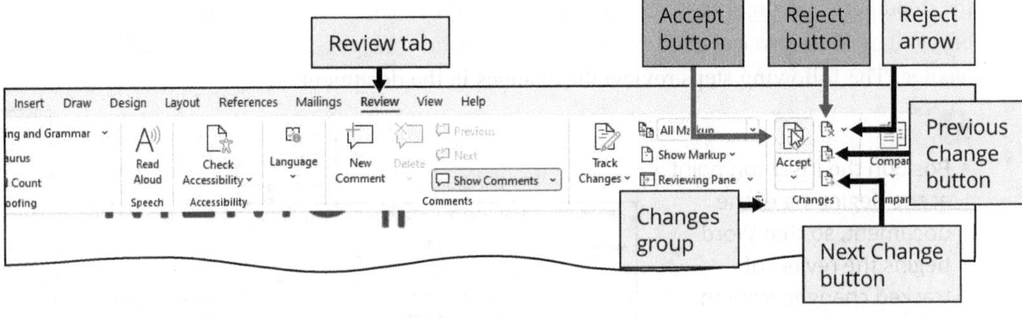

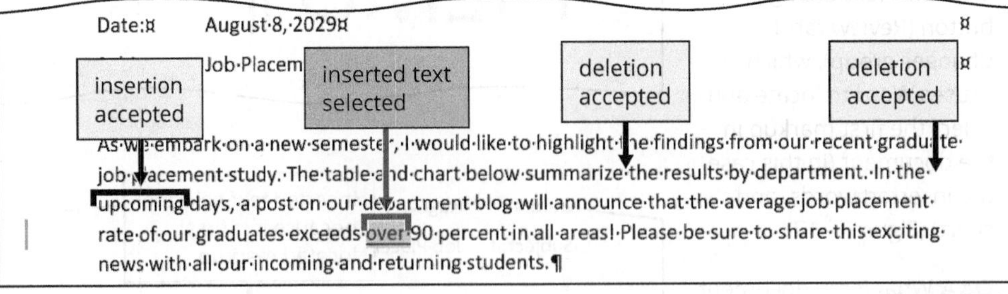

Figure 8–19

4

- Because you do not agree with this change, click the Reject button (Review tab | Changes group) to reject the marked insertion, and instruct Word to locate and select the next markup if one exists.

Q&A What if I accidentally click the Reject arrow (Review tab | Changes group)?
Click 'Reject and Move to Next' on the Reject menu.

What if I wanted to reject the change but not search for the next tracked change?
You would click the Reject arrow (Review tab | Changes group) and then click Reject Change on the Reject menu.

Q&A What if I did not want to accept or reject a change but wanted to locate the next tracked change?
You would click the Next Change button (Review tab | Changes group) to locate the next tracked change. Likewise, to locate the previous tracked change, you would click the Previous Change button (Review tab | Changes group).

- Click OK in the dialog box that appears, which indicates the document contains no more comments or tracked changes.
- **sam** Save the reviewed file on your hard drive, OneDrive, or other storage location using SC_WD_8_FloraVistaCollegeMemo_Reviewed as the file name.

Other Ways

1. Right-click tracked change (or, if using touch, tap 'Show Context Menu' button on Mini toolbar), click desired command on shortcut menu

To Accept or Reject All Tracked Changes

If you wanted to accept or reject all tracked changes in a document at once, you would perform the following step.

1. To accept all tracked changes, click the Accept arrow (Review tab | Changes group) to display the Accept menu and then click 'Accept All Changes' on the menu to accept all changes in the document and continue tracking changes or click 'Accept All Changes and Stop Tracking' to accept all changes in the document and stop tracking changes.

or

1. To reject all tracked changes, click the Reject arrow (Review tab | Changes group) to display the Reject menu and then click 'Reject All Changes' on the menu to reject all changes in the document and continue tracking changes or click 'Reject All Changes and Stop Tracking' to reject all changes in the document and stop tracking changes.

BTW
Creating a Private Document Copy
If you are working on a document that is being shared with others and you want to add comments, annotations, and other notes that will be displayed only in your document, some later versions of Word include a feature that allows you to create a private copy of the document. To use this feature in a shared document, you would click the 'Create a Private Copy' button (SharePoint group).

Changing Tracking Options

If you wanted to change the color and markings reviewers use for tracked changes or change how balloons are displayed, use the Advanced Track Changes Options dialog box (Figure 8–20). To display the Advanced Track Changes Options dialog box, click the Tracking Dialog Box Launcher (Review tab | Tracking group) and then click the Advanced Options button (Track Changes Options dialog box).

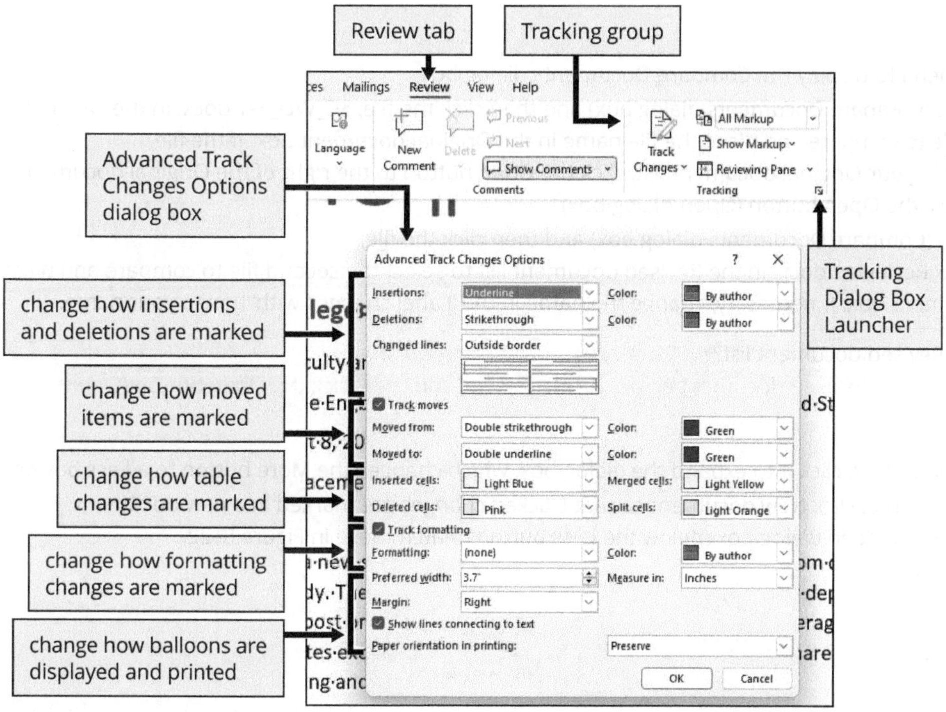

Figure 8–20

BTW
Compare and Merge
If you wanted to compare two documents and merge the changes into an existing document instead of into a new document, you would click the Original document option button (Compare Documents dialog box) to merge into the original document or click the Revised document option button (Compare Documents dialog box) to merge into the revised document (shown in Figure 8–22), and then click OK.

To Compare Documents

With Word, you can compare two documents to each other. **Why?** Comparing documents allows you easily to identify any differences between two files because Word displays the differences between the documents as tracked changes for your review. By comparing files, you can verify that two separate files have the same or different content. If no tracked changes are found, then the two documents are identical.

Assume you want to compare the original SC_WD_8-1.docx document with the SC_WD_8_FloraVistaCollegeMemo_Reviewed.docx document so that you can identify the changes made to the document. The following steps compare two documents.

- If necessary, display the Review tab.
- Click the Compare button (Review tab | Compare group) to display the Compare menu (Figure 8–21).

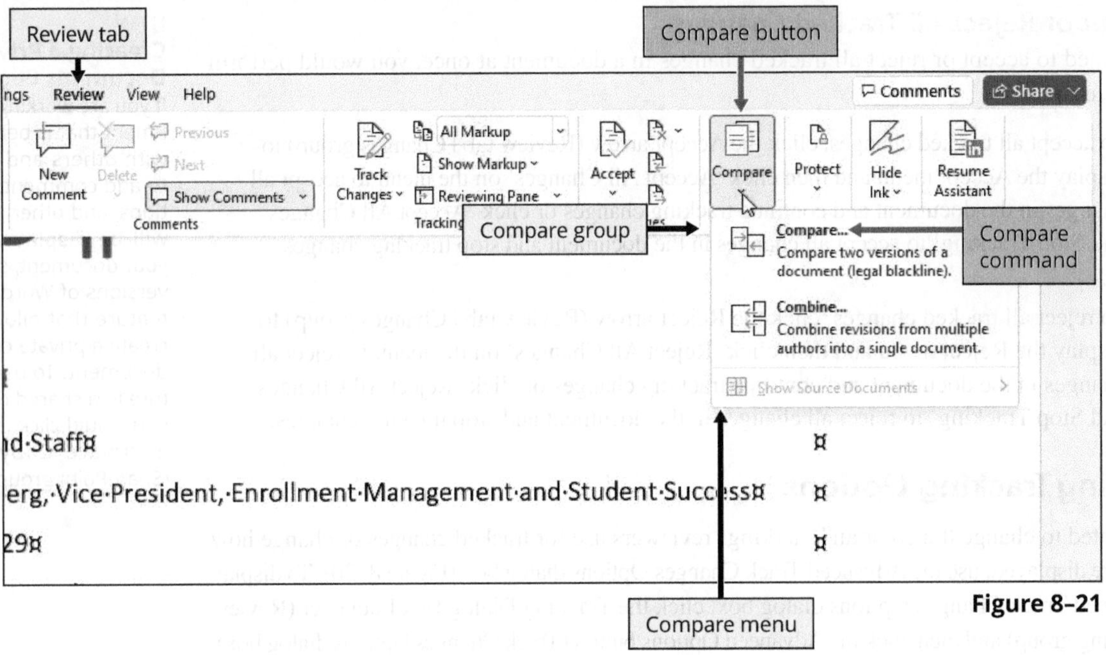

Figure 8–21

- Click Compare on the Compare menu to display the Compare Documents dialog box.
- Click the Original document arrow (Compare Documents dialog box) and then click the file, SC_WD_8-1.docx, in the Original document list to select the first file to compare and place the file name in the Original document box. If the file, SC_WD_8-1.docx, is not displayed in your Original document list, click the Open button to the right of the Original document arrow, locate the file, and then click the Open button (Open dialog box).
- Click the Revised document arrow (Compare Documents dialog box) and then click the file, SC_WD_8_FloraVistaCollegeMemo_Reviewed.docx, in the Revised document list to select the second file to compare and place the file name in the Revised document box. If necessary, change the name in the 'Label changes with' box to your name.

Q&A What if the file is not in the Revised document list?
Click the Open button to the right of the Revised document arrow, locate the file, and then click the Open button (Open dialog box).

- If a More button appears in the dialog box, click it to expand the dialog box, which changes the More button to a Less button.
- If necessary, in the Show changes in area, click New document so that tracked changes are marked in a new document. Ensure that all your settings in the expanded dialog box (below the Less button) match those in Figure 8–22.

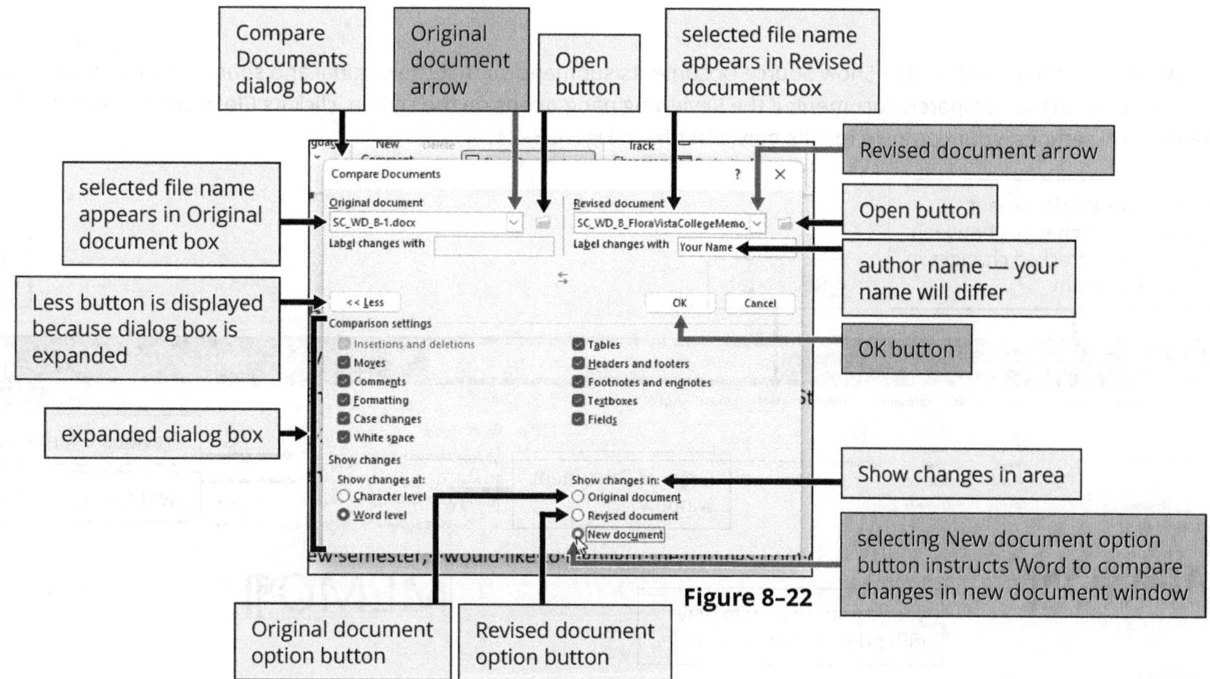

Figure 8-22

- Click OK to open a new document window, labeled Compare Result, and display the differences between the two documents as tracked changes in a Compare Result document window; if the Reviewing pane opens on the screen, click its Close button. Note that, depending on settings, your Compare Result window may differ from Figure 8-23; for example, your screen already may show source documents, which is covered in Step 4.

- Click the Compare button (Review tab | Compare group) to display the Compare menu and then point to 'Show Source Documents' on the Compare menu to display the Show Source Documents submenu (Figure 8-23).

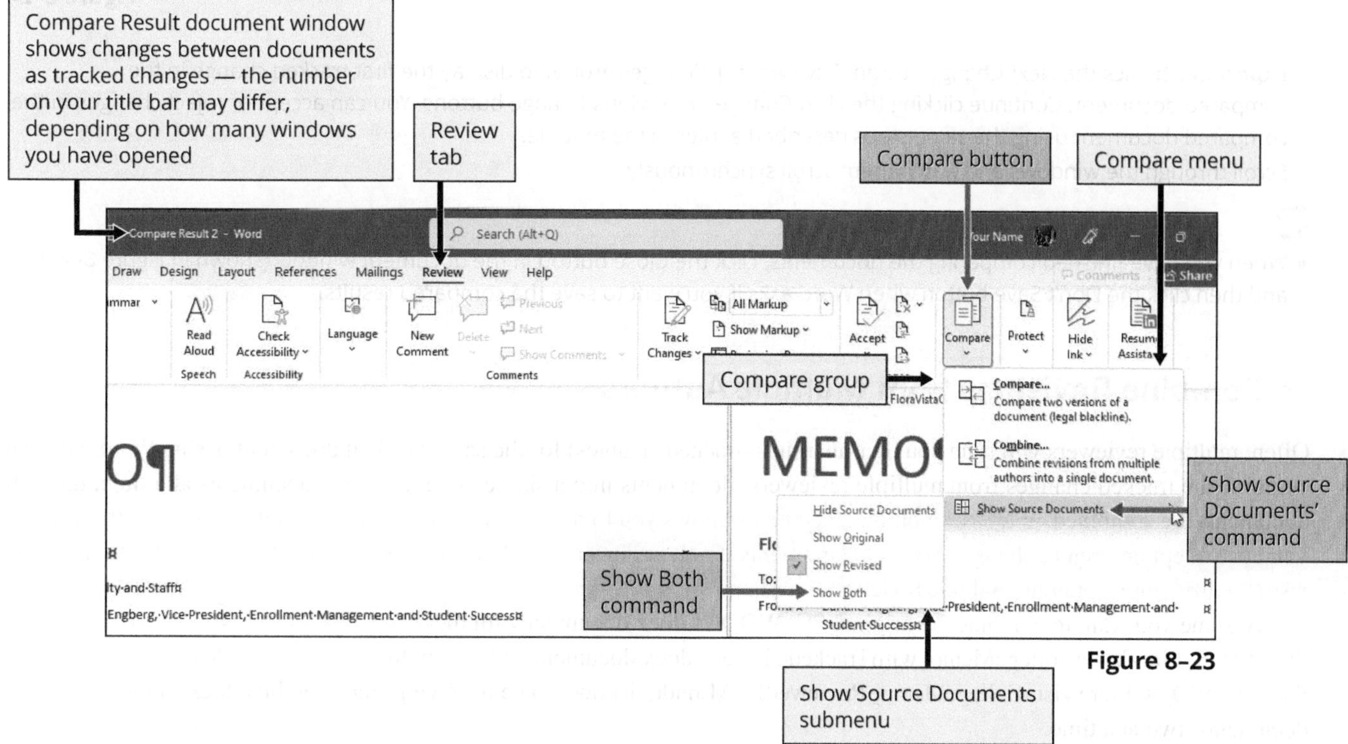

Figure 8-23

- If necessary, click Show Both on the Show Source Documents submenu so that the original and source documents appear on the screen with the compared document; if the Reviewing pane opens on the screen, click its Close button. Note that, depending on settings, your compare results may differ from Figure 8–24.

Figure 8–24

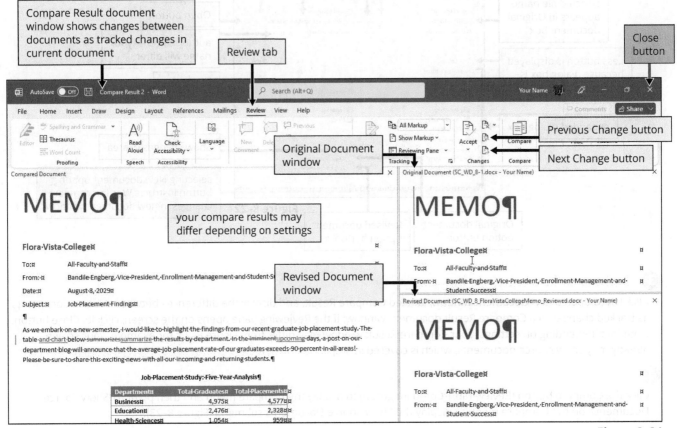

- **Experiment:** Click the Next Change button (Review tab | Changes group) to display the first tracked change in the compared document. Continue clicking the Next Change or Previous Change buttons. You can accept or reject changes in the compared document using the same steps described earlier in the module.
- Scroll through the windows and watch them scroll synchronously.

- When you have finished comparing the documents, click the Close button in the document window (shown in Figure 8–24) and then click the Don't Save button when Word asks if you want to save the compared results.

To Combine Revisions from Multiple Authors

Often, multiple reviewers will send you their markups (tracked changes) for the same original document. Using Word, you can combine the tracked changes from multiple reviewers' documents into a single document, two documents at a time, until all documents are combined. **Why?** Combining documents allows you to review all markups from a single document, from which you can accept and reject changes and read comments. Each reviewer's markups are shaded in a different color to help you visually differentiate among multiple reviewers' markups.

Assume you want to combine the original SC_WD_8-1.docx document with the SC_WD_8_FloraVistaCollegeMemo_withTrackedChanges.docx document and also with a document called Support_WD_8_FloraVistaCollegeMemo_ReviewedByALundquist.docx. The following steps combine these three documents, two at a time.

1

- Click the Compare button (Review tab | Compare group) to display the Compare menu (Figure 8–25).

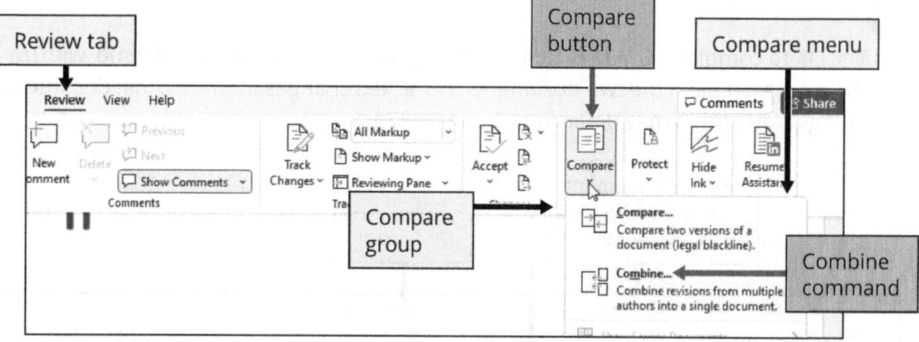

Figure 8–25

2

- Click Combine on the Compare menu to display the Combine Documents dialog box.
- Click the Original document arrow (Combine Documents dialog box) and then click the file, SC_WD_8-1.docx, in the Original document list to select the first file to combine and place the file name in the Original document box.

Q&A What if the file is not in the Original document list?
Click the Open button to the right of the Original document arrow, locate the file, and then click the Open button (Open dialog box).

- Click the Revised document arrow (Combine Documents dialog box) and then click the file, SC_WD_8_FloraVistaCollegeMemo_withTrackedChanges.docx, in the Revised document list to select the second file to combine and place the file name in the Revised document box. (If necessary, double-click the file name in the Revised document list to select it.)

Q&A What if the file is not in the Revised document list?
Click the Open button to the right of the Revised document arrow, locate the file, and then click the Open button (Open dialog box).

- If a More button appears in the dialog box, click it to expand the dialog box, which changes the More button to a Less button.
- In the Show changes in area, if necessary, click Original document so that tracked changes are marked in the original document (SC_WD_8-1.docx). Ensure that all your settings in the expanded dialog box (below the Less button) match those in Figure 8–26.

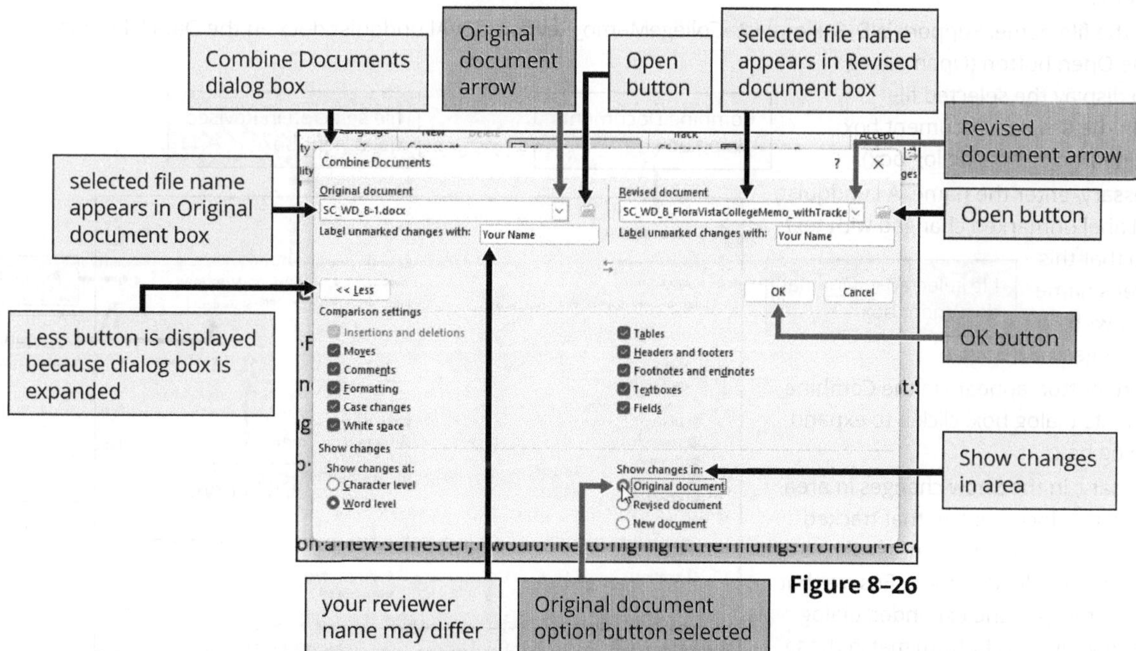

Figure 8–26

- Click OK to combine SC_WD_8-1.docx with SC_WD_8_FloraVistaCollegeMemo_withTrackedChanges.docx and display the differences between the two documents as tracked changes in the original document (Figure 8–27). (Note that depending on settings, you screen may differ from Figure 8–27.)

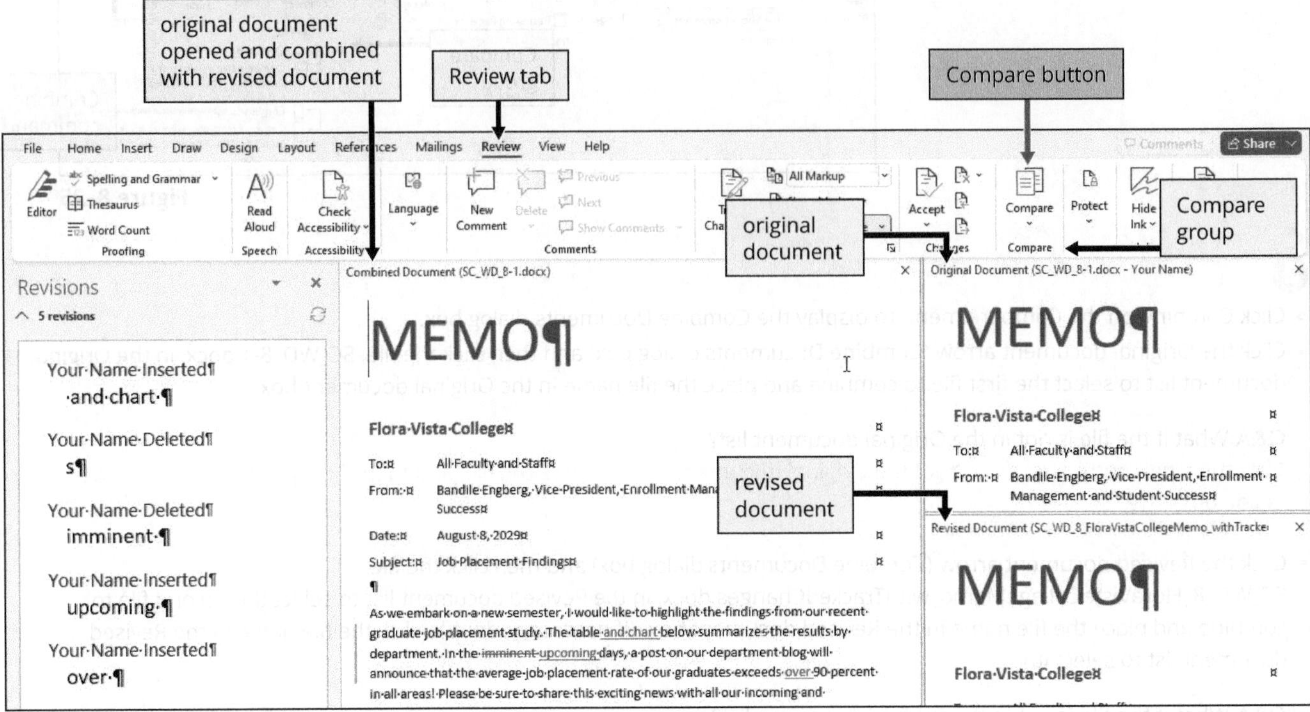

Figure 8–27

- Click the Compare button again (Review tab | Compare group) and then click Combine on the Compare menu to display the Combine Documents dialog box.
- Locate and display the file name, SC_WD_8-1.docx, in the Original document text box (Combine Documents dialog box) to select the first file and place the file name in the Original document box.
- Click the Open button to the right of the Revised document arrow (Combine Documents dialog box) to display the Open dialog box.
- Locate the file name, Support_WD_8_FloraVistaCollegeMemo_ReviewedByALundquist.docx, in the Data Files and then click the Open button (Open dialog box) to display the selected file name in the Revised document box (Combine Documents dialog box).
- If necessary, enter the name, A Lundquist, in the Label unmarked changed with text box, so that this reviewer's name appears with their changes.
- If a More button appears in the Combine Documents dialog box, click it to expand the dialog box.
- If necessary, in the Show changes in area, click Original document so that tracked changes are marked in the original document (SC_WD_8-1.docx). Ensure that all your settings in the expanded dialog box (below the Less button) match those in Figure 8–28.

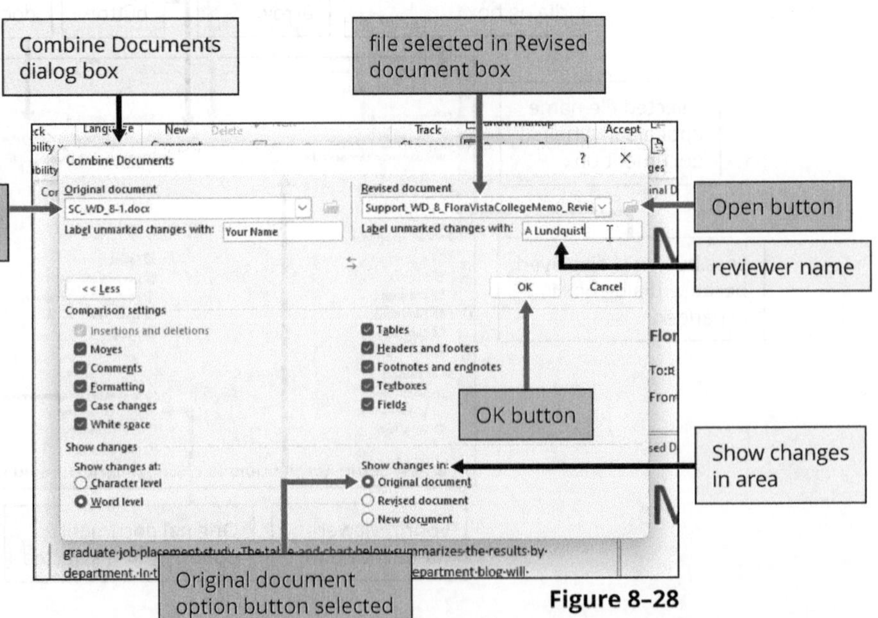

Figure 8–28

- Click OK to combine the Support_WD_8_FloraVistaCollegeMemo_ReviewedByALundquist.docx document with the currently combined document and display the differences among the three documents as tracked changes in the original document (Figure 8–29). If necessary, scroll to view the table in the memo.

Q&A What if my screen does not display the original and source documents?

Click the Compare button (Review tab | Compare group) to display the Compare menu, point to 'Show Source Documents' on the Compare menu, and then click Show Both on the Show Source Documents submenu.

- **Experiment:** Click the Next Change button (Review tab | Changes group) to display the first tracked change in the combined document. Continue clicking the Next Change or Previous Change buttons. You can accept or reject changes in the combined document using the same steps described earlier in the module.

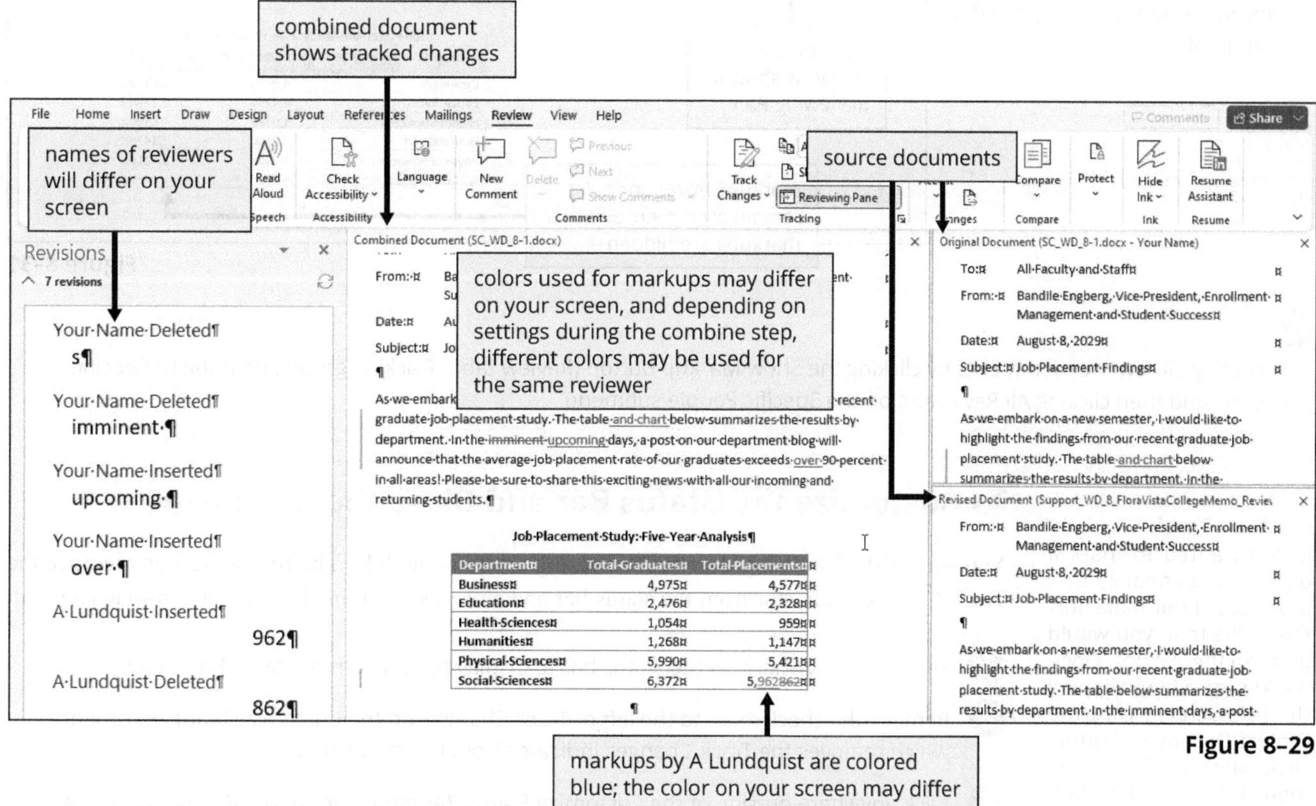

Figure 8–29

To Show Tracked Changes and Comments by a Single Reviewer

Why? Instead of searching through a document for a particular reviewer's markups, you can show markups by reviewer. The following steps show the markups by the reviewer named A Lundquist.

- Click the Show Markup button (Review tab | Tracking group) to display the Show Markup menu and then point to Specific People on the Show Markup menu to display the Specific People submenu (Figure 8–30).

Q&A What if my Specific People submenu differs?

Your submenu may have additional, different, or duplicate reviewer names or colors, depending on your Word settings.

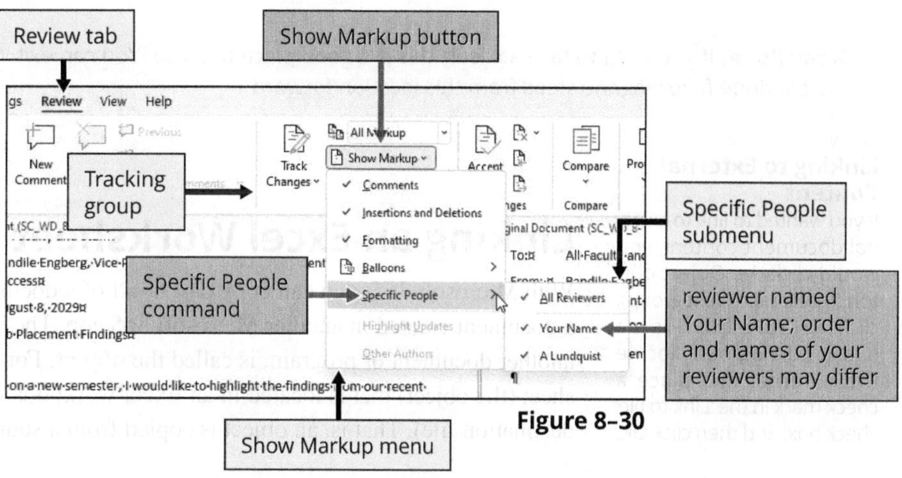

Figure 8–30

- Click Your Name on the Specific People submenu to hide the selected reviewer's markups and leave other markups on the screen (Figure 8–31).

Q&A Are the Your Name reviewer markups deleted?
No. They are hidden from view.

- **Experiment:** Practice hiding and showing reviewer markups in this document.

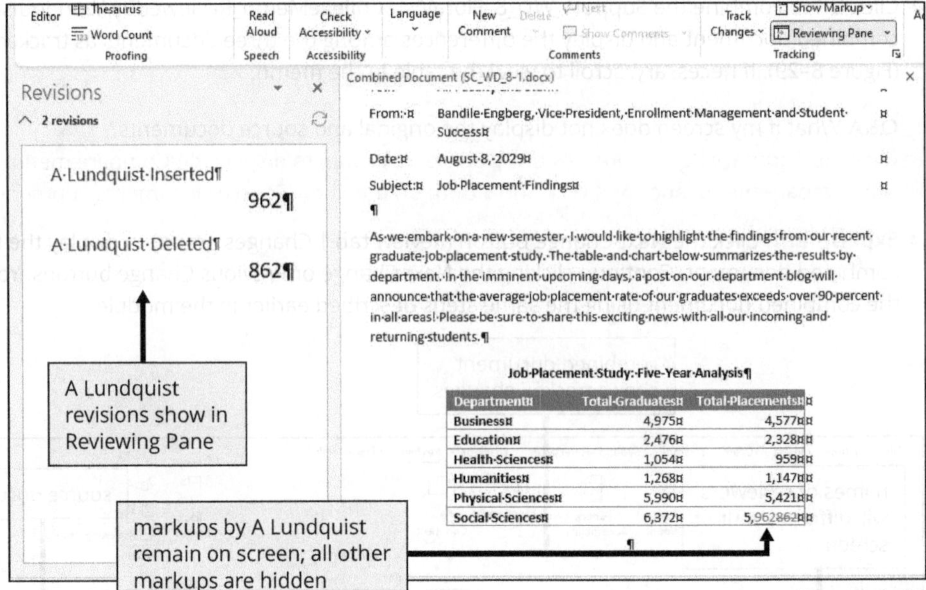

Figure 8–31

- Redisplay all reviewer comments by clicking the Show Markup button (Review tab | Tracking group), pointing to Specific People, and then clicking All Reviewers on the Specific People submenu.

BTW
Mark as Final
If you wanted to mark a document as final so that users could not make further edits to it, you would perform these steps. Open Backstage view, display the Info screen, click the Protect Document button, click 'Mark as Final', and then click OK in the Word dialog box that appears. This makes the document a read-only file, which prevents any further edits.

To Customize the Status Bar and Close the Document

You are finished working with tracked changes in this module. The following steps remove the Track Changes indicator from the status bar and close the combined document without saving it.

1. Right-click anywhere on the status bar to display the Customize Status Bar menu.
2. Remove the check mark to the left of Track Changes on the Customize Status Bar menu, which removes the Track Changes indicator from the status bar.
3. Click anywhere outside of the Customize Status Bar menu, or press ESC, to remove the Customize Status Bar menu from the screen.
4. Close the Word window containing the combined document. When Word displays the dialog box, click the Don't Save button.
5. Close any other open Word documents.

Break Point: If you want to take a break, this is a good place to do so. You can exit Word now. To resume later, start Word and continue following the steps from this location forward.

BTW
Linking to External Content
If you wanted to link to external document content, you would click the Object button (Insert tab | Text group), click the Create from File tab (Object dialog box), locate the external file, place a check mark in the 'Link to file' check box, and then click OK.

Linking an Excel Worksheet to a Word Document

With Microsoft 365, you can copy part or all of a document created in one Microsoft 365 app to a document created in another Microsoft 365 app. The item being copied, or exchanged between another document or program, is called the **object**. For example, you could copy an Excel worksheet (the object) that is located in an Excel workbook (the source file) to a Word document (the destination file). That is, an object is copied from a source to a destination.

You can use one of three techniques to exchange objects from one program to another: copy and paste, embed, or link.

- **Copy and paste:** When you copy an object and then paste it, the object becomes part of the destination document. You edit a pasted object using editing features of the destination app. For example, when you select an Excel worksheet in an Excel workbook, click the Copy button (Home tab | Clipboard group) in Excel, and then click the Paste button (Home tab | Clipboard group) in Word, the Excel worksheet becomes a Word table.
- **Embed:** When you embed an object, like a pasted object, it becomes part of the destination document. The difference between an embedded object and a pasted object is that you edit the contents of an embedded object using the editing features of the source app. The embedded object, however, contains static data; that is, any changes made to the object in the source app are not reflected in the destination document. If you embed an Excel worksheet in a Word document, the Excel worksheet remains as an Excel worksheet in the Word document. When you edit the Excel worksheet from within the Word document, you will use Excel editing features.
- **Link:** A linked object, by contrast, does not become a part of the destination document even though it appears to be a part of it. Rather, a connection is established between the source and destination documents so that when you open the destination document, the linked object appears as part of it. When you edit a linked object, the source app starts and opens the source document that contains the linked object. For example, when you edit a linked worksheet, Excel starts and displays the Excel workbook that contains the worksheet; you then edit the worksheet in Excel. Unlike an embedded object, if you open the Excel workbook that contains the Excel worksheet and then edit the Excel worksheet, the linked object will be updated in the Word document, too.

BTW
Linked Objects
When you open a document that contains linked objects, Word displays a dialog box asking if you want to update the Word document with data from the linked file. Click Yes only if you are certain the linked file is from a trusted source; that is, you should be confident that the source file does not contain a virus or other potentially harmful program before you instruct Word to link the source file to the destination document.

Consider This

How do you determine which method to use: copy/paste, embed, or link?

- If you simply want to use the object's data and have no desire to use the object in the source app, then copy and paste the object.
- If you want to use the object in the source app but you want the object's data to remain static if it changes in the source file, then embed the object.
- If you want to ensure that the most current version of the object appears in the destination file, then link the object. If the source file is large, such as a video clip or a sound clip, link the object to keep the size of the destination file smaller.

The steps in this section show how to link an Excel worksheet (the object), which is located in an Excel workbook (the source file), to a Word document (the destination file). The Word document is similar to the same memo used in the previous section, except that it does not contain the table. To link the worksheet to the memo, you will follow these general steps:

1. Start Excel and open the Excel workbook that contains the object (worksheet) you want to link to the Word document.
2. Select the object (worksheet) in Excel and then copy the selected object to the Clipboard.
3. Switch to Word and then link the copied object to the Word document.

Note: The steps in this section assume you have Microsoft Excel 365 installed on your computer. If you do not have Excel 365, read the steps in this section without performing them.

To Open a Word Document, Start Excel, and Open an Excel Workbook

The first step in this section is to open the memo that is to contain the link to the Excel worksheet object. The memo file, named SC_WD_8-2.docx, is located in the Data Files (this file does not contain the Word table in the memo because this section works with a linked Excel worksheet instead of a Word table). The Excel worksheet to be linked to the memo is in an Excel workbook called Support_WD_8_JobPlacementStudy_inExcel.xlsx, which also is located in the Data Files. Please contact your instructor for information about accessing the Data Files. The following steps open a Word document, start Excel, and open an Excel workbook. (Do not exit Word or close the open Word document during these steps.)

1. In Word, open the file called SC_WD_8-2.docx located in the Data Files.
2. If necessary, change the zoom to 100% so that the content of the memo is displayed in the document window (Figure 8–32).
3. Change the zoom back to page width.
4. Start Excel and open a blank workbook.
5. In Excel, open the file called Support_WD_8_JobPlacementStudy_inExcel.xlsx in the Data Files (shown in Figure 8–34).

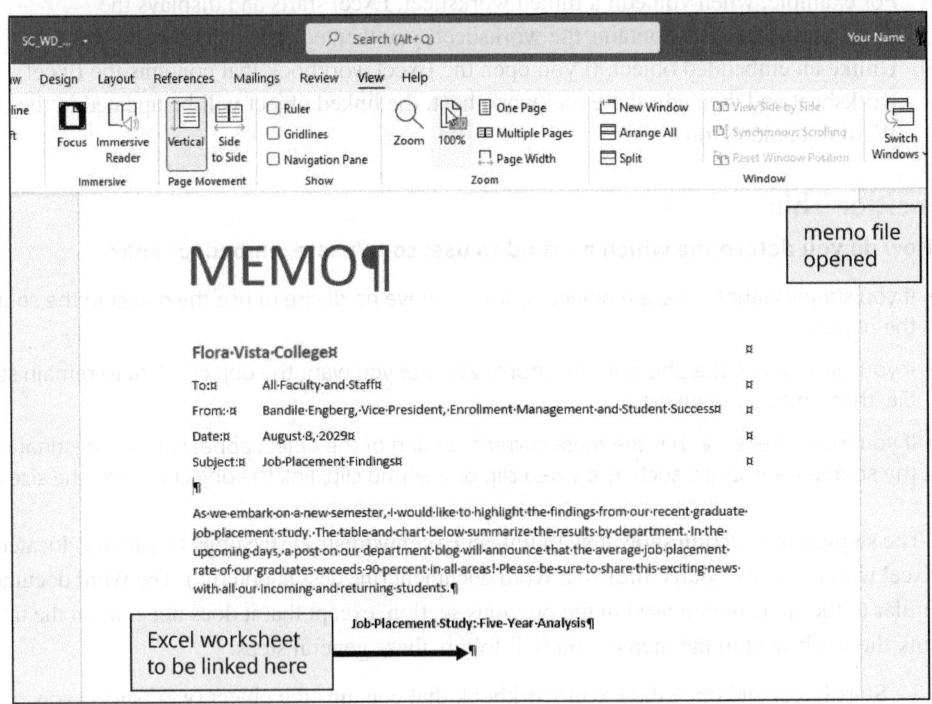

Figure 8–32

BTW
Opening Word Documents with Links
When you open a document that contains a linked object, Word attempts to locate the source file associated with the link. If Word cannot find the source file, open Backstage view, display the Info screen, then click 'Edit Links to Files' in the Related Documents area at the bottom of the right pane to display the Links dialog box. Next, select the appropriate source file in the list (Links dialog box), click the Change Source button, locate the source file, and then click OK.

Excel Basics

The Excel window contains a rectangular grid that consists of columns and rows. A column letter above the grid identifies each column. A row number on the left side of the grid identifies each row. The intersection of each column and row is a cell. A cell is referred to by its unique address, which is the coordinates of the intersection of a column and a row. To identify a cell, specify the column letter first, followed by the row number. For example, cell reference A1 refers to the cell located at the intersection of column A and row 1 (Figure 8–33).

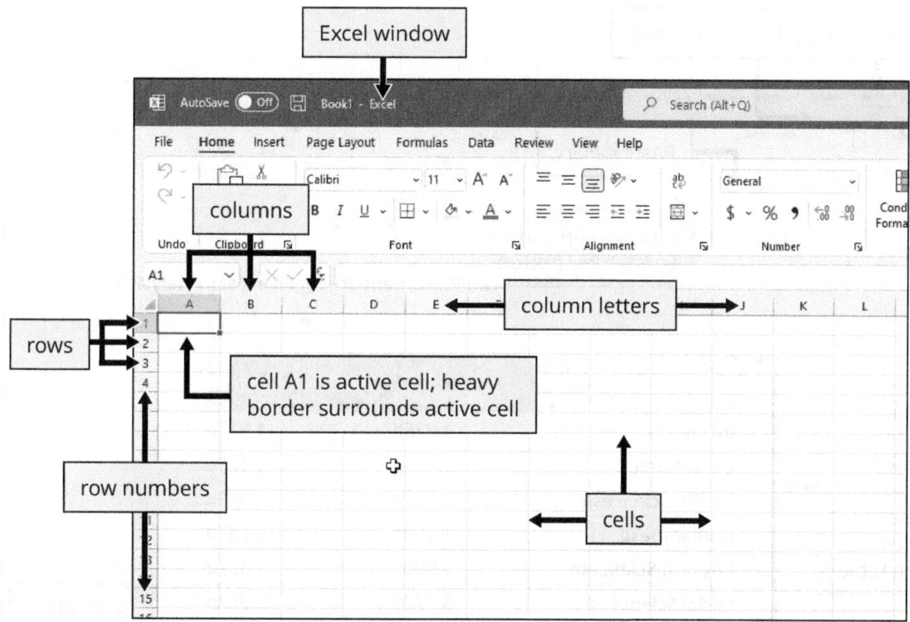

Figure 8–33

To Link an Excel Worksheet to a Word Document

The following steps link an Excel worksheet to a Word document. **Why?** You want to copy the Excel worksheet to the Clipboard and then link the Excel worksheet to the Word document.

1

- In the Excel window, drag through the cells in the range A1 through C7 to select them.
- In the Excel window, click the Copy button (Home tab | Clipboard group) to copy the selected cells to the Clipboard (Figure 8–34).

Q&A What if I click the Copy arrow by mistake?
Click Copy on the Copy menu.

What is the dotted line around the selected cells?
Excel surrounds copied cells with a moving marquee to help you visually identify the copied cells.

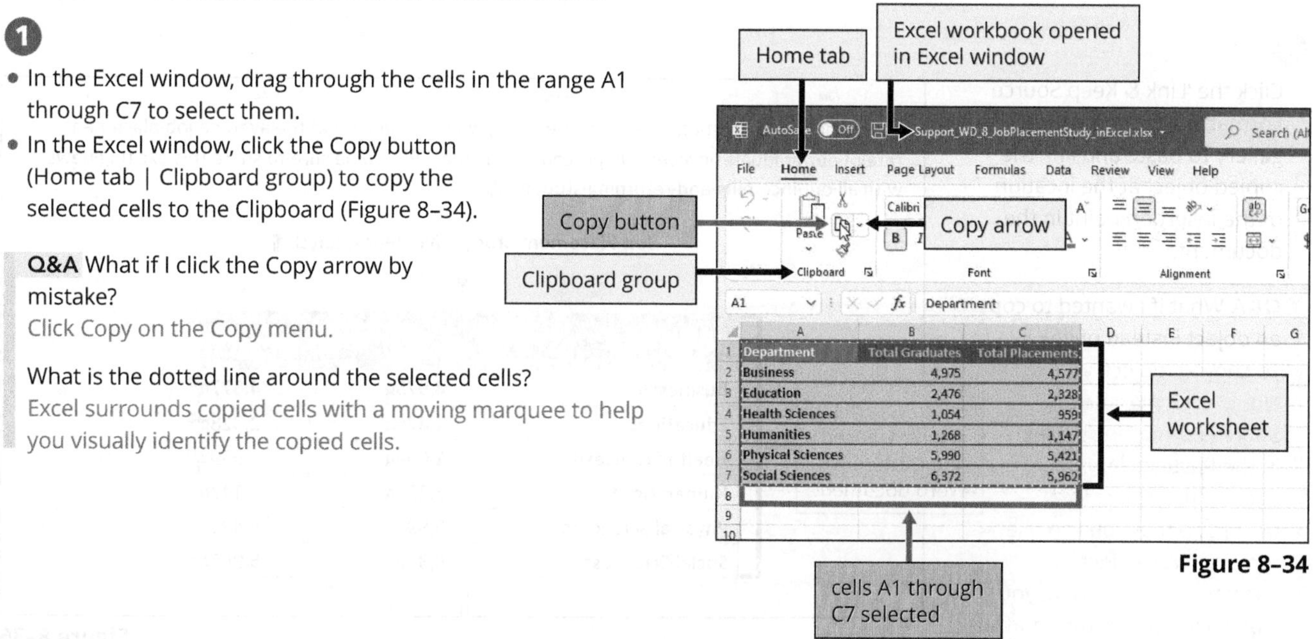

Figure 8–34

2

- Click the Word app button on the taskbar to switch to Word and display the open document in the Word window.
- If necessary, scroll to the end of the memo in the document window and then position the insertion point on the paragraph mark below the table title.
- In Word, display the Home tab and then click the Paste arrow (Home tab | Clipboard group) to display the Paste gallery.

Q&A What if I accidentally click the Paste button instead of the Paste arrow?
Click the Undo button (Home tab | Undo group) and then click the Paste arrow.

- Point to the 'Link & Keep Source Formatting' button in the Paste gallery to display a Live Preview of that paste option (Figure 8–35).
- **Experiment:** Point to the various buttons in the Paste gallery to display a Live Preview of each paste option.

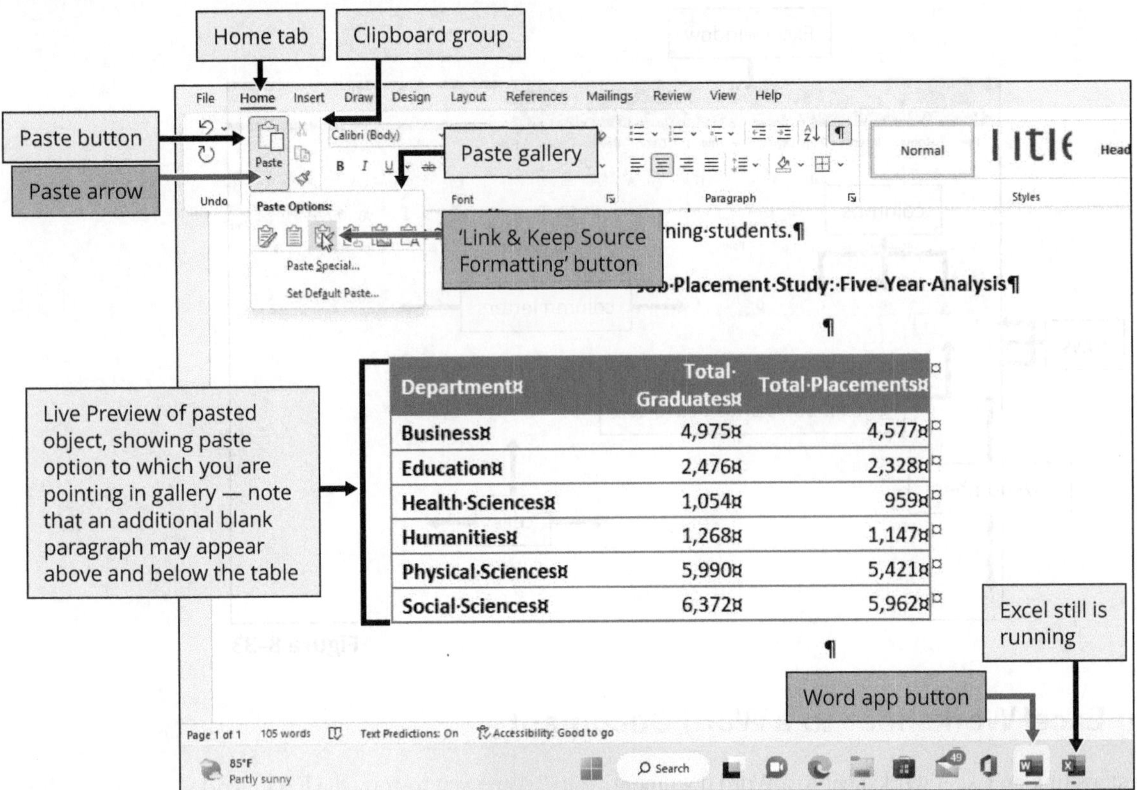

Figure 8–35

- Click the 'Link & Keep Source Formatting' button in the Paste gallery to paste and link the copied object at the location of the insertion point in the document.

Q&A What if I wanted to copy an object instead of link it?
To copy an object, you would click the 'Keep Source Formatting' button in the Paste gallery. To convert the object to a picture so that you can use tools on Word's Picture Format tab to format it, you would click the Picture button in the Paste gallery.

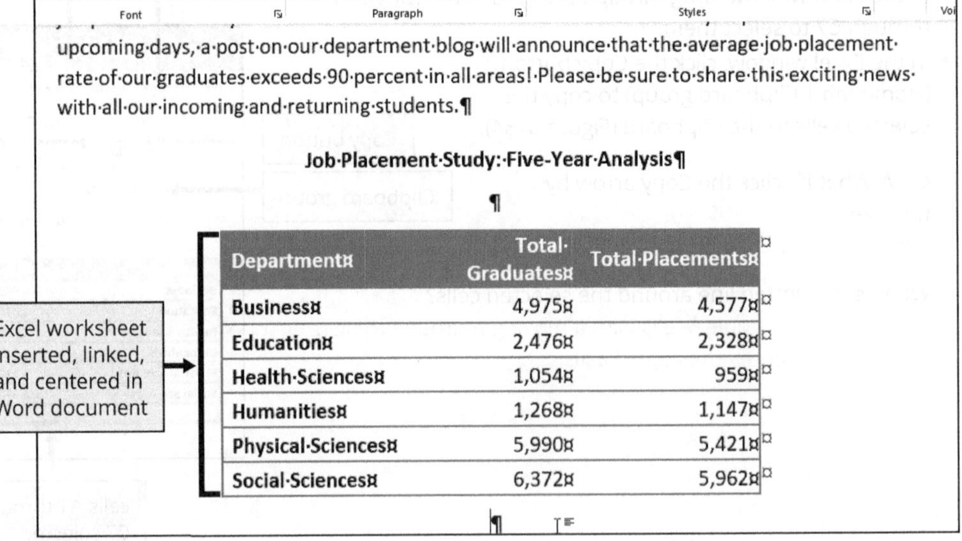

Figure 8–36

- Select and then center the linked Excel table using the same technique you use to select and center a Word table.
- Click outside the table to deselect it (Figure 8–36).

Q&A What if I wanted to delete the linked worksheet?
You would select the linked worksheet and then press DELETE.

Other Ways

1. Click Paste arrow (Home tab | Clipboard group), click Paste Special, click Paste link (Paste Special dialog box), click 'Microsoft Excel Worksheet Object' in As list, click OK
2. To link an entire source file, click Object button (Insert tab | Text group), click Create from File tab (Object dialog box), locate file, click 'Link to file' check box, click OK

To Embed an Excel Worksheet in a Word Document

If you wanted to embed an Excel worksheet in a Word document, instead of link it, you would perform the following steps.

1. Start Excel.
2. In Excel, select the worksheet cells to embed. Click the Copy button (Home tab | Clipboard group) to copy the selected cells to the Clipboard.
3. Switch to Word. In Word, click the Paste arrow (Home tab | Clipboard group) to display the Paste gallery and then click Paste Special in the Paste gallery to display the Paste Special dialog box.
4. Select the Paste option button (Paste Special dialog box), which indicates the object will be embedded.
5. Select 'Microsoft Excel Worksheet Object' as the type of object to embed.
6. Click OK (Paste Special dialog box) to embed the contents of the Clipboard in the Word document at the location of the insertion point.

To Edit a Linked Object

At a later time, you may find it necessary to change the data in the Excel worksheet. Any changes you make to the Excel worksheet while in Excel will be reflected in the Excel worksheet in the Word document because the objects are linked to the Word document. If you wanted to edit a linked object, such as an Excel worksheet, you would perform these steps.

1. In the Word document, right-click the linked Excel worksheet, point to 'Linked Worksheet Object' on the shortcut menu, and then click Edit Link on the Linked Worksheet Object submenu to start Excel and open the source file that contains the linked worksheet.
2. In Excel, make changes to the Excel worksheet.
3. Click the Save button on the Excel title bar to save the changes.
4. Exit Excel.
5. If necessary, redisplay the Word window.
6. If necessary, to update the worksheet with the edited Excel data, click the Excel worksheet in the Word document and then press F9, or right-click the linked object and then click Update Link on the shortcut menu to update the linked object with the revisions made to the source file.

BTW
Editing Embedded Objects
If you wanted to edit an embedded object in the Word document, you would double-click the object to display the source program's interface in the destination program. For example, double-clicking an embedded Excel worksheet in a Word document displays the Excel ribbon in the Word window. To redisplay the Word ribbon in the Word window, double-click outside of the embedded object.

To Break a Link

Why? You can convert a linked or embedded object to a Word object by breaking the link. That is, you break the connection between the source file and the destination file. When you break a linked object, such as an Excel worksheet, the linked object becomes a Word object, a Word table in this case. The following steps break the link to the Excel worksheet.

- Right-click the linked object (the linked Excel worksheet, in this case) to display a shortcut menu.
- Point to 'Linked Worksheet Object' on the shortcut menu to display the Linked Worksheet Object submenu (Figure 8-37).

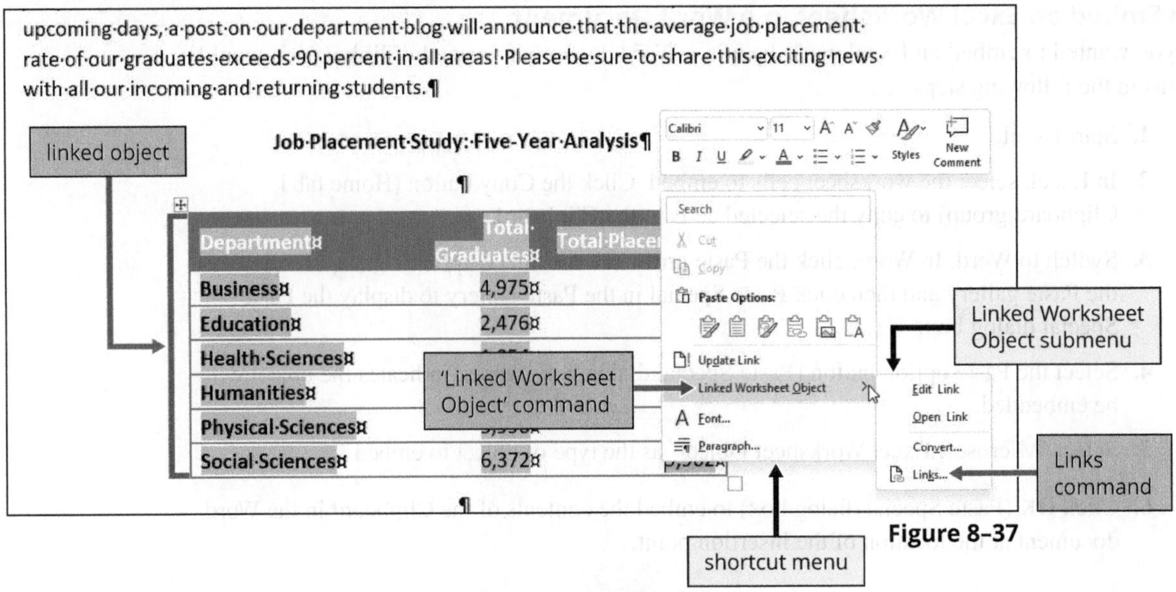

upcoming days, a post on our department blog will announce that the average job placement rate of our graduates exceeds 90 percent in all areas! Please be sure to share this exciting news with all our incoming and returning students.

linked object

Job Placement Study: Five-Year Analysis

Department	Total Graduates	Total Placed
Business	4,975	
Education	2,476	
Health Sciences		
Humanities		
Physical Sciences		
Social Sciences	6,372	

'Linked Worksheet Object' command

Linked Worksheet Object submenu

Links command

shortcut menu

Figure 8–37

2

- Click Links on the Linked Worksheet Object submenu to display the Links dialog box.
- If necessary, click the source file listed in the dialog box to select it (Links dialog box).
- Click the Break Link button, which displays a dialog box asking if you are sure you want to break the selected links (Figure 8–38).

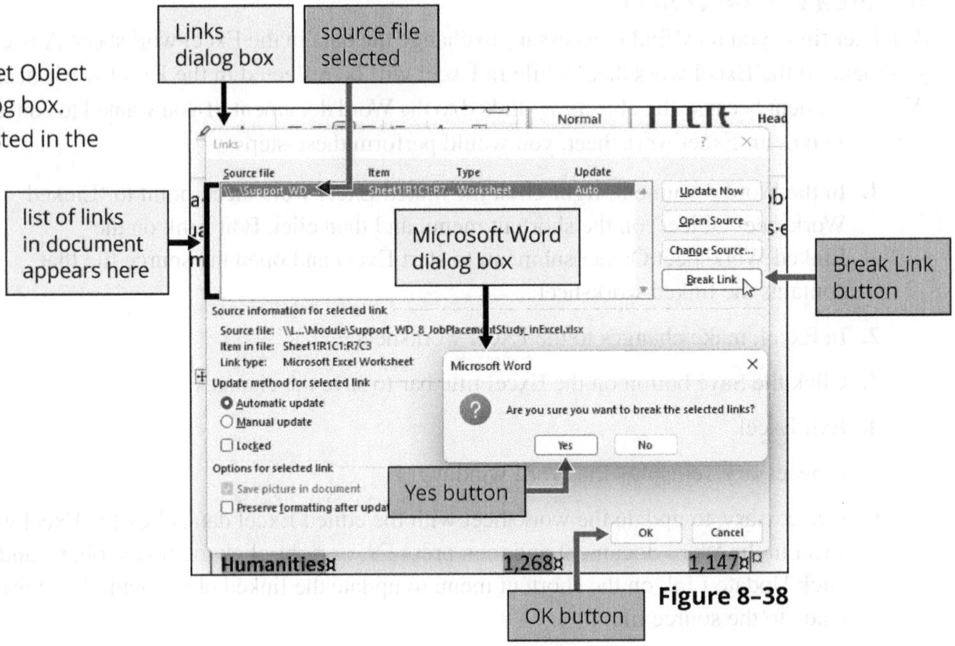

Links dialog box

source file selected

list of links in document appears here

Microsoft Word dialog box

Break Link button

Yes button

OK button

Figure 8–38

- Click Yes in the dialog box to remove the source file from the list (break the link).

Q&A How can I verify the link is broken?

Right-click the table in the Word document to display a shortcut menu. If the shortcut menu does not contain a 'Linked Worksheet Object' command, a link does not exist for the object. Or, when you double-click the table, Excel should not open an associated workbook.

- Close the Word document without saving it.
- Exit Excel without saving changes to the workbook.

Other Ways

1. Select link, press CTRL+SHIFT+F9

Consider This

Why would you break a link?

If you share a Word document that contains a linked object, such as an Excel worksheet, users will be asked by Word if they want to update the links when they open the Word document. If users are unfamiliar with links, they will not know how to answer the question. Further, if they do not have the source program, such as the Excel app, they may not be able to open the Word document. When sharing documents, it is recommended you convert links to a regular Word object; that is, break the link.

Charting a Word Table

Several Microsoft 365 apps, including Word, enable you to create charts from data. In the following pages, you will insert and format a chart of the Job Placement Study Word table using the chart contextual tabs in Word. You will follow these general steps to insert and then format the chart:

1. Create a chart of the table.
2. Remove a data series from the chart.
3. Apply a chart style to the chart.
4. Change the colors of the chart.
5. Add a chart element.
6. Edit a chart element.
7. Format chart elements.
8. Add an outline to the chart.

To Open and Save a Document

The next step is to open the Job Placement Findings Memo file that contains the final wording and the corrected table value for the Social Sciences department so that you can create a chart of the Word table. This file, called SC_WD_8-3.docx, is located in the Data Files. Please contact your instructor for information about accessing the Data Files. The following steps open a document and then save it with a new file name.

BTW
Touch Mode Differences
The Office and Windows interfaces may vary if you are using Touch mode. For this reason, you might notice that the function or appearance of your touch screen differs slightly from this module's presentation.

1 sam Navigate to the Data Files and then open the file called SC_WD_8-3.docx.

2 Save the memo on your hard drive, OneDrive, or other storage location using SC_WD_8_FloraVistaCollegeMemo_withTableandClusteredChart as the file name.

3 Change the zoom to 110%.

To Insert a Chart

The following steps insert a default chart and then copy the data to be charted from the Word table in the Word document to a chart spreadsheet. **Why?** To chart a table, you fill in or copy the data into a chart spreadsheet that automatically opens after you insert the chart.

- Position the insertion point on the centered paragraph mark below the table because the chart will be inserted at the location of the insertion point.
- Display the Insert tab.
- Click the Chart button (Insert tab | Illustrations group) to display the Insert Chart dialog box.
- Click Bar in the left pane (Insert Chart dialog box) to display the available types of bar charts in the right pane.
- **Experiment:** Click the various types of charts in the left pane and watch the subtypes appear in the right pane. When finished experimenting, click Bar in the left pane.

- If necessary, click Clustered Bar in the right pane to select the chart type (Figure 8–39).
- **Experiment:** Click the various types of bar charts in the right pane and watch the graphic change in the right pane. When finished experimenting, click Clustered Bar in the right pane.

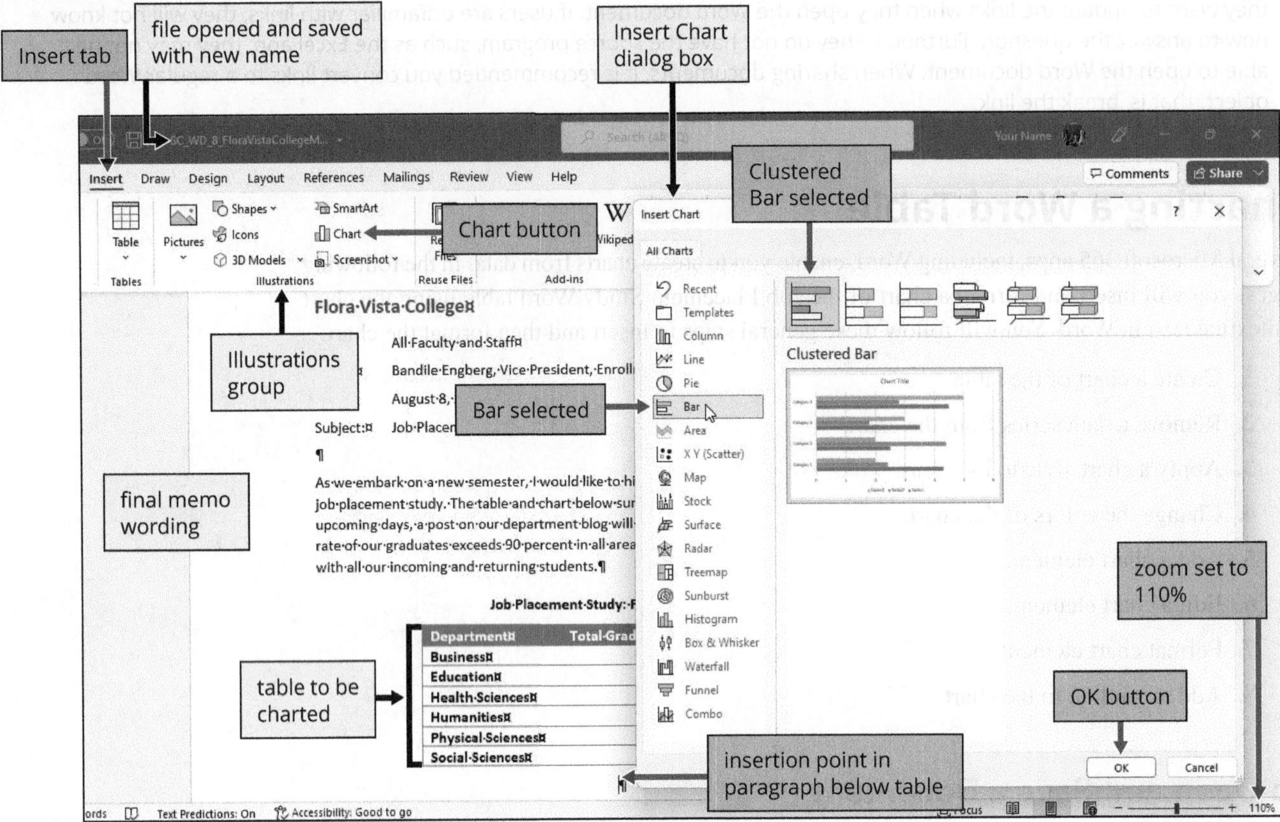

Figure 8–39

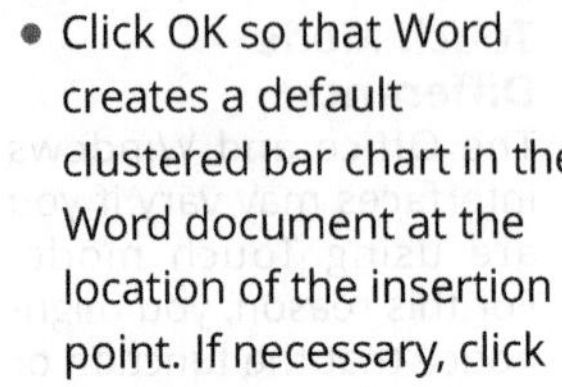

2

- Click OK so that Word creates a default clustered bar chart in the Word document at the location of the insertion point. If necessary, click the chart to select it (Figure 8–40).

Q&A What are the requirements for the format of a table that can be charted?

The chart spreadsheet window shows the layout for the selected chart type. In this case, the categories are in the rows and the series are in the columns. Notice the categories appear in the chart in reverse order.

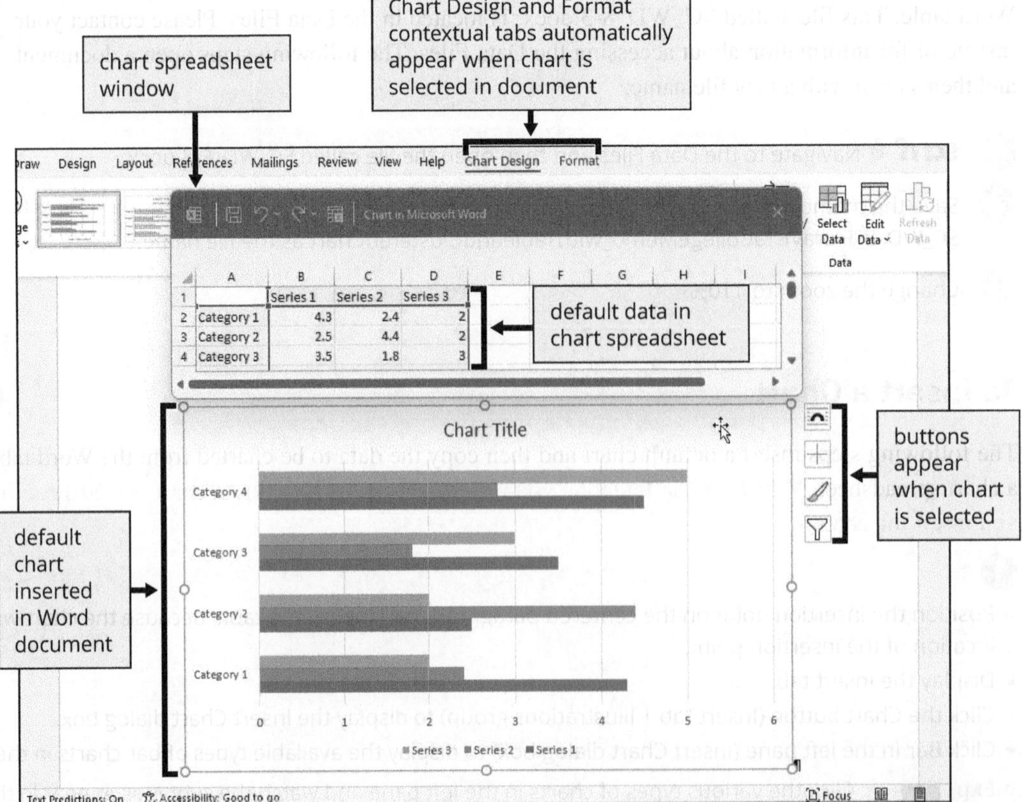

Figure 8–40

- In the Word document, if necessary, select the table to be charted. (If necessary, drag the chart spreadsheet window or scroll in the document window so that the table is visible.)
- Click the Copy button (Home tab | Clipboard group) to copy the selected table to the Clipboard (Figure 8–41).

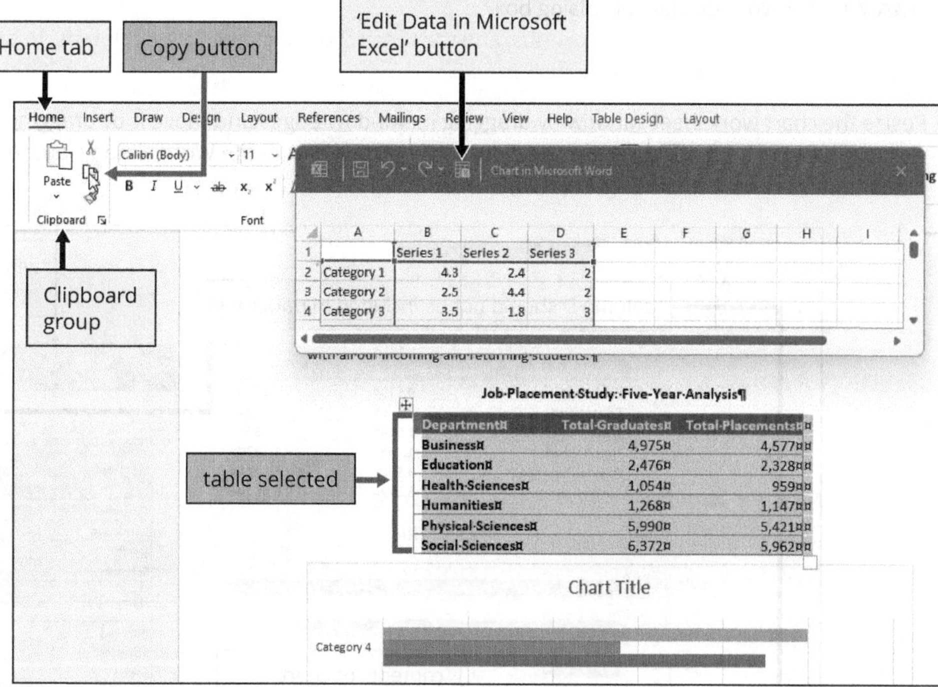

Figure 8–41

Q&A Instead of copying table data to the chart spreadsheet, could I type the data directly into the chart spreadsheet window?

Yes. If the chart spreadsheet window does not appear, click the Edit Data arrow (Chart Design tab | Data group) and then click Edit Data on the menu. You also can click the 'Edit Data in Microsoft Excel' button on the title bar of the chart spreadsheet window to use Excel to enter the data (if Excel is installed on your computer), or click the Edit Data arrow (Chart Design tab | Data group) and then click 'Edit Data in Excel' on the Edit Data menu. You edit (modify) existing data and add new data in rows and columns the same way you would in an Excel worksheet.

4

- In the chart spreadsheet window, if necessary, resize the window by dragging its window edges so that five rows are displayed and then click the Select All button (upper-left corner of worksheet) to select the entire worksheet.
- Right-click the selected worksheet to display a Mini toolbar or shortcut menu (Figure 8–42).

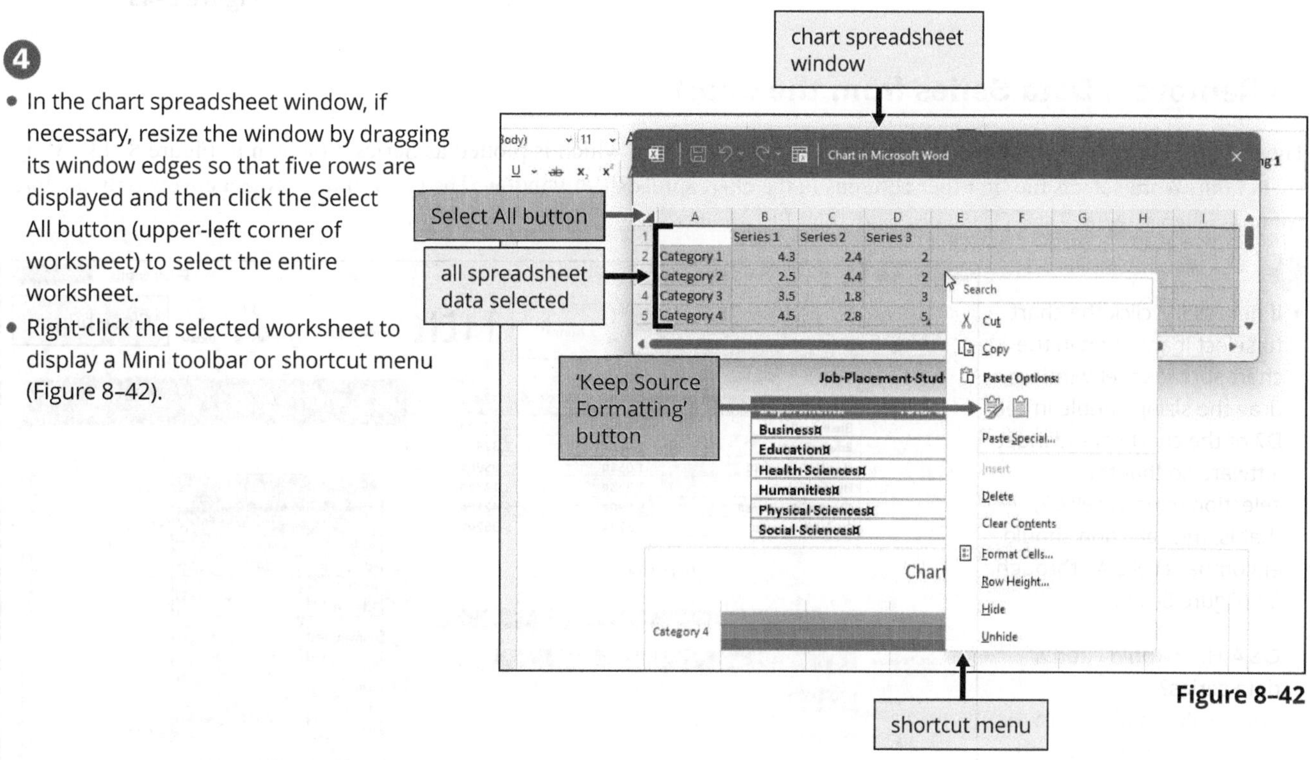

Figure 8–42

- Click the 'Keep Source Formatting' button on the shortcut menu to paste the contents of the Clipboard starting in the upper-left corner of the worksheet.
- When Word displays a dialog box indicating that the pasted contents are a different size from the selection, click OK.

Q&A Why did Word display this dialog box?
The source table contains three columns, and the target worksheet has four columns. In the next section, you will delete the fourth column from the chart spreadsheet.

- Resize the chart worksheet window by dragging its window edges and move it by dragging its title bar so that the worksheet window appears as shown in Figure 8–43. Notice that the chart in the Word window automatically changes to reflect the new data in the chart worksheet (Figure 8–43).

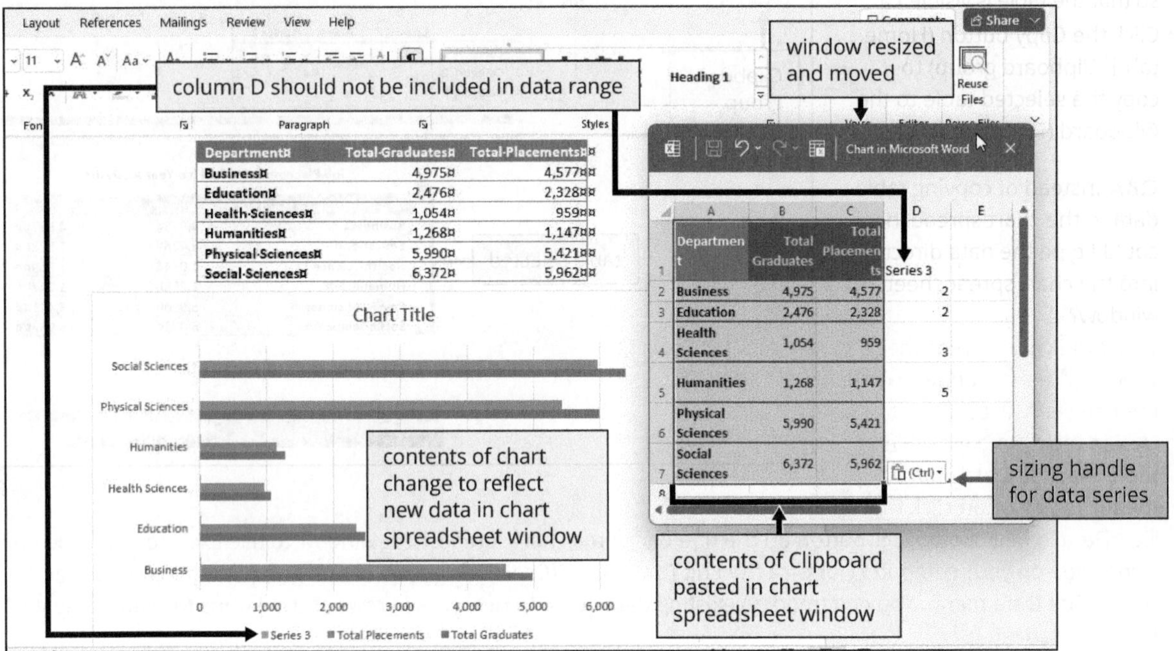

Figure 8–43

To Remove a Data Series from the Chart

The following steps remove the data in column D from the chart, which is plotted as Series 3 (shown in Figure 8–43). **Why?** By default, Word selects the first four columns in the chart spreadsheet window. The chart in this project covers only the three columns: Department, Total Graduates, and Total Placements.

1

- If necessary, click the chart to select it and then in the chart spreadsheet window, drag the sizing handle in cell D7 of the chart spreadsheet leftward so that the selection ends at cell C7; that is, the selection should encompass cells A1 through C7 (Figure 8–44).

Q&A How would I add a data series?
Add a column of data to the chart spreadsheet. Drag the sizing handle outward to include the series, or you could click the Select Data button (Chart Design tab | Data group), click the Add button (Select Data Source dialog box), click the Select Range button (Edit Series dialog box), drag through the data range in the worksheet, and then click OK.

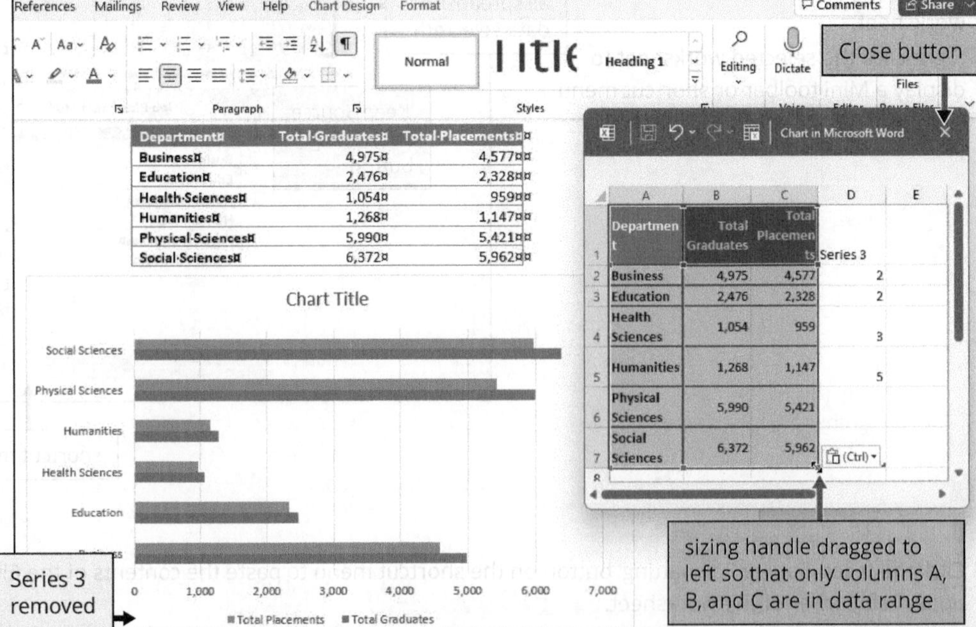

Figure 8–44

Q&A How would I add or remove data categories?
Follow the same steps to add or remove data series, except work with spreadsheet rows instead of columns.

2

- Close the chart spreadsheet window by clicking its Close button.

Q&A How would I copy an existing chart and paste it with source formatting?
To copy the chart, you would select it and then click the Copy button (Home tab | Clipboard group), or right-click the chart and then click Copy on the shortcut menu, or press CTRL+C. To paste the chart with source formatting, you would position the insertion point at the desired paste location, click the Paste arrow (Home tab | Clipboard group) or right-click the chart, and click the 'Keep Source Formatting' button on the Paste menu or shortcut menu.

Other Ways

1. Click Select Data button (Chart Design tab | Data group), click series to remove (Select Data Source dialog box), click Remove button, click OK

To Apply a Chart Style

The next step is to apply a chart style to the chart. **Why?** Word provides a Chart Styles gallery, allowing you to change the chart's format to a more visually appealing style. The following steps apply a chart style to a chart.

1

- If necessary, click the chart to select it and scroll to display the entire chart in the document window.
- If necessary, display the Chart Design tab.
- Point to Style 5 in the Chart Styles gallery (Chart Design tab | Chart Styles group) to display a Live Preview of that style applied to the graphic in the document (Figure 8–45).
- **Experiment:** Point to various styles in the Chart Styles gallery and watch the style of the chart change in the document window.

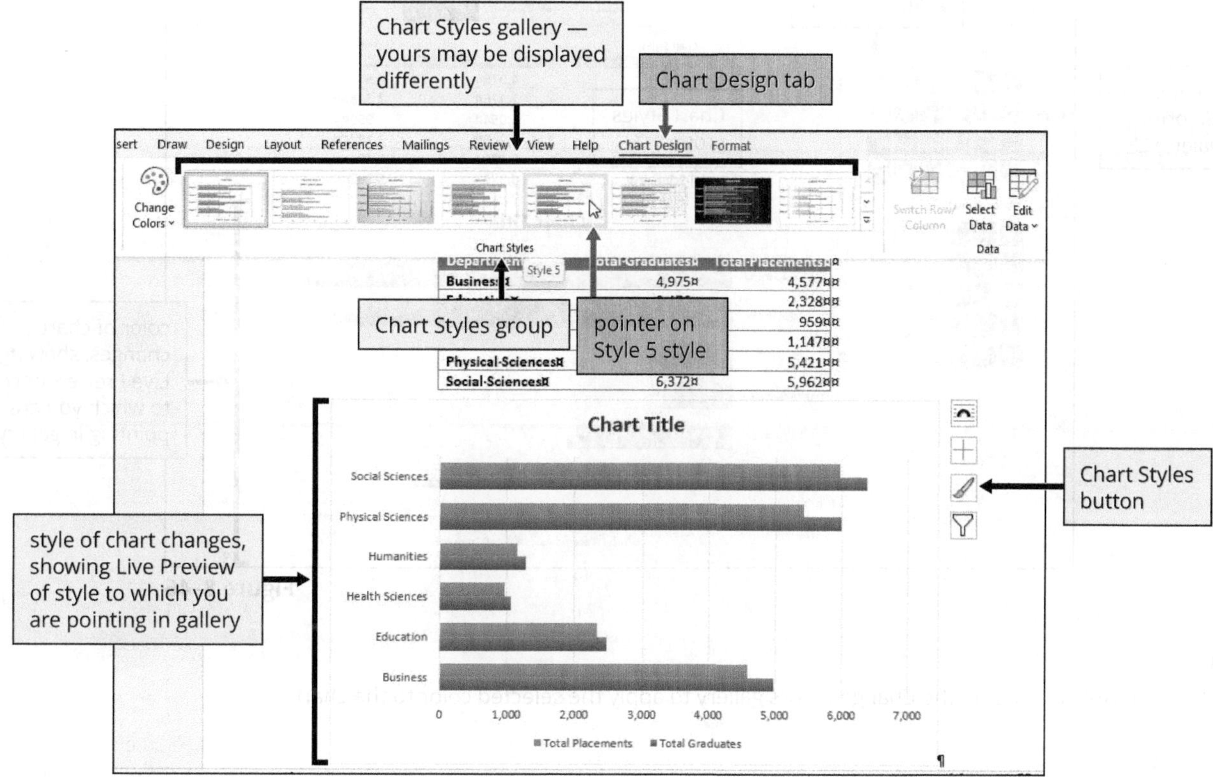

Figure 8–45

• Click Style 5 in the Chart Styles gallery (Chart Design tab | Chart Styles group) to apply the selected style to the chart.

Other Ways

1. Click Chart Styles button attached to chart, click Style tab, click desired style

To Change Colors of a Chart

The following steps change the colors of the chart. **Why?** Word provides a predefined variety of colors for charts. You select one that best matches the colors already used in the letter.

• With the chart selected, click the Change Colors button (Chart Design tab | Chart Styles group) to display the Change Colors gallery.

Q&A What if the chart is not selected?
Click the chart to select it.

• Point to 'Colorful Palette 2' in the Change Colors gallery to display a Live Preview of the selected color applied to the chart in the document (Figure 8–46).

◦ **Experiment:** Point to various palettes in the Change Colors gallery and watch the colors of the chart change in the document window.

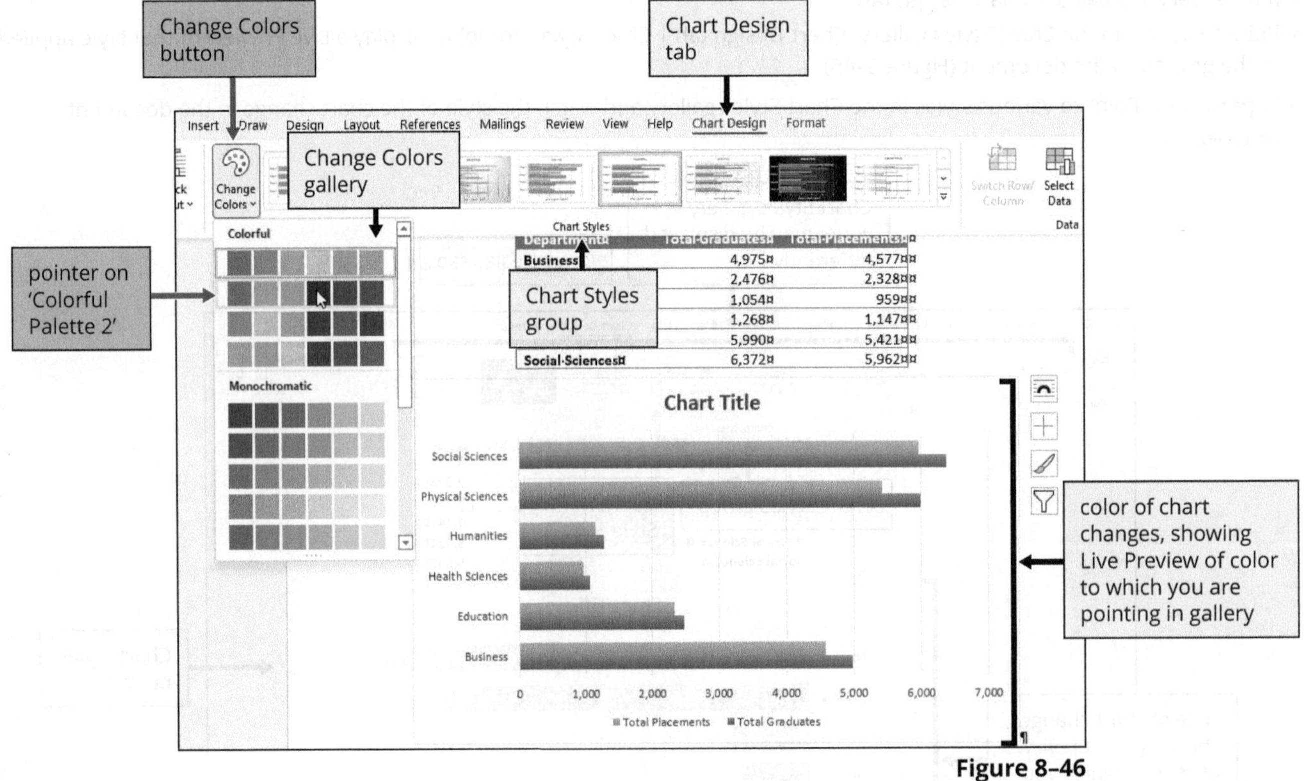

Figure 8–46

2

• Click 'Colorful Palette 2' in the Change Colors gallery to apply the selected color to the chart.

Other Ways

1. Click Chart Styles button attached to chart, click Color tab, click desired palette

To Add a Chart Element

The following steps add minor vertical gridlines to the chart. **Why?** You want to add more vertical lines to the chart so that it is easier to distinguish the total numbers associated with each bar length.

- With the chart selected, click the 'Add Chart Element' button (Chart Design tab | Chart Layouts group) to display the Add Chart Element gallery and then point to Gridlines to display the Gridlines submenu (Figure 8–47).
- **Experiment:** Point to various elements in the Add Chart Element gallery so that you can observe the other types of elements you can add to a chart. When finished, point to Gridlines.

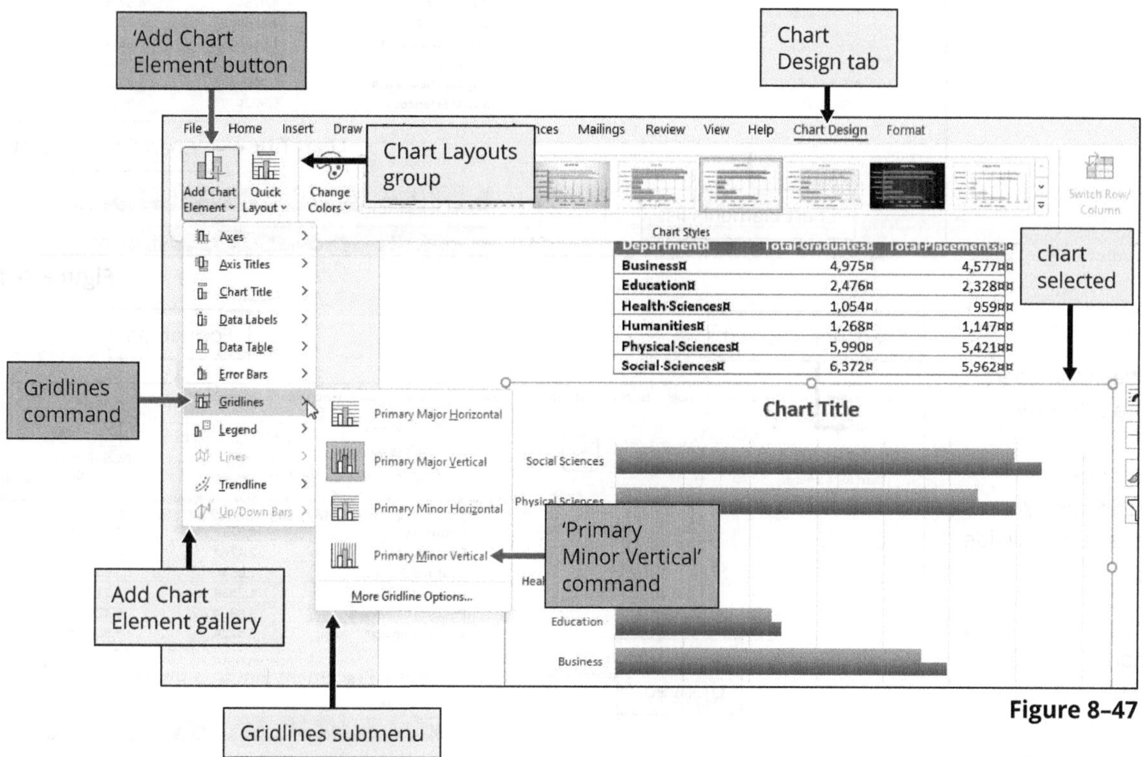

Figure 8–47

2

- Click 'Primary Minor Vertical' on the Gridline submenu to add vertical minor gridlines to the chart (Figure 8–48).

Q&A How would I add data labels to a chart?
Click the 'Add Chart Element' button (Chart Design tab | Chart Layouts group), point to Data Labels, and then click the desired location for the data labels.

How would I remove a chart element?
Select the chart element and then press DELETE.

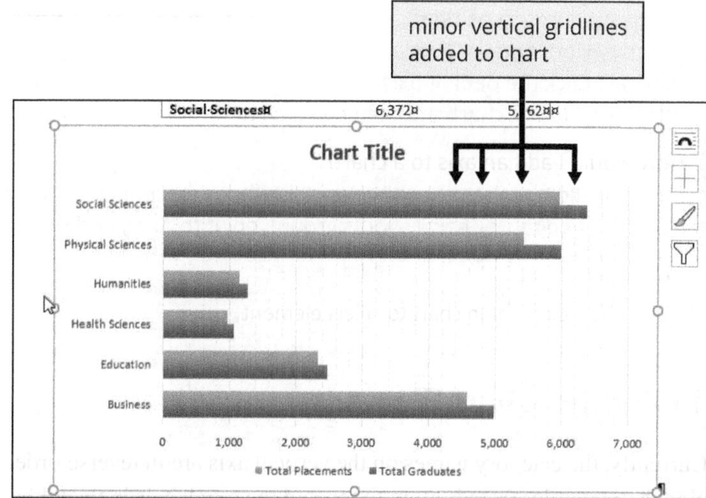

Figure 8–48

To Select a Chart Element and Edit It

The following steps change the chart title. **Why?** You want to change the title from the default to a more meaningful name.

- Display the Format tab.
- With the chart selected, click the Chart Elements arrow (Format tab | Current Selection group) to display the Chart Elements list (Figure 8–49).

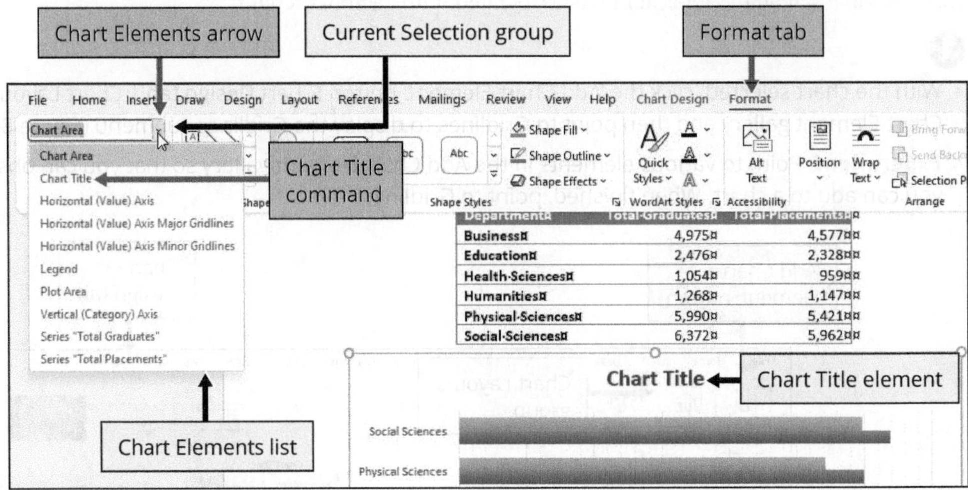

Figure 8–49

- Click Chart Title in the Chart Elements list to select the chart's title.
- Type **Graduate Job Placement Findings by Department** as the new title (Figure 8–50).

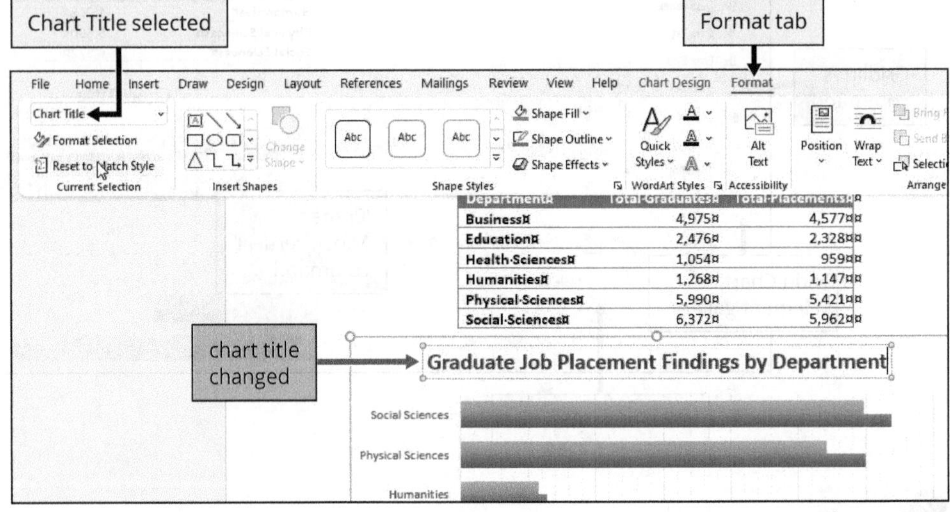

Figure 8–50

Q&A How would I add an axis title to the chart?

Click the 'Add Chart Element' button (Chart Design tab | Chart Layouts group), point to Axis Titles, and then click the desired axis to be titled (Primary Horizontal or Primary Vertical). Click the default axis title added to the chart and then edit it as desired.

How would I add an axis to a chart?

If a chart did not already contain an axis when you created it, you could add one by clicking the 'Add Chart Element' button (Chart Design tab | Chart Layouts group), point to Axes, and then click the desired axis.

Other Ways

1. Click chart element in chart to select element

To Format Chart Elements

Currently, the category names on the vertical axis are in reverse order of the row labels in the table; that is, category names are in alphabetical order from bottom to top and the row labels in the table are in alphabetical order from top to bottom. The following steps format axis elements. **Why?** You want the categories to be displayed in the same order as the table, the maximum value on the horizontal axis to be 6,000 instead of 7,000, and the legend to appear at the top of the chart instead of the bottom.

- If necessary, select the chart by clicking it.
- With the chart selected, if necessary, display the Format tab; click the Chart Elements arrow (Format tab | Current Selection group) to display the Chart Elements list and then click 'Vertical (Category) Axis' to select the vertical axis.

- Click the Chart Elements button attached to the right of the chart to display the Chart Elements gallery.
- Point to and then click the Axes arrow in the Chart Elements gallery to display the Axes fly-out menu (Figure 8–51).

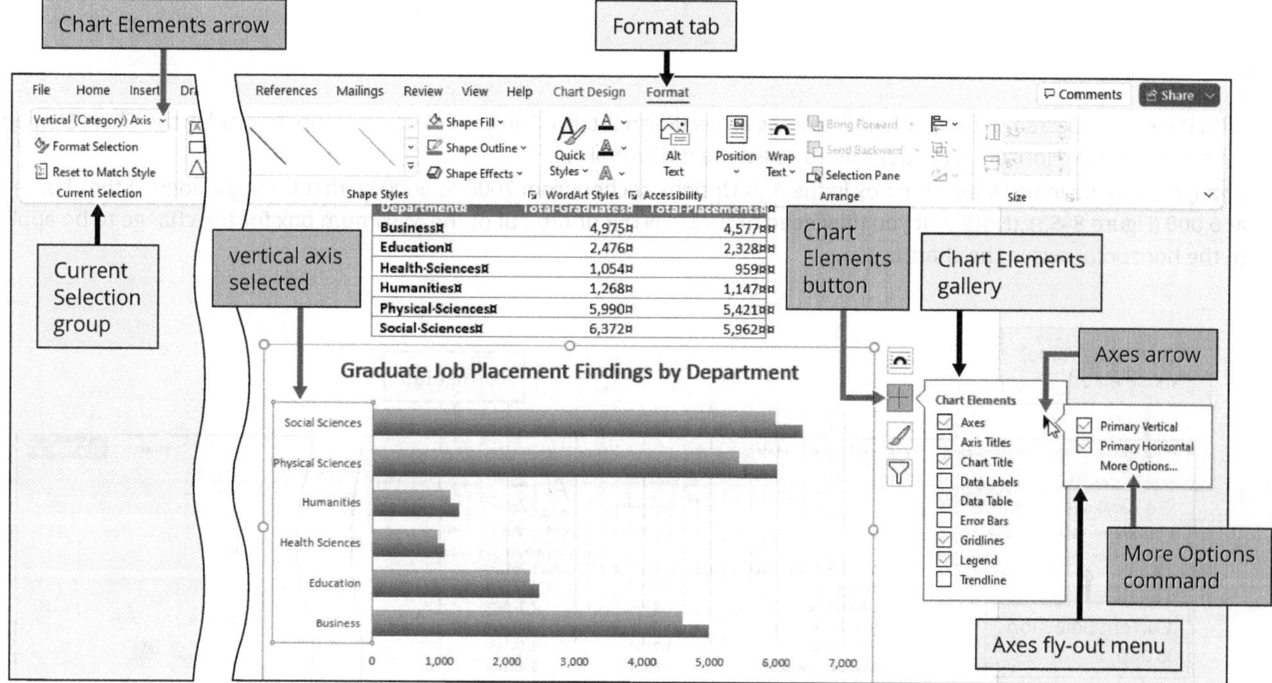

Figure 8–51

2

- Click More Options on the Axes fly-out menu to open the Format Axis pane.
- If necessary, click the Chart Elements arrow (Format tab | Current Selection group) to display the Chart Elements list and then click 'Vertical (Category) Axis' to select the vertical axis.
- If necessary, click Axis Options in the Format Axis pane to expand the section.
- Place a check mark in the 'Categories in reverse order' check box in the Format Axis pane so that the order of the categories in the chart matches the order of the categories in the table (Figure 8–52).

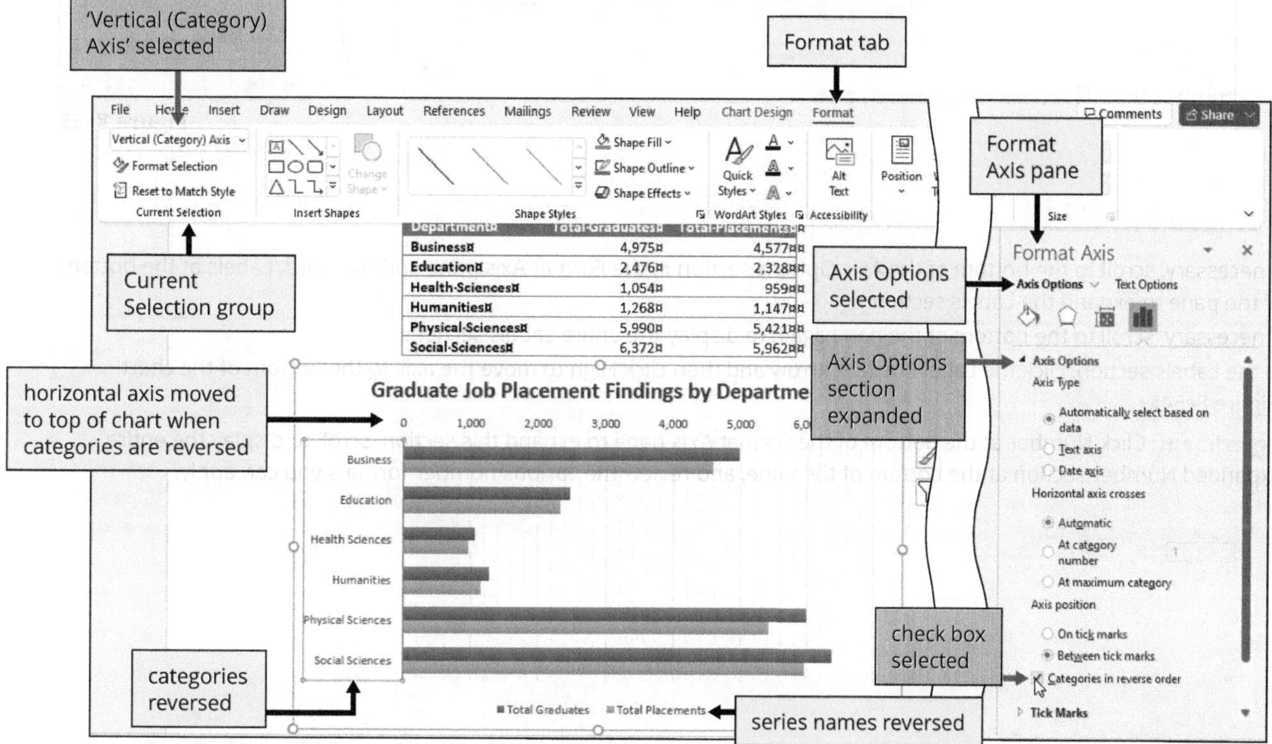

Figure 8–52

Q&A Why did the horizontal axis move from the bottom of the chart to the top?

When you reverse the categories, the horizontal axis automatically moves from the bottom of the chart to the top of the chart. Notice that the series names below the chart also are reversed.

3

- With the chart selected, click the Chart Elements arrow (Format tab | Current Selection group) to display the Chart Elements list and then click 'Horizontal (Value) Axis' to select the horizontal axis.
- Change the value in the Maximum box in the Axis Options section from 7000 to 6000 so that the right edge of the chart ends at 6,000 (Figure 8-53). (Note that you may need to press ENTER or tab out of the Maximum box for the change to be applied to the horizontal axis in the chart.)

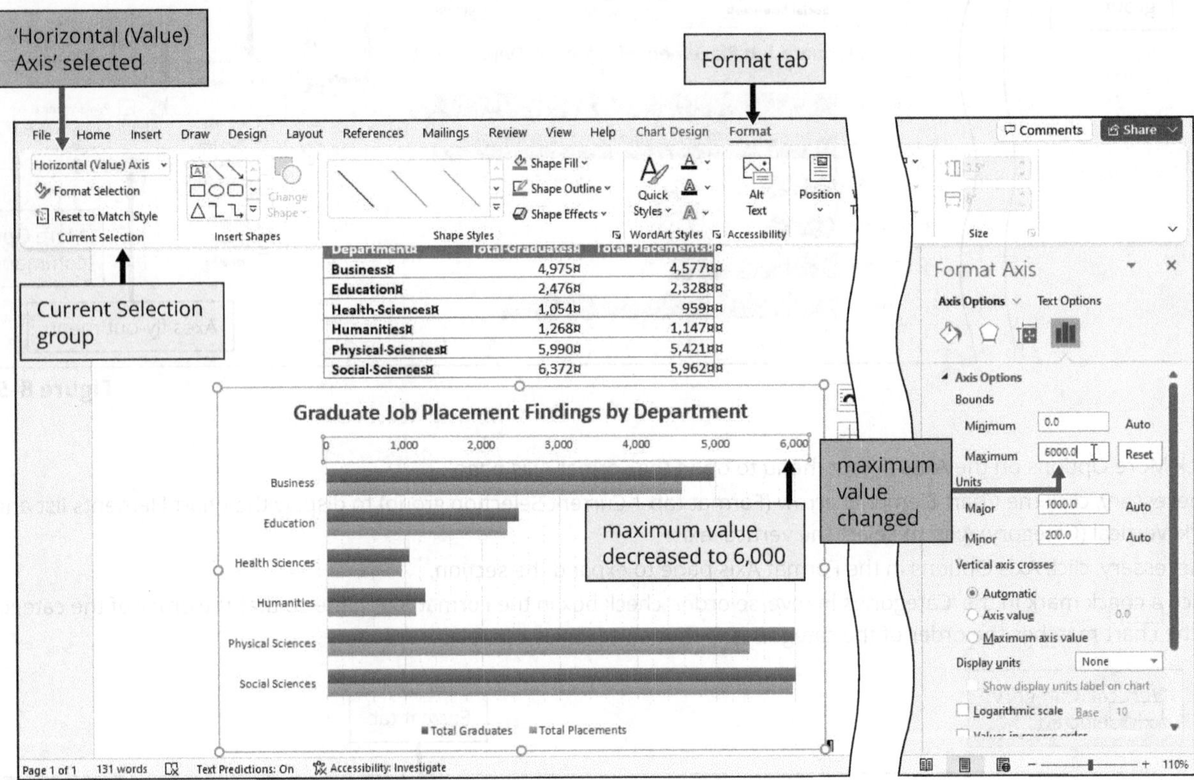

Figure 8-53

4

- If necessary, scroll to the bottom of the Axis Options section in the Format Axis pane and then click Labels at the bottom of the pane to expand the Labels section.
- If necessary, scroll to the bottom of the pane again to display the entire Labels section.
- In the Labels section, click the Label Position arrow and then click High to move the axis to the bottom of the chart (Figure 8-54).
- **Experiment:** Click Number at the bottom of the Format Axis pane to expand this section, scroll to display the entire expanded Number section at the bottom of the pane, and review the various number formats you can apply.

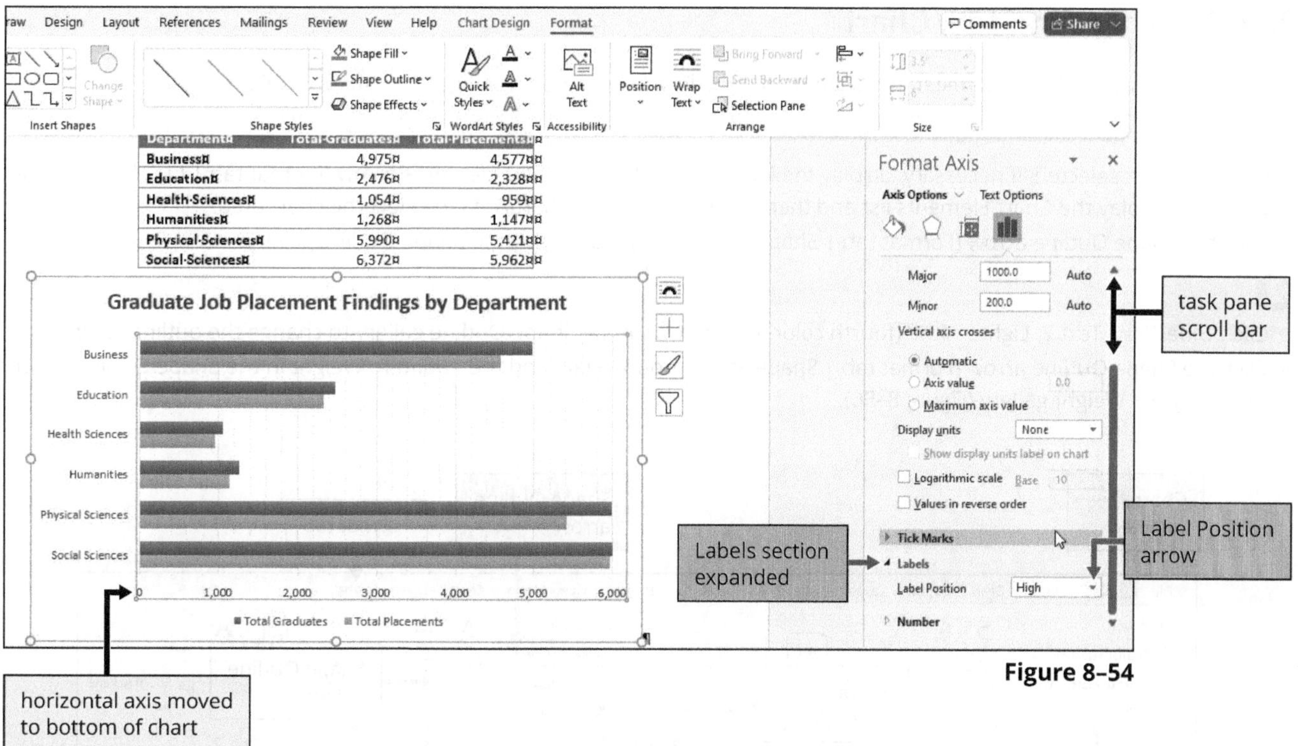

Figure 8-54

5

- With the chart selected, click the Chart Elements arrow (Format tab | Current Selection group) to display the Chart Elements list and then click Legend.

Q&A What happened to the Format Axis pane?
It now is the Format Legend pane. The pane title and options change, depending on the element you are using or formatting.

- If necessary, click Legend Options in the Format Legend pane to expand the section in the pane.
- Click Top to select the option button and move the legend to the top of the chart (Figure 8-55).

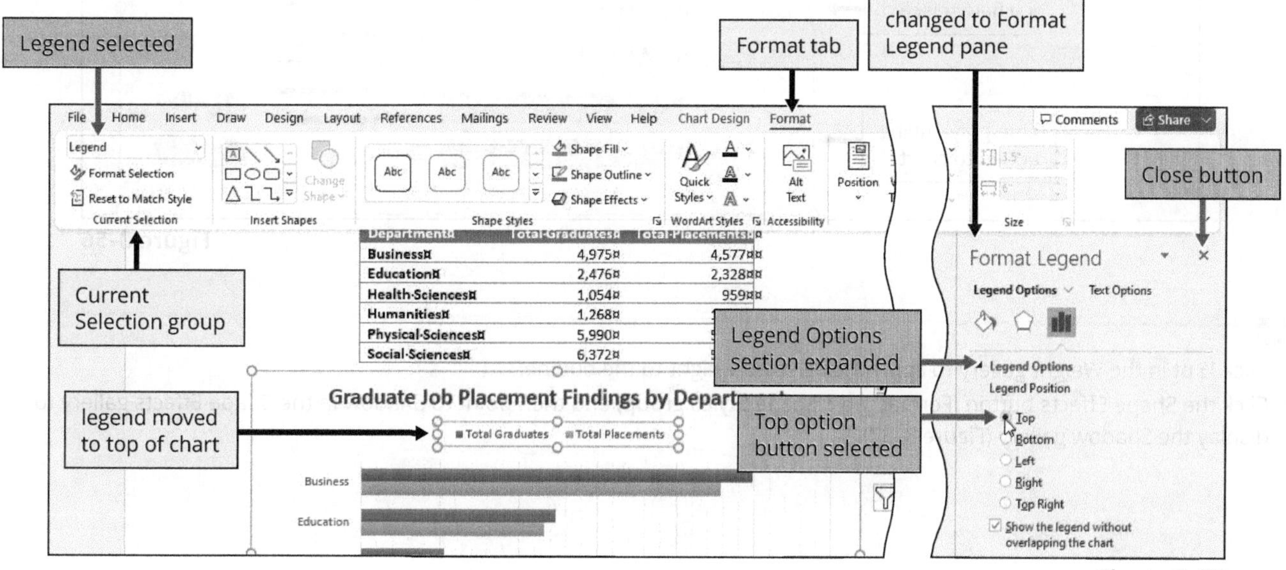

Figure 8-55

6

- Close the Format Legend pane by clicking its Close button.

Q&A How would I add a legend to a chart?
Click the 'Add Chart Element' button (Chart Design tab | Chart Layouts group), point to Legend, and then click the desired location for the legend.

To Add an Outline to a Chart

The following steps add an outline to the chart with a shadow. **Why?** You want a border surrounding the chart.

- With the chart selected, if necessary, display the Format tab; click the Chart Elements arrow (Format tab | Current Selection group) to display the Chart Elements list and then, if necessary, click Chart Area to select the chart area.
- Click the Shape Outline arrow (Format tab | Shape Styles group) to display the Shape Outline gallery.

- Click 'Blue-Gray, Text 2, Lighter 40%' (fourth color, fourth row) in the Shape Outline gallery to change the outline color.
- Click the Shape Outline arrow (Format tab | Shape Styles group) again and then point to Weight in the Shape Outline gallery to display the Weight gallery (Figure 8–56).

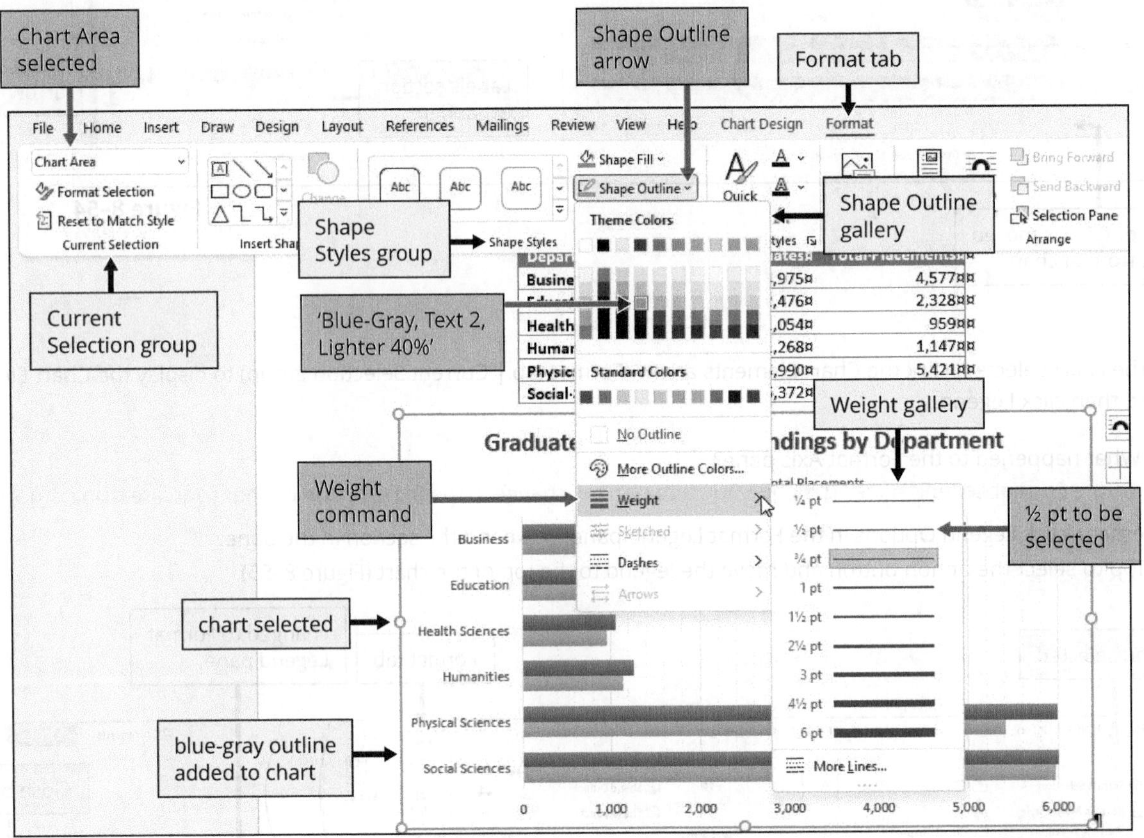

Figure 8–56

- Click ½ pt in the Weight gallery to apply the selected weight to the outline.
- Click the Shape Effects button (Format tab | Shape Styles group) and then point to Shadow in the Shape Effects gallery to display the Shadow gallery (Figure 8–57).

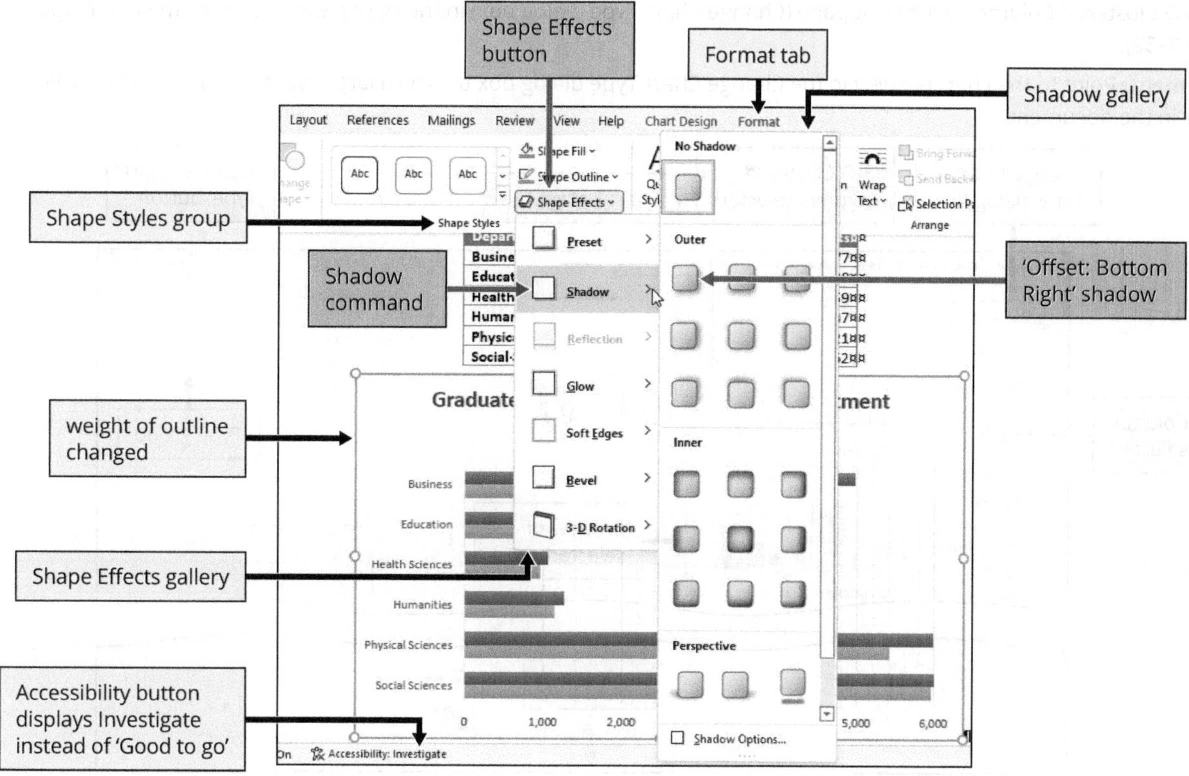

Figure 8–57

- Click 'Offset: Bottom Right' (first shadow in Outer area) in the Shadow gallery to apply the selected shadow to the outline.

To Use the Accessibility Checker and Save the Document Again

Recall that Word includes an Accessibility Checker that identifies potential accessibility issues and presents suggestions to make your documents more inclusive. Notice that instead of the phrase, Good to go, the Accessibility button on the status bar displays the word, Investigate (shown in Figure 8–57). The following steps use the Accessibility Checker.

1. Click the Accessibility button on the status bar to open the Accessibility pane.
2. Add the following description in the Alt Text pane for the chart: Chart comparing total graduates and total job placements by department.
3. If necessary, fix any other identified accessibility issues.
4. Close the Accessibility pane.
5. Save the modified memo in the same storage location using the same file name.

To Change a Chart Type

The following steps change the chart type. **Why?** After reviewing the document, you would like to observe how the chart appears as a 3-D clustered bar chart.

- Display the Chart Design tab.
- Click the 'Change Chart Type' button (Chart Design tab | Type group) to display the Change Chart Type dialog box.
- Click Column in the left pane to change the chart to a column chart.

- Click '3-D Clustered Column' in the right pane (Change Chart Type dialog box) in the right pane to change the chart type (Figure 8–58).
- **Experiment:** Point to the chart preview in the Change Chart Type dialog box to view a larger version how the chart will appear in the document.

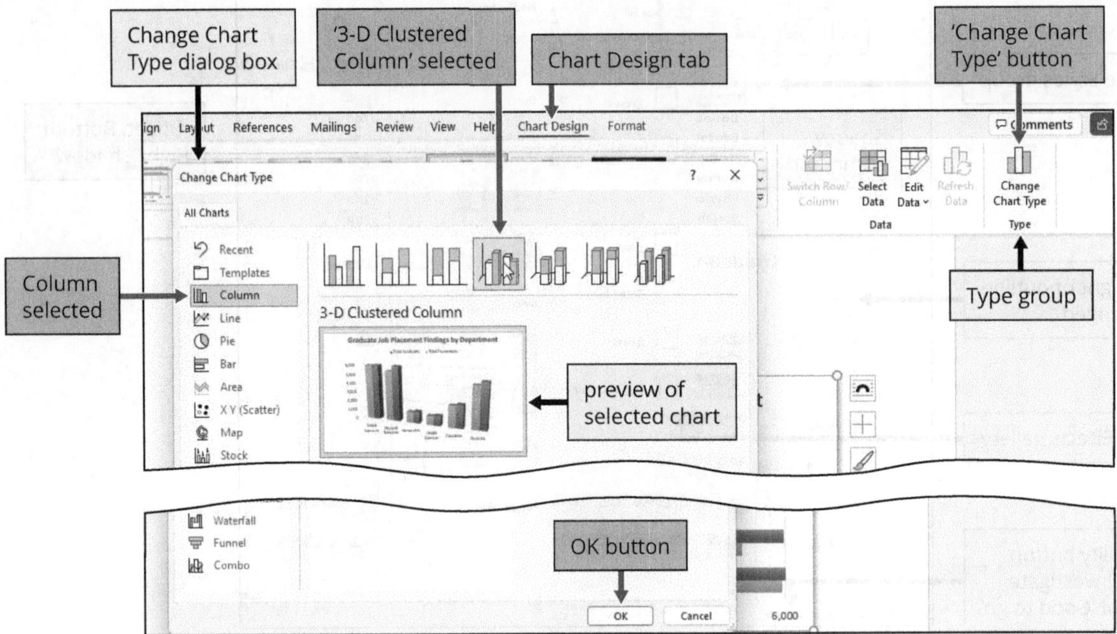

Figure 8–58

2

- Click OK to change the chart type.
- Click outside the chart to deselect it (Figure 8–59).
- **sam** Save the revised memo on your hard drive, OneDrive, or other storage location using the file name, SC_WD_8_FloraVistaCollegeMemo_withTableand3-DColumnChart.

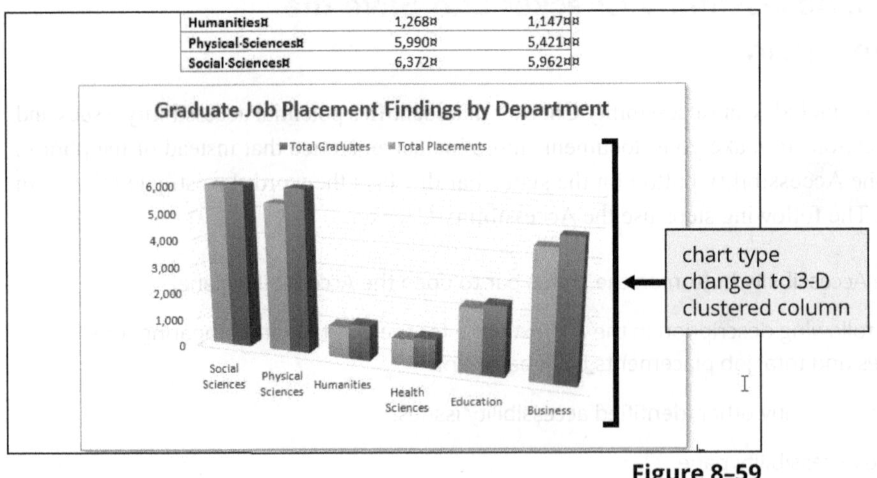

Figure 8–59

BTW

Conserving Ink and Toner

If you want to conserve ink or toner, you can instruct Word to print draft quality documents by clicking File on the ribbon to open Backstage view, clicking Options in Backstage view to display the Word Options dialog box, clicking Advanced in the left pane (Word Options dialog box), scrolling to the Print area in the right pane, placing a check mark in the 'Use draft quality' check box, and then clicking OK. Then, use Backstage view to print the document as usual.

To Chart a Word Table Using Microsoft Graph

In previous versions of Word, you charted Word tables using an embedded program called Microsoft Graph, or simply Graph. When working with the chart, Graph has its own menus and commands because it is a program embedded in Word. Using Graph commands, you can modify the appearance of the chart after you create it. If you wanted to create a chart using the legacy Graph program, you would perform these steps.

1. Select the rows and columns or table to be charted.
2. Display the Insert tab.
3. Click the Object button (Insert tab | Text group) to display the Object dialog box.

4. If necessary, click the Create New tab (Object dialog box).
5. Scroll to and then select 'Microsoft Graph Chart' in the Object type list to specify the object being inserted.
6. Click OK to start the Microsoft Graph program, which creates a chart of the selected table or selected rows and columns.

To View and Scroll through Documents Side by Side

Word provides a way to display two documents side by side, each in a separate window. By default, the two documents scroll synchronously, that is, together. If necessary, you can turn off synchronous scrolling so that you can scroll through each document individually. The following steps display documents side by side. **Why?** You would like to observe how the document with the clustered chart appears alongside the document with the 3-D clustered column chart.

- Position the insertion point at the top of the document because you want to begin viewing side by side from the top of the documents.
- Open the file called SC_WD_8_FloraVistaCollegeMemo_withTableandClusteredChart.docx so that both documents are open in Word.
- Display the View tab (Figure 8–60).

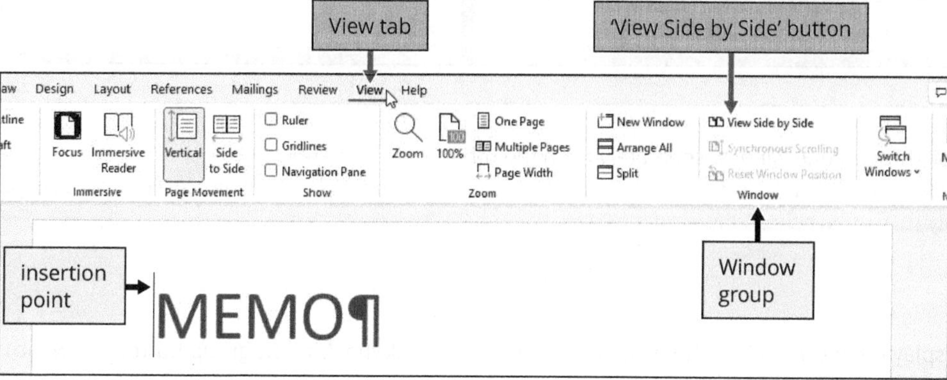

Figure 8–60

2

- Click the 'View Side by Side' button (View tab | Window group) to display each open window side by side (Figure 8–61).

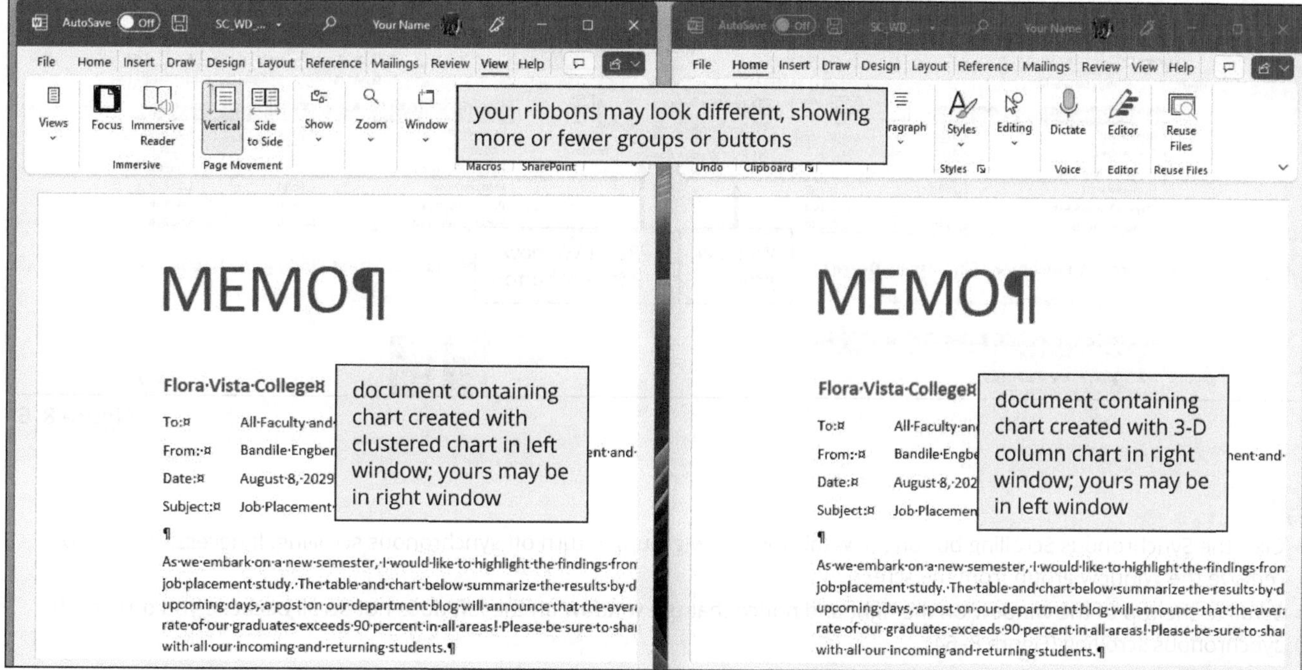

Figure 8–61

- If necessary, adjust the zoom to fit the memo contents in each window.
- Scroll to the bottom of one of the windows and notice how both windows (documents) scroll together (Figure 8–62).

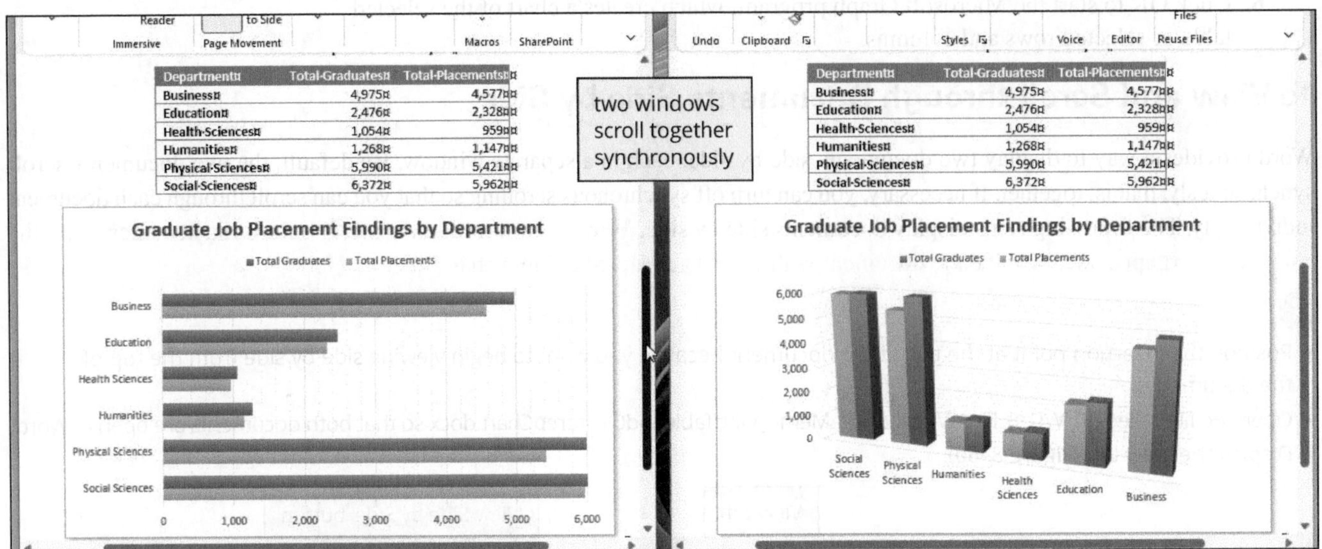

Figure 8–62

Q&A Can I scroll through one window separately from the other?
By default, synchronous scrolling is active when you display windows side by side. If you want to scroll separately through the windows, simply turn off synchronous scrolling.

- If necessary, display the View tab (in either window). If necessary, click the Window group button (View tab) to display the Window group (Figure 8–63).

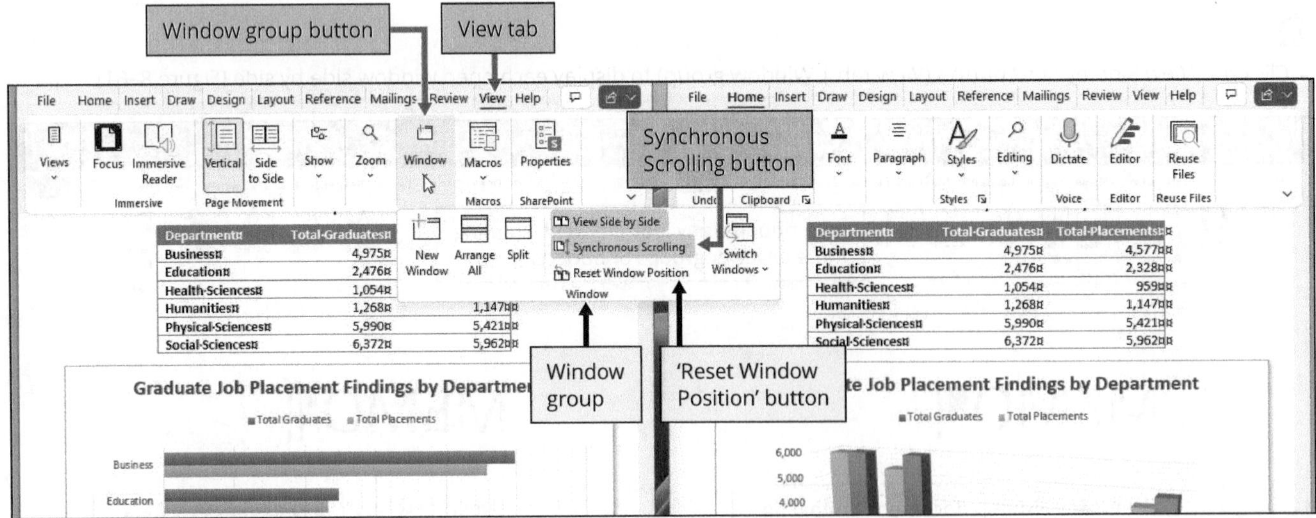

Figure 8–63

- Click the Synchronous Scrolling button (View tab | Window group) to turn off synchronous scrolling. If necessary, click to remove the Window group from the screen.
- Scroll to the top of the window on the right and notice that the window on the left does not scroll because you turned off synchronous scrolling (Figure 8–64).

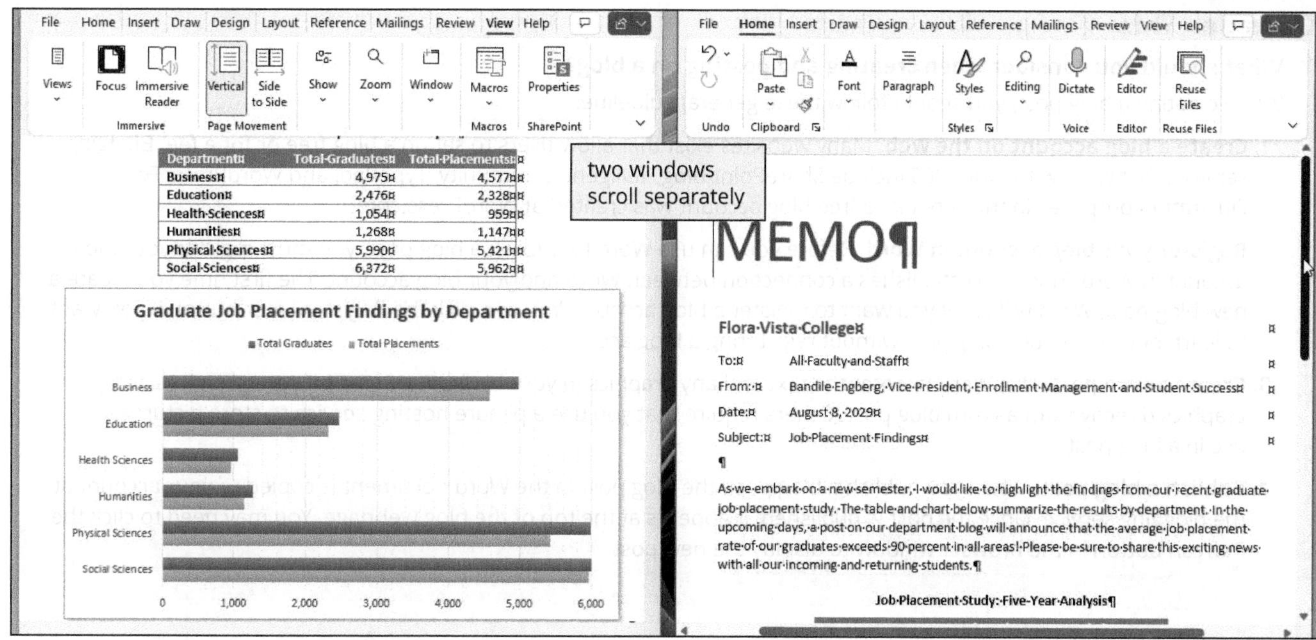

Figure 8–64

Q&A What is the purpose of the 'Reset Window Position' button?

It repositions the side-by-side windows so that each consumes the same amount of screen space.

- Display the View tab (in either window). If necessary, click the Window group button (View tab) to display the Window group and then click the 'View Side by Side' button (View tab | Window group) to turn off side-by-side viewing and display each window in a full screen.
- Close each open Word document, saving them if prompted.

Break Point: If you want to take a break, this is a good place to do so. You can exit Word now. To resume later, start Word and continue following the steps from this location forward.

Creating a Blog Post

A **blog**, short for **weblog**, is an informal website consisting of date- or time-stamped articles, or **posts**, in a diary or journal format, usually listed in reverse chronological order. Blogs reflect the interests, opinions, and personalities of the author, called the **blogger**, and sometimes of the website visitors as well.

Blogs have become an important means of worldwide communications. Businesses create blogs to communicate with employees, customers, and vendors. Teachers create blogs to collaborate with other teachers and students, and home users create blogs to share aspects of their personal life with family, friends, and others.

This section of the module creates a blog post and then publishes it to a registered blog account at WordPress, which is a blogging service on the web. The blog relays messages to faculty and staff at Flora Vista College. This specific blog post is a communication announcing upcoming faculty and staff appreciation events.

Consider This

What should you consider when creating and posting on a blog?

When creating a blog post, you should follow these general guidelines:

1. **Create a blog account on the web.** Many websites exist that allow users to set up a blog free or for a fee. Blogging services that work with Word 365 include SharePoint blog, Telligent Community, TypePad, and WordPress. For illustration purposes in this module, a free blog account was created at WordPress.com.
2. **Register your blog account in Word.** Before you can use Word to publish a blog post, you must register your blog account in Word. This step establishes a connection between Word and your blog account. The first time you create a new blog post, Word will ask if you want to register a blog account. You can click the Register Later button if you want to learn how to create a blog post without registering a blog account.
3. **Create a blog post.** Use Word to enter the text and any graphics in your blog post. Some blogging services accept graphics directly from a Word blog post. Others require that you use a picture hosting service to store pictures you use in a blog post.
4. **Publish a blog post.** When you publish a blog post, the blog post in the Word document is copied to your account at the blogging service. Once the post is published, it appears at the top of the blog webpage. You may need to click the Refresh button in the browser window to display the new post.

To Register a Blog Account

Once you set up a blog account with a blog provider, you must register it in Word so that you can publish your Word post on the blog account. If you wanted to register a blog account, with WordPress for example, you would perform the following steps.

1. Click the Manage Accounts button (Blog Post tab | Blog group) to display the Blog Accounts dialog box.
2. Click the New button (Blog Accounts dialog box) to display the New Blog Account dialog box.
3. Click the Blog arrow (New Blog Account dialog box) to display a list of blog providers and then select your provider in the list.
4. Click the Next button to display the New [Provider] Account dialog box (i.e., a New WordPress Account dialog box would appear if you selected WordPress as the provider).
5. In the Blog Post URL text box, replace the <Enter your blog URL here> text with the web address for your blog account. (Note that your dialog box may differ, depending on the provider you select.)

Q&A What is a URL?
A URL (Uniform Resource Locator), often called a web address, is the unique address for a webpage. For example, the web address for a WordPress blog account might be smith.wordpress.com; in that case, the complete blog post URL might read as http://smith.wordpress.com/xhlrpc.php in the text box.

6. In the Enter account information area, enter the user name and password you use to access your blog account.

Q&A Should I click the Remember Password check box?
If you do not select this check box, Word will prompt you for a password each time you publish to the blog account.

7. If your blog provider does not allow pictures to be stored, click the Picture Options button, select the correct option for storing your posted pictures, and then click OK (Picture Options dialog box).
8. Click OK to register the blog account.
9. When Word displays a dialog box indicating the account registration was successful, click OK.

To Create a Blank Document for a Blog Post

The following steps create a new blank Word document for a blog post. **Why?** Word provides a blog post template you can use to create a blank blog post document.

- Open Backstage view.
- Click New in Backstage view to display the New screen.
- Click the Blog post thumbnail to select the template and display it in a preview window (Figure 8–65).

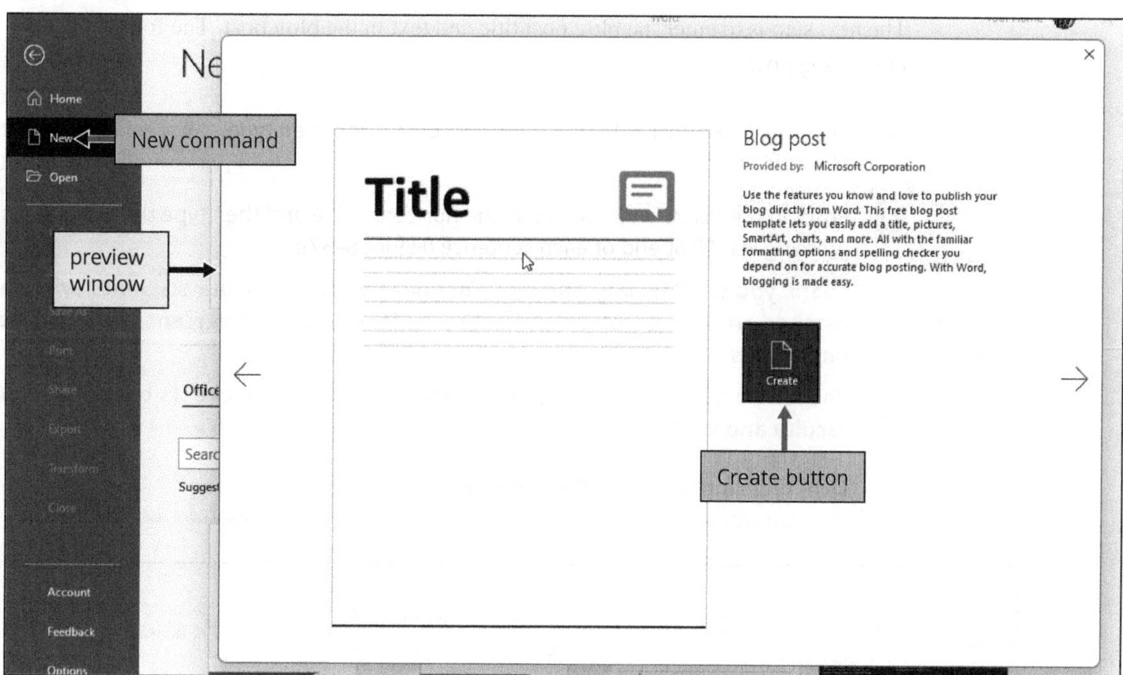

Figure 8–65

Q&A What should I do if the Blog post thumbnail is not listed on the New screen?
Click the 'Search for online templates' box, type **blog post**, and then press ENTER.

- Click the Create button in the preview window to create a new document based on the selected template (Figure 8–66). If necessary, adjust the zoom so that the text is readable on the screen.

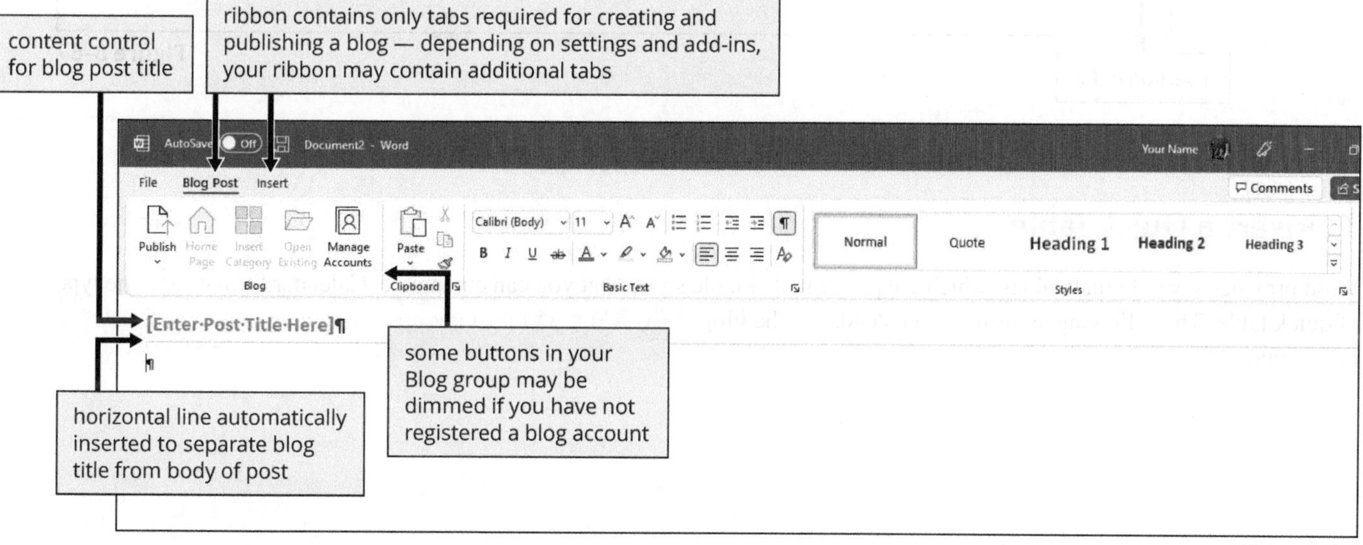

Figure 8–66

Q&A What if a Register a Blog Account dialog box appears?
Click the Register Later button to skip the registration process at this time. Or, if you have a blog account, you can click the Register Now button and follow the instructions to register your account.

Why did the ribbon change?
When creating a blog post, the ribbon in Word changes to display only the tabs required to create and publish a blog post.

To Enter Text

The next step is to enter the blog post title and text in the blog post. The following steps enter text in the blog post.

1. Click the 'Enter Post Title Here' content control and then type **Appreciation Events** as the blog title.

2. Position the insertion point below the horizontal line and then type these two lines of text, pressing ENTER at end of each sentence (Figure 8–67):
   Thank you to all faculty and staff for your dedication to our students, who have reached an average job placement rate of more than 90 percent in every department on campus!
   The following calendar identifies dates for appreciation events to honor all our faculty and staff.

Q&A Can I format text in the blog post?
Yes, you can use the Basic Text and other groups on the ribbon to format the post.

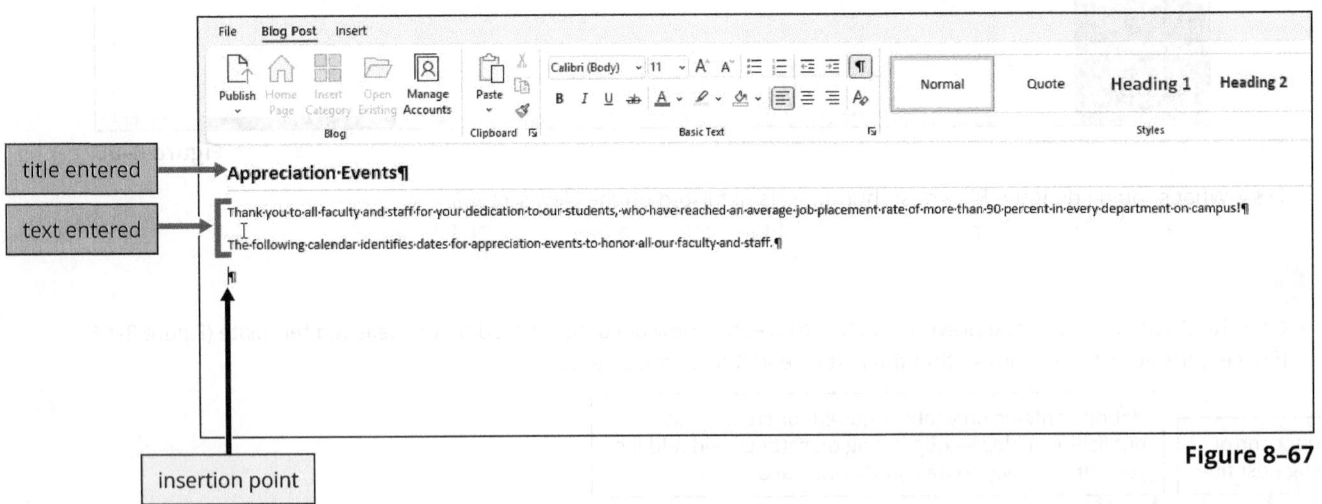

Figure 8–67

To Insert a Quick Table

Word provides several quick tables, which are preformatted table styles that you can customize. Calendar formats are one type of quick table. The following steps insert a calendar in the blog. **Why?** You will post the upcoming appreciate event dates in the calendar.

1

- Display the Insert tab.
- With the insertion point positioned as shown in Figure 8–67, click the Table button (Insert tab | Tables group) to display the Table gallery.
- Point to Quick Tables in the Table gallery to display the Quick Tables gallery (Figure 8–68).

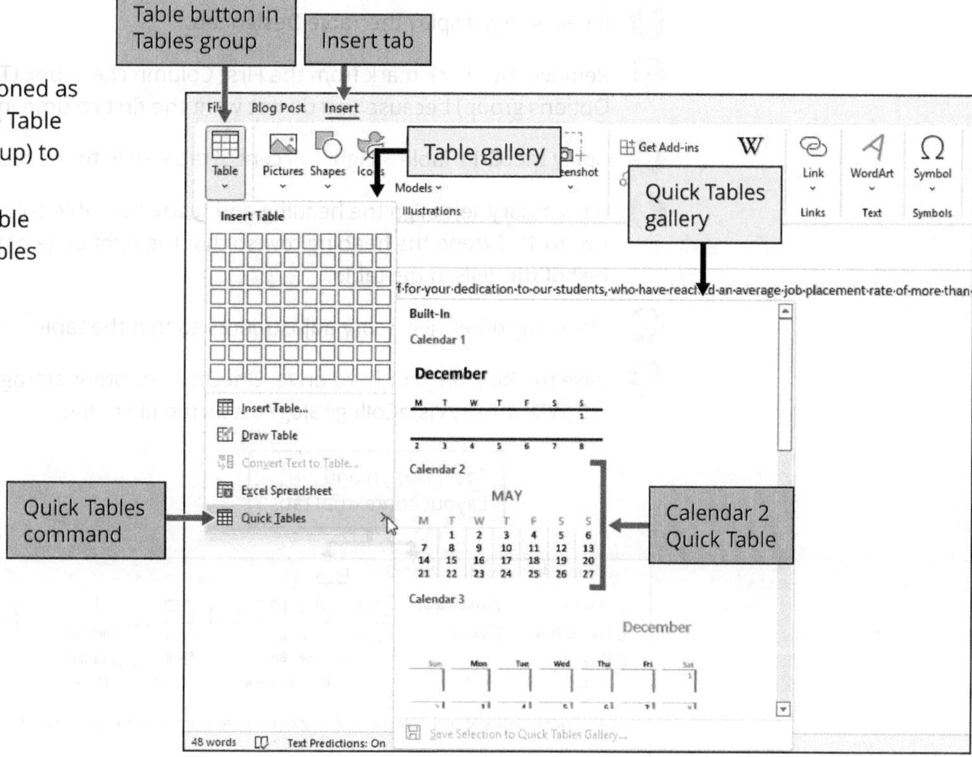

Figure 8–68

- Click Calendar 2 in the Quick Tables gallery to insert the selected Quick Table in the document at the location of the insertion point (Figure 8–69).

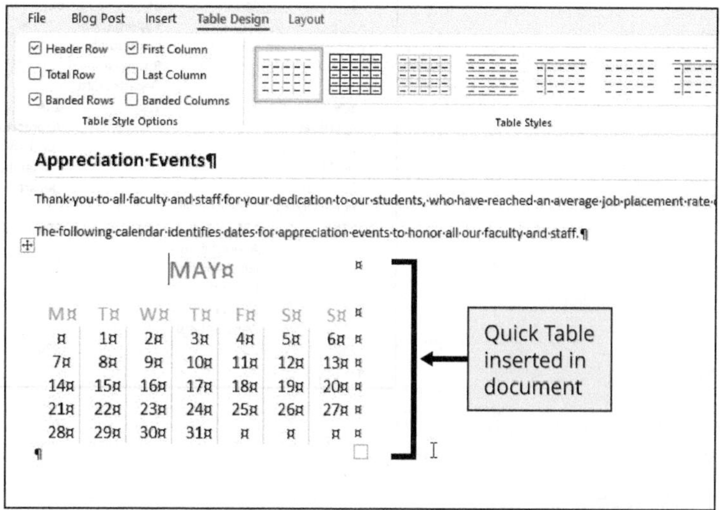

Figure 8–69

To Edit and Format a Table

The calendar in the blog post should show the month of September with a first day of the month starting on Saturday. The following steps edit the table and apply a quick style.

1. Change the month in the first cell of the table from May to September.
2. Edit the contents of the cells in the table so that the first day of the month starts on a Saturday and the 30 (the last day of the month) is on a Sunday.
3. Enter the text in the appropriate cells for September 5, 7, 10, 13, 18, and 21, as shown in Figure 8–70.

4. If necessary, display the Table Design tab.

5. Remove the check mark from the First Column check box (Table Design tab | Table Style Options group) because you do not want the first column in the table formatted differently.

6. Apply the 'Grid Table 1 Light - Accent 5' table style to the table.

7. If necessary, left-align the heading and resize the table column widths below the heading row to 1". Extend the heading row so that the right edge of the row boundary aligns with the rest of the cells in the table.

8. Make any other necessary adjustments so that the table appears as shown in Figure 8–70.

9. Save the blog on your hard drive, OneDrive, or other storage location using SC_WD_8_FloraVistaCollegeBlogPost as the file name.

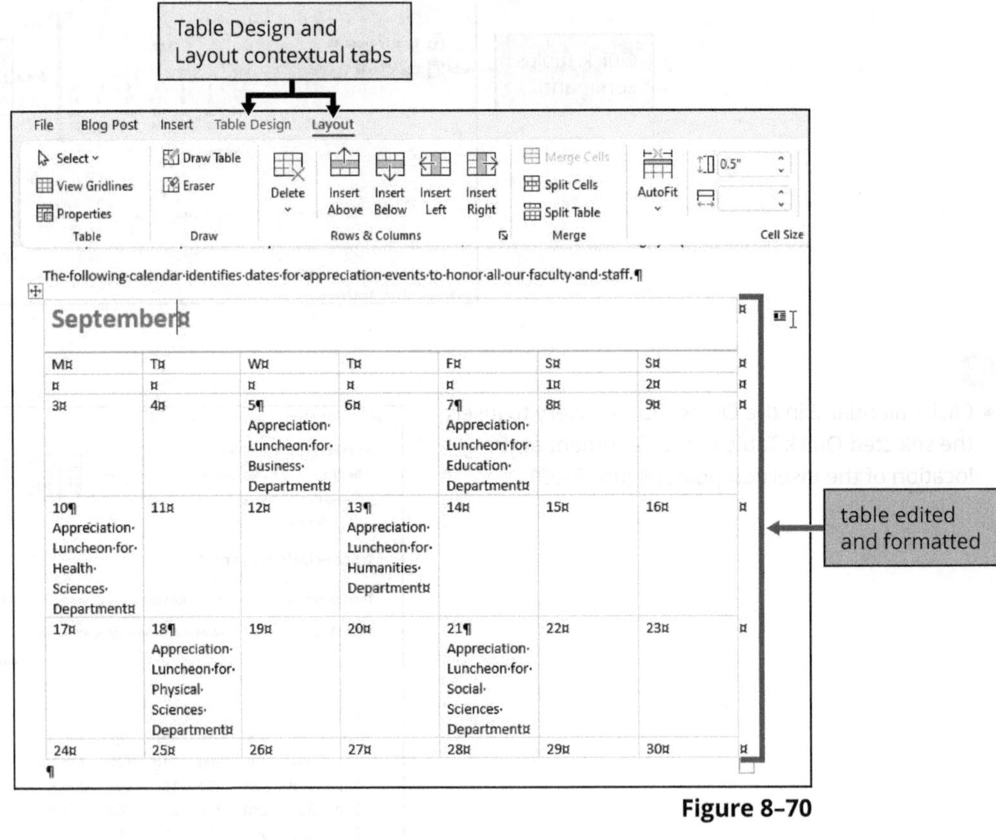

Figure 8–70

Note: If you have not registered a blog account, read the next series of steps without performing them.

To Publish a Blog Post

The following step publishes the blog post. **Why?** Publishing the blog post places the post at the top of the webpage associated with this blog account.

1

- Display the Blog Post tab.
- Click the Publish button (Blog Post tab | Blog group), which causes Word to display a brief message that it is contacting the blog provider and then display a message on the screen that the post was published (Figure 8–71).

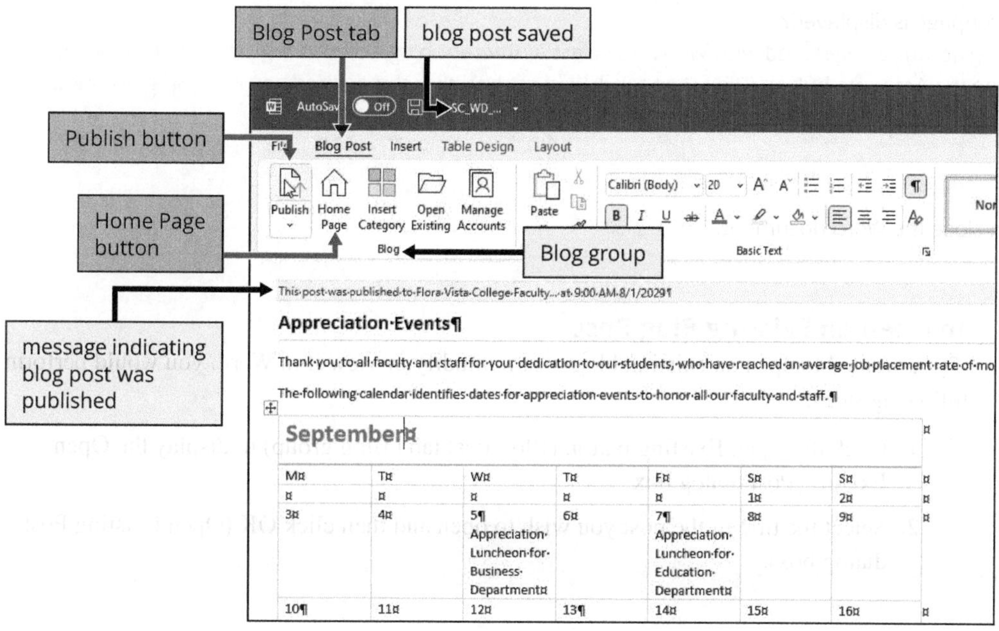

Figure 8–71

To Display a Blog Webpage in a Browser Window

The following steps display the current blog account's webpage in a browser window. **Why?** You can view a blog account associated with Word if you want to verify a post was successful.

- Click the Home Page button (Blog Post tab | Blog group) (shown in Figure 8–71), which starts the default browser (Microsoft Edge, in this case) and displays the webpage associated with the registered blog account in the browser window. You may need to click the Refresh button in your browser window to display the most current webpage contents (Figure 8–72).

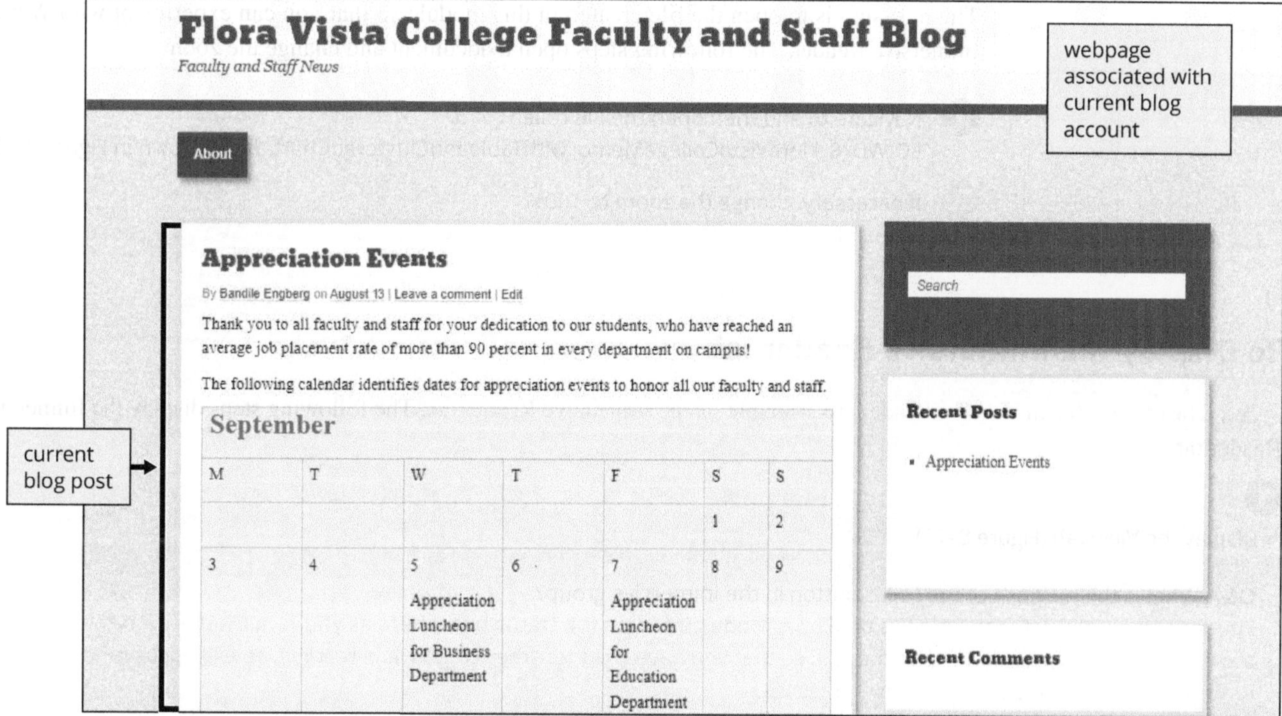

Figure 8–72

Q&A What if the wrong webpage is displayed?
You may have multiple blog accounts registered with Word. To select a different blog account registered with Word, switch back to Word, click the Manage Accounts button (Blog Post tab | Blog group), click the desired account (Blog Accounts dialog box), and then click the Close button. Then, repeat Step 1.

- Exit the browser and then close the Word document.

BTW
Deleting Blog Posts
If you want to delete a blog post from your blog account, sign in to your blog account and then follow the instructions from your blog provider to delete a post from your blog.

To Open an Existing Blog Post

If you wanted to open an existing blog post to modify or view it in Word, you would perform the following steps.

1. Click the Open Existing button (Blog Post tab | Blog group) to display the Open Existing Post dialog box.
2. Select the title of the post you wish to open and then click OK (Open Existing Post dialog box).

Using Immersive Reader

Immersive Reader is a free accessibility tool, built into several Microsoft 365 apps, that is designed to support user reading and writing experiences. Through Immersive Reader, you can customize how Word documents appear on the screen while you are reading or editing them. (Note that any settings you change in Immersive Reader affect only how the document appears on the screen and do not affect how the document will print.)

The following sections use memo document created in this module to present Immersive Reader options available while using Word.

To Open a Document

The next step is to open the file created in this module so that you can experiment with Word's Immersive Reader. The following steps open a document and change the zoom.

1 Navigate to and then open the file called SC_WD_8_FloraVistaCollegeMemo_withTableandClusteredChart.docx (shown in Figure 8–73).

2 If necessary, change the zoom to 100%.

To Display the Immersive Reader Tab

Why? The options for Immersive Reader are available on the Immersive Reader tab. The following steps display the Immersive Reader tab.

- Display the View tab (Figure 8–73).

Q&A What is the purpose of the Focus button in the Immersive group?
This button has the same function as the Focus Mode button on the status bar, which, as you recall, hides everything in the Word window, except for the document, so that you have a clutter-free screen while reading. To exit Focus mode and redisplay the entire document window, press ESC.

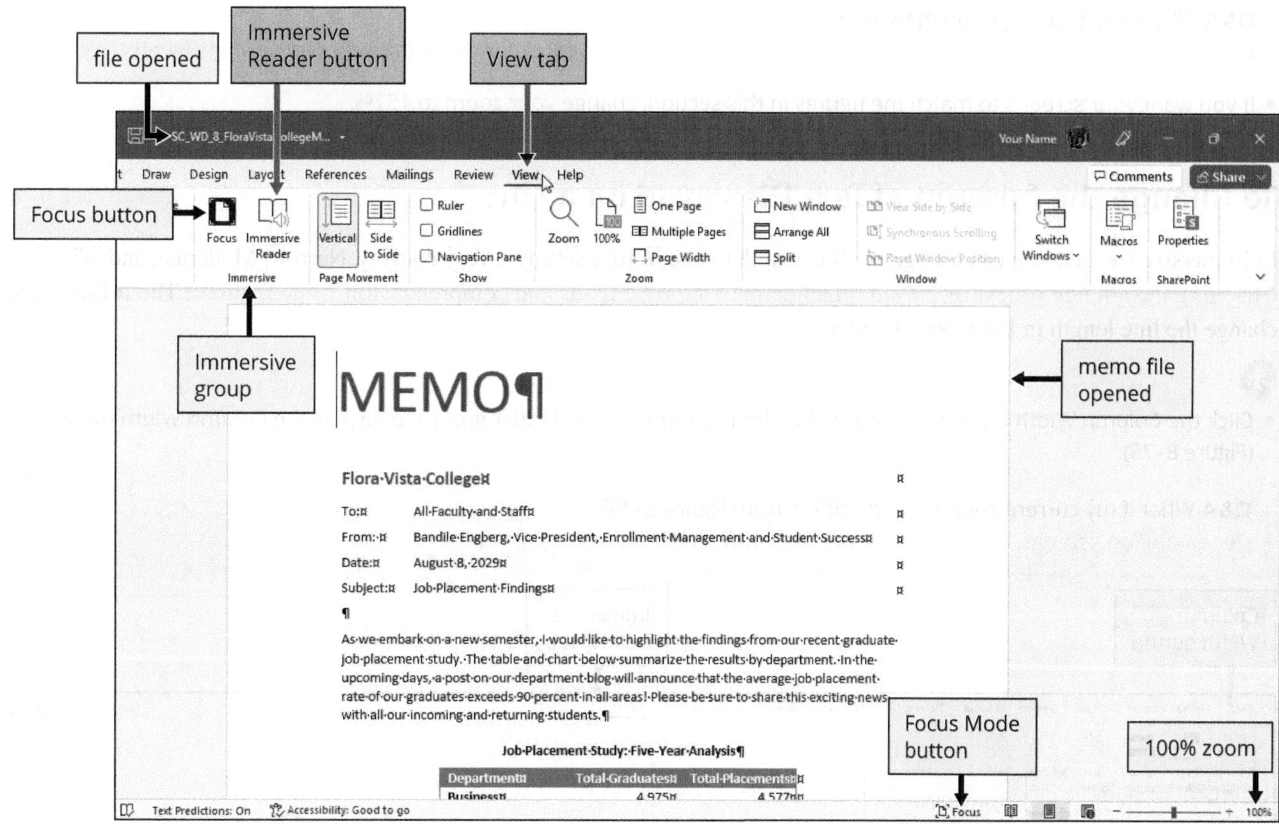

Figure 8–73

2

- Click the Immersive Reader button (View tab | Immersive group) to display the Immersive Reader tab on the ribbon and switch to Immersive Reader view (Figure 8–74). Depending on settings, your screen may differ from Figure 8–74, and some of the buttons on your Immersive Reader tab already may be selected. (Note: If the Text Spacing button (Immersive Reader tab | Immersive Reader group) is selected, click it to deselect it.)

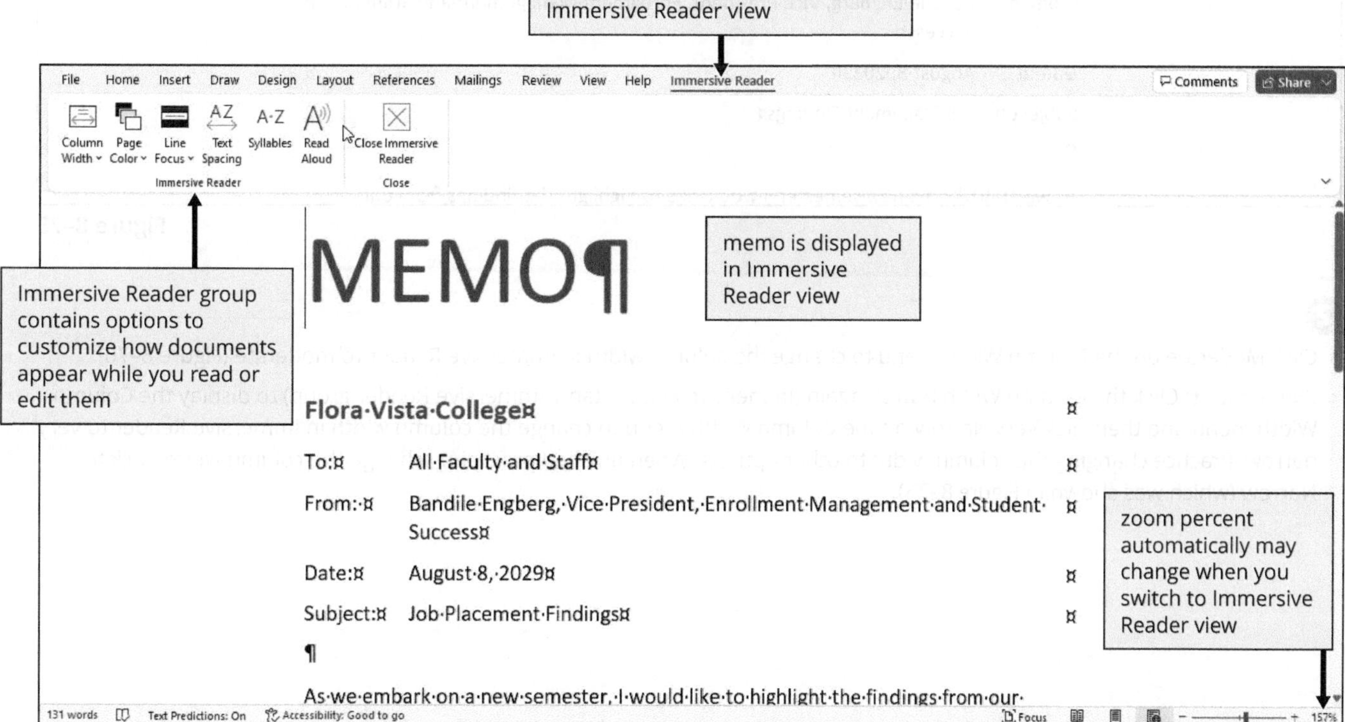

Figure 8–74

Q&A Why is the text bigger on the screen?
Word automatically may change the zoom percentage in Immersive Reader to make document content easier to read.

- If you want your screens to match the figures in this section, change your zoom to 157%.

To Change the Amount of Text Displayed on a Line

In Immersive Reader, you can change the line length to one of four settings: Very Narrow, Narrow, Moderate, and Wide. **Why?** Changing the amount of text displayed on a line may improve focus and comprehension while reading. The following steps change the line length in Immersive Reader.

- Click the Column Width button (Immersive Reader tab | Immersive Reader group) to display the Column Width menu (Figure 8–75).

Q&A What if my current column width differs from Figure 8–75?
Depending on settings, your column width may differ. Proceed to Step 2.

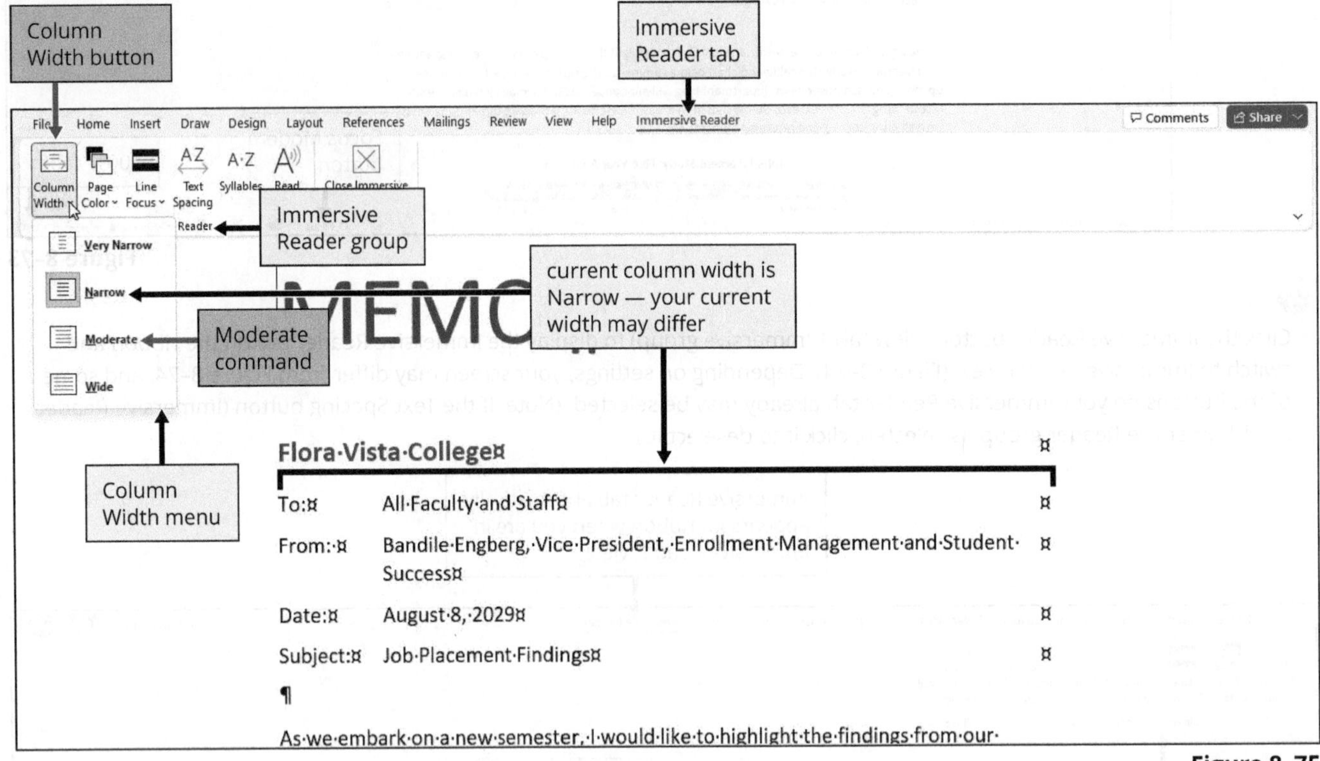

Figure 8–75

- Click Moderate on the Column Width menu to change the column width in Immersive Reader to moderate (Figure 8–76).
- **Experiment:** Click the Column Width button again (Immersive Reader tab | Immersive Reader group) to display the Column Width menu and then click Very Narrow on the Column Width menu to change the column width in Immersive Reader to very narrow. Practice changing the column width to other options. When finished practicing, change the column width back to Narrow (which was shown in Figure 8–75).

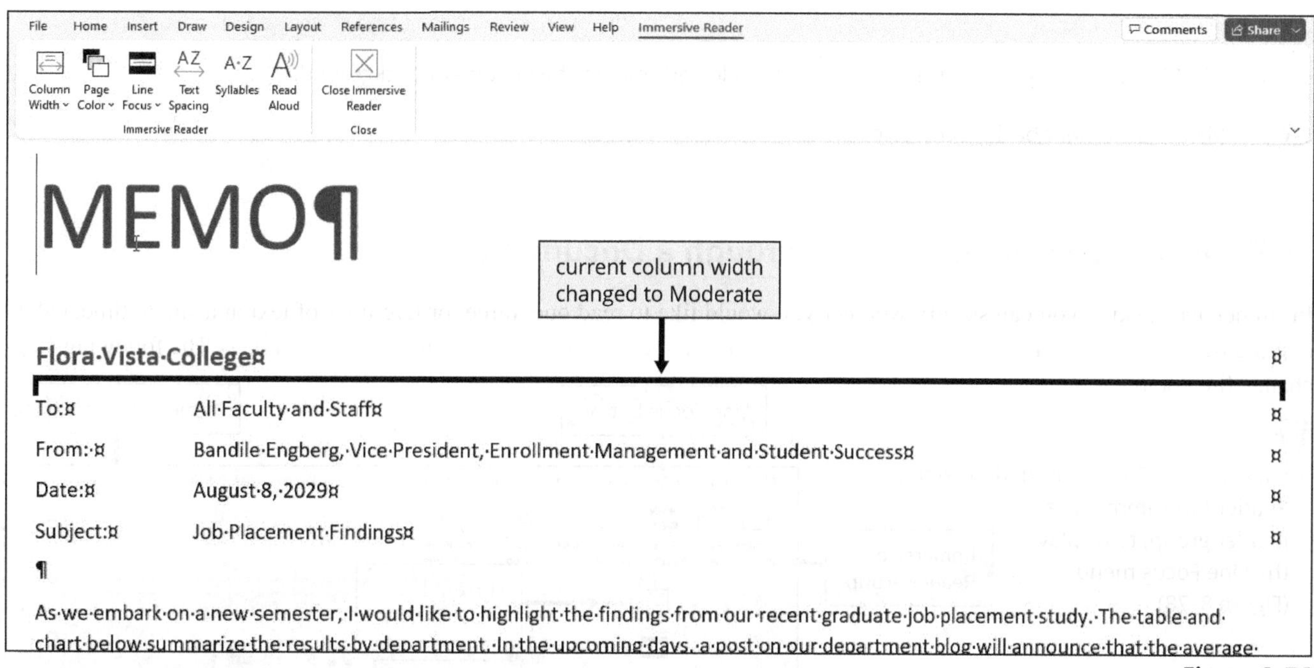

Figure 8–76

To Change the Color of the Document Background

In Immersive Reader, you can change the color of the document background. **Why?** Changing the background color of a document can reduce eye stress. The following steps change the color of the document background.

- Click the Page Color button (Immersive Reader tab | Immersive Reader group) to display the Page Color gallery.
- Point to Light Blue in the Page Color gallery (fourth color in fourth row) to display a Live Preview of the selected color applied to the document background (Figure 8–77).

◦ **Experiment:** Point to various colors in the Page Color gallery and watch the document background color change.

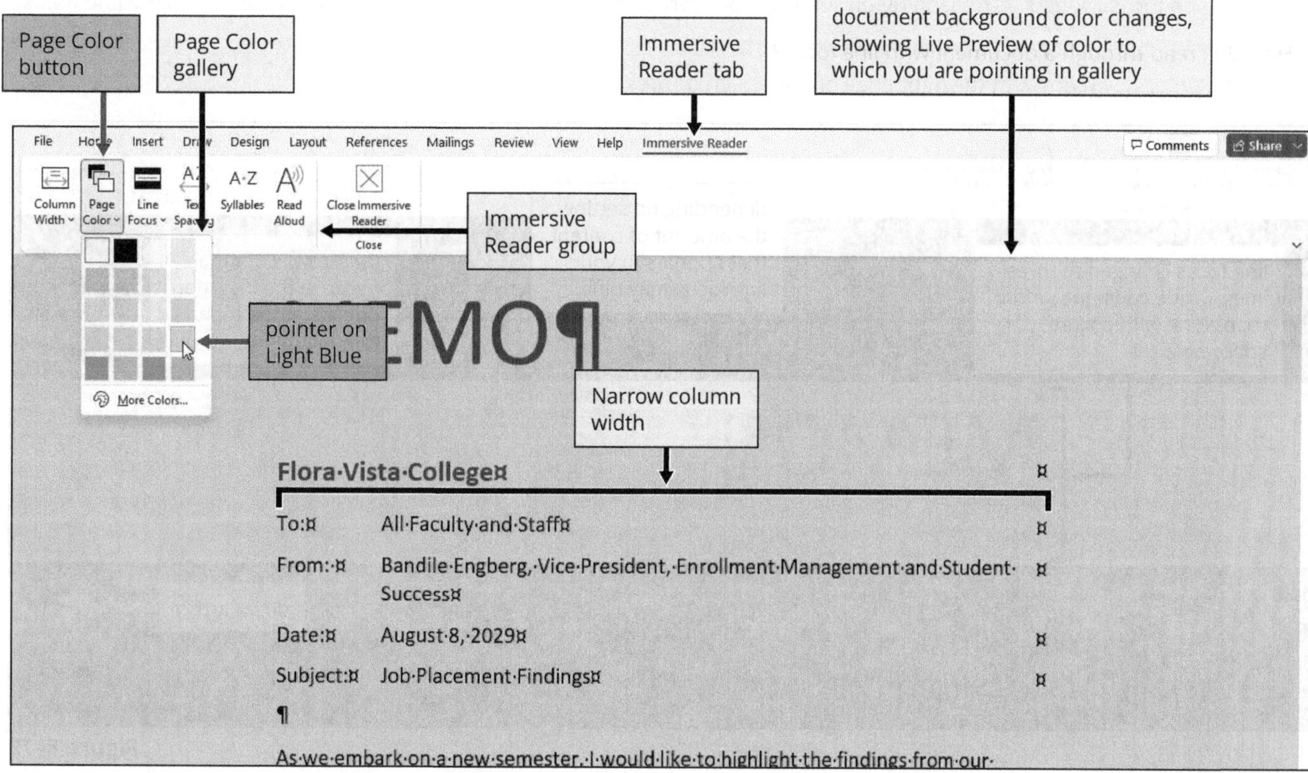

Figure 8–77

• Click Light Blue in the Page Color gallery to apply the selected color to the document background.

Q&A Will the document background color print?
No. Recall that settings changed in Immersive Reader have no impact on how the document will print.

To Focus on Lines as You Scroll Through a Document

In Immersive Reader, you can specify whether you would like to read one, three, or five lines of text at a single time, called line focus. **Why?** Using line focus can reduce distractions on the screen as you read through a document. The following steps change line focus.

1

• Click the Line Focus button (Immersive Reader tab | Immersive Reader group) to display the Line Focus menu (Figure 8–78).

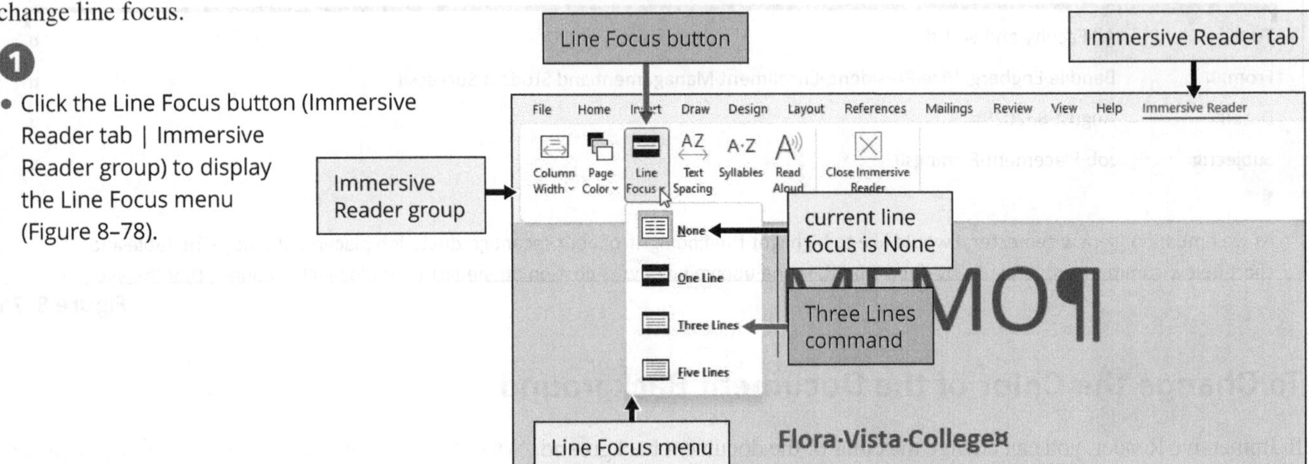

Figure 8–78

• Click Three Lines on the Line Focus menu to change the line focus in Immersive Reader to three lines (Figure 8–79).

Q&A Why does only the title appear?
Because the title is a larger font size than other text in the document and is followed by blank space, only the title appears in the first line focus. Note that, depending on settings, your screen may display a different amount of content in the line focus.

How do I read through a document with line focus?
Click the up or down arrow at the right edge of the screen or press UP ARROW or DOWN ARROW.

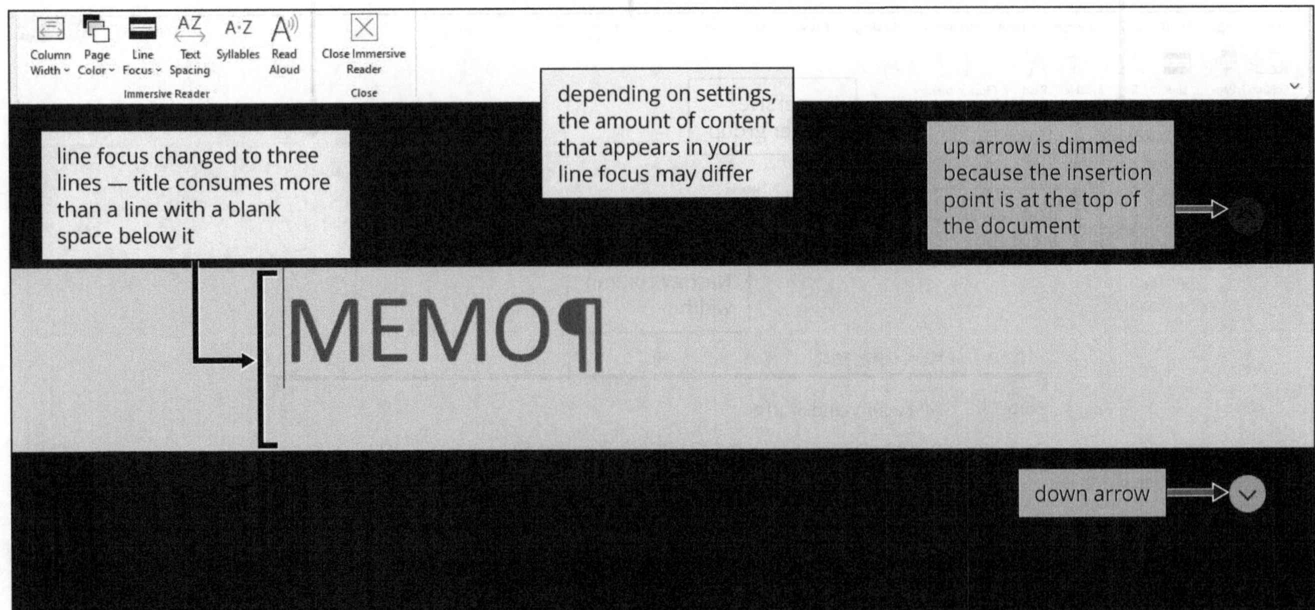

Figure 8–79

- Click the down arrow at the right edge of the screen to move the line focus down to the next three lines in the document (which, in this case, is the college name, the To: line, and the From: line in the menu). Note that, depending on settings, your screen may display a different amount of content in the line focus.
- Click the down arrow at the right edge of the screen again to move the line focus down to the next three lines in the document (which, in this case, is the To: line, and the From: line in the menu, and a blank line). Note that, depending on settings, your screen may display a different amount of content in the line focus.
- Click the down arrow at the right edge of the screen again to move the line focus down to the next three lines in the document (which, in this case, is the first three lines in the body of the memo) (Figure 8–80). Note that, depending on settings, your screen may display a different amount of content in the line focus.

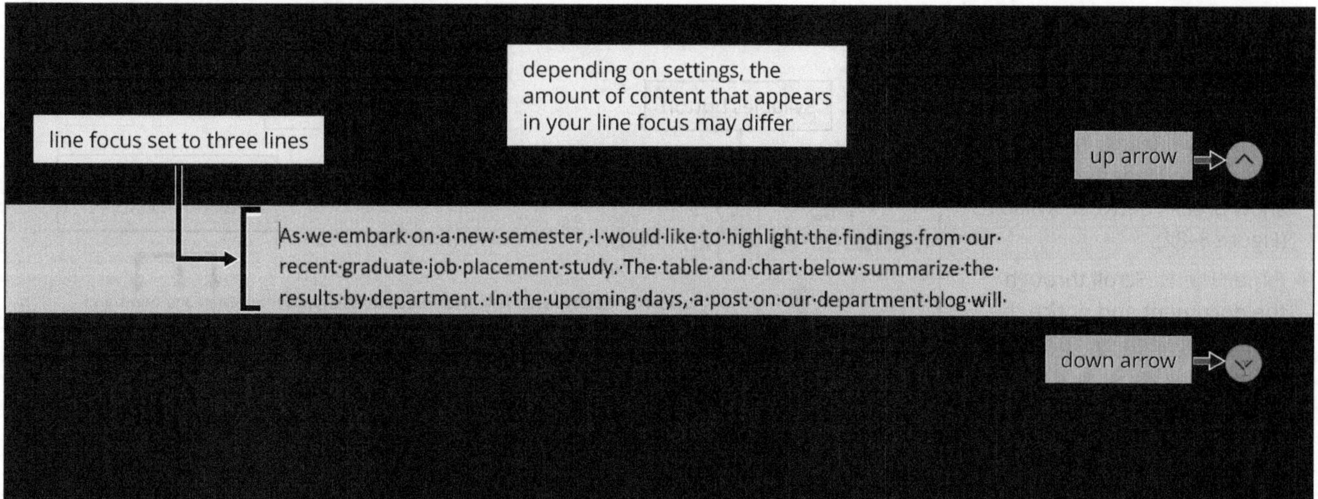

Figure 8–80

- **Experiment:** Practice reading through the document by clicking the up and down arrows at the right edge of the screen or pressing UP ARROW or DOWN ARROW.
- **Experiment:** Change the line focus to one line and practice reading through the document. Change the line focus to five lines and practice reading through the document. When you are finished practicing, change the line focus to None.

To Increase the Space between Words, Characters, and Lines

In Immersive Reader, you can increase text spacing, which adds more space between words, characters, and lines. **Why?** Changing text spacing may make text easier to read. The following steps change text spacing in Immersive Reader.

- Click the Text Spacing button (Immersive Reader tab | Immersive Reader group) to increase the space between words, characters, and lines (Figure 8–81).
- **Experiment:** Scroll through the document and notice the increased text spacing.

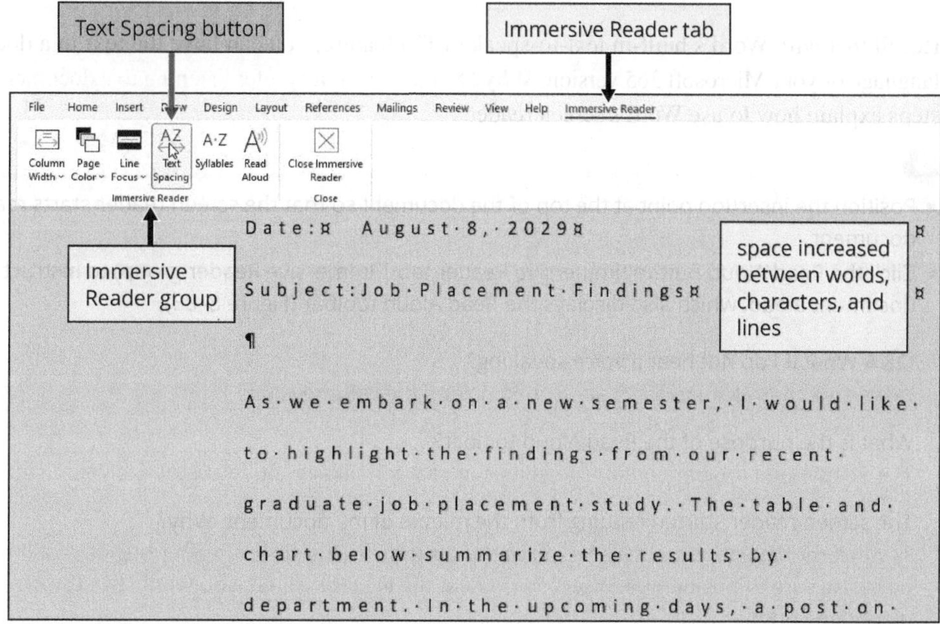

Figure 8–81

- Click the Text Spacing button again (Immersive Reader tab | Immersive Reader group) to remove the increased space between words, characters, and lines.

Q&A Does the text spacing feature work in all languages supported by Word?
This feature may not work in some of the languages.

To Show Breaks Between Syllables

In Immersive Reader, you can divide words into syllables. **Why?** Showing breaks between syllables can help with word identification and pronunciation. The following steps show breaks between syllables in Immersive Reader.

1

- Click the Syllables button (Immersive Reader tab | Immersive Reader group) to show breaks between syllables (Figure 8–82).
- **Experiment:** Scroll through the document and notice the breaks between syllables in the words.

2

- Click the Syllables button again (Immersive Reader tab | Immersive Reader group) to remove the breaks between syllables.

Q&A Does the syllable feature work in all languages supported by Word?
This feature does not work in some of the languages.

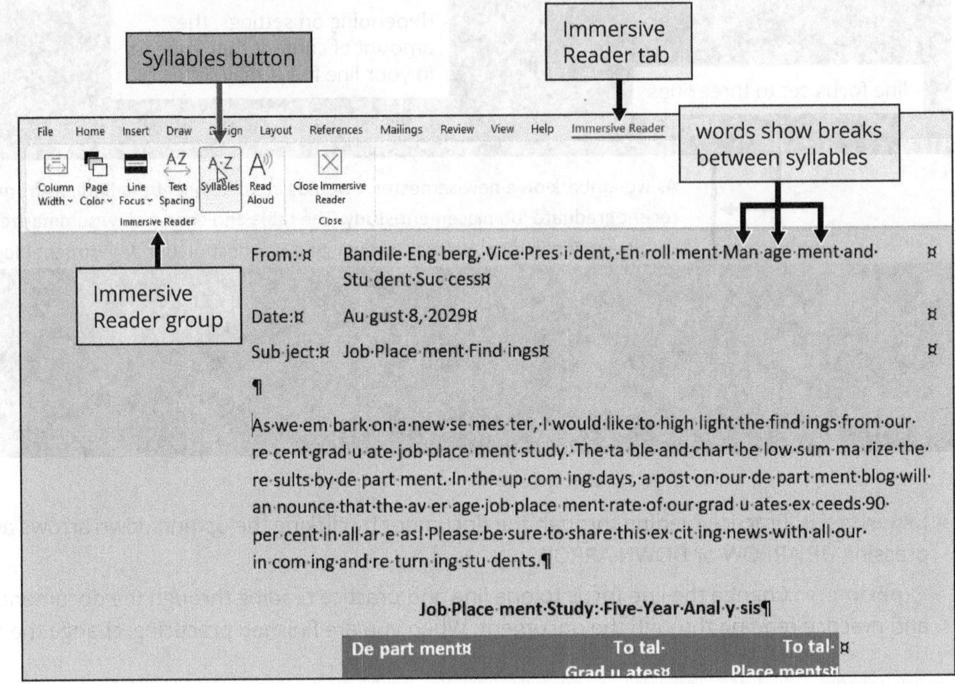

Figure 8–82

To Use Word's Screen Reader

Recall that with Word's built-in text-to-speak (TTS) feature, you can have the text in a document read aloud to you using the language of your Microsoft 365 version. **Why?** Some users may prefer listening to a document instead of reading it. The following steps explain how to use Word's screen reader.

- Position the insertion point at the top of the document so that the screen reader starts reading from the beginning of the document.
- Click the Read Aloud button (Immersive Reader tab | Immersive Reader group) to instruct Word to begin reading your document aloud, which also displays the Read Aloud toolbar (Figure 8–83).

Q&A What if I do not hear a voice speaking?
Make sure that your speakers are turned on and the volume is up.

What is the purpose of the Read Aloud toolbar?
The Read Aloud toolbar contains reading controls and allows you to customize your listening experience.

The screen reader started reading from the middle of my document. Why?
The insertion point was not at the top of the document. The screen reader begins reading from the location of the insertion point. Be sure to position the insertion point at the location where you would like the screen reader to begin reading the document aloud.

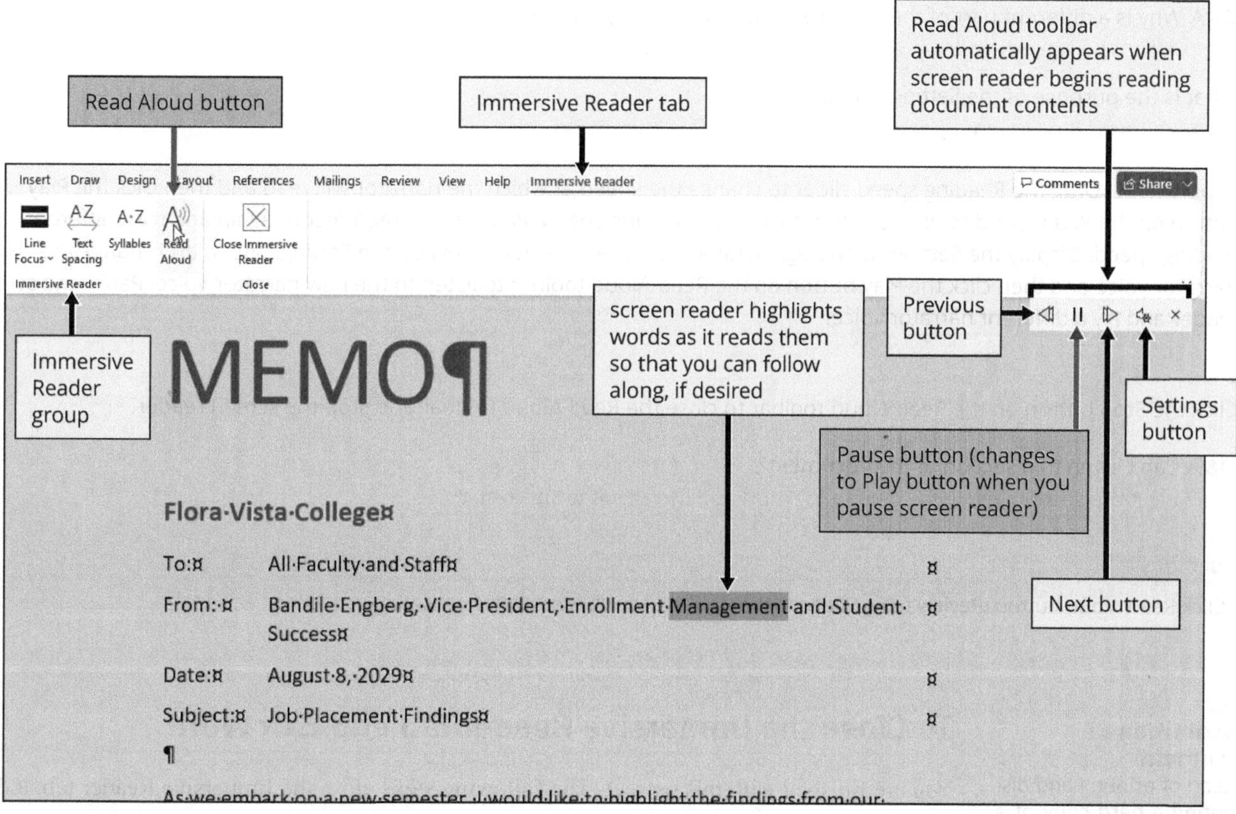

Figure 8–83

- **Experiment:** Click the Pause button on the Read Aloud toolbar to pause the screen reader. Notice the Pause button on the Read Aloud toolbar changes to a Play button. Click the Play button to resume reading aloud. Practice clicking the Previous and Next buttons to move forward and background one paragraph at a time in the document.

2

- Click the Pause button on the Read Aloud toolbar to pause the screen reader.
- Click the Settings button on the Read Aloud toolbar to display the Settings menu. (Figure 8–84).

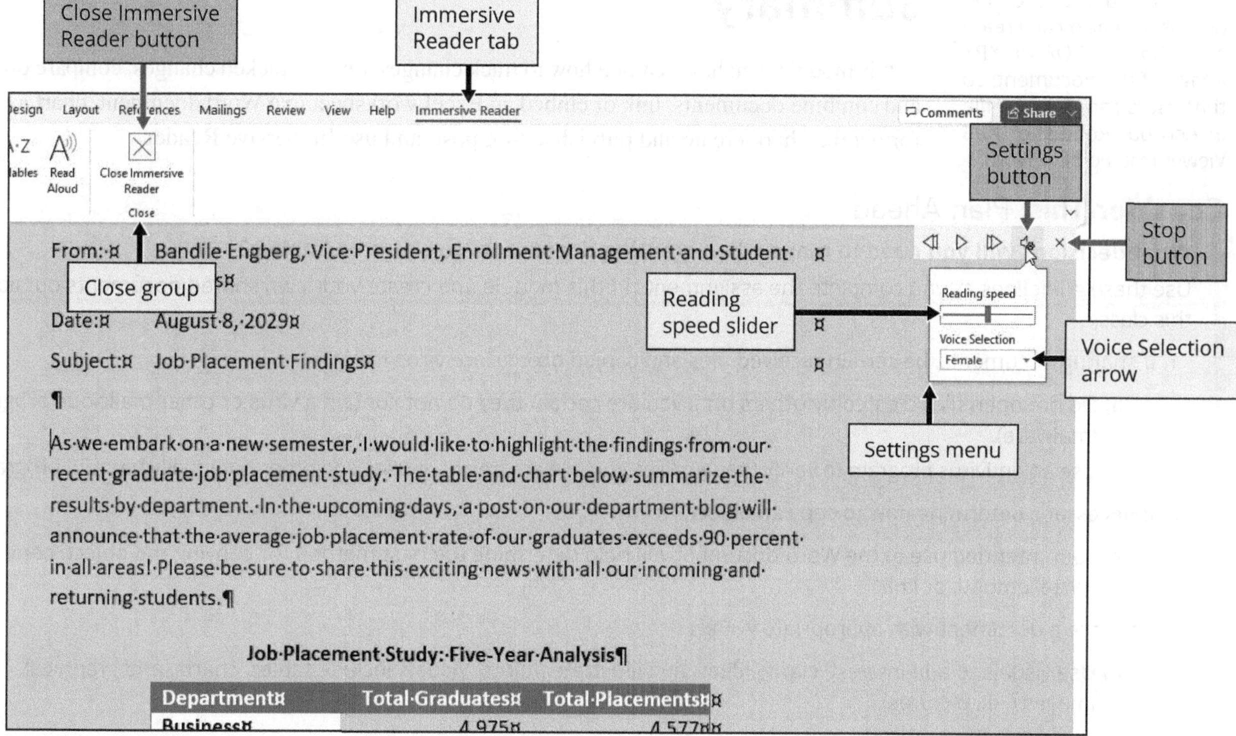

Figure 8–84

Q&A Why is a different part of the document displayed on my screen?
You paused the screen reader in a different location than shown in Figure 8–84.

What is the purpose of the Settings menu?
Through the Settings menu, you can change the reading speed and voice of the narrator.

- **Experiment:** Drag the Reading speed slider to change the speed at which the narrator will read and then click the Play button on the Read Aloud toolbar to listen to the new reading speed. Pause the screen reader again and try a different reading speed. Display the Settings menu again. Click the Voice Selection arrow on the Settings menu and change the narrator voice and then click the Play button on the Read Aloud toolbar to listen to the new narrator voice. Pause the screen reader and try a different narrator voice.

- Click the Stop button on the Read Aloud toolbar to close the Read Aloud toolbar and stop the screen reader.

Q&A Can I listen to a section of the document?
Yes. Select the section you wish to be read aloud and then repeat these steps.

Other Ways

1. Click Read Aloud button (Review tab | Speech group)
2. Press CTRL+ALT+SPACEBAR

BTW
Distributing a Document
Instead of printing and distributing a hard copy of a document, you can distribute the document electronically. Options include sending the document via email; posting it on cloud storage (such as OneDrive) and sharing the file with others; posting it on social media, a blog, or other website; and sharing a link associated with an online location of the document. You also can create and share a PDF or XPS image of the document, so that users can view the file in Acrobat Reader or XPS Viewer instead of in Word.

To Close the Immersive Reader Tab and Exit Word

You are finished with this project. The following steps close the Immersive Reader tab and exit Word.

1. Click the Close Immersive Reader button (Immersive Reader tab | Close group) to close the Immersive Reader and switch back to Print Layout view.
2. Exit Word. (If Word displays a dialog box asking if you want to save changes to your document, click the Don't Save button.)

Summary

In this module, you have learned how to track changes, review tracked changes, compare documents and combine documents, link or embed an Excel worksheet to a Word document, chart a table and format the chart, create and publish a blog post, and use Immersive Reader.

Consider This: Plan Ahead

What decisions will you need to make when creating documents to share or publish?

Use these guidelines as you complete the assignments in this module and create your own shared documents outside of this class.

1. If sharing documents, be certain received files and copied objects are virus free.
   a) Do not open files created by others until you are certain they do not contain a virus or other malicious program (malware).
   b) Use an antivirus program to verify that any files you use are free of viruses and other potentially harmful programs.
2. If necessary, determine how to copy an object.
   a) Your intended use of the Word document will help determine the best method for copying the object: copy and paste, embed, or link.
3. Enhance a document with appropriate visuals.
   a) Use visuals to add interest, clarify ideas, and illustrate points. Visuals include tables, charts, and graphical images (i.e., pictures).
4. If desired, post communications on a blog.

Student Assignments

Apply Your Knowledge

Reinforce the skills and apply the concepts you learned in this module.

Collaborating with Tracked Changes and Other Tools

Note: To complete this assignment, you will be required to use the Data Files. Please contact your instructor for information about accessing the Data Files.

Instructions: Start Word. Open the document, SC_WD_8-4.docx, which is located in the Data Files. Written by the public relations coordinator at Sunrise Financial, the document contains a description of cookies and their uses, with respect to computers and mobile devices. You are to review the document before it is finalized for clients.

Perform the following tasks:

1. Click File on the ribbon and then click Save As and save the document using the new file name, SC_WD_8_Cookies_Reviewed.
2. If necessary, customize the status bar so that it displays the Track Changes indicator.
3. Enable (turn on) tracked changes.
4. If requested by your instructor, change the user name and initials so that your name and initials are displayed in the tracked changes.
5. Open the Reviewing pane. How many tracked changes are in the document? Close the Reviewing pane.
6. If necessary, change the 'Display for Review' box (Review tab | Tracking group) to Simple Markup and then notice how the screen appears. Change it to No Markup and then Original and notice how the screen appears. Change it to All Markup for the remainder of this exercise.
7. Click the Show Markup button (Review tab | Tracking group) and be sure these types of markup are selected so that they show when tracking changes: Insertions and Deletions, and Formatting.
8. If it is not already set, show revisions in balloons. (**Hint:** Use the Show Markup button (Review tab | Tracking group).) Show only formatting in balloons. Practice going back and forth between the two settings. End with showing only formatting in balloons.
9. With the insertion point at the top of the document, use the Next Change button (Review tab | Changes group) to go to the first tracked change in the document. Use the same button to go to the next tracked change. Use the Previous Change button (Review tab | Changes group) to go to the previous tracked change.
10. Keep the tracked changes currently in the document. Track the changes shown in Figure 8–85 as additional tracked changes in the document. What color are the two markups that were in the original document? What color are the additional markups that you tracked in this step?
11. Save the reviewed document with the tracked changes again with the same name and then submit it in the format specified by your instructor.
12. Lock tracked changes in the document — do not enter a password in the dialog box. (**Hint:** Use the Track Changes button (Review tab | Tracking group).) What happens to the Track Changes button when you lock tracked changes? Unlock tracked changes.
13. Print the document with tracked changes.
14. Click File on the ribbon and then click Save As and save the document using the new file name, SC_WD_8_Cookies_Final.
15. Show only your tracked changes in the document. Show all reviewers' tracked changes in the document.
16. Hide tracked insertions and deletions. (**Hint:** Click the Show Markup button (Review tab | Tracking group).) Show tracked insertions and deletions.

Continued on next page

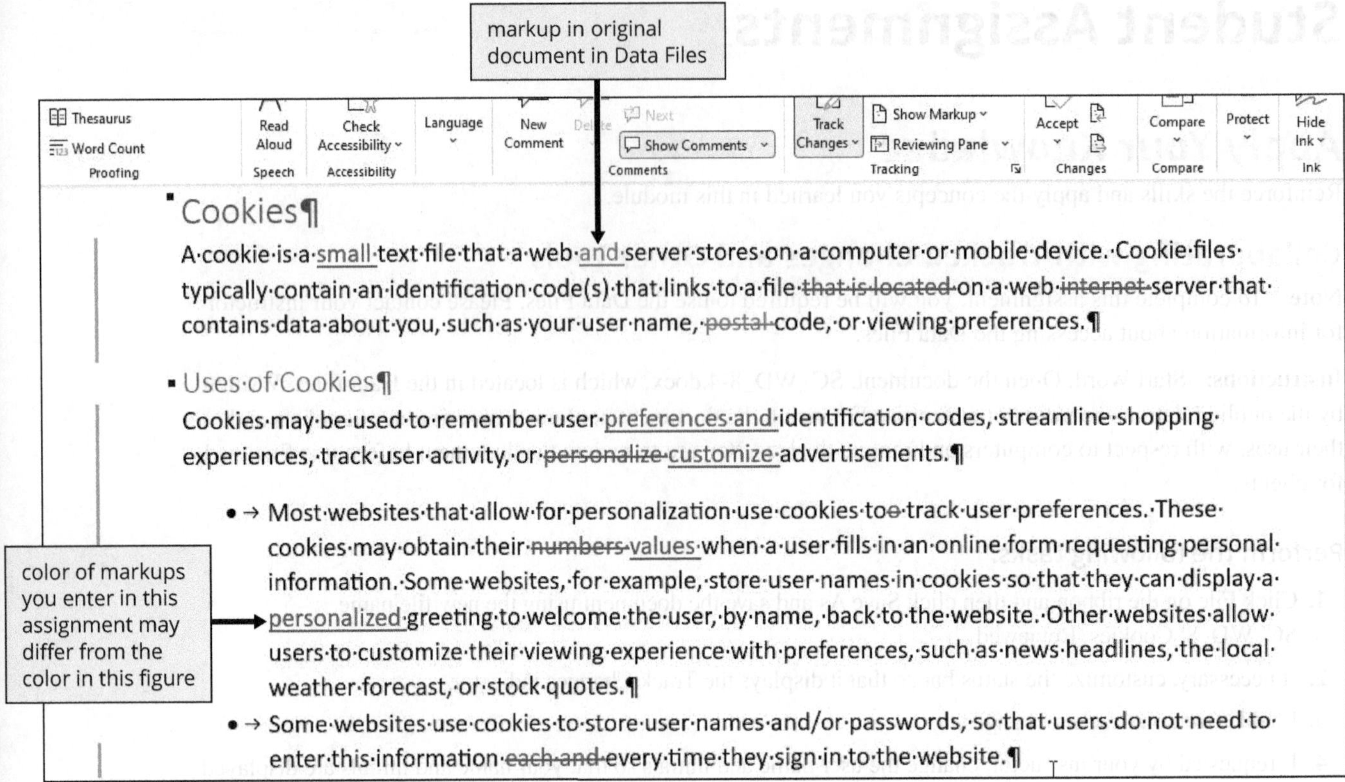

Figure 8–85

17. Reject the tracked change in the document that deleted the word, postal.
18. Reject the tracked change in the document that inserted the word, and.
19. Accept the tracked change in the document that inserted the word, small.
20. Accept the tracked change in the document that deleted the word, internet.
21. Accept all the remaining tracked changes in the document.
22. Disable (turn off) tracked changes. Remove the Track Changes indicator from the status bar.
23. If requested by your instructor, add your name in the header of the document as a document property. (**Hint:** Use the Document Info button (Header & Footer tab | Insert group).)
24. Save the final document again with the same name and then submit it in the format specified by your instructor.
25. Display the Immersive Reader tab and practice using its features. Change the column width to Very Narrow. Change it to Narrow. Change the Page Color to a color of your choice. Which color do you like best? Why? Change the Page Color to None. Change the line focus to five lines and then scroll through the document. Change the line focus to none. Increase text spacing. Turn text spacing off. Do you prefer text spacing on or off? Why? Show breaks between syllables and then turn this feature off. Practice using the screen reader (Read Aloud button) (Immersive Reader tab | Immersive Reader group). Which voice selection do you like best? Close the Immersive Reader tab.
26. Close the document.
27. Compare the SC_WD_8-4.docx file (original document) with the SC_WD_8_Cookies_Final file (revised document) into a new document. Before clicking OK in the Compare Documents dialog box, enter your name in the 'Label changes with' box in the Revised document section. In the Compare Result window, hide source documents. (**Hint:** Click the Compare button (Review tab | Compare group).) In the Compare Result window, show both source documents. Save the compare result with the file name SC_WD_8_Cookies_Compared and then submit it in the format specified by your instructor. Close the document.
28. Combine the SC_WD_8-4.docx file (original document) with the SC_WD_8_Cookies_Final file (revised document) into a new document. Before clicking OK in the Combine Documents dialog box, enter your name in the 'Label changes with' box in the Revised document section. Save the combine result with the file name SC_WD_8_Cookies_Combined and then submit it in the format specified by your instructor. Close the document.

29. Close all open Word documents. Open the SC_WD_8-4.docx file and the SC_WD_8_Cookies_Reviewed file. View the documents side by side. (**Hint:** Use the 'View Side by Side' button (View tab | Window group).) If synchronous scrolling is off, turn it on to scroll the documents at the same time. Scroll through each of the documents. Turn synchronous scrolling off. Scroll through each of the documents. Close both documents and exit Word.
30. Answer the questions posed in #5, #10, #12, and #25. How would you change the color of your tracked changes? How would you determine if two documents contained the same content?

Extend Your Knowledge

Extend the skills you learned in this module and experiment with new skills. You may need to use Help to complete the assignment.

Working with Charts

Note: To complete this assignment, you will be required to use the Data Files. Please contact your instructor for information about accessing the Data Files.

Instructions: Start Word. Open the document, SC_WD_8-5.docx, which is located in the Data Files. The document is a memo draft, written to the director of support services at Brighthill Medical from the community services manager about recent support group registrations. You are to chart the Word table in the memo using Word's charting tools. You also create another similar memo using an Excel table.

Perform the following tasks:

1. Use Help to learn more about charts in Word, linking objects, and embedding objects.
2. Click File on the ribbon and then click Save As and save the document using the new file name, SC_WD_8_SupportGroupRegistrationsMemo.
3. Insert a Line with Markers chart on the centered paragraph below the table. In the Word document window, select the table and then copy the selection. In the chart spreadsheet window, select the entire worksheet and then paste the contents with source formatting.
4. Resize the chart spreadsheet window to display all its data. Remove the Series 3 data series from the chart spreadsheet window by dragging the sizing handle.
5. Resize the column headings in the chart spreadsheet window by dragging their borders. Close the chart spreadsheet window.
6. Remove the primary horizontal axis chart element from the chart by using the 'Add Chart Element' button (Chart Design tab | Chart Layouts group). Use the same procedure to add the horizontal axis back to the chart.
7. Remove the legend chart element from the chart by using the 'Add Chart Element' button (Chart Design tab | Chart Layouts group). Use the same procedure to add the legend back to bottom of the chart.
8. Select the vertical (value) axis chart element. (**Hint:** Use the Current Selection group in the Format tab.) Click the Format Selection button to open the Format Axis pane. Change the value in the Minimum box in the Axis Options section to 350 and the value in the Maximum box to 800.
9. Add data labels to the chart so they appear to the left of each point (Figure 8–86). (**Hint:** Use the 'Add Chart Element' button (Chart Design tab | Chart Layouts group).)
10. Change the value of the Grief and Loss third quarter registrations from 402 to 452 in the chart spreadsheet window by using the Edit Data button (Chart Design tab | Data group). (Note that the change may not occur immediately in the chart.) Change the value in the table in the Word document also.
11. Change the chart style to a style of your choice. (**Hint:** Use the Chart Design tab.)
12. Change the colors of the chart to colors of your choice.
13. Change the position of the chart legend to a location of your choice. (**Hint:** Use the 'Add Chart Element' button (Chart Design tab | Chart Layouts group).)

Continued on next page

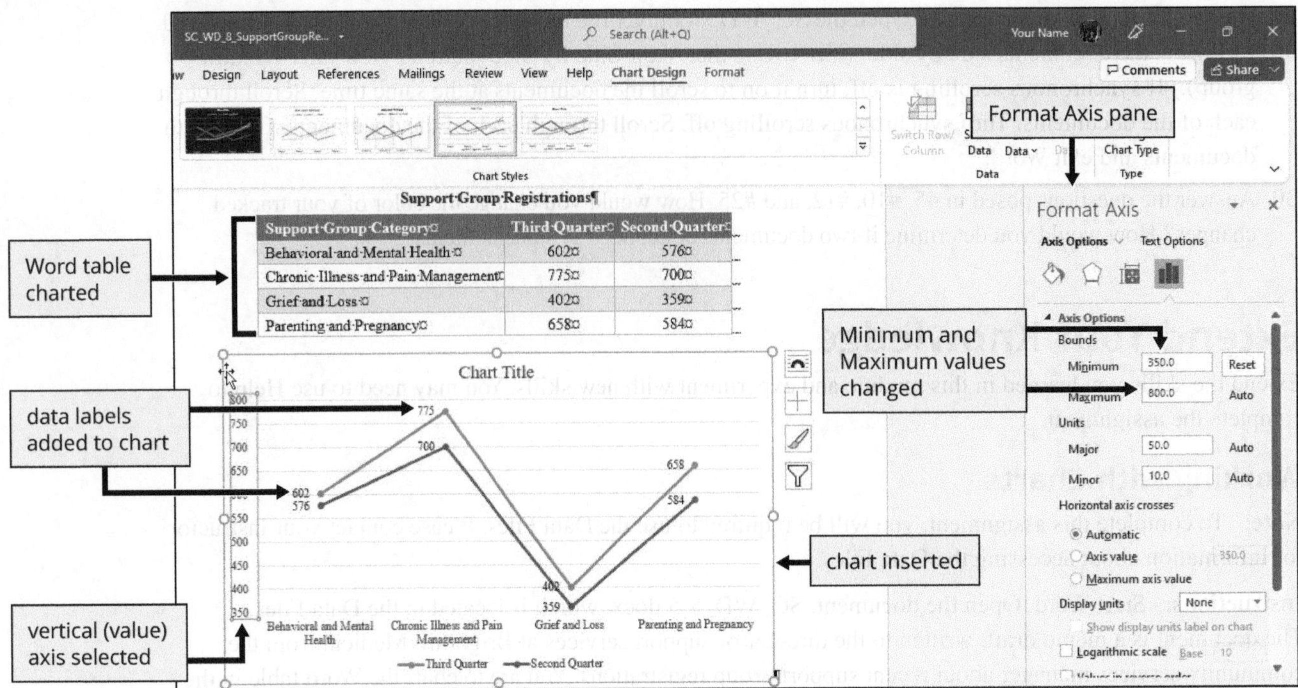

Figure 8–86

14. Remove the chart title from the chart by using the 'Add Chart Element' button (Chart Design tab | Chart Layouts group). Use the same procedure to add the chart title back to the chart. Select the chart title and enter appropriate text as the chart title. Format the title as you deem appropriate.
15. Add a vertical axis title with the text, Number of Registrations. (**Hint:** Use the 'Add Chart Element' button (Chart Design tab | Chart Layouts group).) Add an outline around the vertical axis title using the Shape Outline button (Format tab | Shape Styles group).
16. Add an outline of your choice to border the chart.
17. Check accessibility, adding alt text and fixing any other identified issues. Save the document again with the same name and then submit it in the format specified by your instructor.
18. Copy the chart. Create a new document window and then paste the chart using source formatting (and embed the workbook).
19. Change the chart type to any type of bar chart.
20. Use the chart spreadsheet window to add this row of data to the chart: Stress Management, 503 for third quarter registrations, and 425 for second quarter registrations. Be sure to drag the sizing handle to include the newly added row of data. Close the chart spreadsheet window.
21. Select the vertical (category) axis and then open the Format Axis pane. Select the 'Categories in reverse order' check box.
22. Remove the horizontal axis title. Remove the horizontal axis chart element.
23. Make any additional changes you feel appropriate for the chart.
24. Check accessibility, if necessary, adding alt text and fixing any other identified issues. Save the revised chart document using the file name, SC_WD_8_SupportGroupRegistrationsBarChart. Submit the document in the format specified by your instructor.
25. If you have Excel and your instructor requests, perform the following steps:
    a. In Word, open the document, SC_WD_8-6.docx, which is located in the Data Files. Click File on the ribbon and then click Save As and save the document using the new file name, SC_WD_8_SupportGroupRegistrationsMemo_withExcelTable.
    b. Start Excel and open the workbook, SC_WD_8-7.xlsx, which is located in the Data Files. In Excel, copy the table (the cells in the range A1 through C5). Click File on the ribbon and then click Save As and save the workbook using the new file name, SC_WD_8_SupportGroupRegistrationsTable.

c. In Word, on the blank line below the paragraph, insert the copied object (Excel table) by using the 'Keep Source Formatting' button on the Paste menu. Change one of the registrations values and notice that you edit the inserted object as you edit any other Word element. Delete the copied table.

d. In Word, on the blank line below the paragraph, embed the copied object (Excel table) by clicking Paste Special on the Paste menu, clicking 'Microsoft Excel Worksheet Object' (Paste Special dialog box), and then clicking OK. Try changing one of the enrollment values. Notice that you cannot because the Excel table is embedded. Double-click the embedded table to open an Excel window in the Word window. Change one of the enrollment values in the embedded Excel window. Click outside the embedded Excel window to close it and notice the value changes in the embedded table. Delete the embedded table.

e. In Excel, copy the table (the cells in the range A1 through C5) again. In Word, on the blank line below the paragraph, link the copied object (Excel table) by using the 'Link & Keep Source Formatting' button on the Paste menu.

   i. In Excel, change the Grief and Loss registrations from 402 to 452. Save the modified workbook in Excel. In Word, right-click the linked Excel table and then click Update Link on the shortcut menu to update the linked Excel object in Word.

   ii. Center the linked table. Copy the linked table.

   iii. Insert a chart of your choice of the linked table below the table in the Word document. Format the chart appropriately.

   iv. In Excel, change the Parenting and Pregnancy second quarter registrations from 544 to 584. Save the modified workbook in Excel. In Word, right-click the linked Excel table and then click Update Link on the shortcut menu to update the linked Excel object in Word.

   v. Edit the chart data in Word using the Edit Data button (Chart Design tab | Data group) and then change the Parenting and Pregnancy second quarter registrations from 544 to 584 in the chart spreadsheet window.

   vi. Break the link between the Excel table in the Word document and the Excel worksheet in the Excel workbook. Apply a Word table style of your choice. If necessary, center the table in the Word document. Format the table as you deem appropriate.

   vii. Check accessibility, adding alt text and fixing any other identified issues. Save the document again with the same name and then submit it in the format specified by your instructor. Exit Word and Excel, closing any open documents.

26. Which chart color and styles did you use in this assignment? Why?

Expand Your World

Create a solution that uses cloud or web technologies by learning and investigating on your own from general guidance.

Creating a Blog Account Using a Blogger Service

Instructions: As the web services project manager at Maple Valley's city government center, you have been asked to create a blog account so that blog posts can be used to communicate with the city center's managers and staff. You research a variety of blogging services and select one for use.

Note: You will use a blog account, many of which you can create at no cost, to complete this assignment. If you do not want to create a blog account, perform the first step and then read the remaining steps in this assignment without performing them.

Perform the following tasks:

1. In Word, create the blog post shown in Figure 8–87. Insert a Quick Table using the tabular list option. Delete two rows from the table. Edit the data and format the table as shown in the figure. Use the Grid Table 3 table style. Save the blog file using the file name, SC_WD_8_DonationDriveBlog.

Continued on next page

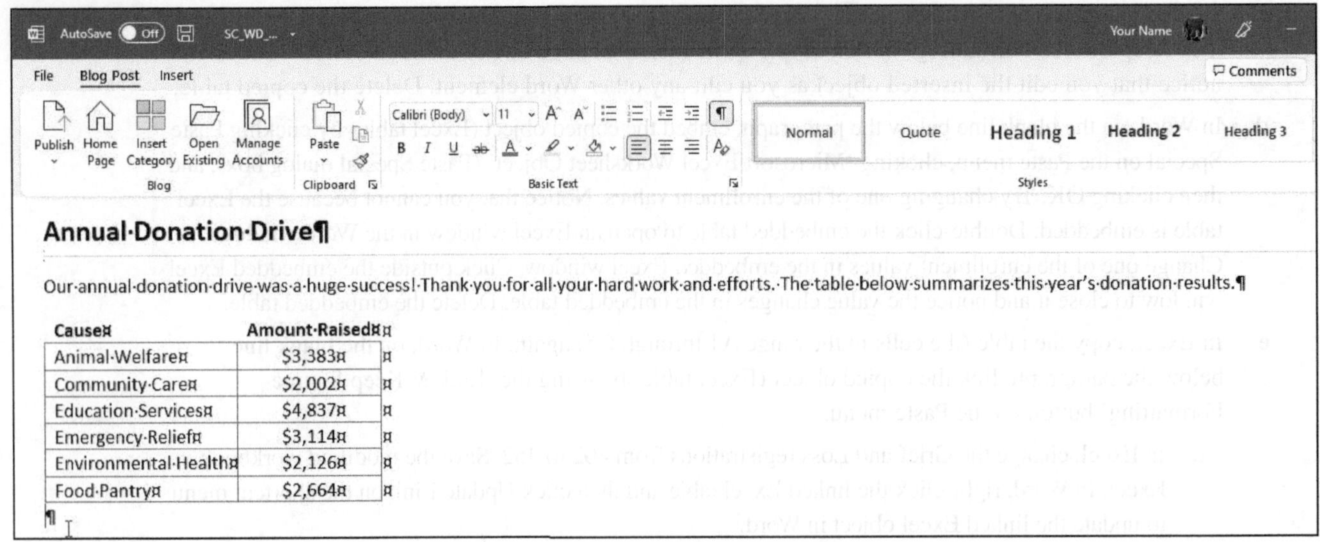

Figure 8–87

2. Start a browser. Research these blogging services: SharePoint blog, Telligent Community, TypePad, and WordPress.
3. Navigate to the blogger service with which you want to set up an account and then follow the instructions to set up an account.
4. Set up your blog in the blogger service.
5. In Word, register your blog account (refer to the section in this module titled To Register a Blog Account).
6. In Word, publish your blog post to your account.
7. Which blogger service did you select and why? Would you recommend this blogger service? Why or why not?

In the Lab

Design and implement a solution using creative thinking and problem-solving skills.

Create a Sales Summary Memo with a Table and Chart for a Party Supply Super Center

Problem: As an accounting clerk at Partyland Super Center, you have been asked to create a memo to sales managers showing the second quarter sales figures by category. The memo should contain a table and chart.

Part 1: You are to create a memo to sales managers with a subject of Second Quarter Sales. Use today's date. The wording for the text in the memo is as follows: Second quarter sales figures have been compiled. The table and chart below show sales by category for the second quarter.

The data for the table is as follows:

- decorations: April $132,217; May $179,268; June $158,839
- gift wrap and gift bags: April $78,546; May $99,687; June $87,983
- tableware and serve ware: April $46,658; May $77,821; June $53,034
- invitations and stationery: April $54,302; May $57,843; June $36,001

Create a chart of all table data.

Use the concepts and techniques presented in this module to create and format the memo and its text, table, and chart. Be sure to check accessibility, adding alt text as requested and fixing any other identified issues. Check spelling and grammar of the finished memo. When you are finished with the memo, save it with the file name, SC_WD_8_SalesMemo. Submit your assignment and answers to the Part 2 critical thinking questions in the format specified by your instructor.

Part 2: **Consider This:** You made several decisions while creating the memo in this assignment: whether to use a memo template or create a memo from scratch; where to position elements in the memo; and how to organize and format the memo, table, and chart (fonts, font sizes, colors, shading, styles, etc.). What was the rationale behind each of these decisions? When you proofread the document, what further revisions did you make, and why?

Creating a Reference Document

Objectives

After completing this module, you will be able to:

- Insert a screenshot
- Insert and edit a caption
- Insert a cross-reference
- Locate items and formats in a document
- Mark index entries
- Insert and link text boxes
- Compress pictures
- Use Outline view and Draft view
- Organize a master document and subdocuments
- Insert a symbol
- Modify page setup in a Word document
- Insert, format, and update a table of contents
- Insert and update a table of figures
- Insert and update an index
- Insert bookmarks

Introduction

During the course of your academic studies and professional activities, you may find it necessary to compose a document that is many pages or even hundreds of pages in length. When composing a long document, you must ensure that the document is organized so that a reader easily can locate material in that document. Sometimes a document of this nature is called a reference document.

Project: Reference Document

A **reference document** is any multipage document organized so that users easily can locate material and navigate through the document. Examples of reference documents include user guides, term papers, pamphlets, manuals, proposals, and plans.

The project in this module uses Word to produce the reference document shown in Figure 9–1. This reference document, titled *Learning Microsoft 365*, is a multipage guide that is distributed by Information Technology Services at Gladstone College to students and staff.

Notice that the inner margin between facing pages has extra space to allow duplicated copies of the printed document to be bound (i.e., stapled or fastened in some manner) — without the binding covering the words.

The *Learning Microsoft 365* reference document begins with a cover page designed to encourage the target audience to open the document and read it. Next is a blank page that will print on the back side of the cover page, then the copyright page, followed by the table of contents. The document then has four pages that contain information about how to insert four types of images in a Word document: online image, picture from a file, shape, and screenshot. The two final pages of this reference document contain a table of figures and an index to assist readers in locating information contained within the document. A miniature version of the *Learning Microsoft 365* reference document is shown in Figure 9–1.

The section of the *Learning Microsoft 365* reference document that is titled Inserting Images is a document that you create from a draft. The draft of this document is located in the Data Files. Please contact your instructor for information about accessing the Data Files. After editing content in the draft document, you will incorporate the final version in the reference document.

You will perform the following general tasks as you progress through this module:

1. Modify a draft of a document.
2. Create a master document with a subdocument for the reference document.
3. Organize the reference document.

To Start Word and Specify Settings

If you are using a computer to step through the project in this module and you want your screens to match the figures in this book, you should change your screen's resolution to 1366 × 768. The following steps start Word and specify settings.

1. Start Word and create a blank document in the Word window. If necessary, maximize the Word window.
2. If the Print Layout button on the status bar is not selected, click it so that your screen is in Print Layout view.
3. Verify that the Ruler check box (View tab | Show group) is not selected. (If it is selected, click it to remove the check mark because you do not want the rulers to appear on the screen.)
4. If you are using a mouse and you want your screens to match the figures in the book, verify that you are using Mouse mode by doing the following: display the Quick Access Toolbar, if necessary, by clicking the 'Ribbon Display Options' button at the right edge of the ribbon and then clicking 'Show Quick Access Toolbar' on the menu; clicking the 'Touch/Mouse Mode' button on the Quick Access Toolbar and then, if necessary, clicking Mouse on the menu (if your Quick Access Toolbar does not display the 'Touch/Mouse Mode' button, click the 'Customize Quick Access Toolbar' button on the Quick Access Toolbar and then click Touch/Mouse Mode on the menu to add the button to the Quick Access Toolbar); then hide the Quick Access Toolbar by clicking the 'Ribbon Display Options' button at the right edge of the ribbon and then clicking 'Hide Quick Access Toolbar' on the menu.

BTW

Touch Mode Differences

The Office and Windows interfaces may vary if you are using Touch mode. For this reason, you might notice that the function or appearance of your touch screen differs slightly from this module's presentation.

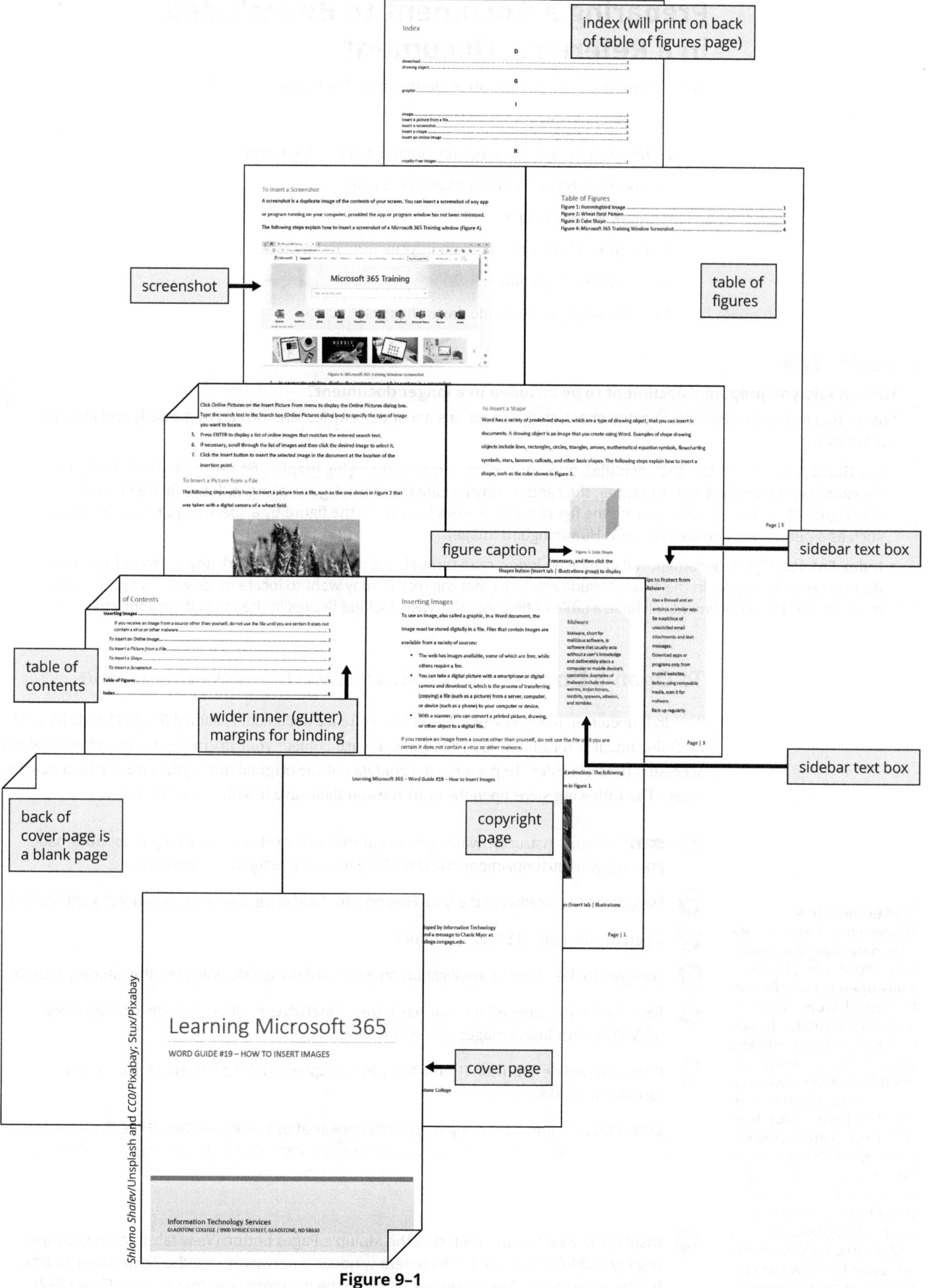
index (will print on back of table of figures page)
screenshot
table of figures
figure caption
sidebar text box
table of contents
wider inner (gutter) margins for binding
sidebar text box
back of cover page is a blank page
copyright page
Learning Microsoft 365
WORD GUIDE #19 – HOW TO INSERT IMAGES
cover page
Information Technology Services
Shlomo Shalev/Unsplash and CC0/Pixabay; Stux/Pixabay

Figure 9–1

Preparing a Document to Be Included in a Reference Document

You will make several modifications to the draft document:

1. Insert a screenshot.
2. Insert captions for the figures (images) in the document.
3. Insert references to the figures in the text.
4. Mark an index entry.
5. Insert text boxes that contain information about malware.
6. Compress the pictures.

The following pages outline these changes.

Consider This:

How should you prepare a document to be included in a longer document?

Ensure that reference elements in a document, such as captions and index entries, are formatted properly and entered consistently.

- **Captions:** A **caption** is text that identifies, titles, or explains an accompanying graphic, figure, or photo. If the figure, for example, is identified with a number, the caption may include the word, Figure, along with the figure number (i.e., Figure 1). In the caption, separate the figure number from the text of the figure by a space or punctuation mark, such as a period or colon (i.e., Figure 1: Hummingbird Image).
- **Index Entries:** If your document will include an index, read through the document and mark any terms or headings that you want to appear in the index. Include any term that the reader may want to locate quickly. Omit figures from index entries if the document will have a table of figures; otherwise, include figures in the index if appropriate.

To Open a Document and Save It with a New File Name

The draft document that you will insert in the reference document is named SC_WD_9-1.docx. The draft document is located in the Data Files. Please contact your instructor for information about accessing the Data Files. To preserve the contents of the original draft, you save it with a new file name. The following steps open the draft file and then save it with a new file name.

1. sam If your instructor wants you to submit your work as a SAM Project for automatic grading, you must download the Data Files from the assignment launch page.
2. Navigate to the location of the Data Files on your hard drive, OneDrive, or other storage location.
3. Open the file named SC_WD_9-1.docx.
4. Navigate to the desired save location on your hard drive, OneDrive, or other storage location.
5. Save the file just opened on your hard drive, OneDrive, or other storage location using SC_WD_9_WordInsertImages as the file name.
6. If the 'Show/Hide ¶' button (Home tab | Paragraph group) is selected, click it to hide formatting marks.

   Q&A What if some formatting marks still appear after I click the 'Show/Hide ¶' button?
   Open Backstage view, click Options to display the Word Options dialog box, click Display in the left pane (Word Options dialog box), remove the check mark from the Hidden text check box, and then click OK.

7. Display the View tab and then click the Multiple Pages button (View tab | Zoom group) to display multiple pages in the document window; if necessary, use the Zoom slider to adjust the zoom so that all four pages are visible in the document window at once (Figure 9–2).

BTW
Protected View
To keep your computer safe from potentially dangerous files, Word may automatically open certain files in Protected view, which is a restricted mode. To see the Protected view settings, click File on the ribbon to open Backstage view, click Options to display the Word Options dialog box, click Trust Center in the left pane (Word Options dialog box), click the 'Trust Center Settings' button in the right pane to display the Trust Center dialog box, and then click Protected View in the left pane to show the current Protected view settings.

8 When you have finished viewing the document, click the Page Width button (View tab | Zoom group) to display the document as wide as possible in the document window.

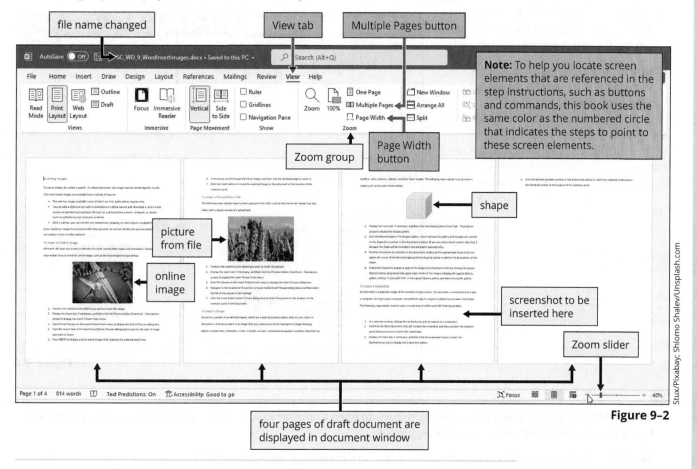

file name changed

View tab

Multiple Pages button

Note: To help you locate screen elements that are referenced in the step instructions, such as buttons and commands, this book uses the same color as the numbered circle that indicates the steps to point to these screen elements.

Zoom group

Page Width button

picture from file

online image

shape

screenshot to be inserted here

Zoom slider

four pages of draft document are displayed in document window

Stux/Pixabay; Shlomo Shalev/Unsplash.com

Figure 9–2

To Insert a Screenshot

A **screenshot** is a duplicate image of the contents of your computer or mobile device's screen or active window. The current document is missing a screenshot of a Microsoft 365 training window. To insert a screenshot, you first must display the screen for which you want a screenshot in a window on your computer or mobile device. **Why?** From within Word, you can insert a screenshot of any app running on your computer, provided the app has not been minimized. You then can resize or position the inserted screenshot as you do any other Word object. The following steps insert a screenshot in a document.

1

- Type **Microsoft 365 training** in the Search box to display search results (Figure 9–3).

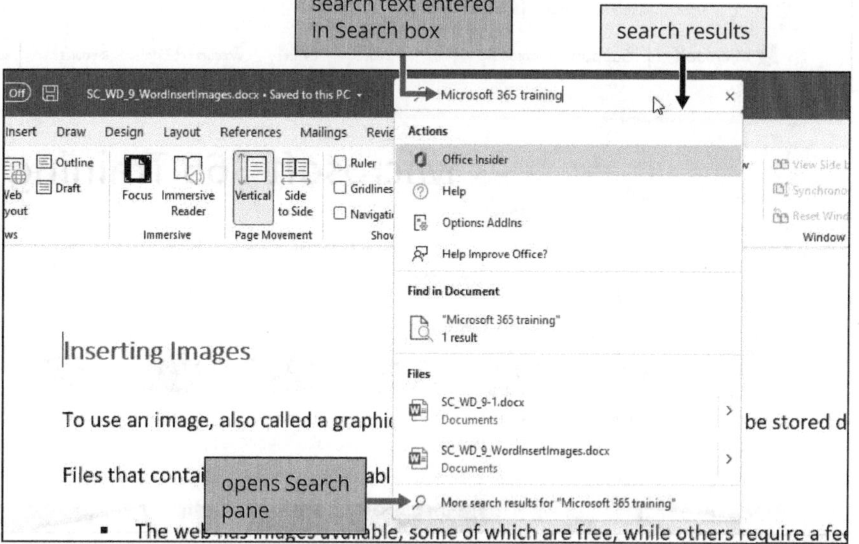

Figure 9–3

2

- Click 'More search results for "Microsoft 365 training"' in the search results to open the Search pane with links to information that matches the search text (Figure 9–4).

Q&A What if 'More search results for "Microsoft 365 training"' does not appear in my search results?
Press ESC to close the search results. Open a browser window, search for the text, Microsoft 365 training, and then click the appropriate link in the search results to display the screen shown in Figure 9–5. If necessary, maximize the browser window. Proceed to Step 4.

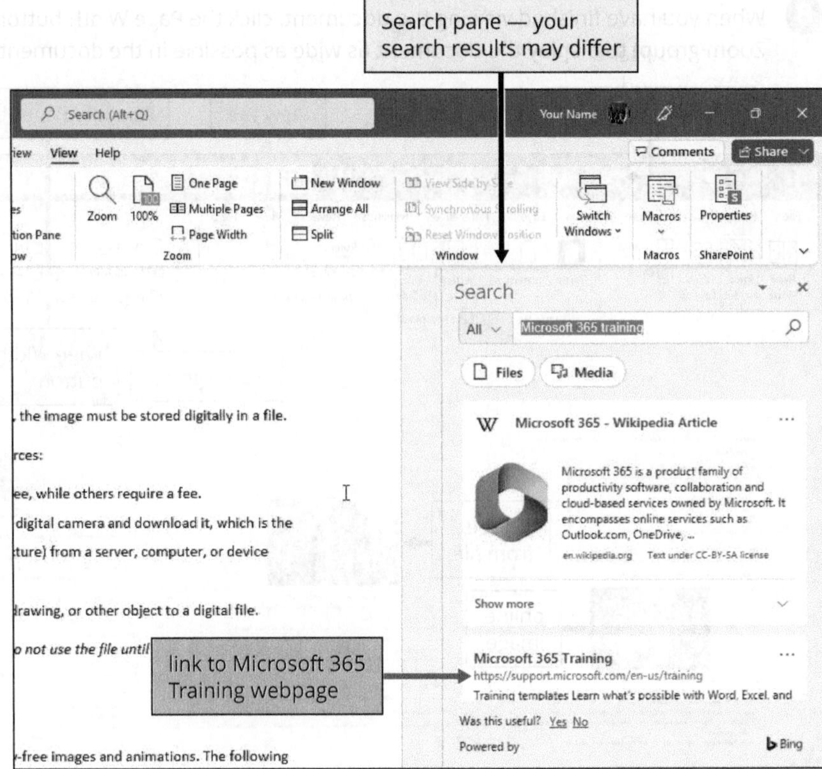

Figure 9–4

3

- Click the 'Microsoft 365 Training' link in the Search pane to open a browser window with the associated webpage displayed; if necessary, maximize the browser window (Figure 9–5).

Q&A What if I do not have access to the Internet or the correct webpage does not appear?
The screenshot is located in the Data Files. Click the Pictures button (Insert tab | Illustrations group), click This Device to display the Insert Picture dialog box, navigate to and select the file called Support_WD_9_Microsoft365TrainingWindow.png in the Data Files, and then click the Insert button (Insert Picture dialog box) to insert the screenshot. Close the Search pane and then proceed to Step 6.

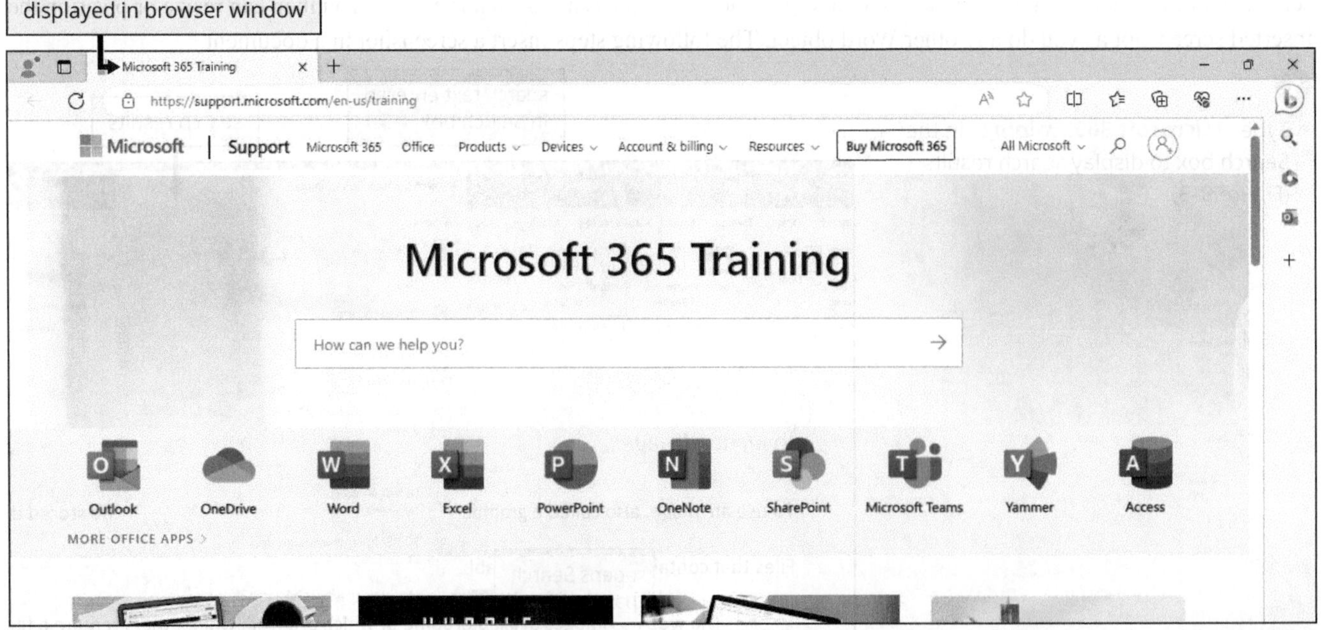

Figure 9–5

- Leave the browser window open, switch to the Word window, close the Search pane, and position the insertion point in the document where the screenshot should be inserted (in this case, on the centered blank line above the numbered list in the To Insert a Screenshot section at the bottom of the document).
- Display the Insert tab.
- Click the Screenshot button (Insert tab | Illustrations group) to display the Microsoft 365 Training window screenshot in the Screenshot gallery (Figure 9–6).

Figure 9–6

Q&A What if my Screenshot gallery does not show the Microsoft 365 Training window screenshot in the Screenshot gallery?
Press ESC to close the Screenshot gallery. The screenshot is located in the Data Files. Click the Pictures button (Insert tab | Illustrations group), click This Device to display the Insert Picture dialog box, navigate to and select the file called Support_WD_9_Microsoft365TrainingWindow.png in the Data Files, and then click the Insert button (Insert Picture dialog box) to insert the screenshot. Skip Step 5 and proceed to Step 6.

What is a screen clipping?
A screen clipping is a section of a window. When you select Screen Clipping in the Screenshot gallery, the window turns opaque so that you can drag through the part of the window to be included in the document.

Why does my Screenshot gallery show more windows?
You have additional programs running on your desktop, and their windows are not minimized.

- Click the Microsoft 365 Training window screenshot in the Screenshot gallery to insert the selected screenshot in the Word document at the location of the insertion point. (If a dialog box appears about hyperlinking the screenshot, click No.)

6

- Verify that the values in the Shape Height and Shape Width boxes (Picture Format tab | Size group) are approximately 3.5" tall by 6.5" wide (Figure 9–7).

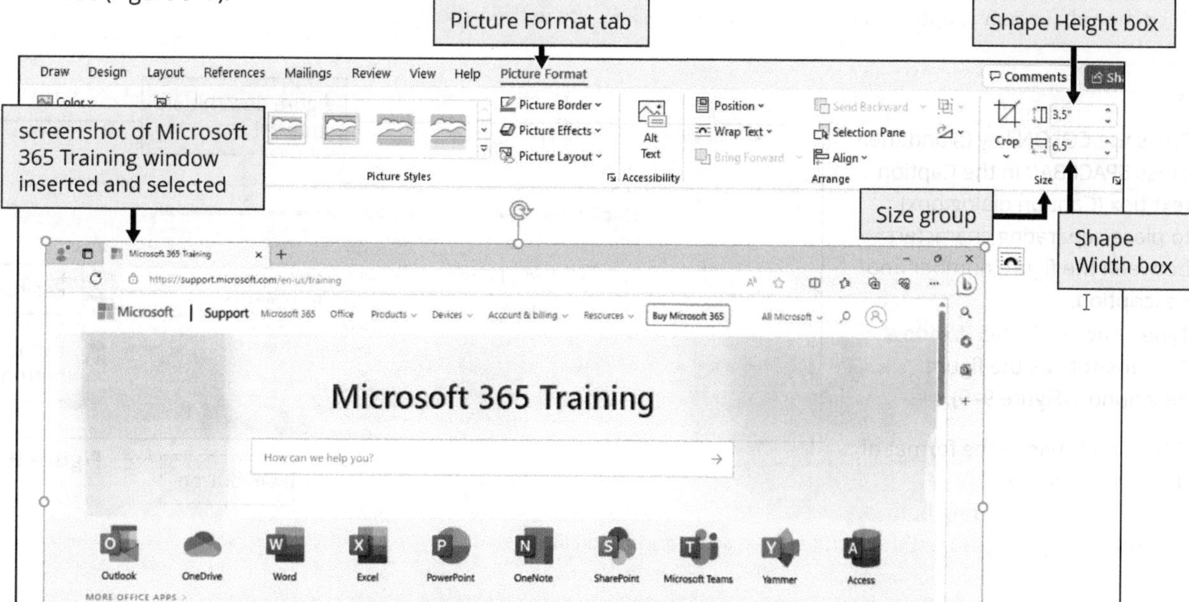

Figure 9–7

Q&A Why can I not set the exact measurements shown above?

You may need to click the Size Dialog Box Launcher (Picture Format tab | Size group) to display the Size sheet in the Layout dialog box and then remove the checkmark from the 'Lock aspect ratio' check box.

Why did the screenshot appear on a new page?

The screenshot is too tall to fit at the bottom of page 3.

To Insert a Caption

In Word, you can insert a caption for an equation, a figure, and a table. If you move, delete, or insert captions in a document, Word renumbers remaining captions in the document automatically (you may need to select the document and then press F9 for the updated fields to be displayed in the document). In this reference document, the captions contain the word, Figure, followed by the figure number, a colon, and a figure description. The following steps insert a caption for an image, specifically, the screenshot. **Why?** The current document contains four images: an image from an online source, a picture from a file, a shape, and a screenshot. All these images should have captions.

- If the screenshot is not selected already, click it to select the image on which you want a caption.
- Display the References tab.
- Click the Insert Caption button (References tab | Captions group) to display the Caption dialog box with a figure number automatically assigned to the selected image (Figure 9–8).

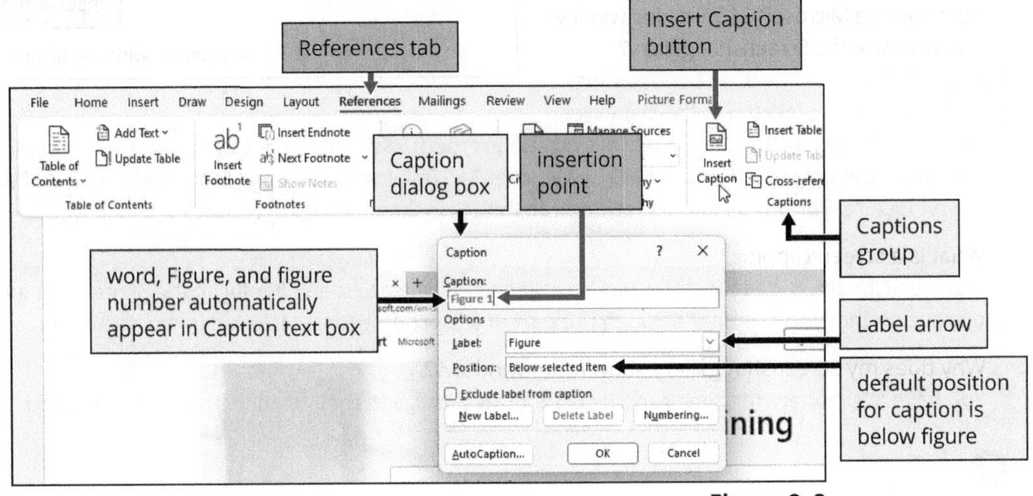

Figure 9–8

Q&A Why is the figure number a 1?

No other captions have been assigned in this document yet. When you insert a new caption, or move or delete items containing captions, Word automatically updates caption numbers throughout the document.

What if the Caption text box has the label Table or Equation instead of Figure?

Click the Label arrow (Caption dialog box) and then click Figure in the Label list.

2

- Press the COLON key (:) and then press SPACEBAR in the Caption text box (Caption dialog box) to place separating characters between the figure number and description.
- Type **Microsoft 365 Window Screenshot** as the figure description (Figure 9–9).

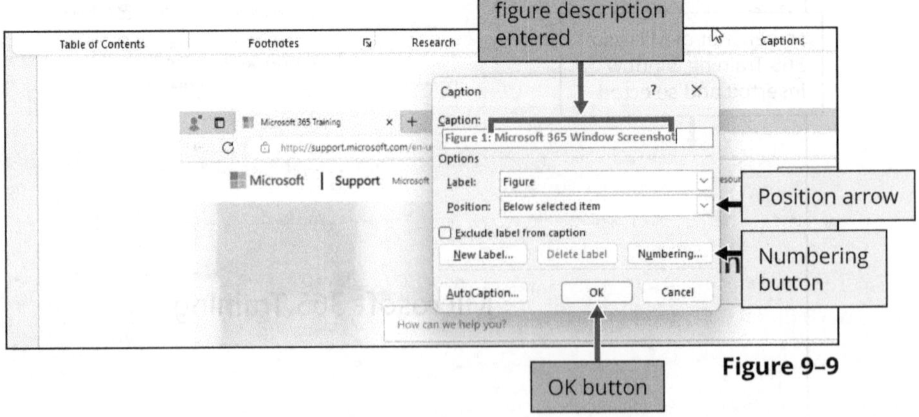

Figure 9–9

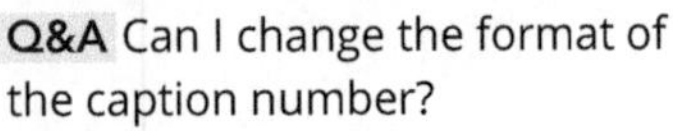

Q&A Can I change the format of the caption number?

Yes, click the Numbering button (Caption dialog box), adjust the format as desired, and then click OK.

- Click OK to insert the caption below the selected image.
- If necessary, scroll to display the caption in the document window (Figure 9–10).

Q&A How do I change the position of a caption?
Click the Position arrow (Caption dialog box) and then select the desired position of the caption.

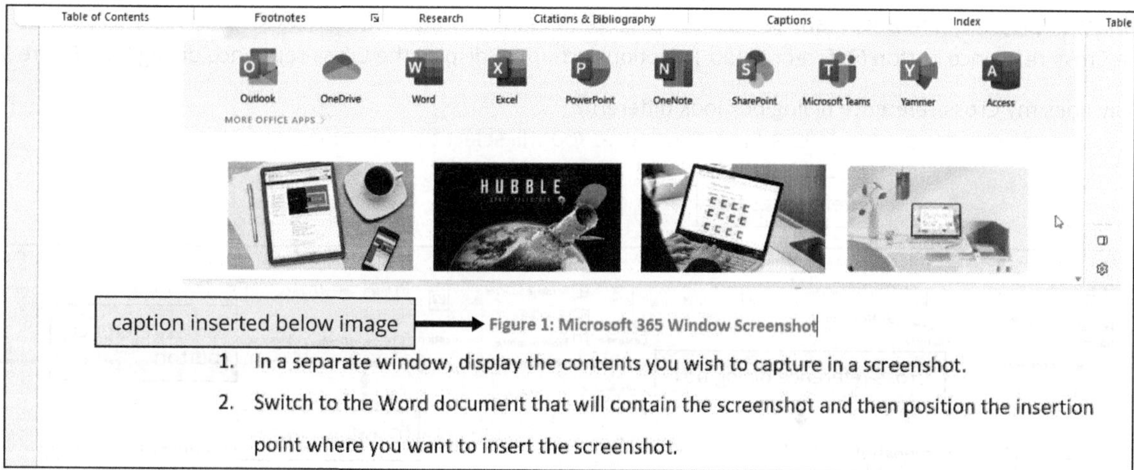

Figure 9–10

Caption Numbers

Each caption number contains a field. Recall that a field is code that serves as a placeholder for data that can change in a document. Examples of fields include page numbers, merge fields, IF fields, the current date, and caption numbers. You update caption numbers using the same technique used to update any other field. That is, to update all caption numbers, select the entire document and then press F9, or right-click the field and then click Update Field on the shortcut menu. When you print a document, Word updates the caption numbers automatically, regardless of whether the document window displays the updated caption numbers.

BTW
Captions
If a caption appears with extra characters inside curly braces ({ }), Word is displaying field codes instead of field results. Press ALT+F9 to display captions correctly as field results. If Word prints field codes for captions, click File on the ribbon to open Backstage view, click Options in Backstage view to display the Word Options dialog box, click Advanced in the left pane (Word Options dialog box), scroll to the Print section in the right pane, remove the check mark from the 'Print field codes instead of their values' check box, click OK, and then print the document again.

To Hide White Space

Recall that white space is the space displayed in the margins at the top and bottom of pages (including any headers and footers) and also space between pages. To make it easier to identify the text in this document as you scroll through it, the following step hides white space.

To hide white space, position the pointer in the document window in the space between the pages or below the last page in the document and then double-click when the pointer changes to a 'Hide White Space' button. (Or, click File on the ribbon to open Backstage view, click Options in Backstage view to display the Word Options dialog box, click Display in the left pane (Word Options dialog box), remove the check mark from the 'Show white space between pages in Print Layout view' check box, and then click OK.)

To Insert a Cross-Reference

The next step in this project is to insert a reference to the new figure. **Why?** In reference documents, the text should reference each figure specifically and, if appropriate, explain the contents of the figure.

Because figures may be inserted, deleted, or moved, you may not know the actual figure number in the final document. For this reason, Word provides a method of inserting a **cross-reference**, which is text that electronically refers the reader to another part of the document, such as a heading, caption, or footnote. You can click a cross-reference to move directly to that specific location in the document. By inserting a cross-reference to the caption, the text that mentions the figure will be updated whenever the caption to the figure is updated. The following steps insert a cross-reference.

- At the end of the last sentence in the first paragraph below the To Insert a Screenshot heading, position the insertion point to the left of the period, press SPACEBAR, and then press the LEFT PARENTHESIS [( ] key.
- If necessary, display the References tab.
- Click the Cross-reference button (References tab | Captions group) to display the Cross-reference dialog box (Figure 9–11).

Q&A Why does my Cross-reference dialog box look different?
It may be displaying contents for a different reference type. You will select the reference type in the next step.

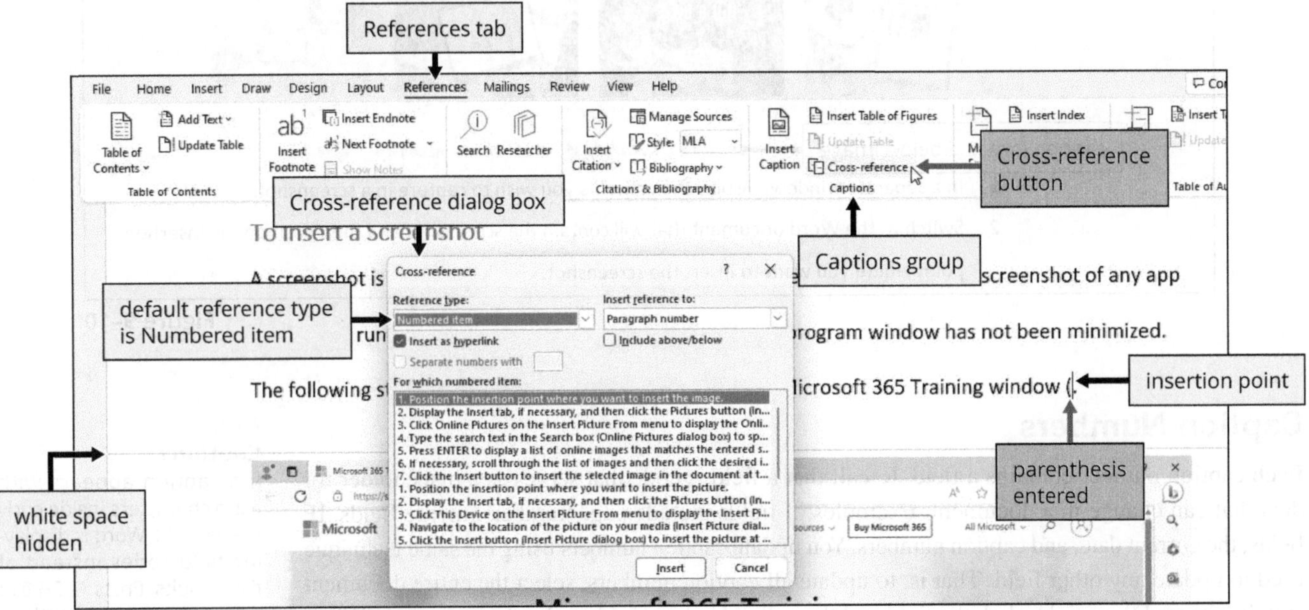

Figure 9–11

2

- Click the Reference type arrow (Cross-reference dialog box) to display the Reference type list; scroll to and then click Figure, which displays a list of figures from the document in the For which caption list (which, at this point, is only one figure).
- If necessary, click 'Figure 1: Microsoft 365 Window Screenshot' in the For which caption list to select the caption to reference.
- Click the 'Insert reference to' arrow and then click 'Only label and number' to instruct Word that the cross-reference in the document should list just the label, Figure, followed by the figure number (Figure 9–12).

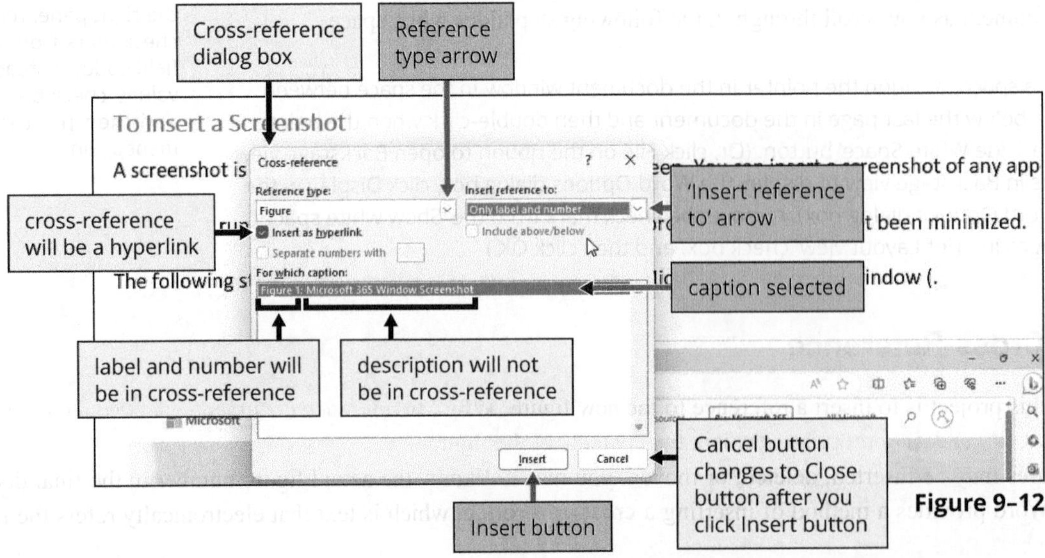

Figure 9–12

- Click the Insert button to insert the cross-reference in the document at the location of the insertion point.

Q&A What if my cross-reference is shaded in gray?
The cross-reference is a field. Depending on your Word settings, fields may appear shaded in gray to help you identify them on the screen.

- Click the Close button (Cross-reference dialog box).
- Press the RIGHT PARENTHESIS [ )] key to close off the cross-reference (Figure 9–13).

Q&A How do I update a cross-reference if a caption is added, deleted, or moved?
In many cases, Word automatically updates a cross-reference in a document if the item to which it refers changes. To update a cross-reference manually, select the cross-reference and then press F9, or right-click the cross-reference and then click Update Field on the shortcut menu.

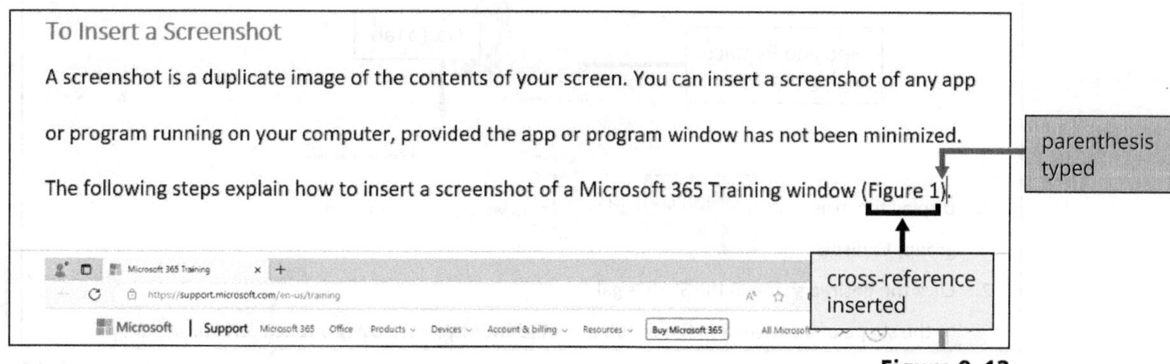

Figure 9–13

Other Ways

1. Click Cross-reference button (Insert tab | Links group)

To Go to an Object

Often, you would like to bring a certain page, image, or other part of a document into view in the document window. Although you could scroll through the document to find a desired page, image, or part of the document, Word enables you to go to a specific location via the Go To sheet in the Find and Replace dialog box.

The following steps go to an image. **Why?** The next step in this module is to add a caption to another image, which is a type of graphic, in the document, so you want to display the image in the document window.

- Display the Home tab.
- Click the Editing group button (Home tab) to the right of the Styles group to display the Editing group and then click the Find arrow (Home tab | Editing group) to display the Find menu (Figure 9–14).

Q&A What if my screen shows an Editing group instead of an Editing group button?
Click the Find arrow (Home tab | Editing group) to display the Find menu.

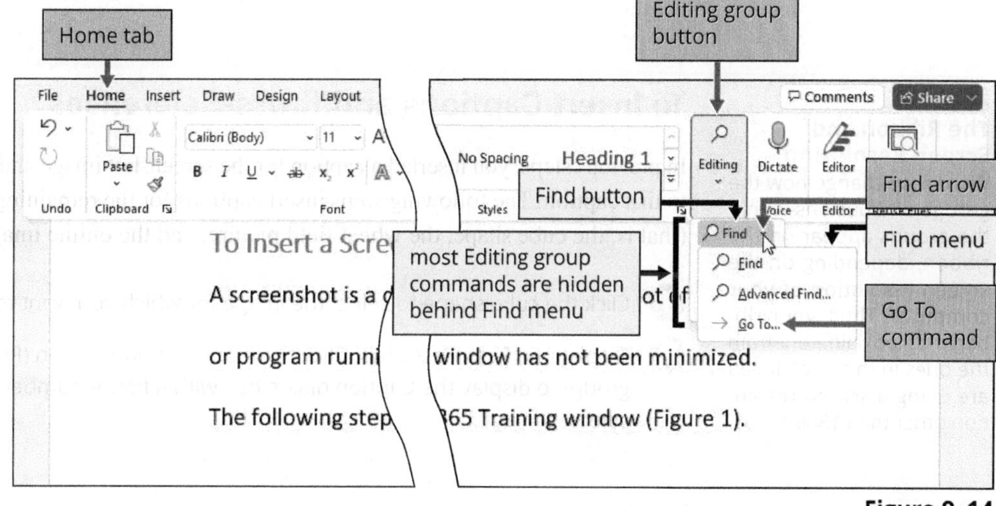

Figure 9–14

Q&A Why did the Navigation pane open on my screen?
You clicked the Find button instead of the Find arrow. Close the Navigation pane and repeat Step 1.

2

- Click Go To on the Find menu to display the Go To sheet in the Find and Replace dialog box.
- Scroll through the Go to what list and then click Graphic to select it.
- Click the Previous button to display the previous graphic in the document window (which is the cube shape, in this case) (Figure 9–15).

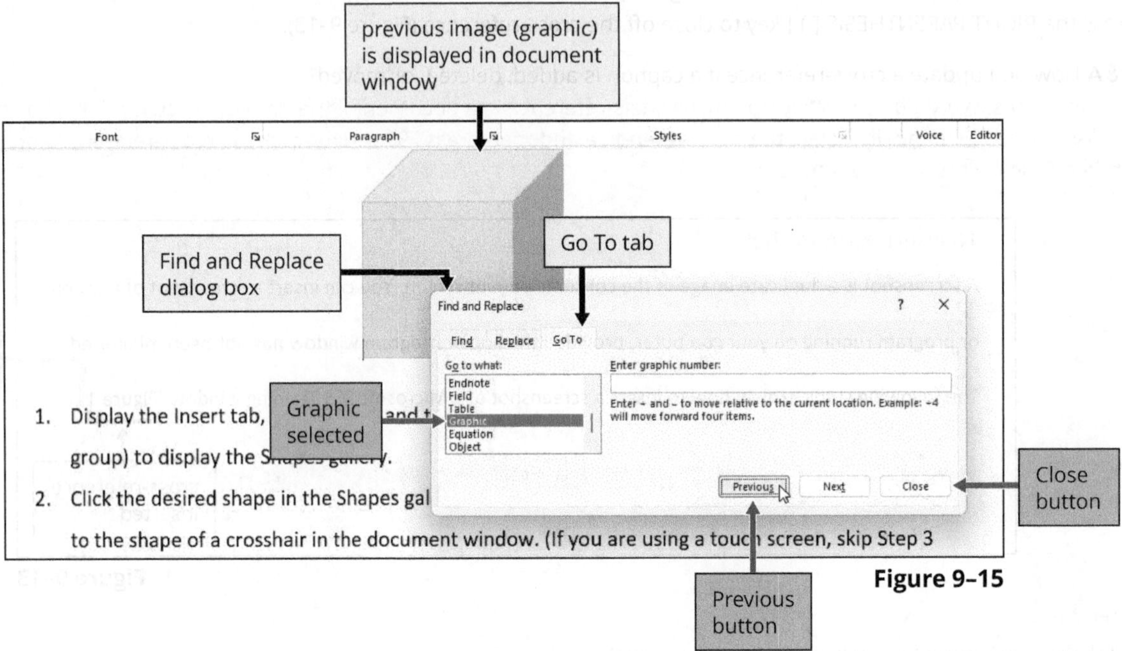

Figure 9–15

3

- Click the Close button to close the dialog box.

Q&A What if I wanted go to the next section or other location in a document?
You can go to any location listed in the Go to what list, including a page, section, line, bookmark, comment, footnote, endnote, field, table, graphic, equation, object, or heading. To go to a section, for example, you would select Section in the Go to what list and then click the Next button in the Go To sheet (Find and Replace dialog box). You also can go to the next section header or footer using the Next button (Header & Footer tab | Header & Footer group).

Other Ways

1. Press CTRL+G

BTW
The Ribbon and Screen Resolution
Word may change how the groups and buttons within the groups appear on the ribbon, depending on the screen resolution of your computer. Thus, your ribbon may look different from the ones in this book if you are using a screen resolution other than 1366 × 768.

To Insert Captions and Cross-References

In previous steps, you inserted a caption for the screenshot image and then inserted a cross-reference to that caption. The following steps insert captions for the remaining three images in the document (that is, the cube shape, the wheat field picture, and the online image of a hummingbird).

1 Click the cube shape to select the image for which you want to insert a caption.

2 Display the References tab. Click the Insert Caption button (References tab | Captions group) to display the Caption dialog box with a figure number automatically assigned to the selected image.

3. Press the COLON (:) key and then press SPACEBAR in the Caption text box (Caption dialog box) to place separating characters between the figure number and description.

4. Type **Cube Shape** as the figure description and then click OK to insert the caption below the selected image.

5. At the end of the last sentence above the cube image, change the word, below, to the word, in, and then press SPACEBAR.

6. Click the Cross-reference button (Insert or References tab | Links or Captions group) to display the Cross-reference dialog box, if necessary, click 'Figure 1: Cube Shape' in the For which caption list to select the caption to reference, click the Insert button (Cross-reference dialog box) to insert the cross-reference at the location of the insertion point, and then click the Close button in the Cross-reference dialog box.

Q&A Why did I not need to change the settings for the reference type and reference to in the dialog box?

Word retains the previous settings in the dialog box.

7. Display the Home tab. Click the Editing group button (Home tab) to display the Editing group. Click the Find arrow (Home tab | Editing group) to display the Find menu and then click Go To on the Find menu (or press CTRL+G) to display the Go To sheet in the Find and Replace dialog box. With Graphic selected in the Go to what list, click the Previous button to display the previous image in the document window (which is the wheat field picture, in this case). Click the Close button to close the dialog box.

8. Repeat Steps 1 through 7 to insert the caption, Wheat Field Picture, for the picture of the wheat field and the caption, Hummingbird Image, for the image of the hummingbird. Also add a cross-reference to the sentence above each image, replacing the word, below, with the word, in, as shown in Figure 9–16.

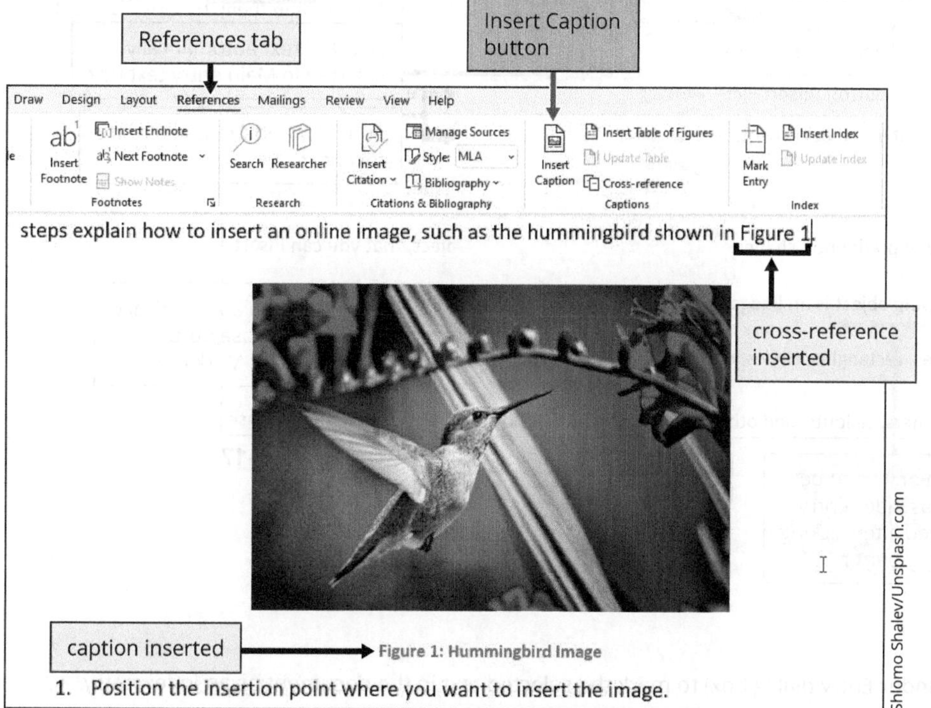

Figure 9–16

BTW

Link to Graphic

If you wanted to link a graphic in a document to a webpage, you would click the Links group button (Insert tab) to display the Links group, click the Link button (Insert tab | Links group), click 'Existing File or Web Page' in the Link to bar, enter the web address in the Address box (Insert Hyperlink dialog box), and then click OK. To display the webpage associated with the graphic, CTRL+click the graphic.

To Mark an Index Entry

The last page of the reference document in this project is an index, which lists important terms discussed in the document along with each term's corresponding page number. For Word to generate the index, you first must mark any text you wish to appear in the index. **Why?** When you mark an index entry, Word creates a field that it uses to build the index. Index entry fields are hidden and are displayed on the screen only when you show formatting marks, that is, when the 'Show/Hide ¶' button (Home tab | Paragraph group) is selected.

In this document, you want the words, drawing object, in the second sentence below the To Insert a Shape heading to be marked as an index entry. The following steps mark an index entry.

- Scroll to, if necessary, and then select the text you wish to appear in the index (the words, drawing object, in the To Insert a Shape section of the document in this case).
- Click the Mark Entry button (References tab | Index group) to display the Mark Index Entry dialog box with the selected text entered in the Main entry text box (Figure 9–17).

Q&A How would I enter a second-level index entry?
Enter the second-level text in the Subentry text box. If you wanted a third-level index entry, you would place a colon after the second-level text in the Subentry text box and then enter the third-level text after the colon. You also can enter a cross-reference to another index entry by entering the text for the other entry in the Cross-reference text box after the text, *See*.

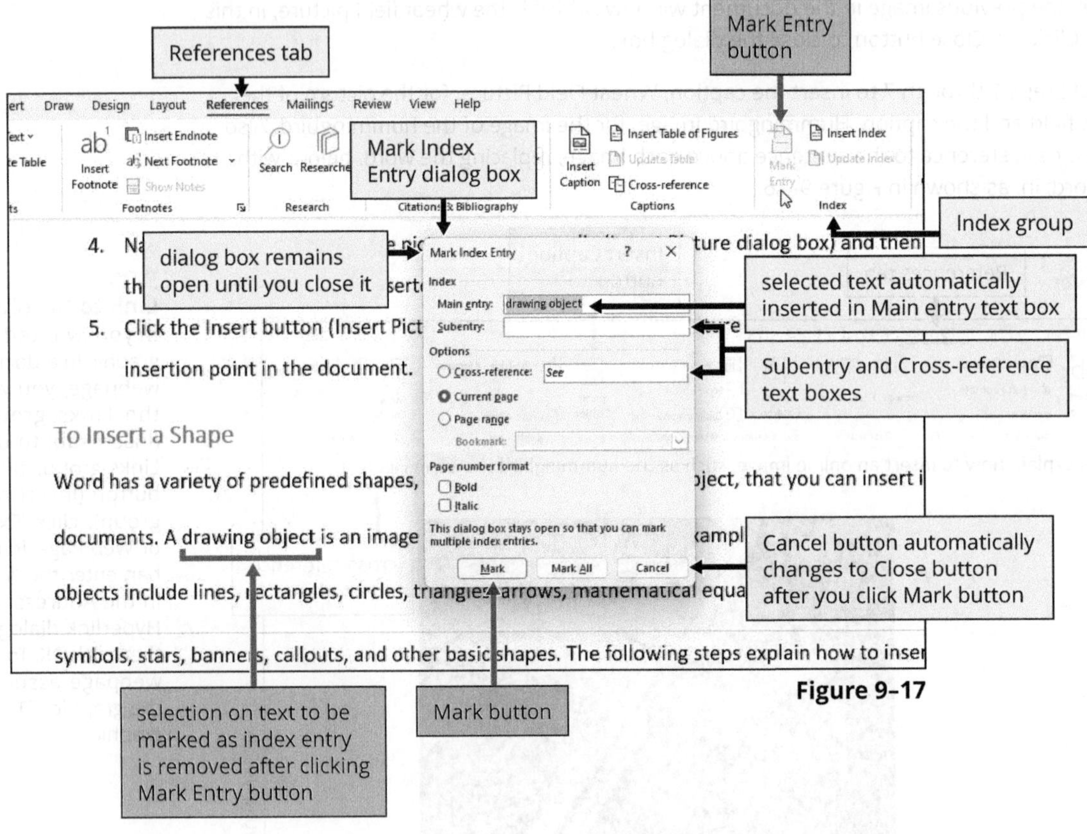

Figure 9–17

- Click the Mark button (Mark Index Entry dialog box) to mark the selected text in the document as an index entry.

Q&A Why do formatting marks now appear on the screen?
When you mark an index entry, Word automatically shows formatting marks (if they are not showing already) so that you can identify the index entry field. Notice that the marked index entry begins with the letters, XE.

- Click the Close button in the Mark Index Entry dialog box to close the dialog box; scroll up, if necessary, to display the To Insert a Shape heading (Figure 9–18).

Q&A How could I see all index entries marked in a document?
With formatting marks displaying, you could scroll through the document, scanning for all occurrences of XE, or you could use the Navigation Pane (that is, place a check mark in the Navigation Pane check box (View tab | Show group)) to find all occurrences of XE.

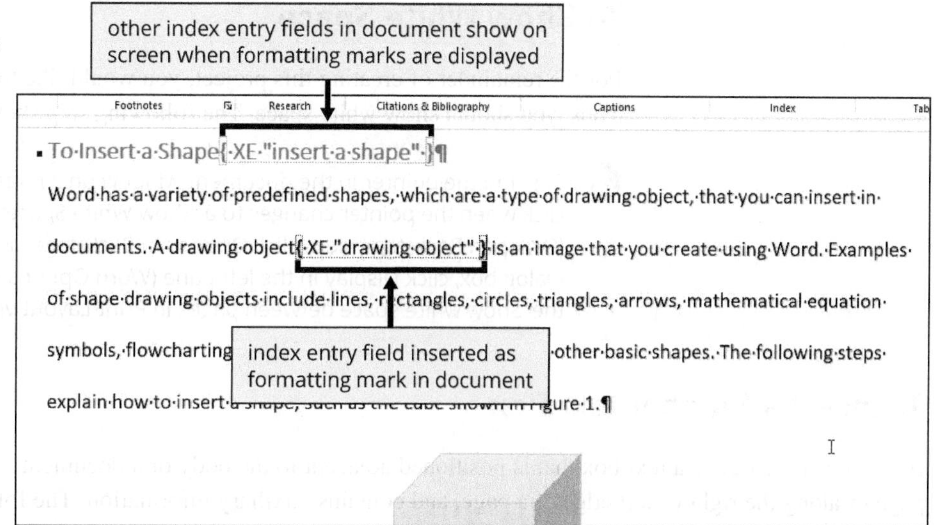

Figure 9–18

Other Ways

1. Select text, press ALT+SHIFT+X

To Mark Multiple Index Entries Word leaves the Mark Index Entry dialog box open until you close it, which allows you to mark multiple index entries without having to reopen the dialog box repeatedly. To mark multiple index entries, you would perform the following steps.

1. With the Mark Index Entry dialog box displayed, click in the document window; scroll to and then select the next index entry.
2. If necessary, click the Main entry text box (Mark Index Entry dialog box) to display the selected text in the Main entry text box.
3. Click the Mark button.
4. Repeat Steps 1 through 3 for all entries. When finished, click the Close button in the Mark Index Entry dialog box.

BTW
Index Entries
Index entries may include a switch, which is a backslash followed by a letter inserted after the field text. Switches include \b to apply bold formatting to the entry's page number, \f to define an entry type, \i to make the entry's page number italic, \r to insert a range of page numbers, \t to insert specified text in place of a page number, and \y to specify that the subsequent text defines the pronunciation for the index entry. A colon in an index entry precedes a subentry keyword in the index.

To Hide Formatting Marks

To remove the clutter of index entry fields from the document, you should hide formatting marks. The following step hides formatting marks.

1. Display the Home tab. If the 'Show/Hide ¶' button (Home tab | Paragraph group) is selected, click it to hide formatting marks.

Q&A What if the index entries still appear after clicking the 'Show/Hide ¶' button?
Open Backstage view, click Options to display the Word Options dialog box, click Display in the left pane (Word Options dialog box), remove the check mark from the Hidden text check box, and then click OK.

To Show White Space

For the remainder of creating this project, you would like to view headers, footers, and margins. Thus, you should show white space. The following step shows white space.

Position the pointer in the document window on a page break notation and then double-click when the pointer changes to a 'Show White Space' button to show white space. (Or, open Backstage view, click Options in Backstage view to display the Word Options dialog box, click Display in the left pane (Word Options dialog box), place a check mark in the 'Show white space between pages in Print Layout view' check box, and then click OK.)

To Insert a Sidebar Text Box

A **sidebar text box** is a text box that is positioned adjacent to the body of a document, running across the top or bottom of a page or along the right or left edge of a page, and contains auxiliary information. The following steps insert a built-in sidebar text box. **Why?** Sidebar text boxes take up less space on the page than text boxes positioned in the middle of the page.

- Be sure the insertion point is near the top of page 1 of the document, as shown in Figure 9–19.

Q&A Does the insertion point need to be at the top of the page?
The insertion point should be close to where you want to insert the text box.

- Display the Insert tab.
- Click the Text Box button (Insert tab | Text group) to display the Text Box gallery.
- **Experiment:** Scroll through the Text Box gallery to view the variety of available text box styles.
- Scroll to display Semaphore Sidebar in the Text Box gallery (Figure 9–19).

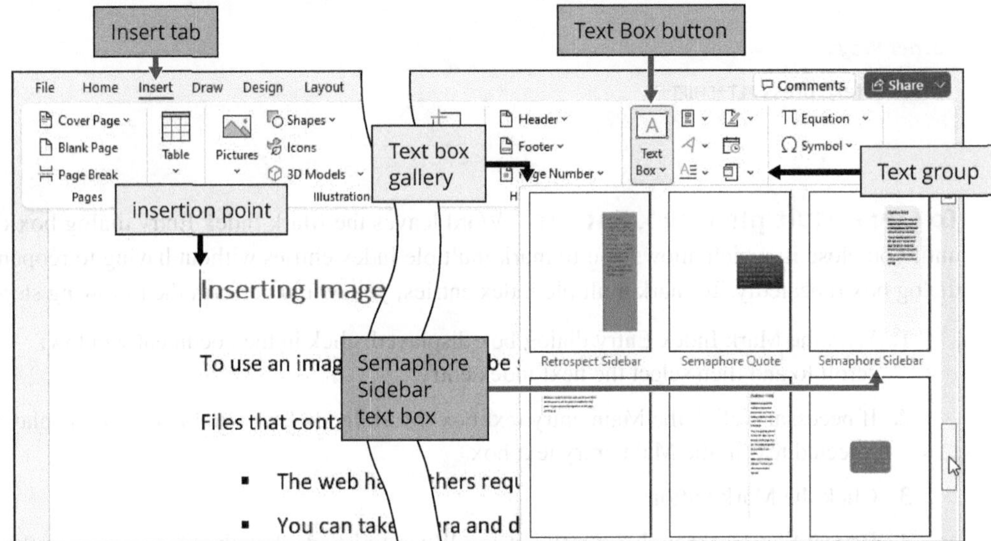

Figure 9–19

- Click Semaphore Sidebar in the Text Box gallery to insert that text box style in the document (Figure 9–20).

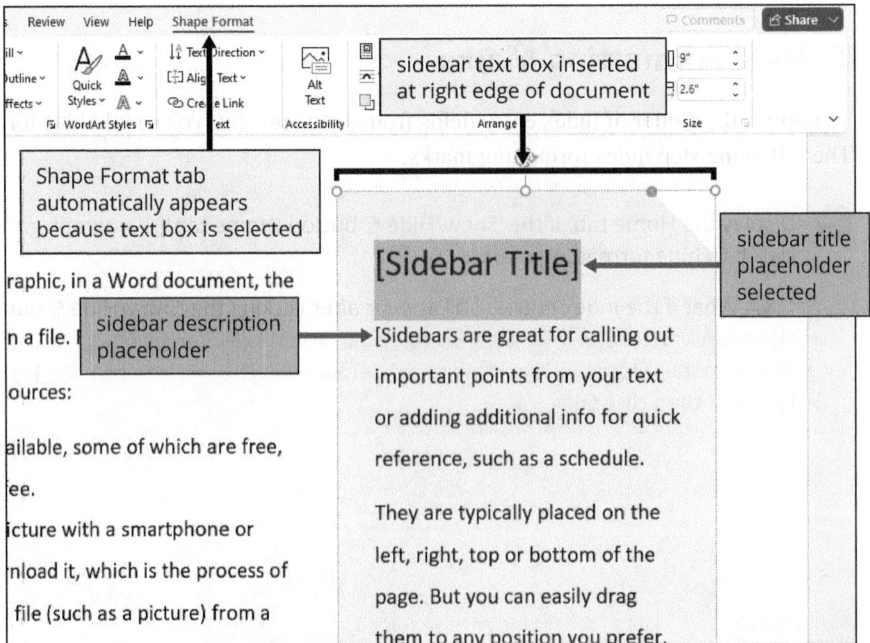

Figure 9–20

Other Ways

1. Click 'Explore Quick Parts' button (Insert tab | Text group), click 'Building Blocks Organizer' on Explore Quick Parts menu, select desired text box name in Building blocks list (Building Blocks Organizer dialog box), click Insert button

To Enter and Format Text in the Sidebar Text Box

The next step is to enter the text in the sidebar text box. The following steps enter text in the text box.

1. If necessary, click the sidebar title placeholder in the text box to select it.
2. Type **Malware** and then change the font size of the entered text to 12 point.
3. Click the sidebar description placeholder and then type the following paragraph: **Malware, short for malicious software, is software that usually acts without a user's knowledge and deliberately alters a computer or mobile device's operations. Examples of malware include viruses, worms, trojan horses, rootkits, spyware, adware, and zombies.** Change the font size of the entered text to 10 point.
4. Press ENTER. Change the font size to 12 point. Type **Tips to Protect from Malware** and then press ENTER.
5. Change the font size to 10 point. Click the Bullets button (Home tab | Paragraph group) to bullet the list. Click the Decrease Indent button (Home tab | Paragraph group) to move the bullet symbol left one-half inch. Type **Use a firewall and an antivirus or similar app.** and then press ENTER.
6. Type **Be suspicious of unsolicited email attachments and text messages.** and then press ENTER.
7. Type **Download apps or programs only from trusted websites.** and then press ENTER.
8. Type **Before using removable media, scan it for malware.** and then press ENTER.
9. Type **Back up regularly.** to enter the last line.
10. Change the line spacing of the paragraphs entered in Steps 3 and 4 to 1.15 using the Line and Paragraph Spacing button (Home tab | Paragraph group).
11. Select the text box by clicking its edge and then change its width to 2.05" using the Shape Width box (Shape Format tab | Size group) and then drag the text box so that it is positioned similarly to Figure 9–21.
12. With the text box selected, change its fill color to 'Green, Accent 6, Lighter 80%' by using the Shape Fill arrow (Shape Format tab | Shape Styles group).
13. Display the View tab and then click the One Page button (View tab | Zoom group) so that you can observe all the entered text at once (Figure 9–21).
14. Change the zoom to page width.

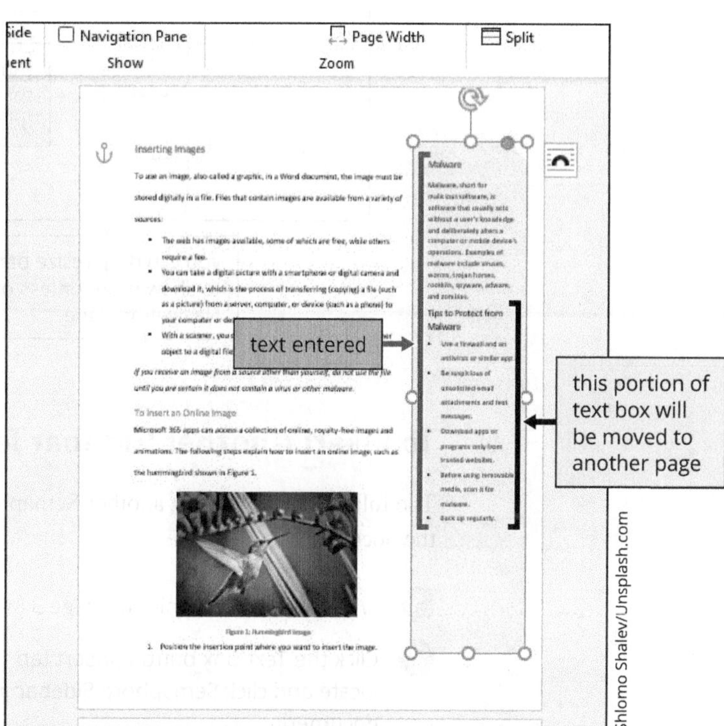

Figure 9–21

BTW
Building Blocks
Many of the objects that you can insert through the Building Blocks gallery are available as built-in objects in galleries on the ribbon. Some examples are cover pages in the Cover Page gallery (Insert tab | Pages group), equations in the Equation gallery (Insert tab | Symbols group), footers in the Footer gallery (Insert tab | Header & Footer group), headers in the Header gallery (Insert tab | Header & Footer group), page numbers in the Page Number gallery (Insert tab | Header & Footer group), text boxes in the Text Box gallery (Insert tab | Text group), and watermarks in the Watermark gallery (Design tab | Page Background group).

BTW
Deleting Building Blocks
To delete an existing building block, click the 'Explore Quick Parts' button (Insert tab | Text group) to display the Explore Quick Parts menu, click 'Building Blocks Organizer' on the Explore Quick Parts menu to display the Building Blocks Organizer dialog box, select the building block to delete (Building Blocks Organizer dialog box), click the Delete button, click Yes in the dialog box that appears, and then close the Building Blocks Organizer dialog box.

To Use the Navigation Pane to Go to a Page

Instead of one long text box, this project splits the text box across the edge of two pages, specifically, the first and third pages of this document. The following steps use the Navigation Pane to display page 3 in the document window so that you can insert another text box on that page.

1. If necessary, display the View tab. Place a check mark in the Navigation Pane check box (View tab | Show group) to open the Navigation Pane at the left edge of the Word window. If desired, drag the edge of the Navigation Pane to widen or narrow the pane so that it is similar to Figure 9–22.
2. Click the Pages tab in the Navigation Pane to display thumbnail images of the pages in the document.
3. Scroll to and then click the thumbnail of the third page in the Navigation Pane to display the top of the selected page in the top of the document window (Figure 9–22).
4. Leave the Navigation Pane open for use in the next several steps.

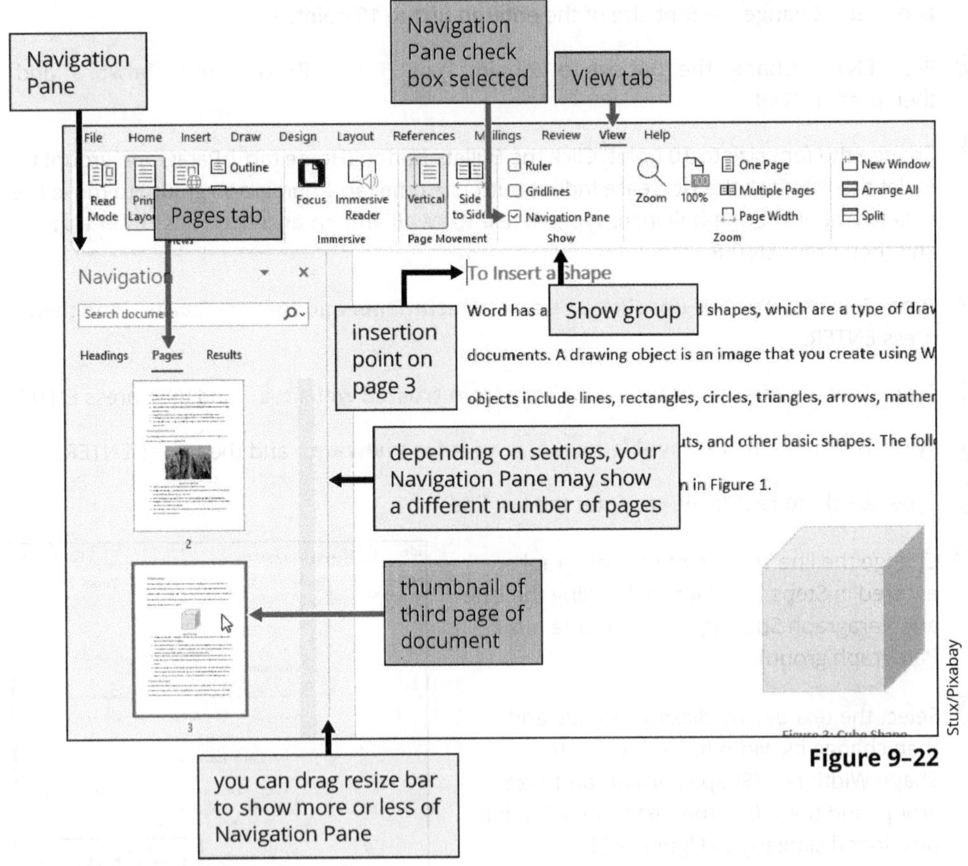

Figure 9–22

To Insert Another Sidebar Text Box

The following steps insert another Semaphor Sidebar text box building block on the third page in the document.

1. With the insertion point on page 3 in the document, display the Insert tab.
2. Click the Text Box button (Insert tab | Text group) to display the Text Box gallery and then locate and click Semaphore Sidebar in the Text Box gallery to insert that text box style in the document.

3 Press DELETE four times to delete the current contents from the text box.

4 With the text box selected, change its width to 2.05" using the Shape Width box (Shape Format tab | Size group) and then, if necessary, drag the text box rightward so that it is positioned similarly to Figure 9–23.

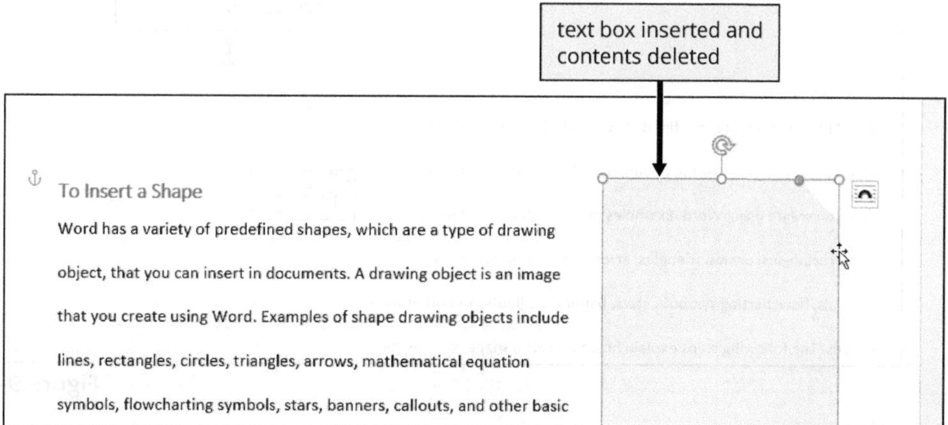

Figure 9–23

To Link Text Boxes

Word allows you to link two separate text boxes. **Why?** You can flow text from one text box into the other. To link text boxes, the second text box must be empty, which is why you deleted the contents of the text box in the previous steps. The following steps link text boxes.

- Click the thumbnail of the first page in the Navigation Pane to display the top of the selected page in the document window.
- Click an edge of the text box on the first page to select it.
- If necessary, display the Shape Format tab.
- Click the Create Link button (Shape Format tab | Text group), which changes the pointer to the shape of a pitcher.
- Move the pointer in the document window to display its new shape (Figure 9–24).

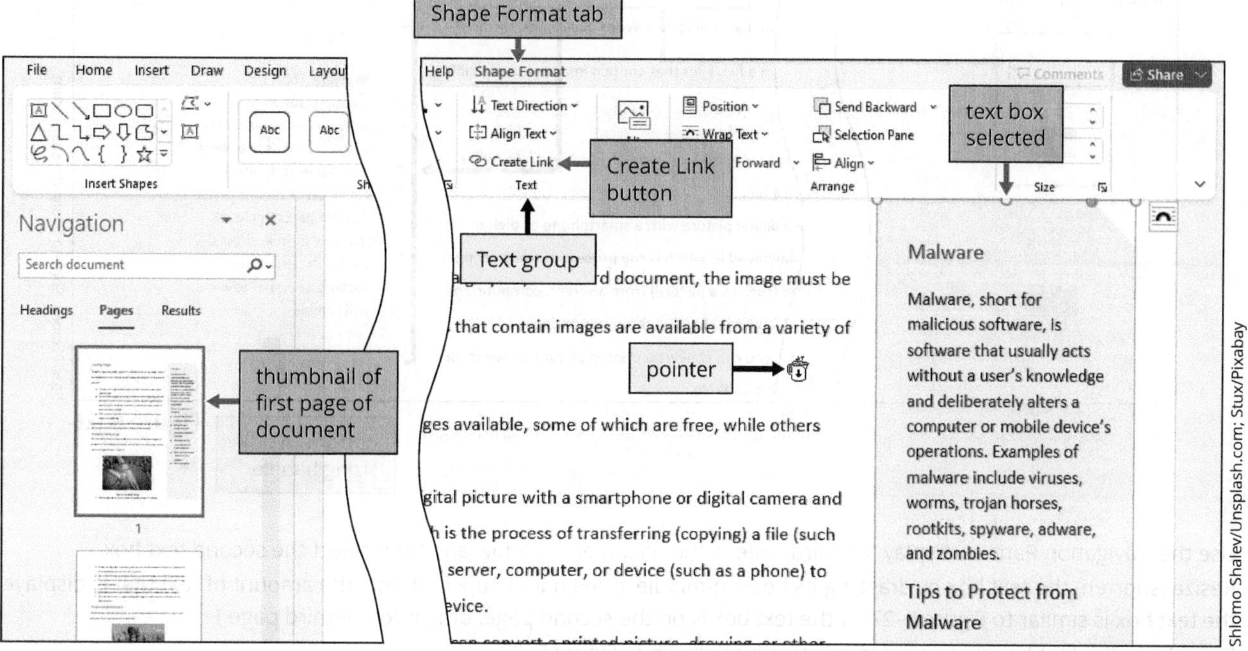

Figure 9–24

- Scroll through the document to display the second text box, which is located on the third page, in the document window.

Q&A Can I use the Navigation Pane to go to the second text box?
No. If you click in the Navigation Pane, the link process will stop and the pointer will return to its default shape.

- Position the pointer in the empty text box, so that the pointer shape changes to a pouring pitcher (Figure 9–25).

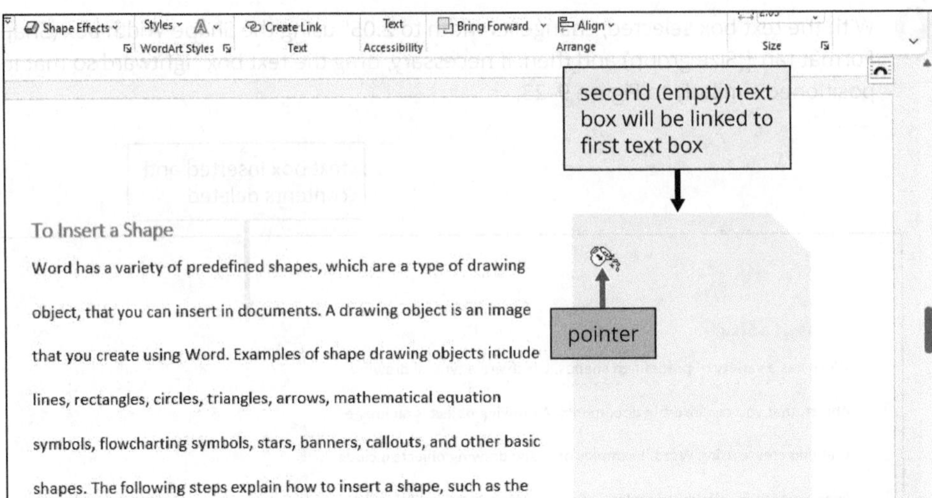

Figure 9–25

3

- Click the empty text box to link it to the first text box (or, if using a touch screen, you will need to use a stylus to tap the empty text box).
- Use the Navigation Pane to display the first text box on the first page in the document window and then, if necessary, select the text box.
- Resize (shorten) the text box by dragging its bottom-middle sizing handle upward until the amount of text that is displayed in the text box is similar to Figure 9–26.
- Drag the text box so that its position is similar to Figure 9–26.

Q&A How would I remove a link?
Select the text box in which you created the link and then click the Break Link button (Shape Format tab | Text group); note the Create Link button changes to a Break Link button when you select a linked text box.

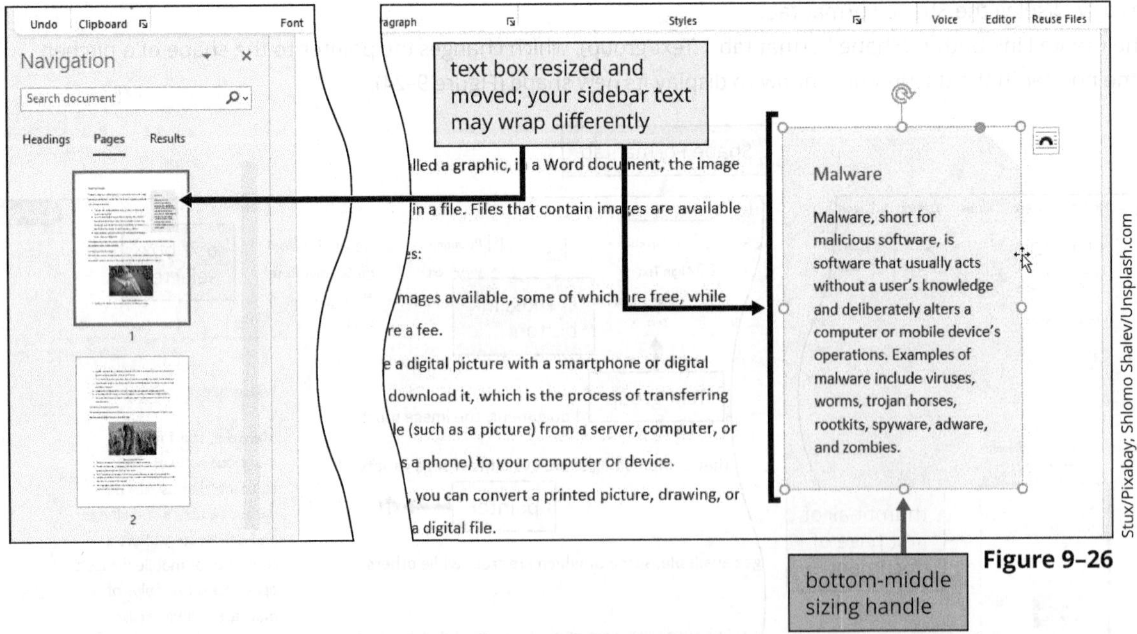

Figure 9–26

4

- Use the Navigation Pane to display the third page in the document window and then select the second text box.
- Resize (shorten) the text box by dragging its bottom-middle sizing handle upward until the amount of text that is displayed in the text box is similar to Figure 9–27. (If the text box is on the second page, drag it to the third page.)
- Drag the entire text box downward to position it as shown in Figure 9–27.
- Verify that all of Step #4 in the document fits on the third page. If it does not, adjust the size or location of the text box or the line and paragraph spacing on the page so that all the To Insert a Shape text fits on the third page.

- Select the text box by clicking its edge and then change its fill color to 'Green, Accent 6, Lighter 80%' by using the Shape Fill arrow (Shape Format tab | Shape Styles group) so that the final text box appears as shown in Figure 9–27.
- If necessary, insert a page break to the left of the To Insert a Shape heading so that the heading begins at the top of the third page.

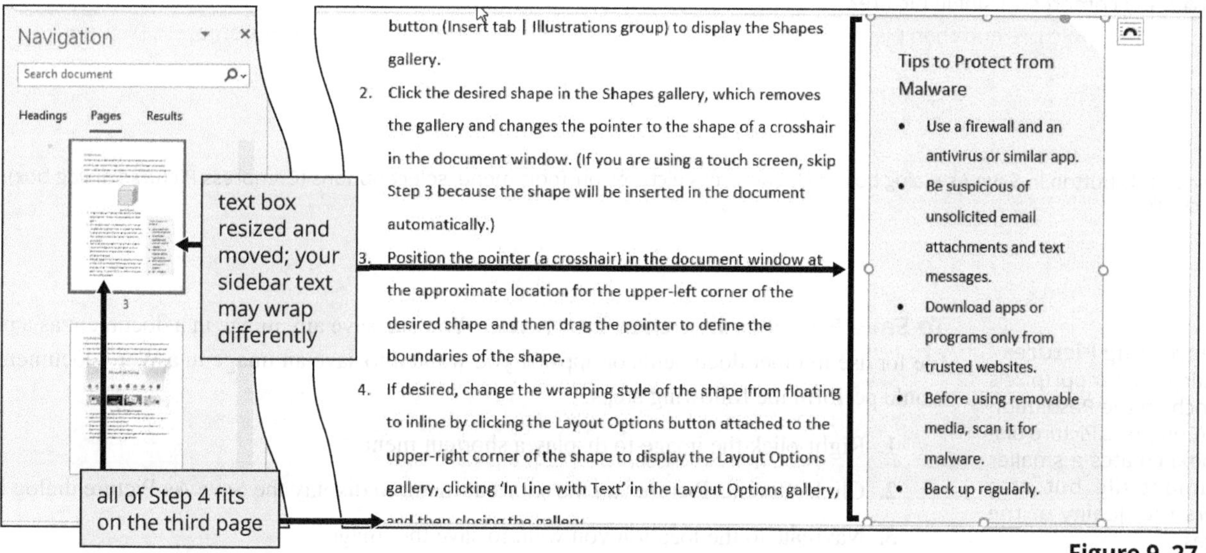

Figure 9–27

To Compress Pictures

If you plan to use email to send a Word document that contains pictures or other images or post it for downloading, you may want to reduce its file size to speed up file transmission time. **Why?** Pictures and other images in Word documents can increase the size of these files. In Word, you can compress pictures, which reduces the size of the Word document. Compressing the pictures in Word does not cause any loss in their original quality. The following steps compress pictures in a document.

- Click a picture in the document to select it, such as the wheat field, and then display the Picture Format tab.
- Click the Compress Pictures button (Picture Format tab | Adjust group) to display the Compress Pictures dialog box.
- If the 'Apply only to this picture' check box (Compress Pictures dialog box) contains a check mark, remove the check mark so that all pictures in the document are compressed.
- If necessary, click 'Use default resolution' in the Resolution area to specify how images should be compressed (Figure 9–28).

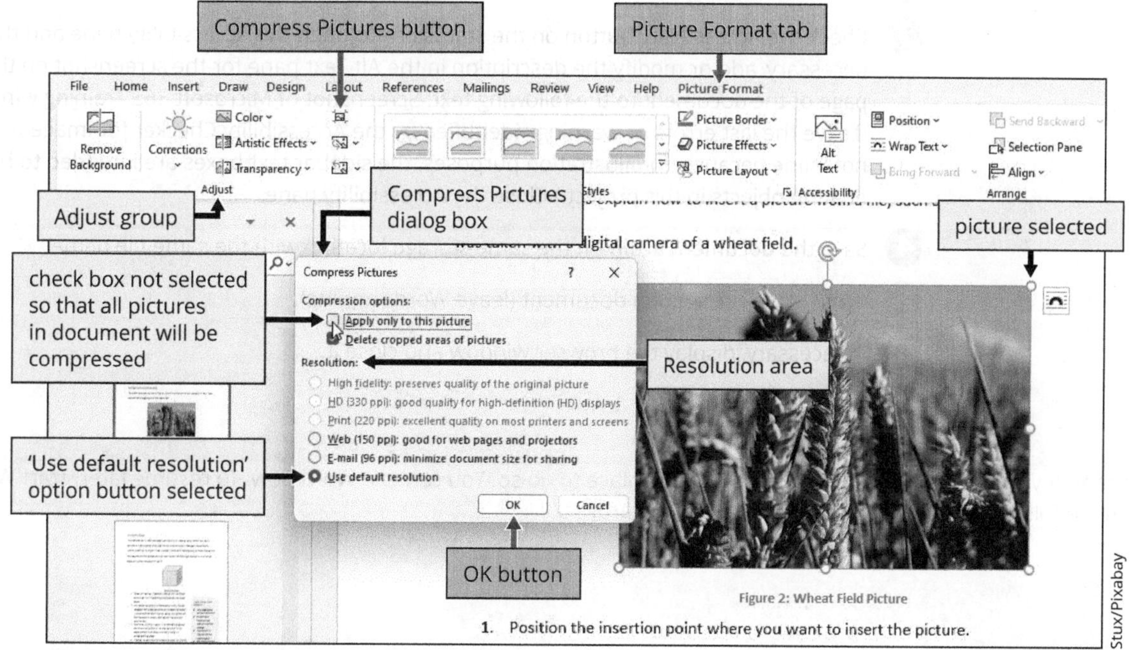

Figure 9–28

• Click OK to compress all pictures in the document.

Q&A Can I compress a single picture?
Yes. Select the picture and then place a check mark in the 'Apply only to this picture' check box (Compress Pictures dialog box).

Other Ways

1. Click Tools button in Save As dialog box, click Compress Pictures on Tools menu, select options (Compress Pictures dialog box), click OK

BTW
Compressing Pictures
Selecting a lower ppi (pixels per inch) in the Resolution area (Compress Picture dialog box) creates a smaller document file but also lowers the quality of the images.

To Save Pictures in Other Formats You can save any image in a document as a picture file for use in other documents or apps. If you wanted to save an image in a Word document, you would perform the following steps.

1. Right-click the image to display a shortcut menu.
2. Click 'Save as Picture' on the shortcut menu to display the Save As Picture dialog box.
3. Navigate to the location you want to save the image.
4. Click the 'Save as type' arrow (Save As Picture dialog box) and then select the image type for the saved image.
5. Click the Save button (Save As Picture dialog box) to save the image in the specified location using the specified image type.

To Finish and Close the Open Document and Window

The following steps update cross references, if necessary, add alt text to the screenshot, save the document again, and then close the open Word document and the browser window.

1. If necessary, update the cross references (right-click them and then click Update Field on the shortcut menu, or select the entire document and then press F9).
2. If necessary, close the Navigation Pane.
3. Check the Accessibility button on the status bar to open the Accessibility pane and then, if necessary, add or modify the description in the Alt Text pane for the screenshot on the last page of the document to the following text: Screenshot of Microsoft 365 Training window. (Leave the last errors or warnings identified by the Accessibility Checker for image or object not inline because, for illustration purposes, the sidebar text boxes are intended to be floating objects in this project.) Close the Accessibility pane.
4. Save the document again on the same storage location with the same file name.
5. sam Close the open document (leave Word running).
6. If necessary, display the browser window and close it.

Break Point: If you want to take a break, this is a good place to do so. You can exit Word now. To resume later, start Word and continue following the steps from this location forward.

Working with a Master Document

When you are creating a document that includes other files, you may want to create a master document to organize the documents. A **master document** is simply a document that contains links to one or more other documents, each of which is called a **subdocument**. In addition to subdocuments, a master document can contain its own text and images.

The master file is SC_WD_9_Microsoft365_WordInsertImages_MasterDocument.docx in this project. This master document file contains a link to one subdocument (the document you created in the first part of this module): SC_WD_9_WordInsertImages.docx. The master document also contains other items: a cover page, a copyright page, and an index. The following sections create this master document and insert the necessary elements in the document to create the finished SC_WD_9_Microsoft365_WordInsertImages_MasterDocument.docx.

BTW
Master Documents
Master documents can be used when multiple people prepare different sections of a document or when a document contains separate elements, such as the modules in a book. If multiple people in a network need to work on the same document simultaneously, each person can work on a section (subdocument); all subdocuments can be stored together collectively in a master document on the network server.

Outlines

To create a master document, Word must be in Outline view. You then enter the headings of the document as an outline using Word's built-in heading styles. In an outline, the major heading is displayed at the left margin with each subordinate, or lower-level, heading indented. In Word, the built-in Heading 1 style is displayed at the left margin in Outline view. Heading 2 style is indented below Heading 1 style, Heading 3 style is indented further, and so on. (Outline view works similarly to multilevel lists.)

You do not want to use a built-in heading style for the paragraphs of text within the document, because when you create a table of contents, Word places all lines formatted using the built-in heading styles in the table of contents. Thus, the text below each heading is formatted using the Body Text style.

Each heading should print at the top of a new page. Because you might want to format the pages within a heading differently from those pages in other headings, you insert next page section breaks between each heading.

To Switch to Outline View

The following steps switch to Outline view. **Why?** To create a master document, Word must be in Outline view.

- sam ↓ If necessary, start Word and create a new blank document.
- Display the View tab (Figure 9–29).

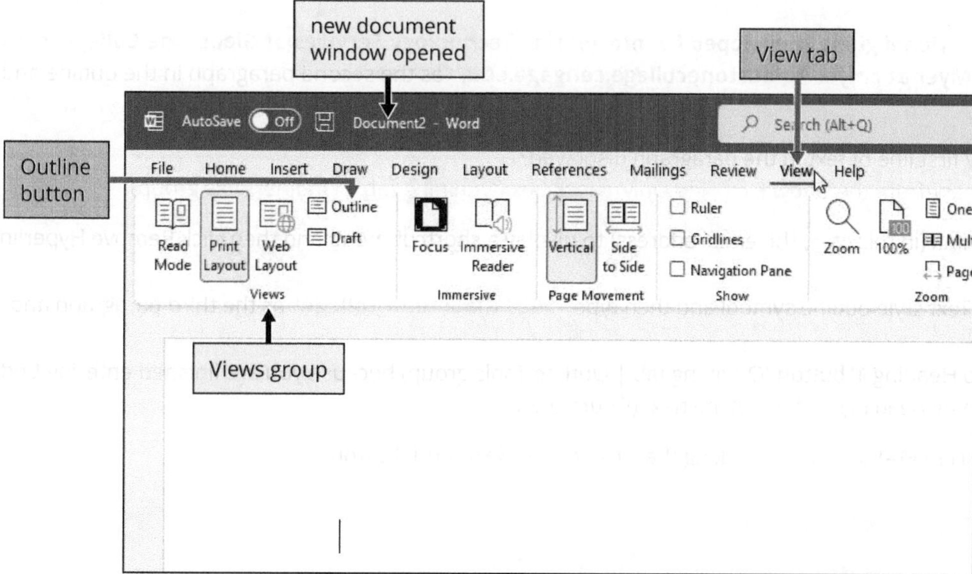

Figure 9–29

- Click the Outline button (View tab | Views group), which displays the Outlining tab on the ribbon and switches to Outline view.
- Be sure the 'Show Text Formatting' check box is selected and the 'Show First Line Only' check box is not selected (Outlining tab | Outline Tools group) (Figure 9–30).

Q&A Can I specify the number of levels (headings) that will be displayed in the outline?
Yes, click the Show Level button (Outlining tab | Outline Tools group) and then select the desired level. The selected level and all higher levels will appear in the outline. To show all levels, select All Levels.

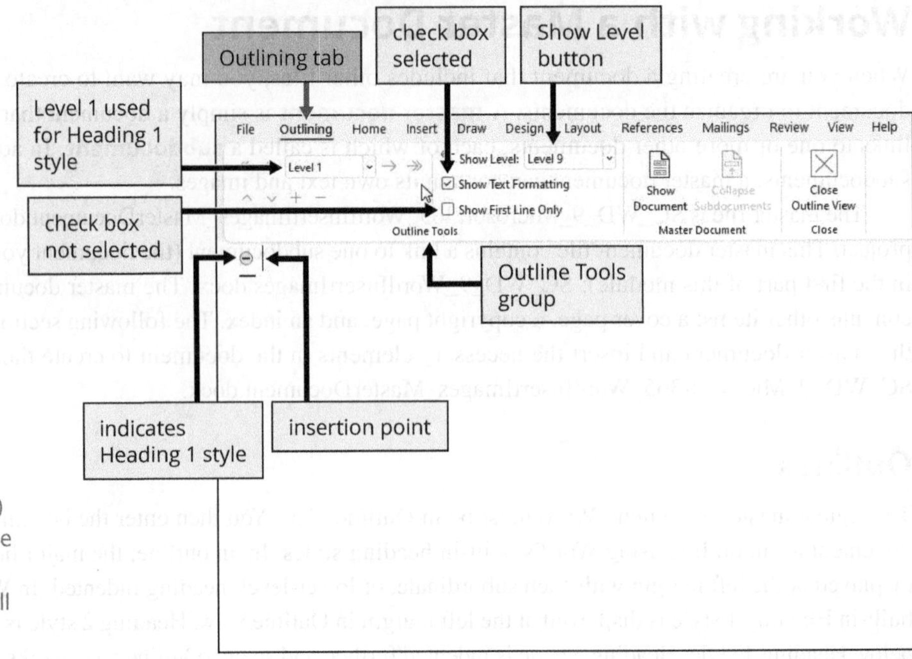

Figure 9–30

To Enter Text in Outline View

The SC_WD_9_Microsoft365_WordInsertImages_MasterDocument.docx document contains these three major headings: Inserting Images, Table of Figures, and Index. The heading, Inserting Images, is not entered in the outline. **Why not?** It is part of the subdocument inserted in the master document.

The copyright page, also in the master document, does not contain a heading; instead it contains three paragraphs of body text, which you enter directly in the outline. The Inserting Images content is inserted from the subdocument. You will instruct Word to create the content for the Table of Figures and Index later in this module. The following steps create an outline that contains headings and body text to be used in the master document.

- Click the 'Demote to Body Text' button (Outlining tab | Outline Tools group), so that you can enter the paragraphs of text for the copyright page.
- Type **Learning Microsoft 365 – Word Guide #19 – How to Insert Images** as the first paragraph in the outline and then press ENTER.
- Type **To receive additional guides developed by Information Technology Services at Gladstone College, send a message to Charis Myer at cmyer@gladstonecollege.cengage.edu.** as the second paragraph in the outline and then press ENTER.

Q&A Why is only my first line of text in the paragraph displayed?
Remove the check mark from the 'Show First Line Only' check box (Outlining tab | Outline Tools group).

- Right-click the hyperlink (in this case, the email address) to display a shortcut menu and then click Remove Hyperlink on the shortcut menu.
- Click the third Body Text style outline symbol and then type **2029 Gladstone College** as the third paragraph and then press ENTER.
- Click the 'Promote to Heading 1' button (Outlining tab | Outline Tools group) because you are finished entering body text and will enter the remaining headings in the outline next (Figure 9–31).

Q&A Could I press SHIFT+TAB instead of clicking the 'Promote to Heading 1' button?
Yes.

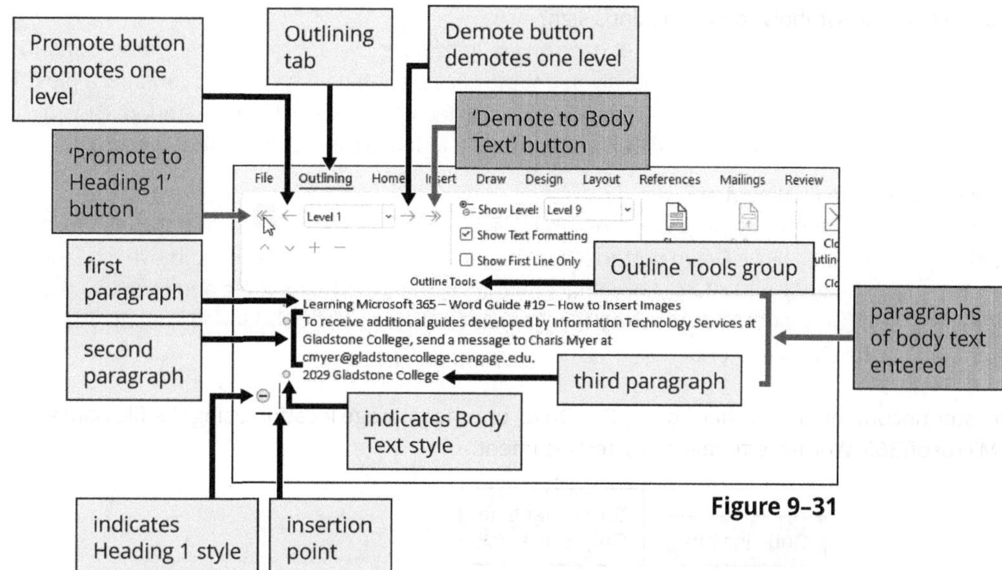

Figure 9–31

- Display the Layout tab.
- With the insertion point positioned as shown in Figure 9–31, click the Breaks button (Layout tab | Page Setup group) and then click Next Page in the Section Breaks area in the Breaks gallery because you want to enter a next page section break before the next heading.

3

- Type **Table of Figures** and then press ENTER.
- Repeat Step 2.

4

- Type **Index** as the last entry (Figure 9–32).

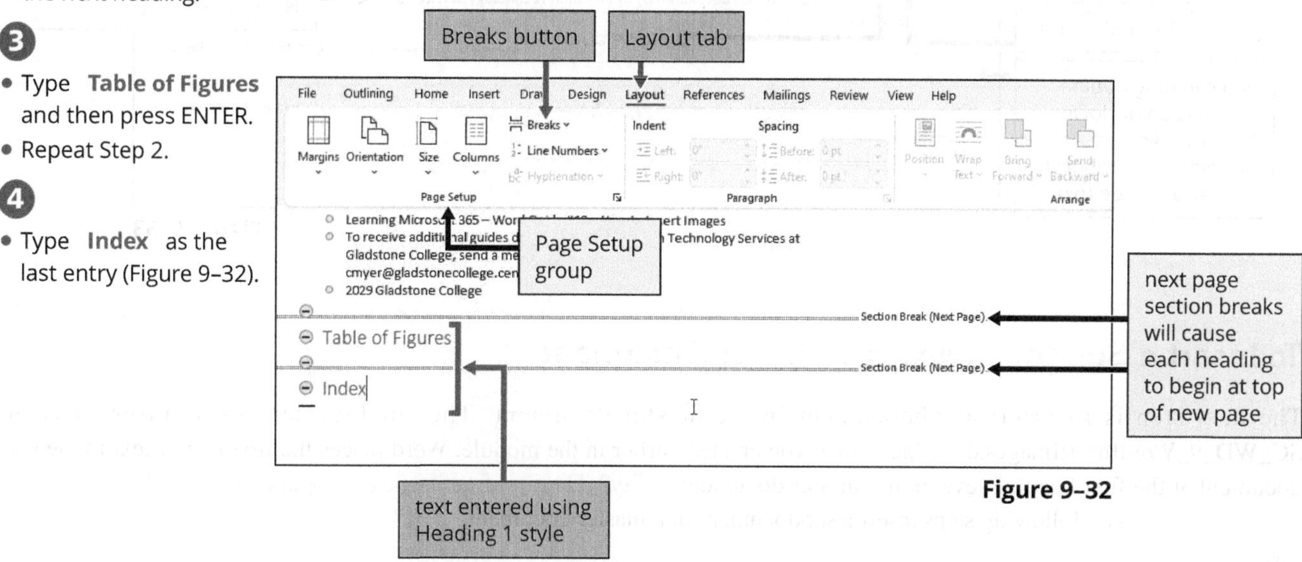

Figure 9–32

To Show Only the First Line of Each Paragraph in Outline View

Users often instruct Word to display just the first line of each paragraph of body text. **Why?** When only the first line of each paragraph is displayed, the outline often is more readable. The following step displays only the first line of body text paragraphs.

- Display the Outlining tab.
- Place a check mark in the 'Show First Line Only' check box (Outlining tab | Outline Tools group), so that Word displays only the first line of each paragraph (Figure 9–33).

Q&A How would I redisplay all lines of the paragraphs of body text?

Remove the check mark from the 'Show First Line Only' check box (Outlining tab | Outline Tools group).

Q&A Why do the outline symbols contain a minus sign?

The minus sign means the outline level does not have any subordinate levels. If an outline symbol contains a plus sign, it means the outline level has subordinate levels. If you double-click an outline symbol that contains a plus sign, the section under the heading will expand (show) if it is collapsed (hidden) and will collapse if it is expanded. Or with the insertion point in the heading, you can click the Expand and Collapse buttons (Outlining tab | Outline Tools group).

How do I move headings in Outline view?

You can drag the outline symbols up or down to rearrange headings. You also can position the insertion point in a heading and then click the Move Up or Move Down button (Outlining tab | Outline Tools group) to move a heading up or down, respectively. To move a heading and all its subordinate headings, collapse the heading and then use the Move Up or Move Down buttons. You also can move headings using the Navigation Pane by right-clicking the heading and then clicking the desired command on the shortcut menu.

- Save this master document on your hard drive, OneDrive, or other storage location using the file name, SC_WD_9_Microsoft365_WordInsertImages_MasterDocument.

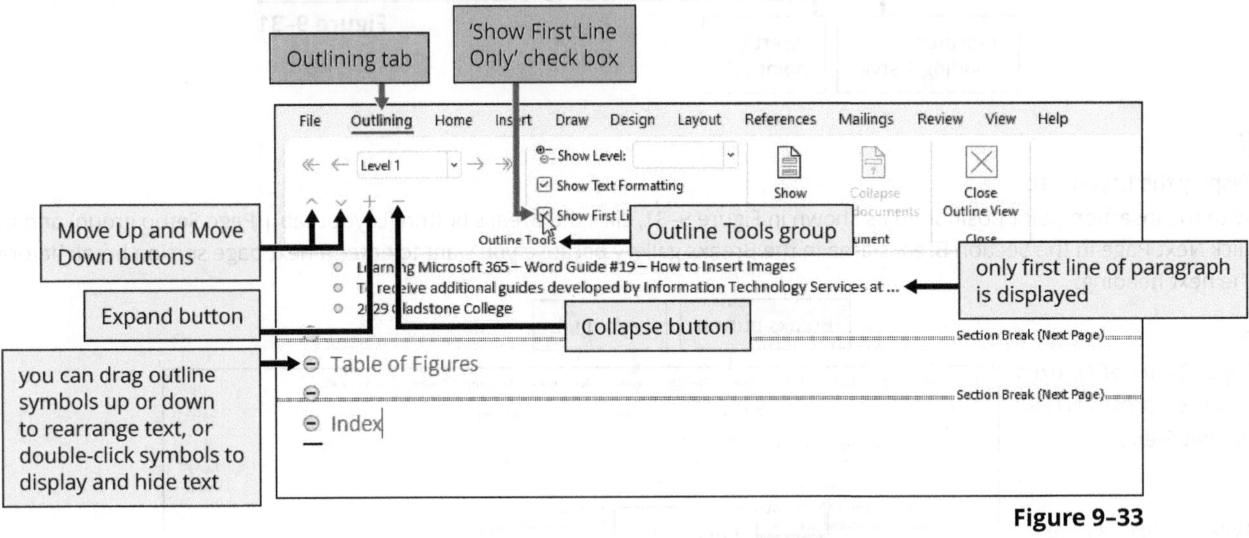

Figure 9–33

To Insert a Subdocument in a Master Document

The next step is to insert a subdocument in the master document. The subdocument to be inserted is the SC_WD_9_WordInsertImages.docx file, which you created earlier in the module. Word places the first line of text in the subdocument at the first heading level in the master document. **Why?** The first line in the subdocument was defined using the Heading 1 style. The following steps insert a subdocument in a master document.

- Display the Home tab. If formatting marks do not appear, click the 'Show/Hide ¶' button (Home tab | Paragraph group) to display formatting marks.
- Position the insertion point where you want to insert the subdocument (on the section break above the Table of Figures heading).
- Display the Outlining tab. Click the Show Document button (Outlining tab | Master Document group) so that all commands in the Master Document group appear.
- Click the Insert button (Outlining tab | Master Document group) to display the Insert Subdocument dialog box.
- Locate and select your SC_WD_9_WordInsertImages.docx file (Insert Subdocument dialog box) (Figure 9–34). (Depending on settings, the file extension of .docx may or may not appear in the dialog box.)

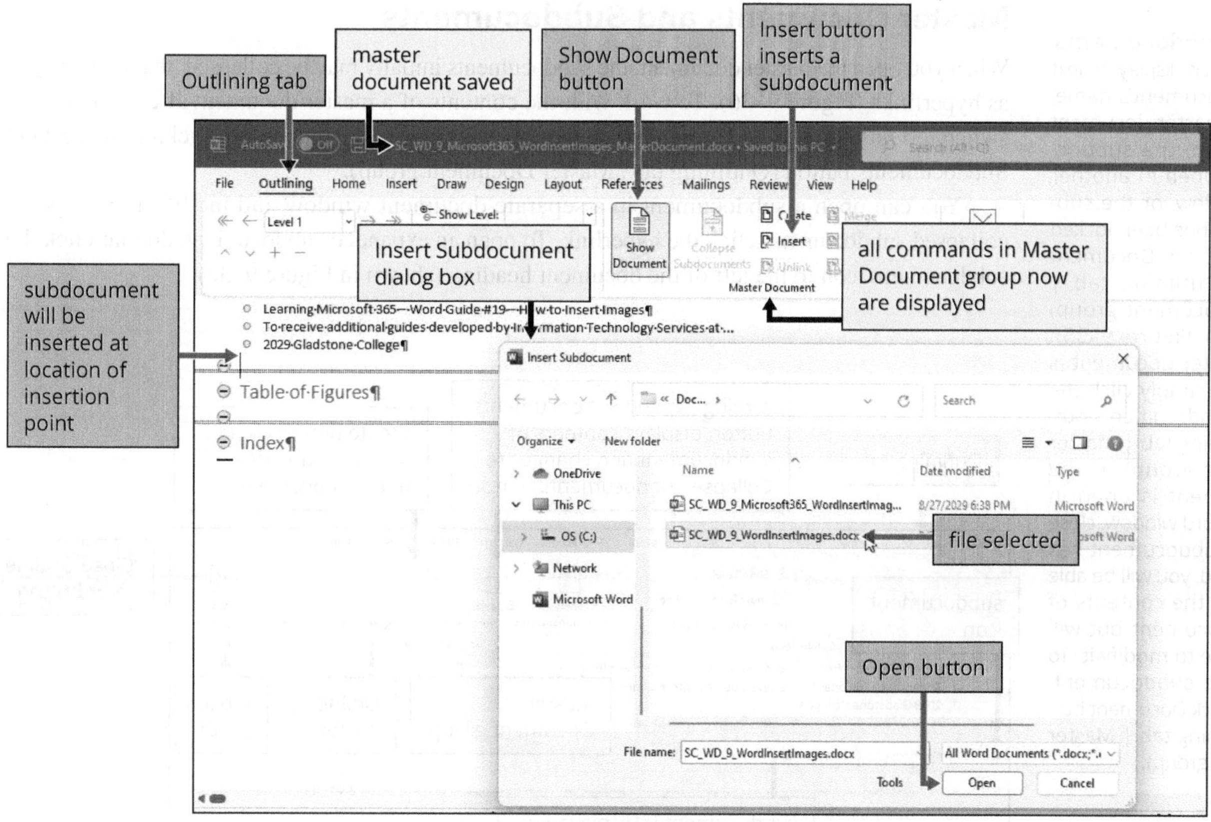

Figure 9–34

2

- Click the Open button (Insert Subdocument dialog box) to insert the selected file as a subdocument.
- If Word displays a dialog box about styles, click the 'No to All' button.
- Press CTRL+HOME to position the insertion point at the top of the document (Figure 9–35).

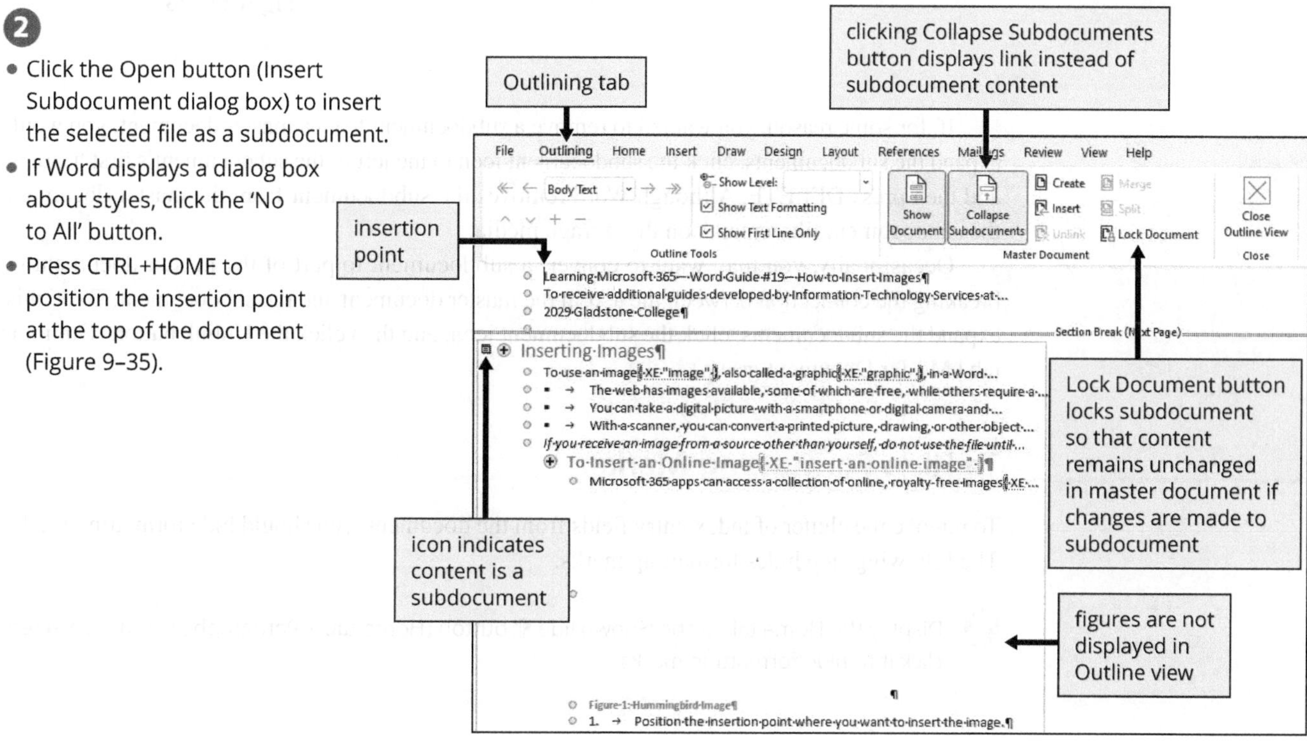

Figure 9–35

BTW

Locked Subdocuments

If a lock icon is displayed next to a subdocument's name, then the master document is collapsed, the subdocument is open in another Word window, or the subdocument has been locked using the Lock Document button (Outlining tab | Master Document group) (shown in Figure 9–35). If the master document is collapsed, simply click the Expand Subdocuments button (Outlining tab | Master Document group). If the subdocument is open in another Word window, close it. If the subdocument has been locked, you will be able to display the contents of the subdocument but will not be able to modify it. To unlock the subdocument, click the Lock Document button (Outlining tab | Master Document group).

Master Documents and Subdocuments

When you open the master document, the subdocuments initially may be collapsed; that is, displayed as hyperlinks (Figure 9–36). To work with the contents of a master document after you open it, switch to Outline view and then, if necessary, expand the subdocuments by clicking the Expand Subdocuments button (Outlining tab | Master Document group).

You can open a subdocument in a separate document window and modify it. To open a collapsed subdocument, click the hyperlink. To open an expanded subdocument, double-click the subdocument icon to the left of the document heading (shown in Figure 9–36).

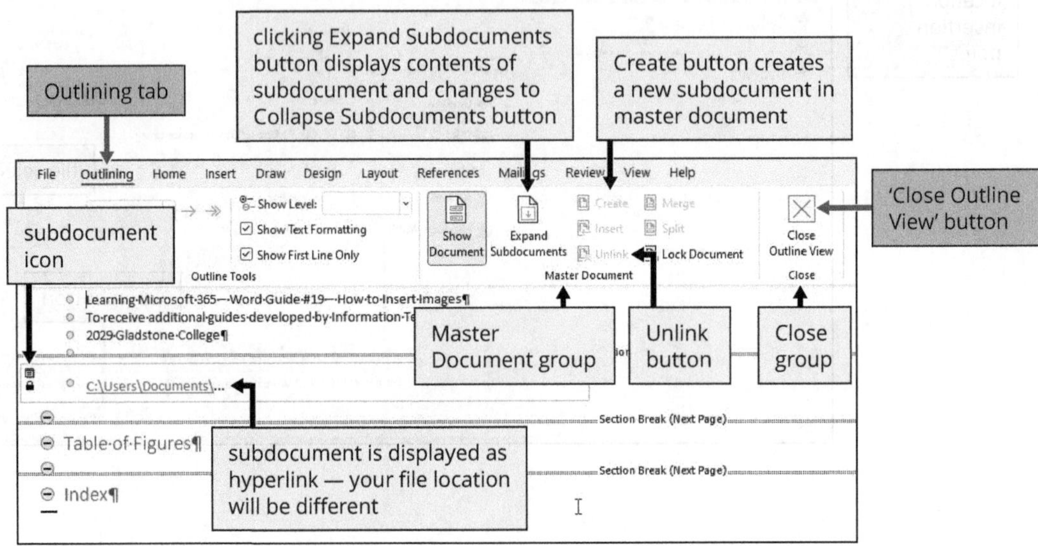

Figure 9–36

If, for some reason, you wanted to remove a subdocument from a master document, you would expand the subdocuments, click the subdocument icon to the left of the subdocument's first heading, and then press DELETE. Although Word removes the subdocument from the master document, the subdocument file remains on the storage media.

Occasionally, you may want to convert a subdocument to part of the master document — breaking the connection between the text in the master document and the subdocument. To do this, expand the subdocuments, click the subdocument icon, and then click the Unlink button (Outlining tab | Master Document group).

To Hide Formatting Marks

To remove the clutter of index entry fields from the document, you should hide formatting marks. The following step hides formatting marks.

Display the Home tab. If the 'Show/Hide ¶' button (Home tab | Paragraph group) is selected, click it to hide formatting marks.

To Close Outline View

The following step closes Outline view. **Why?** You are finished organizing the master document.

- Display the Outlining tab.
- Click the 'Close Outline View' button (shown in Figure 9–36) (Outlining tab | Close group) to redisplay the document in Print Layout view, which selects the Print Layout button on the status bar.
- If necessary, press CTRL+HOME to display the top of the document (Figure 9–37).
- **Experiment:** Scroll through the document to familiarize yourself with the sections. When finished, display the top of the document in the document window.
- Note that the document should contain seven pages. If it contains any extra blank pages, delete the blank pages.
- Save the document again on the same storage location with the same file name.

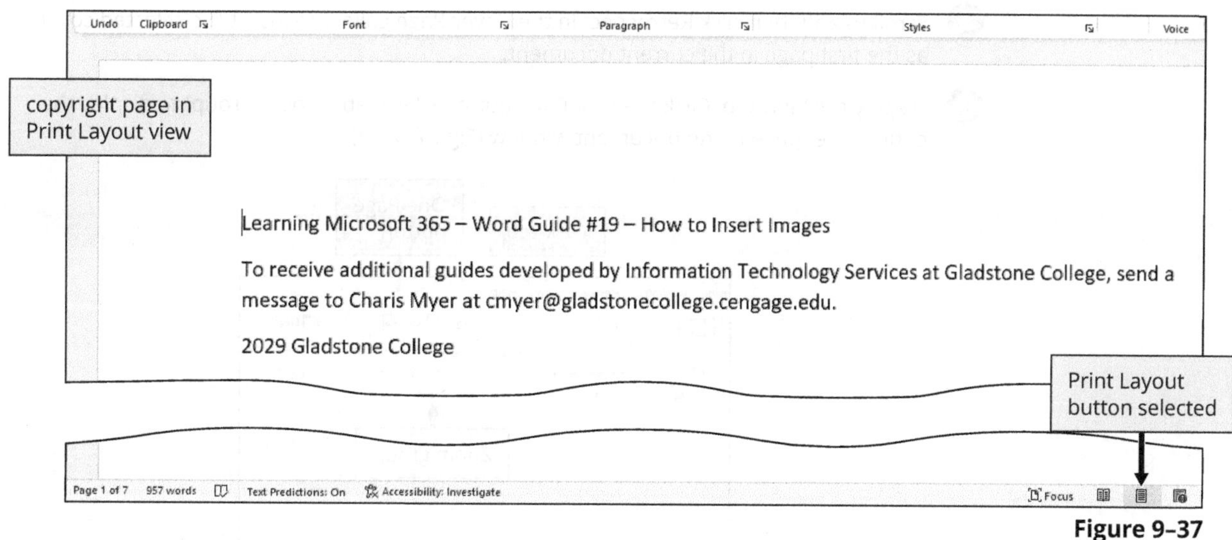

Figure 9–37

Organizing a Reference Document

Reference documents are organized and formatted so that users easily can navigate through and read the document. The reference document in this module includes the following elements: a copyright page, a cover page, a table of contents, a table of figures, an index, odd and even page footers, and a gutter margin. This section illustrates the tasks required to include these elements.

Consider This

What elements are common to reference documents?

Reference documents often include a cover page, a table of contents, a table of figures or list of tables (if one exists), and an index.

- **Cover Page.** A cover page (sometimes called a title page) should contain, at a minimum, the title of the document. Some also contain the author, a subtitle, an edition or volume number, and the date written.
- **Table of Contents.** The table of contents should list the title (heading) of each chapter or section and the starting page number of the chapter or section. You may use a leader character, such as a dot or hyphen, to fill the space between the heading and the page number. Sections preceding the table of contents are not listed in it — list only material that follows the table of contents.
- **Table of Figures or List of Tables.** If you have multiple figures or tables in a document, consider identifying all of them in a table of figures or a list of tables. The format of the table of figures or list of tables should match the table of contents.
- **Index.** The index usually is set in two columns or one column. The index can contain any item a reader might want to look up, such as a heading or a key term. If the document does not have a table of figures or list of tables, also include figures and tables in the index.

To Insert a Cover Page

Word has many predefined cover page formats that you can use for the cover page in a document. The following steps insert a cover page.

1. Display the Insert tab.
2. Click the Cover Page button (Insert tab | Pages group) to display the Cover Page gallery.

Q&A Does it matter where I position the insertion point before inserting a cover page?
No. By default, Word inserts the cover page as the first page in a document.

3. Scroll to and then click Retrospect in the Cover Page gallery to insert the selected cover page as the first page in the current document.
4. Display the View tab. Click the One Page button (View tab | Zoom group) to display the entire cover page in the document window (Figure 9–38).

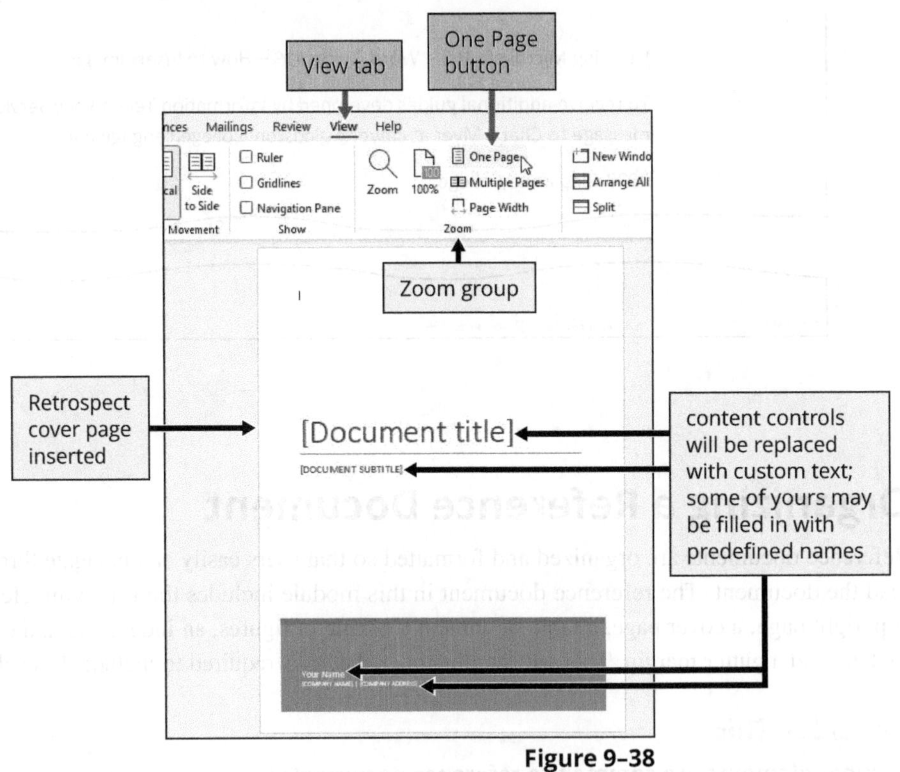

Figure 9–38

BTW
Advanced Paragraph Options
A widow occurs when the last line of a paragraph appears by itself at the top of a page, and an orphan occurs when the first line of a paragraph appears by itself at the bottom of a page. To prevent widows and orphans, click the Paragraph Dialog Box Launcher (Home tab | Paragraph group), click the Line and Page Breaks tab (Paragraph dialog box), place a check mark in the 'Widow/Orphan control' check box, and then click OK. Similarly, you can select the 'Keep with next' check box to keep selected paragraphs together, the 'Keep lines together' check box to keep selected lines together, and the 'Page break before' check box to insert a page break before the selected paragraph.

To Enter Text and Format Content Controls

The next step is to select content controls on the cover page and replace their instructions or text with the cover page information. Keep in mind that the content controls present suggested text. Depending on settings on your computer or mobile device, some content controls already may contain customized text, which you will change. You can enter any appropriate text in any content control. The following steps enter cover page text on the cover page.

1. Change the zoom back to page width.
2. Click the title content control and then type **Learning Microsoft 365** as the title. Change the font size of the entered title to 48 point.
3. Click the subtitle content control and then type **Word Guide #19 – How to Insert Images** as the subtitle.

4 Scroll to the bottom of the cover page and then select the text in the author content control and then type **Information Technology Services** as the name.

> **Q&A** Why is my author content control filled in?
> Depending on settings, your content control already may display an author name.

5 Click the company content control and then type **Gladstone College** for the school name.

6 Click the address content control and then type **9900 Spruce Street, Gladstone, ND 58630** as the address.

7 Select all text in the orange rectangle at the bottom of the cover page (that is, the author, company, and address content controls and the vertical bar separating the company and address content controls) and then change the font color to 'Black, Text 1, Lighter 15%' (second column in fifth row).

8 Select the orange rectangle shape at the bottom of the cover page (be sure to not include the blue band) and then use the Shape Styles gallery (Shape Format tab | Shape Styles group) to change the rectangle shape style to 'Subtle Effect - Gold, Accent 4'.

9 Display the View tab. Click the One Page button (View tab | Zoom group) to display the entire cover page in the document window (Figure 9–39).

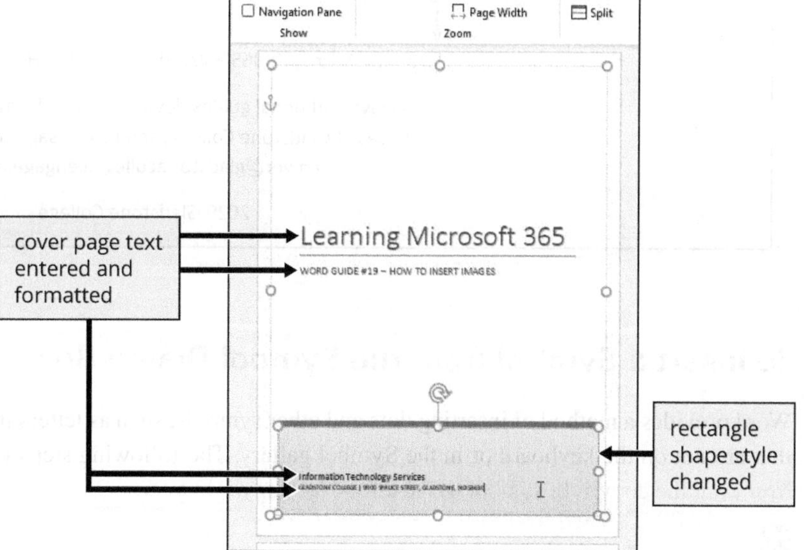

Figure 9–39

To Center Text

The next step is to center the text on the copyright page. The following steps center text.

1 Change the zoom back to page width.

2 Scroll to display the copyright page text in the document window.

3 Select the text on the copyright page and then center it.

4 Deselect the text.

To Insert a Continuous Section Break and Change the Margins in the Section

The margins on the copyright page are wider than the rest of the document. To change margins for a page, the page must be in a separate section. The next steps insert a continuous section break and then change the margins.

1 Position the insertion point at the location for the section break, in this case, to the left of L in Learning on the copyright page.

2 Display the Layout tab. Click the Breaks button (Layout tab | Page Setup group) to display the Breaks gallery.

3 Click Continuous in the Breaks gallery to insert a continuous section break to the left of the insertion point.

BTW
Printing Document Properties
To print document properties, click File on the ribbon to open Backstage view, click Print in Backstage view to display the Print screen, click the first button in the Settings area to display a list of options specifying what you can print, click Document Info in the list to specify you want to print the document properties instead of the actual document, and then click the Print button in the Print screen to print the document properties on the currently selected printer.

Click the Margins button (Layout tab | Page Setup group) to display the Margins gallery and then click Wide in the Margins gallery to change the margins on the copyright page to the selected settings (Figure 9–40).

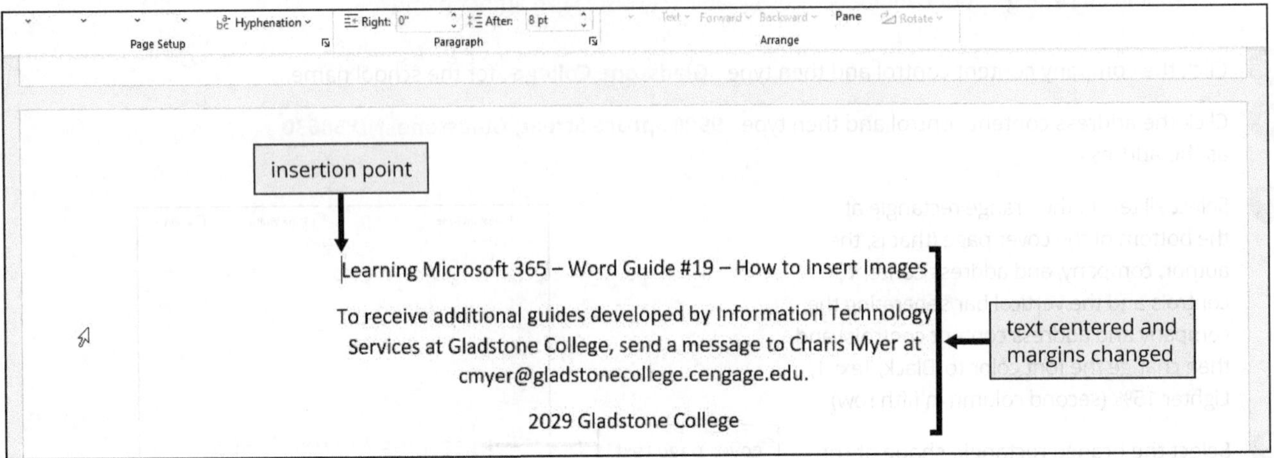

Figure 9–40

To Insert a Symbol from the Symbol Dialog Box

Word provides a method of inserting dots and other symbols, such as letters in the Greek alphabet and mathematical characters, that are not on the keyboard or in the Symbol gallery. The following steps insert a copyright symbol in the document. **Why?** You want the copyright symbol to the left of the copyright year.

- If necessary, position the insertion point at the location where the symbol should be inserted (in this case, to the left of the copyright year).
- Display the Insert tab.
- Click the Symbol button (Insert tab | Symbols group) to display the Symbol gallery (Figure 9–41).

Q&A What if the symbol I want to insert already appears in the Symbol gallery?
You can click any symbol shown in the Symbol gallery to insert it in the document.

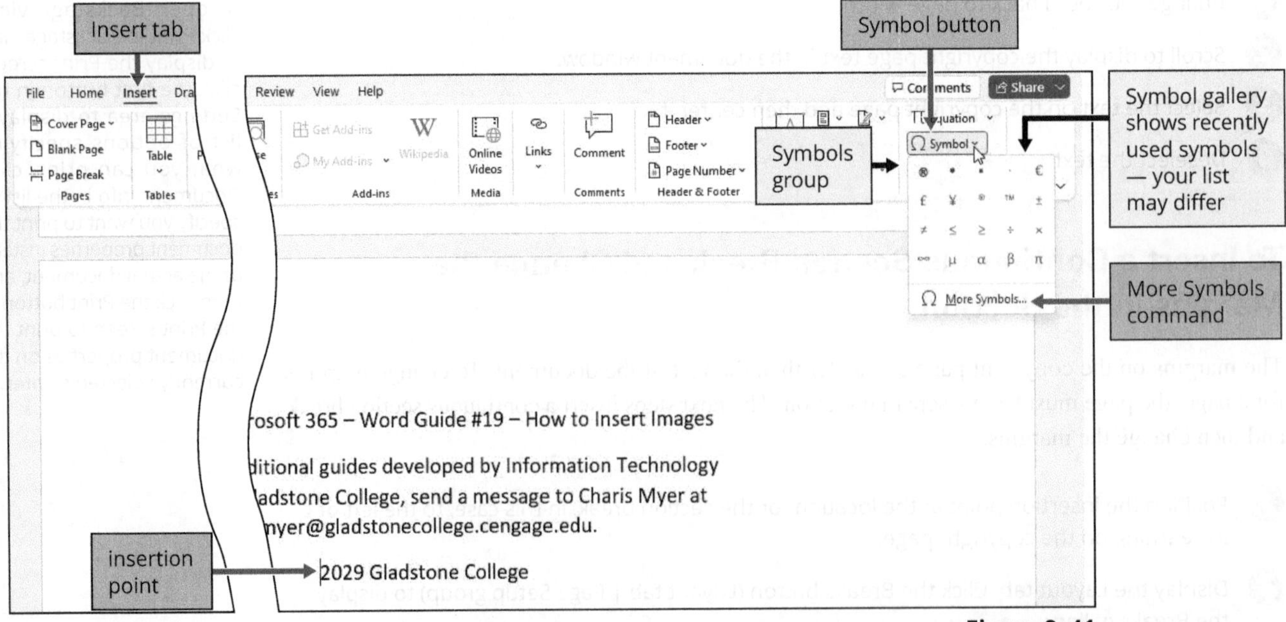

Figure 9–41

2

- Click More Symbols in the Symbol gallery to display the Symbol dialog box.
- If the font in the Font box is not (normal text), click the Font arrow (Symbol dialog box) and then scroll to and click (normal text) to select this font.
- If the subset in the Subset box is not Latin-1 Supplement, click the Subset arrow and then scroll to and click Latin-1 Supplement to select this subset.
- In the list of symbols, if necessary, scroll to the copyright symbol shown in Figure 9–42 and then click the symbol to select it.
- Click the Insert button (Symbol dialog box) to place the selected symbol in the document to the left of the insertion point (Figure 9–42).

Q&A Why is the Symbol dialog box still open?
The Symbol dialog box remains open because often you will need to insert the same or additional symbols elsewhere in the document.

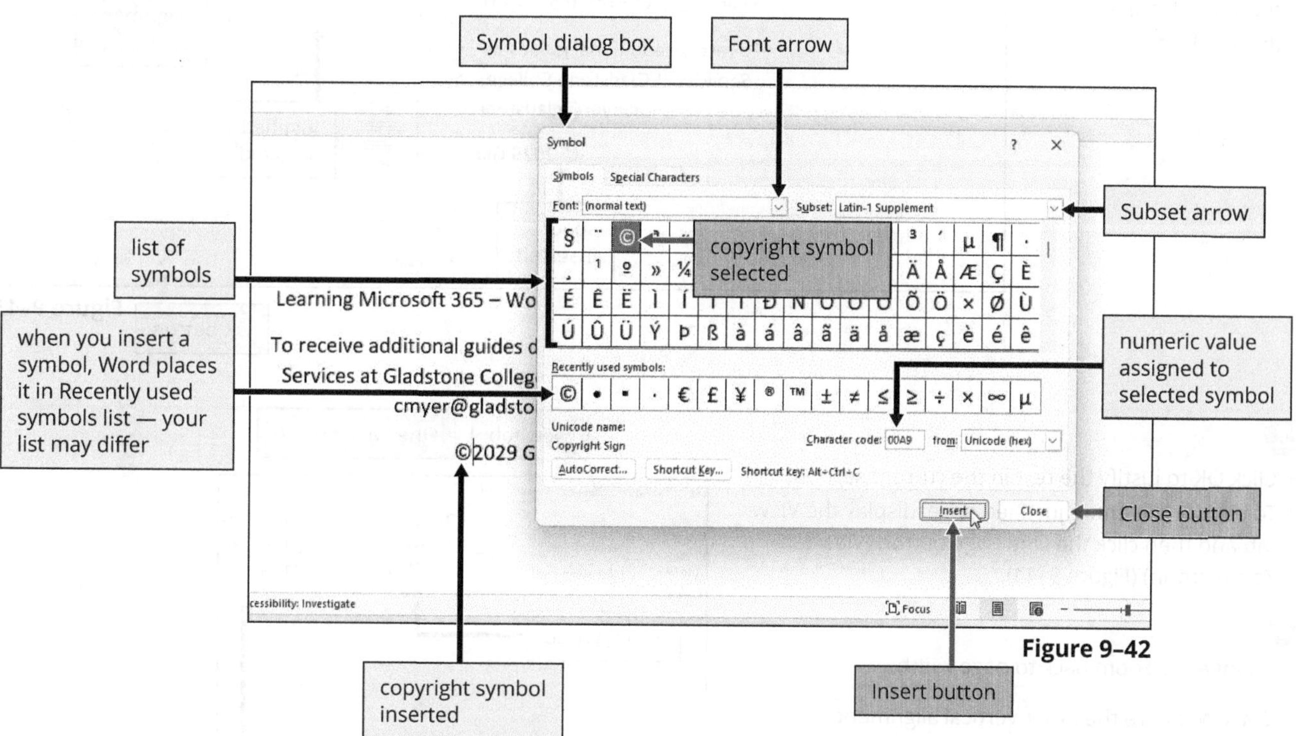

Figure 9–42

- Click the Close button (Symbol dialog box) to close the dialog box.
- Press SPACEBAR to insert a space between the copyright symbol and the year.

To Adjust Vertical Alignment on a Page

You can instruct Word to center the contents of a page vertically using one of two options: place an equal amount of space above and below the text on the page, or evenly space each paragraph between the top and bottom margins. The following steps vertically center text on a page. **Why?** The copyright page in this project evenly spaces each paragraph on a page between the top and bottom margins, which is called justified vertical alignment.

- Display the Layout tab. Click the Page Setup Dialog Box Launcher (Layout tab | Page Setup group) to display the Page Setup dialog box.
- Click the Layout tab (Page Setup dialog box) to display the Layout sheet.
- Click the Vertical alignment arrow and then click Justified (Figure 9–43).

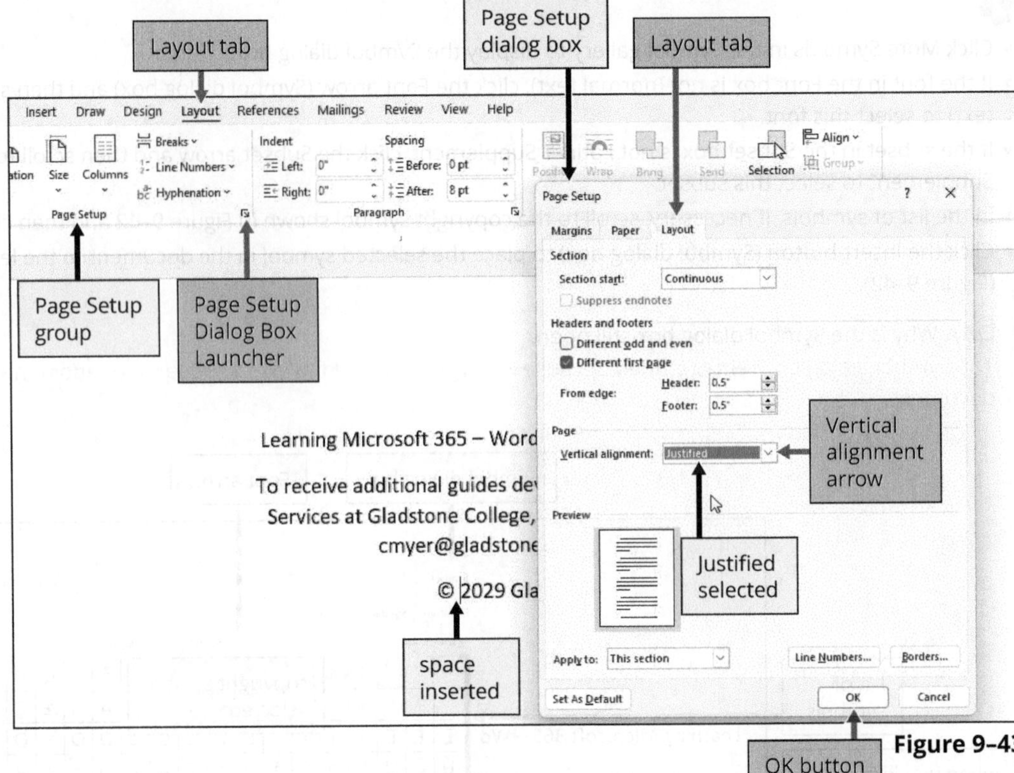

Figure 9–43

- Click OK to justify the text in the current section.
- To display the entire justified page, display the View tab and then click the One Page button (View tab | Zoom group) (Figure 9–44).

3

- Change the zoom back to page width.

Q&A What are the other vertical alignments?
Top, the default, aligns contents starting at the top margin on the page. Center places all contents centered vertically on the page, and Bottom places contents at the bottom of the page.

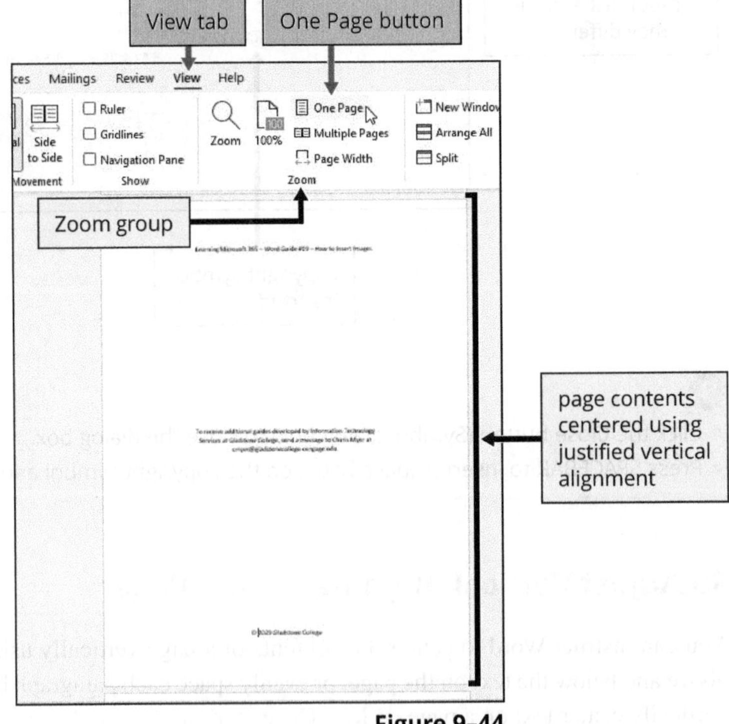

Figure 9–44

To Insert a Blank Page

The following step inserts a blank page. **Why?** In the reference document in this module, the table of contents is on a page after the copyright page.

- Position the insertion point to the left of the word, Inserting, on the first page of the subdocument (as shown in Figure 9–45). (Note that with the insertion point in this location, this blank page that will contain the table of contents will be housed in the subdocument instead of the master document.)
- Display the Insert tab.

Q&A Why are several of the buttons, including the Blank Page button, dimmed on the ribbon?
Your subdocument either is open in another window or is locked. If the subdocument is open in another window, close it. If it is locked, switch to Outline view and then click the Lock Document button (Outlining tab | Master Document group) to unlock it.

- Click the Blank Page button (Insert tab | Pages group) to insert a blank page at the location of the insertion point.
- If necessary, scroll to display the bottom of the blank page in the document window (Figure 9–45).

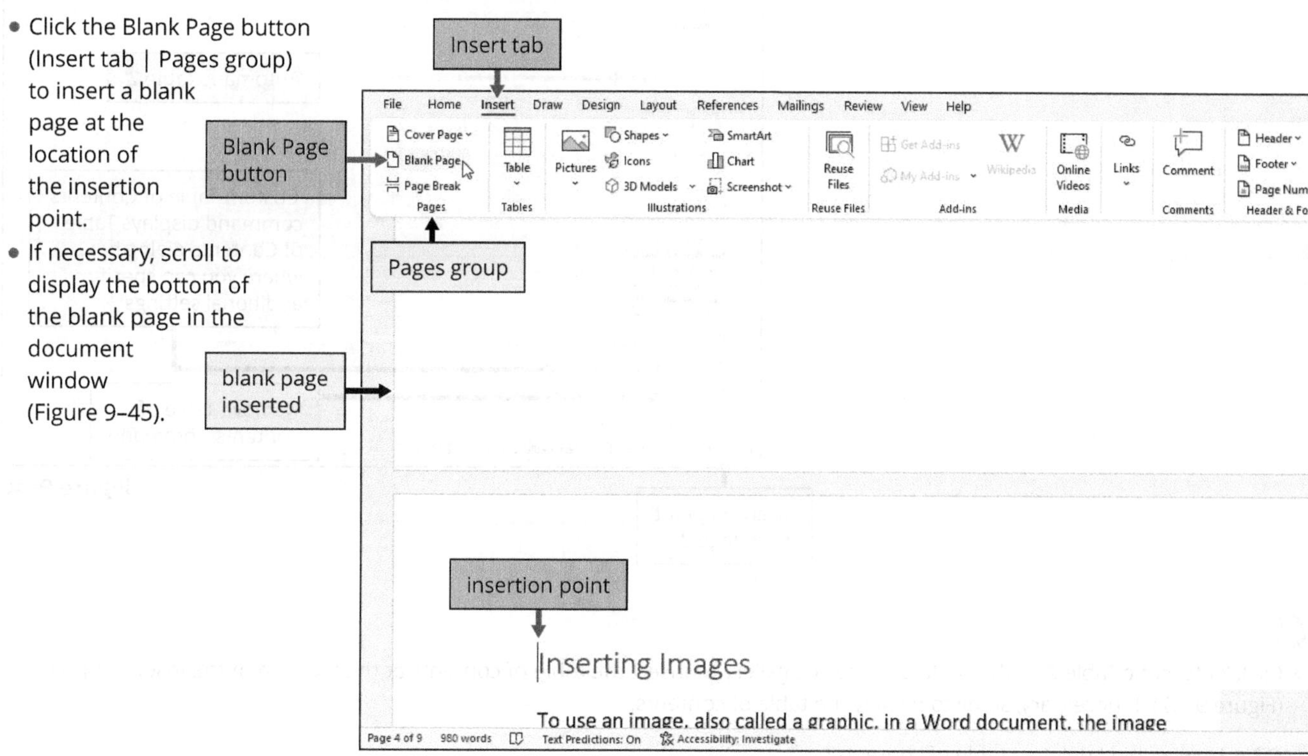

Figure 9–45

To Insert a Table of Contents

A table of contents lists all headings in a document and their associated page numbers. When you use Word's built-in heading styles (for example, Heading 1, Heading 2, and so on), you can instruct Word to insert a table of contents using these headings. In the reference document in this module, the heading of each section uses the Heading 1 style, and subheadings use the Heading 2 style.

The following steps use a predefined building block to insert a table of contents. **Why?** Using Word's predefined table of contents formats can be more efficient than creating a table of contents from scratch.

- Position the insertion point at the top of the blank page 3, which is the location for the table of contents. (If necessary, show formatting marks so that you easily can locate the paragraph mark at the top of the page; then hide formatting marks after you position the insertion point.)
- Ensure that formatting marks do not show.

Q&A Why should I hide formatting marks?
Formatting marks, especially those for index entries, sometimes can cause wrapping to occur on the screen that will be different from how the printed document will wrap. These differences could cause a heading to move to the next page. To ensure that the page references in the table of contents reflect the printed pages, be sure that formatting marks are hidden when you insert a table of contents.

- Display the References tab.
- Click the 'Table of Contents' button (References tab | Table of Contents group) to display the Table of Contents gallery (Figure 9–46).

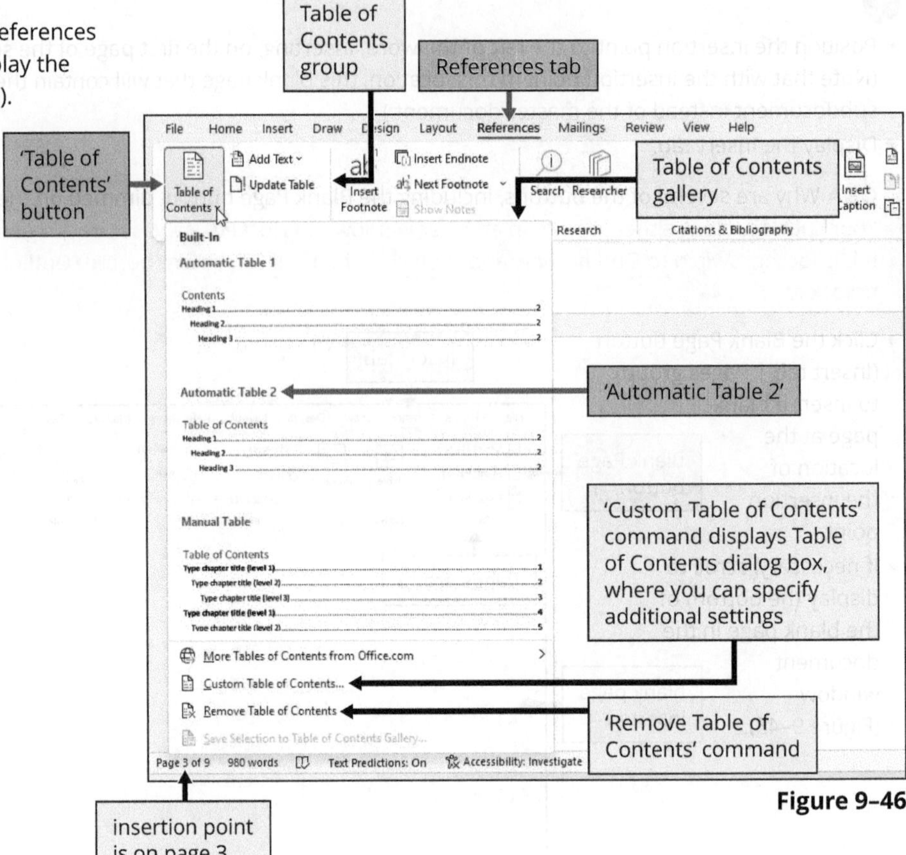

Figure 9–46

- Click 'Automatic Table 2' in the Table of Contents gallery to insert the table of contents at the location of the insertion point (Figure 9–47). If necessary, scroll to display the table of contents.

Q&A How would I delete a table of contents?
You would click the 'Table of Contents' button (References tab | Table of Contents group) and then click 'Remove Table of Contents' in the Table of Contents gallery (shown in Figure 9–46).

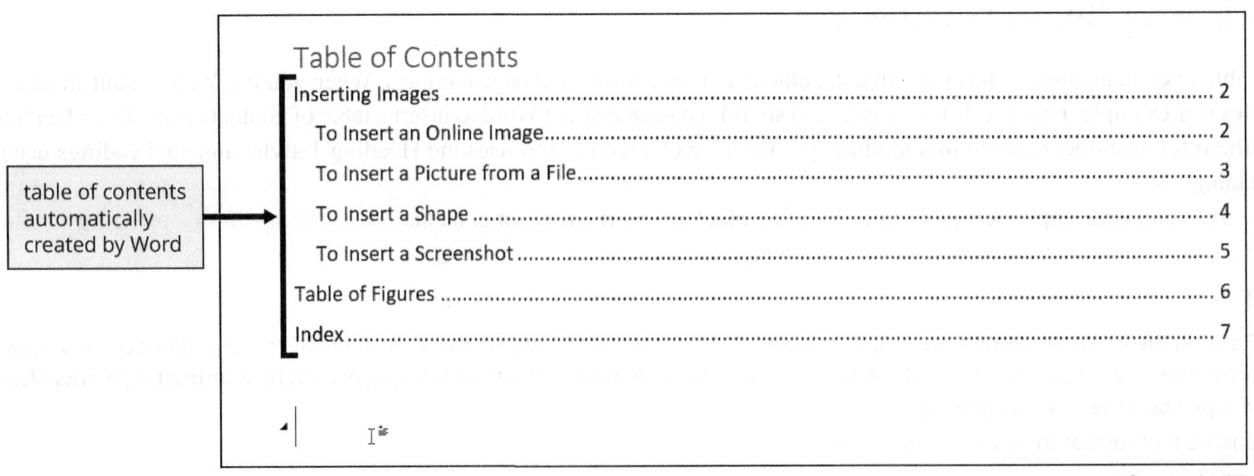

Figure 9–47

Other Ways

1. Click 'Table of Contents' button (References tab | Table of Contents group), click 'Custom Table of Contents', select table of contents options (Table of Contents dialog box), click OK
2. Click 'Explore Quick Parts' button (Insert tab | Text group), click 'Building Blocks Organizer' on Explore Quick Parts menu, select desired table of contents building block (Building Blocks Organizer dialog box), click Insert button, click Close

To Insert a Continuous Section Break and Change the Starting Page Number in a Section

The table of contents should not be the starting page number; instead, the subdocument should be the starting page number in the document. To change the starting page number, the page must be in a separate section. The following steps insert a continuous section break and then change the starting page number for the table of contents.

1. Position the insertion point at the location for the section break, in this case, to the left of I in Inserting Images on page 4 of the document.
2. Display the Layout tab. Click the Breaks button (Layout tab | Page Setup group) to display the Breaks gallery.
3. Click Continuous in the Breaks gallery to insert a continuous section break to the left of the insertion point.
4. Position the insertion point in the table of contents. (Note that your table of contents may appear highlighted when it is selected.)
5. Display the Insert tab. Click the Page Number button (Insert tab | Header & Footer group) to display the Page Number menu and then click 'Format Page Numbers' on the Page Number menu to display the Page Number Format dialog box.
6. Click the Start at down arrow (Page Number Format dialog box) until 0 is displayed in the Start at box (Figure 9–48).
7. Click OK to change the starting page for the current section.

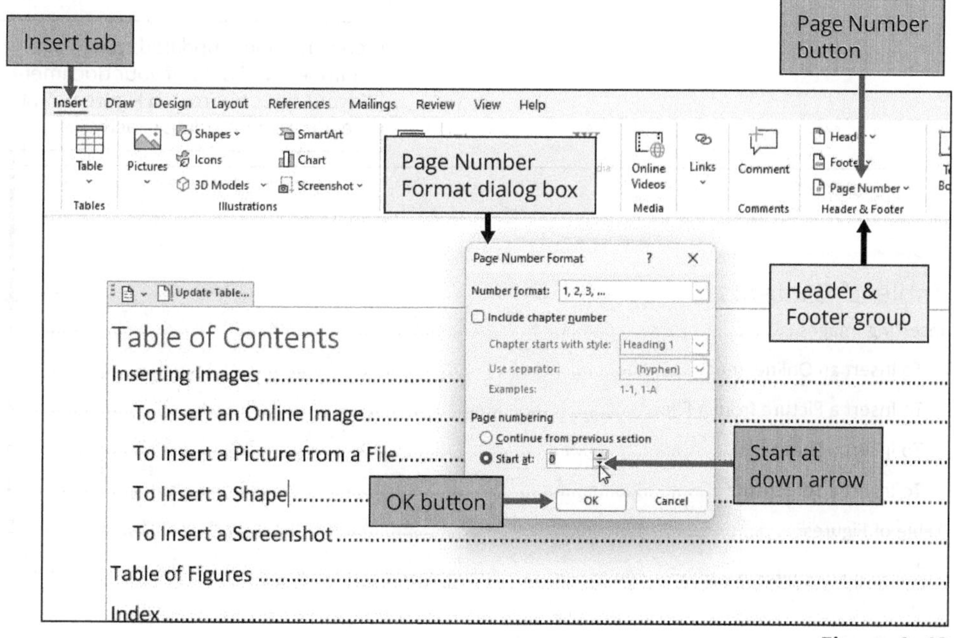

Figure 9–48

To Update Page Numbers in a Table of Contents

When you change a document, you should update the associated table of contents. The following steps update the page numbers in the table of contents. **Why?** The starting page number change will affect the page numbers in the table of contents.

- If necessary, click the table of contents to select it.

Q&A Why does the ScreenTip say 'CTRL+Click to follow link'?
Each entry in the table of contents is a link. If you hold down CTRL while clicking an entry in the table of contents, Word will display the associated heading in the document window.

2

- Click the Update Table button that is attached to the table of contents to display the Update Table of Contents dialog box.
- Ensure the 'Update page numbers only' option button is selected because you want to update only the page numbers in the table of contents (Figure 9–49).

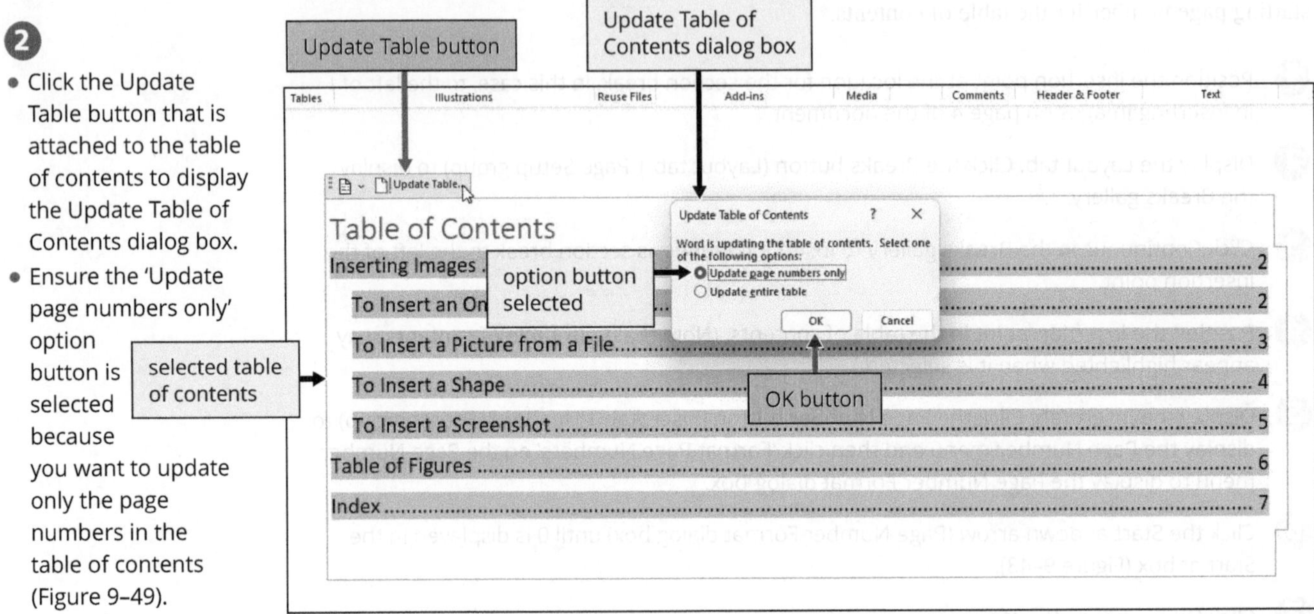

Figure 9–49

- Click OK (Update Table of Contents dialog box) to update the page numbers in the table of contents.
- Click outside the table of contents to remove the selection from the table (Figure 9–50). (Note that depending on Word functionality, part of the table of contents may remain shaded after you click outside the table.)

page numbers updated; your page numbers will differ if your document layout does not match Figure 9–1 at beginning of module exactly

Tables | Illustrations | Reuse Files | Add-ins | Media | Comments | Header & Footer | Text

Table of Contents

Figure 9–50

Other Ways

1. Select table, click Update Table button (References tab | Table of Contents group)
2. Select table, press F9

To Find a Format

The subdocument contains a sentence of text formatted as italic. To find this text in the document, you could scroll through the document until it is displayed on the screen. A more efficient way is to find the italic format using the Find and Replace dialog box. The following steps find a format. **Why?** You want to add the text to the table of contents.

1

- Display the Home tab.
- Click the Editing group button (Home tab) to display the Editing group and then click the Find arrow (Home tab | Editing group) to display the Find menu (Figure 9–51).

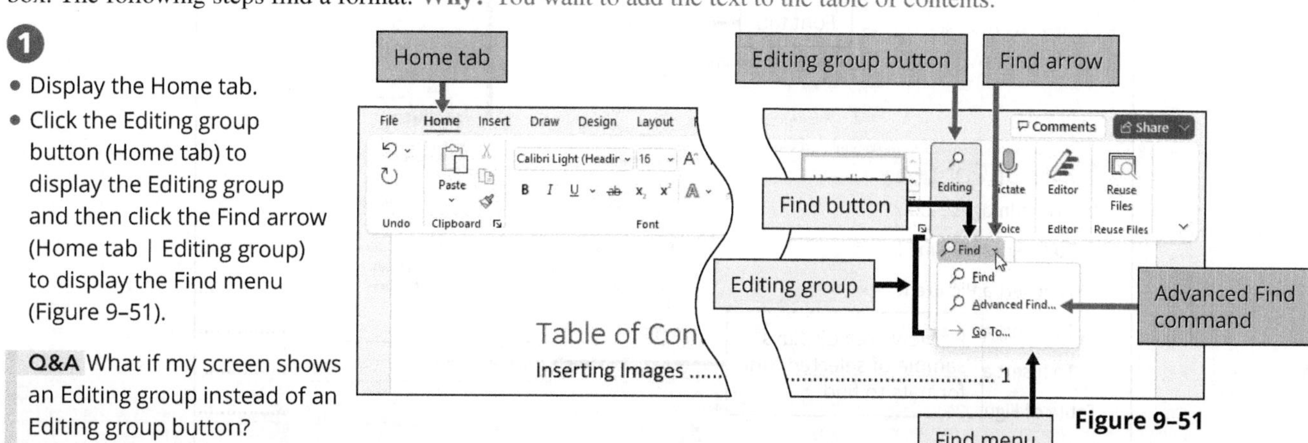

Figure 9–51

Q&A What if my screen shows an Editing group instead of an Editing group button?
Click the Find arrow (Home tab | Editing group) to display the Find menu.

Why did the Navigation Pane open on my screen?
You clicked the Find button instead of the Find arrow. Close the Navigation Pane and repeat Step 1.

2

- Click Advanced Find on the Find menu to display the Find and Replace dialog box.
- If Word displays a More button in the Find and Replace dialog box, click it so that it changes to a Less button and expands the dialog box.
- Click the Format button (Find and Replace dialog box) to display the Format menu (Figure 9–52).

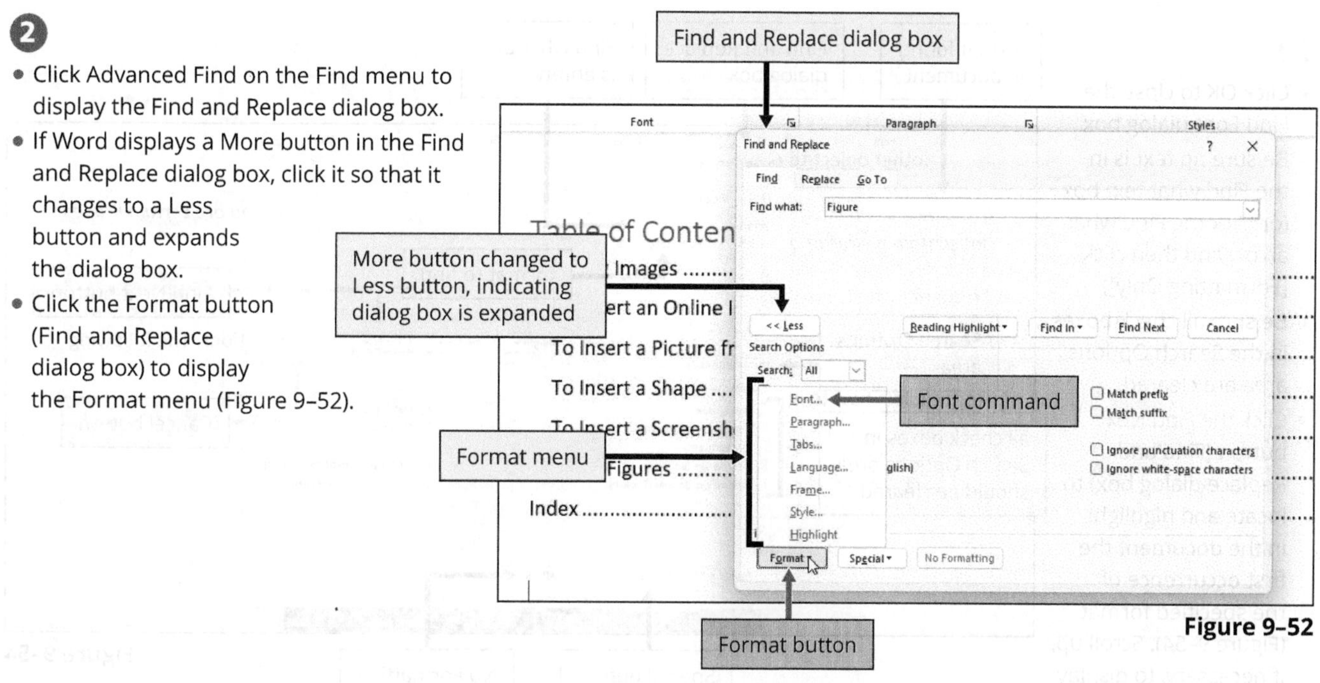

Figure 9–52

3

- Click Font on the Format menu to display the Find Font dialog box. If necessary, click the Font tab (Find Font dialog box) to display the Font sheet.
- Click Italic in the Font style list because that is the format you want to find (Figure 9–53).

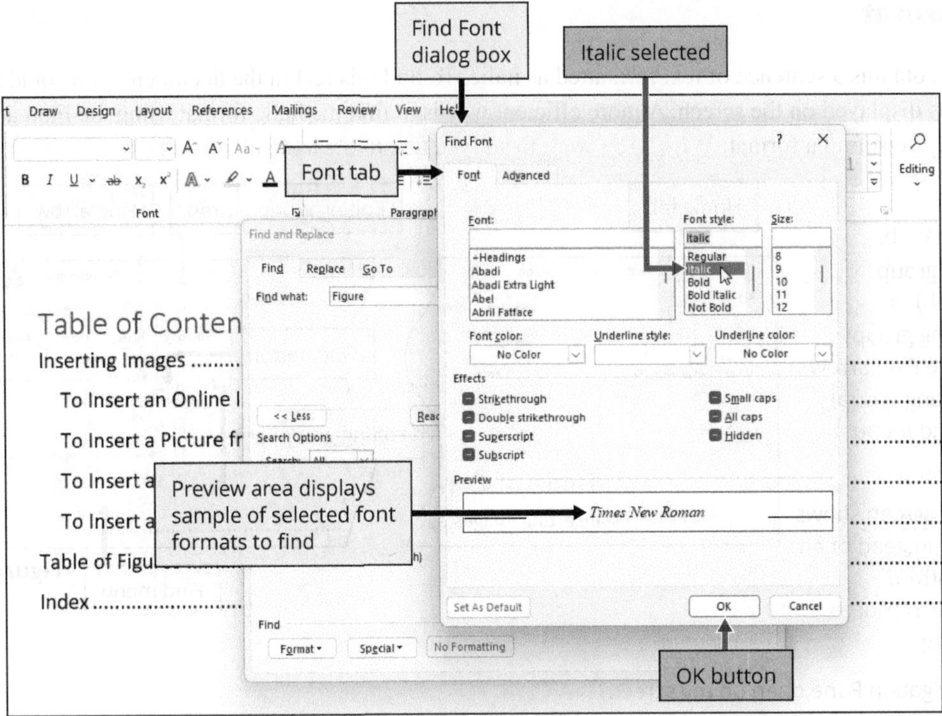

Figure 9–53

4

- Click OK to close the Find Font dialog box.
- Be sure no text is in the Find what text box (or click the Find what arrow and then click [Formatting Only]).
- Be sure all check boxes in the Search Options area are cleared.
- Click the Find Next button (Find and Replace dialog box) to locate and highlight in the document the first occurrence of the specified format (Figure 9–54). Scroll up, if necessary, to display the located format in the document window.

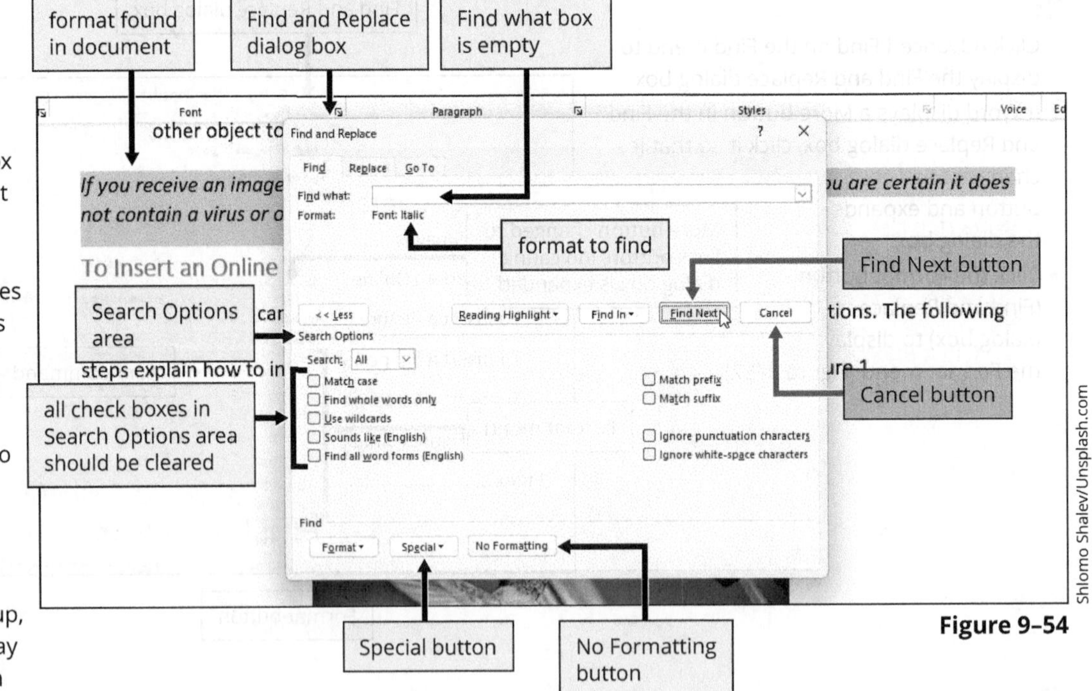

Figure 9–54

Q&A How do I remove a find format?
You would click the No Formatting button in the Find and Replace dialog box.

5

- Click Cancel (Find and Replace dialog box) because the located occurrence is the one you wanted to find.

Q&A Can I search for (find) special characters, such as page breaks?
Yes. To find special characters, you would click the Special button in the Find and Replace dialog box.

To Format Text as a Heading

The following steps format a paragraph of text as a Heading 3 style. Occasionally, you may want to add a paragraph of text, which normally is not formatted using a heading style, to a table of contents. One way to add the text to the table of contents is to format it as a heading style.

1. With the formatted paragraph still selected (shown in Figure 9–54), if necessary, display the Home tab.

2. Located and then click Heading 3 in the Styles gallery (Home tab | Styles group) to apply the selected style to the current paragraph in the document. Click outside the paragraph to deselect it (Figure 9–55).

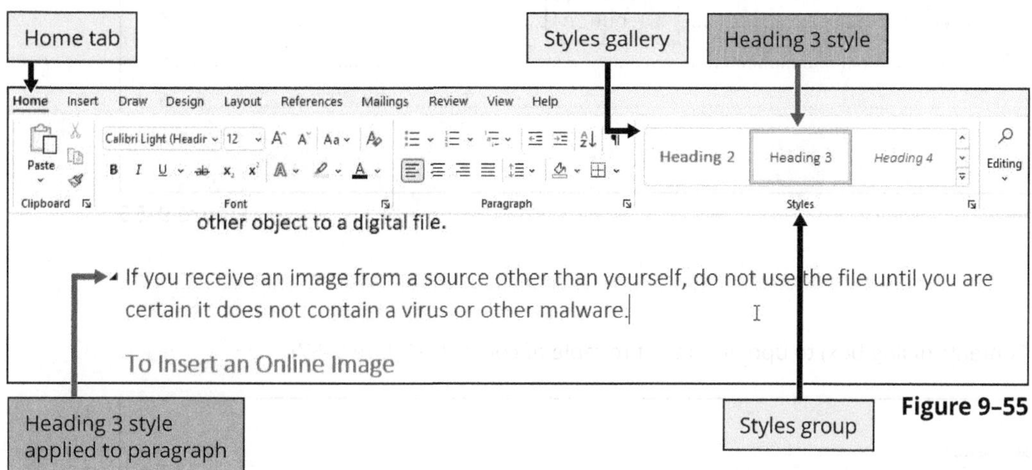

Figure 9–55

BTW
Find and Replace
The expanded Find and Replace dialog box allows you to specify how Word locates search text. For example, selecting the Match case check box instructs Word to find the text exactly as you typed it, and selecting the 'Find whole words only' check box instructs Word to ignore text that contains the search text (i.e., the word, then, contains the word, the). If you select the Use wildcards check box, you can use wildcard characters in a search. For example, with this check box selected, the search text of *ing would search for all words that end with the characters, ing.

To Retain Formatting When Adding Text to the Table of Contents If you wanted to retain formatting of text when adding it to the table of contents, you would perform the following steps.

1. Position the insertion point in the paragraph of text that you want to add to the table of contents.
2. Click the Add Text button (References tab | Table of Contents group) to display the Add Text menu.
3. Click the desired level on the Add Text menu, which adds the format of the selected style to the selected paragraph and adds the paragraph of text to the table of contents.

BTW
Table of Contents Styles
If you wanted to change the level associated with each style used in a table of contents, click the Options button in the Table of Contents dialog box (shown in Figure 9–59), enter the desired level number in the text box beside the appropriate heading or other styled item, and then click OK. To change the formatting associated with a style, click the Modify button in the Table of Contents dialog box.

To Update the Entire Table of Contents

The following steps update the entire table of contents. **Why?** The text changed to the Heading 3 style should appear in the table of contents.

- Display the table of contents in the document window.
- Click the table of contents to select it.
- Click the Update Table button that is attached to the table of contents to display the Update Table of Contents dialog box.
- Click the 'Update entire table' option button (Update Table of Contents dialog box) because you want to update the entire table of contents (Figure 9–56).

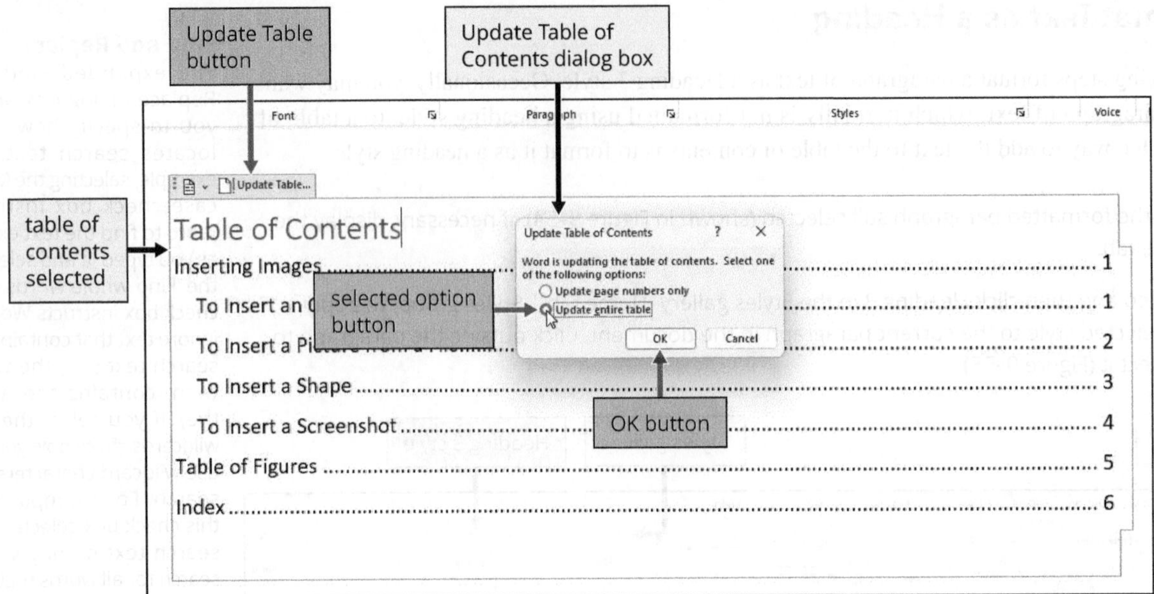

Figure 9–56

2

- Click OK (Update Table of Contents dialog box) to update the entire table of contents (Figure 9–57).

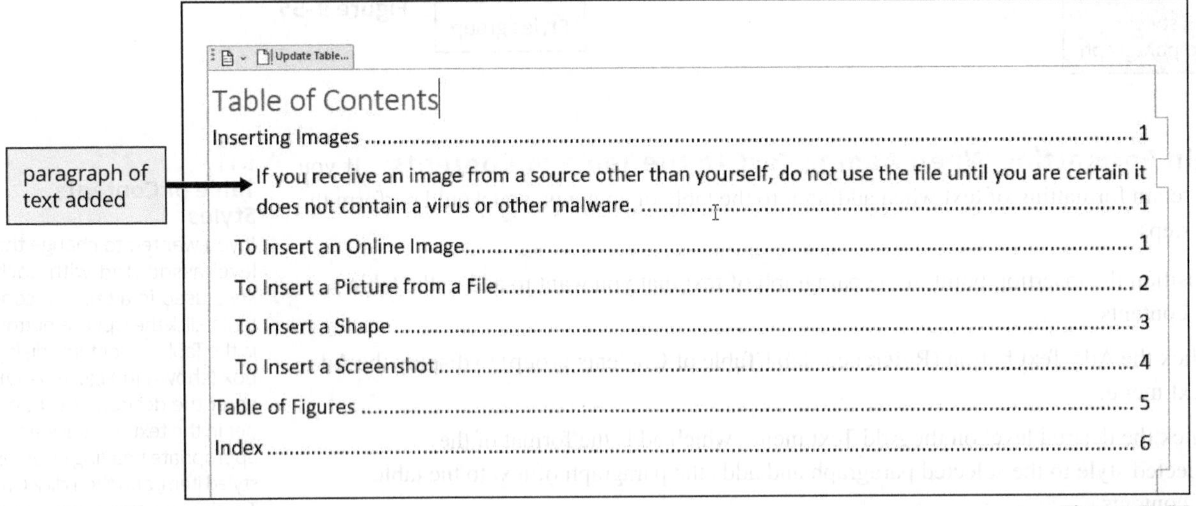

Figure 9–57

Other Ways

1. Select table, click Update Table button (References tab | Table of Contents group)
2. Select table, press F9

To Change the Format of a Table of Contents

You can change the format of the table of contents to any of the predefined table of contents styles or to custom settings. The following steps change the table of contents format. **Why?** In this table of contents, you specify the format, page number alignment, and tab leader character.

1

- Display the References tab.
- Click the 'Table of Contents' button (References tab | Table of Contents group) to display the Table of Contents gallery (Figure 9–58).

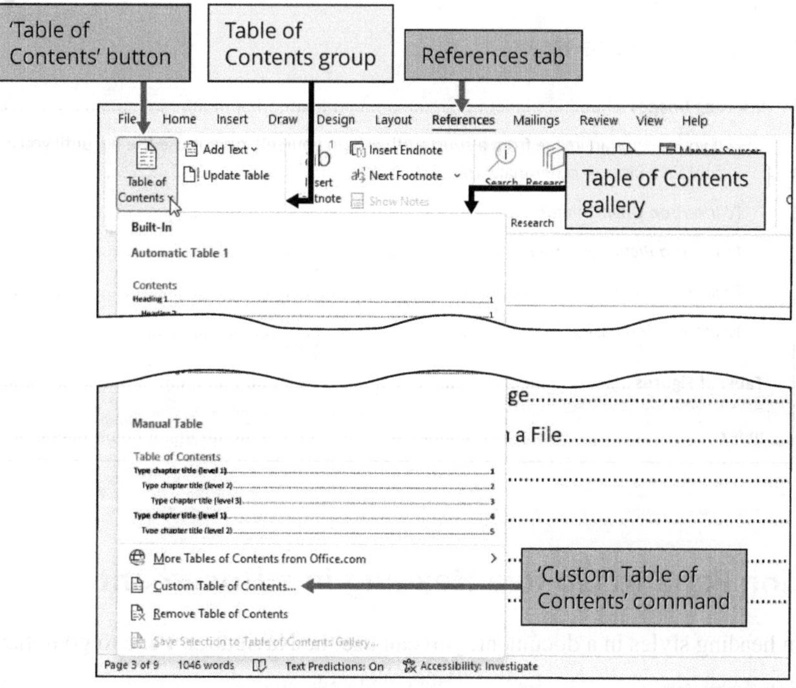

Figure 9–58

2

- Click 'Custom Table of Contents' in the Table of Contents gallery to display the Table of Contents dialog box.
- Click the Formats button (Table of Contents dialog box) and then click Simple to change the format style for the table of contents.
- Place a check mark in the 'Right align page numbers' check box so that the page numbers appear at the right margin in the table of contents.
- If necessary, click the Tab leader button and then click the first leader type in the list so that the selected leader characters appear between the heading name and the page numbers in the table of contents (Figure 9–59).

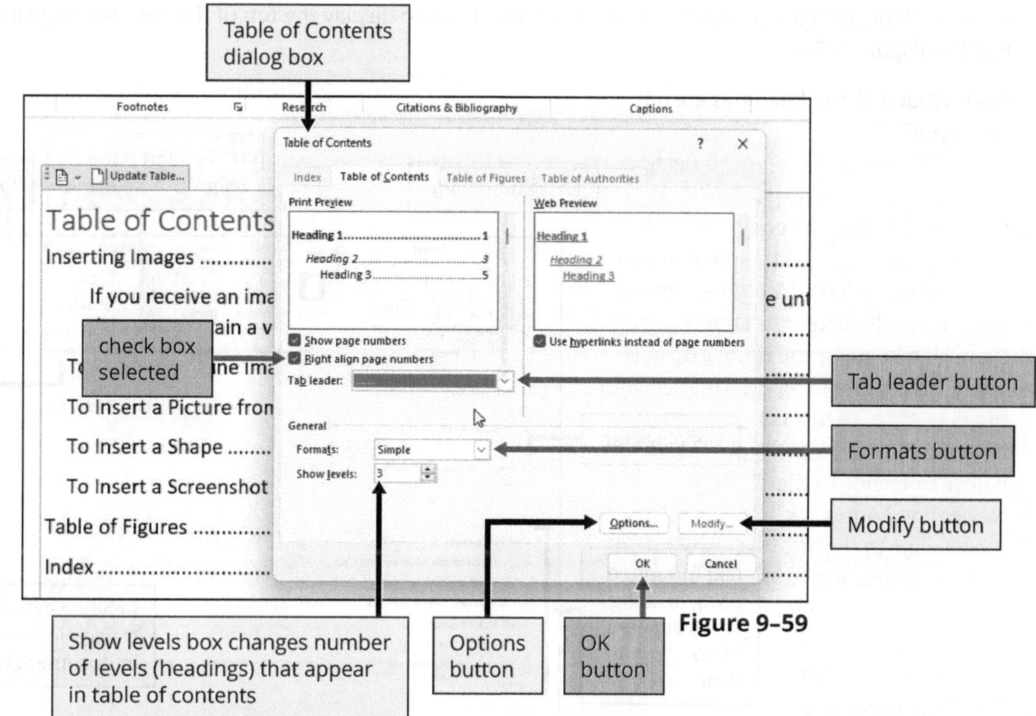

Figure 9–59

- Click OK to modify the table of contents according to the specified settings. When Word displays a dialog box asking if you want to replace the selected table of contents, click OK (Figure 9–60).

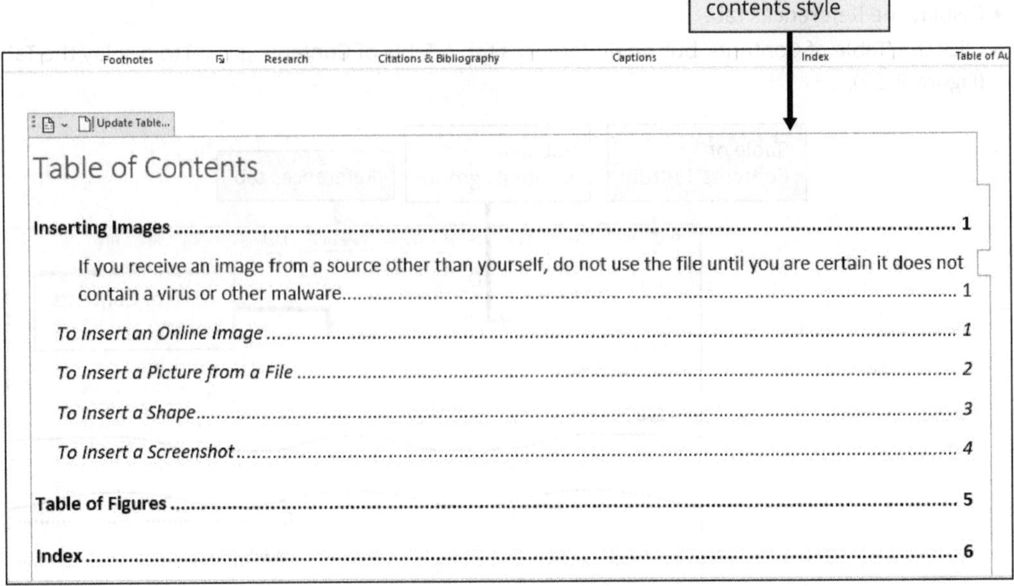

Figure 9–60

To Use the Navigation Pane to Go to a Heading in a Document

When you use Word's built-in heading styles in a document, you can use the Navigation Pane to go to headings in a document quickly. **Why?** When you click a heading in the Navigation Pane, Word displays the page associated with that heading in the document window. The following step uses the Navigation Pane to display an associated heading in the document window.

- Display the View tab. Place a check mark in the Navigation Pane check box (View tab | Show group) to open the Navigation Pane at the left edge of the Word window.
- If necessary, click the Headings tab in the Navigation Pane to display the text that is formatted using Heading styles.
- Click the 'Table of Figures' heading in the Navigation Pane to display the top of the selected page in the top of the document window (Figure 9–61).

Q&A What if all the headings are not displayed?
Right-click a heading in the Navigation Pane and then click Expand All on the shortcut menu to ensure that all headings are displayed. (Note that you can click Collapse All on the shortcut menu to collapse all headings in the Navigation Pane.) If a heading still is not displayed, verify that the heading is formatted with a heading style. To display or hide subheadings below a heading in the Navigation Pane, click the triangle to the left of the heading. If a heading is too wide for the Navigation Pane, you can point to the heading to display a ScreenTip that shows the complete title.

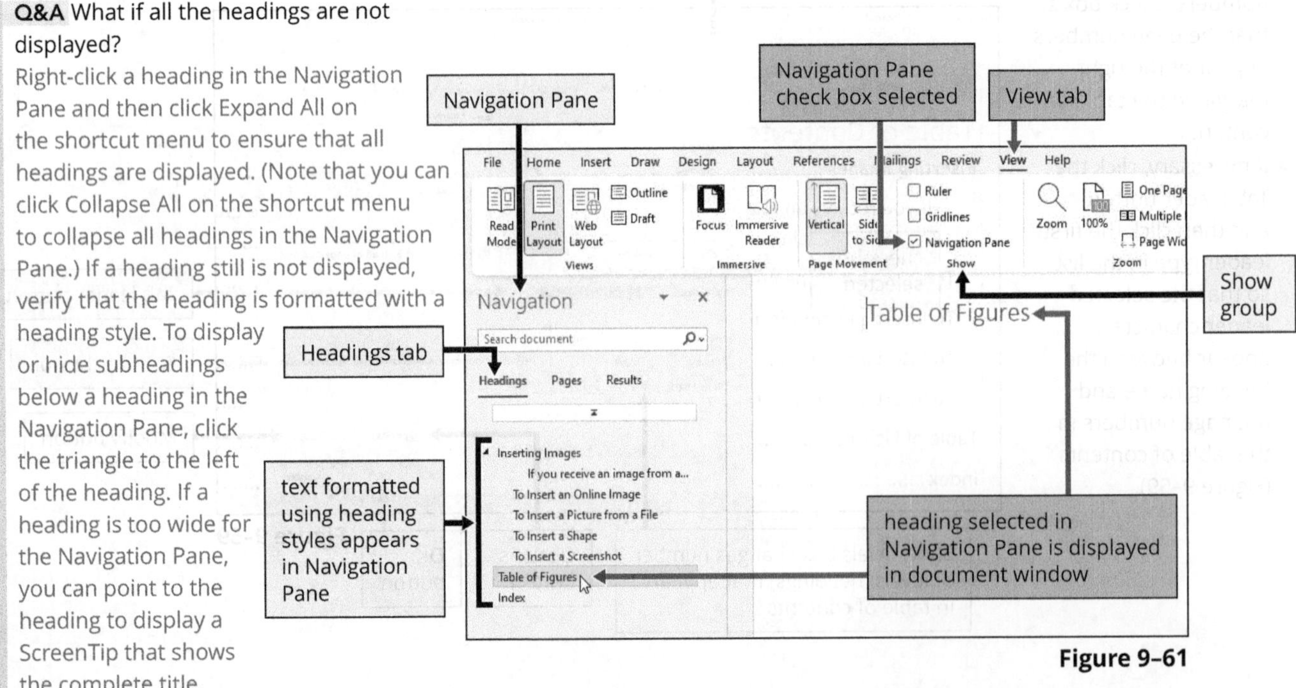

Figure 9–61

To Insert a Table of Figures

The following steps insert a table of figures. **Why?** At the end of the reference document is a table of figures, which lists all figures and their corresponding page numbers. Word generates this table of figures from the captions in the document.

1

- Ensure that formatting marks are not displayed.
- Position the insertion point at the end of the Table of Figures heading (immediately after the s in Figures) and then press ENTER, so that the insertion point is on the line below the heading.
- Display the References tab.
- Click the 'Insert Table of Figures' button (References tab | Captions group) to display the Table of Figures dialog box.
- Be sure that all settings in your dialog box match those in Figure 9–62.

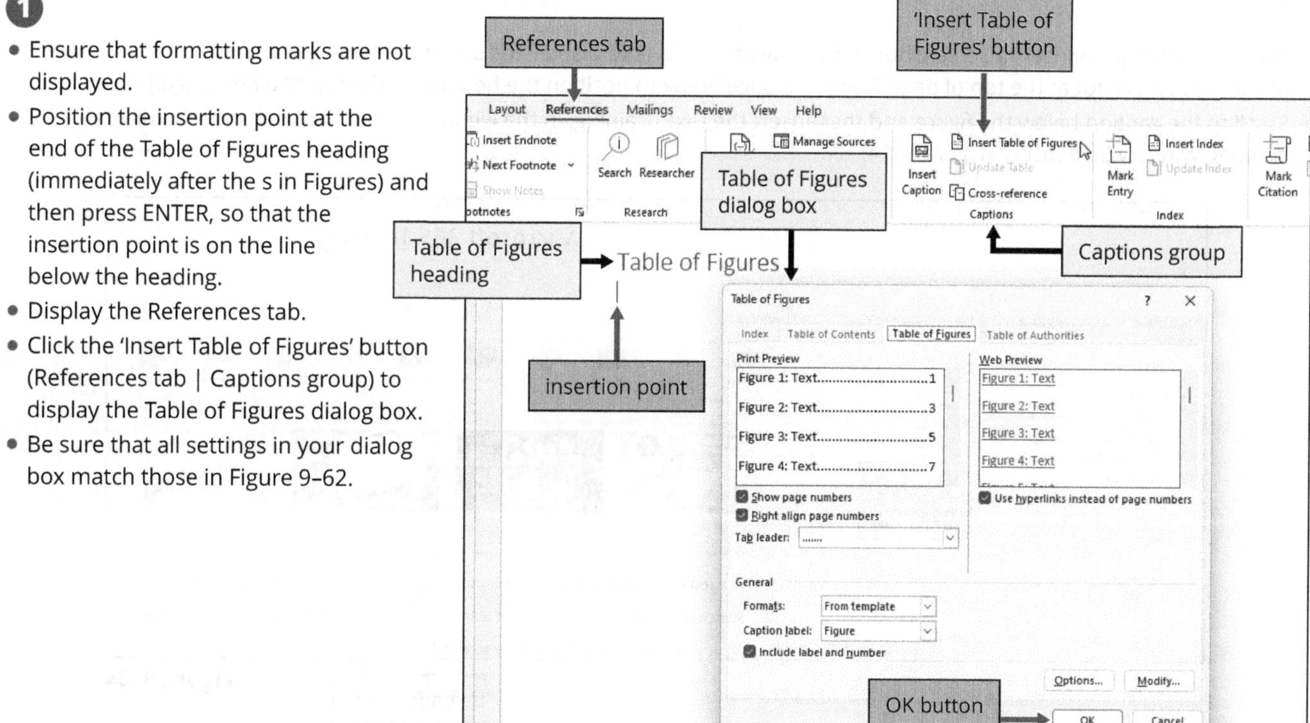

Figure 9–62

- Click OK (Table of Figures dialog box) to insert a table of figures at the location of the insertion point (Figure 9–63).

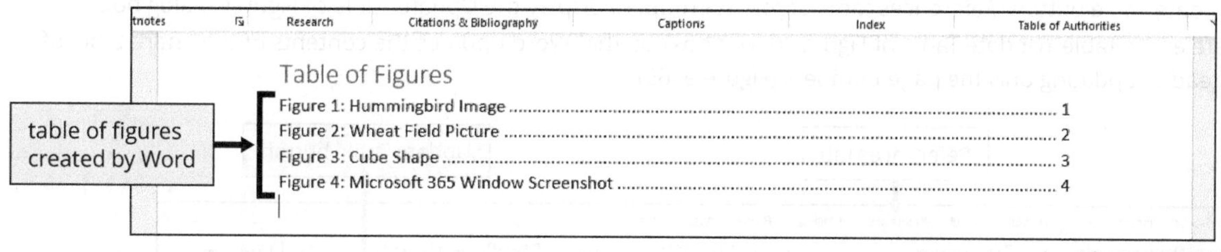

Figure 9–63

To Change the Format of the Table of Figures If you wanted to change the format of the table of figures, you would perform the following steps.

1. Click the table of figures to select it.
2. Click the 'Insert Table of Figures' button (References tab | Captions group) to display the Table of Figures dialog box.
3. Change settings in the dialog box as desired.
4. Click OK (Table of Figures dialog box) to apply the changed settings.
5. Click OK when Word asks if you want to replace the selected table of figures.

BTW

Replace Formats

You can click the Replace tab (Find and Replace dialog box) to find and replace formats. Enter the format to find in the Find what text box and then follow the same steps to enter the format to replace or the format to remove (i.e., Not Bold in the Font style list) in the Replace with text box. Next, click the Replace or Replace All button to replace the next occurrence of the format or all occurrences of the format in the document.

To Edit a Caption and Update the Table of Figures

The following steps change the Figure 4 caption and then update the table of figures. **Why?** When you modify captions in a document or move illustrations to a different location in the document, you will have to update the table of figures.

- Click the heading, To Insert a Screenshot, in the Navigation Pane to display the selected heading in the document window. (If this heading is not at the top of page 7, insert a page break to position the heading at the top of a new page.)
- Scroll to the caption below the figure and then insert the text, Training, in the Figure 4 caption so that it reads: Microsoft 365 Training Window Screenshot (Figure 9–64).

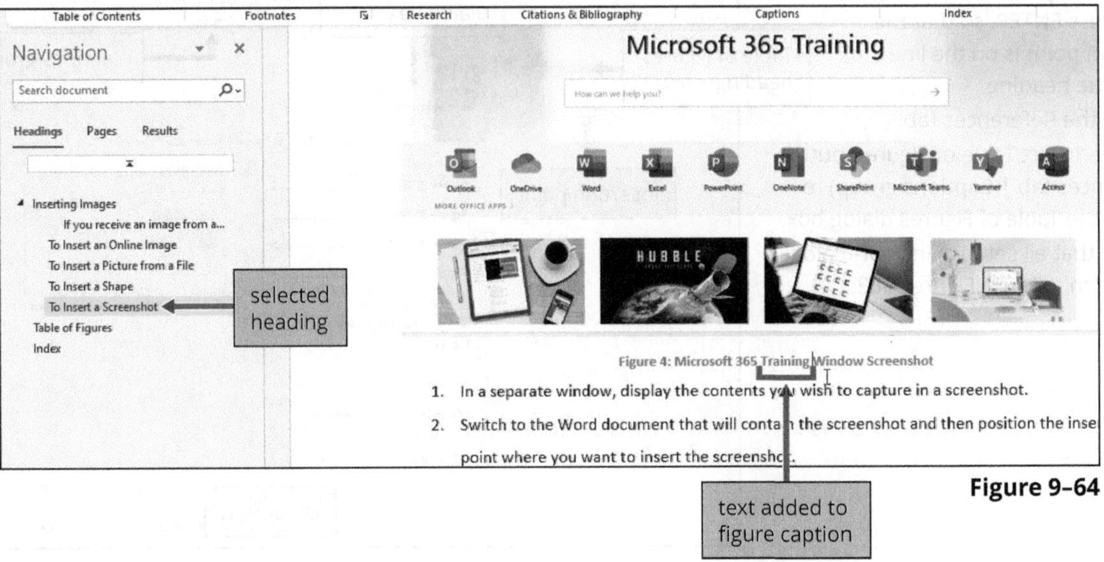

Figure 9–64

- Click the heading, Table of Figures, in the Navigation Pane to display the Table of Figures heading in the document window.
- Click the table of figures to select it.
- Click the Update Table button (References tab | Captions group) to display the Update Table of Figures dialog box.
- Click 'Update entire table' (Update Table of Figures dialog box), so that Word updates the contents of the entire table of figures instead of updating only the page numbers (Figure 9–65).

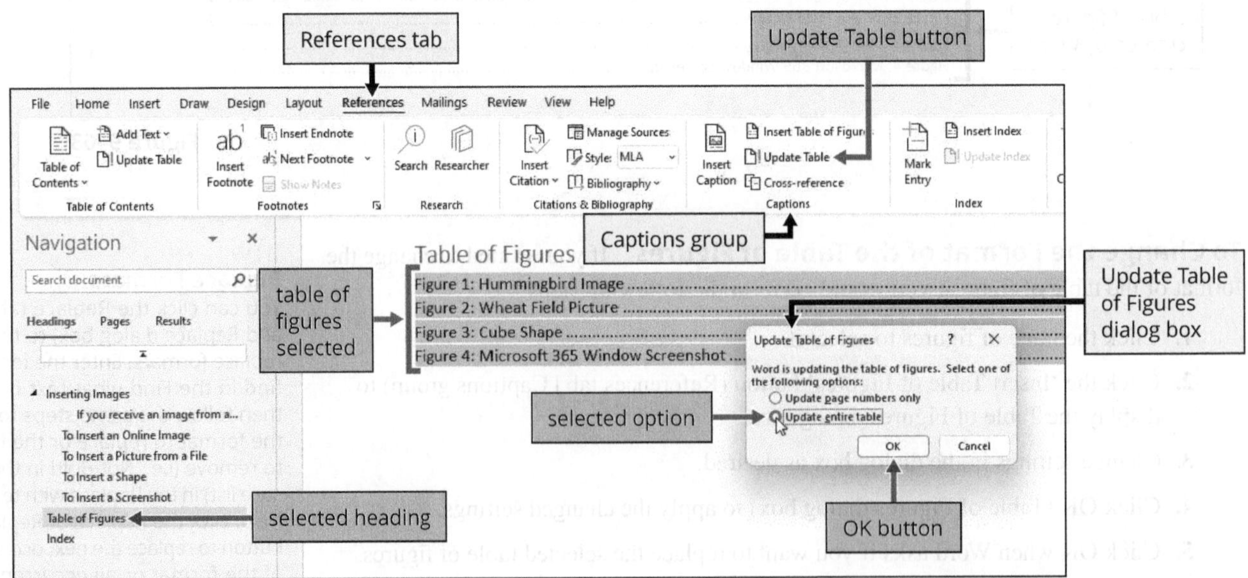

Figure 9–65

- Click OK to update the table of figures and then click outside the table to deselect it (Figure 9–66).

Q&A Are the entries in the table of figures links?
Yes. As with the table of contents, you can CTRL+click any entry in the table of figures and Word will display the associated figure in the document window.

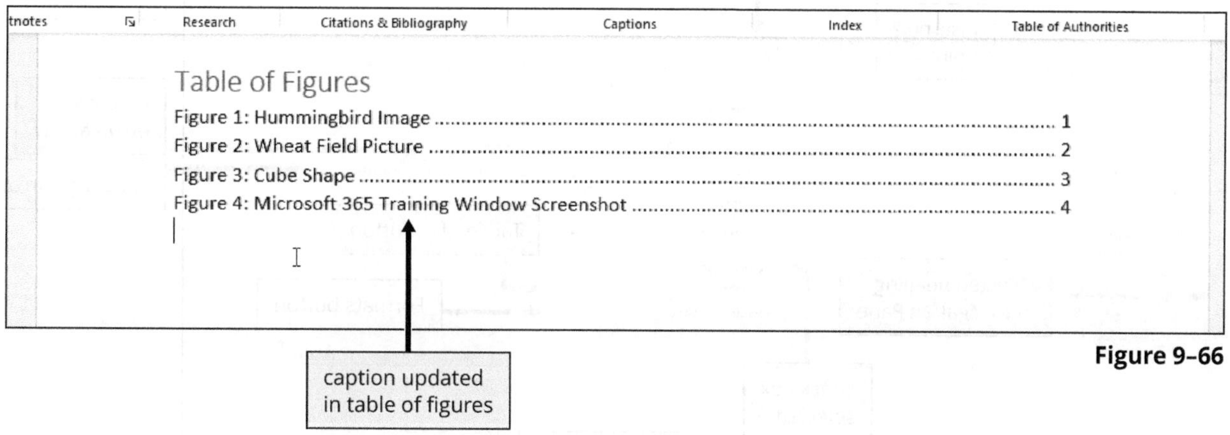

Figure 9–66

Other Ways

1. Select table of figures, press F9

To Insert an Index

The reference document in this module ends with an index. Earlier, this module showed how to mark index entries. **Why?** For Word to generate the index, you first must mark any text you wish to appear in the index.

Once all index entries are marked, Word can insert the index from the index entry fields in the document. Recall that index entry fields begin with XE, which appears on the screen when formatting marks are displayed. When index entry fields show on the screen, the document's pagination probably will be altered because of the extra text in the index entries. Thus, be sure to hide formatting marks before inserting an index. The following steps insert an index.

- Click the heading, Index, in the Navigation Pane to display the Index heading in the document window.
- Position the insertion point at the end of the Index heading (immediately after the x in Index) and then press ENTER, so that the insertion point is on the line below the heading.
- Ensure that formatting marks are not displayed.
- Click the Insert Index button (References tab | Index group) to display the Index dialog box.
- If necessary, click the Formats button in the dialog box and then click Classic in the Formats list to change the index format.
- Place a check mark in the 'Right align page numbers' check box.
- Click the Tab leader button and then click the first leader character in the list to specify the leader character to be displayed between the index entry and the page number.
- Click the Columns down arrow until the number of columns is 1 to change the number of columns in the index (Figure 9–67).

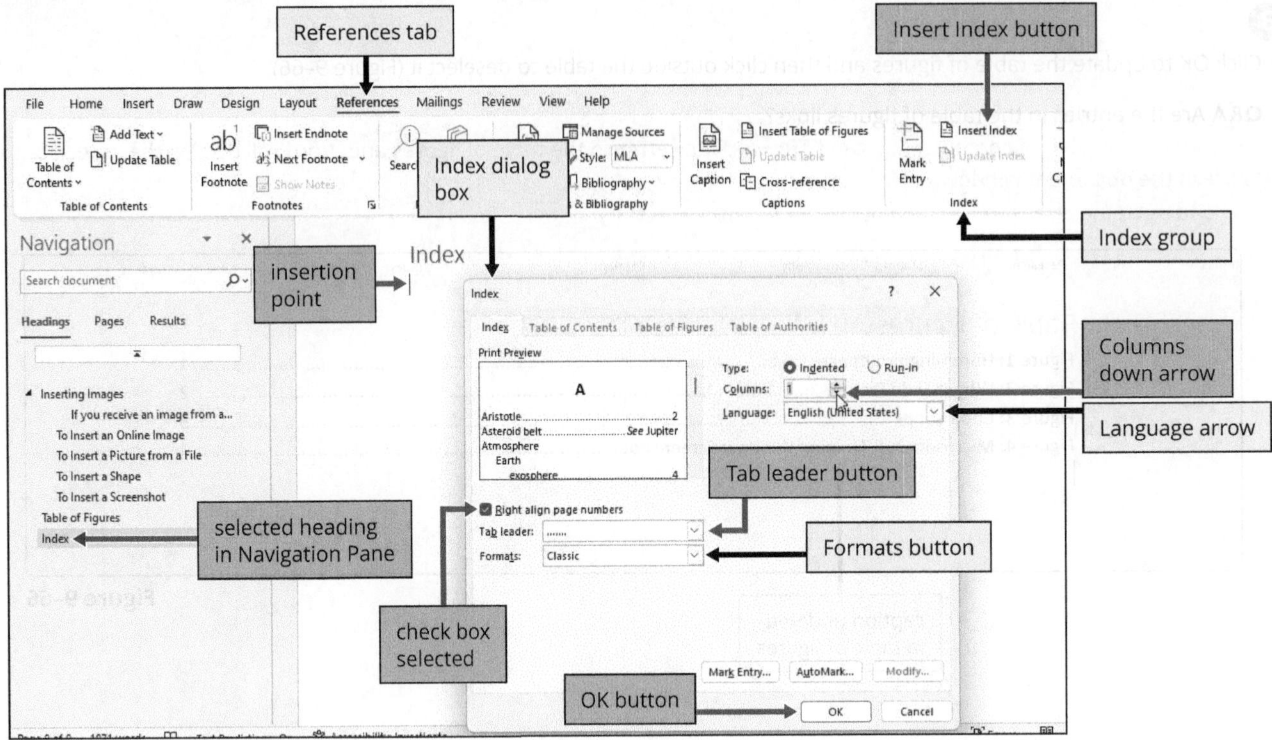

Figure 9–67

2

- Click OK (Index dialog box) to insert an index at the location of the insertion point (Figure 9–68).

Q&A How would I change the language used in the index?
If multiple languages are installed, click the Language arrow (shown in Figure 9–67) (Index dialog box) and then click the desired language.

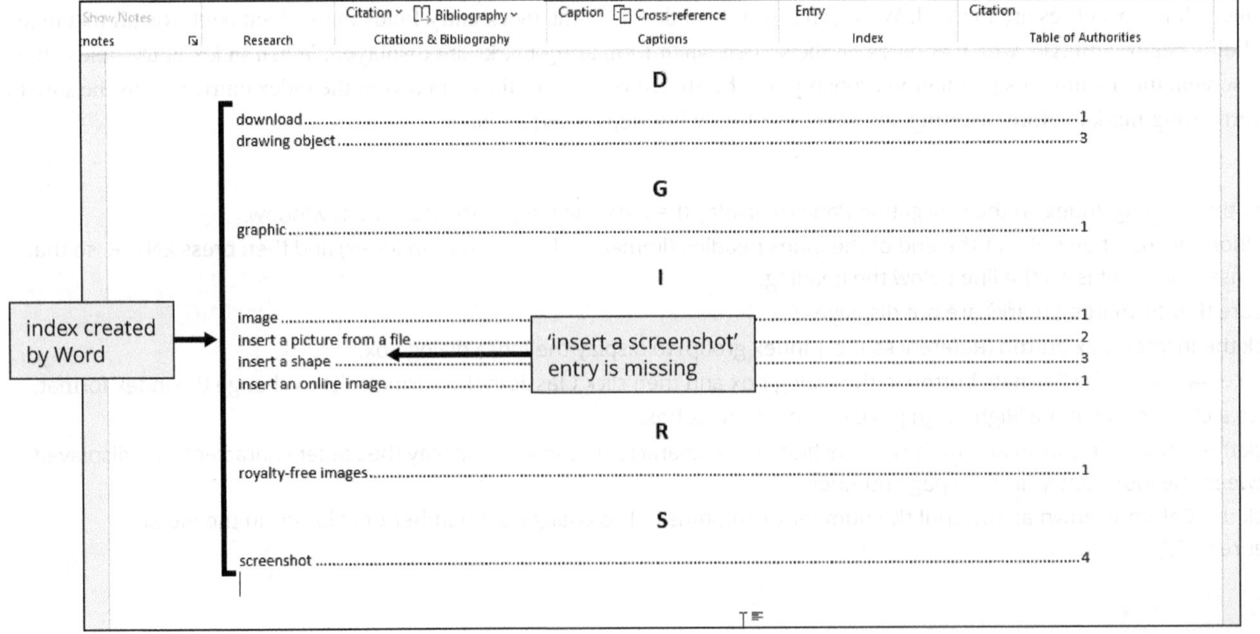

Figure 9–68

To Mark Another Index Entry

Notice in Figure 9–68 that the 'insert a screenshot' index entry is missing. The following steps mark an index entry in the Insert a Screenshot section.

1. Click the heading, To Insert a Screenshot, in the Navigation Pane to display the selected heading in the document window.
2. Select the words, Insert a Screenshot, in the heading.
3. Click the Mark Entry button (References tab | Index group) to display the Mark Index Entry dialog box.
4. Type **insert a screenshot** in the Main entry text box (Mark Index Entry dialog box) so that the entry is all lowercase (Figure 9–69).
5. Click the Mark button to mark the entry.
6. Close the dialog box.
7. Hide formatting marks.

BTW
Index Files
Instead of marking index entries in a document, you can create a concordance file that contains all index entries you wish to mark. A concordance file contains two columns: the first column identifies the text in the document you want Word to mark as an index entry, and the second column lists the index entries to be generated from the text in the first column. To mark entries in the concordance file, click the AutoMark button in the Index dialog box.

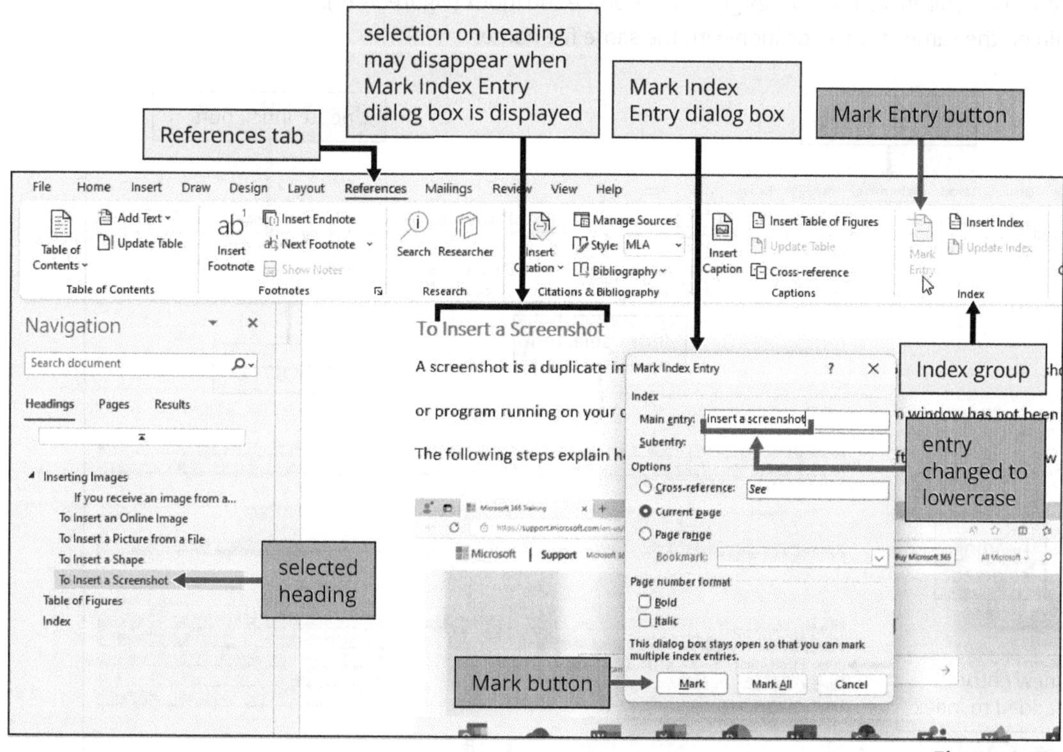

Figure 9–69

To Edit an Index Entry At some time, you may want to change an index entry after you have marked it. For example, you may forget to lowercase the entry for the headings. If you wanted to change an index entry, you would perform the following steps.

1. Display formatting marks.
2. Locate the XE field for the index entry you wish to change (i.e., { XE "Insert a Screenshot" }).
3. Change the text inside the quotation marks (i.e., { XE "insert a screenshot" }).
4. Update the index as described in the steps in the upcoming section titled To Update an Index.

BTW
Navigation Pane
You can drag any heading in the Navigation Pane to reorganize document content. For example, you could drag the To Insert a Screenshot heading upward in the Navigation Pane so that its content appears earlier in the document. You also can promote a heading by right-clicking the heading and then clicking Promote on the shortcut menu. Likewise, you can demote a heading by right-clicking the heading and then clicking Demote on the shortcut menu. To delete a heading and all its contents, right-click the heading and then click Delete on the shortcut menu. If you wanted to print all content in a heading, you would right-click the heading and then click 'Print Heading and Content' on the shortcut menu.

To Delete an Index Entry If you wanted to delete an index entry, you would perform the following steps.

1. Display formatting marks.
2. Select the XE field for the index entry you wish to delete (i.e., { XE "insert a screenshot" }).
3. Press DELETE.
4. Update the index as described in the next set of steps.

To Update an Index

The following step updates an index. **Why?** After marking a new index entry, you must update the index.

- Click the heading, Index, in the Navigation Pane to display the selected heading in the document window.
- In the document window, click the index to select it.
- If necessary, display the References tab.
- Click the Update Index button (References tab | Index group) to update the index (Figure 9–70).
- Save the document again on the same storage location with the same file name.

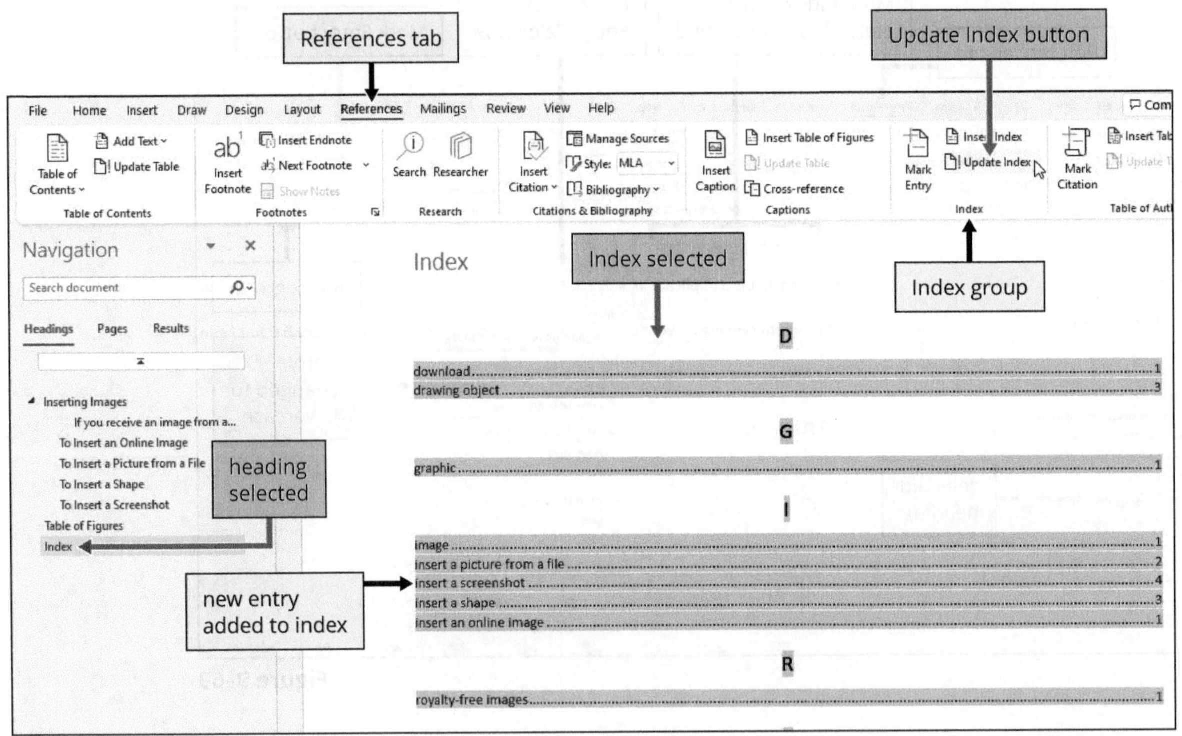

Figure 9–70

Other Ways

1. Select index, press F9

To Change the Format of the Index If you wanted to change the format of the index, you would perform the following steps.

1. Click the index to select it.
2. Click the Insert Index button (References tab | Index group) to display the Index dialog box.

3. Change settings in the dialog box as desired. If you want to modify the style used for the index, click the Modify button.
4. Click OK (Index dialog box) to apply the changed settings.
5. Click OK when Word asks if you want to replace the selected index.

To Delete an Entire Index If you wanted to delete an index, you would perform the following steps.

1. Click the index to select it.
2. Press SHIFT+F9 to display field codes.
3. Drag through the entire field code, including the braces, and then press DELETE.

Table of Authorities

In addition to inserting an index, table of figures, and table of contents, you can use Word to insert a table of authorities. Legal documents often include a **table of authorities** to list references to cases, rules, statutes, etc., along with the page number(s) on which the references appear. To create a table of authorities, you mark the citations first and then insert the table of authorities.

The procedures for marking citations, editing citations, inserting the table of authorities, changing the format of the table of authorities, and updating the table of authorities are the same as those for indexes. The only difference is that you use the buttons in the Table of Authorities group on the References tab instead of the buttons in the Index group.

To Mark a Citation If you wanted to mark a citation, creating a citation entry, you would perform the following steps.

1. Select the long, full citation that you wish to appear in the table of authorities (for example, State v. Smith 220 J.3d 167 (UT, 1997)).
2. Click the Mark Citation button (References tab | Table of Authorities group) or press ALT+SHIFT+I to display the Mark Citation dialog box.
3. If necessary, click the Category arrow (Mark Citation dialog box) and then select a new category type.
4. If desired, enter a short version of the citation in the Short citation text box.
5. Click the Mark button to mark the selected text in the document as a citation.

   Q&A Why do formatting marks now appear on the screen?
   When you mark a citation, Word automatically shows formatting marks (if they are not showing already) so that you can view the citation field. The citation entry begins with the letters, TA.

6. Click the Close button in the Mark Citation dialog box.

   Q&A How could I view all marked citation entries in a document?
   With formatting marks displaying, you could scroll through the document, scanning for all occurrences of TA, or you could use the Navigation Pane (that is, place a check mark in the Navigation Pane check box (View tab | Show group)) to find all occurrences of TA.

To Mark Multiple Citations Word leaves the Mark Citation dialog box open until you close it, which allows you to mark multiple citations without having to redisplay the dialog box repeatedly. To mark multiple citations, you would perform the following steps.

1. With the Mark Citation dialog box displayed, click in the document window; scroll to and then select the next citation.
2. If necessary, click the Selected text text box (Mark Citation dialog box) to display the selected text in the Selected text text box.

BTW
Field Codes
If your index, table of contents, or table of figures displays odd characters inside curly braces ({}), then Word is displaying field codes instead of field results. Press ALT+F9 to display the index or table correctly.

BTW
Inserting Endnotes
To insert an endnote, click the Insert Endnote button (Reference tab | Footnotes group), which places a separator line and the endnote text at the end of the document. Enter desired endnote text to the right of the note reference mark below the separator line.

BTW
Advanced Layout Options
You can adjust Word's advanced layout options by clicking File on the ribbon to open Backstage view, clicking Options in Backstage view to display the Word Options dialog box, clicking Advanced in the left pane (Word Options dialog box), scrolling to the Layout options for area in the right pane, placing a check mark in the desired settings, and then clicking OK.

3. Click the Mark button.
4. Repeat Steps 1 through 3 for all citations you wish to mark. When finished, click the Close button in the dialog box.

To Edit a Citation Entry At some time, you may want to change a citation entry after you have marked it. For example, you may need to change the case of a letter. If you wanted to change a citation entry, you would perform the following steps.

1. Display formatting marks.
2. Locate the TA field for the citation entry you wish to change.
3. Change the text inside the quotation marks.
4. Update the table of authorities as described in the steps at the end of this section.

To Delete a Citation Entry If you wanted to delete a citation entry, you would perform the following steps.

1. Display formatting marks.
2. Select the TA field for the citation entry you wish to delete.
3. Press DELETE, or click the Cut button (Home tab | Clipboard group), or right-click the field and then click Cut on the Mini toolbar or shortcut menu.
4. Update the table of authorities as described in the steps at the end of this section.

To Insert a Table of Authorities Once all citations are marked, Word can build a table of authorities from the citation entries in the document. Recall that citation entries begin with TA, and they appear on the screen when formatting marks are displayed. When citation entries show on the screen, the document's pagination probably will be altered because of the extra text in the citation entries. Thus, be sure to hide formatting marks before inserting a table of authorities. To insert a table of authorities, you would perform the following steps.

1. Position the insertion point at the location for the table of authorities.
2. Ensure that formatting marks are not displayed.
3. Click the 'Insert Table of Authorities' button (References tab | Table of Authorities group) to display the Table of Authorities dialog box.
4. If necessary, select the category to appear in the table of authorities by clicking the desired option in the Category list, or leave the default selection of All so that all categories will be displayed in the table of authorities.
5. If necessary, click the Formats button (Table of Authorities dialog box) and then select the desired format for the table of authorities.
6. If necessary, click the Tab leader button and then select the desired leader character in the list to specify the leader character to be displayed between the marked citation and the page number.
7. If you wish to display the word, passim, instead of page numbers for citations with more than four page references, select the Use passim check box.

Q&A What does the word, passim, mean?
Here and there.

8. Click OK (Table of Authorities dialog box) to create a table of authorities using the specified settings at the location of the insertion point.

BTW
Line Numbers
If you wanted to insert line numbers in a document, click the Line Numbers button (Layout tab | Page Setup group) and then click the desired line number setting on the Line Numbers menu.

BTW
Different First Page Header or Footer
If you wanted only the first page of a document to have a different header or footer, you could place a check mark in the 'Different First Page' check box (Header & Footer tab | Options group). Doing so instructs Word to create a first page header or first page footer that can contain content that differs from the rest of the headers or footers.

To Update a Table of Authorities If you add, delete, or modify citation entries, you must update the table of authorities to display the new or modified citation entries. If you wanted to update a table of authorities, you would perform the following steps.

1. In the document window, click the table of authorities to select it.
2. Click the Update Table button (References tab | Table of Authorities group) or press F9 to update the table of authorities.

To Change the Format of the Table of Authorities If you wanted to change the format of the table of authorities, you would perform the following steps.

1. Click the table of authorities to select it.
2. Click the 'Insert Table of Authorities' button (References tab | Table of Authorities group) to display the Table of Authorities dialog box.
3. Change settings in the dialog box as desired. To change the style of headings, alignment, etc., click the Formats button and then click From template; next, click the Modify button to display the Style dialog box, make necessary changes, and then click OK (Style dialog box).
4. Click OK (Table of Authorities dialog box) to apply the changed settings.
5. Click OK when Word asks if you want to replace the selected category of the table of authorities.

To Delete a Table of Authorities If you wanted to delete a table of authorities, you would perform the following steps.

1. Click the table of authorities to select it.
2. Press SHIFT+F9 to display field codes.
3. Drag through the entire field code, including the braces, and then press DELETE, or click the Cut button (Home tab | Clipboard group), or right-click the field and then click Cut on the Mini toolbar or shortcut menu.

BTW
Inserting Equations
To insert a built-in equation in a document, click the Equation arrow (Insert tab | Symbols group) and then select the desired equation to insert the equation in an equation editor in the document. To enter your own equation, click the Equation button (Insert tab | Symbols group) or click the Equation arrow and then click 'Insert New Equation' on the Equation menu to insert the equation editor in the document. Use buttons and boxes on the Equation tab to enter and format the equation in the equation editor box.

To Specify Different Odd and Even Page Footers Using a Footer Building Block

The *Learning Microsoft 365* document is designed so that it can be duplicated or printed back-to-back. **Why?** Back-to-back duplicating saves resources because, for example, it enables the ten-page document in this project to use only five sheets of paper. That is, the document prints on ten separate pages. When it is duplicated, however, pages are printed on opposite sides of the same sheet of paper. Some printers also have the capability to print back-to-back automatically.

In many books and documents that have back-to-back or facing pages, the page number is always on the same side of the page — often on the outside edge. In Word, you accomplish this task by specifying one type of header or footer for even-numbered pages and another type of header or footer for odd-numbered pages. The following steps specify alternating footers beginning on the fourth page of the document (the beginning of the subdocument).

- If necessary, hide formatting marks.
- Use the Navigation Pane to display the page with the heading, Inserting Images.
- Display the Insert tab.
- Click the Footer button (Insert tab | Header & Footer group) and then click Edit Footer to display the footer area.
- Be sure the 'Link to Previous' button (Header & Footer tab | Navigation group) is not selected. (If it is selected, click it to deselect it.)

Q&A What is the purpose of the 'Link to Previous' button?
If you want to continue using the same header or footer from a previous section, you would select the 'Link to Previous' button. If you want to create a different header or footer from the previous section, you would ensure the 'Link to Previous' button is not selected.

- Place a check mark in the 'Different Odd & Even Pages' check box (Header & Footer tab | Options group), so that you can enter a different footer for odd and even pages.
- If necessary, click the Previous button (Header & Footer tab | Navigation group) to display the desired footer page (in this case, the Even Page Footer -Section 3-) and then, if necessary, delete any text that appears in the section 3 footer.
- If necessary, click the Next button (Header & Footer tab | Navigation group) to display the desired footer page (in this case, the Odd Page Footer -Section 4-).

2

- Click the 'Insert Alignment Tab' button (Header & Footer tab | Position group) to display the Alignment Tab dialog box so that you can set the position of the footer.
- Click Right (Alignment Tab dialog box) because you want to place a right-aligned tab stop in the footer (Figure 9–71).

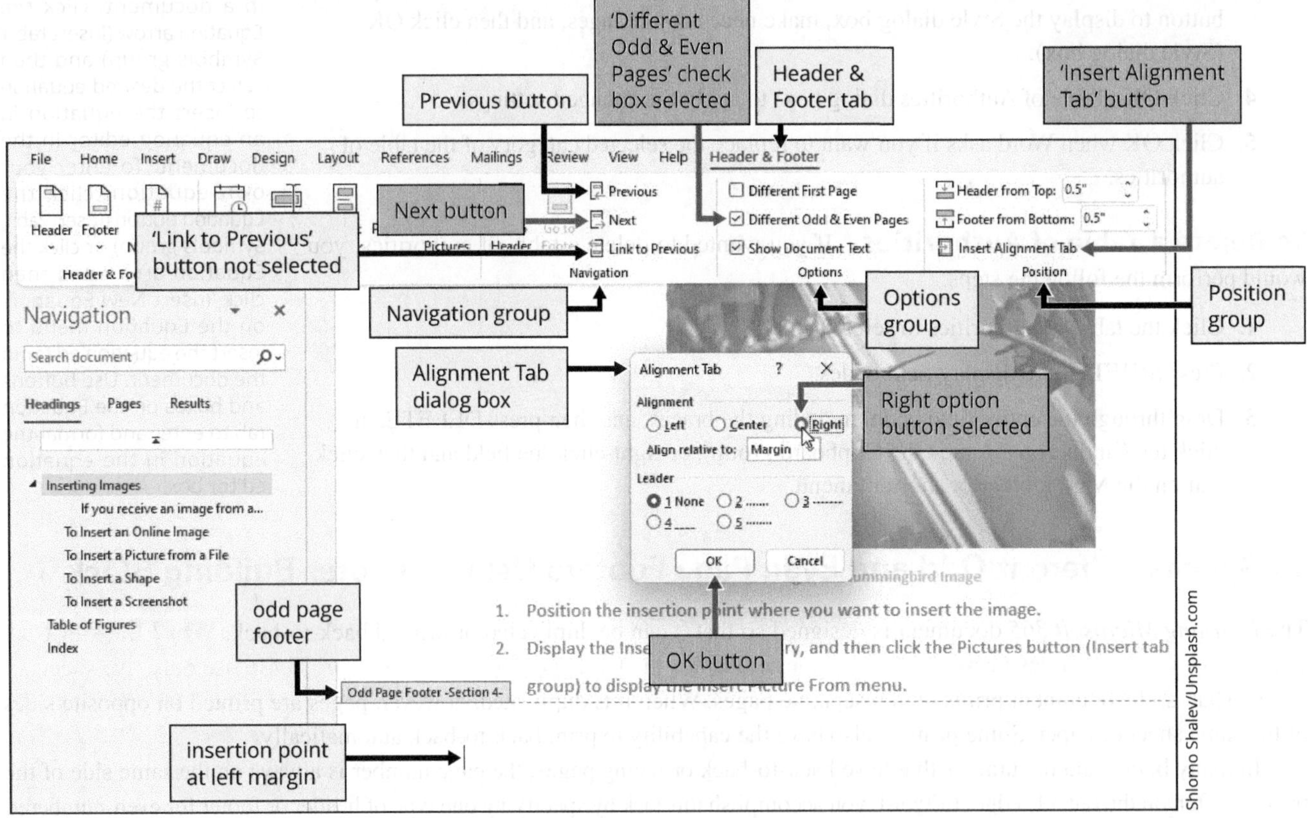

Figure 9–71

3

- Click OK to align the paragraph and insertion point in the footer at the right margin.
- Click the Page Number button (Header & Footer tab | Header & Footer group) to display the Page Number gallery.
- Point to Current Position in the Page Number gallery to display the Current Position gallery and then scroll to display 'Accent Bar 3' in the Current Position gallery (Figure 9–72).

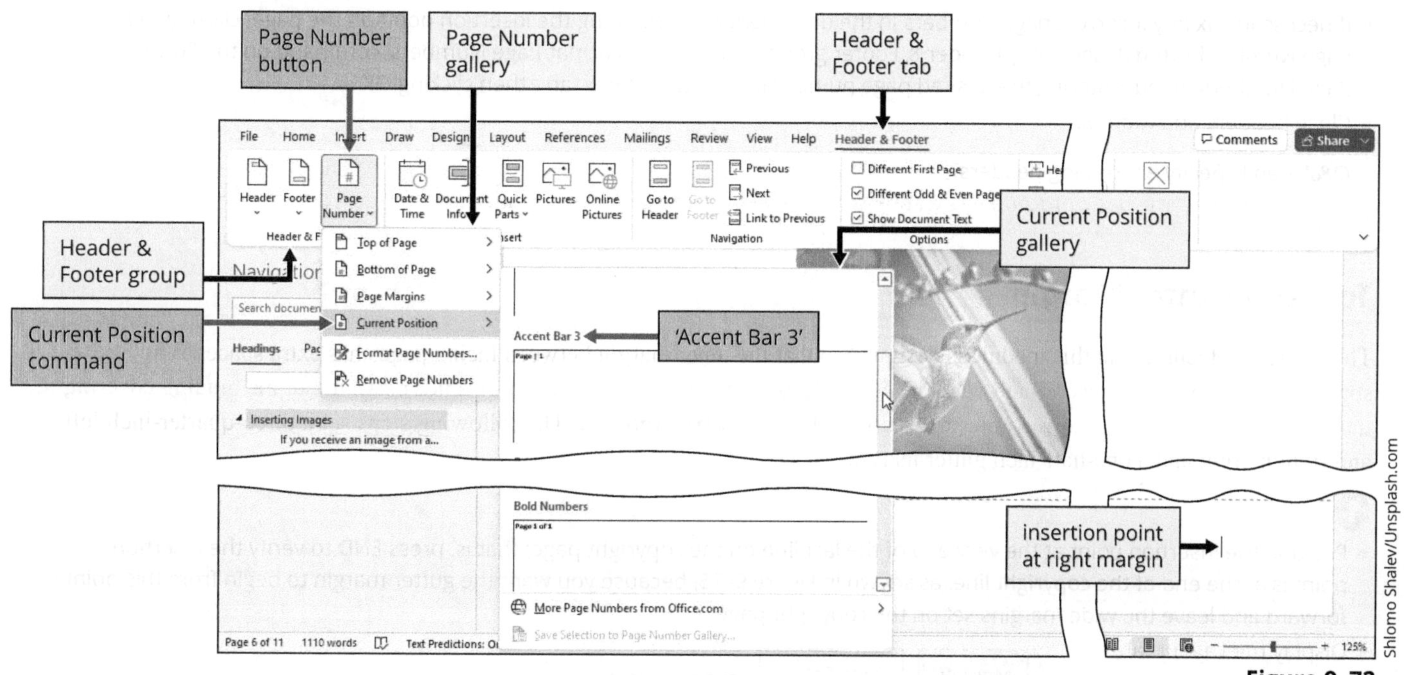

Shlomo Shalev/Unsplash.com

Figure 9–72

4

- Click 'Accent Bar 3' in the Current Position gallery to insert the selected page number in the footer (Figure 9–73).

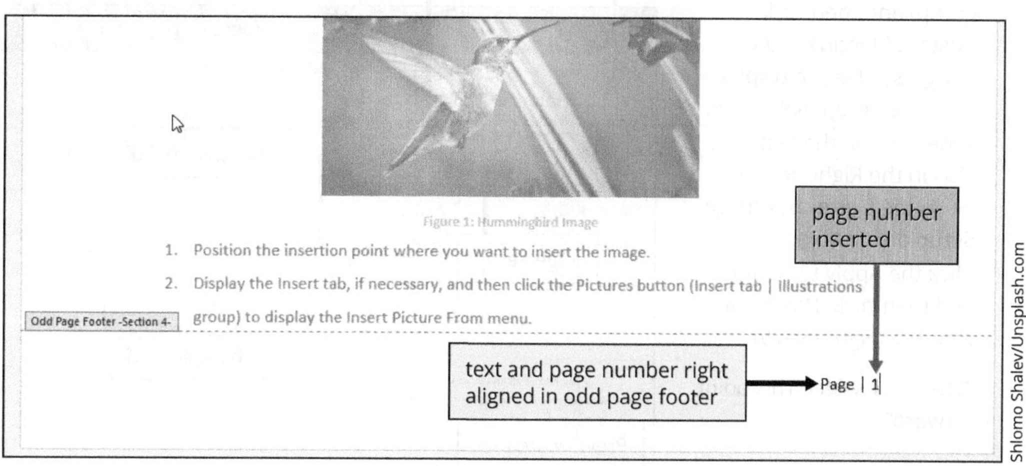

Shlomo Shalev/Unsplash.com

Figure 9–73

5

- Click the Next button (Header & Footer tab | Navigation group) to display the next footer, in this case, Even Page Footer -Section 4-.
- Be sure the 'Link to Previous' button (Header & Footer tab | Navigation group) is not selected. (If it is selected, click it to deselect it.)
- Click the Page Number button (Header & Footer tab | Header & Footer group) to display the Page Number gallery.
- Point to Current Position in the Page Number gallery to display the Current Position gallery and then click 'Accent Bar 3' in the Current Position gallery to insert the selected page number in the footer (Figure 9–74).

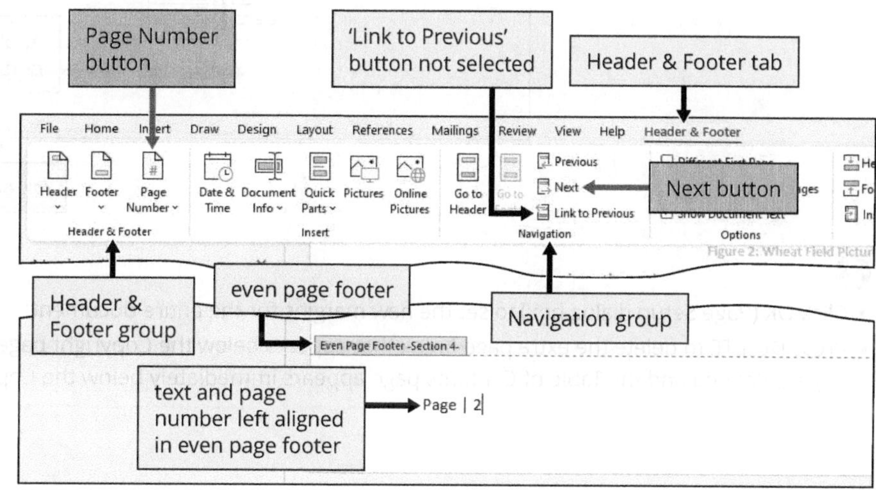

Figure 9–74

- If necessary, fix any incorrect page numbers in the document by positioning the insertion point on the page, clicking the Page Number button (Insert tab | Header & Footer group), clicking the 'Format Page Numbers' command on the Format Page Numbers menu, entering the desired page number in the Start at box, and then clicking OK.
- Close headers and footers.

Q&A Can I specify alternating headers?
Yes. Follow the same basic procedure, except insert a header building block or header text.

To Set a Gutter Margin

The reference document in this module is designed so that the inner margin between facing pages has extra space. **Why?** Extra space on facing pages allows printed versions of the documents to be bound (such as stapled) — without the binding covering the words. This extra space in the inner margin is called the **gutter margin**. The following steps set a three-quarter-inch left and right margin and a one-half-inch gutter margin.

- Position the insertion point at the very end of the last line on the copyright page; that is, press END to verify the insertion point is at the end of the copyright line, as shown in Figure 9–75, because you want the gutter margin to begin from this point forward and leave the wide margins set on the copyright page.
- Display the Layout tab.
- Click the Margins button (Layout tab | Page Setup group) and then click Custom Margins in the Margins gallery to display the Page Setup dialog box.
- Type **.75** in the Left box, **.75** in the Right box, and **.5** in the Gutter box (Page Setup dialog box).
- Click the Apply to button and then click 'This point forward' (Figure 9–75).

Q&A Why select 'This point forward'?
You want to retain the wide margins for the copyright page.

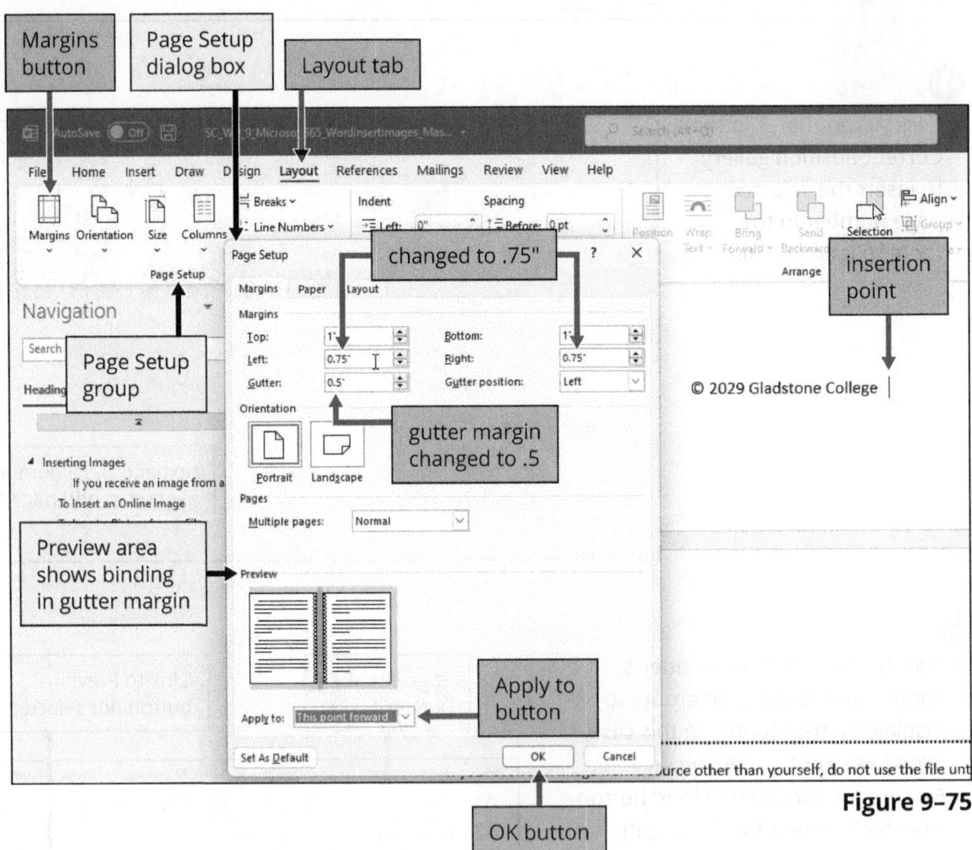

Figure 9–75

- Click OK (Page Setup dialog box) to set the new margins for the entire document.
- Press DELETE to delete the extra page break that appears below the Copyright page (scroll, if necessary, to confirm the extra page is deleted and the Table of Contents page appears immediately below the Copyright page).

To Check the Layout of the Printed Pages

To view the layout of all the pages in the document, the following steps display all the pages as they will print.

1 Open Backstage view.

2 Click Print to display all pages of the document in the right pane, as shown in Figure 9–76. (If all pages are not displayed, change the Zoom level to 10%.)

Q&A Why do blank pages appear in the middle of the document?
When you insert even and odd headers or footers, Word may add pages to fill the gaps.

3 Close Backstage view.

BTW
Break Header or Footer Link
If you do not want the header or footer in a section to be copied to the previous section, you would deselect the 'Link to Previous' button (Header & Footer tab | Navigation group).

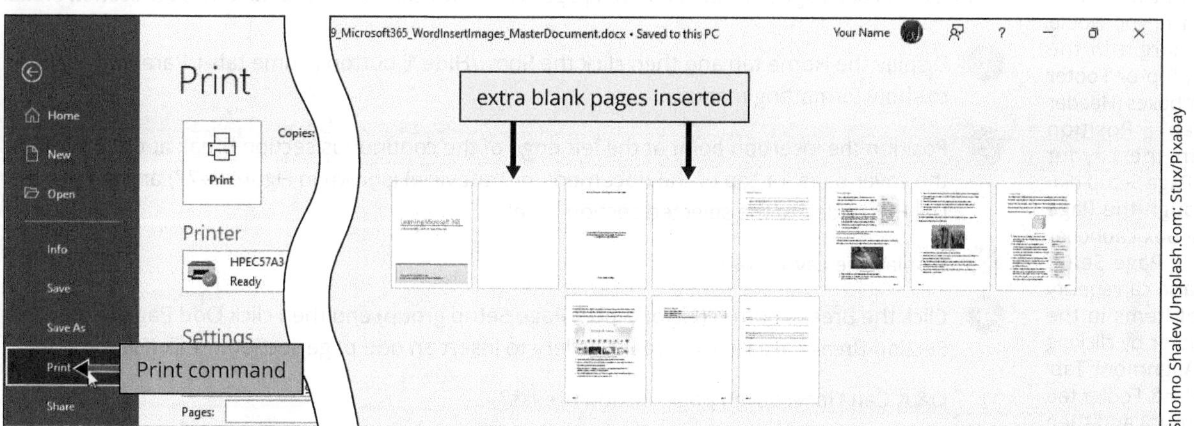

Figure 9–76

To Switch to Draft View

To adjust the blank pages automatically inserted in the printed document by Word, you change the continuous section break at the top of the document to an odd page section break. The following step switches to Draft view. **Why?** Section breaks are easy to see in Draft view.

- Display the View tab. Click the Draft button (View tab | Views group) to switch to Draft view.
- Scroll to the top of the document and notice how different the document appears in Draft view (Figure 9–77).

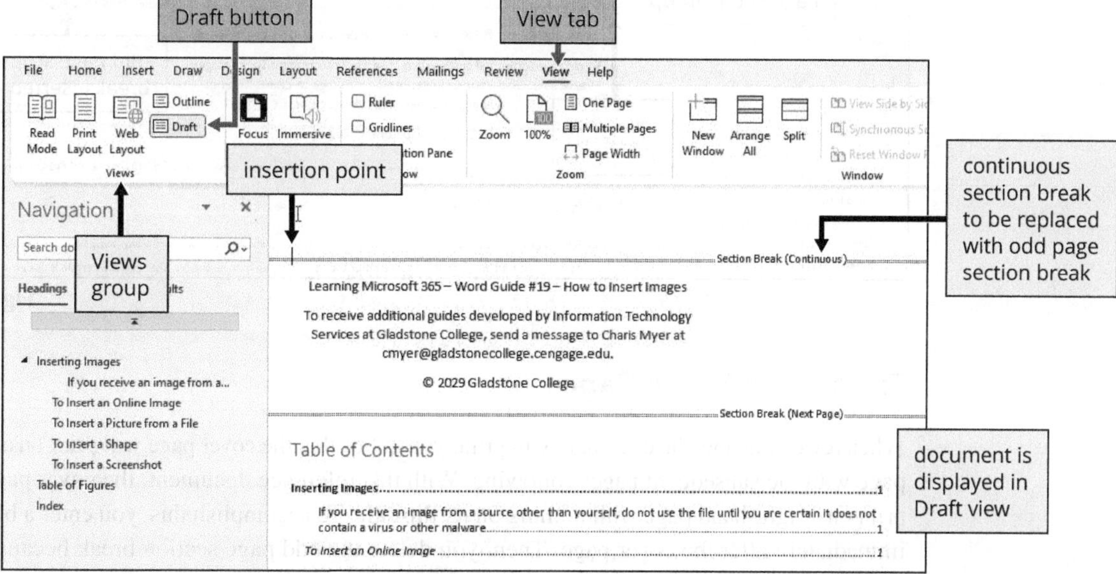

Figure 9–77

Q&A What happened to the images, footers, and other items?
They do not appear in Draft view because Draft view is designed to make editing text in a document easier.

Why is the wordwrap different on my screen?
Wordwrap could differ for a variety of reasons, including zoom settings, the printer being used, or Word Options settings. To verify Word Options settings, open Backstage view, click Options to display the Word Options dialog box, click Advanced in the left pane (Word Options dialog box), be sure the 'Show text wrapped within the document window' check box is not selected, and then click OK.

BTW
Header and Footer Margins
If you want the margins of the header or footer to be different from the default of one-half inch, you would adjust the margin in the 'Header from Top' or 'Footer from Bottom' boxes (Header & Footer tab | Position group) or in the Layout sheet of the Page Setup dialog box through the Page Setup Dialog Box Launcher (Layout tab | Page Setup group). You also can specify alignment of items in the header or footer by clicking the 'Insert Alignment Tab' button (Header & Footer tab | Position group) and then clicking the desired alignment in the Alignment Tab dialog box.

To Insert an Odd Page Section Break

To fix the extra pages in the printed document, you will replace the continuous section break at the end of the cover page with an odd page section break. With an odd page section break, Word starts the next section on an odd page instead of an even page. The following steps insert an odd page section break.

1. Display the Home tab and then click the Show/Hide ¶ button (Home tab | Paragraph group) to show formatting marks.
2. Position the insertion point at the left edge of the continuous section break at the bottom of the cover page (or top of the document in Draft view) (shown in Figure 9–77) and then press DELETE to delete the selected section break.
3. Display the Layout tab.
4. Click the Breaks button (Layout tab | Page Setup group) and then click Odd Page in the Section Breaks area in the Breaks gallery to insert an odd page section break (Figure 9–78).

   Q&A Can I insert even page section breaks?
   Yes. To instruct Word to start the next section on an even page, click Even Page in the Breaks gallery.

5. Check the layout of the printed pages again.

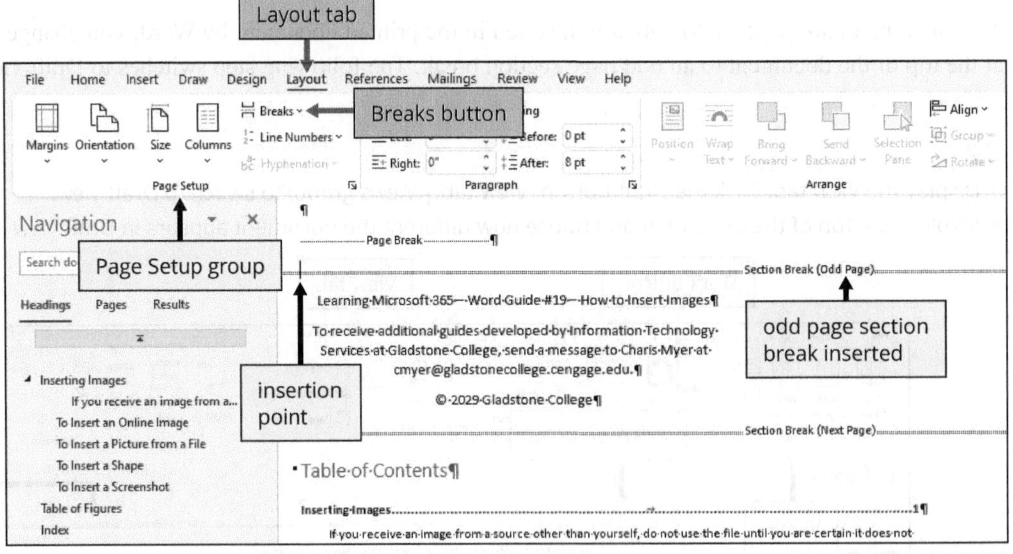

Figure 9–78

To Insert a Blank Page

When reviewing how the document will print, you notice that the cover page will print on a left-hand page with the subsequent pages following. With this reference document, the cover page should print on a right-hand page with nothing on its flip side. To accomplish this, you enter a blank page immediately after the cover page. Then, you delete the odd page section break because it is no longer needed. The following steps insert a blank page.

1. Position the insertion point to the left of the odd page section break notation at the top of the document (shown in Figure 9–78).
2. Display the Insert tab and then click the Blank Page button (Insert tab | Pages group) to insert a blank page (for the blank page that will be on the flip side of the cover page).
3. With the insertion point at the left edge of odd page section break, press DELETE to delete the selected section break (Figure 9–79).
4. Check the layout of the printed pages again to verify one blank page is before the copyright page (the document now contains 10 pages), or view multiple pages using the Multiple Pages button (View tab | Zoom group).
5. Click the Print Layout button on the status bar to switch to Print Layout view.
6. Hide formatting marks.

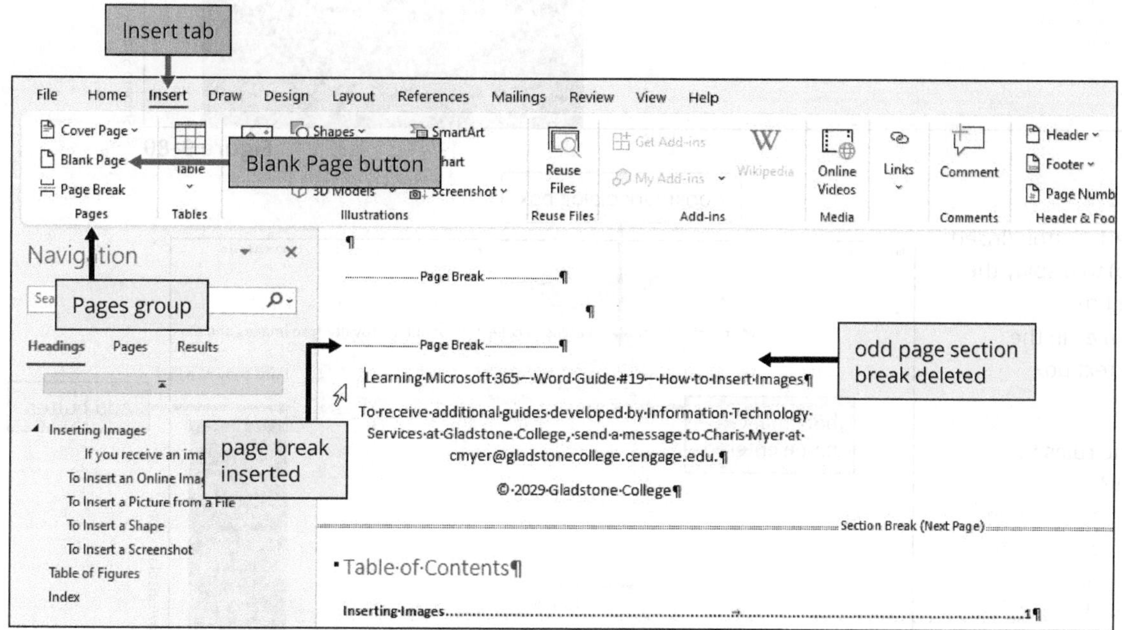

Figure 9–79

To Insert a Bookmark

A **bookmark** is a physical location in a document that you name so that you can reference it later. The following steps insert bookmarks. **Why?** Bookmarks assist users in navigating through a document online. For example, you could bookmark the headings in the document, so that users easily could jump to these areas of the document.

- Use the Navigation Pane to display the To Insert an Online Image heading in the document window and then select the heading in the document.
- Display the Insert tab and then click the Links group button (Insert tab) to display the Links group (Figure 9–80).

Q&A What if my screen shows a Links group instead of a Links group button?
Proceed to Step 2.

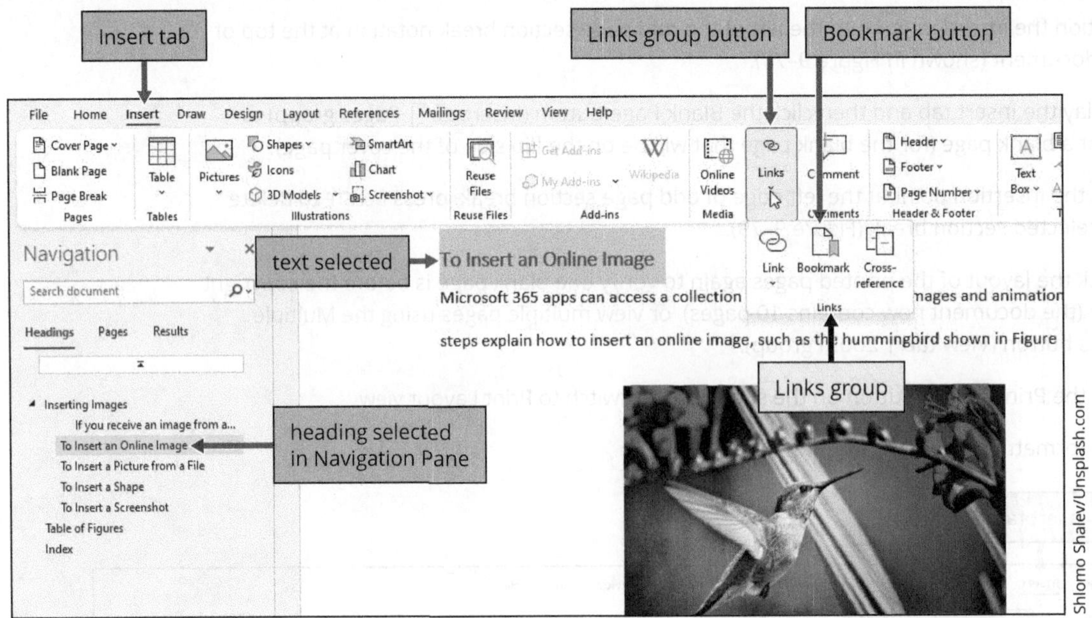

Figure 9–80

- Click the Bookmark button (Insert tab | Links group) to display the Bookmark dialog box.
- Type **OnlineImage** in the Bookmark name text box (Figure 9–81).

Q&A What are the rules for bookmark names?
Bookmark names can contain only letters, numbers, and the underscore character (_). They also must begin with a letter and cannot contain spaces.

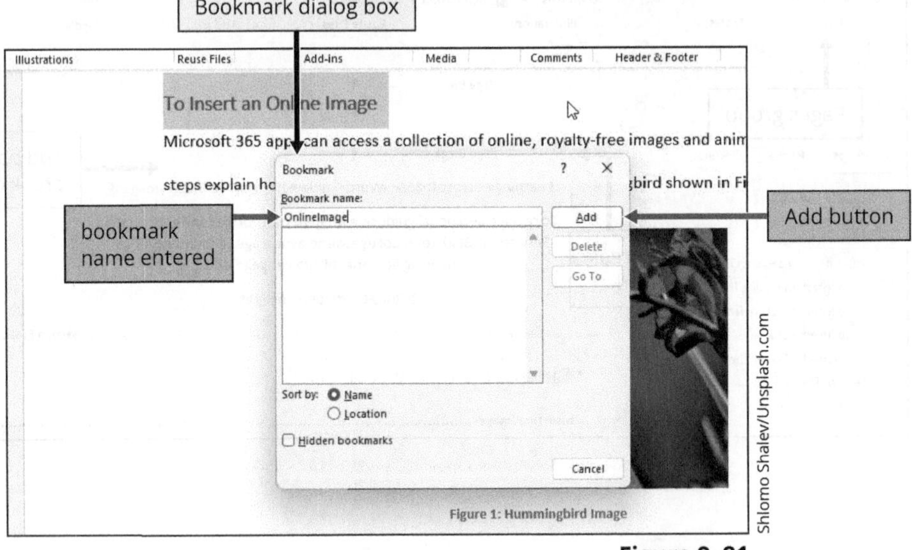

Figure 9–81

- Click the Add button (Bookmark dialog box) to add the bookmark name to the list of existing bookmarks in the document; click anywhere to remove the selection (Figure 9–82).

Q&A What if my screen does not show the brackets around the bookmark?
Click File on the ribbon to open Backstage view, click Options to display the Word Options dialog box, click Advanced in the left pane (Word Options dialog box), scroll to the Show document content area in the right pane, place a check mark in the Show bookmarks check box, and then click OK.

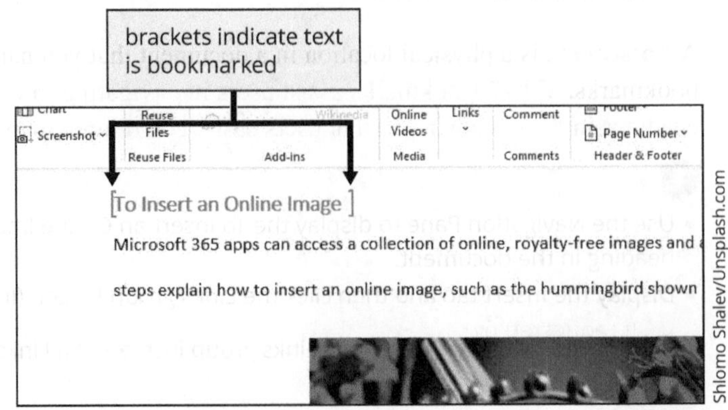

Figure 9–82

- Repeat Steps 1, 2, and 3 for these headings in the document: To Insert a Picture from a File, To Insert a Shape, and To Insert a Screenshot (use bookmark names PictureFromFile, Shape, and Screenshot).

To Go to a Bookmark Once you have added bookmarks, you can jump to them. If you wanted to go to a bookmark, you would perform the following steps.

1. Click the Bookmark button (Insert tab | Links group) to display the Bookmark dialog box (shown in Figure 9–80).
2. Click the bookmark name in the Bookmark name list (Bookmark dialog box) and then click the Go To button.

or

1. Press F5 to display the Go To sheet in the Find and Replace dialog box.
2. Click Bookmark in the 'Go to what' list (Find and Replace dialog box), click the 'Enter bookmark name' arrow, click the desired bookmark in the list, and then click the Go To button.

To Insert a Hyperlink to a Location in the Current Document Instead of or in addition to bookmarks in online documents, you can insert hyperlinks that link one part of a document to another. If you wanted to insert a hyperlink that links to a heading or bookmark in the document, you would follow these steps.

1. Select the text to be a hyperlink.
2. Click the Links group button (Insert tab) to display the Links group, click the Link button (Insert tab | Links group) to display the Insert Hyperlink dialog box.
3. In the Link to bar (Insert Hyperlink dialog box), click 'Place in This Document', so that Word displays all the headings and bookmarks in the document.
4. Click the heading or bookmark to which you want to link.
5. Click OK.

BTW
Hyperlink to Bookmark
If you wanted to insert a hyperlink to a bookmark in a document, click the Cross-reference button (Insert tab | Links group), select Bookmark in the Reference type list (Cross-reference dialog box), select the desired bookmark in the For which bookmark list, be sure the 'Insert as hyperlink' check box is selected, and then click OK. To display the bookmark associated with the link, CTRL+click the link.

To Check Accessibility, Save and Print a Document, and Then Exit Word

The reference document for this project now is complete. The following steps check accessibility, save and print the document, and then exit Word.

1. Click the Accessibility button on the status bar to open the Accessibility pane. Add the following description in the Alt Text pane for the cover page grouped object: Cover page content containing the document title, subtitle, author, school name, and school address. (Leave the last errors or warnings identified by the Accessibility Checker for image or object not inline because, for illustration purposes, the sidebar text boxes are intended to be floating objects.) Close the Accessibility pane.
2. Review the document and, if necessary, adjust line spacing or image sizes as needed so all content is displayed similarly to Figure 9–1 at the beginning of this module.
3. Save the document again as a Word (.docx) file on the same storage location with the same file name.
4. If requested by your instructor, print the finished document (shown in Figure 9–1 at the beginning of this module).
5. If requested by your instructor, save the document as a PDF file and submit the PDF in the format requested by your instructor.

BTW
Conserving Ink and Toner
If you want to conserve ink or toner, you can instruct Word to print draft quality documents by clicking File on the ribbon to open Backstage view, clicking Options in Backstage view to display the Word Options dialog box, clicking Advanced in the left pane (Word Options dialog box), scrolling to the Print area in the right pane, placing a check mark in the 'Use draft quality' check box, and then clicking OK. Then, use Backstage view to print the document as usual.

BTW
Distributing a Document
Instead of printing and distributing a hard copy of a document, you can distribute the document electronically. Options include sending the document via email; posting it on cloud storage (such as OneDrive) and sharing the file with others; posting it on social media, a blog, or other website; and sharing a link associated with an online location of the document. You also can create and share a PDF or XPS image of the document, so that users can view the file in Acrobat Reader or XPS Viewer instead of in Word.

6. sam If requested by your instructor, unlink the subdocument so that it is converted to be part of the master document by clicking the Outline button (View tab | Views group) to switch to Outline view, clicking the Show Document button (Outlining tab | Master Document group) to show all buttons in the Master Document group, click somewhere in the subdocument, and then click the Unlink button (Outlining tab | Master Document group) to break the connection between the text in the master document and the subdocument so that all content is in a single file. Click File on the ribbon, click Save As, save the unlinked document using SC_WD_9_Microsoft365_WordInsertImages_UnlinkedDocument as the Word file name, and then submit the unlinked Word document in the format requested by your instructor. Close Outline view.

7. Exit Word.

Summary

In this module, you learned how to insert a screenshot, insert captions, insert cross-references, insert a sidebar text box, link text boxes, compress pictures, use Outline view, work with master documents and subdocuments, and insert a table of contents, a table of figures, an index, and bookmarks.

Consider This: Plan Ahead

What decisions will you need to make when creating reference documents?

Use these guidelines as you complete the assignments in this module and create your own reference documents outside of this class.

1. Prepare a document to be included in a longer document.
   a) If a document contains multiple images (figures), each figure should have a caption and be referenced from within the text.
   b) All terms in the document that should be included in the index should be marked as an index entry.
2. Include elements common to a reference document, such as a cover page, a table of contents, and an index.
   a) The cover page entices passersby to take a copy of the document.
   b) A table of contents at the beginning of the document and an index at the end help a reader locate topics within the document.
   c) Include a table of figures if the document contains several illustrations.
3. Prepare the document for distribution, including page numbers, gutter margins for binding, bookmarks, and hyperlinks as appropriate.

Student Assignments

Apply Your Knowledge

Reinforce the skills and apply the concepts you learned in this module.

Working with Outline View

Note: To complete this assignment, you will be required to use the Data Files. Please contact your instructor for information about accessing the Data Files.

Instructions: Start Word. Open the document, SC_WD_9-2.docx, which is located in the Data Files. Written by the lead instructor for the Introduction to Information Technology courses at Harbor Valley College, the document is an outline for a reference document that, when complete, will be available to faculty teaching the course for distribution to enrolled students. You are to modify the outline. The final outline is shown in Figure 9–83.

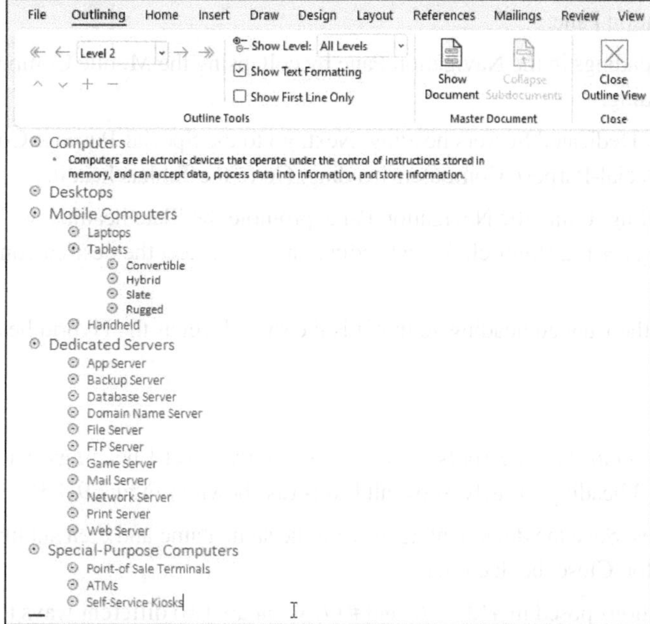

Figure 9–83

Perform the following tasks:

1. Click File on the ribbon and then click Save As and save the document using the new file name, SC_WD_9_Computers.
2. If necessary, switch to Outline view.
3. Practice collapsing and expanding headings in Outline view by collapsing the Desktops heading and then expanding the heading. When finished practicing, expand all headings.
4. In the Dedicated Servers section, move the Game Server heading down three lines so that it is immediately above the Mail Server heading.
5. Promote the Mobile Computers heading so that it is Level 1 instead of Level 2.
6. Demote the Self-Service Kiosks heading so that it is Level 2 instead of Level 1.
7. Demote the Convertible heading so that it is Level 3 instead of Level 2.
8. Move the Dedicated Servers heading and all its subheadings up so that they appear immediately above the Special-Purpose Computers heading. (**Hint:** When you collapse a heading and then move the collapsed heading, all its subheadings move with it.)

Continued on next page

9. Change the word, Notebooks, in the Mobile Computers section to the word, Laptops.
10. Immediately below the Special-Purpose Computers heading, insert a Level 2 heading with the text, Point-of-Sale Terminals.
11. Delete the duplicate Web Server heading in the Dedicated Servers section.
12. Remove the check mark from the 'Show Text Formatting' check box (Outlining tab | Outline Tools group). Place the check mark in the check box again. What is the purpose of this check box?
13. Ensure that the 'Show First Line Only' check box (Outlining tab | Outline Tools group) does not contain a check mark.
14. Add a blank line below the Computers heading. Demote the heading to body text. Enter this sentence as the body text, including the punctuation: Computers are electronic devices that operate under the control of instructions stored in memory, and can accept data, process data into information, and store information.
15. If requested by your instructor, add your name after the sentence entered in the previous step.
16. Place a check mark in the 'Show First Line Only' check box (Outlining tab | Outline Tools group). Remove the check mark from the check box again. What is the purpose of this check box?
17. Close Outline View. How does the document differ when displayed in Print Layout view?
18. Use the View tab to open the Navigation Pane.
19. Practice collapsing and expanding headings in the Navigation Pane by collapsing the Mobile Computers heading and then expanding the heading.
20. Use the Navigation Pane to go to the Dedicated Servers heading. Next, go to the Special-Purpose Computers heading. If necessary, expand the Special-Purpose Computers heading. Go to the Tablets heading.
21. If necessary, expand the Hybrid heading. Using the Navigation Pane, promote the Slate heading so that it is the same level as the Hybrid heading. (**Hint:** Right-click the heading and then select the desired command on the shortcut menu.)
22. Using the Navigation Pane, demote the Rugged heading so that it is the same level as the Hybrid heading.
23. Close the Navigation Pane.
24. Switch to Outline view.
25. Use the Show Level button (Outlining tab | Outline Tools group) to show only Level 1 headings. Show up to Level 2 headings. Show up to Level 3 headings. Lastly, show all levels (as shown in Figure 9–83).
26. Check and fix any accessibility issues. Save the document again with the same name and then submit it in the format specified by your instructor. Close the document.
27. **Consider This:** Answer the questions posed in #12, #16, and #17. What are two different ways to expand and collapse items in an outline, to move items up and down an outline, and to demote and promote items in an outline?

Extend Your Knowledge

Extend the skills you learned in this module and experiment with new skills. You may need to use Help to complete the assignment.

Creating a Reference Document with a Cover Page, a Table of Contents, and an Index

Note: To complete this assignment, you will be required to use the Data Files. Please contact your instructor for information about accessing the Data Files.

Instructions: Start Word. Open the draft document, SC_WD_9-3.docx, which is located in the Data Files. The draft discusses networks and network communications standards and protocols, written by the network management team leader at Communications Equipment Supercenter, for distribution to newly hired employees. As administrative assistant to the network manager, you are to insert a cover page, a table of contents, headers and footers, and an index.

Perform the following tasks:

1. Use Help to expand your knowledge about a cover page, a table of contents, headers and footers, marking index entries, and an index.
2. Click File on the ribbon and then click Save As and save the document using the new file name, SC_WD_9_Networks.
3. Insert the Austin style cover page. Use the following information on the cover page: abstract – Use these employee bulletins to review quick summaries of technology available in our stores.; title – Employee Bulletin #15; subtitle – Networks and Network Communications Standards and Protocols; author – Presented by our Network Management Team. (If the author entry disappears when you save the document, you may need to remove the Author content control and enter the author text again.) Format the text as you deem appropriate. Use the Accessibility pane to mark the shaded and outlined rectangles on the cover page as decorative.
4. If requested by your instructor, use your name as the author instead of Network Management Team.
5. Insert a blank page between the cover page and the Networks heading.
6. Insert a table of contents on the blank page using the Automatic Table 1 style.
7. Mark the following terms in the document as index entries: local area network, wide area network, personal area network, network standard, protocol, Ethernet, token ring, TCP/IP, Wi-Fi, LTE, UWB, Bluetooth, IrDA, RFID, and NFC.
8. Mark the following items in the document as index entries that have the subentry of the text, type of personal area network (Figure 9–84): body area network and body sensor network.

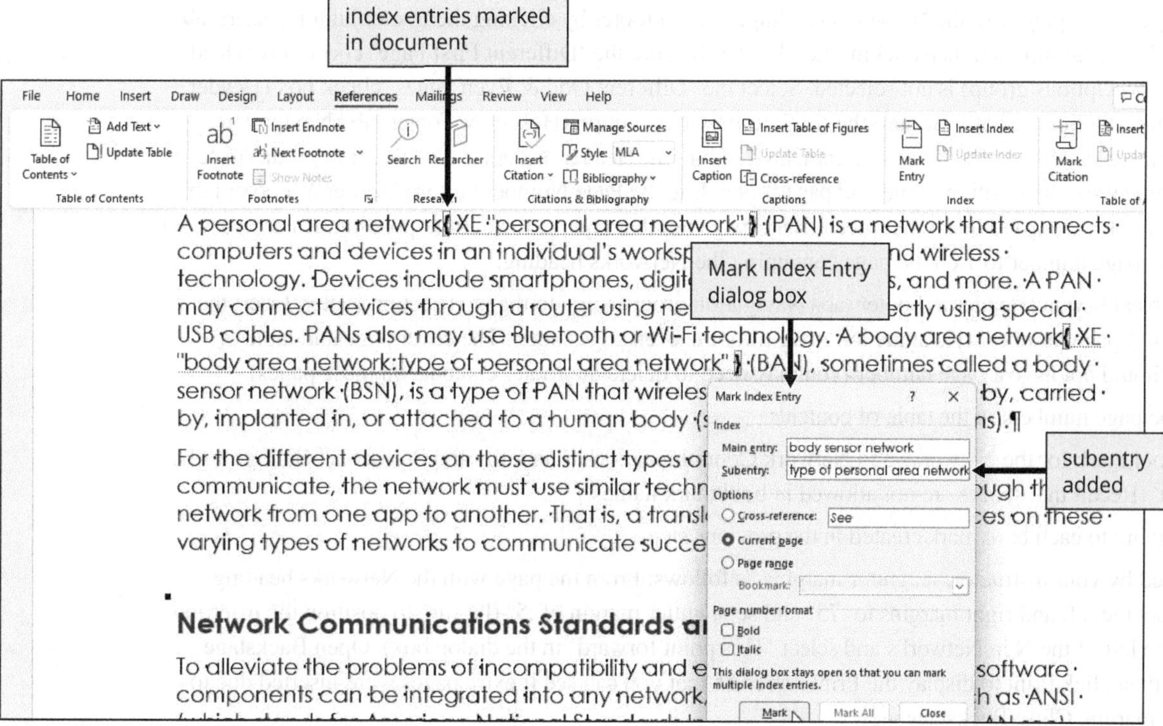

Figure 9–84

9. On a separate page at the end of the document, insert the word, Index, formatted in the Heading 1 style and then insert an index for the document. Remember to hide formatting marks prior to building the index. Use the From template format using one column, with right-aligned page numbers and leader characters of your choice.
10. Update the table of contents so that it includes the index.

Continued on next page

11. Mark another term of your choice in the document as an index entry. Update the index so that it includes this term.
12. Change the format of the table of contents to a format of your choice. (**Hint:** Select the table of contents, click the 'Table of Contents' button (References tab | Table of Contents group), click 'Custom Table of Contents' on the menu, and then select the desired format in the dialog box.) In the Table of Contents dialog box, remove the check mark from the 'Right align page numbers' check box and then notice how the table of contents appears in the document.
13. Redisplay the Table of Contents dialog box and then, if necessary, place a check mark in the 'Right align page numbers' check box. Select a tab leader character of your choice for the table of contents.
14. Find the bold italic format in the document and replace it with just an italic format. (**Hint:** Use the Replace dialog box and find the Bold Italic format and replace with the Not Bold format.)
15. Specify to prevent widows and orphans in the document, if necessary. (**Hint:** Use the Paragraph Dialog Box Launcher and select options in the Line and Page Breaks sheet.)
16. Select the local area network, wide area network, and personal area network paragraphs, and then specify to keep with next and keep lines together so that these paragraph lines stay together. (**Hint:** Use the Paragraph Dialog Box Launcher and select options in the Line and Page Breaks sheet.)
17. Specify that the paragraph containing the Network Communications Standards and Protocols heading should have a page break before it. (**Hint:** Use the Paragraph Dialog Box Launcher and select options in the Line and Page Breaks sheet.)
18. Insert a continuous section break to the left of the N in the Networks heading.
19. Format the page number on the page with the Networks heading to begin on page 1. (**Hint:** Use the Page Number button (Insert tab | Header & Footer group).)
20. On the page that begins with the Networks heading, insert a footer by clicking the Footer button (Insert tab | Header & Footer group) and then clicking Edit Footer. Be sure the 'Different First Page' check box (Header & Footer tab | Options group) is not selected. Select the 'Different Odd & Even Pages' check box (Header & Footer tab | Options group). Be sure the 'Link to Previous' button (Header & Footer tab | Navigation group) is not selected. Use the 'Insert Alignment Tab' button (Header & Footer tab | Position group) to set right alignment for the position of the odd page footer. Use the Page Number button (Header & Footer tab | Header & Footer group) to insert the Accent Bar 3 page number style at the current position. If necessary, set the starting page number to 1 on the page containing the Networks heading.
21. Click the Next button (Header & Footer tab | Navigation group) to go to the next section footer. Insert the Accent Bar 3 page number style at the left margin for the even page footer. The cover page and table of contents should not have a page number (you may need to delete the footer contents on these pages).
22. Update the page numbers in the table of contents.
23. Insert a bookmark for the Networks and Network Communications Standards and Protocols headings in the document. (Recall that spaces are not allowed in bookmark names.)
24. Practice going to each bookmark created in the previous step.
25. If requested by your instructor, set gutter margins as follows: From the page with the Networks heading forward, set the left and right margins to .75" and set a gutter margin of .5" (be sure to position the insertion point to the left of the N in Networks and select 'This point forward' in the dialog box). Open Backstage view and then click Print to display the Print screen so that you can see if extra pages were inserted due to the gutter margin. Close Backstage view.
26. If you performed the previous step, you may need to fix extra pages in the document by switching to Draft view, deleting the continuous section break, and then inserting an even page section break or an odd page section break using the Breaks button (Layout tab | Page Setup group). Practice inserting one, check the pages in the Print screen in Backstage view, undo the insert or delete odd or even section break and then insert the other. When finished, switch to Print Layout view. If necessary, reinsert page numbers in the even or odd footers (be sure the 'Link to Previous' button is not selected).
27. On a blank line below the index, use the Cross-reference button (Insert tab | Links group) to insert a cross-reference to one of the bookmarks as a hyperlink. Then, practice going to the link by CTRL+clicking the link. Delete the inserted cross-reference.

28. On the same blank line, use the Link button (Insert tab | Links group) to insert a hyperlink to a place in the document of your choice. After inserting the link, practice going to the link by CTRL+clicking the link. Delete the inserted link.
29. Position the insertion point on the Networks heading. Use the Line Numbers button (Layout tab | Page Setup group) to display continuous line numbers. Scroll through the document to notice how line numbers are applied. Remove the line numbers from the document.
30. Check accessibility and fix any hard-to-read text contrast warnings; you may need to change the font color of the text in your selected table of contents style. (Leave the last errors or warnings identified by the Accessibility Checker for image or object not inline because, for illustration purposes, the cover page elements are intended to be floating objects.) Save the document again and then submit it in the format specified by your instructor.
31. If required by your instructor or if you would like to practice with citations and a table of authorities, open the draft document again, SC_WD_9-3.docx, which is located in the Data Files. Add this text to the end of the last paragraph: State v. Carstens J.3d 169 (UT, 2021). Select the text just added and then mark the citation using the Mark Citation button (References tab | Table of Authorities group). Insert a new page at the end of the document and then insert a table of authorities on the blank page. At the end of another paragraph in the document, type this text: Barnes v. Wilson 212 F.4d 228 (FL, 2021). Update the table of authorities. Close the document without saving.
32. **Consider This:** If you wanted the index entries to appear in bold in the index but remain not bold in the document, what steps would you take to accomplish this? If your document had multiple pages with headers and footers and you did not want the same headers or footers to appear on different pages, which button would you click to break the link between the sections?

Expand Your World

Create a solution that uses cloud or web technologies by learning and investigating on your own from general guidance.

Inserting Equations, Symbols, Screenshots, and Screen Clippings, and Using an Online Photo Editor

Instructions: As an assistant to the operations manager at Technology Training, you have been asked to insert sample equations and mathematical operators in a Word document, take a screenshot of the screen, and then use an online photo editor to enhance the screenshot. Be creative — the screen shown in Figure 9–85 is only a sample solution. Your document should look different.

Perform the following tasks:

1. Start Word and create a blank document. Change the margins to Narrow. Enter the title, Equations and Mathematical Operators. Format the entered title appropriately at the top of the page.
2. On a line below the title, insert a mathematical symbol of your choice using the Symbol dialog box. (**Hint:** Click the Subset arrow in the Symbol dialog box and then click Mathematical Operators.) Select the entered mathematical symbol and then place it in a text box by clicking the Text Box button (Insert tab | Text group) and then clicking 'Draw Text Box'. Insert five more mathematical operators using this procedure. Position, resize, and format the text boxes as desired.
3. Insert a text box in the document. Delete any text in the text box and insert a built-in equation of your choice using the Equation arrow (Insert tab | Symbols group). Select the equation and format and position it as desired.
4. Insert another text box in the document and delete any text in the text box. So that you can type an equation in the text box, click the Equation button (Insert tab | Symbols group) or click the Equation arrow and then click 'Insert New Equation'. Use the Equation tab to insert an equation of your choice in the equation editor box. Select the equation and format and position it as desired. The title and all text boxes should fit in the document window (Figure 9–85).

Continued on next page

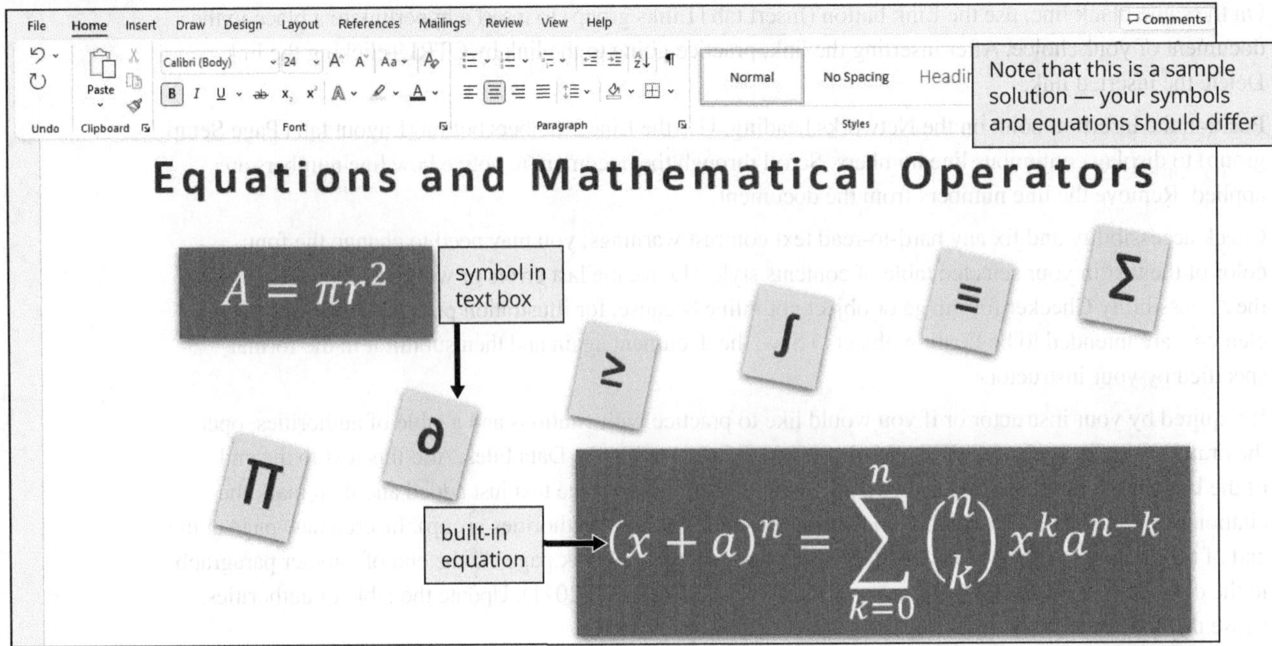

Figure 9–85

5. Save the document with the file name, SC_WD_9_EquationsOperators.
6. From Word, create a blank document so that you have two separate Word windows open. At the top of the blank document, enter the text, Screenshot:, and underline it. Then, insert a screenshot of the window containing the SC_WD_9_EquationsOperators file. Center the screenshot.
7. On a blank line below the inserted screenshot, enter the text, Screen clipping:, and underline it. Then, insert a screen clipping of just the equations and mathematical operators. Center the screen clipping.
8. Add appropriate alt text to the screenshot and screen clipping. Save the document with the screenshot and screen clipping with the file name, SC_WD_9_EquationsOperatorsScreens.
9. Save the Word screenshot as a PNG file with the name, SC_WD_9_EquationsOperatorsScreenshot. (**Hint:** Right-click the image and then click 'Save as Picture' on the submenu.)
10. Save the screen clipping as a PNG file with the file name, SC_WD_9_EquationsOperatorsClipping.
11. Locate the PNG files you saved in the previous two steps and then double-click them. In what program did they open?
12. Submit the documents in the format specified by your instructor.
13. Start a browser. Search for the text, online photo editor, using a search engine. Visit several of the online photo editors and determine which you would like to use to edit an image. Navigate to the desired online photo editor.
14. In the photo editor, open the SC_WD_9_EquationsOperatorsClipping image that you created in Step 10. Use the photo editor to enhance the image. Apply at least five enhancements. Which enhancements did you apply?
15. If requested by your instructor, add your name as a text element to the photo.
16. Save the revised image with the file name, SC_WD_9_EquationsOperatorsClippingEnhanced. In what format did the online photo editor save the file? Submit the image in the format specified by your instructor.
17. **Consider This:** Answer the questions posed in #11, #14, and #16. Which online photo editors did you evaluate? Which one did you select to use, and why? Do you prefer using the online photo editor or Word to enhance images?

In the Lab

Design and implement a solution using creative thinking and problem-solving skills.

Using a Master and Subdocument for a Reference Document

Note: To complete this assignment, you will be required to use the Data Files. Please contact your instructor for information about accessing the Data Files.

Problem: As the assistant to the director at your school's resource center, you have been asked to prepare a basic overview of mobile and game devices to be available to new students in the introductory technology course. You decide to use a master document and a subdocument for this reference document.

Part 1: The subdocument you created is in a file called SC_WD_9-4.docx, which is located in the Data Files. Using the concepts and techniques presented in this module, along with the source content in the Data Files, create and format the master document with the subdocument. While creating the documents, be sure to do the following:

1. Save the subdocument with the file name, SC_WD_9_Mobile-and-GameDevicesSubdocument.
2. In the subdocument, mark at least 10 terms as index entries.
3. Insert the following six images in the Data Files in appropriate locations in the subdocument:
    - Support_WD_9_Smartphone.jpg
    - Support_WD_9_DigitalCamera.jpg
    - Support_WD_9_DigitalMediaPlayer.jpg
    - Support_WD_9_E-BookReader.jpg
    - Support_WD_9_Smartwatch.jpg
    - Support_WD_9_HandheldGameDevice.jpg
4. Insert appropriate captions for each of the six images.
5. Insert a cross-reference to each of the captions.
6. Compress one of the images and then compress all the images.
7. Insert a sidebar text box that contains text about a mobile or game device you use at home or school. Insert another blank text box in the document. Link the two text boxes and then save the file.
8. Create a master document in a new document window in Outline view. Insert appropriate headings for a Table of Figures and an Index. Insert the subdocument file that is called SC_WD_9_Mobile-and-GameDevicesSubdocument in the appropriate location. Be sure to insert a next page section break between each line in the master document in Outline view. Save the master document with the file name, SC_WD_9_Mobile-and-GameDevicesReferenceDocument. Switch to Print Layout view.
9. Insert an appropriate cover page.
10. Insert a table of contents, a table of figures, and an index.
11. Modify one of the figure captions and then update the table of figures.
12. Format the document with a footer that contains a page number. Practice using the 'Link to Previous' button (Header & Footer tab | Navigation group) to continue the footer from a previous section and then create a footer that is different from the previous section.
13. Format the document with a header that is different from the first page.
14. Practice going to the next and previous sections in the document.
15. If requested by your instructor, insert an endnote that contains your name in the document.
16. Be sure to check the accessibility, along with the spelling and grammar of the finished documents.
17. When you are finished with the master document and subdocuments, save them again and then also save the file as a PDF with the file name, SC_WD_9_Mobile-and-GameDevicesReferenceDocument. Submit your documents and answers to the Part 2 critical thinking questions in the format specified by your instructor.

Continued on next page

18. Close all documents and then reopen the master document. In Outline view, expand the document. Collapse the subdocument. Show the subdocument.
19. Practice locking and unlocking a subdocument.
20. Unlink the subdocument. Close the document without saving changes.

Part 2: **Consider This:** You made several decisions while creating the reference document in this assignment: which terms to mark as index entries, what text to use for captions, and how to organize and format the subdocument and master document (table of contents, table of figures, index, etc.). What was the rationale behind each of these decisions? When you proofread the document, what further revisions did you make and why?

Creating an Online Form

Objectives

After completing this module, you will be able to:

- Save a document as a template
- Change paper size
- Add and format a page color
- Insert and format an icon
- Use a table to control document layout
- Show and hide the Developer tab
- Insert plain text, drop-down list, check box, rich text, combo box, and date picker content controls
- Edit placeholder text using Design mode
- Change properties of content controls
- Insert and format a shape
- Restrict editing to filling in a form
- Create a new document based on a template
- Fill in a form

Introduction

During your personal and professional life, you undoubtedly have filled in countless forms. Whether a federal tax form, a time card, a job application, an order, a deposit slip, a request, or a survey, a form is designed to collect information. In the past, forms were printed; that is, you received the form on a piece of paper, filled it in with a pen or pencil, and then returned it manually. An **online form** contains labels and corresponding blank areas in which a user electronically enters the requested information. You use a computer or mobile device to access, fill in, and then return an online form. In Word, you easily can create an online form for electronic distribution; you also can fill in that same form using Word.

Project: Online Form

Today, businesses and individuals are concerned with using resources efficiently. To minimize paper waste, protect the environment, enhance office efficiency, and improve access to data, many businesses have moved toward a paperless office. Thus, online forms have replaced many paper forms. You access online forms on a website, on a company's intranet, or from your inbox if you receive the form via email.

The project in this module uses Word to produce the online form shown in Figure 10–1. Albring Law Offices is a law firm interested in client feedback. Thus, the administrative assistant to the client relations coordinator at Albring Law Offices designed the client survey as a Word online form (shown in the figure). Instead of sending the survey via the postal service, Albring Law Offices will send the survey via email to clients after services are rendered. Upon receipt of the survey (online form), the client fills in the form and then sends it back via email to Albring Law Offices.

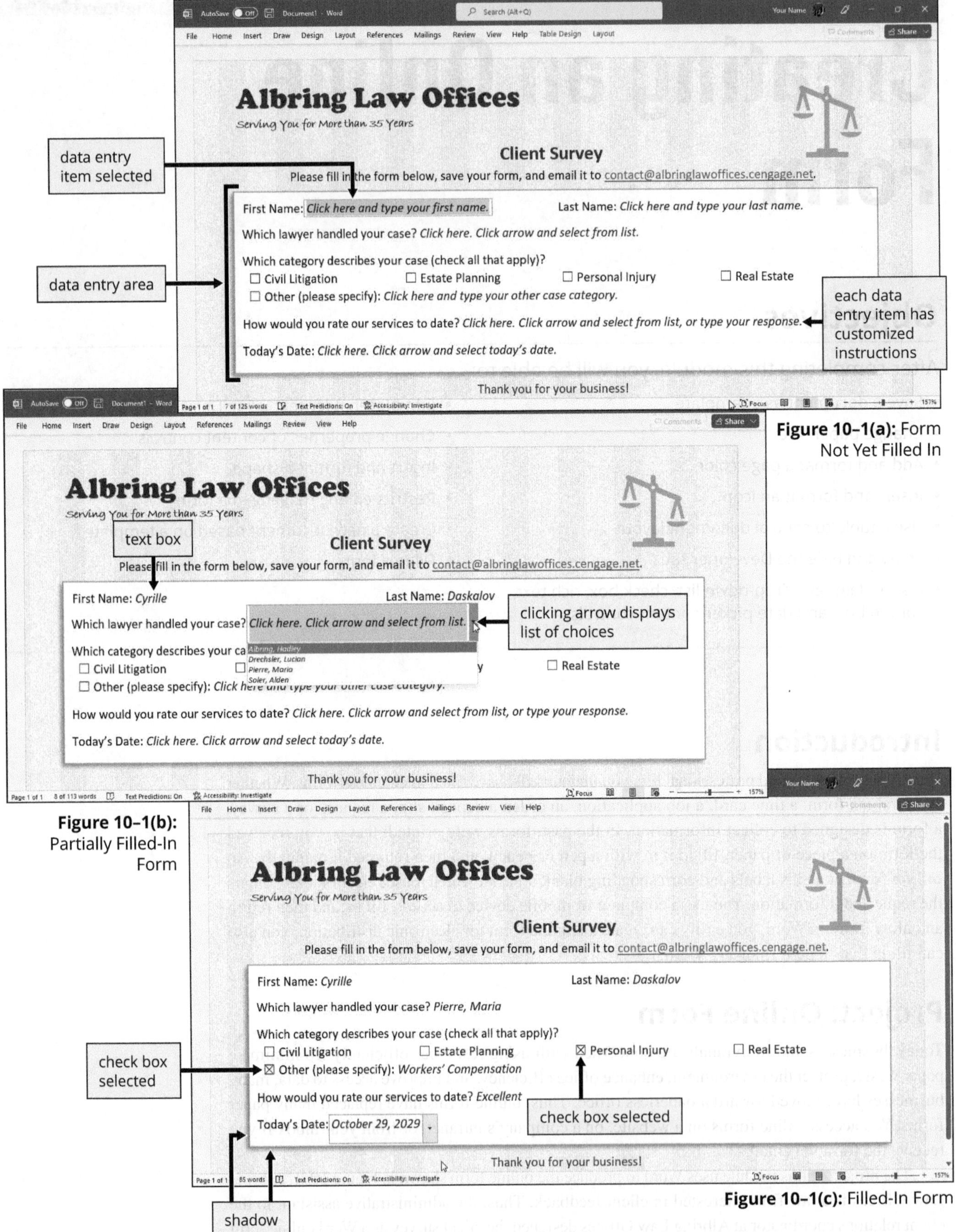

Figure 10–1(a): Form Not Yet Filled In

Figure 10–1(b): Partially Filled-In Form

Figure 10–1(c): Filled-In Form

Figure 10–1a shows how the form is displayed on a user's screen initially, Figure 10–1b shows the form partially filled in by one user, and Figure 10–1c shows how this user filled in the entire form.

The data entry area of the form contains three text boxes (named First Name, Last Name, and Other Case Category), one drop-down list box (named Lawyer Name), five check boxes (named Civil Litigation, Estate Planning, Personal Injury, Real Estate, and Other Case Category), a combination text box/drop-down list box (named Service Rating), and a date picker (named Today's Date).

The form is designed so that it fits completely within a Word window that is set at a page width zoom and has the ribbon collapsed, which reduces the chance a user will have to scroll the window while filling in the form. The data entry area of the form is enclosed by a rectangle that has a shadow on its left and bottom edges.

You will perform the following general tasks as you progress through this module:

1. Save a document as a template.
2. Set form formats for the template.
3. Enter text, graphics, and content controls in the form.
4. Protect the form.
5. Use the form.

To Start Word and Specify Settings

If you are using a computer to step through the project in this module and you want your screens to match the figures in this book, you should change your screen's resolution to 1366 × 768. The following steps start Word and specify settings.

1. sam Start Word and create a blank document in the Word window. If necessary, maximize the Word window.
2. If the Print Layout button on the status bar is not selected, click it so that your screen is in Print Layout view.
3. If the 'Show/Hide ¶' button (Home tab | Paragraph group) is not selected already, click it to display formatting marks on the screen.
4. To display the page the same width as the document window, if necessary, click the Page Width button (View tab | Zoom group).
5. If the rulers are displayed on the screen, click the Ruler check box (View tab | Show group) to remove the rulers from the Word window.
6. If you are using a mouse and you want your screens to match the figures in the book, verify that you are using Mouse mode by doing the following: display the Quick Access Toolbar, if necessary, by clicking the 'Ribbon Display Options' button at the right edge of the ribbon and then clicking 'Show Quick Access Toolbar' on the menu; clicking the 'Touch/Mouse Mode' button on the Quick Access Toolbar and then, if necessary, clicking Mouse on the menu (if your Quick Access Toolbar does not display the 'Touch/Mouse Mode' button, click the 'Customize Quick Access Toolbar' button on the Quick Access Toolbar and then click Touch/Mouse Mode on the menu to add the button to the Quick Access Toolbar); then hide the Quick Access Toolbar by clicking the 'Ribbon Display Options' button at the right edge of the ribbon and then clicking 'Hide Quick Access Toolbar' on the menu.

Saving a Document as a Template

A **template** is a file with a theme applied and that may contain formatted placeholder text, headers and footers, and graphics, some of which you replace with your own information. Every Word document you create is based on a template. When you select the Blank document thumbnail on the Word start screen or in the New screen of Backstage view, Word creates a document based on the Normal template. Word also provides other templates for more specific types of documents, such as memos, letters, and resumes. Creating a document based on these templates can improve your productivity because Word has defined much of the document's appearance for you.

In this module, you create an online form. If you create and save an online form as a Word document, users will be required to open that Word document to display the form on the screen. Next, they will fill in the form. Then, to preserve the content of the original form, they will have to save the form with a new file name. If they accidentally click the Save button on the title bar during the process of filling in the form, Word will replace the original blank form with a filled-in form.

BTW
Saving Templates
When you save a template that contains building blocks, the building blocks are available to all users who access the template.

If you create and save the online form as a template instead, users will open a new document window that is based on that template. This displays the form on the screen as a brand-new Word document; that is, the document does not have a file name. Thus, the user fills in the form and then clicks the Save button on the title bar to save the filled-in form. By creating a Word template for the form, instead of a Word document, the original template for the form remains intact when the user clicks the Save button.

To Save a Document as a Template

The following steps save a new blank document as a template. **Why?** The template will be used to create the online form shown in Figure 10–1.

- With a new blank document in the Word window, open Backstage view and then click Export in the left pane of Backstage view to display the Export screen.
- Click 'Change File Type' in the Export screen to display information in the right pane about various file types that can be saved in Word.
- Click Template in the right pane to specify the file type for the current document (Figure 10–2).

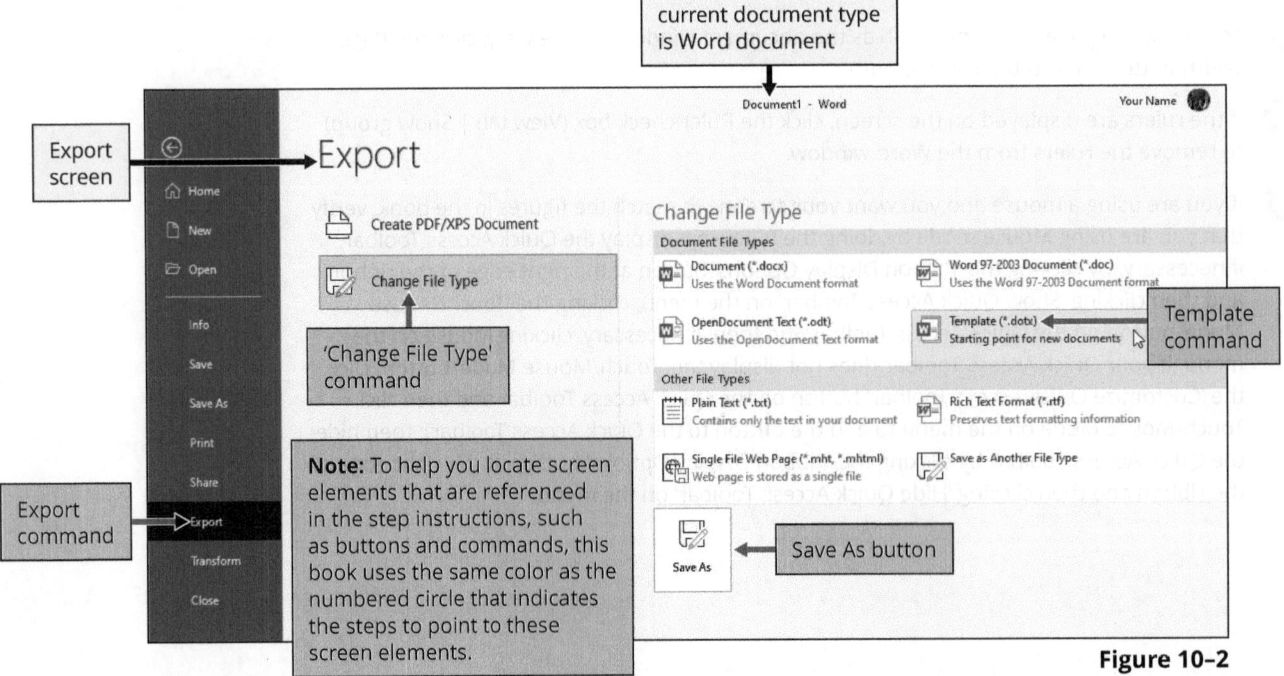

Figure 10–2

- Click the Save As button to display the Save As dialog box with the file type automatically changed to Word Template.

Q&A How does Word differentiate between a saved Word template and a saved Word document?
Files typically have a file name and a file extension. The file extension identifies the file type. The source program often assigns a file type to a file. A Word document has an extension of .docx, whereas a Word template has an extension of .dotx. Thus, a file named JulyReport.docx is a Word document, and a file named JulyReport.dotx is a Word template.

- In the File name box, type **SC_WD_10_AlbringLawOfficesClientSurvey** to change the file name and then navigate to the desired save location (Figure 10–3).

Q&A Why is my save location the Custom Office Templates folder?
The default save location for your templates may be the Custom Office Templates folder. If you are using a home computer, you can save your template in that folder. If you are using a public computer, you should change the save location to your local storage location.

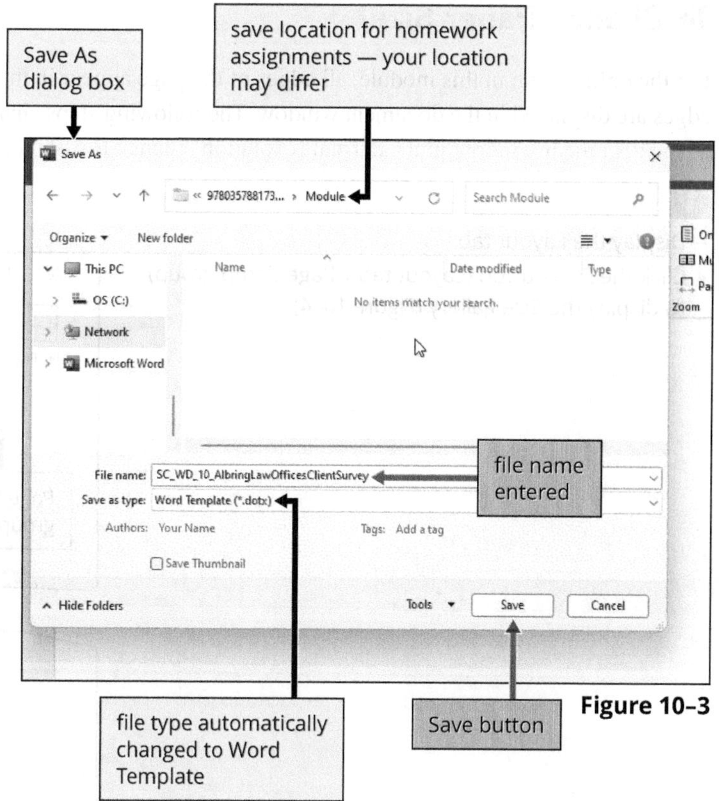

Figure 10–3

- Click Save (Save As dialog box) to save the document as a Word template with the entered file name in the specified location.

Other Ways

1. Press F12, change document type to Word Template
2. Open Backstage view, click Save As, change document type to Word Template

Changing Document Settings

To enhance the appearance of the form, you change several default settings in Word:

1. Display the page as wide as possible in the document window to maximize the amount of space for text and graphics on the form, called page width zoom.
2. Change the size of the paper so that it fits completely within the document window.
3. Adjust the margins so that as much text as possible will fit in the document.
4. Add a light blue page color with a pattern.

The first item was completed earlier in the module. The following sections make the remaining changes to the document.

BTW
The Ribbon and Screen Resolution
Word may change how the groups and buttons within the groups appear on the ribbon, depending on the screen resolution of your computer. Thus, your ribbon may look different from the ones in this book if you are using a screen resolution other than 1366 × 768.

To Change Paper Size

For the online form in this module, all edges of the page appear in the document window. Currently, only the top, left, and right edges are displayed in the document window. The following steps change paper size. **Why?** To display all edges of the document in the document window in the current resolution, change the height of the paper from 11 inches to 4 inches.

1

- Display the Layout tab.
- Click the Size button (Layout tab | Page Setup group) to display the Size gallery (Figure 10–4).

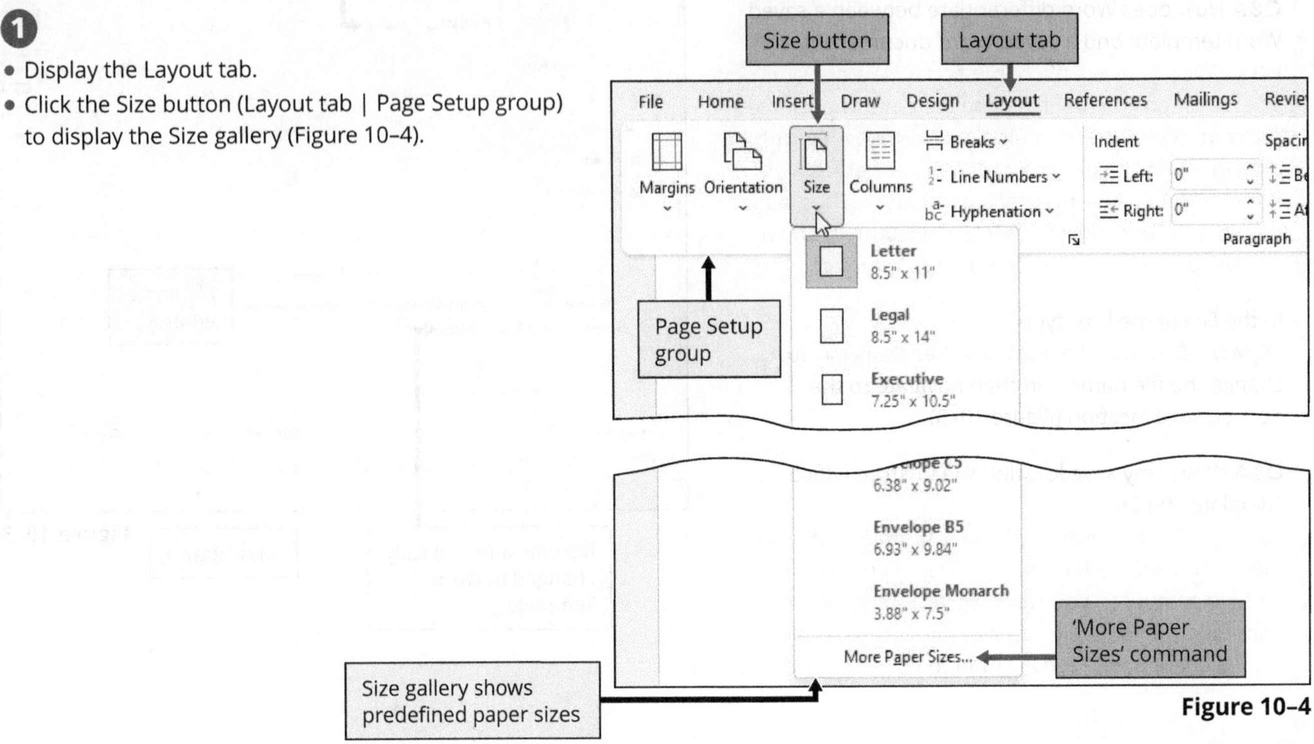

Figure 10–4

2

- Click 'More Paper Sizes' in the Size gallery to display the Paper sheet in the Page Setup dialog box.
- In the Height box (Page Setup dialog box), type **4** as the new height (Figure 10–5).

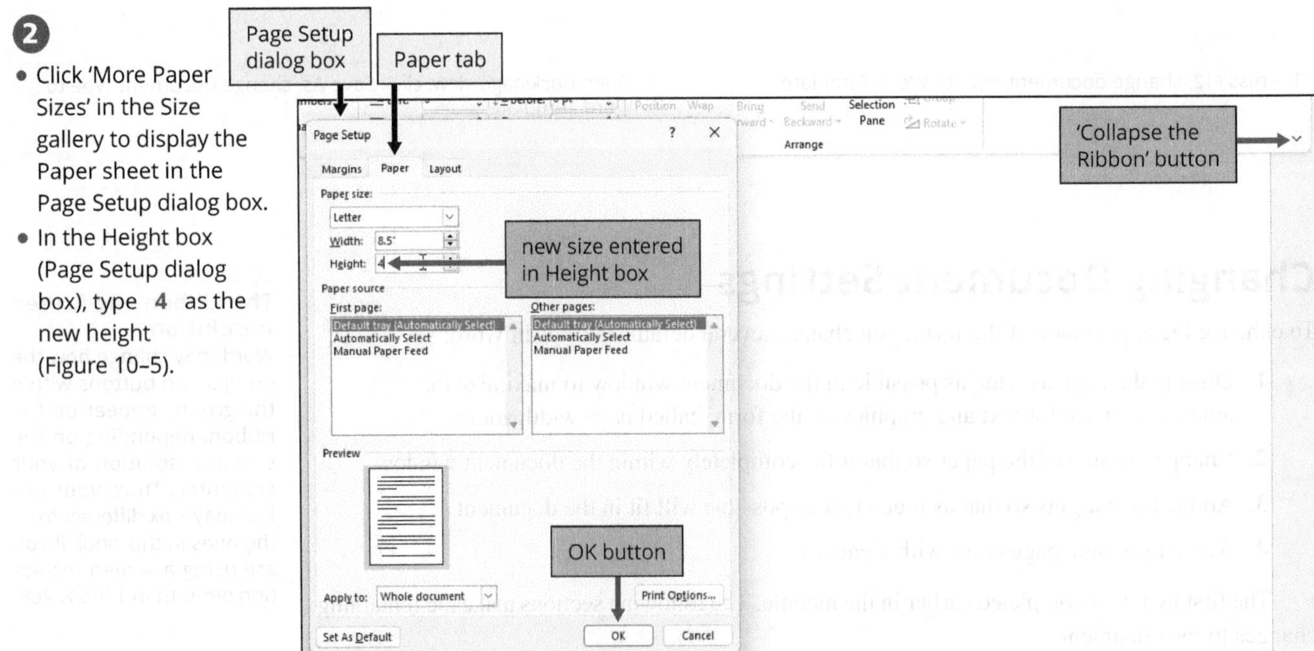

Figure 10–5

3

- Click OK to change the paper size to the entered measurements, which, in this case, are 8.5 inches wide by 4 inches tall (shown in Figure 10–7). If necessary, scroll to display the top of the page in the document window.

To Collapse the Ribbon

To display more of a document or other item in the Word window, you can collapse the ribbon, which hides the groups on the ribbon and displays only the main tabs. For the online form to fit entirely in the Word window, you collapse the ribbon. The following steps collapse the ribbon, sometimes referred to as hide the ribbon, so that you can view the form as it will fit in the document window.

- Click the 'Ribbon Display Options' button at the right edge of the ribbon to display the Ribbon Display Options menu (Figure 10-6).

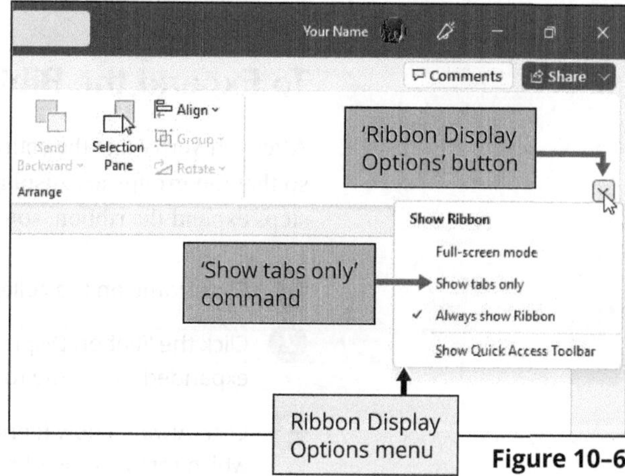

Figure 10-6

- Click 'Show tabs only' on the Ribbon Display Options menu to collapse the ribbon (Figure 10-7). If necessary, scroll slightly to display the entire page in the document window.

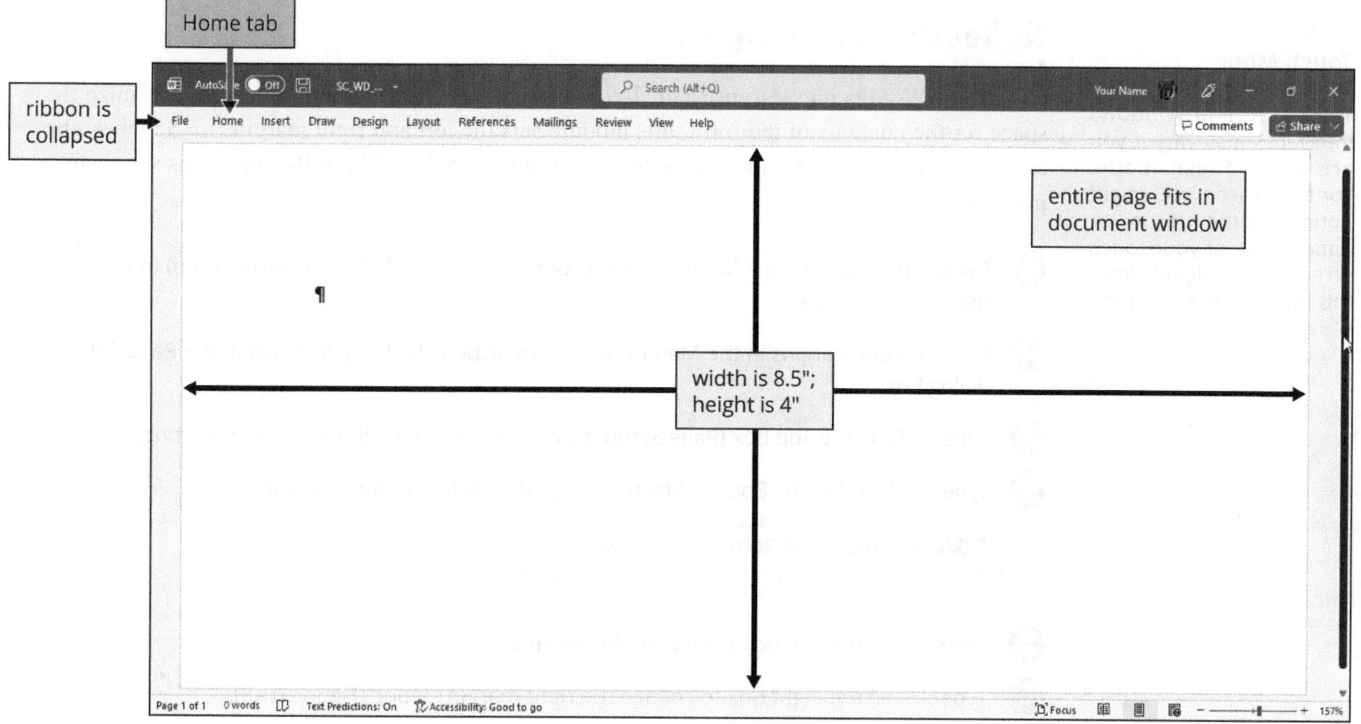

Figure 10-7

Q&A What happened to the 'Ribbon Display Options' button?
The 'Ribbon Display Options' button is not displayed on the screen when the ribbon is collapsed; it is visible only when you expand a ribbon by clicking a tab.

Q&A What if the height of my document does not match the figure or the entire page does not fit in my document window?
You may need to scroll the document slightly in the document window. Or, you may need to show white space. To do this, position the pointer above the top of the page below the ribbon and then double-click when the pointer changes to a 'Show White Space' button (or, if using touch, double-tap below the page). Or, your screen resolution may be different; if so, you may need to adjust the page height or width values (as described in the previous section).

What other ways can I collapse, or hide, the ribbon?
You can double-click any of the tabs on the ribbon, or you can press CTRL+F1.

To Expand the Ribbon

After you verify that the entire form will fit in the document window, you should expand the ribbon so that the groups are displayed on the ribbon while you create the online form. The following steps expand the ribbon, sometimes referred to as show the ribbon.

1. Click Home on the collapsed ribbon to expand the Home tab.
2. Click the 'Ribbon Display Options' button at the right edge of the ribbon showing the expanded Home tab to display the Ribbon Display Options menu.
3. Click 'Always show Ribbon' on the Ribbon Display Options menu to expand the ribbon, which restores the ribbon to display all tabs and commands.

Q&A What other ways can I expand, or show, the ribbon?
You can double-click any of the tabs on the ribbon, or you can press CTRL+F1.

BTW
Touch Mode Differences
The Office and Windows interfaces may vary if you are using Touch mode. For this reason, you might notice that the function or appearance of your touch screen differs slightly from this module's presentation.

To Set Custom Margins

Recall that Word is preset to use 1-inch top, bottom, left, and right margins. To maximize the space for the contents of the form, this module sets the left and right margins to .5 inches, the top margin to .25 inches, and the bottom margin to 0 inches. The following steps set custom margins.

1. Display the Layout tab. Click the Margins button (Layout tab | Page Setup group) to display the Margins gallery.
2. Click Custom Margins in the Margins gallery to display the Margins sheet in the Page Setup dialog box.
3. Type **.25** in the Top box (Page Setup dialog box) to change the top margin setting.
4. Type **0** (zero) in the Bottom box to change the bottom margin setting.

   Q&A Why set the bottom margin to zero?
   This allows you to place form contents at the bottom of the page, if necessary.

5. Type **.5** in the Left box to change the left margin setting.
6. Type **.5** in the Right box to change the right margin setting (Figure 10–8).
7. Click OK to set the custom margins for this document (shown in Figure 10–9).

Q&A What if Word displays a dialog box indicating margins are outside the printable area?
Click the Ignore button because this is an online form that is not intended for printing.

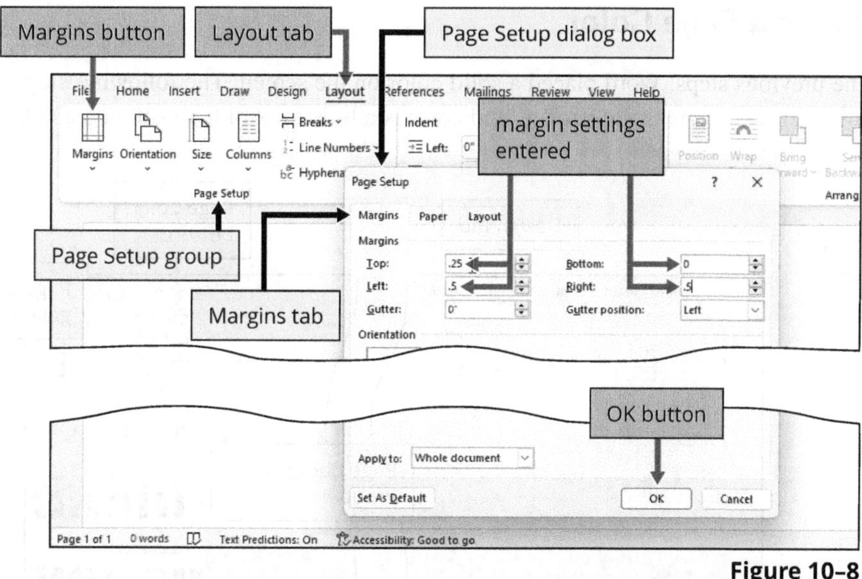

Figure 10–8

To Add a Page Color

The following steps add a page color. **Why?** This online form uses a shade of blue for the page color (background color) so that the form is more visually appealing.

- Display the Design tab. Click the Page Color button (Design tab | Page Background group) to display the Page Color gallery.
- Point to 'Blue, Accent 5, Lighter 40%' (ninth color in the fourth row) in the Page Color gallery to display a Live Preview of the selected background color (Figure 10–9).
- **Experiment:** Point to various colors in the Page Color gallery and watch the page color change in the document window.

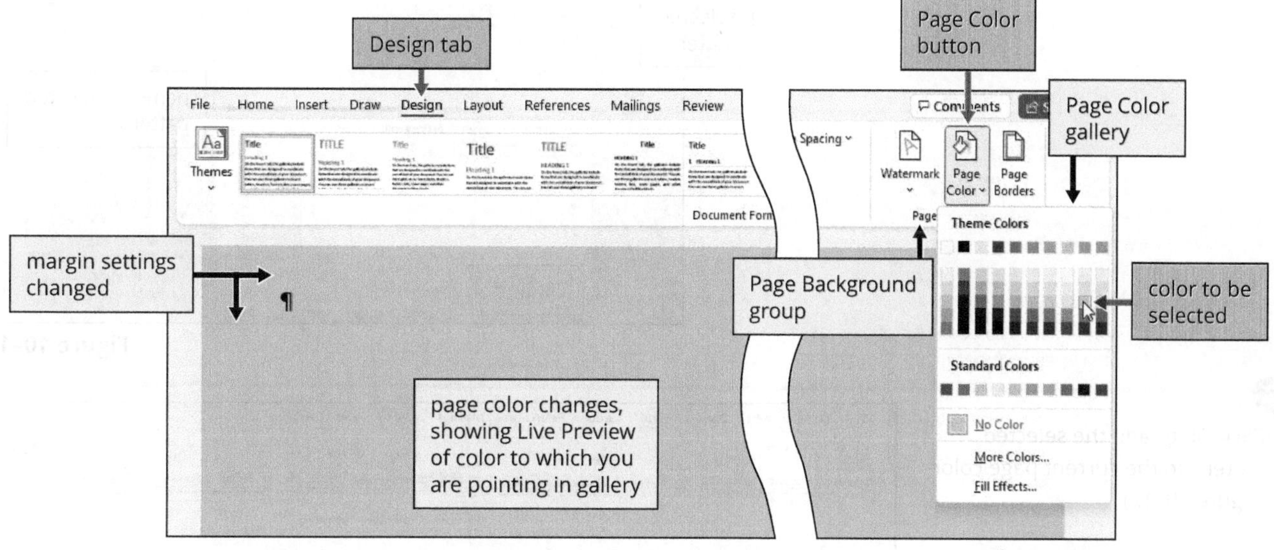

Figure 10–9

- Click 'Blue, Accent 5, Lighter 40%' to change the page color to the selected color.

Q&A Do page colors print?
When you change the page color, it appears only on the screen. Changing the page color does not affect a printed document.

To Apply a Pattern Fill Effect to a Page Color

When you changed the page color in the previous steps, Word placed a solid color on the screen. The following steps add a pattern to the page color. **Why?** For this online form, the solid background color is a little too bold. To soften the color, you can add a pattern to it.

- Click the Page Color button (Design tab | Page Background group) to display the Page Color gallery (Figure 10–10).

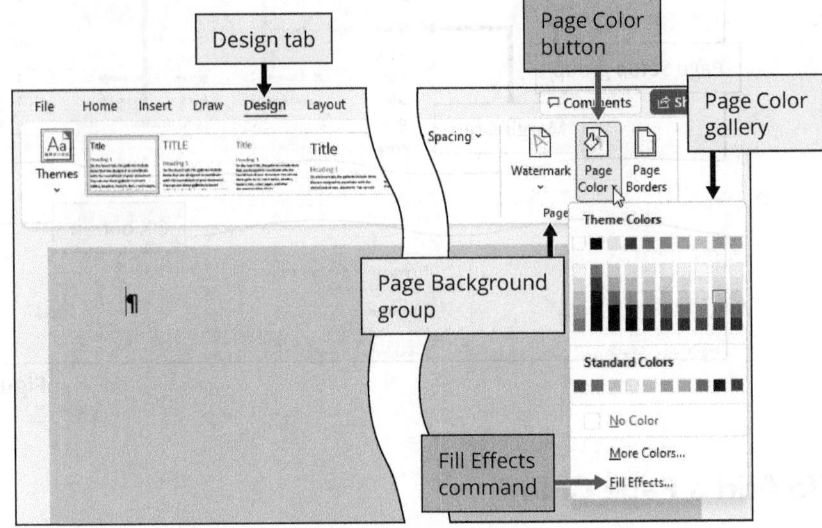

Figure 10–10

2

- Click Fill Effects in the Page Color gallery to display the Fill Effects dialog box.
- Click the Pattern tab (Fill Effects dialog box) to display the Pattern sheet in the dialog box.
- Click the Dotted: 25% pattern (first pattern in the fourth row) to select the pattern (Figure 10–11).

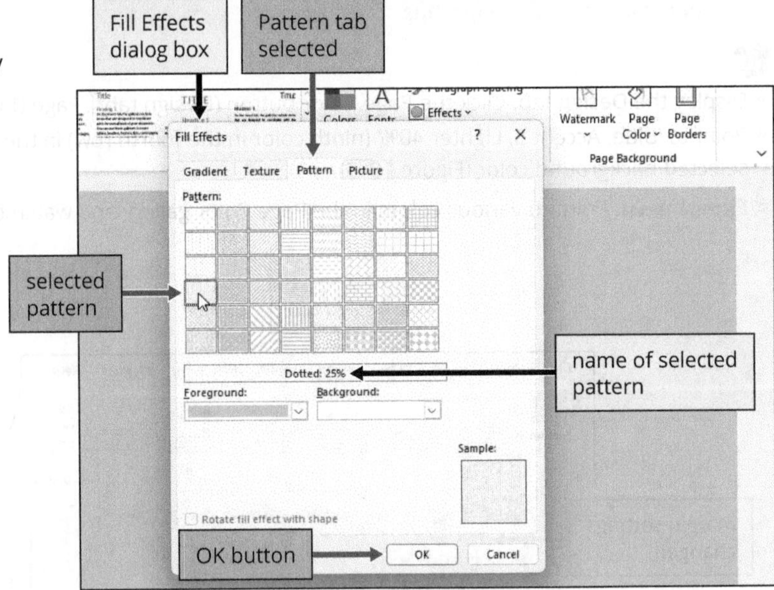

Figure 10–11

- Click OK to add the selected pattern to the current page color (Figure 10–12).

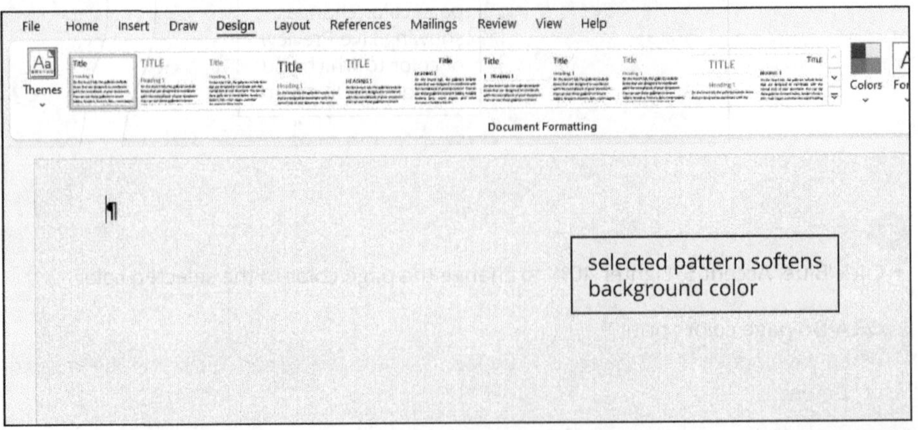

Figure 10–12

Entering Content in the Online Form

The next step in creating the online form in this module is to enter the text, graphics, and content controls in the document. The following sections describe this process.

BTW
Highlighting Text
You can highlight text in online documents. If you click the 'Text Highlight Color' button (Home tab | Font group) without first selecting any text, the highlighter remains active until you turn it off. This allows you to continue selecting text that you want to be highlighted. To deactivate the highlighter, click the 'Text Highlight Color' button (Home tab | Font group) again, click the 'Text Highlight Color' arrow (Home tab | Font group), and then click Stop Highlighting on the Text Highlight Color menu, or press ESC.

To Enter and Format Text

The following steps enter the text at the top of the online form.

1. Type **Albring Law Offices** and then press ENTER.
2. Type **Serving You for More than 35 Years** and then press ENTER.
3. Type **Client Survey** and then press ENTER.
4. Type **Please fill in the form below, save your form, and email it to contact@albringlawoffices.cengage.net.** and then press ENTER.

   Q&A Why did the email address change color?
   In the default Office document theme, the color for a hyperlink is a shade of blue. When you pressed ENTER, Word automatically formatted the hyperlink in this color.

5. Format the characters on the first line to 24-point Cooper Black (or a similar) font with the color of 'Green, Accent 6, Darker 50%' (last color in last row in Theme Colors area). Remove any space before and after this paragraph (that is, spacing before and after should be 0 point).
6. Format the characters on the second line to 10-point bold Bradley Hand ITC (or a similar) font with the color of 'Blue-Gray, Text 2, Darker 25%' (fourth color in fifth row). (Ensure that the spacing after this paragraph is 8 point.)
7. Format the characters on the third line to 16-point bold font with the color of 'Green, Accent 6, Darker 50%' (last color in last row in Theme Colors area) and then center the text on the line. Remove space before and after this paragraph (spacing before and after should be 0 point).
8. Center the text on the fourth line and increase the spacing after this line to 12 point.
9. Be sure that the font size of text entered on the fourth line is 11 point.
10. Position the insertion point on the blank line below the text (Figure 10–13). (Ensure that the font size is 11 point at the location of the insertion point.)

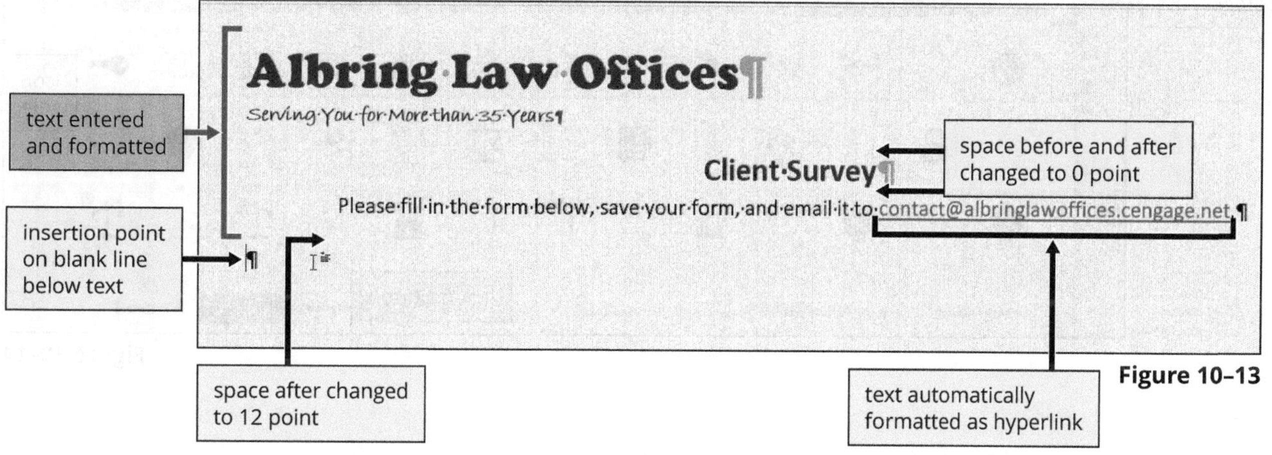

Figure 10–13

To Insert an Icon

Word includes a library of icons that you can insert in documents. The following steps insert an icon that shows an image of the scales of justice. **Why?** You want an image in the form to give it visual appeal.

- Display the Insert tab.
- Click the Icons button (Insert tab | Illustrations group) to display the Icons tab in the Stock Images dialog box.
- Click the right arrow at the right edge of the Category list below the Search box in the dialog box until the Security And Justice category appears and then click the 'Security And Justice' button to display icons associated with the selected category.
- Scroll through the list of Security And Justice icons, if necessary, and then click the scales of justice icon shown in Figure 10–14 to select the icon.

Q&A What if my dialog box does not contain the same category or icon?
Select any appropriate icon in the dialog box.

Can I search for a specific icon instead of using the Category list?
Yes, you can enter text in the Search box to search for a specific icon.

Can I select multiple icons at once in the open dialog box?
Yes, all selected icons will be inserted in the document. The Insert button in the dialog box shows the number of icons you have selected.

What if the Icons button is not available in my version of Word?
A similar image is located in the Data Files. You can click the Pictures button (Insert tab | Illustrations group), click This Device, navigate to the file called Support_WD_10_Scales.png in the Data Files, and then click the Insert button (Insert Picture dialog box) to insert the image. Change the height of the inserted image to .8", change the width to .75" (you may need to use the Size Dialog Box Launcher to turn off Lock Aspect Ratio to set these exact measurements), and then skip Step 2. Note that your image will appear similar to, but not exactly like, the figures in this module.

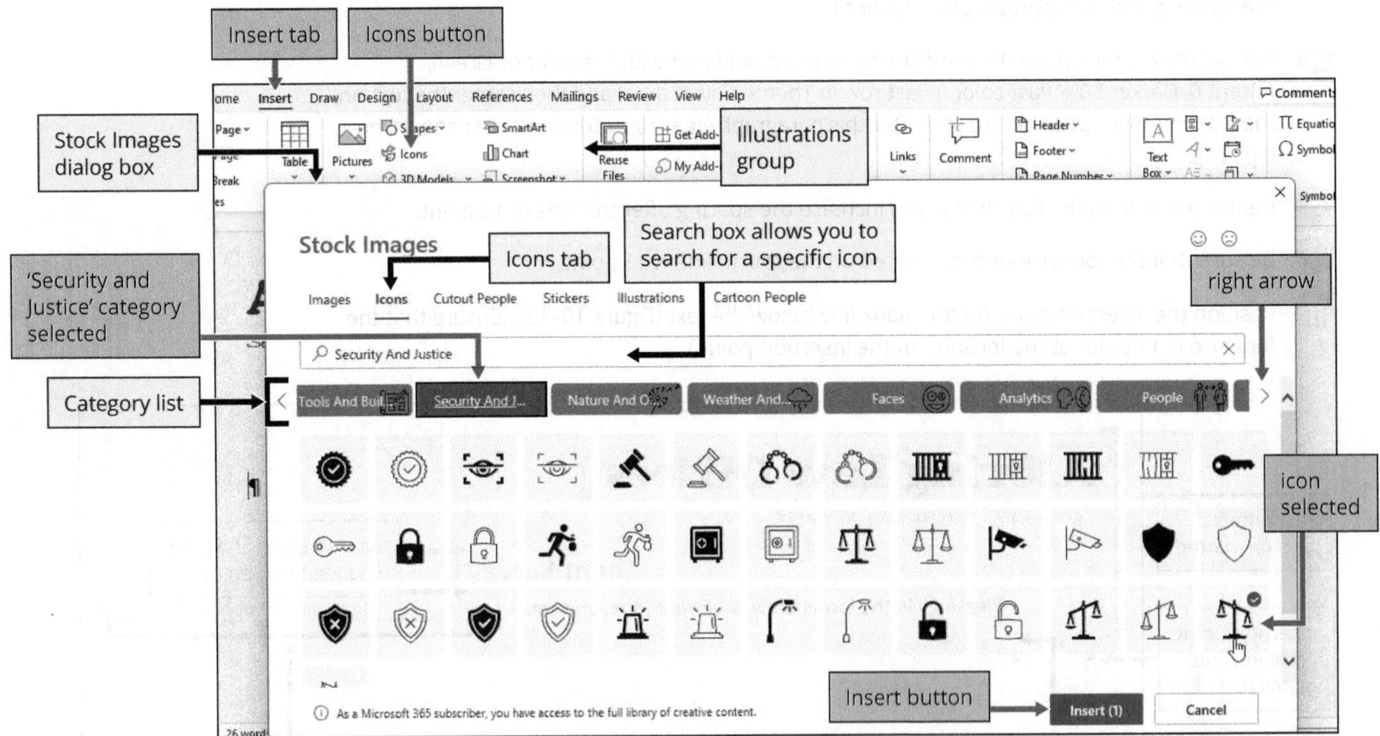

Figure 10–14

2

- Click the Insert button (Stock Images dialog box) to place the selected icon in the document to the left of the insertion point (Figure 10–15).
- If necessary, use the Height and Width boxes (Graphics Format tab | Size group) to change these values to 1".

Q&A What if my icon is inserted in a location different from Figure 10–15?
You will move the icon in a later step.

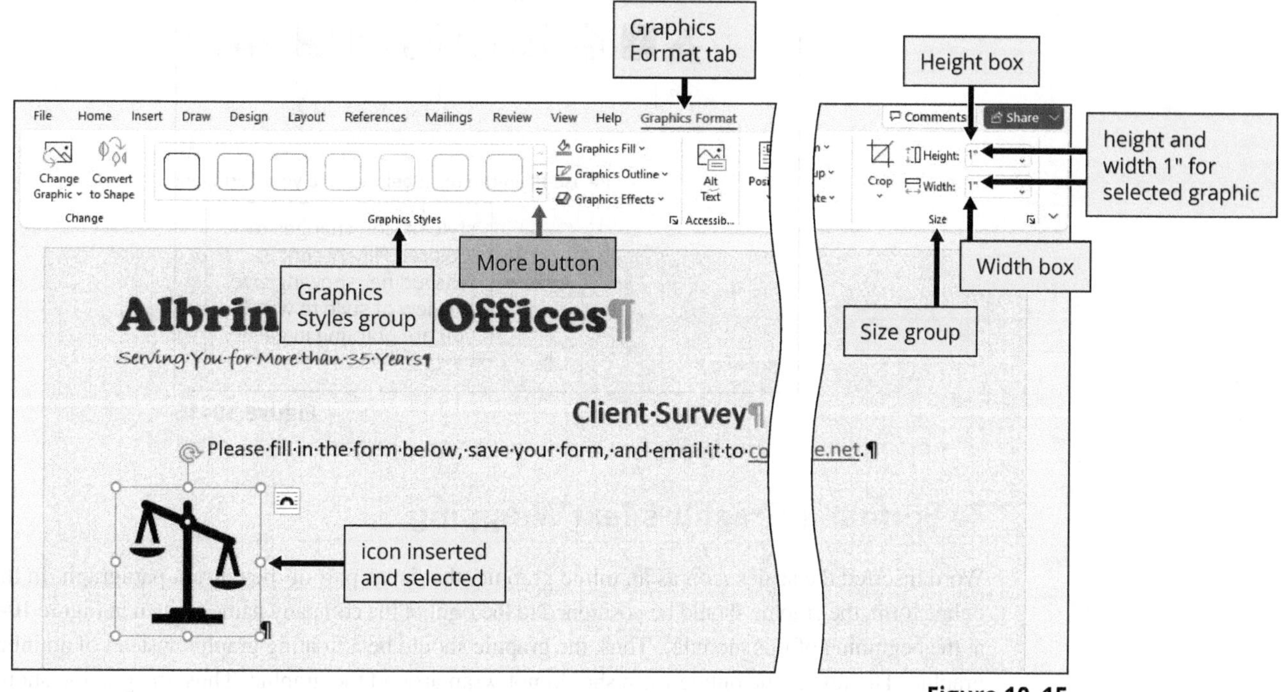

Figure 10–15

To Apply a Graphics Style

Word provides a variety of predefined styles you can apply to graphics. The following steps apply a graphics style to the selected icon.

1 With the icon still selected, click the More button (Graphics Format tab | Graphics Styles group) (shown in Figure 10–15) to display the Graphics Styles gallery.

2 Point to 'Colored Fill - Accent 3, No Outline' (fourth style in second row) in the Graphics Styles gallery to display a Live Preview of the selected graphics style applied to the icon in the document window (Figure 10–16).

- **Experiment:** If you are using a mouse, point to various styles in the Graphics Styles gallery and notice the graphics style change in the document window.

3 Click 'Colored Fill - Accent 3, No Outline' in the Graphics Styles gallery to apply the selected graphics style to the selected icon.

Q&A What if my version of Word did not have the Icons button and I inserted a picture from the Data Files instead?
Click the Color button (Picture Format tab | Adjust group) to display the Color gallery and then click 'Light Gray, Background color 2, Light' in the Recolor area to change the color. Note that your image will appear similar to, but not exactly like, the figures in this module.

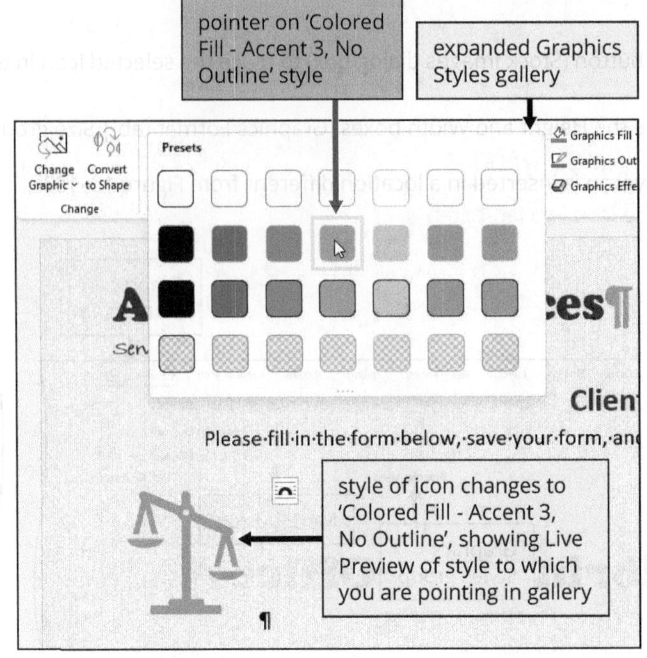

Figure 10–16

To Format a Graphic's Text Wrapping

Word inserted the scales icon as an inline graphic, that is, as part of the current paragraph. In this online form, the graphic should be positioned to the right of the company name (shown in Figure 10–1 at the beginning of this module). Thus, the graphic should be a floating graphic instead of an inline graphic. The text in the online form should not wrap around the graphic. Thus, the graphic should float in front of the text. The following steps change the graphic's text wrapping to In Front of Text.

1. With the graphic selected, click the Layout Options button attached to the graphic to display the Layout Options gallery (Figure 10–17).

2. Click 'In Front of Text' in the Layout Options gallery to change the graphic from inline to floating with the selected wrapping style.

3. Click the Close button in the Layout Options gallery to close the gallery.

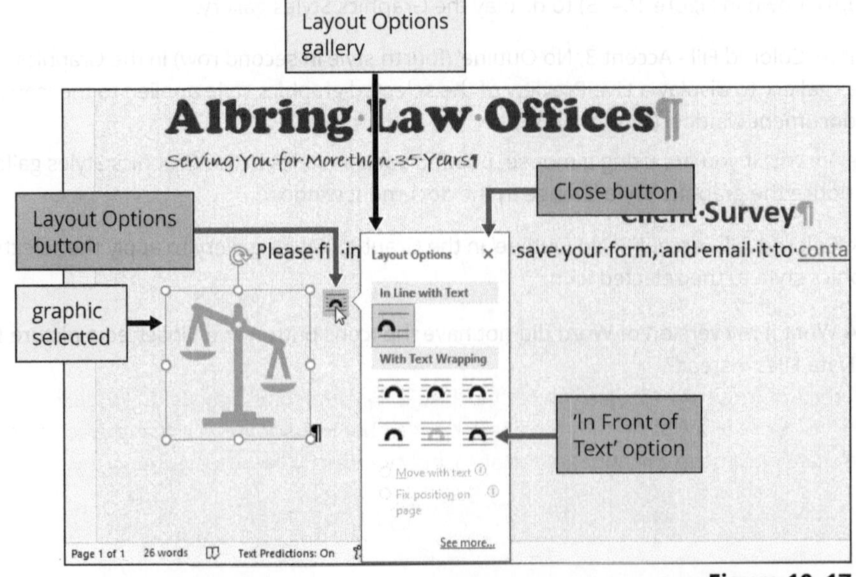

Figure 10–17

BTW

Ordering Graphics

If you have multiple graphics displaying on the screen and would like them to overlap, you can change their stacking order by using the Bring Forward and Send Backward arrows (Graphics Format tab | Arrange group). The 'Bring to Front' command on the Bring Forward menu displays the selected object at the top of the stack, and the 'Send to Back' command on the Send Backward menu displays the selected object at the bottom of the stack. The Bring Forward and Send Backward commands each move the graphic forward or backward one layer in the stack. These commands also are available through the shortcut menu that is displayed when you right-click a graphic.

To Move a Graphic

The final step associated with the graphic is to move it so that it is positioned on the upper-right side of the online form. The following steps move a graphic.

1. If necessary, scroll to display the top of the form in the document window.
2. Drag the graphic to the approximate location shown in Figure 10–18.

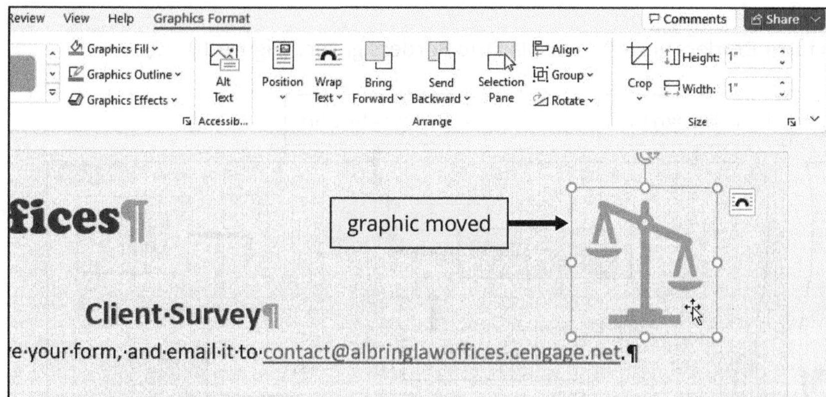

Figure 10–18

To Use a Table to Control Document Layout

The first line of data entry in the form consists of the First Name content control, which begins at the left margin, and the Last Name content control, which begins at the center point of the same line. At first glance, you might decide to set a tab stop at each content control location. This, however, can be a complex task. For example, to place two content controls evenly across a row, you must calculate the location of each tab stop. If you insert a 2 × 1 table instead, Word automatically calculates the size of two evenly spaced columns. Thus, to enter multiple content controls on a single line, insert a table to control document layout.

In this online form, the line containing the First Name and Last Name content controls will be a 2 × 1 table, that is, a table with two columns and one row. By inserting a 2 × 1 table, Word automatically positions the second column at the center point. The following steps insert a 2 × 1 table in the form and remove its border. **Why?** When you insert a table, Word automatically surrounds it with a border. Because you are using the tables solely to control document layout, you do not want the table borders visible.

- Position the insertion point where the table should be inserted, in this case, on the blank paragraph mark below the text on the form.
- Display the Insert tab. Click the Table button (Insert tab | Tables group) to display the Table gallery (Figure 10–19).

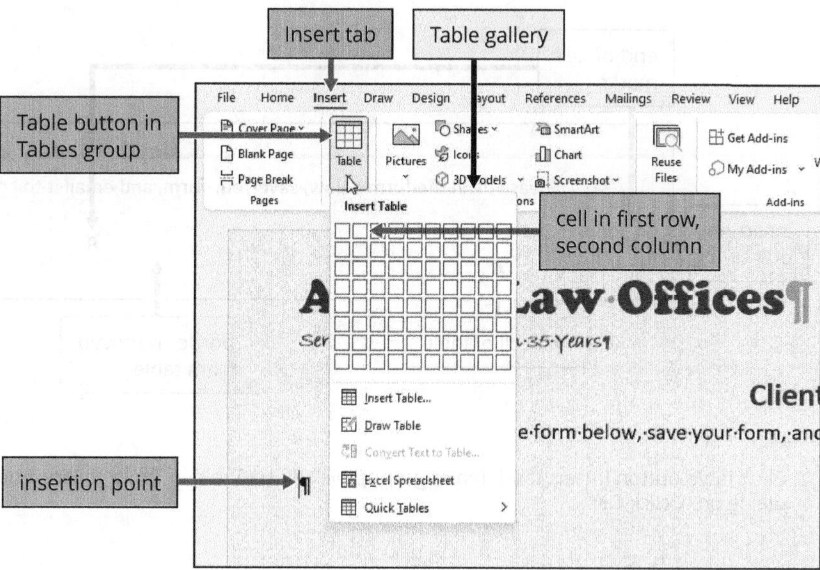

Figure 10–19

- Click the cell in the first row and second column of the grid to insert an empty 2 × 1 table at the location of the insertion point.
- Select the table.

Q&A How do I select a table?
Point somewhere in the table and then click the table move handle that appears in the upper-left corner of the table (or, if using touch, tap the Select button (contextual Layout tab | Tables group) and then tap Select Table on the Select menu).

- If necessary, display the Table Design tab.
- Click the Borders arrow (Table Design tab | Borders group) to display the Borders gallery (Figure 10–20).

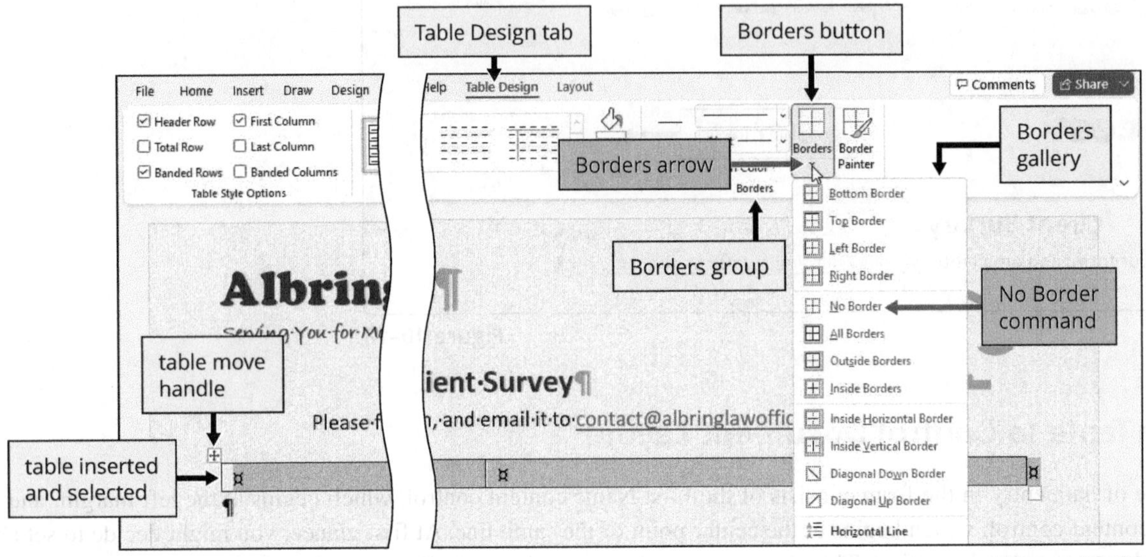

Figure 10–20

3

- Click No Border in the Borders gallery to remove the borders from the table.

4

- Click the first cell of the table to remove the selection (Figure 10–21).

Q&A My screen does not display the end-of-cell marks. Why not?
Display formatting marks by clicking the 'Show/Hide ¶' button (Home tab | Paragraph group).

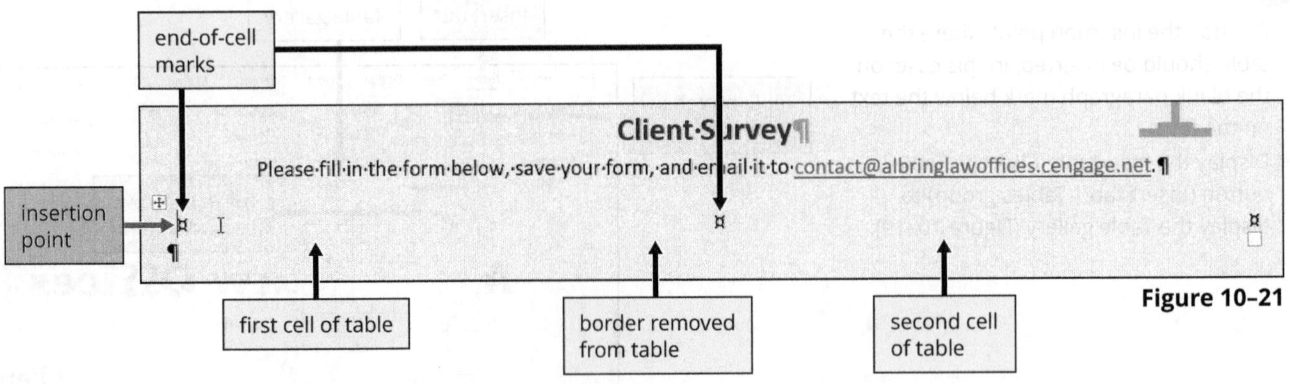

Figure 10–21

Other Ways

1. Click Table button (Insert tab | Tables group), click Insert Table in Table gallery, enter number of columns and rows (Insert Table dialog box), click OK

To Show Table Gridlines

When you remove the borders from a table, you can no longer easily locate the individual cells in the table. To help identify the location of cells, you can display gridlines, which recall are formatting marks that show cell boundaries in a table but do not print. The following steps show gridlines.

1. If necessary, position the insertion point in a table cell.
2. Display the contextual Layout tab.
3. If gridlines do not show already, click the View Gridlines button (contextual Layout tab | Table group) to show table gridlines on the screen (Figure 10–22).

Q&A Is the contextual Layout tab different from the main Layout tab?
Yes, recall that the main Layout tab, which always appears on the ribbon, is used to change page setup, format paragraphs, and arrange objects in a document. The contextual Layout tab appears only when you are working in a table and is used to change the properties and organization of a table and its rows, columns, and cells.

Do table gridlines print?
No. Gridlines are formatting marks that show only on the screen. Gridlines help users easily identify cells, rows, and columns in borderless tables.

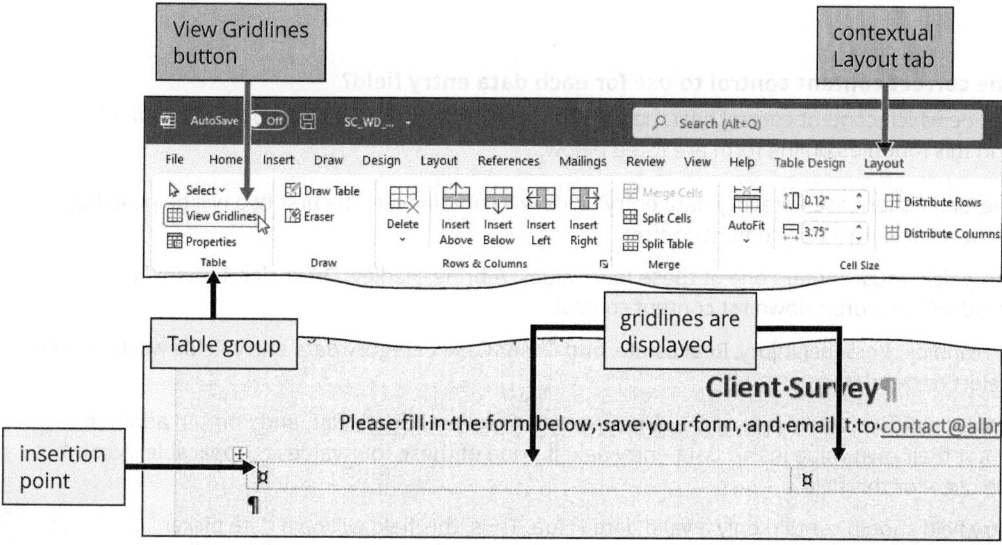

Figure 10–22

Content Controls

To add data entry fields in a Word form, you insert content controls. Word includes nine different content controls you can insert in your online forms. Table 10–1 outlines the use of each of these controls. The following sections insert content controls in the online form for the project in this module.

Table 10-1: Content Controls

Type	Icon	Use
Building Block Gallery		User selects a built-in building block from the gallery.
Check Box		User selects or deselects a check box.
Combo Box		User types text entry or selects one item from a list of choices.
Date Picker		User interacts with a calendar to select a date or types a date in the placeholder.
Drop-Down List		User selects one item from a list of choices.
Picture		User inserts a drawing, a shape, a picture, an image, or a SmartArt graphic.
Plain Text	Aa	User enters text, which may not be formatted.
Repeating Section		Users can instruct Word to create a duplicate of the content control.
Rich Text	Aa	User enters text and, if desired, may format the entered text.

Consider This

How do you determine the correct content control to use for each data entry field?

For each data entry field, decide which content control best maps to the type of data the field will contain. The field specifications for the fields in this module's online form are listed below:

- The First Name, Last Name, and Other Case Category data entry fields will contain text. The first two will be plain text content controls and the last will be a rich text content control.
- The Lawyer Name data entry field must contain one of these four values: Albring, Hadley; Drechsler, Lucian; Pierre, Maria; Soler, Alden. This field will be a drop-down list content control.
- The Civil Litigation, Estate Planning, Personal Injury, Real Estate, and Other Case Category data entry fields will be check boxes that the user can select or deselect.
- The Service Rating data entry field can contain one of these four values: Excellent, Good, Fair, and Poor. In addition, users should be able to enter their own value in this data entry field if none of these four values is applicable. A combo box content control will be used for this field.
- The Today's Date data entry field should contain only a valid date value. Thus, this field will be a date picker content control.

To Show the Developer Tab

To create a form in Word, you use buttons on the Developer tab. The following steps show the Developer tab on the ribbon. **Why?** Because it allows you to perform more advanced tasks not required by everyday Word users, the Developer tab does not appear on the ribbon by default.

1

- Open Backstage view and, if necessary, scroll to display the Options command (Figure 10–23).

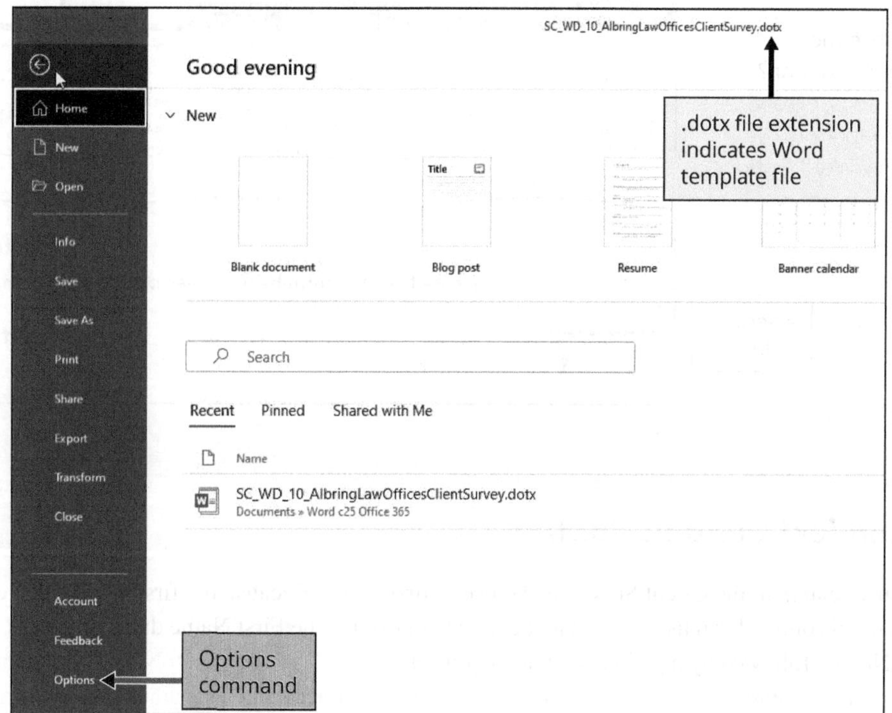

Figure 10–23

2

- Click Options in the left pane of Backstage view to display the Word Options dialog box.
- Click Customize Ribbon in the left pane (Word Options dialog box) to display associated options in the right pane.
- Place a check mark in the Developer check box in the Main Tabs list (Figure 10–24).

Q&A What are the plus symbols to the left of each tab name?
Clicking the plus symbol expands to show the groups.

Can I show or hide any tab in this list?
Yes. Place a check mark in the check box to show the tab, or remove the check mark to hide the tab.

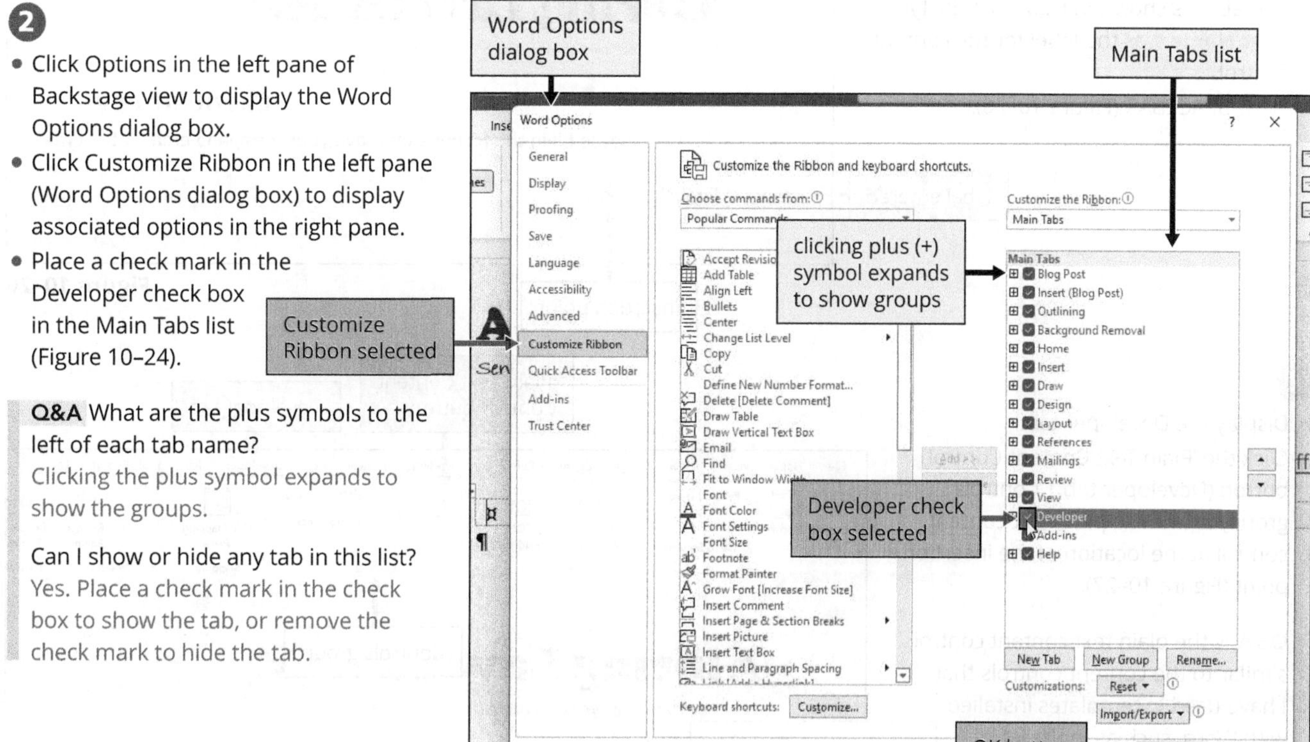

Figure 10–24

- Click OK to show the Developer tab on the ribbon (Figure 10–25).

Q&A How do I remove the Developer tab from the ribbon?
Follow these same steps, except remove the check mark from the Developer check box (Word Options dialog box).

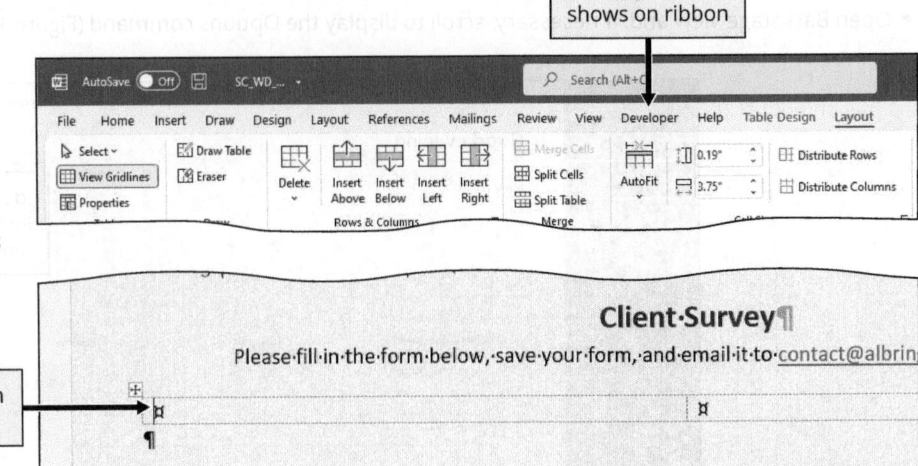

Figure 10–25

To Insert a Plain Text Content Control

The first item that a user enters in the Client Survey is the user's first name. Because the first name entry contains text that the user should not format, this online form uses a plain text content control for the First Name data entry field. The following steps enter the label, First Name:, followed by a plain text content control. **Why?** The label, First Name:, is displayed to the left of the plain text content control. To improve readability, a colon or some other character often separates a label from the content control.

- With the insertion point in the first cell of the table as shown in Figure 10–25, type **First Name:** as the label for the content control.
- Press SPACEBAR (Figure 10–26).

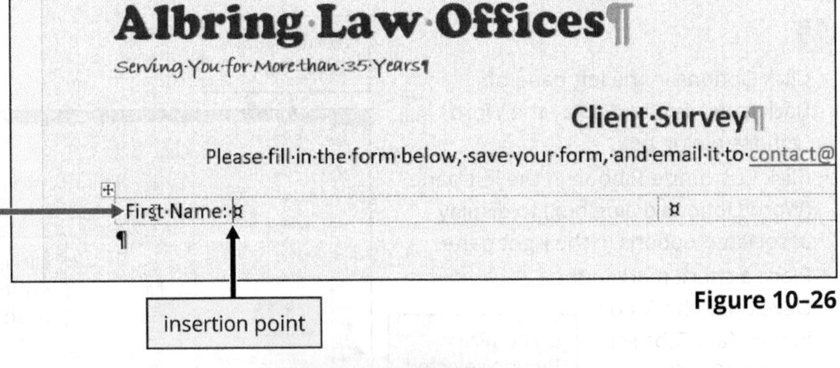

Figure 10–26

- Display the Developer tab.
- Click the 'Plain Text Content Control' button (Developer tab | Controls group) to insert a plain text content control at the location of the insertion point (Figure 10–27).

Q&A Is the plain text content control similar to the content controls that I have used in templates installed with Word, such as in the letter, memo, and resume templates?
Yes. The content controls you insert through the Developer tab have the same functionality as the content controls in the templates installed with Word.

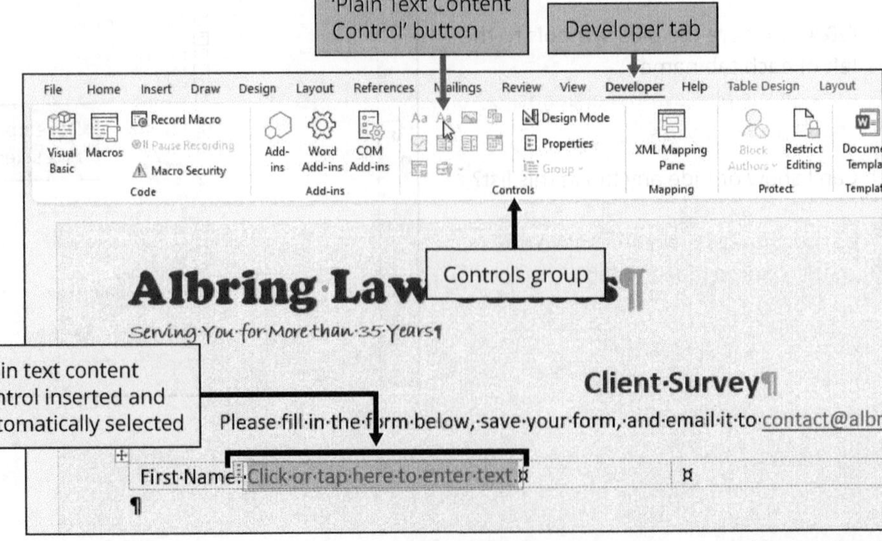

Figure 10–27

To Use Design Mode to Edit Placeholder Text

A content control displays placeholder text, which recall is default text that indicates where text can be typed in documents. The default placeholder text for a plain text content control is the instruction, Click or tap here to enter text. The following steps edit the placeholder text for the plain text content control just entered. **Why?** You can change the wording in the placeholder text so that it is more instructional or applicable to the current form.

- With the plain text content control selected (shown in Figure 10–27), click the Design Mode button (Developer tab | Controls group) to turn on Design mode, which displays tags at the beginning and ending of the placeholder text (Figure 10–28).

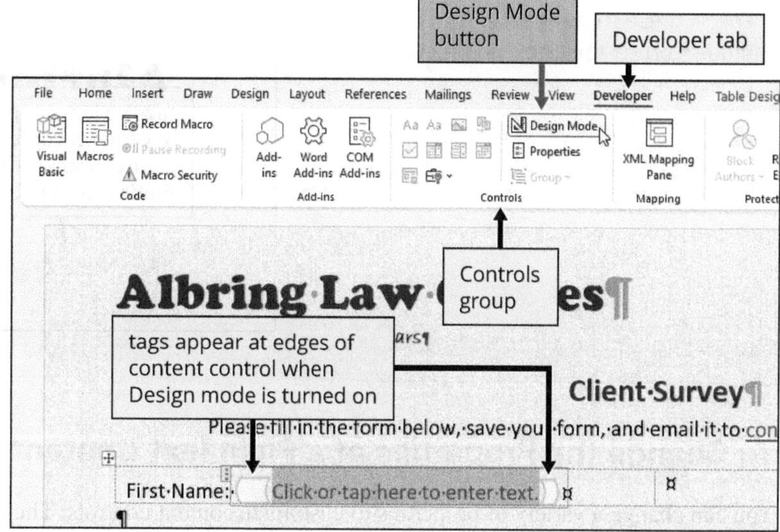

Figure 10–28

2

- Even if it already is selected, drag through the placeholder text, Click or tap here to enter text., because you want to edit the instruction (Figure 10–29).

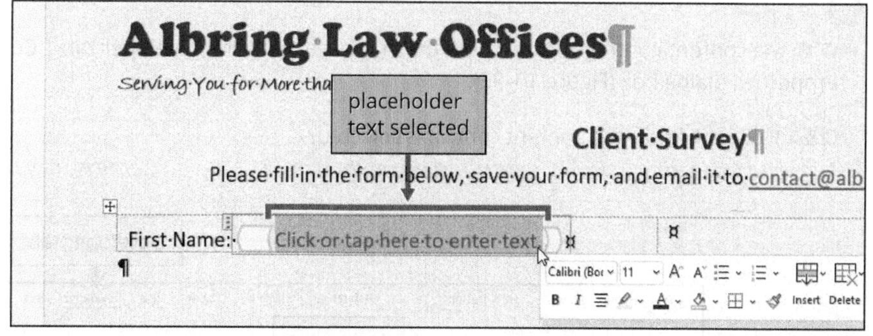

Figure 10–29

3

- Edit the placeholder text so that it contains the text, Click here and type your first name., as the instruction (Figure 10–30).

Q&A What if the placeholder text wraps to the next line?
Because of the tags at each edge of the placeholder text, the entered text may wrap in the table cell. Once you turn off Design mode, the placeholder text should fit on a single line. If it does not, you can adjust the font size of the placeholder text to fit.

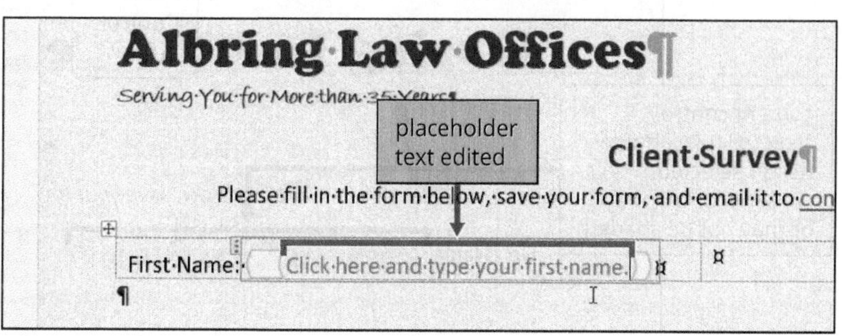

Figure 10–30

- Click the Design Mode button (Developer tab | Controls group) to turn off Design mode (Figure 10–31).

Q&A What if I notice an error in the placeholder text?
Follow these steps again to turn on Design mode, correct the error, and then turn off Design mode.

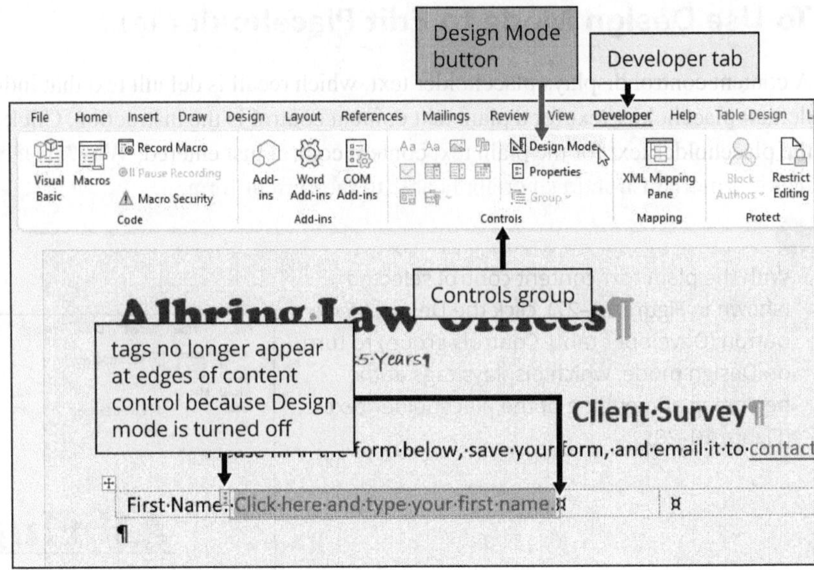

Figure 10–31

To Change the Properties of a Plain Text Content Control

You can change a variety of properties to customize content controls. The following steps change the properties of a plain text content control. **Why?** In this form, you assign a tag name to a content control for later identification. You also apply a style to the content control to define how text will appear as a user types data or makes selections, and you lock the content control so that a user cannot delete the content control during the data entry process.

- With the content control selected, click the Properties button (Developer tab | Controls group) to display the Content Control Properties dialog box (Figure 10–32).

Q&A How do I know the content control is selected?
A selected content control is surrounded by an outline. Its placeholder text may or may not be shaded.

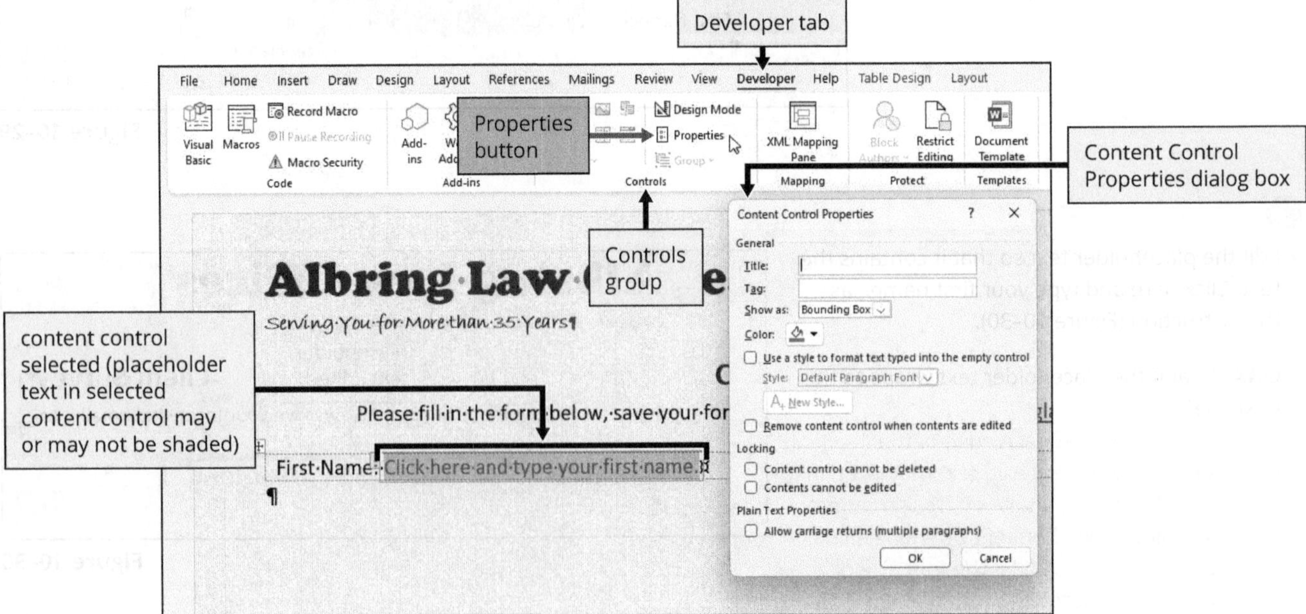

Figure 10–32

2

- Type **First Name** in the Tag text box (Content Control Properties dialog box).
- Place a check mark in the 'Use a style to format text typed into the empty control' check box so that the Style box becomes active.
- Click the Style arrow to display the Style list (Figure 10–33).

Q&A Why leave the Title text box empty?
When you click a content control in a preexisting Word template, the content control may display an identifier in its top-left corner. For templates that you create, you can instruct Word to display this identifier, called the Title, by changing the properties of the content control. In this form, you do not want the identifier to appear.

What is a bounding box?
A bounding box is a rectangle that surrounds the content control on the form. You can show content controls with a bounding box, with tags, or with no visible markings.

What if the Subtle Emphasis style is not displayed in the Style list?
Close the Content Control Properties dialog box. Click the Styles Dialog Box Launcher (Home Tab | Styles group) to open the Styles pane, click the Options button in the Styles pane to display the Style Pane Options dialog box, click the 'Select styles to show' arrow and then click All Styles (Style Pane Options dialog box), click OK to close the dialog box, and then close the Styles pane. Repeat Steps 1 and 2 above.

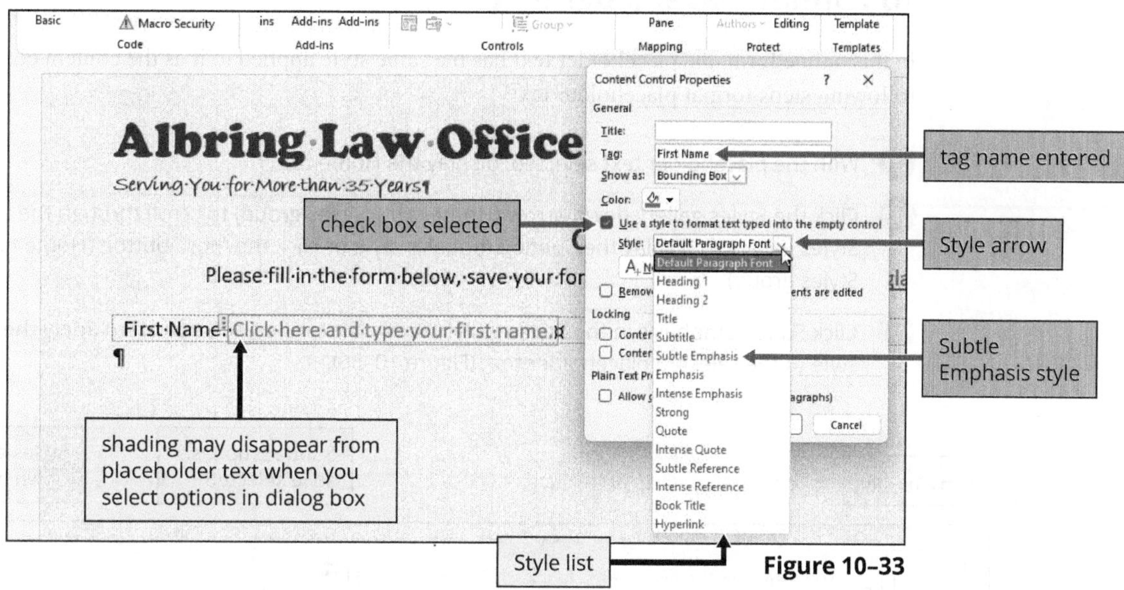

Figure 10–33

3

- Click Subtle Emphasis in the Style list to select the style for the content control.
- Place a check mark in the 'Content control cannot be deleted' check box so that the user cannot delete the content control (Figure 10–34).

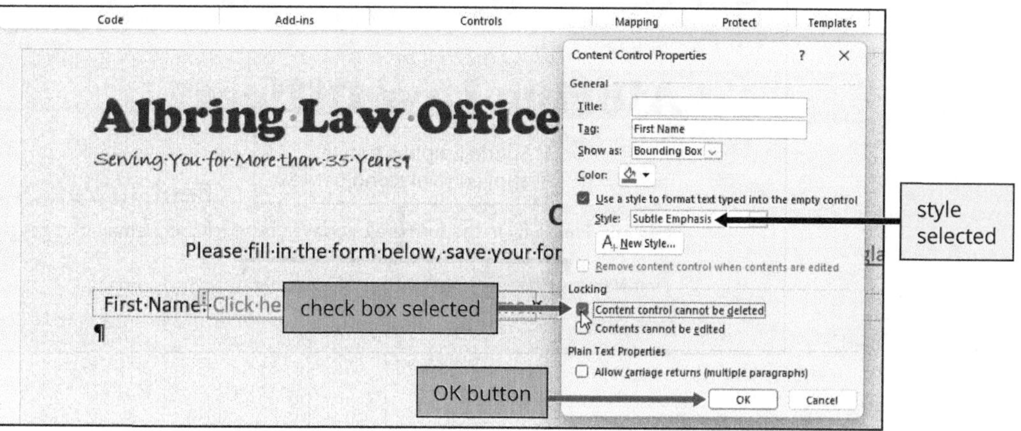

Figure 10–34

- Click OK to assign the modified properties to the content control (Figure 10–35).

Q&A Why is the placeholder text not formatted to the selected style, Subtle Emphasis, in this case?
When you apply a style to a content control, as described in these steps, the style is applied to the text the user types during the data entry process. To change the appearance of the placeholder text, apply a style using the Home tab as described in the next steps.

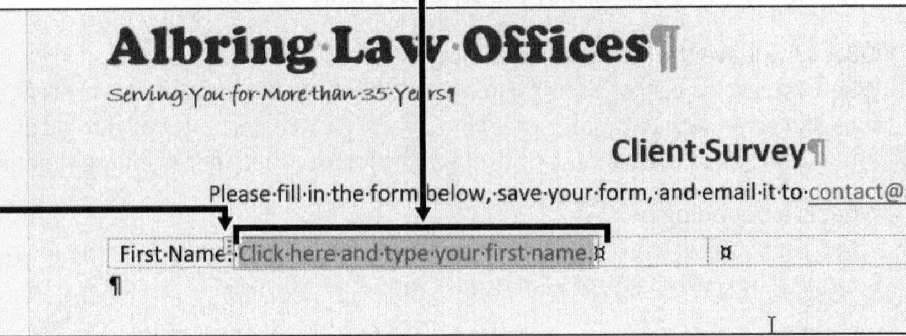

Figure 10–35

To Format Placeholder Text

In this online form, the placeholder text has the same style applied to it as the content control. The following steps format placeholder text.

1. With the placeholder text selected, display the Home tab.
2. Click the Styles gallery down arrow (Home tab | Styles group) to scroll through the Styles gallery to display the Subtle Emphasis style or click the More button (Home tab | Styles group).
3. Click Subtle Emphasis in the Styles gallery (even if it is selected already) to apply the selected style to the selected placeholder text (Figure 10–36).

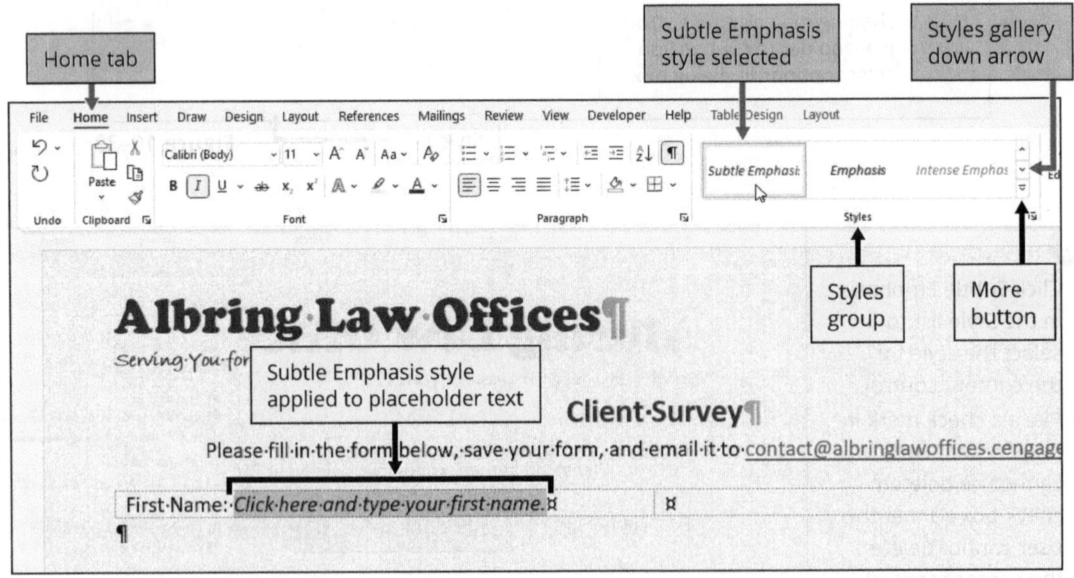

Figure 10–36

To Insert Another Plain Text Content Control and Use Design Mode to Edit Its Placeholder Text

The second item that a user enters in the Client Survey is the user's last name. The steps for entering the last name content control are similar to those for the first name, because the last name also is a plain text content control. The following steps enter the label, Last Name:, and then insert a plain text content control and edit its placeholder text.

1. Position the insertion point in the second cell (column) in the table.
2. With the insertion point in the second cell of the table, type **Last Name:** as the label for the content control and then press SPACEBAR.
3. Display the Developer tab. Click the 'Plain Text Content Control' button (Developer tab | Controls group) to insert a plain text content control at the location of the insertion point.
4. With the plain text content control selected, click the Design Mode button (Developer tab | Controls group) to turn on Design mode (Figure 10–37).
5. Select the placeholder text to be changed (even if it is selected already).
6. Edit the placeholder text so that it contains the text, Click here and type your last name., as the instruction.
7. Click the Design Mode button (Developer tab | Controls group) to turn off Design mode.

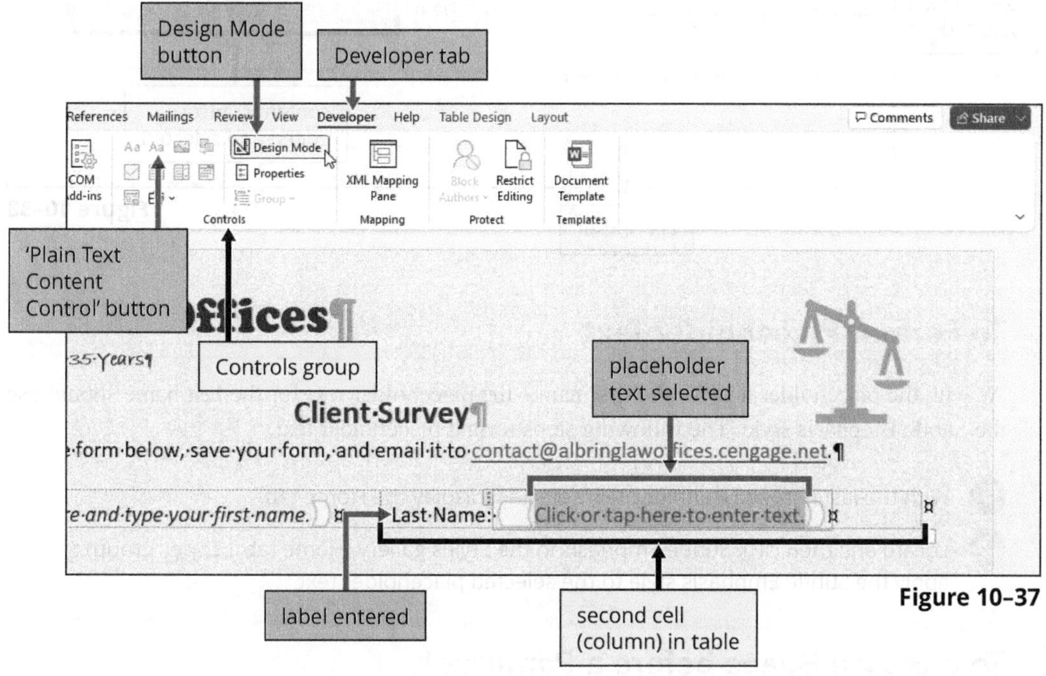

Figure 10–37

BTW

Deleting Content Controls

To delete a content control, right-click it and then click 'Remove Content Control' on the shortcut menu, or click the content control tag at the left edge of the control (shown in Figure 10–35) and then press DELETE. (Note that if the properties of the content control have been set to 'Content control cannot be deleted,' you will not be able to delete the content control using either of these methods. You will need to remove the check mark from that setting in the Content Control Properties dialog box before attempting to delete the content control.)

To Change the Properties of a Plain Text Content Control

The next step is to change the title, style, and locking properties of the Last Name content control, just as you did for the First Name content control. The following steps change properties of a plain text content control.

1. With the content control selected, click the Properties button (Developer tab | Controls group) to display the Content Control Properties dialog box.
2. Type **Last Name** in the Tag text box (Content Control Properties dialog box).

3 Place a check mark in the 'Use a style to format text typed into the empty control' check box to activate the Style box.

4 Click the Style arrow and then select Subtle Emphasis in the Style list to specify the style for the content control.

5 Place a check mark in the 'Content control cannot be deleted' check box (Figure 10–38).

6 Click OK to assign the properties to the content control.

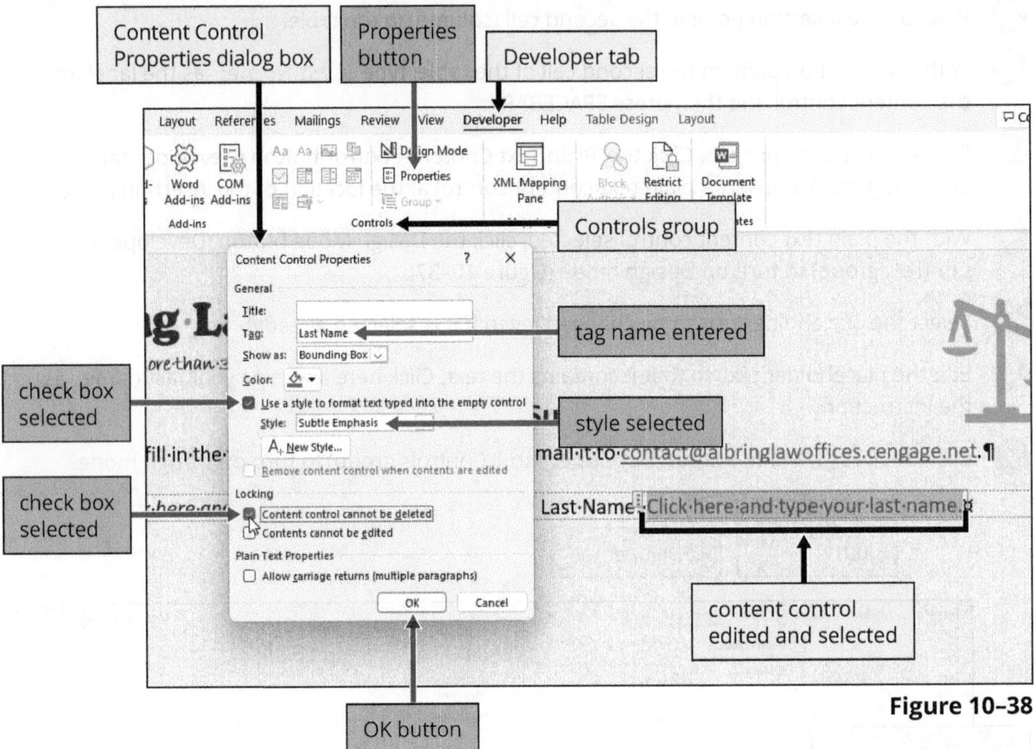

Figure 10–38

To Format Placeholder Text

As with the placeholder text for the first name, the placeholder text for the last name should use the Subtle Emphasis style. The following steps format placeholder text.

1 With the last name placeholder text selected, display the Home tab.

2 Locate and then click Subtle Emphasis in the Styles gallery (Home tab | Styles group) to apply the Subtle Emphasis style to the selected placeholder text.

To Increase Space before a Paragraph

The next step in creating this online form is to increase space before a paragraph so that the space below the table is consistent with the space between other elements on the form. The following steps increase space before a paragraph.

1 Position the insertion point on the blank line below the table.

2 Display the Layout tab.

3 Change the value in the Spacing Before box (Layout tab | Paragraph group) to 8 pt to increase the space between the table and the paragraph (shown in Figure 10–39). (Ensure that the spacing after this paragraph also is 8 point.) (Note that you may need to type the value in the box instead of using the arrow keys.)

To Insert a Drop-Down List Content Control

In the online form in this module, the user selects from one of these four choices for the Lawyer Name content control: Albring, Hadley; Drechsler, Lucian; Pierre, Maria; or Soler, Alden. The following steps insert a drop-down list content control. **Why?** To present a set of choices to a user in the form of a drop-down list, from which the user selects one item in the list, insert a drop-down list content control. To view the set of choices, the user clicks the arrow at the right edge of the content control.

- With the insertion point positioned on the blank paragraph mark below the First Name label and content control, using either the ruler or the Layout tab, change the left indent to 0.06" so that the entered text aligns with the text immediately above it (that is, the F in First).
- Type **Which lawyer handled your case?** and then press SPACEBAR.

- Display the Developer tab.
- Click the 'Drop-Down List Content Control' button (Developer tab | Controls group) to insert a drop-down list content control at the location of the insertion point (Figure 10–39).

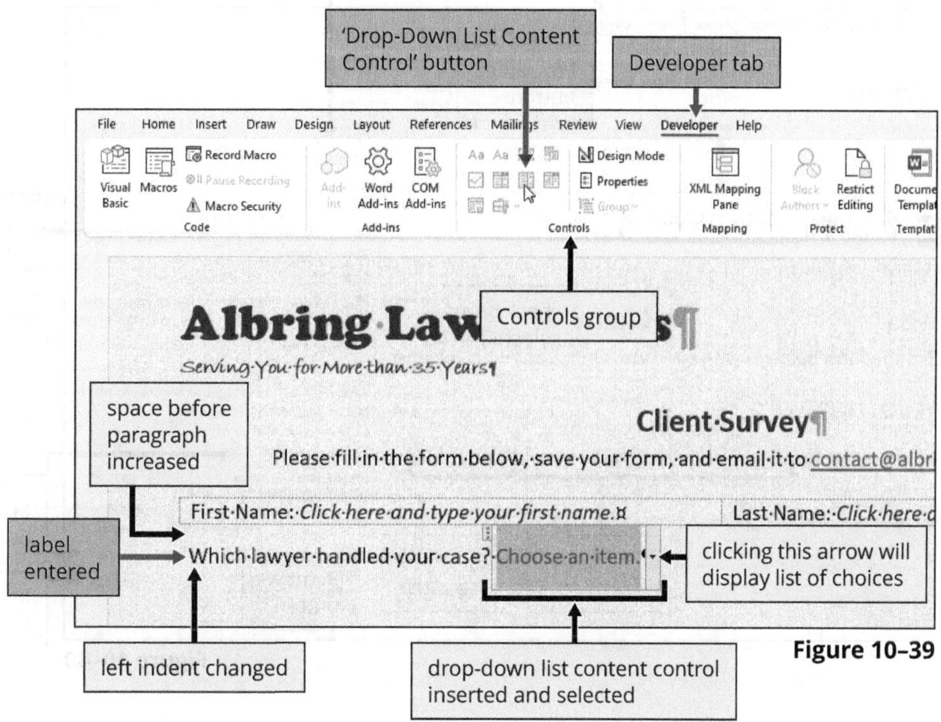

Figure 10–39

To Use Design Mode to Edit Placeholder Text

The following steps edit the placeholder text for the drop-down list content control.

1. With the drop-down list content control selected, click the Design Mode button (Developer tab | Controls group) to turn on Design mode.
2. Edit the placeholder text so that it contains this instruction, which contains two separate sentences: Click here. Click arrow and select from list.
3. Click the Design Mode button (Developer tab | Controls group) to turn off Design mode.

To Change the Properties of a Drop-Down List Content Control

The following steps change the properties of a drop-down list content control. **Why?** In addition to identifying a tag, selecting a style, and locking the drop-down list content control, you can specify the choices that will be displayed when a user clicks the arrow to the right of the content control.

- With the drop-down list content control selected, click the Properties button (Developer tab | Controls group) to display the Content Control Properties dialog box.
- Type **Lawyer Name** in the Tag text box (Content Control Properties dialog box).
- Place a check mark in the 'Use a style to format text typed into the empty control' check box to activate the Style box.
- Click the Style arrow and then select Subtle Emphasis in the Style list to specify the style for the content control.
- Place a check mark in the 'Content control cannot be deleted' check box.
- In the Drop-Down List Properties area, click 'Choose an item.' to select it (Figure 10–40).

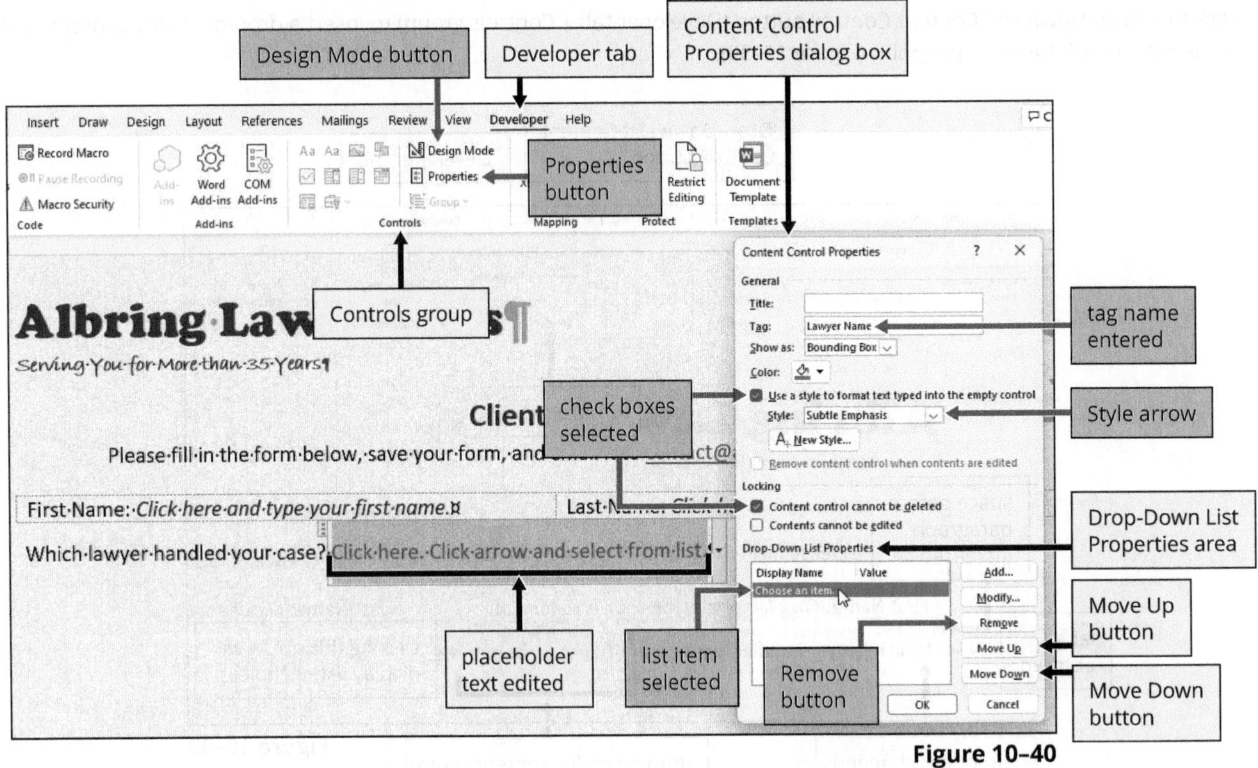

Figure 10–40

- Click the Remove button (Content Control Properties dialog box) to delete the 'Choose an item.' entry.

Q&A Why delete the 'Choose an item.' entry?
If you leave it in the list, it will appear as the first item in the list when the user clicks the content control arrow. You do not want it in the list, so you delete it.

Can I delete any entry in a drop-down list using the Remove button?
Yes, select the entry in this dialog box and then click the Remove button. You also can rearrange the order of entries in a list by selecting the entry and then clicking the Move Up or Move Down buttons.

3

- Click the Add button to display the Add Choice dialog box.
- Type **Albring, Hadley** in the Display Name text box (Add Choice dialog box) and notice that Word automatically enters the same text in the Value text box (Figure 10–41).

Q&A What is the difference between a display name and a value?
Often, they are the same, which is why when you type the display name, Word automatically enters the same text in the Value text box. Sometimes, however, you may want to store a shorter or different value. If the display name is long, entering shorter values makes it easier for separate programs to analyze and interpret entered data.

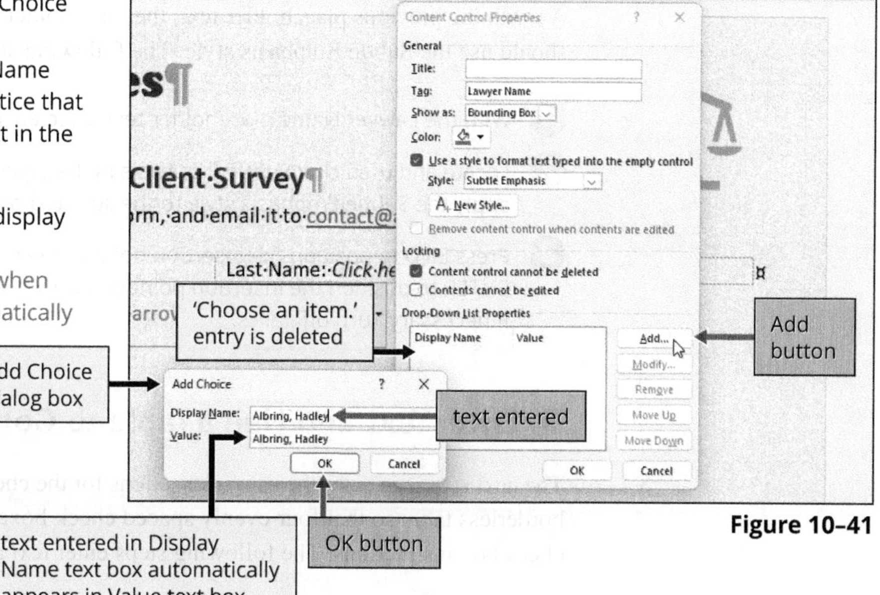

Figure 10–41

- Click OK (Add Choice dialog box) to add the entered display name and value to the list of choices in the Drop-Down List Properties area (Content Control Properties dialog box).

5

- Click the Add button to display the Add Choice dialog box.
- Type **Drechsler, Lucian** in the Display Name text box.
- Click OK to add the entry to the list.
- Click the Add button to display the Add Choice dialog box.
- Type **Pierre, Maria** in the Display Name text box.
- Click OK to add the entry to the list.
- Click the Add button to display the Add Choice dialog box.
- Type **Soler, Alden** in the Display Name text box.
- Click OK to add the entry to the list (Figure 10–42).

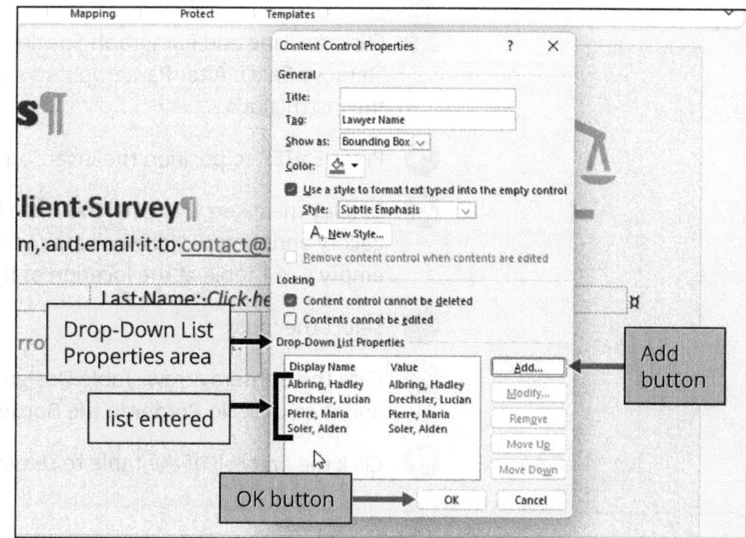

Figure 10–42

- Click OK (Content Control Properties dialog box) to change the content control properties.

Q&A What if I want to change an entry in the drop-down list?
You would select the drop-down list content control, click the Properties button (Developer tab | Controls group) to display the Content Control Properties dialog box, select the entry to change, click the Modify button, adjust the entry, and then click OK.

To Format Placeholder Text

As with the previous placeholder text, the placeholder text for the content Lawyer Name control should use the Subtle Emphasis style. The following steps format placeholder text.

1. With the Lawyer Name placeholder text selected, display the Home tab.
2. Locate and then click Subtle Emphasis in the Styles gallery (Home tab | Styles group) to apply the Subtle Emphasis style to the selected placeholder text.
3. Press END to position the insertion point at the end of the current line and then press ENTER to position the insertion point below the Lawyer Name label and content control. If necessary, turn off italics.

To Enter Text and Use a Table to Control Document Layout

The next step is to enter the user instructions for the check box content controls and insert a 4 × 1 borderless table so that four evenly spaced check boxes can be displayed horizontally below the check box instructions. The following steps enter text and insert a borderless table.

1. With the insertion point positioned on the paragraph below the Lawyer Name label and content control, scroll to, if necessary, and then click Normal in the Styles gallery (Home tab | Styles group) to format the current paragraph to the Normal style.
2. Using either the ruler or the Layout tab, change the left indent to 0.06" so that the entered text aligns with the text immediately above it (that is, the W in Which).
3. Type **Which category describes your case (check all that apply)?** as the instruction.
4. Click the 'Line and Paragraph Spacing' button (Home tab | Paragraph group) and then click 'Remove Space After Paragraph' so that the check boxes will appear one physical line below the instructions.
5. Press ENTER to position the insertion point on the line below the check box instructions.
6. Display the Insert tab. Click the Table button (Insert tab | Tables group) to display the Table gallery and then click the cell in the first row and fourth column of the grid to insert an empty 4 × 1 table at the location of the insertion point.
7. Select the table.
8. Click the Borders arrow (Table Design tab | Borders group) to display the Borders gallery and then click No Border in the Borders gallery to remove the borders from the table.
9. Click the first cell of the table to remove the selection (shown in Figure 10–43).

To Insert a Check Box Content Control

The following step inserts the first check box content control. **Why?** In the online form in this module, the user can select up to five check boxes: Civil Litigation, Estate Planning, Personal Injury, Real Estate, and Other.

- Position the insertion point at the location for the check box content control, in this case, the leftmost cell in the 4 × 1 table.
- Display the Developer tab.
- Click the 'Check Box Content Control' button (Developer tab | Controls group) to insert a check box content control at the location of the insertion point (Figure 10–43).

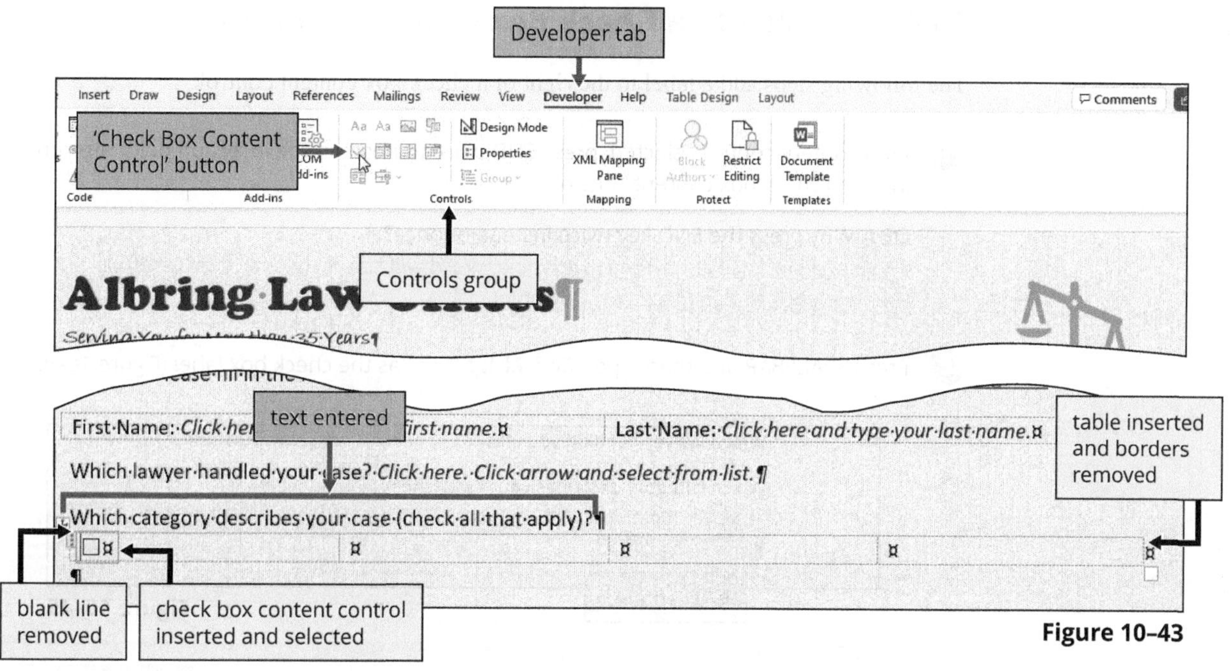

Figure 10–43

To Change the Properties of a Check Box Content Control

The next step is to change the title and locking properties of the content control. The following steps change properties of a check box content control.

1. With the content control selected, click the Properties button (Developer tab | Controls group) to display the Content Control Properties dialog box.
2. Type **Civil Litigation** in the Tag text box (Content Control Properties dialog box).
3. Click the Show as arrow and then select None in the list, because you do not want a border surrounding the check box content control.
4. Place a check mark in the 'Content control cannot be deleted' check box (Figure 10–44).
5. Click OK to assign the properties to the selected content control.

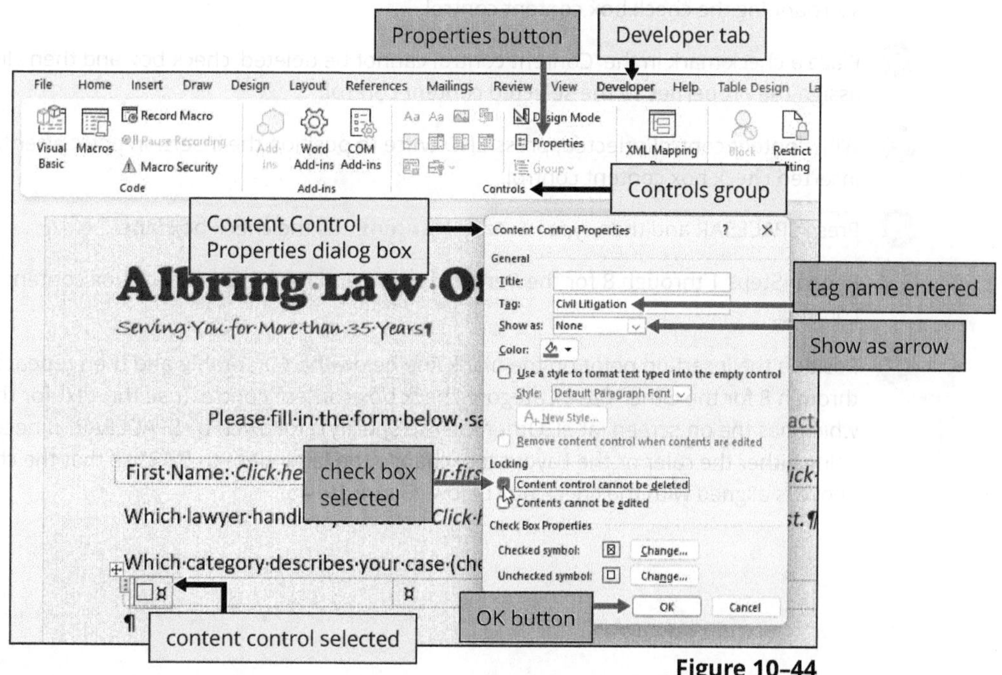

Figure 10–44

To Add a Label to a Check Box Content Control

The following steps add a label to the right of a check box content control.

1. With content control selected, press END twice to position the insertion point after the inserted check box content control.

   Q&A Why press the END key twice instead of once?
   If you press it once and then start typing, Word will select the check box. You do not want the check box to be selected at this point.

2. Press SPACEBAR and then type **Civil Litigation** as the check box label (Figure 10–45).

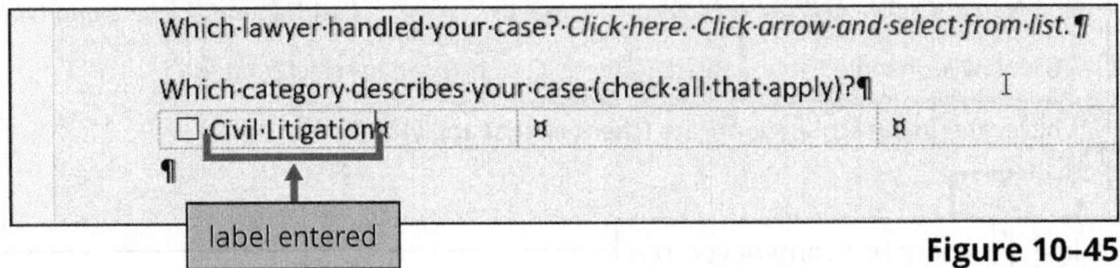

Figure 10–45

To Insert Additional Check Box Content Controls

The following steps insert the remaining check box content controls and their labels.

1. Press TAB to position the insertion point in the next cell, which is the location for the next check box content control.
2. Click the 'Check Box Content Control' button (Developer tab | Controls group) to insert a check box content control at the location of the insertion point.
3. With the content control selected, click the Properties button (Developer tab | Controls group) to display the Content Control Properties dialog box.
4. Type **Estate Planning** in the Tag text box (Content Control Properties dialog box).
5. Click the Show as arrow and then select None in the list, because you do not want a border surrounding the check box content control.
6. Place a check mark in the 'Content control cannot be deleted' check box and then click OK to assign the properties to the selected content control.
7. With content control selected, press END twice to position the insertion point after the inserted check box content control.
8. Press SPACEBAR and then type **Estate Planning** as the check box label.
9. Repeat Steps 1 through 8 for the Personal Injury and Real Estate check box content controls.
10. Position the insertion point on the blank line below the 4 × 1 table and then repeat Steps 2 through 8 for the Other Case Category check box content control (use this text for the tag), which has the on-screen label, Other (please specify):, followed by SPACEBAR. If necessary, using either the ruler or the Layout tab, change the left indent to 0.13" so that the check box above is aligned with the check box below (Figure 10–46).

Client·Survey¶

Please·fill·in·the·form·below,·save·your·form,·and·email·it·to·contact@albringlawoffices.cengage.net.¶

First·Name:·*Click·here·and·type·your·first·name.*¤ Last·Name:·*Click·here·and·type·your·last·name.*¤

Which·lawyer·handled·your·case?·*Click·here.·Click·arrow·and·select·from·list.*¶

Which·category·describes·your·case·(check·all·that·apply)?¶

☐·Civil·Litigation¤ ☐·Estate·Planning¤ ☐·Personal·Injury¤ ☐·Real·Estate¤

☐·Other·(please·specify):·¶

check box content controls and labels inserted

insertion point

Figure 10–46

To Insert a Rich Text Content Control

The next step is to insert the content control that enables users to type in any other case category. The difference between a plain text and rich text content control is that the users can format text as they enter it in the rich text content control. The following step inserts a rich text content control. **Why?** Because you want to allow users to format the text they enter in the Other Case Category content control, you use the rich text content control.

- If necessary, position the insertion point at the location for the rich text content control (shown in Figure 10–46).
- If necessary, display the Developer tab.
- Click the 'Rich Text Content Control' button (Developer tab | Controls group) to insert a rich text content control at the location of the insertion point (Figure 10–47).

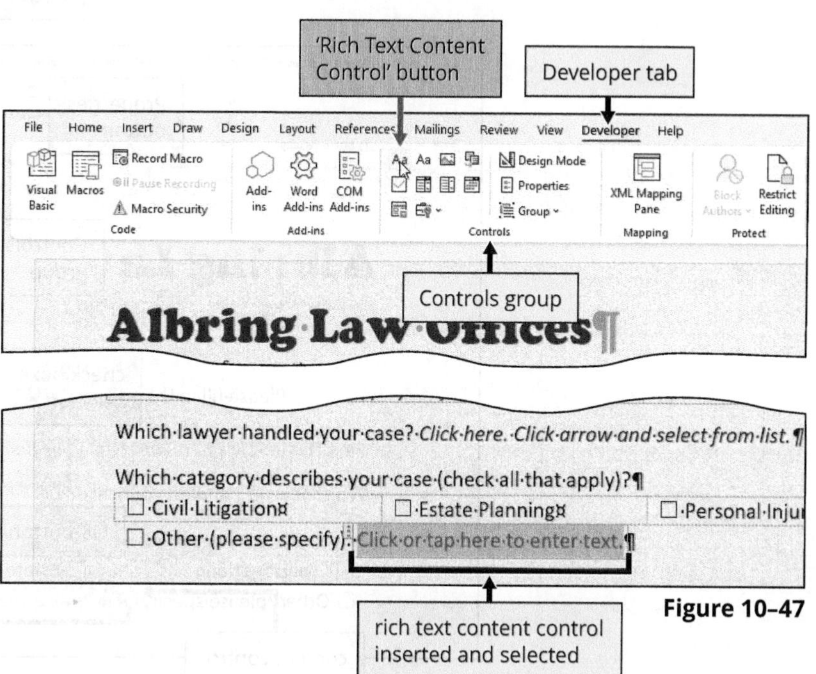

Figure 10–47

To Use Design Mode to Edit Placeholder Text

The following steps edit placeholder text for the rich text content control.

1. With the rich text content control selected, click the Design Mode button (Developer tab | Controls group) to turn on Design mode.
2. If necessary, scroll to display the content control in the document window.
3. Edit the placeholder text so that it contains the text, Click here and type your other case category., as the instruction.
4. Click the Design Mode button (Developer tab | Controls group) to turn off Design mode. If necessary, scroll to display the top of the form in the document window.

To Change the Properties of a Rich Text Content Control

In the online form in this module, you change the same three properties for the rich text content control as for the plain text content control. That is, you enter a tag name, specify the style, and lock the content control. The following steps change the properties of the rich text content control.

1. With the content control selected, click the Properties button (Developer tab | Controls group) to display the Content Control Properties dialog box.
2. Type **Other Case Category** in the Tag text box (Content Control Properties dialog box).
3. Place a check mark in the 'Use a style to format text typed into the empty control' check box to activate the Style box.
4. Click the Style arrow and then select Subtle Emphasis in the list to specify the style for the content control.
5. Place a check mark in the 'Content control cannot be deleted' check box (Figure 10–48).
6. Click OK to assign the properties to the content control.

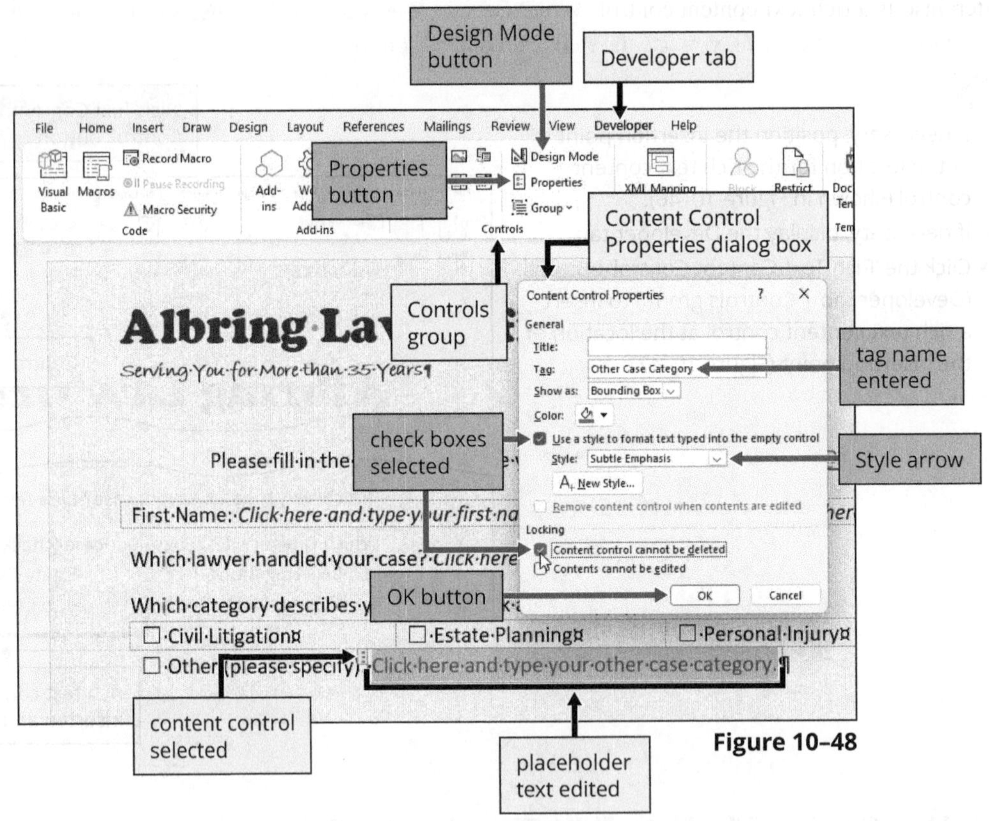

Figure 10–48

To Format Placeholder Text and Add Space before a Paragraph

The placeholder text for the Other Case Category text entry should use the Subtle Emphasis style, and the space below the check boxes should be consistent with the space between other elements on the form. The next steps format placeholder text and increase space before a paragraph.

1. With the Other Case Category placeholder text selected, display the Home tab.
2. Locate and then click Subtle Emphasis in the Styles gallery (Home tab | Styles group) to apply the Subtle Emphasis style to the selected placeholder text.

3 Press END to position the insertion point on the paragraph mark after the Other Case Category content control and then press ENTER to position the insertion point below the Other Case Category label and content control. If necessary, turn off italics.

4 If necessary, display the Home tab. With the insertion point positioned on the paragraph below the Other Case Category label and content control, locate and then click Normal in the Styles gallery (Home tab | Styles group) to format the current paragraph to the Normal style.

5 Using either the ruler or the Layout tab, change the left indent to 0.06" so that the entered text aligns with the text two lines above it (that is, the W in Which).

6 If necessary, display the Layout tab. Change the value in the Spacing Before box (Layout tab | Paragraph group) to 8 pt to increase the space between the Other Case Category check box and the paragraph. If necessary, change the value in the Spacing After box (Layout tab | Paragraph group) to 8 pt.

To Insert a Combo Box Content Control

In Word, a combo box content control allows a user to type text or select from a list. The following steps insert a combo box content control. **Why?** In the online form in this module, users can type their own entry in the Service Rating content control or select from one of these four choices: Excellent, Good, Fair, or Poor.

1

- With the insertion point positioned on the blank paragraph mark, type **How would you rate our services to date?** and then press SPACEBAR.

2

- Display the Developer tab.
- Click the 'Combo Box Content Control' button (Developer tab | Controls group) to insert a combo box content control at the location of the insertion point (Figure 10–49).

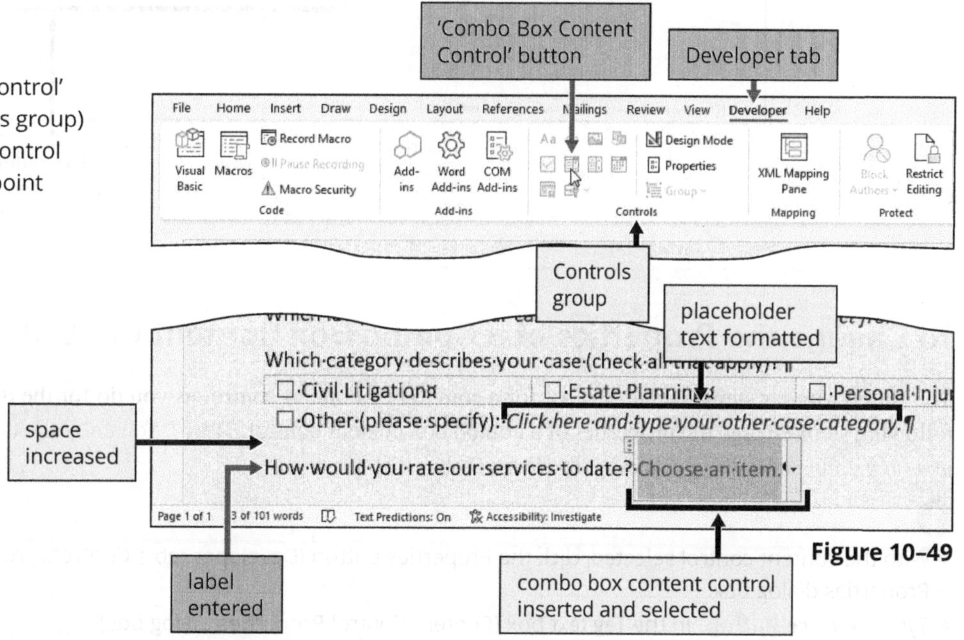

Figure 10–49

To Use Design Mode to Edit Placeholder Text

The following steps edit the placeholder text for the combo box content control.

1 With the combo box content control selected, click the Design Mode button (Developer tab | Controls group) to turn on Design mode.

2 If necessary, scroll to display the combo box content control.

Q&A What if the content control moves to another page?
Because Design mode displays tags, the content controls and placeholder text are not displayed in their proper positions on the screen. When you turn off Design mode, the content controls will return to their original locations and the extra page should disappear.

3 Edit the placeholder text so that it contains this instruction, which contains two sentences (Figure 10–50): Click here. Click arrow and select from list, or type your response.

4 Click the Design Mode button (Developer tab | Controls group) to turn off Design mode.

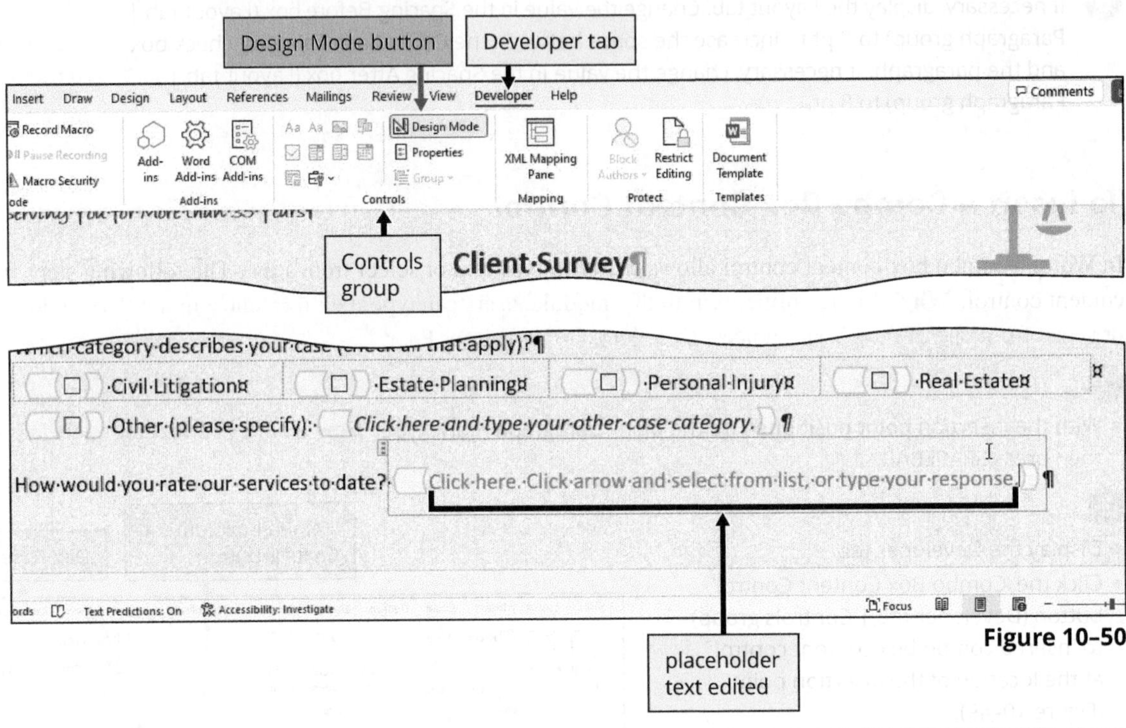

Figure 10–50

To Change the Properties of a Combo Box Content Control

You follow similar steps to enter the list for a combo box content control as you do for the drop-down list content control. The following steps change the properties of a combo box content control. **Why?** You enter the tag name, specify the style for typed text, and enter the choices for the drop-down list.

1

- With the content control selected, click the Properties button (Developer tab | Controls group) to display the Content Control Properties dialog box.
- Type **Service Rating** in the Tag text box (Content Control Properties dialog box).
- Place a check mark in the 'Use a style to format text typed into the empty control' check box to activate the Style box.
- Click the Style arrow and then select Subtle Emphasis in the Style list to specify the style for the content control.
- Place a check mark in the 'Content control cannot be deleted' check box.
- In the Drop-Down List Properties area, click 'Choose an item.' to select it (Figure 10–51).

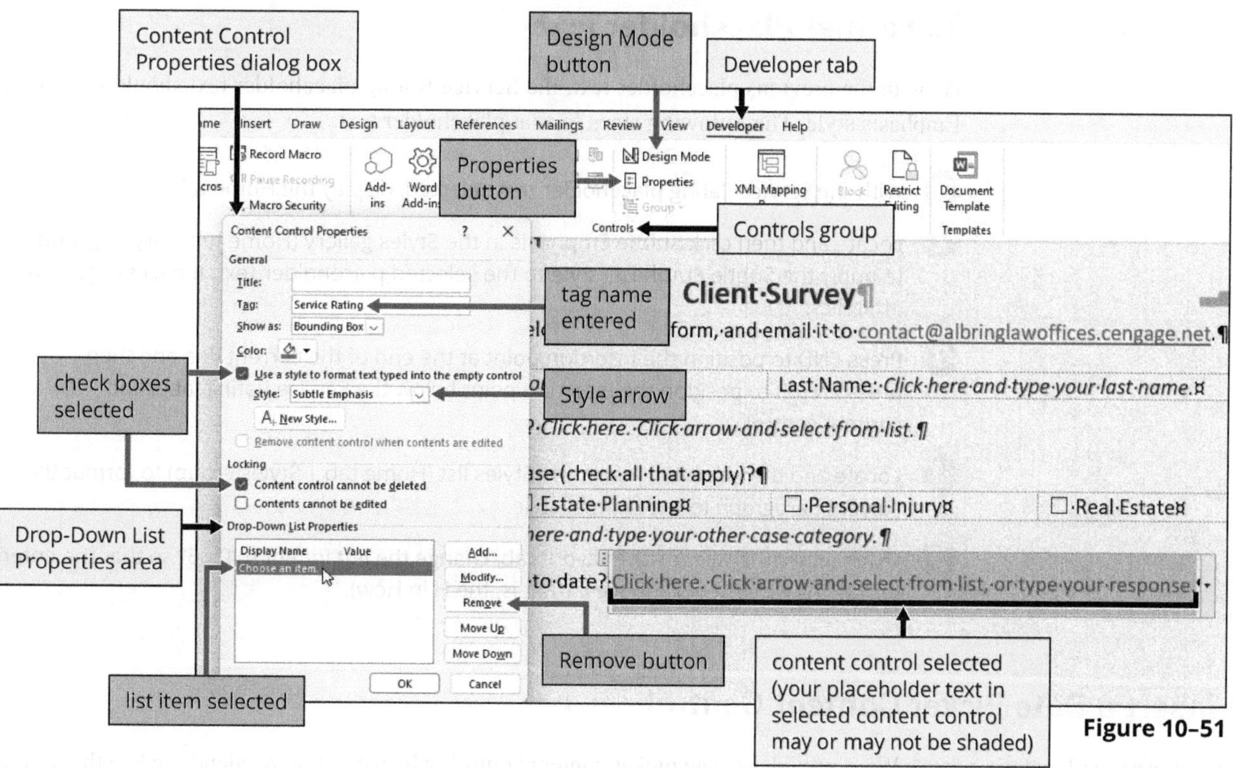

Figure 10–51

2

- Click the Remove button (Content Control Properties dialog box) to delete the selected entry.

3

- Click the Add button to display the Add Choice dialog box.
- Type **Excellent** in the Display Name text box (Add Choice dialog box).
- Click OK to add the entered display name to the list of choices in the Drop-Down List Properties area (Content Control Properties dialog box).
- Click the Add button and add **Good** to the list.
- Click the Add button and add **Fair** to the list.
- Click the Add button and add **Poor** to the list (Figure 10–52).

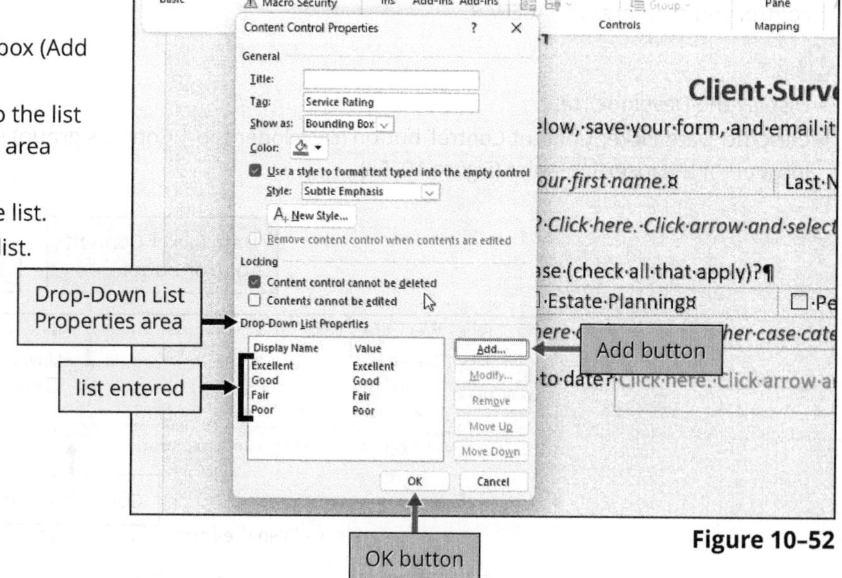

Figure 10–52

4

- Click OK (Content Control Properties dialog box) to change the content control properties.

Q&A How do I make adjustments to entries in the list?

Follow the same procedures as you use to make adjustments to entries in a drop-down list content control.

To Format Placeholder Text

As with the previous placeholder text, the Service Rating placeholder text should use the Subtle Emphasis style. The following steps format placeholder text.

1. With the Service Rating placeholder text selected, display the Home tab.
2. Locate and then click Subtle Emphasis in the Styles gallery (Home tab | Styles group) to apply the Subtle Emphasis style to the selected placeholder text. If necessary, turn off italics.
3. Press END to position the insertion point at the end of the current line and then press ENTER to position the insertion point below the Service Rating label and content control.
4. Locate and then click Normal in the Styles list (Home tab | Styles group) to format the current paragraph to the Normal style.
5. Using either the ruler or the Layout tab, change the left indent to 0.06" so that the entered text aligns with the text above it (that is, the H in How).

To Insert a Date Picker Content Control

To assist users with entering dates, Word provides a date picker content control, which displays a calendar when the user clicks the arrow to the right of the content control. Users also can enter a date directly in the content control without using the calendar. The following steps enter the label, Today's Date:, and a date picker content control. **Why?** The last item that users enter in the Client Survey is today's date.

- With the insertion point below the Service Rating label and content control, type **Today's Date:** as the label for the content control and then press SPACEBAR.

- Display the Developer tab.
- Click the 'Date Picker Content Control' button (Developer tab | Controls group) to insert a date picker content control at the location of the insertion point (Figure 10–53).

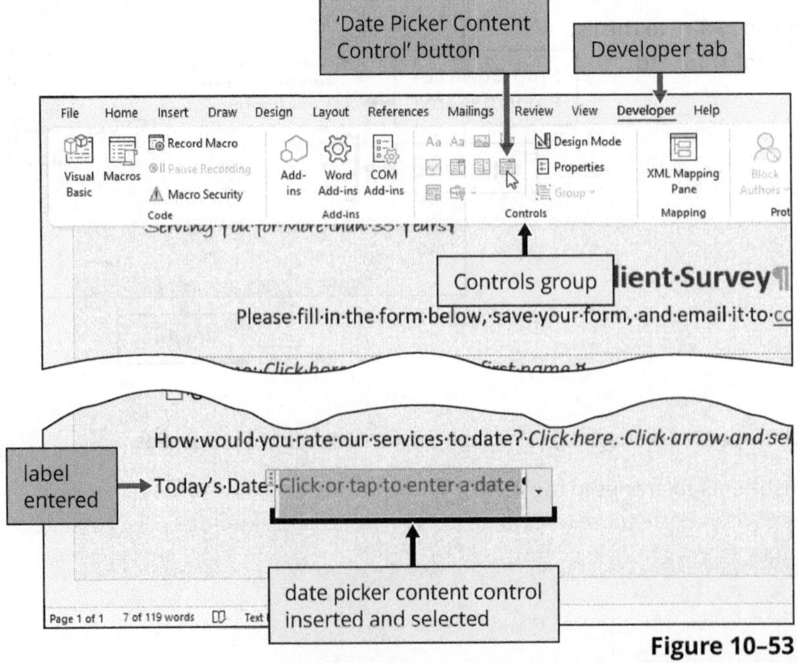

Figure 10–53

To Use Design Mode to Edit Placeholder Text

The following steps edit the placeholder text for the date picker content control.

1. With the date picker content control selected, click the Design Mode button (Developer tab | Controls group) to turn on Design mode.
2. If necessary, scroll to display the date picker content control.
3. Edit the placeholder text so that it contains this instruction, which contains two sentences: Click here. Click arrow and select today's date.
4. Click the Design Mode button (Developer tab | Controls group) to turn off Design mode.
5. If necessary, scroll to display the bottom of the form in the document window.

To Change the Properties of a Date Picker Content Control

The following steps change the properties of a date picker content control. **Why?** In addition to identifying a tag name for a date picker content control, specifying a style, and locking the control, you will specify how the date will be displayed when the user selects it from the calendar.

- With the content control selected, click the Properties button (Developer tab | Controls group) to display the Content Control Properties dialog box.
- Type **Today's Date** in the Tag text box.
- Place a check mark in the 'Use a style to format text typed into the empty control' check box to activate the Style box.
- Click the Style arrow and then select Subtle Emphasis in the list to specify the style for the content control.
- Place a check mark in the 'Content control cannot be deleted' check box.
- In the Display the date like this area, click the desired format in the list (Figure 10–54).

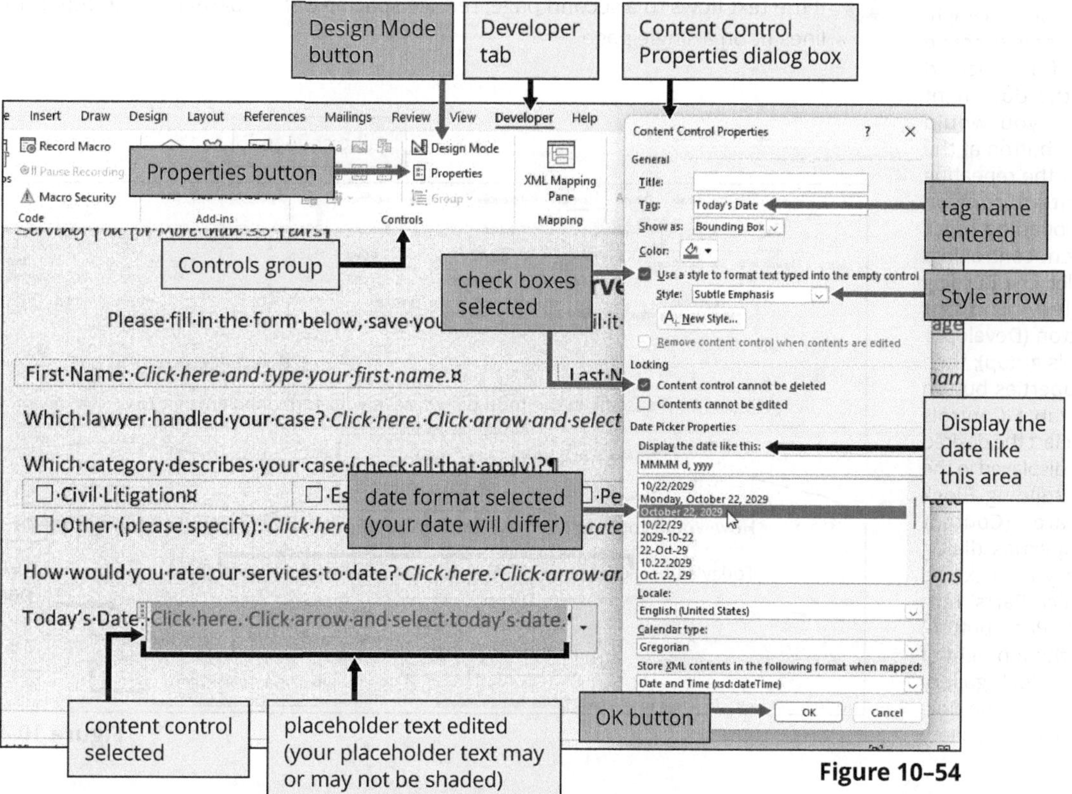

Figure 10–54

- Click OK to change the content control properties.

To Format Placeholder Text

As with the previous placeholder text, the placeholder text for today's date should use the Subtle Emphasis style. The following steps format placeholder text.

1. With the today's date placeholder text selected, display the Home tab.
2. Locate and then click Subtle Emphasis in the Styles gallery (Home tab | Styles group) to apply the Subtle Emphasis style to the selected placeholder text.
3. Press END to position the insertion point at the end of the current line and then press ENTER to position the insertion point below the Today's Date label and content control.
4. Locate and then click Normal in the Styles gallery (Home tab | Styles group) to format the current paragraph to the Normal style.

BTW
Other Content Controls
To insert a picture content control in a document or template, click the 'Picture Content Control' button (Developer tab | Controls group). When the user clicks the icon in the center of the picture content control, the Insert Pictures dialog box is displayed, enabling the user to locate the desired picture. To insert a repeating section content control, select the table or paragraph that you want to repeat and then click the 'Repeating Section Content Control' button (Developer tab | Controls group), which inserts the content control within the selected table or paragraph; then if you wanted to create a duplicate of the selected content in the document or template, you would click the plus button at the right edge of the repeating section content control. To insert a building block gallery content control in a template, select the 'Building Block Gallery Content Control' button (Developer tab | Controls group); then click the Properties button (Developer tab | Controls group) and select the desired gallery to be displayed in the Document Building Block Properties area (Content Control Properties dialog box). When you click the 'Explore Quick Parts' button (or Quick Parts button) attached to the top-right of the building block gallery content control in the document, the selected gallery appears.

To Enter and Format Text

The following steps enter and format the line of text at the bottom of the online form.

1. Be sure the insertion point is on the line below the Today's Date label and content control.
2. Center the paragraph mark.
3. Format the text to be typed with the color of 'Green, Accent 6, Darker 50%'.
4. Type **Thank you for your business!**
5. Change the space before the paragraph to 18 point (Figure 10–55). If necessary, change the space after the paragraph to 8 point.
6. If the text flows to a second page, reduce spacing before paragraphs in the form so that all lines fit on a single page.

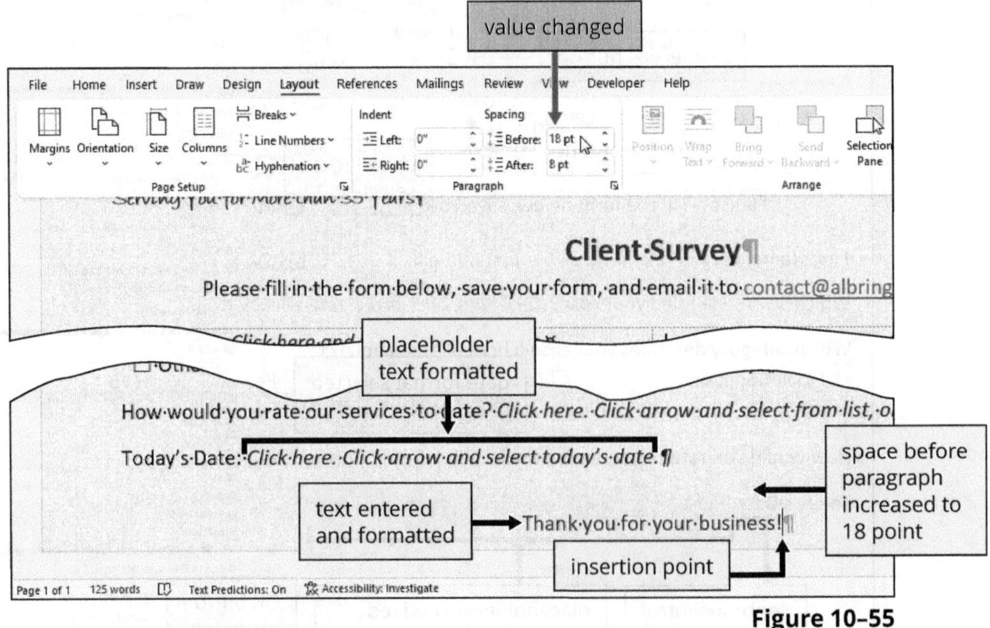

Figure 10–55

To Hide Gridlines and Formatting Marks

Because you are finished with the tables in this form and will not enter any additional tables, you will hide the gridlines. You also are finished with entering and formatting text on the screen. To make the form easier to view, you hide the formatting marks, which can clutter the screen. The following steps hide gridlines and formatting marks.

1. If necessary, position the insertion point in a table cell.
2. Display the contextual Layout tab. If gridlines are showing, click the View Gridlines button (contextual Layout tab | Table group) to hide table gridlines.
3. Display the Home tab. If the 'Show/Hide ¶' button (Home tab | Paragraph group) is selected, click it to remove formatting marks from the screen.
4. Save the template again on the same storage location with the same file name.

Break Point: If you want to take a break, this is a good place to do so. You can exit Word now. To resume later, start Word, open the file called SC_WD_10_AlbringLawOfficesClientSurvey.dotx, and continue following the steps from this location forward.

To Draw a Rectangle

The next step is to emphasize the data entry area of the form. The data entry area includes all the content controls in which a user enters data. The following steps draw a rectangle around the data entry area, and subsequent steps format the rectangle. **Why?** To call attention to the data entry area of the form, this module places a rectangle around the data entry area, changes the style of the rectangle, and then adds a shadow to the rectangle.

1

- Position the insertion point on the last line in the document (shown in Figure 10-55).
- Display the Insert tab.
- Click the Shapes button (Insert tab | Illustrations group) to display the Shapes gallery (Figure 10-56).

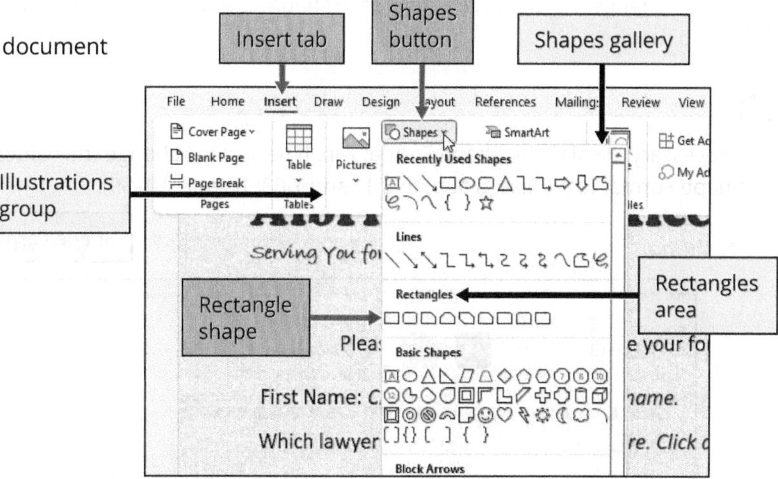

Figure 10-56

2

- Click the Rectangle shape in the Rectangles area of the Shapes gallery, which removes the gallery and changes the pointer to the shape of a crosshair in the document window.

Q&A What if I am using a touch screen?
Proceed to Step 5 because the shape is inserted in the document window after you tap the rectangle shape in the Shapes gallery.

- Position the pointer (a crosshair) in the approximate location for the upper-left corner of the desired shape (Figure 10-57).

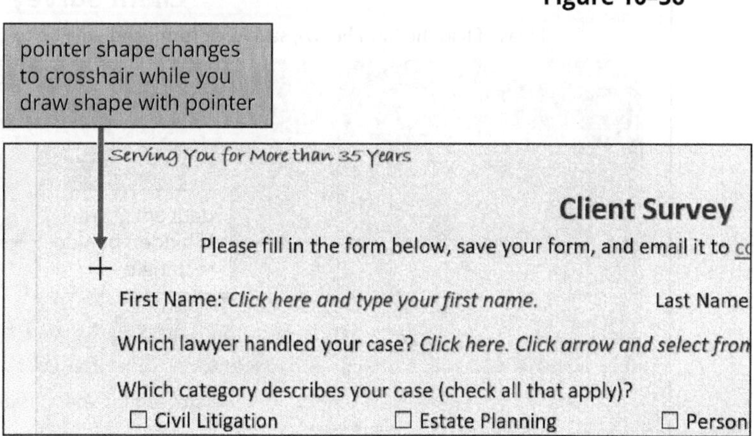

Figure 10-57

- Drag the pointer downward and rightward to form a rectangle around the data entry area, as shown in Figure 10–58.

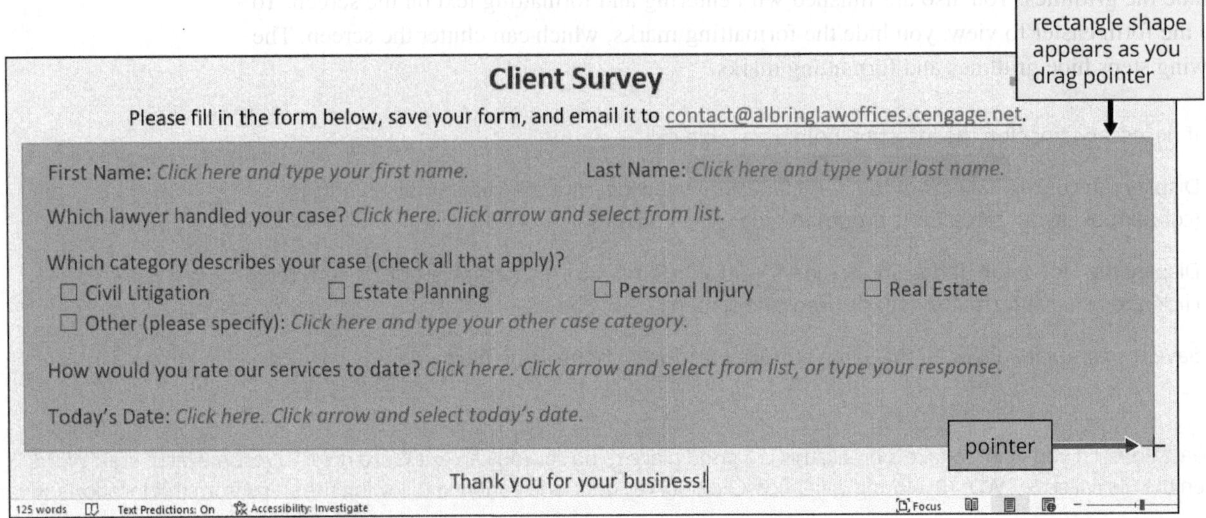

Figure 10–58

- Release the mouse button to draw the rectangle shape on top of the data entry area (shown in Figure 10–59).

Q&A What happened to all the text in the data entry area?
When you draw a shape in a document, Word initially places the shape in front of, or on top of, any text in the same area. You can change the stacking order of the shape so that it is displayed behind the text. Thus, the next steps move the shape behind the text.

- If necessary, display the Shape Format tab. If necessary, change the values in the Shape Height and Shape Width boxes (Shape Format tab | Size group) to 2.1" and 7.63" (Figure 10–59).

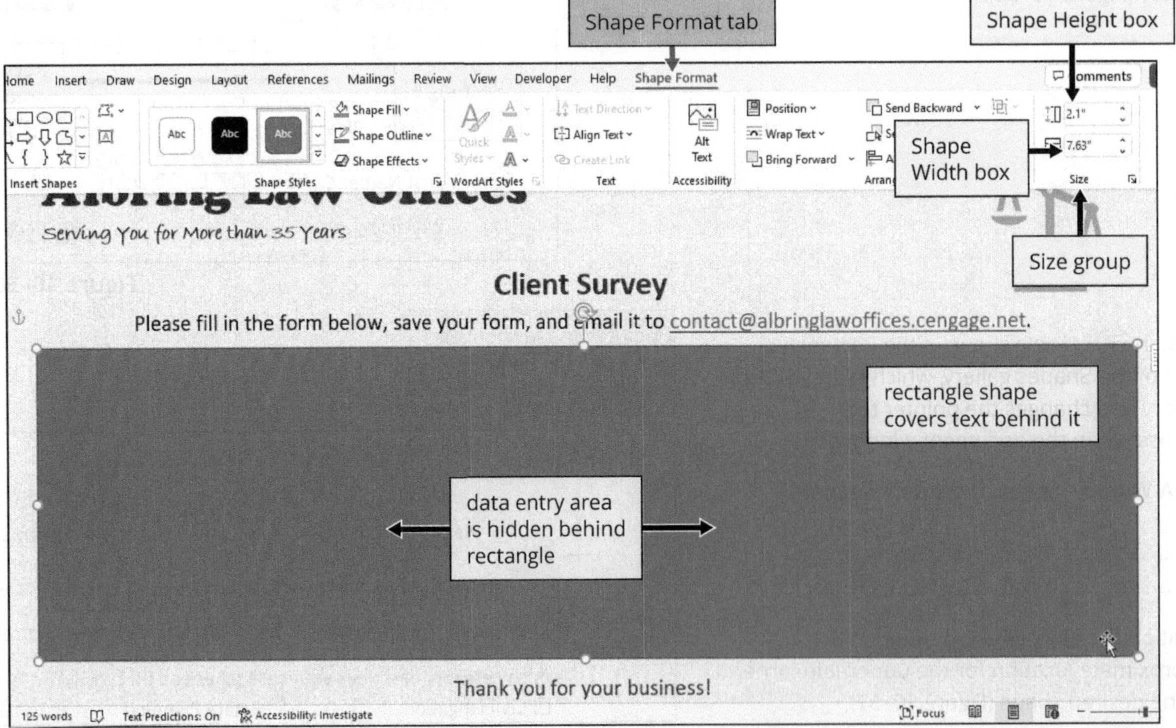

Figure 10–59

To Send a Graphic behind Text

The following steps send a graphic behind text. **Why?** You want the rectangle shape graphic to be positioned behind the data entry area text, so that the text in the data entry area is visible along with the shape.

1

- With the rectangle shape selected, click the Layout Options button attached to the graphic to display the Layout Options gallery (Figure 10–60).

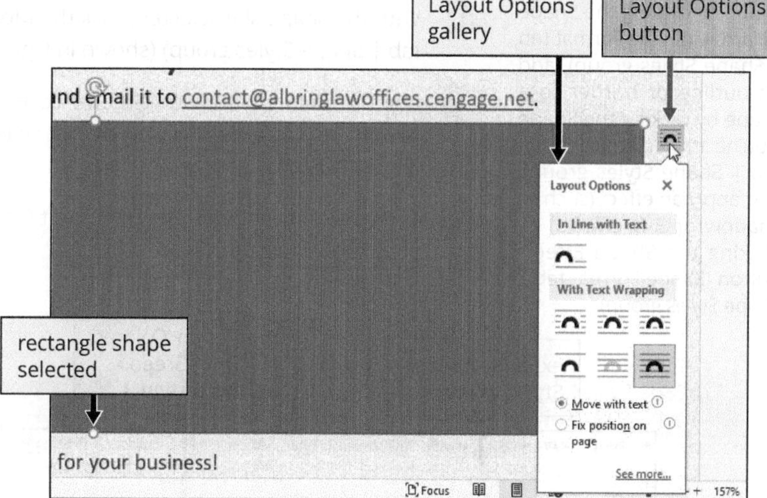

Figure 10–60

2

- Click Behind Text in the Layout Options gallery to position the rectangle shape behind the text (Figure 10–61).

Q&A What if I want a shape to cover text?
You would click 'In Front of Text' in the Layout Options gallery.

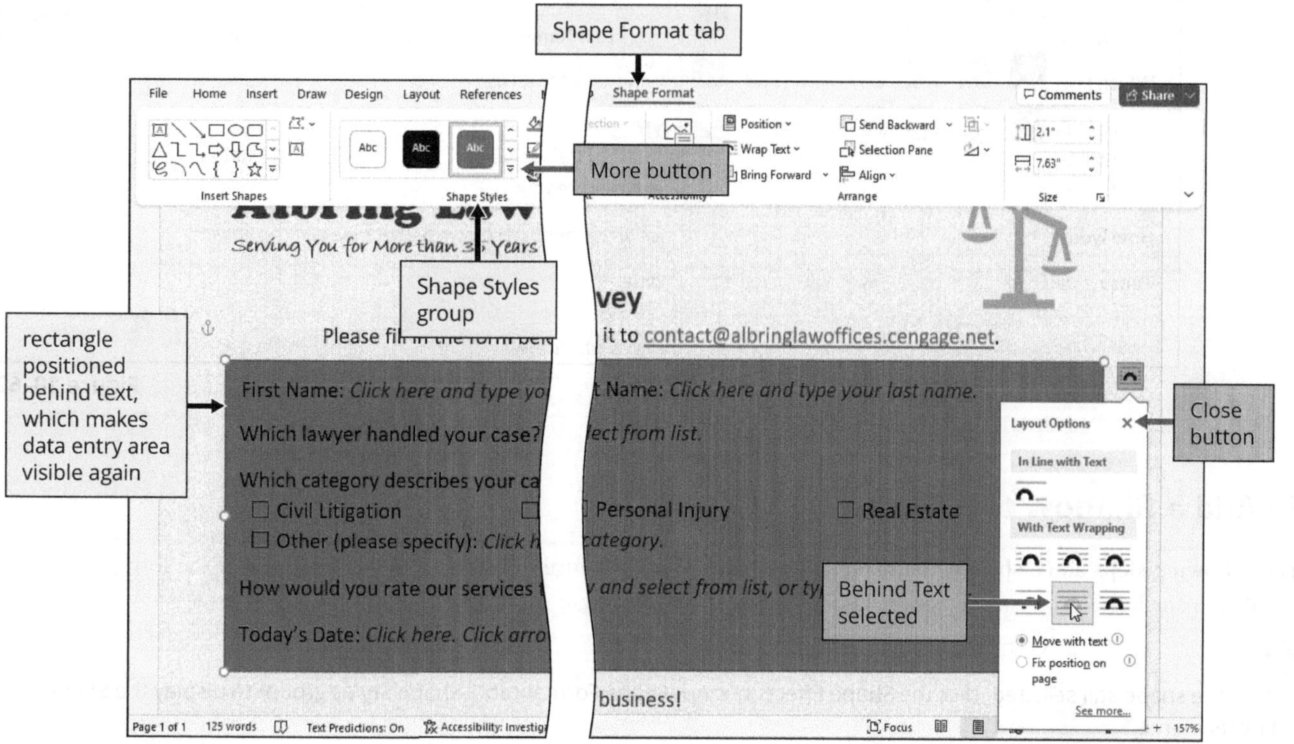

Figure 10–61

3

- Click the Close button in the Layout Options gallery to close the gallery.

Other Ways

1. Click Wrap Text button (Shape Format tab | Arrange group), click desired option
2. Right-click object (or, if using touch, tap 'Show Context Menu' button on Mini toolbar), point to Wrap Text on shortcut menu, click desired option

BTW
Formatting Shapes
Like other drawing objects or pictures, shapes can be formatted or have styles applied. You can change the fill in a shape by clicking the Shape Fill arrow (Shape Format tab | Shape Styles group), add an outline or border to a shape by clicking the Shape Outline arrow (Shape Format tab | Shape Styles group), and apply an effect (such as shadow or 3-D effects) by clicking the Shape Effects button (Shape Format tab | Shape Styles group).

To Apply a Shape Style with an Outline

The next step is to apply a shape style to the rectangle, so that the text in the data entry area is easier to read. The following steps apply a style to the rectangle shape.

1. With the shape still selected, click the More button in the Shape Styles gallery (Shape Format tab | Shape Styles group) (shown in Figure 10–61) to expand the Shape Styles gallery.
2. Point to 'Colored Outline - Green, Accent 6' in the Shape Styles gallery (last style in first row) to display a Live Preview of that style applied to the rectangle shape in the form (Figure 10–62).
3. Click 'Colored Outline - Green, Accent 6' in the Shape Styles gallery to apply the selected style to the selected shape.

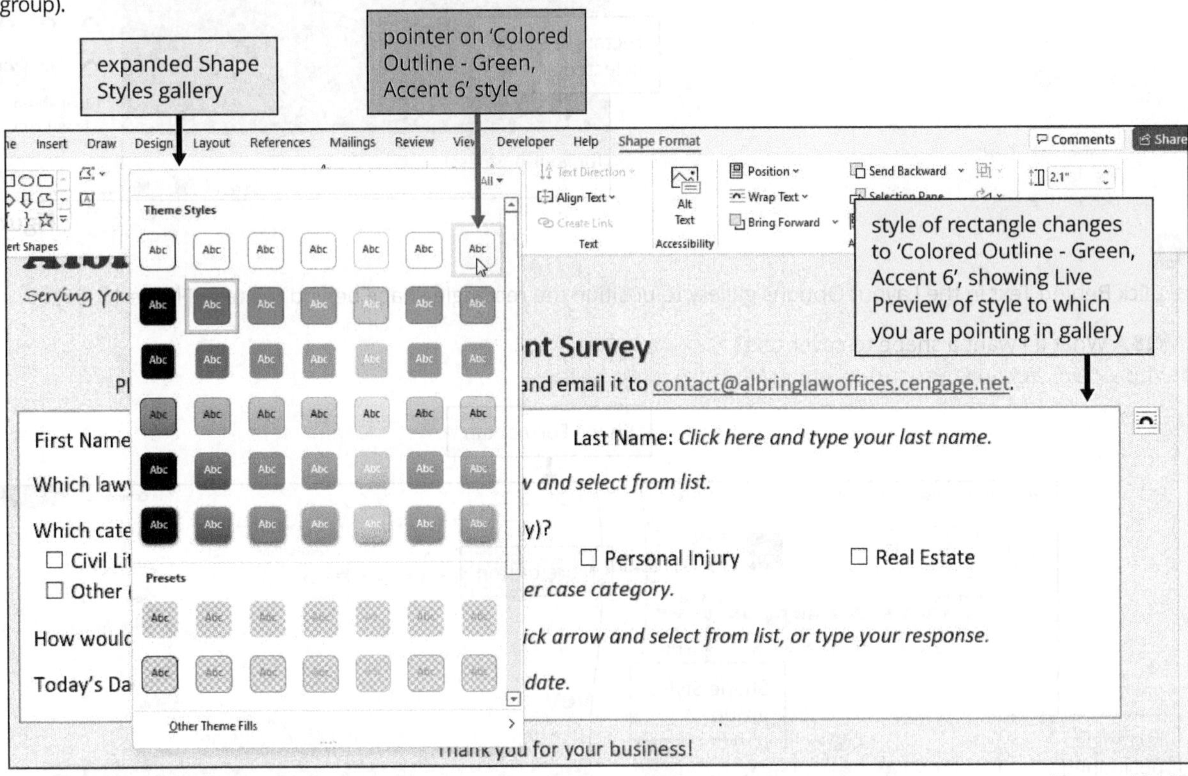

Figure 10–62

To Add a Shadow to a Shape

The following steps add a shadow to the rectangle shape. **Why?** To further offset the data entry area of the form, this online form has a shadow on the outside bottom and left edges of the rectangle shape.

- With the shape still selected, click the Shape Effects button (Shape Format tab | Shape Styles group) to display the Shape Effects menu.

- Point to Shadow on the Shape Effects menu to display the Shadow gallery.
- Point to 'Offset: Bottom Left' in the Outer area in the Shadow gallery to display a Live Preview of that shadow effect applied to the selected shape in the document (Figure 10–63).
- **Experiment:** Point to various shadows in the Shadow gallery and notice the shadow on the selected shape change.

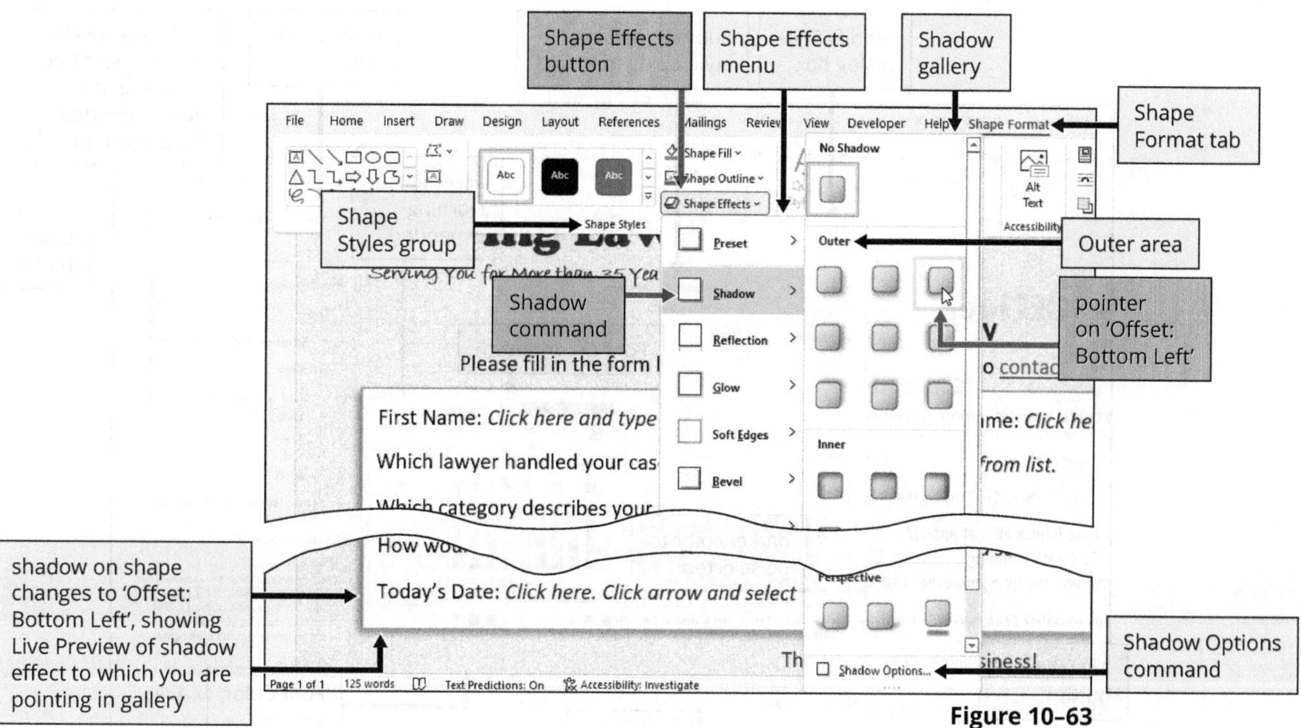

Figure 10–63

- Click 'Offset: Bottom Left' in the Shadow gallery to apply the selected shadow to the selected shape.

Q&A Can I change the color of a shadow?
Yes. Click Shadow Options (shown in Figure 10–63) in the Shadow gallery.

To Check Accessibility and Save the Template

To address issues identified by the accessibility checker, the next steps add alt text to the icon graphic and darken the style for entered text. The following steps check accessibility and save the template.

1. Click the Accessibility button on the status bar to open the Accessibility pane.
2. Fix the 'Missing alternative text' (or similar alt text) issue by adding the following description for the rectangle shape in the template: Rectangle shape surrounding data entry area.
3. If a 'Hard-to-read text contrast' issue also appears, fix it by changing the Subtle Emphasis style of the entered text instructions to a darker shade of gray: click the arrow to the left of the 'Hard-to-read text contrast' warning to expand the warning, click any of the arrows to the right of an identified text issue to display the Recommended Actions menu, click Modified Style on the Recommended Actions menu to display the Modify Style dialog box, click the Font Color button (Modify Style dialog box) to display the Font Color gallery, click 'Light-Gray, Background 2, Darker 75%' (third color in fifth row) (Figure 10–64), click OK to close the dialog box and remove the 'Hard-to-read text contrast' issue from the Accessibility pane.
4. Leave the last errors or warnings identified by the Accessibility Checker for image or object not inline because, for illustration purposes, the icon graphic and the rectangle shape are intended to be floating objects in this project. Close the Accessibility pane.
5. Save the template again on the same storage location with the same file name.

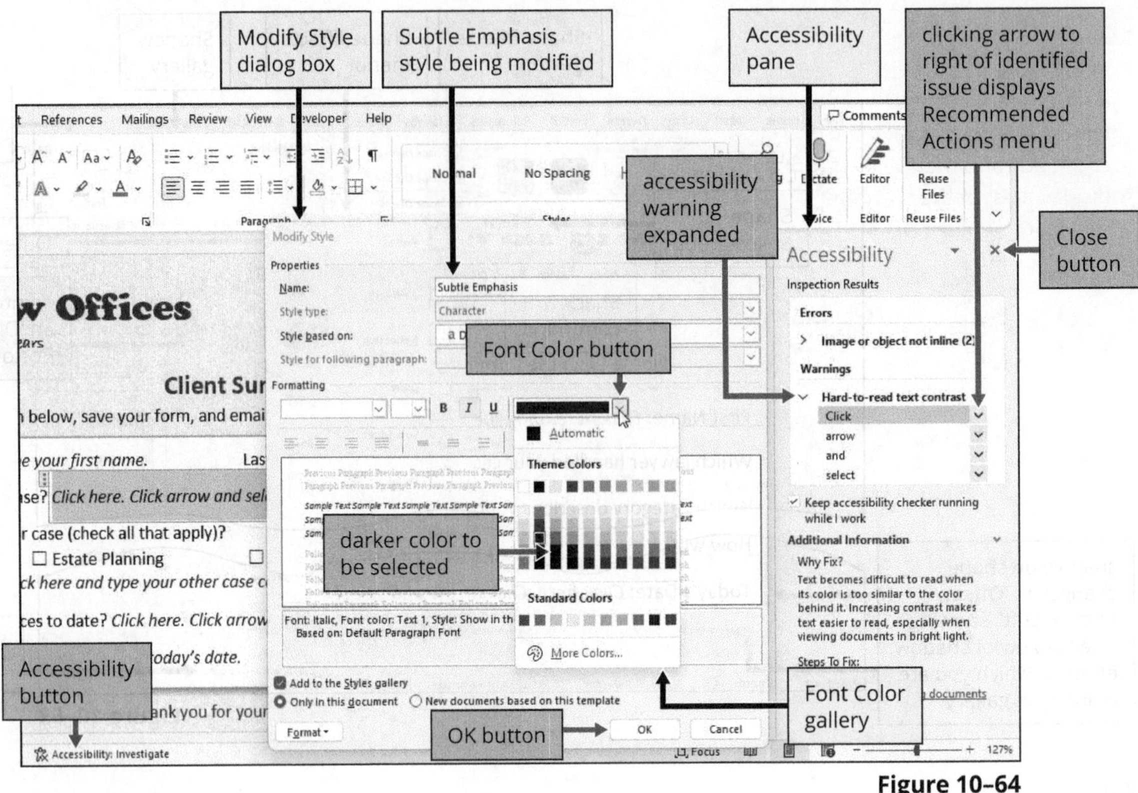

Figure 10-64

To Protect a Form

When you **protect a form**, you are allowing users to enter data only in designated areas — specifically, the content controls. The following steps protect the online form. **Why?** To prevent unwanted changes and edits to the form, it is crucial that you protect a form before making it available to users.

- Display the Developer tab.
- Click the Restrict Editing button (Developer tab | Protect group) to open the Restrict Editing pane (Figure 10–65).

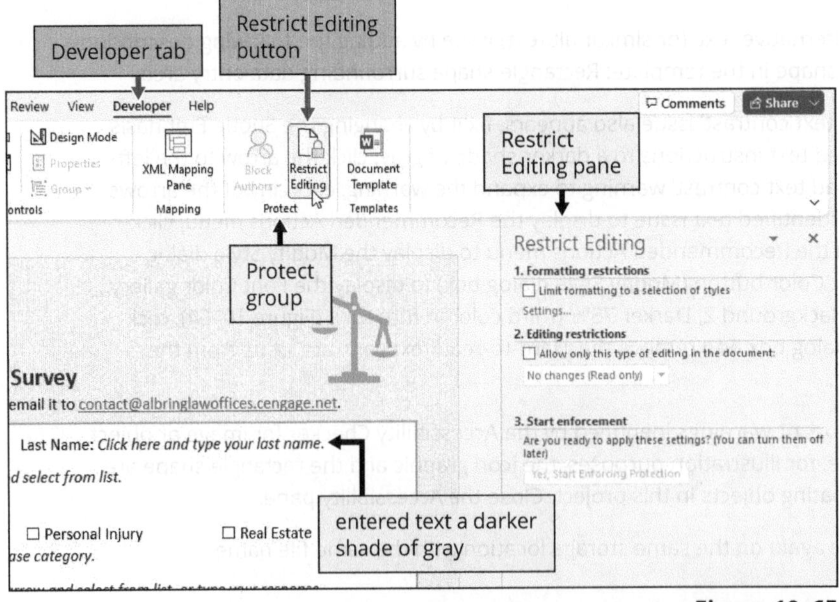

Figure 10-65

2

- In the Editing restrictions area, place a check mark in the 'Allow only this type of editing in the document' check box and then click its arrow to display a list of the types of allowed restrictions (Figure 10–66).

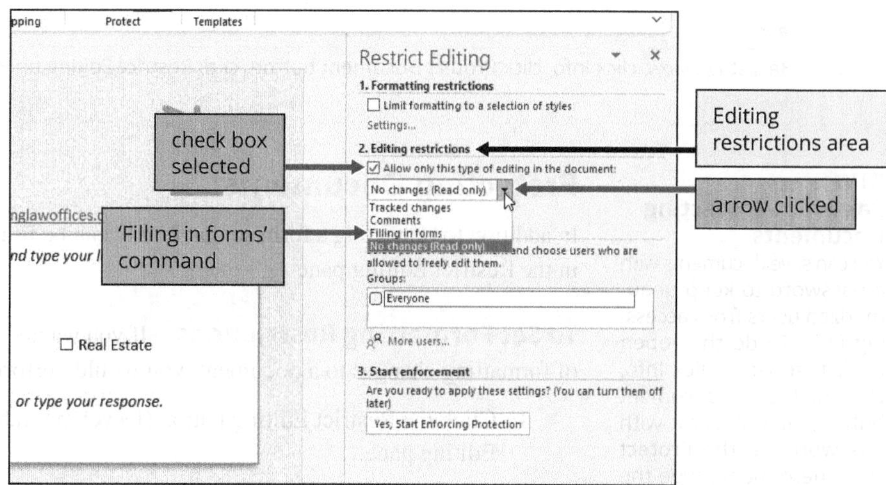

Figure 10–66

3

- Click 'Filling in forms' in the list to instruct Word that the only editing allowed in this document is to the content controls.
- In the Start enforcement area, click the 'Yes, Start Enforcing Protection' button, which displays the Start Enforcing Protection dialog box (Figure 10–67).

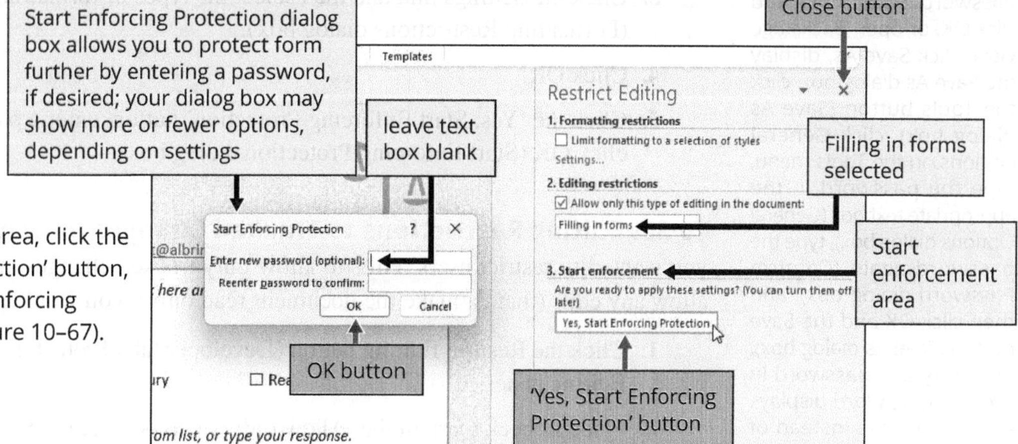

Figure 10–67

4

- Leave the text boxes empty in the Start Enforcing Protection dialog box and then click OK to protect the document without a password.

Q&A What if I enter a password?
If you enter a password, only a user who knows the password will be able to unprotect the document.

- Close the Restrict Editing pane to show the protected form (Figure 10–68).

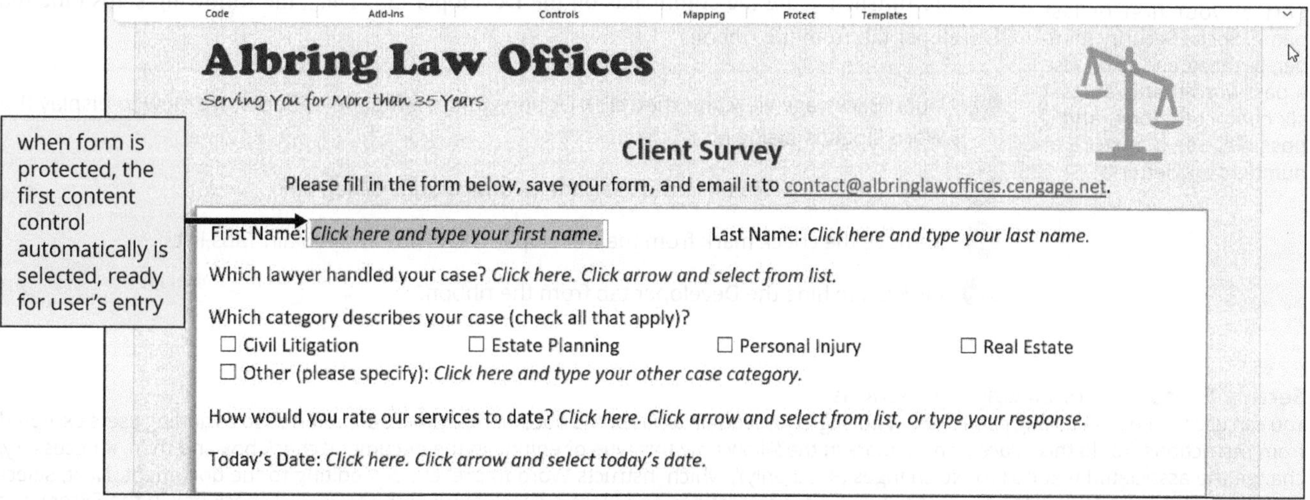

Figure 10–68

Other Ways

1. Open Backstage view, click Info, click Protect Document button, click Restrict Editing on Protect Document menu

BTW
Password-Protecting Documents
You can save documents with a password to keep unauthorized users from accessing files. To do this, open Backstage view, click Info, click the Protect Document button, click 'Encrypt with Password' on the Protect Document menu, type the password in the Encrypt Document dialog box, type the password again (Confirm Password dialog box), and click OK; or open Backstage view, click Save As, display the Save As dialog box, click the Tools button (Save As dialog box), click General Options on the Tools menu, type the password in the appropriate text box (General Options dialog box), type the password again (Confirm Password dialog box), and then click OK and the Save button (Save As dialog box). As you type a password in the text box, Word displays a series of dots instead of the actual characters so that others cannot view your password as you type it. To remove a password from a document, follow these steps, except leave the password text box blank.

Be sure to keep the password confidential. Choose a password that is easy to remember and that no one can guess. Do not use any part of your first or last name, Social Security number, birthday, and so on. Use a password that is at least six characters long, and if possible, use a mixture of numbers and letters.

Protecting Documents

In addition to protecting a form so that it only can be filled in, Word provides several other options in the Restrict Editing pane.

To Set Formatting Restrictions If you wanted to restrict users from making certain types of formatting changes to a document, you would perform the following steps.

1. Click the Restrict Editing button (Developer tab | Protect group) to open the Restrict Editing pane.
2. Place a check mark in the 'Limit formatting to a selection of styles' check box in the Formatting restrictions area.
3. Click the Settings link and then select the types of formatting you want to allow (Formatting Restrictions dialog box).
4. Click OK.
5. Click the 'Yes, Start Enforcing Protection' button, enter a password if desired, and then click OK (Start Enforcing Protection dialog box).

To Set Editing Restrictions to Tracked Changes or Comments or No Edits If you wanted to restrict users' edits to allow only tracked changes, allow only comments, or not allow any edits (that is, make the document read only), you would perform the following steps.

1. Click the Restrict Editing button (Developer tab | Protect group) to open the Restrict Editing pane.
2. Place a check mark in the 'Allow only this type of editing in the document' check box in the Editing restrictions area, click the arrow, and then click the desired option — that is, Tracked changes, Comments, or No changes (Read only) — to specify the types of edits allowed in the document.
3. Click the 'Yes, Start Enforcing Protection' button, enter a password if desired, and then click OK (Start Enforcing Protection dialog box).

To Hide the Developer Tab

You are finished using the commands on the Developer tab. Thus, the following steps hide the Developer tab from the ribbon.

1. Open Backstage view and then click Options in the left pane of Backstage view to display the Word Options dialog box.
2. Click Customize Ribbon in the left pane (Word Options dialog box).
3. Remove the check mark from the Developer check box in the Main Tabs list.
4. Click OK to hide the Developer tab from the ribbon.

BTW
Setting Exceptions to Editing Restrictions
You can use the Restrict Editing pane to allow editing in just certain areas of the document, a procedure referred to as adding users excepted from restrictions. To do this, place a check mark in the 'Allow only this type of editing in the document' check box and then, if necessary, change the associated text box to 'No changes (Read only)', which instructs Word to prevent any editing to the document. Next, select the placeholder text for which you want to waive user restrictions and place a check mark in the Everyone check box in the Exceptions (optional) area to instruct Word that the selected item can be edited — the rest of the form will be read only.

To Hide the Ruler, Collapse the Ribbon, Save the Template, and Exit Word

If the ruler is displayed on the screen, you want to hide it. You also want to collapse the ribbon so that when you test the form in the next steps, the ribbon is collapsed. Finally, the online form template for this project now is complete, so you can save the template again and exit Word. The following steps perform these tasks.

1. If the ruler is displayed on the screen, remove the check mark from the Ruler check box (View tab | Show group).
2. Click the 'Ribbon Display Options' button at the right edge of the ribbon to display the Ribbon Display Options menu and then click 'Show tabs only' on the Ribbon Display Options menu to collapse the ribbon. If necessary, scroll to display the entire form in the document window.
3. Save the template again on the same storage location with the same file name.
4. sam↑ Exit Word.

BTW
Protected Documents
If you open an existing form that has been protected, Word will not allow you to modify the form's appearance until you unprotect it. To unprotect a form (or any protected document), open the Restrict Editing pane by clicking the Restrict Editing button (Developer tab | Protect group) or open Backstage view, display the Info screen, click the Protect Document button, and click Restrict Editing on the Protect Document menu. Then, click the Stop Protection button in the Restrict Editing pane and close the pane. If this unencrypted document has been protected with a password, you will be asked to enter the password when you attempt to unprotect the document.

Working with an Online Form

When you create a template, you use the Open command in Backstage view to open the template so that you can modify it. After you have created a template, you then can make it available to users. Users do not open templates with the Open command in Word. Instead, a user creates a new Word document that is *based* on the template, which means the title bar displays the default file name, Document1 (or a similar name), rather than the template name. When Word creates a new document that is based on a template, the document window contains any text and formatting associated with the template. If a user accesses a letter template, for example, Word displays the contents of a basic letter in a new document window.

To Use File Explorer to Create a New Document That Is Based on a Template

When you save a template on storage media, as instructed earlier in this module, a user can create a new document that is based on the template through File Explorer. **Why?** This allows the user to work with a new document instead of risking the chance of altering the original template. The following steps create a new Word document that is based on the SC_WD_10_AlbringLawOfficesClientSurvey.dotx template.

1.
- Click the File Explorer button on the Windows taskbar to open a File Explorer window.
- Navigate to the location of the saved template (Figure 10-69).

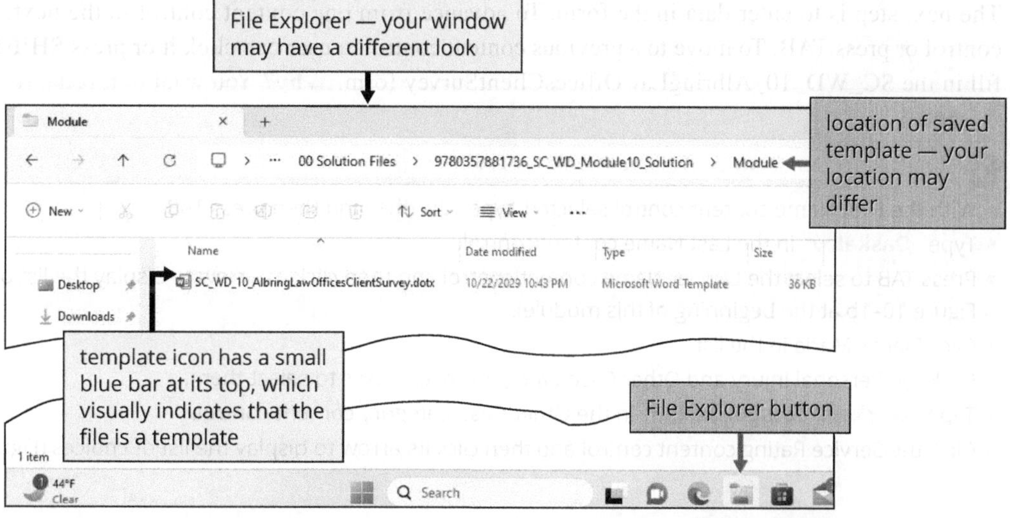

Figure 10-69

- Double-click the SC_WD_10_AlbringLawOfficesClientSurvey.dotx file in the File Explorer window, which starts Word and creates a new document that is based on the contents of the selected template (Figure 10–70). If necessary, scroll slightly so that the entire form is displayed in the document window.

Q&A Why did my background page color disappear?
If the background page color does not appear, open Backstage view, click Options to display the Word Options dialog box, click Advanced in the left pane (Word Options dialog box), scroll to the Show document content section, place a check mark in the 'Show background colors and images in Print Layout view' check box, and then click OK.

Why does my ribbon show only three tabs: File, Tools, and View?
Your screen is in Read mode. Click the View tab and then click Edit Document to switch to Print Layout view.

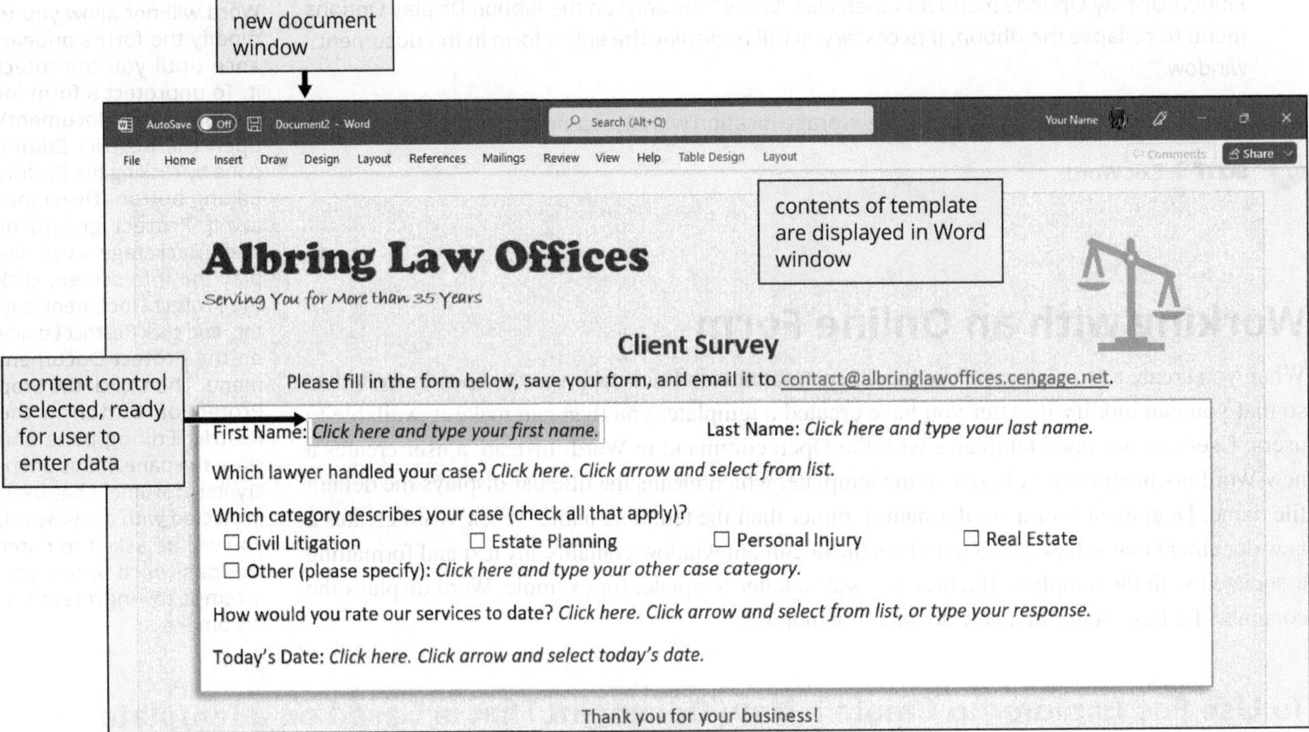

Figure 10–70

To Fill in a Form and Save It

The next step is to enter data in the form. To advance from one content control to the next, a user can click the content control or press TAB. To move to a previous content control, a user can click it or press SHIFT+TAB. The following steps fill in the SC_WD_10_AlbringLawOfficesClientSurvey form. **Why?** You want to test the form to be sure it works as you intended.

- With the First Name content control selected, type **Cyrille** and then press TAB.
- Type **Daskalov** in the Last Name content control.
- Press TAB to select the Lawyer Name content control and then click its arrow to display the list of choices (shown in Figure 10–1b at the beginning of this module).
- Click Pierre, Maria in the list.
- Click the Personal Injury and Other Case Category check boxes to select them.
- Type **Workers' Compensation** in the Other Case Category content control.
- Click the Service Rating content control and then click its arrow to display the list of choices (Figure 10–71).

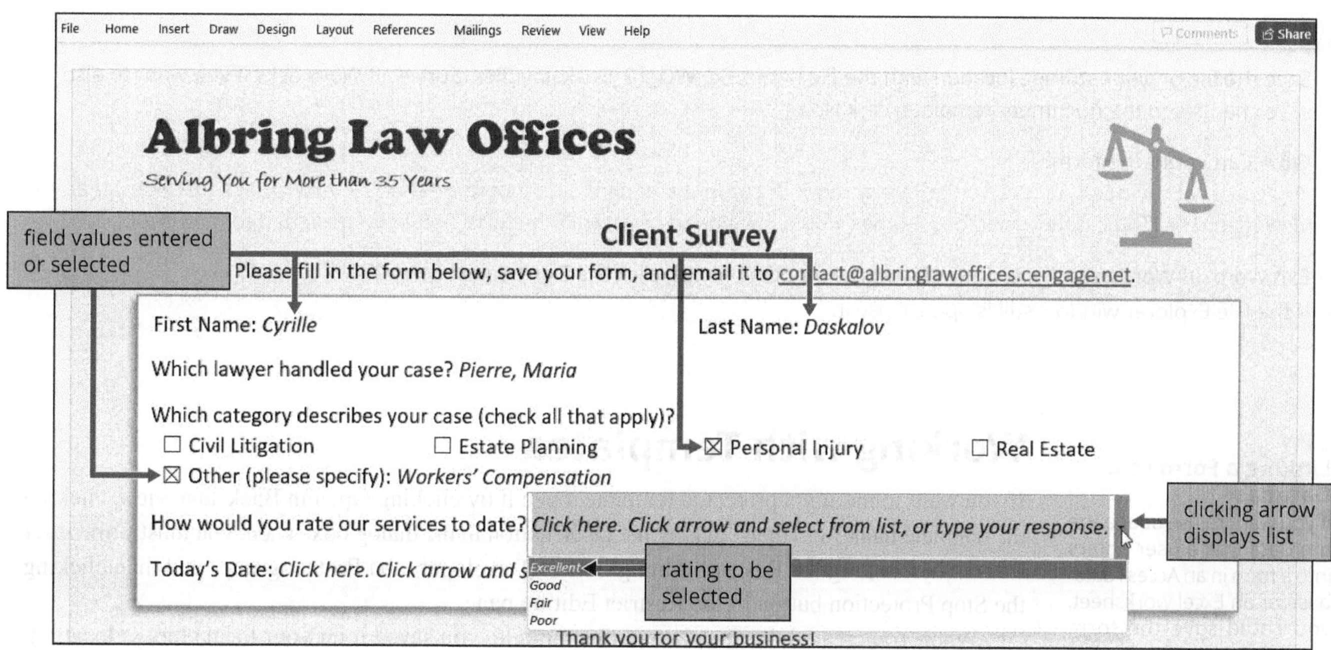

Figure 10–71

- Select Excellent in the list.
- Click the Today's Date content control and then click its arrow to display a calendar (Figure 10–72).

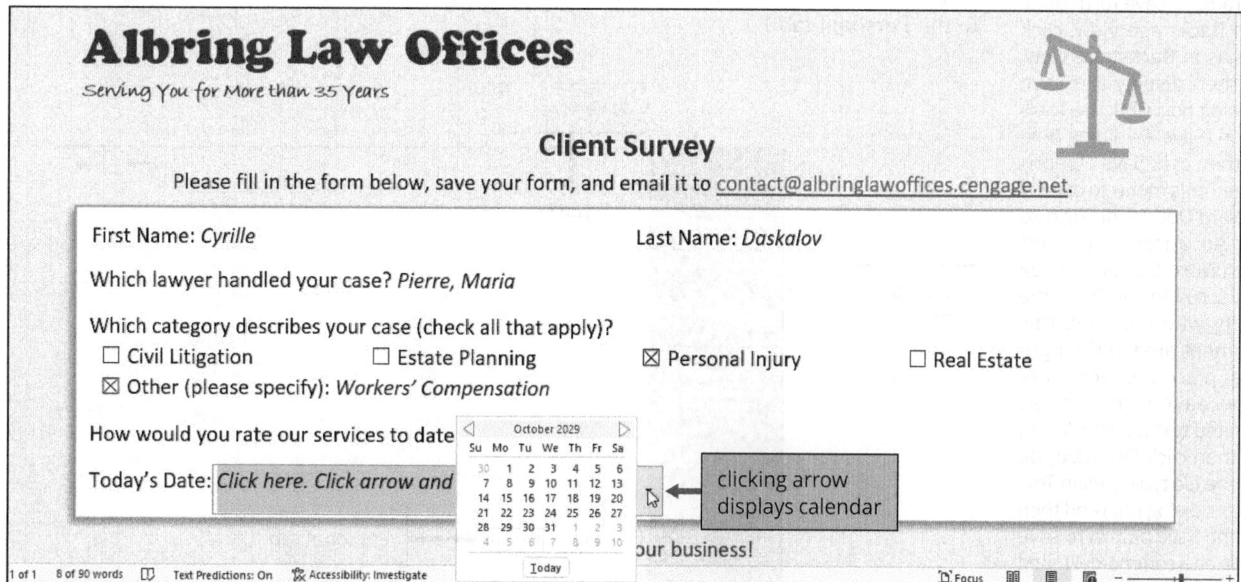

Figure 10–72

3

- Click October 29, 2029 in the calendar to complete the data entry (shown in Figure 10–1c at the beginning of this module).

- Save the file on your storage location with the file name, SC_WD_10_DaskalovClientSurvey. If Word asks if you want to also save changes to the document template, click No.

Q&A Can I print the form?
You can print the document as you print any other document. Keep in mind, however, that the colors used were designed for viewing online. Thus, different color schemes would have been selected if the form had been designed for a printout.

- Exit Word. (If Word asks if you want to save the modified styles, click the Don't Save button.)
- If the File Explorer window still is open, close it.

Working with Templates

If you want to modify a protected template, open it by clicking Open in Backstage view, clicking the template name, and then clicking the Open button in the dialog box. Then, you must **unprotect a form** by clicking the Restrict Editing button (Developer tab | Protect group) and then clicking the Stop Protection button in the Restrict Editing pane.

When you created the template in this module, you saved it on your local storage location. In environments other than an academic setting, you would not save the template on your own storage location; instead, you would save the file in the Custom Office Templates folder. When you save a template in the Custom Office Templates folder, you can locate the template by opening Backstage view, clicking New to display the New screen, and then clicking the Personal tab in the New screen, which displays the template in the New screen (Figure 10–73). (Note that you may need to exit Word and restart the app for the Personal tab to appear. Depending on settings, your templates may be stored in a different location and not appear in the Personal tab.)

BTW
Linking a Form to a Database
If you want to use or analyze the data that a user enters into a form in an Access database or an Excel worksheet, you could save the form data in a comma-delimited text file. This file separates each data item with a comma and places quotation marks around text data items. Then, you can use Access or Excel to import the comma-delimited text file for use in the respective program. To save form data, open Backstage view, click Save As in Backstage view, and then display the Save As dialog box. Click the Tools button (Save As dialog box) and then click Save Options on the Tools menu to display the Word Options dialog box. Click Advanced in the left pane (Word Options dialog box), scroll to the Preserve fidelity when sharing this document area in the right pane, place a check mark in the 'Save form data as delimited text file' check box, and then click OK. Next, be sure the file type is Plain Text (Save As dialog box) and then click the Save button to save the file as a comma-delimited text file. You can import the resulting comma-delimited file in an Access database or an Excel worksheet. To convert successfully, you should use the legacy controls (i.e., text form field, check box form field, etc.), which are available through the Legacy Tools button (Developer tab | Controls group).

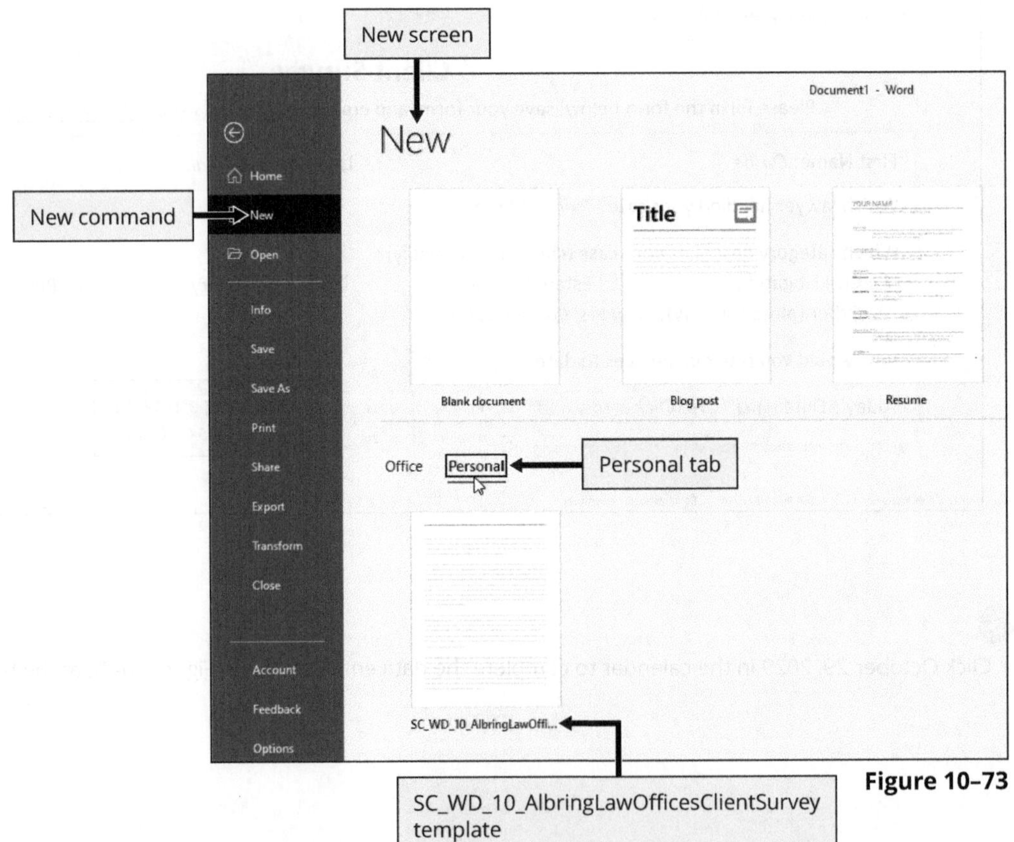

Figure 10–73

Summary

In this module, you learned how to create an online form. Topics covered included saving a document as a template, changing paper size, inserting and formatting icons, using a table to control document layout, showing the Developer tab, inserting and formatting content controls, editing placeholder text, changing properties of content controls, and protecting a form.

BTW
Picture Content Controls
Note that some versions of Word do not allow a picture to be inserted into a picture content control if the form is protected; in this case, you will need to unprotect the form to use the Picture content control.

Consider This: Plan Ahead

What decisions will you need to make when creating online forms?

Use these guidelines as you complete the assignments in this module and create your own online forms outside of this class.

1. Design the form.
   a) To minimize the time spent creating a form while using a computer or mobile device, consider sketching the form on a piece of paper first.
   b) Design a well-thought-out draft of the form — being sure to include all essential form elements, including the form's title, text and graphics, data entry fields, and data entry instructions.
2. For each data entry field, determine its field type and/or list of possible values that it can contain.
3. Save the form as a template, instead of as a Word document, to simplify the data entry process for users of the form.
4. Create a functional and visually appealing form.
   a) Use colors that complement one another.
   b) Draw the user's attention to important sections.
   c) Arrange data entry fields in logical groups on the form and in an order that users would expect.
   d) Data entry instructions should be succinct and easy to understand.
   e) Ensure that users can enter and edit data only in designated areas of the form.
5. Determine how the form data will be analyzed.
   a) If the data entered in the form will be analyzed by a program outside of Word, create the data entry fields so that the entries are stored in separate fields that can be shared with other programs.
6. Test the form, ensuring it works as you intended.
   a) Fill in the form as if you are a user.
   b) Ask others to fill in the form to be sure it is organized in a logical manner and is easy to understand and complete.
   c) If any errors or weaknesses in the form are identified, correct them and test the form again.
7. Publish or distribute the form.
   a) Not only does an online form reduce the need for paper, it saves the time spent making copies of the form and distributing it.
   b) When the form is complete, post it on social media, the web, or your company's intranet, or email it to targeted recipients.

Student Assignments

Apply Your Knowledge

Reinforce the skills and apply the concepts you learned in this module.

Working with an Online Form

Note: To complete this assignment, you will be required to use the Data Files. Please contact your instructor for information about accessing the Data Files.

Instructions: Start Word. Open the template, SC_WD_10-1.dotx, which is located in the Data Files. The template is a draft of an online student survey, created by your school's tutoring center, that will be emailed to students who have used the center. You are to modify the template. The final template is shown in Figure 10–74.

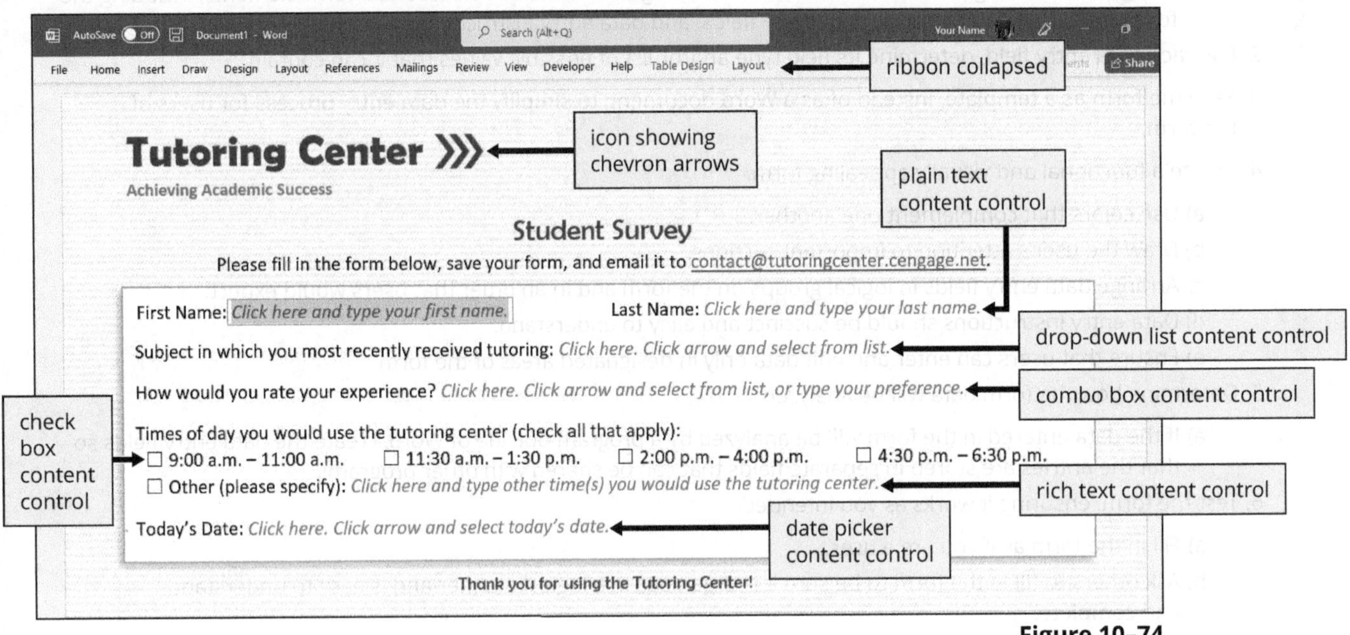

Figure 10–74

1. Click File on the ribbon and then click Save As and save the document using the new file name, SC_WD_10_TutoringCenterStudentSurvey. (**Hint:** If the background page color does not appear, open Backstage view, click Options to display the Word Options dialog box, click Advanced in the left pane (Word Options dialog box), scroll to the Show document content section, place a check mark in the 'Show background colors and images in Print Layout view' check box, and then click OK.)
2. Add the page color 'Gold, Accent 4, Lighter 40%' to the template. Apply the Stripes: Slashes pattern fill effect to the template. (**Hint:** Use the Page Color button (Design tab | Page Background group).)
3. Remove the table border from each of the two tables in the form. (**Hint:** One at a time, select each table using the Select button (contextual Layout tab | Table group) and then use the Borders arrow (Table Design tab | Borders group).)
4. If necessary, use the View Gridlines button (contextual Layout tab | Table group) to show table gridlines.
5. If necessary, show the Developer tab on the ribbon.
6. In the 2 × 1 table in the data entry area, in the cell to the right of the First Name content control, enter the text, Last Name:, followed by a space as the label and then use the Developer tab to insert a plain text content control in the cell after the label.

7. Select the inserted plain text content control and then turn on Design mode. Edit the placeholder text so that it reads: Click here and type your last name. Turn off Design mode.
8. Change the properties of the plain text content control as follows: enter Last Name as the tag, select the 'Use a style to format text typed into the empty control' check box, select the Intense Emphasis style for the text to be typed in the content control, and select the 'Content control cannot be deleted' check box. (Note that Bounding Box should remain in the Show as box.)
9. Use the Styles group in the Home tab to format the placeholder text in the plain text content control to the Intense Emphasis style.
10. In the data entry area, to the right of the type of the subject prompt, insert a drop-down list content control.
11. Select the inserted drop-down list content control and then turn on Design mode. Edit the placeholder text so that it contains two sentences that read: Click here. Click arrow and select from list. When you have finished editing the placeholder text, turn off Design mode.
12. Change the properties of the drop-down list content control as follows: enter Subject as the tag, select the 'Use a style to format text typed into the empty control' check box, select the Intense Emphasis style for the text to be typed in the content control, select the 'Content control cannot be deleted' check box, and set these six choices for the list: Math, English (Language), English (Literature), History, Foreign Language, Science. (Be sure to delete the default choice of Choose an item.)
13. Use the Styles group on the Home tab to format the placeholder text in the drop-down list content control to the Intense Emphasis style.
14. In the data entry area, to the right of the experience rating question, insert a combo box content control.
15. Select the inserted combo box content control and then turn on Design mode. Edit the placeholder text so that it contains two sentences that read: Click here. Click arrow and select from list, or type your preference. When you have finishing editing the placeholder text, turn off Design mode.
16. Change the properties of the combo box content control as follows: enter Experience Rating as the tag, select the 'Use a style to format text typed into the empty control' check box, select the Intense Emphasis style for the text to be typed in the content control, select the 'Content control cannot be deleted' check box, and set these three choices for the list: Extremely Helpful, Fairly Helpful, Not Helpful. (Be sure to delete the default choice of Choose an item.)
17. Use the Styles group in the Home tab to format the placeholder text in the combo box content control to the Intense Emphasis style.
18. In the 4 × 1 table in the data entry area, in the cell to the right of the 11:30 a.m. – 1:30 p.m. content control (the third cell), insert a check box content control.
19. Change the properties of the check box content control as follows: enter 2:00 p.m. – 4:00 p.m. as the tag, select the Show as box and then select None, and select the 'Content control cannot be deleted' check box.
20. One blank space to the right of the inserted check box content control, enter 2:00 p.m. – 4:00 p.m. as the label.
21. In the 4 × 1 table in the data entry area, in the cell to the right of the 2:00 p.m. – 4:00 p.m. content control (the last cell), insert a check box content control.
22. Change the properties of the check box content control as follows: enter 4:30 p.m. – 6:30 p.m. as the tag, select the Show as box and then select None, and select the 'Content control cannot be deleted' check box.
23. One space to the right of the inserted check box content control, enter the text, 4:30 p.m. – 6:30 p.m., as the label.
24. In the data entry area, to the right of the 'Other (please specify):' check box, insert a rich text content control.
25. Select the inserted rich text content control and then turn on Design mode. Edit the placeholder text so that it reads: Click here and type other time(s) you would use the tutoring center. Turn off Design mode.
26. Change the properties of the rich text content control as follows: enter Other Times as the tag, select the 'Use a style to format text typed into the empty control' check box, select the Intense Emphasis style for the text to be typed in the content control, and select the 'Content control cannot be deleted' check box.

Continued on next page

27. Use the Styles group on the Home tab to format the placeholder text in the rich text content control to the Intense Emphasis style.
28. At the bottom of the data entry area, to the right of the Today's Date: label, insert a Date Picker content control.
29. Select the inserted date picker content control and then turn on Design mode. Edit the placeholder text so that it contains two sentences that read: Click here. Click arrow and select today's date. When you have finished editing the placeholder text, turn off Design mode.
30. Change the properties of the date picker content control as follows: enter Today's Date as the tag, select the 'Use a style to format text typed into the empty control' check box, select the Intense Emphasis style for the text to be typed in the content control, select the 'Content control cannot be deleted' check box, and select the date in this format: M/d/yyyy.
31. Use the Styles group on the Home tab to format the placeholder text in the date picker content control to the Intense Emphasis style.
32. If table gridlines show, hide them. (**Hint:** Position the insertion point in one of the two tables in the form and then use the View Gridlines button (contextual Layout tab | Table group).)
33. Collapse the ribbon. If necessary, adjust spacing above and below paragraphs as necessary so that all contents fit on a single screen with the ribbon collapsed.
34. Use the Restrict Editing pane to set editing restrictions to filling in forms and then start enforcing protection (do not use a password). Close the Restrict Editing pane.
35. Check accessibility, leaving the accessibility errors or warnings identified by the Accessibility Checker for image or object not inline because, for illustration purposes, the icon and shape are intended to be floating objects in this assignment. Save the form again with the same file name and then submit it in the format specified by your instructor. Close the template and exit Word.
36. Open a File Explorer window. Locate the SC_WD_10_TutoringCenterStudentSurvey.dotx template you just created and then double-click the template in File Explorer to create a new document based on the template.
37. When Word displays a new document based on the template, if necessary, collapse the ribbon, hide formatting marks, and change the zoom to page width. Your screen should appear like Figure 10–74 and display Document1 (or a similar name) on the title bar instead of the file name.
38. Test your form as follows:
    a. With the First Name content control selected, enter your first name.
    b. Press TAB and then enter your last name in the last name content control.
    c. Click the Subject content control, click its arrow, and then click Science in the list.
    d. Click the Experience Rating content control to select it, click its arrow, and press ESC because you prefer to enter a different response. Enter the text, Helpful, but it was loud in the tutoring center., as the response.
    e. Click the 9:00 a.m. – 11:00 a.m. and 4:30 p.m. – 6:30 p.m. check boxes to select them.
    f. Click the Other check box. If necessary, click the Other text box and then enter 7:00 p.m. – 9:00 p.m. in the text box.
    g. Click the Today's Date content control, click the arrow to display a calendar, and then select today's date in the calendar.
    h. Close the form without saving it. (If any content controls do not work as intended, use Word to open the SC_WD_10_TutoringCenterStudentSurvey.dotx template, unprotect the template, modify it as appropriate, protect the template again, save it, and then retest it as described in this step.)
39. **Consider This:** If the tutoring center wanted the student's middle name on the same line as the first and last names, how would you evenly space the three items across the line?

Extend Your Knowledge

Extend the skills you learned in this module and experiment with new skills. You may need to use Help to complete the assignment.

Working with Icons, Picture Content Controls, Passwords, and More

Note: To complete this assignment, you will be required to use the Data Files. Please contact your instructor for information about accessing the Data Files.

Instructions: Start Word. Open the template, SC_WD_10-2.dotx, which is located in the Data Files. This template is a draft of an online parade entry form for the Hartford Township Pet Palooza.

You will unprotect the form, insert and format icons, group images, insert a picture content control in a text box, practice inserting repeating section and building block gallery content controls, change a shape's shadow color, customize theme colors, and protect a document (form, in this case) with passwords.

Perform the following tasks:

1. Use Help to review and expand your knowledge about these topics: unprotecting documents, picture content controls, text boxes, grouping objects, shadows, shape fill effects, changing theme colors, and protecting forms with passwords.
2. Click File on the ribbon, click Save As, and then save the template using the new file name, SC_WD_10_ParadeEntryForm.
3. Unprotect the document. (**Hint:** Use the Developer tab on the ribbon or the Info screen in Backstage view.) Save the template again.
4. Change the paper size to a width of 8.5 inches and a height of 4 inches.
5. Insert two appropriate icons of your choice in the template. (**Hint:** Use the Icons button (Insert tab | Illustrations group). If your version of Word does not include the Icons button, insert two appropriate images using the Online Picture button or insert the images that are called Support_WD_10_Cat.png and Support_WD_10_Dog.png from the Data Files.)
6. Change the wrapping of each of the inserted images to In Front of Text. For only one of the images, change the color, fill, outline, effects, rotation, size, or style to options of your choice. Move the two images on the page so that they overlap each other. Select the image on the top and send it backward. (**Hint:** Right-click the image and then use commands on the submenu or use buttons in the Arrange group on the ribbon.) Select the image on the bottom and bring it forward. Select the image on top and send it to the back. Select the image on the bottom and bring it to the front.
7. For the image you have not yet formatted, change its color, fill, outline, effects, rotation, size, or style to options of your choice.
8. Move one image on one side of the form title and the other image on the other side. Use gridlines, if necessary, to help position the images. (**Hint:** Click Align button (Graphics Format tab | Arrange group) and then click View Gridlines.) Resize the images as appropriate.
9. Group the two images at the top of the form together. Move the grouped graphics. Return them to their original location.
10. Select the form title (Pet Palooza!) and then use the 'Text Effects and Typography' button (Home tab | Font group) to add a reflection of your choice to the form title. Change the font size of the form title as you deem appropriate. Format the subtitle as you deem appropriate. Adjust spacing above and below paragraphs as necessary so that the entire form fits on a single page.
11. Change the Pet Birthday content control to a format other than M/d/yyyy (i.e., 2/16/2029).
12. Insert a simple text box to the right of the text, Parade Entry Form, and then resize and move the text box into the empty space on the right side of the data entry area. (**Hint:** Click the Text Box button (Insert tab | Text group) and then click 'Simple Text Box' in the Text Box gallery.) Change the wrapping of the inserted text box to In Front of Text. Resize the text box so that it fits completely in the data entry area. Remove space after the paragraph. Delete the rectangle shape and placeholder text in the text box.

Continued on next page

13. In the text box, type the label, Pet Photo:, and then resize and format the text as necessary. (Note that you will need to change case so that the label does not appear in uppercase letters.) Below the label, insert a picture content control in the text box. Resize the picture content control so that it fits in the text box and then center both the picture and label in the text box (Figure 10–75). If necessary, remove the border from the text box. Change the properties of the picture content control as follows: enter Pet Photo: as the tag and select the 'Content control cannot be deleted' check box.

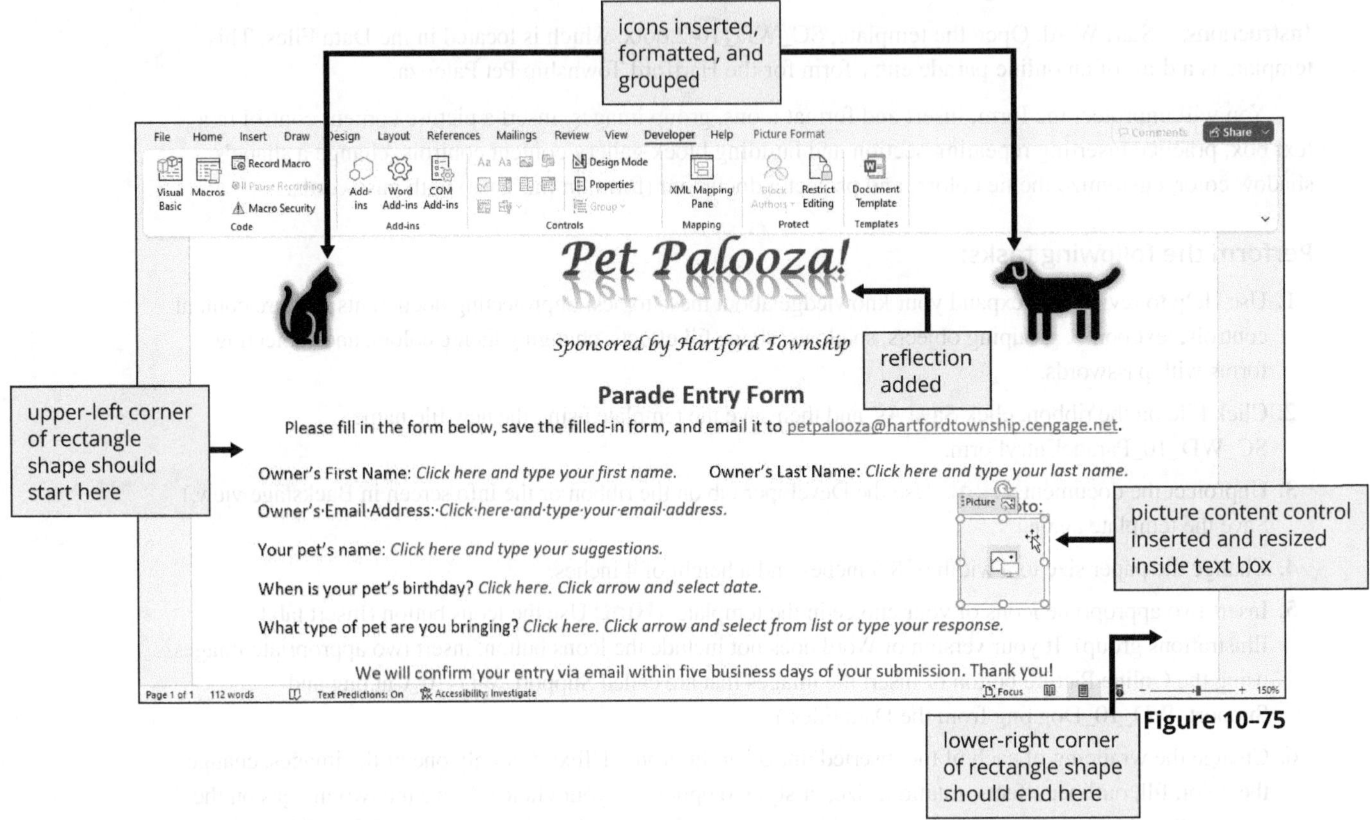

Figure 10–75

14. Save the template again. If necessary, position the insertion point in the text, First Name, and then display table gridlines. Select the table in the data entry area (the owner's first name and last name row) by clicking the Select button (contextual Layout tab | Table group) and then clicking Select Table. Insert a repeating section content control. Click the insert control (the plus sign) at the far-right edge of the table with the repeating section content control. (Depending on your version of Word, the repeating section content control may not display the insert control properly; if this occurs, close the template without saving it again, reopen the template, and proceed to Step 15.) What happens when you click the insert control? Click the Undo button (Home tab | Undo group) to undo the added duplicate table row. Click the Undo button again to undo the insert of the repeating section content control or delete the content control manually.

15. Click to the right of the last line on the template. Insert a building block gallery content control. Click the Properties button (Developer tab | Controls group) to display the Content Control Properties dialog box. Change the value in the Gallery box in the Document Building Block Properties area to Equations and then click OK. In the template, click the 'Explore Quick Parts' button attached to the top of the building block gallery content control. What is displayed when you click this button? Delete the building block gallery content control by right-clicking it and then clicking 'Remove Content Control' on the shortcut menu.

16. Hide table gridlines, if they are showing.

17. Add a page color of your choice to the template. Apply a pattern fill effect of your choice to the page color background.

18. Insert a rectangle shape around the data entry area (starting in the upper-left corner by the First Name label and ending in the lower-right corner to the right of the Pet Type combo box content control).

19. Send the rectangle shape backward, which sends the shape back one layer. Send the rectangle shape behind text. Note that in this case, these two commands may yield the same result.
20. Change the shape fill in the rectangle shape to a color of your choice. Change the shape outline on the rectangle shape to a color or style of your choice. If necessary, change the font color or style of text in the data entry area so that it is readable on the background color.
21. Add a shadow to the rectangle and then change the color of the shadow on the rectangle to a color other than the default.
22. Customize the theme colors for the hyperlink to a color of your choice (**Hint:** Use the Customize Colors command in Colors gallery (Design tab | Document Formatting group).) Save the modified theme colors.
23. Make any necessary formatting changes to the form.
24. If requested by your instructor, change the email address above the data entry area to your email address.
25. Restrict formatting in the document using the 'Limit formatting to a selection of styles' check box. Click the Settings link (Restrict Editing pane) and then select document formatting restrictions. Remove the formatting restrictions just set in the form.
26. Restrict editing in the document to tracked changes. Change the restrict editing selection to comments. Finally, restrict editing to filling in the form and protect the unencrypted form using the word, pet, as the password in the Start Enforcing Protection dialog box. What is the purpose of this password?
27. If requested by your instructor, use the Info screen in Backstage view to encrypt the document with a password. Use the word, pet, as the password. (**Hint:** You will need to use the Restrict Editing pane to remove the password added in the previous step before you can complete this step.) What is the purpose of this password? (Note that to delete the password, you would remove the password in the Password text box in the Encrypt Document dialog box.)
28. Add missing alt text to the images in the template. (Leave the last errors or warnings identified by the Accessibility Checker for image or object not inline because, for illustration purposes, the text box and group are intended to be floating objects in this assignment.) Save the form again with the same name and then submit it in the format specified by your instructor. Close the template and exit Word.
29. Test the form using your own data for the responses. When filling in the form, use your own photo for the pet photo or use the picture called Support_WD_10_PetPhoto in the Data Files for the picture content control. (Note that some versions of Word do not allow a picture to be inserted into a picture content control if the form is protected; in this case, you will need to unprotect the form and then test the form.) If required by your instructor, save the filled-in form and then submit it in the format specified by your instructor.
30. **Consider This:** Answer the questions posed in #14, #15, #26, and #27. What is the advantage of grouping graphics? Besides changing the color of the shadow, what other shadow settings can you adjust?

Expand Your World

Create a solution that uses cloud or web technologies by learning and investigating on your own from general guidance.

Using Microsoft Forms to Create an Online Survey

Instructions: You will use Microsoft Forms, which is part of Microsoft 365, to prepare an online form. As a marketing coordinator at Oakwood County Public Library, you will create an online request for information form. Figure 10–76 shows the bottom portion of the survey. You will enter the questions in Microsoft Forms and then use its tools to enter settings for the responses.

Perform the following tasks:

1. Start a browser. Search for the text, Microsoft Forms, using a search engine. Visit websites to learn about Microsoft Forms. Navigate to the Microsoft Forms website. You will need to sign in to your OneDrive account.
2. Create a new form using Microsoft Forms.

Continued on next page

3. Enter the text, Oakwood County Public Library, as the form title, and the text, Event Survey, as the form description.
4. Click the Add new button. Select Choice as the type of question. Enter the text, Which type of event did you attend at our library?, in the text box. Enter these three options: Author Lecture, Book Discussion, Children's Program. Add an 'Other' option. Make this question required.
5. Click the Add new button. Select Date as the type of question. Enter the text, On what date did you attend the event?, in the text box. Make this question required.
6. Click the Add new button. Select Rating as the type of question. Enter the text, How would you rate the event you attended (with five stars being the highest rating)?, in the text box. Make this question required.
7. Click the Add new button. Select Text as the type of question. Enter the text, What suggestions do you have for future library events?, in the text box. Make this question required.
8. Add an appropriate style to the form.
9. Preview the form on a computer (Figure 10–76). (**Hint:** Adjust the zoom in the browser window to display more of the form in the window at once.) Take a screenshot of the preview (using the Print Screen key or a screen capture app) and submit the screenshot in the format requested by your instructor. Save the screenshot with the file name, SC_WD_10_OakwoodEventSurvey_inForms.

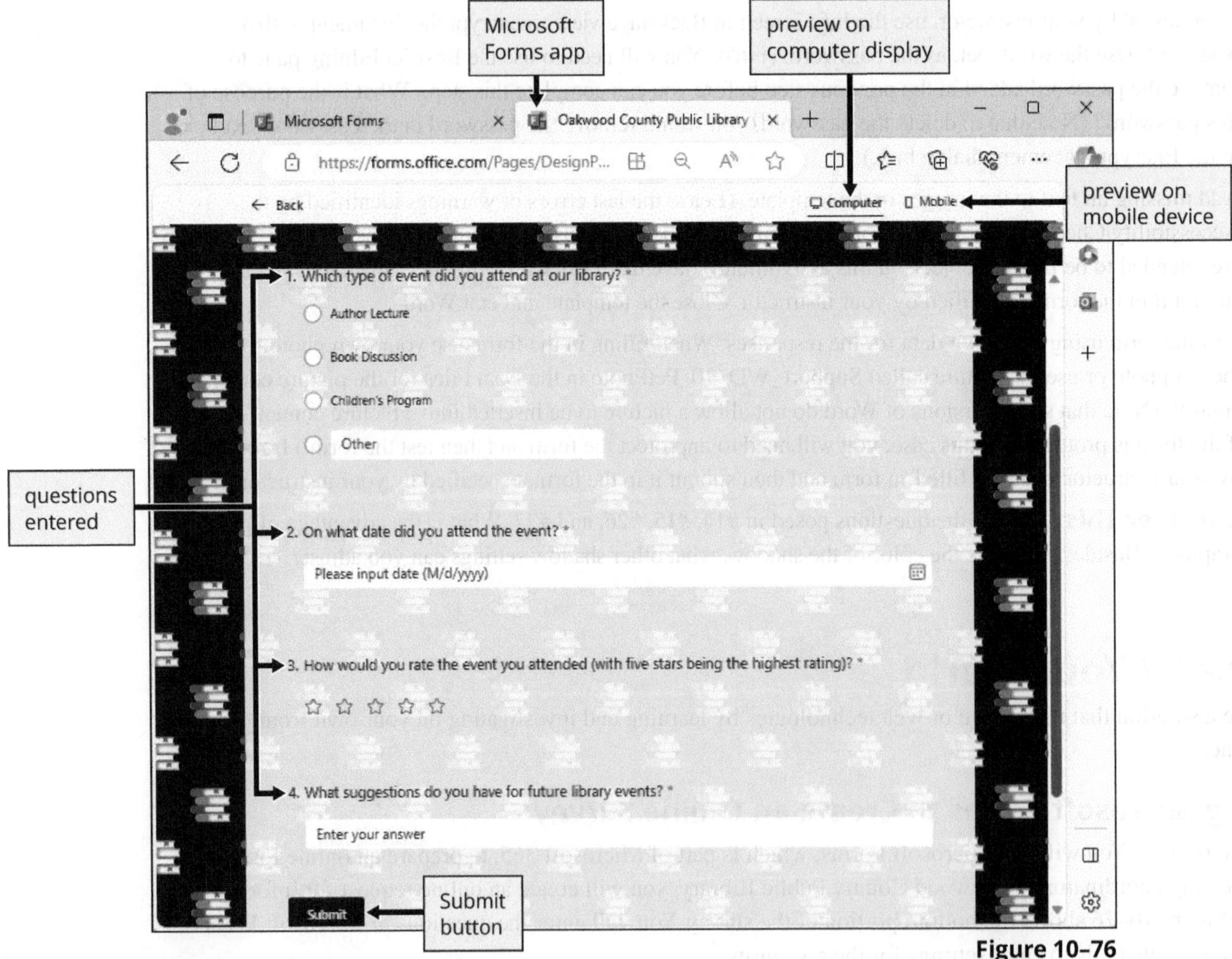

Figure 10–76

10. Preview the form on a mobile device. Click the Back button to return to the form design screen.
11. Click the 'More form settings' button in the upper-right corner of the screen, click Settings on the menu, and review the additional form settings options.

12. Click the Collect responses button and review the options.
13. If requested by your instructor, copy the form link and email it to your instructor.
14. Copy the form link. Open a new browser tab and paste the link into the browser address bar. Fill in the form in the new browser window using responses of your choice and then click the Submit button.
15. Redisplay your form window and then click the Responses tab and notice how Microsoft Forms tabulates results.
16. Close the Microsoft Forms window. If necessary, sign out of your OneDrive account.
17. **Consider This:** What is Microsoft Forms? Do you prefer using Microsoft Forms or the Word desktop app to create online forms? Why?

In the Lab

Design and implement a solution using creative thinking and problem-solving skills.

Create an Online Form for a Retail Store

Note: To complete this assignment, you may be required to use the Data Files. Please contact your instructor for information about accessing the Data Files.

Problem: As the customer relations manager at Natural Surplus, you have been asked to create an online customer survey.

Part 1: Create a template that contains the company name (Natural Surplus), the company's tag line (Get Healthy … Stay Healthy!), and an appropriate image that you obtain from the icons or online images, or use the Support_WD_10_ShoppingCart.png image in the Data Files. The third line should have the text, Customer Survey. The fourth line should read: Please fill in the form below, save the filled-in form, and then email it to survey@naturalsurplus.cengage.net.

The data entry area should contain the following:

- First Name and Last Name are plain text content controls within a table.
- A drop-down list content control with the label, How did you make your most recent purchase?, has these choices: In Store, Online, Phone.
- The following instruction should appear above these check boxes: Product lines you would like to be offered/expanded (check all that apply)?; the check boxes are Gluten Free, Organics, Plant Based, Supplements, Green Cleaning, Cosmetics, Household, Personal Care, and Other (please specify).
- A rich text content control after the Other (please specify) label allows customers to enter their own response.
- A combo box content control with the label, What is your age range?, has these choices: 18-25, 26-35, 36-50, 51-70, over 70.
- A date picker content control with the label, On what date was your most recent purchase at our store?
- On the line below the data entry area, include the text: Thank you for your business!

Use the concepts and techniques presented in this module to create and format the online form. Use meaningful placeholder text for all content controls. (For example, the placeholder text for the First Name plain text content control could be as follows: Click here and type your first name.) Apply a style to the placeholder text. Assign names, styles, and locking to each content control (so that the content controls cannot be deleted). Draw a rectangle around the data entry area of the form and format the rectangle appropriately. Add a page color. Be sure to change the page size and margins, and adjust spacing as necessary above and below paragraphs, so that the entire form fits in the document window.

Continued on next page

Add missing alt text to the images in the template. (Leave the errors or warnings identified by the Accessibility Checker for image or object not inline because, for illustration purposes, some items are intended to be floating objects in this assignment.) When you are finished creating the form, protect it so that editing is restricted to filling in the form and then save it as a template with the file name, SC_WD_10_NaturalSurplusCustomerSurvey. Test the form and make any necessary corrections. Submit the form in the format specified by your instructor.

Part 2: **Consider This:** You made several decisions while creating the online form in this assignment: placeholder text to use, which graphics to use, and how to organize and format the online form (fonts, font sizes, styles, colors, etc.). What was the rationale behind each of these decisions? When you proofread and tested the online form, what further revisions did you make, and why? How would you recommend publishing or distributing this online form?

Enhancing an Online Form and Using Macros

Objectives

After completing this module, you will be able to:

- Save a macro-enabled template
- Unprotect a document
- Specify macro settings
- Convert a table to text
- Insert and edit a field
- Create and modify styles
- Format a page color
- Change a shape
- Format a shape
- Format a picture
- Insert and format a text box and its text
- Group objects
- Create, run, and edit macros
- Customize the Quick Access Toolbar
- Insert and format 3-D models

Introduction

Word provides many tools that allow you to improve the appearance, functionality, and security of your documents. This module discusses tools used to perform the following tasks:

- Modify text and content controls.
- Enhance with color, shapes, effects, and graphics.
- Automate a series of tasks with a macro.

Project: Revised Online Form

In Module 10, you created an online form for Albring Law Offices. Since the form was created, Hadley Albring retired and sold his practice to Maria Pierre, one of his partners. Thus, the name of the firm changed from Albring Law Offices to Pierre Law Offices, and the email address changed accordingly. Due to this transition, Maria also hired Cyrille Daskalov to take over Hadley's case load.

To give the form created in Module 10 a renewed appearance, Maria requested that some of its colors and graphics be changed. Other required updates to the form included changing the firm name, email address, and drop-down list. This module uses Word to improve the visual appearance of and add macros to the updated online form for Pierre Law Offices, producing the online form shown in Figure 11–1a. This project begins with the updated online form for Pierre Law Offices and then enhances it and improves its functionality.

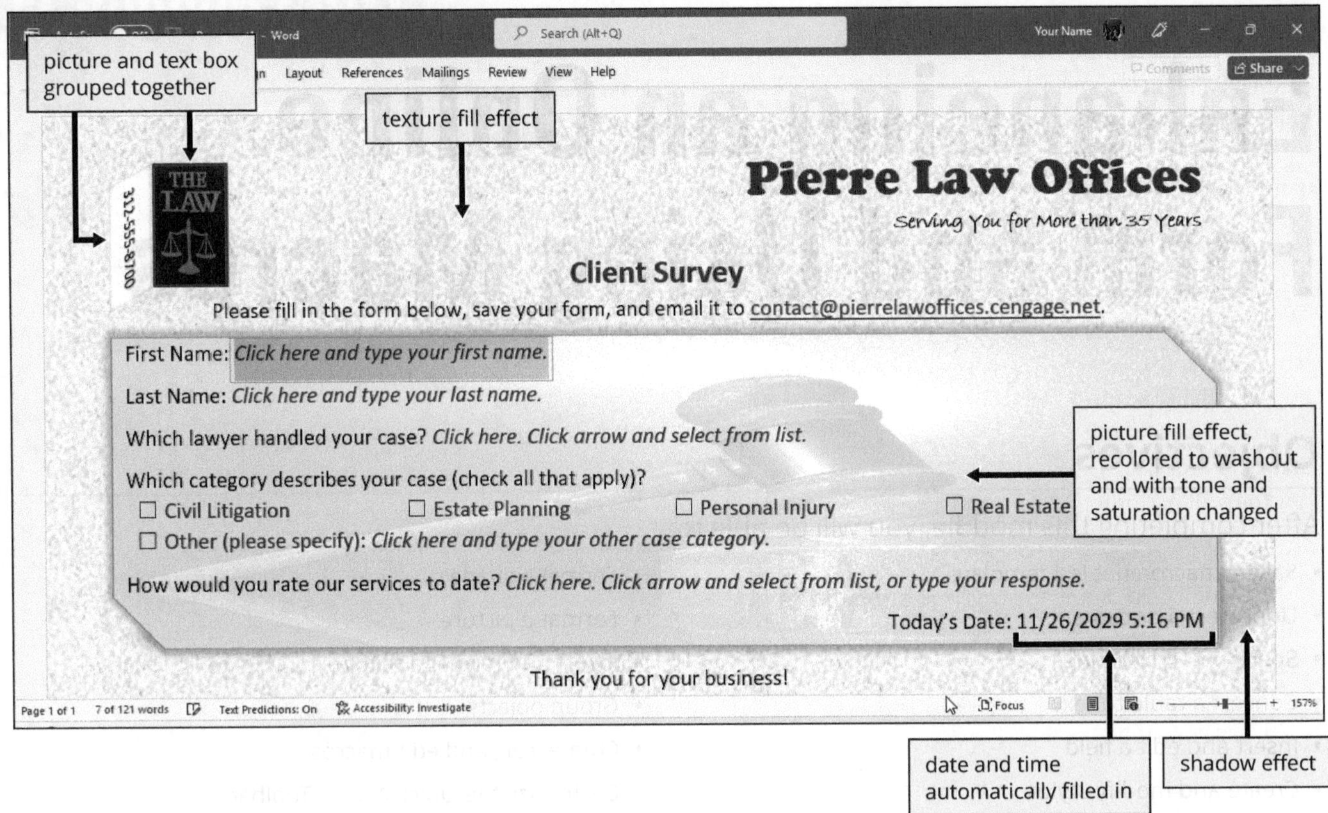

Figure 11–1(a): Modified and Enhanced Online Form

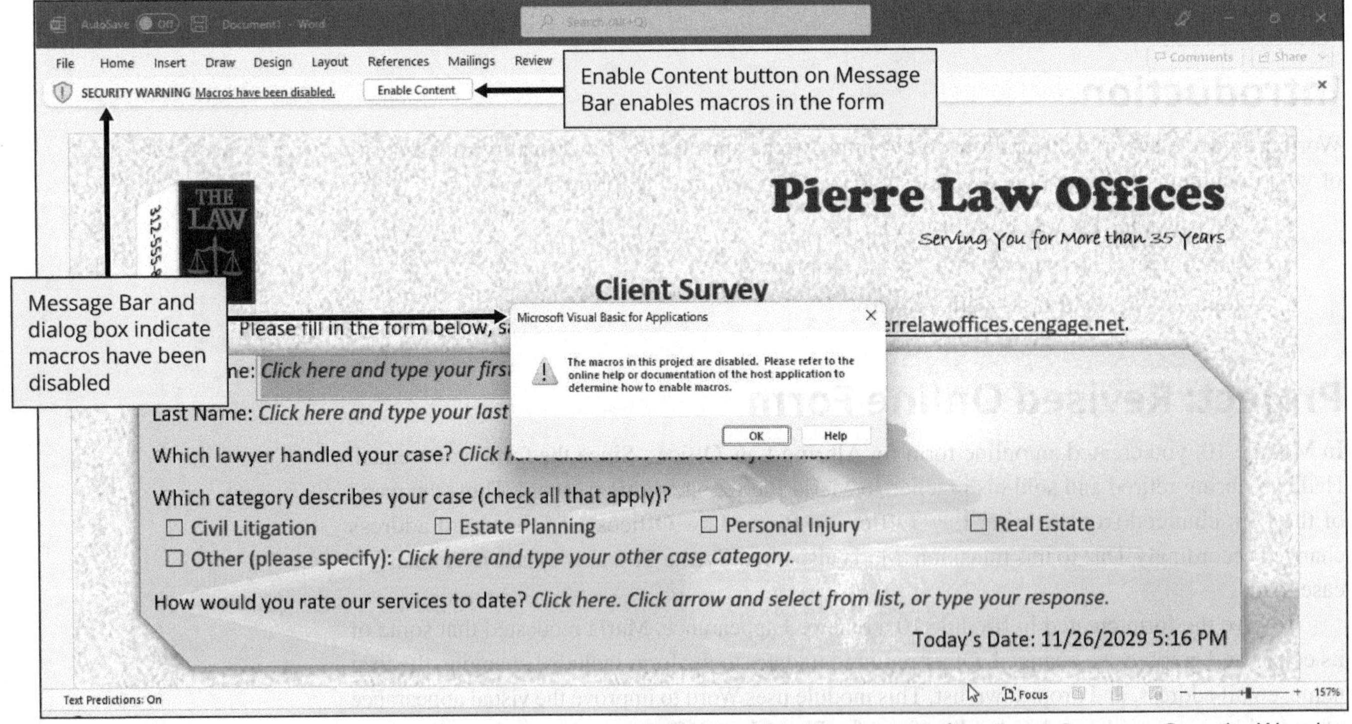

Figure 11–1(b): Macros in Online Form Generate Security Warning

This project modifies the fonts and font colors of the text in the Pierre Law Offices online form and enhances the contents of the form to include a texture fill effect, a picture fill effect, and a text box and picture grouped together. The date in the form automatically displays the computer or mobile device's system date, instead of requiring the user to enter the date.

This form also includes macros to automate tasks. A **macro** is a named set of instructions, written in the Visual Basic programming language, that performs tasks automatically in a specified order. One macro allows the user to hide formatting marks and the ruler by pressing a keyboard shortcut (sometimes called a shortcut key) or clicking a button on the Quick Access Toolbar. Another macro specifies how the form is displayed initially on a user's Word screen.

As shown in Figure 11–1b, when a document contains macros, Word may generate a security warning. If you are sure the macros are from a trusted source and free of viruses, then enable the content. Otherwise, do not enable the content to protect your computer or device from potentially harmful viruses or other malicious software. Steps in this module show how to specify macro settings in Word.

You will perform the following general tasks as you progress through this module:

1. Save a document as a macro-enabled template.
2. Modify the text and form content controls.
3. Enhance the form's visual appeal.
4. Create macros to automate tasks in the form.
5. Insert and format a 3-D model.

BTW
Macros and Trusted Sources
Harmful viruses and other malicious software can be hidden in macros. If you are not sure whether a macro is from a trusted source, do not click the Enable Content button on the Message Bar with the security warning. If you do not enable the content, your computer or mobile device will be protected from potentially harmful viruses or other malicious software that might be embedded in the macro. If you are sure macros are from a trusted source, as are the ones you will be creating in this module, then click the Enable Content button on the Message Bar so that the functionality of the trusted macros will be available in the document or form. Note that if Word does not allow you to enable macros, try enabling them from File Explorer by right-clicking the file in File Explorer, clicking Properties, and the clicking Unblock in the dialog box.

To Start Word and Specify Settings

If you are using a computer to step through the project in this module and you want your screens to match the figures in this book, you should change your screen's resolution to 1366 × 768. The following steps start Word and specify settings.

1. Start Word and create a blank document in the Word window. If necessary, maximize the Word window.
2. If the Print Layout button on the status bar is not selected, click it so that your screen is in Print Layout view.
3. If the 'Show/Hide ¶' button (Home tab | Paragraph group) is selected, click it to hide formatting marks because you will not use them in this project.
4. If the rulers are displayed on the screen, click the Ruler check box (View tab | Show group) to remove the rulers from the Word window because you will not use the rulers in this project.
5. If the edges of the page do not extend to the edge of the document window, display the View tab and then click the Page Width button (View tab | Zoom group).
6. If you are using a mouse and you want your screens to match the figures in the book, verify that you are using Mouse mode by doing the following: display the Quick Access Toolbar, if necessary, by clicking the 'Ribbon Display Options' button at the right edge of the ribbon and then clicking 'Show Quick Access Toolbar' on the menu; clicking the 'Touch/Mouse Mode' button on the Quick Access Toolbar and then, if necessary, clicking Mouse on the menu (if your Quick Access Toolbar does not display the 'Touch/Mouse Mode' button, click the 'Customize Quick Access Toolbar' button on the Quick Access Toolbar and then click Touch/Mouse Mode on the menu to add the button to the Quick Access Toolbar); then hide the Quick Access Toolbar by clicking the 'Ribbon Display Options' button at the right edge of the ribbon and then clicking 'Hide Quick Access Toolbar' on the menu.

BTW
The Ribbon and Screen Resolution
Word may change how the groups and buttons within the groups appear on the ribbon, depending on the screen resolution of your computer. Thus, your ribbon may look different from the ones in this book if you are using a screen resolution other than 1366 × 768.

To Save a Macro-Enabled Template

The project you create in this module will contain macros. Recall that since Maria Pierre took over the law office, several updates were made to the online form created in Module 10. The updated law offices template is located in the Data Files. Please contact your instructor for information about accessing the Data Files.

The first step in this module is to open the updated law offices template and then save the template as a macro-enabled template. **Why?** To provide added security to templates, a basic Word template cannot store macros. Word instead provides a specific type of template, called a **macro-enabled template**, in which you can store macros.

- **sam** Open the template named SC_WD_11-1.dotx from the Data Files. (If necessary, click the Enable or Enable Content button to remove the security warning.)

- Open Backstage view, click Save As to display the Save As screen, display the Save As dialog box, and navigate to the desired save location.
- Type **SC_WD_11_PierreLawOfficesClientSurveyModified** in the File name text box (Save As dialog box) to change the file name.
- Click the 'Save as type' arrow to display the list of available file types and then click 'Word Macro-Enabled Template (*.dotm)' in the list to change the file type (Figure 11-2). (Before proceeding, verify that your file type changed to Word Macro-Enabled Template.) (If the save location changed, adjust it to your desired save location.)

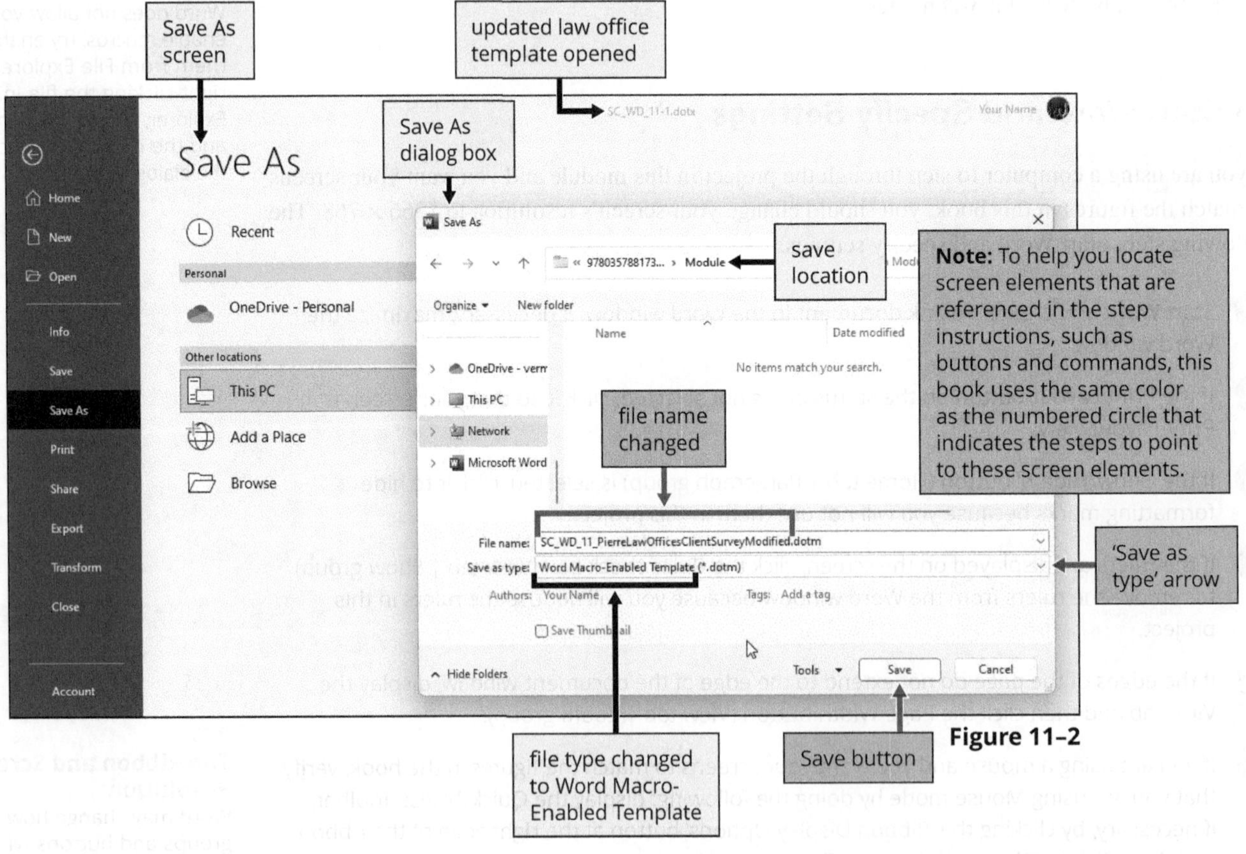

Figure 11-2

- Click the Save button (Save As dialog box) to save the file using the entered file name as a macro-enabled template.

Q&A How does Word differentiate between a Word template and a Word macro-enabled template?
A Word template has an extension of .dotx, whereas a Word macro-enabled template has an extension of .dotm. Also, the icon for a macro-enabled template contains an exclamation point.

To Show the Developer Tab

Many of the tasks you will perform in this module use commands on the Developer tab. Thus, the following steps show the Developer tab on the ribbon.

1. Open Backstage view and then click Options in the left pane of Backstage view to display the Word Options dialog box.
2. Click Customize Ribbon in the left pane (Word Options dialog box) to display associated options in the right pane.
3. If it is not selected already, place a check mark in the Developer check box in the Main Tabs list.
4. Click OK to show the Developer tab on the ribbon.

BTW
Macro-Enabled Documents
The previous set of steps showed how to create a macro-enabled template. If you wanted to create a macro-enabled document, you would click the 'Save as type' arrow (Save As dialog box), click 'Word Macro-Enabled Document', and then click the Save button.

To Unprotect a Document

The SC_WD_11_PierreLawOfficesClientSurveyModified.dotm template is protected. In a protected form, users enter data only in designated areas, specifically, the content controls. The following steps unprotect a document. **Why?** Before this form can be modified, it must be unprotected. Later in this project, after you have completed the modifications, you will protect it again.

- Display the Developer tab.
- Click the Restrict Editing button (Developer tab | Protect group) to open the Restrict Editing pane (Figure 11-3).

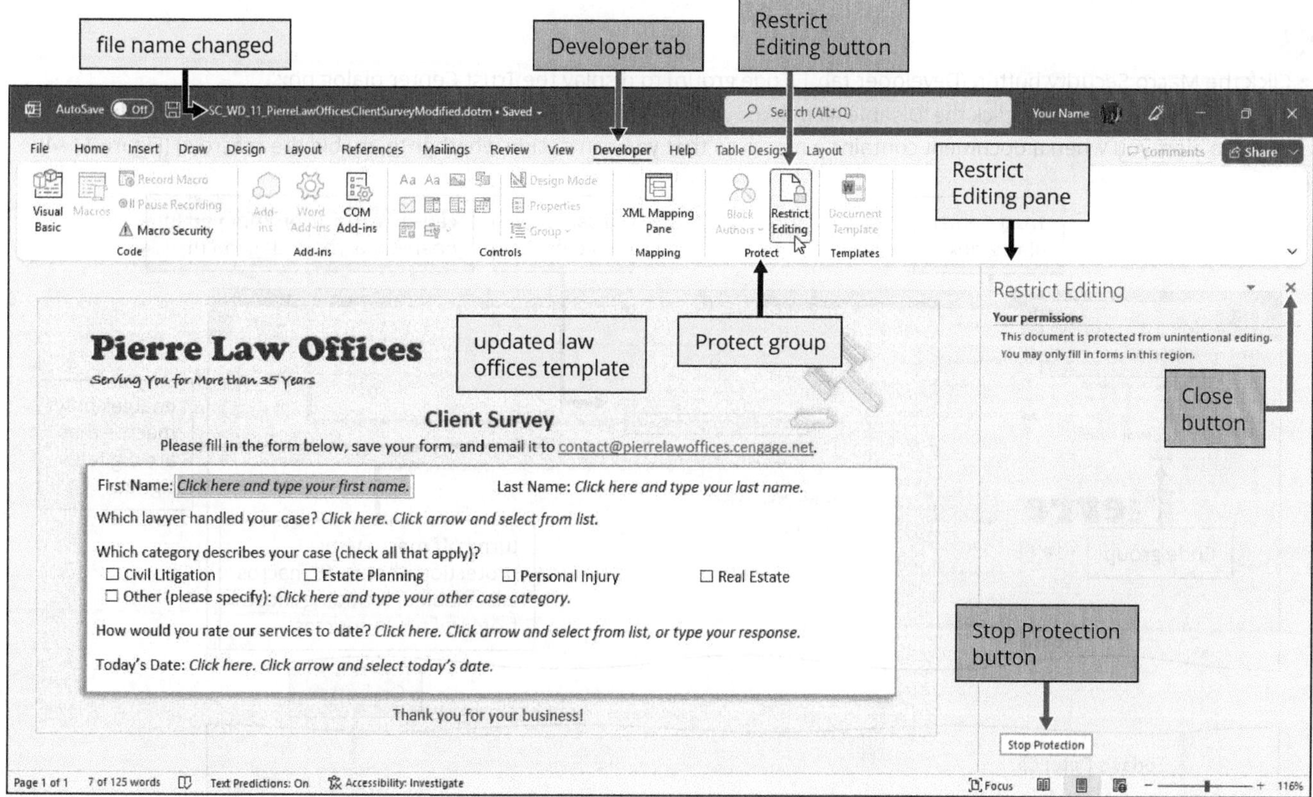

Figure 11-3

- Click the Stop Protection button in the Restrict Editing pane to unprotect the form.
- Click the Close button in the Restrict Editing pane to close the pane.

Other Ways

1. Open Backstage view, click Info in Backstage view, click Protect Document button, click Restrict Editing on Protect Document menu, click Stop Protection button in Restrict Editing pane

Consider This

How do you protect a computer from macro viruses?

Recall that a computer virus is a type of malicious software, or malware, which is a potentially damaging computer program that affects, or infects, a computer or mobile device negatively by altering the way the computer or mobile device works, usually without the user's knowledge or permission. Millions of known viruses and other malicious programs exist. The increased use of networks, the Internet, and email has accelerated the spread of computer viruses and other malicious programs.

- To combat these threats, most computer users run an **antivirus program** that locates viruses and other malware and destroys the malicious programs before they infect a computer or mobile device. Macros are known carriers of viruses and other malware. For this reason, you can specify a macro setting in Word to reduce the chance your computer or mobile device will be infected with a macro virus. These macro settings allow you to enable or disable macros. An **enabled macro** is a macro that Word (or any other Office application) will execute, and a **disabled macro** is a macro that is unavailable to Word (or any other program).
- As shown in Figure 11–1b at the beginning of this module, you can instruct Word to display a security warning on a Message Bar if it opens a document that contains a macro(s). If you are confident of the source (author) of the document and macros, enable the macros. If you are uncertain about the reliability of the source of the document and macros, then do not enable the macros.

To Specify Macro Settings in Word

Why? When you open the online form in this module, you want the macros enabled. At the same time, your computer or mobile device should be protected from potentially harmful macros. Thus, you will specify a macro setting that allows you to enable macros each time you open this module's online form or any document that contains a macro from an unknown source. The following steps specify macro settings.

- Click the Macro Security button (Developer tab | Code group) to display the Trust Center dialog box.
- If it is not selected already, click the 'Disable all macros with notification' option button (Trust Center dialog box), which causes Word to alert you when a document contains a macro so that you can decide whether to enable the macro(s) (Figure 11–4).

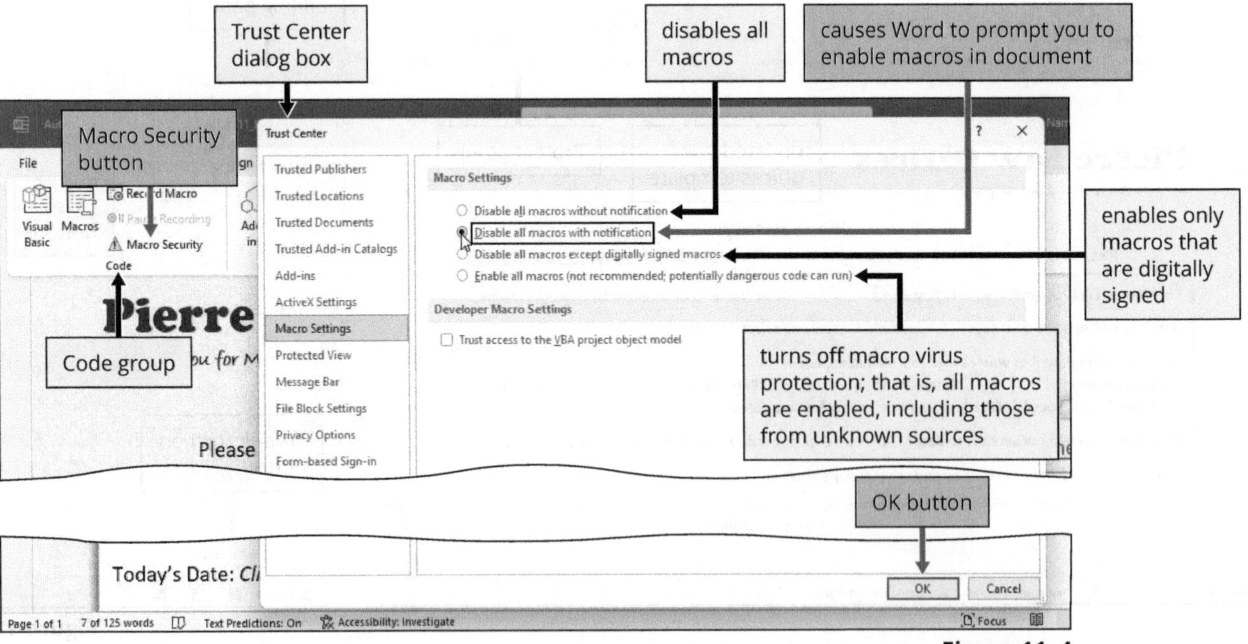

Figure 11–4

2

- Click OK to close the dialog box.

Other Ways

1. Click File on ribbon, click Options in Backstage view, click Trust Center in left pane (Word Options dialog box), click 'Trust Center Settings' button in right pane, if necessary, click Macro Settings in left pane (Trust Center dialog box), select desired setting, click OK in each dialog box

Modifying Text and Form Content Controls

The updated law offices form is enhanced in this module by performing these steps:

1. Delete the current image.
2. Change the fonts, colors, and alignments of the first four lines of text and the last line.
3. Convert the 2 × 1 table containing the First Name and Last Name content controls to text so that each of these content controls is on a separate line.
4. Delete the date picker content control and replace it with a date field.
5. Modify the color of the hyperlink and the check box labels.

The following pages apply these changes to the form.

To Delete a Graphic, Format Text, and Change Paragraph Alignment

The online form in this module contains a different image. It also has different formats for the company name, business tag line, form name, form instructions, date line, and thank you line. The following steps delete the image, format text, and change paragraph alignment.

BTW
Touch Mode Differences
The Office and Windows interfaces may vary if you are using Touch mode. For this reason, you might notice that the function or appearance of your touch screen differs slightly from this module's presentation.

1. Click the image of the gavel to select it and then press DELETE to delete the selected image.
2. Change the color of the first line of text, Pierre Law Offices, and the third line of text, Client Survey, to 'Orange, Accent 2, Darker 50%' (sixth color in sixth row).
3. Change the color of the business tag line and the last line on the form, Thank you for your business!, to 'Black, Text 1' (second color in first row).
4. Right-align the first and second lines of text (company name and business tag line).
5. Right-align the line of text containing the Today's Date content control.
6. If necessary, widen the rectangle surrounding the data entry area to include the entire date placeholder text.
7. If necessary, adjust the zoom to display the entire form on the screen (Figure 11–5).

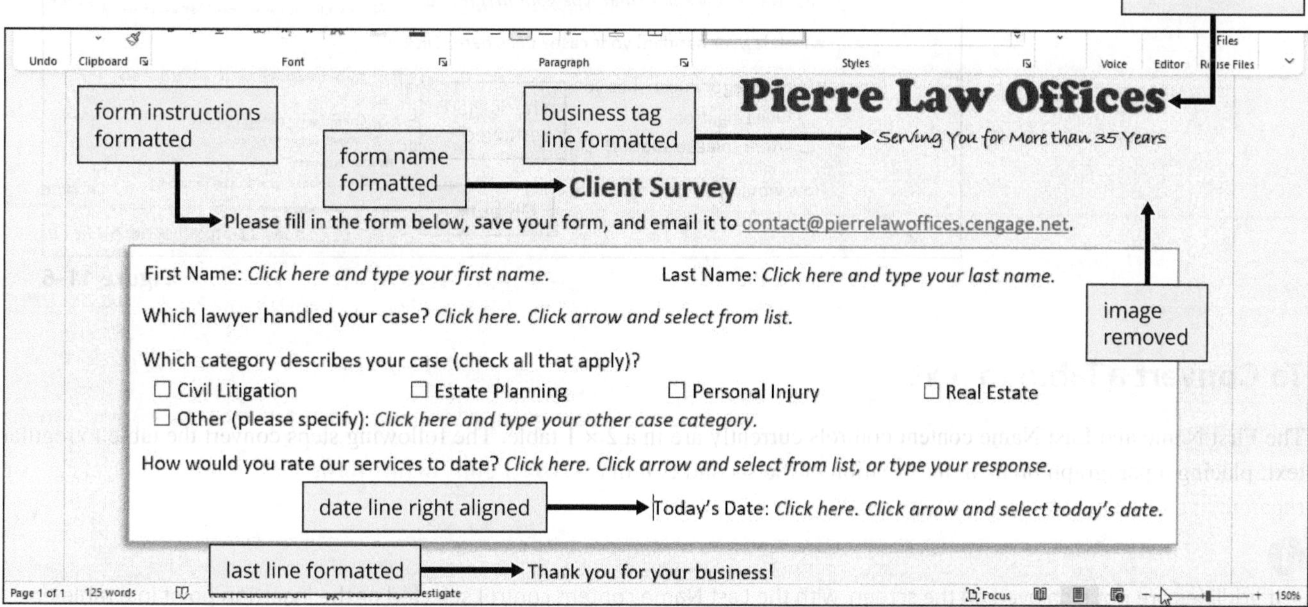

Figure 11–5

BTW
Saving and Resetting Themes
If you have changed the theme colors or theme fonts and want to save this combination for future use, save it as a new theme by clicking the Themes button (Design tab | Document Formatting group), clicking 'Save Current Theme' in the Themes gallery, entering a theme name in the File name box (Save Current Theme dialog box), and then clicking Save. If you want to reset the theme template to the default, you would click the Themes button (Design tab | Document Formatting group) and then click 'Reset to Theme from Template' in the Themes gallery.

To Change the Properties of a Plain Text Content Control

In this online form, the First Name and Last Name content controls are on separate lines. In Module 10, you selected the 'Content control cannot be deleted' check box in the Content Control Properties dialog box so that users could not delete the content control accidentally while filling in the form. With this check box selected, however, you cannot move a content control from one location to another on the form. Thus, the following steps change the locking properties of the First Name and Last Name content controls so that you can rearrange them.

1. Display the Developer tab.
2. Click the First Name content control to select it.
3. Click the Properties button (Developer tab | Controls group) to display the Content Control Properties dialog box.
4. Remove the check mark from the 'Content control cannot be deleted' check box (Content Control Properties dialog box) (Figure 11–6).
5. Click OK to assign the modified properties to the content control.
6. Click the Last Name content control to select it and then click the Properties button (Developer tab | Controls group) to display the Content Control Properties dialog box.
7. Remove the check mark from the 'Content control cannot be deleted' check box (Content Control Properties dialog box) and then click OK to assign the modified properties to the content control.

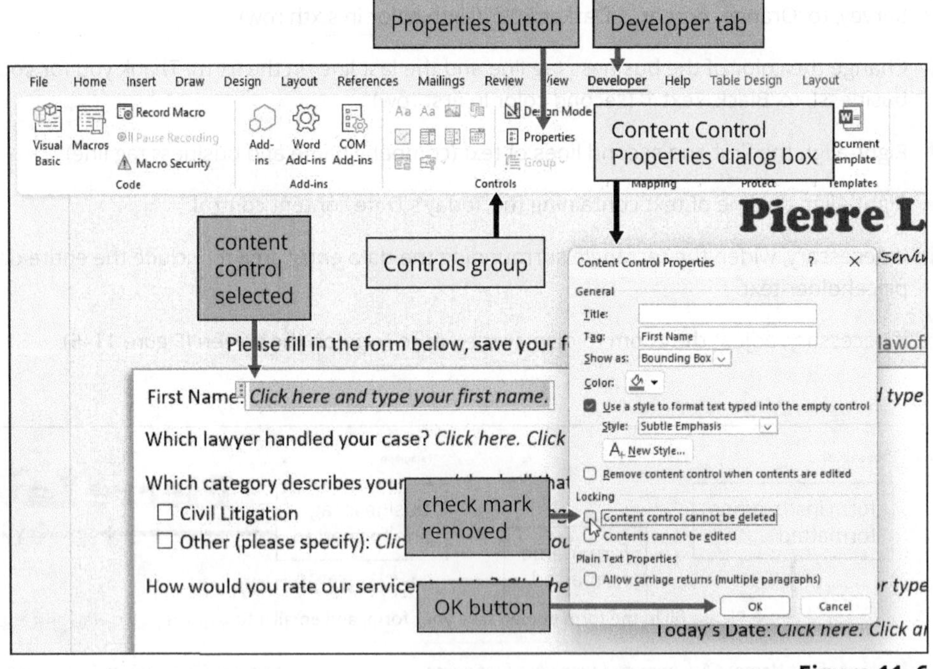

Figure 11–6

To Convert a Table to Text

The First Name and Last Name content controls currently are in a 2 × 1 table. The following steps convert the table to regular text, placing a paragraph break at the location of the second column. **Why?** In this online form, these content controls are on separate lines, one below the other. That is, they are not in a table.

- If gridlines are not displayed on the screen, with the Last Name content control selected or the insertion point in a table on the form, display the contextual Layout tab and then click the View Gridlines button (contextual Layout tab | Table group) to show table gridlines on the screen.

Q&A Is the contextual Layout tab different from the main Layout tab?
Yes, recall that the main Layout tab, which always appears on the ribbon, is used to change page setup, format paragraphs, and arrange objects in a document. The contextual Layout tab appears only when you are working in a table and is used to change the properties and organization of a table and its rows, columns, and cells.

- Position the insertion point somewhere in the table to be converted to text (in this case, in the First Name or Last Name label in the form).
- If necessary, display the contextual Layout tab.
- Click the 'Convert to Text' button (contextual Layout tab | Data group) to display the Convert Table To Text dialog box.
- Click Paragraph marks (Convert Table To Text dialog box), which will place a paragraph mark at the location of each new column in the table (Figure 11–7).

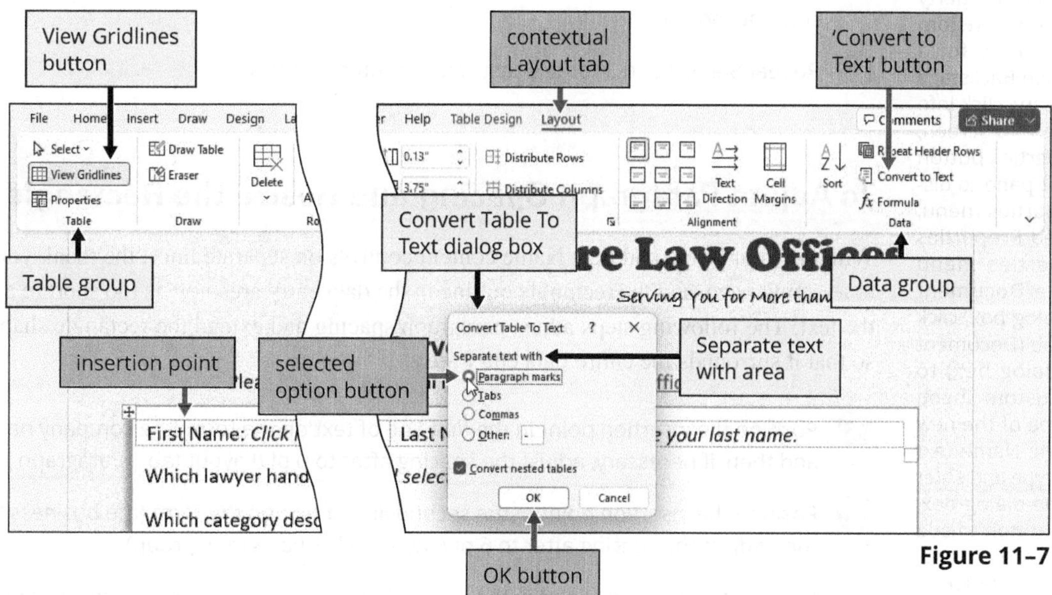

Figure 11–7

2

- Click OK to convert the table to text, separating each column with the specified character, a paragraph mark in this case.

Q&A Why did the Last Name content control move below the First Name content control?
The Separate text with area (Convert Table To Text dialog box) controls how the table is converted to text. The Paragraph marks setting converts each column in the table to a line of text below the previous line. The Tabs setting places a tab character where each column was located, and the Commas setting places a comma where each column was located. If you wanted to place a different character where each column was located, you would enter that character in the Other text box.

3

- With the First Name and Last Name lines selected, using either the ruler or the Layout tab, change the left indent to 0.06" so that the text aligns with the text immediately below it (that is, the W in Which), as shown in Figure 11–8.

4

- Click anywhere to remove the selection from the text.

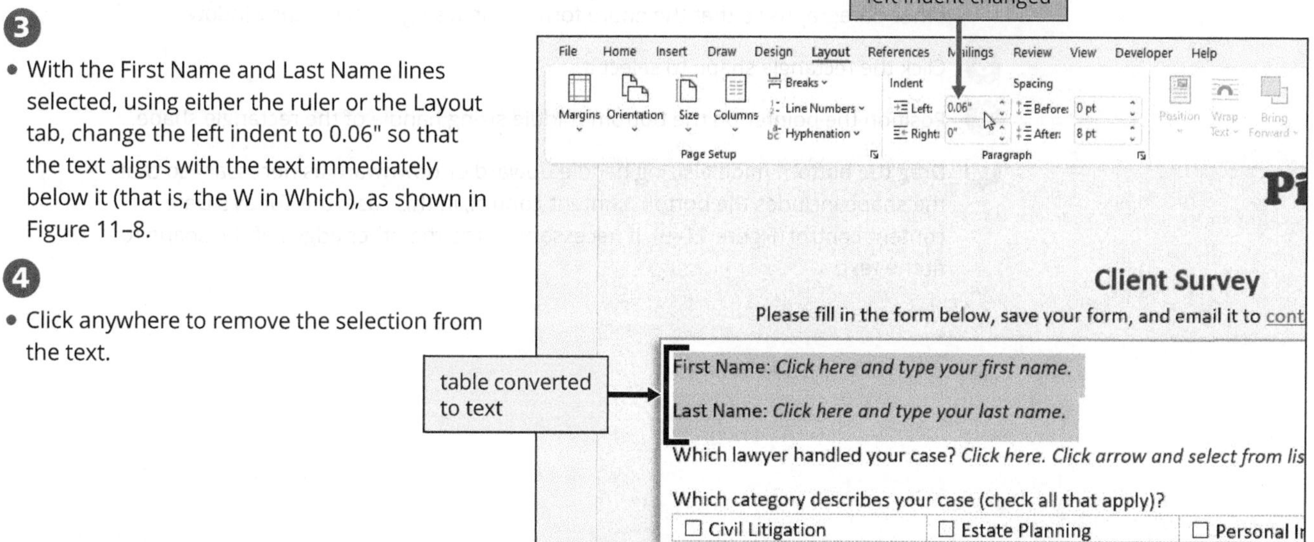

Figure 11–8

BTW
Document Properties
If you wanted to insert document properties in a document, you would click the 'Explore Quick Parts' button (Insert tab | Text group) to display the Explore Quick Parts menu, point to Document Property on the Explore Quick Parts menu, and then click the property you want to insert on the Document Property menu. To create a custom document property for a document, open Backstage view, if necessary, click Info to display the Info screen, click the Properties button in the far right pane to display the Properties menu, click Advanced Properties on the Properties menu to display the Document Properties dialog box, click the Custom tab (Document Properties dialog box) to display the Custom sheet, enter the name of the new property in the Name text box, select its type and enter its value in the dialog box, click the Add button to add the property to the document, and then click OK to close the dialog box.

To Change the Properties of a Plain Text Content Control

You are finished moving the First Name and Last Name content controls. The following steps reset the locking properties of these content controls.

1. Display the Developer tab.
2. Click the First Name content control to select it and then click the Properties button (Developer tab | Controls group) to display the Content Control Properties dialog box.
3. Place a check mark in the 'Content control cannot be deleted' check box (Content Control Properties dialog box) and then click OK to assign the modified properties to the content control.
4. Repeat Steps 2 and 3 for the Last Name content control.

To Adjust Paragraph Spacing and Resize the Rectangle Shape

With the First Name and Last Name content controls on separate lines, the thank you line moved to a second page, and the rectangle outline in the data entry area now is too short to accommodate the text. The following steps adjust paragraph spacing and extend the rectangle shape downward so that it surrounds the entire data entry area.

1. Position the insertion point in the first line of text on the form (the company name) and then, if necessary, adjust the spacing after to 0 pt (Layout tab | Paragraph group).
2. Position the insertion point in the second line of text on the form (the business tag line) and then adjust the spacing after to 6 pt (Layout tab | Paragraph group).
3. Position the insertion point in the fourth line of text on the form (the instruction line that begins, Please fill in the form...) and then adjust the spacing after to 6 pt (Layout tab | Paragraph group).
4. Adjust the spacing after to 6 pt for the First Name and Last Name lines.
5. Adjust the spacing before and after to 6 pt for the line that begins, Which lawyer handled..., and the line that begins, How would you rate....
6. Adjust the spacing before to 12 pt for the thank you line.
7. Scroll to display the entire form in the document window. If necessary, reduce spacing after other paragraphs so that the entire form fits in a single document window.
8. Click the rectangle shape to select it.
9. Position the pointer on the bottom-middle sizing handle of the rectangle shape.
10. Drag the bottom-middle sizing handle upward or downward as necessary so that the shape includes the bottom content control, in this case, the Today's Date content control (Figure 11–9). If necessary, resize the other edges of the shape to fit the text.

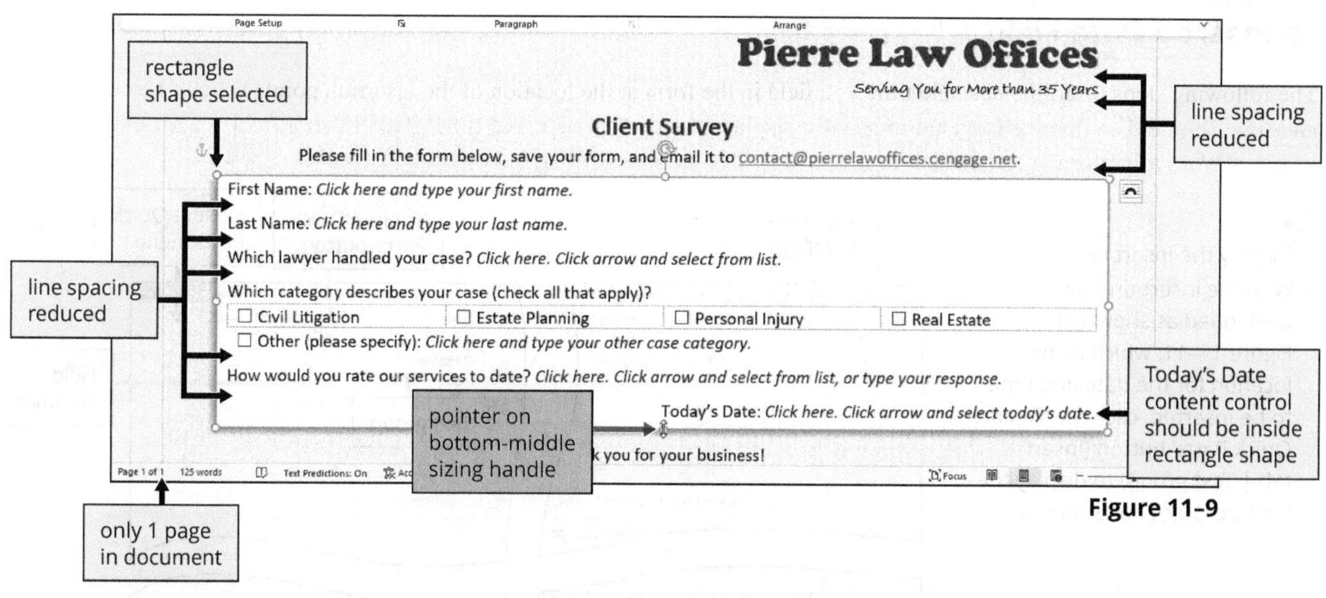

Figure 11-9

To Change the Properties of a Date Picker Content Control

In this online form, instead of the user entering the current date, the computer or mobile device's system date will be filled in automatically by Word. Thus, the Today's Date content control is not needed and can be deleted. To delete the content control, you first will need to remove the check mark from the 'Content control cannot be deleted' check box in the Content Control Properties dialog box. The following steps change the locking properties of the Today's Date content control and then delete the content control.

1. Display the Developer tab.
2. Click the Today's Date content control to select it.
3. Click the Properties button (Developer tab | Controls group) to display the Content Control Properties dialog box.
4. Remove the check mark from the 'Content control cannot be deleted' check box (Content Control Properties dialog box) (Figure 11–10).
5. Click OK to assign the modified properties to the content control.
6. Right-click the Today's Date content control to display a shortcut menu and then click 'Remove Content Control' on the shortcut menu to delete the selected content control.

BTW
Field Formats
If you wanted to create custom field formats, you would click the Field Codes button (Field dialog box) (shown in Figure 11–15) to display advanced field properties in the right pane in the dialog box, click the Options button to display the Field Options dialog box, select the format to apply in the list, click the 'Add to Field' button, and then click OK in each open dialog box.

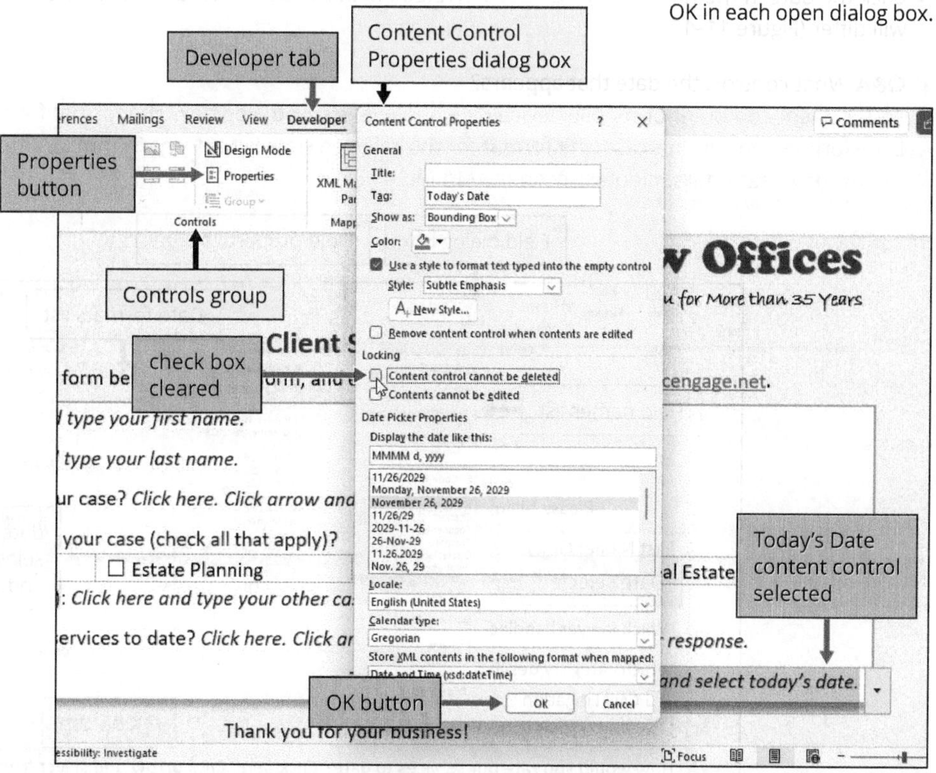

Figure 11–10

To Insert a Date Field

The following steps insert the date and time as a field in the form at the location of the insertion point. **Why?** The current date and time is a field so that the form automatically displays the current date and time. Recall that a field is a set of codes that instructs Word to perform a certain action.

- Display the Insert tab.
- With the insertion point positioned as shown in Figure 11–11, which is the location for the date and time to be inserted, click the 'Explore Quick Parts' button (Insert tab | Text group) to display the Explore Quick Parts menu.

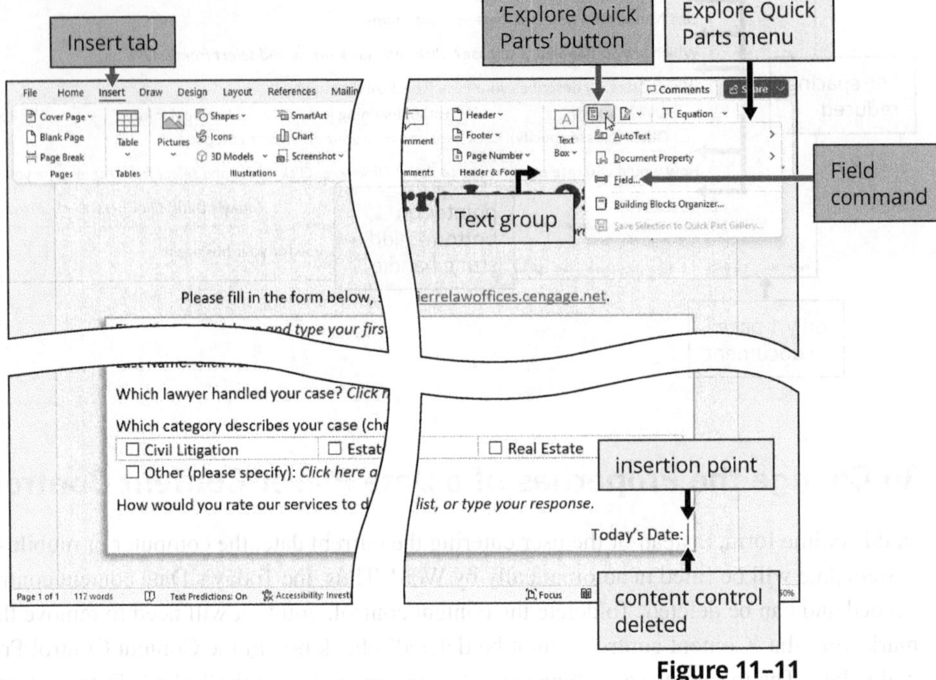

Figure 11–11

2

- Click Field on the Explore Quick Parts menu to display the Field dialog box.
- Scroll through the Field names list (Field dialog box) and then click Date, which displays the Date formats list in the Field properties area.
- Click the date in the format of 11/26/2029 5:12:20 PM in the Date formats list to select a date format — your date and time will differ (Figure 11–12).

Q&A What controls the date that appears?
Your current computer or mobile device date appears in this dialog box. The format for the selected date shows in the Date formats box. In this case, the format for the selected date is M/d/yyyy h:mm:ss am/pm, which displays the date as month/day/year hours:minutes:seconds AM/PM.

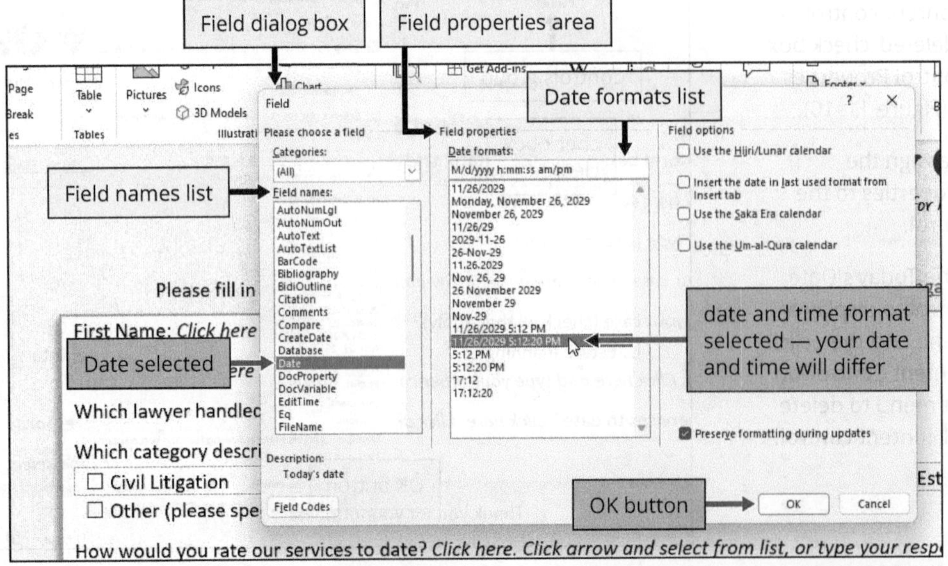

Figure 11–12

- Click OK to insert the current date and time that automatically will be filled in at the location of the insertion point (Figure 11–13).

Q&A How do I delete a field?
Select it and then press DELETE or click the Cut button (Home tab | Clipboard group), or right-click the field and then click Cut on the shortcut menu or Mini toolbar.

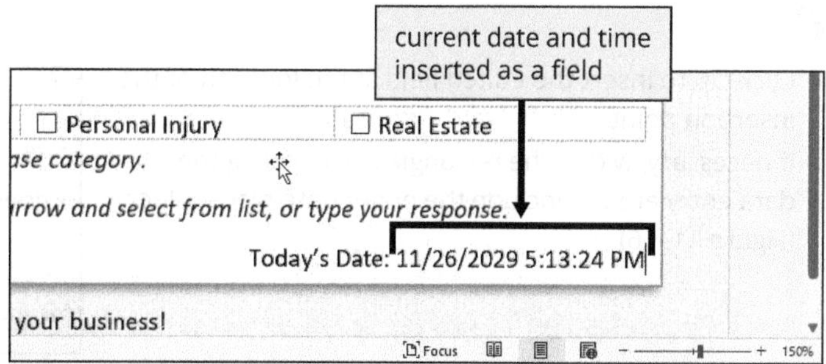

Figure 11–13

Other Ways

1. Click 'Insert Date and Time' button (Insert tab | Text group), select date format (Date and Time dialog box), place check mark in Update automatically check box, click OK

To Edit a Field

The following steps edit the field. **Why?** After reviewing the date and time in the form, you decide not to include the seconds in the time. That is, you want just the hours and minutes to be displayed.

- Right-click the date field to display a shortcut menu (Figure 11–14).

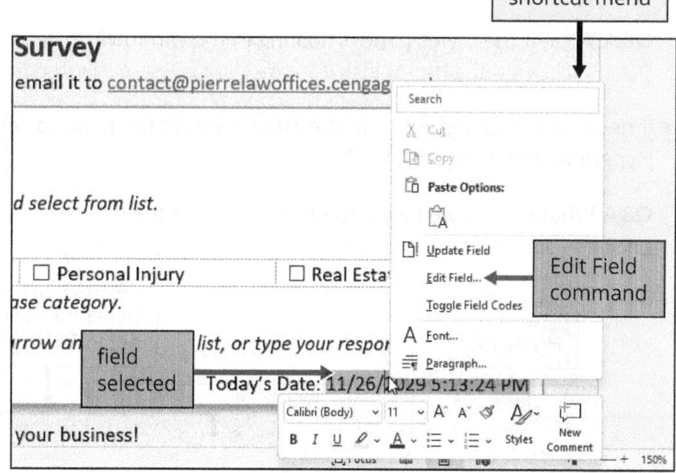

Figure 11–14

- Click Edit Field on the shortcut menu to display the Field dialog box.
- If necessary, scroll through the Field names list (Field dialog box) and then, if necessary, click Date to display the Date formats list in the Field properties area.
- Select the desired date format, in this case 11/26/2029 5:15 PM (Figure 11–15).

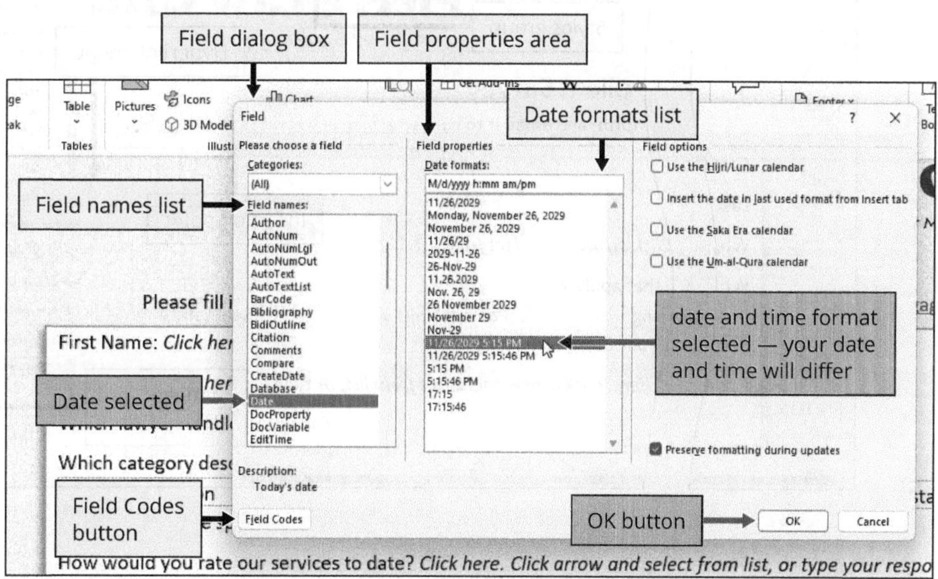

Figure 11–15

- Click OK to insert the edited field at the location of the insertion point.
- If necessary, widen the rectangle surrounding the data entry area to include the entire date placeholder (Figure 11–16).

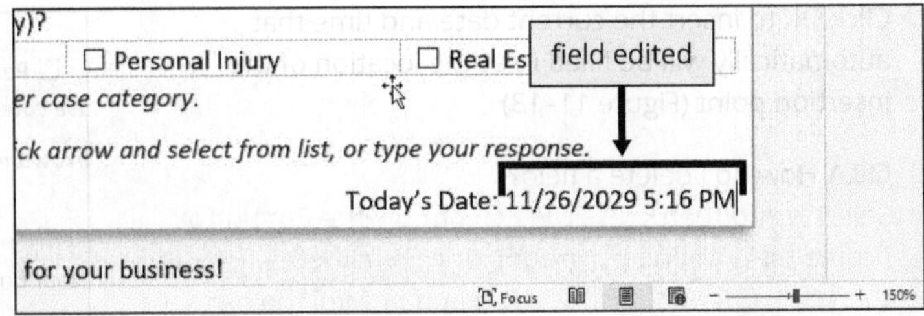

Figure 11–16

To Modify a Style Using the Styles Pane

In this online form, the hyperlink should be the same color as the company name so that it has a complementary color. The following steps modify a style using the Styles pane. **Why?** The Hyperlink style is not in the Styles gallery. To modify a style that is not in the Styles gallery, you can use the Styles pane.

- Position the insertion point in the hyperlink in the form.
- Display the Home tab.
- Click the Styles Dialog Box Launcher (Home tab | Styles group) to open the Styles pane.

Q&A What if the Styles pane is floating in the window?
Double-click its title bar to lock it to the right edge of the document window.

- If necessary, click Hyperlink in the list of styles in the pane to select it and then click the Hyperlink arrow to display the Hyperlink menu (Figure 11–17).

Q&A What if the style I want to modify is not in the list?
Click the Manage Styles button at the bottom of the pane, locate the style, and then click the Modify button in the dialog box.

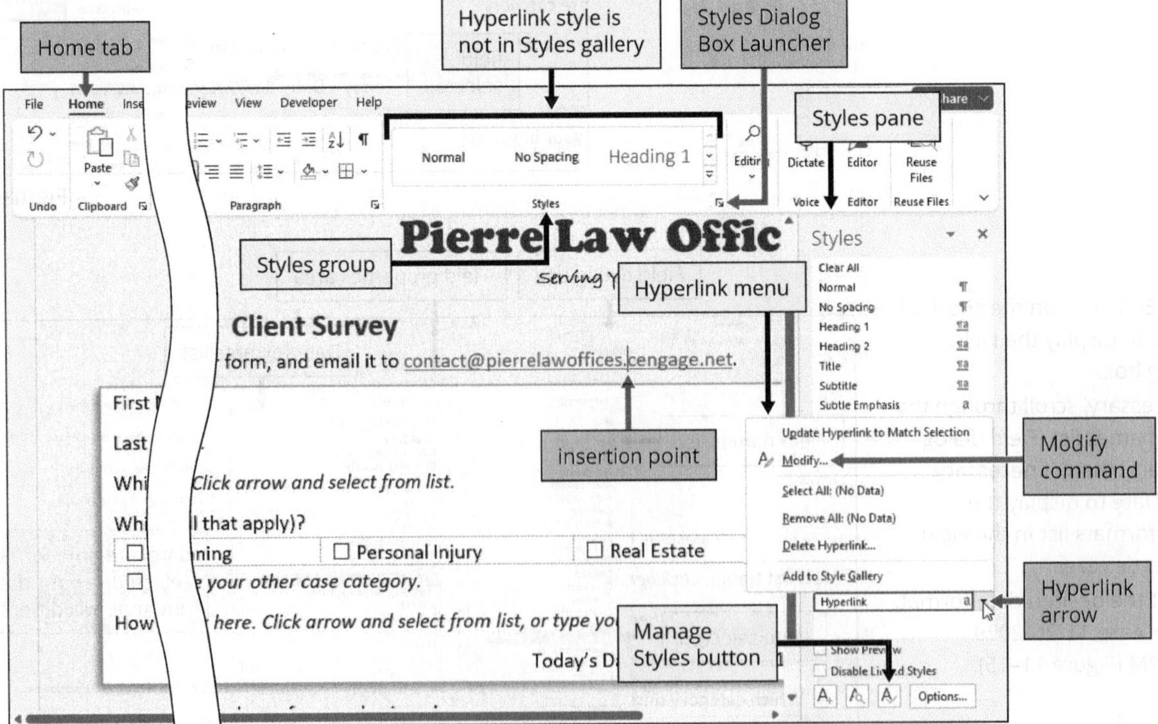

Figure 11–17

2

- Click Modify on the Hyperlink menu to display the Modify Style dialog box.
- Click the Font Color arrow (Modify Style dialog box) to display the Font Color gallery (Figure 11–18).

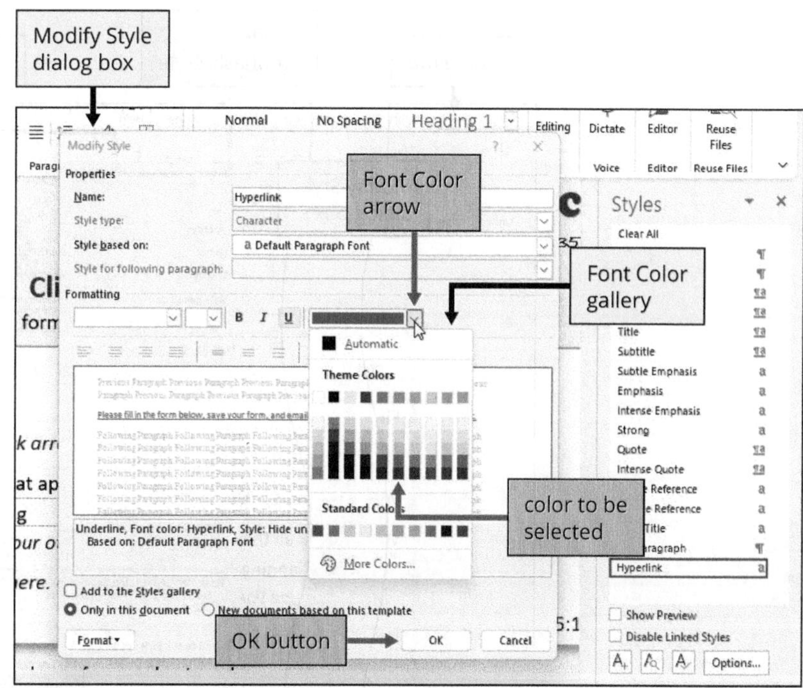

Figure 11–18

3

- Click 'Orange, Accent 2, Darker 50%' (sixth color in sixth row) as the new hyperlink color.
- Click OK to close the dialog box. Close the Styles pane (Figure 11–19).

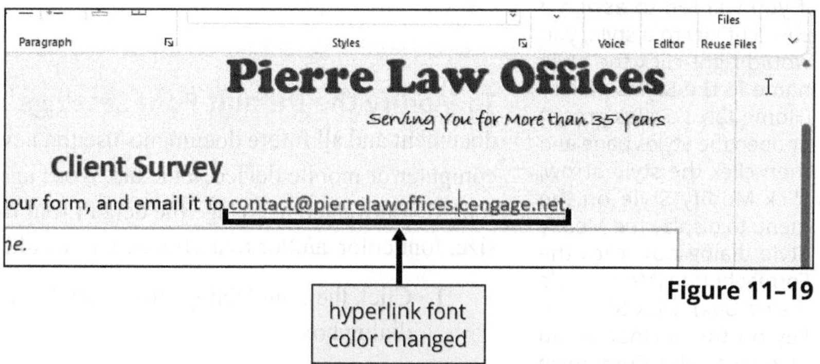

Figure 11–19

To Modify a Style

In this online form, the placeholder text is to be a shade of blue. Currently, the placeholder text is formatted using the Subtle Emphasis style, which uses a shade of gray as the font color. Thus, the following steps modify the color of the Subtle Emphasis style to a shade of blue.

1. Scroll through the Styles gallery (Home tab | Styles group), if necessary, to locate the Subtle Emphasis style.
2. Right-click Subtle Emphasis in the Styles gallery to display a shortcut menu and then click Modify on the shortcut menu to display the Modify Style dialog box.
3. Click the Font Color arrow (Modify Style dialog box) to display the Font Color gallery (Figure 11–20).
4. Click 'Blue, Accent 1, Darker 50%' (fifth color in sixth row) as the new color.
5. Click OK to change the color of the style, which automatically changes the color of every item formatted using this style in the document.

BTW

Hidden Styles and Text

Some styles are hidden, which means they do not appear in the Styles pane. You can display all styles, including hidden styles, by clicking the Manage Styles button in the Styles pane (Figure 11–17), which displays the Manage Styles dialog box. Click the Edit tab, if necessary, and then locate the style name in the Select a style to edit list. To format text as hidden, select the text, click the Font Dialog Box Launcher (Home tab | Font group) to display the Font dialog box, select the Hidden check box in the Effects area, and then click OK (Font dialog box). To view hidden text on the screen, show formatting marks. Hidden text does not print.

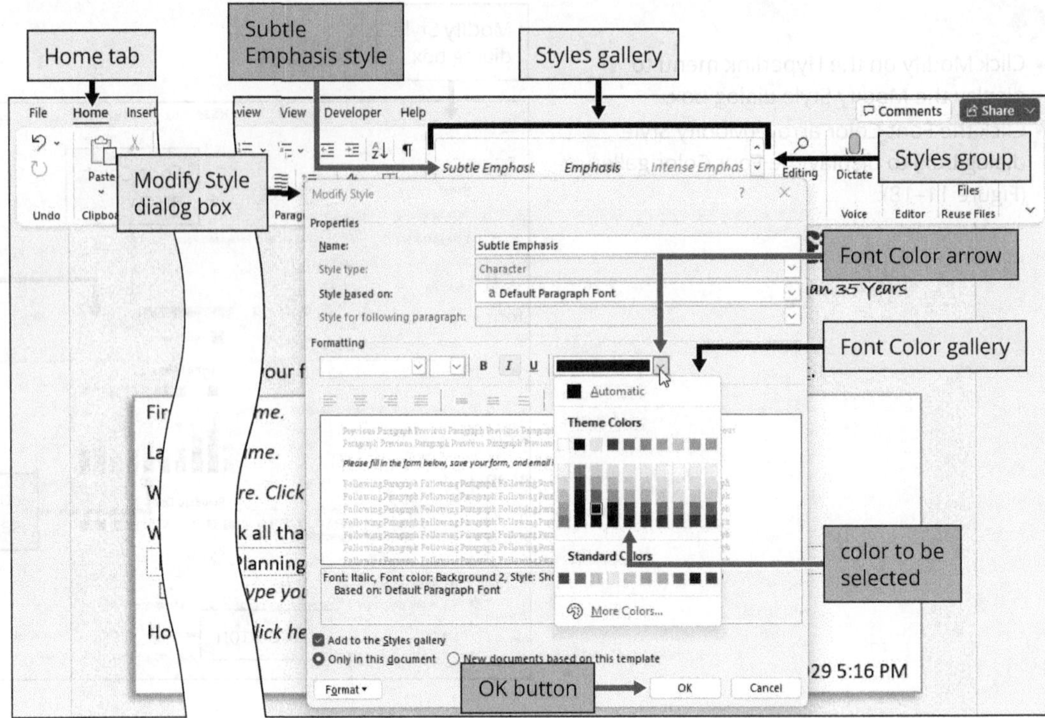

Figure 11–20

BTW

Assign a Shortcut Key to a Style

If you wanted to assign a shortcut key to a style, you would right-click the style name in the Styles gallery (Home tab | Styles group) or open the Styles pane and then click the style arrow, click Modify Style on the menu to display the Modify Style dialog box, click the Format button (Modify Style dialog box), click Shortcut key on the Format menu to display the Customize Keyboard dialog box, press the desired shortcut key(s) (Customize Keyboard dialog box), click the Assign button to assign the shortcut key to the style, click the Close button to close the Customize Keyboard dialog box, and then click OK to close the Modify Style dialog box.

BTW

Advanced Character Attributes

If you wanted to set advanced character attributes, you would click the Font Dialog Box Launcher (Home tab | Font group) to display the Font dialog box, click the Advanced tab (Font dialog box) to display the Advanced sheet, select the desired Character Spacing or OpenType Features settings, and then click OK.

To Modify the Default Font Settings You can change the default font so that the current document and all future documents use the new font settings. That is, if you exit Word, restart the computer or mobile device, and start Word again, documents you create will use the new default font. If you wanted to change the default font from 11-point Calibri to another font, font style, font size, font color, and/or font effects, you would perform the following steps.

1. Click the Font Dialog Box Launcher (Home tab | Font group) to display the Font dialog box.
2. Make desired changes to the font settings in the Font dialog box.
3. Click the 'Set As Default' button to change the default settings to those specified in Step 2.
4. When the Microsoft Word dialog box is displayed, select the desired option button and then click OK.

To Reset the Default Font Settings To change the font settings back to the default, you would follow the steps in the previous section, using the default font settings when performing Step 2. If you do not remember the default settings, you would perform the following steps to restore the original Normal style settings.

1. Exit Word.
2. Use File Explorer to locate the Normal.dotm file (be sure that hidden files and folders are displayed and include system and hidden files in your search), which is the file that contains default font and other settings.
3. Rename the Normal.dotm file to oldnormal.dotm file so that the Normal.dotm file no longer exists.
4. Start Word, which will recreate a Normal.dotm file using the original default settings.

To Create a Character Style

In this online form, the check box labels are to be the same color as the placeholder text. The following steps create a character style called Check Box Labels. **Why?** Although you could select each of the check box labels and then format them, a more efficient technique is to create a character style. If you decide to modify the formats of the check box labels at a later time, you simply change the formats assigned to the style to automatically change all characters in the document based on that style.

- Position the insertion point in one of the check box labels.
- Click the Styles Dialog Box Launcher (Home tab | Styles group) to open the Styles pane.
- Click the Manage Styles button in the Styles pane to display the Manage Styles dialog box (Figure 11–21).

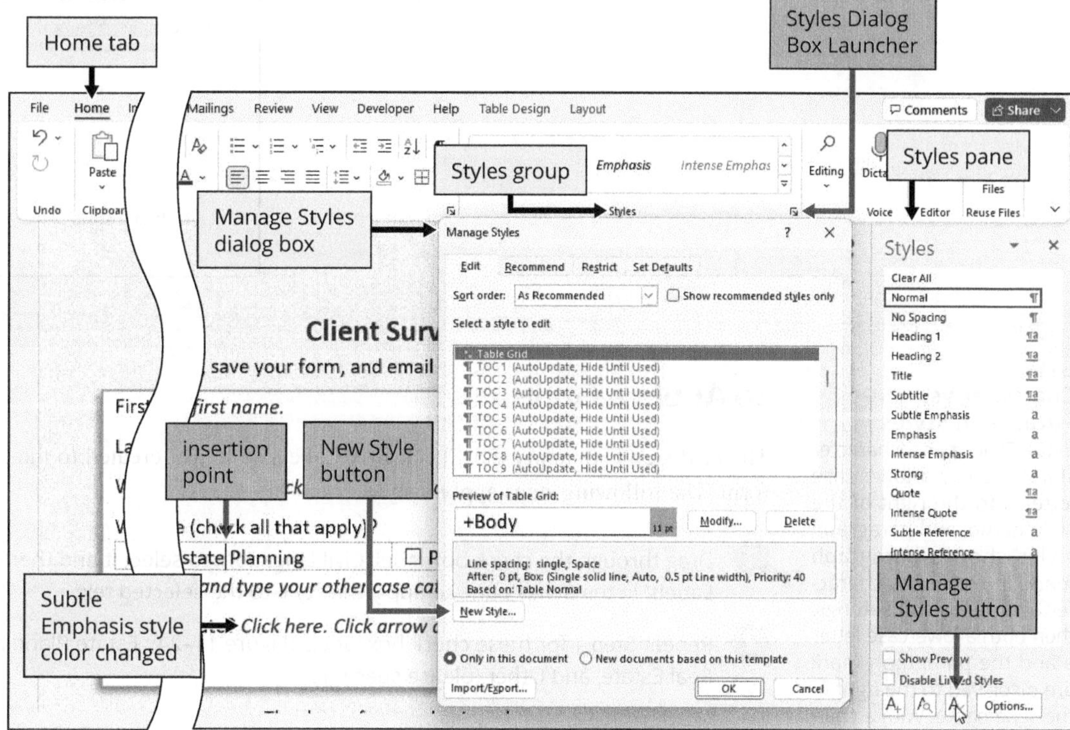

Figure 11–21

- Click the New Style button (Manage Styles dialog box) to display the Create New Style from Formatting dialog box.
- Type **Check Box Labels** in the Name text box (Create New Style from Formatting dialog box) as the name of the new style.
- Click the Style type arrow and then click Character so that the new style does not contain any paragraph formats.
- Click the Font Color arrow to display the Font Color gallery and then click 'Blue, Accent 1, Darker 50%' (fifth color in sixth row) as the new color (Figure 11–22).

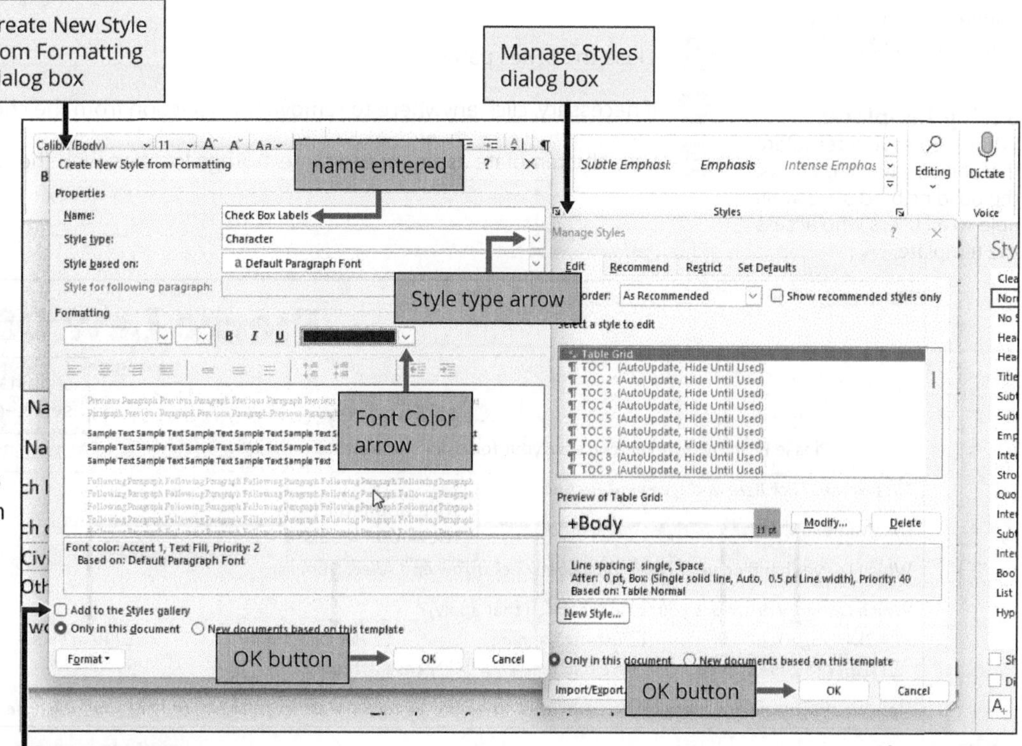

Figure 11–22

- Click OK in each open dialog box to create the new character style, Check Box Labels in this case, and insert the new style name in the Styles pane (Figure 11–23).

Q&A What if I wanted the style to be added to the Styles gallery?
You would place a check mark in the 'Add to the Styles gallery' check box (Create New Style from Formatting dialog box), shown in Figure 11–22.

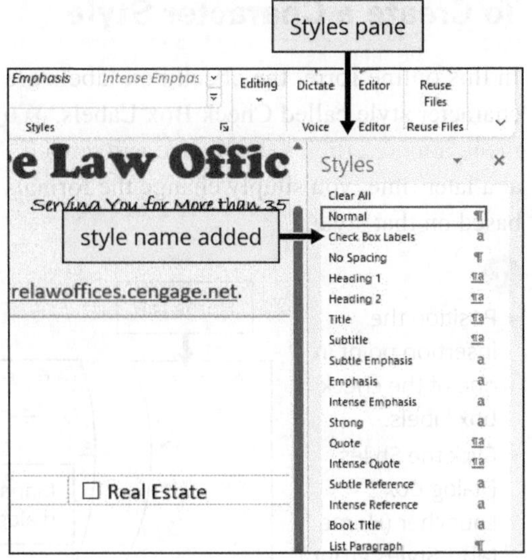

Figure 11–23

BTW
Character vs. Paragraph Styles
In the Styles pane, character styles display a lowercase letter a to the right of the style name, and paragraph styles show a paragraph mark. If a style has character and paragraph settings, then both a lowercase letter a and the paragraph mark are displayed to the right of the style name. With a character style, Word applies the formats to the selected text. With a paragraph style, Word applies the formats to the entire paragraph.

BTW
Saving Templates
When you save a template that contains building blocks, the building blocks are available to all users who access the template.

To Apply a Style

The next step is to apply the Check Box Labels style just created to the check box labels in the form. The following steps apply a style.

1. Drag through the check box label, Civil Litigation, to select it and then click 'Check Box Labels' in the Styles pane to apply the style to the selected text.
2. Repeat Step 1 for these check box labels (Figure 11–24): Estate Planning, Personal Injury, Real Estate, and Other (please specify):.

   Q&A Would I have to drag through one word labels to apply a style?
   No. You simply can position the insertion point in the word before clicking the desired style to apply.

3. Close the Styles pane.
4. If necessary, click anywhere to remove the selection from the check box label.
5. Save the template again on the same storage location with the same file name.

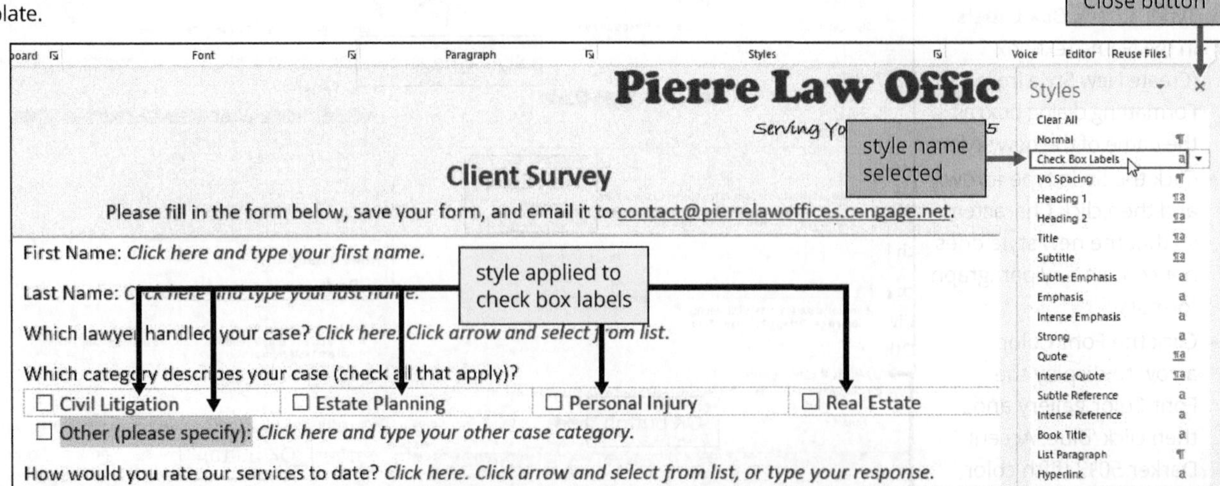

Figure 11–24

Break Point: If you want to take a break, this is a good place to do so. You can exit Word now. To resume later, start Word, open the file called SC_WD_11_PierreLawOfficesClientSurveyModified.dotm, and continue following the steps from this location forward.

Enhancing with Color, Shapes, Effects, and Graphics

You will enhance the updated law offices form by performing these steps:

1. Apply a texture fill effect for the page color.
2. Change the appearance of the shape.
3. Change the color of a shadow on the shape.
4. Fill a shape with a picture.
5. Insert a picture, remove its background, and apply an artistic effect.
6. Insert and format a text box.
7. Group the picture and the text box together.

The following pages apply these changes to the form.

To Use a Fill Effect for the Page Color

Word provides a gallery of 24 predefined textures you can use as a page background. These textures resemble various wallpaper patterns. The following steps change the page color to a texture fill effect. **Why?** Instead of a simple color for the background page color, this online form uses a texture for the page color.

- Display the Design tab.
- Click the Page Color button (Design tab | Page Background group) to display the Page Color gallery (Figure 11–25).

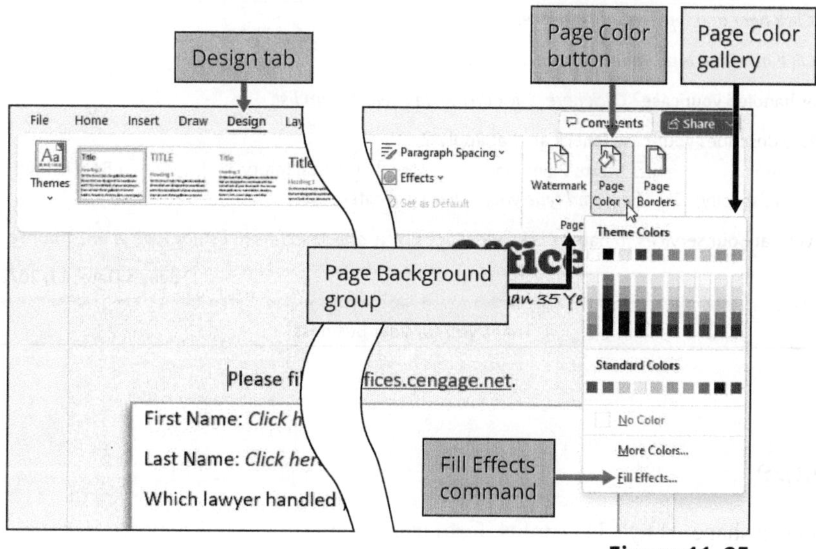

Figure 11–25

2

- Click Fill Effects in the Page Color gallery to display the Fill Effects dialog box.
- Click the Texture tab (Fill Effects dialog box) to display the Texture sheet.
- Scroll to, if necessary, and then click the Newsprint texture in the Texture gallery to select the texture (Figure 11–26).

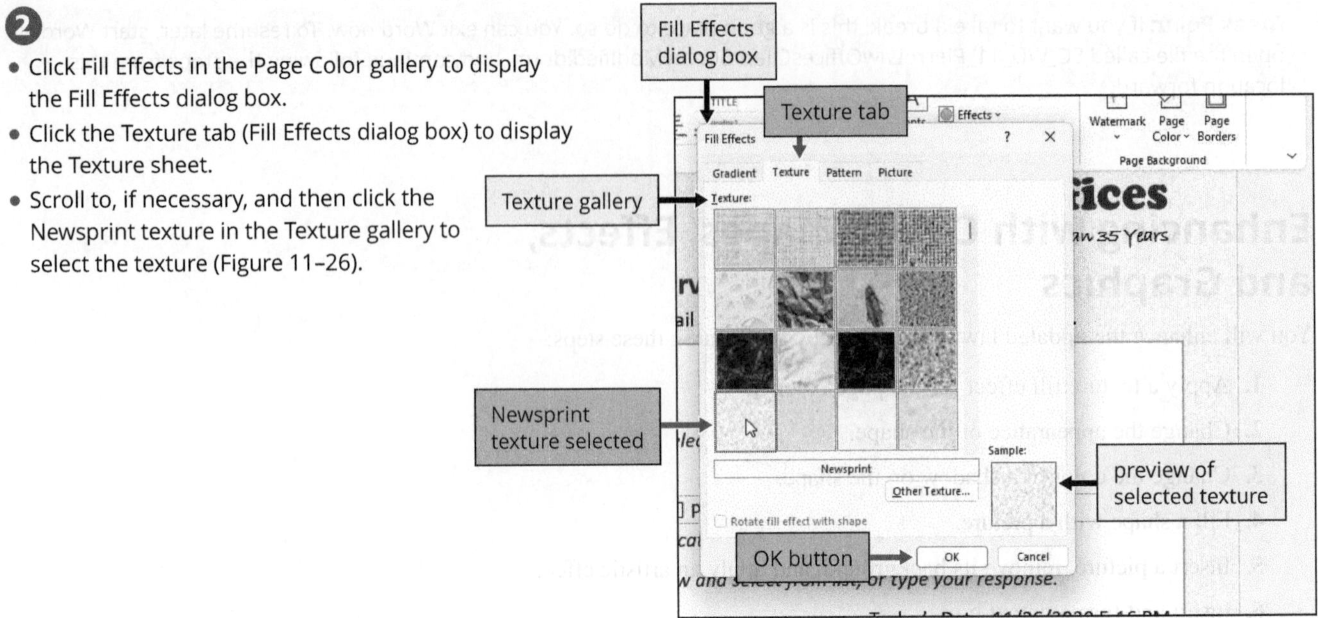

Figure 11–26

3

- Click OK to apply the selected texture as the page color in the document (Figure 11–27).

Q&A How would I remove a texture page color?
You would click the Page Color button (Design tab | Page Background group) and then click No Color in the Page Color gallery.

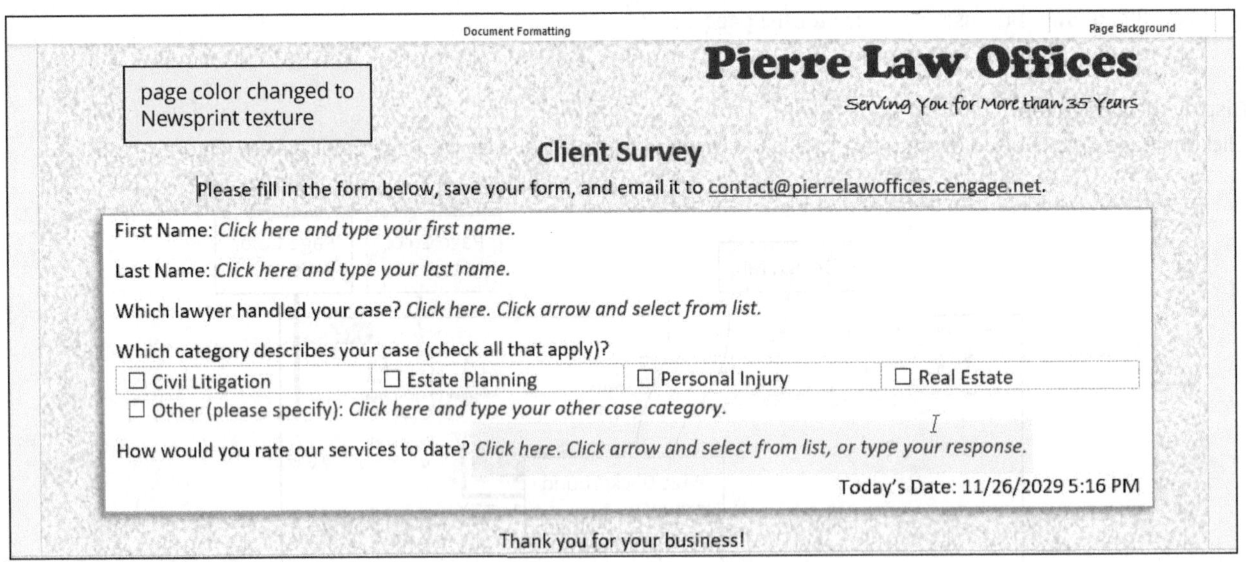

Figure 11–27

To Change a Shape

The following steps change a shape. **Why?** This online form uses a variation of the standard rectangle shape.

- Click the rectangle shape to select it.
- Display the Shape Format tab.

- Click the Edit Shape button (Shape Format tab | Insert Shapes group) to display the Edit Shape menu.
- Point to Change Shape on the Edit Shape menu to display the Change Shape gallery (Figure 11–28).

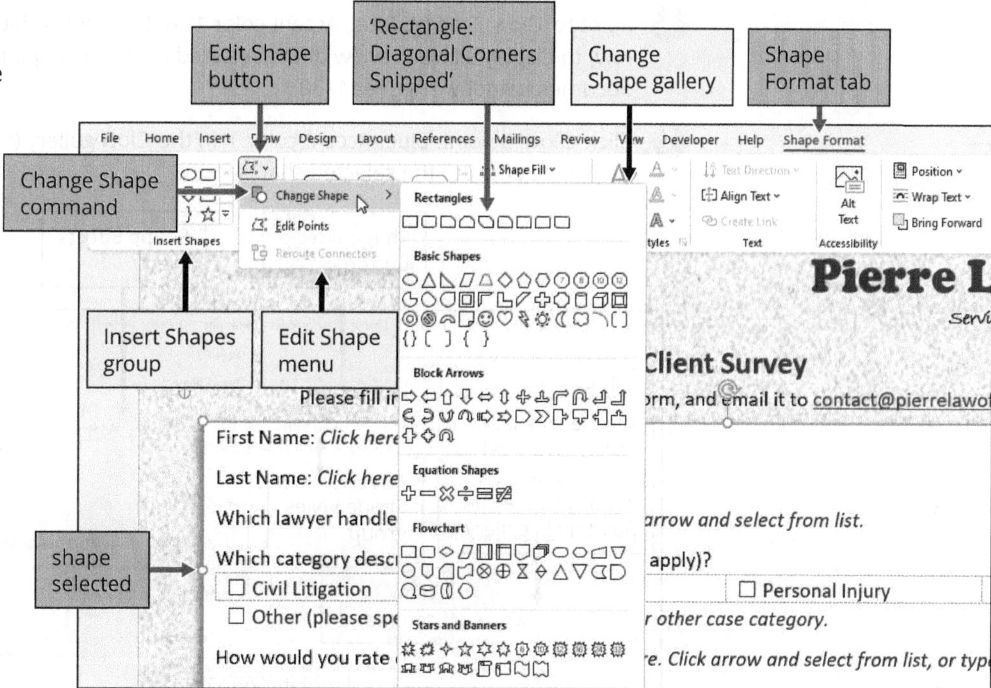

Figure 11–28

2

- Click 'Rectangle: Diagonal Corners Snipped' in the Rectangles area in the Change Shape gallery to change the selected shape (Figure 11–29).

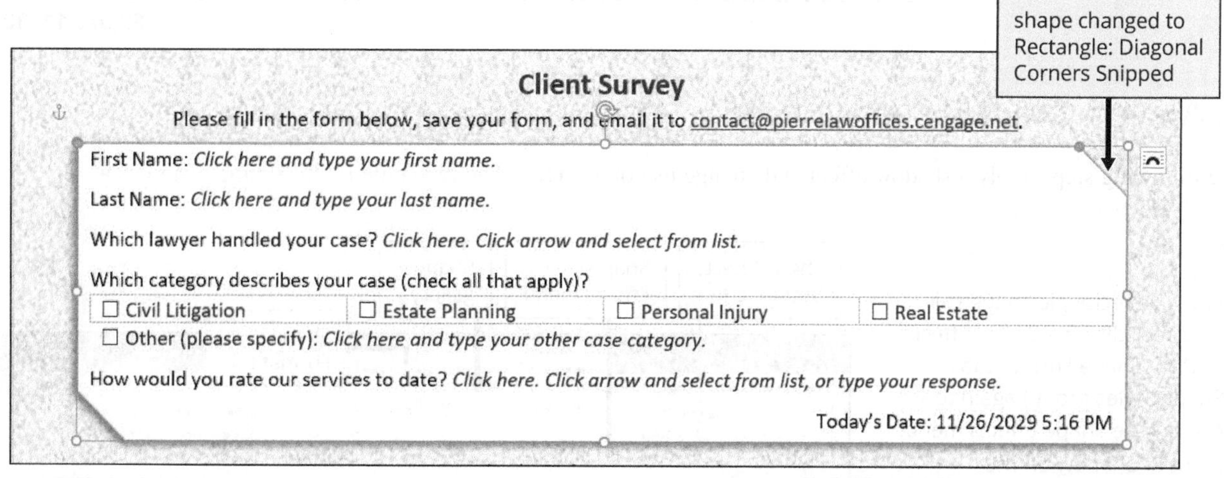

Figure 11–29

To Apply a Glow Shape Effect

The next step is to apply a glow effect to the rectangle shape. You can apply the same effects to shapes as to pictures. That is, you can apply shadows, reflections, glows, soft edges, bevels, and 3-D rotations to pictures and shapes. The following steps apply a shape effect.

1. With the rectangle shape selected, click the Shape Effects button (Shape Format tab | Shape Styles group) to display the Shape Effects menu.
2. Point to Glow on the Shape Effects menu to display the Glow gallery.

3 Point to 'Glow: 5 point; Blue, Accent color 1' in the Glow Variations area (first glow in first row) to display a Live Preview of the selected glow effect applied to the selected shape in the document window (Figure 11–30).

4 Click 'Glow: 5 point; Blue, Accent color 1' in the Glow gallery (first glow in first row) to apply the shape effect to the selected shape.

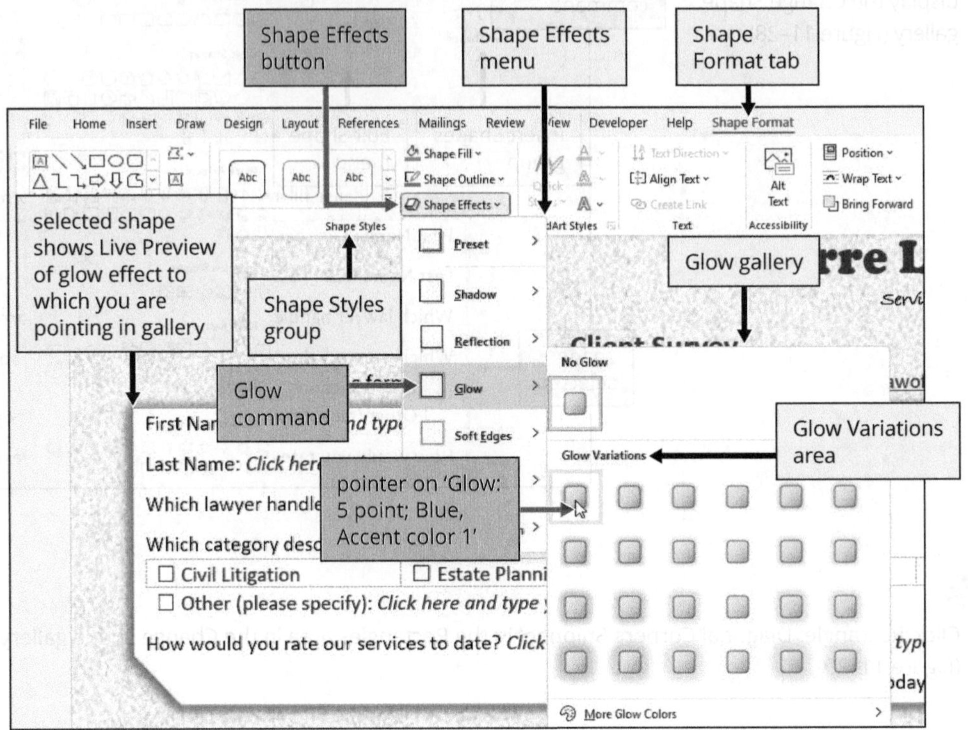

Figure 11–30

To Apply a Shadow Shape Effect

The following steps apply a shadow effect and change its color. **Why?** The rectangle in this online form has a shadow with a similar color to the placeholder text.

1

- With the rectangle shape still selected, click the Shape Effects button (Shape Format tab | Shape Styles group) again to display the Shape Effects menu.
- Point to Shadow on the Shape Effects menu to display the Shadow gallery.
- Point to 'Perspective: Upper Right' in the Perspective area at the bottom of the Shadow gallery to display a Live Preview of that shadow applied to the shape in the document (Figure 11–31).

- **Experiment:** Point to various shadows in the Shadow gallery and notice the shadow on the selected shape change.

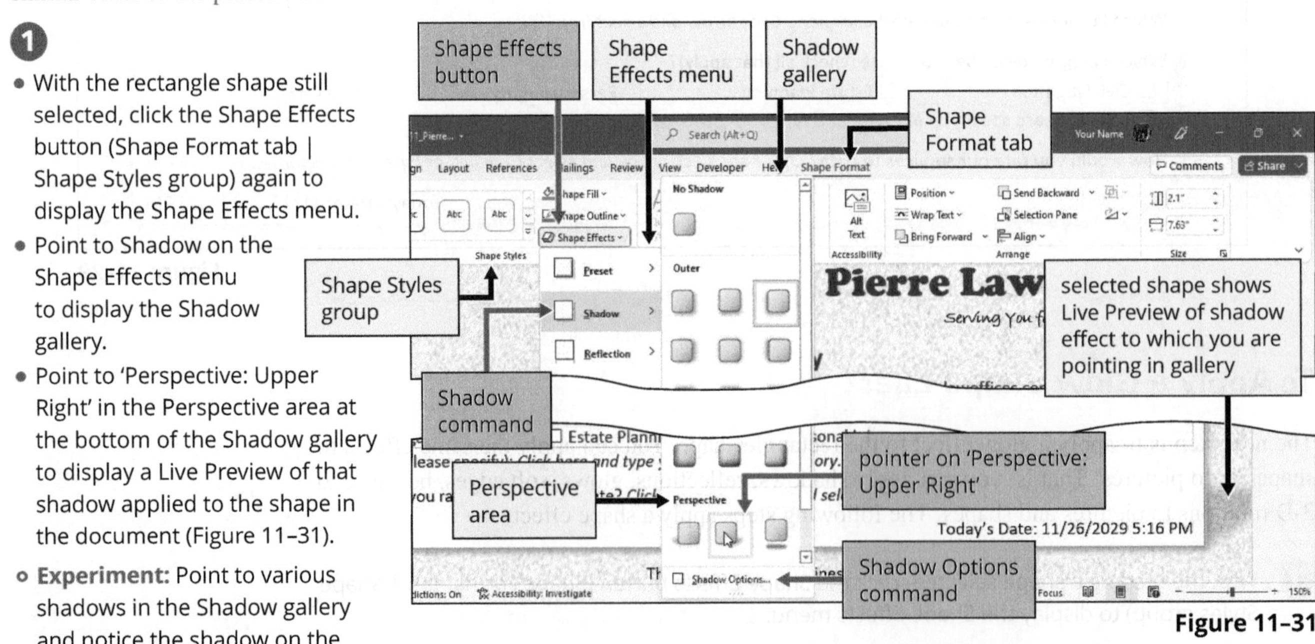

Figure 11–31

2

- Click 'Perspective: Upper Right' in the Shadow gallery to apply the selected shadow to the selected shape.
- Click the Shape Effects button (Shape Format tab | Shape Styles group) again to display the Shape Effects menu.
- Point to Shadow in the Shape Effects menu to display the Shadow gallery.
- Click Shadow Options in the Shadow gallery (shown in Figure 11–31) to open the Format Shape pane. (If necessary, scroll to the right in the document window to display the right edge of the form so that the shadow is visible on the screen.)
- Click the Shadow Color button (Format Shape pane) and then click 'Blue, Accent 1' (fifth color in first row) in the Shadow Color gallery to change the shadow color.
- Click the Transparency down arrow as many times as necessary until the Transparency box displays 60% to change the amount of transparency in the shadow (Figure 11–32).

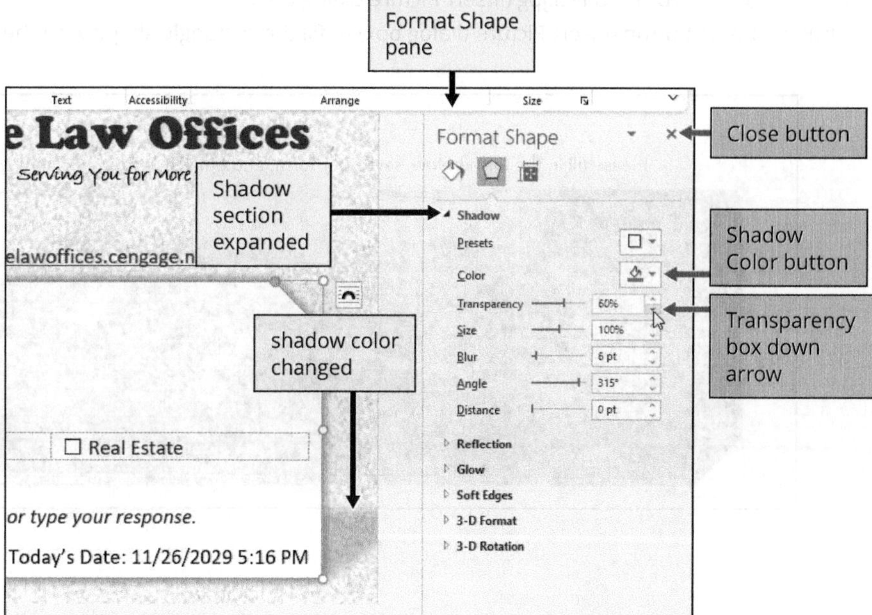

Figure 11–32

- Click the Close button to close the Format Shape pane.

To Fill a Shape with a Picture

The following steps fill a shape with a picture. **Why?** The rectangle in this online form contains a picture of a gavel. The picture, called Support_WD_11_Gavel.jpg, is located on the Data Files. Please contact your instructor for information about accessing the Data Files.

- With the rectangle shape still selected, click the Shape Fill arrow (Shape Format tab | Shape Styles group) to display the Shape Fill gallery (Figure 11–33).

Q&A My Shape Fill gallery did not appear. Why not?
You clicked the Shape Fill button instead of the Shape Fill arrow. Repeat Step 1.

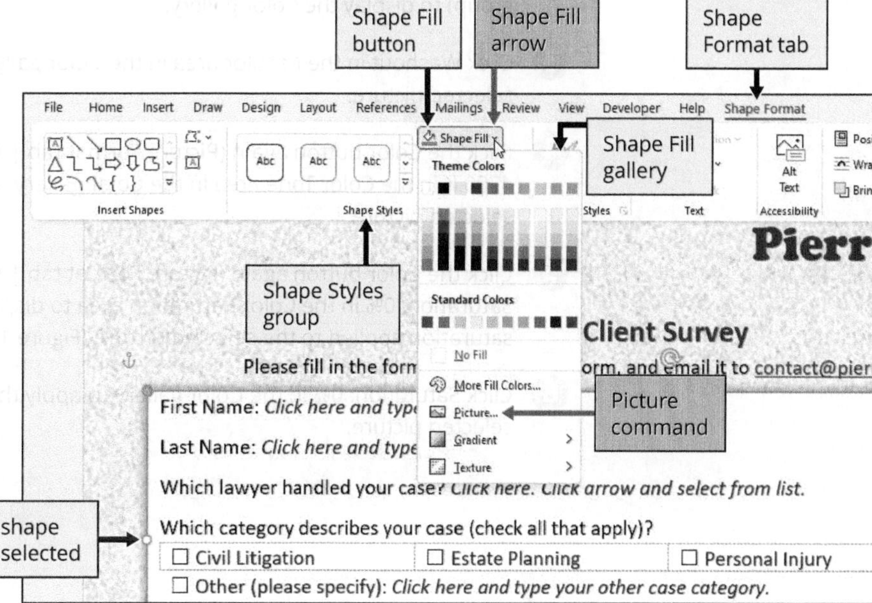

Figure 11–33

- Click Picture in the Shape Fill gallery to display the Insert Pictures dialog box.
- Click the 'From a File' button (Insert Pictures dialog box) to display the Insert Picture dialog box. Locate and then select the file called Support_WD_11_Gavel.jpg (Insert Picture dialog box).
- Click the Insert button (Insert Picture dialog box) to fill the rectangle shape with the picture (Figure 11-34).

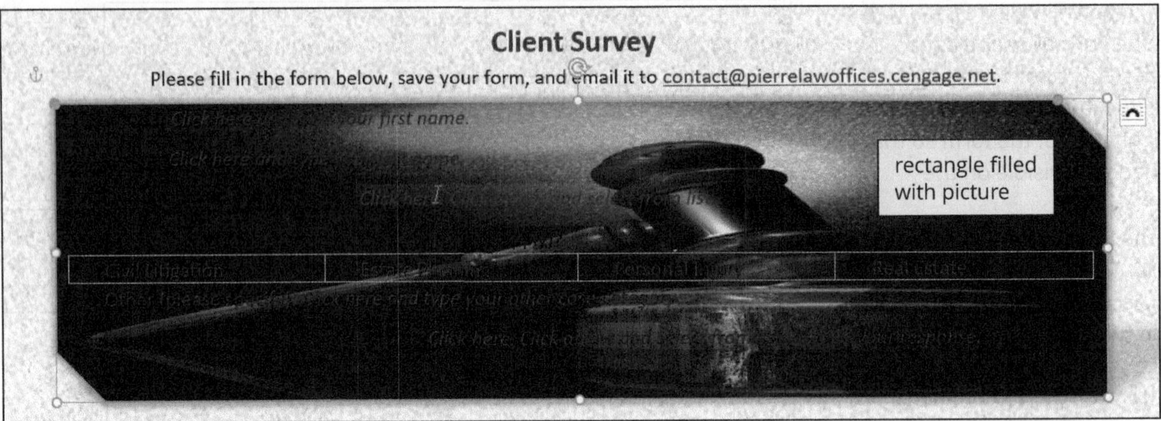

Figure 11-34

To Change the Color of a Picture

The text in the rectangle shape is difficult to read because the picture just inserted is too dark. You can experiment with adjusting the brightness, contrast, and color of a picture so that the text is readable. In this project, the color is changed to the washout setting and the saturation and tone are changed so that the text is easier to read. The following steps change the color, tone, and saturation of the picture.

1. Display the Picture Format tab.
2. With the rectangle shape still selected, click the Color button (Picture Format tab | Adjust group) to display the Color gallery.
3. Click Washout in the Recolor area in the Color gallery to apply the selected color to the selected picture.
4. Click the Color button again (Picture Format tab | Adjust group) and then click Temperature: 4700 K in the Color Tone area in the Color gallery to apply the selected temperature to the selected picture.
5. Click the Color button again (Picture Format tab | Adjust group) and then point to Saturation: 0% in the Color Saturation area to display a Live Preview of the selected saturation applied to the selected picture (Figure 11-35).
6. Click Saturation: 0% in the Color gallery to apply the selected saturation to the selected picture.

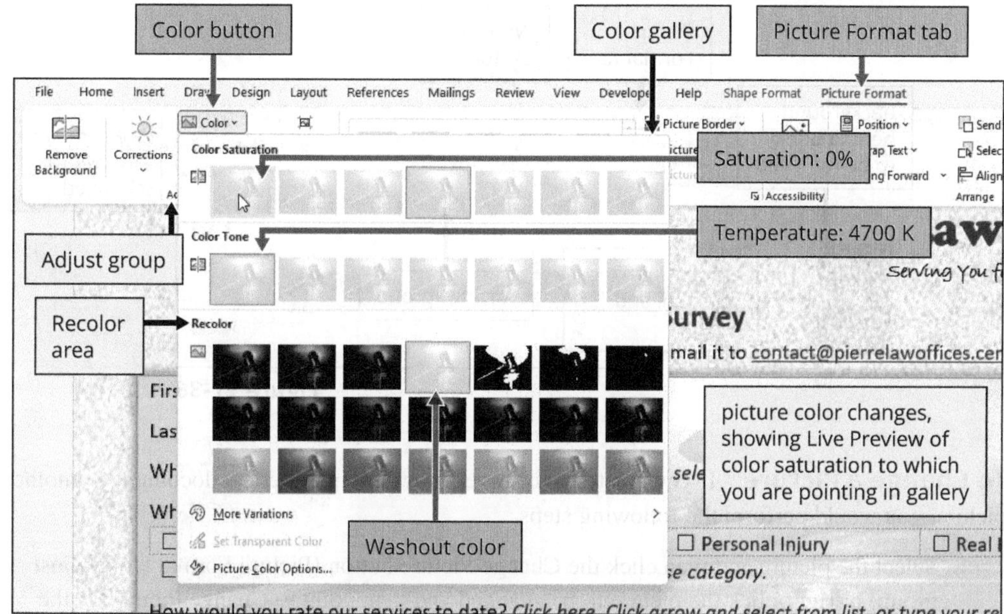

Figure 11-35

To Insert, Change Wrapping Style, and Resize a Picture

The top of the online form in this module contains a picture of the front of a law book. The picture, called Support_WD_11_LawBook.png, is located in the Data Files. Please contact your instructor for information about accessing the Data Files.

You will change the wrapping style of the inserted picture so that it can be positioned in front of the text. Because the graphic's original size is too large, you also will resize it. The following steps insert a picture, change its wrapping style, resize it, and move it to the top of the form.

1. Position the insertion point in a location near where the picture will be inserted, in this case, near the top of the online form.
2. Display the Insert tab. Click the Pictures button (Insert tab | Illustrations group) to display the Insert Picture From menu and then click This Device on the Insert Picture From menu to display the Insert Picture dialog box.
3. Locate and then click the file called Support_WD_11_LawBook.jpg (Insert Picture dialog box) to select the file.
4. Click the Insert button to insert the picture at the location of the insertion point.
5. With the picture selected, click the Wrap Text button (Picture Format tab | Arrange group) and then click 'In Front of Text' so that the graphic can be positioned on top of text.
6. Change the value in the Shape Height box (Picture Format tab | Size group) to 1.05" and the value in the Shape Width box (Picture Format tab | Size group) to 0.7".
7. Drag the graphic to the approximate location shown in Figure 11-36.
8. If necessary, scroll to display the online form in the document window (Figure 11-36).

BTW

Drawing Canvas

Some users prefer inserting graphics on a drawing canvas, which is a rectangular boundary between a shape and the rest of the document; it also is a container that helps you resize and arrange shapes on the page. To insert a drawing canvas, click the Shapes button (Insert tab | Illustrations group) and then click 'New Drawing Canvas' in the Shapes gallery. You can use the Shape Format tab to insert objects in the drawing canvas or format the appearance of the drawing canvas.

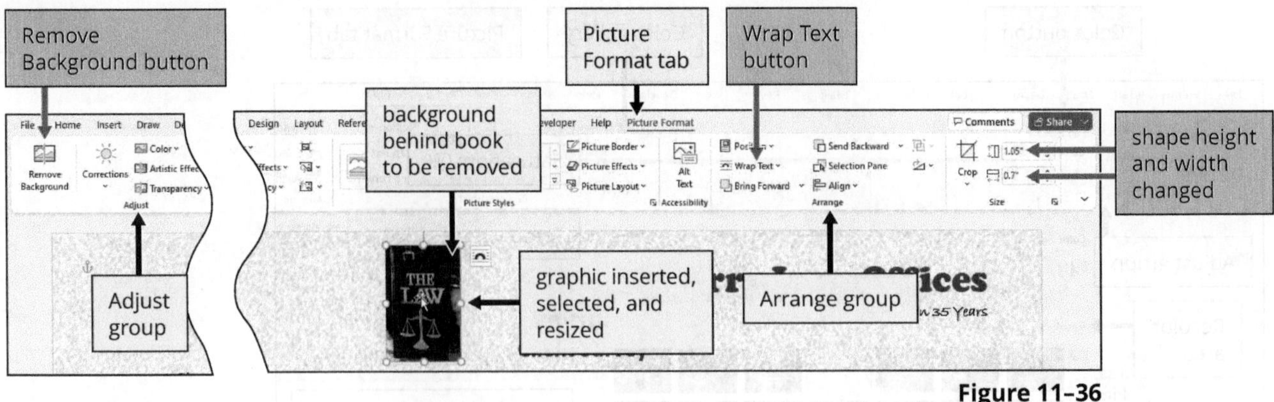

Figure 11-36

To Change a Picture If you wanted to change an existing picture in a document to another picture, you would perform the following steps.

1. Select the picture and then click the Change Picture button (Picture Format tab | Adjust group) or right-click the picture to be changed and then point to Change Picture on the shortcut menu.
2. Click the desired option (From a File, From Stock Images, From Online Sources, From Icons, or From Clipboard) on the Change Picture menu or submenu.
3. Locate the desired replacement picture and then click OK.

To Remove a Background

In Word, you can remove a background from a picture. The following steps remove a background. **Why?** You remove the background behind the book in the picture so that only the book cover is displayed.

- With the law book picture selected, click the Remove Background button (Picture Format tab | Adjust group) (shown in Figure 11-36) to display the Background Removal tab and show the proposed area to be deleted in purple (Figure 11-37). (Note that your proposed areas may differ from the figure.)

Q&A What is the Background Removal tab?
You can draw around areas to keep or areas to remove by clicking the respective buttons on the Background Removal tab. If you mistakenly mark too much, use the 'Mark Areas to Remove' button. When finished marking, click the Keep Changes button, or to start over, click the 'Discard All Changes' button.

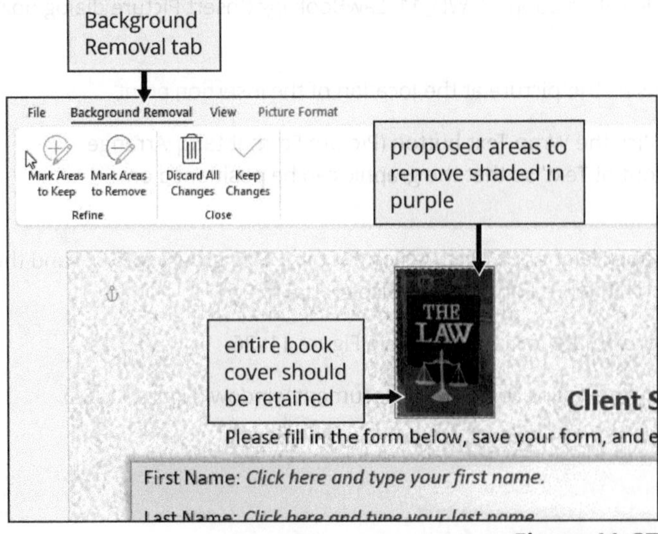

Figure 11-37

- Click the 'Mark Areas to Keep' button (Background Removal tab | Refine group) and then use the pointer to drag over areas that should remain in the image. Repeat as necessary. If necessary, click the 'Mark Areas to Remove' button (Background Removal tab | Refine group) and use the pointer to drag over areas that should be deleted from the image. Your resulting areas to keep and delete should appear similar to Figure 11-38.

Q&A How can you tell from the image which areas will be removed?
The areas in purple will be removed from the image.

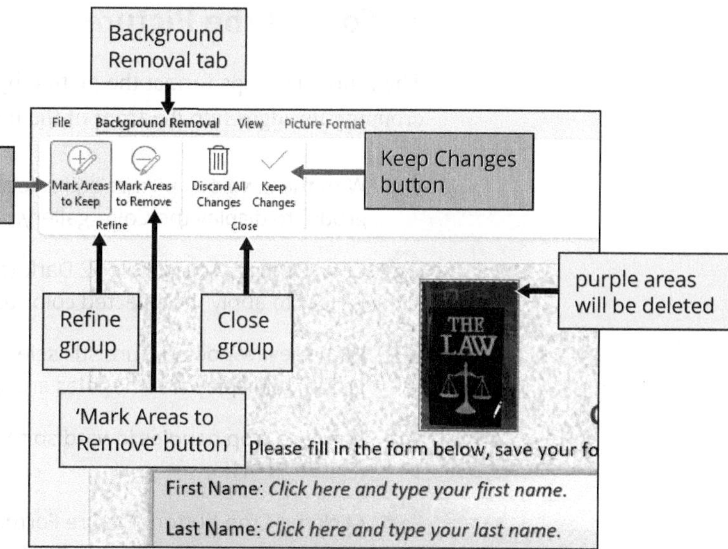

Figure 11-38

- Click the Keep Changes button (Background Removal tab | Close group) to remove the area shaded purple and to close the Background Removal tab (Figure 11-39).

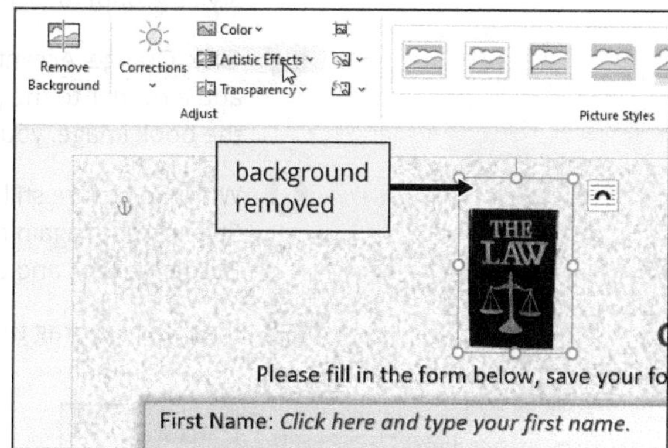

Figure 11-39

To Apply an Artistic Effect

Word provides several different artistic effects, such as blur, line drawing, and paint brush, that alter the appearance of a picture. The following steps apply an artistic effect to the picture. **Why?** You want to soften the appearance of the picture a bit.

- With the picture still selected, click the Artistic Effects button (Picture Format tab | Adjust group) to display the Artistic Effects gallery (Figure 11-40).

- Click Crisscross Etching (third effect in the fourth row) in the Artistic Effects gallery to apply the selected effect to the selected picture (shown in Figure 11-41).

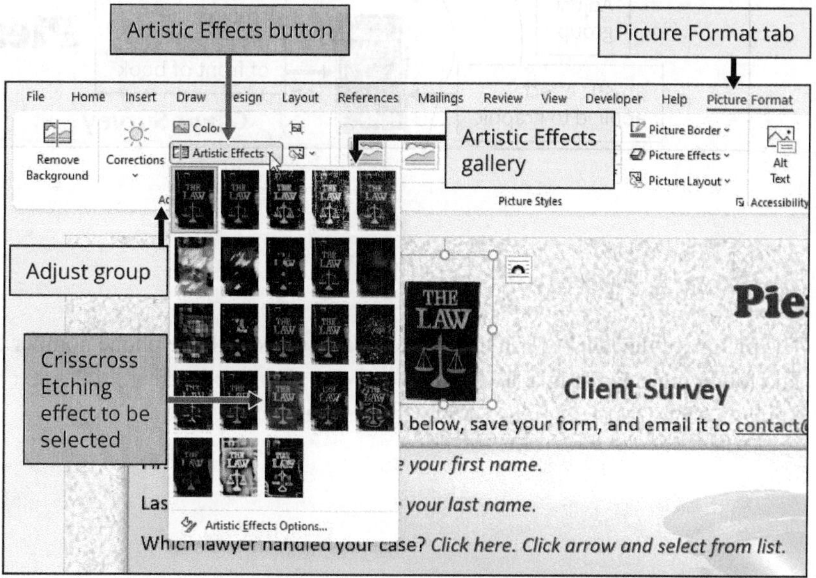

Figure 11-40

To Format the Picture

The following steps format the picture by changing its color to match the name of the law office, cropping its edges into the front of the book cover, and adding a color coordinated border.

1. With the law book picture still selected, click the Color button (Picture Format tab | Adjust group) to display the Color gallery.
2. Click 'Orange, Accent color 2 Dark' (third color in second row in the Recolor area) in the Color gallery to apply the selected color to the selected picture.
3. With the law book picture still selected, click the Crop button (Picture Format tab | Size group) to display crop handles around the picture.
4. Drag the crop handles inward so that they are inside the edges of the front of the book (Figure 11–41).
5. Click the Crop button (Picture Format tab | Size group) again to deactivate the crop tool, which removes the crop handles from the selected picture.
6. With the picture still selected, click the Picture Border arrow (Picture Format tab | Picture Styles group) to display the Picture Border gallery.
7. Click 'Orange, Accent 2, Darker 50%' (sixth color in sixth row) in the Picture Border gallery to add a border to the picture in the selected color. (If the border does not touch the edge of the book image, you need to crop tighter into the book cover image.)
8. With the picture still selected, click the Picture Border arrow (Picture Format tab | Picture Styles group) again to display the Picture Border gallery, point to Weight in the Picture Border gallery, and then click 1½ pt to increase the weight of the border.
9. If necessary, drag the graphic to the approximate location shown in Figure 11–42.

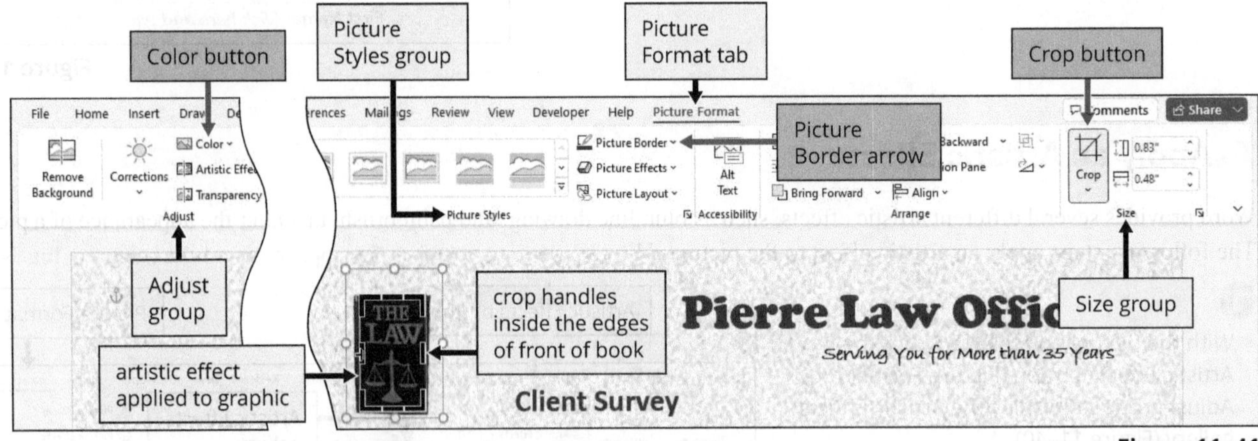

Figure 11–41

To Draw a Text Box

The picture of the law book in this form has a text box with the phone number of the law office positioned along the book spine. The following steps draw a text box. **Why?** The first step in creating the text box is to draw its perimeter. You draw a text box using the same procedure as you do to draw a shape.

1

- Position the insertion point somewhere in the top of the online form.
- Display the Insert tab.
- Click the Text Box button (Insert tab | Text group) to display the Text Box gallery (Figure 11–42).

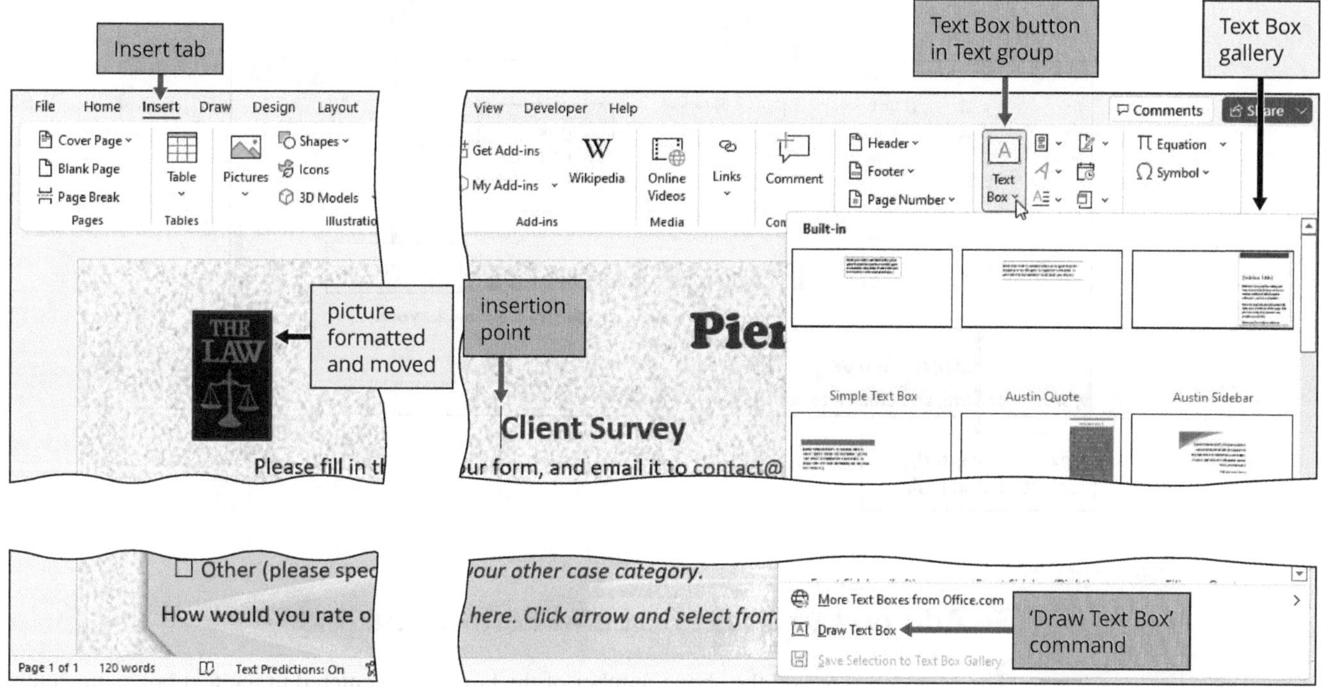

Figure 11–42

2

- Click 'Draw Text Box' in the Text Box gallery, which removes the gallery and changes the shape of the pointer to a crosshair.
- Drag the pointer to the right and downward to form the boundaries of the text box, similar to what is shown in Figure 11–43.

Q&A What if I am using a touch screen?
A text box is inserted in the document window. Proceed to Step 4.

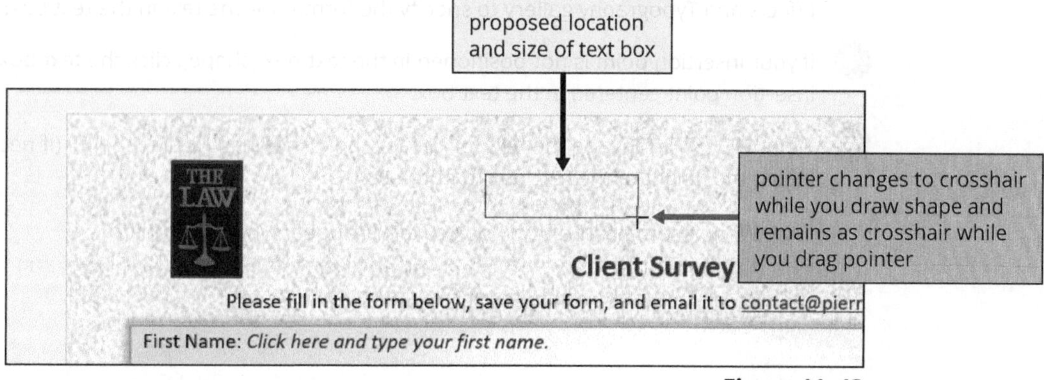

Figure 11–43

- Release the mouse button so that Word draws the text box according to your drawing in the document window.

- Verify your shape is the same approximate height and width as the one in this project by changing the values in the Shape Height and Shape Width boxes (Shape Format tab | Size group) to 0.33" and 1.22", respectively (Figure 11–44).

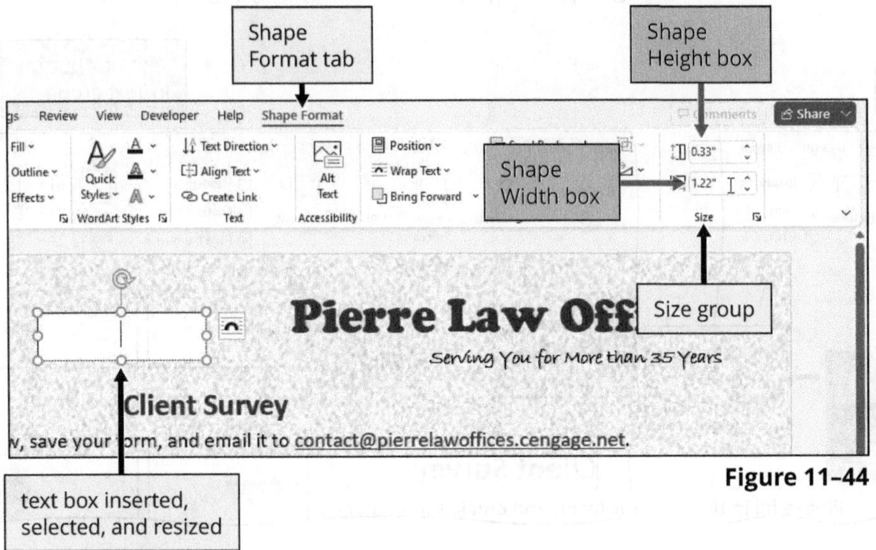

Figure 11–44

To Add Text to a Text Box and Format the Text

The next step is to add the phone number of the law office centered in the text box using a text effect. You add text to a text box using the same procedure you do when adding text to a shape. The following steps add text to a text box.

1. Display the Home tab. With the text box selected, click the Center button (Home tab | Paragraph group) so that the text you enter is centered in the text box.
2. With the text box selected, change the font size to 10.
3. With the text box selected, click the 'Text Effects and Typography' button (Home tab | Font group) and then click 'Fill: Black, Text color 1; Shadow' (first effect in first row) in the Text Effects and Typography gallery to specify the format for the text in the text box.
4. If your insertion point is not positioned in the text box (shape), click the text box to place an insertion point centered in the text box.
5. Type **312-555-8700** as the text for the text box (shown in Figure 11–45). (If necessary, adjust the height of the text box to fit the text.)

Q&A What if some part of the book cover disappears in the graphic?
Repeat the steps discussed earlier in this section to remove a background and mark areas to keep until the entire book cover reappears.

To Change Text Direction in a Text Box

The following steps change text direction in a text box. **Why?** The direction of the text in the text box should be vertical instead of horizontal.

- Display the Shape Format tab.
- With the shape still selected, click the Text Direction button (Shape Format tab | Text group) to display the Text Direction gallery (Figure 11–45).

Q&A What if my text box no longer is selected?

Click the text box to select it.

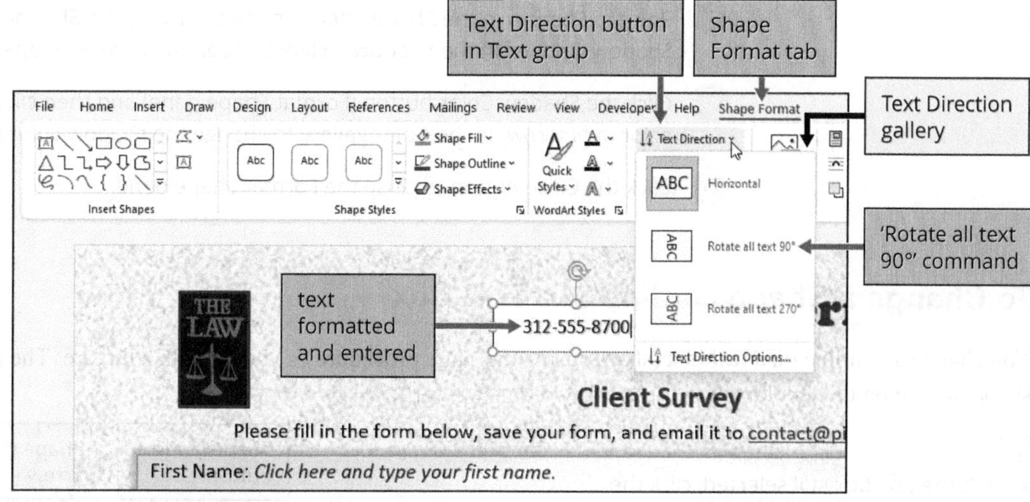

Figure 11–45

2

- Click 'Rotate all text 90°' in the Text Direction gallery to display the text in the text box vertically from top to bottom.
- Resize the text box so that your shape is the same approximate height and width as the one in this project by changing the values in the Shape Height and Shape Width boxes (Shape Format tab | Size group) to 1" and 0.4", respectively (Figure 11–46).

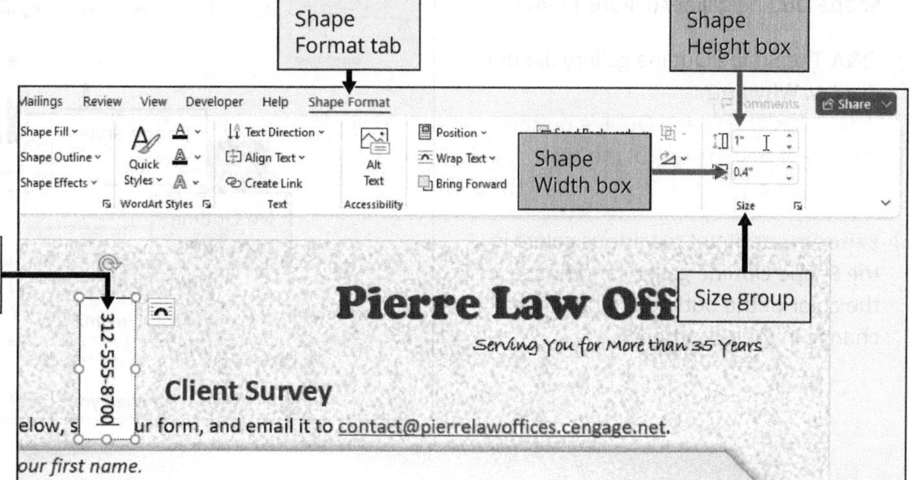

Figure 11–46

Other Ways

1. Right-click text box, click Format Shape on shortcut menu, click Text Options tab (Format Shape pane), click Layout & Properties button, expand Text Box section, click Text direction box, select desired direction, click Close button

To Apply a Shadow Shape Effect to a Text Box

The text box in this online form has an inside shadow that is a shade of orange. The following steps apply a shadow effect and change its color.

1. Move the text box to the right so that it is visible when you change the shadows and colors.
2. With the text box still selected, click the Shape Effects button (Shape Format tab | Shape Styles group) to display the Shape Effects menu.
3. Point to Shadow in the Shape Effects menu to display the Shadow gallery and then click Inside: Center in the Inner area of the Shadow gallery to apply the selected shadow to the selected shape.
4. Click the Shape Effects button (Shape Format tab | Shape Styles group) again to display the Shape Effects menu.

5. Point to Shadow in the Shape Effects menu to display the Shadow gallery and then click Shadow Options in the Shadow gallery to open the Format Shape pane.

6. Click the Shadow Color button (Format Shape pane) and then click 'Orange, Accent 2' (sixth color in first row) in the Color gallery to change the shadow color (shown in Figure 11–47).

7. Click the Close button to close the Format Shape pane.

To Change a Shape Outline of a Text Box

You change an outline on a text box (shape) using the same procedure as you do with a picture. The following steps remove the shape outline on the text box. **Why?** The text box in this form has no outline.

1

- With the text box still selected, click the Shape Outline arrow (Shape Format tab | Shape Styles group) to display the Shape Outline gallery (Figure 11–47).

Q&A The Shape Outline gallery did not display. Why not?
You clicked the Shape Outline button instead of the Shape Outline arrow. Repeat Step 1.

- **Experiment:** Point to various colors in the Shape Outline gallery and notice the color of the outline on the text box change in the document.

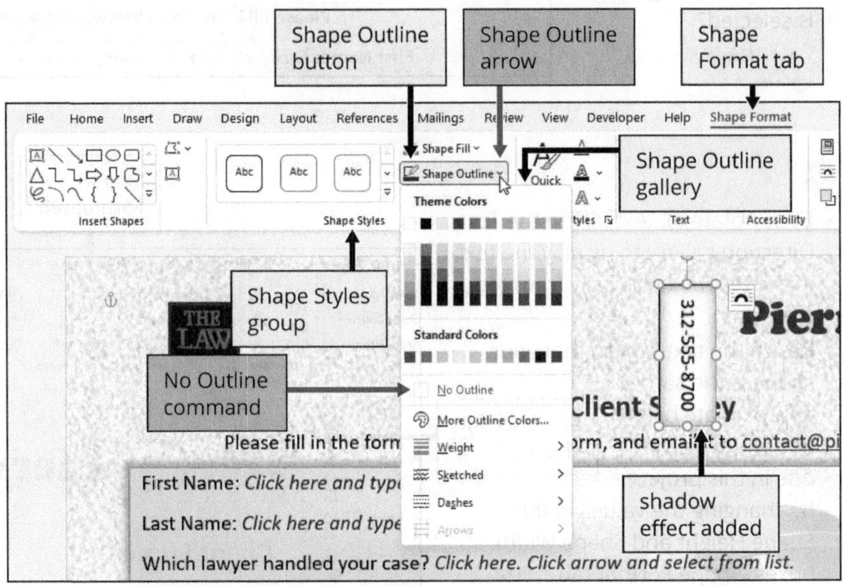

Figure 11–47

- Click No Outline in the Shape Outline gallery to remove the outline from the selected shape (shown in Figure 11–48).

Other Ways

1. Click Shape Styles Dialog Box Launcher (Shape Format tab | Shape Styles group); expand Line section (Format Shape pane); click No line to remove line, or click Solid line, click Outline color button, and select desired color to change line color; click Close button
2. Right-click text box (or, if using touch, tap 'Show Context Menu' button on Mini toolbar), click Format Shape on shortcut menu, expand Line section (Format Shape pane), click No line to remove line, or click Solid line, click Outline color button, and select desired color to change line color; click Close button

To Apply a 3-D Effect to a Text Box

Word provides 3-D effects for shapes (such as text boxes) that are similar to those it provides for pictures. The following steps apply a 3-D rotation effect to a text box. **Why?** In this form, the text box is rotated using a 3-D rotation effect.

- Move the text box to the left so that it is visible when you change to a 3-D effect.
- With the text box selected, click the Shape Effects button (Shape Format tab | Shape Styles group) to display the Shape Effects gallery.

- Point to '3-D Rotation' in the Shape Effects gallery to display the 3-D Rotation gallery.
- Point to 'Isometric: Right Up' in the Parallel area (second rotation in first row) to display a Live Preview of the selected 3-D effect applied to the text box in the document window (Figure 11–48).

◦ **Experiment:** Point to various 3-D rotation effects in the 3-D Rotation gallery and notice the text box change in the document window.

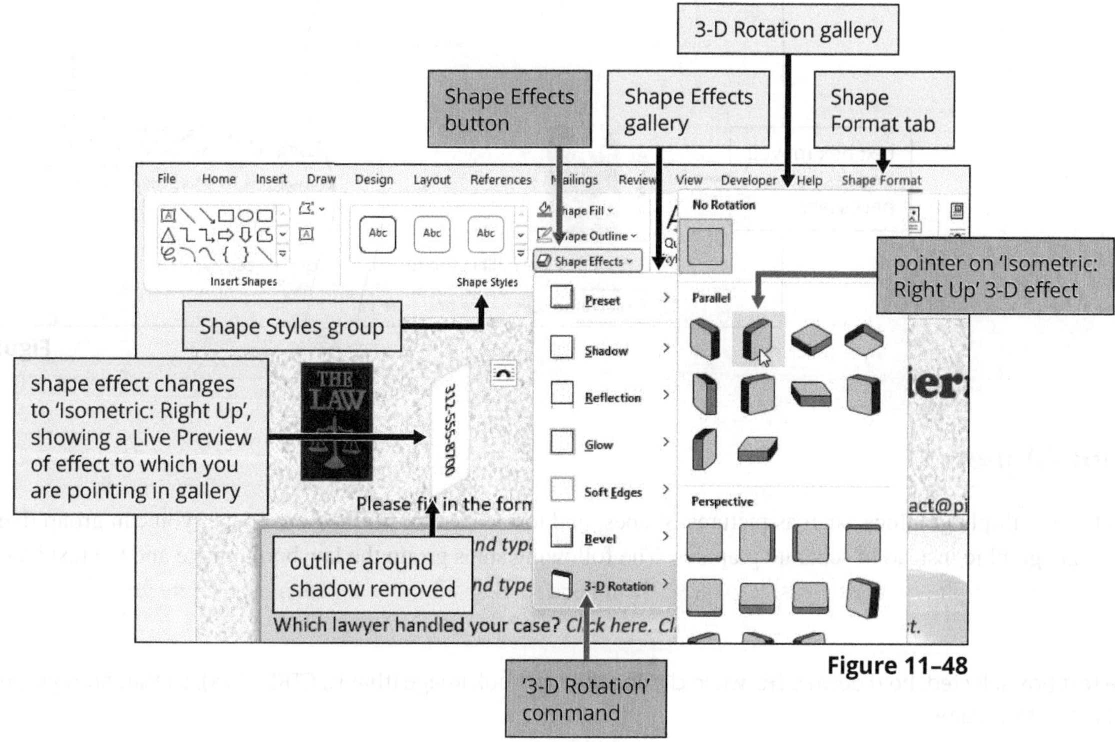

Figure 11–48

- Click 'Isometric: Right Up' in the 3-D Rotation gallery to apply the selected 3-D effect.

Other Ways

1. Click Shape Styles Dialog Box Launcher (Shape Format tab | Shape Styles group), click Text Options tab (Format Shape pane), click Text Effects button, if necessary, expand 3-D Rotation section, select desired options, click Close button
2. Right-click text box (or, if using touch, tap 'Show Context Menu' button on Mini toolbar), click Format Shape on shortcut menu, click Text Options tab (Format Shape pane), click Text Effects button, if necessary, expand 3-D Rotation section, select desired options, click Close button

To Move the Text Box

In this project, the text box is to be positioned near the lower-left of the graphic. The following steps move the text box.

1. With the text box selected, click the Send Backward arrow (Shape Format tab | Arrange group) and then click 'Send to Back' on the Send Backward menu to send the text box behind the book cover image.
2. Drag the text box to the location shown in Figure 11–49. (You may need to drag the text box a couple of times, or use the arrow keys, to position it as shown in the figure.)
3. If necessary, resize the text box so that its right edge is the same height as the left edge of the book cover as shown in Figure 11–49.

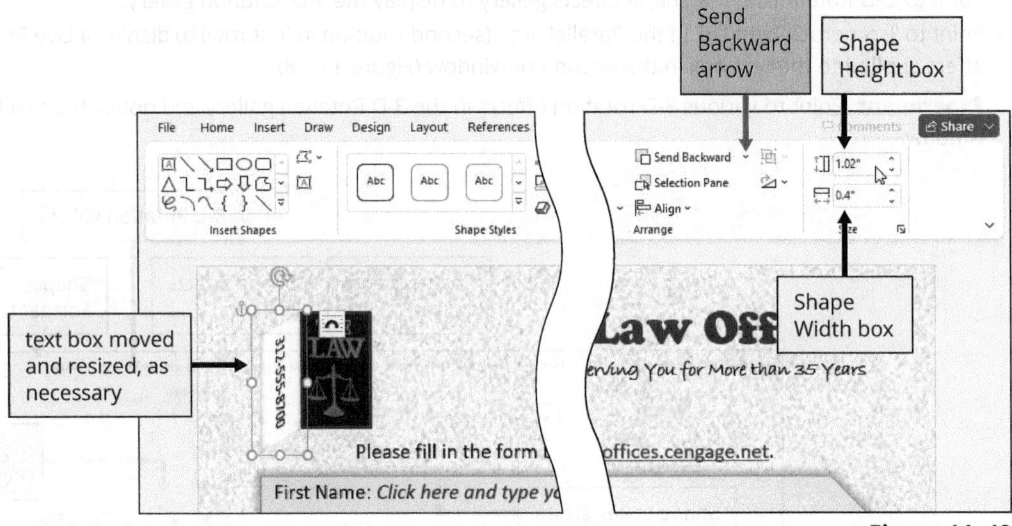

Figure 11–49

To Group Objects

When you have multiple graphics, such as pictures, shapes, and text boxes, positioned on a page, you can group them so that they are a single graphic instead of separate graphics. The following steps group the law book image and the text box together. **Why?** Grouping the graphics makes it easier to move them because they all move together as a single graphic.

- With the text box selected, hold down CTRL while clicking the law book image (that is, CTRL+click), so that both graphics are selected at the same time.

Q&A What if I had more than two graphics (i.e., pictures, shapes, text boxes, etc.) that I wanted to group?
For each subsequent graphic to select, CTRL+click the graphic, which enables you to select multiple objects at the same time.

- Click the Group Objects button (Shape Format tab | Arrange group) to display the Group Objects menu (Figure 11–50).

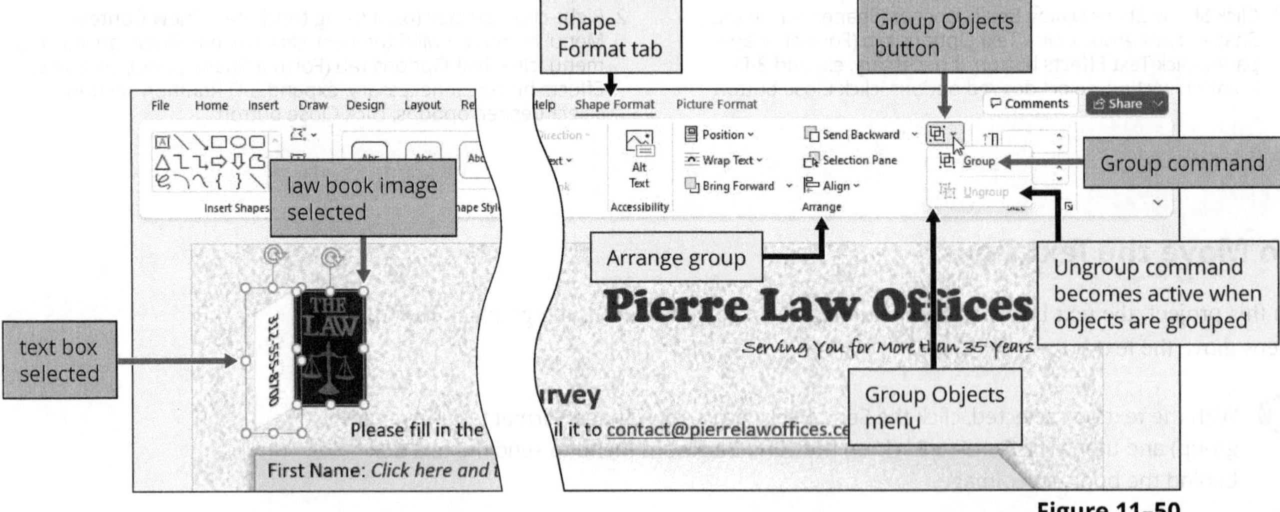

Figure 11–50

- Click Group on the Group Objects menu to group the selected objects into a single selected object (Figure 11–51).

Q&A What if I wanted to ungroup grouped objects (i.e., pictures, shapes, text boxes, etc.)?
Select the object to ungroup, click the Group Objects button (Shape Format tab | Arrange group), and then click Ungroup on the Group Objects menu.

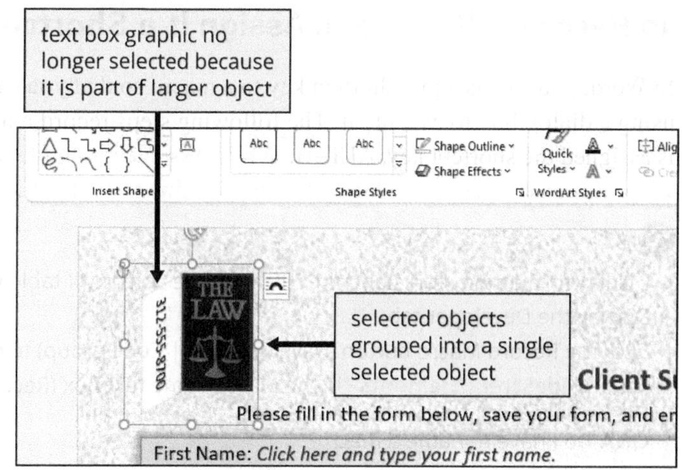

Figure 11–51

- Click outside of the graphic to position the insertion point in the document and deselect the graphic.

To Check Accessibility and Save the Template

The following steps check accessibility and save the template.

1. Click the Accessibility button on the status bar to open the Accessibility pane. Add the following description in the Alt Text pane for the grouped picture and text box object: Law office phone number attached to image of front of law book. (Leave the last errors or warnings identified by the Accessibility Checker for image or object not inline because, for illustration purposes, the grouped object and shape are intended to be floating objects.) Close the Accessibility pane.
2. Save the template again on the same storage location with the same file name.

Break Point: If you want to take a break, this is a good place to do so. You can exit Word now. To resume later, start Word, open the file called SC_WD_11_PierreLawOfficesClientSurveyModified.dotm, and continue following the steps from this location forward.

Using a Macro to Automate a Task

A macro consists of a series of Word commands or instructions that are grouped together as a single command. This single command is a convenient way to automate a difficult or lengthy task. Macros often are used to simplify formatting or editing activities, to combine multiple commands into a single command, or to select an option in a dialog box using a shortcut key.

To create a macro, you can use the macro recorder or the Visual Basic Editor. With the macro recorder, Word generates the VBA instructions associated with the macro automatically as you perform actions in Word. If you wanted to write the VBA instructions yourself, you would use the Visual Basic Editor. This module uses the macro recorder to create a macro and the Visual Basic Editor to modify it.

The **macro recorder** creates a macro based on a series of actions you perform while the macro recorder is recording. The macro recorder works similarly to recording a video: after you start the macro recorder, it records all actions you perform while working in a document and stops recording when you stop the macro recorder. To record a macro, you follow this sequence of steps:

1. Start the macro recorder and specify options about the macro.
2. Execute the actions you want recorded.
3. Stop the macro recorder.

After you record a macro, you can execute the macro, or play it, any time you want to perform the same set of actions.

BTW
Naming Macros
If you give a new macro the same name as an existing built-in command in Microsoft Word, the new macro's actions will replace the existing actions. Thus, you should be careful not to assign a macro a name reserved for automatic macros (refer to Table 11–1) or any Word commands. To view a list of built-in macros in Word, click the Macros button (View tab | Macros group) to display the Macros dialog box. Click the Macros in arrow and then click Word commands.

To Record a Macro and Assign It a Shortcut Key

In Word, you can assign a shortcut key to a macro so that you can execute the macro by pressing the shortcut key instead of using a dialog box to execute it. The following steps record a macro that hides formatting marks and the rulers; the macro is assigned the shortcut key, ALT+H. **Why?** Assume you find that you are repeatedly hiding the formatting marks and rulers while designing the online form. To simplify this task, the macro in this project hides these screen elements.

- Display formatting marks and the rulers on the screen. (If table gridlines appear on the screen, hide them.)
- Display the Developer tab.
- Click the Record Macro button (Developer tab | Code group) to display the Record Macro dialog box.
- Type **HideScreenElements** in the Macro name text box (Record Macro dialog box).

> **Q&A** Do I have to name a macro?
> If you do not enter a name for the macro, Word assigns a default name. Macro names can be up to 255 characters in length and can contain only numbers, letters, and the underscore character. A macro name cannot contain spaces or other punctuation.

- Click the 'Store macro in' arrow and then click 'Documents Based On SC_WD_11_PierreLawOfficesClientSurveyModified.dotm'. Note that, depending on settings, your file name may not show the extension .dotm at the end.

> **Q&A** What is the difference between storing a macro with the document template versus the Normal template?
> Macros saved in the Normal template are available to all future documents; macros saved with the document template are available only with a document based on the template.

- Before proceeding, verify that your Store macro in location is set to 'Documents Based On SC_WD_11_PierreLawOfficesClientSurveyModified'.
- In the Description text box, type this sentence (Figure 11–52): **Hide formatting marks and the rulers.**

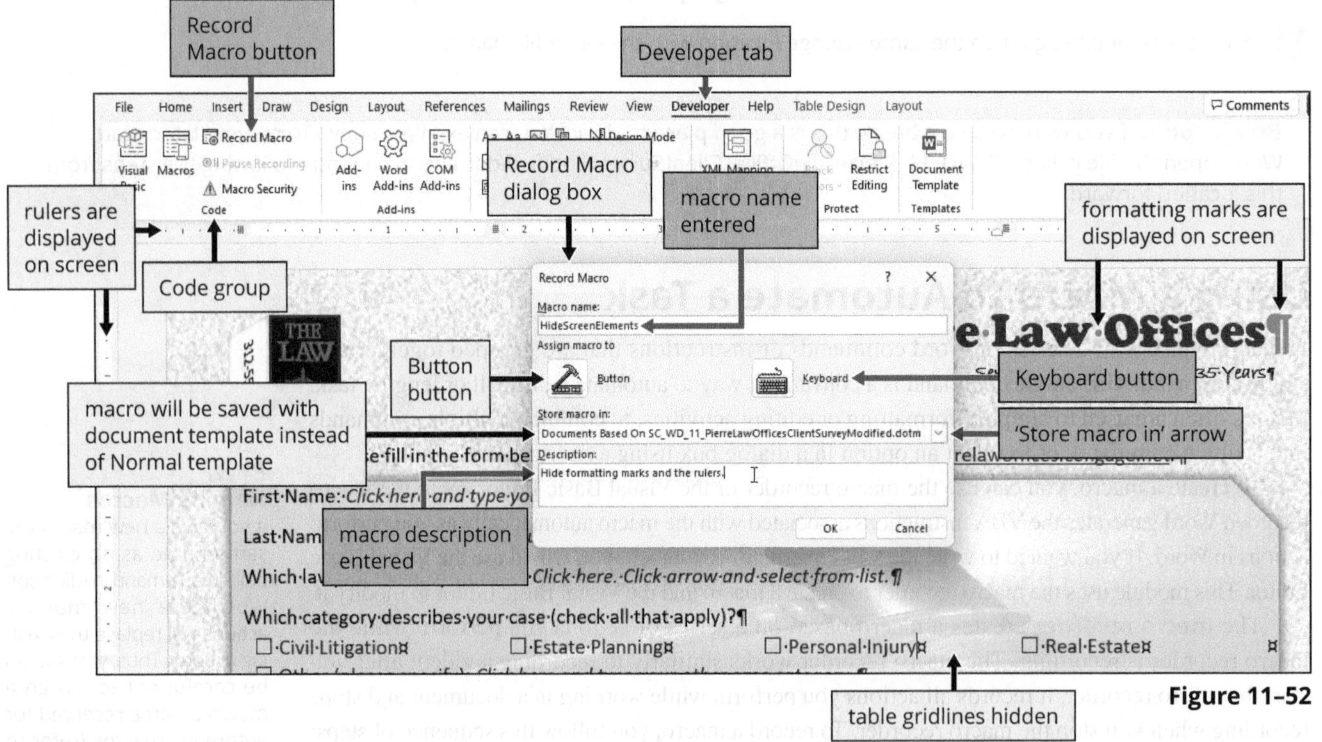

Figure 11–52

2

- Click the Keyboard button (shown in Figure 11–52) to display the Customize Keyboard dialog box.
- Press ALT+H to display the characters, Alt+H, in the 'Press new shortcut key' text box (Customize Keyboard dialog box) (Figure 11–53).

Q&A Can I type the letters in the shortcut key (ALT+H) in the text box instead of pressing them?
No. Although typing the letters places them in the text box, the shortcut key is valid only if you press the shortcut key combination itself.

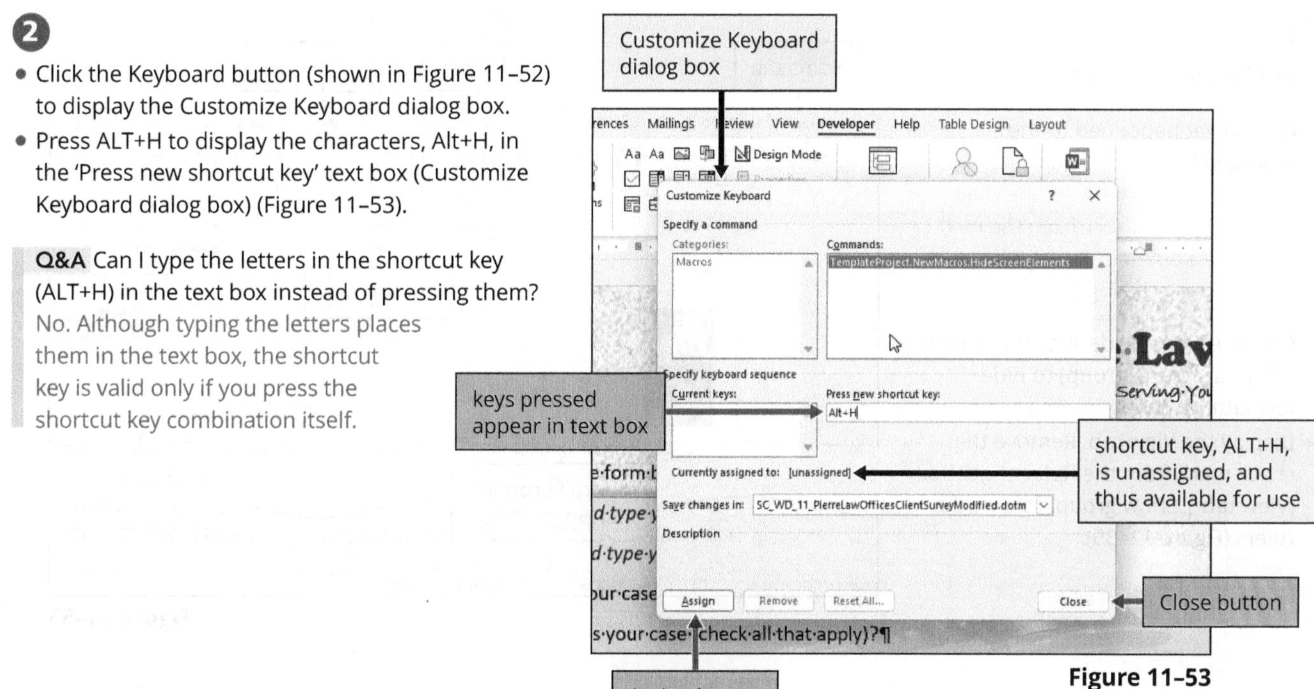

Figure 11–53

3

- Click the Assign button (Customize Keyboard dialog box) to assign the shortcut key, ALT+H, to the macro named HideScreenElements.
- Click the Close button (Customize Keyboard dialog box), which closes the dialog box, displays a Macro Recording button on the status bar, and starts the macro recorder (Figure 11–54).

Q&A How do I record the macro?
While the macro recorder is running, any action you perform in Word will be part of the macro — until you stop or pause the macro.

What is the purpose of the Pause Recording button (Developer tab | Code group)?
If, while recording a macro, you want to perform some actions that should not be part of the macro, click the Pause Recording button to suspend the macro recorder. The Pause Recording button changes to a Resume Recorder button that you click when you want to continue recording.

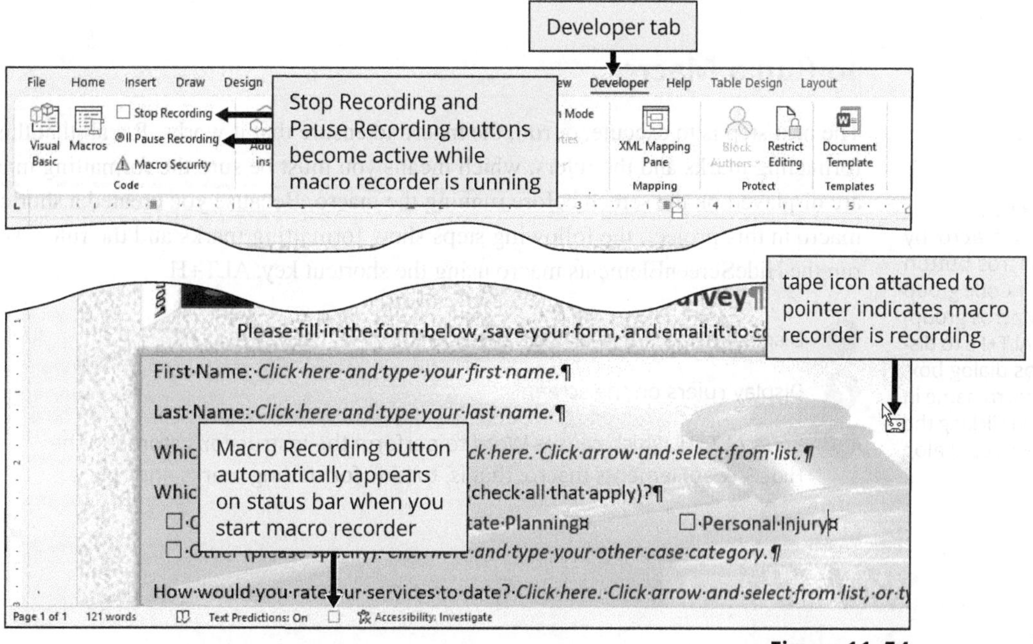

Figure 11–54

- Display the Home tab.

Q&A What happened to the tape icon?
While recording a macro, the tape icon might disappear from the pointer when the pointer is on a menu, on the ribbon, or in a dialog box.

- Click the 'Show/Hide ¶' button (Home tab | Paragraph group) to hide formatting marks.
- Display the View tab. Remove the check mark from the Ruler check box (View tab | Show group) to hide the rulers (Figure 11–55).

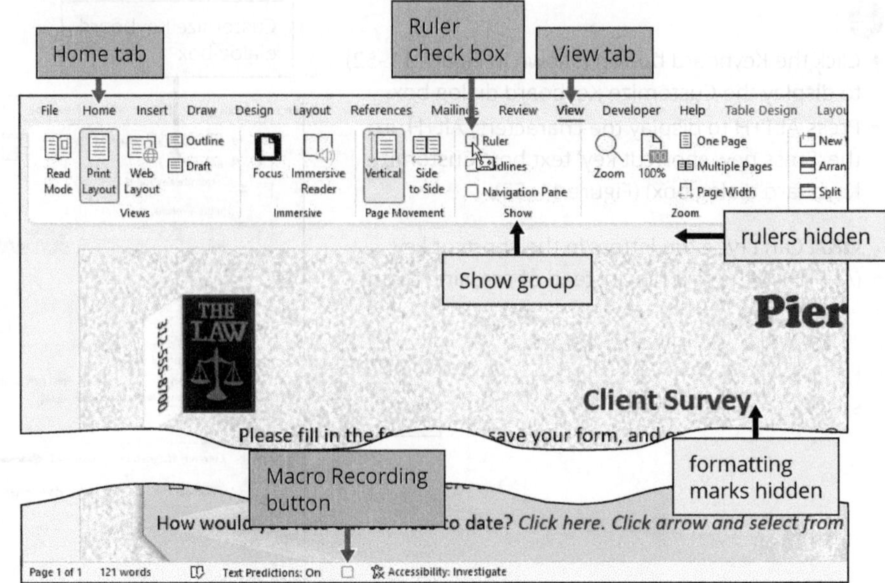

Figure 11–55

- Click the Macro Recording button on the status bar to turn off the macro recorder, that is, to stop recording actions you perform in Word.

Q&A What if I made a mistake while recording the macro?
Delete the macro and record it again. To delete a macro, click the Macros button (Developer tab | Code group), select the macro name in the list (Macros dialog box), click the Delete button, and then click the Yes button.

What if I wanted to assign the macro to a button instead of a shortcut key?
You would click the Button button in the Record Macro dialog box (shown in Figure 11–52) and then follow Steps 4 and 5 in this section.

Other Ways

1. Click Macros arrow (View tab | Macros group), click Record Macro on Macros menu
2. Press ALT+F8, click Create button (Macros dialog box)

To Run a Macro

The next step is to execute, or run, the macro to ensure that it works. Recall that this macro hides formatting marks and the rulers, which means you must be sure the formatting marks and rulers are displayed on the screen before running the macro. Because you created a shortcut key for the macro in this project, the following steps show formatting marks and the rulers so that you can run the HideScreenElements macro using the shortcut key, ALT+H.

BTW
Running Macros
You can run a macro by clicking the Macros button (Developer tab | Code group or View tab | Macros group) or by pressing ALT+F8 to display the Macros dialog box, selecting the macro name in the list, and then clicking the Run button (Macros dialog box).

1. Display formatting marks on the screen.
2. Display rulers on the screen.
3. Press ALT+H, which causes Word to perform the instructions stored in the HideScreenElements macro, that is, to hide formatting marks and rulers.

To Add a Command and a Macro as Buttons on the Quick Access Toolbar

Word allows you to add buttons to and delete buttons from the Quick Access Toolbar. You also can assign a command, such as a macro, to a button on the Quick Access Toolbar. The following steps add an existing command to the Quick Access Toolbar and assign a macro to a new button on the Quick Access Toolbar. **Why?** This module shows how to add the New File command to the Quick Access Toolbar and also shows how to create a button for the HideScreenElements macro so that instead of pressing the shortcut keys, you can click the button to hide formatting marks and the rulers.

1

- Click the 'Ribbon Display Options' button at the right edge of the ribbon to display the Ribbon Display Options menu (Figure 11-56).

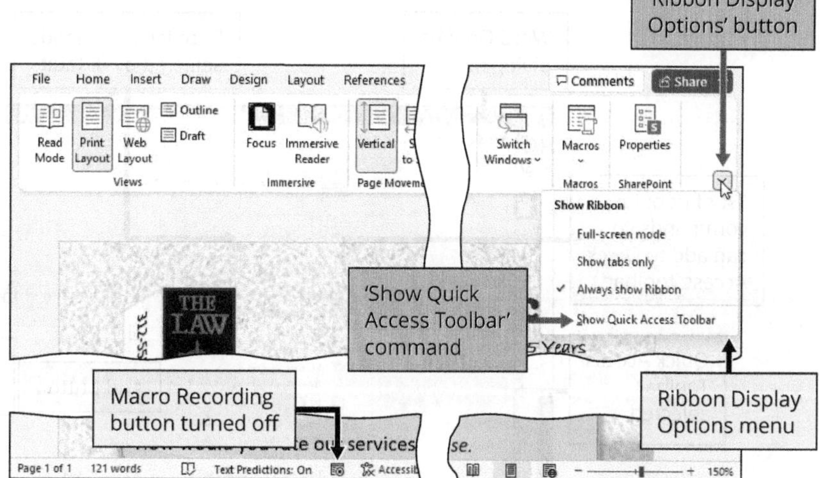

Figure 11-56

2

- Click 'Show Quick Access Toolbar' on the Ribbon Display Options menu to display the Quick Access Toolbar on the screen. (If your menu displays the 'Hide Quick Access Toolbar' command instead of the 'Show Quick Access Toolbar' command, press ESC to remove the menu from the screen and then proceed to Step 3 because the Quick Access Toolbar already appears on your screen.)

3

- Click the 'Customize Quick Access Toolbar' button on the Quick Access Toolbar to display the Customize Quick Access Toolbar menu (Figure 11-57).

Q&A What if my Quick Access Toolbar appears above the ribbon instead of below it?
Right-click the Quick Access Toolbar and then click 'Show Quick Access Toolbar Below the Ribbon' on the shortcut menu.

What happens if I click the commands listed on the Customize Quick Access Toolbar menu?
If the command does not have a check mark beside it and you click it, Word places the button associated with the command on the Quick Access Toolbar. If the command has a check mark beside it and you click (deselect) it, Word removes the command from the Quick Access Toolbar.

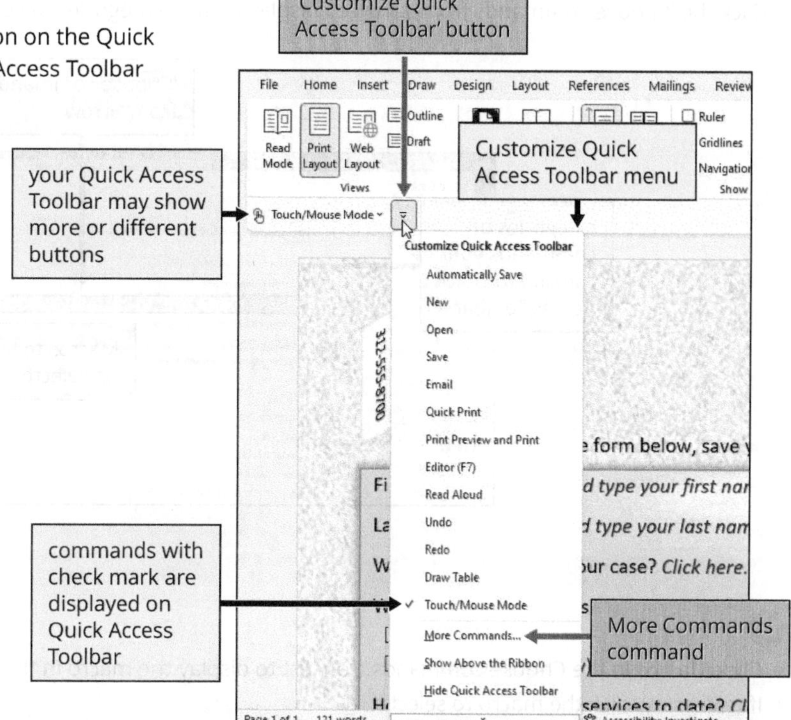

Figure 11-57

- Click More Commands on the Customize Quick Access Toolbar menu to display the Word Options dialog box with Quick Access Toolbar selected in the left pane.
- Scroll through the list of popular commands (Word Options dialog box) and then click New File to select the command.
- Click the Add button to add the selected command (New File, in this case) to the Customize Quick Access Toolbar list (Figure 11–58). Note that the built-in ScreenTip that will appear on the screen for the New File command is New Blank Document.

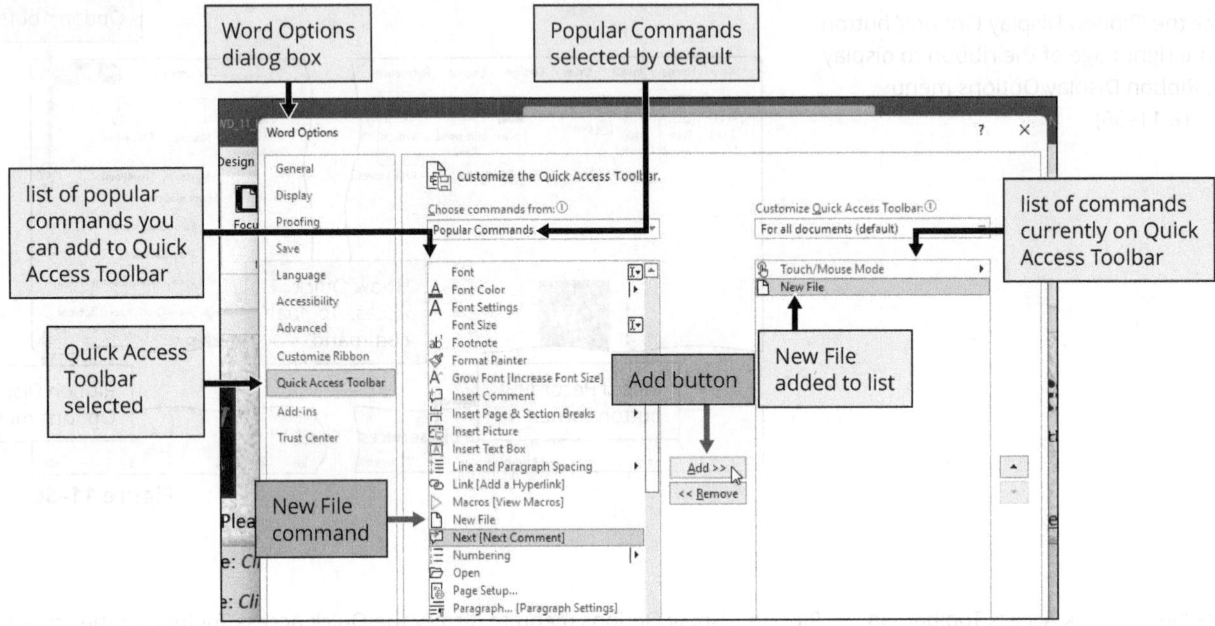

Figure 11–58

- Click the 'Choose commands from' arrow to display a list of categories of commands (Figure 11–59).

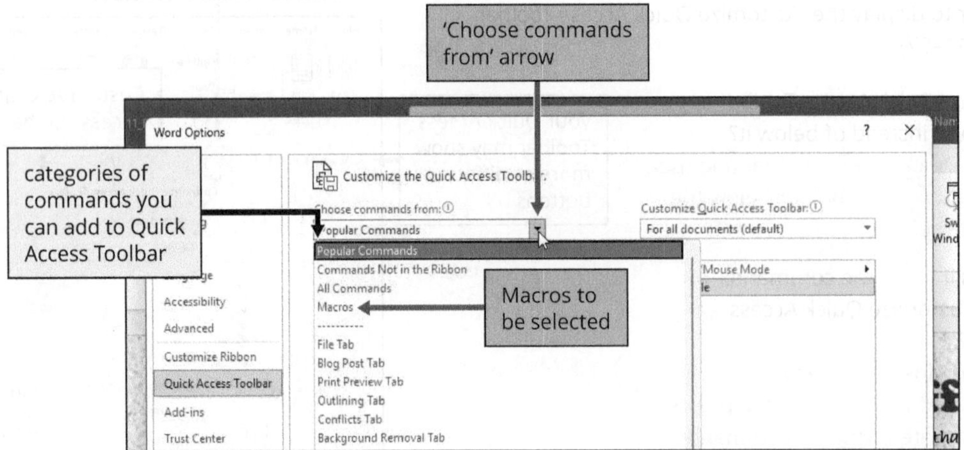

Figure 11–59

- Click Macros in the Choose commands from list to display the macro in this document.
- If necessary, click the macro to select it.
- Click the Add button (Word Options dialog box) to display the selected macro in the Customize Quick Access Toolbar list.

- Click the Modify button to display the Modify Button dialog box.
- Type **Hide Screen Elements** in the Display name text box (Modify Button dialog box) to specify the text that appears in the ScreenTip for the button.
- In the list of symbols, click the screen icon as the new face for the button (Figure 11–60).

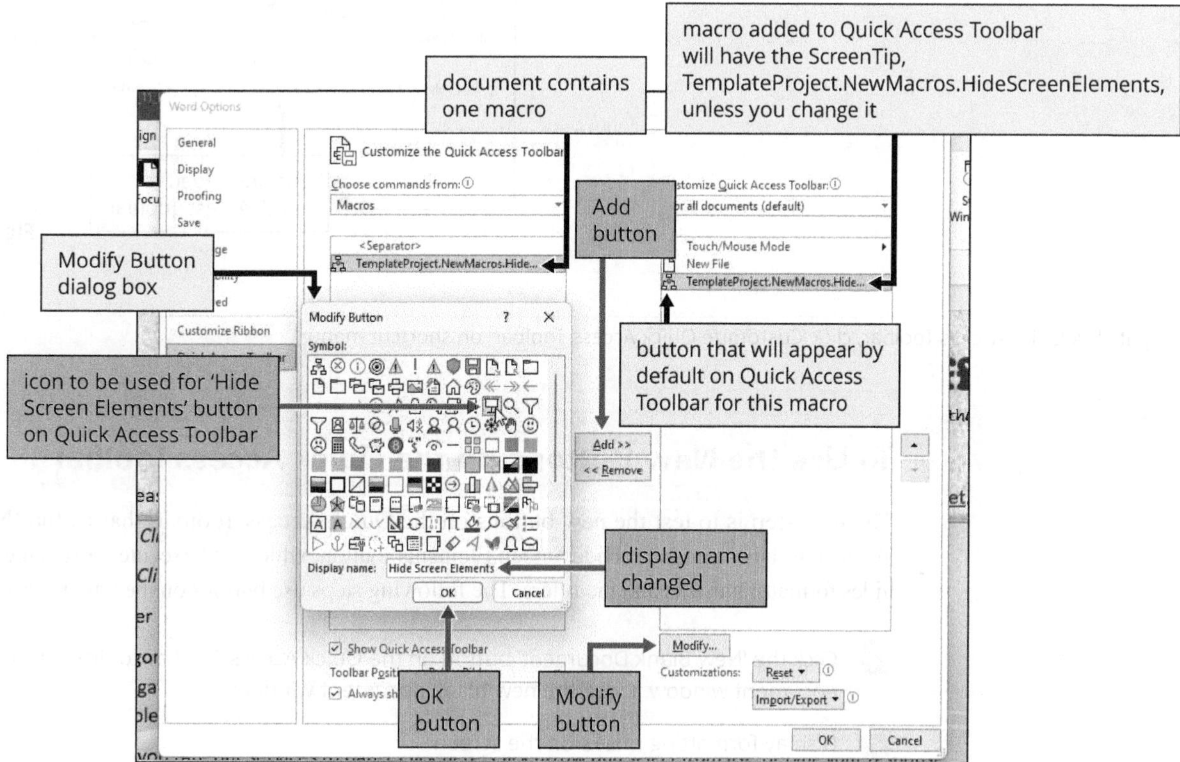

Figure 11–60

7

- Click OK (Modify Button dialog box) to change the button characteristics in the Customize Quick Access Toolbar list (Figure 11–61).

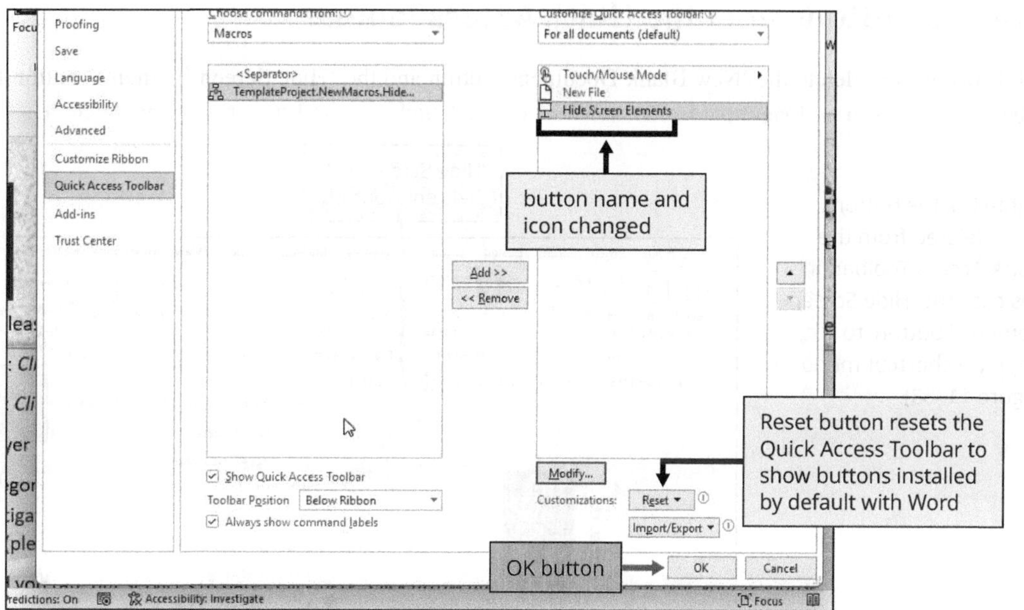

Figure 11–61

- Click OK (Word Options dialog box) to add the buttons to the Quick Access Toolbar (Figure 11–62).

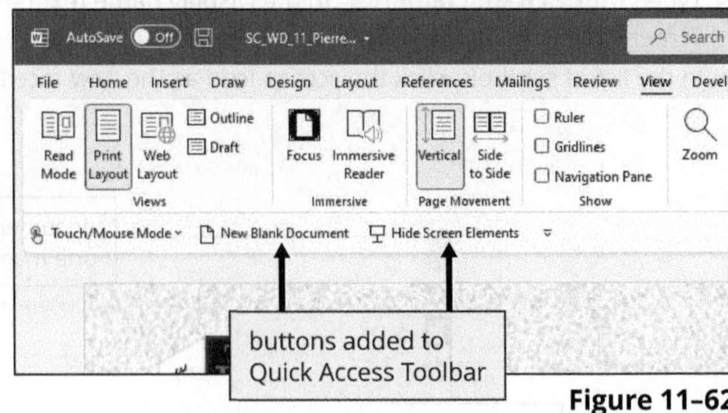

Figure 11–62

Other Ways

1. Right-click Quick Access Toolbar, click 'Customize Quick Access Toolbar' on shortcut menu

To Use the New Buttons on the Quick Access Toolbar

The next step is to test the new buttons on the Quick Access Toolbar, that is, the 'New Blank Document' button and the 'Hide Screen Elements' button, which will execute, or run, the macro that hides formatting marks and the rulers. The following steps use buttons on the Quick Access Toolbar.

1. Click the 'New Blank Document' button on the Quick Access Toolbar to display a new blank document window. Close the new blank document window.
2. Display formatting marks on the screen.
3. Display rulers on the screen.
4. Click the 'Hide Screen Elements' button on the Quick Access Toolbar, which causes Word to perform the instructions stored in the HideScreenElements macro, that is, to hide formatting marks and the rulers.

To Delete Buttons from the Quick Access Toolbar

The following steps delete the 'New Blank Document' button and the 'Hide Screen Elements' button from the Quick Access Toolbar. **Why?** If you no longer plan to use a button on the Quick Access Toolbar, you can delete it.

- Right-click the button to be deleted from the Quick Access Toolbar, in this case the 'Hide Screen Elements' button, to display a shortcut menu (Figure 11–63).

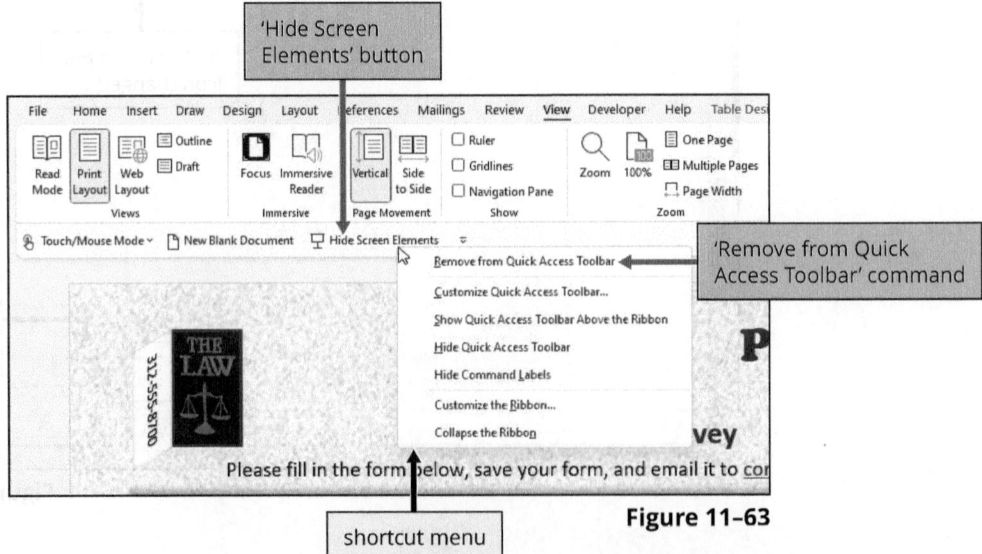

Figure 11–63

2

- Click 'Remove from Quick Access Toolbar' on the shortcut menu to remove the button from the Quick Access Toolbar.

3

- Repeat Steps 1 and 2 for the 'New Blank Document' button on the Quick Access Toolbar.
- Click the 'Ribbon Display Options' button at the right edge of the ribbon to display the Ribbon Display Options menu and then click the 'Hide Quick Access Toolbar' on the Ribbon Display Options menu to hide the Quick Access Toolbar from the screen.

To Delete a Macro If you wanted to delete a macro, you would perform the following steps.

1. Click the Macros button (Developer tab | Code group) to display the Macros dialog box.
2. Click the macro to delete and then click the Delete button (Macros dialog box) to display a dialog box asking if you are sure you want to delete the macro. Click Yes in the dialog box.
3. Close the Macros dialog box.

Automatic Macros

The previous section showed how to create a macro, assign it a unique name (HideScreenElements) and a shortcut key, and then add a button that executes the macro on the Quick Access Toolbar. This section creates an **automatic macro**, which is a macro that executes automatically when a certain event occurs. Word has five prenamed automatic macros. Table 11–1 lists the name and function of these automatic macros.

Table 11–1: Automatic Macros

Macro Name	Event That Causes Macro to Run
AutoClose	Closing a document that contains the macro
AutoExec	Starting Word
AutoExit	Exiting Word
AutoNew	Creating a new document based on a template that contains the macro
AutoOpen	Opening a document that contains the macro

BTW
Automatic Macros
A document can contain only one AutoClose macro, one AutoNew macro, and one AutoOpen macro. The AutoExec and AutoExit macros, however, are not stored with the document; instead, they must be stored in the Normal template. Thus, only one AutoExec macro and only one AutoExit macro can exist for all Word documents.

The automatic macro you choose depends on when you want certain actions to occur. In this module, when a user creates a new Word document that is based on the SC_WD_11_PierreLawOfficesClientSurveyModified.dotm template, you want to be sure that the zoom is set to page width. Thus, the AutoNew automatic macro is used in this online form.

To Create an Automatic Macro

The following steps use the macro recorder to create an AutoNew macro. **Why?** The online form in this module is displayed properly when the zoom is set to page width. Thus, you will record the steps to zoom to page width in the AutoNew macro.

- Display the Developer tab.
- Click the Record Macro button (Developer tab | Code group) to display the Record Macro dialog box.
- Type **AutoNew** in the Macro name text box (Record Macro dialog box).
- Click the 'Store macro in' arrow and then click 'Documents Based On SC_WD_11_PierreLawOfficesClientSurveyModified.dotm'. Note that, depending on settings, your file name may not show the extension .dotm at the end.
- Before proceeding, verify that your Store macro in location is set to 'Documents Based On SC_WD_11_PierreLawOfficesClientSurveyModified'.
- In the Description text box, type this sentence (Figure 11–64): **Specifies how the form initially is displayed.**

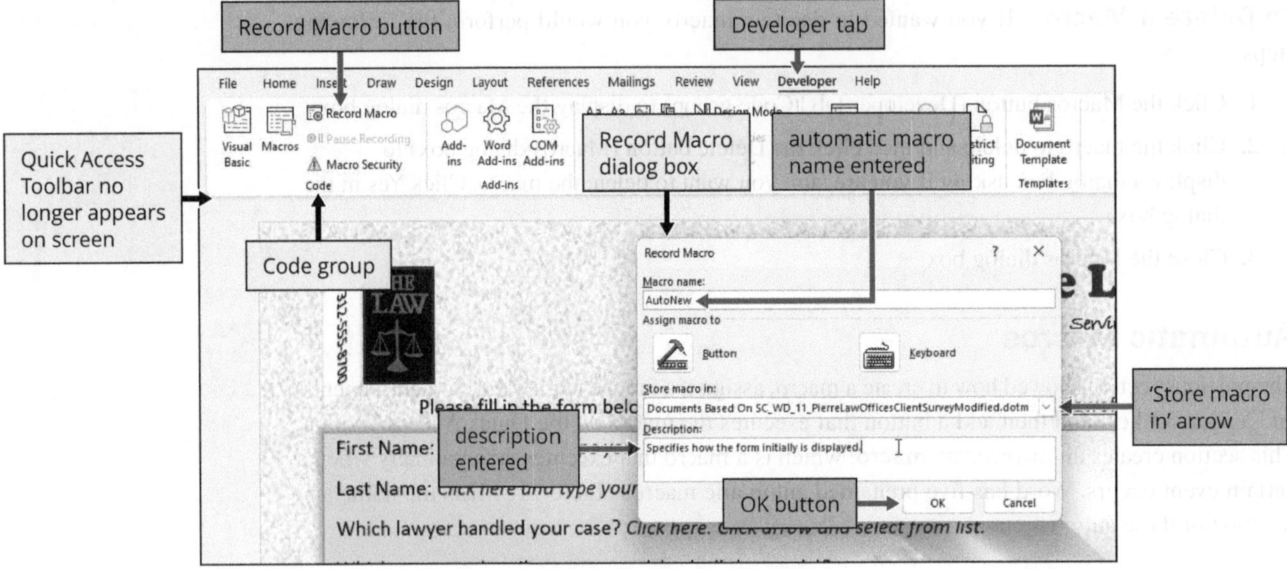

Figure 11–64

2

- Click OK to close the Record Macro dialog box and start the macro recorder.
- Display the View tab.
- Click the Page Width button (View tab | Zoom group) to zoom page width (Figure 11–65).

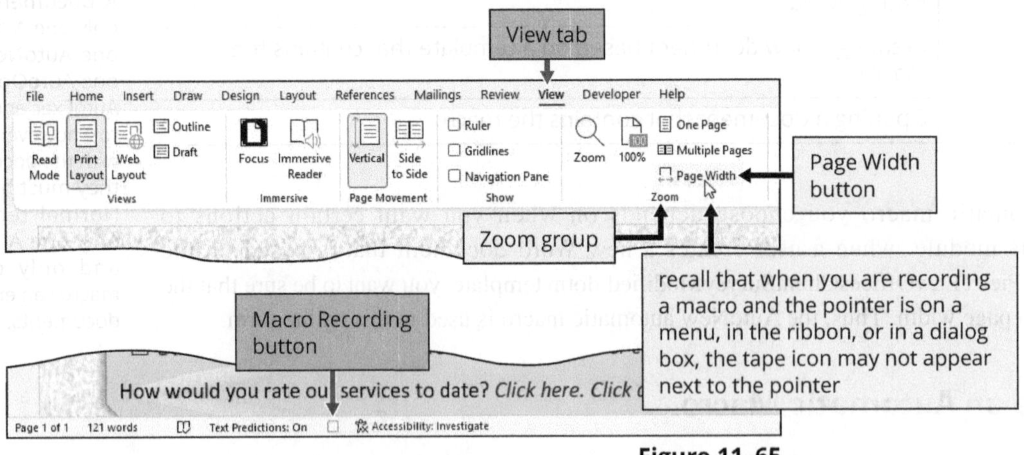

Figure 11–65

- Click the Macro Recording button on the status bar to turn off the macro recorder, that is, stop recording actions you perform in Word.

Q&A How do I test an automatic macro?
Activate the event that causes the macro to execute. For example, the AutoNew macro runs whenever you create a new Word document that is based on the template.

To Run the AutoNew Macro

The next step is to execute, or run, the AutoNew macro to ensure that it works. To run the AutoNew macro, you need to create a new Word document that is based on the template named SC_WD_11_PierreLawOfficesClientSurveyModified.dotm. This macro contains instructions to zoom page width. To verify that the macro works as intended, you will change the zoom to 100% before testing the macro. The following steps run a macro.

1. Use the Zoom Out button on the status bar to change the zoom to 100%.
2. Save the template with the same file name, SC_WD_11_PierreLawOfficesClientSurveyModified.
3. Click the File Explorer button on the taskbar to open the File Explorer window.
4. Locate and then double-click the file SC_WD_11_PierreLawOfficesClientSurveyModified.dotm to display a new document window that is based on the contents of the SC_WD_11_PierreLawOfficesClientSurveyModified.dotm template, which should be zoomed to page width as shown in Figure 11–1a at the beginning of this module. (If Word displays a dialog box about disabling macros, click OK. If the Message Bar displays a security warning, click the Enable Content button.)
5. Close the new document that displays the form in the Word window. Click the Don't Save button when Word asks if you want to save the changes to the new document.
6. Close the File Explorer window.
7. Change the zoom back to page width.

BTW

Display Macros

If you wanted to display macros in a document, you would click the Macros button (View tab | Macros group or Developer tab | Code group) and review the list in the Macro name area (Macros dialog box). To restrict the list to macros saved in only this document or to view all macros in Word, click the Macros in arrow and select the desired option. You also can click the Organizer button (Macros dialog box) to view a list of macros in a document or in Word.

To Edit a Macro's VBA Code

As mentioned earlier, a macro consists of VBA instructions. To edit a recorded macro, you use the Visual Basic Editor. The following steps use the Visual Basic Editor to add VBA instructions to the AutoNew macro. **Why?** In addition to zooming page width when the online form is displayed in a new document window, you would like to be sure that the Developer tab is hidden and the ribbon is collapsed. These steps are designed to show the basic composition of a VBA procedure and illustrate the power of VBA code statements.

- Display the Developer tab.
- Click the Macros button (Developer tab | Code group) to display the Macros dialog box.
- If necessary, select the macro to be edited, in this case, AutoNew (Figure 11–66).

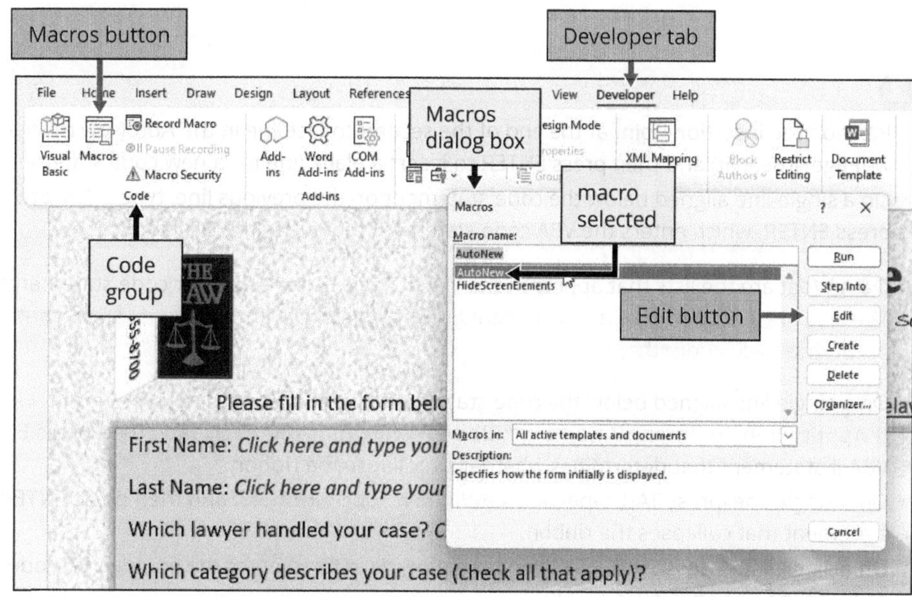

Figure 11–66

- Click the Edit button (Macros dialog box) to open the Visual Basic Editor window and display the VBA code for the AutoNew macro in the Code window — your screen may appear different depending on previous Visual Basic Editor settings (Figure 11–67).

Q&A What if the Code window does not appear in the Visual Basic Editor?
In the Visual Basic Editor, click View on the menu bar and then click Code. If it still does not appear and you are in a network environment, this feature may be disabled for some users.

What are the lines of text (instructions) in the Code window?
The named set of instructions associated with a macro is called a procedure. It is this set of instructions — beginning with the word, Sub, and continuing sequentially to the line with the words, End Sub — that executes when you run the macro. The instructions within a procedure are called code statements.

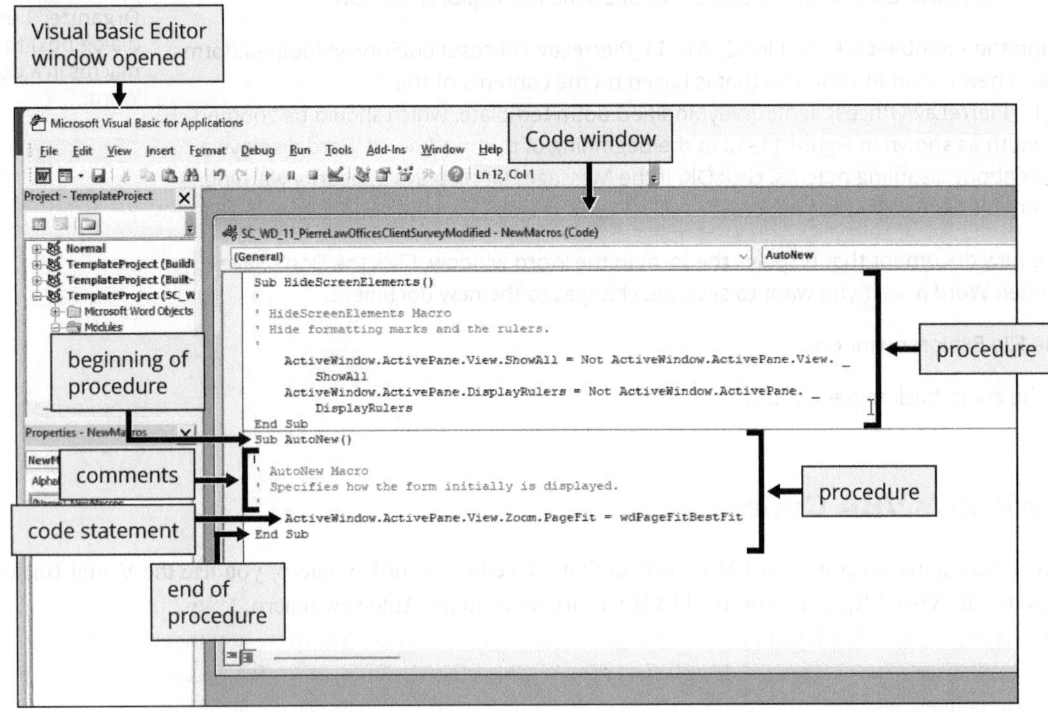

Figure 11–67

- Position the insertion point at the end of the second-to-last line in the AutoNew macro (that is, after the text, wdPageFitBestFit) and then press ENTER to insert a blank line for a new code statement.
- On a single line aligned below the code statement on the previous line, type **Options.ShowDevTools = False** and then press ENTER, which enters the VBA code statement that hides the Developer tab.

Q&A What are the lists that appear in the Visual Basic Editor as I enter code statements?
The lists present valid statement elements to assist you with entering code statements. Because they are beyond the scope of this module, ignore them.

- On a single line aligned below the code statement on the previous line, type **If Application.CommandBars.Item("Ribbon").Height > 100 Then** and then press ENTER, which enters the beginning VBA if statement that determines whether to collapse the ribbon.
- On a single line, press TAB, type **ActiveWindow.ToggleRibbon** and then press ENTER, which enters the beginning VBA code statement that collapses the ribbon.
- On a single line, press SHIFT+TAB and then type **End If** to enter the ending VBA code statement that determines whether to collapse the ribbon (Figure 11–68).

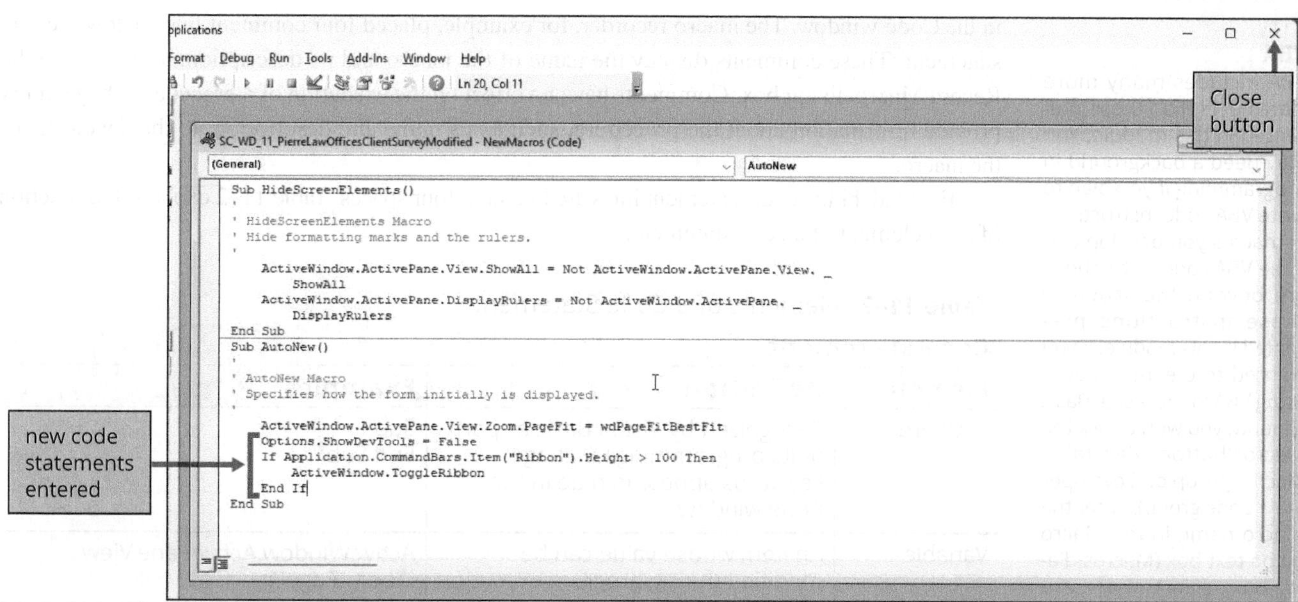

Figure 11-68

4

- Click the Close button on the right edge of the Microsoft Visual Basic window title bar.

To Run the AutoNew Macro

The next step is to execute, or run, the AutoNew macro again to ensure that it works. To be sure the macro works as intended, ensure the Developer tab is displayed on the ribbon. The AutoNew macro should hide the Developer tab. The following steps run the automatic macro.

1. Save the template with the same file name, SC_WD_11_PierreLawOfficesClientSurveyModified.
2. Click the File Explorer button on the taskbar to open the File Explorer window.
3. Locate and then double-click the file SC_WD_11_PierreLawOfficesClientSurveyModified.dotm to open a new document that is based on the contents of this template, which should be zoomed to page width, show a collapsed ribbon, and display no Developer tab. (If Word displays a dialog box about disabling macros, click OK. If the Message Bar displays a security warning, click the Enable Content button.)
4. Close the new document that displays the form in the Word window. Click the Don't Save button when Word asks if you want to save the changes to the new document.
5. Close the File Explorer window.

VBA

As shown in the previous steps, a VBA procedure begins with a Sub statement and ends with an End Sub statement. The Sub statement is followed by the name of the procedure, which is the macro name (AutoNew). The parentheses following the macro name in the Sub statement are required. They indicate that arguments can be passed from one procedure to another. Passing arguments is beyond the scope of this module, but the parentheses still are required. The End Sub statement signifies the end of the procedure and returns control to Word.

Comments often are added to a procedure to help you remember the purpose of the macro and its code statements at a later date. Comments begin with an apostrophe (') and appear in green in the Code window. The macro recorder, for example, placed four comment lines below the Sub statement. These comments display the name of the macro and its description, as entered in the Record Macro dialog box. Comments have no effect on the execution of a procedure; they simply provide information about the procedure, such as its name and description, to the developer of the macro.

For readability, code statement lines are indented four spaces. Table 11–2 explains the function of each element of a code statement.

BTW
VBA
VBA includes many more statements than those presented in this module. You may need a background in programming if you plan to write VBA code instructions in macros you develop and if the VBA code instructions are beyond the scope of those instructions presented in this module. If you wanted to create a macro using VBA in the Visual Basic window, you would click the Macros button (View tab | Macros group or Developer tab | Code group), enter the macro name in the Macro name text box (Macros dialog box), select where you want the macro to be saved in the Macros in list, and click the Create button to open the Visual Basic window, where you can enter VBA code statements.

Table 11–2: Elements of a Code Statement

Code Statement		
Element	**Definition**	**Examples**
Keyword	Recognized by Visual Basic as part of its programming language; keywords appear in blue in the Code window	Sub End Sub
Variable	An item whose value can be modified during program execution	ActiveWindow.ActivePane.View .Zoom.PageFit
Constant	An item whose value remains unchanged during program execution	False
Operator	A symbol that indicates a specific action	=

To Protect a Form Using Backstage View and Exit Word

You now are finished enhancing the online form and adding macros to it. Because the last macro hid the Developer tab on the ribbon, you will use Backstage view to protect the form. The following steps use Backstage view to protect the online form so that users are restricted to entering data only in content controls.

1. Open Backstage view and then, if necessary, display the Info screen.
2. Click the Protect Document button to display the Protect Document menu.
3. Click Restrict Editing on the Protect Document menu to open the Restrict Editing pane.
4. In the Editing restrictions area, if necessary, place a check mark in the 'Allow only this type of editing in the document' check box, click its arrow, and then select 'Filling in forms' in the list.
5. Click the 'Yes, Start Enforcing Protection' button and then click OK (Start Enforcing Protection dialog box) to protect the document without a password.
6. Close the Restrict Editing pane.
7. Save the template again on the same storage location with the same file name.
8. **sam**↑ If the File Explorer window still is open, close it.

BTW
Allowing No Changes in a Document
You can use the Restrict Editing pane to allow no changes to a document. To do this, place a check mark in the 'Allow only this type of editing in the document' check box and then change the associated text box to 'No changes (Read only)', which instructs Word to prevent any editing to the document.

Working with 3-D Models

Some versions of Word enable you to insert and format 3-D models into documents. You can rotate and tilt 3-D models in any direction. This section replaces the graphic currently in the SC_WD_11_PierreLawOfficesClientSurveyModified.dotm file with a 3-D model and then formats the 3-D model. If your version of Word does not include the capability of working with 3-D models, read the steps in these sections without performing them. In the following sections, you will perform these tasks:

1. Save the macro-enabled template with a new file name and then unprotect the template.
2. Delete a graphic.
3. Insert a 3-D model.
4. Format the 3-D model by resizing it, tilting and rotating it, applying a 3-D model view to it, and resetting it.
5. Save and protect the template.

BTW
Unsaved Document Versions
If you wanted to open a previous unsaved version of a document, you could open an automatically saved copy of your document if one is available. To do this, open Backstage view and then, if necessary, click Info to display the Info screen, and then click the desired (autosave) file listed. Or, click the Manage Document button, click 'Recover Unsaved Documents' in the Manage Document list, select the document to open, and then click the Open button (Open dialog box). To change the autosave frequency, open Backstage view, click Options in the left pane, click Save in the left pane (Word Options dialog box), enter the desired number of minutes in the 'Save AutoRecover information every' box, and then click OK. To compare two versions of a document, you could recover them or open automatically saved copies and then use the Compare button (Review tab | Compare group) to identify differences.

To Save the Template with a New File Name and Unprotect It

The following steps save the macro-enabled template with a new file name and then unprotect the template so that you can modify it.

1. With the SC_WD_11_PierreLawOfficesClientSurveyModified.dotm file still open, click File on the ribbon, click Save As, and then save the template using the new file name, SC_WD_11_PierreLawOfficesClientSurveyModified_3-DModel.

   Q&A What if my SC_WD_11_PierreLawOfficesClientSurveyModified.dotm no longer is open?
   Open it and then perform Step 1.

2. If necessary, display the Developer tab and then click the Restrict Editing button (Developer tab | Protect group) to open the Restrict Editing pane.
3. Click the Stop Protection button in the Restrict Editing Pane to unprotect the form.
4. Close the Restrict Editing pane.

To Delete a Graphic

The following steps delete the grouped graphic that contains the text box and the law book image so that you can insert a 3-D model in its location.

1. Click the grouped graphic that contains the text box and the law book image to select the graphic.
2. Press DELETE to delete the selected graphic.

To Insert a 3-D Model

The next step is to insert a 3-D model in the template. Microsoft Office applications can access a collection of free stock 3-D models. The following steps insert a stock 3-D model of a writing pen. **Why?** You want to add a 3-D model to the template for visual appeal. If your version of Word does not support 3-D models, read the steps in this section without performing them.

- If necessary, position the insertion point at the location where you want to insert the picture (in this case, near the top of the online form).
- Display the Insert tab.
- Click the 3D Models arrow (Insert tab | Illustrations group) to display the 3D Models menu (Figure 11–69).

Q&A What if the Online 3D Models dialog box is displayed instead of the 3D Models menu?
You clicked the 3D Models button instead of the 3D Models arrow. Proceed to Step 3.

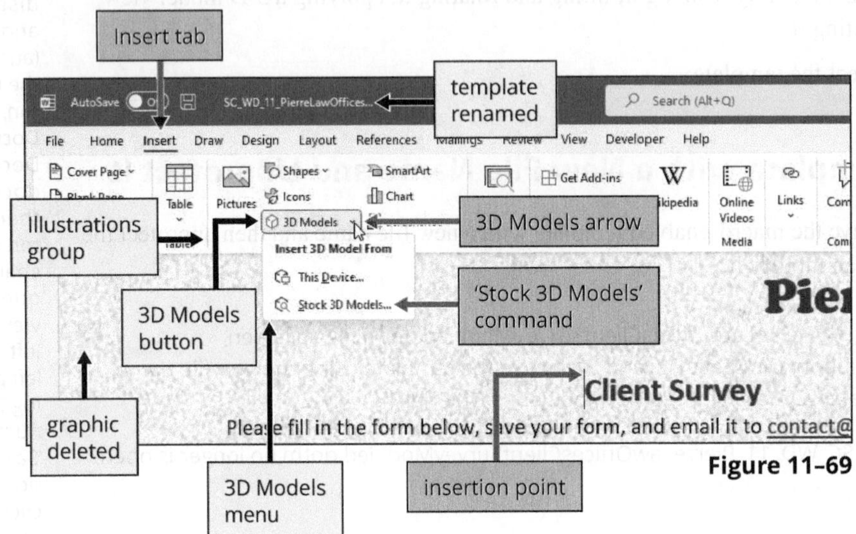

Figure 11–69

2

- Click 'Stock 3D Models' on the 3D Models menu to display the Online 3D Models dialog box with categories of online 3-D models displayed in the dialog box (Figure 11–70).

Q&A Can I click the categories to display 3-D models?
Yes, you can click categories or type search text in the Search box.

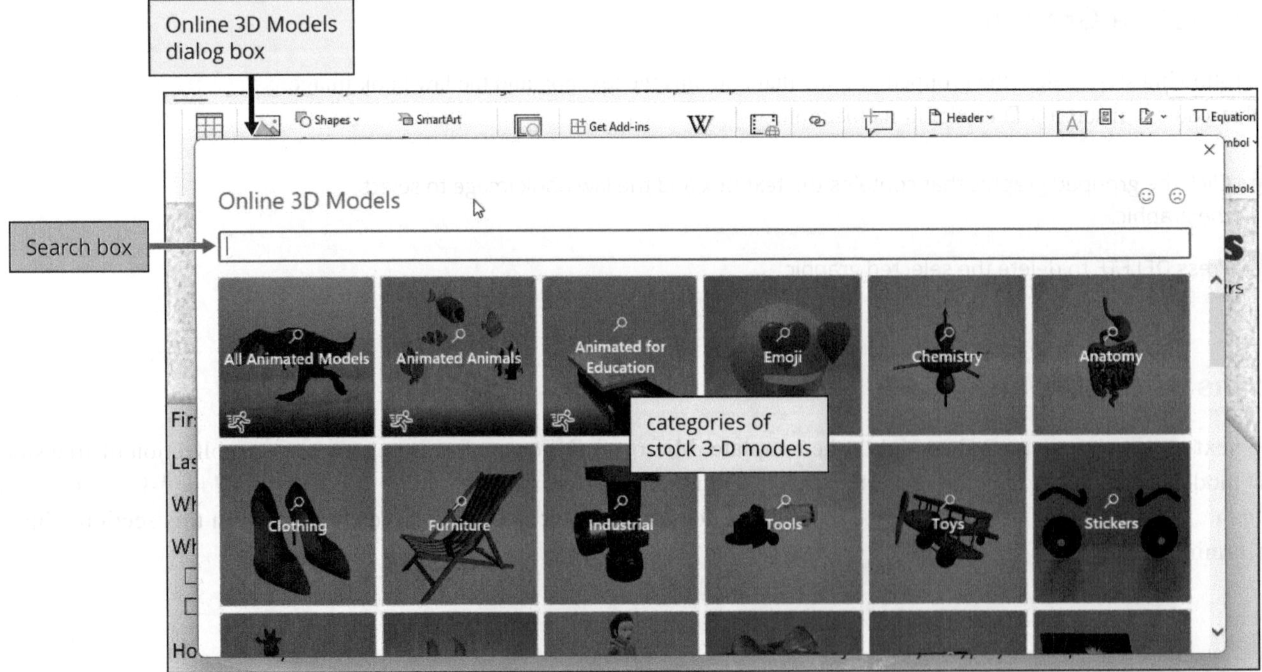

Figure 11–70

3

- Type **pen** in the Search box (Online 3D Models dialog box) to specify the search text.
- Press ENTER to display a list of online 3-D models that matches the entered search text.
- Scroll through the search results and then click the desired 3-D model to select it (Figure 11–71).

Q&A What if I cannot locate the exact 3-D model selected in Figure 11–69?
Select any 3-D model so that you can practice using 3-D models.

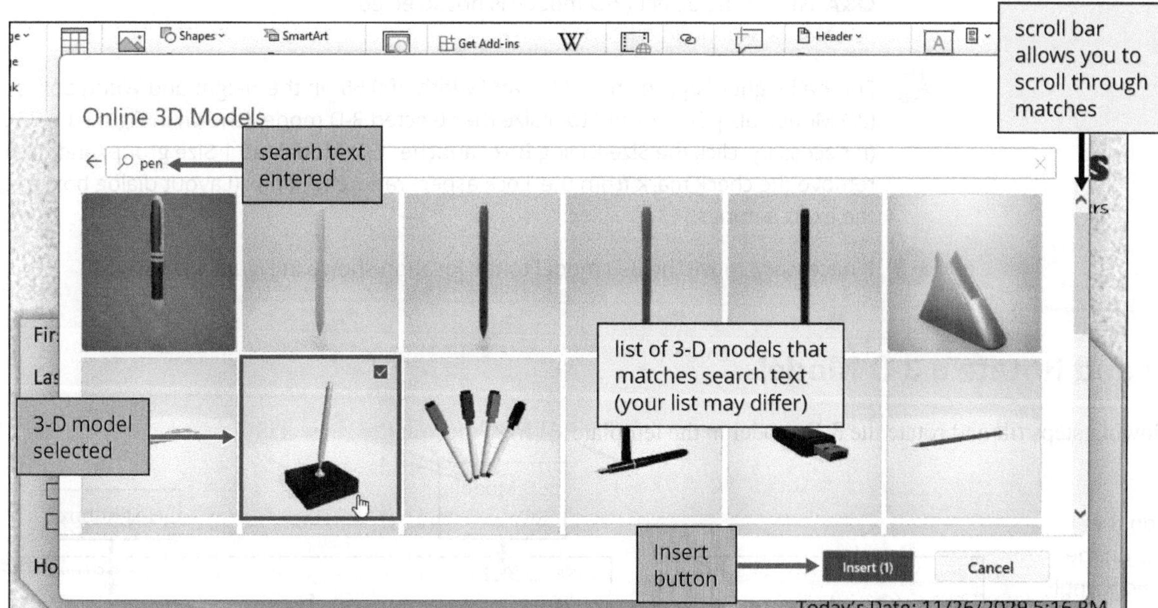

Figure 11–71

4

- Click the Insert button (Online 3D Models dialog box) to insert the selected 3-D model at the location of the insertion point in the document (Figure 11–72).

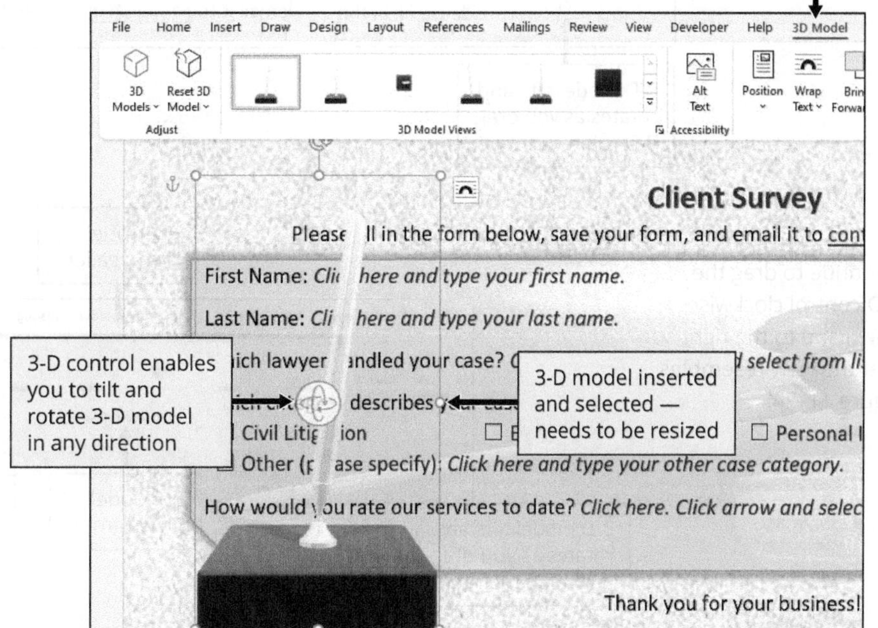

Figure 11–72

To Resize a 3-D Model

You resize a 3-D model the same way you resize any other graphic. You can drag its sizing handles that appear at the corner or middle locations of the selected 3-D model or use the Height and Width buttons (3D Model tab | Size group). The following steps resize a selected 3-D model.

1. Be sure the 3-D model still is selected.

   Q&A What if the object (3-D model) is not selected?
   To select a 3-D model, click it.

2. Enter a height of approximately 1" and width of 0.55" in the Height and Width boxes (3D Model tab | Size group) to resize the selected 3-D model (shown in Figure 11–73). (If necessary, click the Size Dialog Box Launcher (3D Model tab | Size group) and then remove the check mark from the 'Lock aspect ratio' check box (Layout dialog box) to specify the exact settings.)

3. If necessary, move the 3-D model to the location shown in Figure 11–73.

To Tilt and Rotate a 3-D Model

The following steps tilt and rotate the 3-D model in the template. **Why?** You want to show a different view of the pen.

1

- Position the pointer on the 3-D model until the rotate pointer appears and then drag the 3-D model down and to the right in a clockwise motion so that the view resembles Figure 11–73.

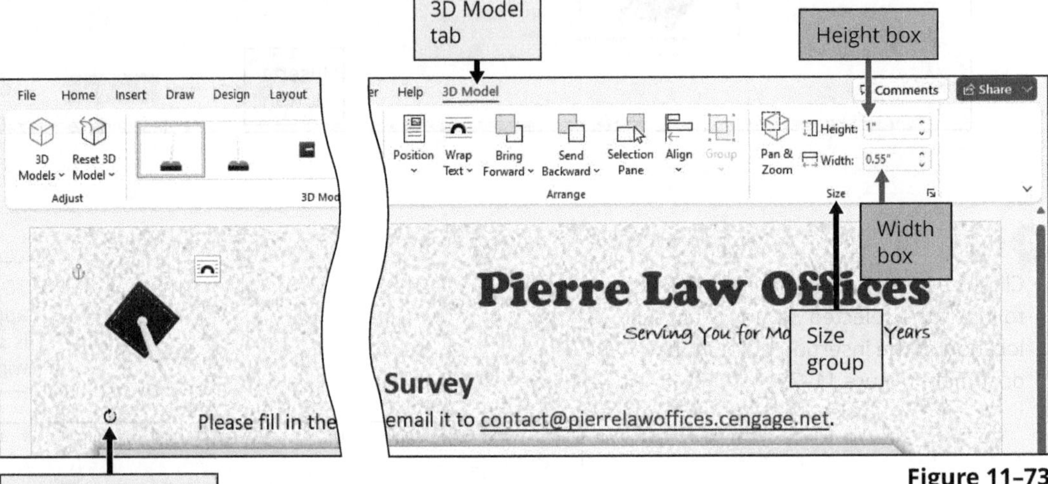

Figure 11–73

2

- Continue to drag the 3-D control clockwise down and to the right so that the view resembles Figure 11–74.

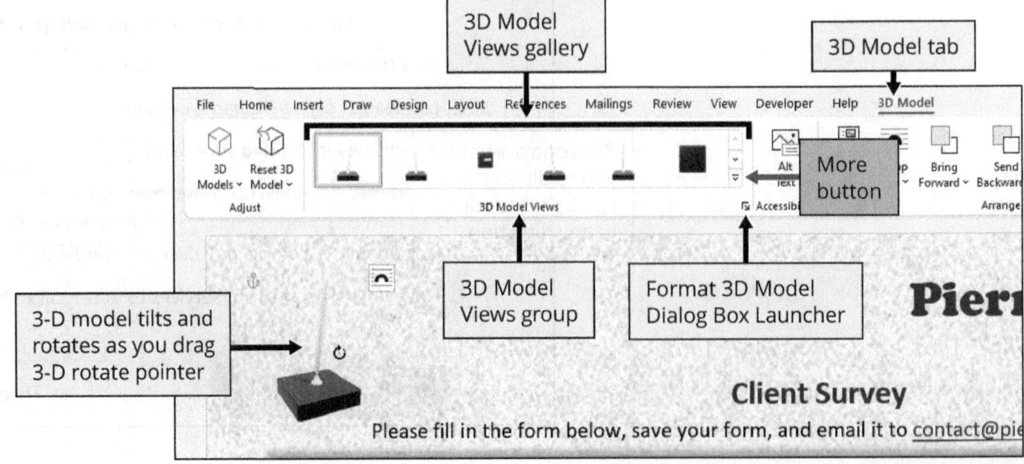

Figure 11–74

To Apply a 3-D Model View

Word provides more than 15 different views of 3-D models. **Why?** The 3-D model views enable you to select a tilted and rotated view of a 3-D model without dragging the 3-D control. The following steps apply a 3-D model view to the selected 3-D model.

- Ensure the 3-D model still is selected and that the 3D Model tab is displayed on the ribbon.

Q&A What if the 3-D model is not selected?
Click it to select it.

- Click the More button in the 3D Model Views gallery (3D Model tab | 3D Model Views group) (shown in Figure 11–74) to expand the gallery.
- Point to 'Above Front Left' in the 3D Model Views gallery to display a Live Preview of that view applied to the 3-D model in the template (Figure 11–75).
- **Experiment:** Point to various 3-D model views in the 3D Model Views gallery and notice the view of the 3-D model change in the document window.

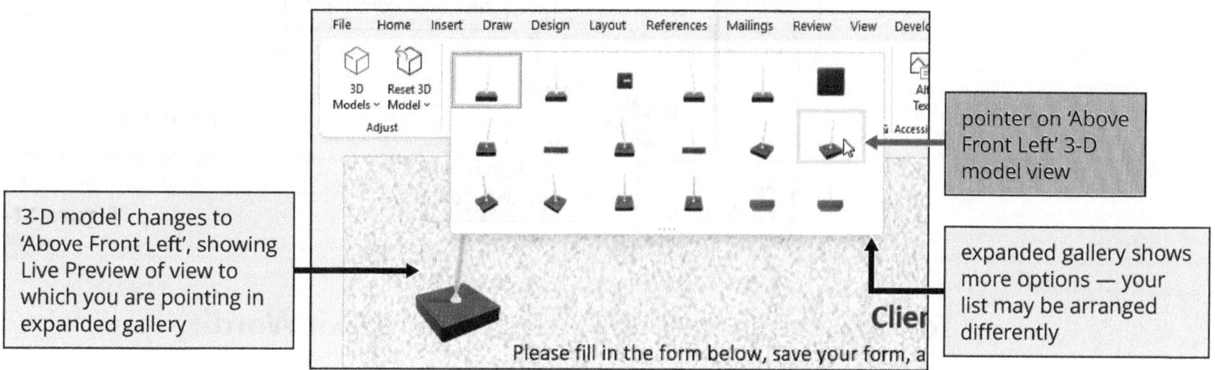

Figure 11–75

- Click 'Above Front Left' in the 3D Model Views gallery to apply the view to the selected 3-D model.

Q&A What if I wanted to format the 3-D model further?
You could open the Format 3D Model pane by clicking the 3D Model Views Dialog Box Launcher (shown in Figure 11–74) and then selecting desired options in the Format 3D Model pane.

Other Ways

1. Right-click 3-D model (or, if using touch, tap 'Show Context Menu' button on Mini toolbar), click 'Format 3D Model' on shortcut menu, if necessary, click 3D Model button (Format 3D Model pane), select desired options, click Close button
2. Click 3D Model Views Dialog Box Launcher (3D Model tab | 3D Model Views group), if necessary, click 3D Model button (Format 3D Model pane), select desired options, click Close button

To Reset a 3-D Model

You can reset a 3-D model by discarding all formatting changes. The following steps reset a selected 3-D model.

1. Be sure the 3-D model still is selected.
2. Click the 'Reset 3D Model' arrow (3D Model tab | Adjust group) to display the Reset 3D Model menu (Figure 11–76).

3. Click 'Reset 3D Model' on the Reset 3D Model menu to discard all formatting changes.
4. Click the Undo button (Home tab | Undo group) to restore the 3-D model with your changes.

> **Q&A** What is the purpose of the 'Reset 3D Model and Size' command on the Reset 3D Model menu?
> In addition to discarding all formatting changes, it resets the size to the 3-D model's original size.

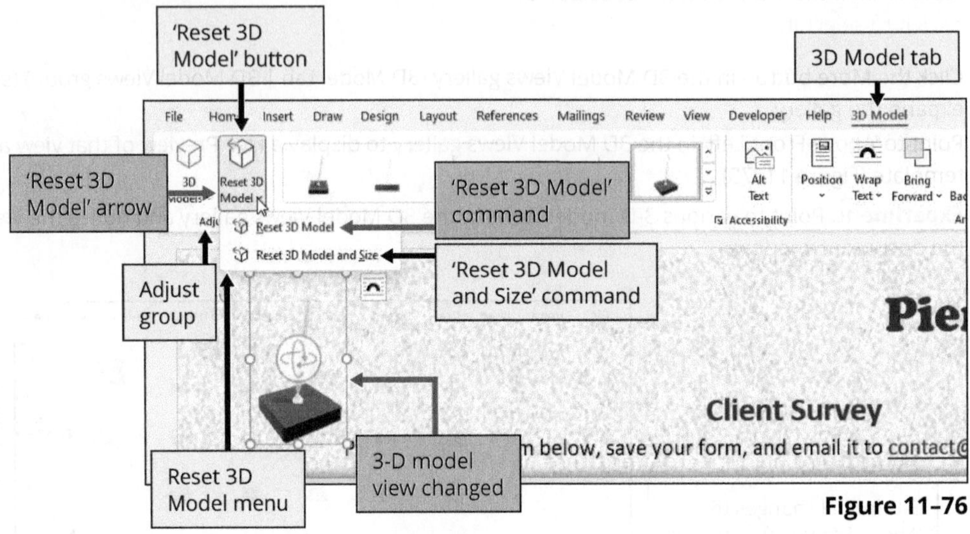

Figure 11-76

To Save the Template, Protect It, and Exit Word

You now are finished with the 3-D model in the online form and with this project. The following steps save the form again, protect it, and then exit Word.

1. Open Backstage view and then, if necessary, display the Info screen.
2. Click the Protect Document button to display the Protect Document menu.
3. Click Restrict Editing on the Protect Document menu to open the Restrict Editing pane.
4. In the Editing restrictions area, if necessary, place a check mark in the 'Allow only this type of editing in the document' check box, click its arrow, and then, if necessary, select 'Filling in forms' in the list.
5. Click the 'Yes, Start Enforcing Protection' button and then click OK (Start Enforcing Protection dialog box) to protect the document without a password.
6. Close the Restrict Editing pane.
7. Save the template again on the same storage location with the same file name.
8. Exit Word.

Supplementary Word Tasks

If you plan to take the certification exam, you should be familiar with the skills in the following sections.

Adding a Digital Signature to a Document

Some users attach a **digital signature** to a document to verify its authenticity. A digital signature is an electronic, encrypted, and secure stamp of authentication on a document. This signature confirms that the file originated from the signer (file creator) and that it has not been altered.

A digital signature references a digital certificate. A **digital certificate** is code attached to a file, macro project, email message, or other digital content that verifies the identity of the creator of the file. Many users who receive online forms enable the macros based on whether they are digitally signed by a developer on the user's list of trusted sources. You can obtain a digital certificate from a commercial certification authority or from your network administrator.

Once a digital signature is added, the document becomes a read-only document, which means that modifications cannot be made to it. Thus, you should create a digital signature only when the document is final. In Word, you can add two types of digital signatures to a document: (1) an invisible digital signature or (2) a signature line.

BTW

Removing Metadata

If you wanted to remove document metadata, such as personal information and comments, you would do the following with the document open in a document window: open Backstage view, if necessary, click Info in Backstage view to display the Info screen, click the 'Check for Issues' button in the Info screen to display the Check for Issues menu, click Inspect Document on the Check for Issues menu to display the Document Inspector dialog box, click the Inspect button (Document Inspector dialog box) to instruct Word to inspect the document, review the results (Document Inspector dialog box), and then click the Remove All button(s) for any item that you do not want to be saved with the document. When you have finished removing information, click the Close button to close the dialog box.

To Add an Invisible Digital Signature to a Document An invisible digital signature does not appear as a tangible signature in the document. If the status bar displays a Signatures button, the document has an invisible digital signature. If you wanted to add an invisible digital signature to a document, you would perform the following steps.

1. If necessary, save the document. Open Backstage view and then, if necessary, display the Info screen.
2. Click the Protect Document button to display the Protect Document menu and then click 'Add a Digital Signature' on the Protect Document menu to display the Sign dialog box. (If a dialog box appears indicating you need a digital ID, click the Yes button and then follow the on-screen instructions. If a dialog box about signature services appears, click OK.)
3. Type the purpose of the digital signature in the 'Purpose for signing this document' text box.
4. Click the Sign button to add the digital signature, show the Signatures button on the status bar, and display Marked as Final on a Message Bar.

> **Q&A** How can I view or remove the digital signatures in a document?
> Open Backstage view, if necessary, display the Info screen, and then click the View Signatures button to open the Signatures pane. To remove a digital signature, click the arrow beside the signature name, click Remove Signature on the menu, and then click Yes in the dialog box.

To Add a Signature Line to a Document A **digital signature line**, which resembles a printed signature placeholder, allows a recipient of the electronic file to type a signature, include an image of the signature, or write a signature using the ink feature on a mobile computer or device. Digital signature lines enable organizations to use paperless methods of obtaining signatures on official documents, such as contracts. If you wanted to add a digital signature line to a document, you would perform the following steps.

1. Position the insertion point at the location for the digital signature.
2. Display the Insert tab. Click the 'Add a Signature Line' button (Insert tab | Text group) to display the Signature Setup dialog box. (If a dialog box appears about signature services, click OK.)
3. Type the name of the person who should sign the document in the appropriate text box.
4. If available, type the signer's title and email address in the appropriate text boxes.

5. Place a check mark in the 'Allow the signer to add comments in the Sign dialog' check box so that the recipient can send a response back to you.
6. Click OK (Signature Setup dialog box) to insert a signature line in the document at the location of the insertion point.

Q&A How does a recipient insert their digital signature?
When the recipient opens the document, a Message Bar appears that contains a View Signatures button. The recipient can click the View Signatures button to open the Signatures pane, click the requested signature arrow, and then click Sign on the menu (or double-click the signature line in the document) to display a dialog box that the recipient then completes.

BTW
Password-Protecting Documents
You can save documents with a password to keep unauthorized users from accessing files. If necessary, save the document. With the document saved, open Backstage view, click Info, click the Protect Document button, click 'Encrypt with Password' on the Protect Document menu, type the password in the Encrypt Document dialog box, type the password again (Confirm Password dialog box), and click OK; or open Backstage view, click Save As, display the Save As dialog box, click the Tools button (Save As dialog box), click General Options on the Tools menu, type the password in the appropriate text box (General Options dialog box), type the password again (Confirm Password dialog box), and then click OK and the Save button (Save As dialog box). As you type a password in the text box, Word displays a series of dots instead of the actual characters so that others cannot view your password as you type it. To remove a password from a document, follow these steps except leave the password text box blank.

Be sure to keep the password confidential. Choose a password that is easy to remember and that no one can guess. Do not use any part of your first or last name, Social Security number, birthday, and so on. Use a password that is at least eight characters long, and if possible, use a mixture of numbers, letters, and at least one special character.

Copying and Renaming Styles and Macros

If you have created a style or macro in one document or template, you can copy the style or a macro to another so that you can use it in a second document or template.

To Copy a Style from One Template or Document to Another If you wanted to copy a style from one template or document to another, you would perform the following steps.

1. Open the document or template into which you want to copy the style.
2. If necessary, click the Styles Dialog Box Launcher (Home tab | Styles group) to open the Styles pane, click the Manage Styles button at the bottom of the Styles pane to display the Manage Styles dialog box, and then click the Import/Export button (Manage Styles dialog box) to display Styles sheet in the Organizer dialog box. Or, click the Document Template button (Developer tab | Templates group) to display the Templates and Add-ins dialog box, click the Organizer button (Templates and Add-ins dialog box) to display the Organizer dialog box, and then, if necessary, click the Styles tab to display the Styles sheet in the dialog box. Notice that the left side of the dialog box displays the style names in the currently open document or template.
3. Click the Close File button (Organizer dialog box) to clear the right side of the dialog box.

Q&A What happened to the Close File button?
It changed to an Open File button.

4. Click the Open File button (Organizer dialog box) and then locate the file that contains the style you wish to copy. Notice that the styles in the located document or template appear on the right side of the dialog box.
5. On the right side of the dialog box, select the style you wish to copy and then click the Copy button to copy the selected style to the document or template on the left. You can continue to copy as many styles as necessary.
6. When finished copying styles, click the Close button to close the dialog box.

To Rename a Style If you wanted to rename a style, you would perform the following steps.

1. Open the document or template that contains the style to rename.
2. If necessary, click the Styles Dialog Box Launcher (Home tab | Styles group) to open the Styles pane, click the Manage Styles button at the bottom of the Styles pane to display the Manage Styles dialog box, and then click the Import/Export button (Manage Styles dialog box) to display the Styles sheet in the Organizer dialog box. Or, click the Document Template button (Developer tab | Templates group) to display the Templates and Add-ins dialog box, click the Organizer button (Templates and Add-ins dialog box) to display the Organizer dialog box, and then, if necessary, click the Styles tab

to display the Styles sheet in the dialog box. Notice that the left side of the dialog box displays the style names in the currently open document or template.

3. Select the style you wish to rename and then click the Rename button (Organizer dialog box) to display the Rename dialog box.
4. Type the new name of the style in the text box and then click OK (Rename dialog box).

Q&A Can I delete styles too?
Yes, click the Delete button (Organizer dialog box) to delete any selected styles.

5. When finished renaming styles, click the Close button (Organizer dialog box) to close the dialog box.

To Copy a Macro from One Template or Document to Another If you wanted to copy a macro from one template or document to another, you would perform the following steps.

1. Open the document or template into which you want to copy the macro.
2. If necessary, click the Macros button (Developer tab | Code group or View tab | Macros group) to display the Macros dialog box and then click the Organizer button (Macros dialog box) to display the Macro Project Items sheet in the Organizer dialog box. Or, click the Document Template button (Developer tab | Templates group) to display the Templates and Add-ins dialog box, click the Organizer button (Templates and Add-ins dialog box) to display the Organizer dialog box, and then, if necessary, click the Macro Project Items tab to display the Macro Project Items sheet in the dialog box. Notice that the left side of the dialog box displays the macro names in the currently open document or template.
3. Click the Close File button (Organizer dialog box) to clear the right side of the dialog box.

Q&A What happened to the Close File button?
It changed to an Open File button.

4. Click the Open File button (Organizer dialog box) and then locate the file that contains the macro you wish to copy. Notice that the macros in the located document or template appear on the right side of the dialog box.
5. On the ride side of the dialog box, select the macro you wish to copy and then click the Copy button to copy the selected macro to the document or template on the left. You can continue to copy as many macros as necessary.
6. When finished copying macros, click the Close button (Organizer dialog box) to close the dialog box.

To Rename a Macro If you wanted to rename a macro, you would perform the following steps.

1. Open the document that contains the macro to rename.
2. If necessary, click the Macros button (Developer tab | Code group or View tab | Macros group) to display the Macros dialog box and then click the Organizer button (Macros dialog box) to display the Macro Project Items sheet in the Organizer dialog box. Or, click the Document Template button (Developer tab | Templates group) to display the Templates and Add-ins dialog box, click the Organizer button (Templates and Add-ins dialog box) to display the Organizer dialog box, and then, if necessary, click the Macro Project Items tab to display the Macro Project Items sheet in the dialog box. Notice that the left side of the dialog box displays the macro names in the currently open document or template.

3. Select the macro you wish to rename and then click the Rename button (Organizer dialog box) to display the Rename dialog box.
4. Type the new name of the macro in the text box and then click OK (Rename dialog box).

Q&A Can I delete macros, too?
Yes, click the Delete button (Organizer dialog box) to delete any selected macros.

5. When finished renaming macros, click the Close button to close the dialog box.

Preparing a Document for Internationalization

Word provides internationalization features you can use when creating documents and templates. Use of features should be determined based on the intended audience of the document or template. By default, Word uses formatting consistent with the country or region selected when installing Windows. In addition to inserting symbols, such as those for currency, and using date and time formats that are recognized internationally or in other countries, you can set the language used for proofing tools and other language preferences.

To Set the Language for Proofing Tools If you wanted to change the language that Word uses to proof documents or templates, you would perform the following steps.

1. If necessary, click the Language group button (Review tab) to display the Language group.
2. Click the Language button (Review tab | Language group) to display the Language menu.
3. Click 'Set Proofing Language' on the Language menu to display the Language dialog box. (If you want to set this language as the default, click the 'Set As Default' button.)
4. Select the desired language to use for proofing tools and then click OK.

To Set Language Preferences If you wanted to change the language that Word uses for editing, display, Help, and ScreenTips, you would perform the following steps.

1. If necessary, click the Language group button (Review tab) to display the Language group.
2. Click the Language button (Review tab | Language group) to display the Language menu and then click Language Preferences on the Language menu to display the language settings in the Word Options dialog box. Or, open Backstage view, click Options in the left pane to display the Word Options dialog box, and then click Language in the left pane (Word Options dialog box) to display the language settings.
3. Select preferences for the display language and the authoring languages and proofing, then click OK.

BTW
Opening Files
In addition to current and previous versions of Word documents and templates, XML and PDF files, and web-page files, you can open a variety of other types of documents through the Open dialog box, including rich text format, text files, OpenDocument text, and WordPerfect files. To open these documents, open Backstage view, click Open to display the Open screen, click the Browse button to display the Open dialog box, click the file type arrow (Open dialog box), click the desired file type to open, locate the file, and then click the Open button to open the file and display its contents in a Word window. Through the Save dialog box, you can save the open file in its native format or save it as a Word document or template.

Working with XML

You can convert an online form to the XML format so that the data in the form can be shared with other programs, such as Microsoft Access. XML is a popular format for structuring data, which allows the data to be reused and shared. **XML**, which stands for Extensible Markup Language, is a language used to mark up structured data so that it can be more easily shared between different computer programs. An **XML file** is a text file containing XML tags that identify field names and data. Each data item is called an **element**. Businesses often create standard XML file layouts and tags to describe commonly used types of data.

In Word, you can save a file in a default XML format, in which Word parses the document into individual components that can be used by other programs. Or, you can identify specific sections of the document as XML elements; the elements then can be used in other programs, such as Access. This feature may not be available in all versions of Word.

To Save a Document in the Default XML Format If you wanted to save a document in the XML format, you would perform the following steps.

1. Open the file to be saved in the XML format (for example, a form containing content controls).
2. Open Backstage view and then click Save As to display the Save As screen.
3. Navigate to the desired save location and then display the Save As dialog box.
4. Click the 'Save as type' arrow (Save As dialog box), click 'Word XML Document' in the list, and then click the Save button to save the template as an XML document. (Note that depending on settings, your list also may display the extension (*.xml) after 'Word XML Document'.)

> **Q&A** How can I identify an XML document?
> XML documents typically have an .xml extension.

To Attach a Schema File To identify sections of a document as XML elements, you first attach an XML schema to the document, usually one that contains content controls. An **XML schema** is a special type of XML file that describes the layout of elements in other XML files. Word users typically do not create XML schema files. Software developers or other technical personnel create an XML schema file and provide it to Word users. XML schema files, often simply called **schema files**, usually have an extension of .xsd. Once the schema is attached, you can use the 'XML Mapping Pane' button (Developer tab | Mapping group) to insert controls from the schema into the document. If you wanted to attach a schema file to a document, such as an online form, you would perform the following steps.

1. Open the file to which you wish to attach the schema, such as an online form that contains content controls.
2. Open Backstage view and then use the Save As command to save the file with a new file name, to preserve the contents of the original file.
3. Click the Document Template button (Developer tab | Templates group) to display the Templates and Add-ins dialog box.
4. Click the XML Schema tab (Templates and Add-ins dialog box) to display the XML Schema sheet and then click the Add Schema button to display the Add Schema dialog box.
5. Locate and select the schema file (Add Schema dialog box) and then click the Open button to display the Schema Settings dialog box.
6. Enter the URI and alias in the appropriate text boxes (Schema Settings dialog box) and then click OK to add the schema to the Schema Library and to add the namespace alias to the list of available schemas in the XML Schema sheet (Templates and Add-ins dialog box).

> **Q&A** What is a URI and an alias?
> Word uses the term, URI, also called a namespace, to refer to the schema. Because these names are difficult to remember, you can define a namespace alias. In a setting outside of an academic environment, a computer administrator would provide you with the appropriate namespace entry.

7. If necessary, place a check mark in the desired schema's check box.
8. Click OK, which causes Word to attach the selected schema to the open document and open the XML Structure pane in the Word window.

To Delete a Schema from the Schema Library To delete a schema from a document, you would remove the check mark from the schema name's check box in the XML Schema sheet in the Templates and Add-ins dialog box. If you wanted to delete a schema altogether from the Schema Library, you would perform the following steps.

1. Click the Document Template button (Developer tab | Templates group) to display the Templates and Add-ins dialog box.
2. Click the XML Schema tab (Templates and Add-ins dialog box) to display the XML Schema sheet and then click the Schema Library button to display the Schema Library dialog box.
3. Click the schema you want to delete in the Select a schema list (Schema Library dialog box) and then click the Delete Schema button.
4. When Word displays the Schema Library dialog box asking if you are sure you want to delete the schema, click Yes.
5. Click OK (Schema Library dialog box) and then click the Cancel button (Templates and Add-ins dialog box).

Summary

In this module, you learned how to enhance the appearance of text and graphics, create and modify styles, automate a series of tasks with a macro, customize the Quick Access Toolbar, and work with 3-D models. You also learned about several supplementary tasks that you should know if you plan to take the certification exam.

Consider This: Plan Ahead

What decisions will you need to make when creating macro-enabled and enhanced online forms?

Use these guidelines as you complete the assignments in this module and create your own online forms outside of this class.

1. Save the form to be modified as a macro-enabled template, if you plan to include macros in the template for the form.
2. Enhance the visual appeal of a form.
   a) Arrange data entry fields in logical groups on the form and in an order that users would expect.
   b) Draw the user's attention to important sections.
   c) Use colors and images that complement one another.
3. Add macros to automate tasks.
   a) Record macros, if possible.
   b) If you are familiar with computer programming, write VBA code to extend capabilities of recorded macros.
4. Determine how the form data will be analyzed.
   a) If the data entered in the form will be analyzed by a program outside of Word, create the data entry fields so that the entries are stored in a format that can be shared with other programs.

Student Assignments

Apply Your Knowledge

Reinforce the skills and apply the concepts you learned in this module.

Working with Images, Shapes, and Fields

Note: To complete this assignment, you will be required to use the Data Files. Please contact your instructor for information about accessing the Data Files.

Instructions: Start Word. Open the template, SC_WD_11-2.dotx, which is located in the Data Files. The template is an updated version of the tutoring center student survey online form you created in the Apply Your Knowledge Student Assignment in Module 10. In this assignment, you enhance the updated tutoring center online form by changing colors and pictures, removing an image background, adding an artistic effect to an image, changing saturation and tone, grouping images, using a texture fill effect, changing a shape, inserting a date field, rotating text in a shape, and applying 3-D effects to a shape (Figure 11–77).

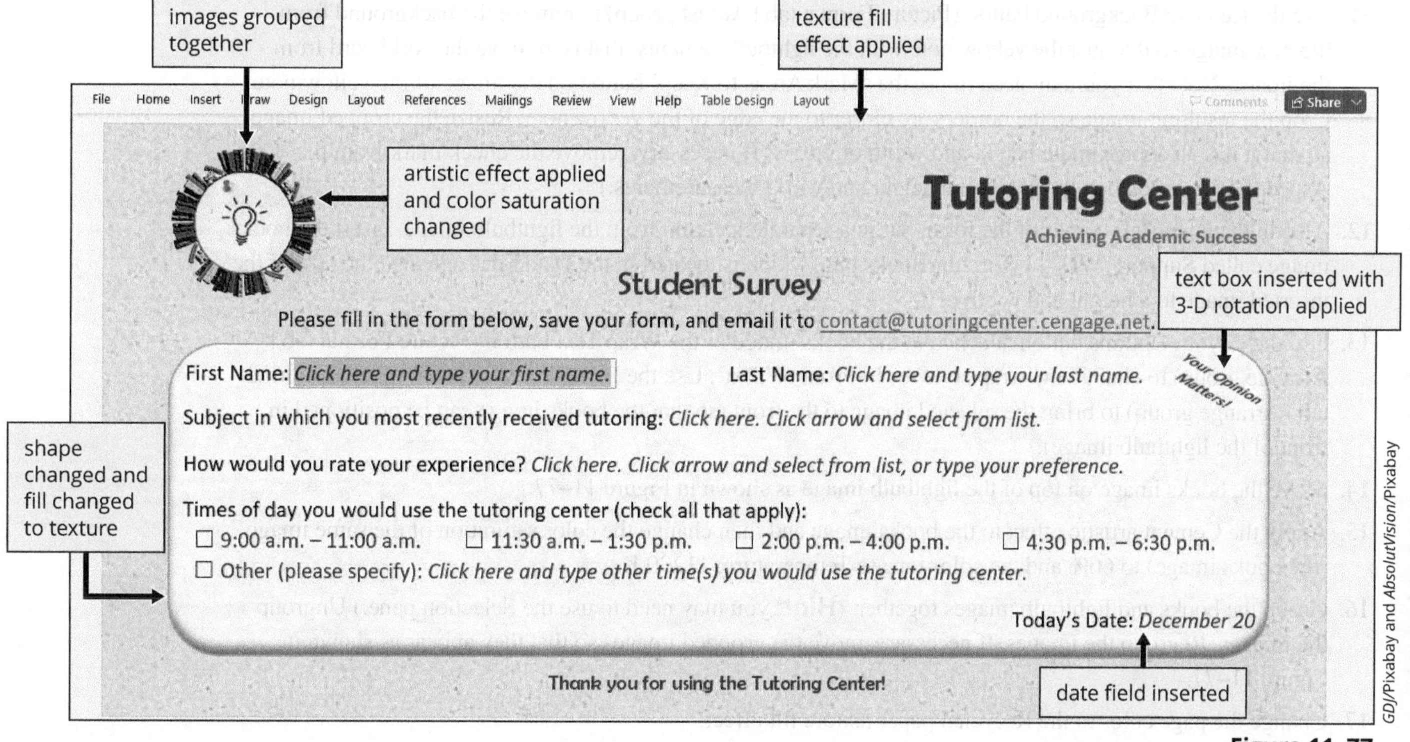

Figure 11–77

Note: Data file graphic is from *Tumisu*/Pixabay

Perform the following tasks:

1. Click File on the ribbon, click Save As, and then save the template using the new file name, SC_WD_11_UpdatedTutoringCenterStudentSurveyModified.
2. Unprotect the template.
3. Change the font color of the first line (Tutoring Center), the third line (Student Survey), and the last line on the form (Thank you for using the Tutoring Center!) to 'Orange, Accent 2, Darker 50%'.
4. Change the font color of the tag line (Achieving Academic Success) to 'Green, Accent 6, Darker 25%'. Modify the hyperlink style so that the email address (contact@tutoringcenter.cengage.net) is the same color as the tag line ('Green, Accent 6, Darker 25%').
5. Modify the Intense Emphasis style to use the color 'Green, Accent 6, Darker 50%'.

Continued on next page

6. Create a character style with the name Check Box Labels for all check boxes in the data entry area that uses a font color of 'Green, Accent 6, Darker 50%' (be sure the font is 11-point Calibri (Body) and the font is not bold). Apply the new character style to the check box labels in the form: 9:00 a.m. – 11:00 a.m., 11:30 a.m. – 1:30 p.m., 2:00 p.m. – 4:00 p.m., 4:30 p.m. – 6:30 p.m., and Other (please specify):.
7. Select the image in the upper-right corner and then open the Selection pane, which you may use throughout this assignment. Use the Layout Options button attached to the image or the Wrap Text button (Picture Format tab | Arrange group) to change the layout to 'In Front of Text'.
8. Right-align the first two lines of text (the center name and the tag line). Click anywhere to remove the selection. Move the image in the upper-right corner of the form to the upper-left corner. Remove the reflection picture effect from the picture.
9. Change the image in the upper-left corner of the form with the lightbulb image called Support_WD_11_Lightbulb.jpg, which is located in the Data Files. (**Hint:** Use the Change Picture button (Picture Format tab | Adjust group) and then click 'From a File' (or This Device) on the Change Picture menu, or right-click the image, point Change Picture on the shortcut menu, and then click 'From a File' (or This Device) on the Change Picture submenu.)
10. Use the Send Backward arrow (Picture Format tab | Arrange group) to send the selected image to the back (so that the lightbulb image can be positioned behind the circular books image later in this assignment).
11. Use the Remove Background button (Picture Format tab | Adjust group) to remove the background from the new image so that just the yellow note with the lightbulb remains; that is, remove the corkboard from the image. Note that you may need to use the 'Mark Areas to Keep' button on the image of the yellow note. Crop the resulting image so the borders are closer to the edge of the yellow note. Resize the cropped image so that it has an approximate height and width of 0.65". (If necessary, remove the check mark from the 'Lock Aspect Ratio' check box to specify the height and width measurements.)
12. Also in the upper-left corner of the form, but in a separate location from the lightbulb image, insert the books image called Support_WD_11_CircularBooks.png, which is located in the Data Files. Change the size of the inserted image to a height and width of 1".
13. Use the Layout Options button attached to the books image or the Wrap Text button (Picture Format tab | Arrange group) to change the wrap style to 'In Front of Text'. Use the Bring Forward arrow (Picture Format tab | Arrange group) to bring the selected image to the front (so that the books image can be positioned in front of the lightbulb image).
14. Move the books image on top of the lightbulb image as shown in Figure 11–77.
15. Apply the Cement artistic effect to the books image and then change the color saturation of the same image (the books image) to 66% and the color tone to Temperature: 11200 K.
16. Group the books and lightbulb images together. (**Hint:** you may need to use the Selection pane.) Ungroup the images. Regroup the images. If necessary, move the grouped images so that they appear as shown in Figure 11–77.
17. Change the page color to the Recycled paper texture fill effect.
18. Change the shape around the data entry area to Rectangle: Rounded Corners.
19. Change the fill of the rectangle shape to the Parchment texture fill effect.
20. Apply the Inside: Bottom shadow effect to the rectangle shape.
21. If necessary, display the Developer tab. Change the properties of the date picker content control so that its contents can be deleted and then delete the content control. Use the 'Explore Quick Parts' button (Insert tab | Text group) to insert a date field after the Today's Date: label in the format month day (i.e., December 20), so that the date field is automatically filled in on the form. (**Hint:** You may need to adjust the date format to MMMM dd.) Right-align the line containing the date. If necessary, change the format of the displayed date field to Intense Emphasis. Hide the Developer tab.
22. Draw a text box that is approximately 1" × 0.72" that contains the text, Your Opinion Matters!, centered in the text box. Decrease the font size to 10 point. Remove the outline from the text box (shape). Change the direction of text in the text box (shape) to 'Rotate all text 90°'. Select the text and use the 'Text Effects and

Typography' button (Home tab | Font group) to apply the effect called 'Fill: Gray, Accent color 3; Sharp Bevel'. Change the font color to 'Gray, Accent 3, Darker 50%'. Be sure the text is bold. Select the text box and then apply the 3-D rotation shape effect called 'Isometric: Top Up' to the text box (shape). Then, apply the Offset: Center shadow shape effect to the text box. Remove the fill from the text box (shape). Move the text box to the upper-right corner of the data entry area as shown in Figure 11–77.

23. Select the text box, click the Send Backward arrow (Shape Format tab | Arrange group), and then click 'Send Behind Text' on the Send Backward menu to send the text box behind text. (Note this step is necessary so that you can group the rectangle and text box shapes together.) Select the rectangle shape and then the text box shape. With both shapes selected, group the two shapes together. Ungroup the shapes. Regroup the shapes. If necessary, close the Selection pane.
24. If requested by your instructor, change the email address on the form to your email address.
25. If necessary, adjust spacing above and below paragraphs so that all contents fit on a single screen.
26. Check accessibility. Add this alt text to the grouped image in the upper-left corner of the form: Image of lightbulb surrounded by books. Add this alt text to the grouped rectangle shape and text box: Your Opinion Matters! graphic in data entry area. Leave the accessibility errors or warnings identified by the Accessibility Checker for image or object not inline because, for illustration purposes, the grouped objects are intended to be floating objects in this assignment. Protect the form to restrict editing to filling in forms. Save the form again with the same file name and then submit it in the format specified by your instructor. Collapse the ribbon.
27. Access the template through File Explorer and test it using your own data for the responses. If necessary, make necessary corrections to the form.
28. **Consider This:** What is the advantage of creating a style for the check box labels?

Extend Your Knowledge

Extend the skills you learned in this module and experiment with new skills. You may need to use Help to complete the assignment.

Enhancing a Form and Working with Macros

Note: To complete this assignment, you will be required to use the Data Files. Please contact your instructor for information about accessing the Data Files.

Instructions: Start Word. Open the template, SC_WD_11-3.dotx, which is located in the Data Files. The template is an updated version of the parade entry form you created in the Extend Your Knowledge Student Assignment in Module 10. In this assignment, you enhance the updated parade entry form created by changing colors and pictures, converting a table to text, and working with macros.

Perform the following tasks:

1. Click File on the ribbon and then click Save As and save the template as a macro-enabled template using the new file name, SC_WD_11_ParadeEntryFormModified.
2. Unprotect the password-protected template. Enter the password, pet, when prompted. (Note that you may need to click the Enable Content button on the Word Message Bar, or right-click the file in File Explorer, click Properties, and then click Unblock in the dialog box to use the file.)
3. In the rectangle that surrounds the data entry area, use the Shape Fill arrow (Shape Format tab | Shape Styles group) to insert the picture called Support_WD_11_PawPrints.jpg, which is located in the Data Files, in the rectangle shape. Change the color of the picture in the rectangle to 'Lavender, Background color 2 Light'.
4. Convert the table to text for the 2 × 1 table containing the First Name: and Last Name: labels and associated First Name and Last Name content controls, separating the text with paragraph marks. (**Hint:** You will need to change the properties of the content controls so that their contents can be deleted before you can convert the table to text. When finished, reset the content controls so that their contents cannot be deleted.) Change the left indent to 0.06" on these two lines.

Continued on next page

5. If necessary, adjust spacing above and below paragraphs so that all contents fit on a single screen.
6. Adjust the size of the rectangle shape so that it covers all content controls in the data entry area.
7. Change the page background to a texture or color of your choice.
8. Change the font color of the form name (Pet Palooza!) to a color of your choice. If desired, change the color of other text on the form.
9. If necessary, customize macro security settings to the 'Disable all macros with notification' option.
10. Show formatting marks and rulers on the screen. Record a macro that hides the formatting marks and the rulers. Name it HideScreenElements. Store it in Documents Based On SC_WD_11_ParadeEntryFormModified template and enter an appropriate description (Figure 11–78). Assign it the shortcut key, ALT+H. Run the macro to test it.

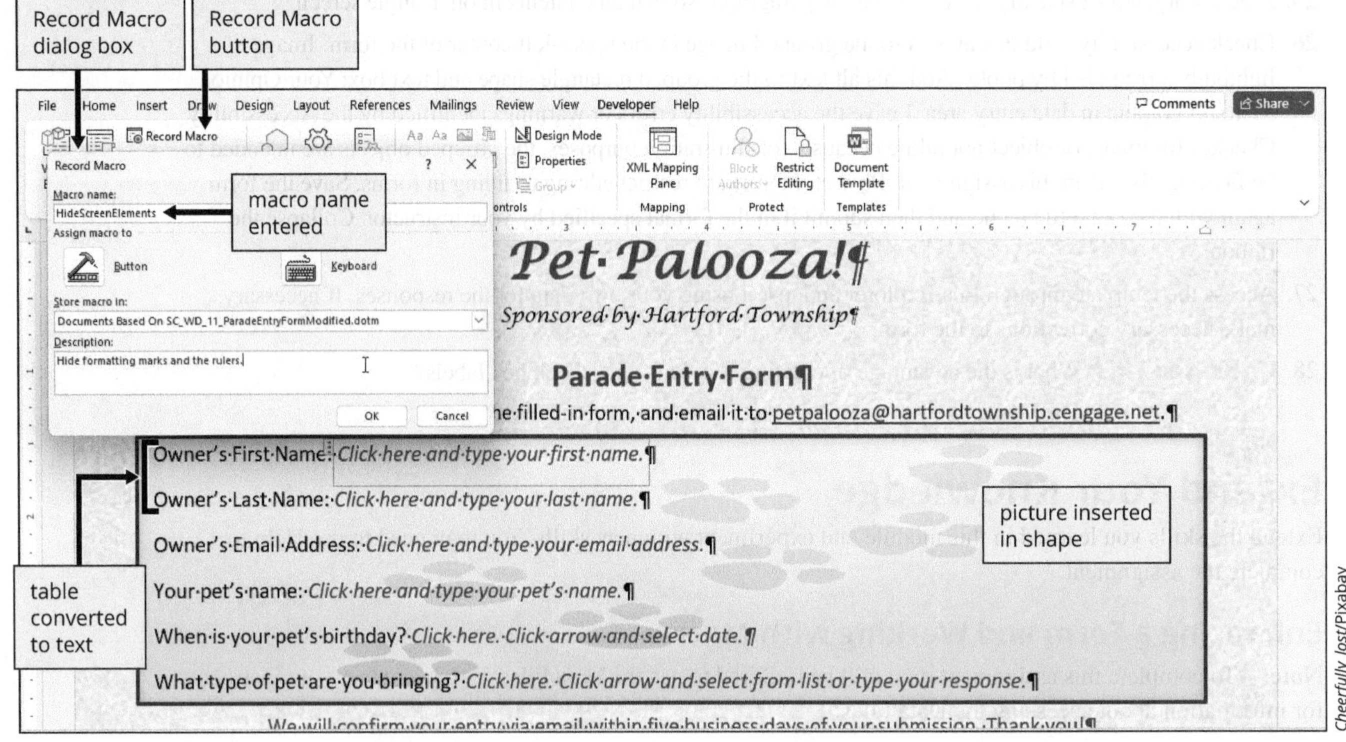

Figure 11–78

11. Add a button to the Quick Access Toolbar for the macro created in Step 10. Test the button and then delete the button from the Quick Access Toolbar.
12. Create an automatic macro called AutoNew using the macro recorder. Store it in Documents Based On SC_WD_11_ParadeEntryFormModified template. The macro should change the view to page width. While recording the macro, practice pausing the recording and resuming recording the macro.
13. Edit the AutoNew macro so that it also hides the Developer tab and the ribbon. (**Hint:** You will need to open the Visual Basic Editor window from the Macros dialog box to display the VBA code for the AutoNew macro and then enter the appropriate VBA code statements in the Visual Basic Editor.)
14. Display all macros.
15. If requested by your instructor, create a macro of your choice using the Visual Basic window.
16. If requested by your instructor, display the Organizer dialog box. Close the file on the right side and then open another template of your choice. Copy the Intense Emphasis style from the SC_WD_11_ParadeEntryFormModified file to the template you opened on the right side. Then, delete the Intense Emphasis style from the template on the right side. Copy the macros from the SC_WD_11_ParadeEntryFormModified file to the template on the right side. Then, delete the copied macros from the template on the right side. Close the Organizer dialog box.

17. If requested by your instructor, add a custom document property by opening Backstage view, clicking Info, clicking the Properties button in the right pane, clicking Advanced Properties, clicking the Custom tab, entering the text, My Name, in the Name text box, selecting Text in the Type box if necessary, typing your name as the value, clicking the Add button, and then clicking OK (Properties dialog box). Then, in the form, in place of the township name (Hartford), insert the custom field by clicking the 'Explore Quick Parts' button (Insert tab | Text group), clicking Field, selecting Document Information in the Categories area, clicking DocProperty in the Field names list, selecting My Name in the Property list, and then clicking OK.
18. Check accessibility and fix any issues as necessary. In the Restrict Editing pane, select 'No changes (Read only)' in the Editing restrictions area. Next, change the protection on the form in the Restrict Editing pane to filling in forms and then protect the unencrypted form using the word, pet, as the password. Save the form again and submit it in the format specified by your instructor.
19. Access the template through File Explorer and test it using your own data for the responses. If necessary, make corrections to the form.
20. **Consider This:** If a recorded macro does not work as intended when you test it, how would you fix it?

Expand Your World

Create a solution that uses cloud or web technologies by learning and investigating on your own from general guidance.

Working with Document Security and Digital IDs

Note: To complete this assignment, you will be required to use the Data Files. Please contact your instructor for information about accessing the Data Files.

Instructions: Start Word. Open the document, SC_WD_11-4.docx, which is located in the Data Files. As a client of Forestview Insurance, you are submitting a change of address to your agent. To secure the document, you will add a digital signature line, encrypt the document with a password, remove the password, digitally sign the document, and mark the document as final.

Perform the following tasks:

1. Use Help to review and expand your knowledge about these topics: signature lines, passwords, document encryption, marking the document as final, and digital IDs.
2. Click File on the ribbon, click Save As, and then save the document using the new file name, SC_WD_11_NewAddressLetter.
3. Position the insertion point on the blank line at the end of the document and then click the 'Add a Signature Line' button (Insert tab | Text group) to display the Signature Setup dialog box. Fill in the information to add a signature line to the document. If requested by your instructor, use your personal information in the signature line; otherwise, use the recipient's name and title.
4. Encrypt the document with the password, fun.
5. Save the document again on the same storage location with the same file name. Then, close the document and reopen it. Enter the password when prompted.
6. Click the View Signatures button on the Signatures Bar that appears in the document to open the Signatures pane. Close the Signatures pane.
7. Remove the password from the document. (**Hint:** To delete a password, follow the same steps as to add a password, except delete all content from the password text box so that it is blank.)
8. Double-click the digital signature to sign the document.
9. Click the Edit Anyway button on the Message Bar, which removes the digital signature.
10. Select the signature line in the document and then use the Font dialog box to format the text as hidden. If formatting marks are showing, hide formatting marks so that the hidden text is not visible in the document. Show formatting marks, select the hidden signature line, and then use the Font dialog box to unhide the text.

Continued on next page

11. Click the 'Add a Signature Line' arrow (Insert tab | Text group) and then click 'Add Signature Services' on the menu, which starts a browser and opens an Office Help window with a list of services that issue digital IDs (Figure 11–79). (If Word displays a Get a Digital ID dialog box, click Yes.) If a list of services does not appear, search for the text, digital ID, in the Office Help window.

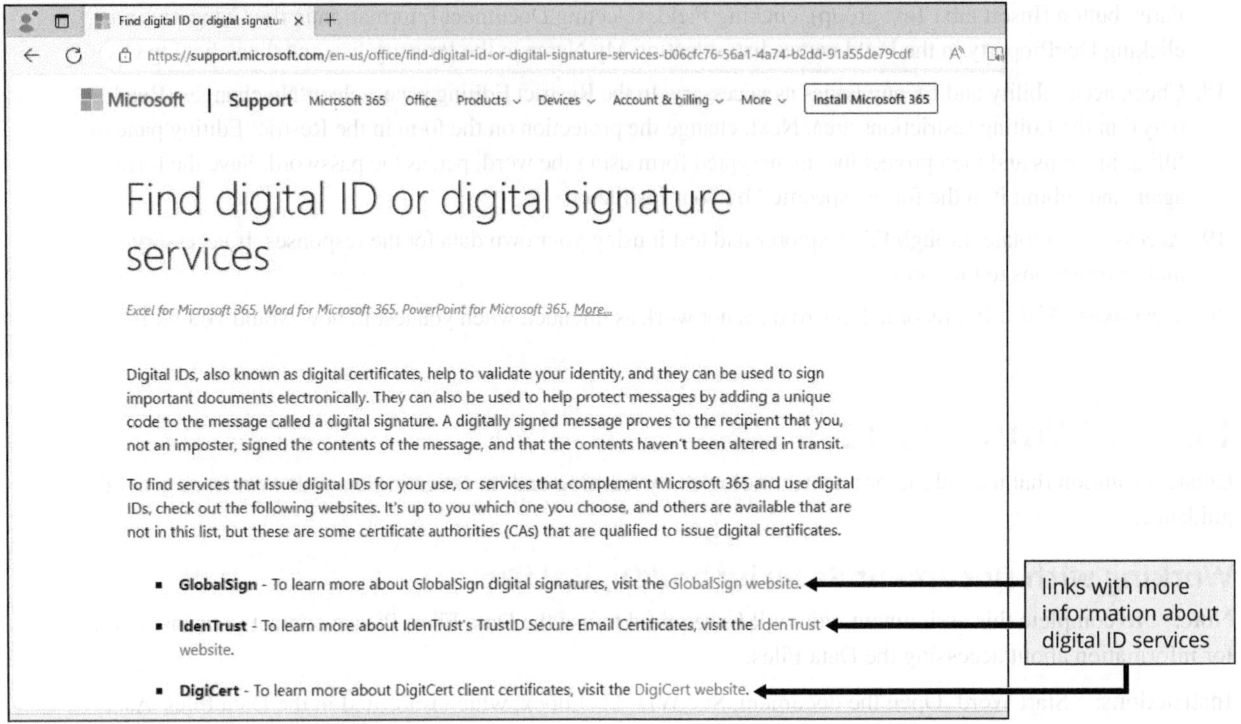

Figure 11–79

12. Click the link beside each service to learn more about each one.
13. Use a search engine to read reviews about these services and determine which digital ID service you would recommend. Close the browser window.
14. Use Backstage view to add a digital signature to the document. Click the Edit Anyway button on the Message Bar.
15. If requested by your instructor, set the proofing language to English (United States).
16. If necessary, mark the document as final. (**Hint:** Use the Protect Document button in Backstage view.)
17. Submit the document in the format specified by your instructor.
18. **Consider This:** Which digital ID services did you evaluate? When you read the reviews, were there other services not listed on the Office website? If so, what were their names? Which digital ID service would you recommend? Why? When you marked the document as final, what text appeared on the title bar? What text appeared on the Message Bar? What appeared on the status bar?

In the Lab

Design and implement a solution using creative thinking and problem-solving skills.

Modifying an Online Form for a Retail Store

Problem: As customer relations manager at Natural Surplus, you created the online customer survey that was defined in the In the Lab Student Assignment in Module 10. Although you were pleased with the initial design, you believe the form can be improved by enhancing its appearance and adding macros to it.

Part 1a: Open the template called SC_WD_10_NaturalSurplusCustomerSurvey.dotx that you created in the In the Lab Student Assignment in Module 10. Click File on the ribbon and then click Save As and save the template as a macro-enabled template using the new file name, SC_WD_11_NaturalSurplusCustomerSurveyModified and then proceed to Part 1b.

If you did not complete the In the Lab Student Assignment in Module 10, create a template that contains the company name (Natural Surplus), the company's tag line (Get Healthy … Stay Healthy!), and an appropriate image that you obtain from the icons or online images, or use the Support_WD_11_ShoppingCart.png image in the Data Files. The third line should have the text, Customer Survey. The fourth line should read: Please fill in the form below, save the filled-in form, and then email it to survey@naturalsurplus.cengage.net.

The data entry area should contain the following:

- First Name and Last Name are plain text content controls within a table.
- A drop-down list content control with the label, How did you make your most recent purchase?, has these choices: In Store, Online, Phone.
- The following instruction should appear above these check boxes: Product lines you would like to be offered/expanded (check all that apply)?; the check boxes are Gluten Free, Organics, Plant Based, Supplements, Green Cleaning, Cosmetics, Household, Personal Care, and Other (please specify).
- A rich text content control after the Other (please specify) label allows customers to enter their own response.
- A combo box content control with the label, What is your age range?, has these choices: 18-25, 26-35, 36-50, 51-70, over 70.
- A date picker content control with the label, On what date was your most recent purchase at our store?
- On the line below the data entry area, include the text: Thank you for your business!

Use meaningful placeholder text for all content controls. (For example, the placeholder text for the First Name plain text content control could be as follows: Click here and type your first name.) Apply a style to the placeholder text. Assign names, styles, and locking to each content control (so that the content controls cannot be deleted). Draw a rectangle around the data entry area of the form and format the rectangle appropriately. Add a page color. Be sure to change the page size and margins, and adjust spacing as necessary above and below paragraphs, so that the entire form fits in the document window.

Add missing alt text to the images in the template. (Leave the errors or warnings identified by the Accessibility Checker for image or object not inline because, for illustration purposes, some items are intended to be floating objects in this assignment.) When you are finished creating the form, protect it so that editing is restricted to filling in the form and then save it as a template with the file name, SC_WD_10_NaturalSurplusCustomerSurvey. Test the form and make any necessary corrections. Click File on the ribbon and then click Save As and save the template as a macro-enabled template using the new file name, SC_WD_11_NaturalSurplusCustomerSurveyModified and then proceed to Part 1b.

Part 1b: Next, enhance the Natural Surplus online customer survey as follows. Change the font and color of the company name, tag line, and form title. Change the page color to a texture. Change the font and color of the last line. Apply an artistic effect to the image that you used on the form. Change the rectangle shape around the data entry area. In the rectangle, add a picture fill effect using the image of a shopping cart (if desired, one is available in the Data Files for use called Support_WD_11_ShoppingCart.png) and recolor it as necessary. Change the color of the shadow in the rectangle. Draw a text box with the text, See you again soon!, and apply a 3-D effect to the text box.

Specify the appropriate macro security level. Record a macro that hides screen elements and then assign the macro to a button on the Quick Access Toolbar. Record another macro of your choice for a task you would like to automate. Add a button to the Quick Access Toolbar for any Word command not on the ribbon.

Use the concepts and techniques presented in this module to modify the online form. Be sure to save it as a macro-enabled template. Protect the form, test it, and submit it along with the answers to the Part 2 critical thinking questions in the format specified by your instructor.

Continued on next page

If working with a 3-D model is required by your instructor, save the form using a new file name, SC_WD_11_NaturalSurplusCustomerSurveyModified_3-DModel. Delete the current image at the top of the form and then insert an appropriate 3-D model in its place. Resize and position the 3-D model as needed. Practice rotating and tilting the 3-D model. Format the 3-D model using additional formatting options of your choice. Protect the form, test it, and submit it in the format specified by your instructor.

Part 2: Consider This: You made several decisions while enhancing the online form in this assignment: formats to use (i.e., fonts, font sizes, colors, styles, etc.), graphics to use, which task to automate, and which button to add to the Quick Access Toolbar. What was the rationale behind each of these decisions? When you proofread and tested the online form, what further revisions did you make, and why?

Creating Photo Albums and Delivering Presentations

Objectives

After completing this module, you will be able to:

- Create a custom slide show
- Save a slide as a picture
- Create handouts by exporting to Word
- Record slide timings and narration
- Save a presentation as a PowerPoint show
- Use the Accessibility Checker to inspect design, colors, contrast, and fonts
- Encrypt a presentation with a password
- Print handouts and notes
- Customize the Notes Master
- Change slide orientation and resolution
- Insert a summary zoom slide

Introduction

Sharing pictures has become a part of our everyday lives. We use smartphones, digital cameras, and mobile devices, and we visit social media websites to share our adventures, special occasions, and business activities. PowerPoint has the ability to create custom slide shows with these pictures so you can show particular slides to specific audiences. For example, one large presentation created for students interested in enrolling in classes internationally can be separated into custom shows describing particular cities where study abroad programs are offered.

In addition, the PowerPoint photo album feature allows you to organize and enhance your pictures. These photo albums can be shared with people who do not have PowerPoint installed on their devices. You can create custom handouts to distribute to audience members and develop notes to help you deliver your presentation effectively.

BTW
Using Photographs
A carefully selected image can convey an engaging message that your audience will remember long after the presentation has ended. One picture can evoke emotions and create a connection between the speaker and the listeners. The adage, "A picture is worth a thousand words," is relevant when audience members view PowerPoint slides.

Project: Presentation with a Custom Slide Show and Photo Album

In this module's project, you will follow proper design guidelines and learn to use PowerPoint to create the slides and printouts shown in Figure 8–1a through 8–1g. The objective is to produce a presentation for a seminar on campus for students considering studying abroad. You will create a custom slide show highlighting two cities: Paris and London. You will save one slide as a picture, create handouts to distribute to audience members, and save the presentation as a PowerPoint show. You then will create a photo album with all the slides in the presentation.

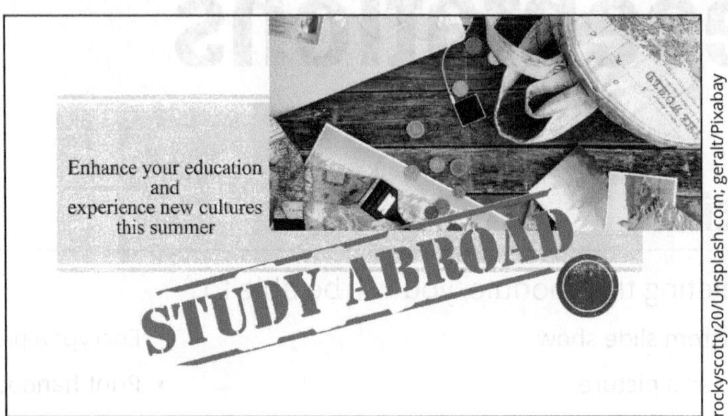

rockyscotty20/Unsplash.com; geralt/Pixabay

Figure 8–1(a): Custom Slide Show Title Slide

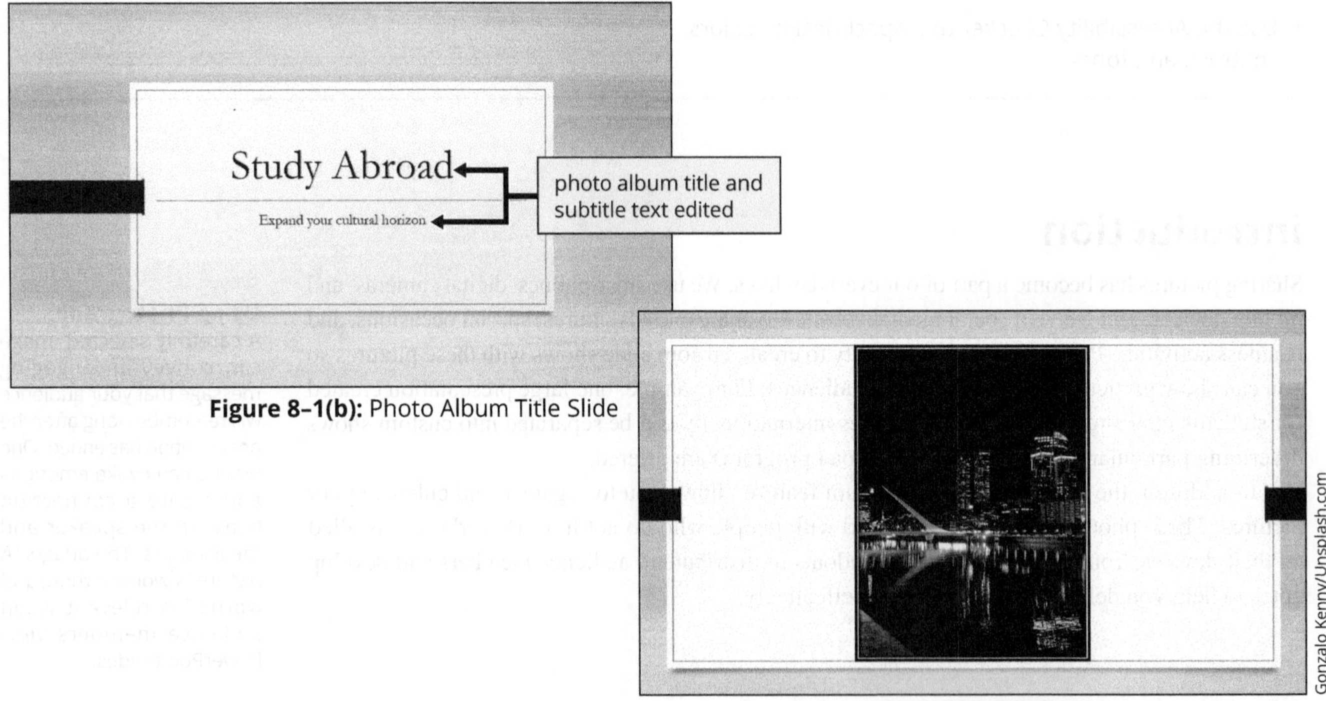

Figure 8–1(b): Photo Album Title Slide

Gonzalo Kenny/Unsplash.com

Figure 8–1(c): Photo Album Slide

STUDY ABROAD

title edited

iankelsall1/Pixabay; Alexas_Fotos/Pixabay; Andrea De Santis/Unsplash; cmmellow/Pixabay; Gonzalo Kenny/unsplash; matcuz/Pixabay; DUCTINH91/Pixabay; scharfsascha/Pixabay; Pharaoh_EZYPT/Pixabay; Ledoc/Pixabay; acheemete/Pixabay

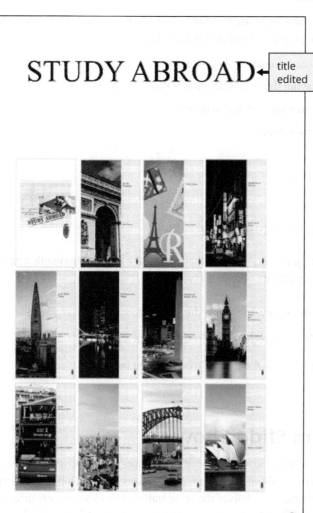

Figure 8–1(d): Summary Zoom Slide

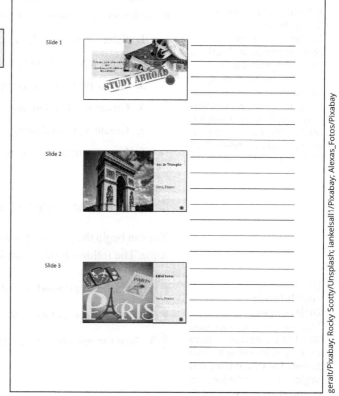

Slide 1

Slide 2

Arc de Triomphe

Paris, France

Slide 3

Eiffel Tower

Paris, France

geralt/Pixabay; Rocky Scotty/Unsplash; iankelsall1/Pixabay; Alexas_Fotos/Pixabay

Figure 8–1(e): Microsoft Word Handout

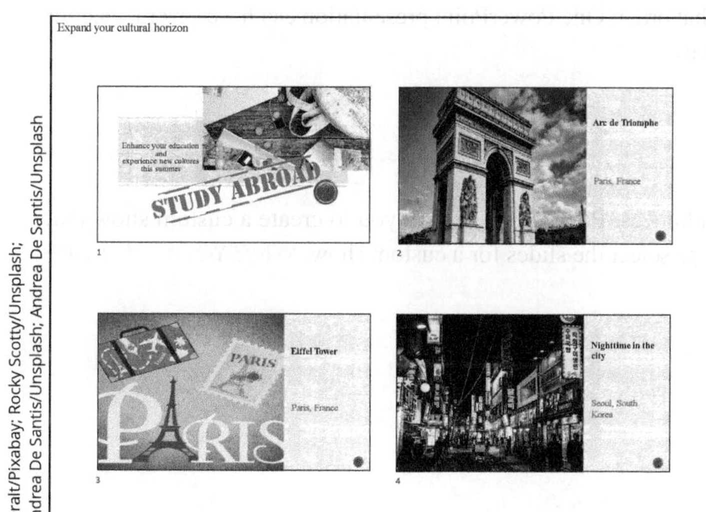

geralt/Pixabay; Rocky Scotty/Unsplash; Andrea De Santis/Unsplash; Andrea De Santis/Unsplash

Figure 8–1(f): Handout in Landscape Orientation

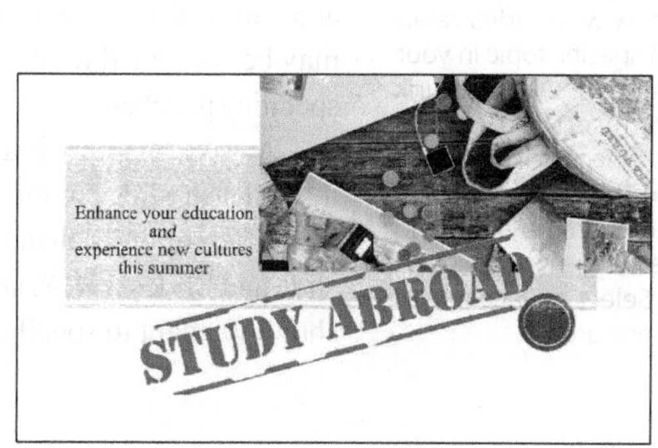

The Study Abroad program is a once-in-a-lifetime opportunity to expand your cultural horizon. Experience life in an immersion setting.

rockyscotty20/Unsplash.com; geralt/Pixabay

Figure 8–1(g): Speaker Notes in Portrait Orientation

In this module, you will learn how to create the slides shown in Figure 8–1. You will perform the following general tasks as you progress through this module:

1. Select specific slides to create a custom slide show.
2. Share a presentation by saving the presentation as a PowerPoint show.
3. Check presentation compatibility and accessibility.
4. Customize handout and notes pages.
5. Create a photo album.
6. Insert a summary zoom slide.

BTW
Ribbon and Screen Resolution
PowerPoint may change how the groups and buttons within the groups appear on the ribbon, depending on the screen resolution of your computer. Thus, your ribbon may look different from the ones in this book if you are using a screen resolution other than 1920 × 1080.

To Start PowerPoint and Save a File

You can begin the project by starting PowerPoint and then saving the presentation with a new file name. The following steps start PowerPoint and then save a file.

1. sam Start PowerPoint. If necessary, maximize the PowerPoint window.
2. Open the presentation, SC_PPT_8_International, from the Data Files.
3. Save the presentation using **SC_PPT_8_Study_Abroad** as the file name.

BTW
Touch Mode Differences
The Microsoft 365 and Windows interfaces may vary if you are using a touch screen. For this reason, you might notice that the function or appearance of your touch screen differs slightly from this module's presentation.

Creating a Custom Slide Show

Quality PowerPoint presentations are tailored toward specific audiences, and experienced presenters adapt the slides to meet the listeners' needs and expectations. Speakers can develop one slide show and then modify the content each time they deliver the presentation. For example, the director of human resources may present one set of slides for new employees, another set for potential retirees, and a third for managers concerned with new regulations and legislation. Slides for all these files may be contained in one file, and the presenter can elect to show particular slides to accompany specific speeches.

A **custom show** is a subset of slides in a presentation that can be reordered without affecting the order of slides in the original presentation. This can be useful when you want to show slides in a different order than in the original presentation. For example, you may desire to show a title slide and Slides 2, 4, 8, and 9, in that order. One PowerPoint presentation can have several custom shows to adapt to specific audiences.

BTW
Hyperlinking Custom Shows
You can hyperlink to a custom show with slides relating to a specific topic in your presentation. Click the Link button (Insert tab | Links group), if necessary click the 'Place in This Document' button in the Link to area, and then select the custom show in the 'Select a place in this document' area.

To Select Slides for a Slide Show

Many presenters deliver their speeches in front of targeted audiences. PowerPoint allows you to create a custom show that displays only selected slides for these people. The following steps select the slides for a custom show. **Why?** You decide to use the slides that showcase two cities: Paris and London.

- Click the Slide Show tab and then click the 'Custom Slide Show' button (Slide Show tab | Start Slide Show group) to display the 'Custom Slide Show' menu (Figure 8–2).

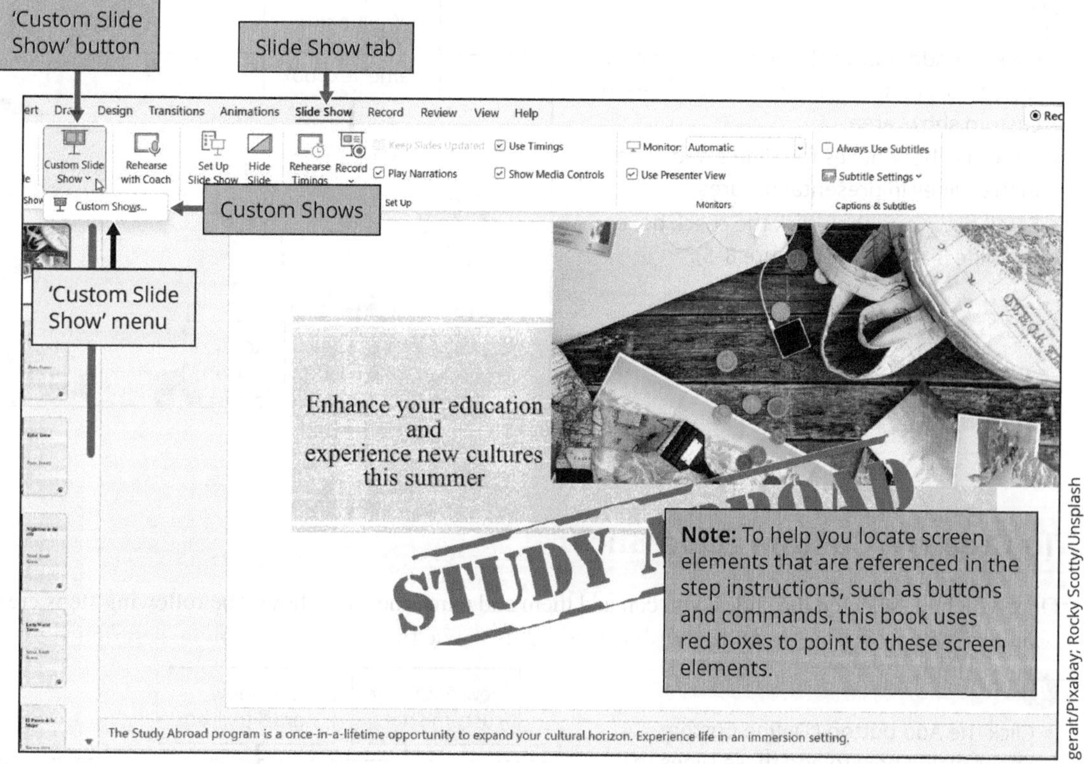

geralt/Pixabay; Rocky Scotty/Unsplash

Figure 8–2

2

- Click Custom Shows to open the Custom Shows dialog box (Figure 8–3).

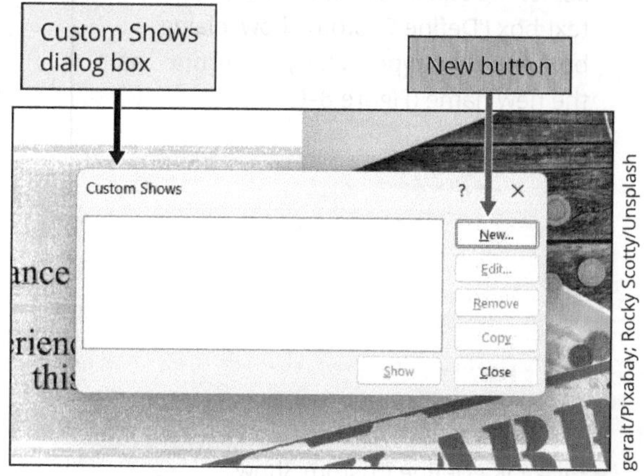

geralt/Pixabay; Rocky Scotty/Unsplash

Figure 8–3

3

- Click the New button (Custom Shows dialog box) to display the 'Define Custom Show' dialog box.
- Click '1. Enhance your education and experience' in the 'Slides in presentation' area to place a check mark in the check box and select this slide (Figure 8–4).

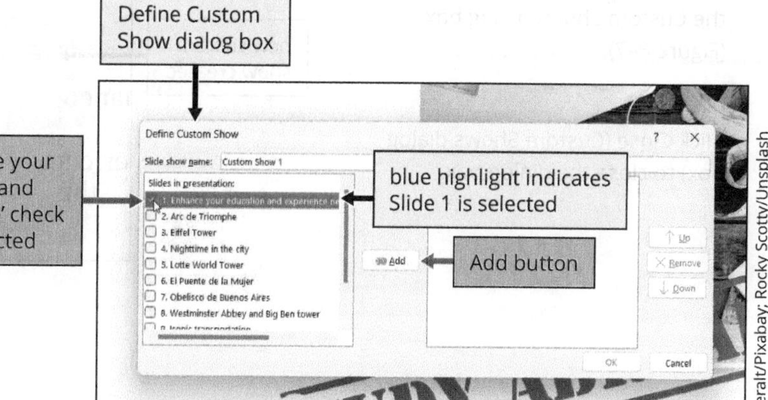

geralt/Pixabay; Rocky Scotty/Unsplash

Figure 8–4

- Click the Add button ('Define Custom Show' dialog box) to add this slide to the 'Slides in custom show' area.
- Click the check boxes for Slide 2 and Slide 3 in the 'Slides in presentation' area.
- Scroll down and then click the check boxes for Slide 8 and Slide 9 (Figure 8–5).

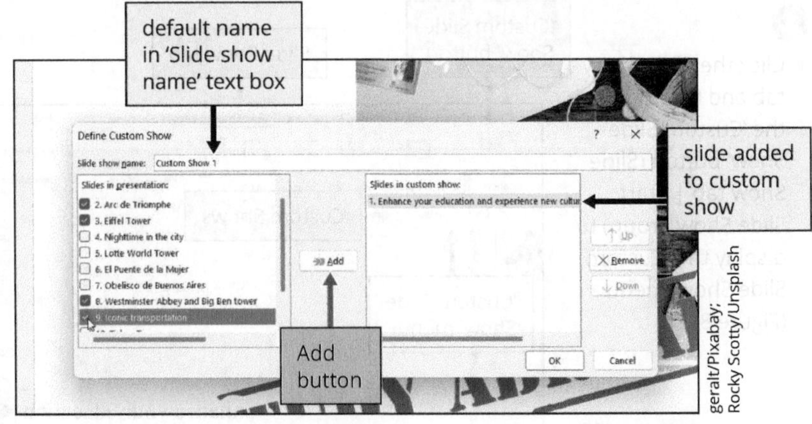

Figure 8–5

To Create a Custom Slide Show

Once you have selected the slides, you can add them and name the slide show. The following steps create this show. **Why?** You want to finish adding the slides you wish to use and then give the presentation a more descriptive name.

- Click the Add button ('Define Custom Show' dialog box) to add these slides to the 'Slides in custom show' area.
- Select the text in the 'Slide show name' text box ('Define Custom Show' dialog box) and then type **Study in Europe** as the new name (Figure 8–6).

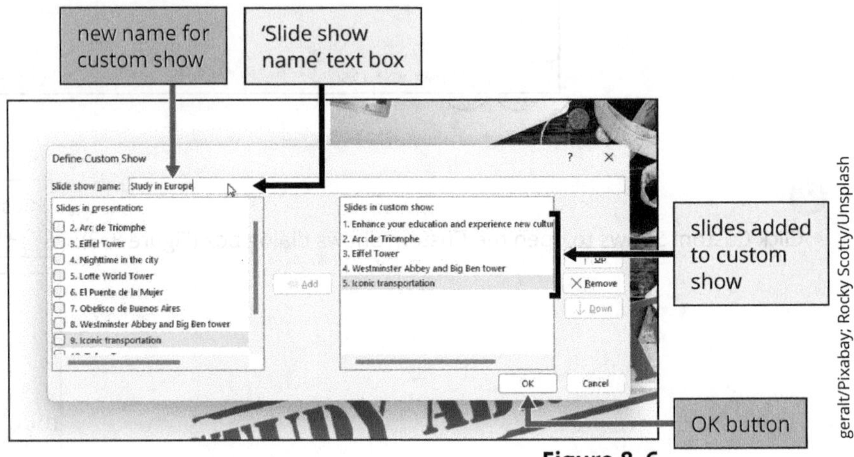

Figure 8–6

- Click OK ('Define Custom Show' dialog box) to create the new Study in Europe custom show and display the Custom Shows dialog box (Figure 8–7).

- Click Close (Custom Shows dialog box) to close the dialog box.

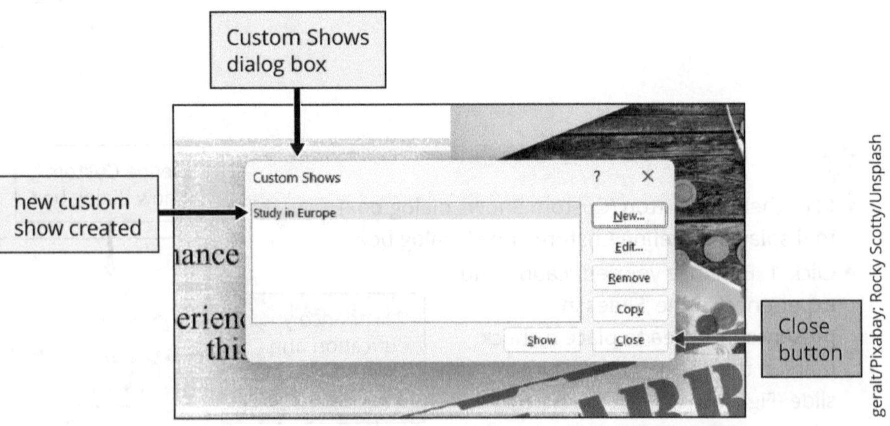

Figure 8–7

To Open and Edit a Custom Slide Show

A PowerPoint file can have several custom slide shows. You can elect to display one of them at any time. **Why?** If you need to reorder the slides based on the particular needs of your audience, you can change the sequence easily. The following steps open a custom show and edit the slide sequence.

- With the Slide Show tab displayed, click the 'Custom Slide Show' button (Slide Show tab | Start Slide Show group) to display the 'Custom Slide Show' menu (Figure 8–8).

Q&A Why does 'Study in Europe' display in the 'Custom Slide Show' menu?

The names of any custom shows will display in the menu. If desired, you could click this custom show name to run the slide show and display the selected slides.

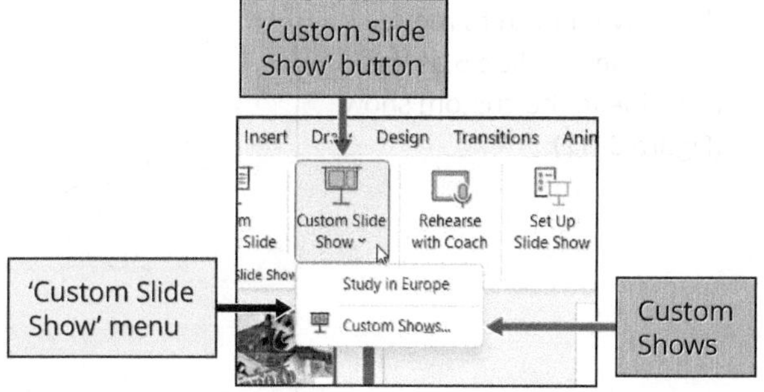

Figure 8–8

- Click Custom Shows to display the Custom Shows dialog box (Figure 8–9).

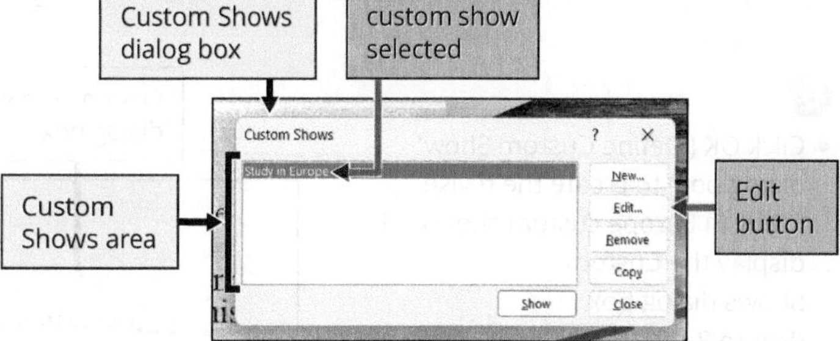

Figure 8–9

- With the Study in Europe custom show name displayed in the Custom Shows area, click the Edit button (Custom Shows dialog box) to display the 'Define Custom Show' dialog box.
- Click '3. Eiffel Tower' in the 'Slides in custom show' area to select it (Figure 8–10).

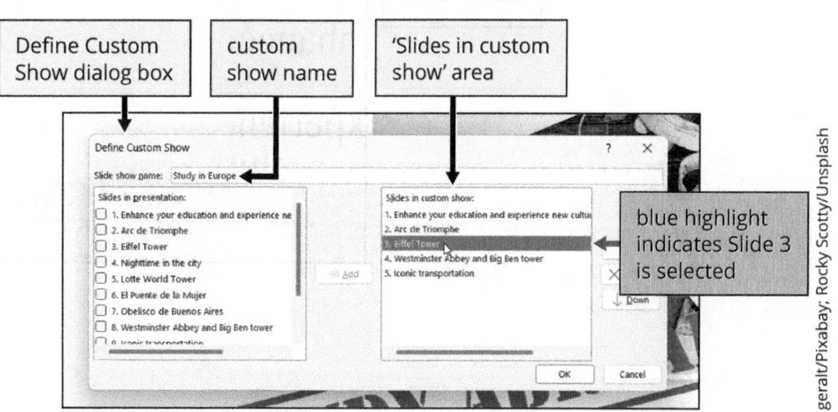

Figure 8–10

- Click the Up button to move Slide 3 below Slide 1 as the second slide in the custom show (Figure 8–11).

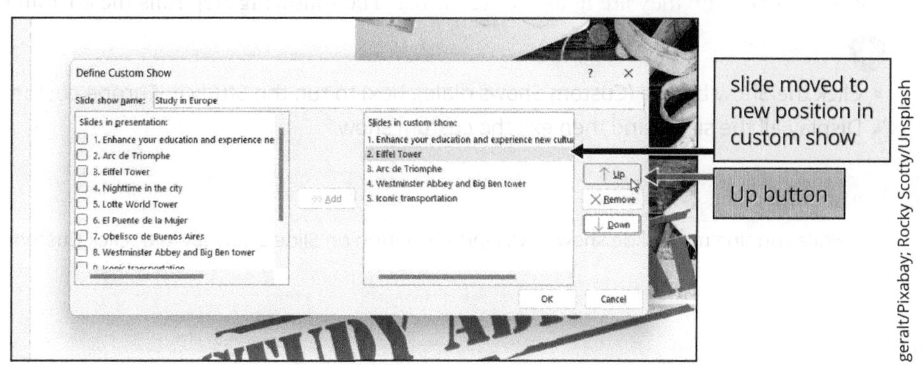

Figure 8–11

geralt/Pixabay; Rocky Scotty/Unsplash

geralt/Pixabay; Rocky Scotty/Unsplash

5

- Click '4. Westminster Abbey and Big Ben tower' in the 'Slides in custom show' area to select it and then click the Down button to move Slide 4 below Slide 5 as the last slide in the custom show (Figure 8–12).

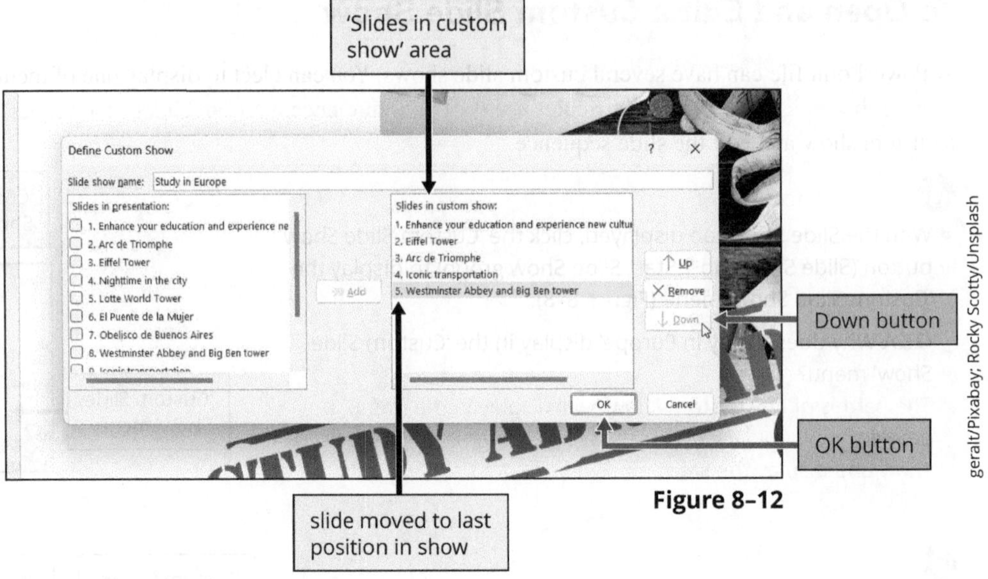

Figure 8–12

6

- Click OK ('Define Custom Show' dialog box) to create the revised Study in Europe custom show and display the Custom Shows dialog box (Figure 8–13).

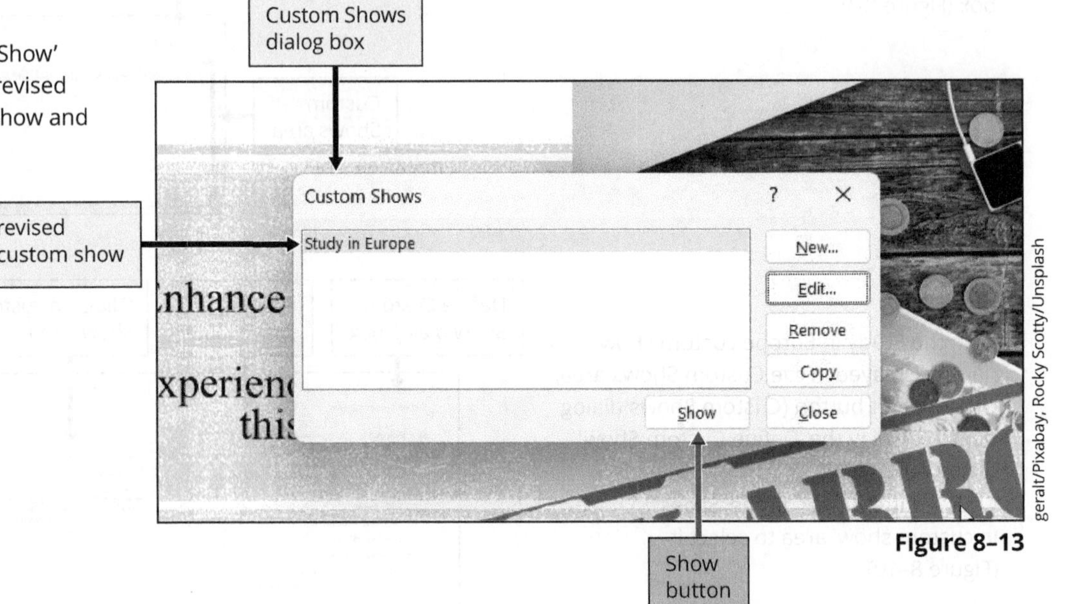

Figure 8–13

To Run a Custom Slide Show

Once the custom show is created, you can run the show from within the Custom Shows dialog box. **Why?** You want to review the slides to ensure they are in the desired order. The following step runs the custom slide show.

- Click the Show button (Custom Shows dialog box) to run the Study in Europe custom show.
- Display all the slides and then exit the custom show.

Other Ways

1. While running main slide show, click Options button on Slide Show toolbar, click Custom Shows, select desired custom show

3D Models

If you have a Microsoft 365 subscription, you can enhance your creativity and productivity by embedding 3D models in your presentations. A **3D model** is an illustration created using 3D animation techniques, which you can rotate in three dimensions. The Online 3D Models gallery of stock 3D models contains hundreds of free 3D models in a wide variety of categories, many of them animated. Once you have inserted a 3D model into your slide, you can rotate and tilt the image. If an image isn't already animated, you can add animation with PowerPoint's animation features. The 3D objects can be matched with 2D content to illustrate your points.

To Insert a 3D Model You insert 3D images into your slide in the same manner that you insert pictures or other content. To insert a 3D model, you would perform the following steps.

1. Click the Insert tab and then click the 3D Models arrow (Insert tab | Illustrations Group) to display the 3D Models menu. If you have a model already created, click This Device. Otherwise, click 'Stock 3D Models' to display the 'Online 3D Models' dialog box.
2. Select a category and then click a picture to place a check mark in that model.
3. Click the Insert button to insert the model into your slide.

BTW
Embedding Animated 3D Graphics
Microsoft 365 subscribers can embed an animated 3D graphic in Word or PowerPoint for Windows. Each one has preset animations, or scenes. When you display the 'Online 3D Models' dialog box, look for the categories that have a runner badge, which indicates the graphics in it are animated. Each graphic has multiple scenes, or animations, from which to choose.

To Modify a 3D Model PowerPoint's controls help you manipulate a 3D model to focus on an area you want to highlight. These controls are available on the contextual tab that is displayed when you insert the image. The 3D Model Views gallery has a collection of views you can use, such as head-on or top-down. The Align tool helps you position the image in a precise area of the slide, in the same manner that you position pictures and other slide objects. The Pan & Zoom control allows you to click and drag the object within the frame, and the Zoom icon that displays on the right side of the frame when you click the Pan & Zoom button makes the object larger or smaller within the frame. To modify a 3D model, you would perform the following steps.

1. With the model selected, click a view (3D Model tab | 3D Model Views group) to change the view.
2. Click the 'Pan & Zoom' button (3D Model tab | Size group) and then click the Pan & Zoom 3D control in the middle of the image to rotate and tilt the model in any direction.
3. Click the Zoom icon on the right side of the image to increase or decrease the size of the image.

To Animate a 3D Model You can add animation effects to your 3D model. Along with the effects available to animate 2D content, 3D options include Arrive, Turntable, Swing, Jump & Turn, and Leave. All the animations have options to adjust the direction, intensity, or movement. For example, the Turntable animation allows you to showcase the object slowly and smoothly. You also can have two animations play simultaneously. To animate a 3D model, you would perform the following steps.

1. Display the Animations tab and then click one of the animation effects (Animations tab | Animation group) to see a preview of that animation and apply the animation to the model.
2. Click the Effect Options button to view the Effect Options menu and then choose a property related to the movement direction, amount, or rotation axis.
3. Click the Preview button (Animations tab | Preview group) to view the effect.

Saving and Sharing a Presentation

Many people design PowerPoint presentations to accompany a speech given in front of an audience, and they also develop slide shows to share with family, work associates, and friends in a variety of ways. PowerPoint saves files by default as a PowerPoint Presentation with a .pptx file extension. You can, however, select other file types that allow other users to view your slides if they do not have one of the newer PowerPoint versions installed. You also can save the file as a PowerPoint show so that it runs automatically when opened and does not require the user to have the PowerPoint program. Another option is to save one slide as an image that can be inserted into another program, such as Word, or emailed.

To Save a Slide as a Picture

To create visually interesting slides, you insert pictures, clips, and video files into your presentation. Conversely, you may want to insert a PowerPoint slide into another document, such as a file you created in Word. **Why?** A slide may have information that you want to share with an audience and include with other material that is not part of the PowerPoint presentation. You can save one slide as an image and then insert this file into another document. The following steps save Slide 1 as a JPEG File Interchange Format (.jpg) image.

- With Slide 1 of the SC_PPT_8_Study_Abroad presentation displayed, open Backstage view, display the Export tab, and then click 'Change File Type' in the Export section to display the 'Change File Type' section.
- Click 'JPEG File Interchange Format (*.jpg)' in the 'Image File Types' section (Figure 8–14).

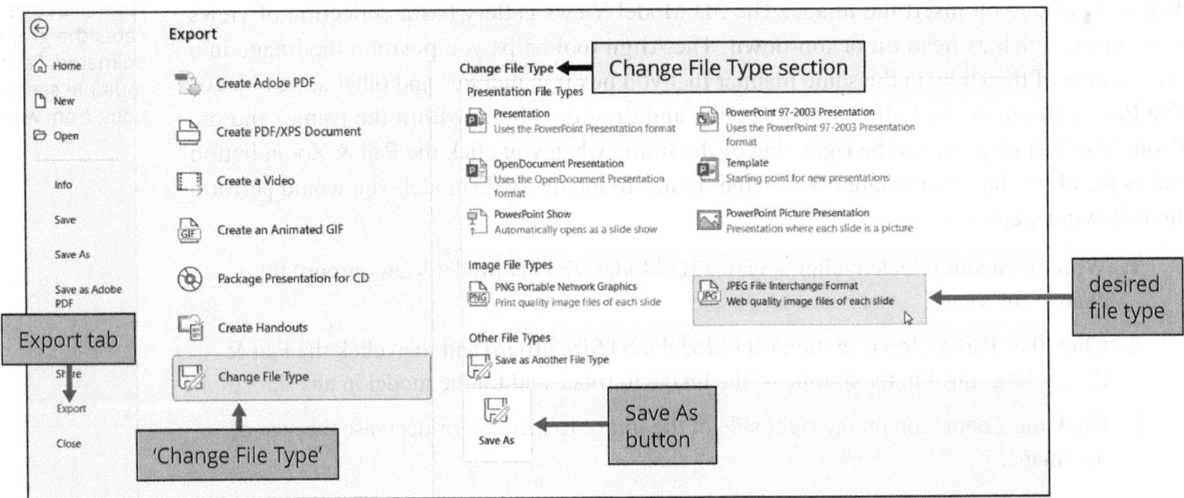

Figure 8–14

2

- Click the Save As button to display the Save As dialog box.
- Change the file name to **SC_PPT_8_Study_Abroad_Slide** in the File name box (Figure 8–15).

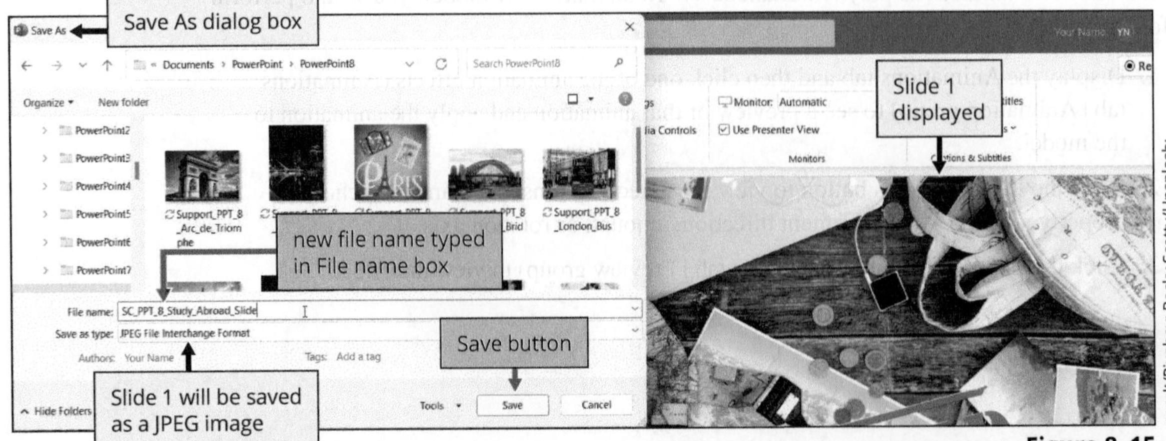

geralt/Pixabay; Rocky Scotty/Unsplash; ianke'sall1/Pixabay; Gonzalo Kenny/unsplash; Alexas_Fotos/Pixabay; DUCTINH91/Pixabay

Figure 8–15

3

- Click the Save button (Save As dialog box) to display the Microsoft PowerPoint dialog box (Figure 8–16).

4

- Click the 'Just This One' button to save only Slide 1 as a file in JPEG (.jpg) format.

Q&A What would happen if I clicked All Slides?
PowerPoint would save each slide as a separate file in a folder with the file name you specified.

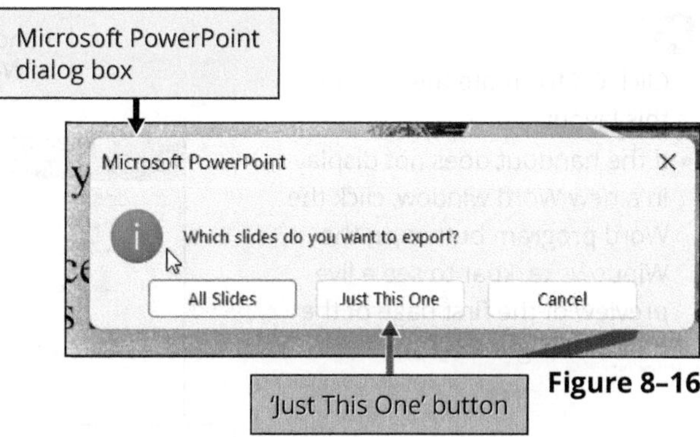

Figure 8–16

Other Ways

1. Click File on ribbon, click Save As in Backstage view, click Browse button to locate save location, click 'Save as type' arrow, select 'JPEG File Interchange Format (*.jpg)', click Save button

To Create Handouts by Exporting to Word

The handouts you create using PowerPoint are useful to distribute to audiences. Each time you need to create these handouts, however, you need to open the file in PowerPoint and then print from Backstage view. As an alternative, it might be convenient to save, or export, the file as a Word document if you are going to be using Word to type a script or lecture notes. **Why?** The handout can have a variety of layouts; for example, the notes you type in the Notes pane can display to the right of or beneath the slide thumbnails, blank lines can display to the right of or beneath the slide thumbnails, or just an outline can display. The following steps export the presentation to Word and then create a handout.

- Open Backstage view, display the Export tab, and then click Create Handouts in the Export section to display the 'Create Handouts in Microsoft Word' section (Figure 8–17).

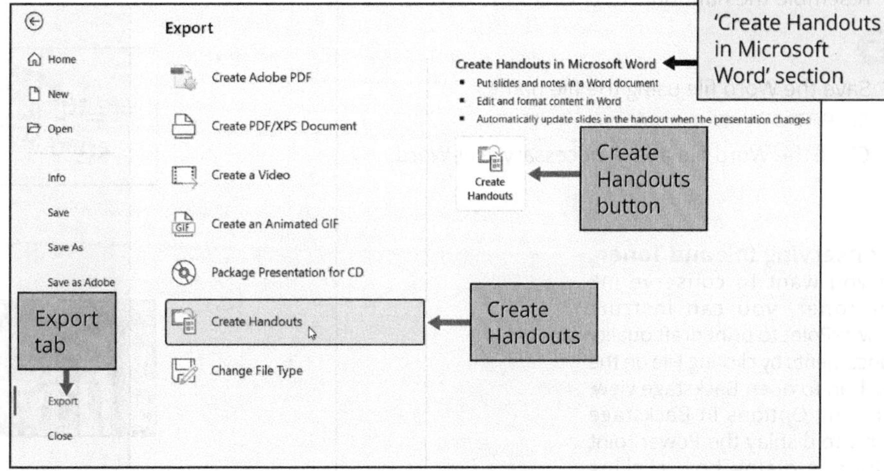

Figure 8–17

2

- Click the Create Handouts button to display the 'Send to Microsoft Word' dialog box.
- Click 'Blank lines next to slides' to add blank lines next to the slides when the handout is printed (Figure 8–18).

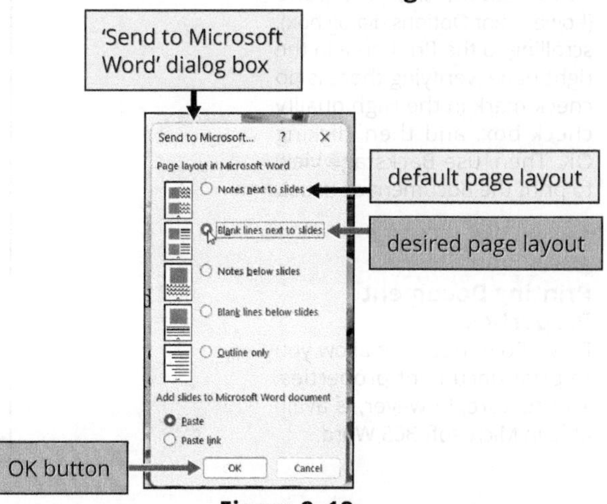

Figure 8–18

3

- Click OK to create the file with this layout.
- If the handout does not display in a new Word window, click the Word program button on the Windows taskbar to see a live preview of the first page of the handout (Figure 8–19).

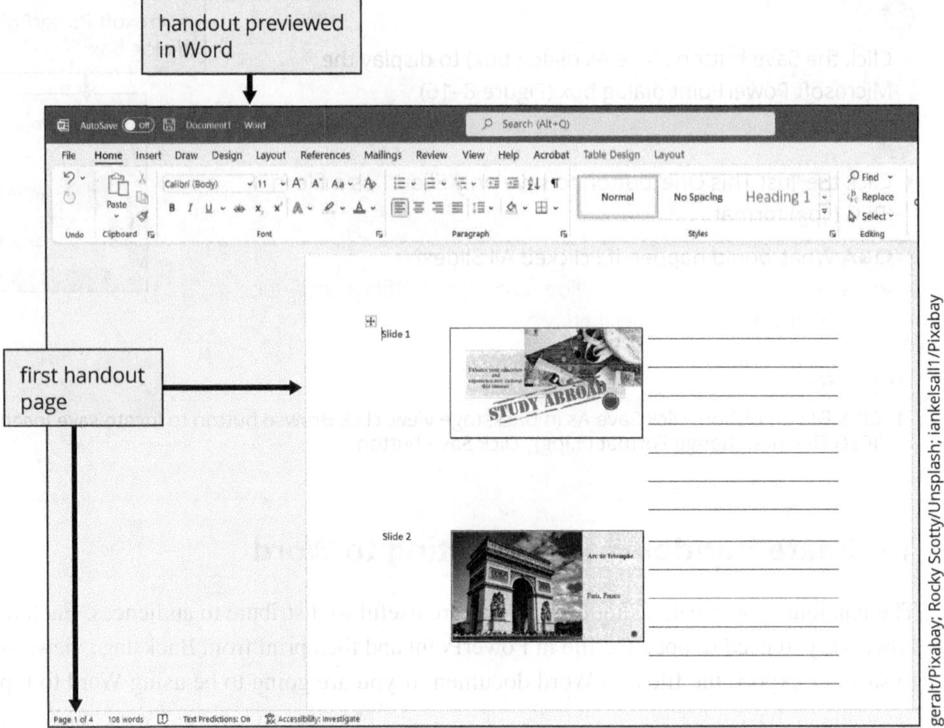

geralt/Pixabay; Rocky Scotty/Unsplash; iankelsall1/Pixabay

Figure 8–19

4

- If you print the handouts, the first page will resemble the handout shown in Figure 8–20.

5

- Save the Word file using the file name, **SC_PPT_8_Word.**
- Close the Word file and, if necessary, exit Word.

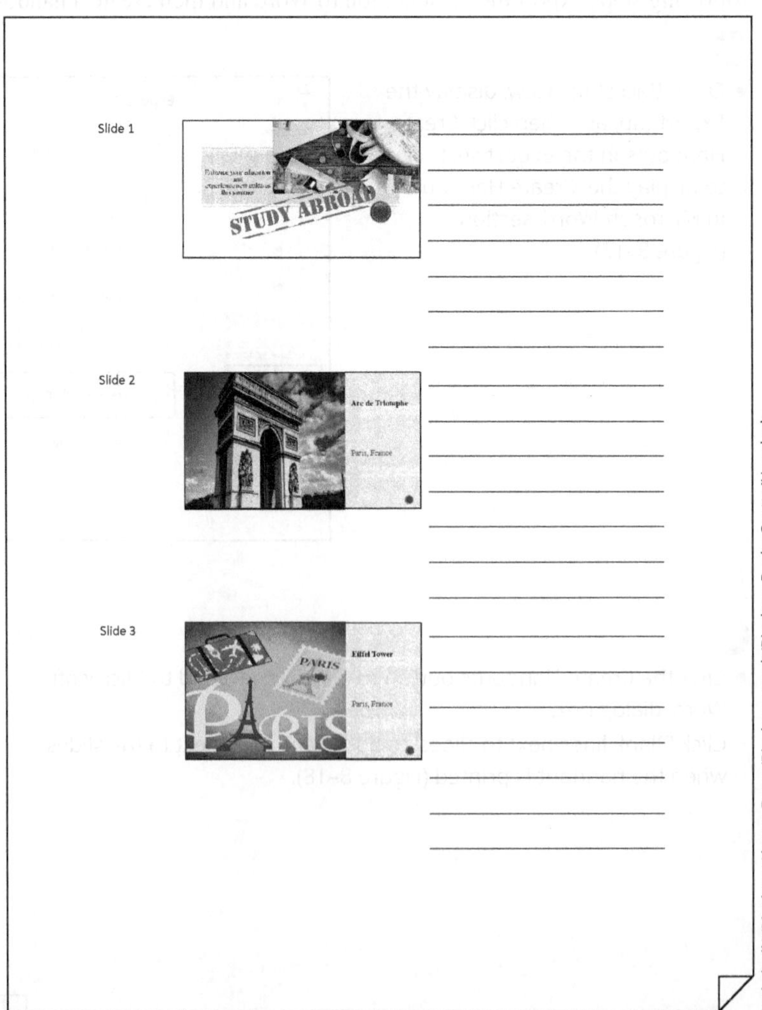

iankelsall1/Pixabay; Alexas_Fotos/Pixabay; geralt/Pixabay; Rocky Scotty/Unsplash

Figure 8–20

BTW
Conserving Ink and Toner
If you want to conserve ink or toner, you can instruct PowerPoint to print draft quality documents by clicking File on the ribbon to open Backstage view, clicking Options in Backstage view to display the PowerPoint Options dialog box, clicking Advanced in the left pane (PowerPoint Options dialog box), scrolling to the Print area in the right pane, verifying there is no check mark in the High quality check box, and then clicking OK. Then, use Backstage view to print the document as usual.

BTW
Printing Document Properties
PowerPoint does not allow you to print document properties. This feature, however, is available in Microsoft 365 Word.

To Record Slide Timings and Narration In some situations, you may want your viewers to hear recorded narration that accompanies slides. You can record narration separately and then add this file to the slide. You also can record narration while the slide show is running. To record this narration, you would perform the following steps.

1. Display the Record tab and then click From Beginning (Record tab | Record group) if you want to begin with the first slide or click 'From Current Slide' (Record tab | Record group) if you want to begin with the slide that is displayed on your screen.
2. Click the red Start recording button.
3. When you have finished speaking, click the red Stop recording button.

Other Ways

1. Display Slide Show tab, click Record arrow (Slide Show tab | Set Up group), click 'From Beginning' or 'From Current Slide', click Start recording, right-click slide, click End Show on shortcut menu

BTW
Digital Inking
Digital inking allows you to draw and write anywhere on your slides, even during a presentation. The pens in the Drawing Tools group on Draw tab can have a variety of thicknesses, colors, and textures. Once you write on your slide, you can use the Lasso tool to convert the ink to an equation, shape, or formatted text. The Ink Replay button allows you to play back your animated drawing.

To Preview Narration Once you have recorded some narration, you can play the audio to review the sound. To preview this narration, you would perform the following steps.

1. In Normal view, click the sound icon on the slide.
2. Display the Playback tab and then click the Play button (Playback tab | Preview group).

To Show a Presentation with or without Narration If you have recorded narration to accompany your slides, you can choose whether to include this narration when you run your slide show. To run the slide show either with or without narration, you would perform the following steps.

1. Display the Slide Show tab and then click the Play Narrations check box (Slide Show tab | Set Up group) to remove the check from the box.
2. If you have chosen to show the presentation without narration and then desire to allow audience members to hear this recording, click the Play Narrations check box (Slide Show tab | Set Up group) to check this option.

To Save a Presentation as a PowerPoint Show

Why? To simplify giving a presentation in front of an audience, you may want to start your slide show without having to start PowerPoint, open a file, and then click the Slide Show button. When you save a presentation as a **PowerPoint Show (.ppsx)**, it automatically begins running when opened. The following steps save the SC_PPT_8_Study_Abroad presentation as a PowerPoint show.

- Open Backstage view, display the Export tab, and then click 'Change File Type' to display the 'Change File Type' section.
- Click PowerPoint Show in the Presentation File Types section (Figure 8–21).

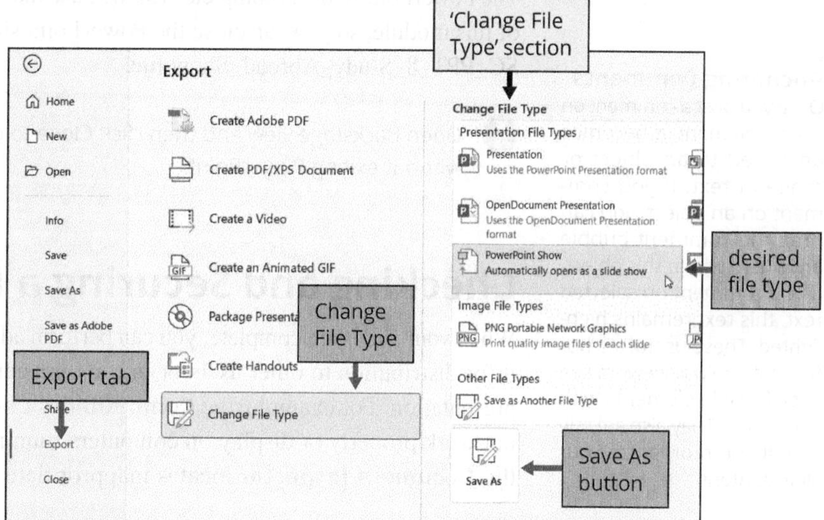

Figure 8–21

- Click the Save As button to display the Save As dialog box.
- Change the file name to **SC_PPT_8_Study_Abroad_Show** in the File name box (Figure 8–22).

- Click the Save button to close the Save As dialog box.

- Close the file and then reopen it to see it as a PowerPoint show.

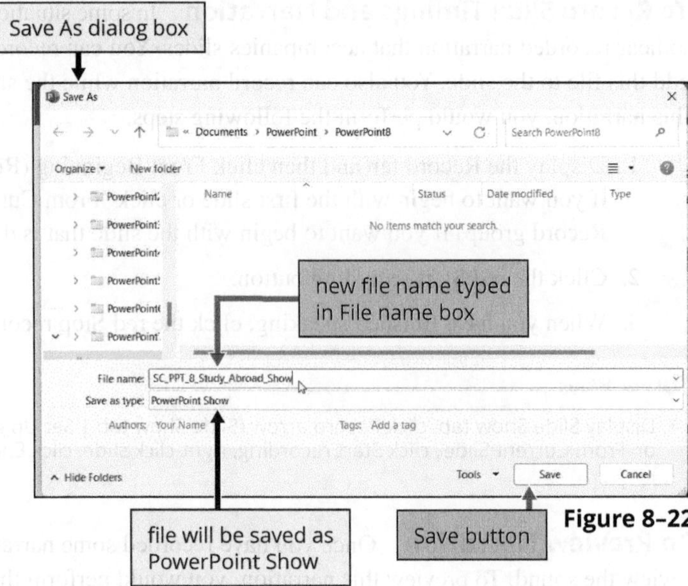

Figure 8–22

Other Ways

1. Click Save As, click Browse, click 'Save as type' arrow, select PowerPoint Show, click Save

To Share a Presentation on OneDrive You can save a presentation in your OneDrive account and then share this file with specific individuals. To share a presentation, you first upload it to your OneDrive account and then determine the individuals who can access this file. To share a presentation, you would perform the following steps.

1. Display Backstage view, click the Share tab, and then click 'Share with People' in the Share area.
2. If necessary, select your OneDrive account, choose a permission level, and then click Apply.
3. Click the 'Share with People' button in the Share with People area, enter the names of the individuals with whom you want to share the file, and then add a message.
4. Click Send.

To Close a Presentation

The PowerPoint show is complete. You will use the SC_PPT_8_Study_Abroad file for the remainder of this module, so you can close the PowerPoint show presentation. The following step closes the SC_PPT_8_Study_Abroad_Show file.

Open Backstage view and then click Close to close the SC_PPT_8_Study_Abroad_Show file without exiting PowerPoint.

BTW
Anchoring Comments
Once you post a comment on a slide element, it becomes anchored to an object or range of text. If you comment on an object, you can drag the comment bubble anywhere within this object. If you comment on selected text, this text remains highlighted. These useful anchor features help reviewers see specific slide elements with comments. They also are reliable if you reorganize your slide content.

Checking and Securing a Presentation

When your slides are complete, you can perform additional functions to finalize the file and prepare it for distribution to other users or to run on a computer other than the one used to develop the presentation. For example, the **Compatibility Checker** reviews the file for any feature that will not work properly or display on computers running a previous PowerPoint version. In addition, the **Document Inspector** locates inappropriate information, such as comments, in a file and allows you to delete these slide elements. You also can set passwords so only authorized people can distribute, view, or modify your slides. When the review process is complete, you can indicate this file is the final version.

To Check Presentation Compatibility

This version of PowerPoint has many new features not found in some previous versions, especially versions older than PowerPoint 2007. If you give your file to people who have a previous PowerPoint version installed on their computers, they will be able to open the file but may not be able to see or edit some special features and effects. The following steps run the Compatibility Checker. **Why?** You can use the Compatibility Checker to see if any presentation elements will not function in earlier versions of PowerPoint and display a summary of any elements in your presentation that will be lost if your file is opened in some earlier PowerPoint versions.

- Open the SC_PPT_8_Study_Abroad presentation.
- Open Backstage view, if necessary click the Info tab, and then click the 'Check for Issues' button to display the 'Check for Issues' menu (Figure 8-23).

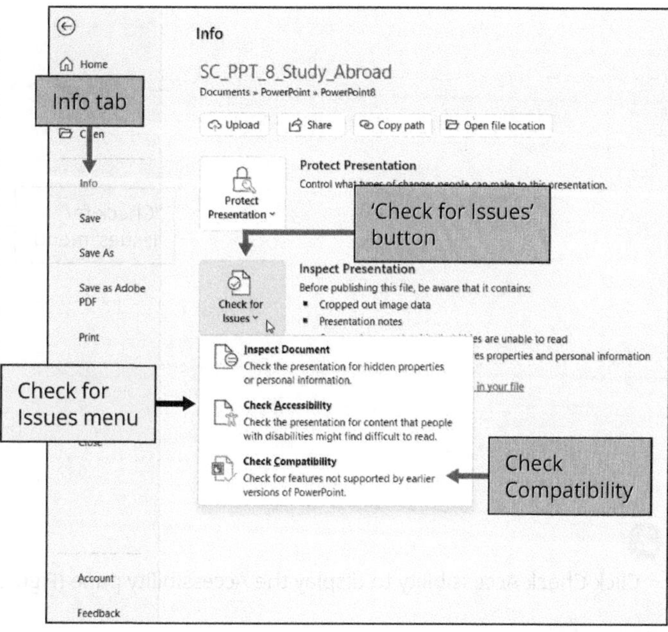

Figure 8-23

- Click Check Compatibility to display the 'Microsoft PowerPoint Compatibility Checker' dialog box.
- If any features are not supported by earlier versions of PowerPoint, they are displayed in the Summary box (Figure 8-24).

3

- Click OK ('Microsoft PowerPoint Compatibility Checker' dialog box) to close the dialog box and return to the presentation.

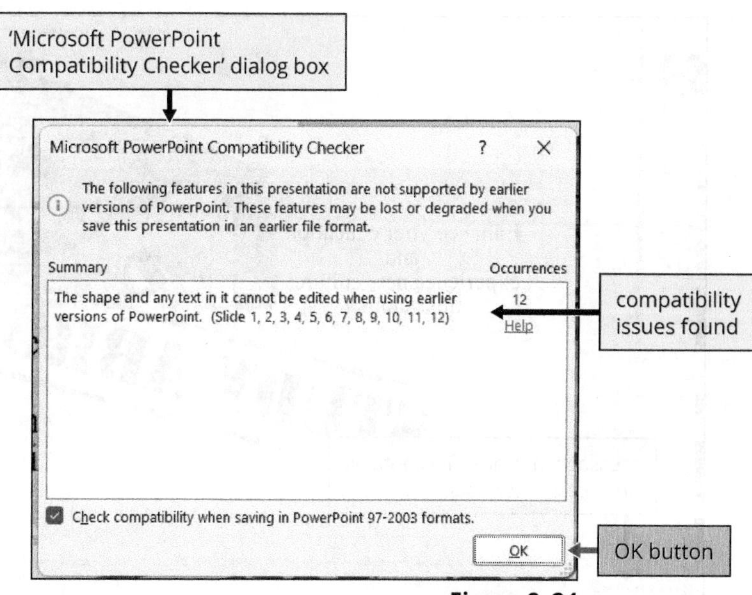

Figure 8-24

To Check Presentation Accessibility

An effective PowerPoint presentation is highly visual, so a good designer creates slides that people with disabilities such as those who are visually impaired can understand easily. PowerPoint includes an **Accessibility Checker** to identify potential issues. This feature scans the slides and finds missing alternative text, possible problems with the reading order, insufficient color contrast, slides without titles, and complex tables. The following steps run the Accessibility Checker. **Why?** This feature can identify slide elements that may not be accessible and provide advice on how to fix these issues.

1

- Open Backstage view, click the Info tab, and then click the 'Check for Issues' button to display the Check for Issues menu (Figure 8–25).

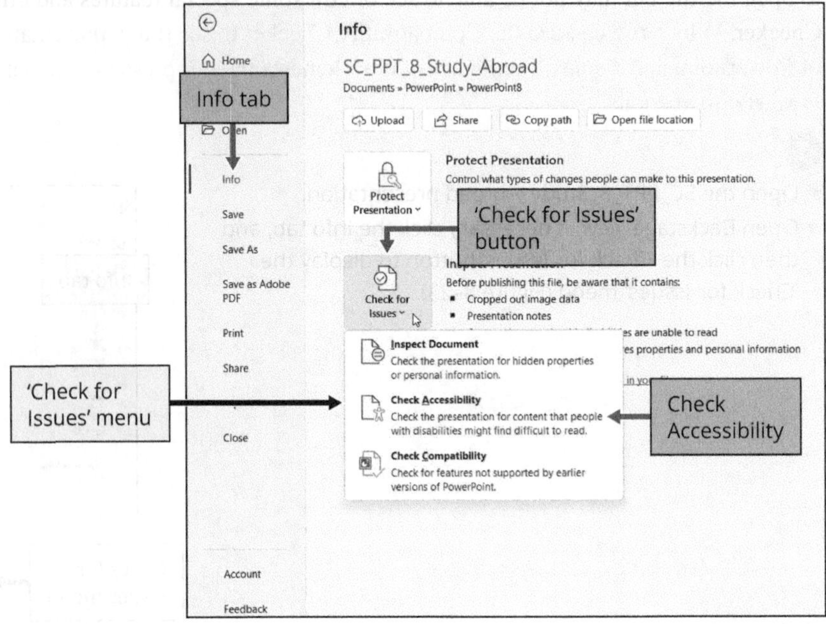

Figure 8–25

2

- Click Check Accessibility to display the Accessibility pane (Figure 8–26).

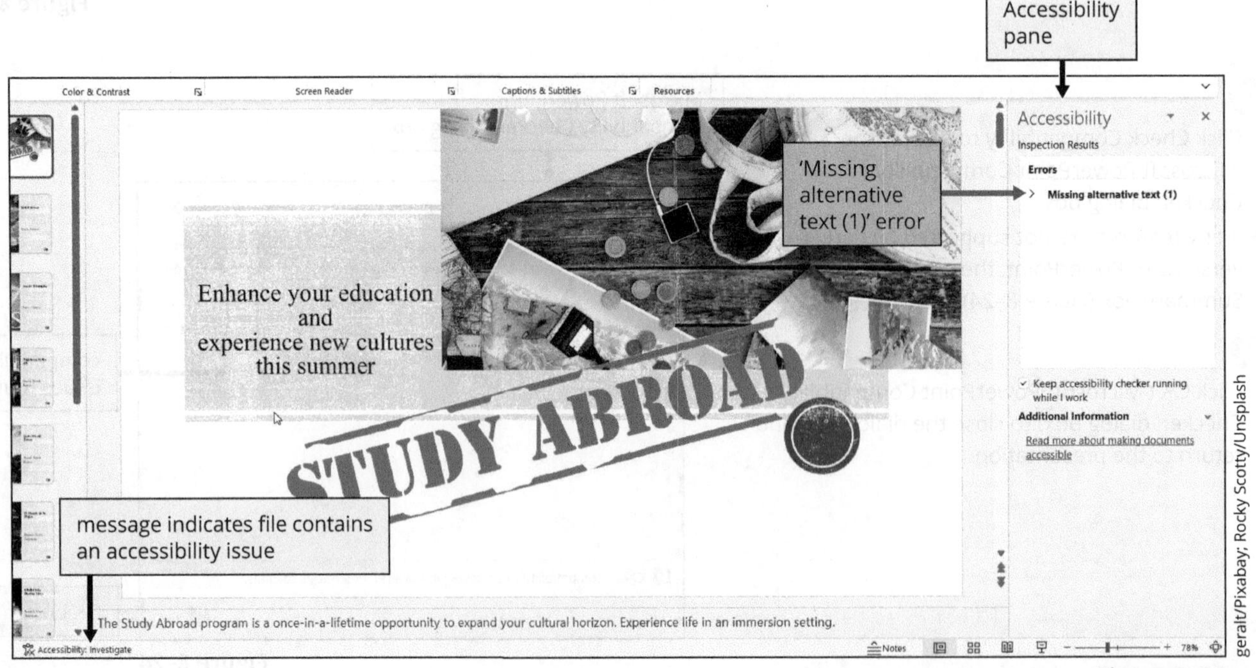

geralt/Pixabay; Rocky Scotty/Unsplash

Figure 8–26

3

- Click the 'Missing alternative text (1)' error and then click the Picture 6 (Slide 1) arrow (Figure 8–27).

Q&A Can PowerPoint generate sample alternative text?
Yes. Click the 'Suggest a description for me' link to obtain possible wording. You can verify or modify this text if necessary.

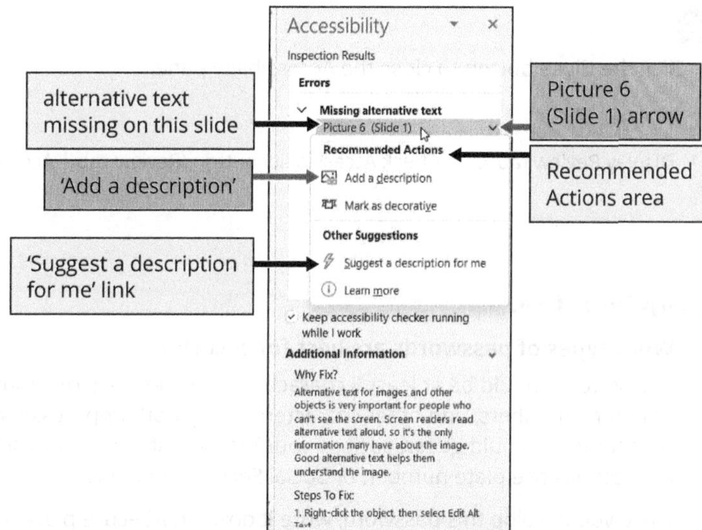

Figure 8–27

4

- Click 'Add a description' in the Recommended Actions area and then type **Computer, camera, coins, tote bag, photos, and an ID on a table** as the alt text description (Figure 8–28).

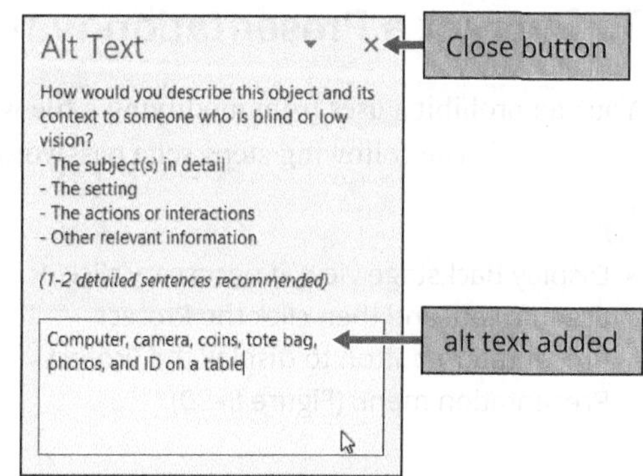

Figure 8–28

5

- Click the Close button to close the Alt Text pane and display the Accessibility Pane (Figure 8–29). Note that there are now no Accessibility issues.

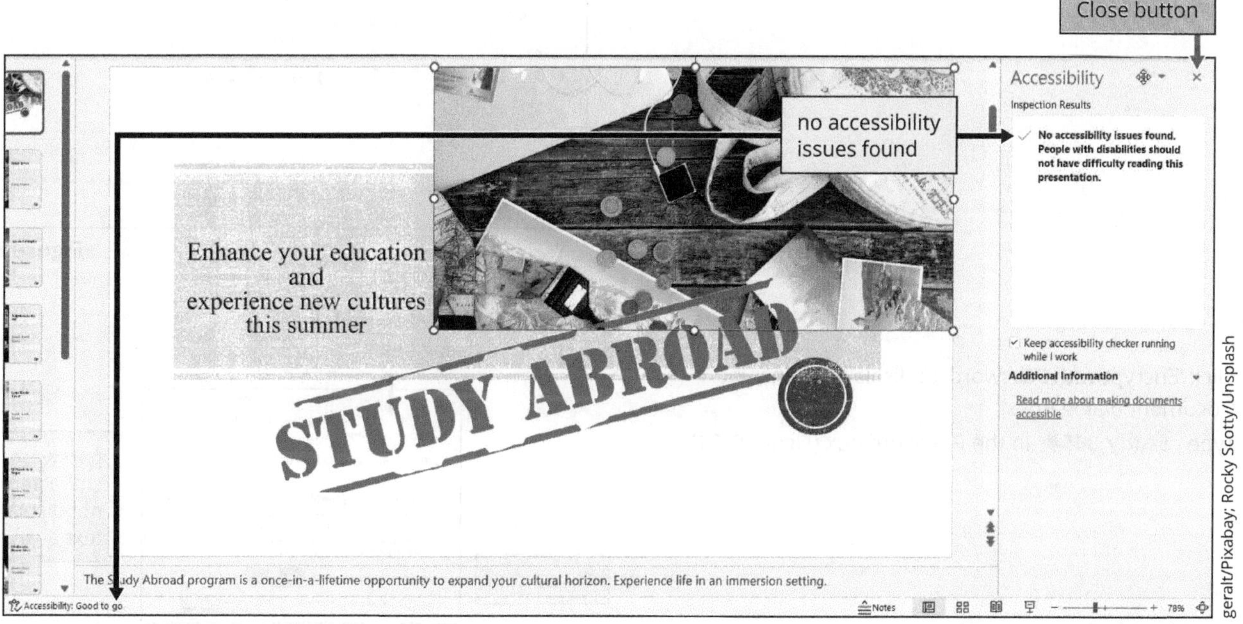

geralt/Pixabay; Rocky Scotty/Unsplash

Figure 8–29

- Click the Close button to close the Accessibility pane.

Other Ways

1. Display Review tab, click Check Accessibility button (Review tab | Accessibility group)

BTW

Finding a Definition

If you need the definition of a word or phrase, select the Microsoft Search box (or press ALT+Q), type it in the Microsoft Search box and then click 'More search results' for that term. The right pane will display articles, files, and other media.

Consider This

What types of passwords are best for security?

A password should be at least 8 characters (some experts recommend at least 20 characters) and contain a combination of letters, numbers, and other characters. Using both uppercase and lowercase letters is advised. Do not use a password that someone could guess, such as your first or last name, spouse's or child's name, telephone number, birth date, street address, license plate number, or Social Security number.

Once you develop this password, write it down in a secure place. Underneath your keyboard is not a secure place, nor is your middle desk drawer. You also can use a password manager program for added security.

To Encrypt a Presentation with a Password

You can prohibit a user from modifying a file without entering the password. **Why?** You can protect your slide content by using a password. The following steps set a password for the SC_PPT_8_Study_Abroad file.

- Display Backstage view, if necessary click the Info tab, and then click the Protect Presentation button to display the Protect Presentation menu (Figure 8–30).

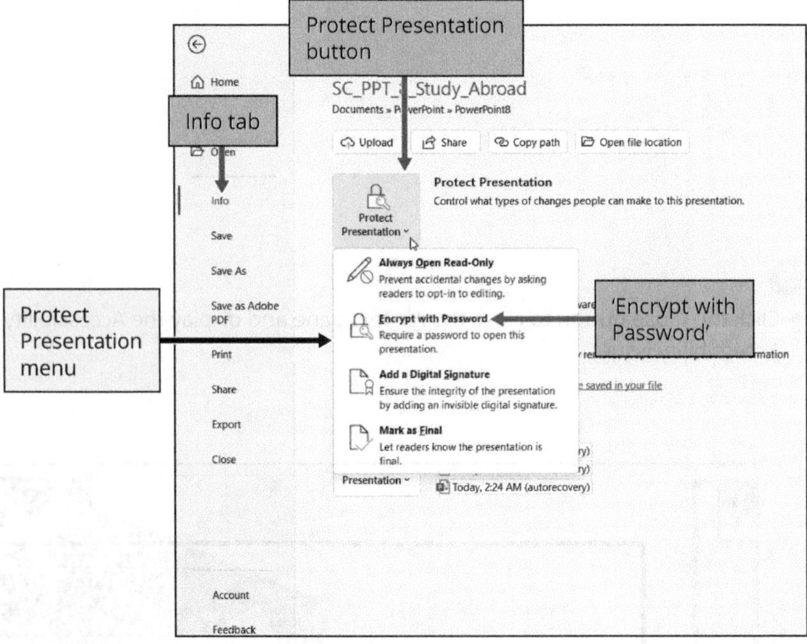

Figure 8–30

- Click 'Encrypt with Password' to display the Encrypt Document dialog box.
- Type **Study_365#** in the Password box (Figure 8–31).

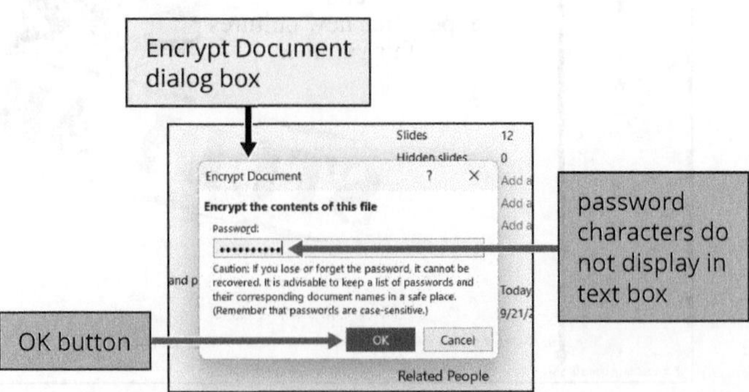

Figure 8–31

- Click OK to display the Confirm Password dialog box.
- Type **Study_365#** in the Reenter password box (Figure 8–32).

Q&A What if I forget my password?
You will not be able to open your file. For security reasons, Microsoft or other companies cannot retrieve a lost password.

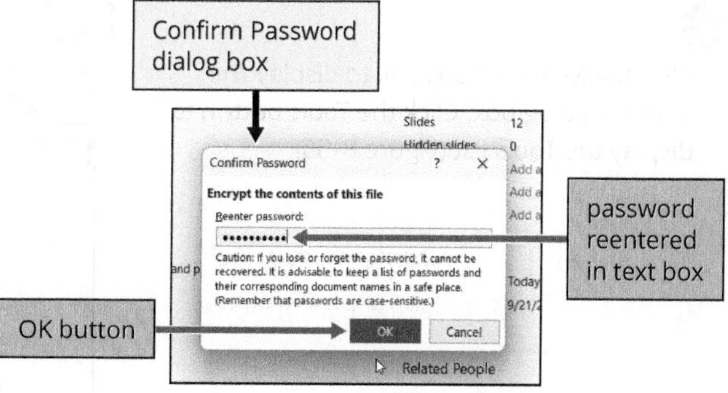

Figure 8–32

- Click OK in the Confirm Password dialog box to encrypt the file with a password and display a message that the file is protected (Figure 8–33).

Q&A When does the password take effect?
You will need to enter your password the next time you open your presentation.

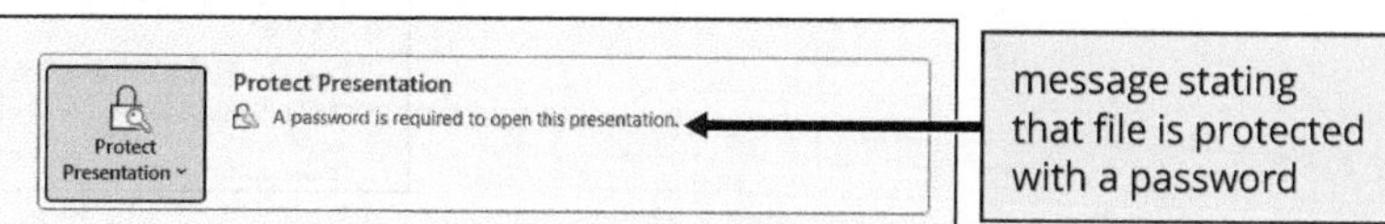

Figure 8–33

To Open a Presentation with a Password To open a file that has been protected with a password, you would perform the following steps.

1. Display the Open dialog box, locate the desired file, and then click the Open button to display the Password dialog box.
2. When the Password dialog box appears, type the password in the Password box and then click OK to display the presentation.

BTW
Searching for Help
Microsoft Search can provide help with performing a particular task. Type your question in the Microsoft Search box. Then view Microsoft Support articles in the Get Help section or click 'More search results' for that particular question and review additional support articles displayed in the right pane.

To Change or Remove Password Protection

You can change a password that you added to a file or remove all password protection from the file. **Why?** Another password may be more secure or password protection may be unnecessary. The following steps remove the password from the SC_PPT_8_Study_Abroad file.

1

- With Backstage view open, click Save As to display the Save As gallery (Figure 8–34).

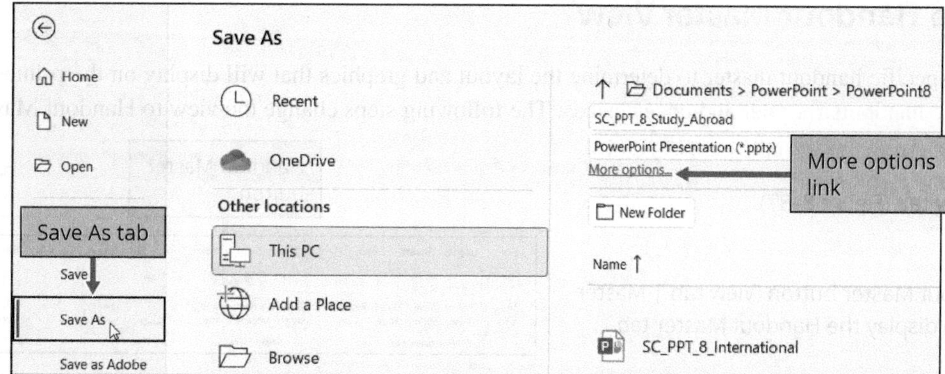

Figure 8–34

- Click the More options link to display the Save As dialog box. Click the Tools button to display the Tools list (Figure 8–35).

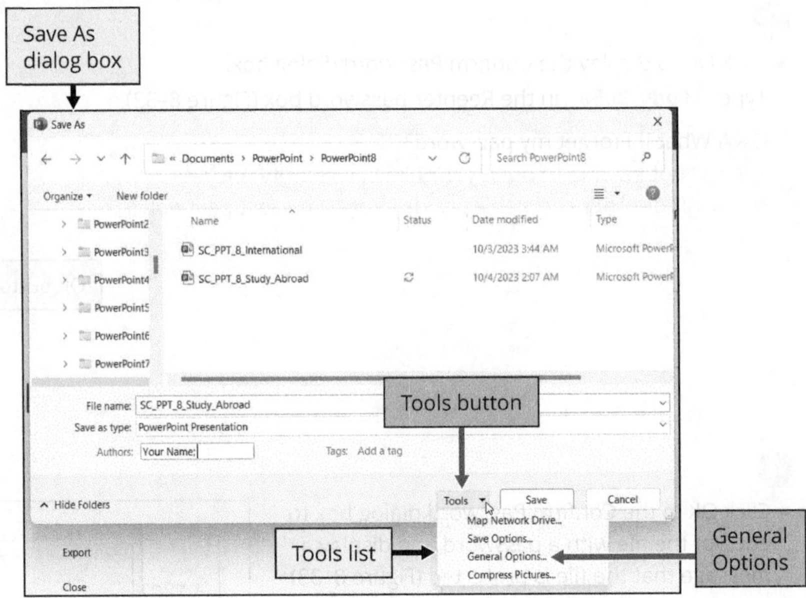

Figure 8–35

- Click General Options in the Tools list to display the General Options dialog box.
- Delete the contents of the 'Password to open' box (Figure 8–36).

- Click OK (General Options dialog box), click the Save button (Save As dialog box), and then click Yes ('Confirm Save As' dialog box) to resave the presentation.

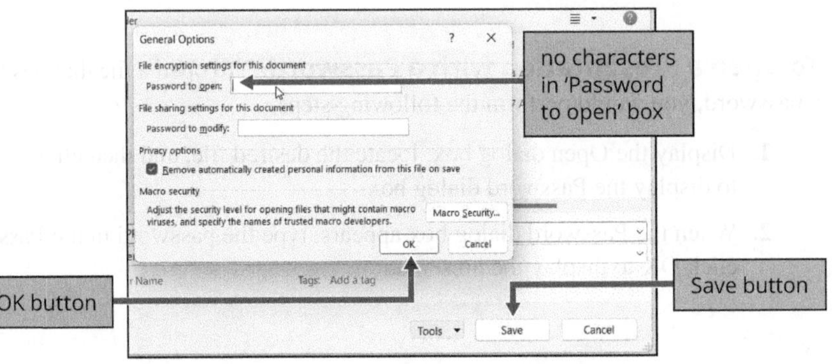

Figure 8–36

Customizing Handout and Notes Masters

PowerPoint has master template files to create handouts and notes. If you are going to distribute handouts to your audience, you can customize the handout master so that it coordinates visually with the presentation slides and reinforces your message. In addition, if you are going to use speaker notes to guide you through a presentation, you can tailor the notes master to fit your needs.

To Switch to Handout Master View

You can create a specific handout master to determine the layout and graphics that will display on the printed handout. **Why?** You can customize handouts for your audience's needs. The following steps change the view to Handout Master.

- Display the View tab (Figure 8–37).

- Click the Handout Master button (View tab | Master Views group) to display the Handout Master tab.

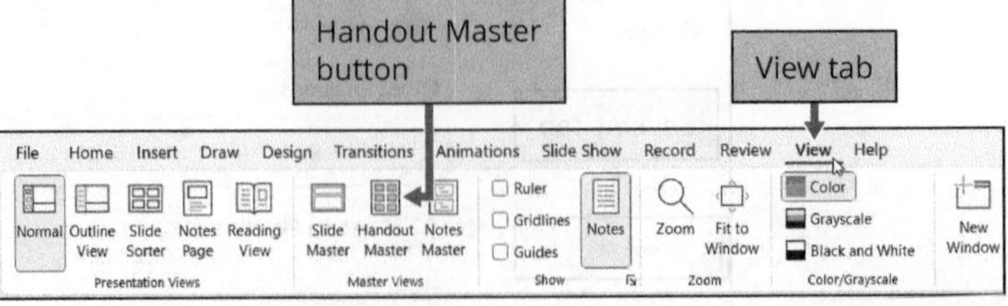

Figure 8–37

To Customize the Handout Master

The Handout Master tab has buttons and controls that allow you to design a custom handout master. **Why?** You can format the header and footer placeholders, set the page number orientation, add graphics, and specify the number of slides to print on each page. The following steps customize the handout master to create a custom handout.

- With the Handout Master tab displayed, click the 'Slides Per Page' button (Handout Master tab | Page Setup group) to display the 'Slides Per Page' gallery (Figure 8–38).

Q&A Is 6 Slides the default layout for all themes?

Yes. If you have fewer than six slides in your presentation or want to display slide details, then choose a handout layout with 1, 2, 3, or 4 slides per sheet of paper.

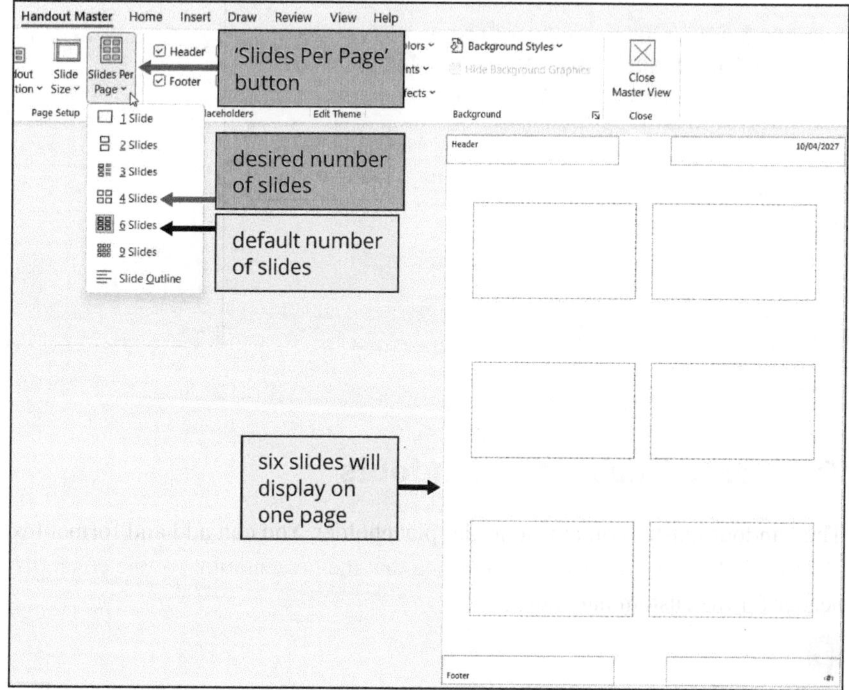

Figure 8–38

- Click 4 Slides in the list to change the layout from six slides to four slides.
- Click the Handout Orientation button (Handout Master tab | Page Setup group) to display the Handout Orientation gallery (Figure 8–39).

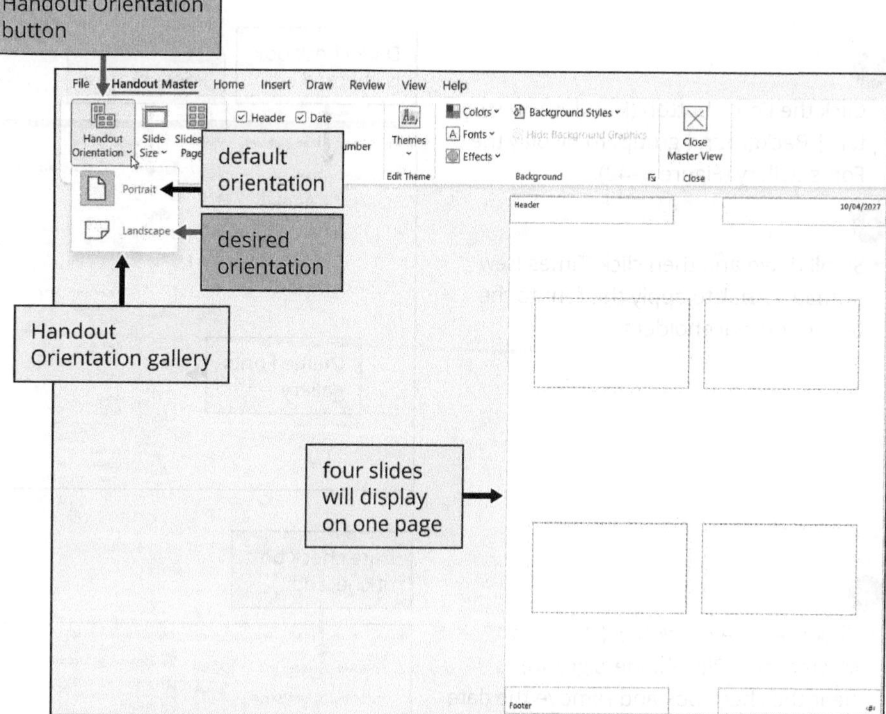

Figure 8–39

- Click Landscape in the gallery to display the page layout in landscape orientation (Figure 8–40).

Q&A How do I decide between portrait and landscape orientation?
If your slide content is predominantly vertical, such as an athlete running or a skyscraper in a major city, consider using the default portrait orientation. If, however, your slide content has long lines of text or pictures of four-legged animals, landscape orientation may be more appropriate.

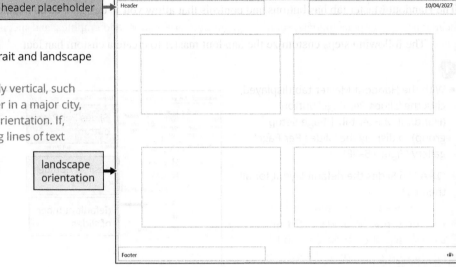

Figure 8–40

To Insert a Header for Handouts

The handout master contains a header placeholder. You can add and format text in that box and also position it on the slide. **Why?** The header informs your audience that the presentation's topic concerns studying abroad. The following steps insert a header for the custom handout.

- Click the Header placeholder and then type **Study Abroad** as the header text (Figure 8–41).

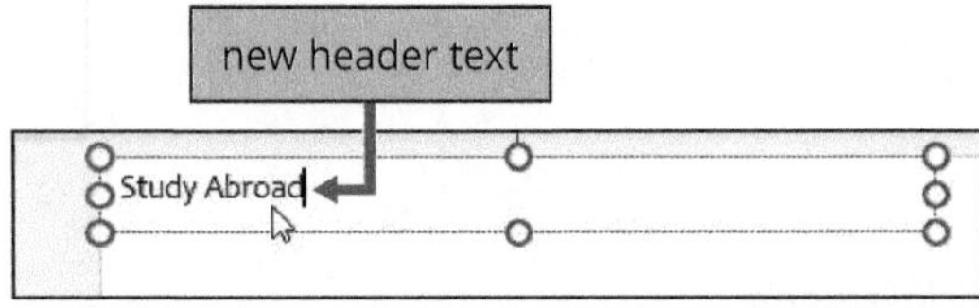

Figure 8–41

- Click the Fonts button (Handout Master tab | Background group) to display the Fonts gallery (Figure 8–42).

- Scroll down and then click 'Times New Roman – Arial' to apply the font to the text in the placeholders.

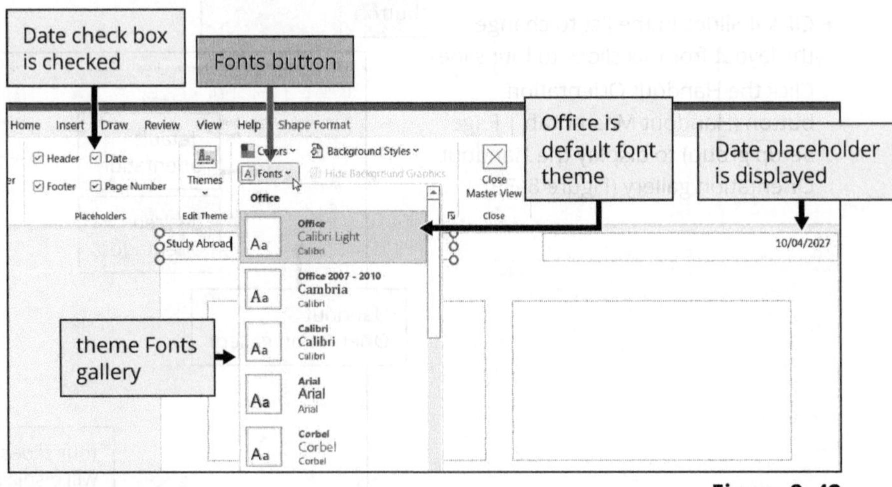

Figure 8–42

- Click the Date check box (Handout Master tab | Placeholders group) to clear the check box and remove the date display (Figure 8–43).

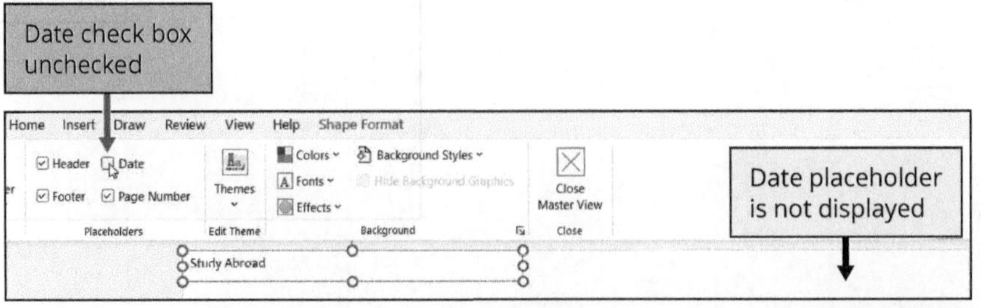

Figure 8–43

To Switch to Notes Page View

If you type notes in the Notes pane, you can print them for yourself or your audience. The basic format found in Backstage view generally suffices for handouts. **Why?** This format includes placeholders for the header, date, slide image, footer, body, and page number. The following steps change the view to Notes Page.

- Display the View tab (Figure 8-44).

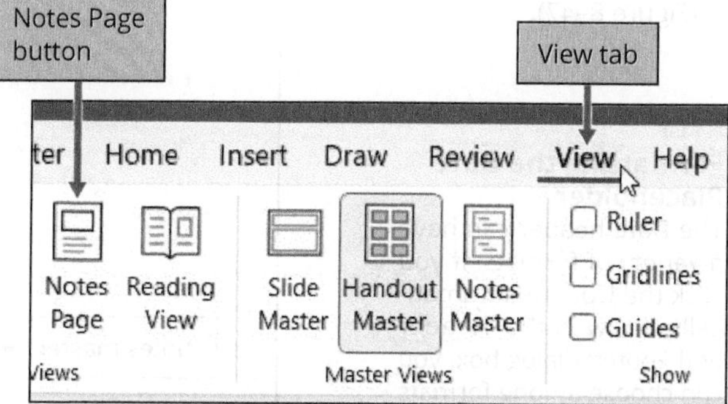

Figure 8-44

- Click the Notes Page button (View tab | Presentation Views group) to display Notes Page view.
- Press RIGHT ARROW repeatedly to view all 12 notes pages (Figure 8-45).

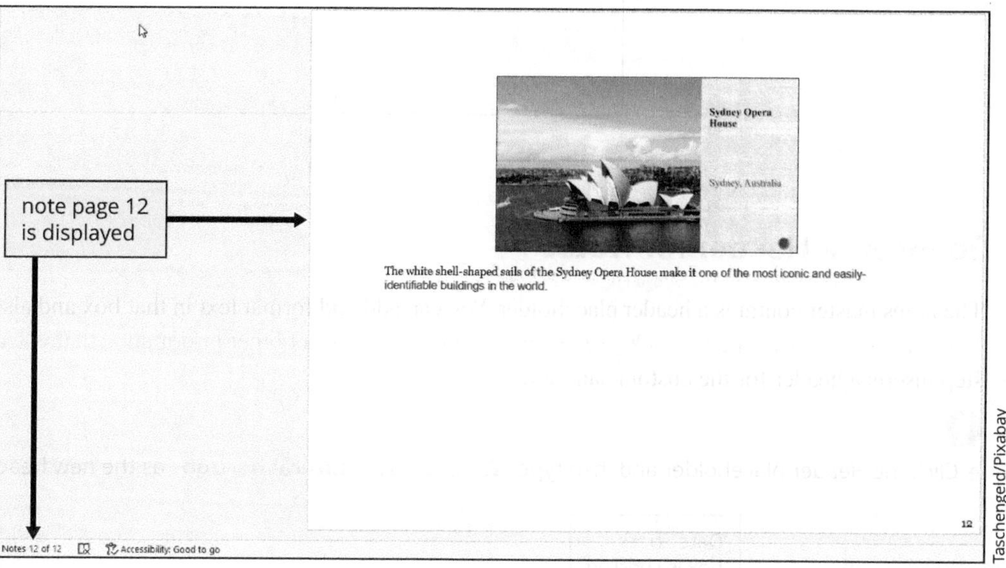

Figure 8-45

To Switch to Notes Master View

You may desire to alter the layout using the notes master. **Why?** You can add graphics and rearrange and format the header, footer, and page number placeholders. The following steps use the notes master to create a custom handout.

- Display the View tab (Figure 8-46).

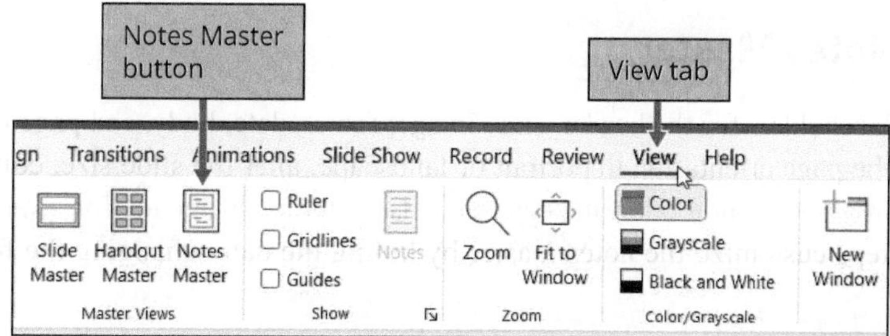

Figure 8-46

- Click the Notes Master button (View tab | Master Views group) to display the Notes Master tab (Figure 8–47).

BTW
Formatting the Date Placeholder
The Date header can have a variety of formats. If you click the Update automatically arrow in the 'Header and Footer' dialog box, you can choose among formats that display the date in a variety of combinations.

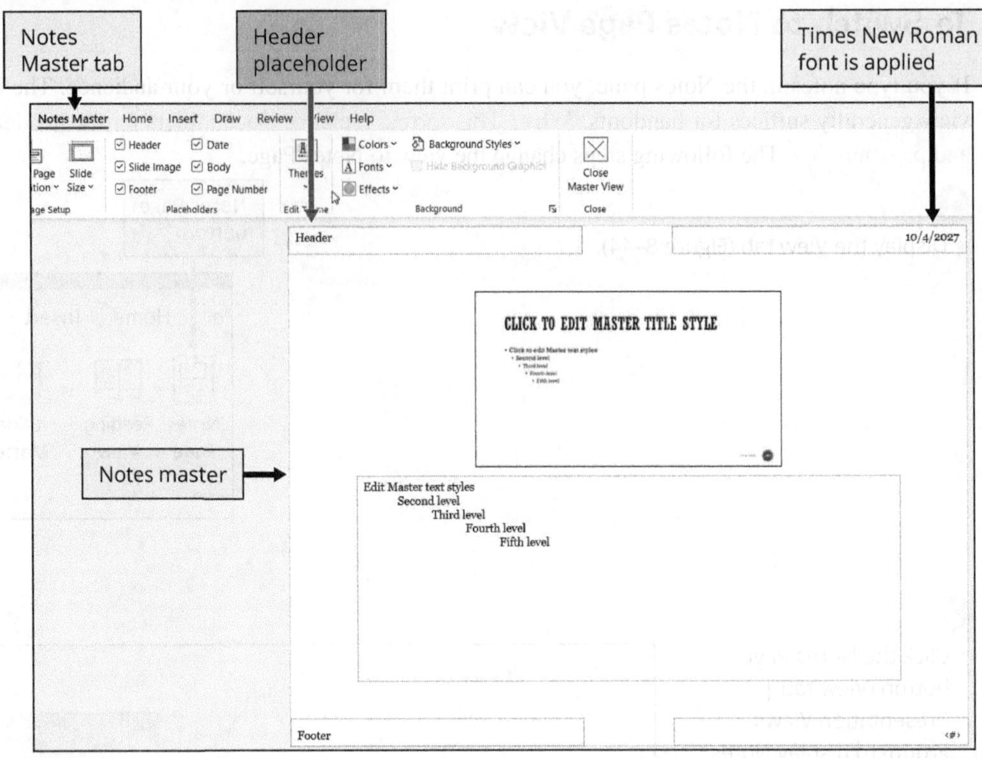

Figure 8–47

To Insert a Header for Notes

The notes master contains a header placeholder. You can add and format text in that box and also position it on the slide. **Why?** You can view the header and quickly see your presentation's topic or other information that you added to this box. The following step inserts a header for the custom handout.

- Click the Header placeholder and then type **Expand your cultural horizon** as the new header text (Figure 8–48).

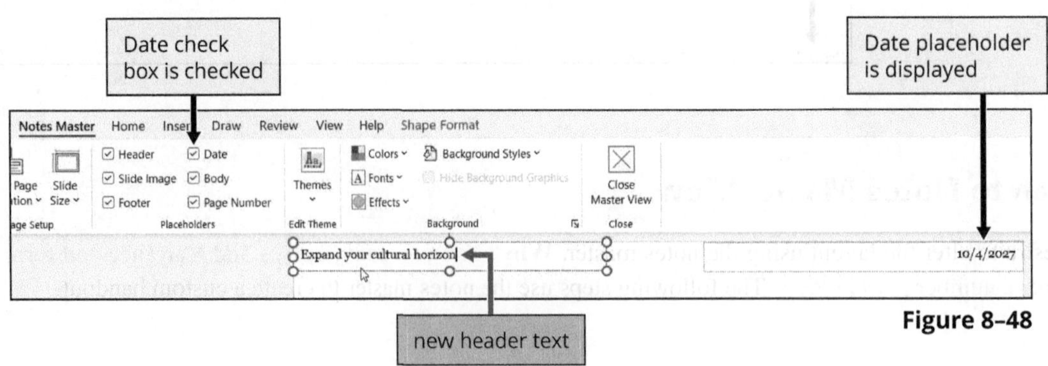

Figure 8–48

To Customize the Notes Master

The notes master contains placeholders for the header, slide image, footer, date, body, and page number. You can hide any of these placeholders, change the page orientation to portrait or landscape, alter the slide size, edit the theme, and change the fonts and colors. **Why?** It is not important to view the date. You also want to change the font and change the page orientation to portrait. The following steps customize the notes master by hiding the date, changing the font, and changing the page orientation to portrait.

- Click the Date check box to remove the check mark.
- Click the Fonts button to display the Fonts gallery (Figure 8–49).

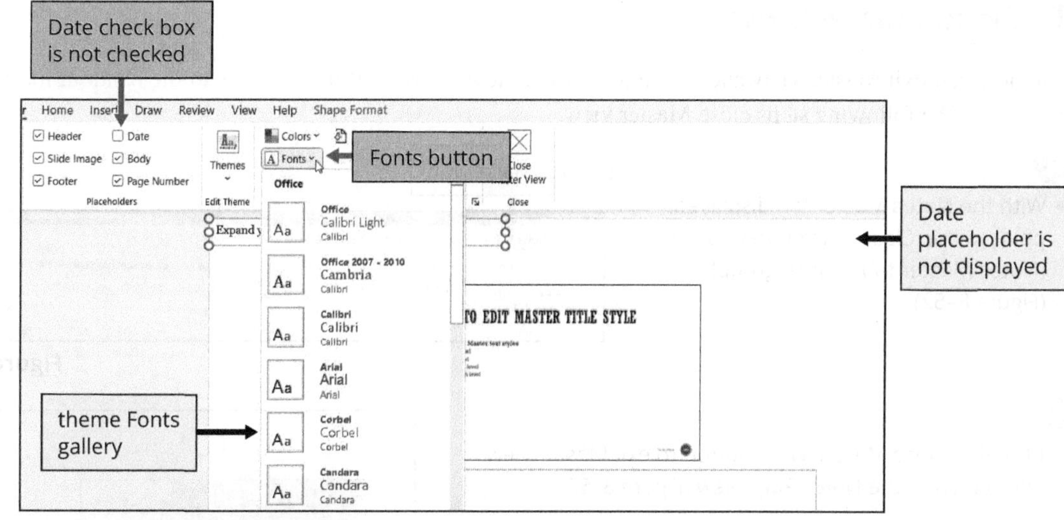

Figure 8–49

- Scroll down and then click 'Times New Roman – Arial' in the Fonts gallery to apply that font to the text in the header and page number placeholders.
- Click the 'Notes Page Orientation' button (Notes Master tab | Page Setup group) to display the 'Notes Page Orientation' gallery (Figure 8–50).

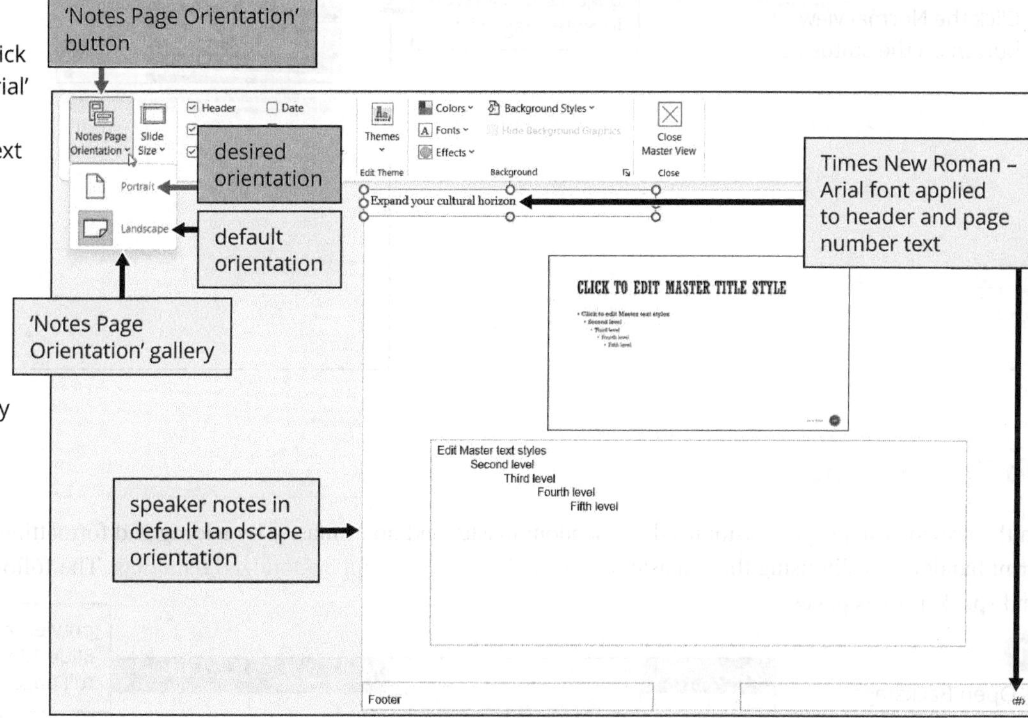

Figure 8–50

- Click Portrait in the gallery to display the page layout in portrait orientation (Figure 8–51).

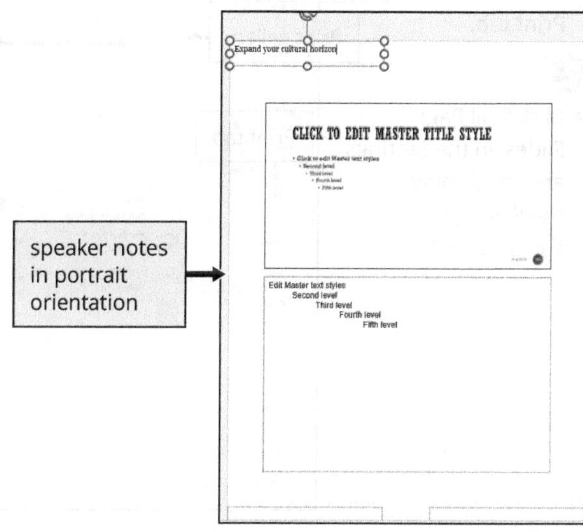

Figure 8–51

To Close Master View

You now can exit Master view and return to Normal view. **Why?** All the changes to the handout master and notes master are complete. The following steps close Master view.

- With the Notes Master tab displayed, point to the 'Close Master View' button (Notes Master tab | Close group) (Figure 8–52).

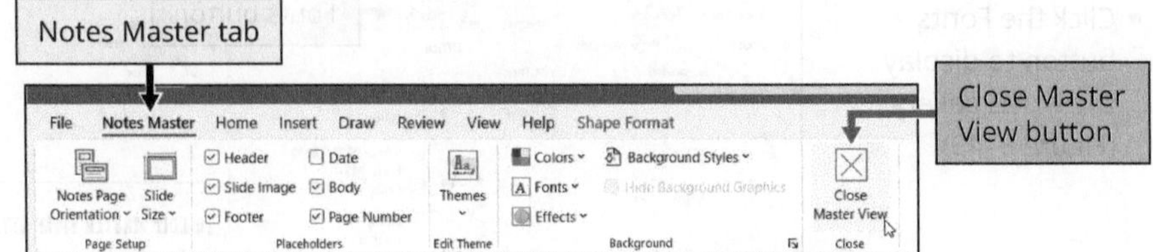

Figure 8–52

- Click the 'Close Master View' button to exit Master view and return to the Notes Page view (Figure 8–53).

- Click the Normal view button on the status bar.

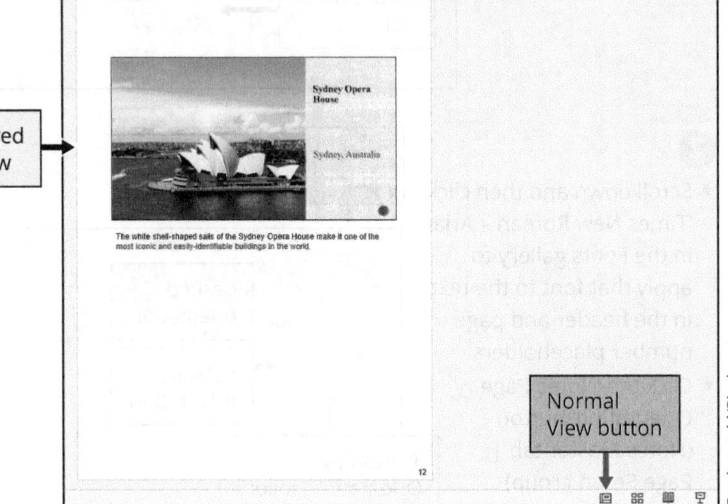

Figure 8–53

To Print Handouts

In the previous steps, you customized the handout master and notes master by adding and formatting header text. You now can print handouts easily using these masters. **Why?** You want to print customized handouts. The following steps print handouts and speaker notes pages.

1

- Open Backstage view and then click the Print tab.

2

- Click 'Full Page Slides' in the Settings area to display the Print gallery (Figure 8–54).

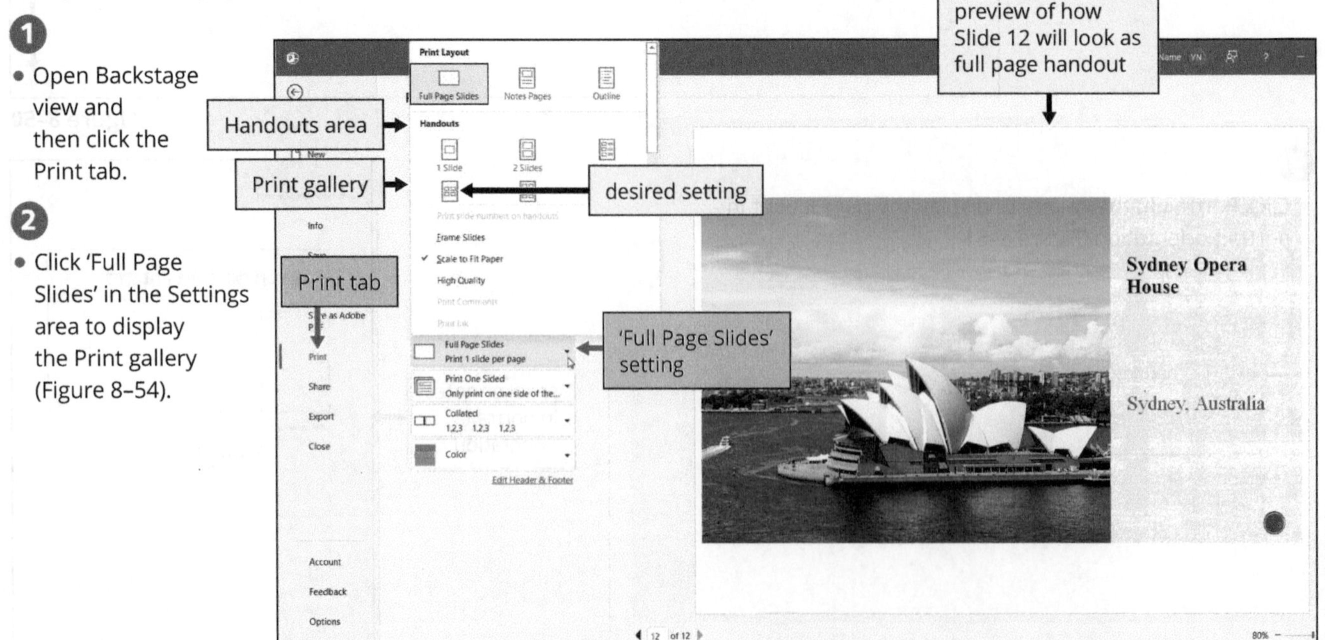

Figure 8–54

3

- Scroll down and then click '4 Slides Horizontal' in the Handouts area.
- Click Portrait Orientation in the Settings area to display the Orientation gallery (Figure 8–55).

Print button
preview of handout in portrait orientation
header text
Settings area
'4 Slides Horizontal' setting
Orientation gallery
Portrait Orientation
desired orientation
page number
Previous Page button
Next Page button

acheemete/Pixabay; scharfsascha/Pixabay; Ledoc/Pixabay; cmmellow/Pixabay

Figure 8–55

- Click Landscape Orientation to change the setting.
- Verify that '4 Slides Horizontal' is selected as the option in the Settings area and that the preview shows the header text, page number, and four slides in landscape orientation.
- Click the Previous Page and Next Page buttons to display previews of the other pages and then display Page 1.
- Click the Print button in the Print gallery to print the handout. Figure 8–56 shows the first page of the printout.

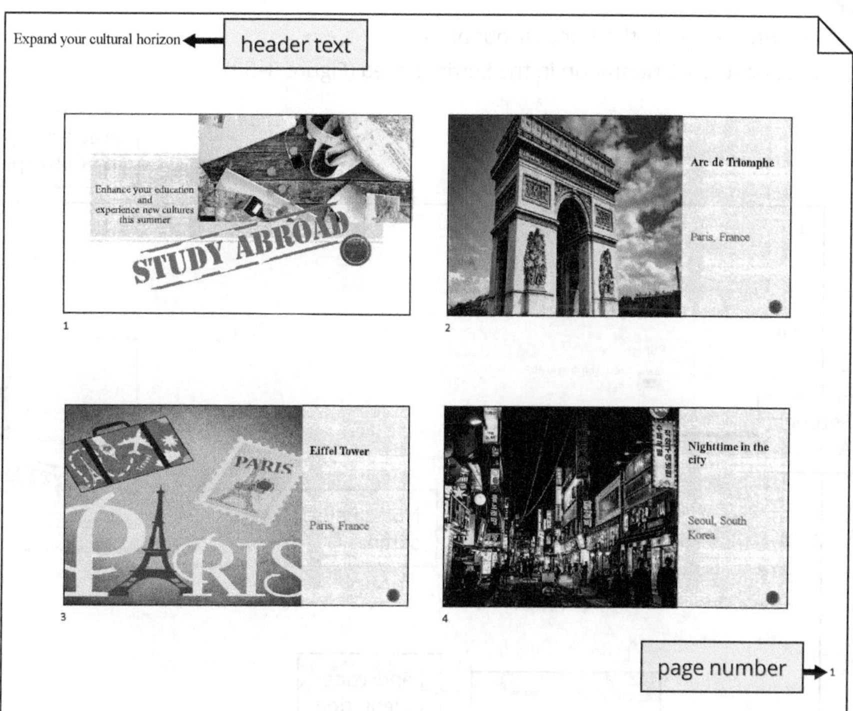

geralt/Pixabay; Rocky Scotty/Unsplash; iankelsall1/Pixabay; Alexas_Fotos/Pixabay; Andrea De Santis/Unsplash

Figure 8–56: Handout in Landscape Orientation – Page 1

BTW
Printing Selections
When you are developing slides or creating handouts for a particular audience, you may not want to print every slide in your presentation. To print specific slides, select the desired slides in the Slide pane. Then, open Backstage view, display the Print tab, click the first button in the Settings area, click Print Selection in the list to specify you want to print the slides you have selected, and then click the Print button in the Print gallery to print these slides.

- Open Backstage view, click the Print tab, and then click '4 Slides Horizontal' in the Settings area to display the Print gallery (Figure 8–57).

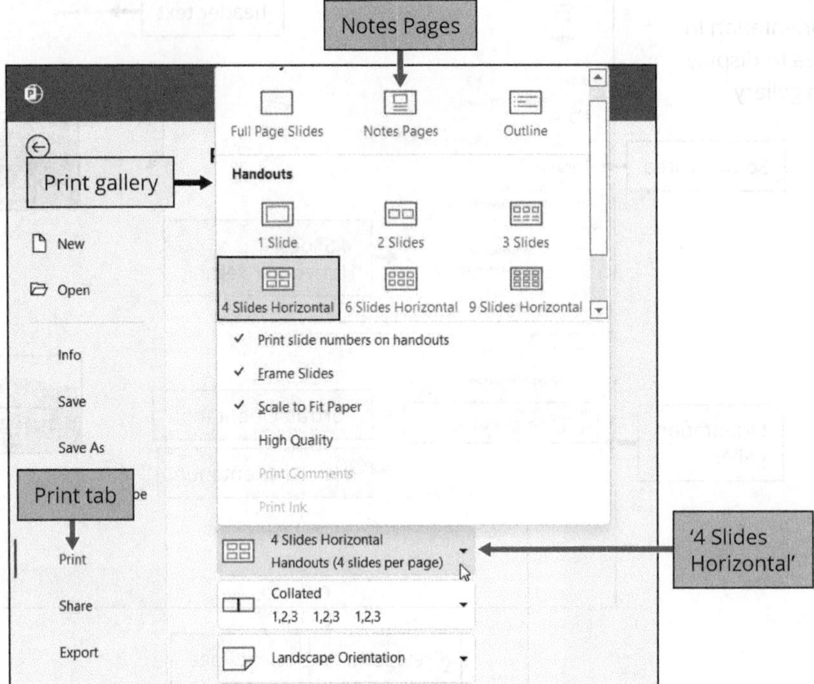

Figure 8–57

- Click Notes Pages in the Print Layout area.
- Click Landscape Orientation in the Settings area (Figure 8–58).

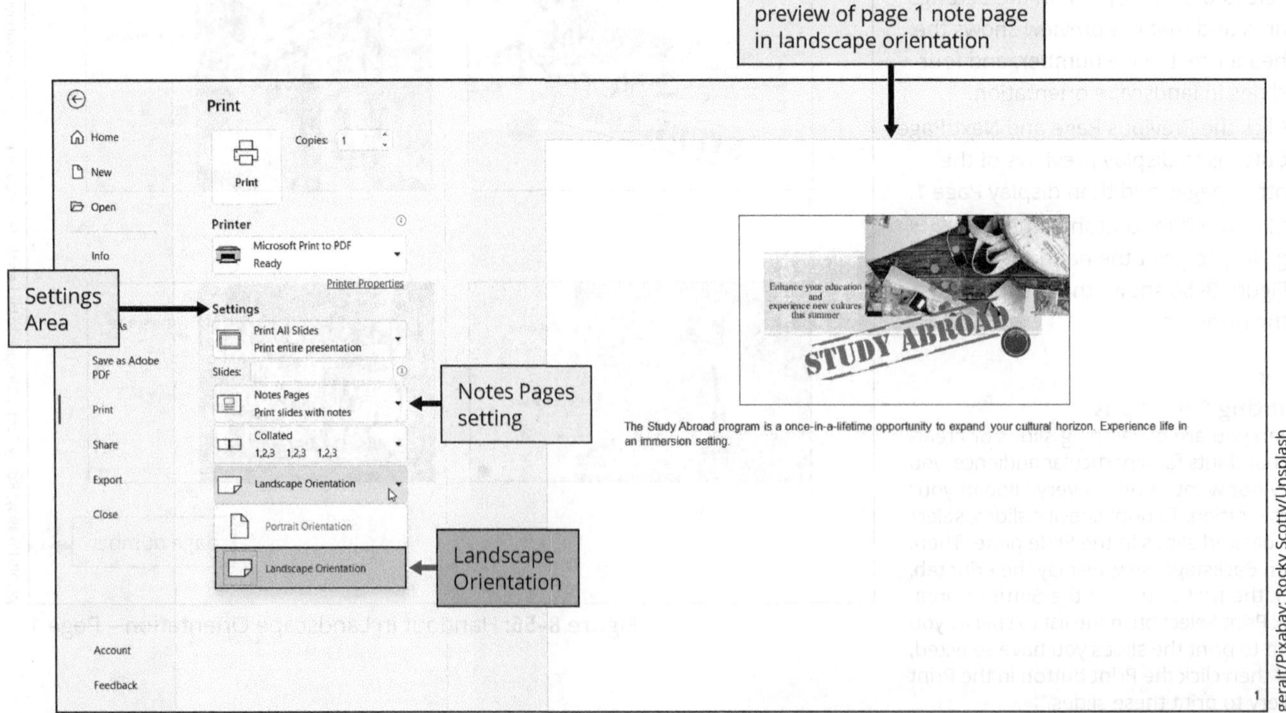

Figure 8–58

7

- Click Portrait Orientation in the gallery to change the setting.
- Verify that the page preview shows the speaker notes and page number in portrait orientation (Figure 8–59).

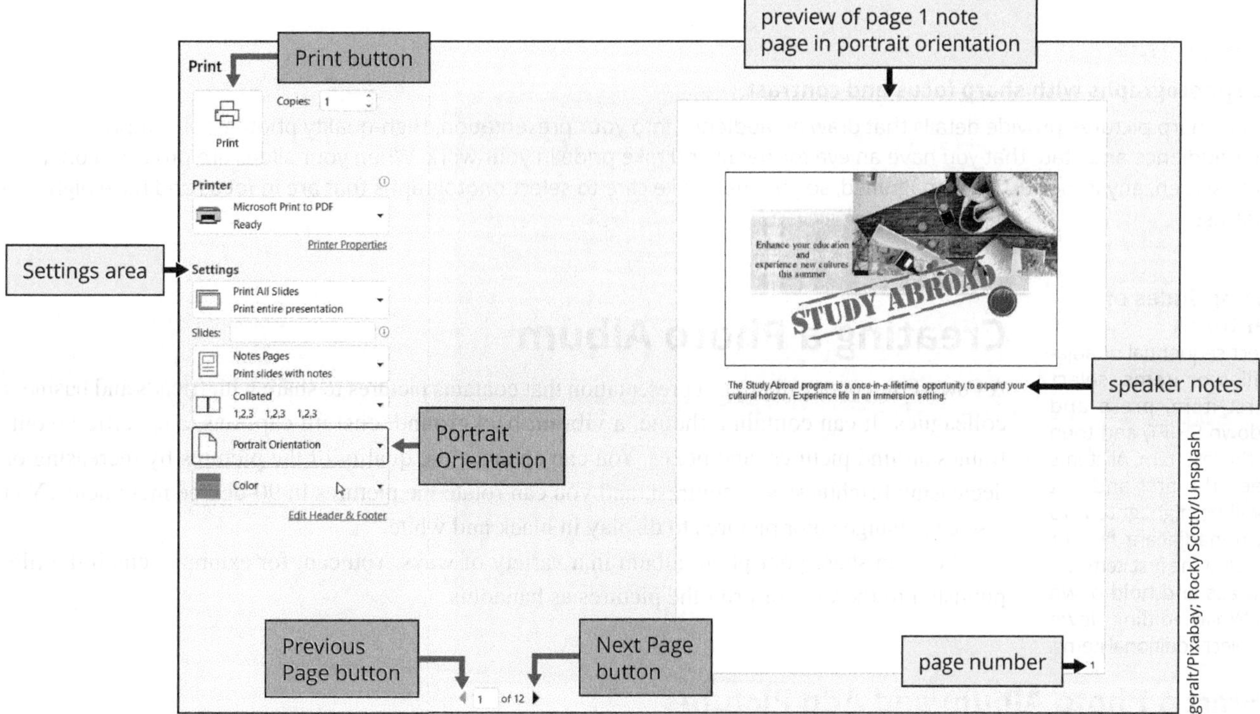

geralt/Pixabay; Rocky Scotty/Unsplash

Figure 8–59

- Click the Previous Page and Next Page buttons to display previews of the other pages.
- Click the Print button to print the notes. Figure 8–60 shows the first page of the printout.

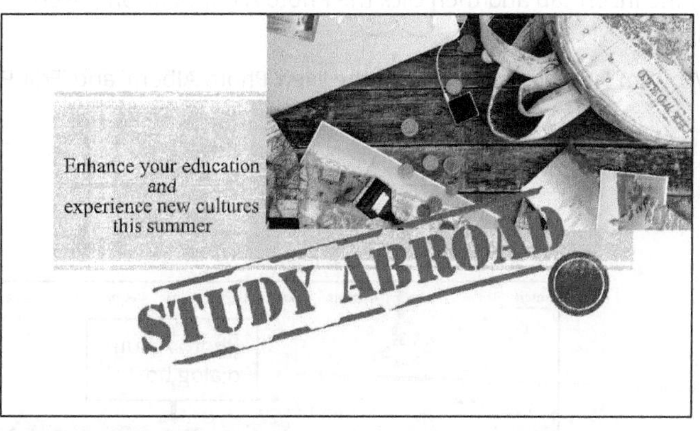

geralt/Pixabay; Rocky Scotty/Unsplash

Figure 8–60: Speaker Notes in Portrait Orientation – Page 1

BTW

Printing in Grayscale

If you desire to keep your images in color but do not have a color printer or do not require a color printout, choosing Grayscale will print all the slide objects in shades of gray. In grayscale, some objects on the slides will appear crisper and cleaner than if you choose the Color option on a non-color printer. Open Backstage view, click the Print tab to display the Print pane, click the Color button in the Settings area, click Grayscale, and then click Print. If you then want to print in color, click the Grayscale button and then click Color.

Break Point: If you wish to take a break, this is a good place to do so. Be sure the Study Abroad file is saved and then you can exit PowerPoint. To resume later, start PowerPoint, open the file called SC_PPT_8_Study_Abroad.pptx, and continue following the steps from this location forward.

Consider This

Use photographs with sharp focus and contrast.

Clear, sharp pictures provide details that draw an audience into your presentation. High-quality photographs impress your audience and state that you have an eye for detail and take pride in your work. When your slides are projected on a large screen, any imperfection is magnified, so you must take care to select photographs that are in focus and have high contrast.

BTW
Selecting Slides or Other Items
To select sequential or adjacent files or items, select the first item, press and hold down SHIFT, and then select the last item. All items between the first and last item will be highlighted. To select nonadjacent files or items, select the first item and then press and hold down CTRL. While holding down CTRL, select additional items.

Creating a Photo Album

A PowerPoint photo album is a presentation that contains pictures to share with friends and business colleagues. It can contain a theme, a vibrant background, custom captions, a specific layout, frames around pictures, and boxes. You can enhance the quality of the pictures by increasing or decreasing brightness and contrast, and you can rotate the pictures in 90-degree increments. You also can change color pictures to display in black and white.

You can share your photo album in a variety of ways. You can, for example, email the file, publish it to the web, or print the pictures as handouts.

To Start a Photo Album and Add Pictures

You initially create the album and then later enhance its appearance. **Why?** Once you have gathered files of digital pictures, you can begin building a photo album. The following steps start a photo album and add pictures.

- Display the Insert tab and then click the Photo Album button (Insert tab | Images group) to display the Photo Album dialog box (Figure 8–61).

Q&A Why am I viewing a menu with the 'New Photo Album' and 'Edit Photo Album' commands instead of the Photo Album dialog box?
You mistakenly clicked the 'New Photo Album' arrow instead of the 'New Photo Album' button.

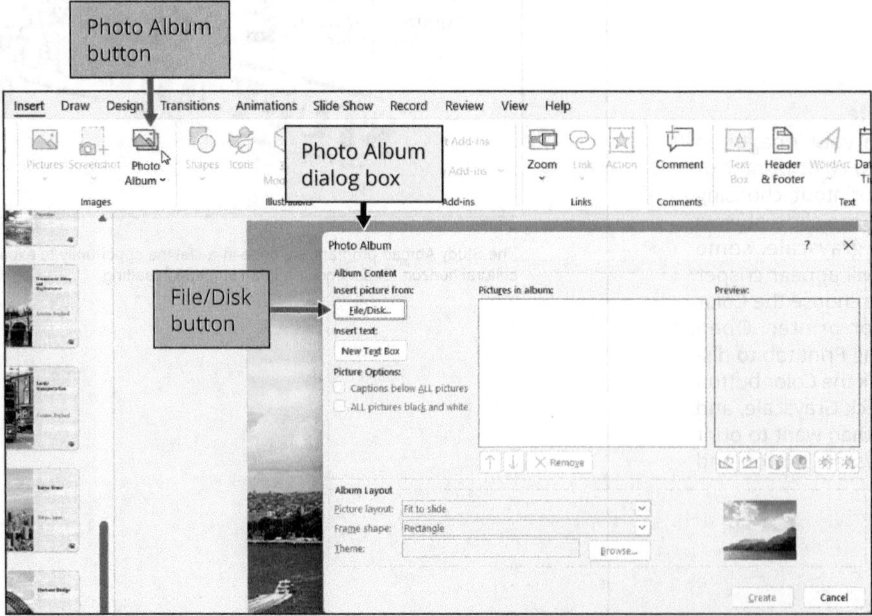

Figure 8–61

- Click the File/Disk button to display the 'Insert New Pictures' dialog box.
- If necessary, navigate to the location where your Data Files are stored (Figure 8–62).

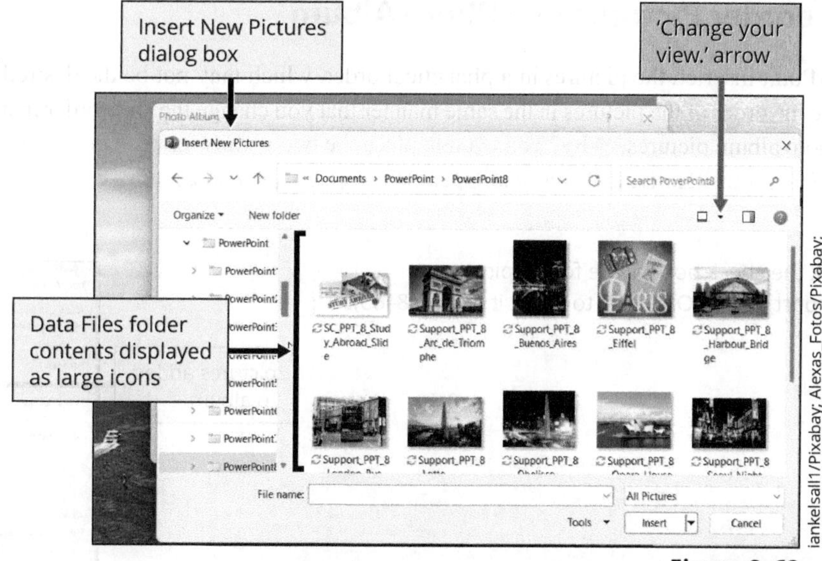

Figure 8–62

iankelsall1/Pixabay; Alexas_Fotos/Pixabay; Andrea De Santis/Unsplash; cmmellow/Pixabay; Gonzalo Kenny/unsplash; matcuz/Pixabay; DUCTINH91/Pixabay; scharfsascha/Pixabay; Pharaoh_EZYPT/Pixabay; Ledoc/Pixabay; acheemete/Pixabay

- If necessary, display only the picture file names by clicking the 'Change your view.' arrow (shown in Figure 8–62), on the toolbar ('Insert New Pictures' dialog box) to display the view settings (Figure 8–63).
- Click List in the view settings to change the view setting and display only the picture file names.

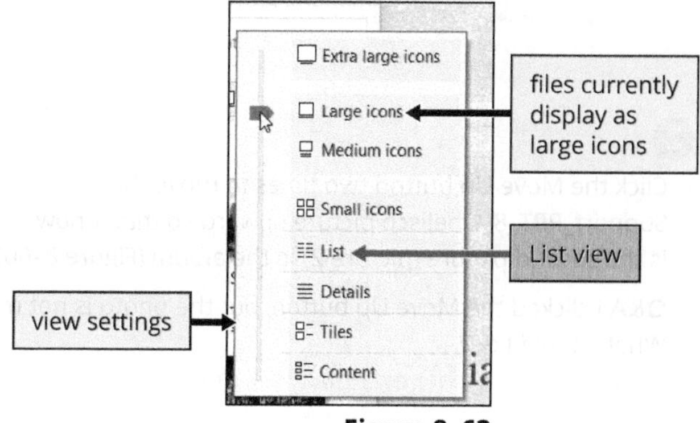

Figure 8–63

- Click Support_PPT_8_Buenos_Aires to select the file name. Press and hold down CTRL and then select the file names Support_PPT_8_Harbour_Bridge, Support_PPT_8_Lotte, Support_PPT_8_Obelisco, Support_PPT_8_Opera_House, and Support_PPT_8_Seoul_Night as additional files to insert (Figure 8–64).

Q&A If I mistakenly select a file name, how can I remove the selection?

Click the file name again to remove the check mark.

I'm using a touch screen and am having trouble selecting multiple files. What can I do?

You may need to use a mouse in combination with the onscreen keyboard CTRL, or you can select and insert each file individually.

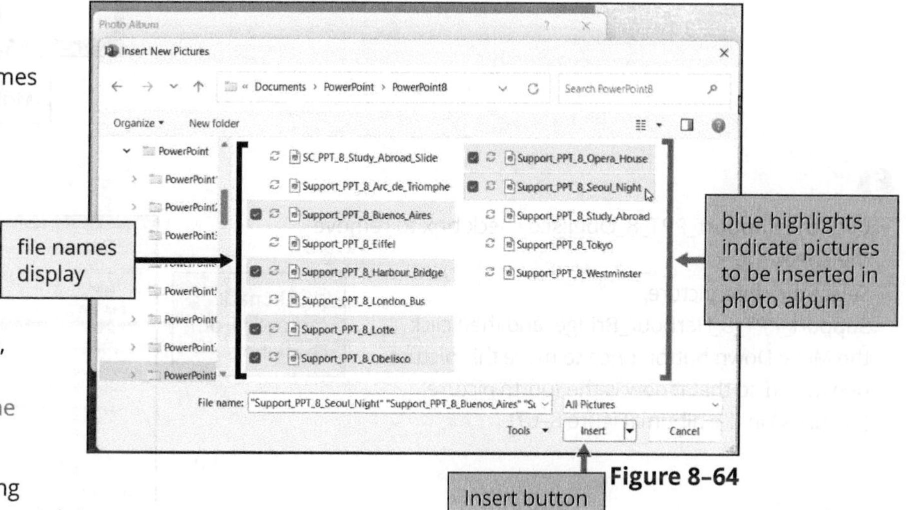

Figure 8–64

- Click Insert ('Insert New Pictures' dialog box) to add the pictures to the album and display the Photo Album dialog box showing the inserted pictures.

To Reorder Pictures in a Photo Album

PowerPoint inserted the pictures in alphabetical order, which may not be the desired sequence for your album. You easily can change the order of the pictures in the same manner that you change the slide order in a custom show. The following steps reorder the photo album pictures. **Why?** You want to place the two photos for each destination together. For example, you want the two Australia photos (Harbour Bridge and Opera House) to appear adjacent to each other in the middle of the album.

- Click the check box for the fourth picture, Support_PPT_8_Obelisco, to select it (Figure 8–65).

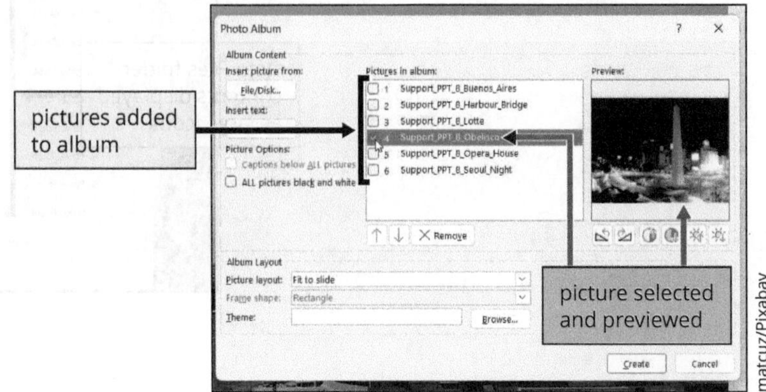

Figure 8–65

2

- Click the Move Up button two times to move the Support_PPT_8_Obelisco picture upward so that it now is the second picture (picture 2) in the album (Figure 8–66).

Q&A I clicked the Move Up button, but the photo is not moving. What should I do?
Be patient. The photo eventually will move.

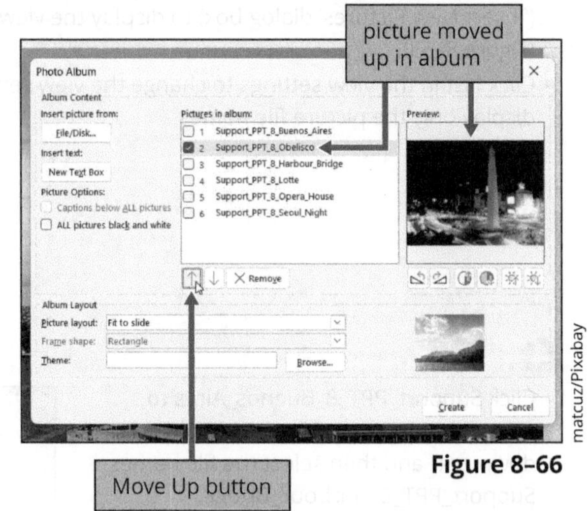

Figure 8–66

3

- Click the Support_PPT_8_Obelisco check box to remove the check mark.
- Select the third picture, Support_PPT_8_Harbour_Bridge, and then click the Move Down button once to move this picture downward so that it now is the fourth picture (picture 4) in the album (Figure 8–67).

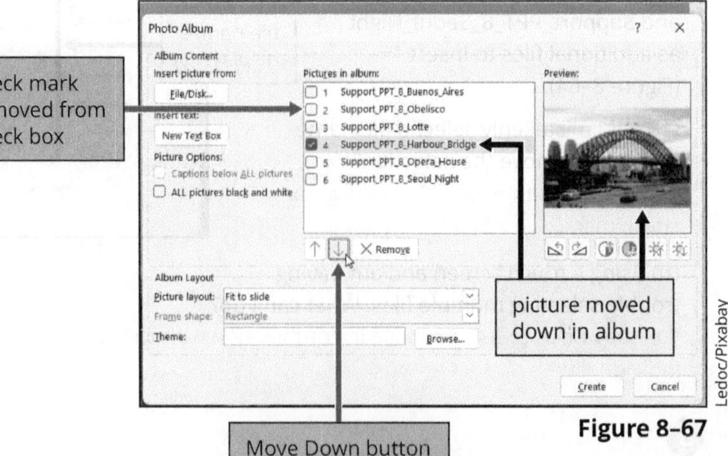

Figure 8–67

4

- Click the Support_PPT_8_Harbour_Bridge check box to remove the check mark.
- Select the third picture, Support_PPT_8_Lotte, and then click the Move Down button three times to move this picture downward so that it now is the last picture (picture 6) in the album.
- Click the Support_PPT_8_Lotte check box to remove the check mark (Figure 8–68).

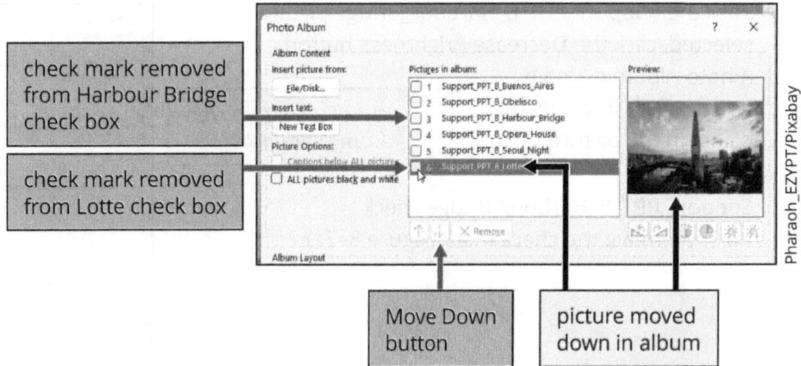

Pharaoh_EZYPT/Pixabay

Figure 8–68

To Format Photos in an Album

A picture you insert may need correcting to enhance its visual appeal. You can adjust the difference between the darkest and lightest areas of the picture by increasing or decreasing the contrast. If a picture in the photo album is too light or too dark, you can adjust its brightness to enhance its appearance. The following steps adjust the brightness and contrast of a photo album picture. **Why?** The Harbour Bridge picture is somewhat dark, so increasing the brightness would help the colors stand out on the slide and give more depth to the image. In addition, it lacks contrast and would be more dramatic if it had a wide variety of dark and light regions.

- Click the check box for the third picture, Support_PPT_8_Harbour_Bridge, to select it and display a preview (Figure 8–69).

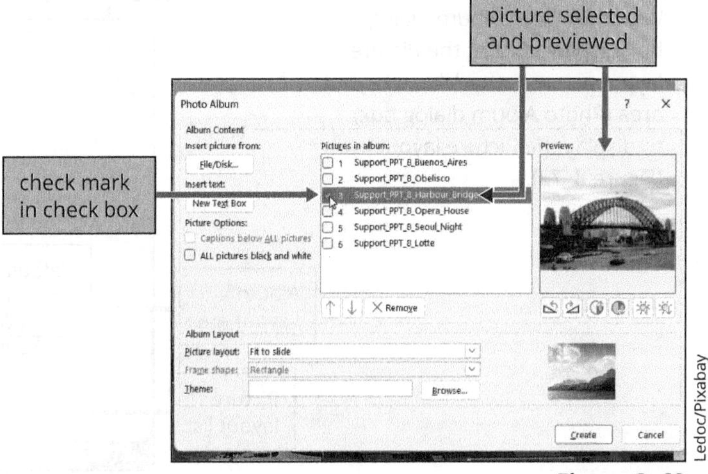

Ledoc/Pixabay

Figure 8–69

- Click the Increase Contrast button (Photo Album dialog box) four times to increase the contrast of this picture (Figure 8– 70).

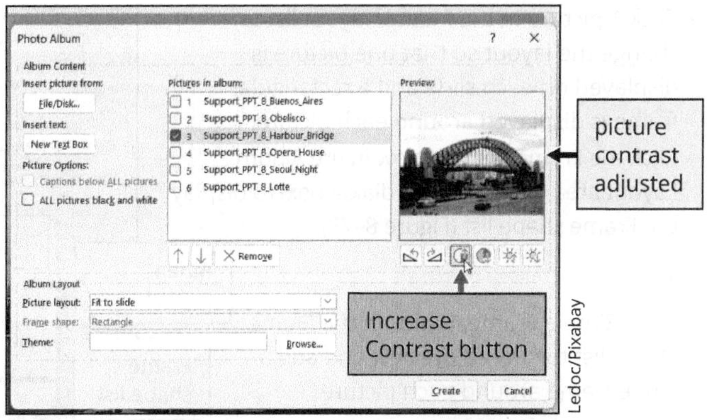

Ledoc/Pixabay

Figure 8–70

- With the Support_PPT_8_Harbour_Bridge picture selected, click the Decrease Brightness button (Photo Album dialog box) two times to intensify the colors in the picture.
- Click the Support_PPT_8_Harbour_Bridge check box to remove the check mark (Figure 8–71).

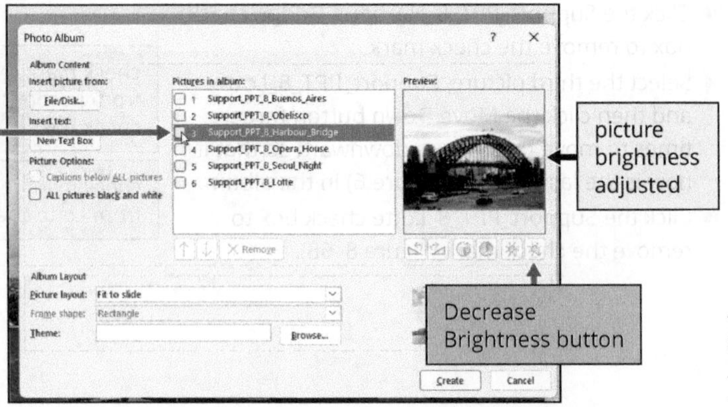

Figure 8–71

To Change a Photo Album Layout

PowerPoint inserts each photo album picture so that it fills, or fits, one entire slide. You can modify this layout to display two or four pictures on a slide, display a title, or add white space between the image and the slide edges. You also can add a white or black frame around the perimeter of each picture. The following steps change an album layout. **Why?** You want to display only one picture on each slide so that you can discuss each destination thoroughly during your presentation. Adding a frame provides contrast between the photos and the background.

- With the Photo Album dialog box displayed, click the Picture layout arrow in the Album Layout area (Photo Album dialog box) to display the Picture layout list (Figure 8–72).

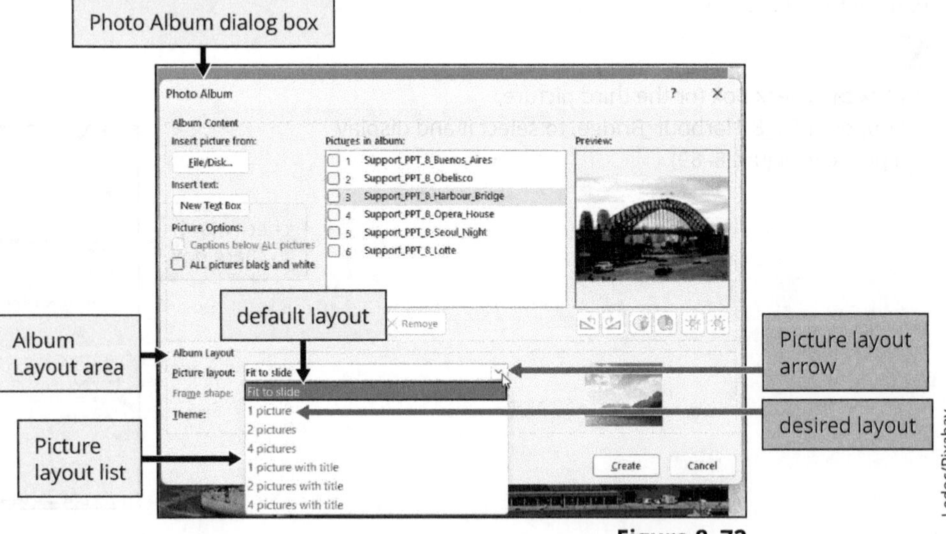

Figure 8–72

- Click 1 picture in the Picture layout list to change the layout so that one picture is displayed on each slide and a rectangular frame is displayed around each picture.
- Click the Frame shape arrow in the Album Layout area (Photo Album dialog box) to display the Frame shape list (Figure 8–73).

- Click 'Simple Frame, White' in the Frame shape list to show a preview and add a white frame around each picture.

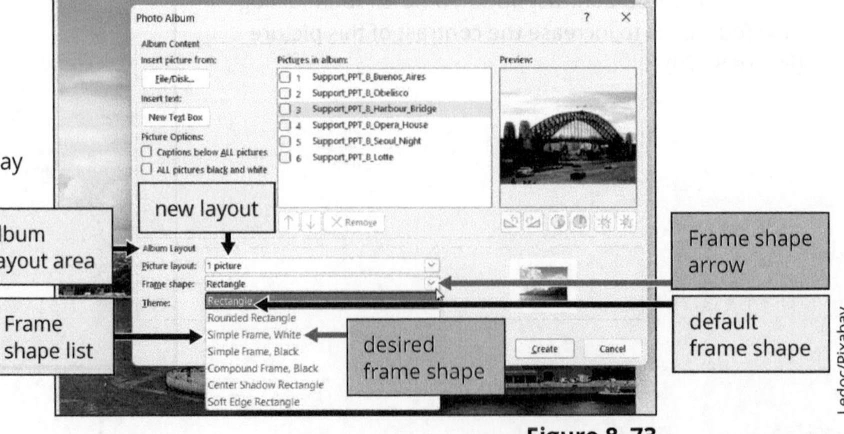

Figure 8–73

To Add a Photo Album Theme

The themes that are used to design a presentation also are available to add to a photo album. These themes determine the colors and fonts that complement each other and increase the visual appeal of the slides. The following steps add a theme to the photo album. **Why?** You want to select a simple theme that has an uncluttered layout and font that will complement the pictures.

- Click the Browse button in the Album Layout area (Photo Album dialog box) to display the Choose Theme dialog box.
- Click Organic in the theme list to select this theme (Figure 8–74).

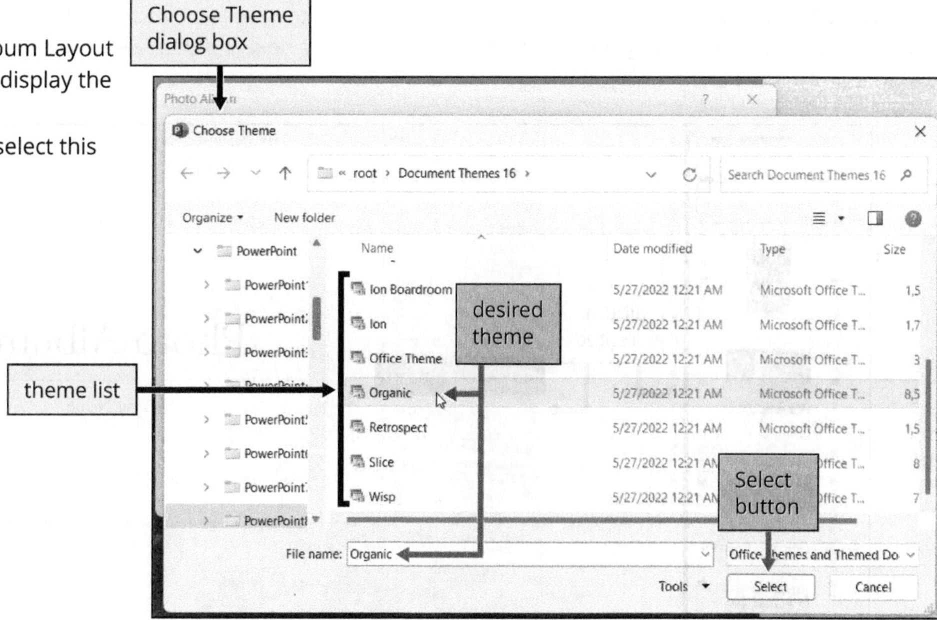

Figure 8–74

- Click the Select button (Choose Theme dialog box) to apply this theme to the presentation (Figure 8–75).

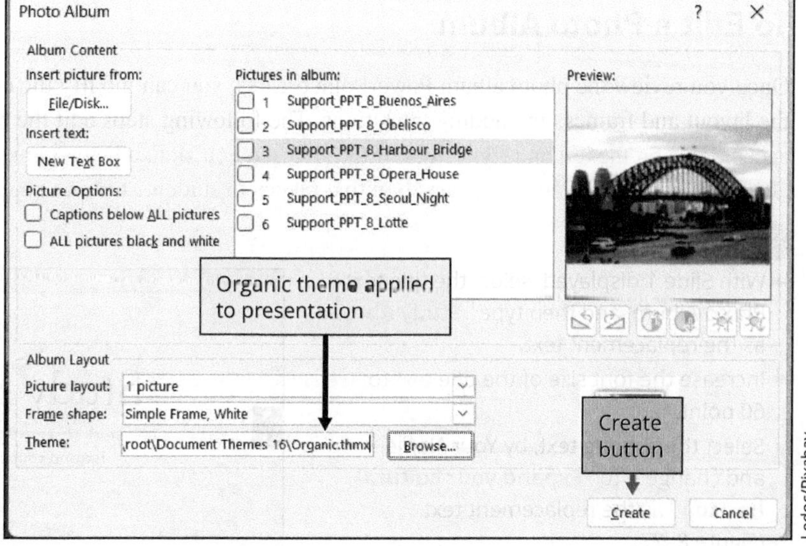

Figure 8–75

To Create a Photo Album

Once you have inserted the pictures and determined the picture sequence, layout, frame shape, and theme, you are ready to make the photo album. **Why?** You have specified all the information PowerPoint needs to create this album. The following step creates the photo album.

- Click the Create button (Photo Album dialog box) to close the dialog box and create a photo album with a title slide and six pictures (Figure 8–76).
- If the Design Ideas pane is displayed, close it.

Q&A Why does a particular name display below the Photo Album title?
PowerPoint displays the user name that was entered when the program was installed. To see this name, display Backstage view, click Options to display the 'PowerPoint Options' dialog box, and then view or change the name entered in the User name box in the Personalize your copy of Microsoft Office area.

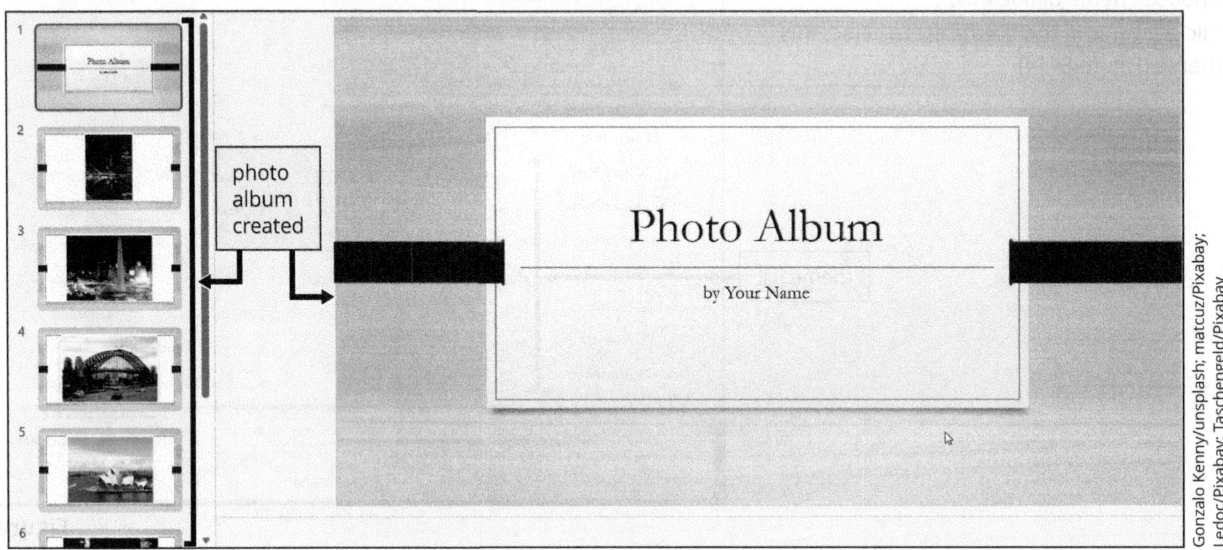

Figure 8–76

To Edit a Photo Album

Once you review the photo album PowerPoint creates, you can modify the contents by adding and deleting pictures, changing the layout and frames, and adding transitions. The following steps edit the photo album. **Why?** The Organic theme has black accent lines on the left and right sides of the slide, so you want a black picture frame to coordinate with this slide element. You also want to add the Page Curl transition that relates to students turning pages in a book.

- With Slide 1 displayed, select the title text, Photo Album, and then type **Study Abroad** as the replacement text.
- Increase the font size of the title text to 60 point.
- Select the subtitle text, by Your Name, and change it to **Expand your cultural horizon** as the replacement text (Figure 8–77).

Figure 8–77

2

- Display the Insert tab and then click the Photo Album arrow (Insert tab | Images group) to display the Photo Album menu (Figure 8–78).

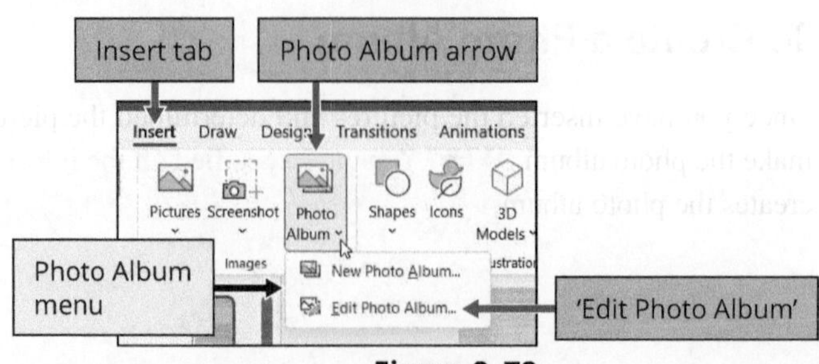

Figure 8–78

3

- Click 'Edit Photo Album' in the menu to display the 'Edit Photo Album' dialog box.
- Click the Frame shape arrow to display the Frame shape list and then click 'Compound Frame, Black' in the list to change the frame from a single white border to a double black border (Figure 8–79).

- Click the Update button (Edit Photo Album dialog box) to make the frame change to the photo album.
- If the Design Ideas pane displays, close it.
- Apply the Page Curl transition and then change the duration to 03.00 seconds for all slides.
- Save the file using **SC_PPT_8_Photo_Album** as the file name.
- Close the SC_PPT_8_Photo_Album presentation to return to the open Study Abroad presentation.

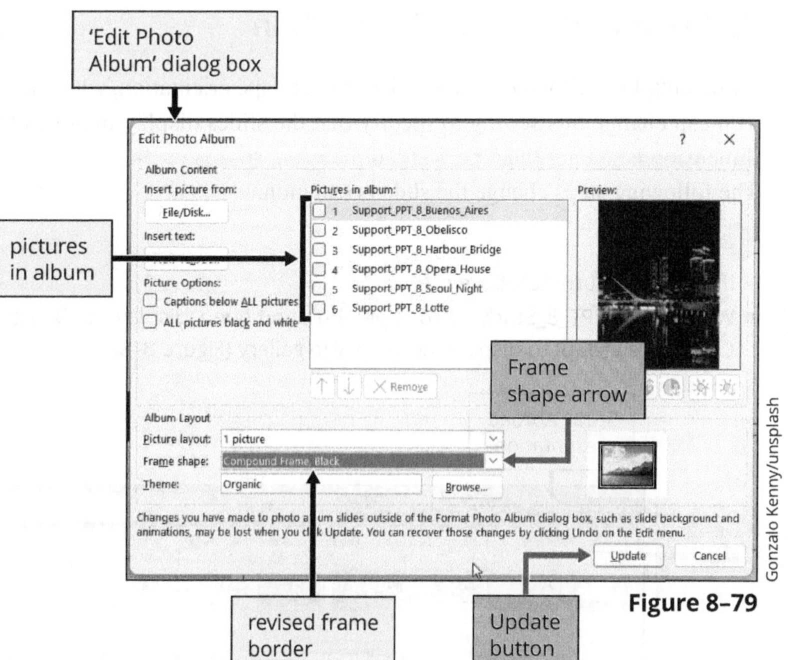

Figure 8–79

Modifying and Presenting Slides

PowerPoint's default settings generally suffice for most presentations. At times, however, the slide content can be presented more effectively in a different perspective or resolution. You easily can modify these settings to tailor the slides to your specific needs. In addition, many designers create one comprehensive slide deck and then elect to display particular parts of that file when presenting to varied audiences. They create a **summary zoom** slide as the first slide in their presentation, which allows them to jump to a specific slide or section and then return to this initial slide.

Speakers often deliver a presentation using two monitors: one to display their speaker notes privately, and a second to display the slides and project them on a large screen for the audience to view. PowerPoint's **Presenter view** supports the use of two monitors connected to one computer so presenters can view the slide currently being projected while viewing the slide thumbnails, seeing a preview of the next slide or animation, reading their speaker notes, viewing the elapsed time, lightening or darkening the audience's screen, or customizing the presentation by skipping the next slide or reviewing a slide previously displayed. A computer must support the use of multiple monitors and must be configured to use this feature.

BTW
Zoom Availability
Zoom for PowerPoint is available only in Microsoft 365 and PowerPoint 2019 and later. Summary zoom also is supported for Microsoft 365 for Mac.

BTW
Speaker Coach
PowerPoint Speaker Coach (called Presenter Coach in some earlier versions of PowerPoint) can help you become a more confident presenter. It uses AI to give feedback about a speaker's body language, including eye contact and distance from the camera. Also, it identifies repeated words and phrases and provides a list of synonyms. Another feature detects perceived mispronounced words. This feedback is detailed in a Summary Report provided at the end of each rehearsal, and it includes statistics and suggested recommendations. To rehearse your presentation with Speaker Coach, click the Slide Show tab, click the 'Rehearse with Coach' button (Slide Show tab | Rehearse group), and then click Get Started.

Consider This

Use hyperlinks to show slides with landscape and portrait orientations.

When you are creating your presentation, you have the option to display all your slides in either the default landscape orientation or portrait orientation. You may, however, desire to have slides with both orientations during a single presentation. Using hyperlinks is one solution to mixing the orientations. Apply a hyperlink to an object on the last slide in one orientation and then hyperlink to another presentation with slides in the other orientation. If you desire to hyperlink to one particular slide in a second presentation, click the Bookmark button in the Insert Hyperlink dialog box and then select the title of the slide you want to use as your link. Once you have displayed the desired slides in the second presentation, create another hyperlink from that presentation back to a slide in your original presentation.

To Change the Slide Orientation

By default, PowerPoint displays slides in landscape orientation, where the width dimension is greater than the height dimension. You can change this setting to specify that the slides display in portrait orientation. **Why?** In portrait orientation, the height dimension is greater than the width dimension, so it is useful to display tall objects, people who are standing, or monuments. The following steps change the slide orientation.

- If necessary, turn AutoSave off.
- With the SC_PPT_8_Study_Abroad presentation open, display the Design tab and then click the Slide Size button (Design tab | Customize group) to display the Slide Size gallery (Figure 8–80).

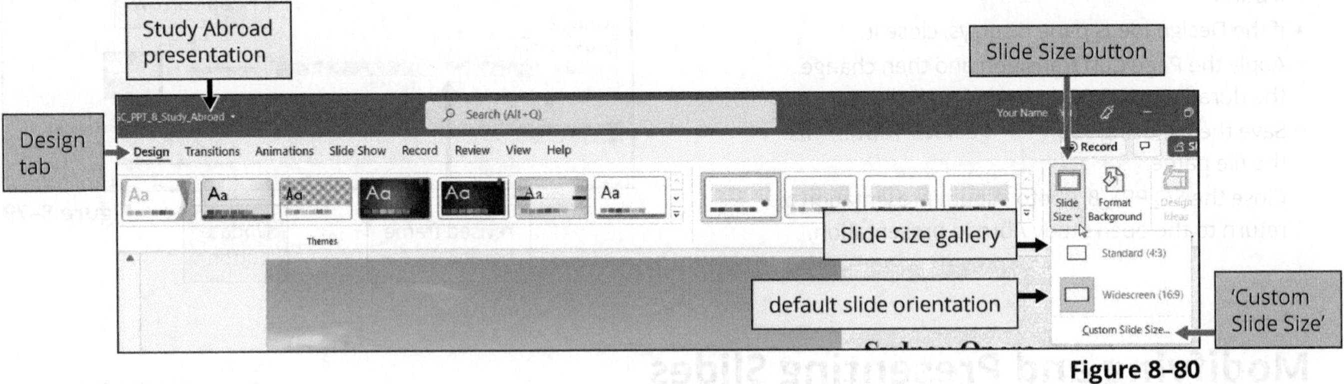

Figure 8–80

- Click 'Custom Slide Size' to display the Slide Size dialog box and then click Portrait in the Slides area of the Orientation section to change the slide orientation from Landscape to Portrait (Figure 8–81).

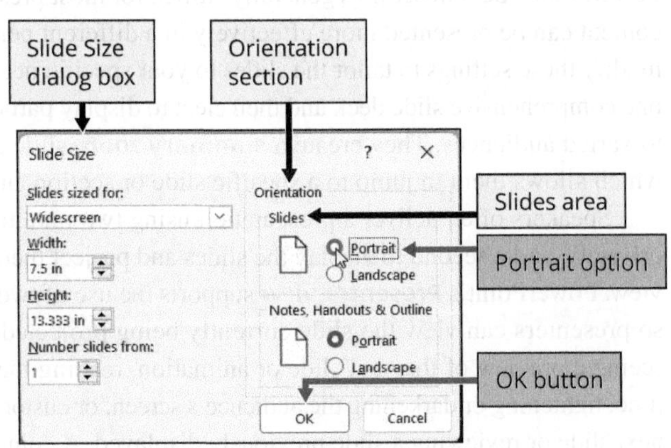

Figure 8–81

- Click OK to display the Microsoft PowerPoint dialog box (Figure 8–82).

- Click Ensure Fit to scale the slide content to fit on each slide.

Q&A I see an Ensure Fit icon and an Ensure Fit button. Can I click either one to scale the slide content?
Yes.

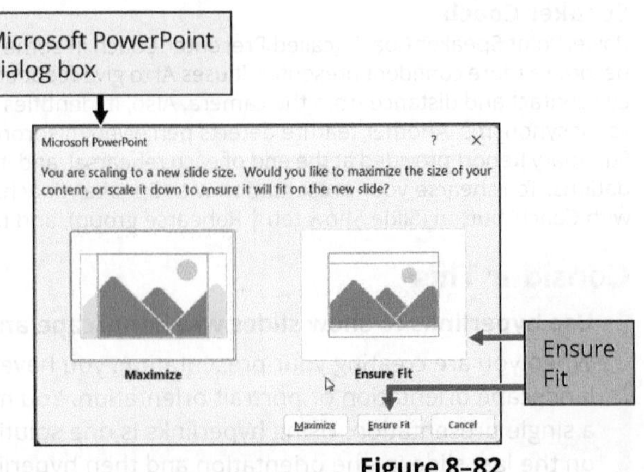

Figure 8–82

To Change the Slide Show Resolution

Screen resolution affects the number of pixels that are displayed on your screen. When screen resolution is increased, more information is displayed, but it is decreased in size. Conversely, when screen resolution is decreased, less information is displayed, but that information is increased in size. You can change the resolution you want to use to display your presentation. This feature is valuable when your computer is connected to two different monitors, when you are delivering your presentation using a computer other than the one used to create the slides, or when the projector does not support the resolution you specified when you saved the presentation. Throughout this book, the screen resolution has been set to 1920 × 1080. The following steps change the presentation resolution to 1360 × 768. **Why?** You may need to run your presentation on a monitor that has a different resolution.

- Display the Slide Show tab and then click the 'Set Up Slide Show' button (Slide Show tab | Set Up group) to display the 'Set Up Show' dialog box.

2

- If necessary, click the 'Slide show monitor' arrow in the Multiple monitors section and then choose Primary Monitor.
- Click the Resolution arrow in the Multiple monitors section to display the Resolution list (Figure 8–83).

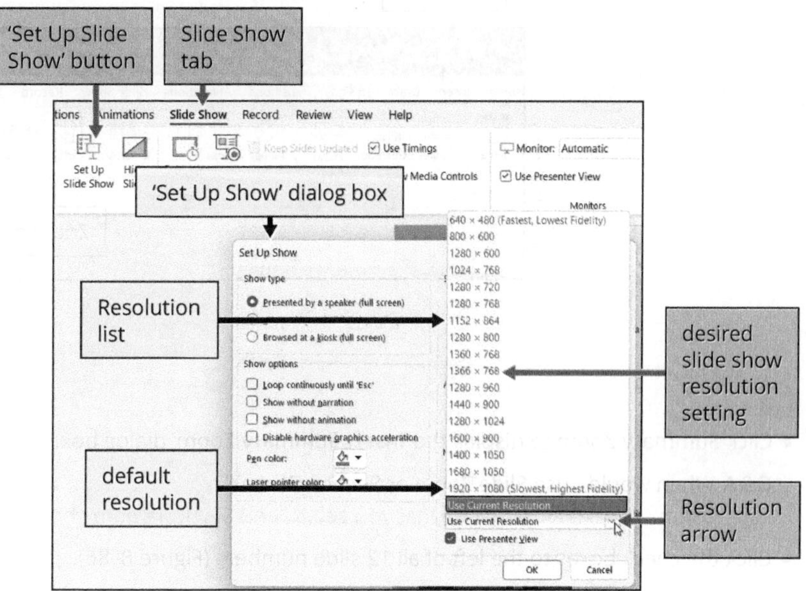

Figure 8–83

- Click 1360 × 768 (or a similar resolution) to change the slide show resolution setting.
- If necessary, click the 'Use Presenter View' check box to clear the check box (Figure 8–84).

Q&A What is Presenter view?

When you use Presenter view, you control the slide show using one screen only you can see, but your audience views the slides on another main screen.

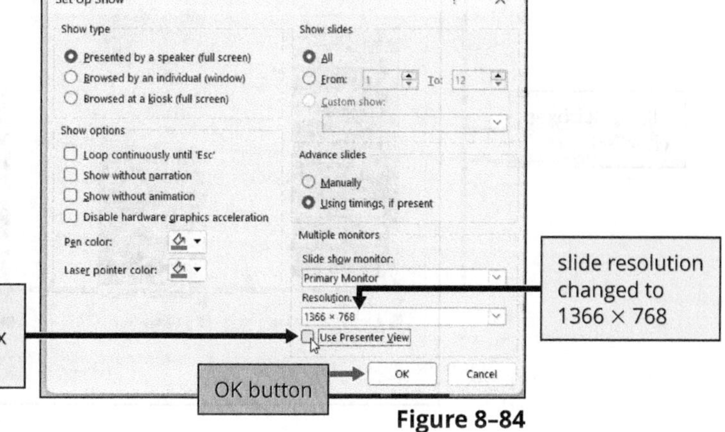

Figure 8–84

- Click OK to close the 'Set Up Show' dialog box and apply the new resolution to the slides.
- Save the presentation using **SC_PPT_8_Study_Abroad_Portrait** as the file name.

To Insert a Summary Zoom Slide

Speakers often use their PowerPoint files in many venues for different types of audiences. They may, for example, need to condense the presentation and display only a few slides when time is short. Or, in another situation, the audience may be familiar with the topic and need to know only specific information located on slides near the end of the slide deck. When a Zoom is created in PowerPoint, a speaker can decide which slides, sections, and portions of a presentation to display in a nonlinear way depending upon the audience's needs. The following steps insert a summary zoom slide in the SC_PPT_8_Study_Abroad_Portrait file. **Why?** When this slide is displayed during the presentation, you will see thumbnails of all the slides on one slide and then interactively can decide which slide to display next in any order.

- Display the Insert tab and then click the Zoom button (Insert tab | Links group) to display the Zoom menu (Figure 8–85).

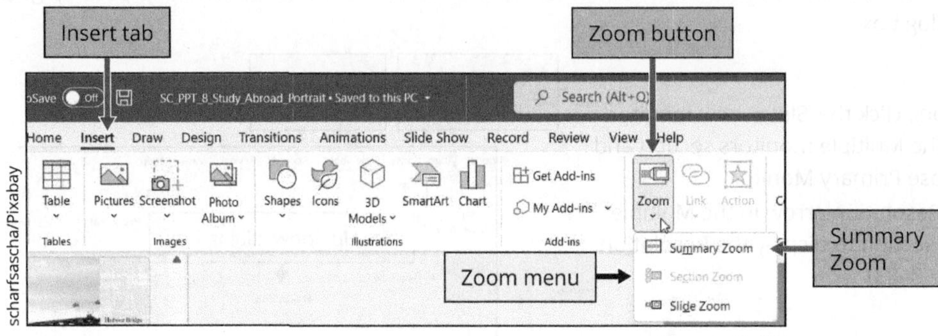

Figure 8–85

- Click Summary Zoom to display the 'Insert Summary Zoom' dialog box.

Q&A When would I use Slide Zoom or Section Zoom?
Slide Zoom shows specific slides that you select, and Section Zoom shows slides contained in a single section.

- Click the check boxes to the left of all 12 slide numbers (Figure 8–86).

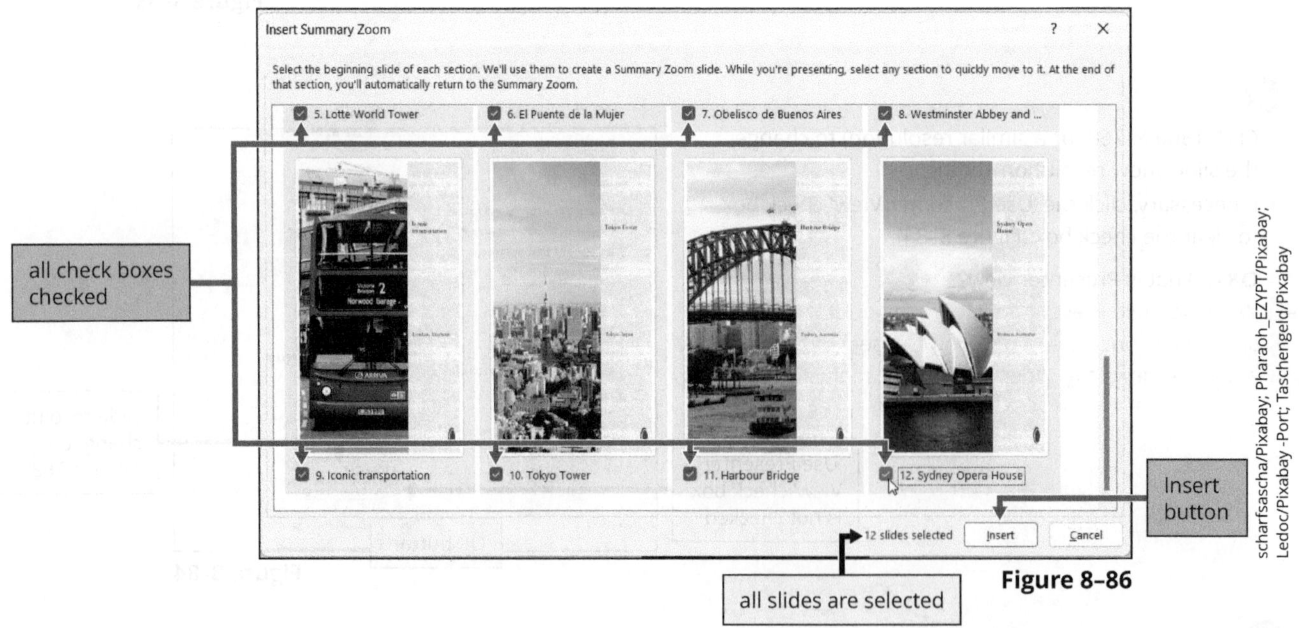

Figure 8–86

BTW
Updating Summary Zoom
If you make changes to your presentation after you have created the summary zoom, you can update the summary zoom by clicking the Edit Summary button (Zoom tab | Zoom Options), selecting the sections you want to include in your summary zoom, and then clicking the Update button.

- Click the Insert button ('Insert Summary Zoom' dialog box) to create the summary zoom slide and insert it as a new Slide 1 in the slide deck.
- Click the text box at the top of the summary zoom slide and then type **Study Abroad** as the slide title.
- Change the font to Times New Roman, increase the font size to 48 point, and then center the title (Figure 8–87).

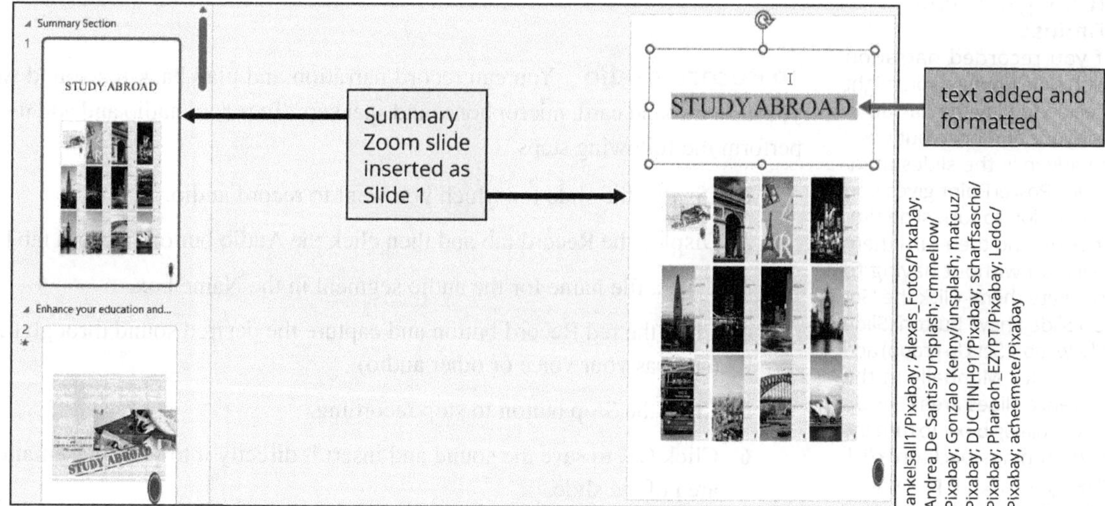

Figure 8–87

- Save the presentation again.

Consider This

Rehearse, rehearse, rehearse.

Speakers should spend as much time practicing their presentations as they do preparing their PowerPoint slides. Frequently, however, they use the majority of their preparation time designing and tweaking the slides. Audience members expect to see a presenter who is prepared, confident, and enthusiastic. Practicing the presentation helps convey this image. As you rehearse, focus on a strong introduction that grasps the audience's attention and previews the main points of your talk. You have only one chance to make a good first impression, so begin the speech by establishing eye contact with audience members in various parts of the room. Resist the urge to stare at the slides projected on the screen. Consider rehearsing using PowerPoint's Speaker Coach to help you deliver a high-quality talk that exceeds your audience's expectations.

To Create and Insert Screen Recordings You can create screen recordings in your PowerPoint presentations if you have a sound card, microphone, and speakers. To create and insert a screen recording in your presentation, you would perform the following steps.

1. Display the slide you would like to record at the beginning of the presentation.
2. Display the Record tab and then click the Screen Recording button (Record tab | Record group).
3. Select an area of your screen to record and then click the Record button.
4. Capture the desired information, including voice narrations, slide timings, and pointer gestures.

5. When you have finished recording, click the Stop button and save the presentation.
6. The recording is directly inserted into your presentation in the desired area of the slide

Other Ways

1. Display Insert tab, click Screen Recording button (Insert tab | Media group), select area to record, click Record button, capture information, click Stop

BTW
Turning Off Slide Timings
If you recorded narration with slide timings, you might decide to play the narration for your audience but want to advance the slides manually. PowerPoint gives you the option to turn slide timings off and then turn them back on without having to recreate them. Click the 'Set Up Slide Show' button (Slide Show tab | Set Up group) and then click Manually in the Advance slides area ('Set Up Show' dialog box). To turn the slide timings back on, click 'Using timings, if present' in the Advance slides area ('Set Up Show' dialog box).

To Record Audio You can record narration and play back the sound within PowerPoint if you have a sound card, microphone, and speakers. To record audio and add it to a slide, you would perform the following steps.

1. Display the slide for which you want to record audio.
2. Display the Record tab and then click the Audio button (Record tab | Record group).
3. Type a file name for the audio segment in the Name box.
4. Click the red Record button and capture the desired sound through the microphone (such as your voice or other audio).
5. Click the Stop button to stop recording.
6. Click OK to save the sound and insert it directly into your presentation in the desired area of the slide.
7. Drag the audio icon to the desired location on the slide.

Other Ways

1. Display Insert tab, click Audio button (Insert tab | Media group), click Record Audio (Insert tab | Media group), type file name, click Record button, capture sound, click Stop

BTW
Using Reading View
Most people reviewing a PowerPoint presentation without a presenter will want to use Reading view. It displays the presentation in a full screen like Slide Show view, and it includes a few simple controls to make it easy to flip through the slides.

To Display All Slides in Presenter View Presenter view allows a speaker to use dual monitors: one that displays what the audience is seeing, and another with controls to aid the presenter. You can rehearse using Presenter view with one monitor so that you are comfortable using the features. You will not be able to edit the slides while using Presenter view. To use Presenter view, you would perform the following steps.

1. Display the Slide Show tab and then if necessary click the 'Use Presenter View' check box to place a check in the box (Slide Show tab | Monitors group).
2. Press ALT+F5.

BTW
Using Your Mouse as a Laser Pointer
When you are presenting, you can emphasize an important point in your slide by using your mouse as a laser pointer. In Slide Show view, click either the From Beginning or the 'From Current Slide' button (Slide Show tab | Start Slide Show group), press and hold CTRL, and then click and drag the left mouse button to point to specific slide contents. To change the laser pointer color, click the 'Set Up Slide Show' button (Slide Show tab | Set Up group) to display the 'Set Up Show' dialog box. Then, in the Show options area, click the 'Laser pointer color' button, select the desired color in the gallery, and then click OK.

To Zoom Using the Magnifying Glass in Presenter View While using Presenter view, you can magnify part of the slide on the screen. When you click the magnifying glass icon, a bright rectangle is displayed on the slide and the mouse pointer changes to a hand. To zoom using this magnifying glass, you would perform the following steps.

1. In Slide Show view, click the magnifying glass icon in the Control bar on the lower edge of Presenter view.
2. Position your mouse pointer over the area of the slide that you want to magnify and then click to zoom in on that location.
3. Press ESC or click the magnifying glass icon again to turn off the zoom effect.

To Run a Presentation with Slide Zoom Links

All changes are complete. You now can view the Study Abroad Portrait presentation with zoom links. The following steps run the slide show.

1. Display Slide 1 and then run the presentation.
2. Click the Eiffel Tower slide to display it and then click the slide to return to Slide 1.
3. Click the title slide and then click this slide to return to Slide 1.
4. Continue displaying the slides in the presentation using the summary zoom slide. When the last slide (Sydney Opera House) is displayed, press ESC to end the presentation.

BTW
Using a Laser Pointer on a Smartphone
You can use your smartphone as a laser pointer. Open the file in Presenter view on your mobile device and then emphasize content with the laser pointer. This feature requires that your smartphone has a gyroscope. If you do not have a Microsoft 365 subscription or your phone does not have a gyroscope, you still can use the laser pointer by pressing and holding on the slide area and moving your finger around the slide.

To Save the Presentation

With the presentation completed, you should save the file. The following steps save the Study Abroad Portrait file and then exit PowerPoint.

1. Save the presentation again in the same storage location with the same file name.
2. sam Because the project now is complete, you can exit PowerPoint.

Summary

In this module, you learned how to create a custom slide show by selecting specific slides and then reordering their sequence. You also saved a slide as a .jpg file and saved a presentation as a PowerPoint show. You created handouts by exporting the file to Word and customized handouts and notes pages. You checked the presentation for compatibility and accessibility and then protected it with a password. Next, you created a photo album, formatted a photo, and changed the album theme and slide borders. Finally, you modified the slide show orientation and resolution and inserted a summary zoom slide.

Consider This: Plan Ahead

What decisions will you need to make when creating your next presentation?

Use these guidelines as you complete the assignments in this module and create your own slide show decks outside of this class.

1. **Use secure passwords.** A password should be at least 8 characters and contain a combination of letters, numbers, and other characters. Using both uppercase and lowercase letters is advised. Do not use a password that someone could guess, such as your first or last name, spouse's or child's name, telephone number, birth date, street address, license plate number, or Social Security number. Once you develop this password, write it down in a secure place. Underneath your keyboard is not a secure place, nor is your middle desk drawer. You also can use a password manager program for added security.
2. **Use photographs with sharp focus and contrast.** The adage, "A picture is worth a thousand words," is relevant in a PowerPoint presentation. When your audience can see a visual representation of the concept you are describing during your talk, they are apt to understand and comprehend your message. Be certain your pictures are sharp and clear.
3. **Use hyperlinks to show slides with landscape and portrait orientations.** All slides in one presentation must display in either landscape or portrait orientation. If you want to have variety in your slide show or have pictures or graphics that display best in one orientation, consider using hyperlinks to mix the two orientations during your presentation.
4. **Rehearse, rehearse, rehearse.** Outstanding slides lose their value when the presenter is unprepared to speak. Always keep in mind that the visual aspects are meant to supplement a speaker's verbal message. Practice your presentation before different types of audiences to solicit feedback and use their comments to improve your speaking style. You also can use PowerPoint's Speaker Coach to obtain a critique and suggested recommendations.

Student Assignments

Apply Your Knowledge

Reinforce the skills and apply the concepts you learned in this module.

Creating a Custom Show and Notes

Note: To complete this assignment, you will be required to use the Data Files. Please contact your instructor for information about accessing the Data Files.

Instructions: Start PowerPoint. Open the presentation called SC_PPT_8-1.pptx, which is located in the Data Files.

Nature centers rely upon and value volunteers to help care for their valuable resources. These people give back to their communities by offering their time and skills while enjoying the mental and physical benefits of being outdoors. They can help in many ways, such as removing invasive species, planting and mulching trees, or leading a family-friendly seminar. Your local nature center's naturalists want to inform the community about the programs available for all ages. You have received a PowerPoint presentation with 10 slides, and you need to develop two custom shows and the notes shown in Figure 8–88.

Perform the following tasks:

1. Create a custom slide show with slides 1, 2, 4, 6, 7, and 8.
2. Type **Restore the forest** as the new custom show name.
3. Edit the custom show by moving the last slide (6. Prune a tree) up below the third slide (3. Restore the forest) and the second slide (2. Volunteers make a difference) down to the end of the custom show.
4. Create a second custom show with slides 1, 3, 5, 11, and 12.
5. Type **Share your knowledge** as the new custom show name (Figure 8–88a).
6. Edit the custom show by moving Slide 3 (3. Help our feathered friends) down to the end of the custom show.
7. Display the notes master. Change the font to Arial Black-Arial and do not display the date.
8. Display the notes page in Landscape orientation and then print the notes pages (Figure 8–88b).
9. Create a handout in Word with notes below the slides. Save the Word file using the file name, **SC_PPT_8_Volunteer_Word** (Figure 8–88c).
10. Save Slide 2 as a .jpg picture using the file name, **SC_PPT_8_Volunteer_Slide** (Figure 8–88d). If requested by your instructor, insert the day of the week you were born after the word, swim, in the title text placeholder on the last slide.
11. Insert a summary zoom slide with all 12 slides in the presentation. Type **Become a Volunteer** as the title text for the new slide and then center this text in the placeholder (Figure 8–88e).
12. Check the presentation accessibility and compatibility.
13. Run the presentation using the summary zoom slide to display various slides.
14. Run the presentation showing the two custom slide shows.
15. Save the presentation using the file name, **SC_PPT_8_Volunteer**.
16. Submit the presentation in the format specified by your instructor.
17. **Consider This:** Where would a presenter use the two custom shows? What were the Accessibility Checker's inspection results? Did the Compatibility Checker summary display any features not supported by earlier versions of PowerPoint? If so, what were they?

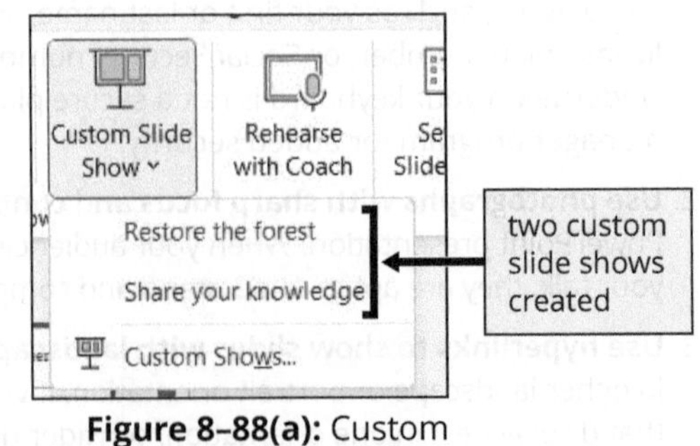

Figure 8–88(a): Custom Slide Shows

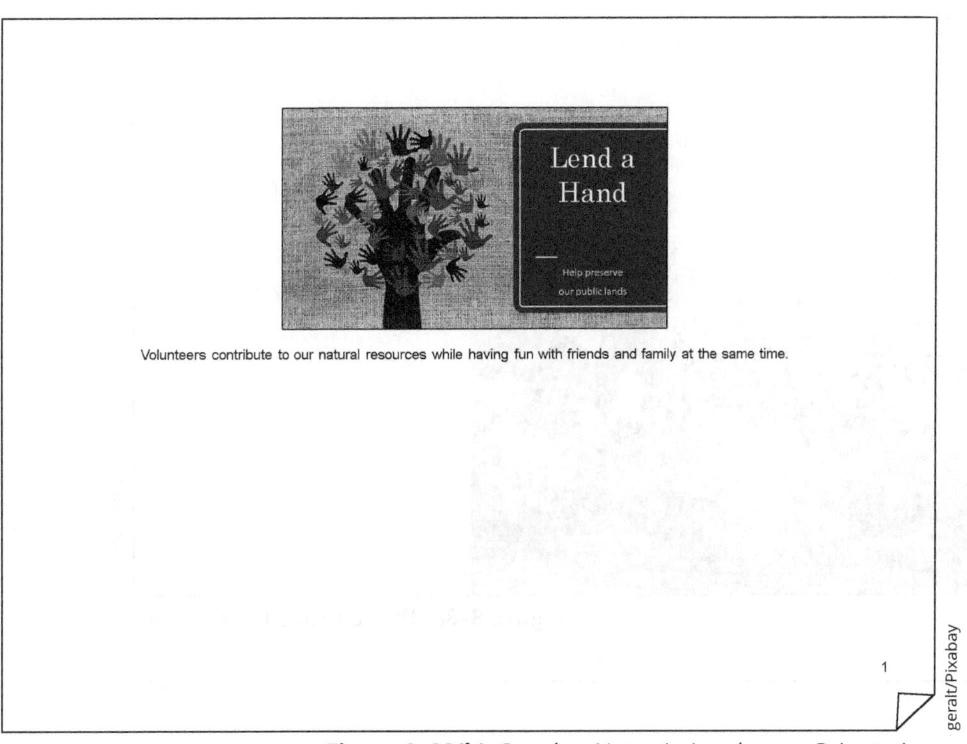

Figure 8–88(b): Speaker Notes in Landscape Orientation

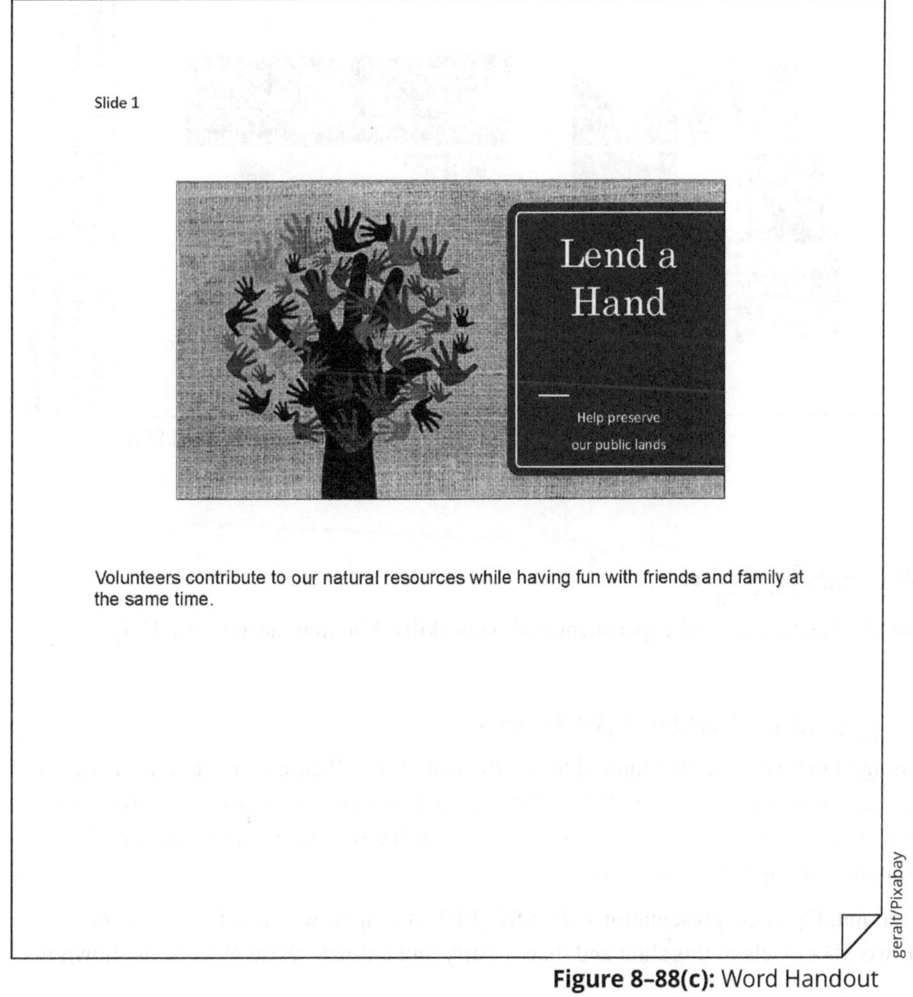

Figure 8–88(c): Word Handout

Continued on next page

Matheus Bertelli/Pexels

Figure 8–88(d): Slide Saved as a Picture

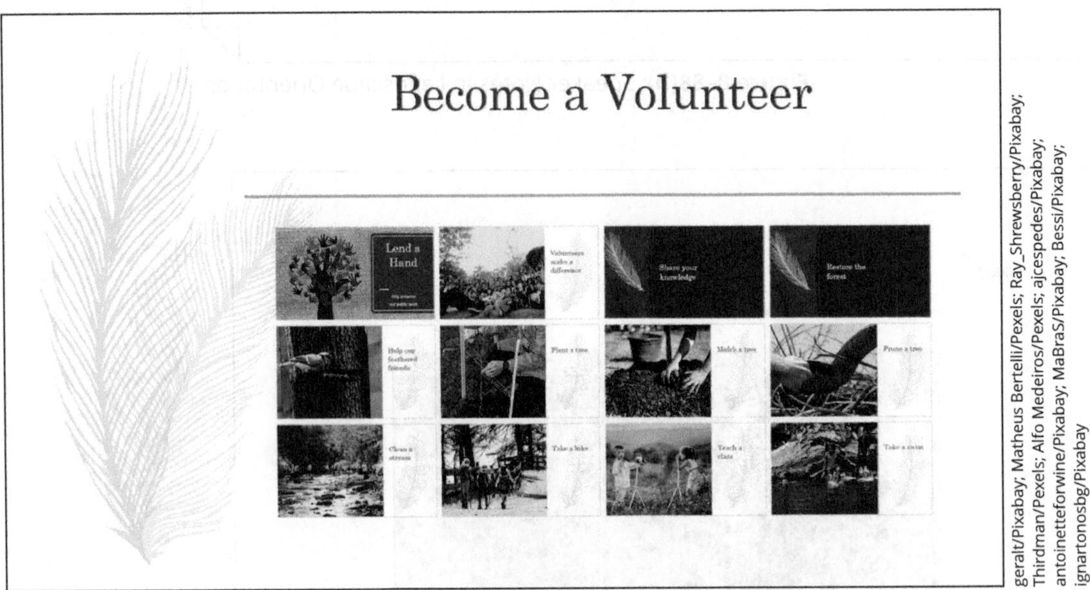

geralt/Pixabay; Matheus Bertelli/Pexels; Ray_Shrewsberry/Pixabay; Thirdman/Pexels; Alfo Medeiros/Pexels; ajcespedes/Pixabay; antoinetteforwine/Pixabay; MaBraS/Pixabay; Bessi/Pixabay; ignartonosbg/Pixabay

Figure 8–88(e): Summary Zoom Slide

Extend Your Knowledge

Extend the skills you learned in this module and experiment with new skills. You may need to use Help to complete the assignment.

Inserting, Modifying, and Animating 3D Models

Note: To complete this assignment, you will be required to use the Data Files. Please contact your instructor for information about accessing the Data Files. You will need Internet access and a Microsoft 365 subscription to obtain the 3D models and complete this assignment. If you do not have Internet access and a subscription, read this assignment without performing the instructions.

Instructions: Start PowerPoint. Open the presentation called SC_PPT_8-2.pptx, which is located in the Data Files. You will insert two 3D models in this slide and then modify and animate these objects, as shown in Figure 8–89.

Perform the following tasks:

1. Display the Insert tab and then click the 3D Models arrow (Insert tab | Illustrations group) to display the 3D Models menu. Click 'Stock 3D Models' to display a window with galleries of 3D models.
2. Click the Animated Animals gallery to view the models and then click the five fish (or similar fish) to place a check mark in that model.
3. Click the Insert button on the search results page to insert the selected fish model on the slide. Resize the fish height to approximately 7" and the width to approximately 11", and then align it on the right and in the middle of the slide.
4. With the fish selected, click the Right 3D model view (fifth model in the first row) to turn the fish and have them swim around the slide.
5. Display the Insert tab, click the 3D Models button, click the Animated Animals gallery, type **shark** after the words, Animated Animals, in the search box, and then press ENTER to display shark models. Click the shark that looks like the one in Figure 8-89 to place a check mark in that model and then click the Insert button.
6. Resize the shark's height to approximately 6". Click the 'Above Front Right' 3D model view (fifth view in the second row) and then position the shark in the upper-right corner of the slide.
7. With the shark selected, display the Animations tab and then click the Swing animation (Animations tab | Animation group). Click the Effect Options button (Animations tab | Animation group) and then click Subtle in the Intensity area and Continuous in the Amount area.
8. Click Preview (Animations tab | Preview group) to view the animations.

   If requested by your instructor, add the city in which you were born to the Notes pane.
9. Save the presentation using the file name, **SC_PPT_8_Fish_3D.**
10. Submit the revised document in the format specified by your instructor.
11. **Consider This:** In this assignment, you searched for and selected two 3D models. Were these models appropriate for this presentation? Which other models would be suitable? Does the animation add interest to the slide, or is the shark animation a distraction and should be eliminated? What are the advantages and disadvantages of adding 3D models to a slide?

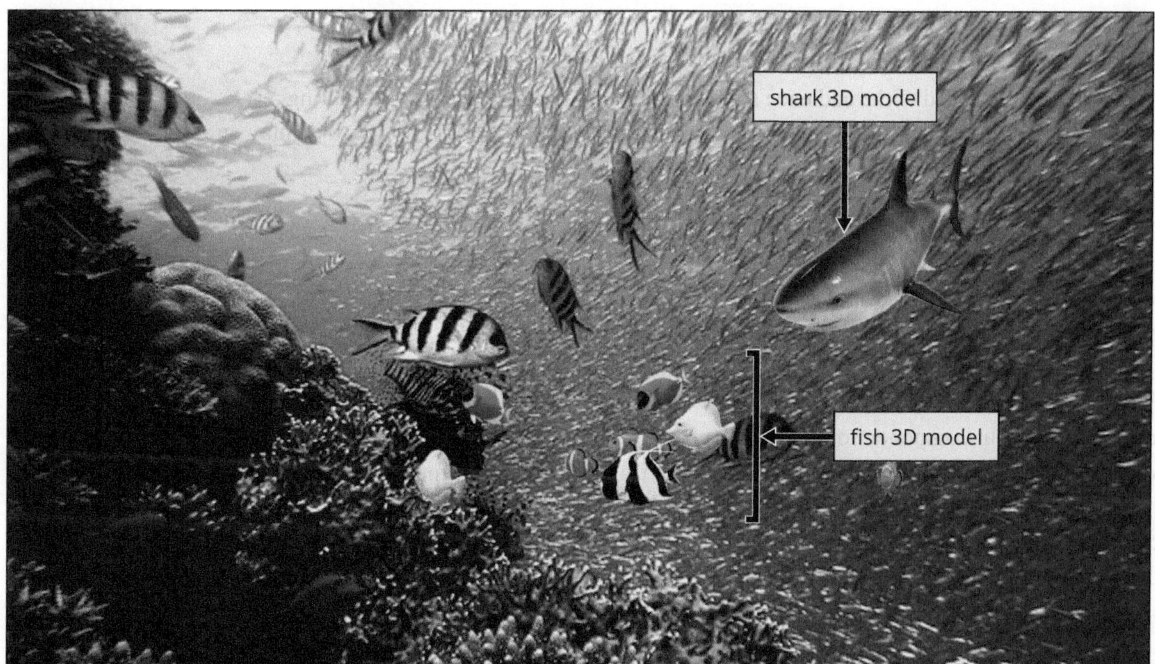

Figure 8–89

Expand Your World

Create a solution that uses cloud or web technologies by learning and investigating on your own from general guidance.

Linking to an Online Video

Note: You will need Internet access to complete this assignment. If you do not have Internet access, read this assignment without performing the actions specified in the instructions.

Instructions: You have created a presentation and want to play a video from an online website, such as YouTube, SlideShare, Vimeo, Stream, or Flip, as part of your slide show. Some websites encourage users to share video clips, while others restrict users from performing this process. The videos are not downloaded and inserted, or embedded, in the file; instead, they are linked to the presentation so that when the slide show is running and an Internet connection is present, the user can click the Play button to begin watching the video. PowerPoint includes instructions to insert a video clip from video providers.

Perform the following tasks:

1. Start PowerPoint and then open the SC_PPT_8_Study_Abroad presentation you created in this module. At the end of the presentation, insert one slide using the Title and Content layout and then type the title text, **Studying Abroad Advice** on Slide 13. Change the font to Times New Roman
2. Display the Insert tab and then click the Video button (Insert tab | Media group) to display the Video menu. Click Online Videos in the menu to display a dialog box with an Address bar where you can enter a Web address.
3. Locate a video in your web browser, copy the web address of the webpage from the browser's Address bar, switch back to PowerPoint, and then paste the web address of the online video in the Address bar.
4. Click the Insert button to display the selected clip on Slide 13. Increase the clip size and then align it in the center and the bottom of the slide. Add a border and an effect.

   If requested by your instructor, change the word, Napoleon, in the Notes pane on Slide 2 to your grandmother's or guardian's first name.
5. Run the presentation. If you see a yellow security warning at the top of the presentation, click Enable Content and then click Yes on the Security Warning dialog to make the file a trusted document and view the video.
6. Save the file with the new file name, **SC_PPT_8_Study_Abroad_Video.**
7. **Consider This:** Do videos add to the audience's ability to retain information presented during a presentation? Do they increase interest in the topic? Why did you select this specific video to display on Slide 13?

In the Lab

Apply your creative thinking and problem-solving skills to design and implement a solution.

Design and Create a Presentation about Nature Programs

Part 1: Public lands are a vital component of the overall ecosystem. They clean our air, purify our water, and provide food and habitat for wildlife. In addition, they help us reduce stress, stimulate the imagination, and promote a sense of community. The naturalists and programming teams at the nature center in your community are creating a new campaign directed toward residents of all ages, and they have asked you to create a PowerPoint photo album highlighting the variety of events offered.

Perform some research to learn about events and sessions at your local park district, woodlands, or forest. These programs could include disc golf, ziplining, guided hikes, and bird walks. Perhaps seminars are offered on the topics of seed collecting, invasive plant species, therapy walks, and owl prowls. Possible pictures to use for your slides are available in your Data Files folder. Use these files and other pictures to create a photo album. Format at least two pictures in the album by changing the contrast and brightness. Add a frame and a theme. Save the photo album file using the file name, **SC_PPT_8_Nature_Photo_Album**. Review and revise your presentation as needed and then save the file as a PowerPoint show using the file name, **SC_PPT_8_Nature_Show**. Submit your assignment in the format specified by your instructor.

Part 2: **Consider This:** You made several decisions while creating the presentation in this assignment: what content to include, how to format the album with a frame and theme, and which pictures to format. What was the rationale behind each of these decisions? Where would you recommend distributing this album? When you reviewed the document, what changes did you make?

Working with Trendlines, PivotTables, PivotCharts, and Slicers

Objectives

After completing this module, you will be able to:

- Analyze worksheet data using a trendline
- Create a PivotTable report
- Format a PivotTable report
- Apply filters to a PivotTable report
- Change the summary functions in a PivotTable
- Create a PivotChart report
- Format a PivotChart report
- Change the display of a PivotChart
- Drill down into a PivotTable
- Create calculated fields
- Create slicers to filter PivotTable and PivotChart reports
- Format slicers
- Examine other statistical and process charts
- Create a Box and Whisker Chart

Introduction

In both academic and business environments, people are presented with large amounts of data they need to analyze and interpret. Data is increasingly available from a wide variety of sources and can be gathered with ease. Analysis of data and interpretation of the results are important skills that can serve you in many disciplines Learning how to ask questions that identify patterns in data is a skill that enables you to make sense of large data sets and to make more informed decisions.

Project: City Museums

The City Museums is a civic organization consisting of three local museums, named Art, History, and Science. Each museum features three different types of exhibits and sells four different types of tickets to select age groups. The organization has been collecting visitor data for the past ten years, and the data reflects these exhibit and ticket types.

The advisory board in charge of the City Museums is interested in reviewing this visitor data. They also have requested a comparison of the last two years of ticket revenue figures for the museums. In this module, you will learn how to use the trendline charting feature in Excel to examine data for trends. You also will analyze revenue data for the City Museums using PivotTable and PivotChart reports. The results of this analysis are shown in Figure 8–1.

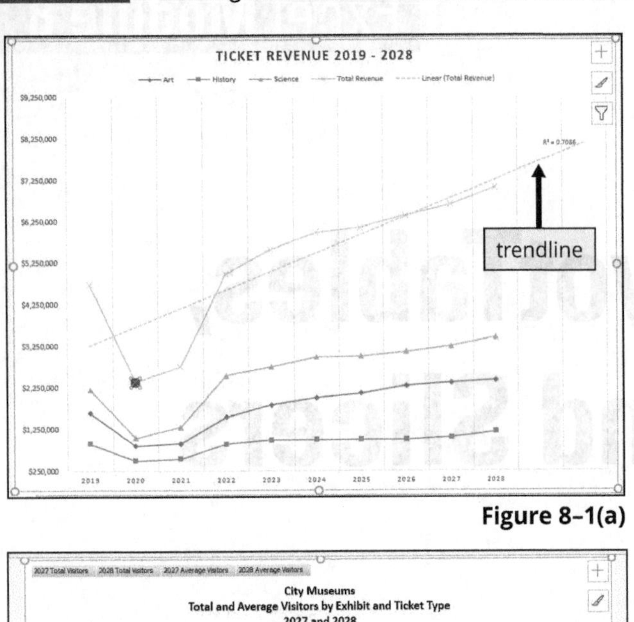

Figure 8–1(a)

PivotTable

	Ticket Type	Museum	2027 Total Visitors	2028 Total Visitors	20
2					
3					
4	Ticket Type	Museum	2027 Total Visitors	2028 Total Visitors	20
5	⊟Adult	Art	148,968	155,277	
6	Adult	History	61,839	71,032	
7	Adult	Science	246,665	254,434	
8	**Adult Total**		**457,472**	**480,743**	
9	⊟Child	Art	91,037	94,324	
10	Child	History	35,074	41,470	
11	Child	Science	131,422	141,638	
12	**Child Total**		**257,533**	**277,432**	
13	⊟Senior	Art	43,596	45,871	
14	Senior	History	32,140	34,584	
15	Senior	Science	45,766	56,221	
16	**Senior Total**		**121,502**	**136,676**	
17	⊟Student	Art	138,516	138,269	
18	Student	History	51,795	59,015	
19	Student	Science	199,791	217,455	
20	**Student Total**		**390,102**	**414,739**	
21	**Grand Total**		**1,226,609**	**1,309,590**	
22					

Figure 8–1(b)

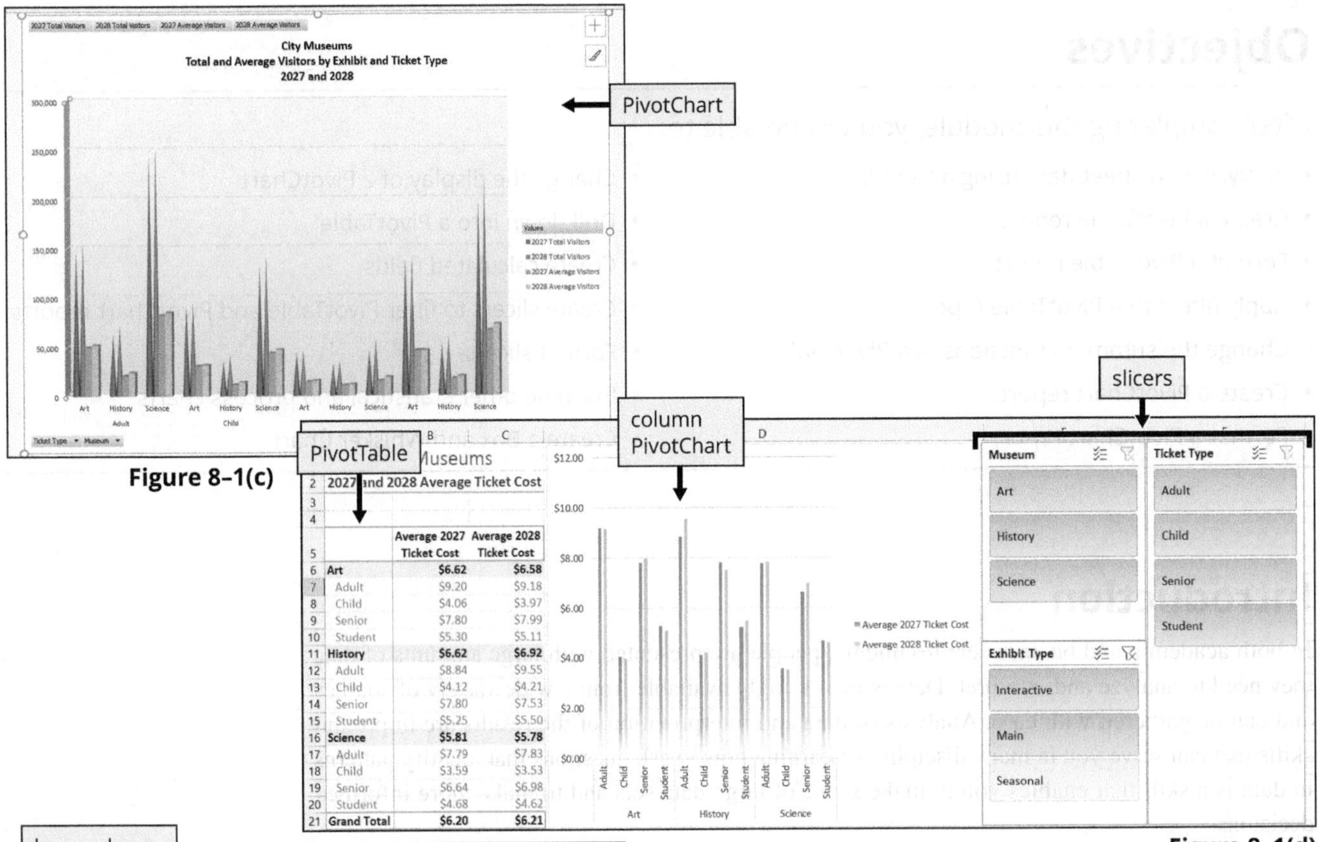

Figure 8–1(c)

	A	B	C
1	City Museums		
2	2027 and 2028 Average Ticket Cost		
3			
4			
5		Average 2027 Ticket Cost	Average 2028 Ticket Cost
6	**Art**	**$6.62**	**$6.58**
7	Adult	$9.20	$9.18
8	Child	$4.06	$3.97
9	Senior	$7.80	$7.99
10	Student	$5.30	$5.11
11	**History**	**$6.62**	**$6.92**
12	Adult	$8.84	$9.55
13	Child	$4.12	$4.21
14	Senior	$7.80	$7.53
15	Student	$5.25	$5.50
16	**Science**	**$5.81**	**$5.78**
17	Adult	$7.79	$7.83
18	Child	$3.59	$3.53
19	Senior	$6.64	$6.98
20	Student	$4.68	$4.62
21	**Grand Total**	**$6.20**	**$6.21**

Figure 8–1(d)

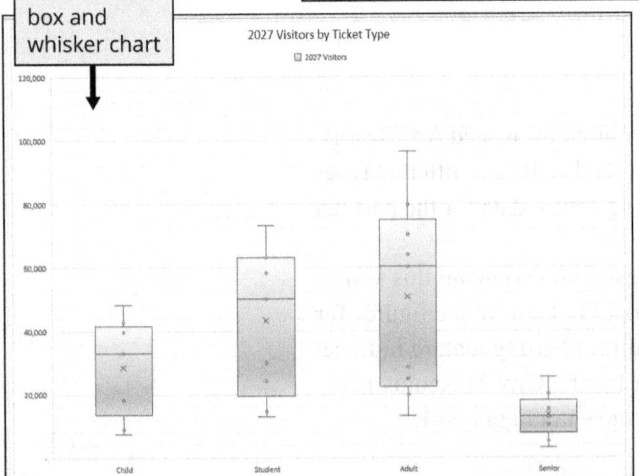

Figure 8–1(e)

A **trendline** (Figure 8–1a) is a line that represents the general direction in a series of data. Trendlines often are used to represent changes in one set of data over time. Excel can overlay a trendline on certain types of charts, allowing you to compare changes in one set of data with overall trends.

In addition to trendlines, PivotTable reports and PivotChart reports provide methods to manipulate and visualize data. A **PivotTable report** (Figure 8–1b) is a workbook table designed to create meaningful data summaries that analyze worksheets containing large amounts of data. As an interactive display of worksheet data, a PivotTable report lets users summarize data by selecting and grouping categories. When using a PivotTable report, you can change, or pivot, selected categories quickly without needing to manipulate the worksheet itself. You can examine and analyze several complex arrangements of the data and may spot relationships you might not otherwise. For example, you can learn the number of visitors at each museum, broken down by ticket type and then display the yearly ticket revenue for certain subgroupings without having to reorganize your worksheet.

A **PivotChart report** (Figure 8–1c) is an Excel feature that lets you summarize worksheet data in the form of a chart and rearrange parts of the chart structure to explore new data relationships. Also called simply a PivotChart, these reports are visual representations of PivotTables. For example, if the advisory board of the City Museums wanted to have a pie chart showing percentages of total visitors for each exhibit type, a PivotChart could show that percentage categorized by museum without having to rebuild the chart from scratch for each view. When you create a PivotChart report, Excel creates and associates a PivotTable with that PivotChart.

Slicers (Figure 8–1d) are graphic objects that you click to filter the data in PivotTables and PivotCharts. Each slicer button clearly identifies its purpose (the applied filter), making it easy to interpret the data displayed in the PivotTable report.

Figure 8–1e displays a box and whisker chart. You will create that chart later in this module as you learn about various kinds of statistical and process charts.

Using trendlines, PivotTables, PivotCharts, slicers, and other charts, a user with little knowledge of formulas, functions, and ranges can perform powerful what-if analyses on a set of data.

Figure 8–2 illustrates the requirements document for the City Museums ticket analysis. It includes the needs, source of data, calculations, and other facts about the worksheet's development.

Worksheet Title	City Museums Ticket Analysis
Needs	Evaluate different sets of data: 1. Total ticket revenue for 2019–2028. Provide a visual representation of ticket revenue over the past ten years and a forecast for the next two years based on the current trend. 2. Revenue data for 2027 and 2028 for all three museums, with details identifying the museum, ticket type, exhibit type, number of visitors, and ticket revenue. For this data, use PivotTables and PivotCharts to search for patterns and anomalies in the data, based on different arrangements of data to discover relationships. Some specific items of interest include Total Visitors and Average Ticket Cost per ticket and exhibit type. 3. Set up slicers to facilitate easy examination of various subgroupings for users with little or no Excel experience. 4. Create a box and whisker chart to search for the distribution of numerical data, including the highs and lows for 2027 visitors by ticket type.
Calculations	In addition to total revenue for the various groupings, calculations will include comparisons of average ticket cost for groupings. Create calculations of the average ticket cost for various combinations.
Source of Data	The advisory board will supply the data in the workbook SC_EX_8-1.xlsx.

Figure 8–2

To Start Excel and Open a Workbook

The following steps start Excel and open a workbook named SC_EX_8-1.xlsx. The workbook currently has two worksheets, one showing detailed ticket and revenue data, named Ticket Revenue Data, and one summarizing the data, named 10-Year Revenue.

To complete these steps, you will be required to use the Data Files. Please contact your instructor for information about accessing the Data Files.

1. **sam** Start Excel.
2. Open the file named SC_EX_8-1.xlsx from the Data Files.
3. If the Excel window is not maximized, click the Maximize button on its title bar to maximize the window. If necessary, change the magnification to 100%.
4. Save the file on your storage device with the name, **SC_EX_8_CityMuseums**.

BTW
Touch Mode Differences
The Office and Windows interfaces may vary if you are using Touch Mode. For this reason, you might notice that the function or appearance of your touch screen differs slightly from this module's presentation.

Line Charts and Trendlines

A **line chart** is a chart that displays data as lines across categories. A line chart illustrates the amount of change in data over a period of time, or it may compare multiple items. Some line charts contain data points that usually are plotted in evenly spaced intervals to emphasize the relationships between the points. A 2-D line chart has two axes but can contain multiple lines of data, such as two data series over the same period of time. A 3-D line chart may include a third axis, illustrated by depth, to represent the second data series or even a new category.

Using a trendline on certain Excel charts allows you to illustrate the behavior of a set of data to determine if there is a pattern. Trends most often are thought about in terms of how a value changes over time, but trends also can describe the relationship between two variables, such as height and weight. In Excel, you can add a trendline to most types of charts, such as unstacked 2-D area, bar, column, line, inventory, scatter (X, Y), and bubble charts, among others. Chart types that do not examine the relationship between two variables, such as pie and doughnut charts that examine the contribution of different parts to a whole, cannot include trendlines.

BTW
Ribbon and Screen Resolution
Excel may change how the groups and buttons within the groups appear on the ribbon, depending on the screen resolution of your computer. Thus, your ribbon may look different from the ones in this book if you are using a screen resolution other than 1920 × 1080.

Consider This

How do you determine which trends to analyze?

Before you add a trendline to a chart, you need to determine which data series to analyze. If the chart displays only one data series, Excel uses it automatically. If the chart involves more than one data series, you select the one you want to use as a trendline. Then you can analyze current or future trends.

To analyze a current trend, make sure you have enough data available for the period you want to analyze. For example, two years of annual sales totals might not provide enough data to analyze sales performance. Five years of annual sales totals or two years of monthly sales totals are more likely to present a trend.

To analyze a future trend, you use a trendline to project data beyond the values or scope of the data set in a process called forecasting. **Forecasting** is an analysis tool that helps predict data values that are outside of a data set. For example, if a data set is for a 10-year period and the data show a trend in that 10-year period, Excel can predict values beyond that period or estimate what the values may have been before that period.

When you add a trendline to a chart, you can set the number of periods to forecast forward or backward in time. For example, if you have six years of sales data, you can forecast two periods forward to show the trend for eight years: six years of current data and two years of projected data. You also can display information about the trendline on the chart itself to help guide your analysis. For example, you can display the equation used to calculate the trend and show the **R-squared value**, which is a number from 0 to 1 that measures the strength of the trend. An R-squared value of 1 means the estimated values in the trendline correspond exactly to the actual data.

To Create a 2-D Line Chart

Why? Line charts are suited to charting a variable, in this case, ticket sales over the past ten years. The following steps create a 2-D line chart of combined ticket sales for the City Museums. You will add a trendline to the chart later in the module.

- Click the '10-Year Revenue' sheet tab.
- Select cells A3:K7 to select the range to be charted (Figure 8–3).

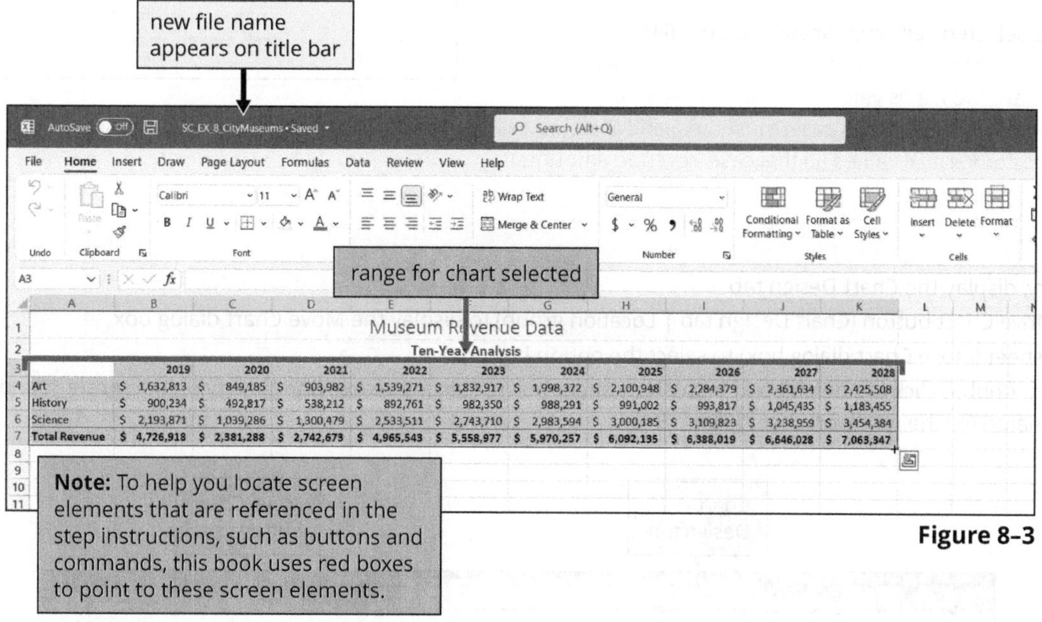

Figure 8–3

- Click Insert on the ribbon to display the Insert tab.
- Click the 'Insert Line or Area Chart' button (Insert tab | Charts group) to display the Insert Line and Area Chart gallery (Figure 8–4).

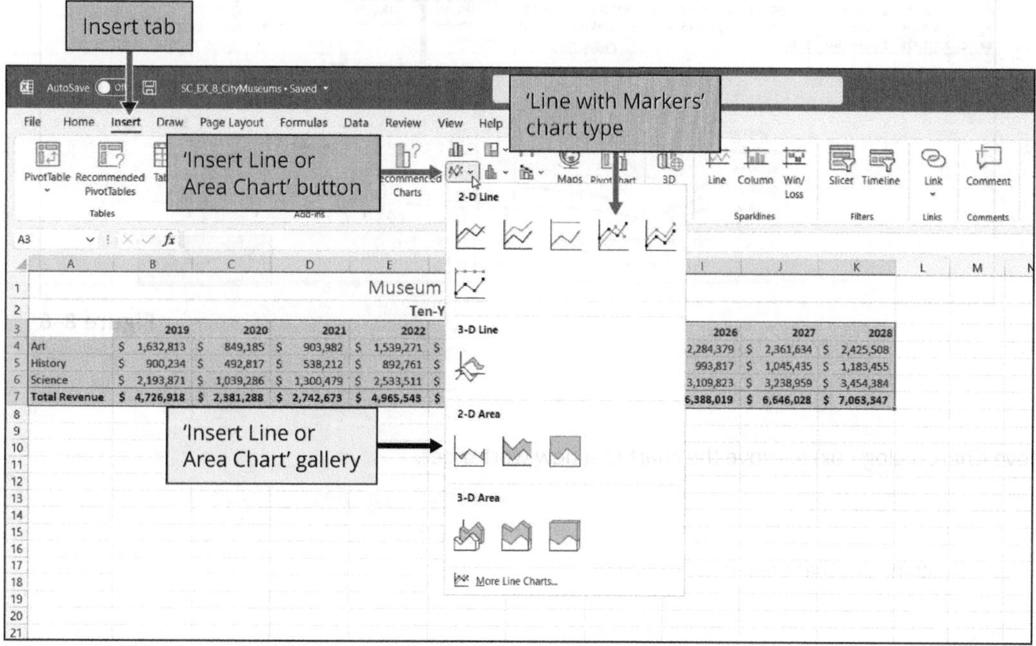

Figure 8–4

- Click 'Line with Markers' in the 2-D Line area to insert a 2-D line chart with data markers (Figure 8–5).

Q&A What are data markers?
A data marker is the symbol in a chart that represents a single value from a worksheet cell. In this case, the data markers are circles that represent each year of ticket revenue.

Why do the selected cells appear with colored fill?
Excel uses colors to identify chart elements. In this case, the purple cells are the x-axis values (in this case, years), the red cells are the categories (in this case, museums) and the blue cells are the y-axis or vertical values (in this case, revenue amounts).

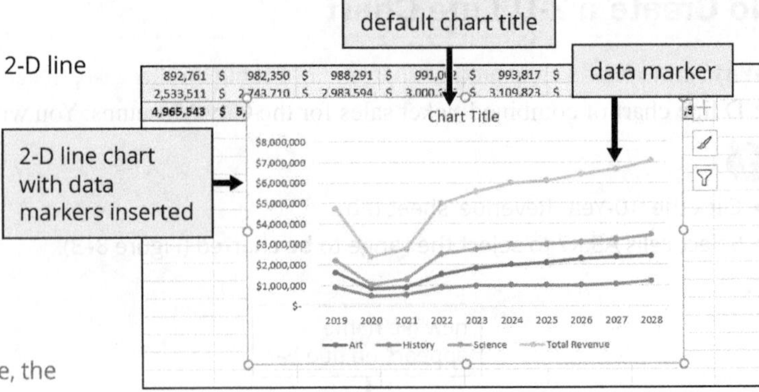

Figure 8–5

- If necessary, display the Chart Design tab.
- Click the Move Chart button (Chart Design tab | Location group) to display the Move Chart dialog box.
- Click New sheet (Move Chart dialog box) to select the option button.
- If necessary, double-click the default text in the New sheet box to select the text, and then type **Revenue Trendline Chart** to enter a name for the new worksheet (Figure 8–6).

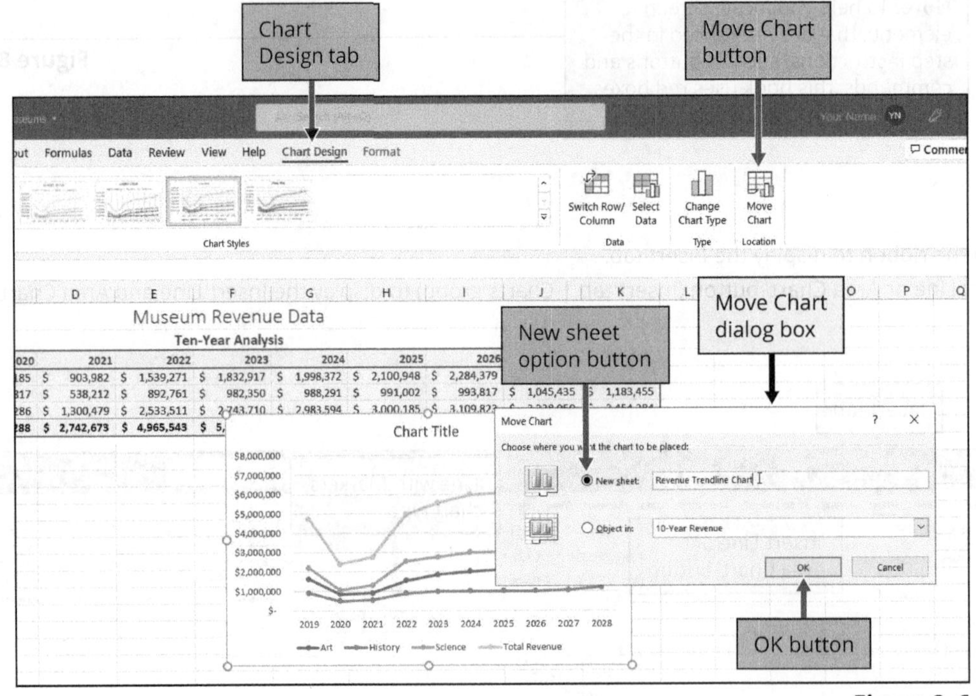

Figure 8–6

- Click OK (Move Chart dialog box) to move the chart to a new worksheet.

Other Ways

1. Click Quick Analysis button, click Charts tab, click Line button

To Format a 2-D Line Chart

You can format 2-D line charts by editing various chart elements, changing the style or color of the chart, or formatting the data series. In the following steps, you will edit the title, format the y-axis, and change the chart style. **Why?** Customizing the chart will make the data easier to read. You also will change the **bounds** of the chart axis, which are the beginning or ending values on an axis.

- Click the chart title.
- Edit the text by entering **Ticket Revenue 2019 – 2028** as the new chart title.
- Bold the text (Figure 8–7).

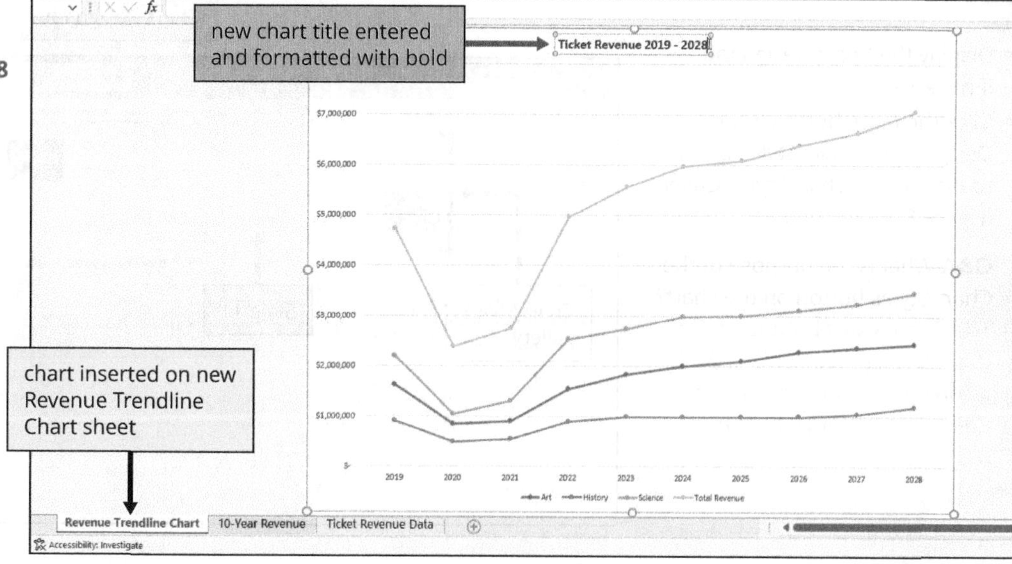

Figure 8–7

- Double-click the y-axis to display the Format Axis pane.
- If necessary, click the Axis Options tab and expand the Axis Options menu.
- In the Minimum box (Axis Options area), type **250000**, and then press ENTER to set a value for the y-axis (Figure 8–8).

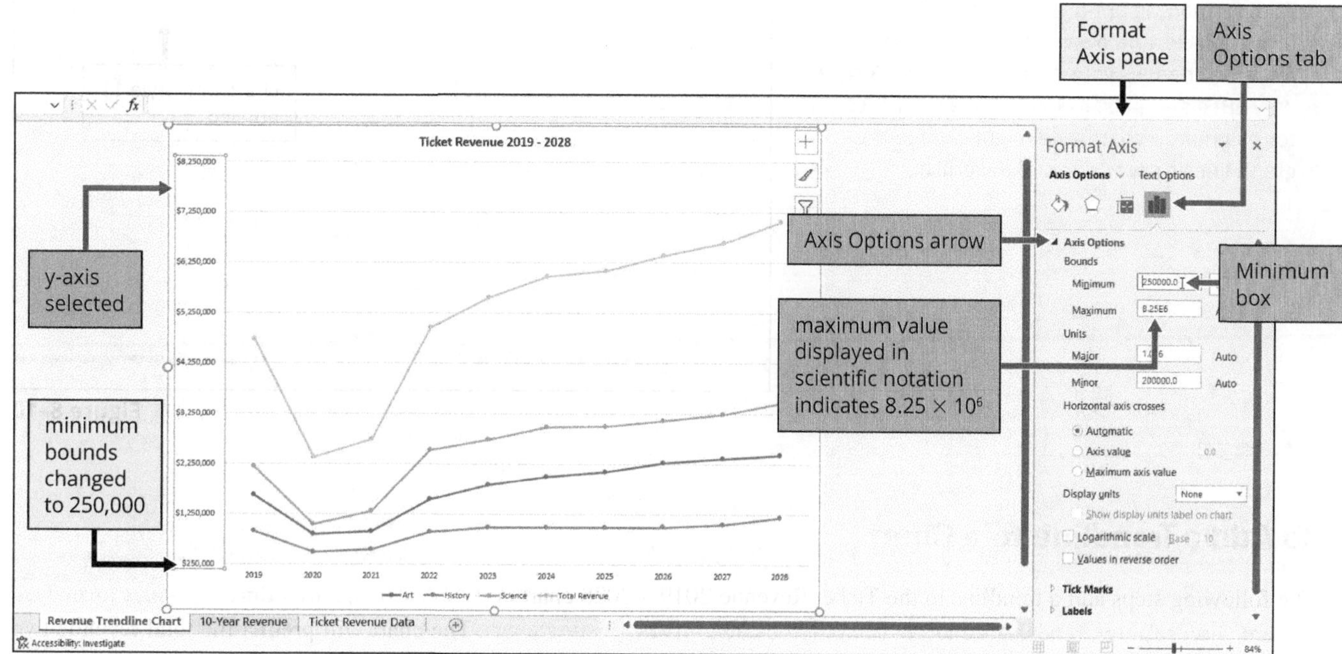

Figure 8–8

Q&A Why should I change the minimum value?
If you adjust the minimum value to a position slightly below the lowest data point, you will have less white space in your chart, making it more legible. Be aware, however, that trends represented in line charts may appear exaggerated when the lowest data point is not zero. Do not change the value if you are confident your data will change.

What is the purpose of the Reset button?
When you click the Reset button, Excel automatically adjusts the lower bounds to back to zero.

- Display the Chart Design tab if necessary.
- Click the More button (Chart Design tab | Chart Styles group) to display the Chart Styles Gallery (Figure 8–9).

Q&A What is the purpose of the Chart Styles button on the chart?
The Chart Styles button on the chart displays the same styles as on the ribbon, as well as a Color gallery from which you may choose.

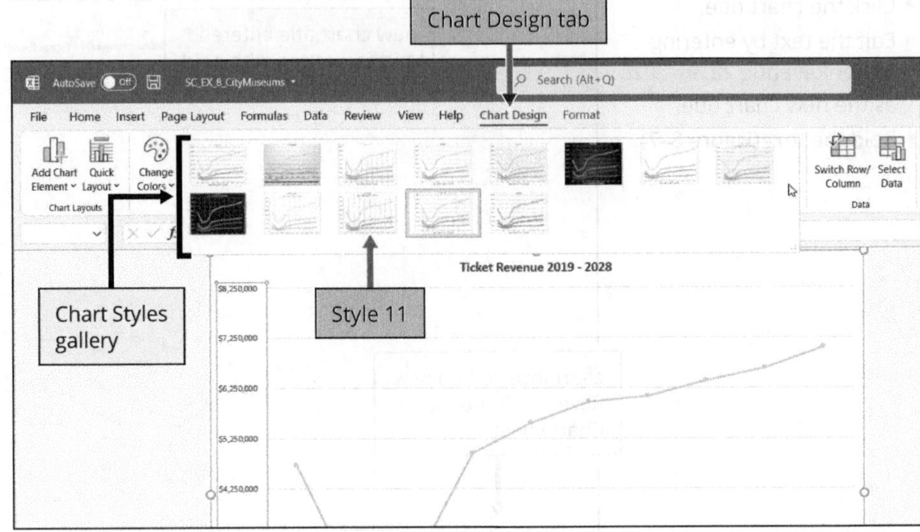

Figure 8–9

- Click Style 11 to choose a chart style (Figure 8–10).

Q&A What is the difference between a theme and a style?
Both formatting options change the color, fonts, effects, and overall appearance and feel. A theme changes your entire workbook. A style only affects a specific element in a worksheet; for example, a chart style might change the graph lines from horizontal to vertical.

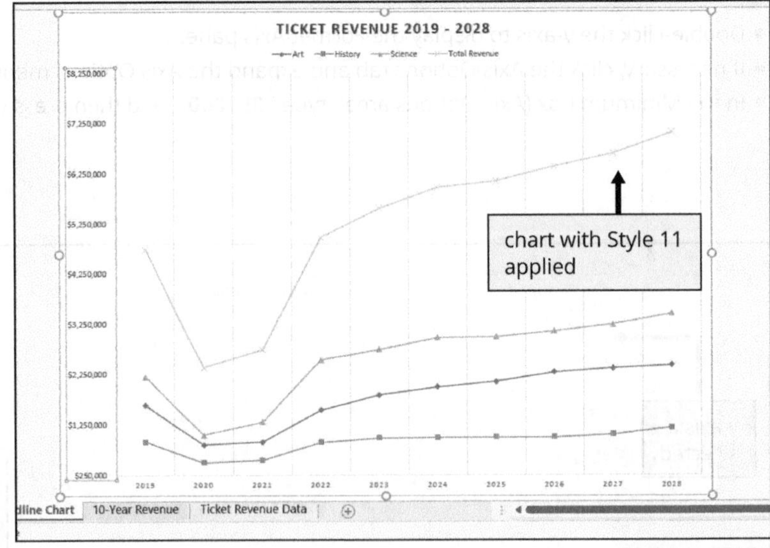

Figure 8–10

To Add a Trendline to a Chart

The following steps add a trendline to the Ticket Revenue 2019 – 2028 chart. **Why?** You add a trendline to a chart to analyze current and/or future trends. A trendline can only be added to an existing chart. The chart will predict the total revenue two years beyond the data set in the ten-year revenue worksheet.

1

- Click the 'Add Chart Element' button (Chart Design tab | Chart Layouts group) to display the Add Chart Element menu.
- Point to Trendline to display the Trendline gallery (Figure 8–11).

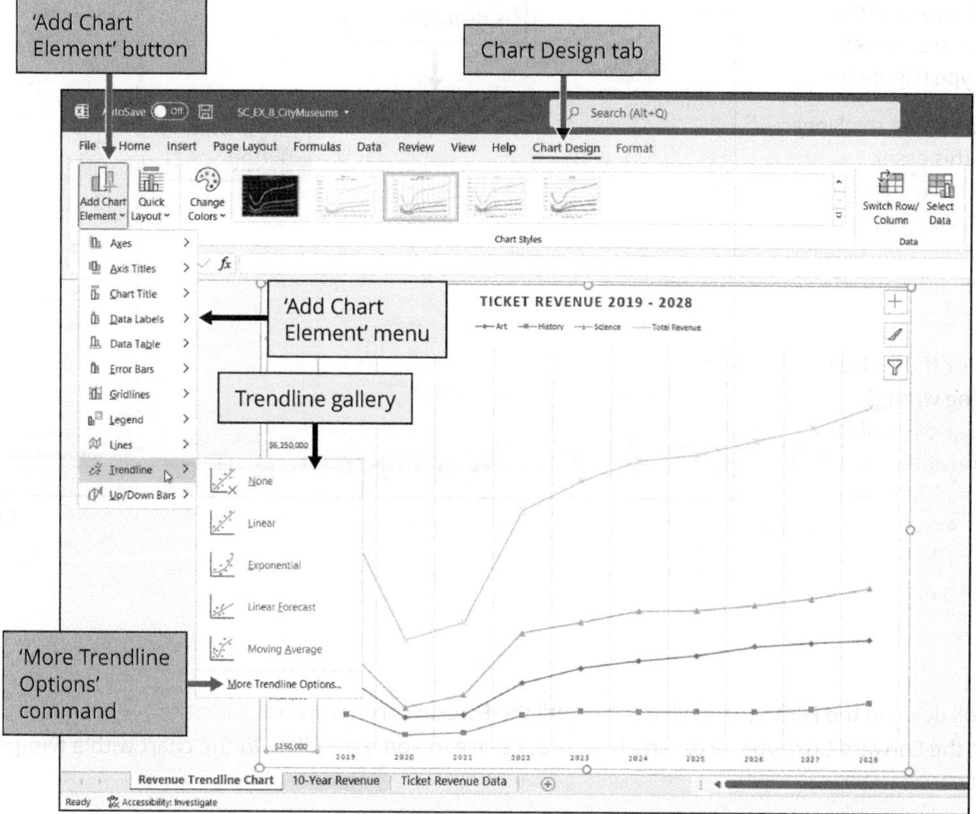

Figure 8–11

2

- Click 'More Trendline Options' (Trendline gallery) to display the Add Trendline dialog box.
- Click 'Total Revenue' in the Add Trendline box (Figure 8–12).
- Click OK.

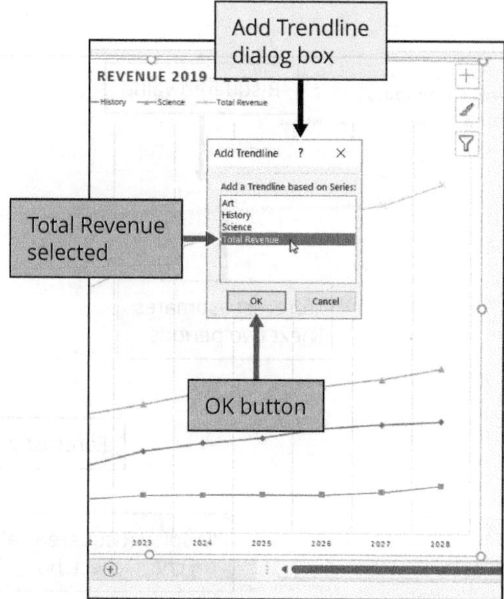

Figure 8–12

3

- If necessary, in the Format Trendline pane, click the Trendline Options button.
- If necessary, click Linear in the Trendline Options area to select a linear trendline type (Figure 8–13).

Q&A Why should I select the Linear option button in this case?
The 2-D line chart you created is a basic line chart, so it is appropriate to apply a linear trendline, which shows values that are increasing or decreasing at a steady rate.

My trendline runs off the chart. Did I do something wrong?
It may be that your chart did not adjust the bounds automatically. To resolve this, right-click the vertical axis, click Format Axis on the shortcut menu, and then click the upper bounds Reset button.

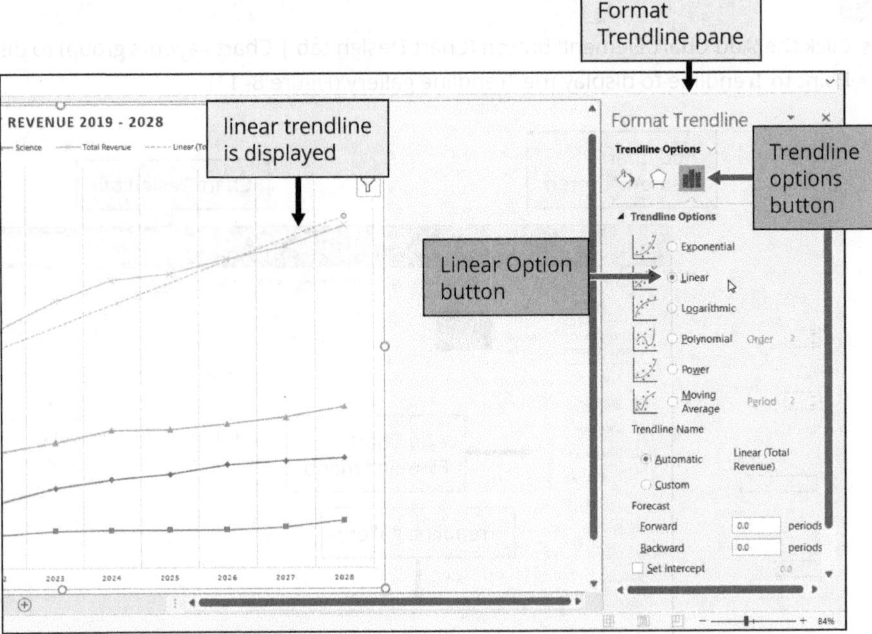

Figure 8–13

4

- If necessary, scroll down in the Format Trendline pane until the Forecast area is visible.
- Select the text in the Forward box, type **2.0**, and then press ENTER to add a trendline to the chart with a two-period forward forecast.

Q&A What does it mean to enter a two-period forward forecast?
A two-period forward forecast estimates the values for the two time periods that follow the data you used to create the line chart. In this case, it will estimate the total ticket sales for the next two years.

- Click the 'Display R-squared value on chart' check box to display the R-squared value on the chart (Figure 8–14).

Q&A What is the R-squared value?
The R-squared value is a measure of how well the trendline describes the relationship between total ticket revenue and time. The closer the value is to 1, the more accurate the trendline.

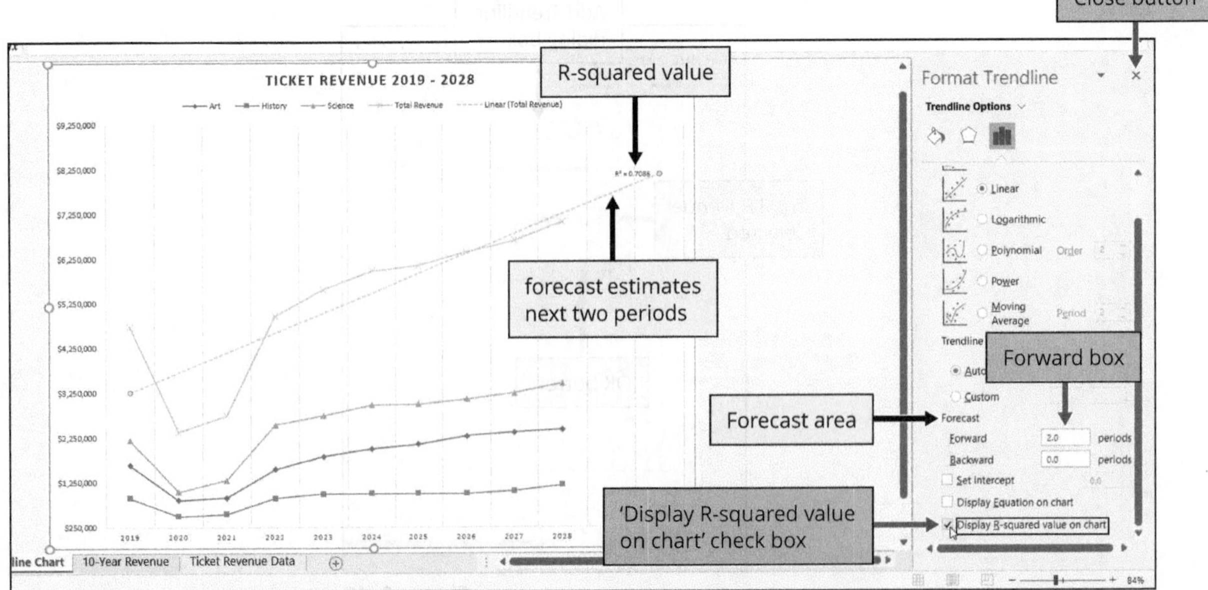

Figure 8–14

- Click the Close button (Format Trendline pane) to close the pane.

Other Ways

1. Right-click graphed line, click Add Trendline on shortcut menu

More about Trendlines

It is important to take note of the axes when displaying trendlines. Charts with trendlines are often reformatted to start the vertical axis at a number other than zero, particularly when the values on the vertical axis are high. When interpreting a trendline, you should refer to the vertical axis to know if it starts at zero. If it does not, be aware that trends represented by the trendline may appear exaggerated. Figure 8–15 shows a chart with a trendline that uses the same data as the chart in Figure 8–14. The difference between the two charts is in the vertical axis, which starts at zero in Figure 8–15 and at 250,000 in Figure 8–14. The difference between the values for the two projected periods is slightly larger in Figure 8–14 where the axis starts at 250,000. While not a major issue in this chart, this can prove problematic in displaying other charts. When reviewing charts, always check the axes to be sure that the differences shown in the chart are not being overstated visually.

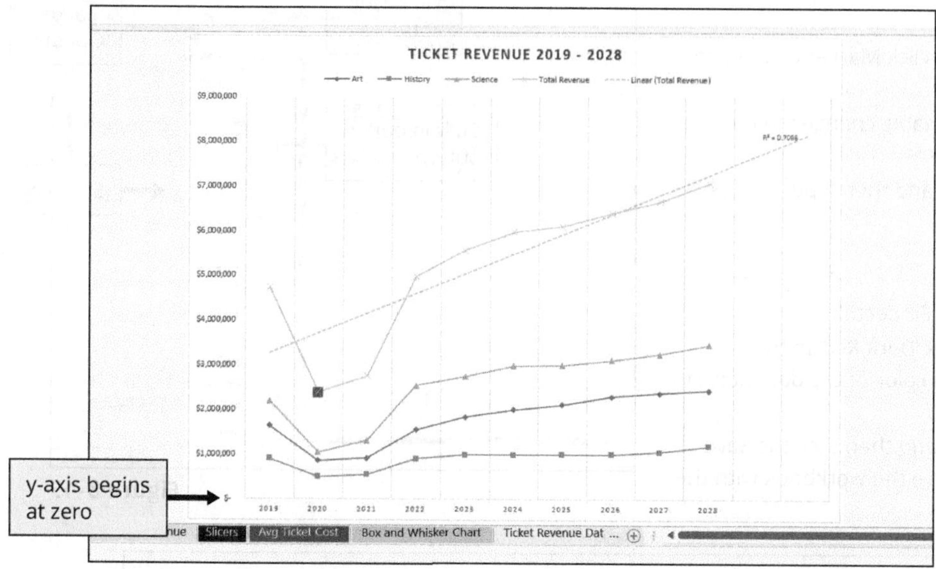

Figure 8–15

To Change the Format of a Data Point

The following steps change the format of the 2020 total revenue data point. **Why?** When graphing data, you may want to call visual attention to a particular data point or points.

- Slowly click the 2020 total revenue data point twice to select the single point. Do not double-click.
- Right-click the selected data point to display the shortcut menu (Figure 8–16).

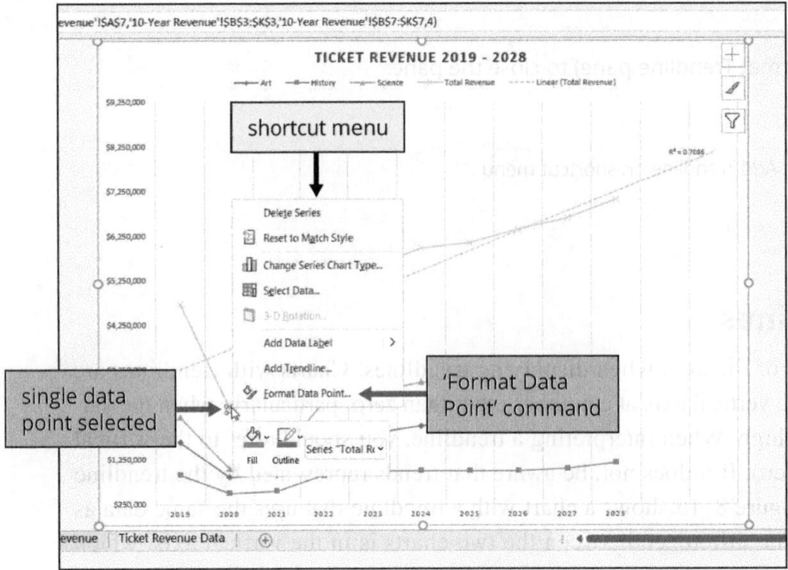

Figure 8–16

- Click 'Format Data Point' on the shortcut menu to display the Format Data Point pane.
- Click the 'Fill & Line' button (Format Data Point pane) to display the Fill & Line options.
- Click Marker, and then if necessary, click Marker Options to expand the section.
- Click the Built-in option button to enable changes to the data point.
- Select the contents of the Size box, and then type **10** as the new size (Figure 8–17).

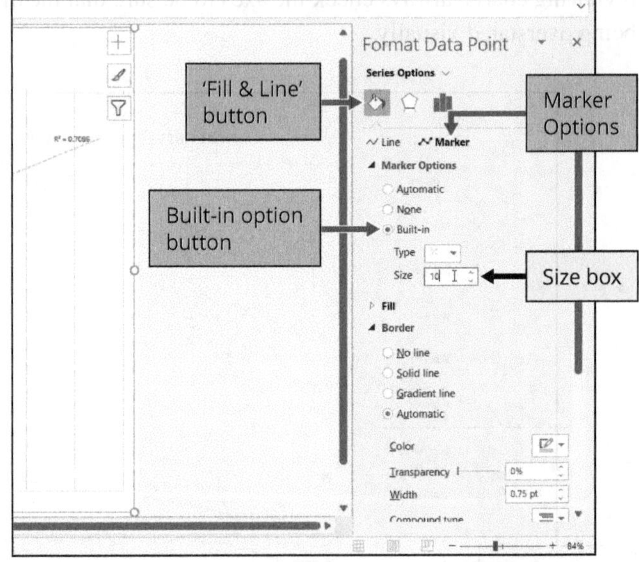

Figure 8–17

3

- If necessary, click Fill to expand the Fill section.
- Click the Color button and then click 'Dark Red' in the Standard Colors area to change the color of the data point to dark red (Figure 8–18).
- Close the Format Data Point pane, and then click the Save button (Quick Access Toolbar) to save the workbook with the same name in the same location.

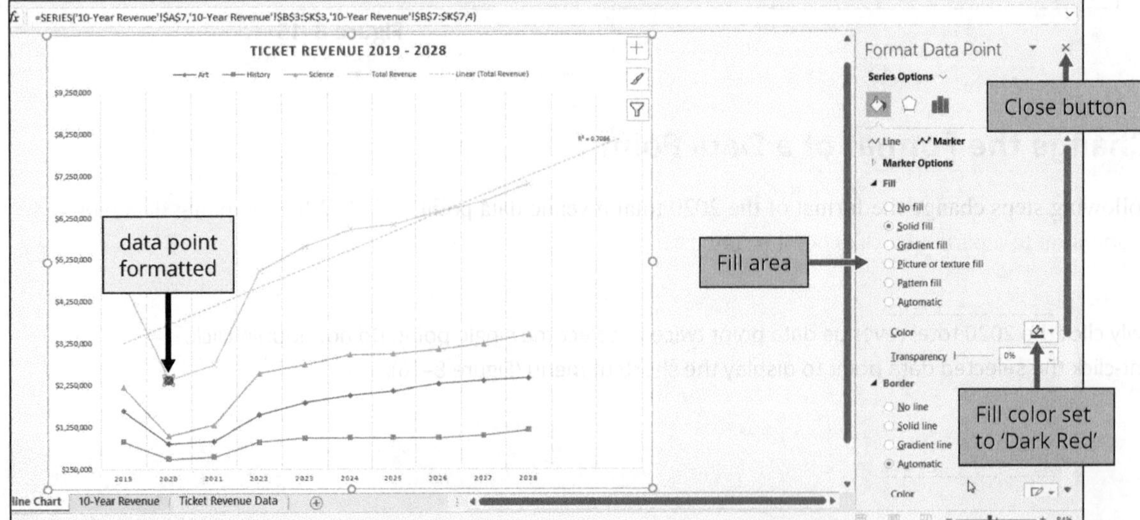

Figure 8–18

Break Point: If you want to take a break, this is a good place to do so. You can exit Excel now. To resume later, start Excel, open the file called SC_EX_8_CityMuseums.xlxs, and continue following the steps from this location forward.

Creating and Formatting PivotTable Reports

A PivotTable report, also called a PivotTable, is an interactive tool that summarizes worksheet data. It uses filter buttons in the cells and a pane to change the way the data is presented without changing any of the original data. Normally, when working with data tables or lists of data, each different reorganization of the data requires a new table or list. In contrast, you can reorganize data and examine summaries in a PivotTable report with a few clicks. PivotTable reports allow you to display different summaries of the data quickly and easily, using just a single table.

BTW
Selecting PivotTable Ranges
When creating PivotTables, you can click anywhere in the range that contains the data. You do not have to select the range.

When creating a PivotTable report, you can use categories in the data to summarize different groups or totals. PivotTables use two types of fields: data fields, which contain values that the PivotTable will summarize, and category fields, which describe the data by categorizing it. Category fields typically correspond to columns in the original data, and data fields correspond to summary values across categories. You can change row and column groupings quickly to summarize the data in different ways or to ask new questions. Reorganizing the table reveals different levels of detail and allows you to analyze specific subgroups.

One PivotTable created in this project is shown in Figure 8–19. It summarizes the City Museum data to show the total visitors and average visitors in 2027 and 2028 for each museum (Art, History, and Science) by ticket type (Adult, Child, Senior, and Student). The filter button in cell A4 filters the results by ticket type, and the filter button in cell B4 filters the results by museum. Columns C and D show the values for the total number of visitors in 2027 and 2028, and columns E and F show the values for the average number of visitors in 2027 and 2028.

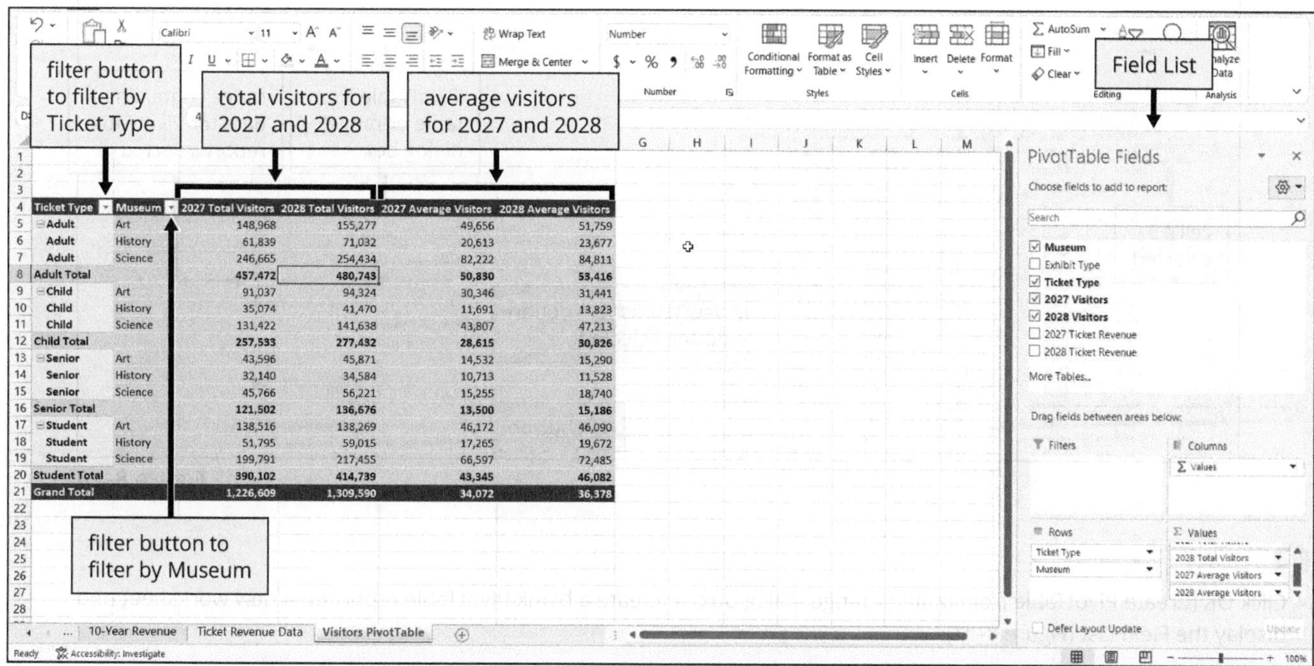

Ticket Type	Museum	2027 Total Visitors	2028 Total Visitors	2027 Average Visitors	2028 Average Visitors
Adult	Art	148,968	155,277	49,656	51,759
Adult	History	61,839	71,032	20,613	23,677
Adult	Science	246,665	254,434	82,222	84,811
Adult Total		457,472	480,743	50,830	53,416
Child	Art	91,037	94,324	30,346	31,441
Child	History	35,074	41,470	11,691	13,823
Child	Science	131,422	141,638	43,807	47,213
Child Total		257,533	277,432	28,615	30,826
Senior	Art	43,596	45,871	14,532	15,290
Senior	History	32,140	34,584	10,713	11,528
Senior	Science	45,766	56,221	15,255	18,740
Senior Total		121,502	136,676	13,500	15,186
Student	Art	138,516	138,269	46,172	46,090
Student	History	51,795	59,015	17,265	19,672
Student	Science	199,791	217,455	66,597	72,485
Student Total		390,102	414,739	43,345	46,082
Grand Total		1,226,609	1,309,590	34,072	36,378

Figure 8–19

Consider This

How do you determine which fields to use in a PivotTable?

You can create PivotTable and PivotChart reports in almost any configuration of your existing data. To use this powerful tool effectively, you need to create these reports with various questions in mind. Refer to the categories you can use to describe your data and think about how the various categories can interact. Common questions relate to how the data changes over time and how the data varies in geographical locations, such as states or regions, different functional groups within an organization, different product groupings, and demographic groupings, such as age.

To Create a Blank PivotTable

The following steps create a blank PivotTable report using the ribbon. **Why?** Creating a blank PivotTable allows you to create a framework within which to analyze the available data. When you create a PivotTable, each column heading from your original data will represent a field accessible via the Field List.

- Click the Ticket Revenue Data sheet tab to make the worksheet active.
- Click cell A3 to select a cell containing data for the PivotTable.
- Display the Insert tab.
- **Experiment:** Click the Recommended PivotTables button (Insert tab | Tables group). Scroll down the list to check out the various ways the data might be represented as a PivotTable. Click Cancel (Recommended PivotTables dialog box) to continue.
- Click the PivotTable button (Insert tab | Tables group) to display the 'PivotTable from table or range' dialog box (Figure 8–20).

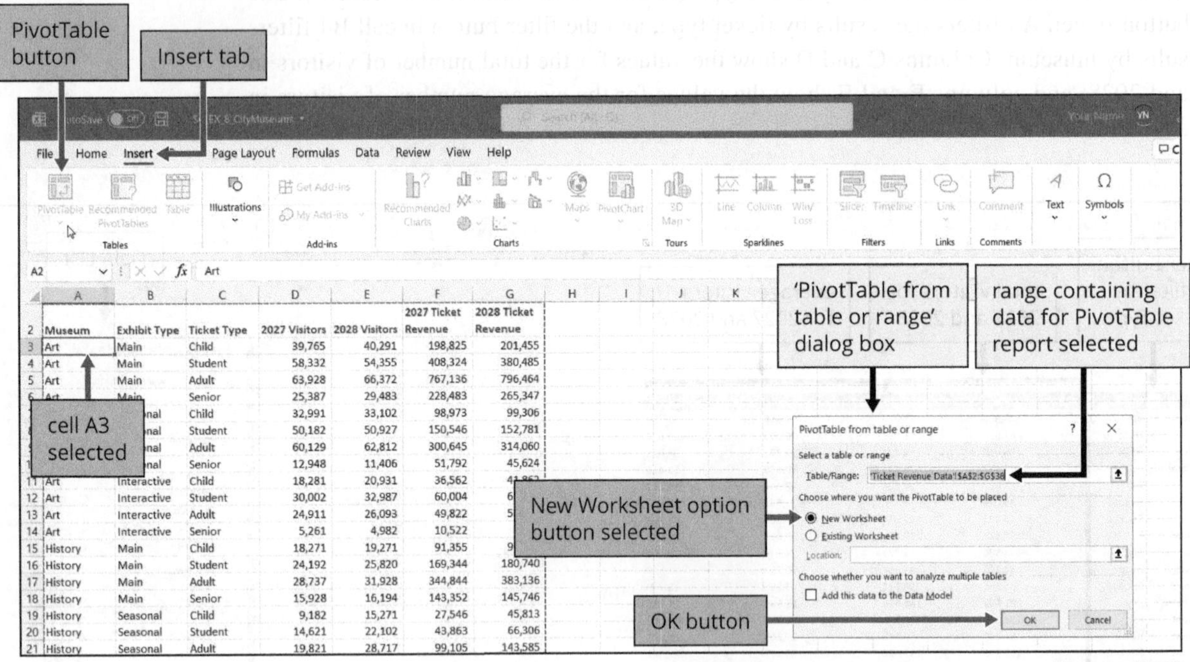

Figure 8–20

- Click OK (Create PivotTable from table or range dialog box) to create a blank PivotTable report on a new worksheet and display the Field List (Figure 8–21).

Q&A Why is the PivotTable blank?

When you create a PivotTable, you first create the structure. The resulting PivotTable is blank until you add fields to it, which you will do in the next set of steps.

My Field List just disappeared. What happened?

If you click outside of the PivotTable, the pane no longer will appear. To redisplay the pane, click in the PivotTable.

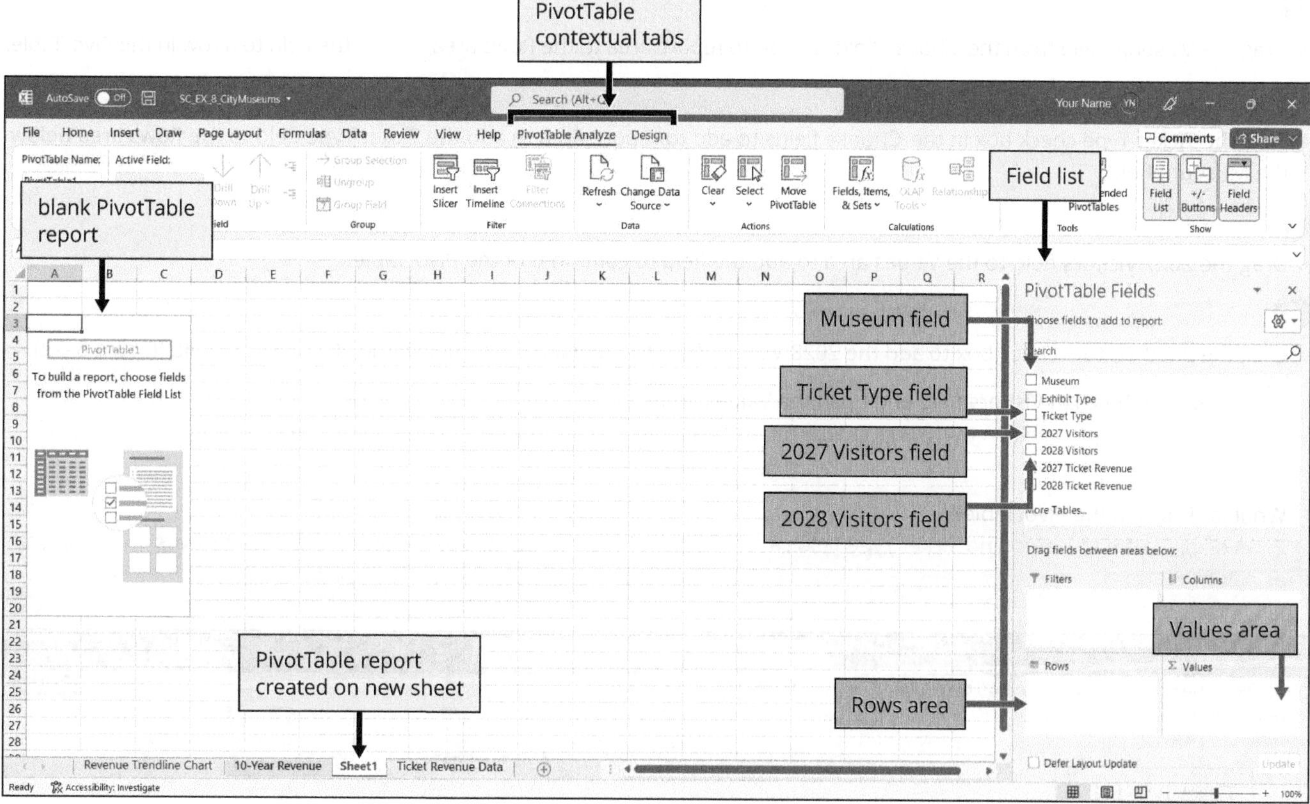

Figure 8–21

Other Ways

1. Click the cell in range, click Recommended PivotTables (Insert tab | Tables group), click Blank PivotTable button (Recommended PivotTables dialog box), click OK

To Add Data to the PivotTable

Why? Once the blank PivotTable is created, it needs to be populated using any or all of the fields in the Field List. You can add data by selecting check boxes in the Field List or by dragging fields from the Choose fields area to the one of the four boxed areas in the lower part of the pane. Once you add a field, it becomes a button in the pane, with its own button menu. Table 8–1 describes the four areas in the Field List and their common usage.

Table 8–1: Field Areas in the PivotTable Fields Pane

Areas	Use
Filters	Fields added to the Filters area create a report filter and filter button in the PivotTable, representing a subset that meets a selection criterion.
Columns	Normally, Excel creates a field in the Columns area when multiple fields are dragged to the Values area. Fields directly added to the Columns area should contain summary numeric data.
Rows	Fields added to the Rows area become rows in the PivotTable. Subsequent fields added to the Rows area become subsets of the first field.
Values	Fields added to the Values area must contain numeric data from the source data.

The following steps add data to the PivotTable. The rows will show the type of museum and, within that, the types of tickets purchased. As you add the 2027 Visitors and 2028 Visitors fields to the Values area, Excel will create columns.

1

- Drag the Museum field from the 'Choose fields to add to report' area to the Rows area, to add the field to a row in the PivotTable.

2

- Click the Ticket Type check box in the 'Choose fields to add to report' area to add the Ticket Type field to the Rows area below the Museum field.

3

- Drag the 2027 Visitors field to the Values area to add the field to column B of the PivotTable.

4

- Click the 2028 Visitors check box to add the 2028 Visitors field to the Values area below the 2027 Visitors field (Figure 8–22).

Q&A How did the 2028 Visitors field end up in the Values area?
Excel places a checked field in the group it determines is correct for that field. You can drag the field to a different group if you choose.

What is shown in the PivotTable?
Excel displays the Museum and Ticket Type fields as rows in the PivotTable. The 2027 Visitors and 2028 Visitors are displayed as columns.

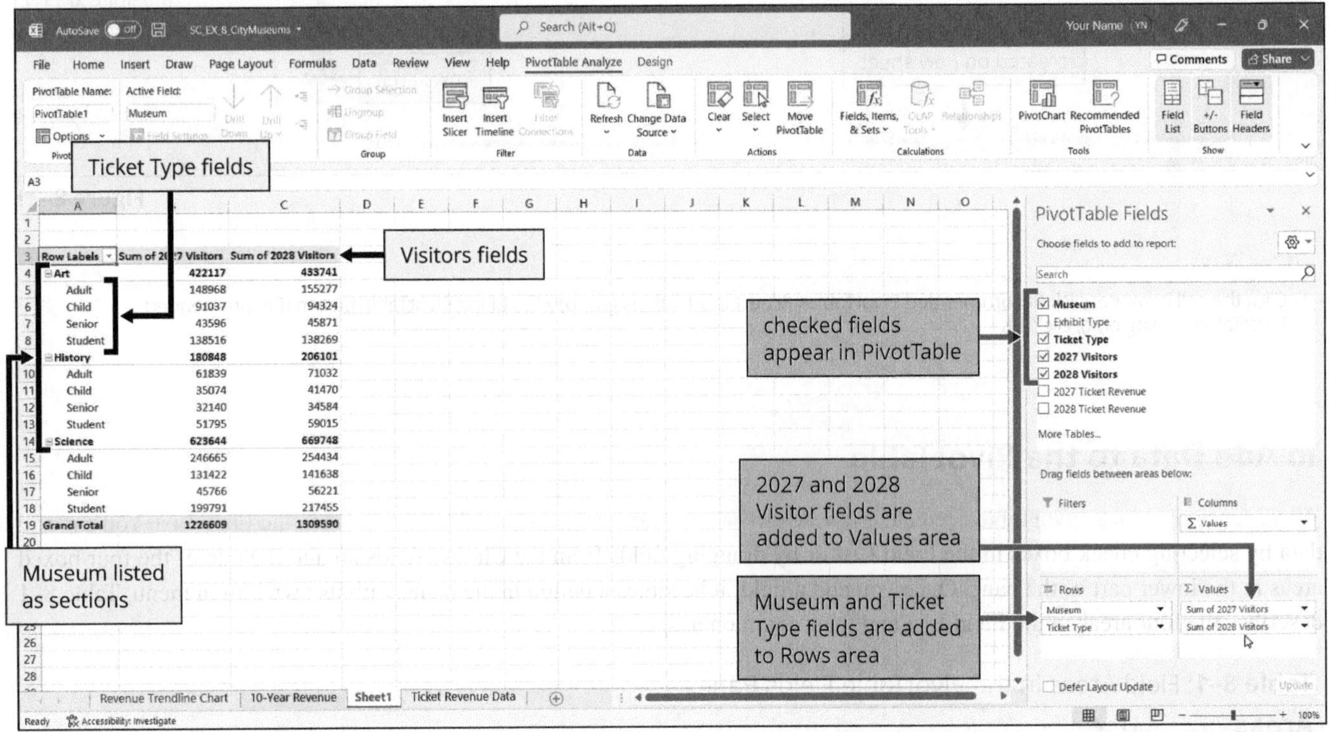

Figure 8–22

Other Ways

1. Click the check box for each field name (Field List)

To Change the Layout of a PivotTable

You can display a PivotTable in one of three layouts; however, sometimes you may want to change the layout. **Why?** When using multiple-row labels, a different layout can make identifying the groups and subgroups easier for the reader. By default, PivotTable reports are presented in a compact layout. The following steps change the layout of the PivotTable report to the tabular layout and then add item labels to all rows. The tabular layout will display totals below each museum type.

1

- If necessary, display the Design tab.
- Click the Report Layout button (Design tab | Layout group) to display the Report Layout menu (Figure 8–23).

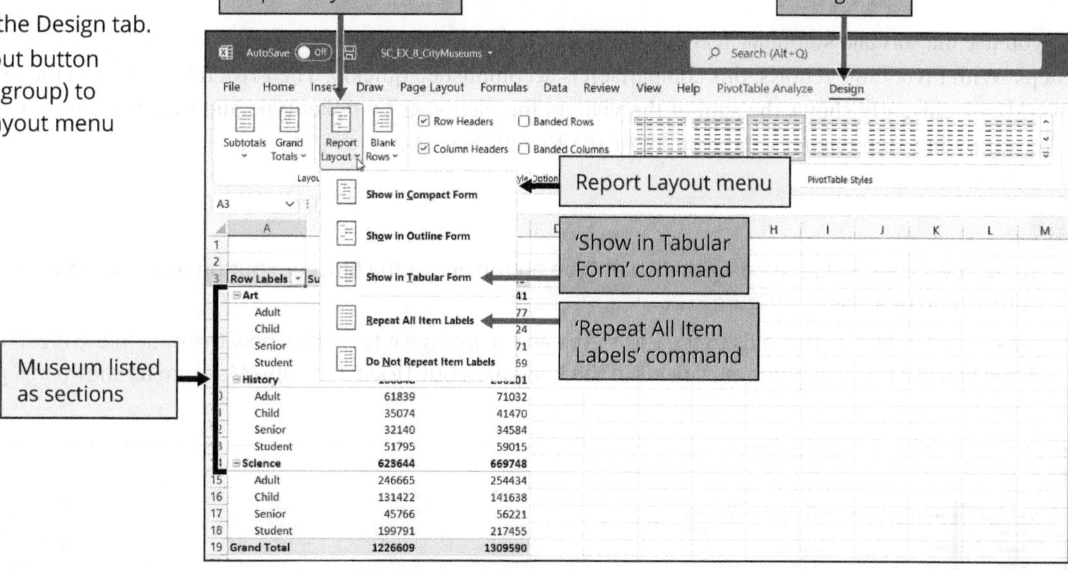

Figure 8–23

2

- Click 'Show in Tabular Form' to display the PivotTable report in a tabular format (Figure 8–24).
- **Experiment:** Click all the layout options to review the differences in the layout. When done, click 'Show in Tabular Form' once again.

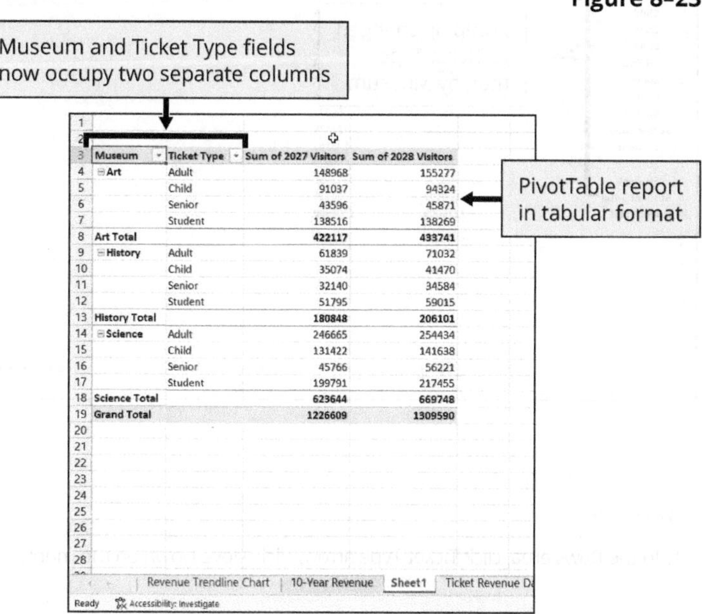

Figure 8–24

3

- Click the Report Layout button (Design tab | Layout group) again, and then click 'Repeat All Item Labels' to display Museum labels for all Ticket Type entries (Figure 8–25).
- **Experiment:** Point to any cell in column C or D to reveal the ScreenTip that displays information about the value.

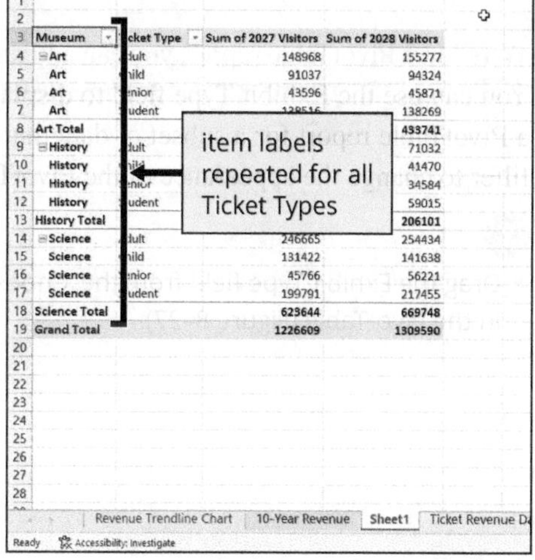

Figure 8–25

To Change the Display of a PivotTable Report

If you use the sort and summary features in Excel, comparing the revenue for each service type and region would require many steps. With PivotTable reports, this comparison is accomplished quickly. The PivotTable report in the SC_EX_8_CityMuseums workbook currently shows the sum of the visitors for each year by ticket type and then by museum. (Refer to Figure 8–25.) The following step changes the display of the PivotTable. **Why?** You decide to show the visitors by ticket type for each museum.

- In the Rows area (Field List), drag the Ticket Type button above the Museum button to group total sales by Ticket Type (rather than by Museum) (Figure 8–26).
- **Experiment:** Drag other fields to the Rows area and rearrange it to display how the data in the PivotTable changes. When you are finished, remove all fields in the Rows area but Ticket Type and Museum as shown in Figure 8–26.

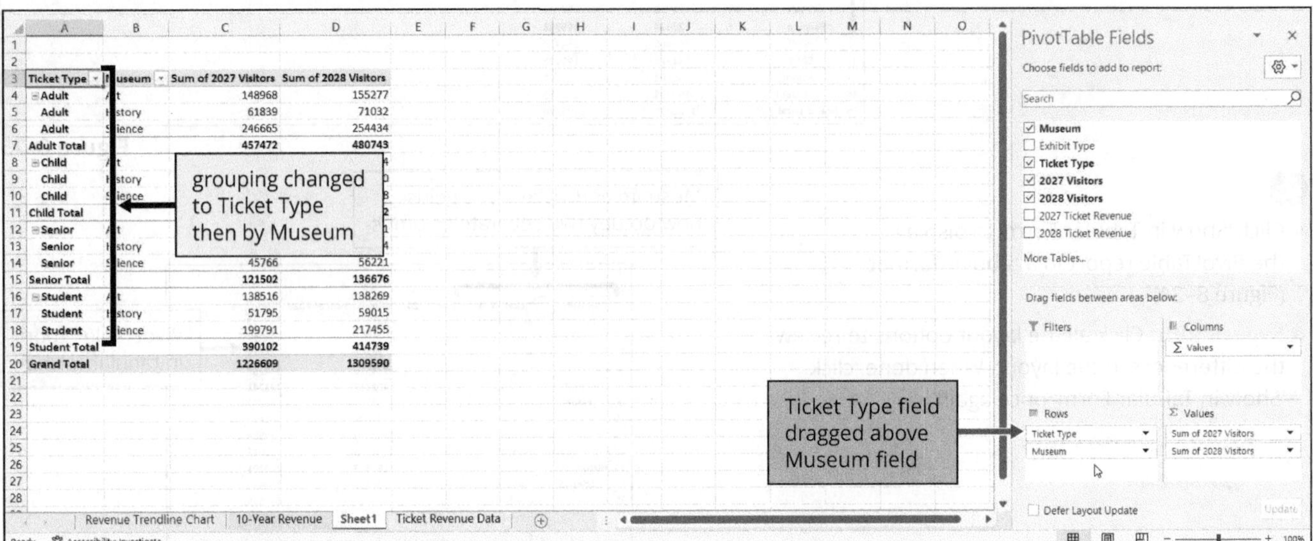

Figure 8–26

Other Ways

1. In the Rows area, click Ticket Type arrow, click Move Down on the menu

To Filter a PivotTable Report Using a Report Filter

Why? In a PivotTable report, you can add detail by further categorizing the data to focus on a particular subgroup or subgroups. You can use the Exhibit Type field to display the number of visitors with a specific ticket type to a specific museum. Viewing a PivotTable report for a subset of data that meets a selection criterion is known as filtering. The following steps add a report filter to change the appearance of the PivotTable and then filter the PivotTable by Exhibit Type.

- Drag the Exhibit Type field from the 'Choose fields to add to report' area (Field List) to the Filters area to create a report filter in the PivotTable (Figure 8–27).

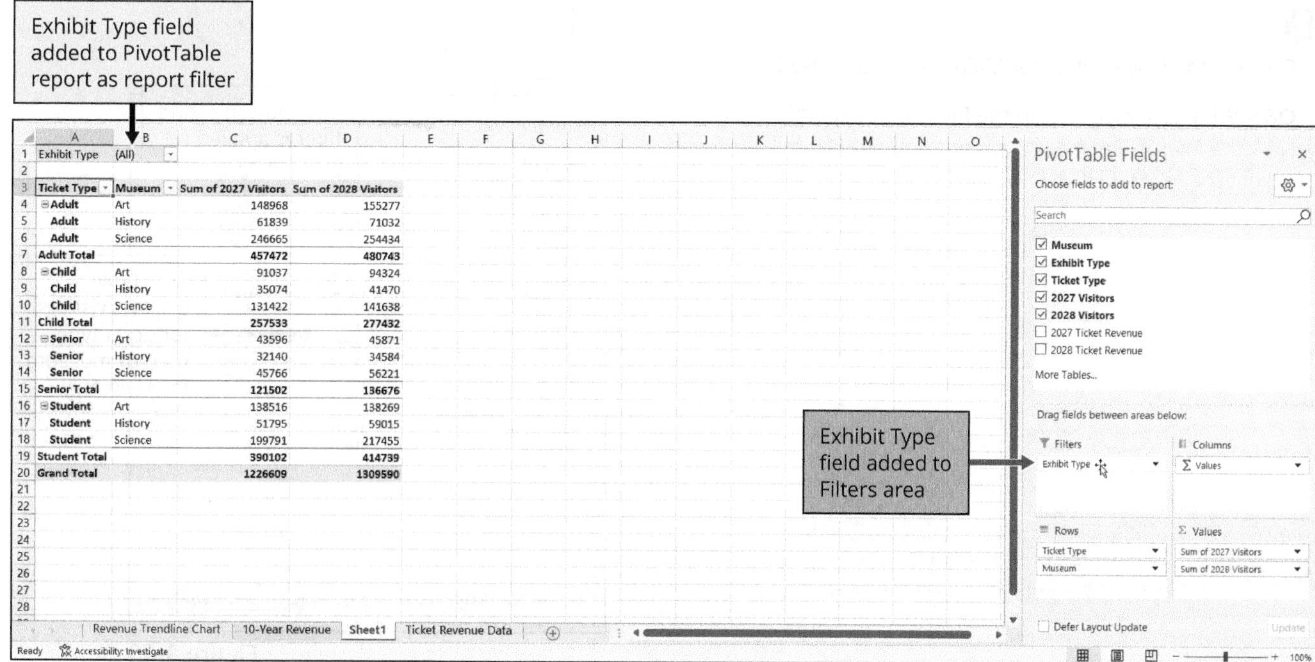

Figure 8–27

2

- Click the filter button in cell B1 to display the filter menu for column B, Exhibit Type in this case.
- Click Main on the filter menu to select the Main criterion (Figure 8–28).

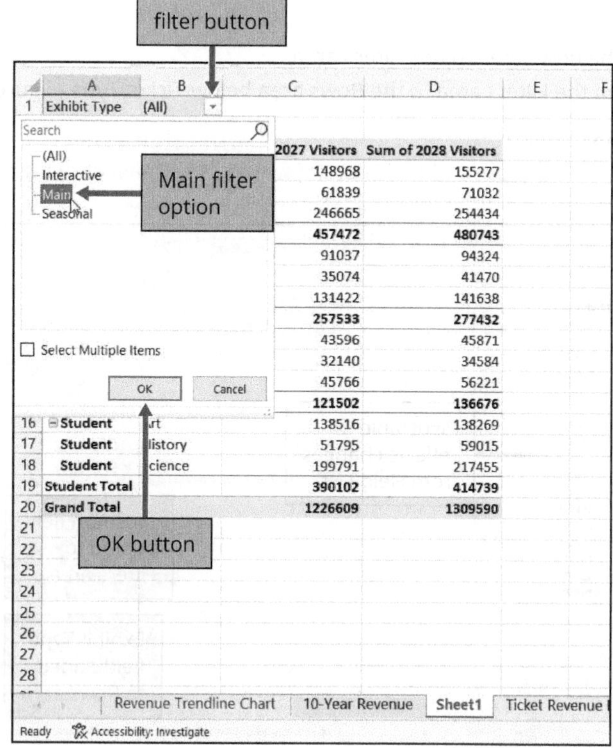

Figure 8–28

- Click OK to display totals for Main only (Figure 8–29).

Q&A What is shown now in the PivotTable report?
Now the PivotTable shows total visitors for each museum and ticket type for Main only.

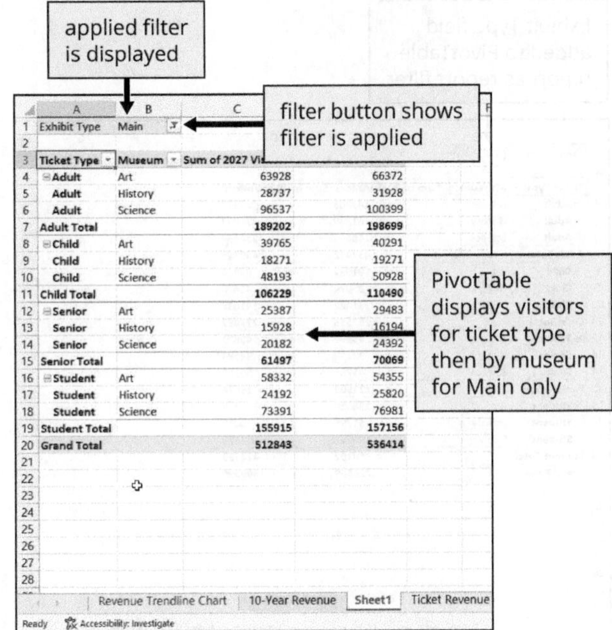

Figure 8–29

To Filter a PivotTable Report Using Multiple Selection Criteria

Why? You may need to identify a subset that is defined by more than one filter criterion. The following steps change the filter field and select multiple criteria on which to filter. This filtering allows for a different display of the data, which allows for further analyzing of ticket sales by exhibit type for the art and history museums.

- Drag the Museum button from the Rows area to the Filters area.
- Drag the Exhibit Type button from the Filters area to the Rows area below Ticket Type (Figure 8–30).

Q&A What does the PivotTable now show?
Excel now filters the entire report by Museum and does not show that as a detail line within the report.

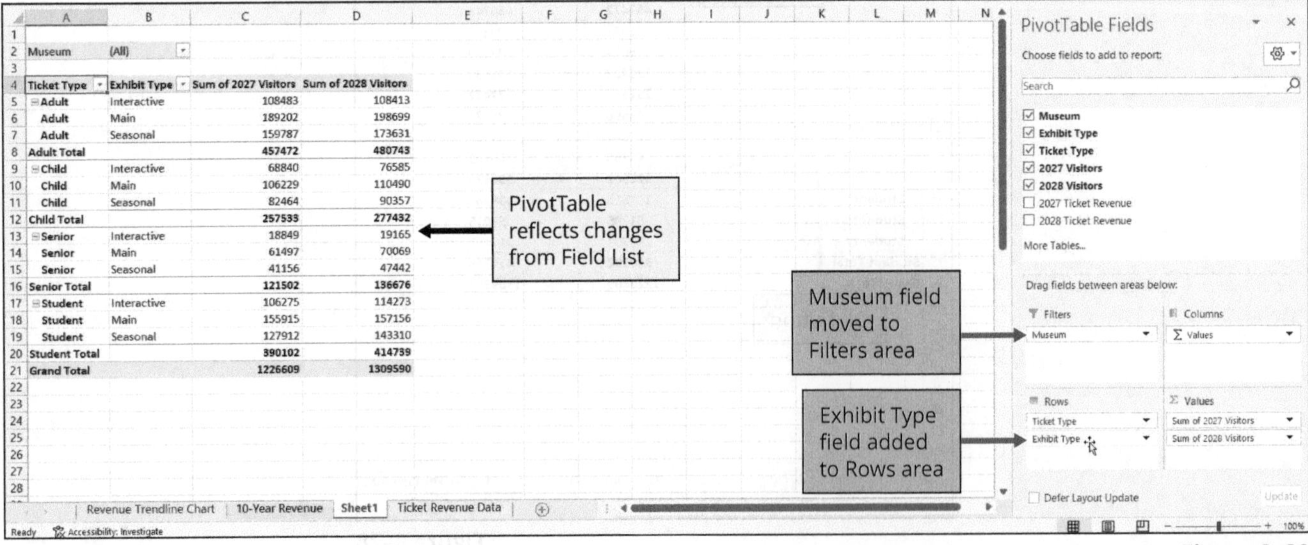

Figure 8–30

- Click the filter button in cell B2 to display the filter menu for the Museum field.
- Click the 'Select Multiple Items' check box to prepare to select multiple criteria.
- Click to remove the checkmark in the Science check box to deselect the criteria and leave only the Art and History criteria selected (Figure 8–31).

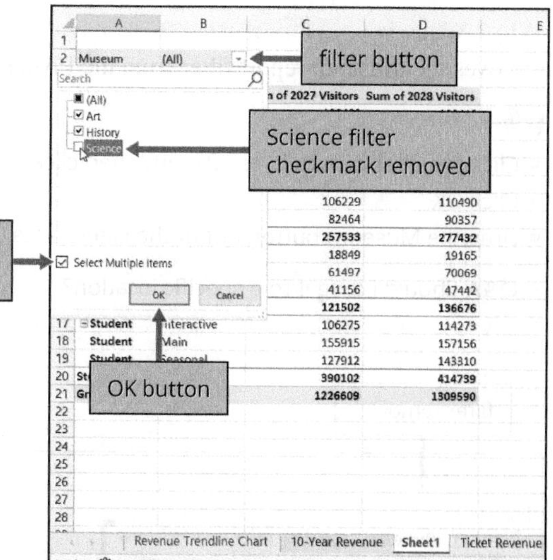

Figure 8–31

- Click OK to display visitor totals for the Art and History museums (Figure 8–32).

Q&A How do I know which criteria have been selected?

With a multiple-item filter, you need to click the filter button to display which criteria have been selected.

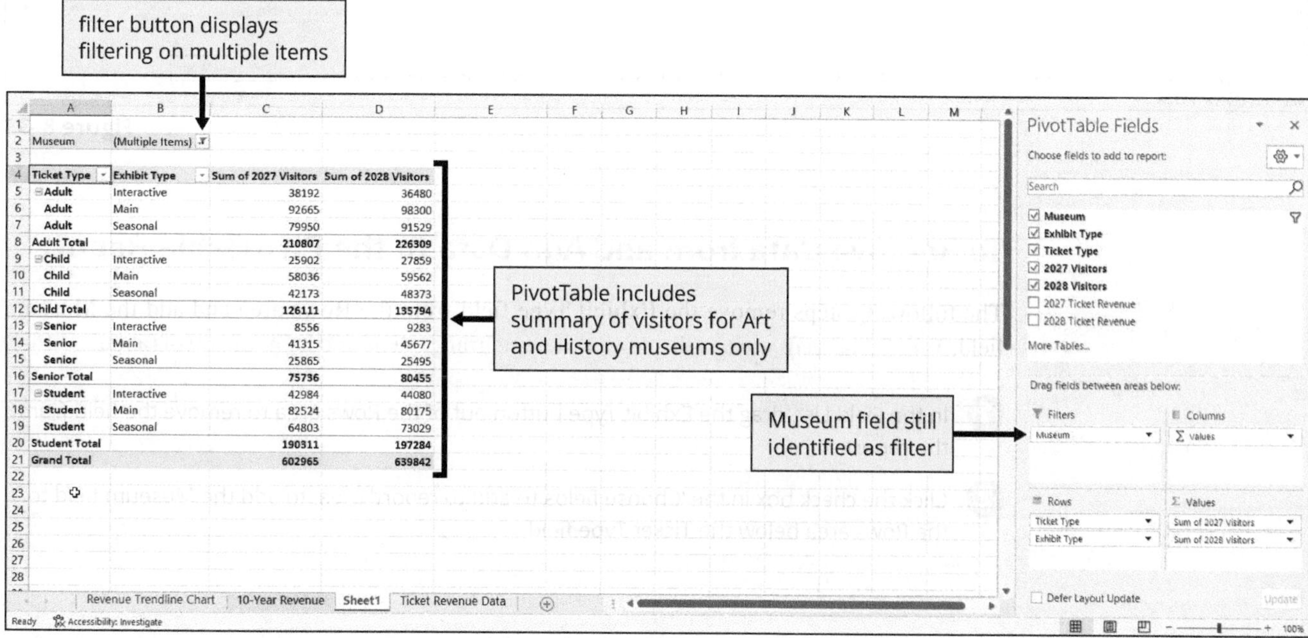

Figure 8–32

To Remove a Report Filter from a PivotTable Report

Why? When you no longer need to display filtered data in a PivotTable, you can remove the filter easily. The following step removes the Museum report filter from the PivotTable report.

- Click the filter button in cell B2, and then click the (All) check box to include all museum type criteria in the PivotTable report.
- Click OK.
- Drag the Museum button out of the Filters area (Field List) to remove the field from the PivotTable report (Figure 8–33).

Q&A Should I drag it to a specific location?
No. You can drag it out of the box to any blank area on the worksheet.

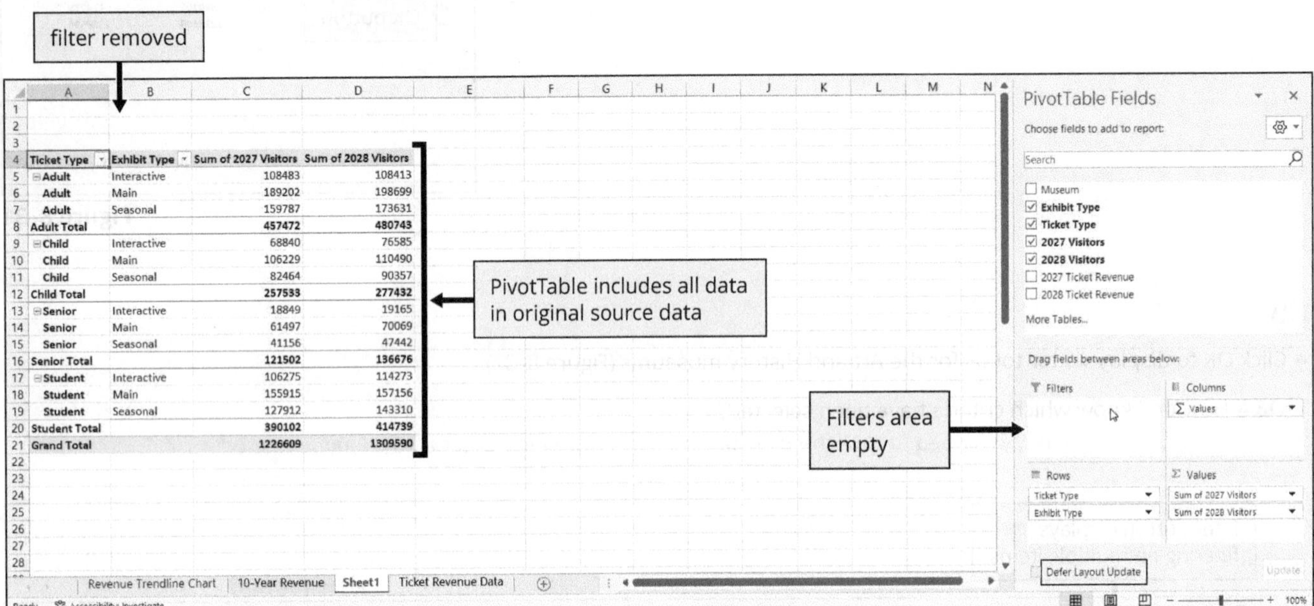

Figure 8–33

To Remove Data from and Add Data to the PivotTable Report

The following steps remove the Exhibit Type field from the Rows area and add the Museum field. **Why?** You may want to display a different arrangement of data in the PivotTable.

1. In the Field List, drag the Exhibit Type button out of the Rows area to remove the field from the report.
2. Click the check box in the 'Choose fields to add to report' area, to add the Museum field to the Rows area below the Ticket Type field.

To Filter a PivotTable Report Using the Row Label Filter

Report filters are added to the PivotTable report by adding a field to the Filters area of the Field List. **Why?** In a PivotTable report, you may want to display a subset of data based on fields that are already in use. When the field of interest is already part of the PivotTable and included in the Rows area of the Field List, you can use row label filters to check out a subset of the data. Like other filter buttons, row label filters display within the column heading. When you click the filter button, Excel displays a menu of available fields. The following steps use a row label filter for Museum to restrict data in the PivotTable to the History and Science museums.

- Click the filter button in cell B4 to display the filter menu for the Museum field.

> **Q&A** I do not have a filter button in cell B4. How do I access the filter?
> The filter buttons may be hidden. Click the Field Headers button (PivotTable Analyze tab | Show group) to turn on the field headers and make the filter buttons visible.
>
> Why does cell B4 not appear selected when I use the filter button?
> Filtering happens independently of cell selection. You do not need to select the cell in which the filter button is located in order to use the filter.

- Click the Art check box on the filter menu to leave only the History and Science museums selected (Figure 8–34).

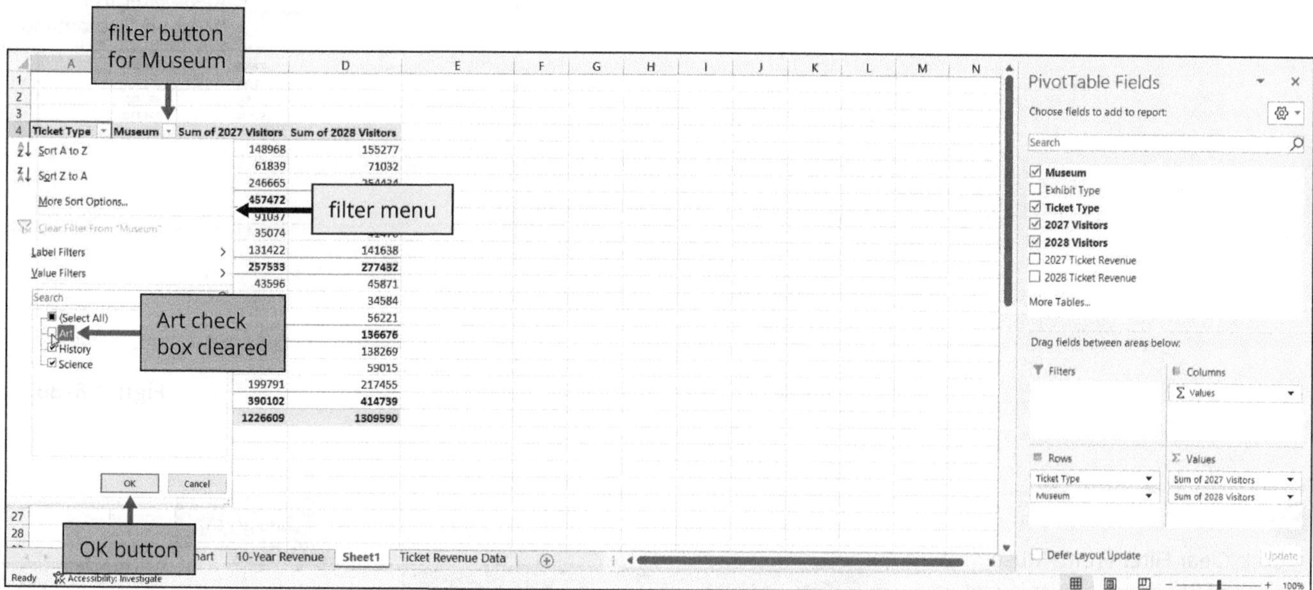

Figure 8–34

- Click OK to display totals for History and Science museums only, categorized by ticket type (Figure 8–35).

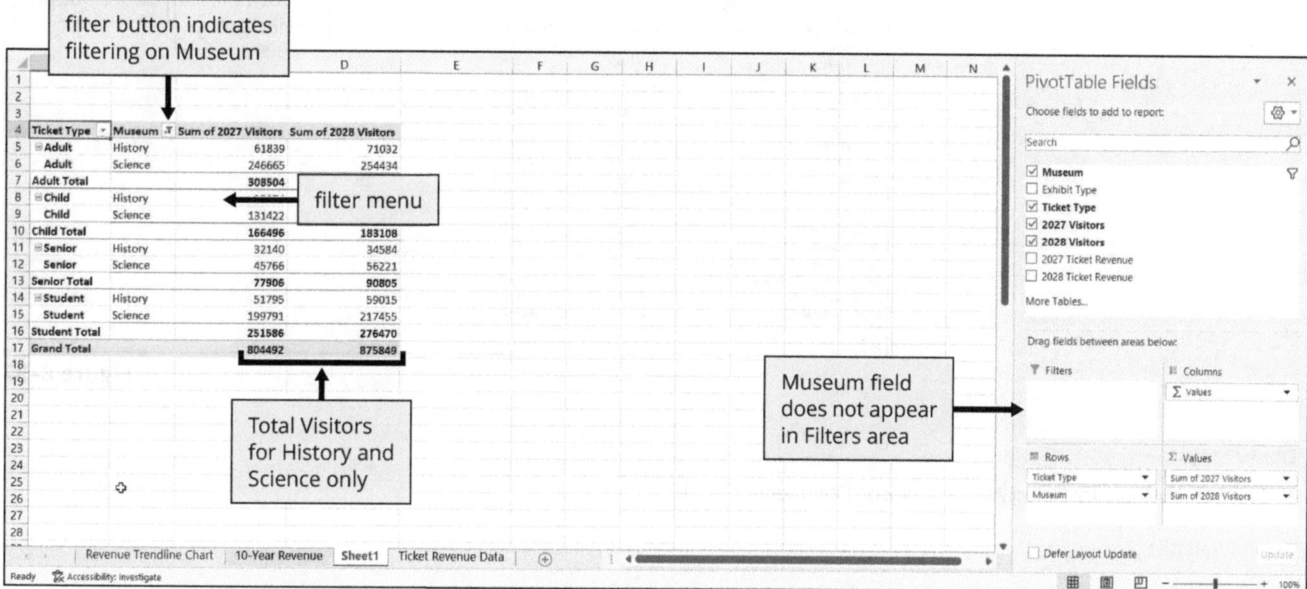

Figure 8–35

To Clear the Filter

Why? Once you have reviewed the subset of data, you may want to remove the criteria using the Row Label filter to display all records. The following steps clear the filter in order to display all records.

- Click the filter button in cell B4 again to display the filter menu for the Museum field (Figure 8–36).

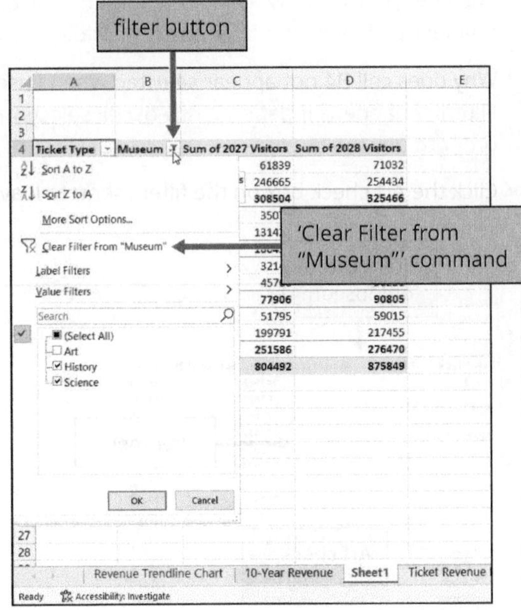

Figure 8–36

- Click 'Clear Filter From "Museum"' on the filter menu to display totals for all ticket types in all museums (Figure 8–37).

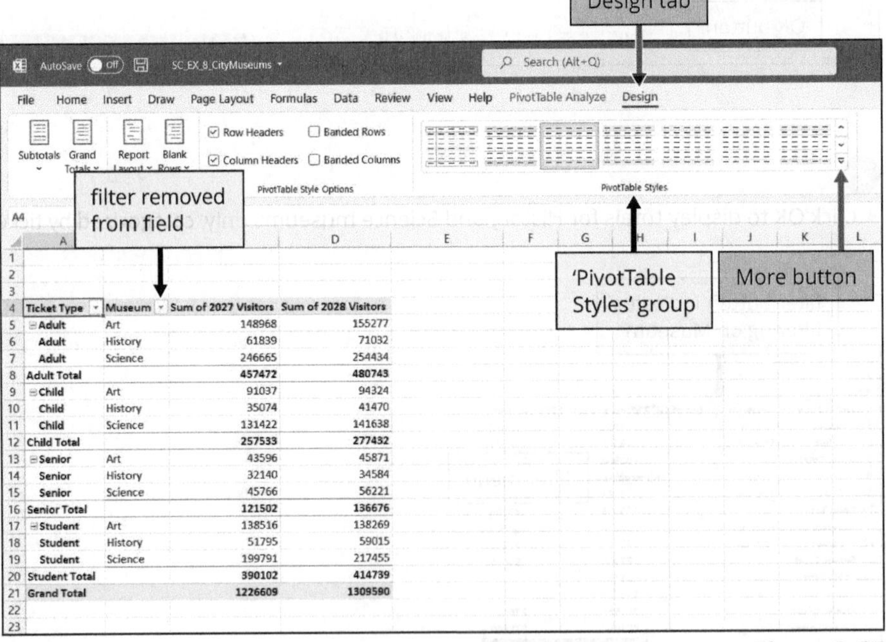

Figure 8–37

Other Ways

1. Click filter button, click (Select All) check box on filter menu, click OK

Formatting PivotTable Reports

You can use several formatting options to enhance the appearance of PivotTable reports and make the content easier to read. Excel includes a number of preset PivotTable report styles to simplify this task. These styles function in a similar fashion to the Excel table styles. Take care when formatting PivotTable reports, however, because formatting techniques that work for regular tables of data do not behave in the same fashion in PivotTable reports. Adjusting the formatting in a PivotTable without using a PivotTable style will prove challenging, as the formatting will change if you change any of the data displayed in the PivotTable. PivotTable report formatting requires the use of PivotTable styles and field settings.

Consider This

How do you choose a particular PivotTable style?

When you plan PivotTables and PivotCharts, consider what information you want to display in each report. As you are developing a report, review the galleries of PivotTable and PivotChart styles to find the best one to display your data. For example, some PivotTable styles include banded rows and columns, which can make it easier to scan and interpret the report.

To Format a PivotTable Report

Why? Thoughtful formatting can enhance the readability of a PivotTable report. The following steps format a PivotTable report by applying a PivotTable style and specifying number formats for the fields.

- Rename the Sheet1 tab, entering **Visitors PivotTable** as the new name and set the color to Orange, Accent 2 in the Theme colors.
- Drag the Visitors PivotTable sheet to after the Ticket Revenue Data sheet.
- Click cell A4 to select a cell in the PivotTable.
- Click the More button in the PivotTable Styles group (Design tab | PivotTable Styles group) to expand the gallery.
- Scroll down to the Dark section of the gallery.
- Point to 'Brown, Pivot Style Dark 3' (PivotTable Styles gallery) to display a preview of the style in the PivotTable (Figure 8–38).

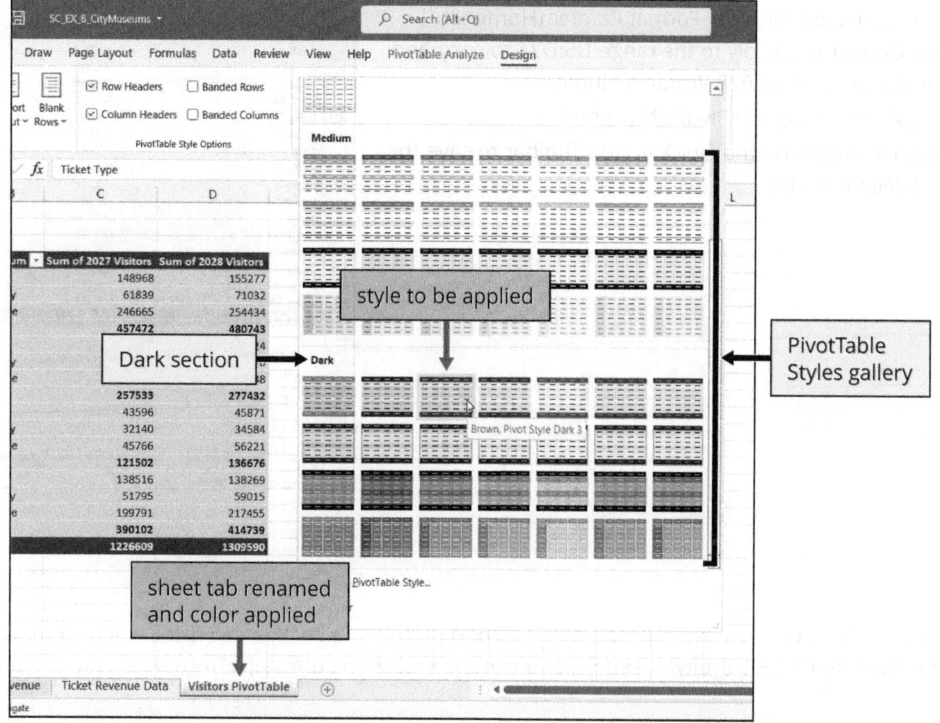

Figure 8–38

2

- Click 'Brown, Pivot Style Dark 3' in the PivotTable Styles gallery to apply the style to the PivotTable report.
- Right-click cell C5, and then click Number Format on the shortcut menu to display the Format Cells dialog box.
- Click Number in the Category list (Format Cells dialog box) to select the Number format.
- Type **0** in the Decimal places box to specify no decimal places.
- Click the check box next to Use 1000 Separator (,) to apply commas to the formatting (Figure 8–39).

Q&A Can I use the formatting options on the Home tab?
Yes, but you would have to highlight all of the cells first and then apply the formatting. Using the Number Format command is easier.

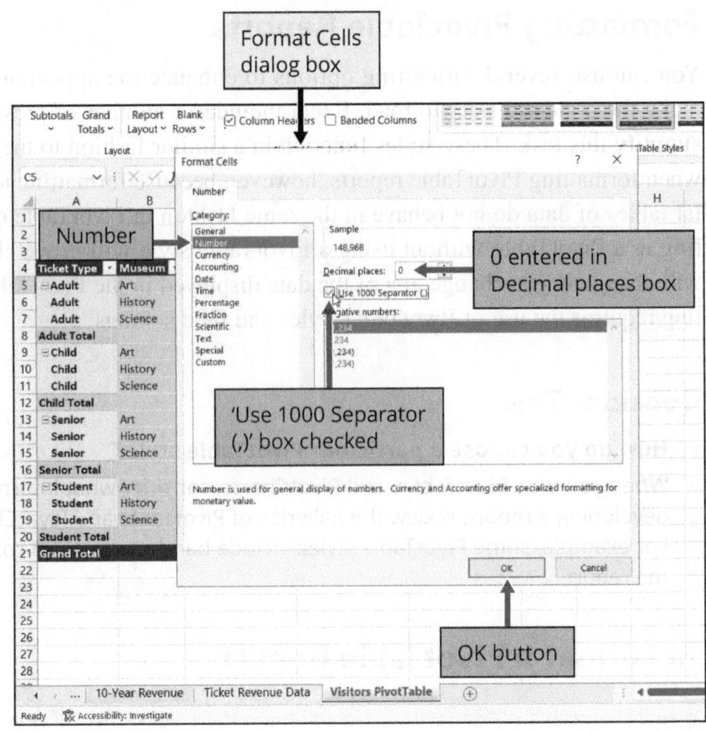

Figure 8–39

3

- Click OK to apply the Number style with commas and no decimal places to all 2027 visitor values in the PivotTable report.

Q&A Why does the number format change apply to all Visitor values?
In a PivotTable, when you format a single cell using Number Format, that formatting is applied to the entire set of values to which that single cell belongs.

4

- With cell C5 selected, click the Format Painter (Home tab | Clipboard Group) and apply to the range D5:D21 to copy and paste the format to the 2028 Visitors column.
- Click cell E7 to deselect the PivotTable report.
- Click the Save button on the Quick Access Toolbar to save the workbook (Figure 8–40).

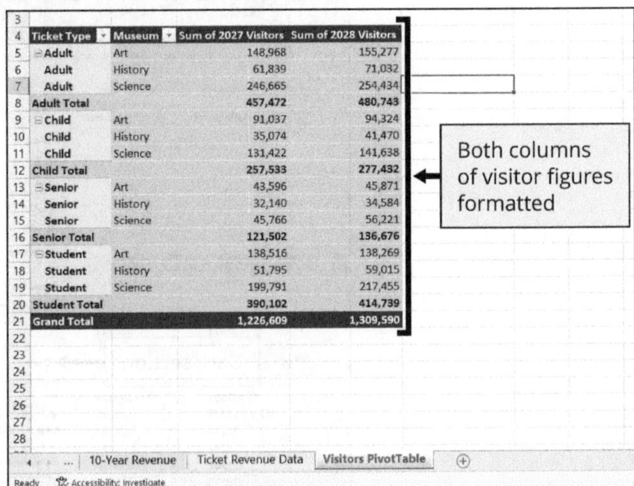

Ticket Type	Museum	Sum of 2027 Visitors	Sum of 2028 Visitors
Adult	Art	148,968	155,277
Adult	History	61,839	71,032
Adult	Science	246,665	254,434
Adult Total		457,472	480,743
Child	Art	91,037	94,324
Child	History	35,074	41,470
Child	Science	131,422	141,638
Child Total		257,533	277,432
Senior	Art	43,596	45,871
Senior	History	32,140	34,584
Senior	Science	45,766	56,221
Senior Total		121,502	136,676
Student	Art	138,516	138,269
Student	History	51,795	59,015
Student	Science	199,791	217,455
Student Total		390,102	414,739
Grand Total		1,226,609	1,309,590

Figure 8–40

Break Point: If you want to take a break, this is a good place to do so. You can exit Excel now. To resume later, start Excel, open the file called SC_EX_8_CityMuseums, and continue following the steps from this location forward.

Summary Functions

In PivotTable reports, you easily can change the **summary function**, the function that determines the type of calculation applied to PivotTable data, such as SUM or COUNT. For example, in Figure 8–40, the data is totaled for 2027 and 2028 Visitors using a SUM function. You can change that to a different summary function. Summary functions can be inserted in one of three ways: by using the shortcut menu of a cell in the PivotTable, by using the field button menu in the Values area (Field List), or by using the Field Settings button (PivotTable Analyze tab | Active Field group).

Table 8–2 lists the summary functions Excel provides for the analysis of data in PivotTable reports. These functions also apply to PivotChart Reports.

Table 8–2: Summary Functions for PivotTable Report and PivotChart Report Data Analysis

Summary Function	Description
Sum	Sum of the values (default function for numeric source data)
Count	Number of data values
Average	Average of the values
Max	Largest value
Min	Smallest value
Product	Product of the values
Count Numbers	Number of data values that contain numeric data
StdDev.s	Estimate of the standard deviation of all of the data to be summarized, used when data is a sample of a larger population of interest
StdDev.p	Standard deviation of all of the data to be summarized, used when data is the entire population of interest
Var.s	Estimate of the variance of all of the data to be summarized, used when data is a sample of a larger population of interest
Var.p	Variance of the data to be summarized, used when data is the entire population of interest

To Switch Summary Functions

Why? The default summary function in a PivotTable is the SUM function. For some comparisons, using a different summary function will yield more useful measures. In addition to analyzing the total visitors for each museum and ticket type, you are interested in displaying the average visitors by museum and ticket type. Currently, the PivotTable report for City Museums displays the total number of visitors for each museum by ticket type. Average visitors by museum and then by ticket type might be a better measure for comparing the visitors. The following steps switch summary functions in a PivotTable using the shortcut menu.

- Right-click cell C5 to display the shortcut menu and then point to 'Summarize Values By' to display the Summarize Values By submenu (Figure 8–41).

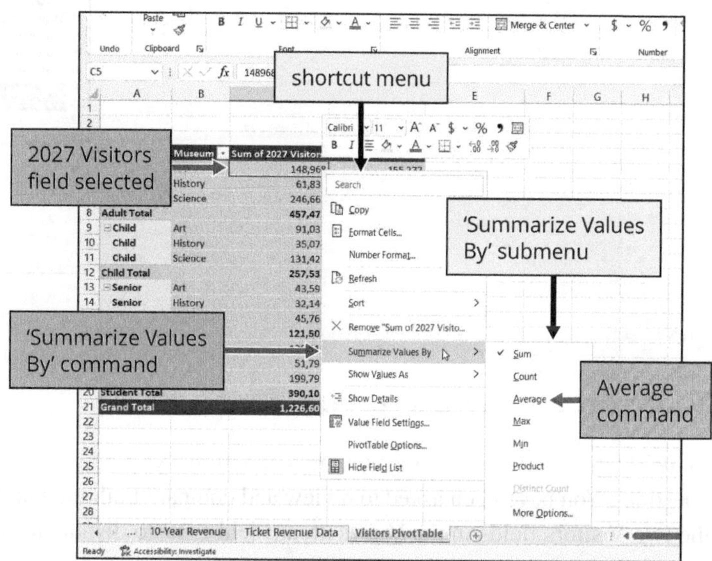

Figure 8–41

- Click Average on the Summarize Values By submenu to change the summary function from Sum to Average (Figure 8–42).

Q&A Why did the column title in cell C4 change?
When you change a summary function, the column heading automatically updates to reflect the new summary function chosen.

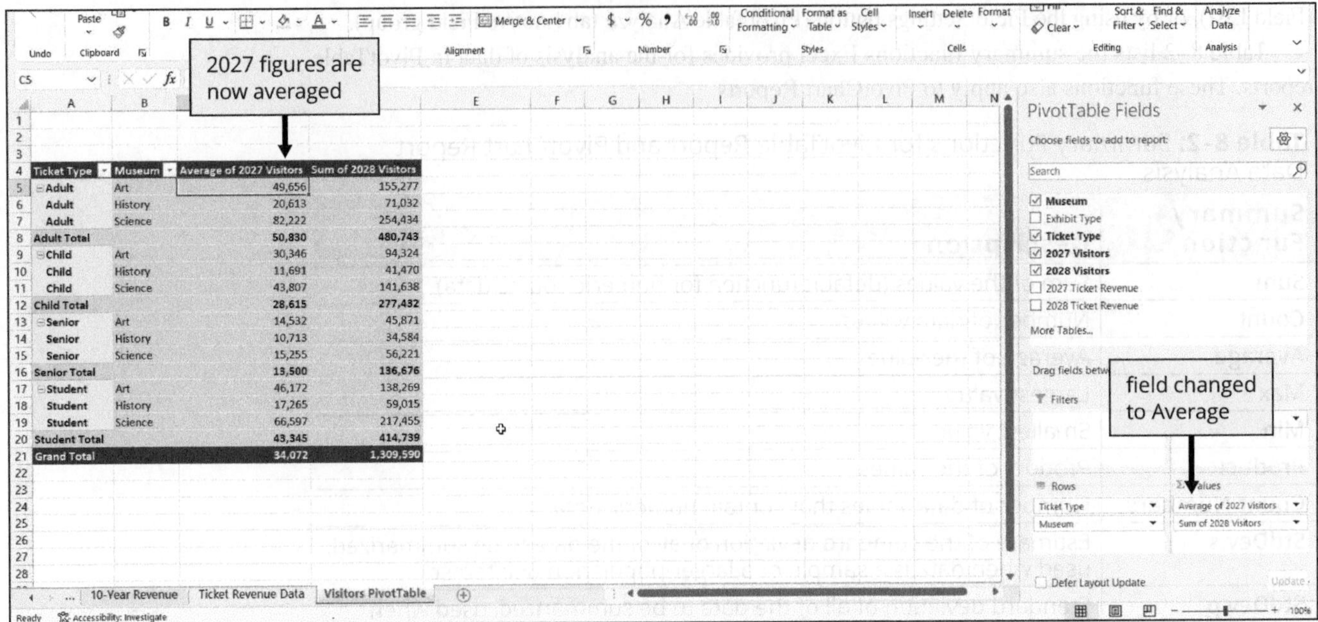

Figure 8–42

3

- Repeat Steps 1 and 2 to change the summary function used in column D from Sum to Average.
- If necessary, reapply the Number style with commas and no decimal places to all 2027 and 2028 visitor values (Figure 8–43).

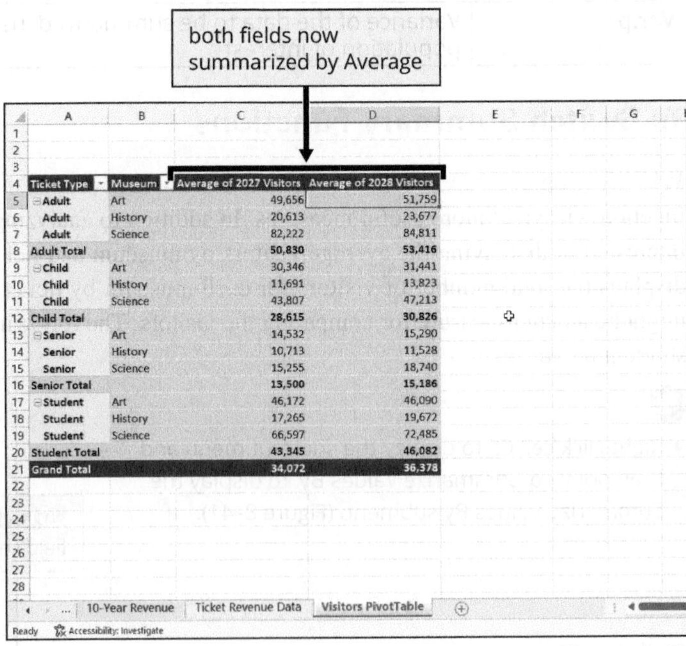

Figure 8–43

To Insert a New Summary Function

Why? In addition to changing summary functions, you may need to add new fields to analyze additional or more complex questions. You have been asked to review and compare both total and average visitors for 2027 and 2028. Earlier you changed the two Visitors fields in the Values area (Field List) to display averages. Because you now want the totals as well, you will need to drag another copy of the two Visitors fields to the Values area, creating a total of four sets of data. The following steps add a second value calculation for each of the two years and use these fields to add a summary function in the PivotTable report. This time, you will use the menu displayed when you click the value field button to access the Value Field Settings dialog box.

- In the Field List, drag the 2027 Visitors field to the Values area above the 'Average of 2027 Visitors' button to add a third field to the PivotTable.
- In the Values area, click the 'Sum of 2027 Visitors' button to display the Sum of 2027 Visitors menu (Figure 8–44).

Q&A Why did I place the new field above the other items in the Values area?
Dragging the new field to a location above the other fields will place the data in a new column before the others in the PivotTable report, in this case in column C.

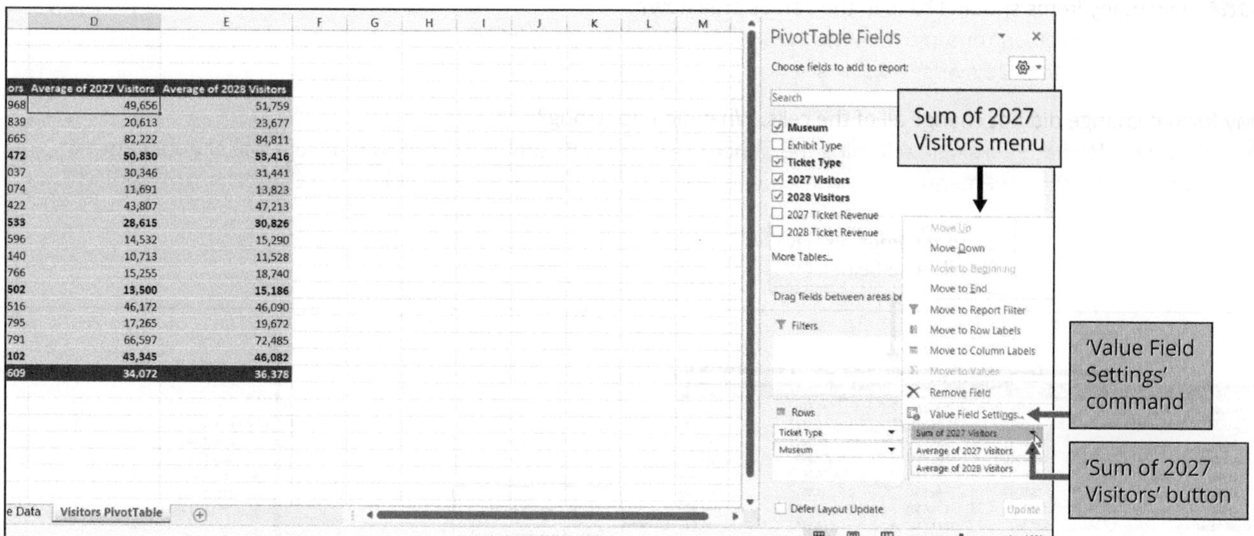

Figure 8–44

- Click 'Value Field Settings' to display the Value Field Settings dialog box.
- In the Custom Name text box (Value Field Settings dialog box), type **2027 Total Visitors** to change the field name (Figure 8–45).

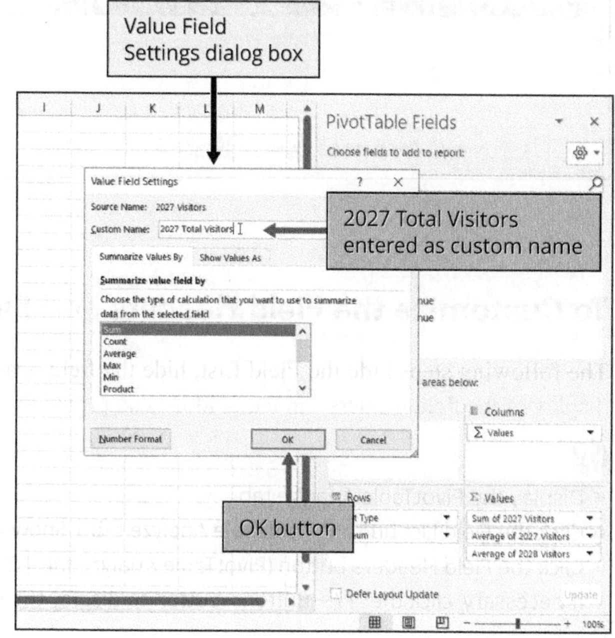

Figure 8–45

- Click OK (Value Field Settings dialog box) to apply the custom name.
- In the Field List, drag the 2028 Visitors field to the Values area to add a fourth field. Place it between the '2027 Total Visitors' button and the 'Average of 2027 Visitors' button.
- In the Values area, click the 'Sum of 2028 Visitors' button to display its menu, and then click 'Value Field Settings' to display the Value Field Settings dialog box.
- In the Custom Name text box, type **2028 Total Visitors** and then click OK (Value Field Settings dialog box) to rename the field.
- Using the buttons in the Values area, rename the other two fields to customize the column headings in cells E4 and F4 as shown in Figure 8–46.
- Using the shortcut menu, if necessary, format the values in columns C and then D to the Number category, 0 decimal places, and commas (Figure 8–46).

Q&A How many items should I have in the Values area now?
You can use the scroll buttons in the Values area to display the four fields: 2027 Total Visitors, 2028 Total Visitors, 2027 Average Visitors, and 2028 Average Visitors.

My format change did not change all of the cells. What did I do wrong?
You may have formatted a single cell using the ribbon. To format all numbers in the column, use the Number Format command on the shortcut menu.

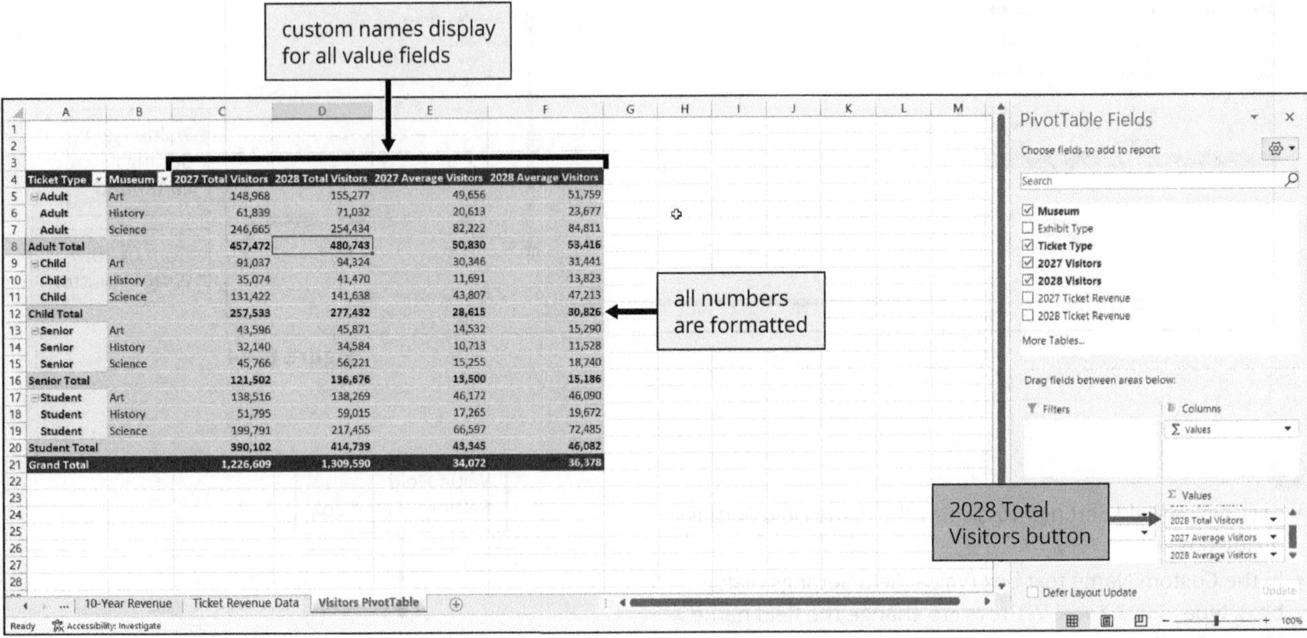

Figure 8–46

To Customize the Field Headers and Field List

The following steps hide the Field List, hide the field headers, and then turn off column autofitting. **Why?** Customizing the display of the field headers and the field list can provide a less cluttered worksheet.

- Display the PivotTable Analyze tab.
- Click the Field List button (PivotTable Analyze tab | Show group) to hide the Field List.
- Click the Field Headers button (PivotTable Analyze tab | Show group) to hide the field headers.
- If necessary, click the '+/– Buttons' button to display the expand and collapse buttons in the PivotTable (Figure 8–47).

Q&A How can I display the Field List and field headers after hiding them?
The Field List and Field Headers buttons (PivotTable Analyze tab | Show group) are toggle buttons—clicking them again turns the display back on.

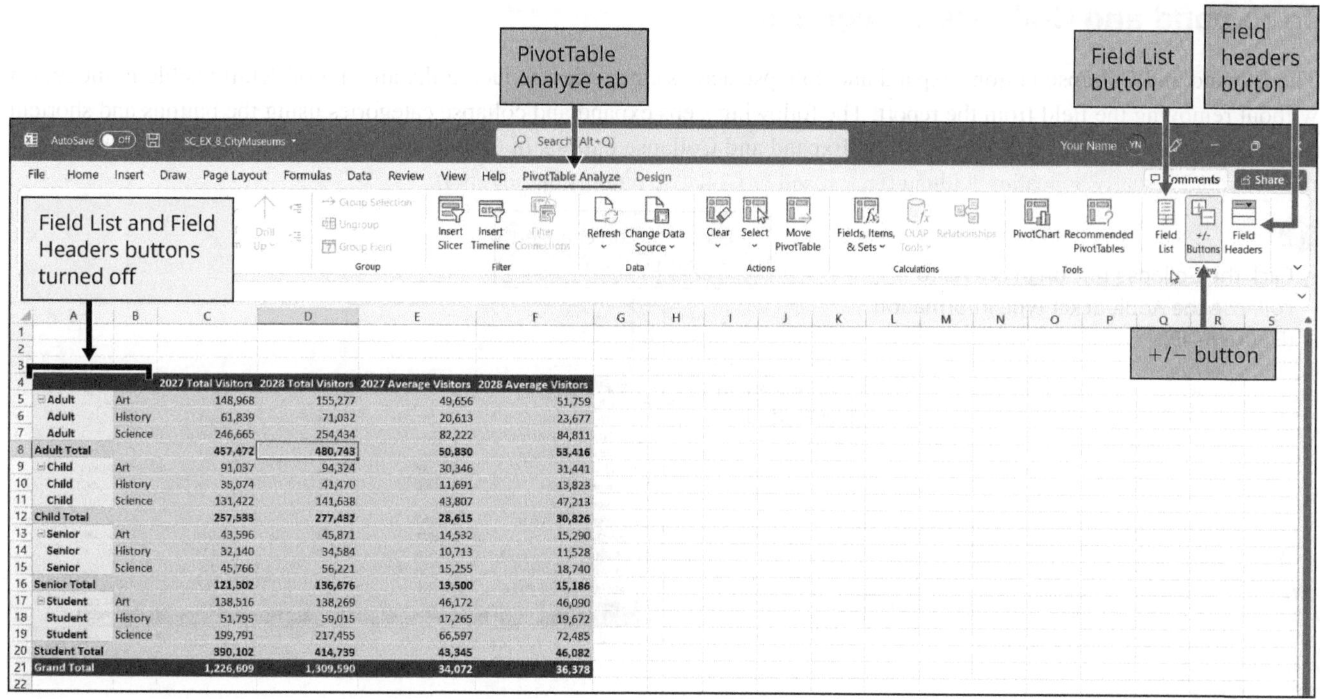

Figure 8–47

2

- Click the Options button (PivotTable Analyze tab | PivotTable group) to display the PivotTable Options dialog box.
- Click the 'Autofit column widths on update' check box to remove the checkmark (Figure 8–48).

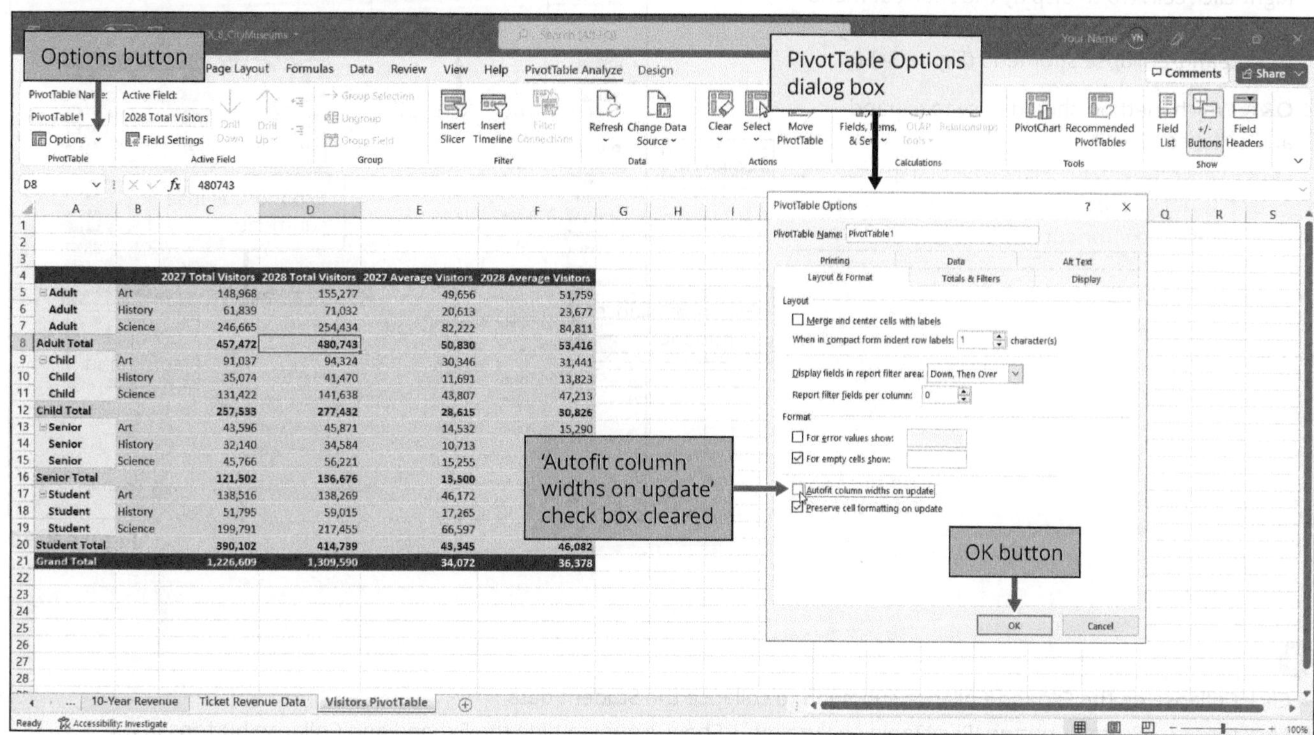

Figure 8–48

- Click OK (PivotTable Options dialog box) to turn off the autofitting of column widths if updates should take place.

To Expand and Collapse Categories

The Expand and Collapse buttons expand and collapse across categories, reducing the amount of detail visible in the report without removing the field from the report. The following steps expand and collapse categories using the buttons and shortcut menus, and then suppress the display of the Expand and Collapse buttons in the report. **Why?** In some instances, the report may be more visually appealing without the Expand or Collapse buttons in the report.

1

- Click the Collapse button in cell A5 to collapse the Adult ticket type information (Figure 8–49).

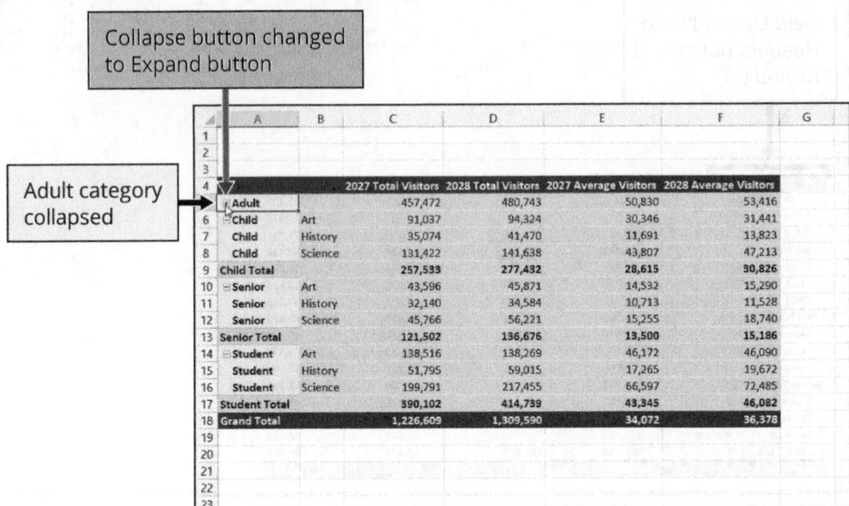

Figure 8–49

2

- Right-click cell A10 to display the shortcut menu and then point to Expand/Collapse to display the Expand/Collapse submenu (Figure 8–50).

Q&A Which method should I use to expand and collapse?
Either way is fine. Sometimes the Collapse button is not visible, in which case you would have to use the shortcut menu.

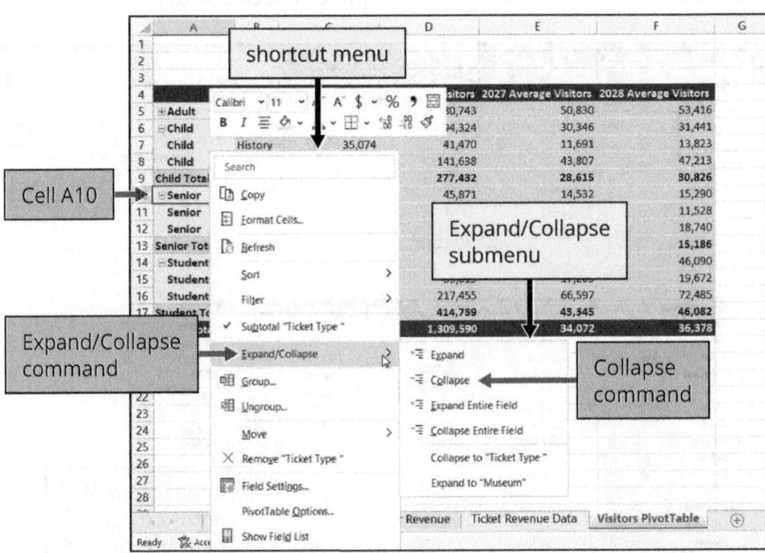

Figure 8–50

- Click Collapse on the Expand/Collapse submenu to collapse the Student data.
- Click the '+/– Buttons' button (PivotTable Analyze tab | Show group) to hide the Expand and Collapse buttons in the PivotTable (Figure 8–51).

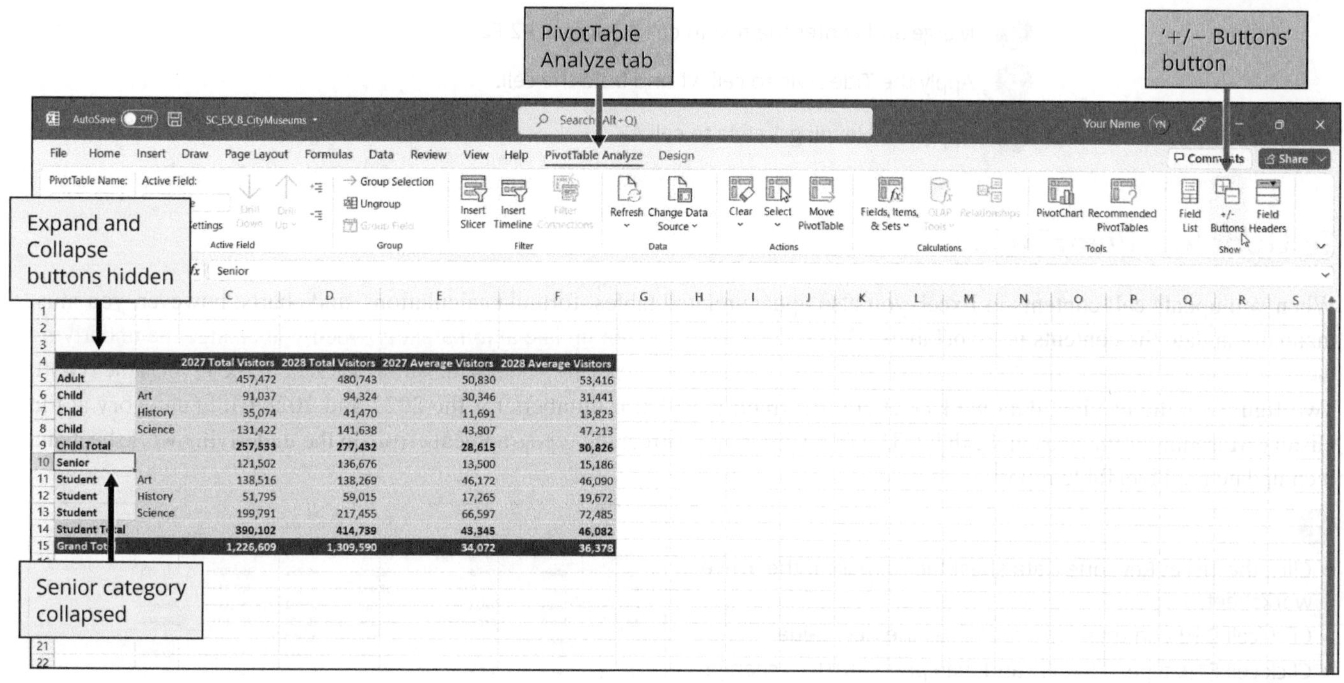

Figure 8–51

- Right-click cell A5 and then point to Expand/Collapse on the shortcut menu to display the Expand/Collapse submenu.
- Click 'Expand Entire Field' on the Expand/Collapse submenu to redisplay all data.
- If necessary, repeat the last two steps with cell A13 (Figure 8–52).

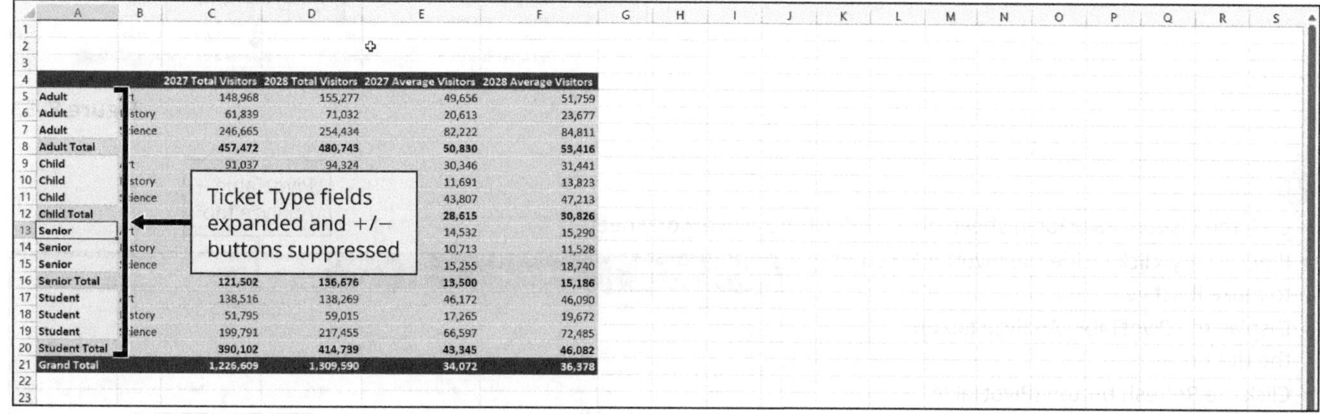

Figure 8–52

To Create a Title

In the following steps, insert two blank rows and create a title for the PivotTable. You must insert new rows because Excel requires the two rows above the PivotTable to be reserved for extra filters.

1. Insert two blank rows above row 1 for the title and subtitle.
2. In cell A1, enter the title **City Museums Visitors Report** and then enter the subtitle **2027 and 2028** in cell A2.
3. Merge and center the text in cell A1 across A1:F1.

4. Merge and center the text in cell A2 across A2:F2.
5. Apply the Title style to cell A1 and bold the cell.
6. Apply the Heading 1 style to cell A2.

To Update a PivotTable

When you update cell contents in Excel, you also update related tables, formula calculations, and charts; however, you must manually update the contents in PivotTables. **Why?** PivotTables do not update automatically when you change the underlying data for the PivotTable report. You must refresh the PivotTable manually to recalculate summary data in the PivotTable report. Two figures in the original data worksheet are incorrect: the Visitor numbers for the 2027 and 2028 Child category at the History Museum for the Seasonal exhibit. The following steps correct the typographical errors in the underlying worksheet and then update the PivotTable report.

- Click the Ticket Revenue Data sheet tab to make it the active worksheet.
- Click cell D19 and then type **9010** as the new value.
- Click cell E19, type **15765**, and then press ENTER to change the contents of the cell (Figure 8–53).

	A	B	C	D	E	F	G
2	Museum	Exhibit Type	Ticket Type	2027 Visitors	2028 Visitors	2027 Ticket Revenue	2028 Ticket Revenue
3	Art	Main	Child	39,765	40,291	198,825	201,455
4	Art	Main	Student	58,332	54,355	408,324	380,485
5	Art	Main	Adult	63,928	66,372	767,136	796,464
6	Art	Main	Senior	25,387	29,483	228,483	265,347
7	Art	Seasonal	Child	32,991	33,102	98,973	99,306
8	Art	Seasonal	Student	50,182	50,927	150,546	152,781
9	Art	Seasonal	Adult	60,129	62,812	300,645	314,060
10	Art	Seasonal	Senior	12,948	11,406	51,792	45,624
11	Art	Interactive	Child	18,281	20,931	36,562	41,862
12	Art	Interactive	Student	30,002	32,987	60,004	65,974
13	Art	Interactive	Adult	[illegible]	[illegible]	49,822	52,186
14	Art	Interactive	Senior	[illegible]	[illegible]	10,522	9,964
15	History	Main	Child	[illegible]	[illegible]	91,355	96,355
16	History	Main	Student	24,192	25,820	169,344	180,740
17	History	Main	Adult	28,737	31,928	344,844	383,136
18	History	Main	Senior	15,928	16,194	143,352	145,746
19	History	Seasonal	Child	9,010	15,765	27,546	45,813
20	History	Seasonal	Student	14,621	22,102	43,863	66,306
21	History	Seasonal	Adult	19,821	28,717	99,105	143,585
22	History	Seasonal	Senior	12,917	14,089	51,668	56,356
23	History	Interactive	Child	[illegible]	[illegible]	[illegible]	13,856
24	History	Interactive	Student	[illegible]	[illegible]	[illegible]	22,186
25	History	Interactive	Adult	[illegible]	[illegible]	[illegible]	20,774
26	History	Interactive	Senior	[illegible]	[illegible]	[illegible]	8,602
27	Science	Main	Child	[illegible]	[illegible]	[illegible]	254,640
28	Science	Main	Student	73,391	76,981	513,737	538,867

updated values

Ticket Revenue Data sheet tab

Revenue Trendline Chart | 10-Year Revenue | Ticket Revenue Data | Visitors PivotTable

Ready Accessibility: Investigate

Figure 8–53

2.
- Click the Visitors PivotTable sheet tab to make it the active worksheet.
- If necessary, click inside the PivotTable report to make it active.
- Display the PivotTable Analyze tab on the ribbon.
- Click the Refresh button (PivotTable Analyze tab | Data group) to update the PivotTable report to reflect the change to the underlying data (Figure 8–54).

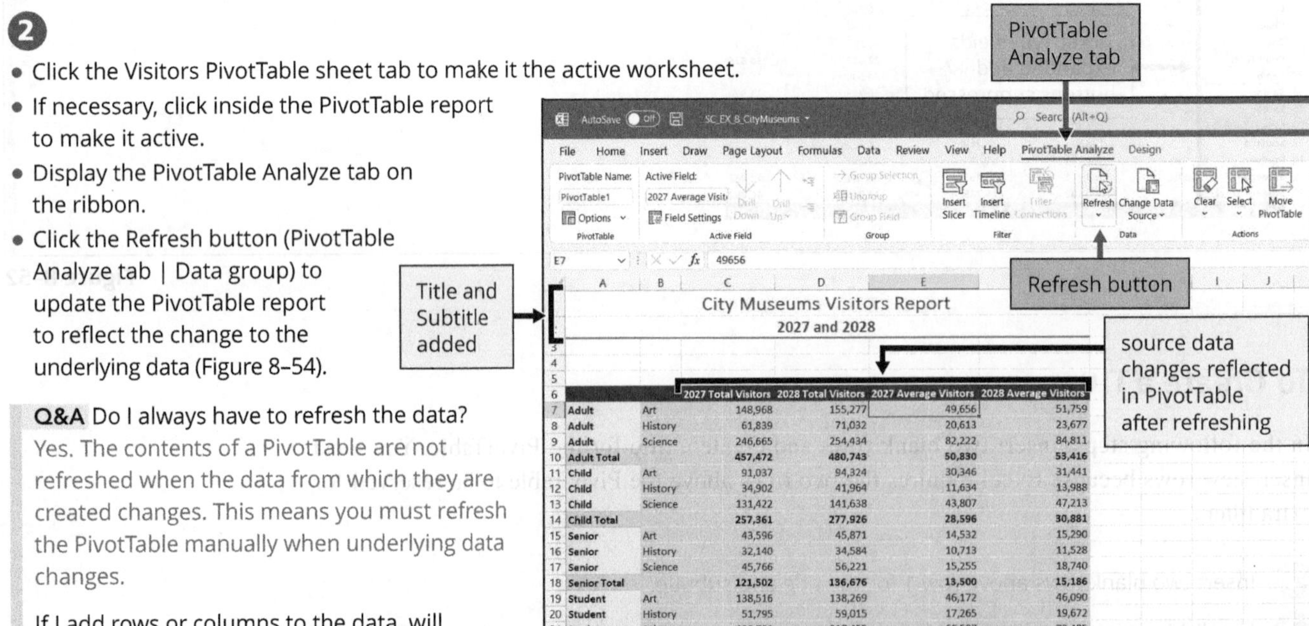

	A	B	C	D	E	F
6			2027 Total Visitors	2028 Total Visitors	2027 Average Visitors	2028 Average Visitors
7	Adult	Art	148,968	155,277	49,656	51,759
8	Adult	History	61,839	71,032	20,613	23,677
9	Adult	Science	246,665	254,434	82,222	84,811
10	Adult Total		457,472	480,743	50,830	53,416
11	Child	Art	91,037	94,324	30,346	31,441
12	Child	History	34,902	41,964	11,634	13,988
13	Child	Science	131,422	141,638	43,807	47,213
14	Child Total		257,361	277,926	28,596	30,881
15	Senior	Art	43,596	45,871	14,532	15,290
16	Senior	History	32,140	34,584	10,713	11,528
17	Senior	Science	45,766	56,221	15,255	18,740
18	Senior Total		121,502	136,676	13,500	15,186
19	Student	Art	138,516	138,269	46,172	46,090
20	Student	History	51,795	59,015	17,265	19,672
21	Student	Science	199,791	217,455	66,597	72,485
22	Student Total		390,102	414,739	43,345	46,082
23	Grand Total		1,226,437	1,310,084	34,068	36,391

Q&A Do I always have to refresh the data?
Yes. The contents of a PivotTable are not refreshed when the data from which they are created changes. This means you must refresh the PivotTable manually when underlying data changes.

If I add rows or columns to the data, will refreshing update the PivotTable?
If your data is in a data table, yes. Otherwise, you will have to create a new PivotTable.

Figure 8–54

To Drill Down into a PivotTable

An easy way to display the underlying data associated with a PivotTable value is to drill down, a visualization that lets the user drill into, or go to deeper levels in, the data. To drill down, you simply double-click a PivotTable value. Excel creates a new worksheet with the details of the value. The following steps drill down into the PivotTable. **Why?** You want to display detailed information about a value, in this case, the 2027 and 2028 visitor information for the senior tickets at the Art Museum.

- In the Revenue PivotTable report, double-click cell C15 to drill down in the data. Click away from the data to remove the selection (Figure 8–55).

Q&A What did Excel do?
Excel found all of the data related to the value in C15 and displayed it in a new worksheet.

What should I do with the data?
Sometimes you may just want to display the data or use the filter buttons to drill down further; other times, you may want to print it. If it is important to have a permanent record of the data behind a value, rename the new worksheet and save it with the workbook.

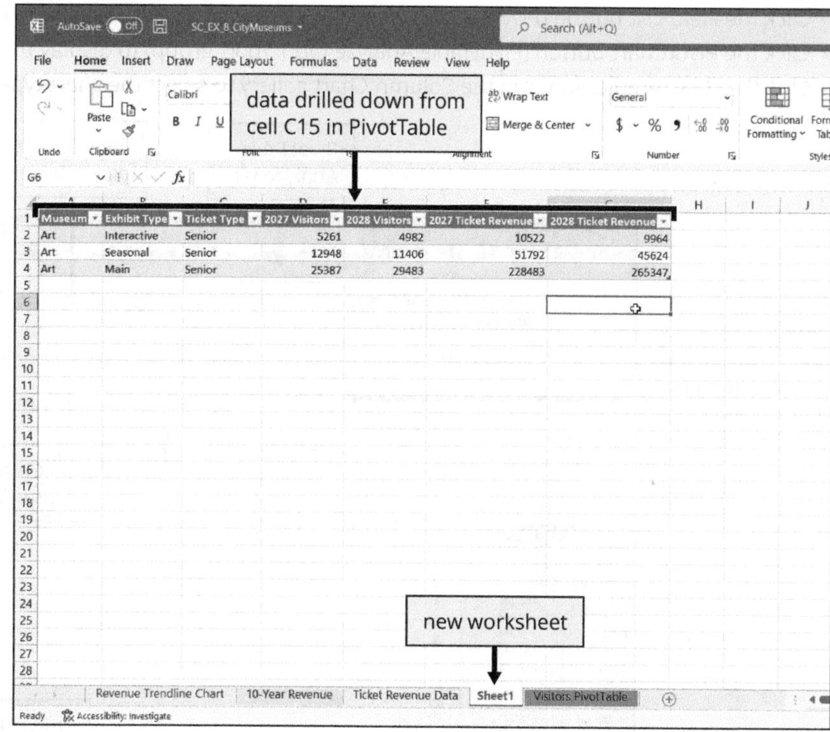

Figure 8–55

- Rename the sheet **Drill Down Data** and set the tab color to Purple in the Standard colors.

Q&A Could I use the Drill Down and Drill Up buttons on the PivotTable Analyze tab?
No. Those buttons are only available with Power Pivot or for PivotTables associated with a data model. You will learn about data models in a later module.

- Click the Save button on the Quick Access Toolbar to save the workbook.

Break Point: If you want to take a break, this is a good place to do so. You can exit Excel now. To resume later, start Excel, open the file called SC_EX_8_CityMuseums, and continue following the steps from this location forward.

Creating and Formatting PivotChart Reports

A PivotChart report, also called a PivotChart, is an interactive chart that allows users to change, with just a few clicks, the groupings that graphically present the data in chart form. As a visual representation of PivotTables, each PivotChart Report must be associated or connected with a PivotTable report. Most users create a PivotChart from an existing PivotTable; however, you can create a new PivotTable and PivotChart at the same time. If you create the PivotChart first, Excel will create the PivotTable automatically.

To Create a PivotChart Report from an Existing PivotTable Report

If you already have created a PivotTable report, you can create a PivotChart report for that PivotTable using the PivotChart button (PivotTable Analyze tab | Tools group). The following steps create a 3-D clustered column PivotChart report from the existing PivotTable report. **Why?** You want the PivotChart to show the two-year data for each museum by ticket type side by side.

- Display the Visitors PivotTable sheet. Click cell A7 to select it in the PivotTable report.
- Click the Field List button (PivotTable Analyze tab | Show group) to display the Field List.
- Click the PivotChart button (PivotTable Analyze tab | Tools group) to display the Insert Chart dialog box.
- Click '3-D Clustered Column' in the Column Chart gallery to select the chart type (Figure 8–56).

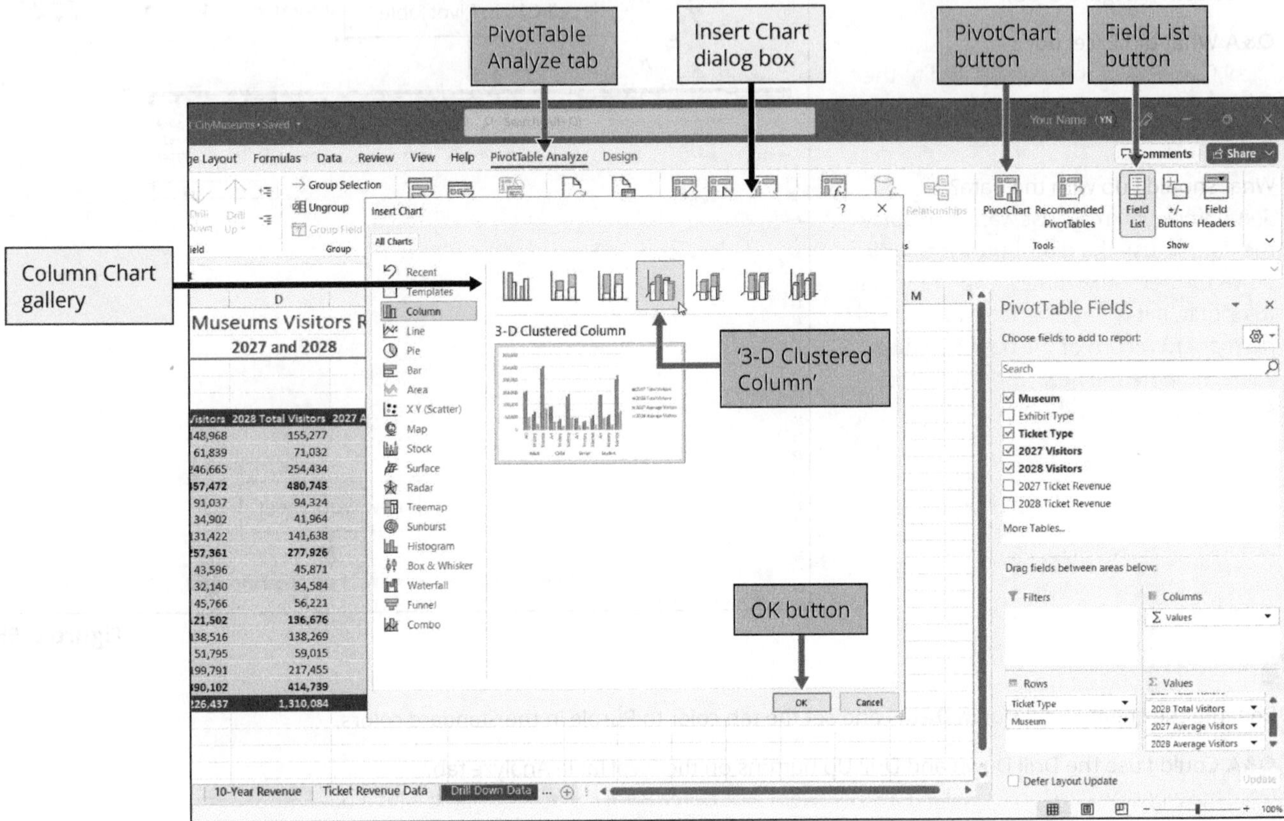

Figure 8–56

2

- Click OK (Insert Chart dialog box) to add the chart to the Visitors PivotTable worksheet (Figure 8–57).

Q&A My chart does not display field buttons across the top. Did I do something wrong?
It may simply be that the field buttons are turned off. Click the Field Buttons button (PivotChart Analyze tab | Show/Hide Group) to turn them on.

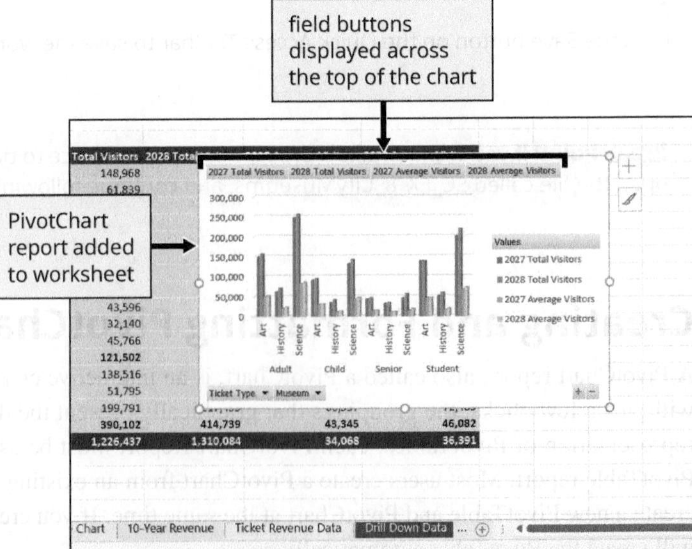

Figure 8–57

Other Ways

1. Click Insert PivotChart button (Insert tab | Charts group), select chart type (Insert Chart dialog box), click OK
2. Select a cell in PivotTable, press F11 to create default chart

To Move the PivotChart Report

By default, a PivotChart report will be created on the same page as the associated PivotTable report. **Why?** Moving the PivotChart report to a new sheet allows users to display each separately, which can be used for better sharing of the PivotChart and Pivot Table. The following steps move the PivotChart report to a separate worksheet and then change the tab color to match that of the PivotTable report tab.

1. Display the Design tab.
2. With the 3-D Clustered Column chart selected, use the Move Chart button (Design tab | Location group) to move the chart to a new sheet named **Visitors PivotChart.**
3. Move the Visitors PivotChart sheet to the right of the Visitors PivotTable sheet.
4. Set the tab color to Blue, Accent 1.

To Change the PivotChart Type and Reset Chart Elements

Why? Selecting a chart type instead of using the default type provides variety for the reader and may enhance the impact of the graphic. The default chart type for a PivotChart is a clustered column chart. However, PivotCharts can support most chart types, except scatter (X, Y), stock, and bubble. The following steps change the PivotChart type to Full Cone, add a title to the PivotChart report, and apply formatting options to the chart.

- Click one of the orange '2028 Total Visitors' columns to select the data series.
- Right-click to display the shortcut menu (Figure 8–58).

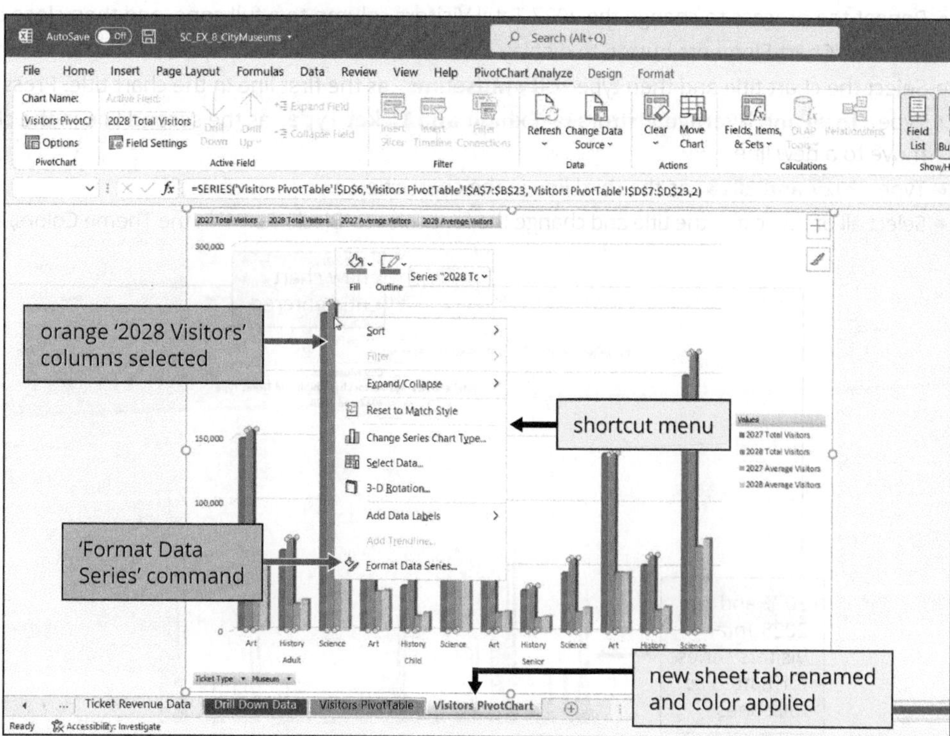

Figure 8–58

- Click 'Format Data Series' on the shortcut menu to open the Format Data Series pane.
- If necessary, click the Series Options button.
- In the Column shape section (Series Options area), click Full Cone (Figure 8–59).

- **Experiment:** One at a time, click each of the column shapes in the Format Data Series pane and notice the difference in the PivotChart column. When you are finished, click Full Cone again.

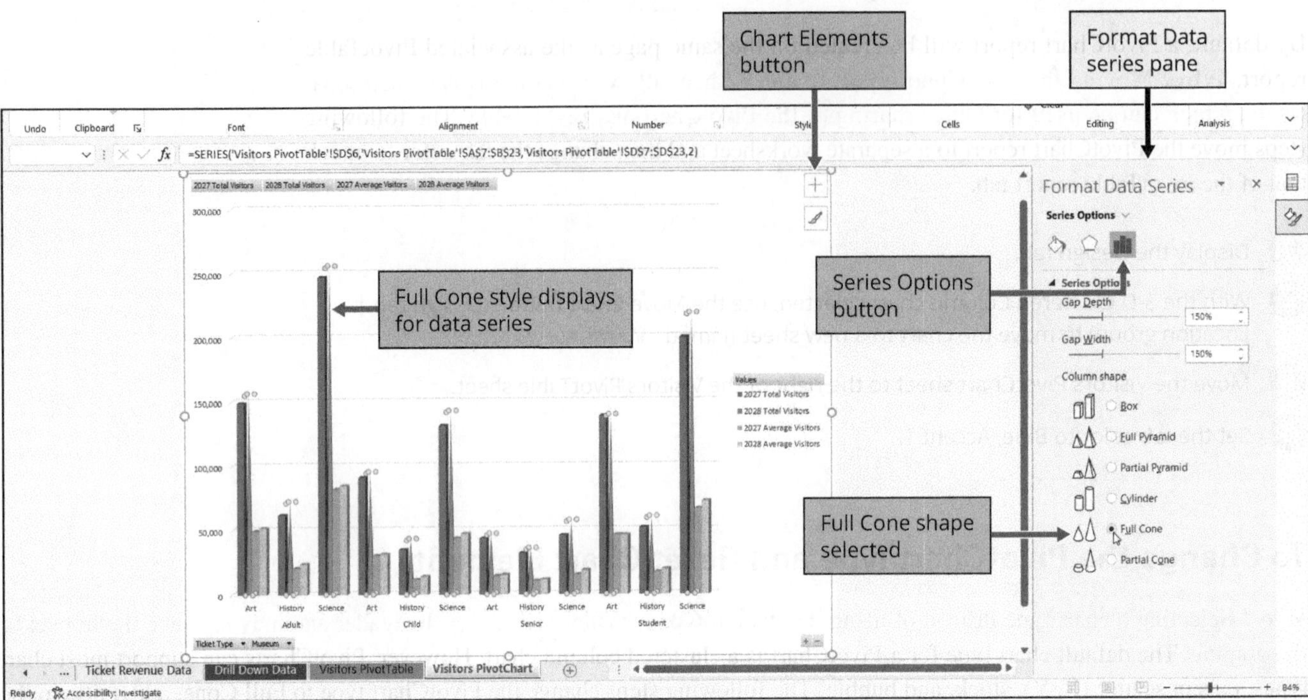

Figure 8–59

- Repeat the process to change the 2027 Total Visitors column to a full cone, and then close the Format Data Series pane.
- Click the Chart Elements button to display the menu, and then click to place a checkmark in the Chart Title check box.
- Select the chart title and then type **City Museums** as the first line in the chart title. Press ENTER to move to a new line.
- Type **Total and Average Visitors by Exhibit and Ticket Type** as the second line in the chart title and then press ENTER to move to a new line.
- Type **2027 and 2028** as the third line in the chart title.
- Select all of the text in the title and change the font color to 'Black, Text 1' in the Theme Colors, and then bold the text (Figure 8–60).

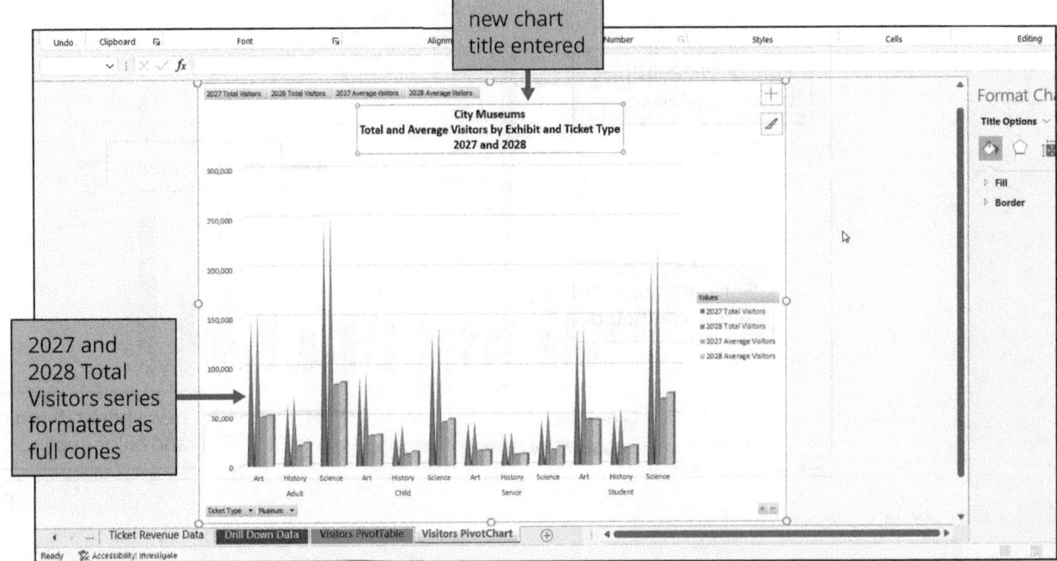

Figure 8–60

4

- Display the Format tab.
- Click the Chart Elements arrow (Format tab | Current Selection group) to display the Chart Elements menu (Figure 8–61).

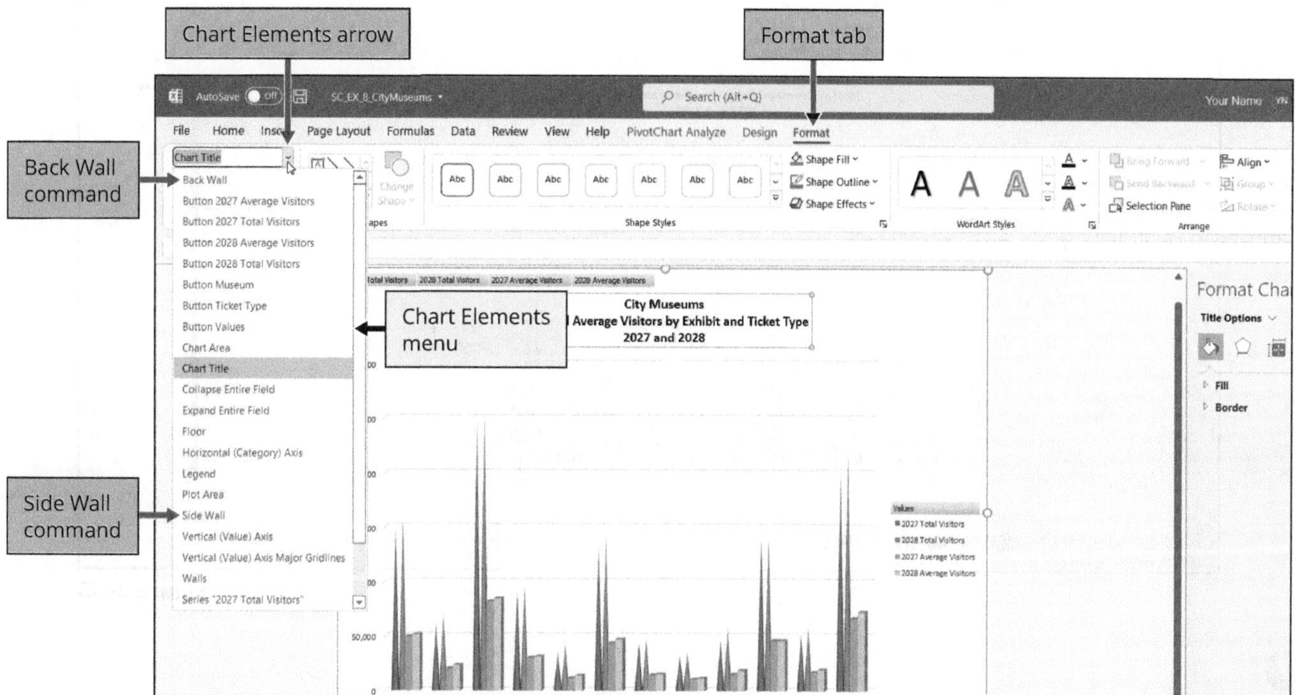

Figure 8–61

- Click Back Wall on the Chart Elements menu to select the back wall of the chart.
- Click the Shape Fill button (Format tab | Shape Styles group) to display the Shape Fill gallery and then click Green, Accent 6.
- Click the Shape Fill arrow again and then point to Gradient in the Shape Fill gallery to display the Gradient submenu (Figure 8–62).

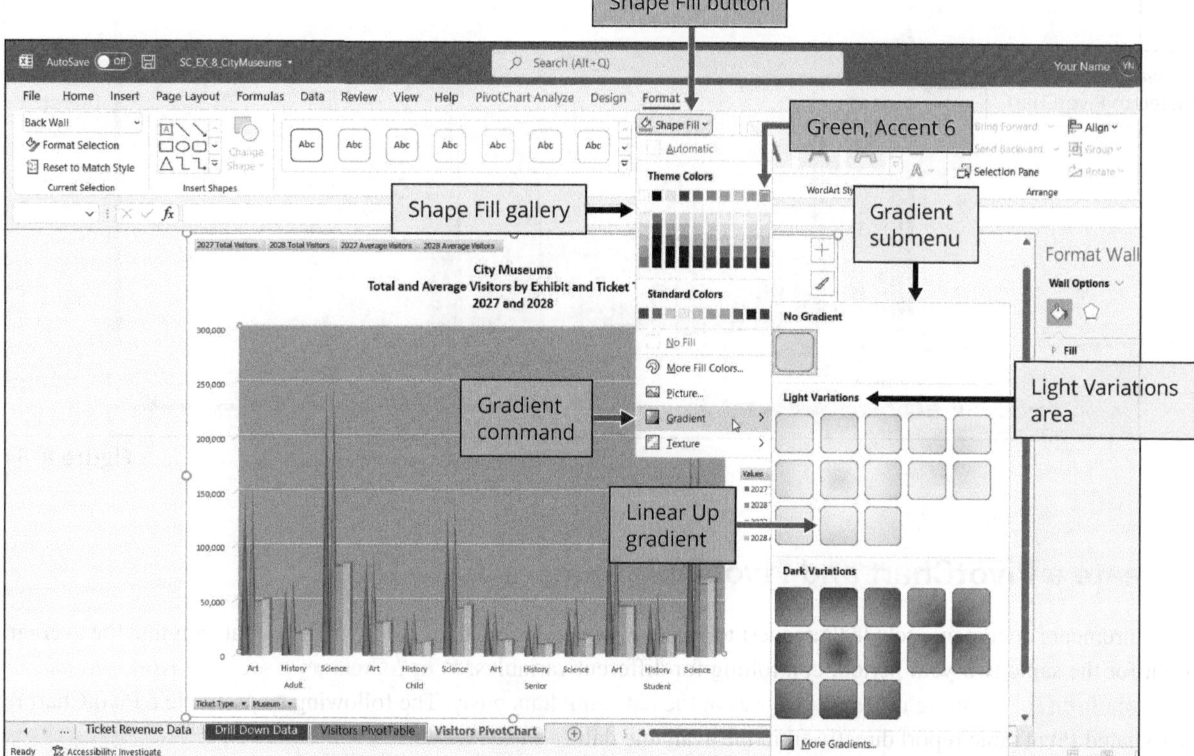

Figure 8–62

- Click Linear Up in the Light Variations area to apply a gradient fill to the back wall of the chart (Figure 8–63).

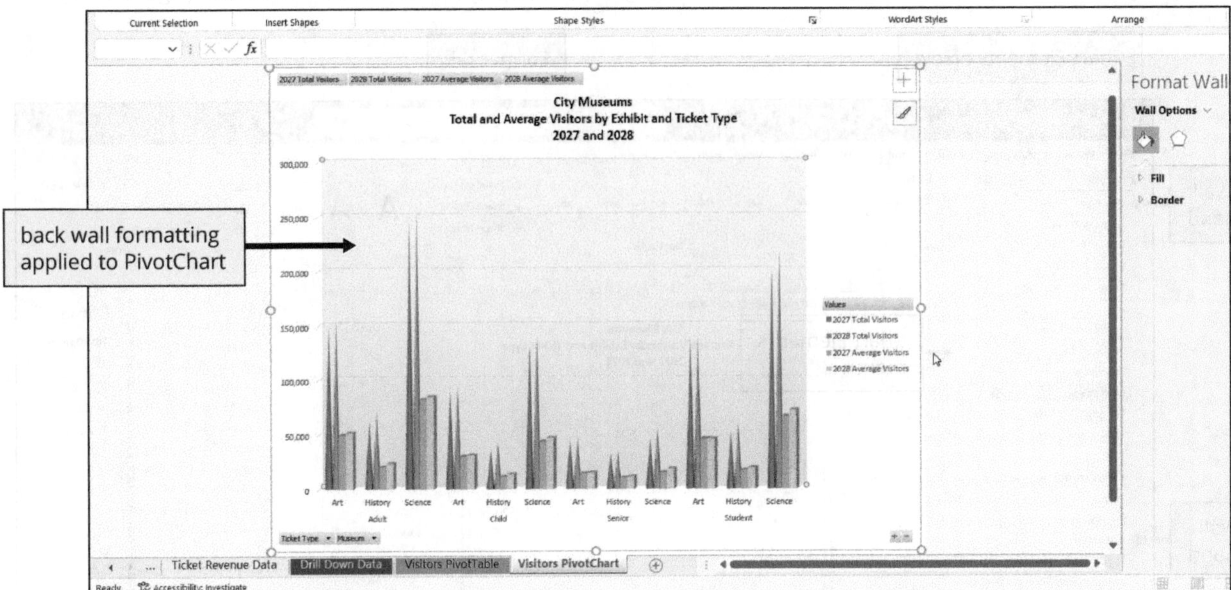

Figure 8–63

- Select the Side Wall element on the Chart Elements menu, and then repeat Steps 5 and 6 (Figure 8–64).
- Close the Format Wall pane.

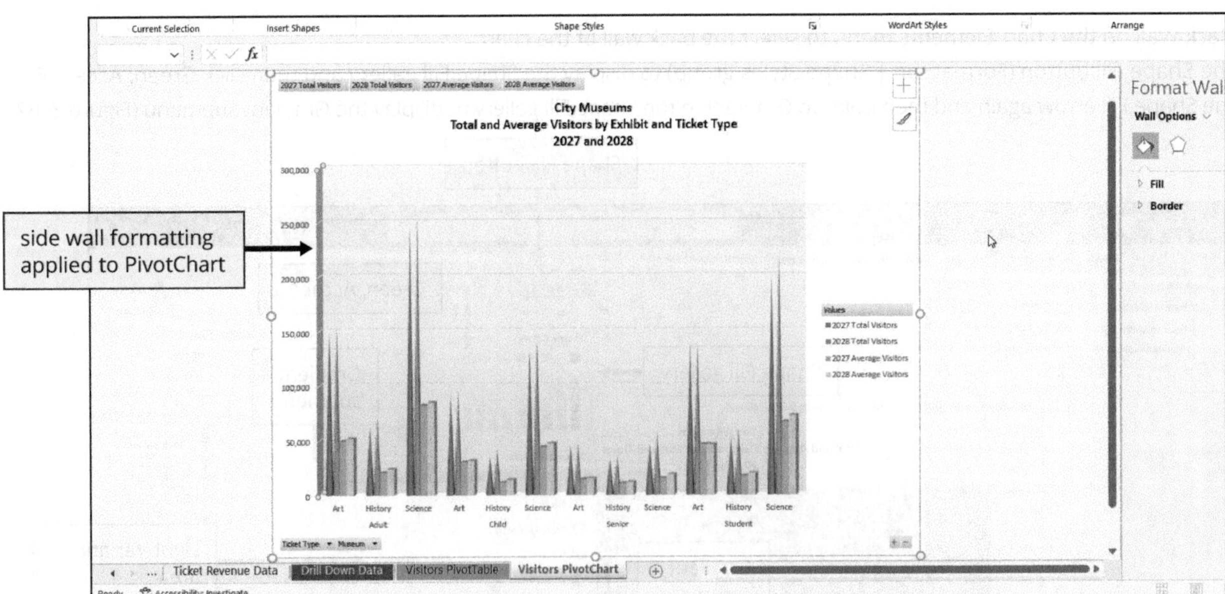

Figure 8–64

To Create a PivotChart and PivotTable Directly from Data

The requirements document included a request to create a second PivotChart and PivotTable that examine the average revenue amount for the same two-year period, controlling for different variables. **Why?** Creating a second PivotChart and PivotTable offers a platform for pursuing multiple inquiries of the data simultaneously. The following steps create a PivotChart report and an associated PivotTable report directly from the available data.

1

- Click the Ticket Revenue Data sheet tab to display the worksheet.
- Click cell A3 and then display the Insert tab.
- Click the PivotChart arrow (Insert tab | Charts group) to display the PivotChart menu (Figure 8–65).

Q&A Can I select specific data for a PivotChart?
Yes, you can highlight the cells before creating the PivotChart. By default, Excel includes the table around the chosen cell; or, if the data is not a table, Excel assumes all contiguous data.

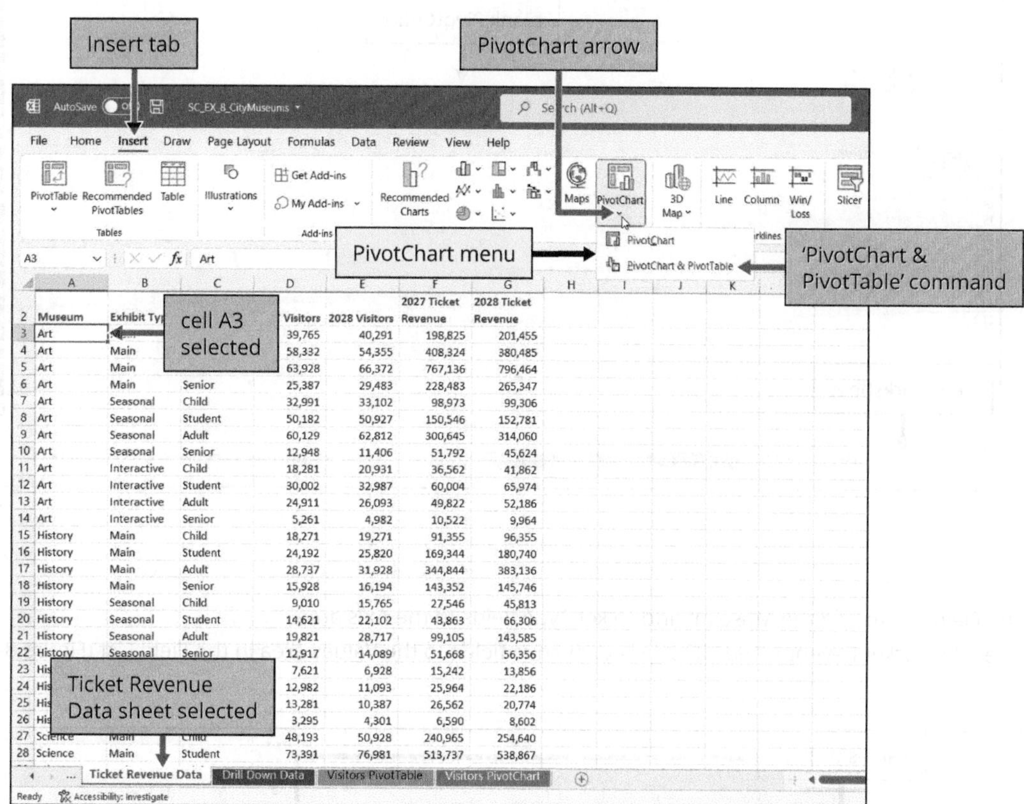

Figure 8–65

- Click 'PivotChart & PivotTable' on the PivotChart menu to display the Create PivotTable dialog box.
- If necessary, click the New Worksheet option button (Create PivotTable dialog box) (Figure 8–66).

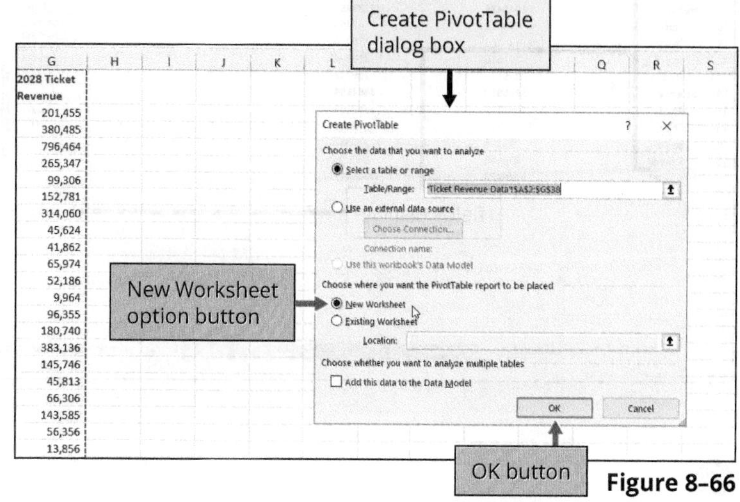

Figure 8–66

- Click OK to add a new worksheet containing a blank PivotTable and blank PivotChart (Figure 8–67).

Q&A What does the Field List display when creating a blank PivotChart?
Based on the location of your selected cell when you started the process, the Field List displays the available fields for you to place in the Filters and Axis areas.

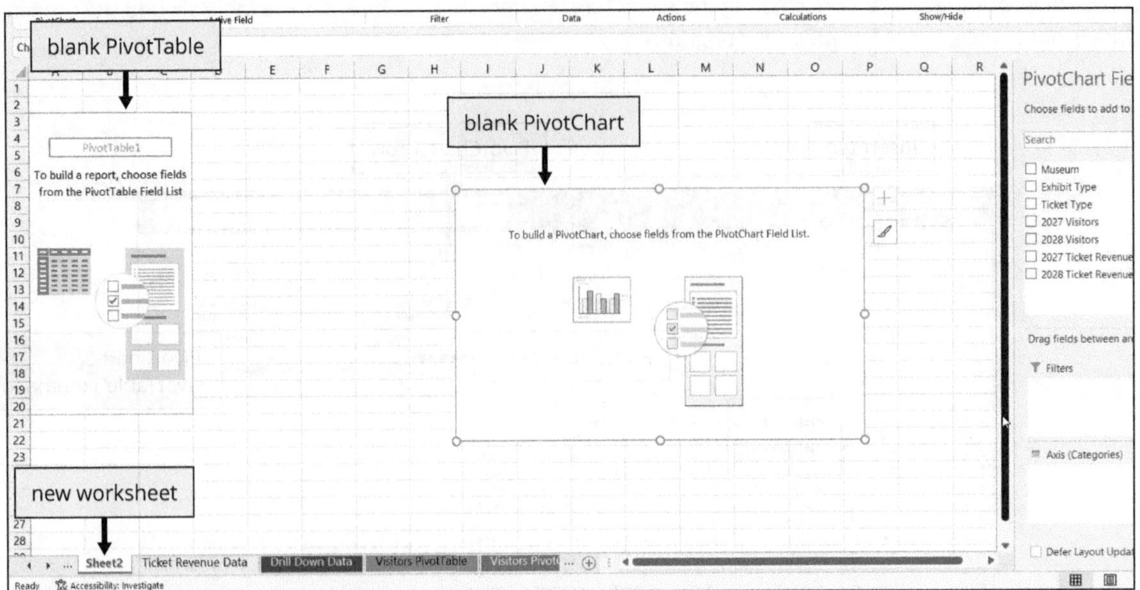

Figure 8–67

- Use the Field List to add the Museum and Ticket Type fields to the Axis area.
- Add the 2027 Ticket Revenue and 2028 Ticket Revenue fields to the Values area in the Field List (Figure 8–68).

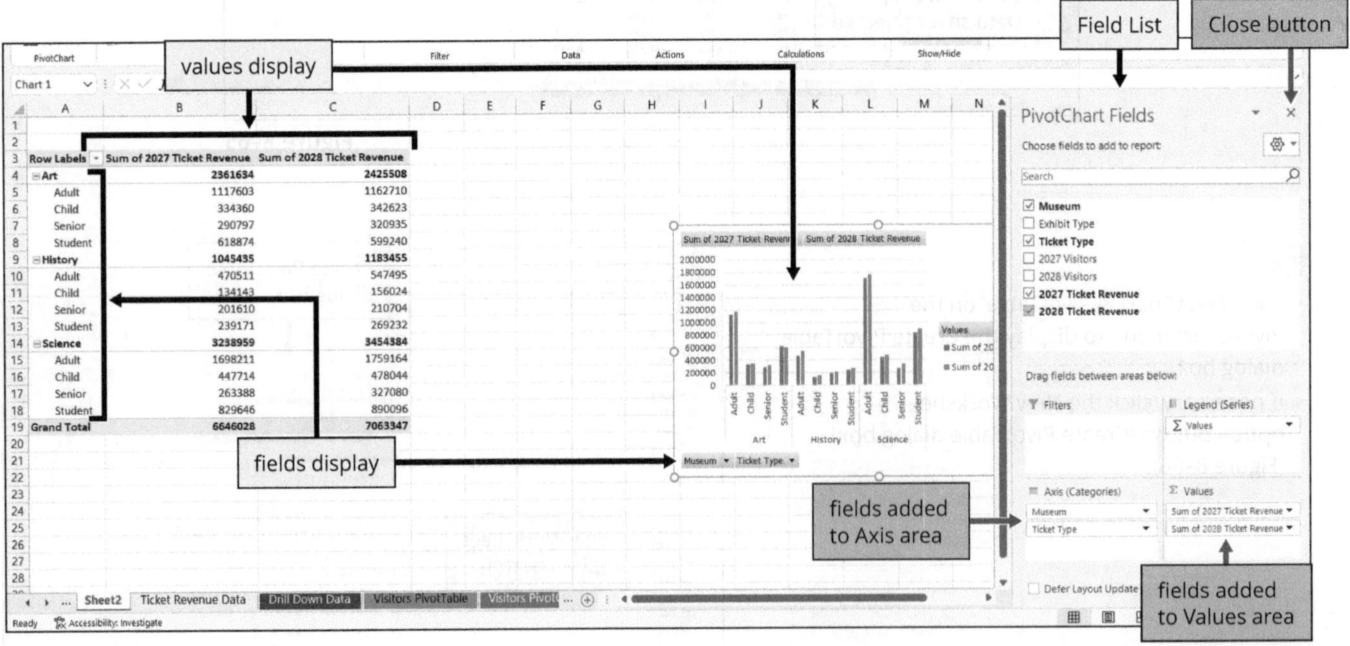

Row Labels	Sum of 2027 Ticket Revenue	Sum of 2028 Ticket Revenue
Art	2361634	2425508
Adult	1117603	1162710
Child	334360	342623
Senior	290797	320935
Student	618874	599240
History	1045435	1183455
Adult	470511	547495
Child	134143	156024
Senior	201610	210704
Student	239171	269232
Science	3238959	3454384
Adult	1698211	1759164
Child	447714	478044
Senior	263388	327080
Student	829646	890096
Grand Total	6646028	7063347

Figure 8–68

- Close the Field List.
- Rename the new worksheet **Avg Ticket Cost**, in preparation for creating ticket cost averages in the next steps, and then change the sheet tab color to the Dark Red tab color in the Standard Colors.

To Create a Calculated Field to a PivotTable Report

The following steps create calculated fields to use in the PivotTable and PivotChart reports. **Why?** You would like to review the average ticket cost by museum and ticket type for 2027 and 2028, but this information currently is not part of the data set with which you are working. You will need to calculate the values you need through the use of a calculated field. A **calculated field** is a field or table column whose values are not entered but are calculated based on other fields. A calculated field may contain a formula, function, cell reference, structured reference, or condition. In this case, 2027 Average Ticket Cost and 2028 Average Ticket Cost will be newly calculated fields, based on dividing the existing values of the 2027 Ticket Revenue and 2028 Ticket Revenue by the total visitors for 2027 and 2028, respectively.

- If necessary, click the PivotTable to make it active and then display the PivotTable Analyze tab.
- Click the 'Fields, Items, & Sets' button (PivotTable Analyze tab | Calculations group) to display the Fields, Items, & Sets menu (Figure 8–69).

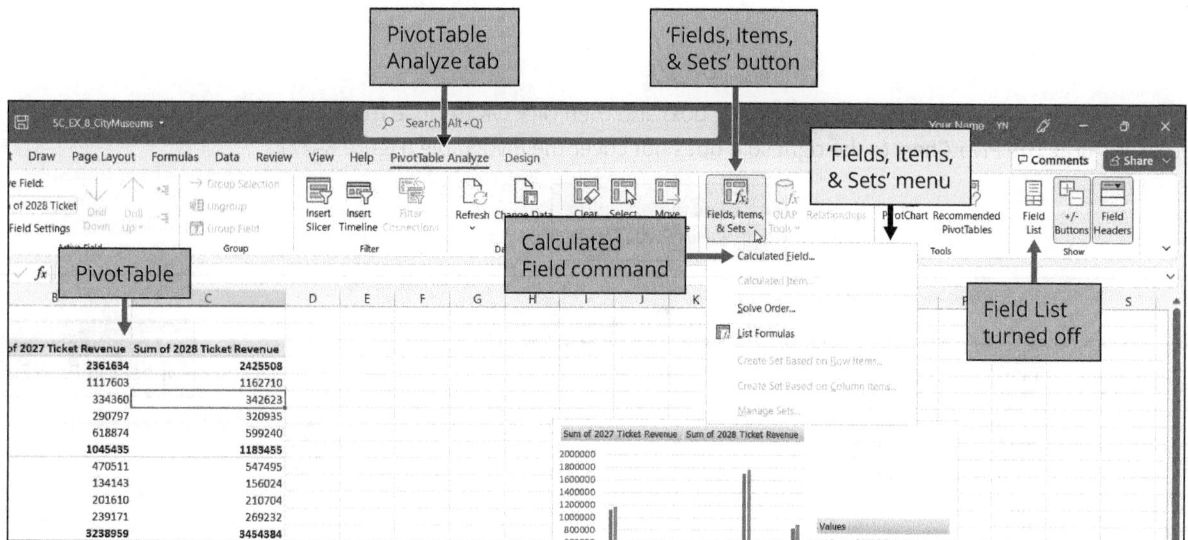

Figure 8–69

2

- Click Calculated Field to display the Insert Calculated Field dialog box.
- In the Name box, type **2027 Average Ticket Cost**.
- In the Formula box, delete the value to the right of the equal sign, in this case, 0.
- In the Fields list, double-click the 2027 Ticket Revenue field to insert it in the Formula text box.
- Type / (slash), and then double-click the 2027 Visitors field to complete the formula, which should read, = '2027 Ticket Revenue' / '2027 Visitors' (Figure 8–70).

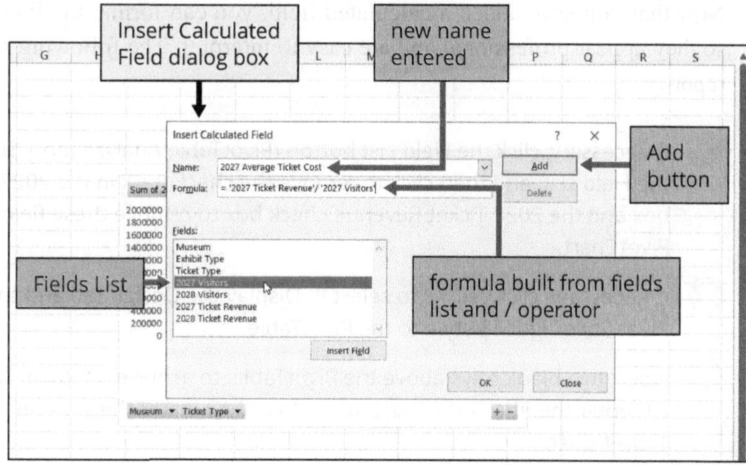

Figure 8–70

- Click the Add button (Insert Calculated Field dialog box) to add the calculated field to the Fields list.
- Repeat Step 2 to create a calculated field named 2028 Average Ticket Cost, calculated using 2028 Ticket Revenue divided by 2028 Visitors (Figure 8–71).

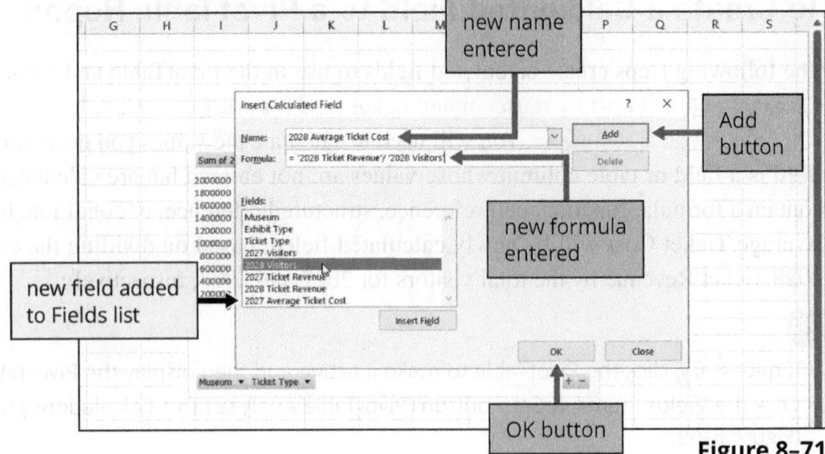

Figure 8–71

- Click the Add button (Insert Calculated Field dialog box) and then click OK to close the dialog box.
- If necessary, drag the PivotChart to the right so it does not cover the PivotTable (Figure 8–72).

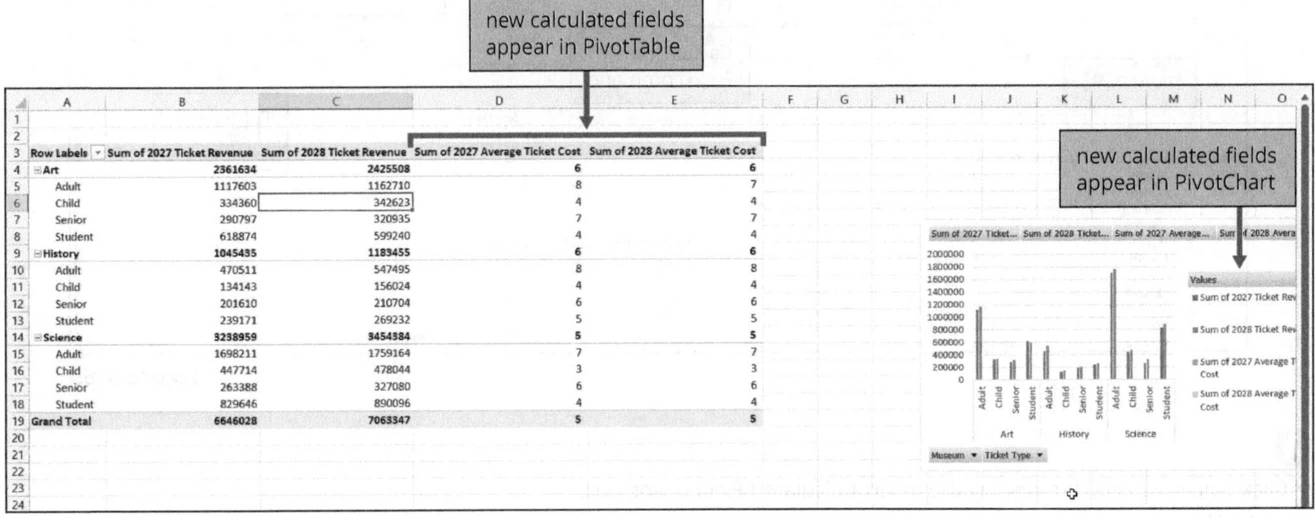

Row Labels	Sum of 2027 Ticket Revenue	Sum of 2028 Ticket Revenue	Sum of 2027 Average Ticket Cost	Sum of 2028 Average Ticket Cost
Art	2361634	2425508	6	6
Adult	1117603	1162710	8	7
Child	334360	342623	4	4
Senior	290797	320935	7	7
Student	618874	599240	4	4
History	1045435	1183455	6	6
Adult	470511	547495	8	8
Child	134143	156024	4	4
Senior	201610	210704	6	6
Student	239171	269232	5	5
Science	3238959	3454384	5	5
Adult	1698211	1759164	7	7
Child	447714	478044	3	3
Senior	263388	327080	6	6
Student	829646	890096	4	4
Grand Total	6646028	7063347	5	5

Figure 8–72

To Format the PivotTable

Now that you have added a calculated field, you can format the PivotTable and the PivotChart so they appear professional and are easy to interpret. The following steps format the PivotTable report.

1. If necessary, click the Field List button (PivotTable Analyze tab | Show/Hide group) to display the Field List, and then click to remove the checkmark in the 2027 Ticket Revenue check box and the 2028 Ticket Revenue check box to remove these fields from the PivotTable and PivotChart.

2. If necessary, click cell A3 to select it. Display the Design tab and then apply the 'Light Blue, Pivot Style Light 13 style to the PivotTable.

3. Insert two blank rows above the PivotTable, to achieve a total of four blank rows. In cell A1, enter the title **City Museums.** In cell A2, enter the subtitle **2027 and 2028 Average Ticket Cost.**

4. Merge and center the text across cells A1:C1 and cells A2:C2. Apply the Title style to cell A1. Apply the Heading 2 style to cell A2.

5. Change the field name in cell B5 to **Average 2027 Ticket Cost**. Change the field name in cell C5 to **Average 2028 Ticket Cost**.

6. Apply the Currency number format with two decimal places and the $ symbol to the Average 2027 Ticket Cost and Average 2028 Ticket Cost field columns, excluding the headers.

7. Use the Field List button, the '+/– Buttons' button, and the Field Headers button (PivotTable Analyze tab | Show group) to hide the field list, the Expand/Collapse buttons, and the field headers.

8. Change the column widths for columns B and C to **15.00**, and change the width for column D, which is currently blank, to **70**.

9. Wrap and center the field names in cells B5 and C5 (Figure 8–73).

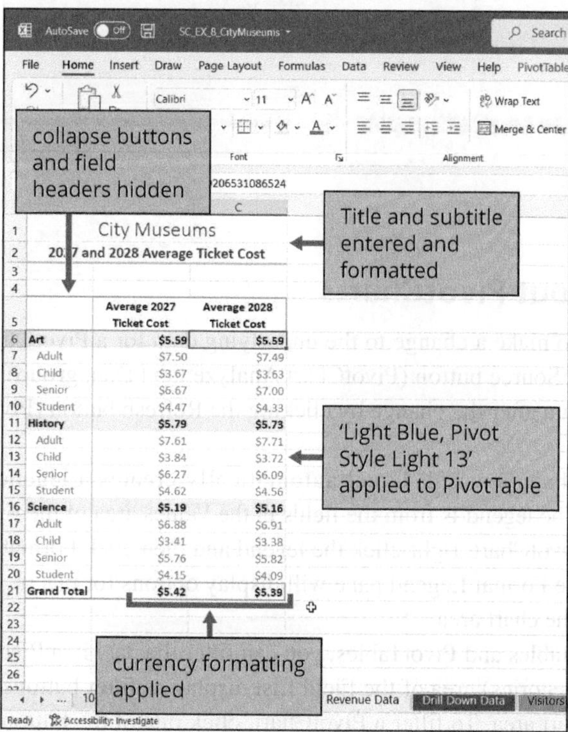

Figure 8–73

To Format the PivotChart

The following steps format the PivotChart report.

1. Click on the PivotChart report to select it.

2. Move and resize the PivotChart report so that it fills the range D1:D21.

3. Apply Style 11 in the Chart Styles gallery (Design tab | Chart Styles group).

4. Use the 'Change Colors' button (Design tab | Chart Styles group) to change the colors to 'Monochromatic Palette 5' in the Monochromatic area.

5. Click the Field Buttons button (PivotChart Analyze tab | Show/Hide group) to hide the field buttons.

6. Increase the worksheet magnification to 110%.

7. Save the workbook (Figure 8–74).

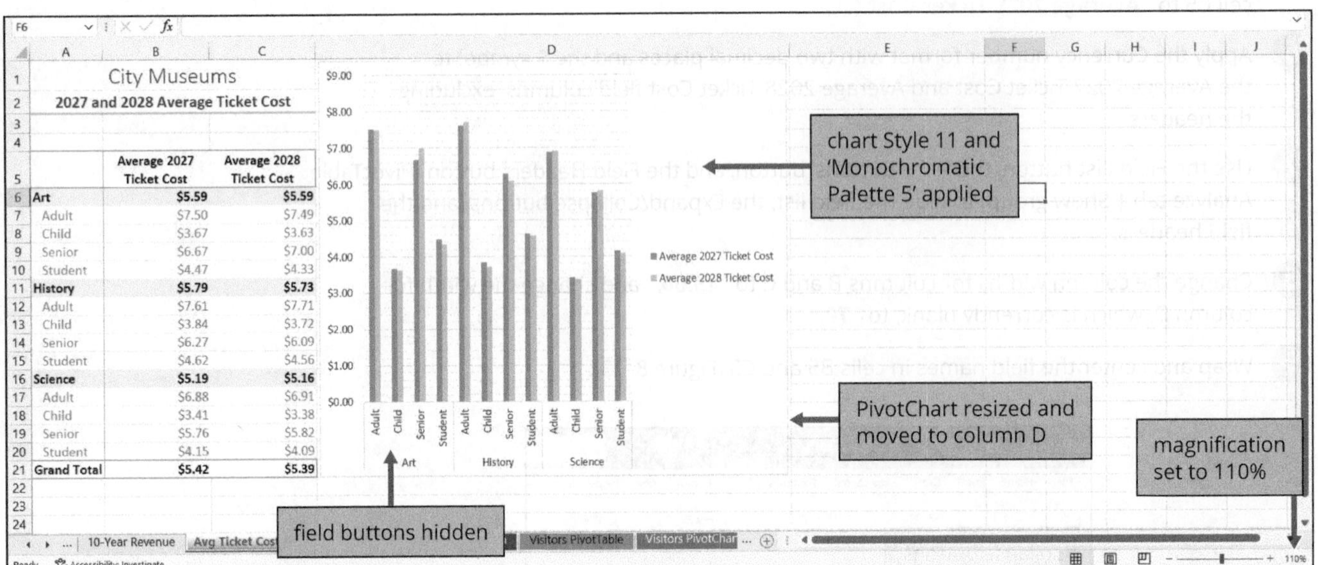

Figure 8–74

BTW
Distributing a Workbook
Instead of printing and distributing a hard copy of a workbook, you can distribute the workbook electronically. Options include sending the workbook via email; posting it on a cloud storage location (such as OneDrive) and sharing the file with others; posting it on social media, a blog, or other websites; and sharing a link associated with an online location of the workbook. You also can create and share a PDF or XPS image of the workbook so that users can check out the file in Acrobat Reader or XPS Viewer instead of in Excel.

BTW
Printing
If you want to improve the quality of Excel printouts that contain graphical elements, such as images, charts, and tables, you can instruct Excel to print high-quality graphics in workbooks by clicking File on the ribbon to open Backstage view, clicking the Options tab in Backstage view to display the Excel Options dialog box, clicking Advanced in the left pane (Excel Options dialog box), scrolling to the Print area in the right pane, placing a checkmark in the 'High quality mode for graphics' check box, and then clicking OK. Then, use Backstage view to print the workbook as usual.

More About PivotCharts

If you need to make a change to the underlying data for a PivotChart, you can click the Change Data Source button (PivotChart Analyze tab | Data group). You also can refresh PivotChart data after the change by clicking the Refresh button (PivotChart Analyze tab | Data group).

As you have learned, Excel automatically creates a legend when you create a PivotChart. The legend is from the fields in the Values area of the Field List. To move the legend in a PivotChart, right-click the legend and then click Format Legend on the shortcut menu. The Format Legend pane will display options for placing the legend at various locations in the chart area.

As with tables and PivotTables, you can filter the data in a Pivot Chart. Any fields in the Axis (Categories) area of the Field List display as filter buttons in the lower-left corner of the chart area. To filter a PivotChart, click one of the buttons; the resulting menu will allow you to sort, search, and select.

Working with Slicers

One of the strengths of PivotTables is that you can ask questions about the data by using filters. Being able to identify and examine subgroups is a useful analytical tool; however, when using filters and autofilters, the user cannot always tell which subgroups have the filters and autofilters selected without clicking the filter buttons. Slicers are easy-to-use buttons that you can click to filter the data in PivotTables and PivotCharts, making the data easier to interpret. With slicers, the subgroups are immediately identifiable and can be changed with a click of a button or buttons.

Consider This

Why would you use slicers rather than row, column, or report filters?

One effective way to analyze PivotTable data is to use slicers to filter the data in more than one field. They offer the following advantages over filtering directly in a PivotTable:

- In a PivotTable, you use the filter button to specify how to filter the data, which involves a few steps. After you create a slicer, you can perform this same filtering task in one step.
- You can filter only one PivotTable at a time, whereas you can connect slicers to more than one PivotTable to filter data.
- Excel treats slicers as graphic objects, which means you can move, resize, and format them as you can any other graphic object. As graphic objects, they invite interaction.
- Slicers are intuitive—users without knowledge of Excel can use them to interact with the data.
- Slicers make it easy for users to understand exactly what is shown in a filtered PivotTable or PivotChart.

The advisory board of the City Museums has asked you to set up a PivotChart and PivotTable with a user-friendly way for anyone to explore the average ticket cost data. You can use slicers to complete this task efficiently.

To Copy a PivotTable and PivotChart

To create a canvas for exploratory analysis of revenue data, you first need to create a new PivotTable and a PivotChart. The following steps copy an existing PivotTable and PivotChart to a new worksheet, format the PivotTable, and rename the worksheet.

1. Create a copy of the Avg Ticket Cost worksheet and then move the copy so that it precedes the Avg Ticket Cost worksheet.
2. Rename the new worksheet, **Slicers**, and apply the Dark Blue tab color from the Standard Colors area.
3. Apply chart Style 9 to the PivotChart.
4. Set the column widths of column E and column F to 25.00.
5. If necessary, turn off the display of field headers and +/– buttons for the PivotTable (Figure 8–75).

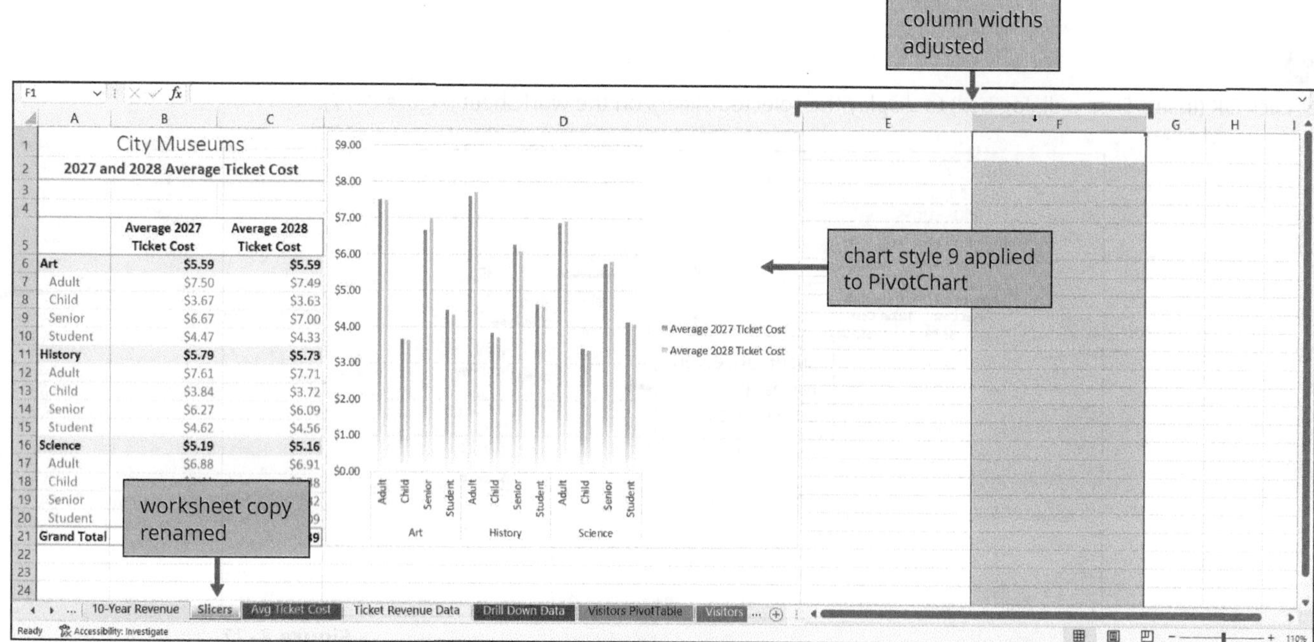

Figure 8–75

To Add Slicers to the Worksheet

The following steps add slicers to the new PivotTable and PivotChart. **Why?** To analyze ticket cost data for specific subgroups, you can use slicers instead of PivotTable filters.

- If necessary, click to make the PivotChart active and then display the PivotChart Analyze tab.
- Click the Insert Slicer button (PivotChart Analyze tab | Filter group) to display the Insert Slicers dialog box.
- Click to place checkmarks in the Museum, Exhibit Type, and Ticket Type check boxes (Figure 8–76).

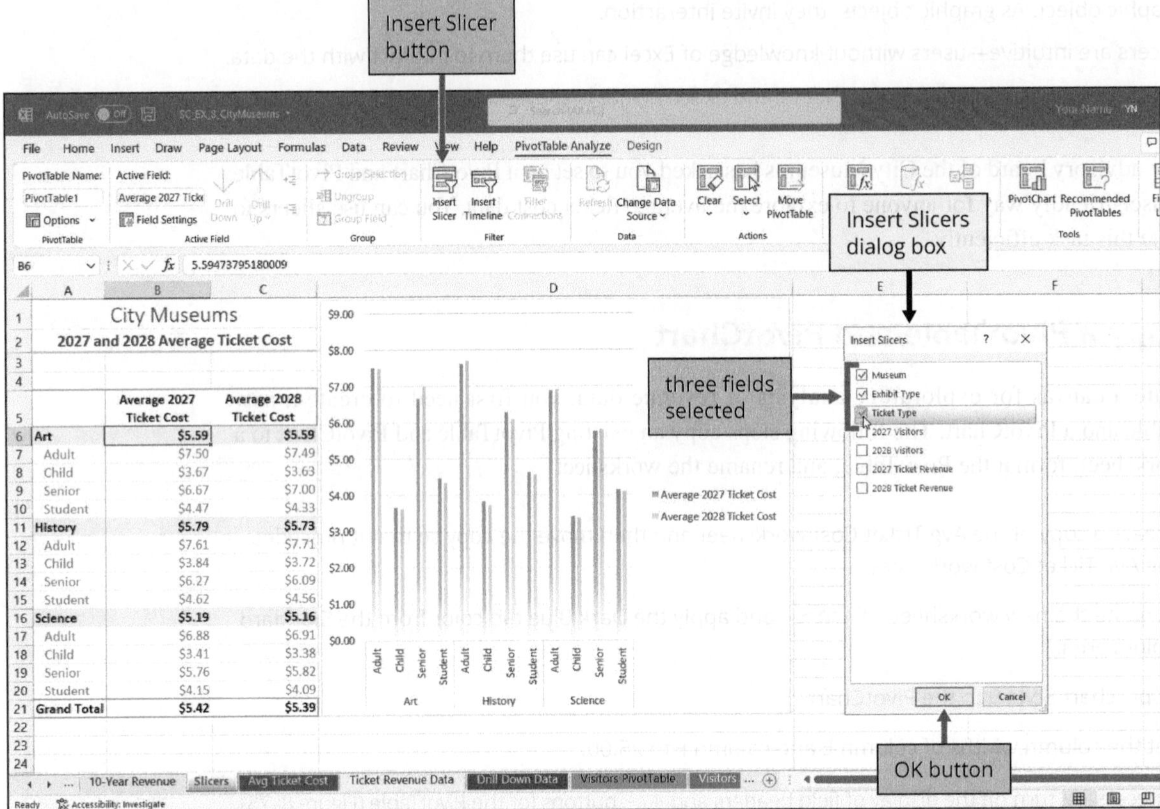

Figure 8–76

2

- Click OK (Insert Slicers dialog box) to display the selected slicers on the worksheet (Figure 8–77).

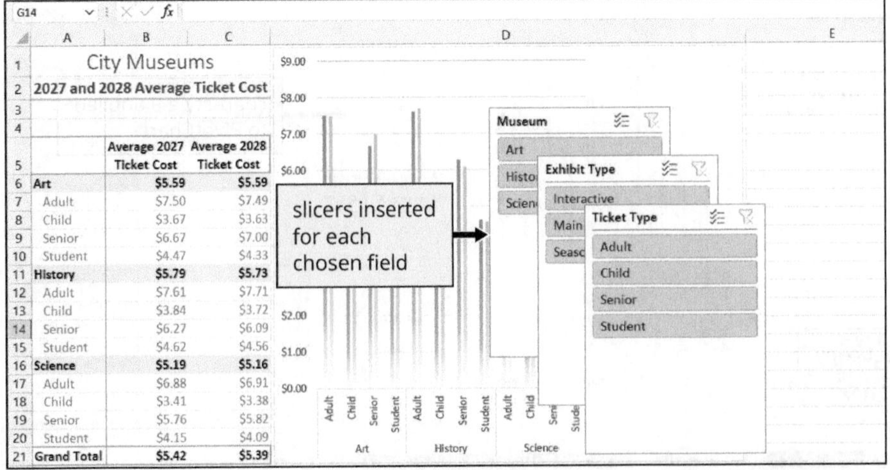

Figure 8–77

To Format Slicers

You can format slicers in a variety of ways. Using the Slicer tab, you can customize slicer settings, resize slicer buttons to exact dimensions, change the number of columns in a slicer, or connect a slicer to a different PivotChart using the Report Connections button (Slicer tab | Slicer group). The following steps move the slicers to the right of the PivotChart and then format them. **Why?** The slicers need to be moved and formatted so that they do not obscure the PivotTable or PivotChart, and so they are easy to read and use.

- Click the title bar of the Museum slicer and then drag the slicer to column E. Use the sizing handles to adjust the length of the slicer so that it ends at the bottom of row 10 and fits the width of the slicer so that it ends at the right edge of column E.
- Click and drag the Ticket Type slicer to column F. Use the sizing handles to adjust the length of the slicer so that it ends at the bottom of row 21 and the width so that it fits in column F.
- Click and then drag the Exhibit Type slicer to column E, just below the Museum slicer. Use the sizing handles to change the length of the slicer so that it ends at the bottom of row 21 and the width so that it fits in column E.
- Hold down CTRL and then, one at a time, click each of the slicer title bars to select all three.
- Select the text in the Height box (Slicer tab | Buttons group), type **.5** and then press ENTER to set the button height (Figure 8–78).

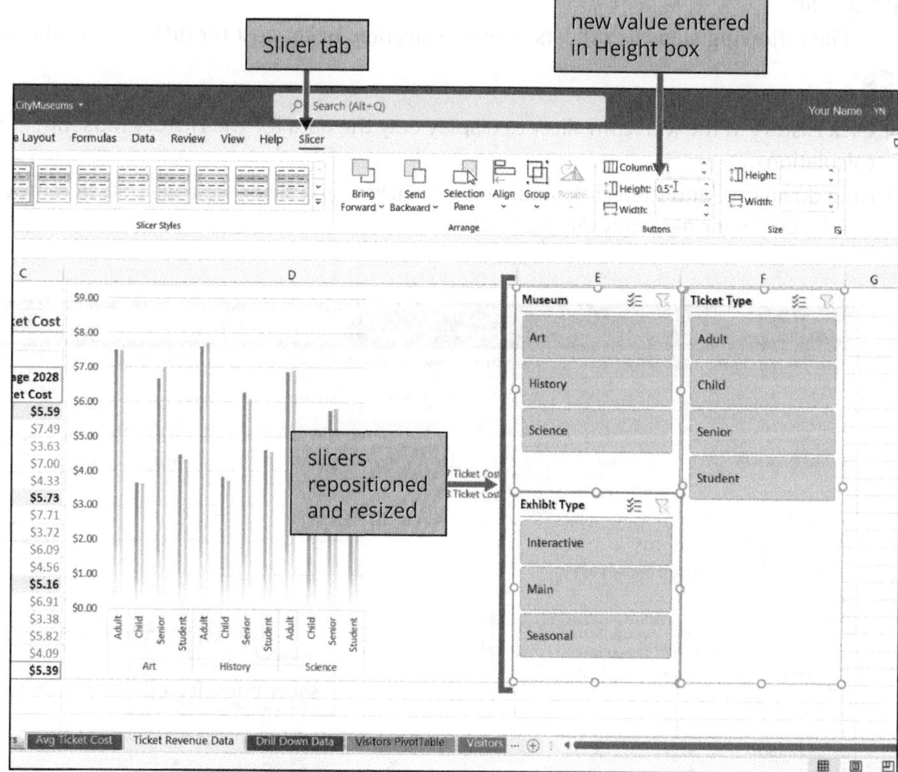

Figure 8–78

- Click the 'White, Slicer Style Other 2' Slicer style in the Light area (Slicer tab | Slicer Styles group) to apply it to the slicers (Figure 8–79).

- Click any cell to deselect the slicers.

Q&A How do you resize slicers and slicer buttons to exact dimensions?
Use the Height and Width boxes (Slicer tab | Size group and Buttons group) to change the size of a slicer or of slicer buttons.

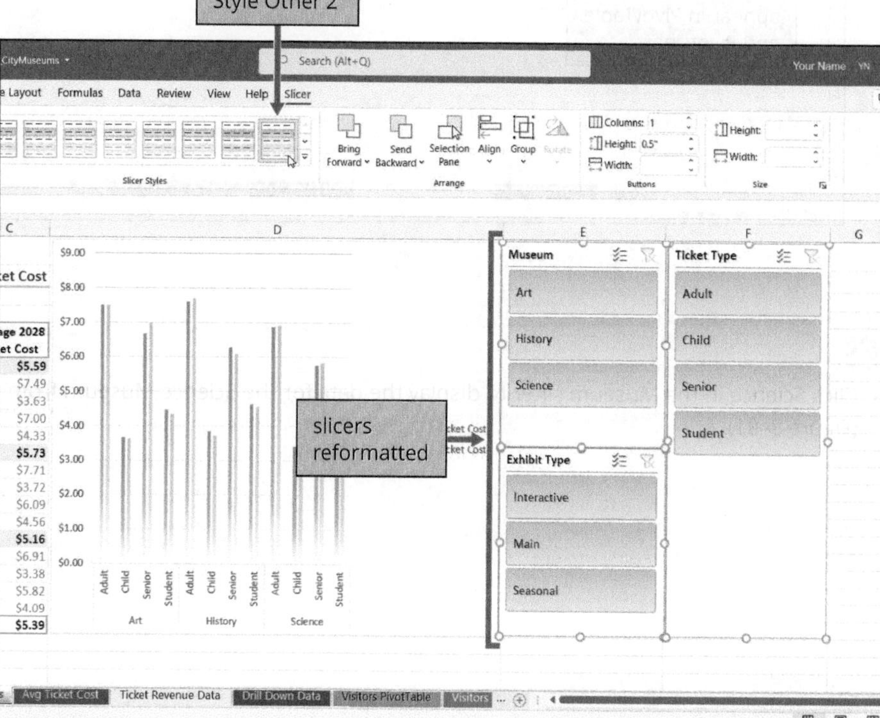

Figure 8–79

To Use the Slicers

Why? Slicers provide you with a visual means of filtering data by simply clicking subgroups of interest to change the data displayed in the PivotTable and PivotChart. Slicers based on row label fields provide the same results as filters in a PivotTable. They narrow the table down to a visible subgroup or subgroups. Clicking a slicer button displays only the data that corresponds to the variable name on the slicer. You can select multiple fields by using the Multi-Select button in the slicer title bar or by using CTRL+click to add a button (in the same slicer) to the display. Note that slicers filter data in both the PivotTable and the PivotChart.

The following steps use slicers to review average ticket cost for different combinations of Ticket Type and Museum.

- Click History in the Museum slicer to display only the data for the History Museum in the PivotTable and PivotChart calculations.
- Hold down CTRL and then click Student in the Ticket Type slicer. Release CTRL to remove the student data and show the Adult, Child, and Senior data only (Figure 8–80).

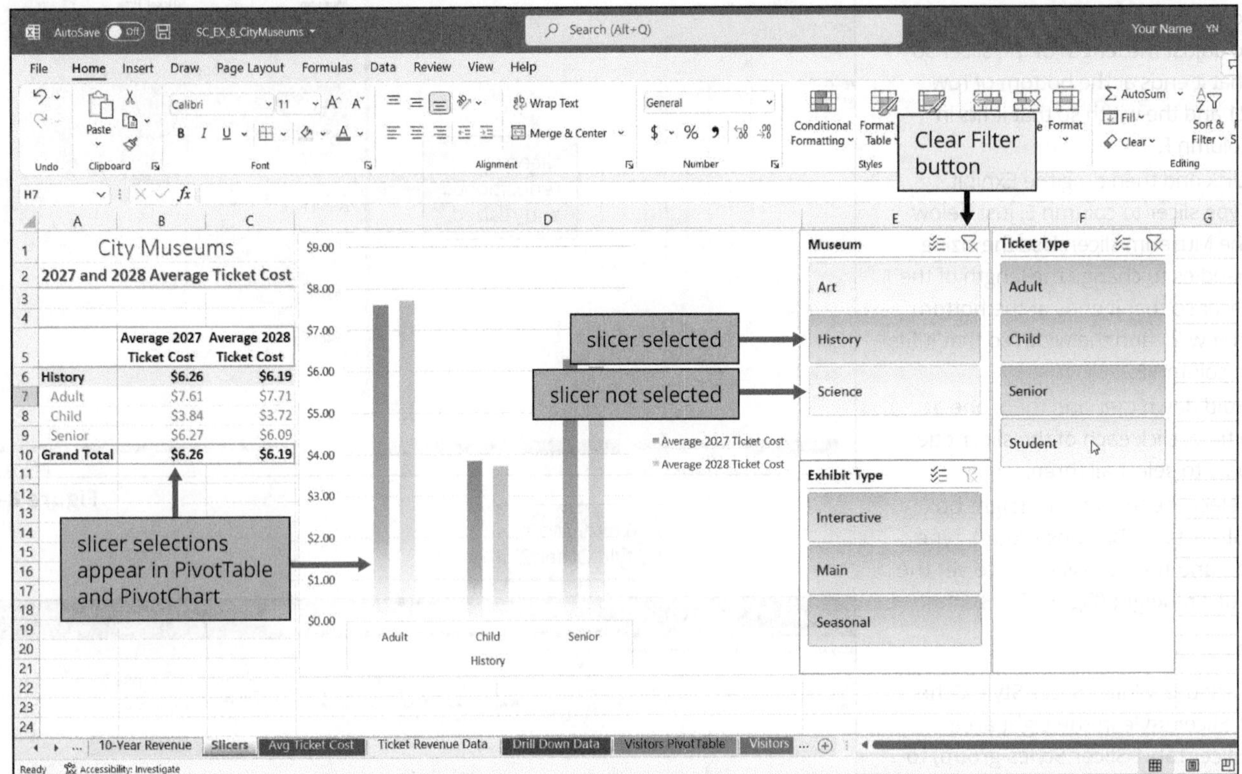

Figure 8–80

- Click Science in the Museum slicer to display the data for the Science Museum from the Adult, Child, and Senior data only (Figure 8–81).

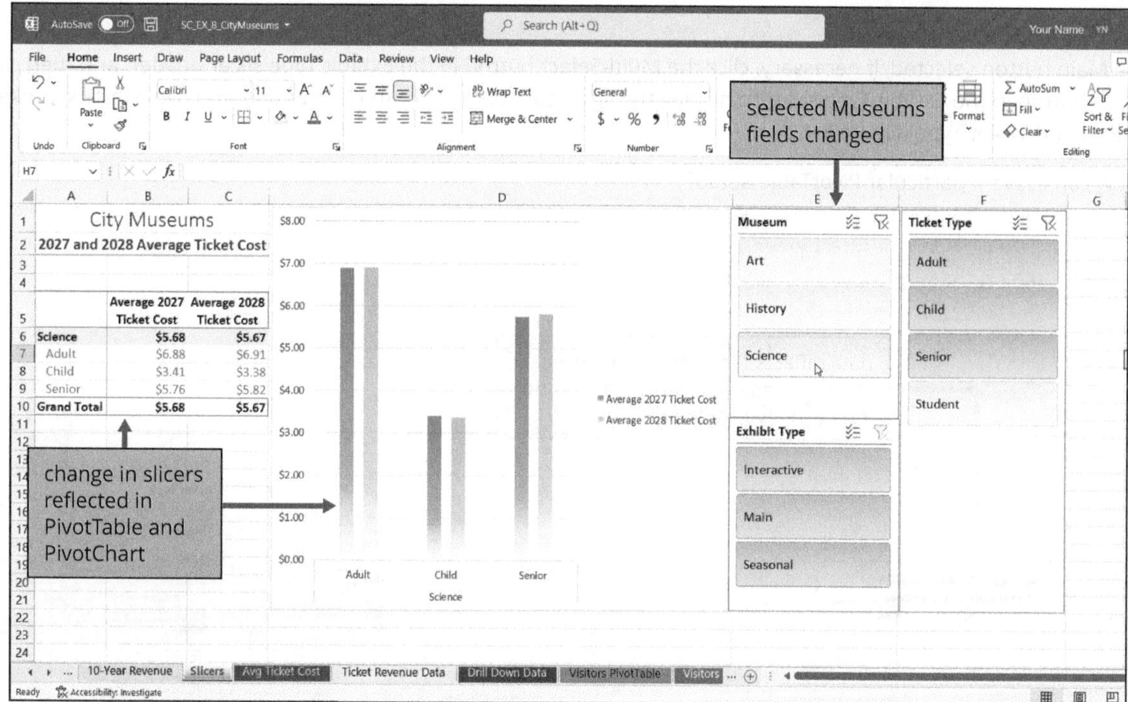

Figure 8–81

To Use Slicers to Review Data Not in a PivotTable

You can search for possible explanations of patterns by using slicers to analyze data other than that which is displayed in the PivotTable. **Why?** Slicers based on fields not included in the PivotTable provide the same results as report filters. Slicers regroup and narrow the PivotTable content to groups not visible in the PivotTable. The following steps use slicers to review data not currently visible in the PivotTable.

- Click the Clear Filter button on the Museum slicer and on the Ticket Type slicer to remove the filters and return the PivotTable and PivotChart to their unfiltered states.
- Click the Main button in the Exhibit Type slicer to display the aggregate data for the average ticket cost for visitors, broken down by Museum and Ticket Type (Figure 8–82).
- **Experiment:** Click different service types and combinations of service types to display how the aggregate data changes.

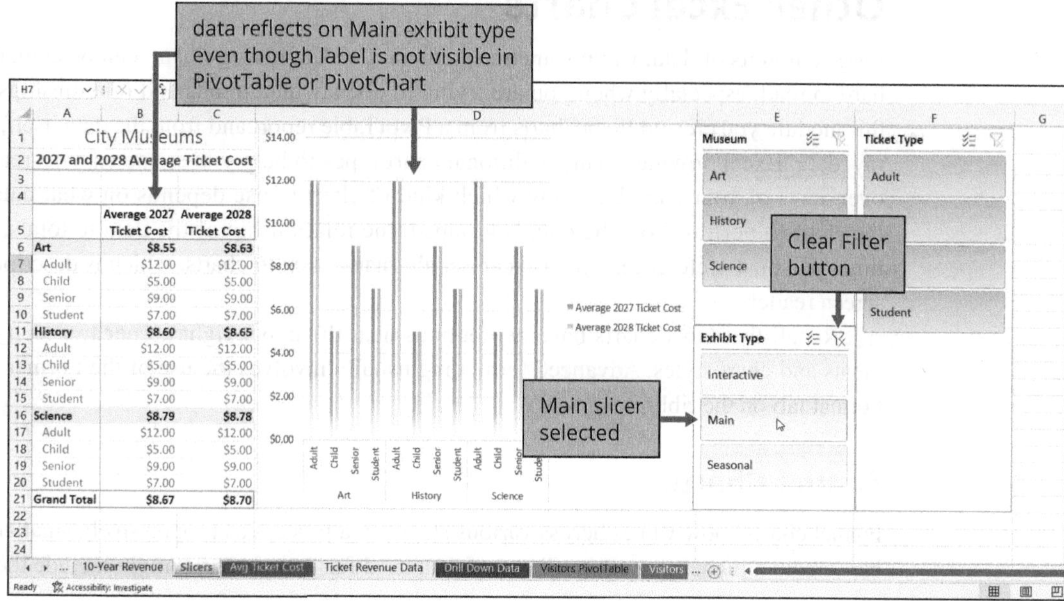

Figure 8–82

- With the Main button selected, if necessary, click the Multi-Select button in the Exhibit Type slicer header, and then click the Interactive button in the Exhibit Type slicer to display the aggregate data for both Main and Interactive exhibits, broken down by Museum and Ticket Type (Figure 8–83).

Q&A How can I save a particular PivotTable setup?
PivotTables are dynamic by nature. To save a particular configuration, make a copy of the worksheet, and use the Protect Sheet command (Review tab | Protect group) to keep changes from being made to the worksheet copy. You can continue to use the PivotTable on the original worksheet to analyze the data.

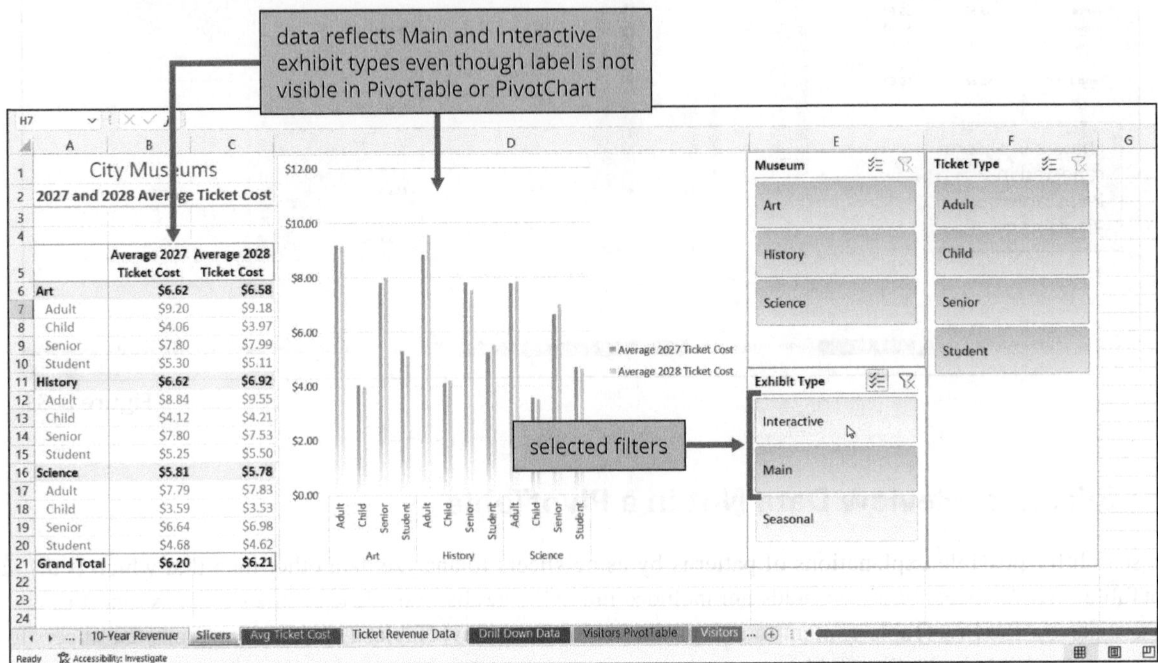

Figure 8–83

- Save the workbook.

Other Excel Charts

Large amounts of data, while sometimes crucial for data management, can be cumbersome and hard to read, especially when you are trying to display data trends and relationships. Earlier in this module you created PivotCharts from a PivotTable report and from the data itself, also called raw data. Excel provides many additional chart types to help you create easy-to-read, intuitive overviews of your data. Deciding which kind of chart to use depends on what data you want the chart to portray, how the data is grouped, the relationship of the data to totals, and sometimes personal preference. You also can set alternative text to charts, which is descriptive text for screen readers.

Recall that most charts have two buttons near the upper-right corner to specify chart elements and chart styles. Advanced formatting usually involves the use of the Format pane or the Format tab on the ribbon.

Funnel Charts

Funnel charts show values across various stages in a process as progressively smaller horizontal bars create a funnel-like effect. Types of data used for funnel charts might include the process of narrowing down a pool of job applicants to hired employees, a sales pipeline, or an order fulfillment process. Figure 8–84 uses data from an e-commerce software website to show how website hits drill down into licensed users.

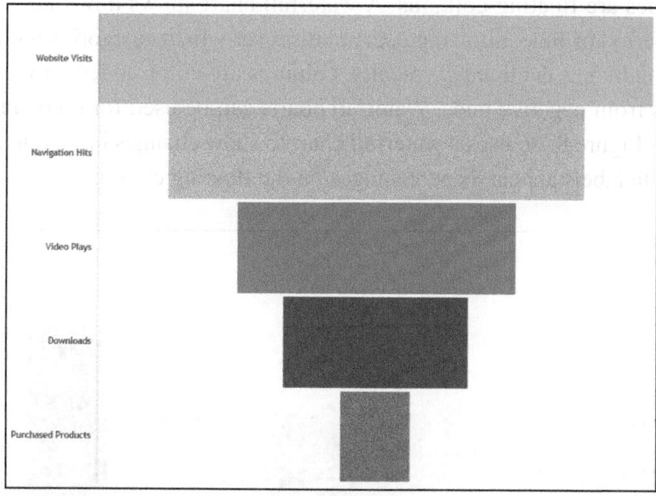

Figure 8–84

Besides the typical color schemes, styles, fills, borders, axis formatting, and editing that you can perform on most charts, funnel charts let you set a gap width, which is the distance between bars or levels in the funnel.

Sunburst Charts

The sunburst chart is used to show hierarchical data. Similar to a multilevel pie or donut chart, each level of the hierarchy is represented by a ring or circle. The innermost circle is the top of the hierarchy; relationships are shown via the outer rings. Types of data used for sunburst charts might include the reporting relationships in an organization, taxonomies, or sales or events shown by time (month-weeks-days) or locations (country-state-city). Figure 8–85 uses a sunburst chart to display the number of invoices submitted throughout the year, by quarter, month, and date.

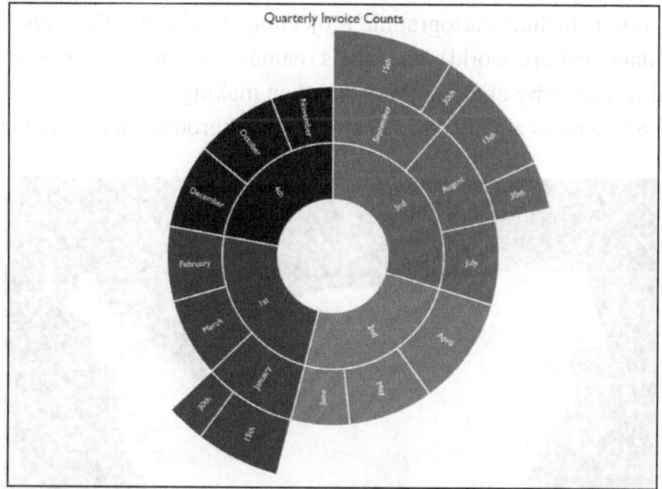

Figure 8–85

Colors in a sunburst chart are based on the theme and color style of the worksheet. Interesting effects can be created by adjusting the size of shadows, soft edges, and glows. With numeric data, you can add values to the sunburst chart in the same manner you do with a treemap.

Waterfall Charts

A waterfall chart shows how an initial value is affected by a series of positive and negative changes. The initial and the final value columns often start on the horizontal axis, while the intermediate values are floating columns. A waterfall chart shows how one data point grew or declined over a period of time, allowing users to discover which categories within the data point improved and which ones declined. Typically, columns are color-coded so you quickly can tell positive numbers from negative ones. Waterfall charts can be used for company growth, profit/loss, or inventory. Figure 8–86 uses a waterfall chart to show changes in regional sales over a six-month period. Data labels appear as percentages on the floating columns.

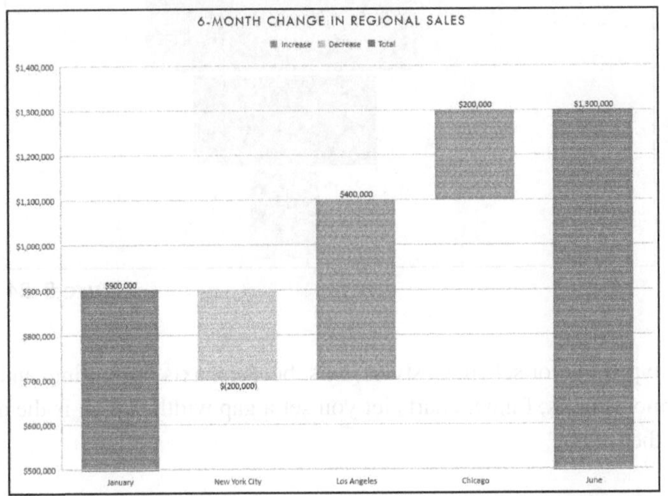

Figure 8–86

Map Charts

If your data has geographical regions or postal codes, you can create a map chart to compare values and show categories across those regions. To do so, highlight the list of locations and the matching data such as populations, land masses, or other statistical information. Then, when you choose to insert a map chart, Excel executes a Bing search to create a map. Figure 8–87 displays a map of the United States with statistical data about heart-related deaths.

Formatting options include cartographic projections (including flat, spherical, and others), area (displays of data, regions, world), and labels (names of countries, states, etc.). You even can format individual locations by clicking them and then making changes in the Format pane. The chart in Figure 8–87 displays a solid color chart area (background) and a gradient legend.

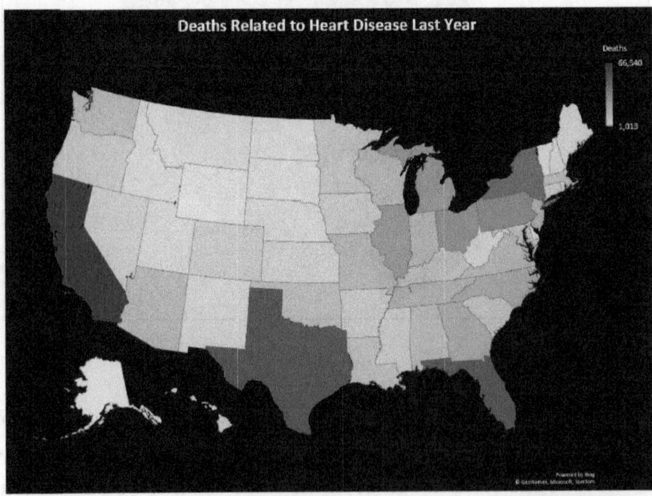

Figure 8–87

Scatter Charts

Scatter charts display two value axes to show one set of numerical data along a horizontal (x) axis and another set of numerical values along a vertical (y) axis. The chart displays points at the intersection of x and y numerical values. These data points may be distributed evenly or unevenly across the horizontal axis, depending on the data. Scatter charts, also called X-Y scatter charts or scatter plots, should be used when there are many different data points and you want to highlight the similarities or display the distribution of your data.

Figure 8–88 shows sales data—the days of the month along the horizontal axis at the bottom, and the amount of sales on the vertical axis on the side. The plot area (area inside the chart) displays a gradient pattern.

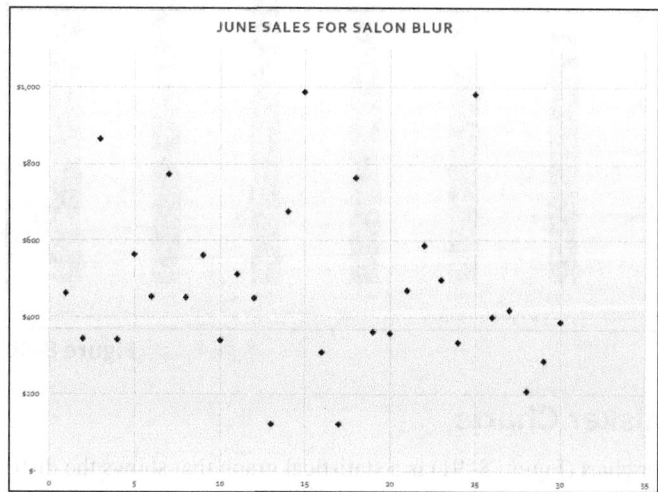

Figure 8–88

Histogram Charts

A histogram is a type of column chart that shows the frequency of data. It consists of rectangles whose height is proportional to the frequency of a variable. The x-axis across the bottom contains ranges of data values called bins. The y-axis is the frequency. Figure 8–89 displays the temperature on July 4th in Chicago from years 1970–2019, with a picture chart area (background) and a gap width between columns.

Ken Koskela/Alamy Stock Photo

Figure 8–89

Combo Charts

A **combo chart** is a chart consisting of two charts, such as a column chart combined with a line chart, that together graph related but dissimilar data. Other combinations might include bar charts or area charts. Combo charts emphasize the differences between sets of data; for example, in-store sales are down but online sales are up, or comparing projections versus actual figures. Figure 8–90 uses a column chart to display attendance at an amusement park for 2027 and a line chart to display attendance for 2028. While a clustered column chart could show the same data, a combo chart emphasizes the difference by presenting the data in a completely different way. Figure 8–90 displays a colored background in the chart area with a thick border.

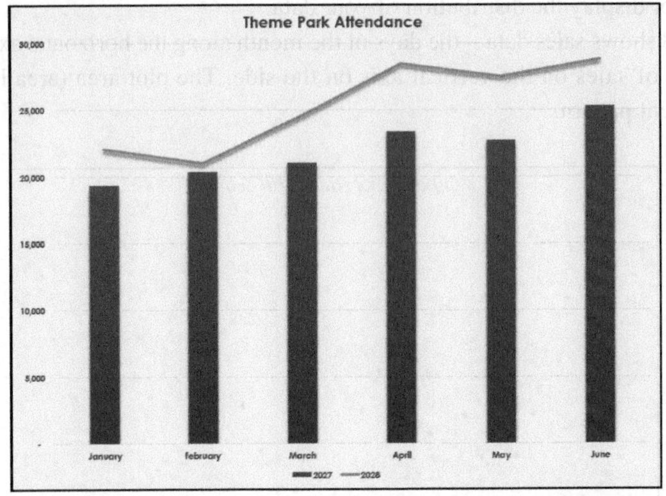

Figure 8–90

Box and Whisker Charts

A box and whisker chart (Figure 8–91) is a statistical graph that shows the distribution of numerical data into quartiles. A **quartile** is a way to divide ordered data into equal groups based on finding the median. Simply put, the box part of the chart shows the median and the two groups around the median with equal sets of numbers. The high and low values in the ordered data are displayed by lines extending vertically, called whiskers. Any value that is 1.5 times below or above the box is called an outlier and is represented by a dot in the box and whisker chart.

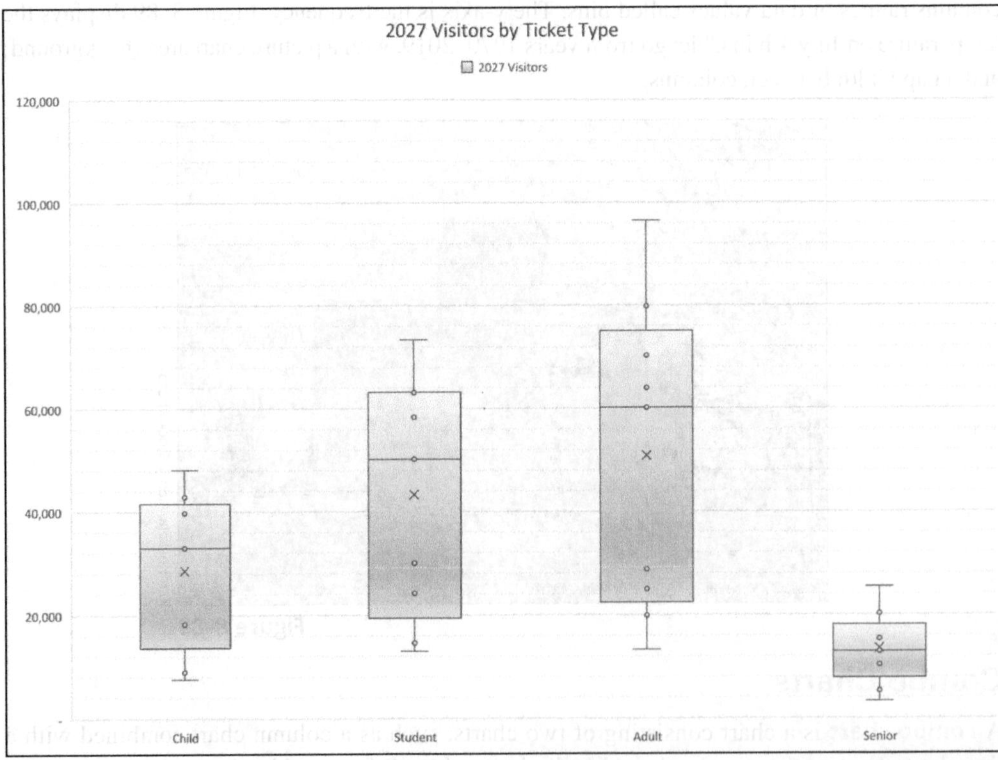

Figure 8–91

To Create a Box and Whisker Chart

The City Museums advisory board would like to compare the visitors in 2027 by using the ticket type: Senior, Adult, Student, and Child. In each category, the company would like to display the box and whisker notation. **Why?** The company is searching for the median visitors by ticket type and any visitor data that is extremely high or low in each category. The following steps create a box and whisker chart.

- Click the Ticket Revenue Data tab to display the Ticket Revenue Data sheet.
- Select cells C2:D38.
- Click the 'Insert Statistic Chart' button to display its gallery (Insert tab | Charts group) (Figure 8–92).

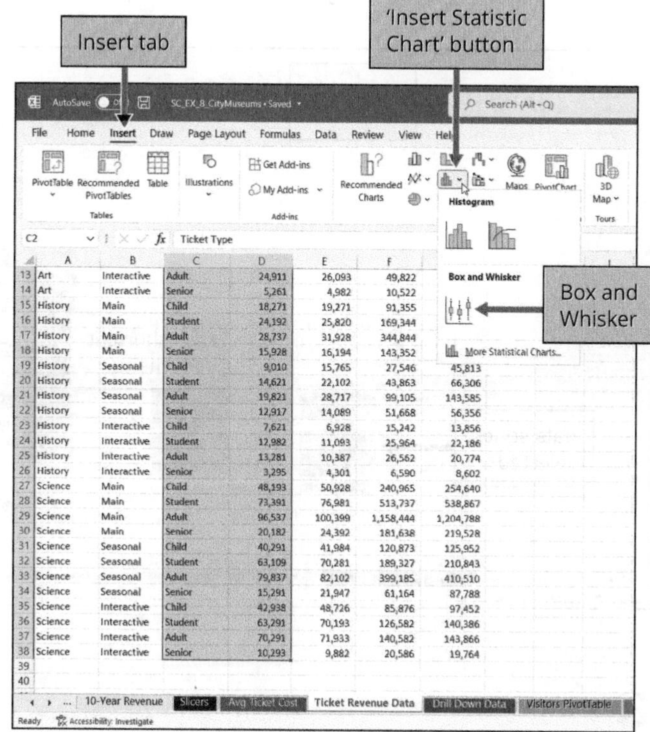

Figure 8–92

2

- Click Box and Whisker to create the chart.
- Click the Move Chart button (Chart Design tab | Location group) to display the Move Chart dialog box.
- Click New sheet (Move Chart dialog box) to select the option button.
- If necessary, double-click the default text in the New sheet box to select the text, and then type **Box and Whisker Chart** to enter a name for the new worksheet.
- Click OK (Move Chart dialog box) to move the chart to a new worksheet.
- Change the color of the worksheet tab to Light Green in the Standard Colors area (Figure 8–93).

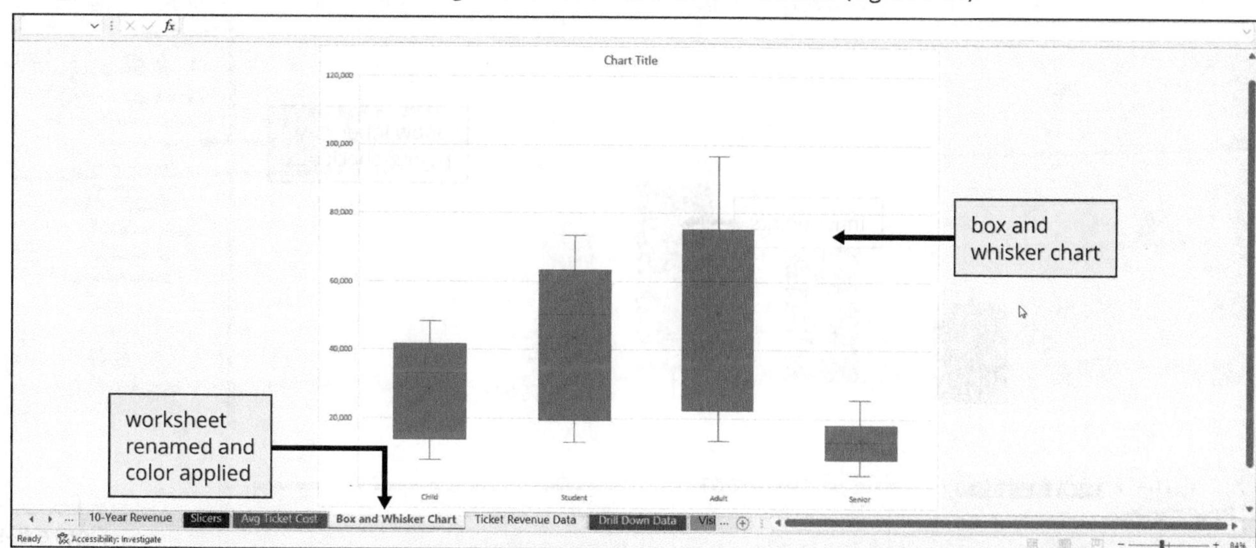

Figure 8–93

To Format a Box and Whisker Chart

The following steps edit the chart title, apply a chart style, and format the box and whisker data series.

- Select the text in the chart title and then type **2027 Visitors by Ticket Type**.
- In the plot area, right-click any of the boxes to display the shortcut menu (Figure 8–94).

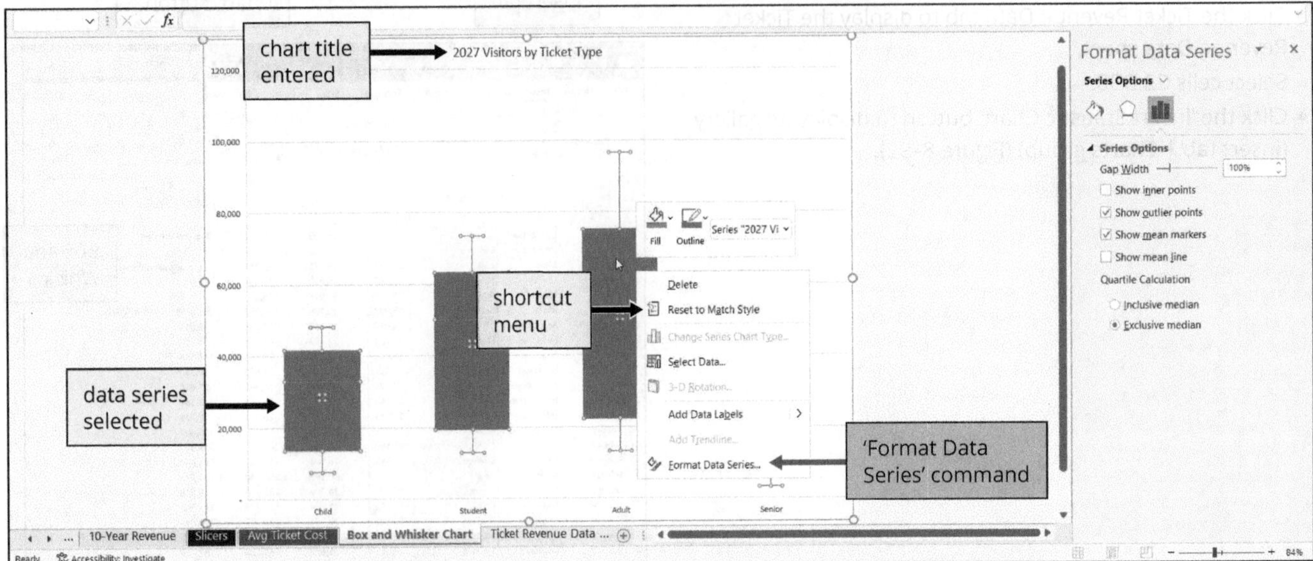

Figure 8–94

2

- Click 'Format Data Series' to display the Format Data Series pane.
- If necessary, click the Series Options button to display the Series Options sheet.
- Click the 'Show Inner Points' check box to display the various data values as dots on the chart (Figure 8–95).
- **Experiment:** Click other combinations of checkboxes to display how the chart changes. When you are finished, click the checkboxes shown in Figure 8–95.

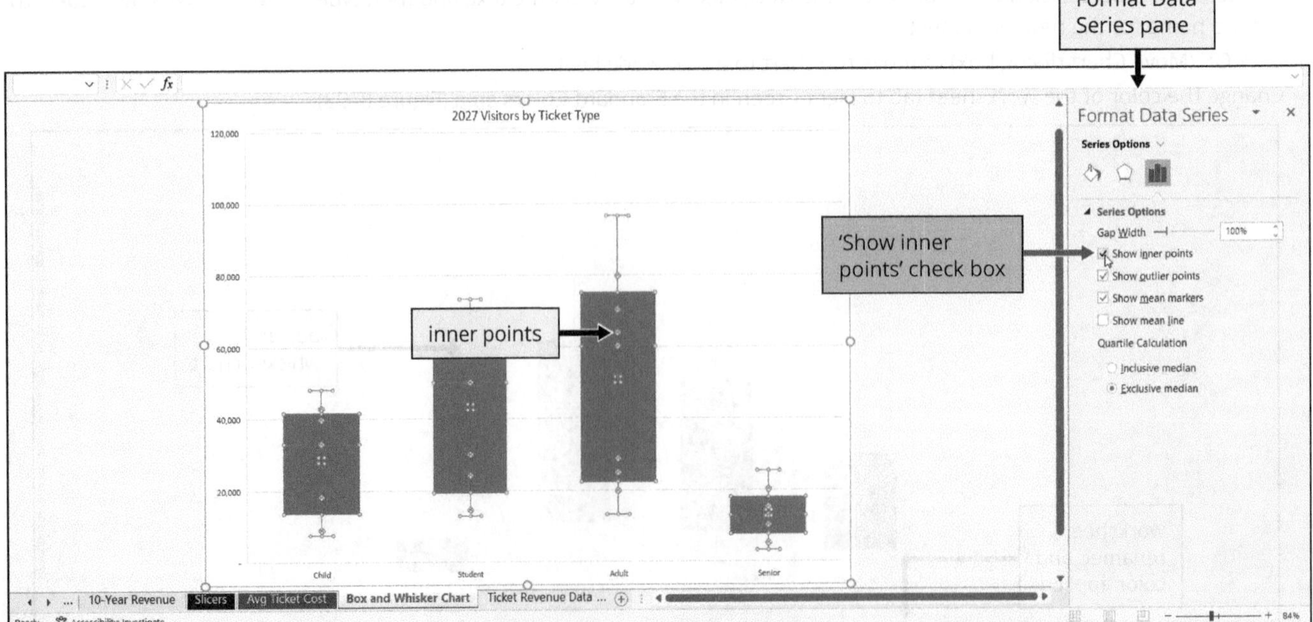

Figure 8–95

- In the Format Data Series pane, click the 'Fill & Line' button to display the Fill & Line sheet.
- Click Fill if necessary to display the choices for filling the boxes in the chart.
- Click the Gradient fill option button (Figure 8–96).

- **Experiment:** One at a time, click each of the other option buttons to display how the chart changes. When you are finished, click the Gradient option button.

Q&A What are the other gradient settings?
You can choose from various preset gradients and types. The Gradient stops bar lets you customize the amount of color from darkest to lightest. As you click each stop, you can set its color, position, amount of transparency, and brightness.

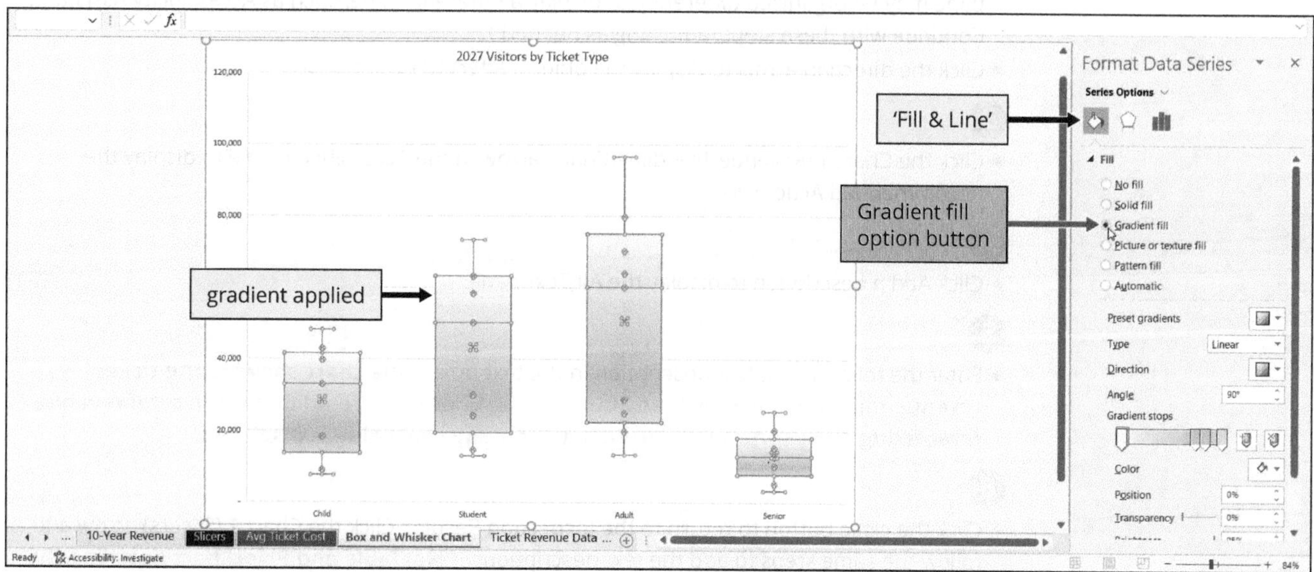

Figure 8–96

4

- Click Style 6 in the Chart Styles gallery (Chart Design tab | Chart Styles group) (Figure 8–97).

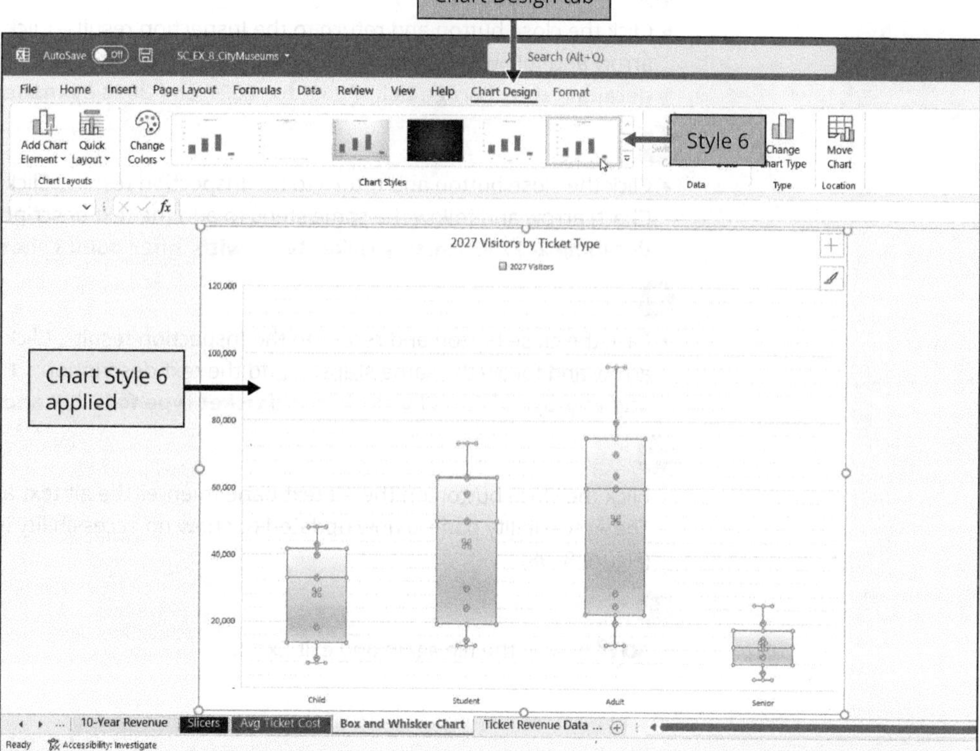

Figure 8–97

To Use the Accessibility Checker

The following steps use the Accessibility Checker to identify and fix accessibility issues.

- Click the Review tab and then click the 'Check Accessibility' arrow (Review tab | Accessibility group) to display the Accessibility menu.

2

- Click Check Accessibility to display the Accessibility pane with a list of Errors or Warnings in the Inspection Results box. (Note that depending on your version of Excel, your Accessibility pane may be organized differently or display a different name, such as Accessibility Assistant. Continue with these steps, adjusting as needed.)
- Click the direction arrow to display the objects affected by the issue.

3

- Click the Chart 1 (Revenue Trendline Chart) arrow in the Accessibility pane to display the Recommended Actions list.

4

- Click Add a description to display the Alt Text pane.

5

- Enter the following alt text description in the text box: **Line chart showing the ticket revenue for each museum from 2019 to 2028. There is a trendline for the total revenue forecasting two years in the future, and an r-squared value is displayed.**

6

- Click the close button to return to the Inspection Results. Click the Chart 1 (Slicers) arrow and follow the same steps to add the text description: **PivotTable and PivotChart detailing the average ticket cost for 2027 and 2028. Slicers are displayed to filter by museum, ticket type, and exhibit type.**

7

- Click the close button and return to the Inspection results. Click the Chart 1 (Avg Ticket Cost) arrow and follow the same steps to add the text description: **PivotTable and PivotChart detailing the average ticket cost for 2027 and 2028 by museum and ticket type.**

8

- Click the close button and return to the Inspection results. Click the Chart 1 (Box and Whisker Chart) arrow and follow the same steps to add the text description: **Box and whisker chart detailing 2027 visitors by ticket type, with inner points shown.**

9

- Click the close button and return to the Inspection results. Click the Chart 1 (Visitors PivotChart) arrow and follow the same steps to add the text description: **PivotChart detailing the total and average visitors by exhibit and ticket type for 2027 and 2028.**

10

- Click the close button on the Alt text pane to enter the alt text and close the pane.
  The Accessibility pane is now updated to show no accessibility issues in the worksheet (Figure 8–98).

11

- **sam** Save the file again and exit Excel.

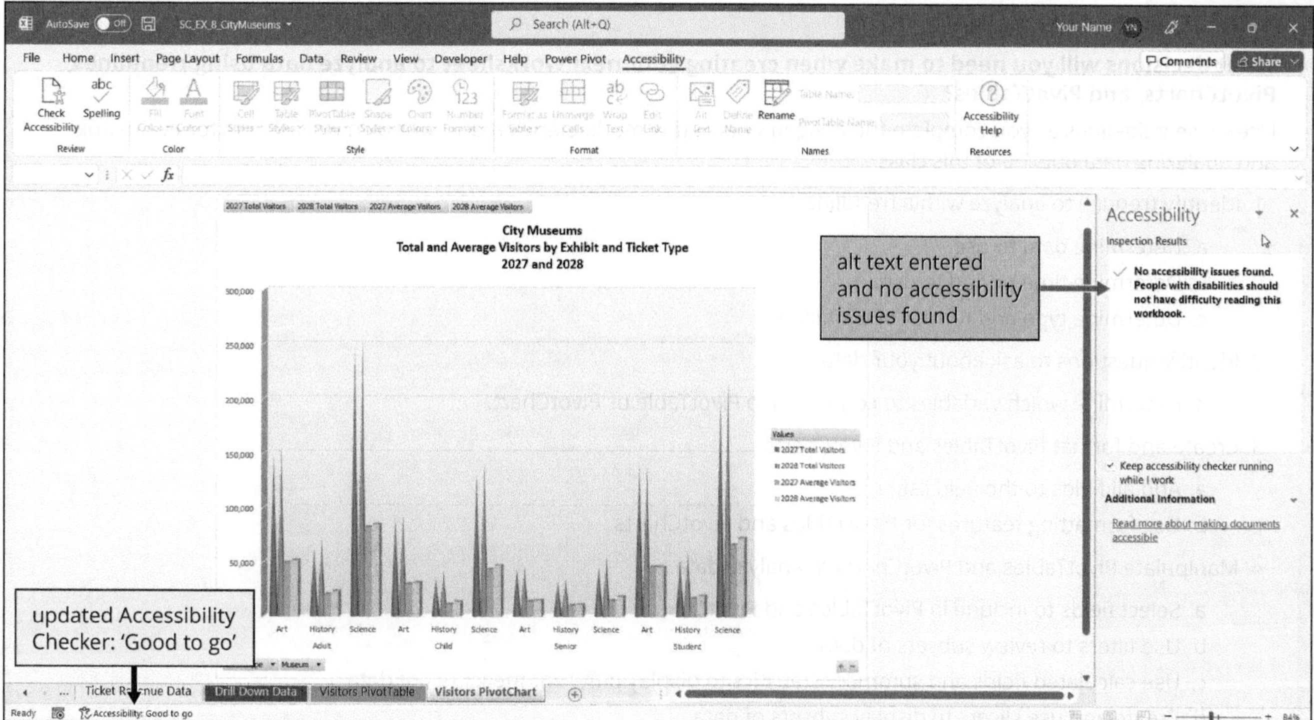

Figure 8–98

Summary

In this module, you learned how to create a 2-D line chart and add a trendline to extend the trend to two more time periods. You added an R-squared (R^2) value to the trendline to measure the strength of the trend and formatted a data point. You created and formatted a PivotTable report based on raw data. Using the Field List, you added row fields and columns to the PivotTable. You created calculated fields in the PivotTable using summary functions. To experience the power of the PivotTable, you inserted, deleted, and organized fields to display the data in different ways. You created and formatted a PivotChart Report from a PivotTable, filtering and analyzing data. You then created both a PivotTable and PivotChart from scratch and added a calculated field. You created slicers to make manipulating PivotTables and PivotCharts easier and added a box and whisker chart. Finally, you added alternative text to each chart to improve the accessibility of the workbook.

Consider This: Plan Ahead

What decisions will you need to make when creating your next worksheet to analyze data using trendlines, PivotCharts, and PivotTables?

Use these guidelines as you complete the assignments in this module and create your own worksheets for evaluating and analyzing data outside of this class.

1. Identify trend(s) to analyze with a trendline.
   a. Determine data to use.
   b. Determine time period to use.
   c. Determine type and format of trendline.
2. Identify questions to ask about your data.
   a. Determine which variables to combine in a PivotTable or PivotChart.
3. Create and format PivotTables and PivotCharts.
   a. Add all fields to the field list.
   b. Use formatting features for PivotTables and PivotCharts.
4. Manipulate PivotTables and PivotCharts to analyze data.
   a. Select fields to include in PivotTables and PivotCharts.
   b. Use filters to review subsets of data.
   c. Use calculated fields and summary statistics to display different measures of data.
   d. Create and use slicers to display subsets of data.

Student Assignments

Apply Your Knowledge

Reinforce the skills and apply the concepts you learned in this module.

Creating a PivotTable and PivotChart

Note: To complete these steps, you will be required to use the Data Files. Please contact your instructor for information about accessing the Data Files.

Instructions: Start Excel. Open the workbook SC_EX_8-2.xlsx, which is located in the Data Files. The workbook you open contains quarterly employee data for a medical sales company. You are to create a PivotTable and PivotChart from Quarterly Employee Data. Figure 8–99 shows the completed Sales Analysis worksheet.

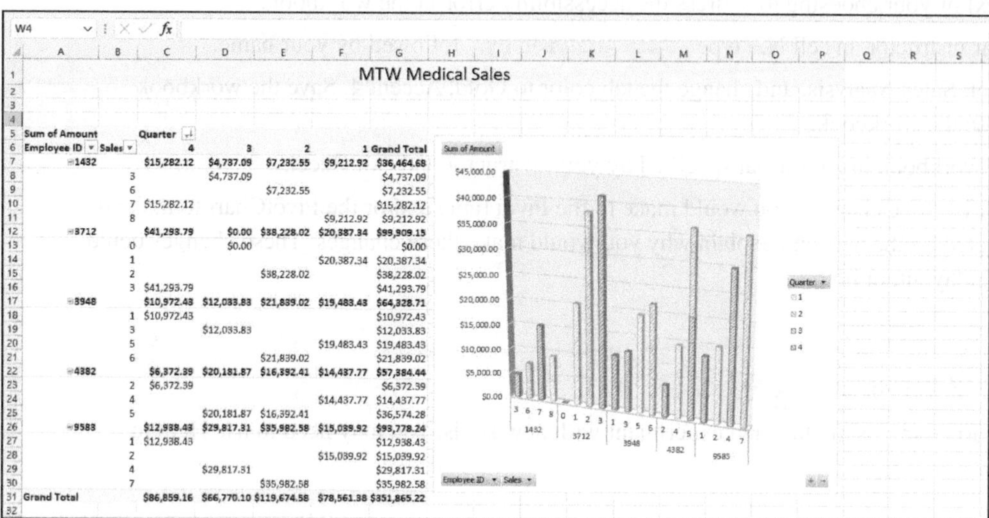

Sum of Amount		Quarter				
Employee ID	Sales	4	3	2	1	Grand Total
1432		$15,282.12	$4,737.09	$7,232.55	$9,212.92	$36,464.68
	3		$4,737.09			$4,737.09
	6			$7,232.55		$7,232.55
	7	$15,282.12				$15,282.12
	8				$9,212.92	$9,212.92
3712		$41,293.79	$0.00	$38,228.02	$20,387.34	$99,909.15
	0		$0.00			$0.00
	1				$20,387.34	$20,387.34
	2			$38,228.02		$38,228.02
	3	$41,293.79				$41,293.79
3948		$10,972.43	$12,033.83	$21,839.02	$19,483.43	$64,328.71
	1	$10,972.43				$10,972.43
	3		$12,033.83			$12,033.83
	5				$19,483.43	$19,483.43
	6			$21,839.02		$21,839.02
4382		$6,372.39	$20,181.87	$16,392.41	$14,437.77	$57,384.44
	2	$6,372.39				$6,372.39
	4				$14,437.77	$14,437.77
	5		$20,181.87	$16,392.41		$36,574.28
9583		$12,938.43	$29,817.31	$35,982.58	$15,039.92	$93,778.24
	1	$12,938.43				$12,938.43
	2				$15,039.92	$15,039.92
	4		$29,817.31			$29,817.31
	7			$35,982.58		$35,982.58
Grand Total		$86,859.16	$66,770.10	$119,674.58	$78,561.38	$351,865.22

Figure 8–99

Perform the following tasks:

1. Save the workbook with the filename, SC_EX_8_MedicalSales. Select range A3:D23 and then click the PivotTable button (Insert tab | Tables group) to display the 'PivotTable from table or range' dialog box. Make sure New Worksheet is selected and the range 'Employee Sales'!$A$3:$D$23 is selected, and then click OK.
2. Drag the Employee ID and Sales fields from the 'Choose fields to add to report' area to the Rows area to add the fields to the PivotTable.
3. Drag the Amount field from the 'Choose fields to add to report' area to the Values area to add the sum of the Amount field to the PivotTable.
4. Drag the Quarter field from the 'Choose fields to add to report' area to the Columns area.
5. Click the More button (Design tab | PivotTable Styles group), and then choose the 'Light Yellow, Pivot Style Light 19' style.
6. Format the Amount data in columns B through F as currency with dollar signs and two decimal places. If necessary, widen columns so all data and headings display correctly.
7. Click the Report Layout button (Design tab | Layout group) to display the Report Layout menu. Change the PivotTable report layout to outline form.
8. Click the PivotChart button (PivotTable Analyze tab | Tools group) and select the 3-D Stacked Column.

Continued on next page

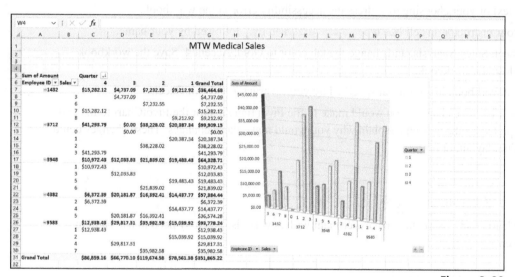

9. Move the PivotChart to a location beside the PivotTable and resize it as shown in Figure 8–99. Change chart style to Style 2 (Design tab | Chart Styles group). In the PivotChart, click the Quarter filter button and then click 'Sort Largest to Smallest' on the menu.
10. Insert two more blank lines at the top of the worksheet. Type **MTW Medical Sales** as the title. Merge and center it across both the PivotTable and PivotChart, columns A through P. Change the font color and fill color to match the PivotTable headers. Change the font size to 20.
11. Change the magnification of the worksheet to 85%.
12. Click the PivotChart. Click the Chart Elements arrow (Format tab | Current Selection group) and choose Back Wall. Click the Shape Fill button (Format tab | Shape Styles group) and apply a fill color of Blue, Accent 5, Lighter 80%. Click the Shape Effects button (Format tab | Shape Styles group), click 3-D Rotation, and then, in the Perspective area, click 'Perspective: Contrasting Left'.
13. Click the Chart Elements arrow (Format tab | Current Selection group) and choose Side Wall. Click the Shape Fill button (Format tab | Shape Styles group) and apply a fill color of Blue, Accent 5, Lighter 80%. Click the Shape Fill button (Format tab | Shape Styles group) and apply a Linear Down gradient.
14. Enter alternative text of your choosing to address the accessibility error in the workbook.
15. If requested by your instructor, in cell N2, type **Data Analyzed by,** followed by your name.
16. Name the worksheet, Sales Analysis, and change the tab color to Gold, Accent 4. Save the workbook again, and then close the workbook.
17. Submit the revised workbook in the format specified by your instructor and exit Excel.
18. **Consider This:** List three changes you would make to the PivotTable and/or the PivotChart to make it more easily interpreted by the user and explain why you would make these changes. These changes could be to the formatting, layout, or both.

Extend Your Knowledge

Extend the skills you learned in this module and experiment with new skills. You may need to use Help to complete the assignment.

Grouping Content in PivotTables

Note: To complete this assignment, you will be required to use the Data Files. Please contact your instructor for information about accessing the Data Files.

Instructions: Start Excel. Open the workbook SC_EX_8-3.xlsx from the Data Files. The workbook you open contains data about the number of candies sold twice monthly for a year. You are to create a PivotTable and PivotChart for Chocolate Holiday Candy Inc. that analyzes sales in 2029.

Perform the following tasks:

1. Save the workbook using the file name, SC_EX_8_ChocolateSales.
2. Use Help to learn to group or ungroup data in a PivotTable.
3. Select the data in the Sales Data worksheet (cells A3:B27). Create a PivotTable on a new worksheet. Use Date as the Rows field and use Units as the Values field. Note that Excel breaks the date field down into months.
4. Name the new worksheet **Sales PivotTable**. Color the sheet tab purple. Change the PivotTable style to 'Dark Gray, Pivot Style Dark 10'.
5. In cell A1, type **Chocolate Holiday Candies Inc.** to create a title. In cell A2, type **2029 Sales** to create a subtitle. Merge and center the titles across columns A and B. Format range A1:A2 using the Title cell style and bold. Change the font size in cell A2 to 15. Change the font color in both cells to black, if necessary.
6. Format the Units sold data values to be Number with commas, but no decimal places. Remove the Field Header for column A.
7. Click cell A4 and use the Group Field command (PivotTable Analyze tab | Group group) to group the daily figures by days and months.
8. Change the width of columns A and B to 23 (Figure 8–100).

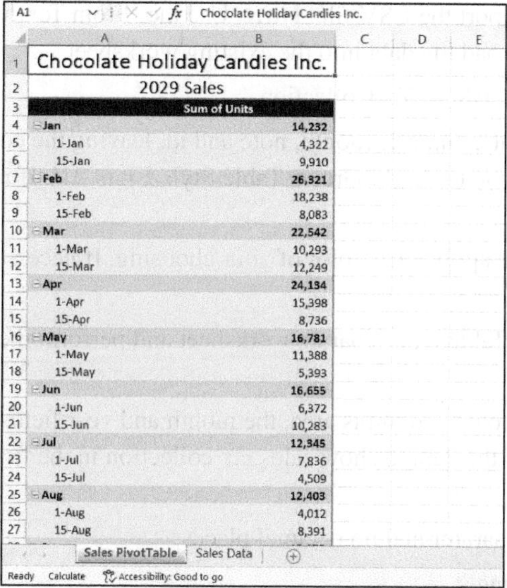

Figure 8–100

9. Create a PivotChart and locate it on the same worksheet as the PivotTable. Use the Line with Markers chart type and set up the chart to have no legend.
10. Right-click the vertical axis, and then choose 'Format Axis' on the shortcut menu. In the Format Axis pane, set the minimum bound to 2000 and the major units to 2500.
11. Edit the chart title text to match the PivotTable title and subtitle. Change the chart color to Monochromatic Palette 2 (Design tab | Chart Styles group) and apply chart style 10. Resize the chart to fill the area between cell C2 and L27.
12. Enter alternative text of your choosing to address the accessibility error in the workbook.
13. If requested by your instructor, add a worksheet header with your name and course number.
14. Because Excel changes the column width of the PivotTable as you change the grouping, double-check that the column widths of A and B are still 23.
15. Save the workbook.
16. Submit the revised workbook in the format specified by your instructor and exit Excel.
17. **Consider This:** What other chart type would you use to present this data for the user? Why would you choose that particular chart type?

Expand Your World

Create a solution that uses cloud and web technologies by learning and investigating on your own from general guidance.

Creating PivotTable Reports and PivotCharts with Web Data

Instructions: Start Excel. You are to create a PivotTable, PivotChart, and map chart from data you obtain from the web.

Perform the following tasks:

1. Open a browser and navigate to https://www.data.gov/, a searchable, open database of files stored by the U.S. government.
2. In the search box, type **Sales Tax Collection** and then press ENTER.
3. In the search results, navigate to the link, 'Sales Tax Collection by State', and then click the CSV (Comma Separated Values) button. Save the file on your storage device.

Continued on next page

4. Start Excel and open a blank workbook. Import the CSV file. **Hint:** Use the 'From Text/CSV' button (Data tab | Get & Transform Data group). Load the data into the existing worksheet.
5. Save the workbook using the file name, SC_EX_8_TaxCollection.
6. Delete the columns named tax type, fips state, numeric month, note and id, leaving the columns state, month, year, and value. Change the table style to 'Light Green, Table Style Light 21'. If necessary, close the Queries & Connections pane.
7. Rename the worksheet, Sales Tax Data, and apply a tab color of your choosing. If necessary, delete Sheet1.
8. Click any cell in the data and insert a PivotTable on a separate worksheet and perform the following analysis:
   a. Using the Field list, drag the state field to the Columns area, the month and year fields to the rows area, and value to the Values area. Filter the data to show sales tax collection in the first quarter of the year: January, February, and March.
   b. Format the numbers with the comma separator and no decimal places.
   c. Apply a PivotTable Style of your choosing.
   d. Experiment by dragging fields to various PivotTable areas to show different views of the data.
   e. Rename the worksheet and apply a tab color.
9. Create a Line PivotChart from the PivotTable and do the following:
   a. Move the chart to a new worksheet with a unique name and apply a tab color.
   b. Format the PivotChart with a title, style, and an appropriate legend.
   c. Filter the PivotChart to show only data for your state and the states that border it, or a region of the United States (Figure 8–101).
   d. Return to the PivotTable.

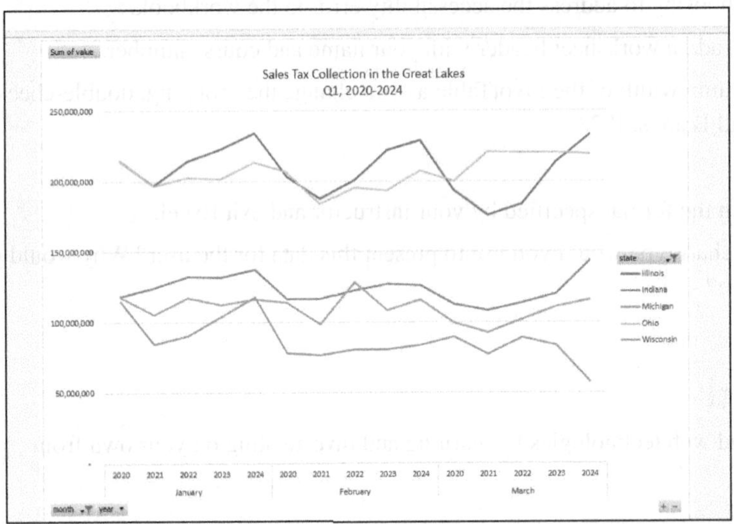

Figure 8–101

10. Go back to the original web data. Use the Year filter button to select only the most recent year and the month filter button to select January. Filter the State column with the region you chose in Step 9.
11. Select the resulting State and Deaths data. Create a map chart similar to Figure 8–87 from the filtered data. **Hint:** Click the Maps button (Insert tab | Charts group).
    a. If Bing prompts you to allow its search, click the I Accept button.
    b. Move the map to a new worksheet. Name the worksheet, Great Lakes Chart.
    c. Apply a tab color of your choosing to the worksheet.
    d. Right-click the legend, click Select Data, and delete the year and month values.

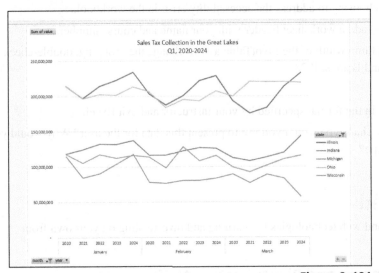

e. Display the Format Data Series Pane and the Series Options sheet. Click the Map Area button and then click 'Only Regions with Data'.

f. Edit the title and color. Remove the legend and apply data labels. Format the data labels to include Category Name and Value. Change the font size and color as necessary to ensure readability.

12. Enter alt text of your choosing for the PivotChart and Great Lakes Chart in the accessibility pane.
13. Save the workbook again.
14. Submit the revised workbook as specified by your instructor.
15. **Consider This:** In this data, you dealt with 5 states and four years of monthly data. With large amounts of data, what are the advantages to using PivotTables? What are the problems with PivotCharts?

In the Lab

Design and implement a solution using creative thinking and problem-solving skills.

Create Charts

Problem: A local law firm would like a detailed summary from their last month of cases. A sample of the weekly data has been compiled and supplied to you in a table, provided below, as shown in Table 8–3.

Table 8–3: Weekly Case Data

Case Number	County	Charge Code	Hourly Rate ($)
573	Elmhurst	2	320
473	Wakan	6	300
313	Southern	6	310
499	Elmhurst	2	300
321	Elmhurst	2	320
039	Wakan	8	120
318	Southern	11	400
281	Wakan	3	300
367	Wakan	2	320
462	Elmhurst	4	180

Perform the following tasks:

Part 1: Enter the data in a new workbook. Save the workbook. Create a PivotTable with slicers and instructions for use. The PivotTable should show average hourly rates by county and case number, with a slicer utilizing the charge codes. Submit your assignment in the format specified by your instructor.

Part 2: **Consider This:** Would a PivotChart provide a useful depiction of this data, and if so, why? What type of PivotChart would you use?

Formula Auditing, Data Validation, and Complex Problem Solving

Objectives

After completing this module, you will be able to:

- Use formula auditing techniques to analyze a worksheet
- Trace precedents and dependents
- Use error checking to identify and correct errors
- Add data validation rules to cells
- Use trial and error to solve a problem on a worksheet
- Use goal seeking to solve a problem
- Circle invalid data on a worksheet
- Enable the Solver add-in
- Use Solver to solve a complex problem
- Use the Scenario Manager to record and save sets of what-if assumptions
- Create a Scenario Summary report
- Create a Scenario Summary PivotTable

Introduction

Excel offers many tools that can be used to correct errors in a spreadsheet and solve complex business problems. In previous modules, simple what-if analyses have demonstrated the effect of changing one value on another value of interest. This module introduces you to auditing the formulas in a worksheet, validating data, and performing complex problems involving multiple values of interest. **Formula auditing** allows you to examine formulas to determine which cells are referenced by those formulas and examine cells to determine which formulas are built upon those cells. Auditing the formulas in a worksheet can give insight into how a worksheet is structured and how cells are related to each other. Formula auditing is especially helpful when you are working with a workbook created by someone else.

Data validation allows you to set cells so that the values they accept are restricted in terms of type and range of data. This feature can be set up to display prompts and error messages when users select a cell or enter invalid data. You also can use data validation to circle cells containing data that does not meet the criteria you specified.

When using Excel to project possible outcomes, you can make an educated guess if you are familiar with the data and the structure of the workbook. **Trial and error** is a way to perform what-if analysis by changing one or more of the input values to understand how they affect the other cells in the workbook. For simpler problems such as cases where you are considering a change in a price or quantity, you may find a solution using this process. For more complex problems, you might need to use the error and validation techniques in Excel to find a satisfactory solution.

One of the tools that Excel provides to solve complex, multi-variable problems is **Solver**, which allows you to specify up to 200 cells that can be adjusted to find a solution to a problem. Solver also lets you place limits or constraints on allowable values for some or all of those cells. A **constraint** is a limitation on the possible values that a cell can contain. Solver will try many possible solutions to find one that solves the problem subject to the constraints placed on the data.

Project: Restaurant Wholesale Supply

BTW
Ribbon and Screen Resolution
Excel may change how the groups and buttons within the groups appear on the ribbon, depending on the screen resolution of your computer. Thus, your ribbon may appear different from the ones in this book if you are using a screen resolution other than 1366 × 768.

Restaurant Wholesale Supply (RWS) is a company that receives shipments of industrial equipment for restaurants from manufacturers, which it then distributes to wholesalers around the country. The items RWS receives are at a discount to regular prices and usually include close-outs and overstocked items. To ship its goods, the company purchases extra space on trucks from trucking firms. This week they are wanting to ship three types of equipment currently in stock: heavy duty countertop meat and cheese slicers, double basket fryers, and programmable countertop mixers with accessories. These item descriptions will be shortened to slicer, fryer, and mixer for the workbook in this module. Typically, the company deals with the following for each item: physical volume in cubic feet, the weight in pounds, the profit per item, and the number of items in stock. The company will need to enter the quantity of each item to ship, making sure it is one or more, and less than or equal to the number in stock (to ensure the order can be fulfilled). The objective is to maximize the profit while filling up as much of the truck as possible. In this module, you will learn how to use the RWS Analysis workbook displayed in Figure 9–1.

The Weekly Shipment worksheet, displayed in Figure 9–1a, was created to determine the most cost-effective way of scheduling trucks to meet existing needs. The worksheet includes the details of the requirements for the three items, taking into account the truck capacities as well as the weight and volume of the items.

The details of the first solution determined by Solver are displayed in Figure 9–1b. Solver was given the goal of maximizing the total profits (cell E13) while also accommodating the following constraints: the number of items assigned to each truck (range B9:D9) cannot be negative or fractional. The total volume and weight must not exceed the truck constraints displayed in cells B16:B17. The company wants to ship at least one of each item per truck. Applying these constraints, Solver calculated the optimal items to ship displayed in the range B9:D9 to achieve the goal of maximizing total profit and filling the truck. Solver modified the shipping quantities for each item (B9:D9) that resulted in changes in the total volume and weight per truck (E11:E12). If you applied a different set of constraints, Solver would determine a new solution.

BTW
Touch Mode Differences
The Office and Windows interfaces may vary if you are using Touch Mode. For this reason, you might notice that the function or appearance of your touch screen differs slightly from this module's presentation.

When Solver finishes solving a problem, you can create an Answer Report. An Answer Report (Figure 9–1c) summarizes the answer found by Solver, identifying which constraints were in place and which values in the worksheet were manipulated in order to solve the problem within the constraints.

The Excel **Scenario Manager** is a what-if analysis tool that allows you to record and save different sets, or scenarios, of what-if assumptions for the same worksheet. In this case, you will use Scenario Manager to manage the two sets of Solver data for the Weekly Shipment Worksheet. The Scenario Manager also allows you to create reports that summarize the scenarios on your worksheet. Both the Scenario Summary report (Figure 9–1d) and the Scenario PivotTable (Figure 9–1e) concisely present the differences among different shipping scenarios. Like any PivotTable, the Scenario PivotTable allows you to interact with the data easily.

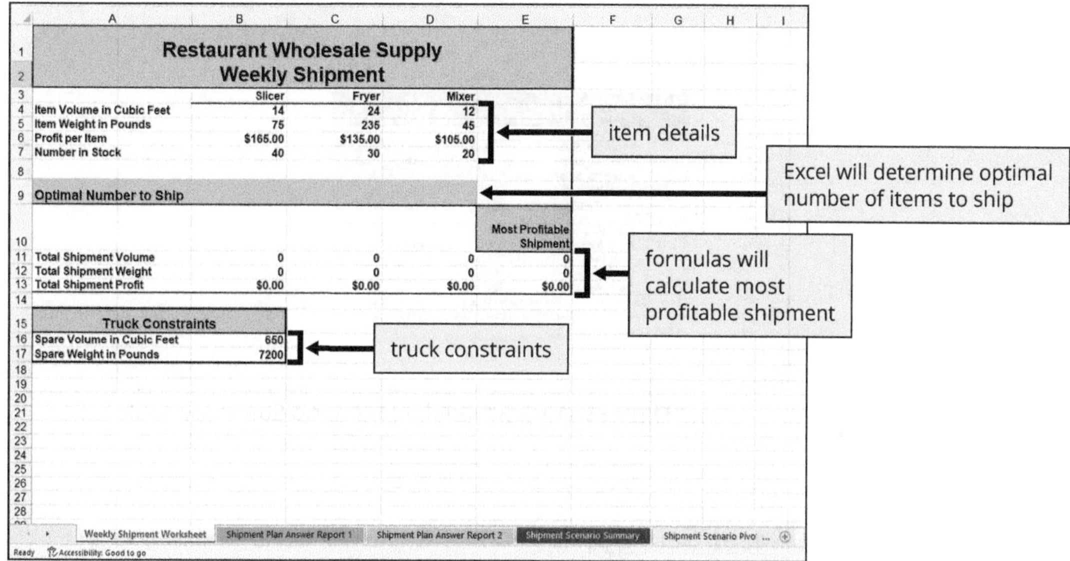

	Slicer	Fryer	Mixer	
Restaurant Wholesale Supply Weekly Shipment				
Item Volume in Cubic Feet	14	24	12	
Item Weight in Pounds	75	235	45	
Profit per Item	$165.00	$135.00	$105.00	
Number in Stock	40	30	20	
Optimal Number to Ship				
				Most Profitable Shipment
Total Shipment Volume	0	0	0	0
Total Shipment Weight	0	0	0	0
Total Shipment Profit	$0.00	$0.00	$0.00	$0.00

Truck Constraints	
Spare Volume in Cubic Feet	650
Spare Weight in Pounds	7200

Figure 9–1(a): Scheduling Plan Worksheet

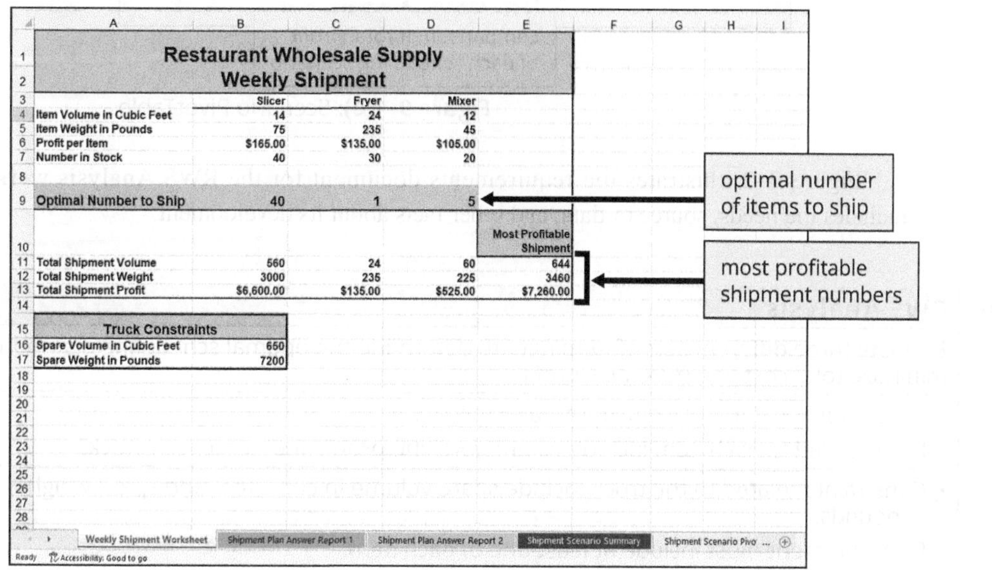

	Slicer	Fryer	Mixer	
Restaurant Wholesale Supply Weekly Shipment				
Item Volume in Cubic Feet	14	24	12	
Item Weight in Pounds	75	235	45	
Profit per Item	$165.00	$135.00	$105.00	
Number in Stock	40	30	20	
Optimal Number to Ship	40	1	5	
				Most Profitable Shipment
Total Shipment Volume	560	24	60	644
Total Shipment Weight	3000	235	225	3460
Total Shipment Profit	$6,600.00	$135.00	$525.00	$7,260.00

Truck Constraints	
Spare Volume in Cubic Feet	650
Spare Weight in Pounds	7200

Figure 9–1(b): Solver Solution

A1 Microsoft Excel 16.0 Answer Report

Microsoft Excel 16.0 Answer Report
Worksheet: [SC_EX_9_RWSAnalysis.xlsx]Weekly Shipment Worksheet
Report Created: 7/8/2029 6:52:10 AM
Result: Solver found a solution. All Constraints and optimality conditions are satisfied.
Solver Engine
Engine: Simplex LP
Solution Time: 0.016 Seconds.
Iterations: 1 Subproblems: 14
Solver Options
Max Time Unlimited, Iterations Unlimited, Precision 0.000001, Use Automatic Scaling
Max Subproblems Unlimited, Max Integer Sols Unlimited, Integer Tolerance 0%

Objective Cell (Max)

Cell	Name	Original Value	Final Value
$E$13	Total_Profit	$7,260.00	$7,260.00

Variable Cells

Cell	Name	Original Value	Final Value	Integer
$B$9	Slicers_to_Ship	40	40	Integer
$C$9	Fryers_to_Ship	1	1	Integer
$D$9	Mixers_to_Ship	5	5	Integer

Constraints

Cell	Name	Cell Value	Formula	Status	Slack
$E$11	Total_Volume	644	$E$11<=$B$16	Not Binding	6
$E$12	Total_Weight	3460	$E$12<=$B$17	Not Binding	3740
$B$9	Slicers_to_Ship	40	$B$9>=1	Not Binding	2
$C$9	Fryers_to_Ship	1	$C$9>=1	Binding	0
$D$9	Mixers_to_Ship	5	$D$9>=1	Not Binding	4
$C$9	Fryers_to_Ship	1	$C$9<=$C$7	Binding	0
$D$9	Mixers_to_Ship	5	$D$9<=$D$7	Binding	0
$B$9	Slicers_to_Ship	40	$B$9<=$B$7	Binding	0
$B$9:$D$9=Integer					

Figure 9–1(c): Scheduling Plan Answer Report

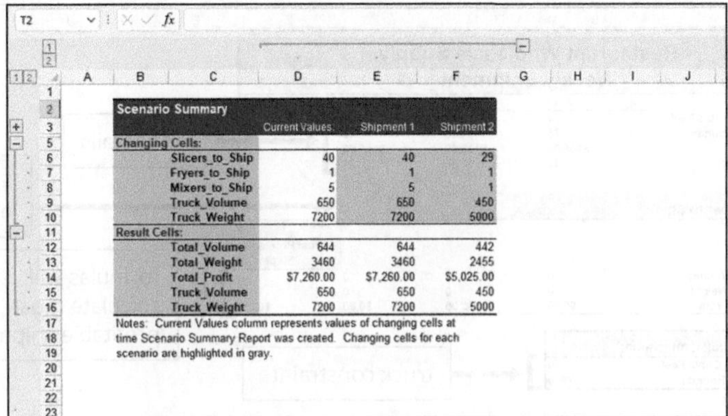

Scenario Summary	Current Values:	Shipment 1	Shipment 2
Changing Cells:			
Slicers_to_Ship	40	40	29
Fryers_to_Ship	1	1	1
Mixers_to_Ship	5	5	1
Truck_Volume	650	650	450
Truck_Weight	7200	7200	5000
Result Cells:			
Total_Volume	644	644	442
Total_Weight	3460	3460	2455
Total_Profit	$7,260.00	$7,260.00	$5,025.00
Truck_Volume	650	650	450
Truck_Weight	7200	7200	5000

Notes: Current Values column represents values of changing cells at time Scenario Summary Report was created. Changing cells for each scenario are highlighted in gray.

Figure 9–1(d): Scheduling Scenario Summary Table

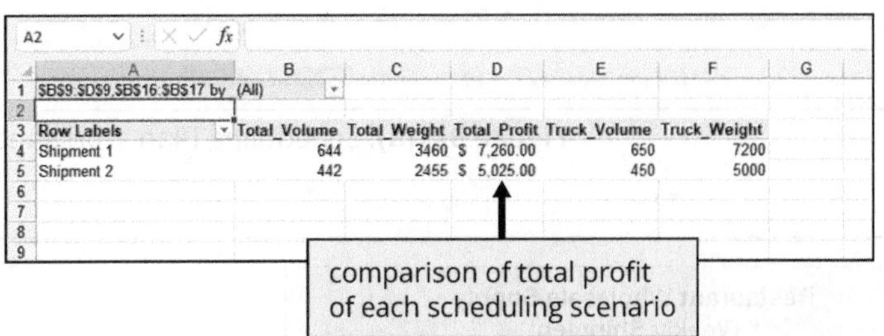

$B$9:$D$9,$B$16:$B$17 by (All)

Row Labels	Total_Volume	Total_Weight	Total_Profit	Truck_Volume	Truck_Weight
Shipment 1	644	3460	$ 7,260.00	650	7200
Shipment 2	442	2455	$ 5,025.00	450	5000

Figure 9–1(e): Scenario PivotTable

Figure 9–2 illustrates the requirements document for the RWS Analysis workbook. It includes the needs, source of data, and other facts about its development.

Worksheet Title	RWS Analysis
Needs	Evaluate three different sets of item data to determine the optimal scheduling distribution to minimize total cost and maximize profits.
Data	• Three types of items: slicers, fryers, and mixers. • Data related to each item include volume, weight, profit, and number in stock.
Constraints	• Constraints related to the truck include spare volume in cubic feet and spare weigh in pounds. • Each shipment must include at least one of each item. • Item numbers cannot be fractional of negative.
Source of Data	All item information is available in the SC_EX_9-1.xlsx workbook, on the Weekly Shipment Worksheet.
Calculations	All formulas are set up in the workbook with some errors. The worksheets in the workbook should be reviewed to familiarize yourself with the following calculations. • Total Shipment Volume is volume times number of items to ship. • Total Weight Volume is the weight times the number of items to ship. • Total Profit is the profit per item times the number of items to ship.
Other Requirements	• Create a Shipment Scenario Summary. • Create a Shipment Scenario Pivot Table. • Create two Shipment Plan Answer Reports.

Figure 9–2

With a good understanding of the requirements document and an understanding of the necessary decisions, the next step is to use Excel to create the workbook. In this module, you will learn how to create the RWS Analysis workbook displayed in Figure 9–1.

To Open a Blank Workbook and Format the Rows and Columns

The following steps start Excel and open a workbook named SC_EX_9-1. The Weekly Shipment Worksheet tab displays the overall shipping plan and constraints for the items and trucks. To complete these steps, you will be required to use the Data Files. Please contact your instructor for information about accessing the Data Files.

1. sam Start Excel.
2. Open the file named SC_EX_9-1.xlsx from the Data Files.
3. If the Excel window is not maximized, click the Maximize button on its title bar to maximize the window.
4. Save the workbook on your hard drive, OneDrive, or other storage location using **SC_EX_9_RWSAnalysis** as the file name.
5. Select cell A20 if necessary and zoom to 120% (Figure 9–3).

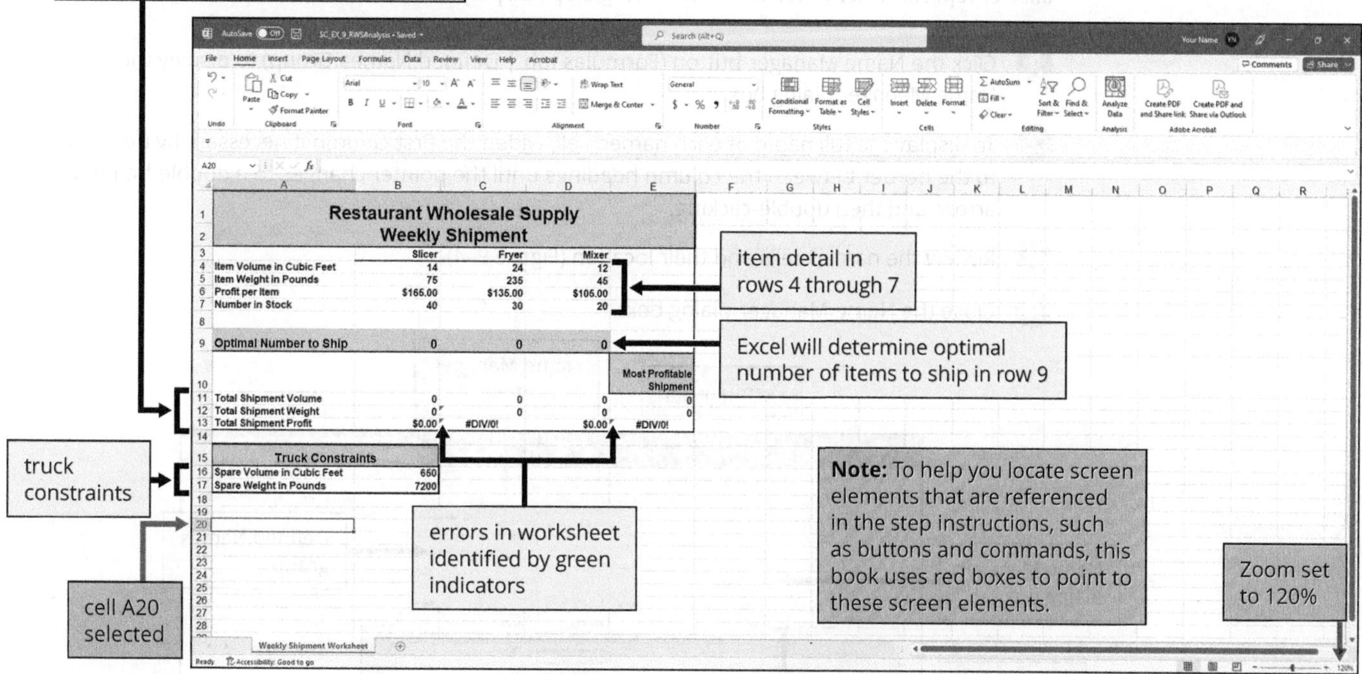

Figure 9–3

About the Weekly Shipment Worksheet

The Weekly Shipment Worksheet displayed in Figure 9–3 provides information about three items and four types of data: volume, weight, stock levels, and profits. Rows 4 and 5 contain the volume and weight for each of the three items. Row 6 contains the profit per item; row 7 displays the number in stock. The range B9:D9 will display the optimal number of each item to ship that maximizes the total profit to RWS, which is the problem that needs to be solved in this module. The total volume, weight, and profits for each item (rows 11 to 13) are based on the number of each item to ship—displayed in the range B9:D9—multiplied by the corresponding values in rows 4 through 6. As the number of each item changes, the values in the range B11:D13 are updated.

BTW
Getting Familiar with a Worksheet
When working with a new worksheet, you should try to become familiar with the formulas, functions, and errors it may contain. You also should click the Name Manager button (Formulas tab | Defined Names group) to learn what ranges or cells may have useful predefined names.

Your goal is to determine the optimal number of items to ship in each category without exceeding the maximum volume (650) and weight (7200) per truck (cells B16:B17), while maximizing total profits for the company (cell E13). In the worksheet, the "spare" volume and weight will be the difference between the maximum volume and weight for the truck, and the volume and weight of the items already loaded into the truck for other purposes. In other words, the spare volume and weight is the leftover volume and weight not being used and therefore available to RWS.

As outlined in the requirements document in Figure 9–2, a second set of constraints also must be analyzed. Thus, the information in the range B16:B17 will be modified to reflect the constraints associated with the different scenario, for a truck with a maximum volume of 450 and a maximum weight of 5500.

The worksheet also contains some errors which will be addressed in the following sections.

To Access Named Cells

In workbooks prepared by others, it is always a good idea to double-check for named cells and ranges. The Weekly Shipment Worksheet contains several named cells. Named cells help identify concepts in the worksheet and can be used in formulas, for data validation, and as bookmarks. Later in the module, you will learn that named cells are used by Excel to make constraints and answer reports easier to read. The following steps display named cells.

1. Click the Name Manager button (Formulas tab | Defined Names Group) to display the Name Manager dialog box.
2. To display the full name of each named cell, widen the first column if necessary by pointing to the border between the column headings until the pointer changes to a double-headed arrow, and then double-clicking.
3. Review the named cells and their location (Figure 9–4).
4. Close the Name Manager dialog box.

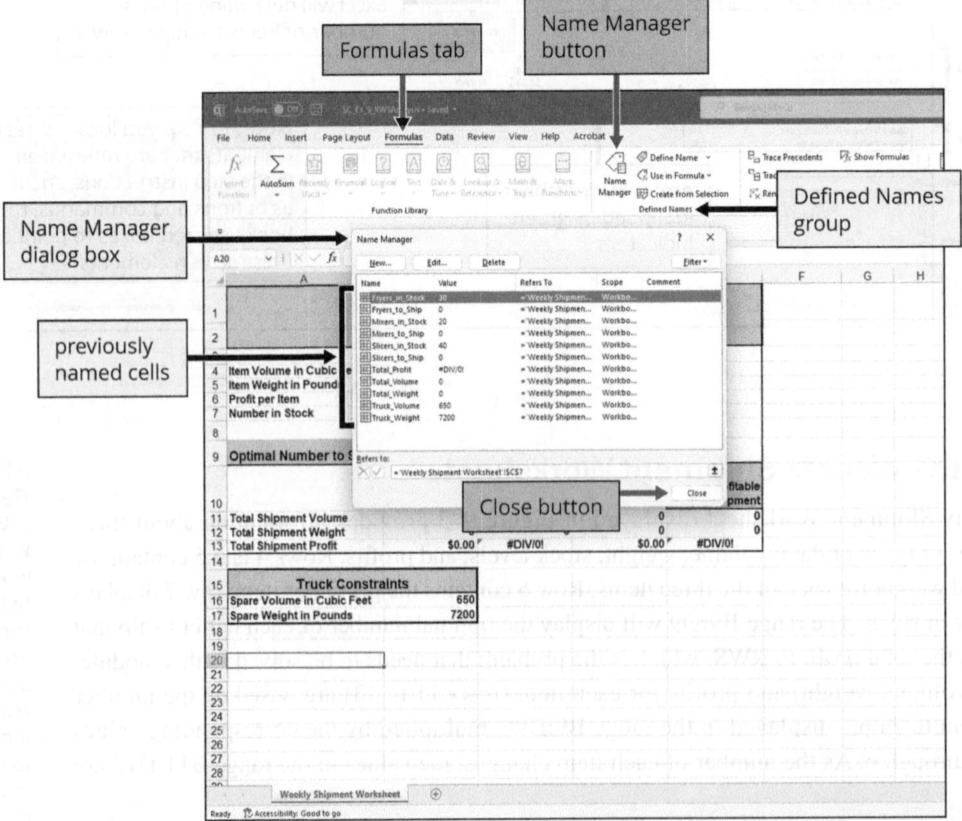

Figure 9–4

Formula Auditing

Formula auditing is the process of tracking errors, checking worksheet logic, and reviewing formulas for errors. Errors may be obvious, with results that indicate that a formula is incorrect. For example, in Figure 9–3, cells C12, C13, and E13 display error codes. These errors are flagged by the error indicator, a green triangle, in the upper-left corner of those cells, and two of the three cells also display an error code, #DIV/0!. Errors also may be less obvious, introduced through formulas that, while technically correct, result in unintended results in the worksheet or formulas that are inconsistent with other similar formulas. Error indicators with no accompanying error code, such as that found in cell C12, should be examined for these less-obvious errors. A complex worksheet should be reviewed to correct obvious errors and to correct formulas that do not produce error indicators but still do not produce the intended results.

Excel provides formula auditing tools, found in the Formula Auditing group on the Formulas tab, that can be used to review the formulas in a worksheet. Some tools, such as the Error Checking command, deal with identified errors. Other auditing tools provide visual cues to identify how cells in a worksheet relate to each other. **Tracer arrows** are blue, worksheet auditing arrows that point from cells that might have caused an error to the active cell containing an error. Tracer arrows identify cells that are related to other cells through their use in a formula. Red tracer arrows indicate that one of the referenced cells contains an error.

A formula that references other cells is said to have precedents. A **precedent** is a cell referenced in a formula that references other cells. For example, cell C24 might contain the formula, = C23/$B$1. Cells C23 and B1 are precedents of cell C24. Cells C23 and B1 may contain their own precedents, and these cells also would be precedents of cell C24. Oppositely, cell C24 is considered dependent upon C23 and B1. A **dependent** cell relies on references to another cell and usually contains a formula whose value changes depending on the values in the input cells. Tracing precedents and dependents can indicate where a formula may be incorrect.

BTW
Naming Cell Ranges
Naming ranges for use with input variables is helpful when dealing with multiple input variables. Assign names to all the input variables before creating your first scenario. Named ranges will make scenario reports easier to understand and interpret.

BTW
Tracing Precedents and Dependents
When all levels of precedents or dependents have been identified, Excel will sound a beep if you try to trace another level.

BTW
Tracer Arrow Lines
If a tracer arrow line appears as a black dashed line connected to a small worksheet icon, it indicates that precedent cells exist on another worksheet. You can double-click a dashed tracer line to move to the connected worksheet.

To Trace Precedents

Why? Tracing precedents in Excel allows you to identify upon which cells a particular formula is based, not only directly by the formula in the cell, but indirectly via precedents. The following steps trace the precedent cells for cell E13, which displays the Total Shipment Profit for accommodating the shipping needs.

- Display the Formulas tab, if necessary, and then select cell E13.
- Click the Trace Precedents button (Formulas tab | Formula Auditing group) to draw a tracer arrow across precedents of the selected cell (Figure 9–5).

Q&A How do I interpret the precedent arrows?
The arrow in Figure 9–5 terminates with an arrowhead on the traced cell, in this case cell E13. The arrow that runs through the range of cells B13:D13 indicates that all cells in the range are precedents of the traced cell.

Is it always red?
No. If a referenced cell contains a formula and that formula also contains an error, then a red line is drawn between the formula cells; otherwise the arrow is blue.

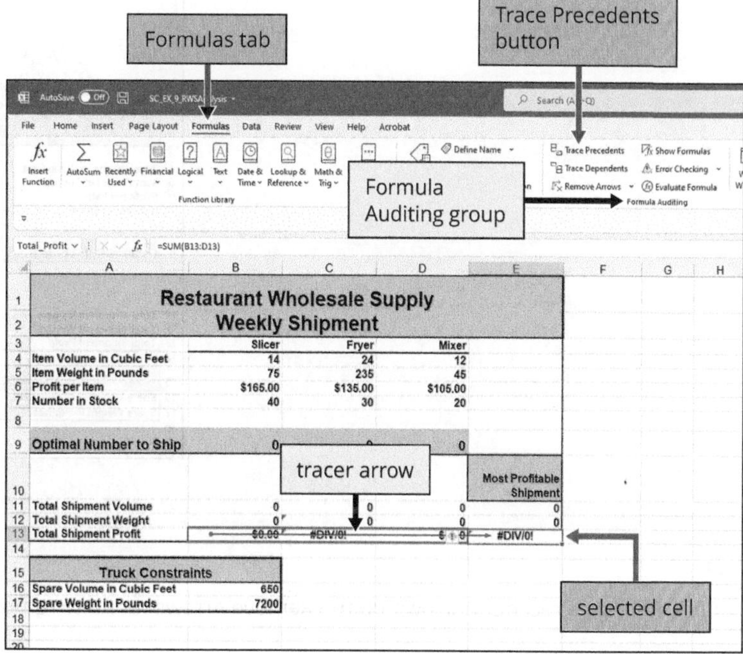

Figure 9–5

- Click the Trace Precedents button (Formulas tab | Formula Auditing group) again to draw arrows indicating precedents of cells B13:D13 (Figure 9–6).

Q&A How do I interpret the new precedent arrows?
The new arrows in Figure 9–6 have arrowheads on traced cells and dots on cells that are direct precedents of the cells with arrowheads. For instance, cell B13 has a tracer arrow pointing to it with a blue line appearing in the range B6:B12 and dots in cell B6 and B9. This indicates that the cells containing dots are precedents of cell B12, while the other cells, without dots, are not.

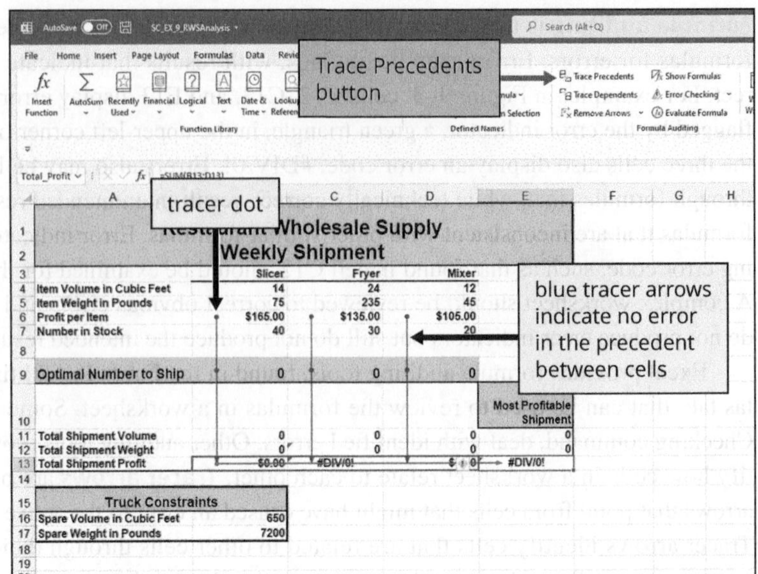

Figure 9–6

To Remove the Precedent Arrows

Why? Reducing visual clutter makes the worksheet easier to edit. The following steps remove the precedent arrows level by level. The formula will be corrected later in the module.

- Click the 'Remove Arrows' arrow (Formulas tab | Formula Auditing group) to display the 'Remove Arrows' menu (Figure 9–7).

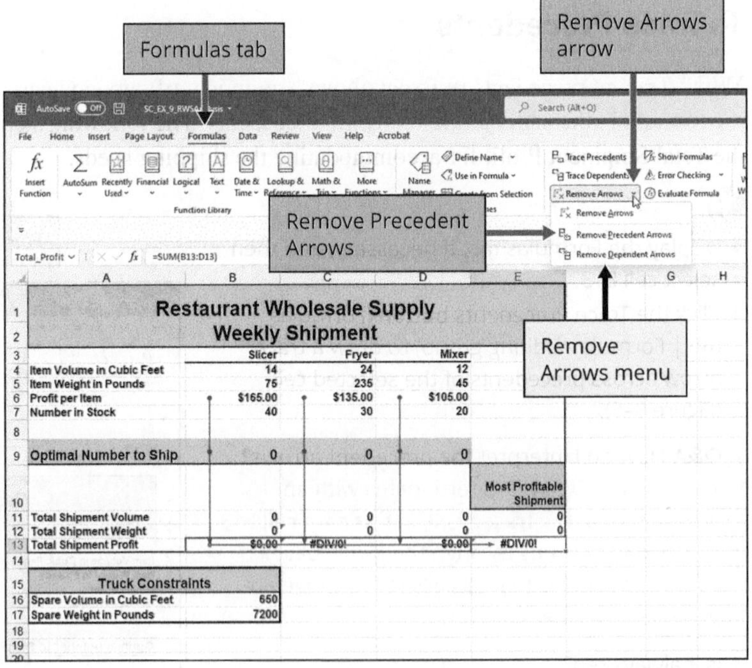

Figure 9–7

- Click 'Remove Precedent Arrows' on the Remove Arrows menu to remove precedent arrows.

- Repeat steps 1 and 2 to remove any remaining precedent arrows (Figure 9–8).

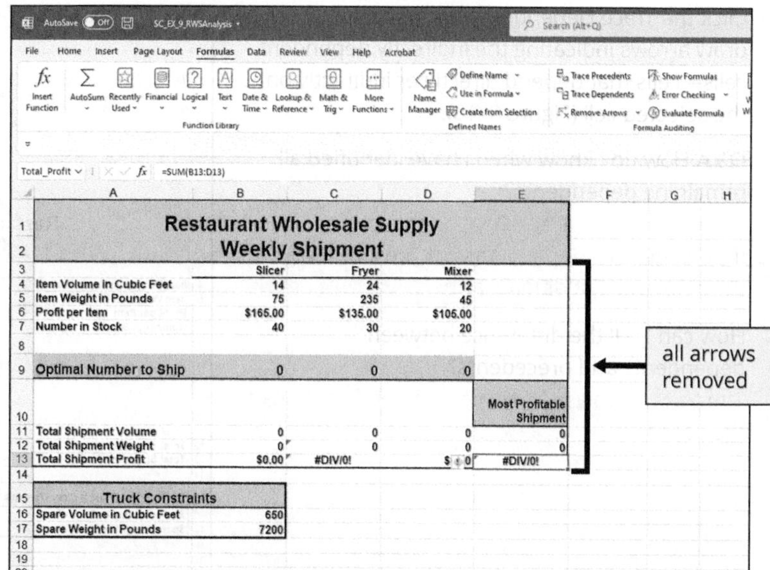

Figure 9–8

To Review Precedents on a Different Worksheet using the Go To Command

You can use precedent arrows to navigate directly to precedents on a different worksheet or different workbook. If you choose to use this feature, you would use the following steps:

1. Double-click on the dashed precedent arrow to display the Go To dialog box.
2. Select the cell reference you wish to navigate to, from the Go To list (Go To dialog box).
3. Click OK (Go To dialog box) to navigate to the selected cell reference.

To Trace Dependents

Why? Identifying dependents highlights where changes will occur in the worksheet as a result of changing the value in the referenced cell. The following steps trace the dependents of cell C9, which will display the optimal number of fryers to ship.

- Select cell C9.
- Click the Trace Dependents button (Formulas tab | Formula Auditing group) to draw arrows to dependent cells (Figure 9–9).

Q&A What is the meaning of the dependent arrows?

As displayed in Figure 9–9, the arrowheads indicate which cells directly depend on the selected cell. In this case, cell C9 is explicitly referenced in formulas located in cells C11, C12, and C13, indicated by the arrow tips.

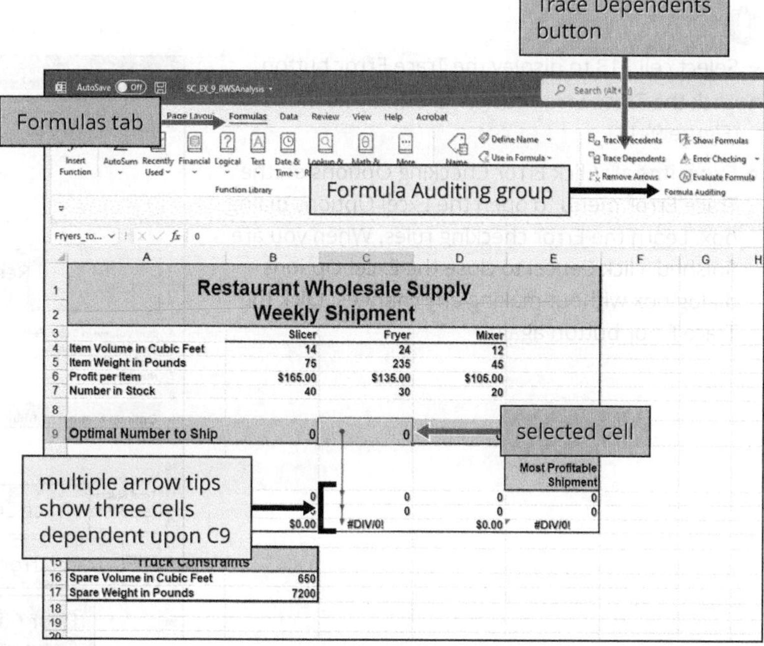

Figure 9–9

- Click the Trace Dependents button again to draw arrows indicating the indirectly dependent cells—cells that depend directly or indirectly on the selected cell (Figure 9–10).

Q&A How do I know when I have identified all remaining dependents?
You can click the Trace Dependents button again. If no additional dependents are present, Excel does not draw additional arrows.

How can I tell the difference between dependents and precedents?
The tracer arrows always point in the direction of the data flow.

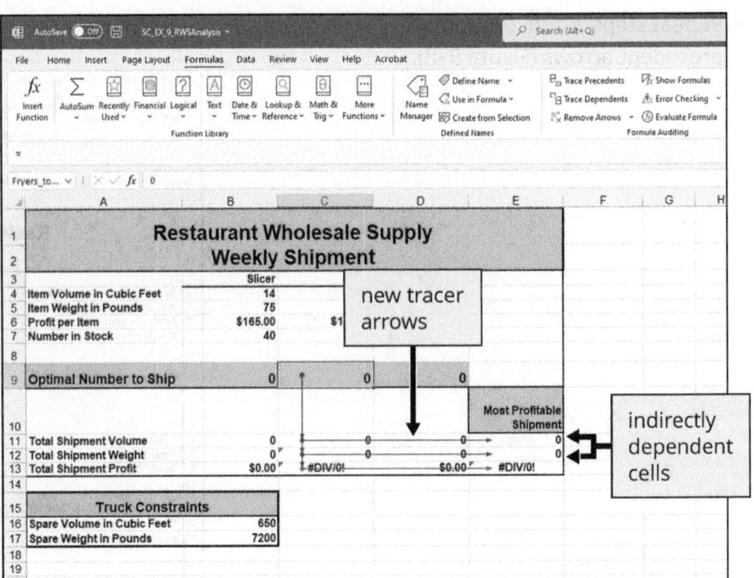

Figure 9–10

To Remove the Dependent Arrows

The following step clears the dependent arrows from the worksheet.

Click the 'Remove Arrows' button (Formulas tab | Formula Auditing group) as necessary to remove all of the dependent arrows.

To Use the Trace Error Button

Another way to trace errors is to the use the Trace Error button that appears in the worksheet itself. **Why?** The Trace Error button offers commands that may help identify the error further. The following steps use the Trace Error button and the Trace Error command to identify the error.

- Select cell E13 to display the Trace Error button.
- Click the Trace Error button to display its menu (Figure 9–11).
   - **Experiment:** Click Error Checking Options on the Trace Error menu to open the Excel Options dialog box. Learn the Error checking rules. When you are finished, click Cancel to close the Excel Options dialog box without making any changes. Click the Trace Error button again.

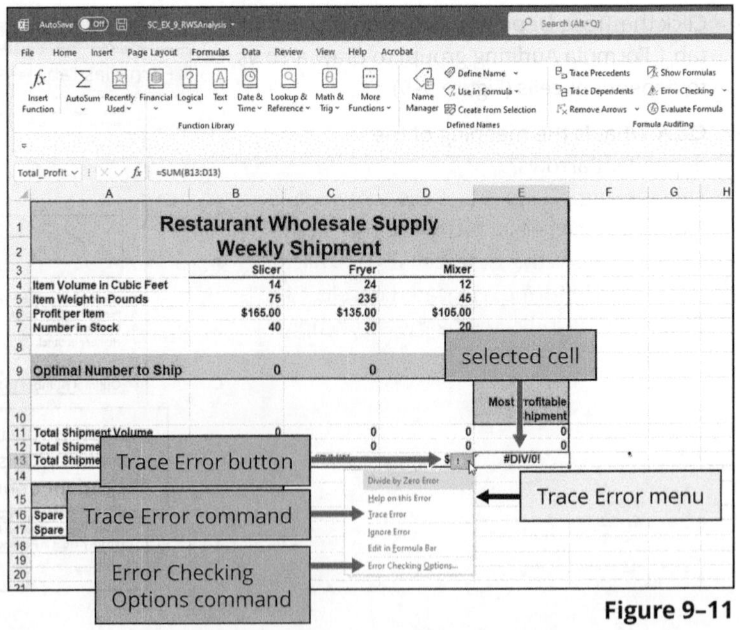

Figure 9–11

- Click Trace Error on the menu to display precedent arrows directly involved in the error (Figure 9–12).

Q&A How is tracing the error different from tracing precedents?
The Trace Error command displays only the precedent arrows involved in the error. Depending on the kind of error, the Trace Error command also moves the selection to the probable erroneous cell.

- Click the Remove Arrows button (Formulas tab | Formula Auditing group) to remove all of the arrows.

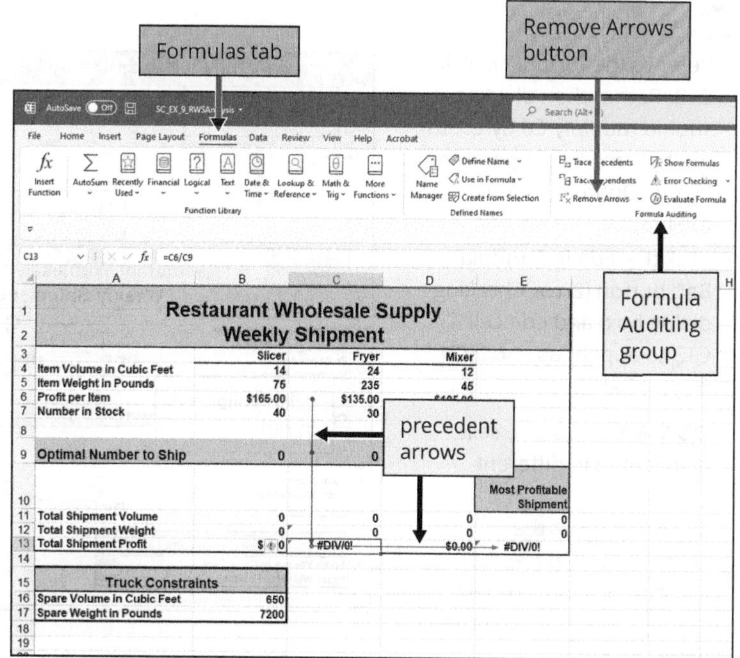

Figure 9–12

Other Ways

1. Click Error Checking arrow (Formulas tab | Formula Auditing Group), click Trace Error on menu

To Use Error Checking to Correct Errors

After tracing the precedents and dependents, and using the Trace Error command, you decide to correct the #DIV/0! in cell C13 first. **Why?** All the arrows indicate that C13 may be causing the error displayed in E13.

The following steps use error checking features to find the source of these errors and correct them.

1

- Select cell C13, if not already selected.
- Click the Error Checking button (Formulas tab | Formula Auditing group) to display the Error Checking dialog box. If necessary, drag the dialog box away from the cells containing data so those cells are visible.
- Refer to the message in the Error Checking dialog box that identifies that the formula is dividing by zero or empty cells (Figure 9–13).

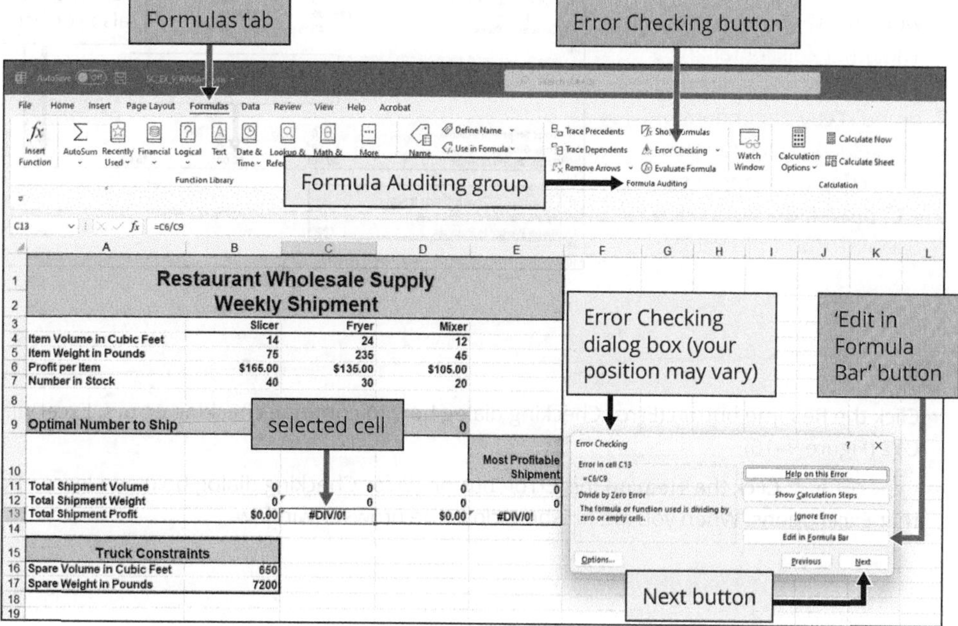

Figure 9–13

Q&A What is the purpose of the Next button?
Excel will move to the next cell in which it finds an error code or an error indicator.
Excel moves forward or backward through the workbook, row by row, when you click the Next or Previous button. Clicking the Next button does not move to a precedent or dependent cell.

- Refer to the formula in cell C13. Rather than dividing, it should multiply C6 by C9, to multiply the 'Profit per Item' by the 'Optimal Number to Ship'.
- Click the 'Edit in Formula Bar' button (Error Checking dialog box) and edit cell C13 to appear as **=C6*C9** (Figure 9–14).

Q&A Why are some cells highlighted in different colors?
Excel highlights the cells involved in the current formula. The cell highlighted in red indicates a possible error.

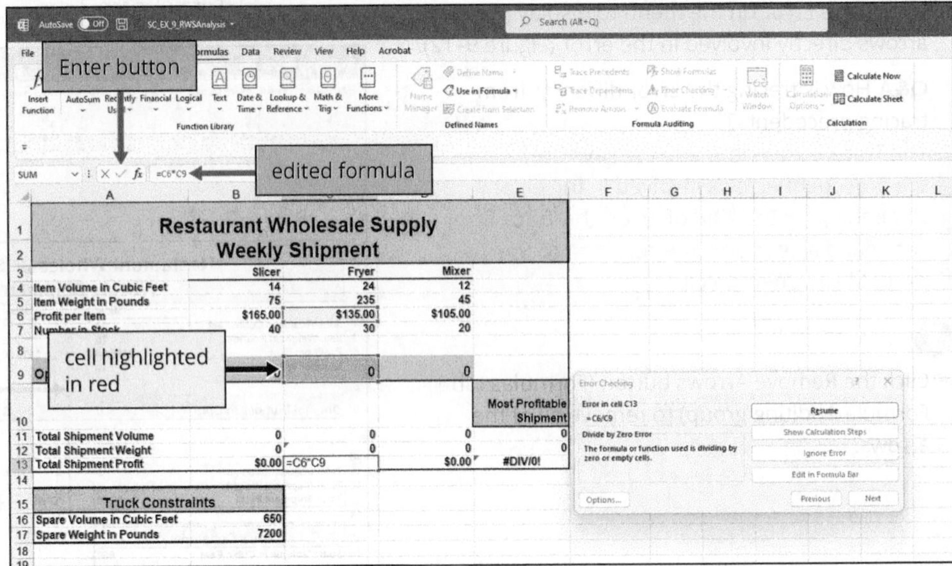

Figure 9–14

- Click the Enter button in the formula bar to complete the edit of the cell and to correct the error in cell C13 and the dependent error in cell E13 (Figure 9–15).

Q&A Why did correcting one error in cell C13 correct the other #DIV/0! error in the worksheet?
The other cell containing a #DIV/0! error was directly or indirectly dependent on the value in cell C13; thus, correcting the error in cell C13 provided a valid value for use in the other formulas.

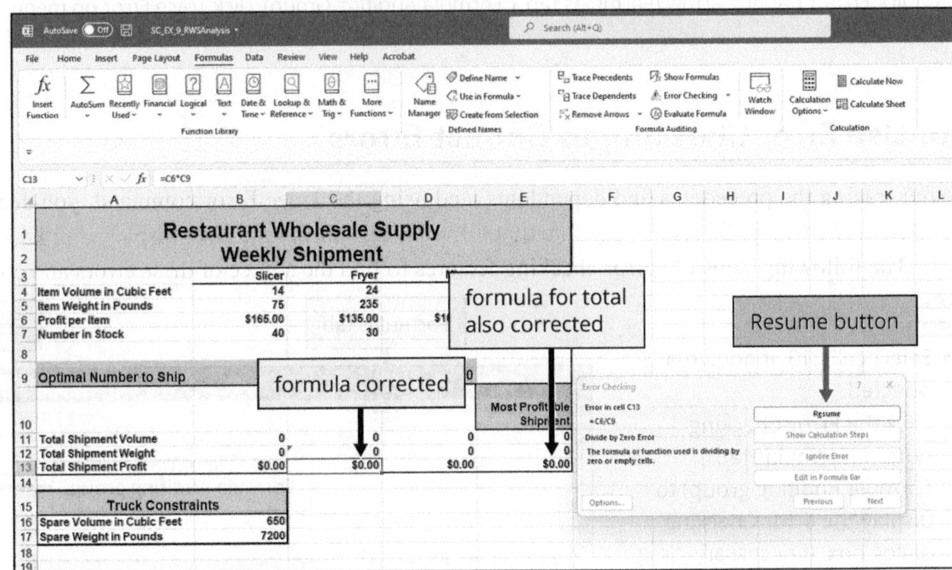

Figure 9–15

- Click the Resume button (Error Checking dialog box) to continue checking errors. Excel will move to the error in cell C12 (Figure 9–16).
- **Experiment:** Click the 'Help on this Error' button (Error Checking dialog box) and learn about the error in the browser window that Excel opens. When you are finished, close the browser window.

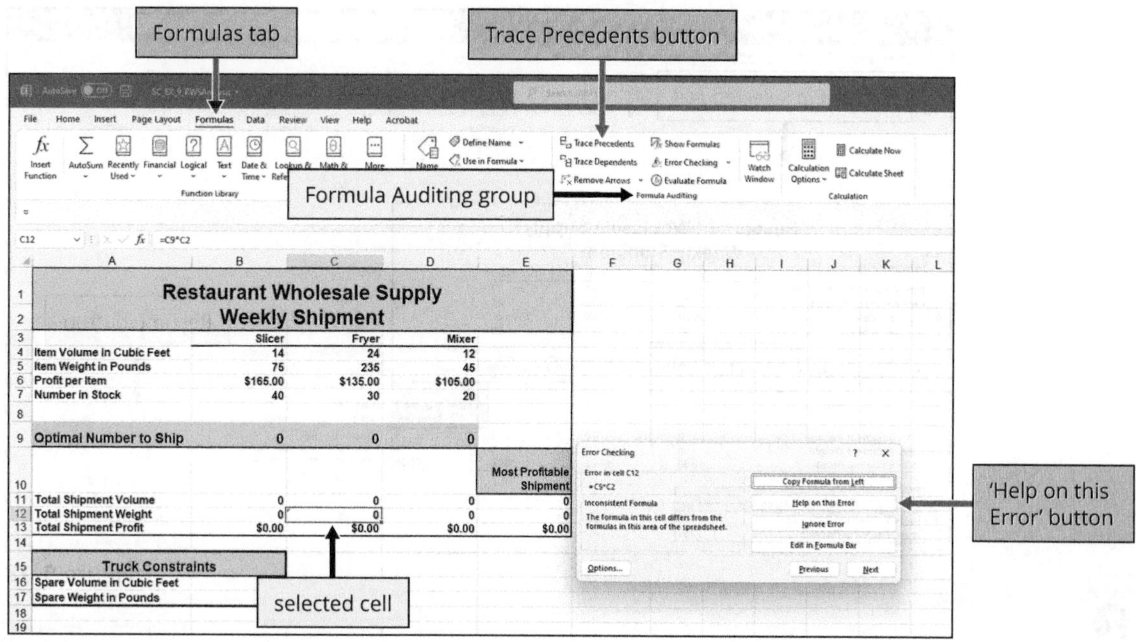

Figure 9–16

- Click the Trace Precedents button (Formulas tab | Formula Auditing group) to display the tracer arrow (Figure 9–17).
  - **Experiment:** Refer to the formula in the formula bar. Notice the formula and the tracer arrow both reference C2, which is text and is incorrect.

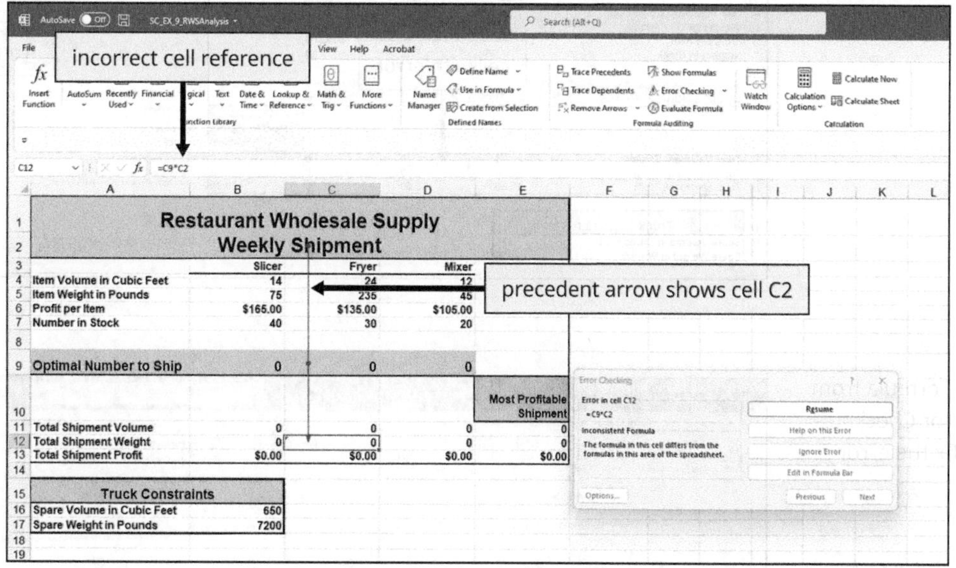

Figure 9–17

- Click cell B12 to display the formula (Figure 9–18).
  - **Experiment:** Notice this formula is =B9*B5, which correctly multiplies the 'Optimal Number to Ship' by the 'Item Weight in Pounds'.

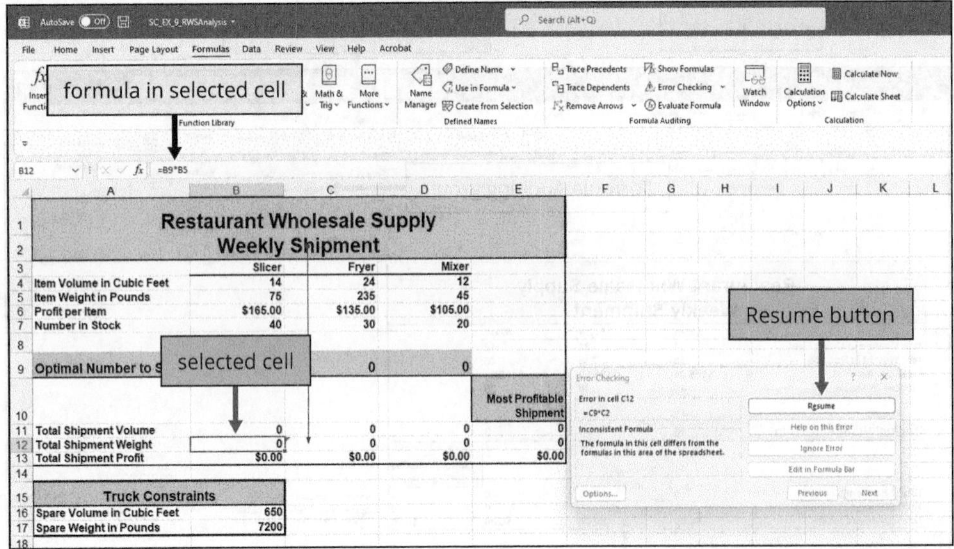

Figure 9–18

7

- Click the Resume button (Error Checking dialog box) to move to the error in cell C12 (Figure 9–19).

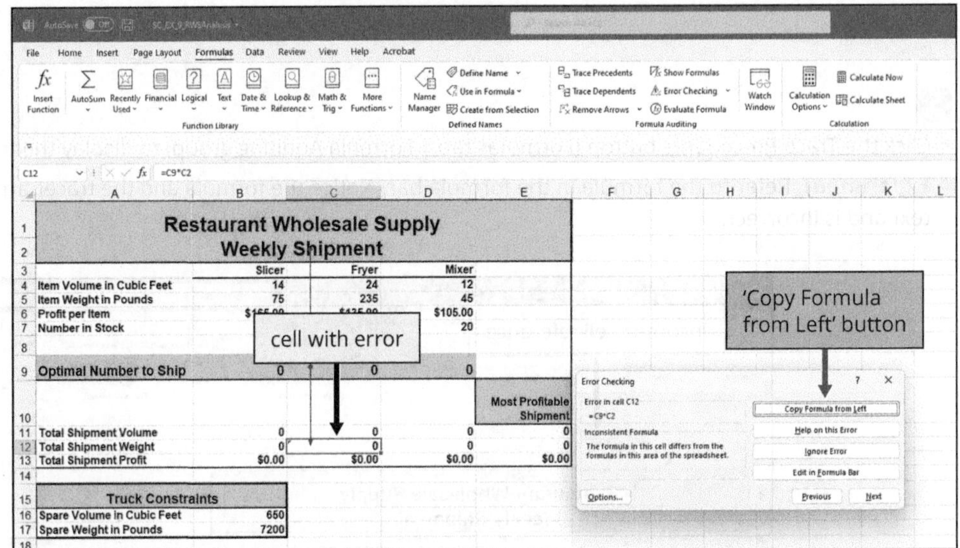

Figure 9–19

8

- Click the 'Copy Formula from Left' button (Error Checking dialog box) to fix the error (Figure 9–20).

9

- Click OK (Microsoft Excel dialog box) as the error correction is complete.
- Click the Save button on the Quick Access Toolbar to save the file.

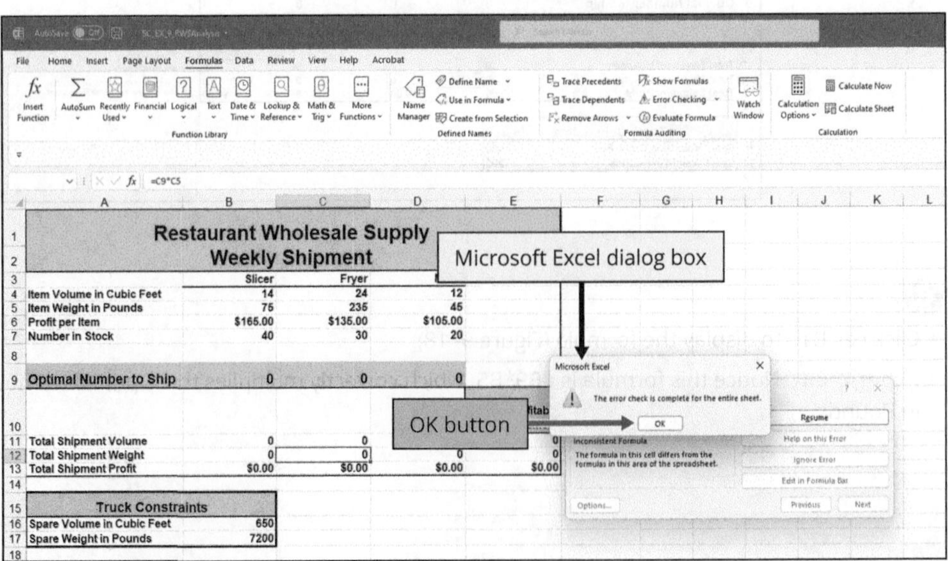

Figure 9–20

More about the Formula Auditing Group

In the previous steps, you used some of the buttons in the Formula Auditing group on the Formulas tab to identify and correct errors in your worksheet. You already have used the Trace Precedents, Trace Dependents, and 'Remove All Arrows' buttons to gain insight into the structure of the worksheet. You used the Trace Error button in the worksheet and the Trace Error command to display red arrows to highlight the precedents of the selected cell, to help you identify the source of the error. You also used the Error Checking button to check for errors throughout the worksheet. When the Error Checking button is clicked, Excel highlights each error in the worksheet in sequence and displays options for correcting the error.

If you click the Error Checking arrow (Formulas tab | Formula Auditing group), you have an option to fix a circular reference, if your worksheet contains one. A **circular reference** occurs when one of the defining values in a cell is itself. For example, if you type =B2/A2 in cell B2, you have created a circular reference. Excel displays an error message when you create a circular reference and provides you with access to the appropriate Help topic. In complex worksheets with multiple precedent levels, these errors are not uncommon.

Table 9–1 lists other common error codes identified in Excel.

Table 9–1: Common Excel Error Codes

Error Code	Description
#DIV/0!	Indicates that a formula divides a number by zero
#N/A!	Indicates that a formula cannot locate a referenced value
#NAME?	Indicates use of an invalid function name
#NULL!	Indicates that a formula incorrectly contains a space between two or more cell references
#NUM!	Indicates that a formula contains invalid numeric values
#REF!	Indicates that a cell reference in a formula is not valid; it may be pointing to an empty cell, for instance
#VALUE!	Indicates that a calculation includes nonnumeric data

The Formula Auditing group contains three other commands you can use when auditing formulas. The Evaluate Formula button allows you to move through a formula step by step, which can be a useful tool when working with long, complex formulas. The Show Formulas button displays formulas instead of values in the active worksheet. The Watch Window button opens a separate window that displays values and formulas for specific cells that you choose to monitor.

BTW

Setting Iterative Calculation Options

In certain situations, you will want Excel to recalculate a formula that contains a circular reference, to enable Excel to converge upon an acceptable solution. Changing the iterative calculation option allows Excel to recalculate a formula a specified number of times after the initial circular reference error message is dismissed. To allow Excel to recalculate a formula, display the Excel Options dialog box and then click the Formulas tab. In the Calculation options area, click to select the 'Enable iterative calculation' check box. You can specify the maximum number of iterations and maximum amount of change between iterations. Be aware that turning on this option will slow down the worksheet due to the additional computations.

Using the Watch Window

The **Watch Window** (Figure 9–21a) displays values of cells located throughout the workbook and allows you to keep an eye on cells that you have identified as being related; this allows you to observe changes to the cells even when reviewing a different worksheet or workbook. For example, if you were reviewing cell E13, which displays 'Total Shipment Profit' for the most profitable shipment, and you changed the value in cell B13, the Watch Window would display the updated value of cell E13 on the Weekly Shipment Worksheet. You add cells to the Watch Window using the Add Watch button and the Add Watch dialog box (Figure 9–21b). The Watch Window continues to display the values of watched cells even as you navigate the worksheet and the cells no longer are displayed. Similarly, if you change the display to another worksheet or workbook, the Watch Window allows you to continue to monitor the cell values.

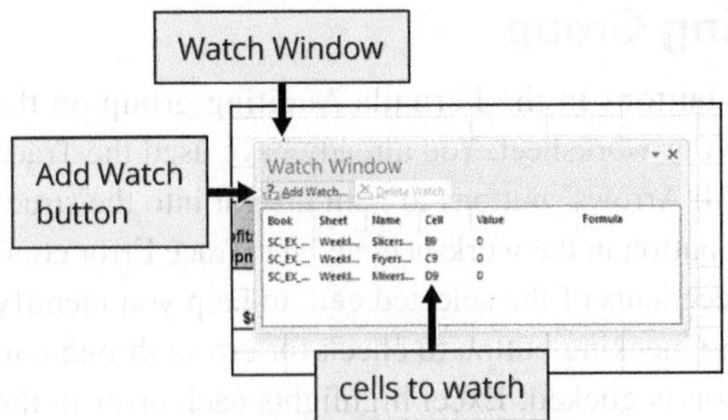

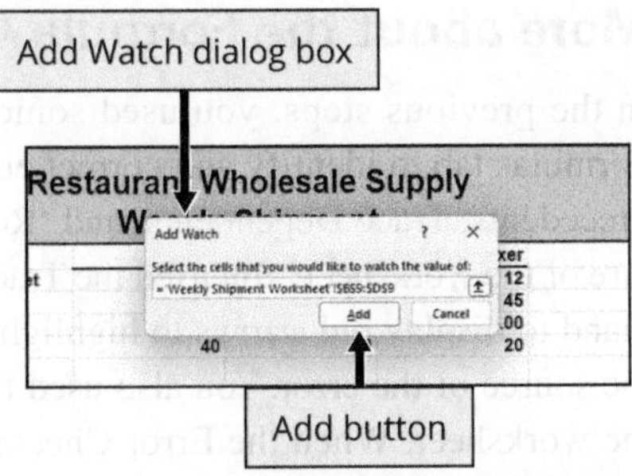

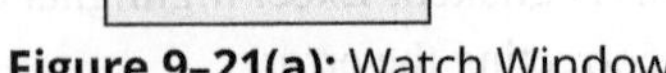

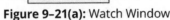

Figure 9–21(a): Watch Window

Figure 9–21(b): Add Watch dialog box

To Open the Watch Window

If you wanted to open the Watch Window, you would perform the following steps:

1. If necessary, display the Formulas tab.
2. Click the Watch Window button (Formulas tab | Formula Auditing group) to open the Watch Window (Figure 9–21a).
3. If necessary, move the Watch Window to a location where it does not obscure cells you may want to edit.

To Add Cells to the Watch Window

If you wanted to add cells to the Watch Window, you would perform the following steps:

1. Click the Add Watch button on the Watch Window toolbar to display the Add Watch dialog box (Figure 9–21b).
2. Select the cell or cells to be watched.
3. Click the Add button (Add Watch dialog box) to add the selected cells to the Watch Window.

To Delete Cells from the Watch Window

If you wanted to delete cells from the Watch Window, you would perform the following steps:

1. In the Watch Window dialog box, select the cell you want to stop watching.
2. Click the Delete Watch button in the Watch Window to delete the selected cell from the Watch Window (Figure 9–21a).

Data Validation

When creating advanced worksheets, some user-entered values my need to fall within certain ranges or contain specific types of data. For example, cells B9:D9 in the Weekly Shipment Worksheet display the optimal number of each item to ship. Recall from the requirements that shipment amounts must be whole numbers and at least one of each type of item must be included in each shipment but no more than are in stock of each type of item. Excel provides you with tools to restrict the values that can be placed in cells to valid values. You can place restrictions on values, provide a message to the user when a cell with restrictions is selected, and create an error message that is displayed when an invalid value is entered.

Excel data validation rules apply only when you enter data into the cell manually. Excel does not check the validation rules if a cell is calculated by a formula or set in a way other than by direct input by the user.

The types of data validation criteria you can use include specific values, whole numbers, a value in a list (such as a text value), dates, and custom values. When using the custom validation type, you can use a formula that evaluates to either true or false. If the value is false, users may not enter data in the cell. Suppose, for example, you have a cell that contains an employee's salary. If the salary is zero, which indicates the employee no longer is with the company, you may want to prohibit a user from entering a percentage in another cell that contains the employee's raise for the year.

BTW
Errors and Data
Excel cannot identify cells that contain formulas that are mathematically correct but logically incorrect without the use of data validation rules. It is up to the user to create validation rules that restrict solutions to logical values based on the goals of the formula.

To Add Data Validation to Cells

Why? In the Weekly Shipment Worksheet, the numbers of each type of equipment to ship must be nonnegative whole numbers. The cells that need to be restricted are cells B9:D9. You can use data validation to apply these conditions and restrictions to the cells. The following steps add data validation to cells in the range B9:D9.

- Display the Data tab and then select cells B9:D9.
- Click the Data Validation button (Data tab | Data Tools group) to display the Data Validation dialog box. If necessary, drag the dialog box away from the cells containing data so those cells are displayed.
- Click the Allow arrow (Data Validation dialog box | Settings tab) to display the list of allowed restrictions on the input data (Figure 9–22).

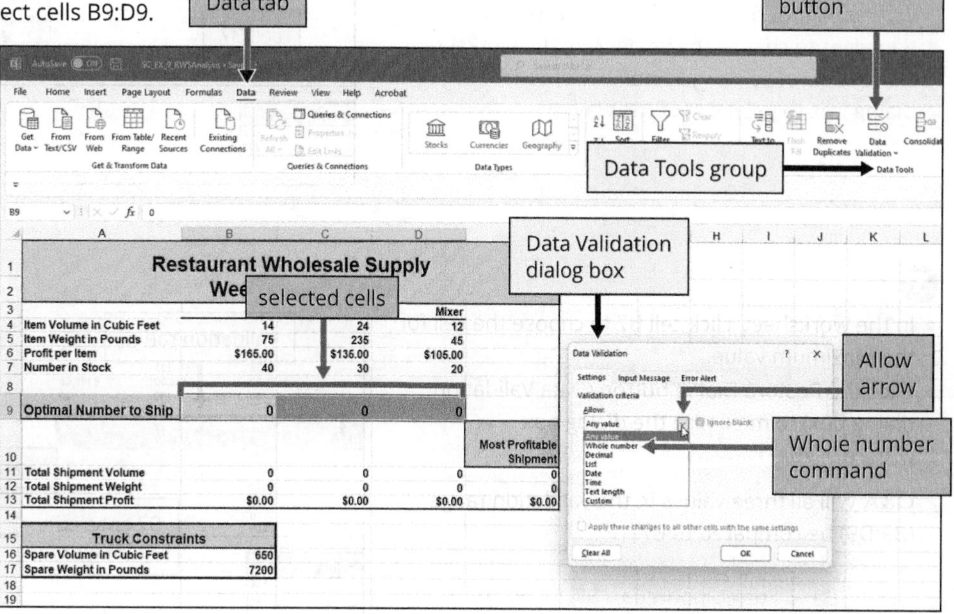

Figure 9–22

Q&A What are the allowed restrictions?
The Any value selection allows you to enter any value but still allows you to specify an input message for the cell. The Whole number, Decimal, Date, and Time selections permit only values of those types to be entered in the cell. The List selection allows you to specify a range that contains a list of valid values for the cell. The Text length selection allows only a certain length of text string to be entered in the cell. The Custom selection allows you to specify a formula that validates the data entered by the user. Each selection displays its own set of options.

2

- Click Whole number in the Allow list to display options for whole numbers.
- Click the Data arrow to display its list (Figure 9–23).

Q&A What is in the Data list?
The Data list includes the standard logical operators for numeric, date, and time data. The list is not available for other data types.

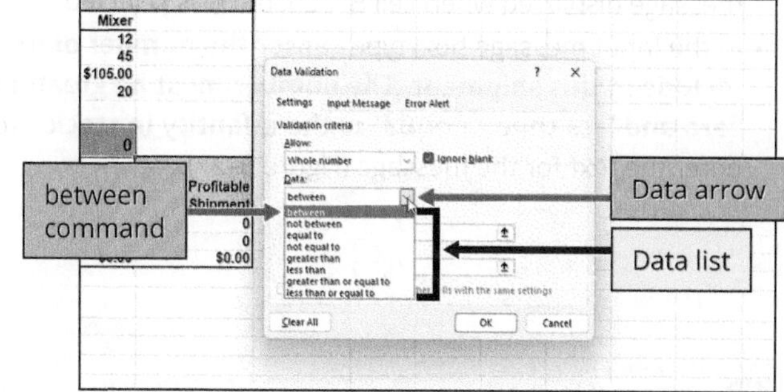

Figure 9–23

- Click between in the Data list to select it and close the list.
- Type 1 in the Minimum box to specify that the values in the selected cells must be whole numbers greater than or equal to one (Figure 9–24).

Q&A Why am I entering 1?
Recall that the requirements document specifies that at least one of each item should be shipped.

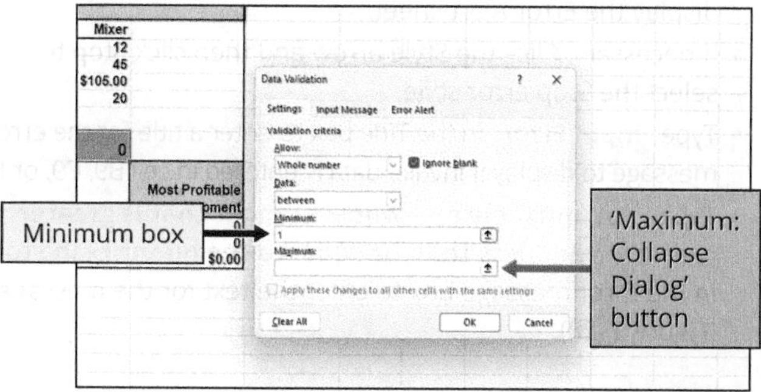

Figure 9–24

- Click the 'Maximum: Collapse Dialog' button to collapse the dialog box and go to the worksheet (Figure 9–25).

Q&A Why is the dialog box collapsed?
When you click a Collapse Dialog button associated with any input box, you are telling Excel that you want to choose the value from the worksheet rather than type it in yourself. Excel collapses the dialog box to get it out of the way.

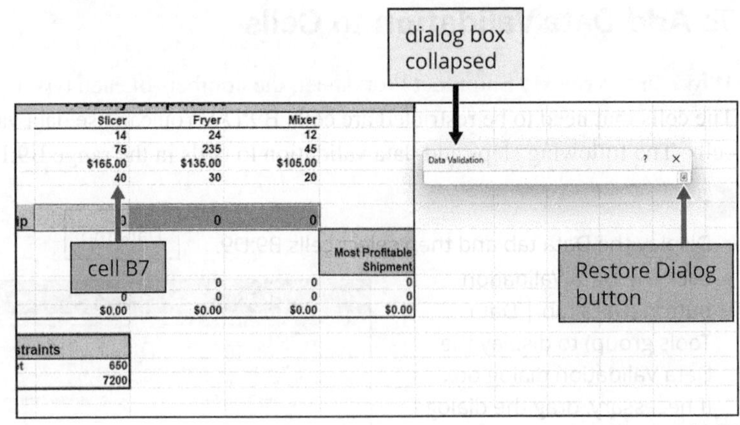

Figure 9–25

- In the worksheet, click cell B7 to choose the cell for the Maximum value.
- Click the Restore Dialog button (Data Validation dialog box) to maximize the dialog box (Figure 9–26).

Q&A Will all three values in the validation range (B9:D9) be compared to B7?
No. Excel will apply a relative reference; in other words, B9 will be compared to B7, C9 will be compared to C7, and D9 will be compared to D7. If you wanted to compare to an absolute, nonchanging reference, you would input =$B$7.

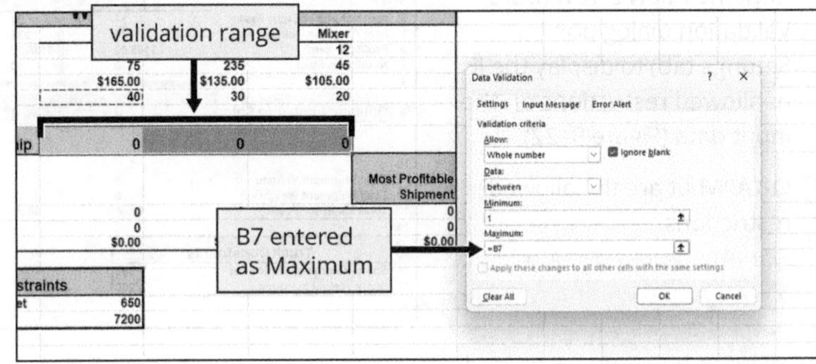

Figure 9–26

- Click the Input Message tab (Data Validation dialog box) to display the Input Message sheet.
- Type **Item to Ship** in the Title box to enter a title for the message displayed when cell B9, C9, or D9 is selected.
- In the Input message box, type **Enter the number of items to include in this shipment. The number must be greater than zero and less than or equal to the quantity in stock.** to enter the text for the message (Figure 9–27).

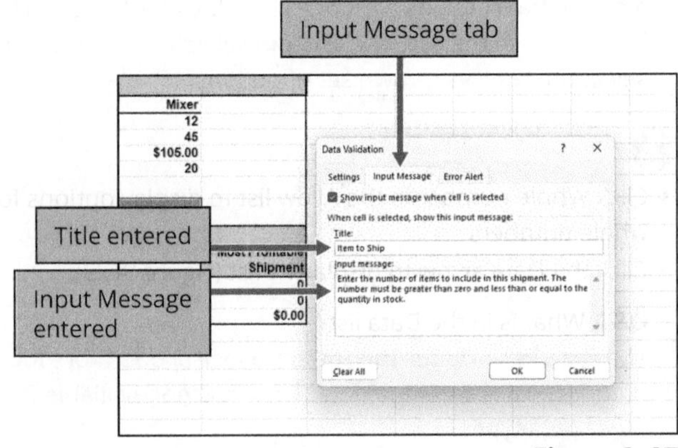

Figure 9–27

- Click the Error Alert tab (Data Validation dialog box) to display the Error Alert sheet.
- If necessary, Click the Style arrow and then click Stop to select the Stop error style.
- Type **Input Error** in the Title box to enter a title for the error message to display if invalid data is entered in cell B9, C9, or D9.
- Type **You must enter a whole number that is greater than zero and less than or equal to the quantity in stock.** in the Error message box to enter the text for the message (Figure 9–28).

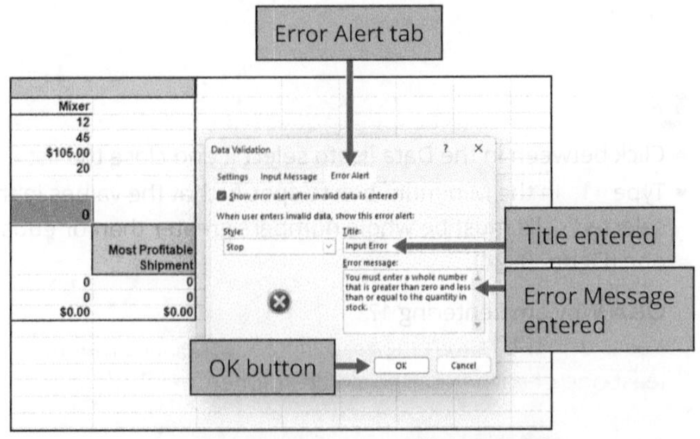

Figure 9–28

Q&A What is a Stop error style?
You can select one of three types of error styles. Stop prevents users from entering invalid data in a cell. Warning displays a message that the data is invalid and lets users accept the invalid entry, edit it, or remove it. Information displays a message that the data is invalid but still allows users to enter it.

- Click OK (Data Validation dialog box) to accept the data validation settings for cells B9:D9.
- Click outside the data range to remove the selection.

To Test the Validation

The following steps test the validation rules. **Why?** It is always a good idea to test validation rules to make sure they work as you expect them to.

- Click cell B9 to make it the active cell and display the 'Items to Ship' input message (Figure 9–29).
- **Experiment:** Click cells C9 and D9 to make sure the same input message appears. Click cell B9.

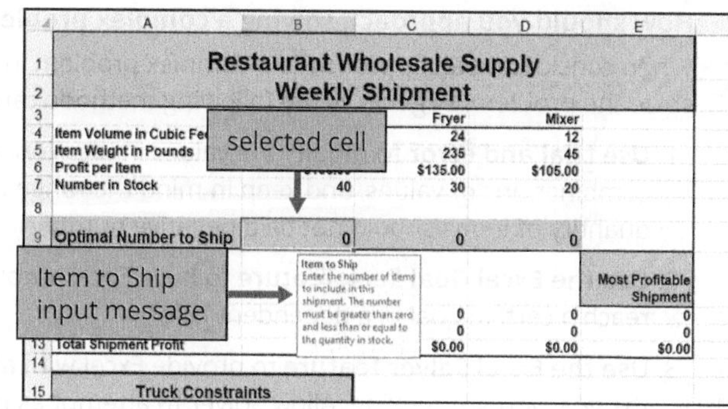

Figure 9–29

2

- Type **23.5** and then press ENTER to enter the number of slicers to ship and to display the Input Error dialog box (Figure 9–30).

Q&A Why does the Input Error dialog box appear after entering 23.5 in cell B9?
You set a data validation rule in cell B9 that accepts only whole numbers greater than or equal to zero. Because 23.5 is not a whole number, Excel displays the Input Error dialog box with the title and error message you specified when you set the data validation rule.

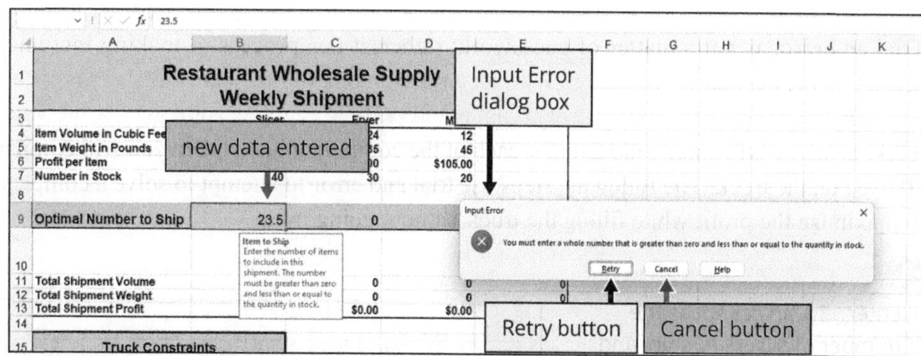

Figure 9–30

3

- Click Cancel (Input Error dialog box) to return to cell B9.
- **Experiment:** Repeat Step 1 using values that are negative and values that are more than the number in stock. When you are finished, click Cancel (Input Error dialog box).
- Click the Save button on the Quick Access Toolbar to save the file. If Excel displays an Input Error dialog box, click Cancel.

Break Point: If you want to take a break, this is a good place to do so. You can exit Excel now. To resume later, start Excel, open the file called SC_EX_9_RWSAnalysis.xlsx, and continue following the steps from this location forward.

BTW

Copying Validation Rules

You can copy validation rules from one cell to other cells using the Paste Special command. Select the cell that contains the validation rules you want to copy and then click Copy. Select the cell or cells to which you want to apply the validation rules, click the Paste button arrow, and then click Paste Special. Click Validation in the Paste area and then click the OK button (Paste Special dialog box).

Solving Complex Problems

In the RWS Analysis workbook, the problem of determining how to schedule trucks to maximize weight, volume, and profit within the constraints provided is complex due to the number of variables involved. You can attempt to solve the problem manually through trial and error, or you can use an Excel tool to automate some or all of the solution. To solve the problem manually, you could try adjusting values in the ranges B9, C9, and D9 until the goal for the schedule is met. Remember that RWS wants to identify the best logistics of items to trucks that will maximize the company's total profit. Because so many possible combinations could meet the criteria, you could hold one or more of the cells affected by constraints constant and adjust the other cells to attempt to meet the rest of the criteria.

Consider This

How should you approach solving a complex problem?

When considering an approach to a complex problem in Excel, start with the least complex method of attempting to solve the problem. In general, the following methods can be useful in the following order:

1. **Use trial and error** to modify the values in the worksheet. Use a commonsense approach to entering different combinations of values, and keep in mind the range of acceptable answers to your problem. For example, the quantity of items should not be a negative number.
2. **Use the Excel Goal Seek feature** to have Excel automatically modify a cell's value in a worksheet in an attempt to reach a certain goal in a dependent cell.
3. **Use the Excel Solver feature** to provide Excel with all of the known rules, or constraints, of your problem, as well as the goal you are seeking. Allow Solver to attempt as many different solutions to your problem as possible.

To Use Trial and Error to Attempt to Solve a Complex Problem

Trial and error is not a matter of guesswork; rather, it is a process of making incremental changes in order to observe the impact on the desired result. **Why?** With an understanding of how the worksheet is set up and how the various values interact, you can make informed changes, or trials, based on how each decision affects the worksheet. In the first trial for the RWS workbook, you will enter valid data for each of the equipment items; then you will compare the total weight and volume to that allowed on the truck. The following steps use trial and error to attempt to solve a complex problem. In this case, you are trying to maximize the profit while filling the truck without going over.

- Enter **16** in cell B9 as the number of slicers to ship, and then press TAB.
- Enter **25** in cell C9 as the number of fryers sets to ship, and then press TAB.
- Enter **15** in cell D9 as the number of mixers to ship, and then press ENTER (Figure 9–31).

Q&A Do the values entered in Step 1 solve the scheduling problem?

No. Both the Volume and Weight in cells E11:E12 exceed the truck constraints displayed in cells B16:B17.

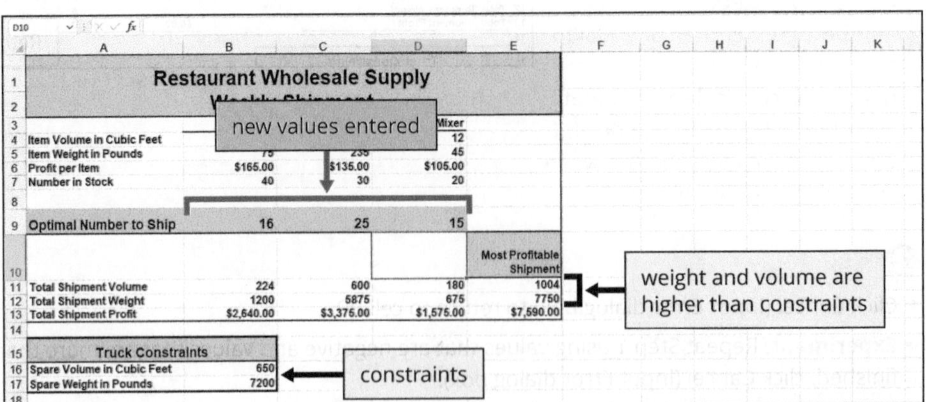

Figure 9–31

2

- Click cell C9 to make it the active cell.
- Enter **20** and then press ENTER to reduce the number of fryers to ship (Figure 9–32).

Q&A Does the value entered in Step 2 solve the scheduling problem?
No. The volume is still too high. Compare cells E11 and B16.

What are some problems with using trial and error?
While trial and error can be used on simple problems, it has many limitations when used to solve complex problems. Endless combinations of values could be entered in cells B7, C7, D7, C9, B9, and D9 to try to come up with a solution. Using trial and error, it is difficult to determine if a solution you reach satisfies the goal of maximizing the total profit.

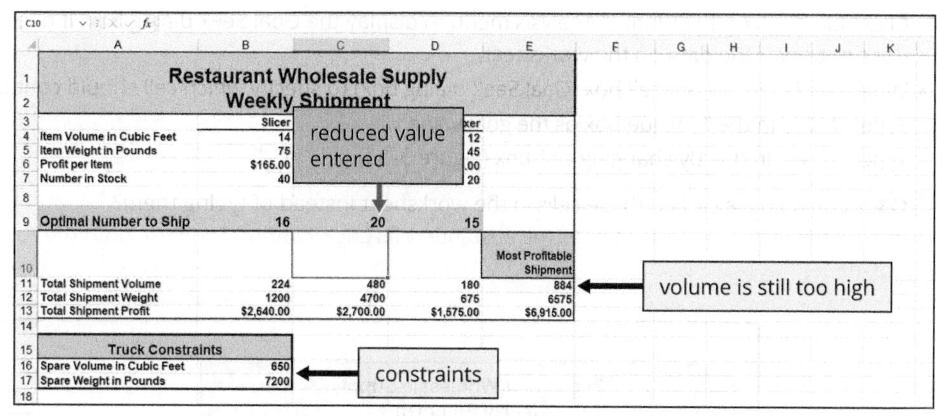

Figure 9–32

To Use Goal Seek to Attempt to Solve a Complex Problem

If you know the result you want a formula to produce, recall that you can use **Goal Seek** to determine the value of a cell on which a formula depends. Goal seeking takes trial and error one step further by automatically changing the value of a cell until a single criterion is met in another cell.

In the Weekly Shipment Worksheet, the number of shipped items cannot exceed the number in stock, and, with the various weights and volumes, the shipment must fit in the truck. With Goal Seek, you can manipulate one of these precedent cells—that is, a cell containing the quantity of a particular item to ship—to find a solution that meets the constraints. You decide to have Goal Seek manipulate the number of mixers. **Why?** You want to try to achieve the goal of 7200 pounds, the total weight for the shipment.

The following steps use Goal Seek to change the number of mixers to keep the total weight close to but under or equal to 7200 pounds.

- If necessary, display the Data tab.
- Click the 'What-If Analysis' button (Data tab | Forecast group) to display the What-If Analysis menu (Figure 9–33).

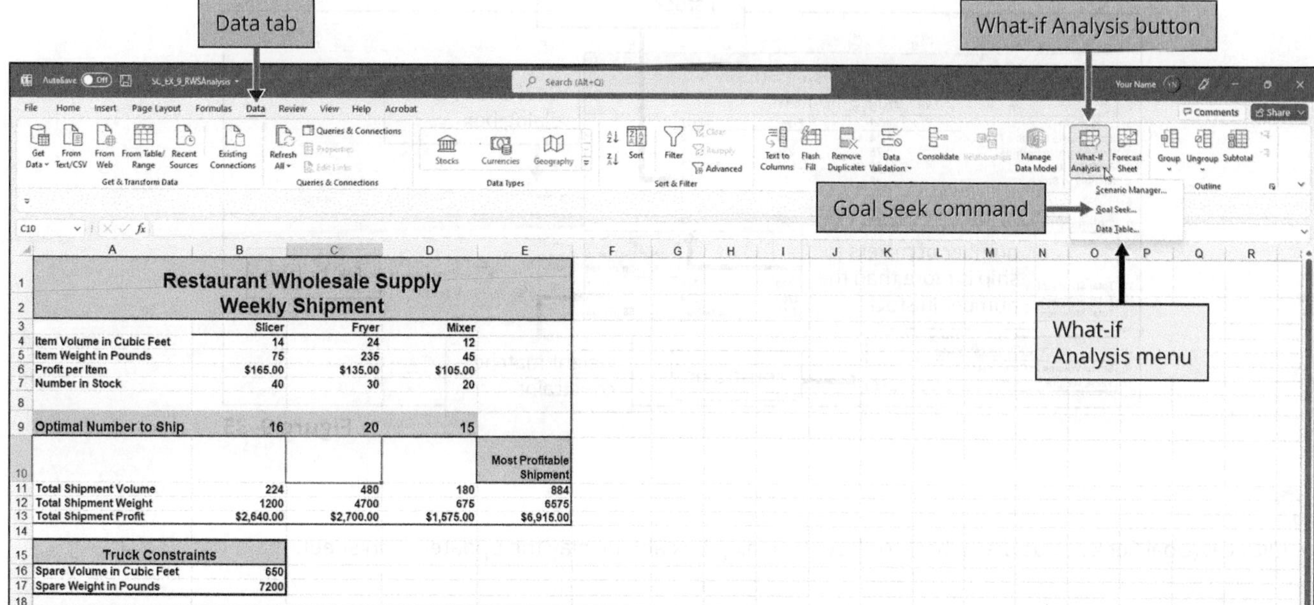

Figure 9–33

- Click Goal Seek on the What-If Analysis menu to display the Goal Seek dialog box. If necessary, drag the dialog box so that it does not cover the data on the worksheet.
- Type **$E$12** in the Set cell box (Goal Seek dialog box) to specify which cell should contain the goal value.
- Type **7200** in the To value box as the goal value.
- Type **$D$9** in the 'By changing cell' box (Figure 9–34).

Q&A Could I have clicked those cells in the worksheet instead of typing them?
Yes, just be sure that Excel applies the absolute reference symbol ($) before both the row and column so no replications are made.

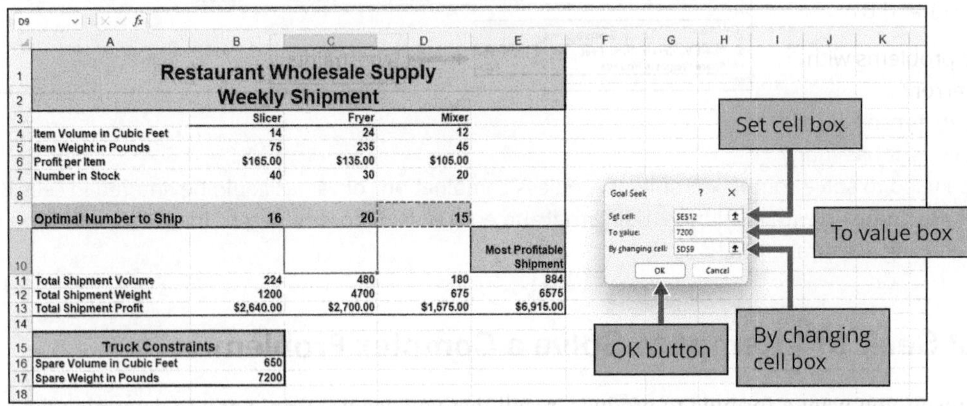

Figure 9–34

- Click OK (Goal Seek dialog box) to seek the goal of 7200 pounds in cell E12 and display the Goal Seek Status dialog box (Figure 9–35).
  - **Experiment:** Check out Excel create iterations in trying to come close to 7200.

Q&A How can the number of mixers to ship (D9) be more than the number in stock (D7) when the data validation rule disallowed numbers greater than the number in stock?
Data validation rules are applied only to data that is entered into a cell. Entries that are the result of calculations and goal seeking will not produce a data validation error.

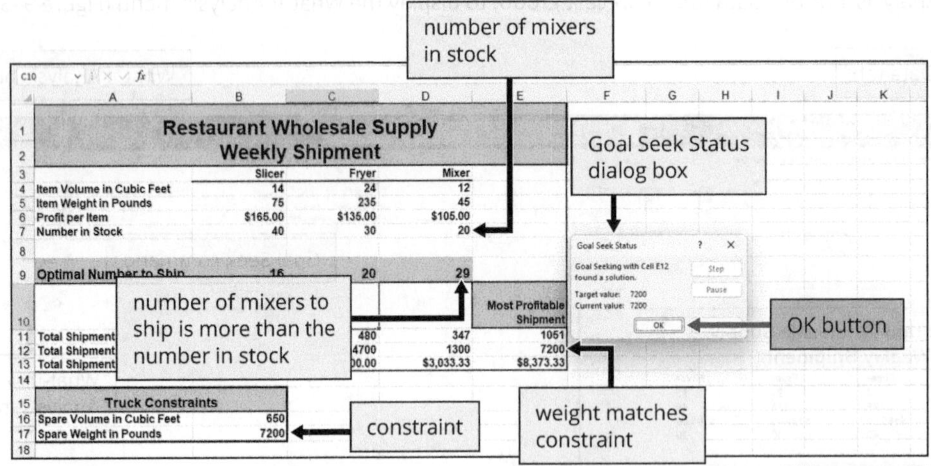

Figure 9–35

- Click OK (Goal Seek Status dialog box) to close the dialog box and display the updated worksheet.

To Circle Invalid Data

The 'Circle Invalid Data' command checks for invalid data entered as the result of a formula or automated tool, such as Goal Seek. In this case, Goal Seek found a solution that satisfied the criteria specified for the goal, but that solution violated the conditions specified for data validation. It is good practice to check your worksheet for invalid data periodically through use of the 'Circle Invalid Data' command. **Why?** The previous set of steps illustrates how the data validation rules apply only to data directly entered into a cell, not to the results of actions such as Goal Seek. The following steps check for and circle any invalid data on the Weekly Shipment Worksheet.

- Click the Data Validation arrow (Data tab | Data Tools group) to display the Data Validation menu (Figure 9–36).

Q&A What are some limitations of using goal seeking?
Goal seeking allows you to manipulate only one cell in order to reach a goal. In this example, Goal Seek produced a result that is acceptable mathematically, but not logically, as is the case here.

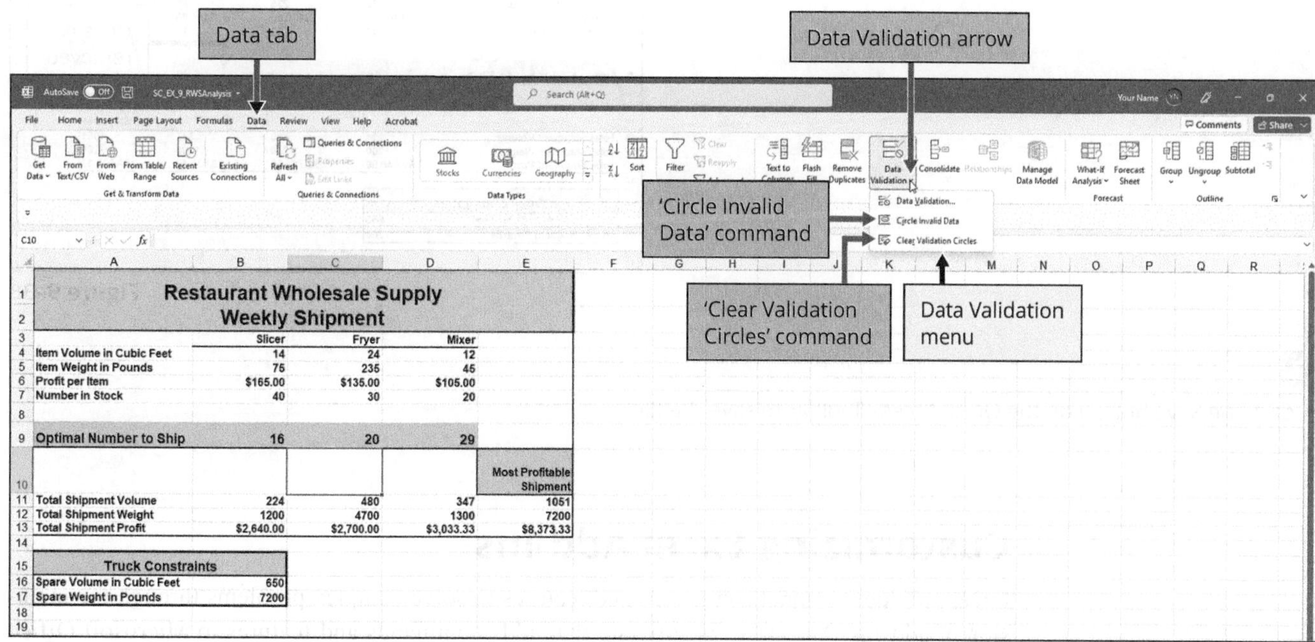

Figure 9–36

- Click 'Circle Invalid Data' on the Data Validation menu to place a red validation circle around any invalid data, in this case cell D9 (Figure 9–37).

Q&A How does Excel determine invalid data?
Excel only can identify data you have specified in the data validation process earlier in the module. In this case, the optimal number to ship is greater than the quantity in stock.

Now that I have identified invalid data, what do I do with that information?
Once you identify invalid data in a worksheet, you should determine how to correct the data.

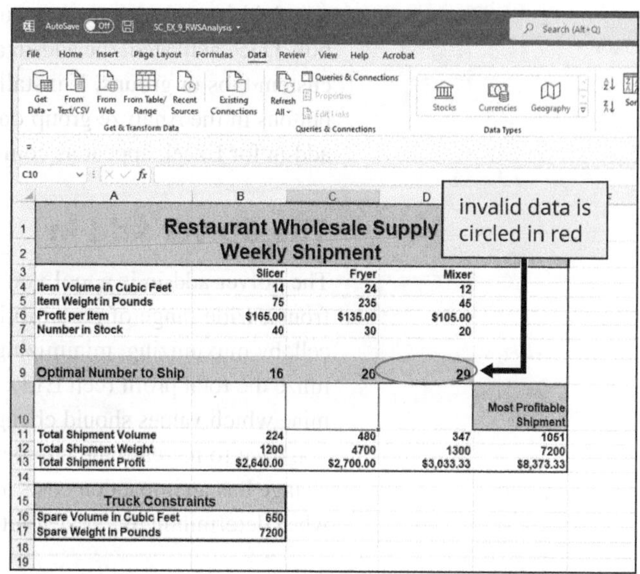

Figure 9–37

To Clear Validation Circles

Why? Once the invalid data has been identified, it is easier to work when the worksheet is clear of extraneous marks. The following step clears the validation circles.

- Click the Data Validation arrow (Data tab | Data Tools group) to display the Data Validation menu (displayed in Figure 9–36).
- Click 'Clear Validation Circles' on the Data Validation menu to remove the red validation circle (Figure 9–38).

Q&A Has the scheduling problem been solved?
No. As noted previously, the number of mixers is more than the number in stock. Also, the volume is significantly over the truck constraint.

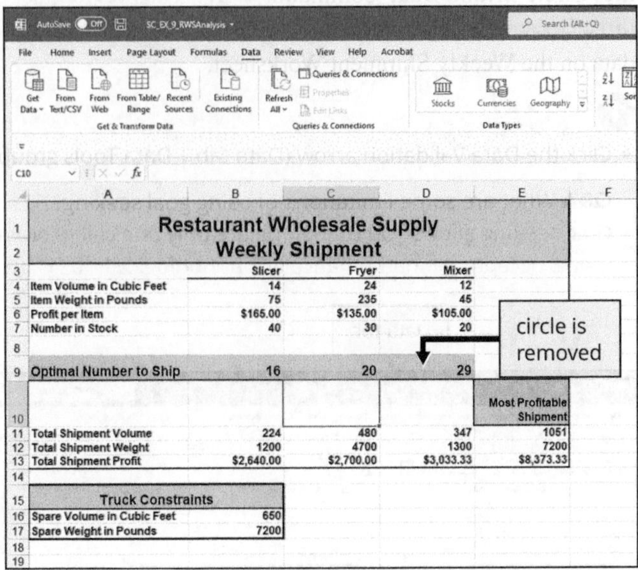

Figure 9–38

- Click the Save button on the Quick Access Toolbar to save the file.

Customizing Excel Add-Ins

Excel provides optional commands and features to solve complex problems through the inclusion of add-ins. An **add-in** is software that adds commands and features to Microsoft Office applications. Although some add-ins are built into Excel, including the Solver add-in used in this module, you may need to download and install others as needed. In any case, add-ins for Excel must be installed before they are available for use.

Add-ins are managed through the Add-ins tab accessible through the Excel Options dialog box. Once activated, the add-in and related commands are accessible through the ribbon, often in custom tabs or groups. If installed, the Solver and Analysis ToolPak add-ins are represented by buttons in the Analyze group on the Data tab. If installed, Euro Currency Tools, another built-in add-in for Excel, appear as commands in the Solutions group on the Formulas tab.

The Solver Add-In

The Solver add-in is a tool you use to generate the best possible solution for complex problems from a wide range of possibilities. Solver works to optimize a specific cell, called an objective cell, by maximizing, minimizing, or setting it to a specific value. For example, you want to maximize the total profit (cell E13). Because of the number of precedents, it can be difficult to determine which values should change. When you decrease the number of items to ship for one item, you have to increase the number assigned to another item, to ensure that all trucks are full. This change has an impact on costs and resulting profit. Solver considers all of the various constraints when determining the best solution.

To Enable the Solver Add-In

Many of the advanced features of Excel, such as the Solver add-in, are hidden until the user adds the feature to the user interface. **Why?** Excel is a powerful application with many features that the average user does not need to access on a regular basis. These features are hidden to keep the interface from becoming too overwhelming. The following steps will add the Solver add-in to Excel and verify the additional features on the Data tab of the ribbon. If Solver is added to your Data tab already, you can skip these steps.

- Click the File tab to display Backstage view.
- Click the Options tab at the bottom of Backstage view to display the Excel Options dialog box (Figure 9–39).

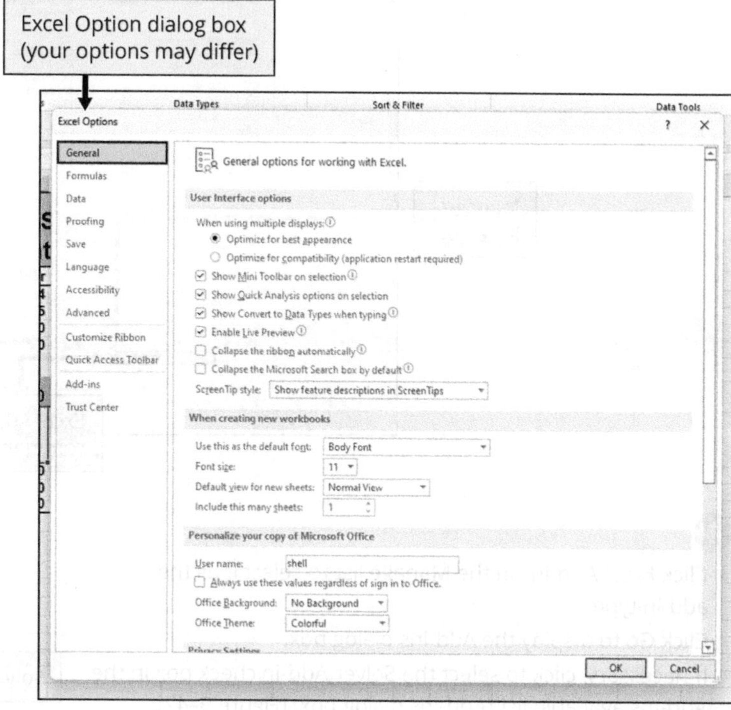

Figure 9–39

- Click the Add-ins tab to display the 'View and manage Microsoft Office Add-ins' screen (Figure 9–40).

Q&A Why is my list of add-ins different?
Depending on the applications installed and enabled for use in Excel, your list of active, inactive, and available add-ins may differ.

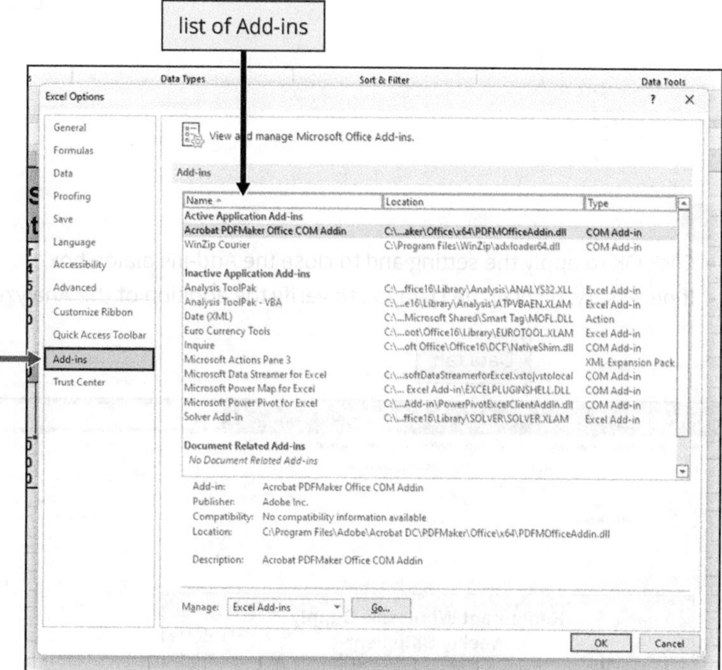

Figure 9–40

- Click the Manage list arrow to display the list of add-in types (Figure 9–41).

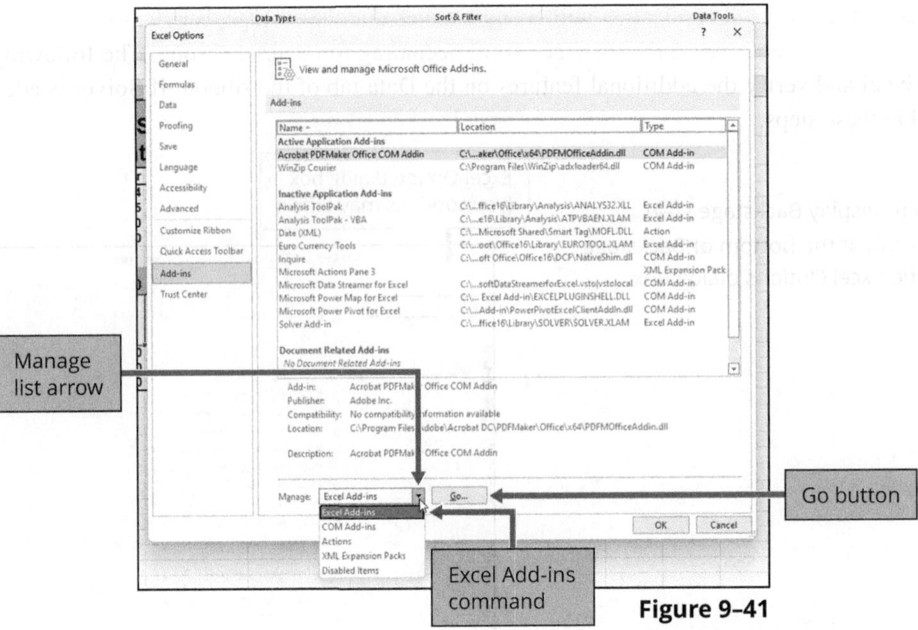

Figure 9–41

- Click Excel Add-ins in the Manage list to select it as the add-in type.
- Click Go to display the Add-ins dialog box.
- If necessary, click to select the Solver Add-in check box in the Add-ins available list (Add-ins dialog box) (Figure 9–42).

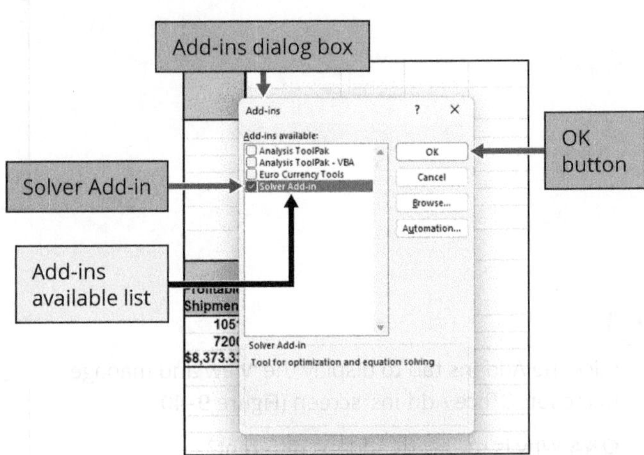

Figure 9–42

- Click OK to apply the setting and to close the Add-ins dialog box.
- If necessary, display the Data tab to verify the addition of the Analyze group and the Solver button (Figure 9–43).

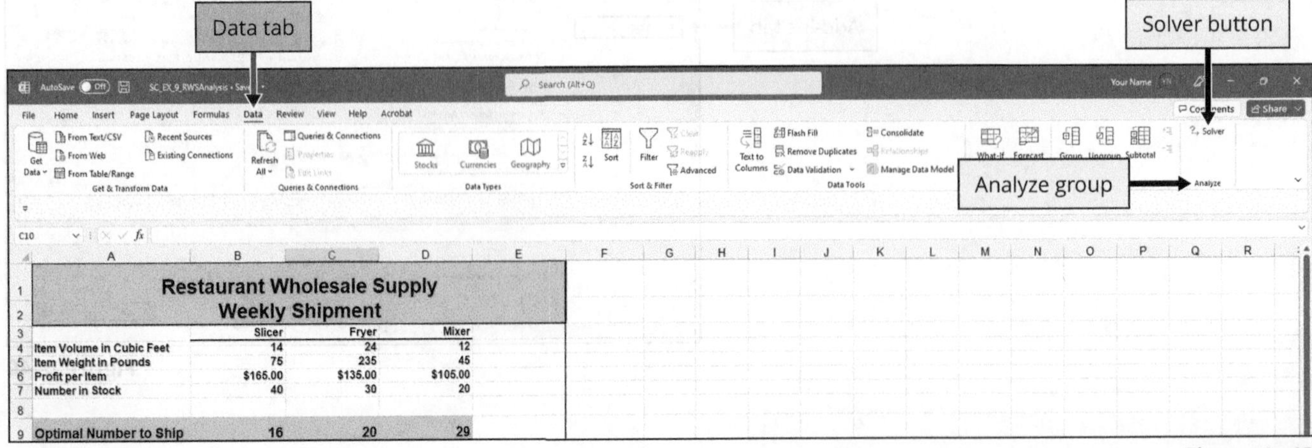

Figure 9–43

Solver Requirements

Regardless of the technique Solver uses to solve a problem, it requires three different types of inputs from the user: the objective, or the result you need for the target cell; variable cells, the values that can change; and constraints, the conditions that the solution has to meet.

The technique Solver uses to solve a problem depends on the model that the user selects as best representing the data. For the current scheduling problem, you will use LP Simplex, a technique in Solver associated with linear programming. **Linear programming** is a complex mathematical process used to solve problems that include multiple variables and the minimizing or maximizing of result values. Solver essentially tries as many possible combinations of solutions as it can. On each attempt to solve the problem, Solver checks whether it has found a solution.

In order for Solver to solve the scheduling problem, Solver must modify data until an optimum value is reached for the selected cell. The cells modified by Solver are called **decision variable cells**, also known as changing cells or adjustable cells. In this case, these are cells in the ranges B9:D9. The cell that Solver is working to optimize, either by finding its maximum or its minimum value, is known as the **objective cell**, or target cell. In this case, Solver is trying to maximize the total profit of the shipment, which makes cell E13 the objective cell. Solver will attempt to maximize the value of cell E13 by varying the values in the decision variable cells within the constraints set by Item Logistics.

Recall that constraints have been placed on certain values in the problem and are listed in the requirements document. For example, one constraint in the Weekly Shipment Worksheet is that each truck must contain at least one of each type of equipment. Other constraints include the truck volume and weight limits as well as the number of items in stock. The constraints are summarized in Table 9–2. In the table, the word, int, applies an integer constraint which means Solver must use a positive whole number.

BTW
Using Solver to Solve Complex Problems
Solver allows you to solve complex problems where a number of variables can be changed in a worksheet in order to meet a goal in a particular cell. Unlike Goal Seek, Solver is not restricted to changing one cell at a time and can efficiently evaluate many combinations for a solution.

Table 9–2: Constraints for Solver

Cell or Range or Named Cell	Operator	Constraint
$B$9:$D$9	>=	1
$B$9:$D$9	int	integer
Fryers_to_Ship	<=	Fryers_in_Stock
Mixers_to_Ship	<=	Mixers_in_Stock
Slicers_to_Ship	<=	Slicers_in_Stock
$E$11	<=	$B$16
$E$12	<=	$B$17

When Solver reaches a solution to a problem, it generates an Answer Report. An **Answer Report** is a Solver report summarizing the results of a successful solution. It displays the answer for the objective cell, the values used in the changing cells to arrive at that answer, and the constraints that were applied to the calculation. By creating an Answer Report, you satisfy the requirement to document the results of the scheduling calculation.

To Enter Constraints with Solver

To solve the shipping problem for RWS, you give Solver the goal of maximizing the total profit of the shipment, displayed in cell E13, within the constraints set in the requirements document. To accomplish this goal, Solver can modify the number of each item (represented by cells B9, C9, and D9). **Why use Solver?** Solver allows Excel to evaluate multiple combinations of values and constraints for changing variables to find an optimal solution to a complex problem.

The following steps use Solver to find the optimal solution to the scheduling problem in the Weekly Shipment Worksheet within the given constraints.

- Click the Solver button (Data tab | Analyze group) to display the Solver Parameters dialog box. If necessary, drag the title bar to move the dialog box so it doesn't obscure the data in the worksheet.
- If necessary, click the Set Objective box (Solver Parameters dialog box) and then, in the worksheet, click cell E13 to set the objective cell, in this case the total shipment profit (Figure 9–44).

Q&A Are there any restrictions on which cell can be the objective?
The value in the Set Objective box must be a single cell reference or name, and the cell must contain a formula.

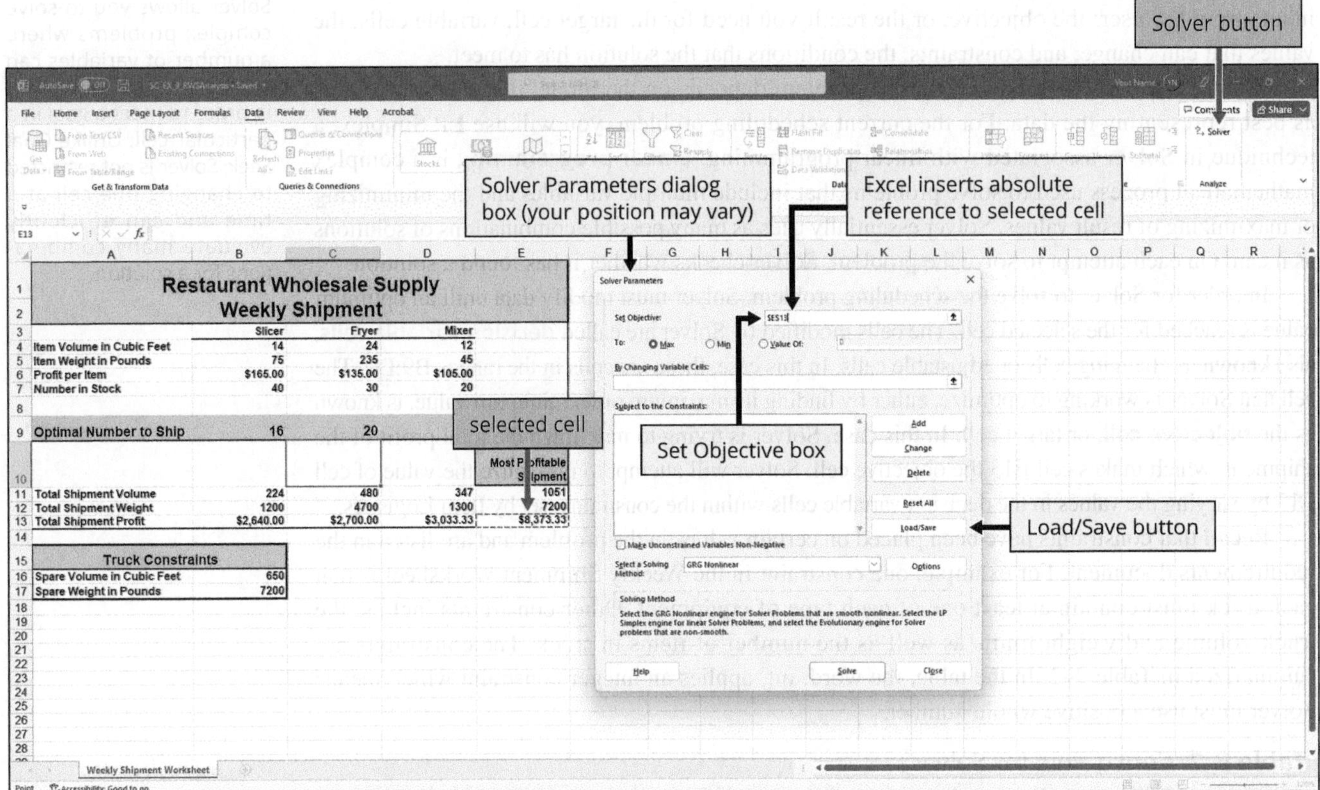

Figure 9–44

2

- Click the Max option button in the To area (Solver Parameters dialog box) if necessary to specify that the value of the target cell should be as large as possible, maximizing the total profit.
- Click the 'By Changing Variable Cells' box and then, in the worksheet, select the range B9:D9 to set the cells that you want Solver to manipulate (Figure 9–45).

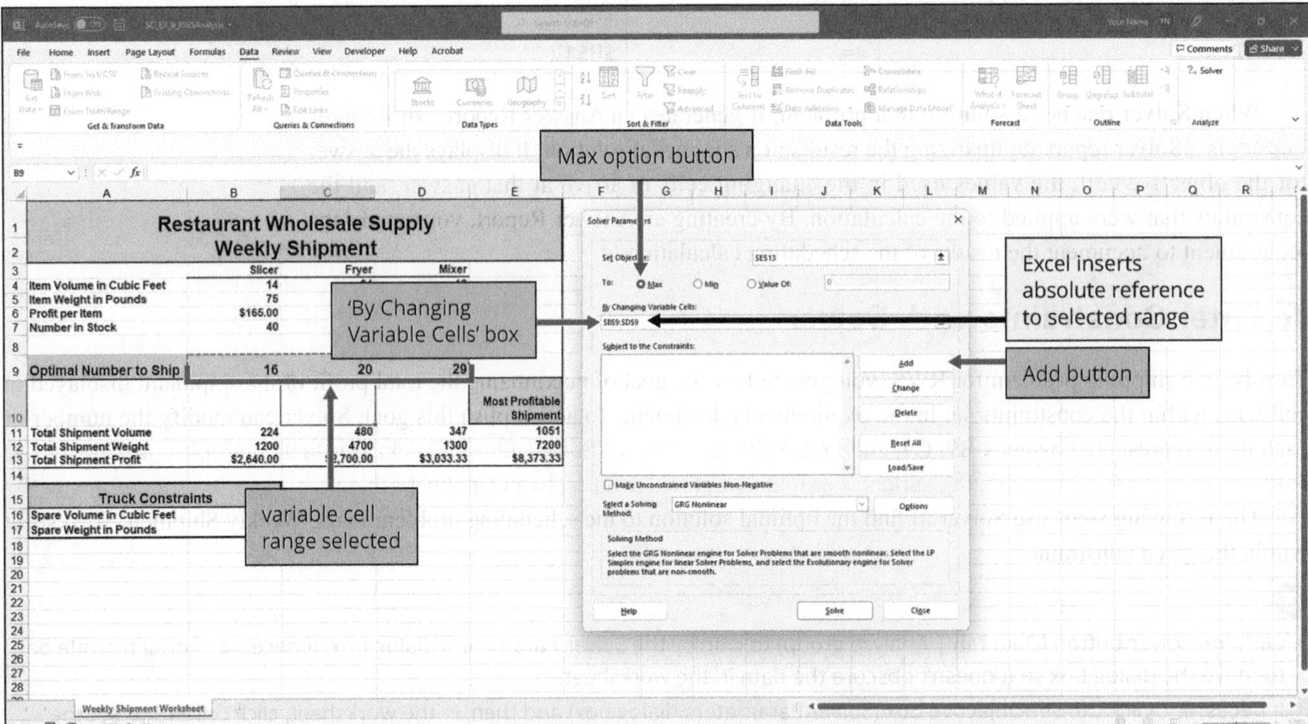

Figure 9–45

Q&A Can you save the constraints you add to the Solver?
Yes. You can click the Load/Save button (Solver parameters dialog box) to load constraints you have saved previous or to save a new one, called a Solver model. Models are saved to an empty part of the worksheet, but do not print or display.

- Click the Add button (Solver Parameters dialog box) to display the Add Constraint dialog box.
- If necessary, click the 'Cell Reference: Collapse Dialog' button. Select the range B9:D9 to set the value of the Cell Reference box. Click the Expand Dialog button, if necessary.
- Click the middle arrow to display the list of constraint operators (Figure 9–46).

Q&A What does the Add Constraint dialog box do?
It is a way to set limitations on the possible values that a cell or range can contain.

What happened to the dialog box while I selected the range?
Excel collapsed the dialog box to give you more room to select cells.

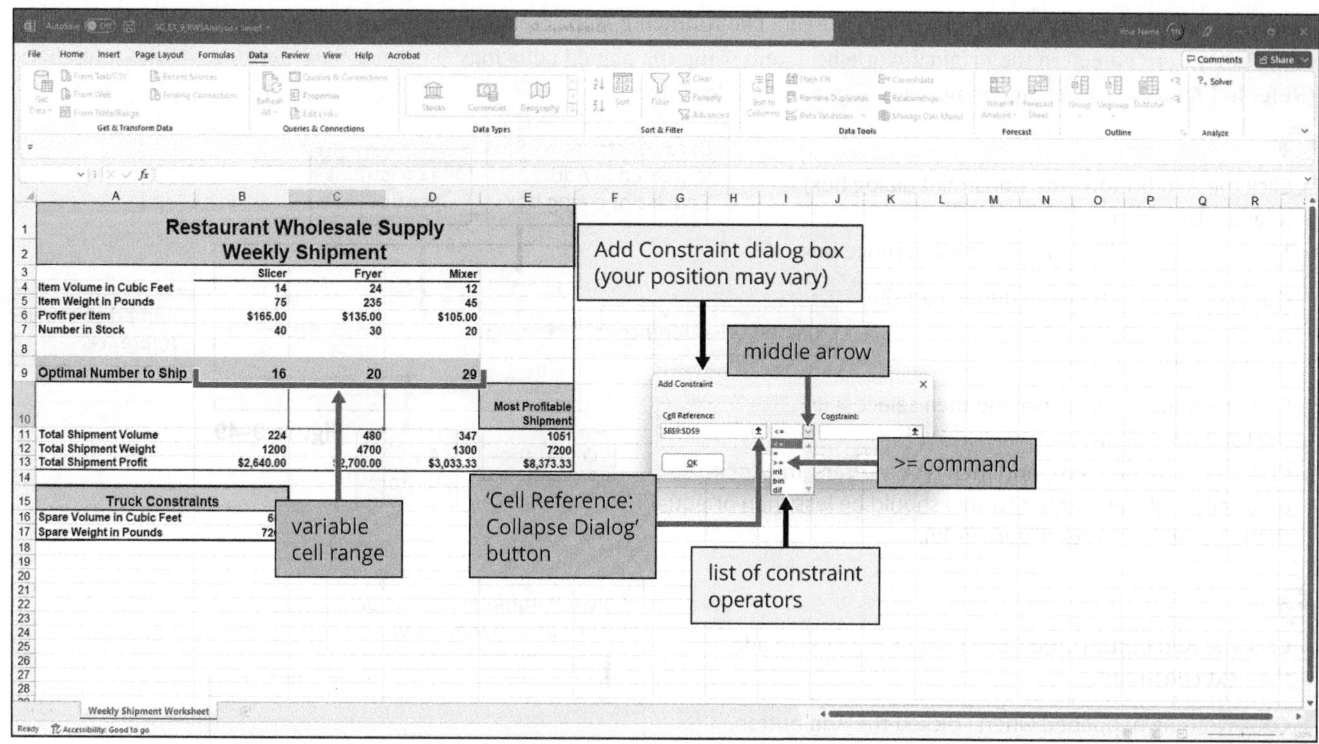

Figure 9–46

- Select >= in the list to specify greater than or equal to.
- Type **1** in the Constraint box to set the constraint so at least one of each item will be included in the solution, per the requirements document (Figure 9–47).

Q&A How do I use the Constraint box?
After entering a cell reference, you must select an operator. If the operator is <=, >=, or =, then you enter a constraint value or cell reference. Other valid operators are int, for an integer value; bin, for cells that contain a binary value of only one of two values, such as yes/no or true/false; or dif, for an all different constraint where no two values are the same.

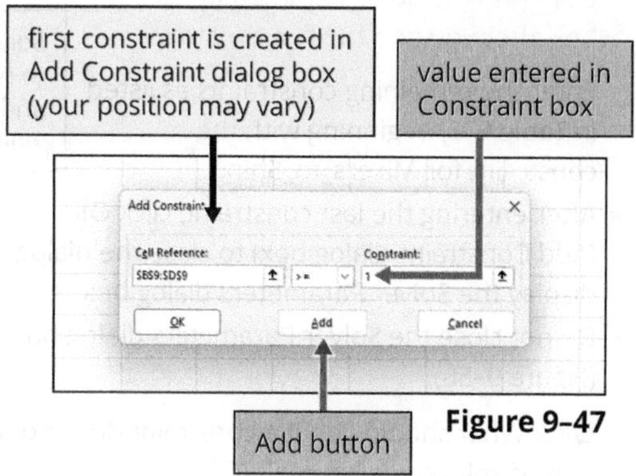

Figure 9–47

- Click the Add button (Add Constraint dialog box) to add a second constraint.
- Select the range B9:D9 to set the value of the Cell Reference box.
- Click the middle box arrow and then select int in the list to set a constraint on the cells in the range B9:D9 to be assigned only integer values.
- Do not close the Add Constraint dialog box (Figure 9–48).

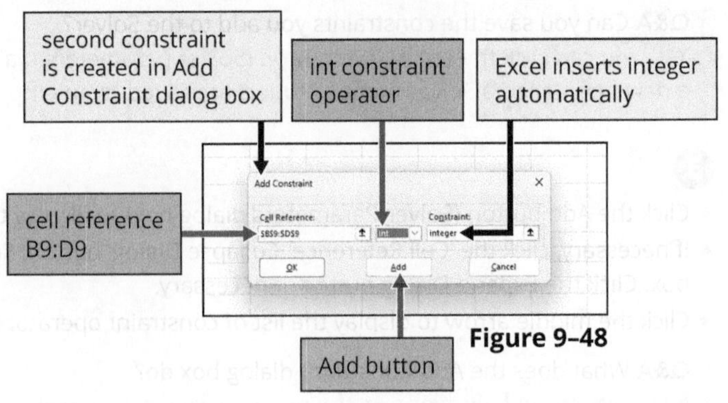

Figure 9–48

To Enter Constraints with Named Cells

You also can use cell and range names with Solver. The following steps create a constraint using named cells. **Why?** Many of the cells were named in the original worksheet, and using the named cells may be easier than figuring out the references. (Refer to Figure 9–4.) Cell and range names carry over into Solver.

- Click the Add button (Add Constraint dialog box) to add a third constraint.
- Type **Fryers_to_Ship** in the Cell Reference box.

Q&A Do I have to type the underscores?
Yes. Named cells and ranges cannot have spaces.

- Click the middle box arrow and then select <= in the list if necessary.
- Click the Constraint box, and then type **Fryers_in_Stock** to specify that the number to ship should be less than or equal to the number in stock (Figure 9–49).

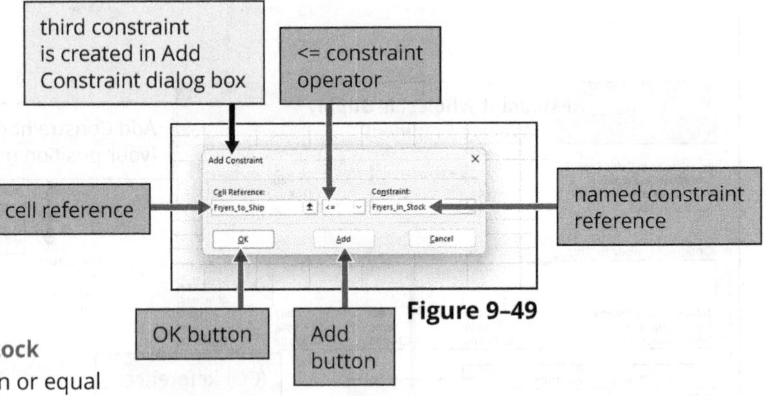

Figure 9–49

- Click the Add button (Add Constraint dialog box) to add the next constraint.

Q&A Nothing happened when I clicked the Add button. Did I do something wrong?
No. The constraint is added behind the scenes and will display in the Solve Parameters dialog box after you add the last constraint.

- Enter the remaining constraints as listed in Table 9–2, beginning with the constraint for Mixers_to_Ship.
- After entering the last constraint, click OK (Add Constraint dialog box) to close the dialog box and display the Solver Parameters dialog box.
- Do not close the Solver Parameters dialog box. (Figure 9–50).

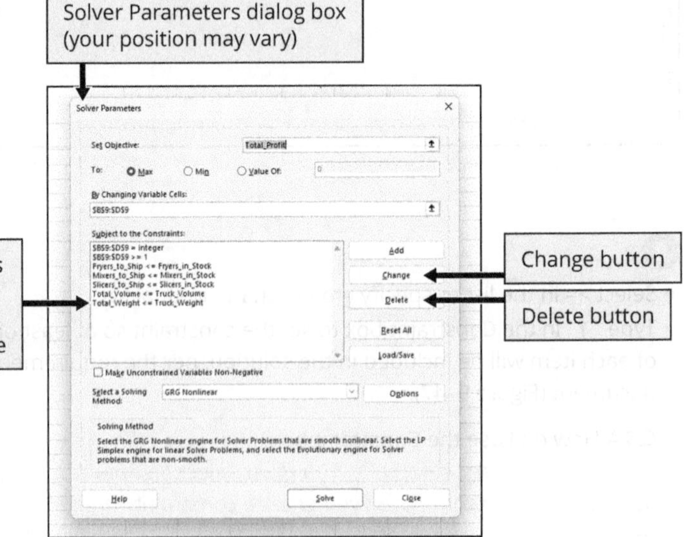

Figure 9–50

Q&A What should I do if a constraint does not match the ones displayed in Figure 9–49?
Your order may differ, but the constraints should be the same. If they are not, select the constraint in error, click the Change button (Solver Parameters dialog box), and then enter the constraint as displayed in Table 9–2. To delete a constraint, select the constraint you want to delete, and then click the Delete button.

To Set Solver Options

Now that you have entered all of the constraints for the problem, the following steps set options in order to obtain the optimal solution. You will choose the Simplex LP solving method. LP stands for linear progression, and Simplex refers to the basic problem-solving method used to solve linear problems. Linear problems are ones in which a "straight-line" approach of cause and effect can seek to determine a goal value by modifying values that impact the goal. For example, a decrease in costs results in an increase in profits.

To ensure that Solver finds the true optimal solution—possibly at the expense of more solution time—you will set the Integer Optimality % tolerance to zero. **Why?** Setting the value to zero will help Solver to find an optimal solution when one of the constraints says that a value must be an integer.

- With the Solver Parameters dialog box still open, click the 'Select a Solving Method' arrow to display the choices (Figure 9–51).
- Click Simplex LP in the list to select the linear progression method (Figure 9–52).

Q&A What are the other choices?
GRG Nonlinear is the Generalized Reduced Gradient optimizing algorithm in which the change of the objective cell is not proportional to the change of the dependent cells. The Evolutionary method finds a better solution, but because it does not rely on derivative or gradient information, it usually requires running Solver several times as you search for the best one.

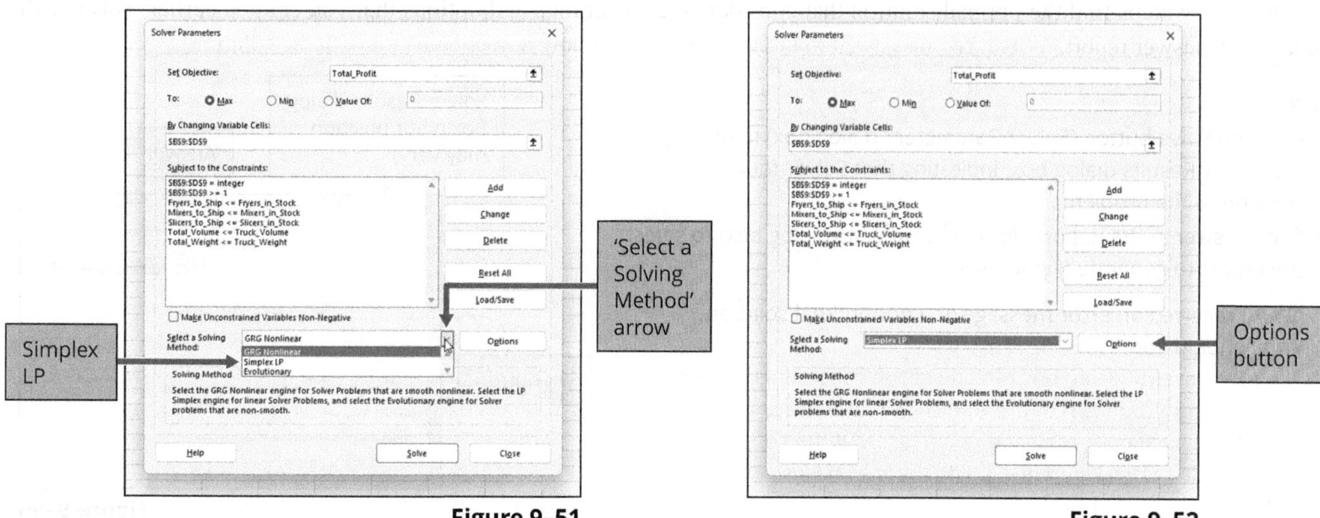

Figure 9–51

Figure 9–52

2

- Click the Options button (Solver parameters dialog box) to display the Options dialog box.
- If necessary, click the 'Use Automatic Scaling' check box to select it.
- Set the 'Integer Optimality (%)' to **0** to extend the amount of time that Solver takes to find an optimal solution.
- Verify that all other dialog box settings match those in Figure 9–53.
- In particular, ensure that only the Use Automatic Scaling checkbox contains a checkmark, and that the boxes in the Solving Limits area are all blank.

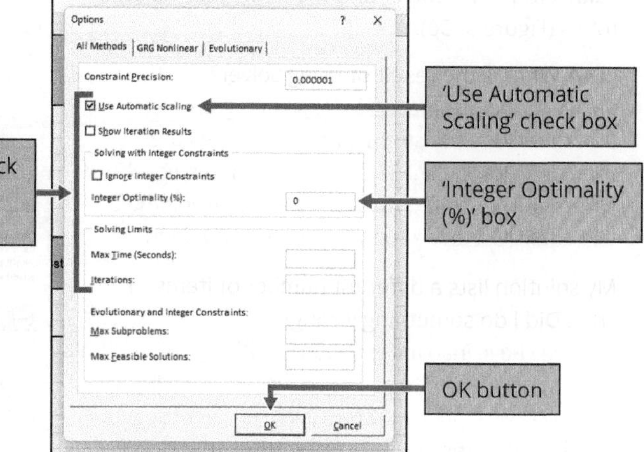

Figure 9–53

- Click OK (Options dialog box) to return to the Solver Parameters dialog box (Figure 9–54).
- **Experiment:** Click the Help button (Solver Parameters dialog box) to open Help related to Solver in a browser window. Learn about the general explanation and click on various links to access specific instruction. When you are finished, close the browser window and return to Excel.

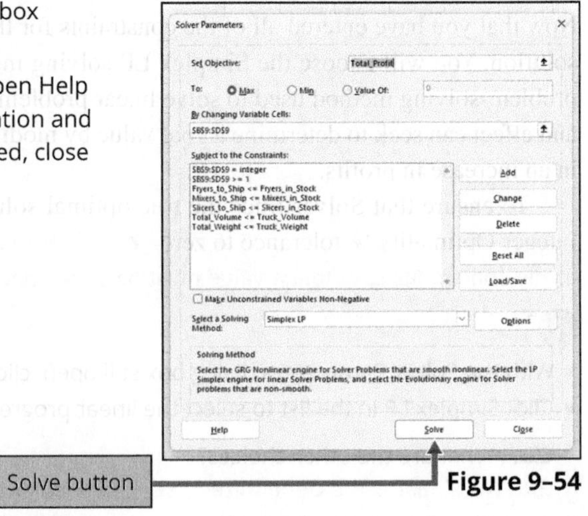

Figure 9–54

To Find the Optimal Solution

The following steps find the optimal solution that considers the constraints and options that you entered earlier. Solver will produce an answer report. **Why?** You may want to know a summary of how Solver came up with the solution.

- Click the Solve button (Solver Parameters dialog box) to display the Solver Results dialog box, indicating that Solver found a solution to the problem.
- Click Answer in the Reports list (Solver Results dialog box) to select the report to generate (Figure 9–55).

Q&A I received an error message or a nonoptimal solution. What should I do?
You may have made an error in one of the constraints. Click the Cancel button to return to the worksheet. Click the Solver button (Data tab | Analyze group) and refer closely at the constraints. They should match Figure 9–51. Edit them as necessary.

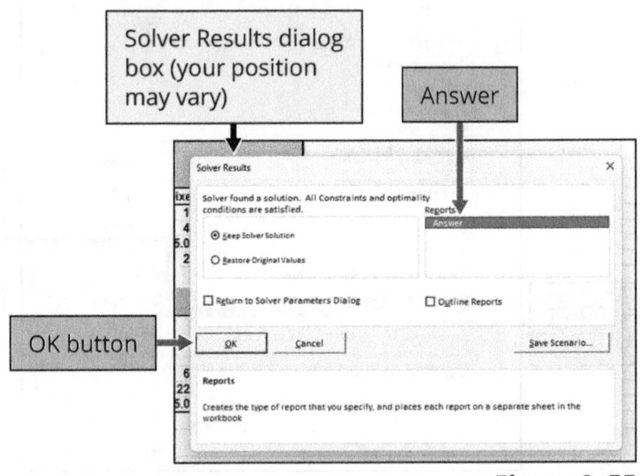

Figure 9–55

- Click OK (Solver Results dialog box) to display the values found by Solver and the newly recalculated totals (Figure 9–56).

Q&A What is the result of using Solver?
Solver found a solution to the shipping problem that meets the constraints and maximizes the total profit of the shipment. The solution ships 40 slicers, 1 fryer, and 5 mixers, with a total volume of 644 cubic feet and a total weight of 3460 pounds.

My solution lists a different number of items to ship. Did I do something wrong?
You may have inadvertently turned off integer constraints. Return to the Solver Parameters dialog box, click the Options button, and then click the All Methods tab. Remove the checkmark for 'Ignore Integer Constraints'. The 'Use Automatic Scaling' check box should be checked. Click OK and then solve again.

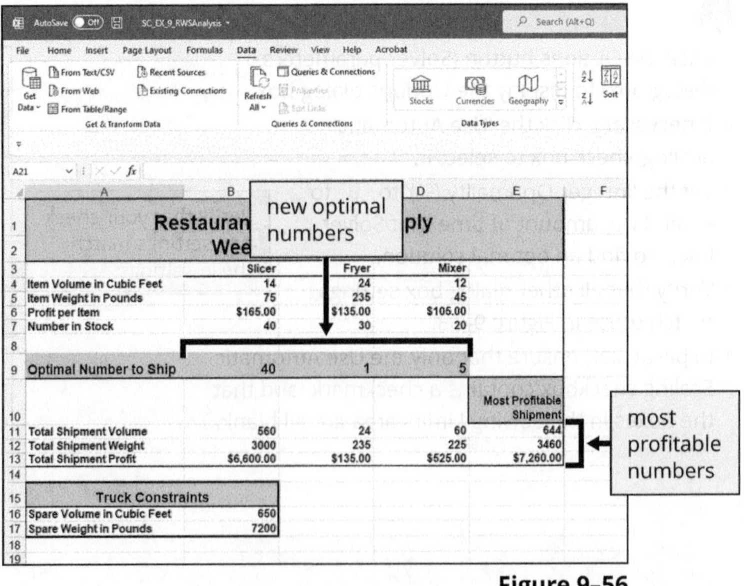

Figure 9–56

To Access the Solver Answer Report

Solver generates the requested Answer Report on a separate worksheet after it finds a solution. The Answer Report summarizes the problem that you have presented to Solver. It displays the original and final values of the objective cell along with the original and final values of the changing cells that Solver modified to find the answer. Additionally, it lists all of the constraints that you entered.

Why? The Answer Report documents that a particular problem has been solved correctly. Because it lists all of the relevant information in a concise format, you can use the Answer Report to make certain that you have entered all of the constraints and allowed Solver to modify all the necessary values to solve the problem. You also can use the report to reconstruct the Solver model in the future.

The following steps will access the Solver Answer Report.

- Click the Answer Report 1 sheet tab to display the Solver Answer Report (Figure 9–57).

Q&A What is contained in the Answer Report?
The Answer Report provides additional information about the constraints and how they were used to solve the problem. The Status column, beginning in cell F28, indicates whether a constraint was binding. A constraint that is **binding** is one that limits the final solution in some way and must be included in the Solver model. A constraint that is not binding is one that is not a limiting factor in the solution that Solver provides.

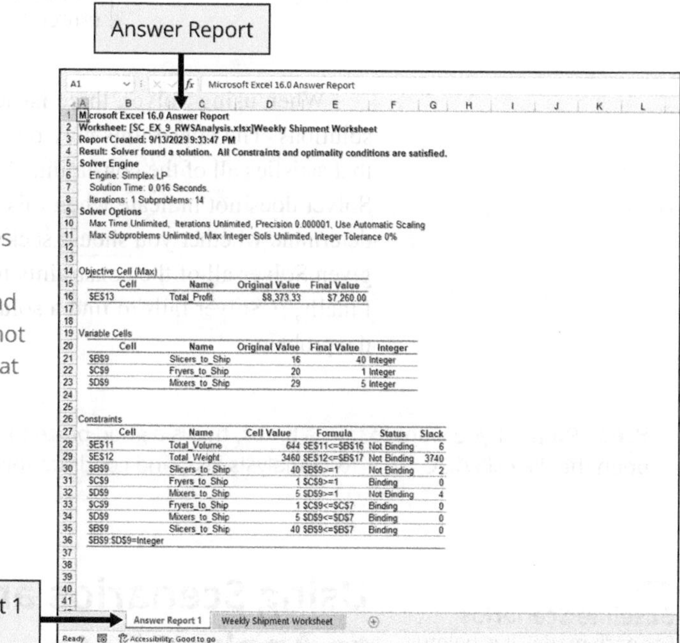

Figure 9–57

- Drag the Answer Report 1 sheet tab to the right of the Weekly Shipment Worksheet tab to move the worksheet in the workbook.
- Double-click the Answer Report 1 sheet tab to select the name.
- Type **Shipment Plan Answer Report 1** and then press ENTER to rename the worksheet.
- Change the color of the sheet tab to Light Blue in the Standard Colors.

- Click the Save button on the Quick Access Toolbar to save the file.

More about Solver Options

When you selected the Simplex LP method of solving the production problem in the Solver Parameters dialog box, you selected a linear programming method that assumes the problem follows a cause and effect relationship. Changes to one value have a direct impact on another value. After choosing the Solver method, you can select various options to further configure the inner workings of Solver. Note that Excel saves the most recently used Solver parameters and options. Table 9–3 presents some of the more commonly used Solver options.

BTW
Accessing Other Solutions
If you want to view solutions other than the one Solver identifies as optimal, select the Show Iteration Results check box in the Options dialog box. After each iteration, the Show Trial Solution dialog box will be displayed, and you will have the option of saving that scenario and then stopping Solver or continuing on to the next solution.

Table 9–3: Commonly Used Solver Parameters

Parameter	Meaning
Max Time	The total time that Solver should spend trying different solutions, expressed in seconds
Iterations	The number of possible answer combinations that Solver should try
Constraint Precision	Instructs Solver in how close it must come to the target value in order to consider the problem to be solved. For example, if the target value is 100 and you set tolerance to 5%, then generating a solution with a target value of 95 is acceptable.
Use Automatic Scaling	Selected by default, specifies that Solver should internally rescale values of variables, constraints, and the objective to reduce the effect of outlying values

When using Solver, three issues must be kept in mind. First, some problems do not have solutions. The constraints may be constructed in such a way that Solver cannot find an answer that satisfies all of the constraints. Second, sometimes multiple answers solve the same problem. Solver does not indicate when this is the case, and you will have to use your own judgment to determine whether you should seek another solution. As long as you are confident that you have given Solver all of the constraints for a problem, however, all answers should be equally valid. Finally, if Solver fails to find a solution, more time or more iterations may be required to solve the problem.

Break Point: If you want to take a break, this is a good place to do so. You can exit Excel now. To resume later, start Excel, open the file called SC_EX_9_RWSAnalysis.xlsx, and continue following the steps from this location forward.

BTW
Baseline Scenarios
For each model, it is helpful to define a baseline scenario that represents the starting assumptions. Even if the results of the baseline scenario do not figure prominently in the final analysis, they represent the starting point and should be saved.

Using Scenarios and Scenario Manager to Analyze Data

A **scenario** is a named set of values you use in a what-if analysis; the Excel Scenario Manager lets you store and manage different scenarios. In this project, you will create different shipping plans, or scenarios, based on different assumptions. For example, you have created a shipping plan that required finding the optimal number of items to ship based on several constraints, one of which was the free space on the truck. Changing the truck volume or weight would create a new scenario. Each set of values in these examples represents a what-if assumption. You use the Scenario Manager to keep track of various scenarios and produce a report detailing the what-if assumptions and results for each scenario.

The primary uses of the Scenario Manager are to:

1. Create different scenarios with multiple sets of changing cells.
2. Build summary worksheets that contain the different scenarios.
3. Review the results of each scenario on your worksheet.

You will use the Scenario Manager for each of these primary applications. After you create the scenarios, you will instruct Excel to build the summary worksheets, including a Scenario Summary worksheet and a Scenario PivotTable worksheet.

To Save the Current Data as a Scenario

Why? The current data on the Weekly Shipment Worksheet consists of constraints and values that correctly solve the shipping problem. These values can be saved as a scenario that can be accessed later or compared with other scenarios. The following steps save the current data using the Scenario Manager dialog box.

1

- Make the Weekly Shipment Worksheet the active sheet.
- Click the 'What-If Analysis' button (Data tab | Forecast group) to display the What-If Analysis menu (Figure 9–58).

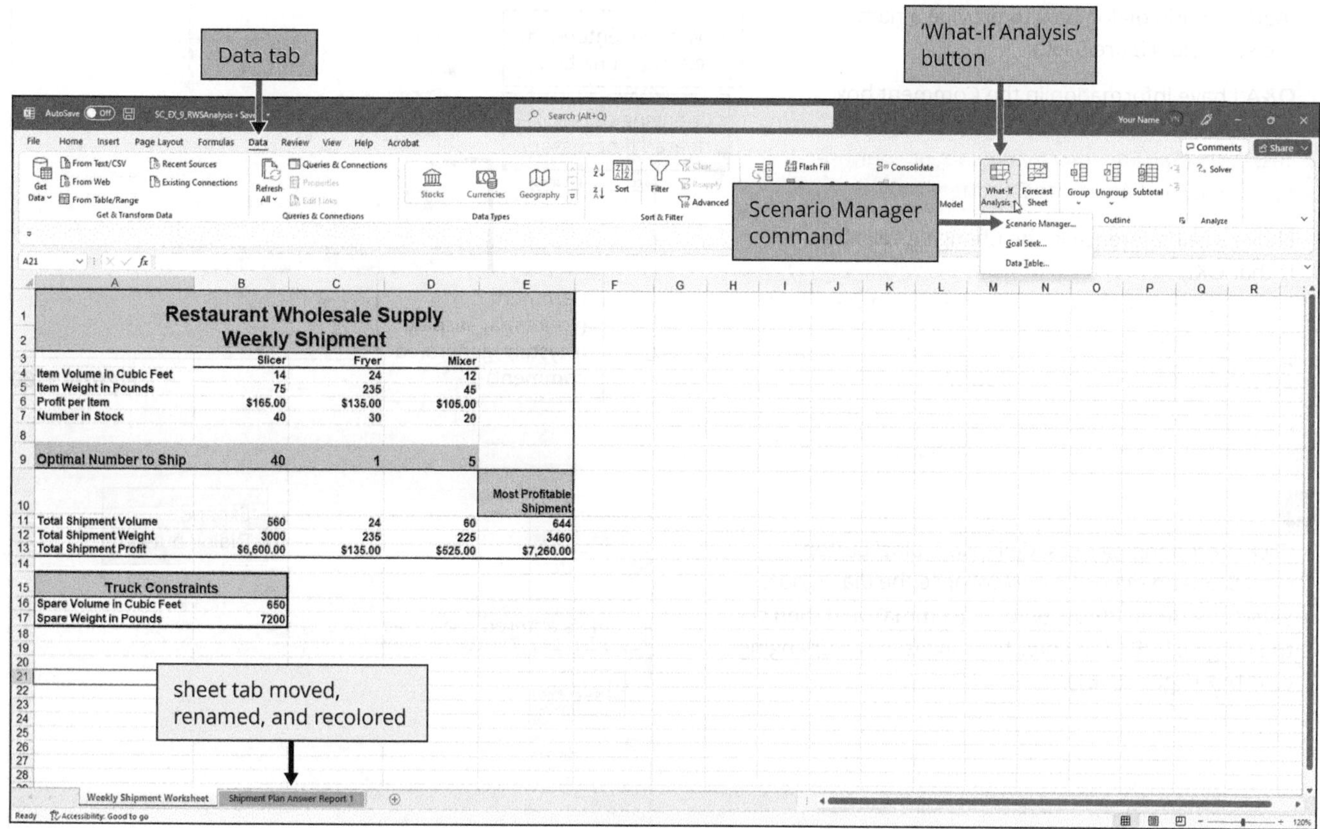

Figure 9–58

2

- Click Scenario Manager on the What-If Analysis menu to display the Scenario Manager dialog box, which indicates that no scenarios are defined (Figure 9–59).

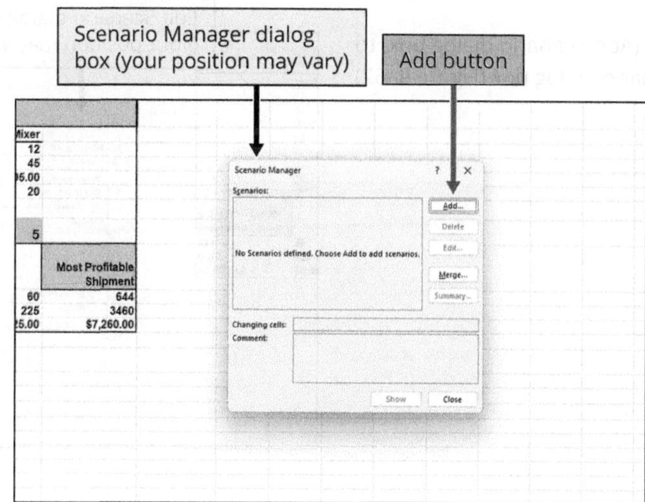

Figure 9–59

- Click the Add button (Scenario Manager dialog box) to open the Add Scenario dialog box.
- Type **Shipment 1** in the Scenario name box (Add Scenario dialog box) to provide a name for the scenario (Figure 9–60).

Q&A I have information in the Comment box. Is that OK?

Yes. Excel may add information about your user name and the date in the Comment box.

I have a cell reference in the Changing cells box. Is that OK?

If a cell currently has focus, the cell reference will be displayed here. If this is the case, you simply delete the cell reference and leave the box empty.

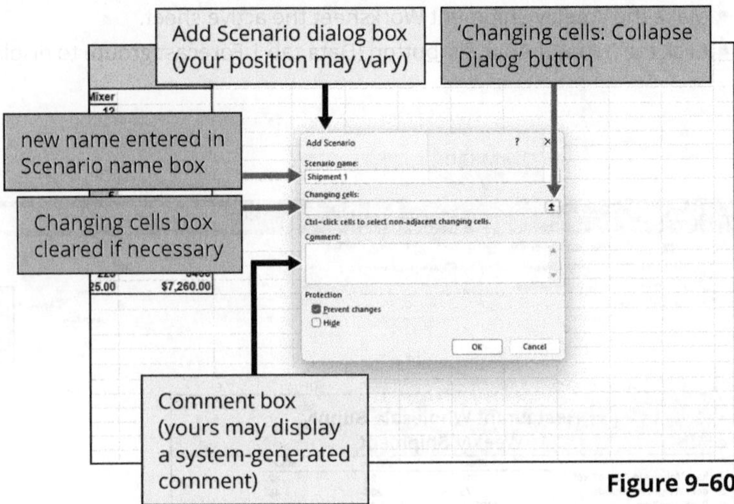

Figure 9–60

- Click the 'Changing Cells: Collapse Dialog' button (Add Scenario dialog box) to collapse the dialog box.
- Select the range B9:D9, type , (comma), and then select the range B16:B17 to enter the ranges in the Changing cells box (Figure 9–61).

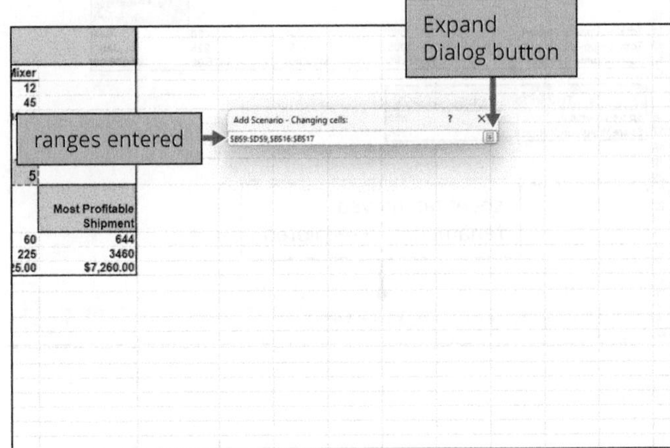

Figure 9–61

5

- Click the Expand Dialog button (Add Scenario dialog box) to display the expanded Edit Scenario dialog box (Figure 9–62).

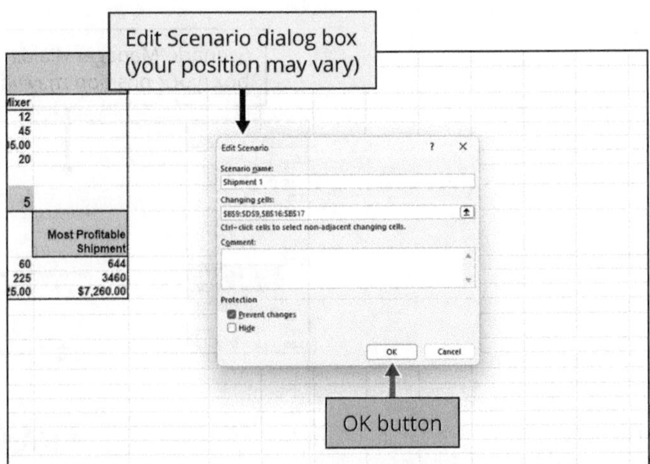

Figure 9–62

- Click OK (Edit Scenario dialog box) to accept the settings and display the Scenario Values dialog box.
- Click OK (Scenario Values dialog box) to display the Scenario Manager dialog box with the Shipment 1 scenario selected in the Scenarios list (Figure 9–63).

Q&A What can I do with the scenario?

After a scenario has been saved, you can recall it at any time using the Scenario Manager or create a Scenario Summary, as you will do later in this module.

7

- Click Close (Scenario Manager dialog box) to save the Shipment 1 scenario in the workbook.

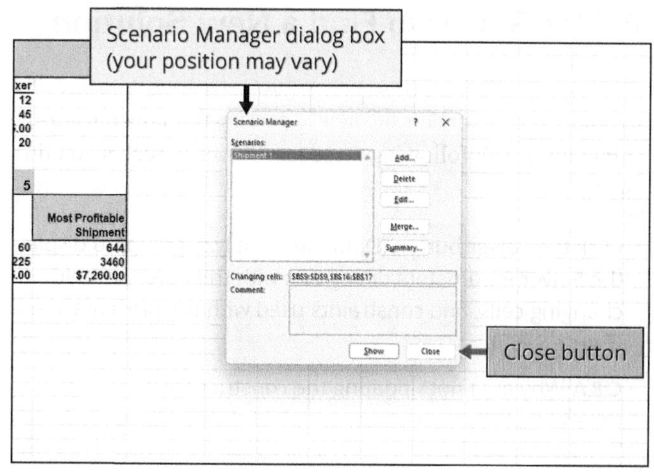

Figure 9–63

Other Ways

1. When running Solver, click Save Scenario (Solver Results dialog box), enter scenario name, click OK (Save Scenario dialog box), click OK (Solver Results dialog box)

Creating a New Scenario

After saving the Shipment 1 scenario, you will enter new data for the Shipment 2 scenario directly in the worksheet and then use Solver to solve the problem in the same way that you solved the Shipment scenario. Because both scenarios are based on the same model, you do not need to reenter the constraints into the Scenario Manager. A second Answer Report will solve the needs of the requirements document.

To Add the Data for a New Scenario

A truck with less room has become available. The shipping manager would like to know the difference in profit should the company fill this smaller load. The constraints for the Shipment 2 scenario therefore require a change in spare truck volume and weight. These values must be entered into the appropriate cells before you can use Solver. The following steps add the data for a new scenario.

1. Click cell B16 and then type **450** as the spare volume.
2. Click cell B17 and then type **5000** as the spare weight.
3. Click cell C17 to deselect cell B17 (Figure 9–64).

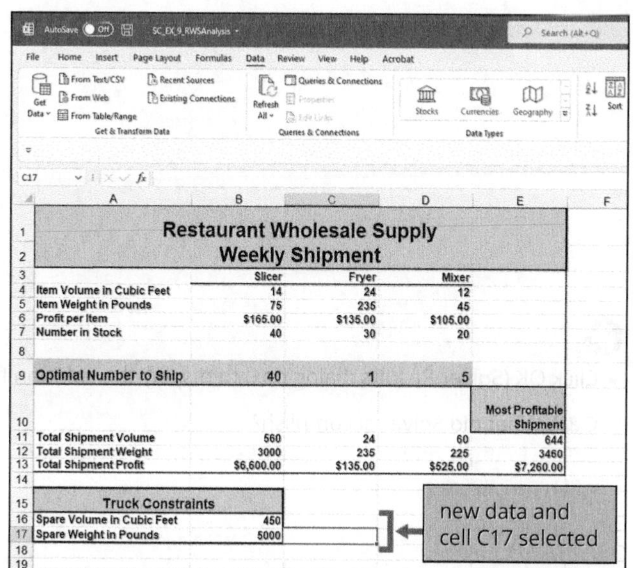

Figure 9–64

To Use Solver to Find a New Solution

Why? After entering the new values, the total volume and weight displayed in the range B16:B17 no longer satisfy the shipping constraints for the new scenario. You now must use Solver again to determine if a solution exists for the constraints of Shipment 2. The following steps use Solver to seek a solution.

- Click the Solver button (Data tab | Analyze group) to display the Solver Parameters dialog box with the objective cell, changing cells, and constraints used with the previous scenario (Figure 9–65).

Q&A Why am I not updating the constraints?
When you set up the constraints in Solver for Shipment 1, you used cell references and named cells rather than actual values for the number of each type of item. Entering the new values in cells B16:B17 automatically updated the constraints.

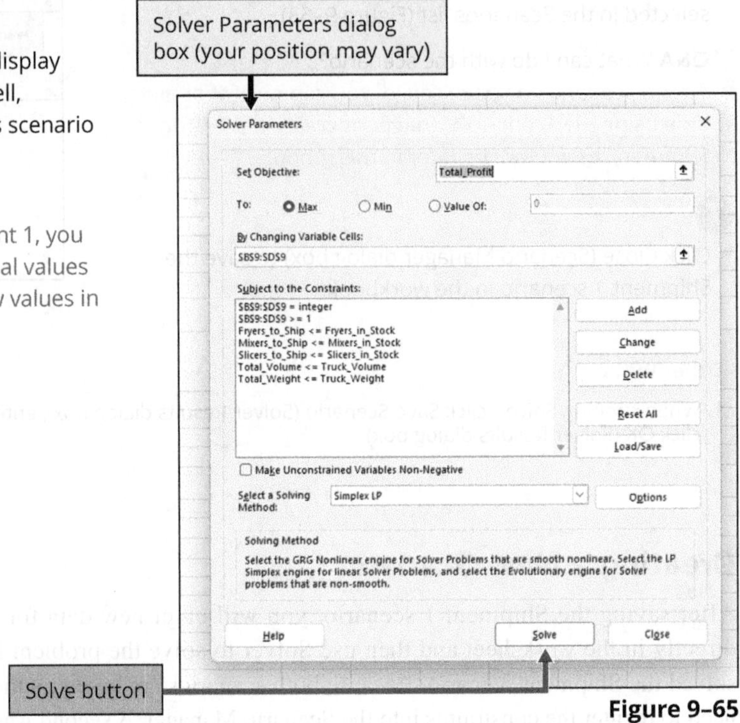

Figure 9–65

- Click the Solve button (Solver Parameters dialog box) to solve the problem and display the Solver Results dialog box.
- Click Answer in the Reports list to select a report type (Figure 9–66).

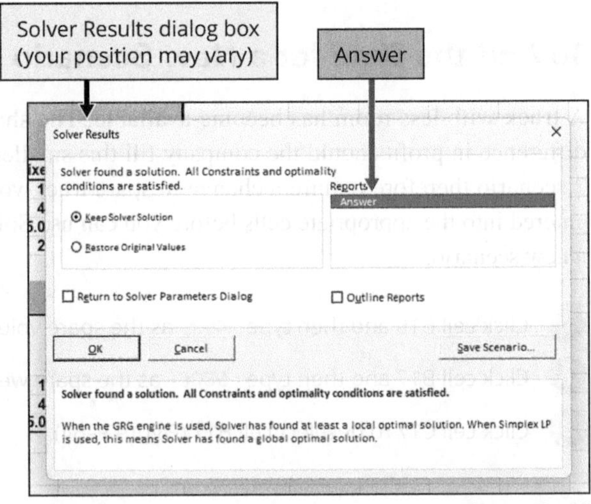

Figure 9–66

- Click OK (Solver Results dialog box) to display the solution found by Solver (Figure 9–67).

Q&A What did Solver accomplish?
Solver found a solution that satisfies all of the constraints and maximizes the total profit. In this new scenario, total profit will be $5,025.00.

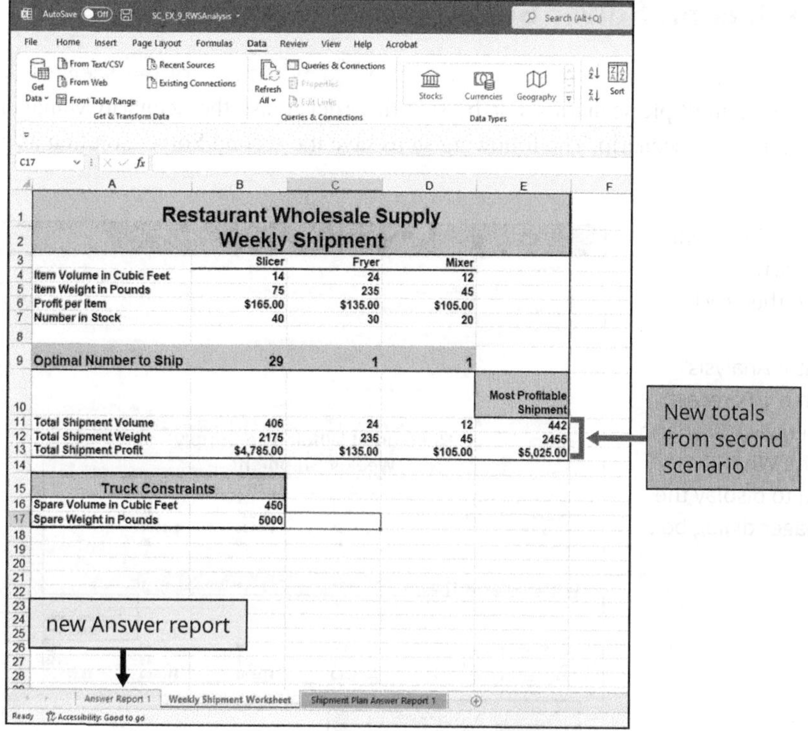

Figure 9–67

To Access the Solver Answer Report for the Shipment 2 Solution

The next step displays the Answer Report for the Shipment 2 solution.

1. Drag the new Answer Report 1 sheet tab to the right of the Shipment Plan Answer Report 1 sheet tab to move the worksheet.
2. Rename the Answer Report 1 worksheet, entering **Shipment Plan Answer Report 2** as the new name.
3. Change the sheet tab color to Light Green in the Standard Colors (Figure 9–68).
4. Click the Save button on the Quick Access Toolbar to save the file.

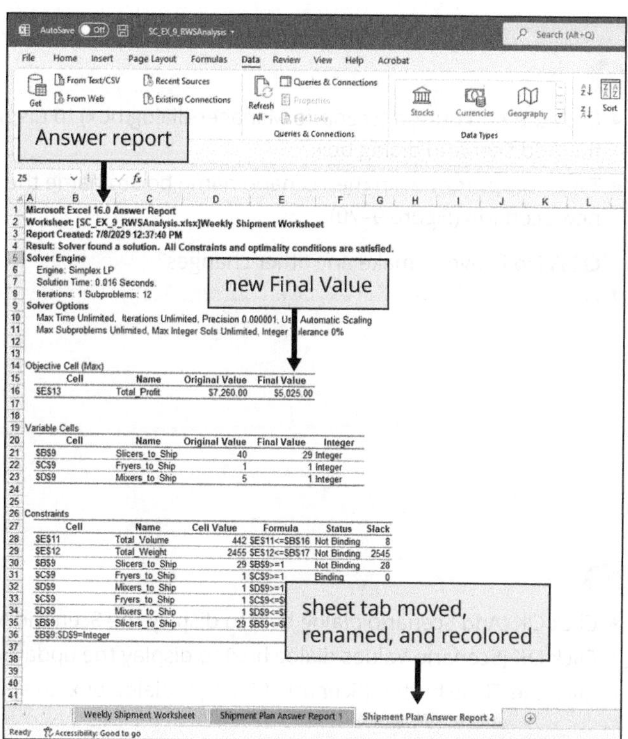

Figure 9–68

To Save the Second Solver Solution as a Scenario

Why? With a second scenario created, you can begin to take advantage of the Scenario Manager. The Scenario Manager allows you to compare multiple scenarios side by side. In order to use the Scenario Manager for this, you first must save the second Solver solution as a scenario. The following steps save the second Solver solution as a scenario.

- Make the Weekly Shipment Worksheet the active worksheet, and then click cell A1.
- Click the 'What-If Analysis' button (Data tab | Forecast group) and then click Scenario Manager on the What-If Analysis menu to display the Scenario Manager dialog box (Figure 9–69).

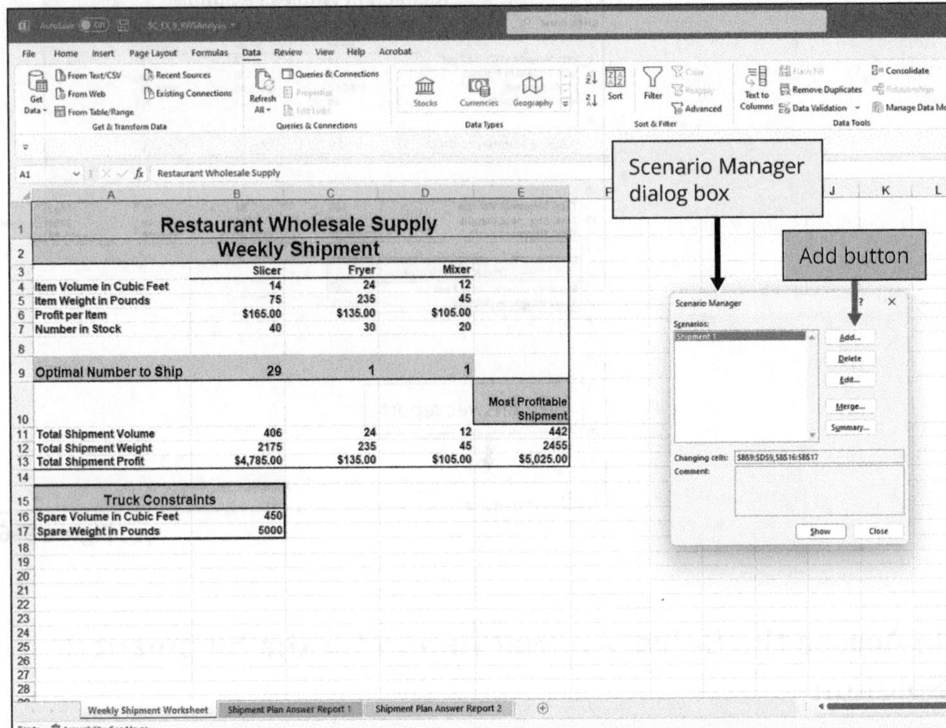

Figure 9–69

- Click the Add button (Scenario Manager dialog box) to display the Add Scenario dialog box.
- Type **Shipment 2** in the Scenario name box to name the new scenario (Figure 9–70).

Q&A Do I have to make any other changes?
No. The new figures will be saved automatically with the scenario.

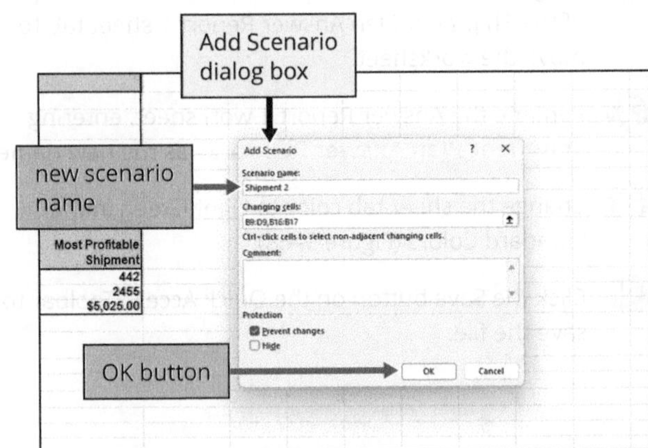

Figure 9–70

- Click OK (Add Scenario dialog box) to display the Scenario Values dialog box with the current values.
- Click OK (Scenario Values dialog box) to display the updated Scenarios list in the Scenario Manager dialog box.
- Click the Close button (Scenario Manager dialog box) to save the Shipment 2 scenario and close the dialog box.

To Display a Saved Scenario

Why? You can display and review any scenario in the workbook by using the Show button in the Scenario Manager dialog box. The following steps display the Shipment 1 scenario created earlier.

- Click the 'What-If Analysis' button (Data tab | Forecast group) to display the What-If Analysis menu.
- Click Scenario Manager on the What-If Analysis menu to display the Scenario Manager dialog box.
- Click the scenario of interest, Shipment 1 in this case, to select it (Figure 9–71).

Q&A Can I edit a scenario?

Yes. Select the scenario (Scenario Manager dialog box) and then click the Edit button. Excel will display the Edit Scenario dialog box, allowing you to change the scenario name, edit the cells, or add a comment.

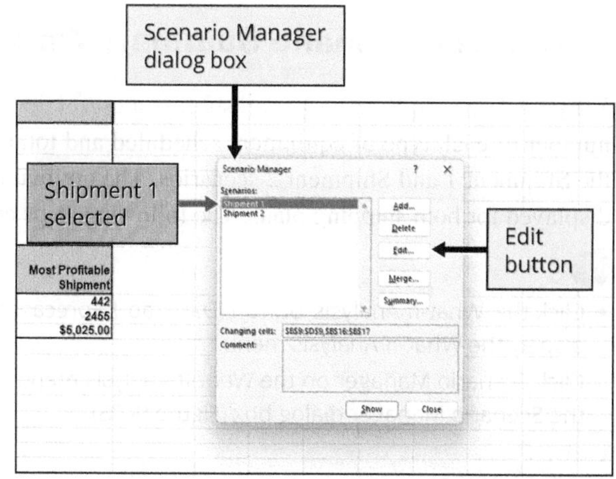

Figure 9–71

- Click the Show button (Scenario Manager dialog box) to display the data for the selected scenario in the worksheet (Figure 9–72).
- Click the Close button (Scenario Manager dialog box) to close the dialog box.

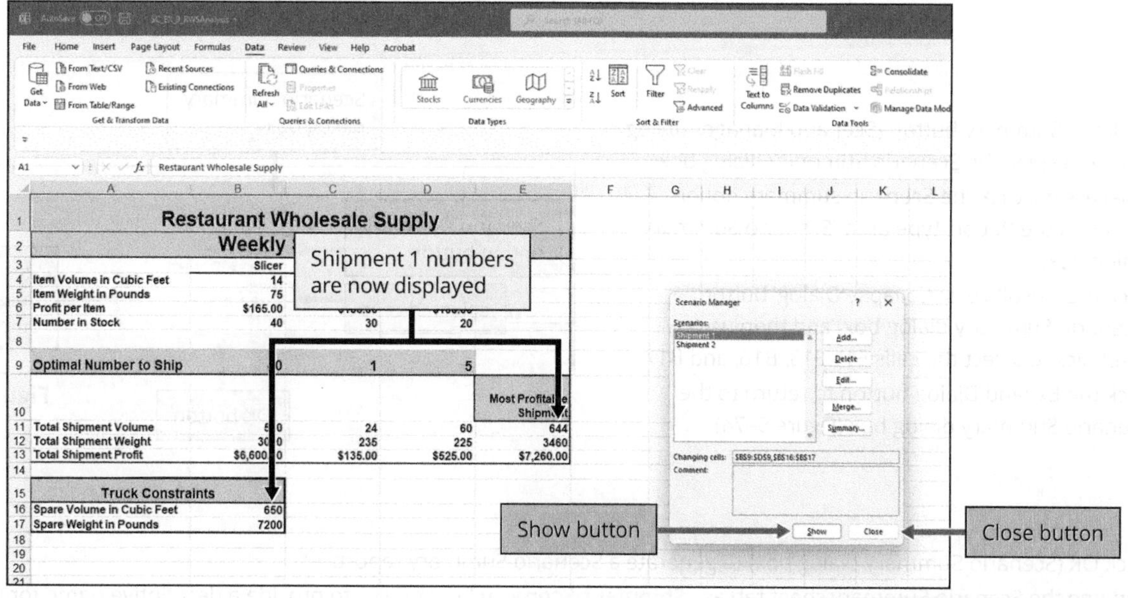

Figure 9–72

Summarizing Scenarios

You can create a Scenario Summary worksheet or a Scenario PivotTable worksheet to review and analyze various what-if scenarios when making decisions. A Scenario Summary worksheet, generated by the Scenario Manager, is a worksheet in outline format that you can print and manipulate just like any other worksheet. Recall that you worked with outlines in a previous module.

The Scenario PivotTable worksheet generated by the Scenario Manager also is a worksheet that you can print and manipulate like other worksheets. PivotTables summarize large amounts

BTW

Scenario Summary Details

Clicking the show detail button on the Scenario Summary worksheet will display any information entered in the Comments box of the Scenario Manager dialog box, along with creation and modification information.

of data and can be rearranged and regrouped to display the data in various forms. Recall that you worked with PivotTables in a previous module. The Scenario PivotTable worksheet allows you to compare the results of multiple scenarios.

To Create a Scenario Summary Worksheet

Why? A Scenario Summary worksheet is a useful decision-making tool. The Scenario Summary worksheet will display the number of each type of equipment scheduled and total profit of the shipment for the current worksheet values, followed by the Shipment 1 and Shipment 2 scenarios. The optimal number of each type of item to be shipped, as calculated by Solver, is displayed for both shipping plans. The following steps create a Scenario Summary worksheet.

- Click the 'What-If Analysis' button (Data tab | Forecast group) to display the What-If Analysis menu.
- Click Scenario Manager on the What-If Analysis menu to display the Scenario Manager dialog box (Figure 9–73).

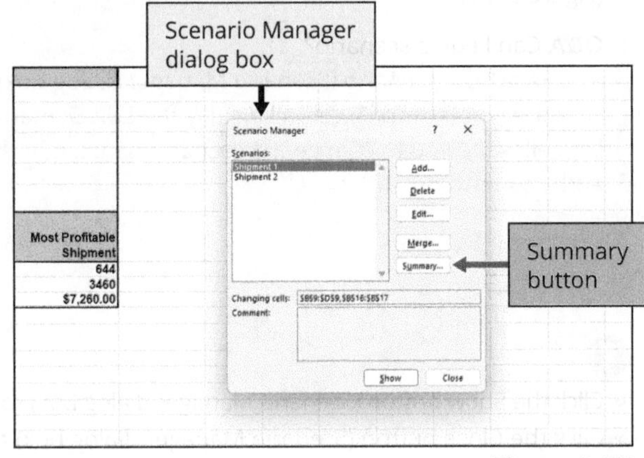

Figure 9–73

- Click the Summary button (Scenario Manager dialog box) to display the Scenario Summary dialog box.
- If necessary, click the Scenario summary option button in the Report type area (Scenario Summary dialog box).
- Click the 'Result cells: Collapse Dialog' button (Scenario Summary dialog box) and then use CTRL+click to select the cells E11:E13, B16, and B17.
- Click the Expand Dialog button to return to the Scenario Summary dialog box (Figure 9–74).

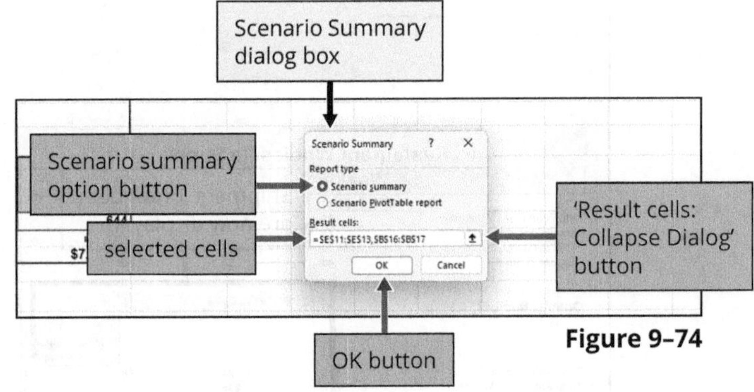

Figure 9–74

3

- Click OK (Scenario Summary dialog box) to generate a Scenario Summary report.
- Rename the Scenario Summary sheet tab as **Shipment Scenario Summary** to provide a descriptive name for the sheet.
- Change the sheet tab color to Purple in the Standard Colors.
- Drag the Shipment Scenario Summary sheet tab to the right of the Shipment Plan Answer Report 2 sheet tab to reposition the worksheet in the workbook (Figure 9–75).

Q&A What is contained in the Scheduling Scenario Summary worksheet?
The current values are displayed in column D, and scenarios Shipment 1 and Shipment 2 are displayed side by side (in columns E and F), allowing you to compare results and determine the best available option. As you might expect, less truck space equals less profit (row 14) and greatly reduces the number of fryers to ship (row 7).

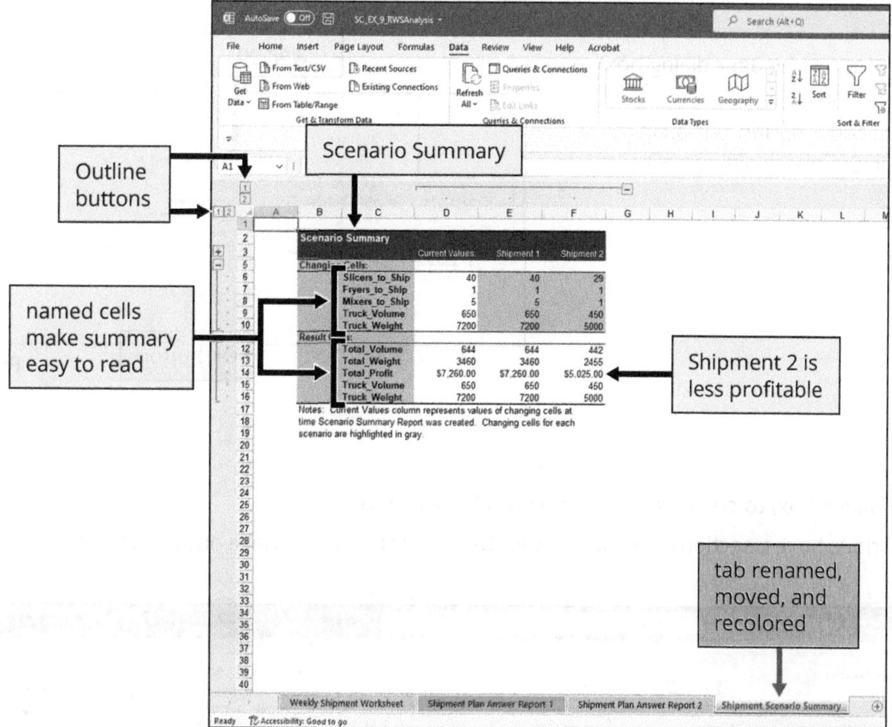

Figure 9–75

Working with an Outline Worksheet

Excel automatically outlines the Scheduling Scenario Summary worksheet. The symbols for expanding and collapsing the rows appear above and to the left of the worksheet. You can hide or display levels of detail by using the hide detail and show detail symbols. You can also use the row- and column-level show detail buttons to collapse or expand rows and columns.

The outline feature is especially useful when working with very large worksheets. With smaller worksheets, the feature may not provide any real benefits. You can remove an outline by clicking the Ungroup arrow (Data tab | Outline group) and then clicking Clear Outline on the Ungroup menu.

To Create a Scenario PivotTable Worksheet

Excel also can create a Scenario PivotTable report worksheet to help analyze and compare the results of multiple scenarios. **Why?** A Scenario PivotTable report worksheet gives you the ability to summarize the scenario data and reorganize the rows and columns to obtain different displays of the summarized data. The Scenario PivotTable summarizes the Shipment 1 and Shipment 2 scenarios and displays the result cells for the two scenarios for easy comparison. The following steps create the Scenario PivotTable worksheet.

- Click the Weekly Shipment Worksheet tab to make it active. You may have to scroll through the sheet tabs to locate the worksheet.
- Click the 'What-If Analysis' button (Data tab | Forecast group) to display the What-If Analysis menu.
- Click Scenario Manager on the What-If Analysis menu to display the Scenario Manager dialog box (Figure 9–76).

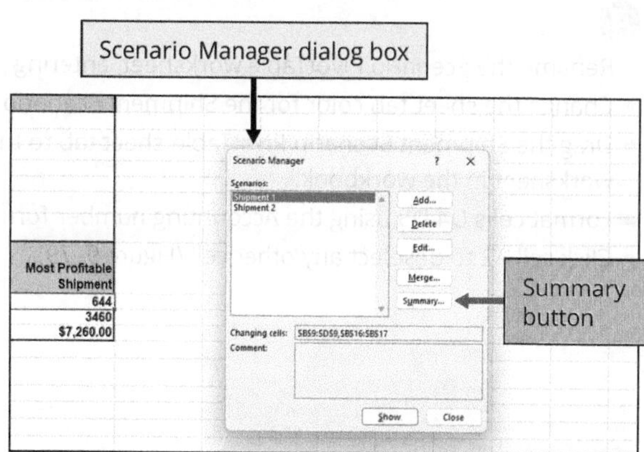

Figure 9–76

2

- Click the Summary button (Scenario Manager dialog box) to display the Scenario Summary dialog box.
- Click the 'Scenario PivotTable report' option button in the Report type area (Scenario Summary dialog box) (Figure 9–77).

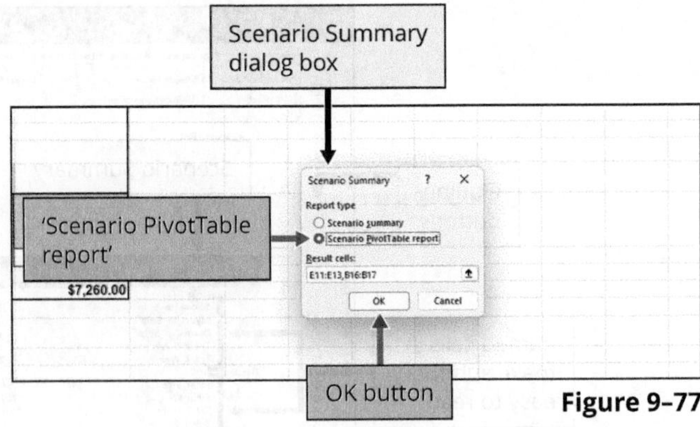

Figure 9–77

3

- Click OK (Scenario Summary dialog box) to create the Scenario PivotTable (Figure 9–78).
- **Experiment:** Examine the various boxes, sections, and settings in the Field List. Do not make any selections.

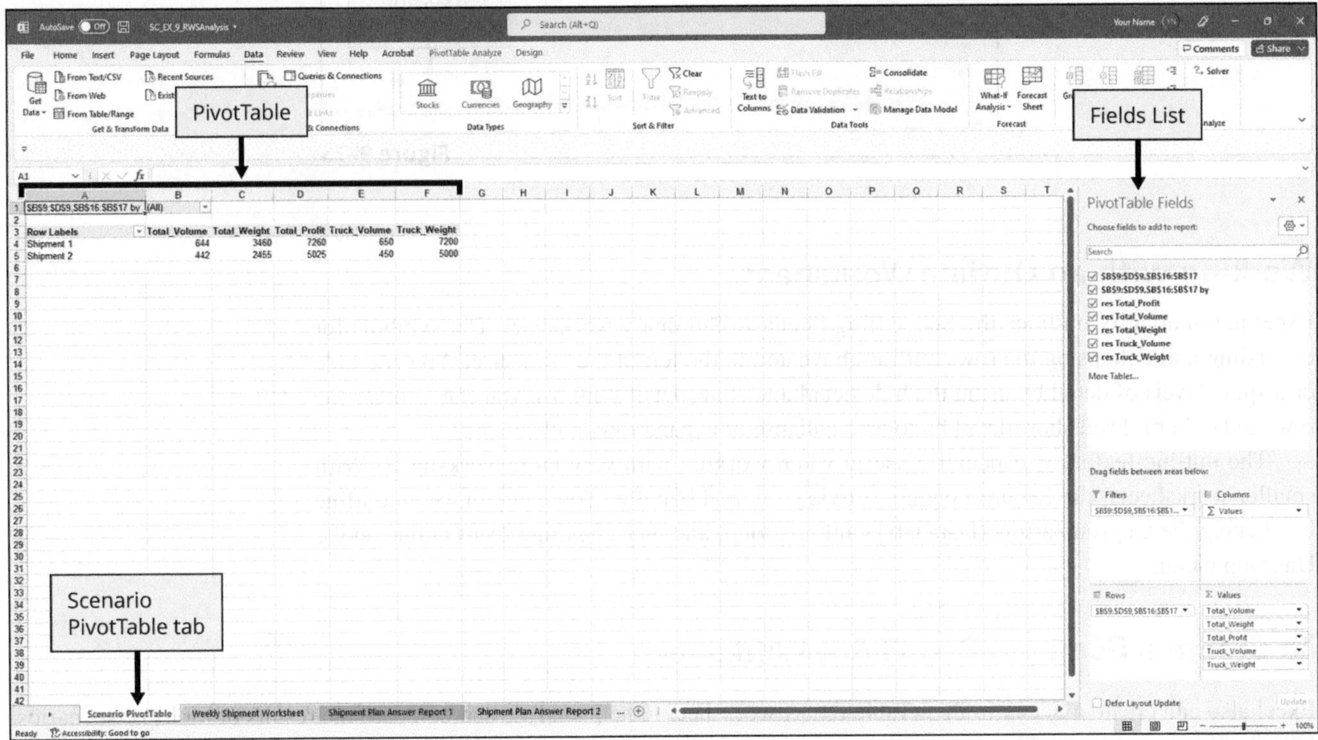

Figure 9–78

4

- Rename the Scenario PivotTable worksheet, entering **Shipment Scenario PivotTable** as the new name of the sheet.
- Change the sheet tab color for the Shipment Scenario PivotTable worksheet to Yellow in the Standard Colors.
- Drag the Shipment Scenario PivotTable sheet tab to the right of the Shipment Scenario Summary sheet tab to reposition the worksheet in the workbook.
- Format cells D4:D5 using the Accounting number format.
- Click cell A2 to deselect any other cell (Figure 9–79).

Q&A How can I use the PivotTable?
After creating the PivotTable, you can treat it like any other worksheet. Thus, you can print or chart a PivotTable. If you update the data in one of the scenarios, click the Refresh All button (Data tab | Queries & Connections group) to update the PivotTable. Note that if you merely change values on a scenario worksheet, it is not the same as changing the scenario. If you want to change the data in a scenario, you must enter the new data using the Scenario Manager.

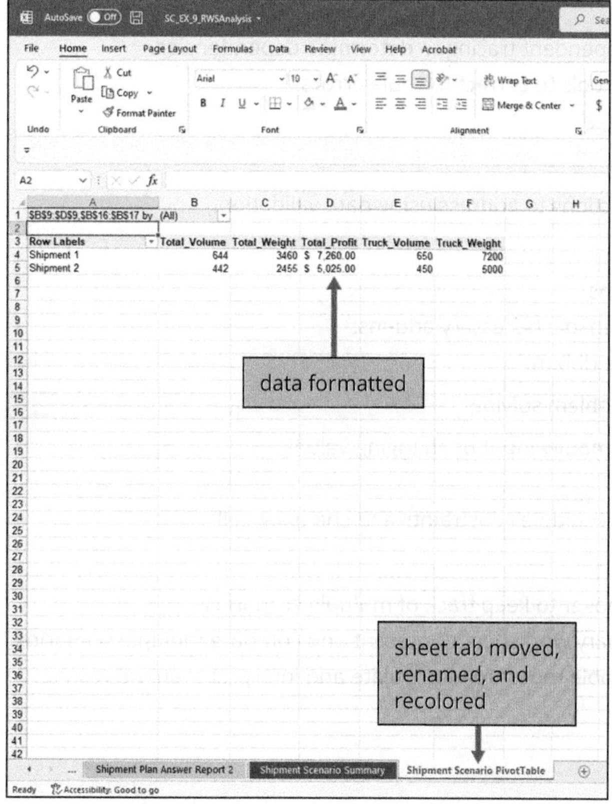

Figure 9–79

- Click the Save button on the Quick Access Toolbar to save the file.
- **sam** Because the project is now complete, you can exit Excel.

Summary

In this module, you learned how to analyze a worksheet using formula auditing techniques and tracer arrows. You used error checking features to determine how to fix errors in the worksheet. You established data validation rules and informed users with input messages about the validation rules. You solved a complex business problem with Excel, using trial and error, Goal Seek, and Solver. Finally, you used the Scenario Manager to manage different problems on the same worksheet and then summarized the results of the scenarios with a Scenario Summary worksheet and a Scenario PivotTable worksheet.

Consider This: Plan Ahead

What decisions will you need to make when creating your next worksheet to solve a complex problem?

Use these guidelines as you complete the assignments in this module and create your own worksheets for evaluating and analyzing data outside of this class.

1. Review and analyze workbook structure and organization.
   a) Review all formulas.
   b) Use precedent and dependent tracing to determine dependencies.
   c) Use formula auditing tools to correct formula errors.
2. Establish data validation rules.
   a) Identify changing cells.
   b) Determine data restrictions to address using data validation.
3. Configure useful add-ins.
   a) Identify missing add-ins.
   b) Use Excel Options to enable necessary add-ins.
   c) Verify inclusion on the ribbon.
4. Determine strategies for problem solving.
   a) Use trial and error to modify input or changing values.
   b) Use Goal Seek.
   c) Use Solver to address multiple constraints and changing cells.
5. Create and store scenarios.
   a) Use the Scenario Manager to keep track of multiple scenarios.
   b) Use a Scenario Summary worksheet to present and compare multiple scenarios.
   c) Use a Scenario PivotTable report to manipulate and interpret scenario results.

Student Assignments

Apply Your Knowledge

Reinforce the skills and apply the concepts you learned in this module.

Using Solver to Plan Charity Concert Advertising

Note: To complete this assignment, you will be required to use the Data Files. Please contact your instructor for information about accessing the Data Files.

Instructions: Start Excel. Open the workbook called SC_EX_9-2.xlsx, which is located in the Data Files. The workbook you open contains information about two charity concerts benefiting children's charities throughout the county, one in the spring and one in the fall. You are to determine how best to promote the charity concerts, making the most of the county's advertising budget. The budget amount has been graciously donated by a county resident. Figure 9–80a displays the completed Answer Report. Figure 9–80b displays the completed Scenario Summary.

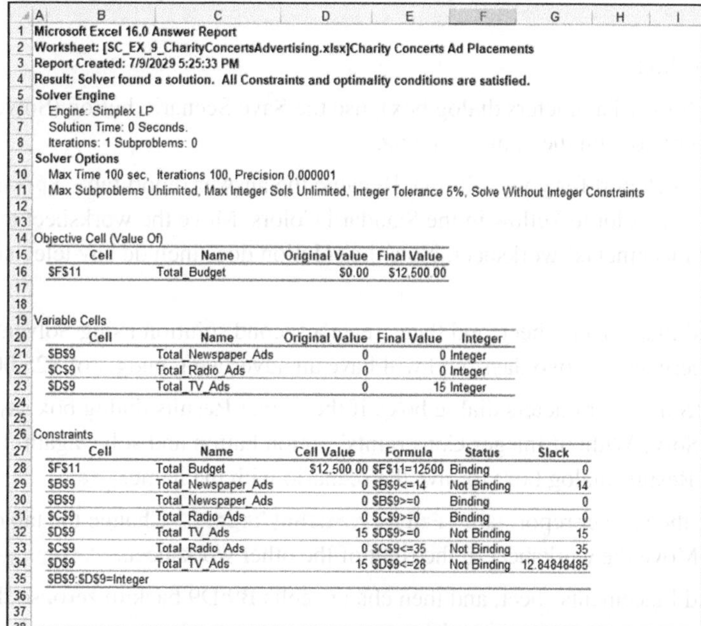

Microsoft Excel 16.0 Answer Report
Worksheet: [SC_EX_9_CharityConcertsAdvertising.xlsx]Charity Concerts Ad Placements
Report Created: 7/9/2029 5:25:33 PM
Result: Solver found a solution. All Constraints and optimality conditions are satisfied.
Solver Engine
Engine: Simplex LP
Solution Time: 0 Seconds.
Iterations: 1 Subproblems: 0
Solver Options
Max Time 100 sec, Iterations 100, Precision 0.000001
Max Subproblems Unlimited, Max Integer Sols Unlimited, Integer Tolerance 5%, Solve Without Integer Constraints

Objective Cell (Value Of)

Cell	Name	Original Value	Final Value
$F$11	Total_Budget	$0.00	$12,500.00

Variable Cells

Cell	Name	Original Value	Final Value	Integer
$B$9	Total_Newspaper_Ads	0	0	Integer
$C$9	Total_Radio_Ads	0	0	Integer
$D$9	Total_TV_Ads	0	15	Integer

Constraints

Cell	Name	Cell Value	Formula	Status	Slack
$F$11	Total_Budget	$12,500.00	$F$11=12500	Binding	0
$B$9	Total_Newspaper_Ads	0	$B$9<=14	Not Binding	14
$B$9	Total_Newspaper_Ads	0	$B$9>=0	Binding	0
$C$9	Total_Radio_Ads	0	$C$9>=0	Binding	0
$D$9	Total_TV_Ads	15	$D$9>=0	Not Binding	15
$C$9	Total_Radio_Ads	0	$C$9<=35	Not Binding	35
$D$9	Total_TV_Ads	15	$D$9<=28	Not Binding	12.84848485

$B$9:$D$9=Integer

Figure 9–80(a): Answer Report

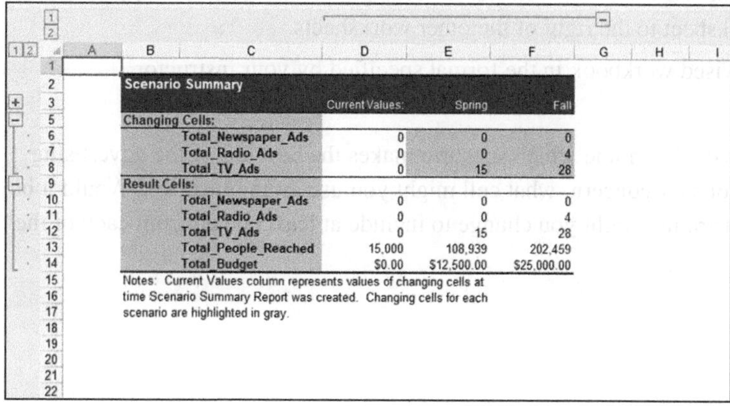

Scenario Summary

	Current Values:	Spring	Fall
Changing Cells:			
Total_Newspaper_Ads	0	0	0
Total_Radio_Ads	0	0	4
Total_TV_Ads	0	15	28
Result Cells:			
Total_Newspaper_Ads	0	0	0
Total_Radio_Ads	0	0	4
Total_TV_Ads	0	15	28
Total_People_Reached	15,000	108,939	202,459
Total_Budget	$0.00	$12,500.00	$25,000.00

Notes: Current Values column represents values of changing cells at time Scenario Summary Report was created. Changing cells for each scenario are highlighted in gray.

Figure 9–80(b): Scenario Summary

Continued on next page

Perform the following tasks:

1. Save the file using the file name, SC_EX_9_CharityConcertsAdvertising.
2. Trace precedents and dependents on the two cells with errors: F9 and E7.
3. Use Error Checking to evaluate the error in cell F9. Use the solution suggested by Error Checking.
4. Trace the error in cell E7. Because the Social Media cost of zero is valid, the division error appears. In cell E7, type **=E5** because all people might be reached using social media at no added cost.
5. Use Solver to determine the best mix of advertising for the advertising dollars. The costs for the spring concert are already entered in the worksheet (B6:D6).
   a. The objective is an advertising budget of $12,500 (the Value Of parameter), which should be displayed in cell F11.
   b. Set the Value Of parameter to 12500.
   c. The changing variables cells are B9:D9.
   d. The constraints are as follows: the newspaper allows a maximum of 14 ads during the advertising period, the radio station allows a maximum of 35 advertisement spots during the advertising period, and the TV station allows a maximum of 28 ads during the advertising period. The Ads Placed values must be positive whole numbers. (**Hint:** Use the int operator as well as the >= operator, and turn on 'ignore integer constraints.')
   e. Use the Simplex LP solving method.
6. After you click the Solve button (Solver Parameters dialog box), use the Save Scenario button (Solver Results dialog box) to save the scenario with the name, **Spring**.
7. Instruct Solver to create the Answer Report for your solution. Rename the answer report tab, **Spring Advertising Report**. Change the tab color to Yellow in the Standard Colors. Move the worksheet to the right of the 'Charity Concerts Ad Placements' worksheet. Note the solution does include any television or newspaper ads.
8. Switch to the Charity Concerts Ad Placements sheet, and then create a second solution using Solver. This solution is for the larger, fall concerts lasting two days, and will have an advertising budget of $25,000.
9. After you click the Solve button (Solver Parameters dialog box), if the Solver Results dialog box says it cannot find a solution, click the 'Solve Without Integer Constraints' option button and solve again. Use the Save Scenario button (Solver Results dialog box) to save the scenario with the name, **Fall**.
10. Create an answer report. Rename the answer report tab, **Fall Advertising Report**. Change the tab color to Green in the Standard Colors. Move the worksheet to the right of the other worksheets.
11. Switch to the Charity Concerts Ad Placements sheet, and then change cells B9:D9 back to zero, so the summary report you create in the next step will begin with zeroes.
12. Use Scenario Manager to create a summary report. When Excel displays the Scenario Summary dialog box, enter **B9:D9,F10:F11** in the Result cells box.
13. Name the resulting summary tab, **Advertising Summary**. Change the tab color to Purple in the Standard Colors. Move the worksheet to the right of the other worksheets.
14. Save the file, and submit the revised workbook in the format specified by your instructor.
15. Exit Excel.
16. **Consider This:** How would you determine which scenario makes the best use of the advertising dollars? If the budget was a secondary concern, what cell might you use as an objective? Would it be a max, min, or value? What constraints might you change to include at least one ad from each of the three ad types?

Extend Your Knowledge

Extend the skills you learned in this module and experiment with new skills. You may need to use Help to complete the assignment.

Validating Loan Calculator Data for New Furniture

Note: To complete this assignment, you will be required to use the Data Files. Please contact your instructor for information about accessing the Data Files.

Instructions: Start Excel. Open the workbook SC_EX_9-3.xlsx, which is located in the Data Files. There is a new business in town that sells new and refurbished furniture, as well as allows you to trade-in any existing furniture you may have for them to refurbish and resell. This new business model appeals to many families in the community. The workbook you open contains a template that calculates the monthly payment for a furniture loan using this business model. The workbook has some errors. You are to correct these errors and create data validation rules. Figure 9–81 displays the worksheet with the errors fixed and an input message for the price of the furniture.

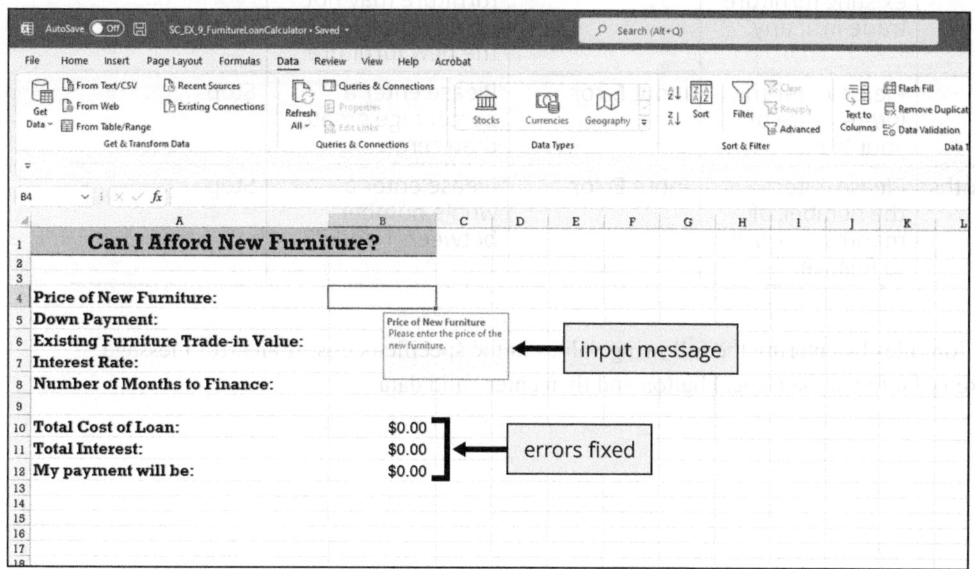

Figure 9–81

Perform the following tasks:

1. Save the file using the file name, SC_EX_9_FurnitureLoanCalculator.
2. To validate the data in cells B10:B12, first do the following:
   a. Examine the formula in cell B10. Trace the error. Check for both precedent and dependent cells. Remove the tracer arrows.
   b. Examine the formula in cell B11. Trace the error. Check for both precedent and dependent cells. Remove the tracer arrows.
   c. Examine the formula in cell B12. Trace the error. Check for both precedent and dependent cells. Remove the tracer arrows.
3. Use Help to review the IF() function. In cells B10 and B11, use the IF() function to execute the formula only when the dependent value is greater than 0. (Note that cell B10 may still display a #NUM error until you fix other errors.)
4. Use Help to review the IFERROR() function, and then use it in cell B12 to display zero if any other errors occur. (**Hint:** Use the current PMT() function as the first argument in the IFERROR() function and use 0 as the second argument.)

Continued on next page

5. Create data validation constraints and messages for each of the cells displayed in Table 9–4. (**Hint:** cells B4:B6 should be formatted in the Accounting style with two decimal places.) Use the Error message column to help you determine the constraint.

Table 9–4: Data Constraints and Messages

Cell	Input Message Title	Input Message	Error Alert Title	Error Message	Error Alert Style
B4	Price of New Furniture	Please enter the price of the new furniture.	Input Error	The price of the furniture must be greater than zero.	Stop
B5	Down Payment	Please enter the amount of your down payment, if any.	Input Error	Your down payment may not exceed the price of the new furniture.	Stop
B6	Trade-in Value	Please enter the amount for your existing furniture trade-in, if any.	Input Error	Your trade-in value for existing furniture may not exceed the price of the new furniture.	Stop
B7	Interest Rate	Please enter the interest rate of your loan.	Input Error	Please enter a percentage greater than zero.	Stop
B8	Number of Months	Please enter the number of months you wish to finance.	Input Error	Please enter a whole number between 1 and 72.	Stop

6. Test the data validation rules by entering the following values in the specified cells. If an error message appears, click the Retry button or the Cancel button and then enter valid data.

   B4: 12000

   B5: 500

   B6: 1125

   B7: 7

   B8: 36

7. Apply appropriate number formatting to the cells in the range B4:B8.
8. Save the file, and submit the revised workbook in the format specified by your instructor.
9. **Consider This:** In step 4, why did you need to use the IFERROR() function, rather than the IF() function? Was there another way you could have solved the errors other than using those functions? What effect would locking the cells with the formulas have on the rest of the spreadsheet?

Expand Your World

Create a solution that uses cloud and web technologies by learning and investigating on your own from general guidance.

Add-Ins for Excel Online in Data Analytics and Visualization

You use Excel Online through your OneDrive account and understand that there are limitations to the online versions of the Office apps compared to the desktop applications. You are interested in discovering add-ins that can improve your overall productivity with Excel Online. Two of the more advanced topics in technology today involve data analytics and visualization. You will explore the add-ins for these topics in the following tasks, along with one in an area of interest to you:

Instructions:

1. Sign into OneDrive and create a new workbook using Excel Online.
2. Explore the Office Add-ins collection available from the Insert tab of the ribbon in the new workbook under the Get Add-ins button.
3. Browse options in the Data Analytics and Visualization categories of the Store as well as those in another category of your choice.
4. Create a document that summarizes the features of an add-in from each of the three categories.
5. Save the file using the file name, SC_EX_9_ExcelAddIns, and submit the revised workbook in the format specified by your instructor.
6. **Consider This:** Compare the add-ins available in Excel to those available for Excel Online. Choose two add-ins and evaluate the strengths and weaknesses of each. Which would you recommend, and why?

In the Lab

Design and implement a solution using creative thinking and problem-solving skills.

Planning for Travel in Retirement

Note: To complete this assignment, you will be required to use the Data Files. Please contact your instructor for information about accessing the Data Files.

Problem: You are currently age 45 and plan to retire at age 60. You have already planned for living expenses in retirement and will have your home paid off; however, you want to travel extensively when you retire but have not yet built that into your plan. You have estimated that at age 60, you will need approximately $75,000 to travel to the destinations you have always wanted to visit, including projected price increases, without impacting your existing retirement savings plan. You decide to use a financial calculator to find out how much you might have to save each year to add to your existing financial plans to cover your future travels.

Perform the following tasks:

Part 1: Start Excel and open the file named SC_EX_9-4.xlsx. Save the file using the file name, SC_EX_9_TravelPlanningCalculator. Examine the Travel Planning Calculator worksheet and examine the various calculations. The worksheet, displayed in Figure 9–82, makes the following assumptions:

a. The starting balance deposited in the travel account is stored in cell B3.

b. The first annual contribution is in cell C3. The calculator assumes a $200 increase in contributions to this account each year.

c. The rate of return (column D) is based on a moderate investment strategy of 5 percent.

Use Goal Seek to set the final ending balance (E18) to $75,000 by changing cell B3, the initial starting balance. Write down the new B3 value on a piece of paper. Click Cancel to undo the changes and return to the original values.

Use Goal Seek again by changing cell C3, the annual contribution. Write down the new value in cell C3. Click Cancel to undo the changes.

Use Solver to set the objective in cell E18 to **75000** by changing the values in cells B3:D3. Set constraints for cells B3 and C3 to be greater than or equal to one. Select the GRG Nonlinear solving method (because you are dealing with a percentage rate of return). When Excel displays the Solver Results dialog box, choose to produce an answer report. Move the new worksheet to the right of the original one and change the tab color to Blue in the Standard Colors.

Continued on next page

Experiment with other constraints. For example, suppose the most you can start the account with is $5,000. Perhaps you can only add a maximum of $500 a year. Will Solver find a solution with those constraints? Submit your assignment in the format specified by your instructor.

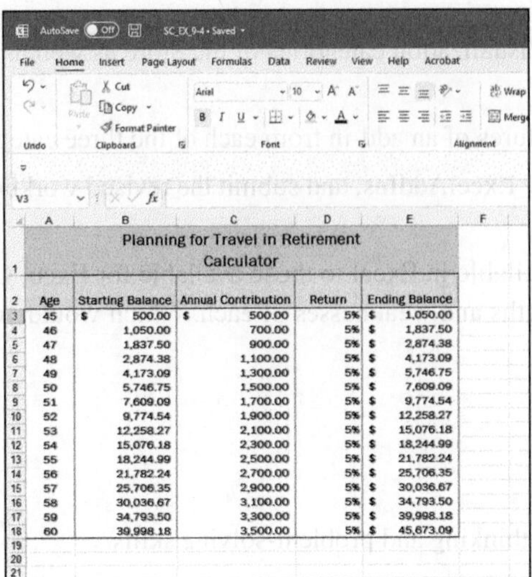

Planning for Travel in Retirement Calculator

Age	Starting Balance	Annual Contribution	Return	Ending Balance
45	$ 500.00	$ 500.00	5%	$ 1,050.00
46	1,050.00	700.00	5%	$ 1,837.50
47	1,837.50	900.00	5%	$ 2,874.38
48	2,874.38	1,100.00	5%	$ 4,173.09
49	4,173.09	1,300.00	5%	$ 5,746.75
50	5,746.75	1,500.00	5%	$ 7,609.09
51	7,609.09	1,700.00	5%	$ 9,774.54
52	9,774.54	1,900.00	5%	$ 12,258.27
53	12,258.27	2,100.00	5%	$ 15,076.18
54	15,076.18	2,300.00	5%	$ 18,244.99
55	18,244.99	2,500.00	5%	$ 21,782.24
56	21,782.24	2,700.00	5%	$ 25,706.35
57	25,706.35	2,900.00	5%	$ 30,036.67
58	30,036.67	3,100.00	5%	$ 34,793.50
59	34,793.50	3,300.00	5%	$ 39,998.18
60	39,998.18	3,500.00	5%	$ 45,673.09

Figure 9–82

Save the file, and submit the revised workbook in the format specified by your instructor.

Part 2: **Consider This:** You made several decisions while creating the worksheet in this assignment: initial starting balance, annual contribution, and constraints. What was the rationale behind each of these decisions? Which of the solutions seemed the most feasible to you? Why?

Data Analysis with Power Tools and Creating Macros

Objectives

After completing this module, you will be able to:

- Explain the Excel power tools
- Customize the ribbon and enable data analysis
- Use the Get & Transform data commands
- Create a query using Power Query Editor
- Build a PivotTable using Power Pivot
- Explain data modeling
- Create a measure
- Display cube functions
- Use 3D Maps
- Save a tour as an animation
- Create hyperlinks
- Use the macro recorder to create a macro
- Execute a macro

Introduction

Excel has a wide range of interlinked power tools for data analysis—Get & Transform, Power Pivot, Power BI (Business Intelligence), and 3D Maps—which enable you to perform tasks such as to exporting data for business intelligence, pivoting or manipulating data to find trends, creating data models, and showing data more visually.

Table 10–1 describes the power tools available to analyze Excel data. In this module, you will only touch on some of the power tools. The topic is vast and would require a lot of time and data modeling experience to explore all of the features associated with each tool. Power BI is a separate program available as a free download and is designed to analyze Excel data. Power Pivot may not be available in all versions of Excel. While you may have limited access to these tools, you will be able to work through most of the steps in this module.

Table 10–1: Power Tools

Tool	Purpose
Get & Transform (also called Power Query)	The Get & Transform commands enable you to extract, connect, refine, and transform large amounts of data into an accessible Excel file. You can use Get & Transform to exert greater control over columns, formulas, and filtering tools, and also to modify data types and extract PivotTables.
Power Pivot	Power Pivot enables you to import and compare large amounts of data from multiple sources to analyze relationships between tables of data. You can use Power Pivot to create and model data tables, feed data to other Power Tools, and use data analysis expressions. Power Pivot is not available with all versions of Excel.
Power BI	Power BI, or Power Business Intelligence, is a collection of tools that enables you to understand and communicate large amounts of data in the form of visualizations. Power BI includes a range of tools for report generation, data modeling, sharing and collaboration, including a free desktop app and an online service.
3D Maps (formerly called Power Map)	3D Maps let you plot and visualize geographic or temporal data on a three-dimensional map. With filtering, you can compare how different factors affect your data. You can use a 3D Map to build custom regions, capture screenshots, and build cinematic time tours or animations through your data.

In addition to using Excel power tools, you will create hyperlinks to move quickly to other parts of the workbook, animations, and external websites. You also will record a macro to automate a task.

Project: Business Decisions Demographics

The project in this module follows proper design guidelines and uses Excel to create the workbook displayed in Figures 10–1 and 10–2. The Department of Family Health Services (DFHS) of the state health department in Tennessee wants to address the needs of growing counties by building new child care centers. They are hiring an analytics firm to find the best locations for new child care centers based mainly on population and new births. The business analytics firm specializes in examining raw data, searching for patterns, correlations, and other associations to help companies and organizations make better business decisions. Using data from the U.S. Census Bureau, the firm plans to present several forms of visual data to its client using Excel power tools. Not every county in Tennessee is included in the data, as not all counties are eligible. Figure 10–1a shows the opening worksheet that includes a screen capture, a symbol, and hyperlinks to the other pages. Figure 10–1b queries the external data to display the 10 most populous counties. Figure 10–1c lists all counties, along with the number of child care centers from a different data table.

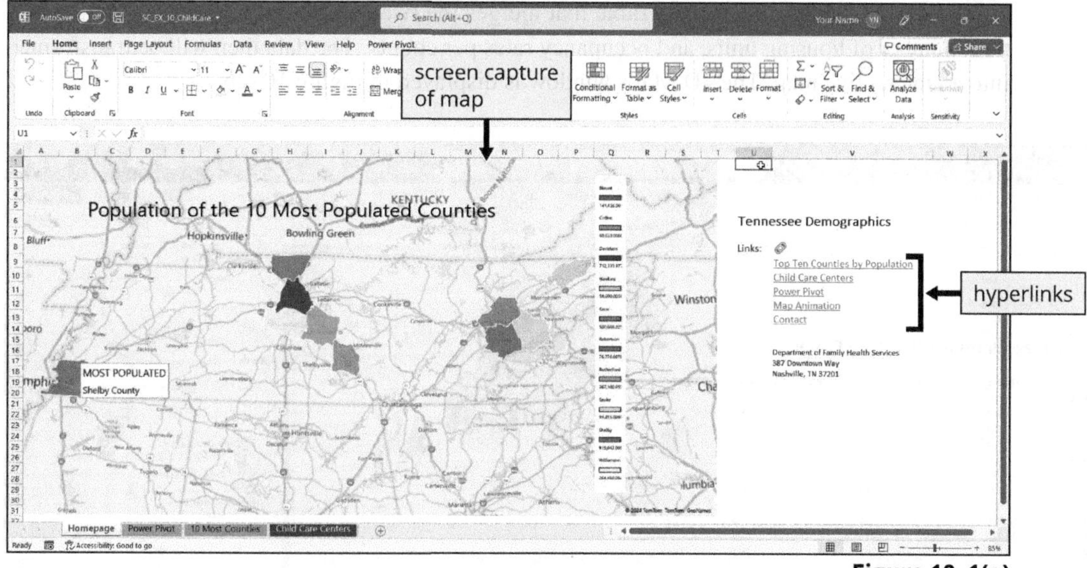

Figure 10–1(a)

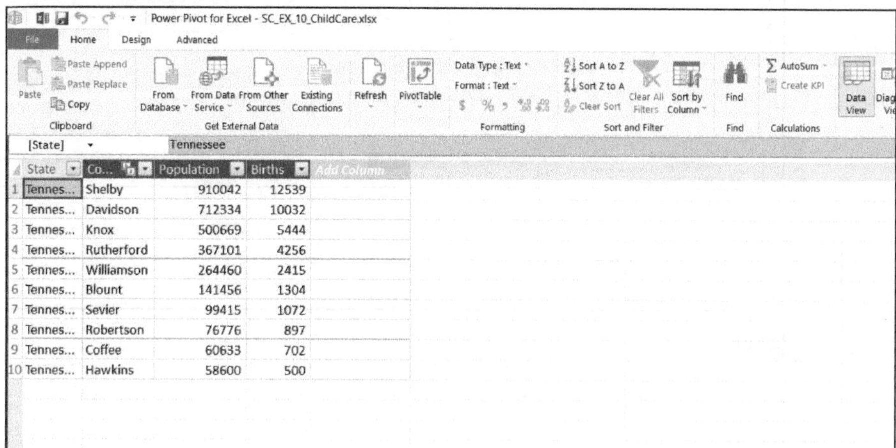

Power Pivot for Excel - SC_EX_10_ChildCare.xlsx

[State] Tennessee

	State	Co...	Population	Births
1	Tennes...	Shelby	910042	12539
2	Tennes...	Davidson	712334	10032
3	Tennes...	Knox	500669	5444
4	Tennes...	Rutherford	367101	4256
5	Tennes...	Williamson	264460	2415
6	Tennes...	Blount	141456	1304
7	Tennes...	Sevier	99415	1072
8	Tennes...	Robertson	76776	897
9	Tennes...	Coffee	60633	702
10	Tennes...	Hawkins	58600	500

Figure 10–1(b)

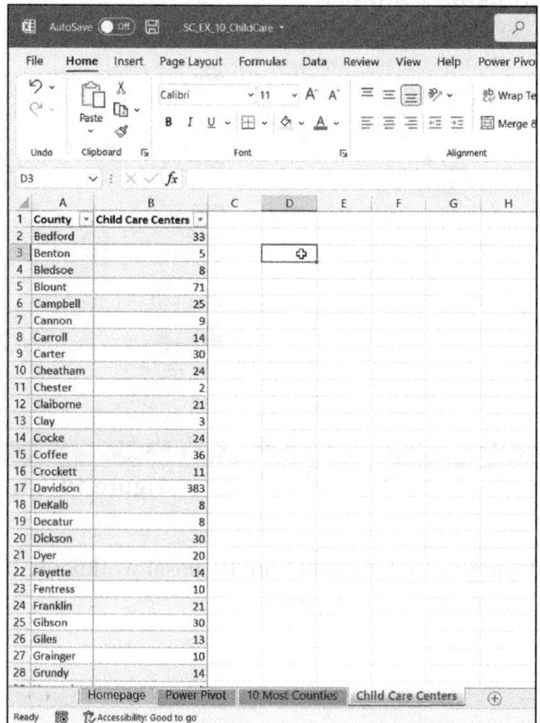

	A	B
1	County	Child Care Centers
2	Bedford	33
3	Benton	5
4	Bledsoe	8
5	Blount	71
6	Campbell	25
7	Cannon	9
8	Carroll	14
9	Carter	30
10	Cheatham	24
11	Chester	2
12	Claiborne	21
13	Clay	3
14	Cocke	24
15	Coffee	36
16	Crockett	11
17	Davidson	383
18	DeKalb	8
19	Decatur	8
20	Dickson	30
21	Dyer	20
22	Fayette	14
23	Fentress	10
24	Franklin	21
25	Gibson	30
26	Giles	13
27	Grainger	10
28	Grundy	14

Figure 10–1(c)

Figure 10–2a displays a PivotTable that merges the two data sources to display the population, number of housing units, and occupancy rates per county. The data then will be transformed into an interactive map. The 3D Maps window is displayed in Figure 10–2b.

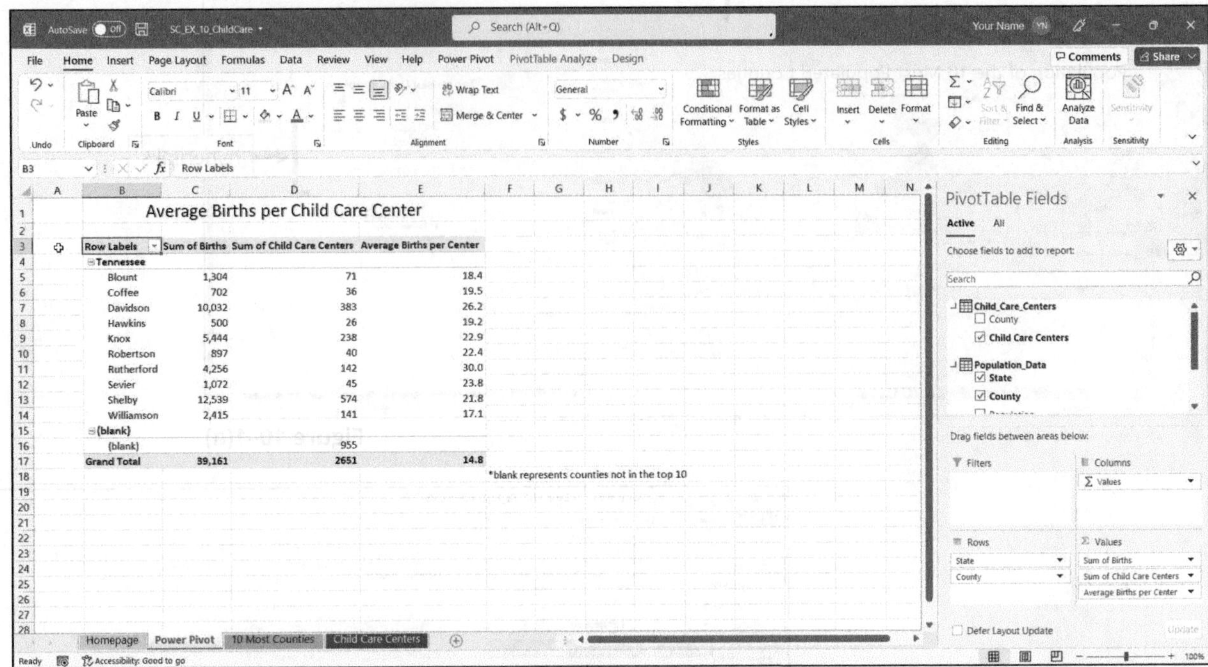

Figure 10–2(a)

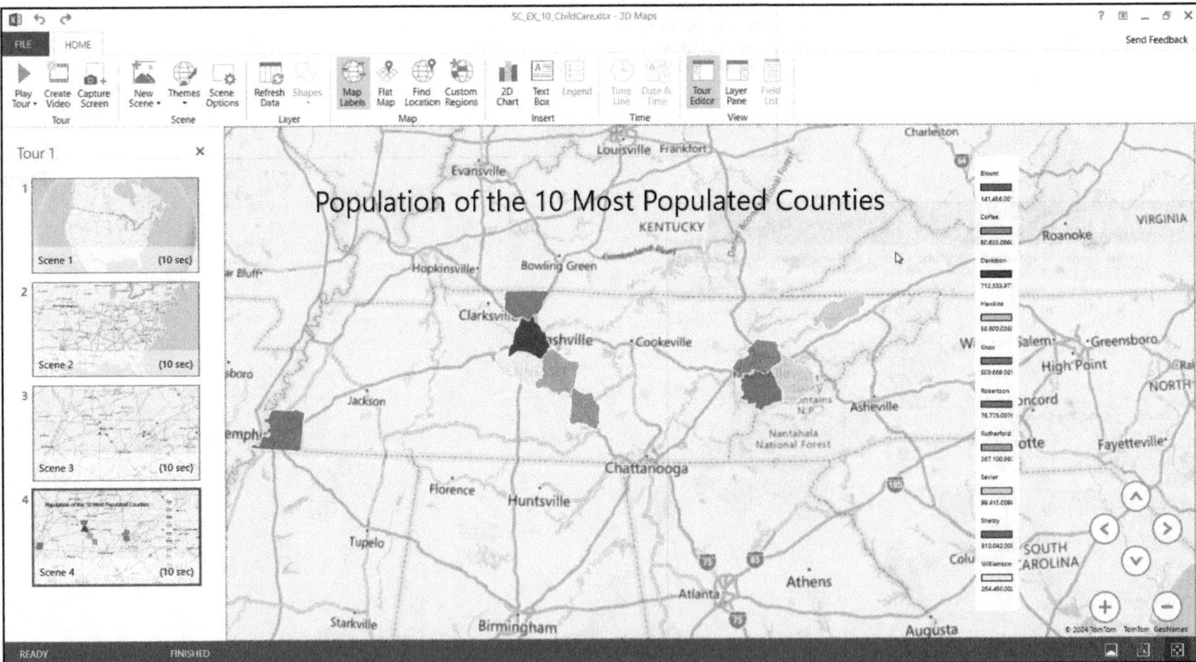

Figure 10–2(b)

Figure 10–3 illustrates the requirements document for the Child Care Proposal workbook. It includes the needs, source of data, and other facts about its development.

Worksheet Title	Demographic Analysis for Child Care Centers Proposal
Needs	The analytics firm would like to present a variety of data visualizations to the health department, including: 1. The 10 most populous counties in order from most to least, and number of births for each. 2. A list of all of eligible counties in the state, along with the number of child care centers in each. 3. A Power Pivot report combining the data sources to show the relationship between county, births, and child care centers. 4. An animated map showing the counties with the most population. 5. An attractive opening worksheet with hyperlinks to each of the above items, 1 through 4, and a decorative link symbol.
Calculations	Average births per child care center for each county, which is calculated by dividing the number of births of the county by the number of child care centers. This calculation will appear in the Power Pivot report.
Source of Data	The health department will supply the data in the workbook SC_EX_10-1.xlsx to the analytics firm.

Figure 10-3

Workflow

Recall that in previous modules you imported data from a variety of sources including an Access database, a Word table, a comma-delimited text file, and a table from the web. The workflow to create connections for use with the power tools is similar:

- Connect to the data: Make connections to data in the cloud, in a service, or from local sources. You can work with the connected data by creating a permanent connection from your workbook to that data source, ensuring that the data you work with is always up to date.
- Transform the data: Shape the data locally to meet your needs; the original source remains unchanged.
- Combine data from various sources: Create a data model from multiple data sources and get unique insights into the data.
- Share the data: Save, share, or use transformed data for reports and presentations.

With a good understanding of the requirements and an understanding of the necessary decisions, the next step is to use Excel to create the workbook. In this module, you will learn how to create the workbook displayed in Figures 10–1 and 10–2.

To Create a Workbook

The following steps start Excel and open a blank workbook. Then, you will use the Save As dialog box to save the workbook on your storage device.

1. **sam** Start Excel.
2. Click the Blank workbook from the template gallery in Backstage view.
3. If necessary, maximize the Excel window.
4. Display Backstage view, click Save As, and then click Browse to open the Save As dialog box.
5. Browse to your storage device.
6. In the File name box, type **SC_EX_10_ChildCare** as the file name.
7. Click Save (Save As dialog box) to save the file.

To Copy Data Files

Sometimes data sources move to different locations. You probably have noticed while browsing the web that some webpages no longer exist or have been redirected. On your computer, you may have links that no longer work after moving a file to a different folder. Therefore, if you are using local data—that is, the data stored on your computer—it is a good idea to store the workbook and any connected data sources in the same folder location.

The following steps copy two files from the Data Files to your storage location. Consult your instructor for more information about this process. If you already have downloaded the Data Files to the same storage location that you are using to create and save files in this module, you can skip these steps.

To complete these steps, you will be required to use the Data Files. Please contact your instructor for information about accessing the Data Files.

1. Click the File Explorer button on the Windows taskbar to open a File Explorer window.
2. Navigate to the location of the Data Files for this module.
3. Select both the Support_EX_10-1.xlsx file and the Support_EX_10-2.xlsx file, and then copy and paste the files into your storage location folder.
4. Close the File Explorer window.

To Enable Data Analysis

The following steps verify that Data Analysis has been enabled in the version of Excel that you are running. **Why?** Data analysis commands are required in order to use the power tools and they are not enabled by default in a standard Excel installation.

- Display Backstage view, and then click Options to open the Excel Options dialog box.
- In the left pane of the Excel Options dialog box, click Data to display the Data options area.
- If necessary, click to display a check mark in the 'Enable Data Analysis add-ins: Power Pivot, Power View and 3D Maps' check box (Figure 10–4).
- Click OK button to close the Excel Options dialog box.

Q&A I do not have access to the Enable option. What should I do?
You may have a version of Excel that does not support data analysis and the power tools. Continue with the steps and contact your instructor or IT administrator.

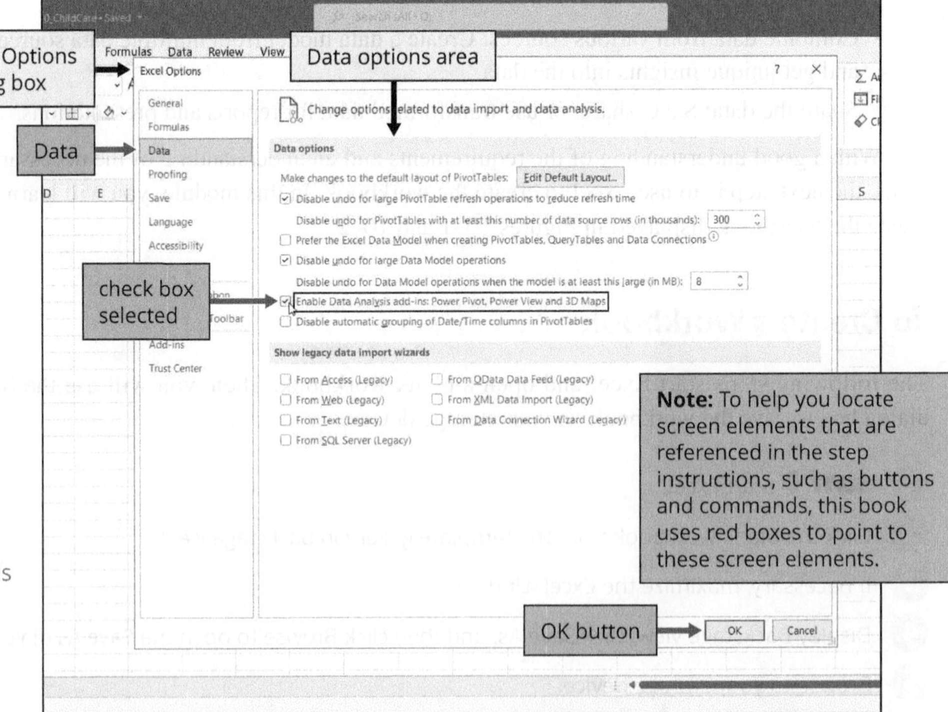

Figure 10–4

To Add in Power Map

If you could not enable data analysis in the previous steps, you may need to add Power Map to your version of Excel in order to run 3D Maps. Recall from a previous module that you used the Add-ins option to add Solver to Excel. The following steps add in Power Map.

1. Display Backstage view, and then click Options to open the Excel Options dialog box.
2. In the left pane of the Excel Options dialog box, click Add-ins to display the Add-ins options.
3. Near the bottom of the dialog box, click the Manage arrow and then click COM Add-ins.
4. Click the Go button to open the COM Add-ins dialog box.
5. If necessary, click to display a check mark in the 'Microsoft Power Map for Excel' check box. If you have a check box for Power Pivot, select that as well.
6. Click OK (COM Add-ins dialog box).

Customizing the Ribbon

It is easy to customize, or personalize, the ribbon the way that you want it. You can

- Create custom groups and custom tabs to contain frequently used commands.
- Rearrange or rename buttons, groups, and tabs to fit your work style.
- Rename or remove buttons and boxes from an existing tab and group.
- Add new buttons to a custom group or to the Quick Access Toolbar.

When you add new buttons to the ribbon, you can choose from a list that includes 1) commands that you use elsewhere in Excel, such as those on shortcut menus; 2) commands from Backstage view; or 3) other commands that are not on the ribbon. Or, you can create a new button that executes a command or set of commands that you record. In this module, you will enable the Power Pivot tab on the ribbon and then enable the Developer tab.

You can customize the ribbon in all of the Microsoft Office applications, but the customizations only apply to the application you are using. The changes you make to the Excel ribbon will not change the ribbon in any other Microsoft Office application. When you no longer need the customization, it can be removed individually, or the entire ribbon can be reset to its default settings, removing all customizations.

BTW
Touch Screen Differences
The Office and Windows interfaces may vary if you are using Touch Mode. For this reason, you might notice that the function or appearance of your touch screen differs slightly from this module's presentation.

Consider This

What should I keep in mind when customizing the ribbon?

- Customize the ribbon when you need to access new features of Excel, or when you regularly need to access commands that are not part of the ribbon already.
- If the new command will be used at various times, with different tabs, consider adding the command or button to the Quick Access Toolbar.
- If you need to add a single command to the ribbon, choose a tab with plenty of room to hold the new command and its new group.
- If you need to add several commands, consider creating a new tab on the ribbon.
- If you are using a computer in a lab situation, you may not have permission to change the ribbon. Check with your instructor or IT administrator.
- If you are using a computer in a lab situation, reset the ribbon when you are done.

To Customize the Ribbon

The following steps customize the ribbon. **Why?** Due to space constraints on the ribbon and the advanced nature of the power tools, some of the commands do not appear automatically. You will enable the Power Pivot tab on the ribbon and then enable the Developer tab that you will use later in the module.

The Power Pivot tool is not available in all versions of Excel. If you do not have access to the Power Pivot tab in the following steps, contact your instructor or IT administrator to find out whether your version of Excel can run Power Pivot; you may have to use an Add-in process.

- Right-click a blank area of the ribbon to display the shortcut menu (Figure 10–5).

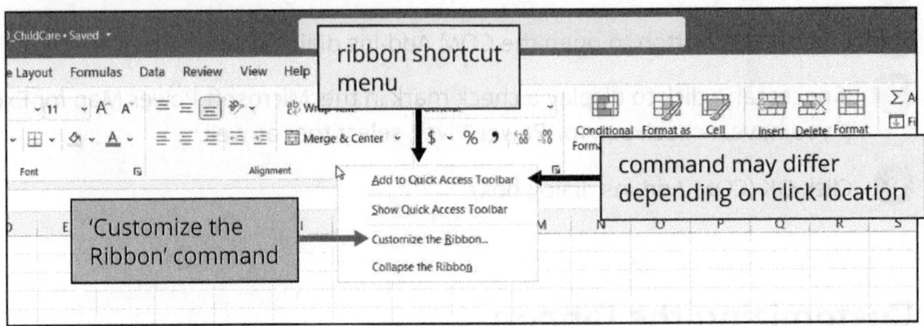

Figure 10–5

- Click the 'Customize the Ribbon' command on the shortcut menu to display the Customize Ribbon area of the Excel Options dialog box.
- In the Main Tabs area, scroll as necessary, and then click to display a check mark in both the Developer and the Power Pivot check boxes, if necessary (Figure 10–6).

Q&A I do not have access to Power Pivot. What should I do?
Contact your instructor or IT administrator to find out if your version of Excel can run Power Pivot. If not, you can still continue with these steps and create a regular Pivot Table.

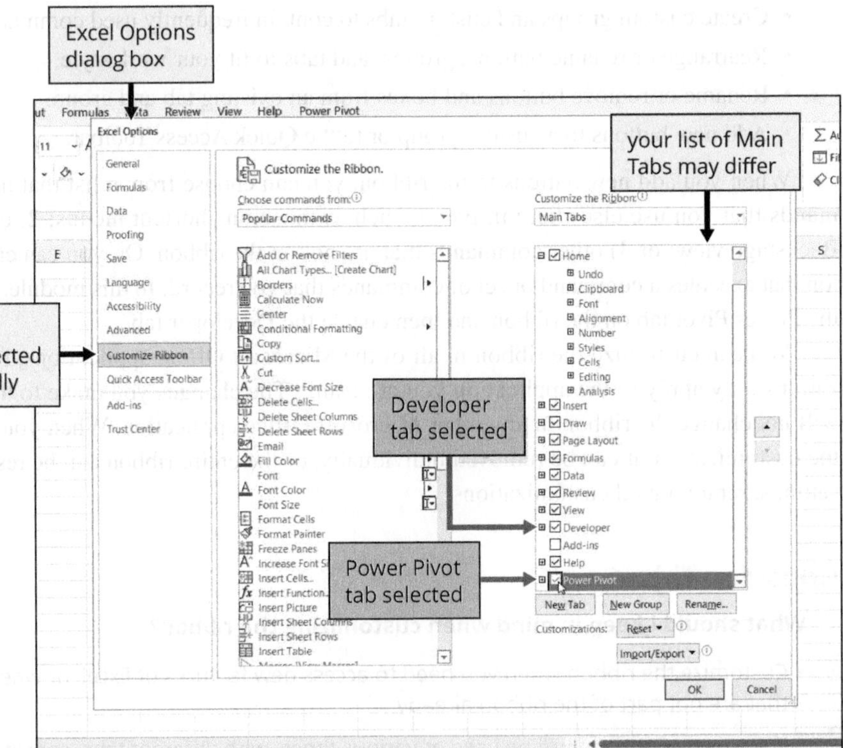

Figure 10–6

- Click OK (Excel Options dialog box) to display the customization on the ribbon (Figure 10–7).

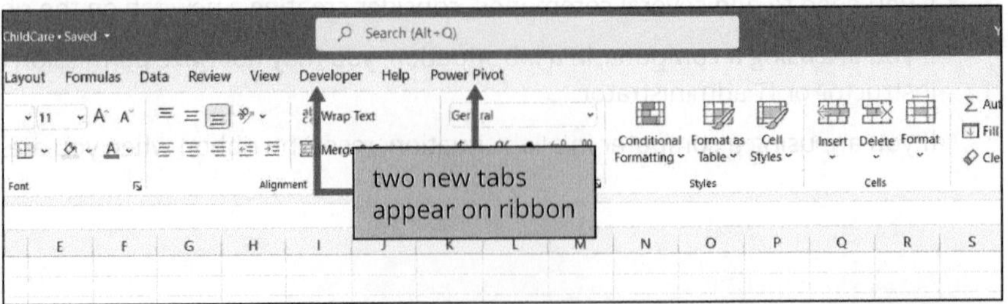

Figure 10–7

Other Ways

1. Display Backstage view, click Options, click Customize Ribbon (Excel Options dialog box), click appropriate check box in main Tabs list, click OK

To Add a New Group If you wanted to add a new group to customize the ribbon, you would perform the following steps.

1. Right-click a blank area of the ribbon to display the shortcut menu.
2. Click the 'Customize the Ribbon' command on the shortcut menu to display the Excel Options dialog box.
3. In the Main Tabs area, navigate to and then select the tab where you want the New Group to be added.
4. Click the New Group button to insert a New Group in the selected
5. Select the command(s) you want to add in the new group from the column on the left.
6. Click the Add button to add the new command(s) to the New Group.
7. To Rename the New Group, select the New Group and click the Rename button.
8. Enter a display name and click OK (Rename dialog box).
9. Click OK (Excel Options dialog box).

Get & Transform

Also called Power Query, the Get & Transform commands located on the Data tab allow you to extract, connect, clean, and transform large amounts of data into an accessible Excel table. Recall that when you get data using a Get & Transform command, Excel provides advanced editing and querying techniques to use with that data. When you use the Power Query Editor, you are provided with tools to group rows, filter, replace values, remove duplicates, and edit columns to facilitate transformations. The resulting query table then becomes a displayed subset of the actual data. When loaded into your workbook, the Queries & Connections pane shows all of the files connected to your workbook.

BTW

Getting Data from Access Databases

When you click the Get Data button (Data Tab | Get & Transform Data group) and choose to import an Access database, the Navigator window opens so you can select which table (or tables) you want to use in your query. When you select a table, a preview of its data is displayed in the right pane of the Navigator window.

To Get Data

The following steps connect to a table with data provided by the U.S. Census Bureau for the state of Tennessee. The table is located in the Data Files. **Why?** Connecting with the U.S. Census Bureau website is somewhat cumbersome and requires many steps. You will use the Get Data button (Data tab | Get & Transform Data group) to connect to the data. When you bring the data into Excel, you are working with a local copy; you will not change the original data source in any way. Should the data source be updated externally, however, you easily can refresh your local copy. The local data becomes a table, also called a query table in Excel.

To complete these steps, you will be required to use the Data Files. Please contact your instructor for information about accessing the Data Files.

1

- Display the Data tab.
- Click the Get Data button (Data tab | Get & Transform Data group) to display the Get Data menu.
- Point to the From File command to display the From File submenu (Figure 10–8).

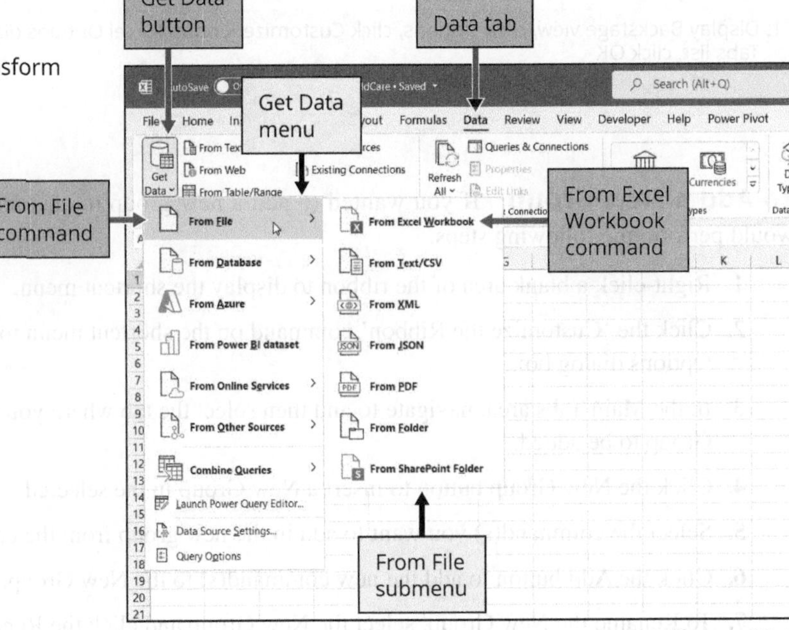

Figure 10–8

- Click From Excel Workbook on the From File submenu to display the Import Data dialog box.
- If necessary, navigate to your storage location to display the files.
- Double-click the file named Support_EX_10–1.xlsx to display the Navigator dialog box.
- Click the table named Child Care Centers to preview the data (Figure 10–9).

Q&A Could I have clicked From Web and navigated to the census data?
Yes; however, you would have had to perform many additional steps to drill down to the desired data for this project.

Why does the Navigator dialog box display two available tables?
The Support_EX_10–1.xlsx file contains only one table, Child Care Centers, but Excel may identify additional tables in a workbook and assign default names such as Table1, Table2, etc. This ensures that you can easily load any identifiable table data and transform it as needed.

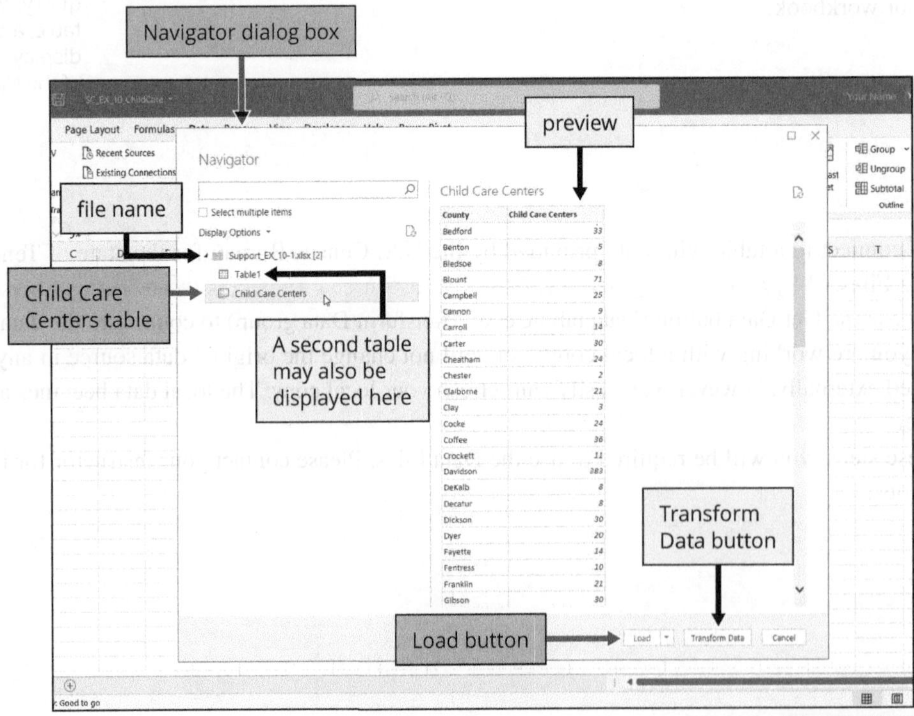

Figure 10–9

3

- Click the Load button (Navigator dialog box) to import the data (Figure 10–10).

Q&A How is the data displayed?
Excel shows one row of column headings and 79 rows of data for the counties in Tennessee in a table format.

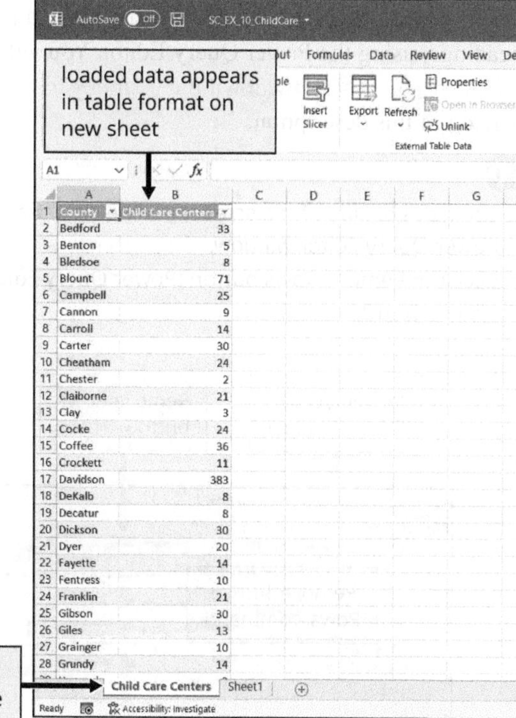

Figure 10–10

To Get Another Data Source

The following steps add a second data source to the workbook. **Why?** The information we need is stored in two different files.

1. In the Excel window, click the Get Data button (Data tab | Get & Transform Data group), point to From File to display the From File submenu, and then click From Workbook (or 'From Excel Workbook') to display the Import Data dialog box.
2. If necessary, navigate to your storage location.
3. Click the file named Support_EX_10-2.xlsx to select it and then click the Import button to display the Navigator dialog box.
4. If necessary, click the 'Population Data' table to preview the data.
5. Click the Load button (Navigator dialog box) to import the data (Figure 10–11).

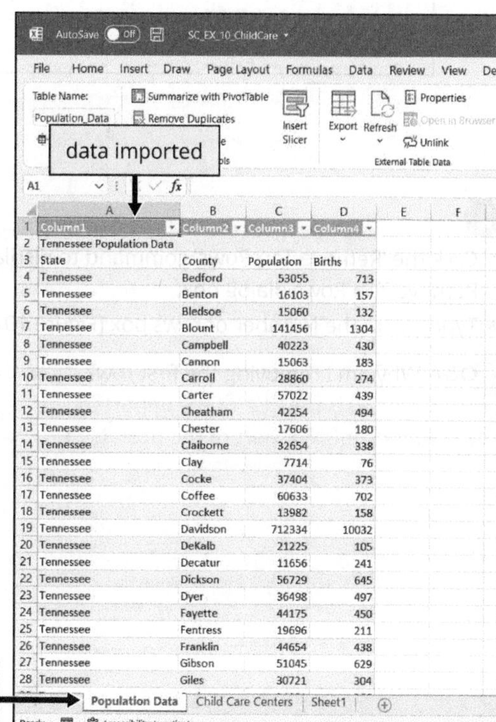

Figure 10–11

To Edit Data Using the Power Query Editor

The following steps edit the query to remove a heading from the imported data and to convert the second row into column headings, using the Power Query Editor. You will also sort the data and display the 10 most populated counties. **Why?** The DFHS wants to narrow down the counties to those with the most people. You will rename the sheet tab using a shortened version of this description.

- On the right side of the screen, double-click the 'Population Data' query in the Queries & Connections pane to display the Power Query Editor window.
- Click the Remove Rows button (Power Query Editor Home tab | Reduce Rows group) to display the Remove Rows menu (Figure 10–12).

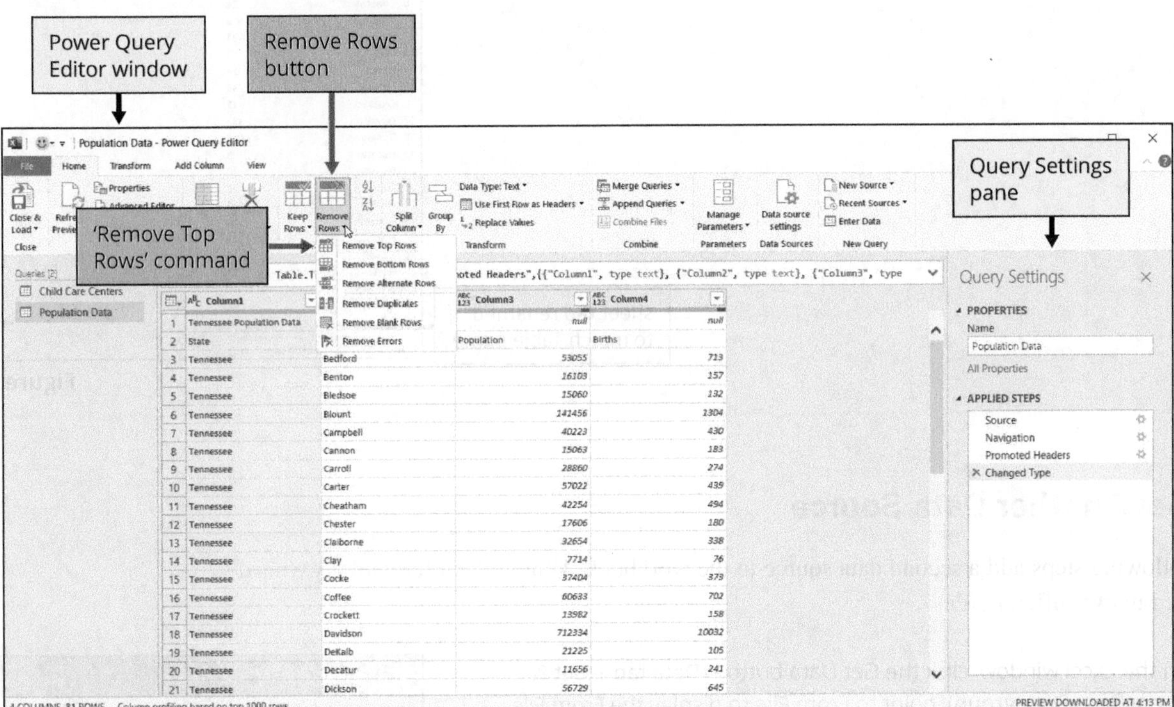

Figure 10–12

- Click the 'Remove Top Rows' command to display the Remove Top Rows dialog box.
- Type **1** in the Number of rows box (Figure 10–13).

Q&A Why am I removing the first row?
The first row is the title of the imported worksheet; it is not part of the data itself.

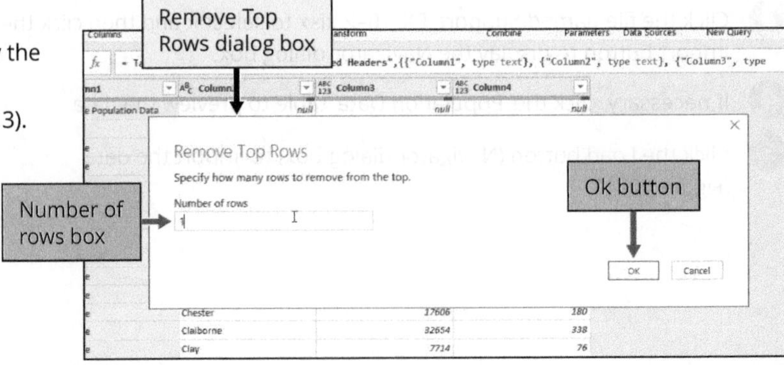

Figure 10–13

3

- Click OK (Remove Top Rows dialog box) to remove the first row.
- Click the 'Use First Row as Headers' button (Home tab | Transform group) to use the imported table's column headings (Figure 10–14).

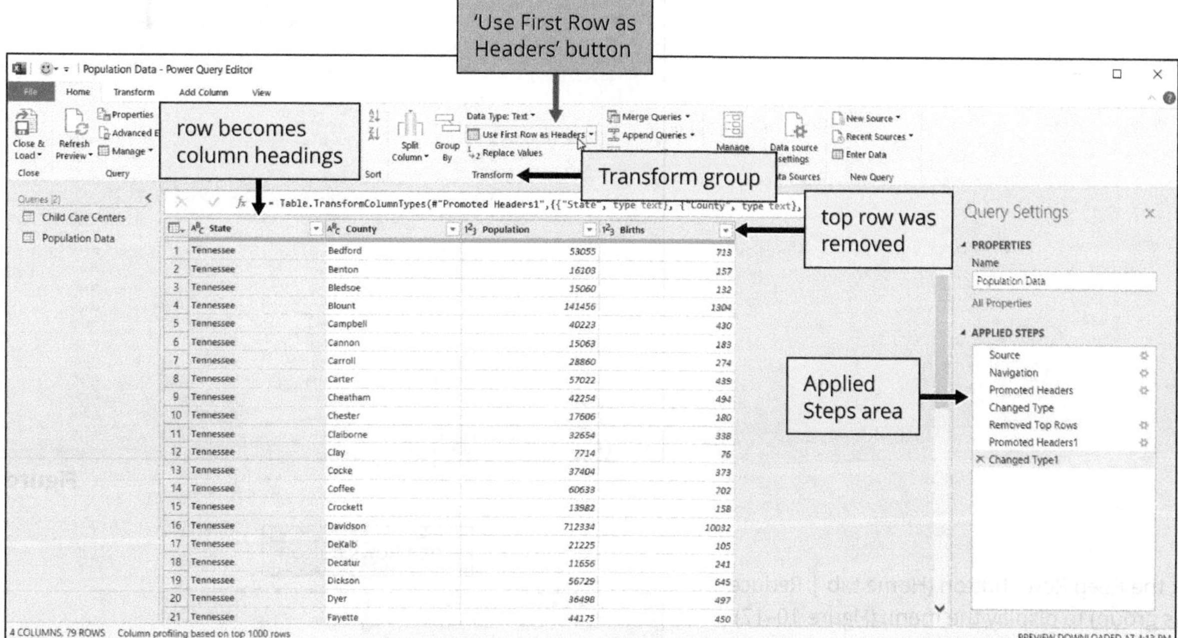

Figure 10–14

- In the third column, click the Population column filter button to display the filter menu (Figure 10–15).

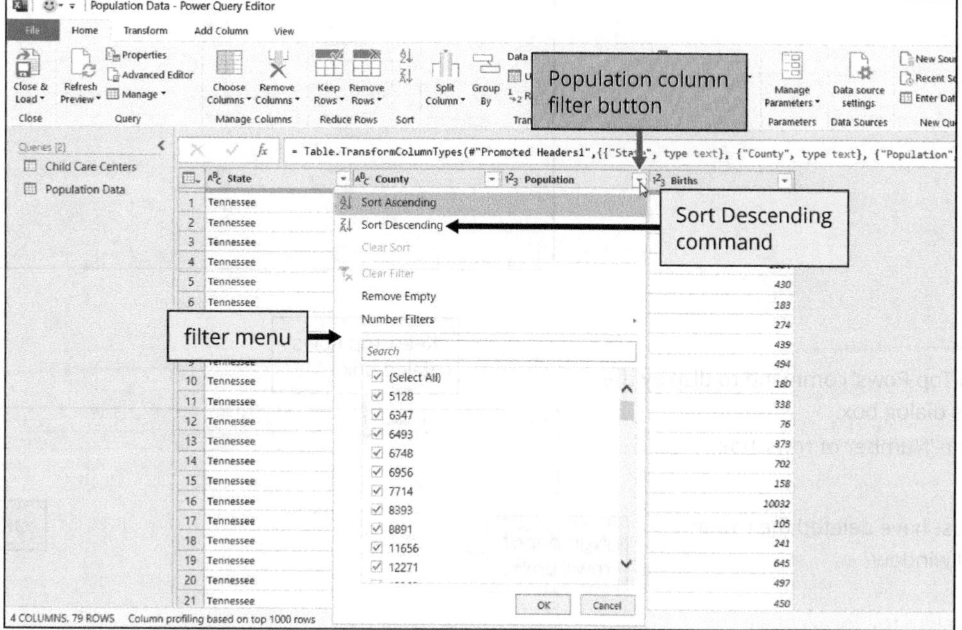

Figure 10–15

5

- On the filter menu, click Sort Descending to sort the data in order by population with the most populous county first (Figure 10–16).

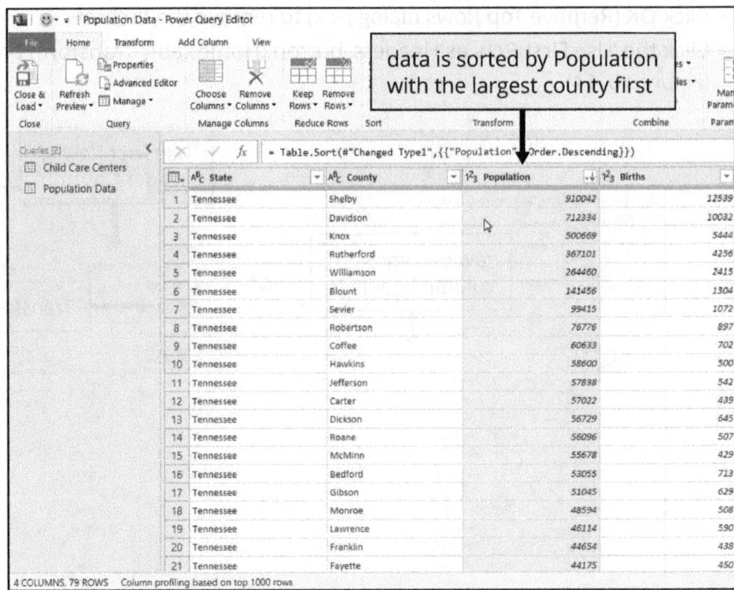

Figure 10–16

6

- Click the Keep Rows button (Home tab | Reduce Rows group) to display the menu (Figure 10–17).

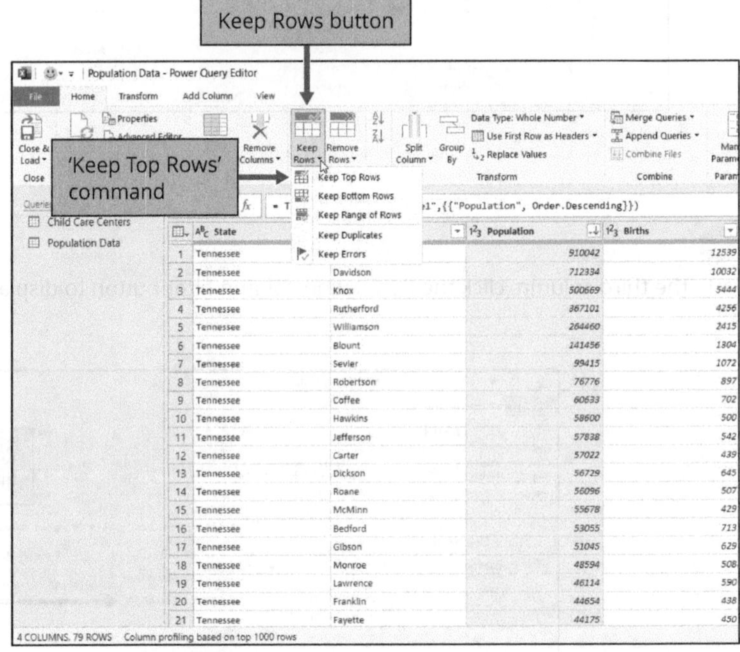

Figure 10–17

7

- Click the 'Keep Top Rows' command to display the Keep Top Rows dialog box.
- Type **10** in the 'Number of rows' box (Figure 10–18).

Q&A Could I just have deleted the row in the main Excel window?

You could have; however, that would permanently delete the local copy of the data. By using the Power Query Editor, you can restore the data if you need it later. The first row is the title of the imported worksheet; it is not part of the data itself.

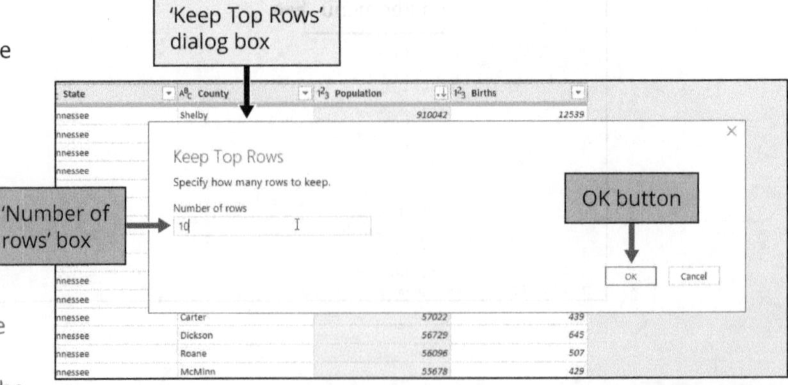

Figure 10–18

8

- Click OK (Keep Top Rows dialog box) to return to the Power Query Editor window (Figure 10–19).

Q&A What happens if my data source data moves?
If you suspect that your source data has moved, display the Power Query Editor window and then click the Refresh Preview button (Power Query Editor window | Home tab | Query group). If an error message appears, click the 'Go To Error' button, click the Edit Details button, and then navigate to the new location of the file. When your table appears, click the final step in the Applied Steps area. You may have to click the Expand Data filter button in the Data column and remove extraneous columns.

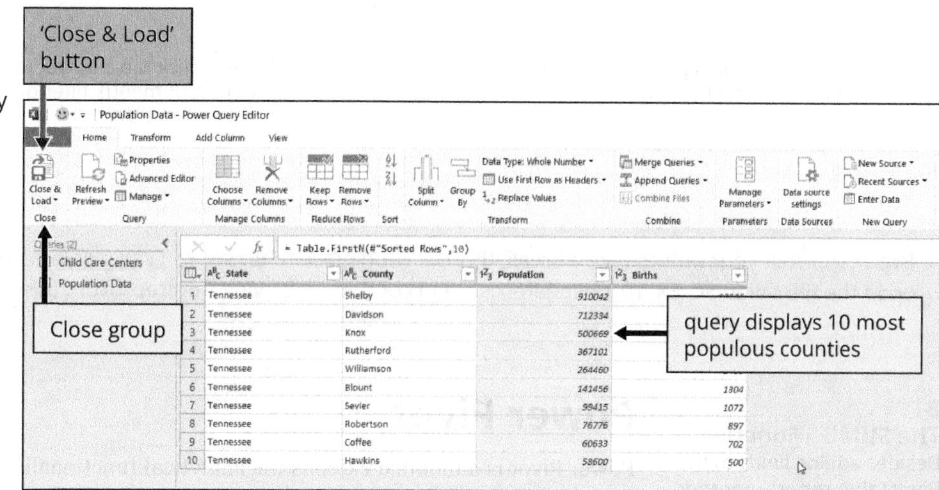

Figure 10–19

9

- Click the 'Close & Load' button (Home tab | Close group) to load the transformed data into the worksheet in the Excel window.
- Rename the sheet tab, entering **10 Most Counties** as the new name.
- Recolor the sheet tab with the color Blue, Accent 5 in the Theme colors (Figure 10–20). If Blue, Accent 5 is not displayed in the Theme colors, choose the available Accent 5 color, the second option from the right in the top row of Theme colors.
- Save the workbook.

Q&A What is the new tab on the ribbon?
It is the Query tab (displayed in Figure 10–20), which allows you to make additional queries easily. The tab appears when you click anywhere in the data itself.

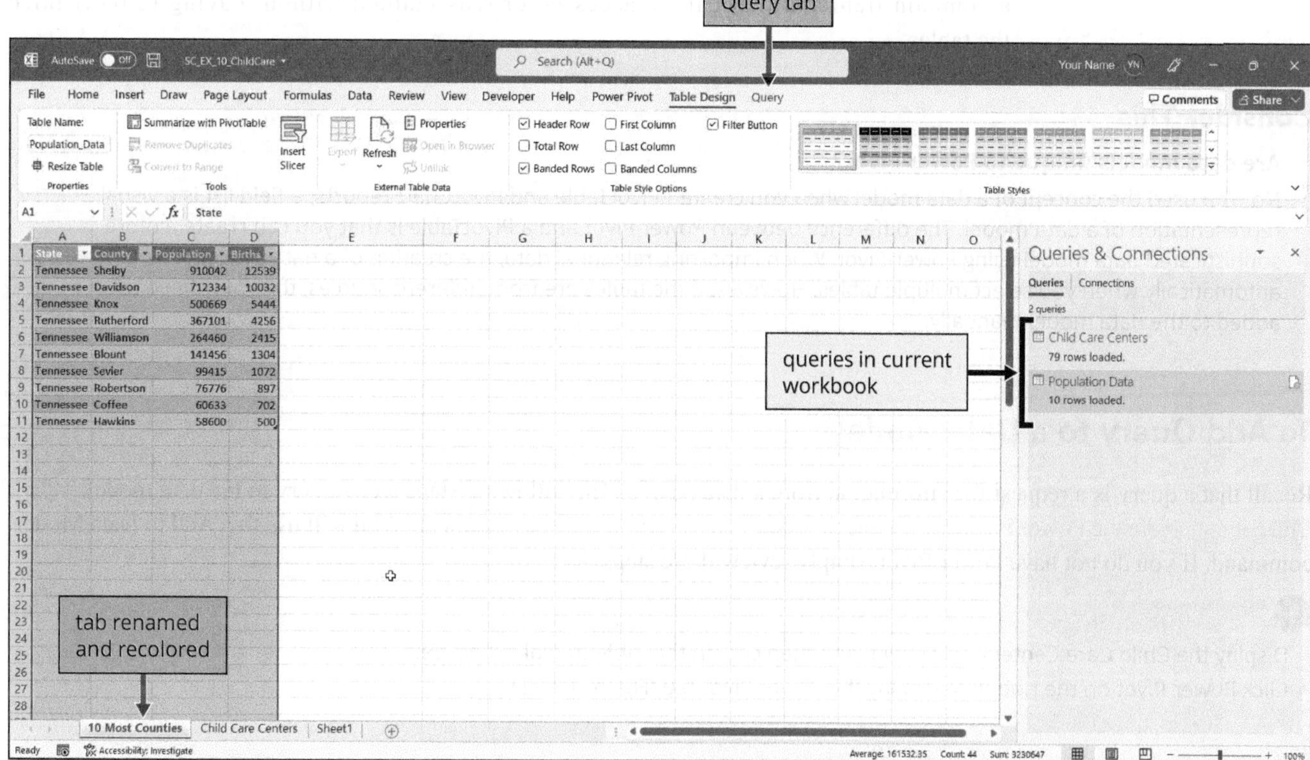

Figure 10–20

Other Ways

1. Click Edit button (Query tab | Edit group), filter data, edit columns and rows, click 'Close & Load' button
2. Right-click table in Queries & Connections pane, click Edit (shortcut menu), filter data, edit columns and rows, click 'Close & Load' button

Break Point: If you want to take a break, this is a good place to do so. You can exit Excel now. To resume later, start Excel, open the file called SC_EX_10_ChildCare.xlsx, and continue following the steps from this location forward.

BTW
The SUMIFS Function
Besides adding fields to the PivotTable report, another way to find multi-criteria sums is to use the SUMIFS function with arguments of range, criteria, range, criteria, etc.

Power Pivot

Power Pivot is a tool that extends the analytical functionality of PivotTables in Excel. It includes the capability of combining data from multiple data sources into one PivotTable. Valued as a business intelligence (BI) tool by the business community, Power Pivot especially is helpful when analyzing large, complex sets of related tables. Using Power Pivot, you can import some or all of the tables from a relational database into Excel in order to analyze the data using PivotTables and the enhanced features.

Data Models

Power Pivot, along with the other power tools, provides data modeling capability to help you explore, analyze, and manage your data. Data modeling is the process of creating a model, simulation, or small-scale representation of data and the relationships among pieces of data. Data modeling often includes multiple ways to display the same data and ensure that all data and processes are identified. A **data model** documents the processes and events to capture and translate complex data into easy-to-understand information. It is an approach for integrating data from multiple tables, effectively building a relational database inside Excel. A **relational database** consists of a collection of tables that can be joined through a common field and that can be accessed or reassembled without having to reorganize the tables.

Consider This

Are data models unique to Power Pivot?

No. You used the concept of a data model when you created PivotTable and PivotChart reports; a field list is a visual representation of a data model. The difference between Power Pivot and a PivotTable is that you can create a more sophisticated data model using Power Pivot. When importing relational data, the creation of a data model occurs automatically when you select multiple tables. However, if the tables are from different sources, they may have to be added to the data model manually.

To Add Query to a Data Model

Recall that a query is a request for information from a data source. The following steps add a query to the data model. **Why?** You cannot create the Power Pivot PivotTable unless queries are added to the data model. You will use the 'Add to Data Model' command. If you do not have Power Pivot, simply review these steps.

- Display the Child Care Centers worksheet, and then click in the table to make it active.
- Click Power Pivot on the ribbon to display the Power Pivot tab (Figure 10–21).

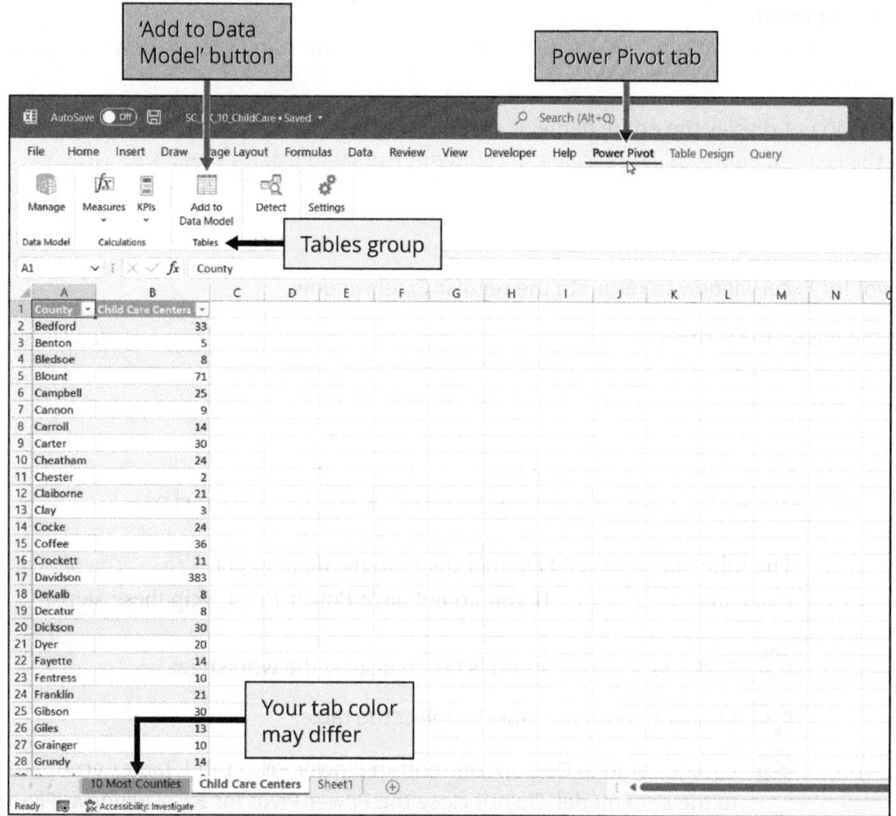

Figure 10–21

2

- Click the 'Add to Data Model' button (Power Pivot tab | Tables group) to add the data on the current worksheet to the data model and to display the Power Pivot for Excel window. Maximize the window, if necessary (Figure 10–22).

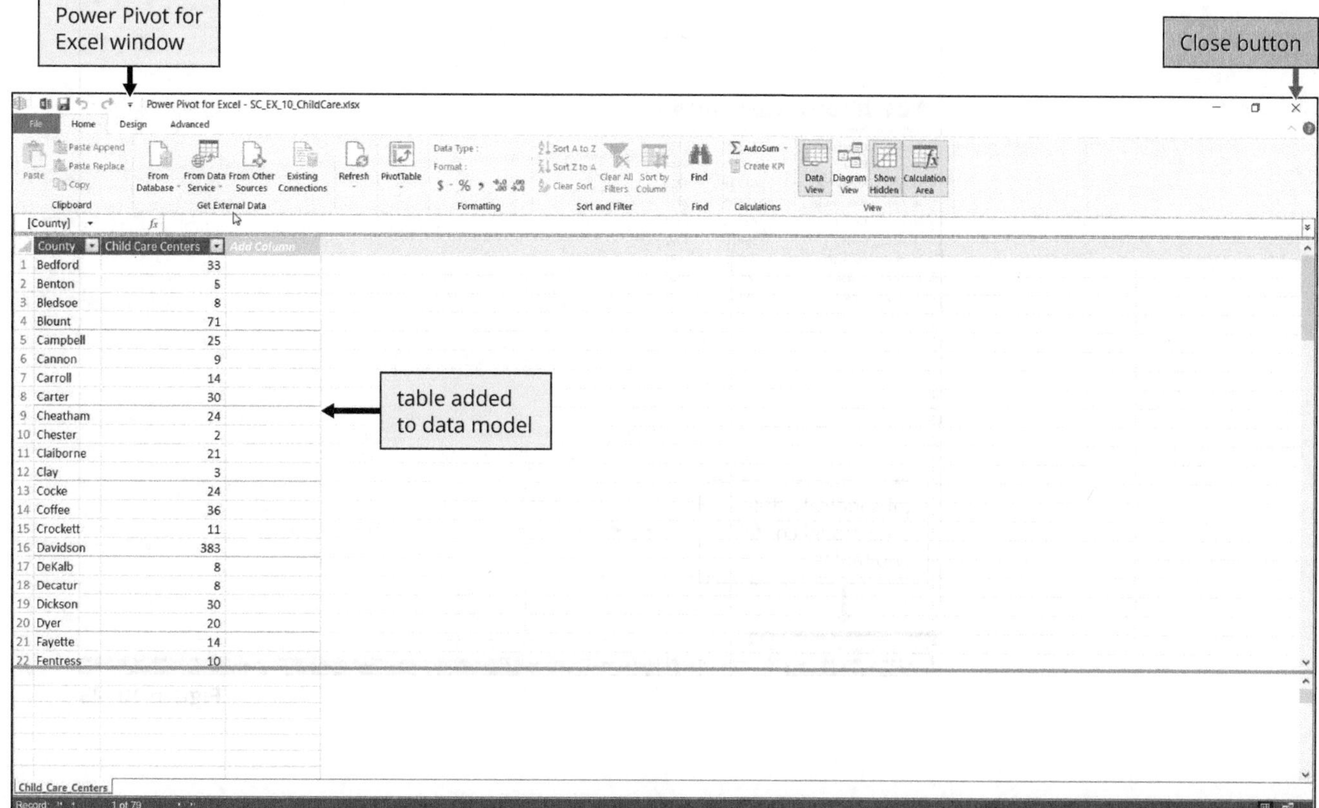

Figure 10–22

Q&A What window is displayed?
Excel displays the maximized Power Pivot for Excel window that contains tabs and groups used when working with multiple tabs from multiple sources.

My columns headings do not display the entire name. Is that a problem?
No. You can widen the column, however, by dragging the column heading border to the right.

- Close the Power Pivot for Excel window to return to the regular Excel window.

Q&A Did anything change on the screen?
No, but behind the scenes Excel added the file to the data model.

To Add Another Query to the Data Model

The following steps add another query to the data model. **Why?** You also need to add the population table to the model. **If you do not have Power Pivot, skip these steps.**

1. Click the 10 Most Counties tab to display the worksheet.
2. Click any cell in the table to select the table.
3. Click the 'Add to Data model' button (Power Pivot tab | Tables group) to add a second query to the data model. Do not close the Power Pivot for Excel window (Figure 10–23).

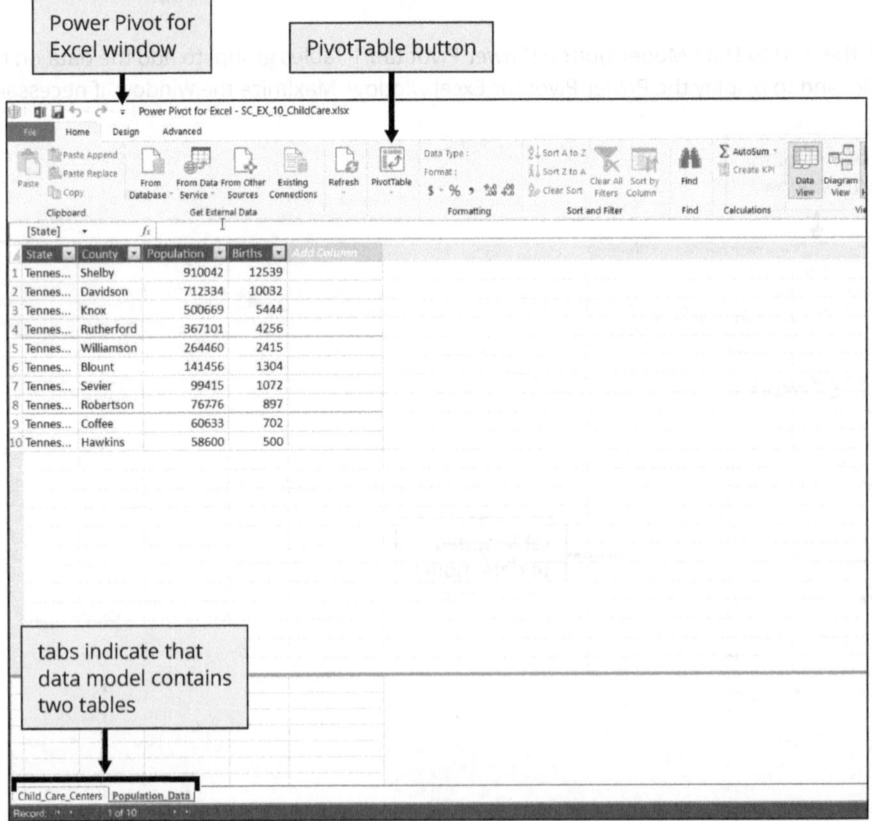

Figure 10–23

To Build a PivotTable Using Power Pivot

The following steps create a PivotTable using Power Pivot, based on the two queries. **Why?** Using Power Pivot provides you with the most flexibility and functionality when building a PivotTable. Once created, you can update a Power Pivot PivotTable in the same way you update regular PivotTables. Simply click the Refresh button (Power PivotTable Analyze tab | Data group). If you do not have access to Power Pivot, you can create a regular PivotTable report.

- With the Power Pivot for Excel window still open, select any cell in the Population Data table, and then click the PivotTable button (Power Pivot for Excel | PivotTable group) to display the Create PivotTable dialog box.
- If necessary, click the New Worksheet option button to select it (Figure 10–24).

Q&A Can I make a PivotTable without Power Pivot?
Yes. Click the PivotTable button (Insert tab | Tables group). In the Create PivotTable dialog box, click to display a check mark in the 'Add this data to the Data Model' check box.

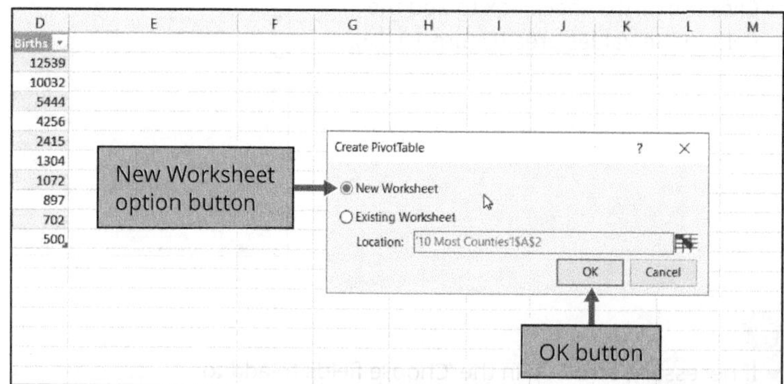

Figure 10–24

2

- Click OK (Create PivotTable dialog box) to create a PivotTable on a new sheet and to display the PivotTable Fields pane (Figure 10–25).
- Close the Queries & Connections pane, if necessary

Q&A Why do I not have access to both of my tables?
You may not have all fields displayed. To remedy this, in the PivotTable Fields pane, click the All tab.

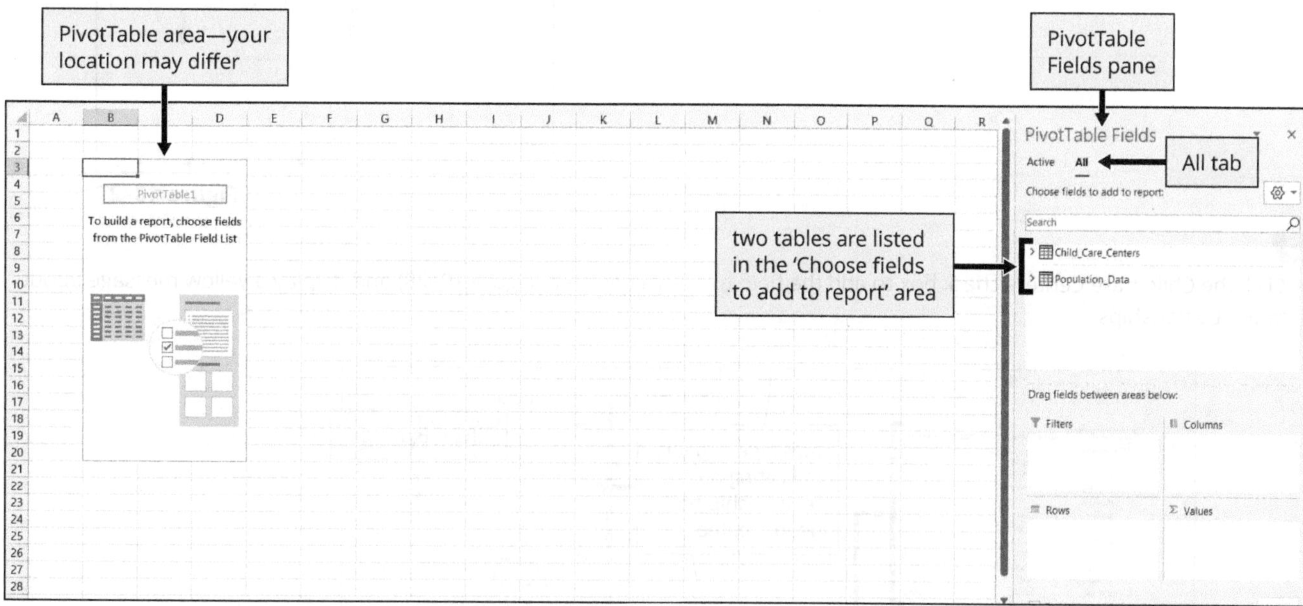

Figure 10–25

- In the PivotTable Fields pane, click Population_Data to display the fields from the query table.
- Click the check boxes beside State and County to add the fields to the Rows area.
- Click the Births check box to add the field to the Values area (Figure 10–26).

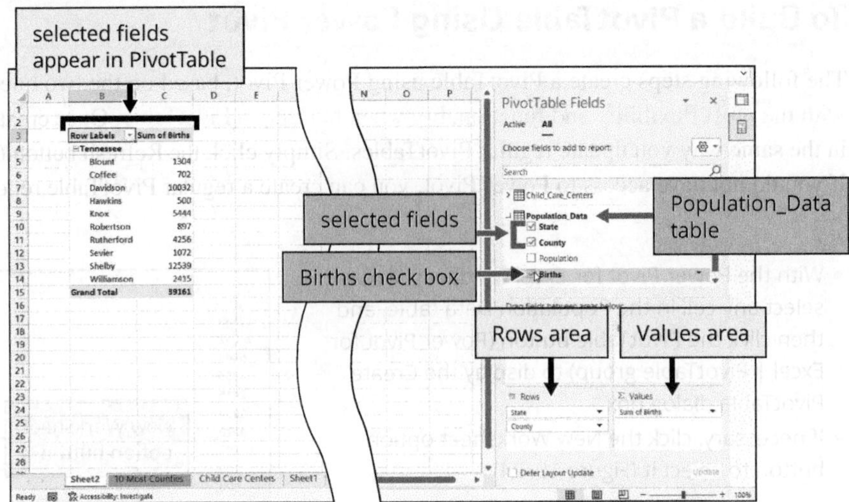

Figure 10–26

- If necessary, scroll up in the 'Choose fields to add to report' area (PivotTable Fields pane) and then click Child_Care_Centers to display the fields from the query (Figure 10–27).

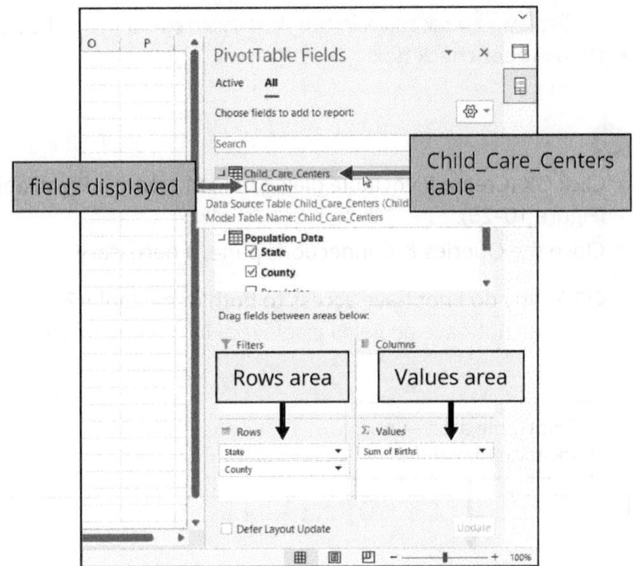

Figure 10–27

- Click the Child Care Centers check box to add the field to the Values area (Figure 10–28) and display a yellow message about table relationships.

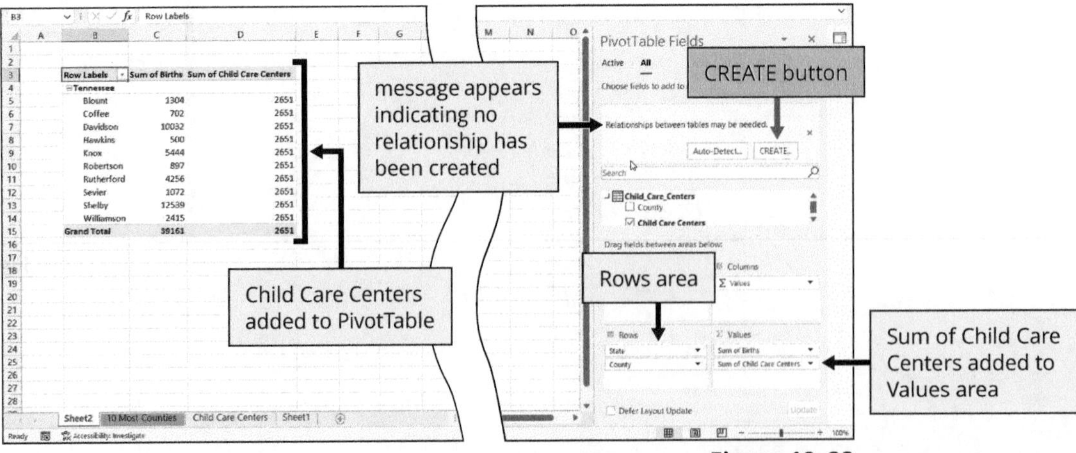

Figure 10–28

Q&A Why do all of the counties have the same number of child care centers?

The PivotTable does not associate the child care centers with the counties automatically. You will create that relationship in the next series of steps.

To Create a Relationship

A **relationship** is a field or column that two data sources have in common. For example, a payroll file and a human resource file might each have a field named employee_number. Sometimes that field is named identically in the two files and has the same number of rows; other times the name is different. One file might use the field name last_name and another file might call it LastName. Those two fields would have to be manually associated.

When the number of rows is different, the relationship is said to be **one-to-many**; in that case, the relationship between two tables is created by a common field that links the tables together, and one table value can have many options from another table. For example, both a client file and an employee file might have a field named salesperson. In the employee file, there is only one record for each salesperson; however, in the client file, several clients might be assigned to the same salesperson.

The following steps create a relationship using the County field. **Why?** Both query tables have a column named County.

1

- Click the CREATE button in the yellow relationships message (Figure 10–28) to display the Create Relationship dialog box (Figure 10–29).

Q&A I do not have a CREATE button, or it did not work. What should I do?

Click the Relationships button (Data tab | Data Tools) to display the Manage Relationships dialog box. Click the New button.

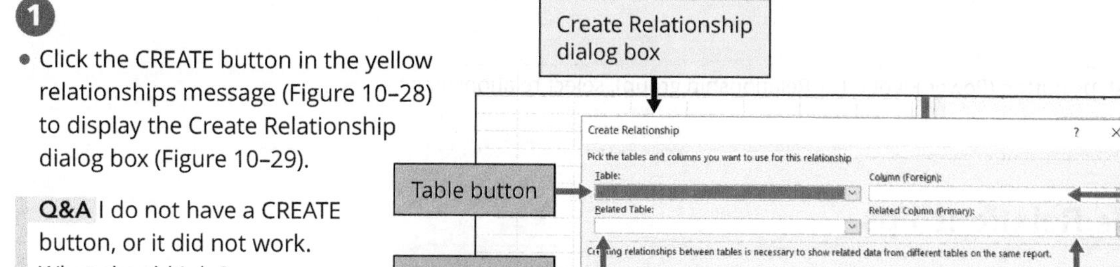

Figure 10–29

- Click the Table list arrow and then click Data Model Table: Child_Care_Centers
- Click the Related Table list arrow and then click Data Model Table: Population_Data (Figure 10–30).

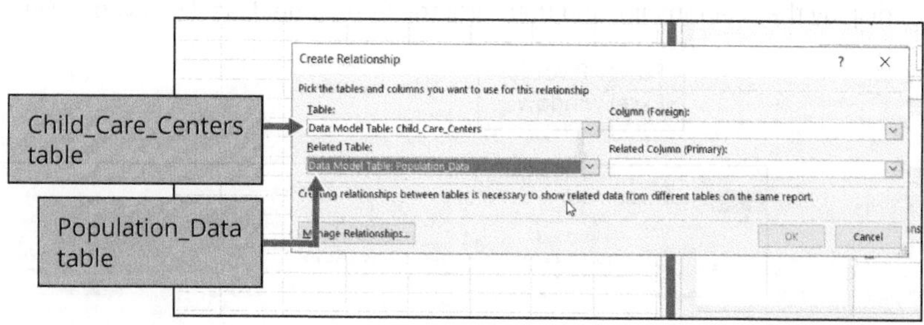

Figure 10–30

- Click the Column (Foreign) list arrow and then click County (Figure 10–31).

Q&A Why is it called a foreign column?

Foreign, or foreign key, refers to a field in one table that uniquely identifies a row in a different table. Even though the names may be the same, the field is foreign to the second table. For most Excel purposes, it does not matter which table you use for the foreign versus the primary key.

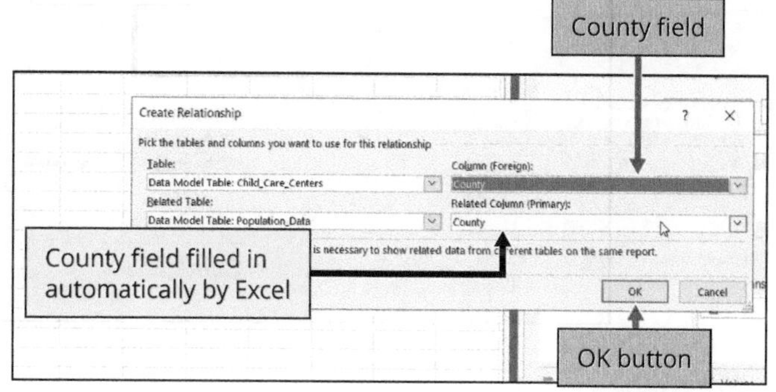

Figure 10–31

- Click OK (Create Relationship dialog box) to create the relationship between the tables and adjust the numbers in the PivotTable (Figure 10–32).

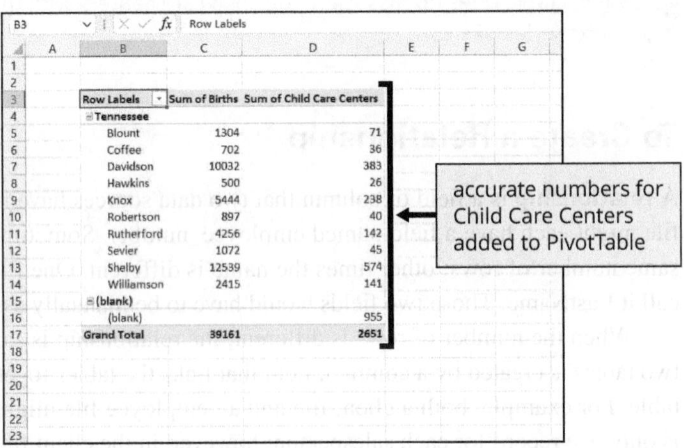

B3
Row Labels
Row Labels
Sum of Births
Sum of Child Care Centers
Tennessee
Blount 1304 71
Coffee 702 36
Davidson 10032 383
Hawkins 500 26
Knox 5444 238
Robertson 897 40
Rutherford 4256 142
Sevier 1072 45
Shelby 12539 574
Williamson 2415 141
(blank)
(blank) 955
Grand Total 39161 2651
accurate numbers for Child Care Centers added to PivotTable

Figure 10–32

Other Ways

1. Click Detect Relationships button (Power Pivot tab | Relationship group), select relationships

To Manage Table Relationships

The following steps graphically display the relationship that you created in the previous steps using the Power Pivot window. **Why?** Sometimes reviewing a picture makes the concept clearer. If you do not have Power Pivot, simply review these steps.

- Click the Manage button (Power Pivot tab | Data Model group) to make the Power Pivot for Excel window active.
- Click the Diagram View button (Home tab | View group) to access a visual display.
- If necessary, resize each of the tables to display all of the fields in each table, drag the tables by their title bars to clearly display the relationship, and then click the County field, as displayed in Figure 10–33. Your field order may differ.

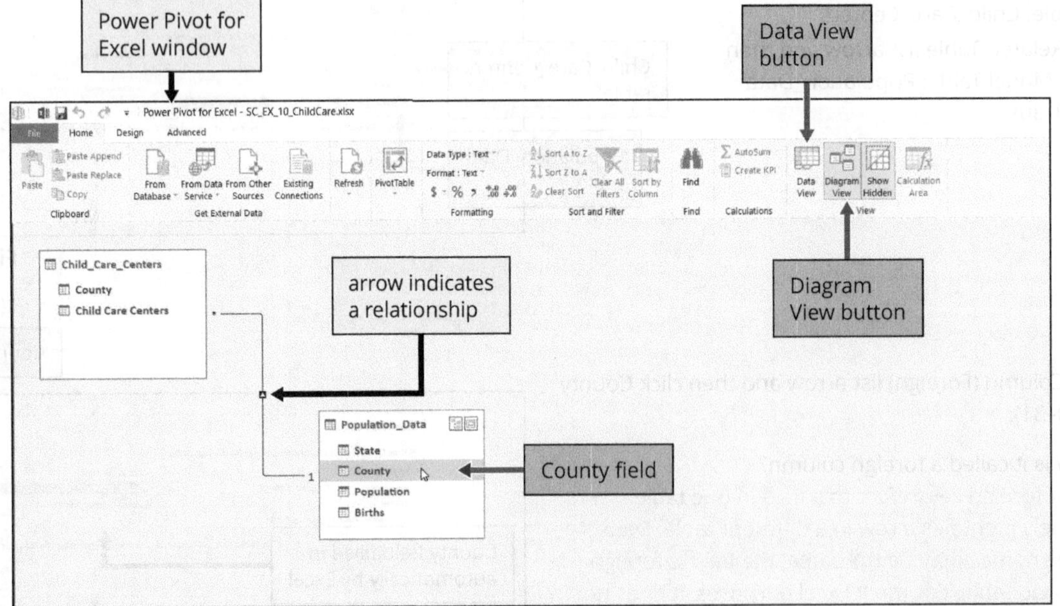

Figure 10–33

2

- Click the Data View button (Home tab | View group) to return to Data View.

To Manage Relationships You may need to add, edit, or delete relationships at some point. You can set up multiple relationships using Power Pivot. To do this, you would use the Manage Relationships command in the Power Pivot window, as demonstrated in the following steps.

1. Click the Manage button (Power Pivot tab | Data Model group) to make the Power Pivot for Excel window active.
2. Display the Design tab and then click the Manage Relationships button in the Power Pivot for Excel window (Design tab | Relationships group) to display the Manage Relationships dialog box.
3. Use the Create, Edit, and Delete buttons as needed to make changes to the selected relationship, and then click Close (Manage Relationships dialog box) to close the dialog box.
4. Minimize the Power Pivot for Excel window.

To Create a Measure

A **measure** is a calculated, named field in Power Pivot. Measures are created by a special set of functions and commands called **data analysis expressions (DAX)**. Measures have several advantages over simple formulas and other calculated fields. **Why?** With measures, you can create aggregate formulas that use one or multiple rows from multiple sources, which will adjust as you rearrange the PivotTable. You can format measures as you create them, this way, the formatting is applied globally across future elements in the PivotTable. Measures become fields in pivot field lists and can be used in multiple reports and across multiple worksheets. In regular PivotTables, you cannot create calculated fields using multiple data sources.

The following steps create a measure to calculate the average number of births per child care center for the 10 most populated counties. If you do not have Power Pivot, simply review these steps.

- If necessary, minimize the Power Pivot for Excel window.
- Click any cell in the Sum of Births column and then click the Measures button (Power Pivot tab | Calculations group) to display the menu (Figure 10–34).

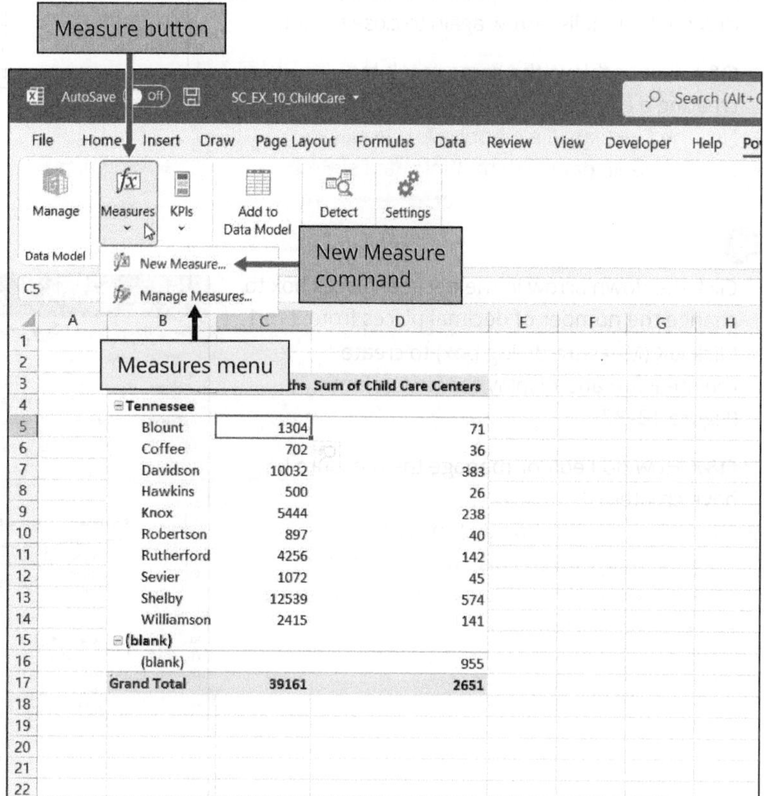

Figure 10–34

- Click New Measure in the Measures menu to display the Measure dialog box. If necessary, click the Table name list arrow and then click Population_Data in the list.
- In the Measure name box, select any default text and then type **Average Births per Center** to name the column.
- In the Description box, select any default text and then type **Average number of births per child care center** to create a description.
- In the Formula box, following the equal sign, type **[** (left bracket) to prompt Excel to display the available fields that exist in the PivotTable (Figure 10–35).

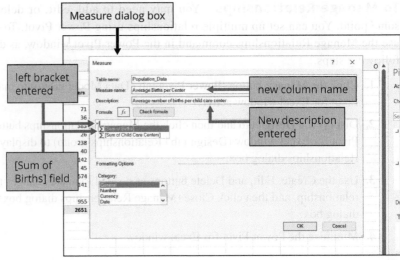

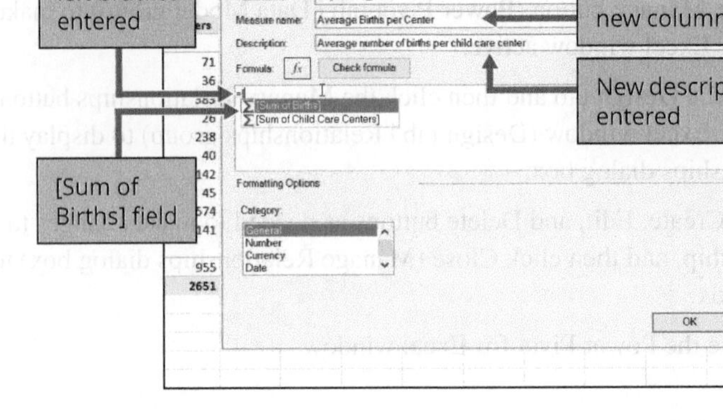

Figure 10–35

- Double-click the [Sum of Births] field to insert it into the formula.
- Type **/[** to enter the division symbol and to display again the available fields.
- Double-click the [Sum of Child Care Centers] field to insert it into the formula.
- In the Category box, click Number (Figure 10–36).
- **Experiment:** Click the Format list arrow and then check out the various number formats that are available. When you are finished, click the Format list arrow again to close the list.

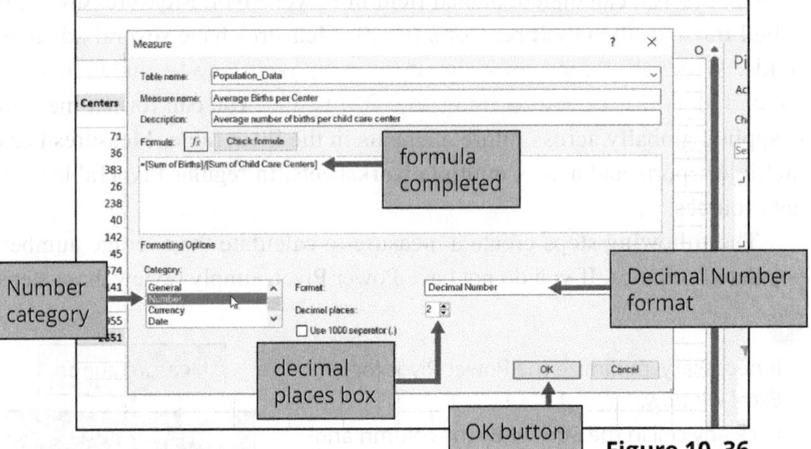

Figure 10–36

Q&A Can I achieve the same result by creating a calculated field in the PivotTable?
No. The Calculate Field option is unavailable for PivotTable data with multiple data sources.

- Click the down arrow in the decimal places box to change the number of decimal places from 2 to 1.
- Click OK (Measure dialog box) to create the measure and display the new column (Figure 10–37).

Q&A How do I edit or manage the measure I have created?
Click the Measures button (Power Pivot tab | Calculations group) to display the Manage Measures dialog box. Then select the measure and click the Edit button.

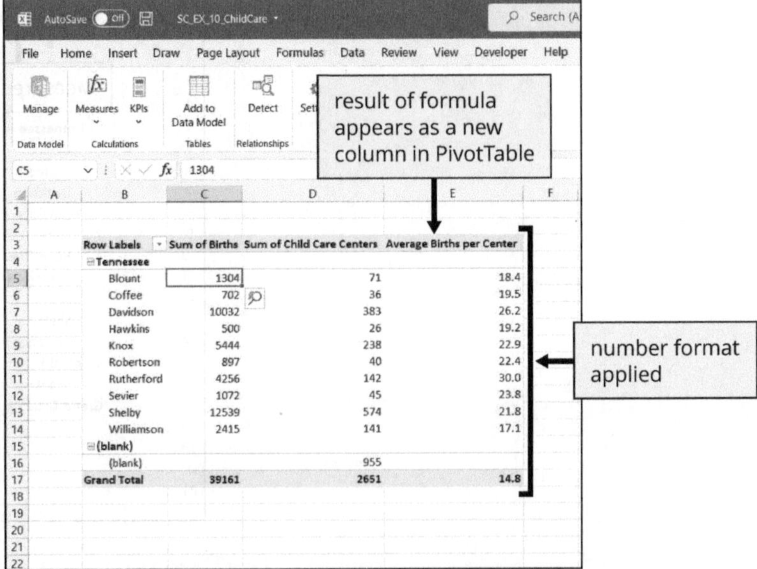

Row Labels	Sum of Births	Sum of Child Care Centers	Average Births per Center
Tennessee			
Blount	1304	71	18.4
Coffee	702	36	19.5
Davidson	10032	383	26.2
Hawkins	500	26	19.2
Knox	5444	238	22.9
Robertson	897	40	22.4
Rutherford	4256	142	30.0
Sevier	1072	45	23.8
Shelby	12539	574	21.8
Williamson	2415	141	17.1
(blank)			
(blank)		955	
Grand Total	39161	2651	14.8

Figure 10–37

To Finish Formatting the PivotTable

The following steps format the other columns of numbers, insert a heading for the page, add a footnote, and save the file.

1. Right-click any number in the 'Sum of Births' column and then click Number Format on the shortcut menu to display the Format Cells dialog box.
2. In the Category area (Format Cells dialog box), click Number. Change the decimal places to 0 and then click to select the 'Use 1000 Separator (,)' check box.
3. Click OK (Format Cells dialog box) to return to the PivotTable.
4. Click cell B1. If necessary, change the font color to black (Home tab | Font group). Change the font to Calibri and the font size to 18. Type **Average Births per Child Care Center** and then press ENTER to complete the text.
5. Drag through cells B1 through E1 and then click the Merge & Center button (Home tab | Alignment group) to merge and center the title.
6. Click cell F18. Type ***blank represents counties not in the top 10** to create a footnote.
7. Rename the worksheet tab, entering **Power Pivot** as the tab name.
8. Recolor the worksheet tab with the color, Green, Accent 6 in the Theme Colors.
9. Save the file again (Figure 10–38).

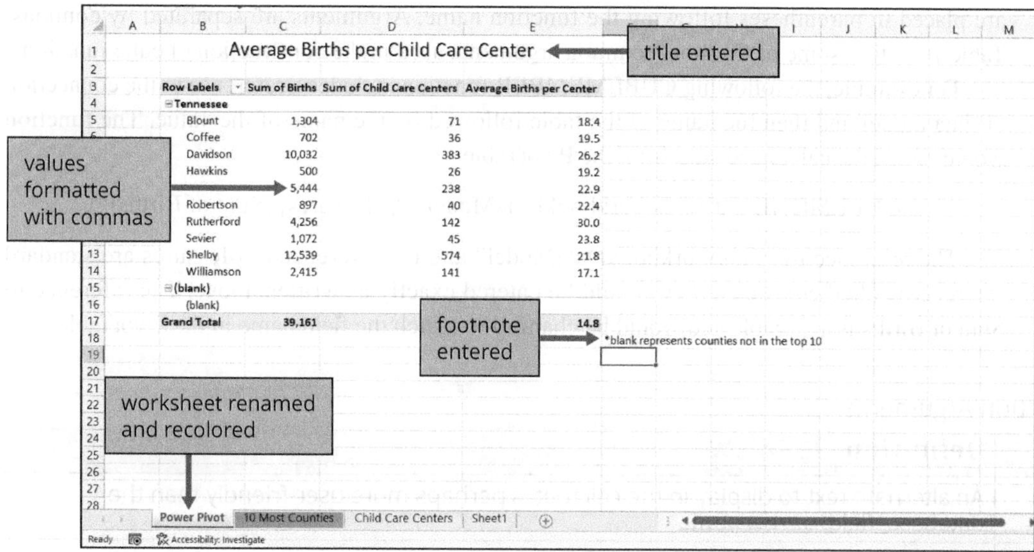

Figure 10–38

Cube Functions

Normally if you want to reference a piece of data, you use a cell reference such as B4. If the data in that cell changes, your reference will reflect that change as well. And, when you want to replicate a formula containing a reference that should not change, you use an absolute reference, such as $B$4. In PivotTables, however, neither of those cell references work. The data is prone to change dramatically, from numeric values to text values, from field to field, or even to blank. Formulas or other references to that data immediately become invalid or display errors when the data is pivoted.

The solution to that problem is to use cube functions. **Cube functions** are a set of advanced analytic functions that you can use with multidimensional data, which are also called **data cubes**. A Power Pivot report is considered a data cube because of its 3-D cube-like structure.

With a cube function, you can reference any piece of data in the PivotTable to use in formulas or in other functions or merely to display the data in other places in the workbook. The cube function will adjust automatically if you change the way your data pivots.

Table 10–2 lists the cube functions.

Table 10–2: Cube Functions

Function	Return Value	Purpose
CUBEKPIMEMBER	Returns the name of a key performance indicator (KPI)	Produces a quantifiable measure such as net income
CUBEMEMBER	Returns a member or tuple from the cube	Validates that the member or tuple exists in the cube
CUBEMEMBERPROPERTY	Returns the value of a member property from the cube	Validates that a member name exists within the cube and returns the specified property for this member
CUBERANKEDMEMBER	Returns the nth, or ranked, member in a set	Returns one or more elements in a set, such as the top salesperson or the top 10 athletes
CUBESET	Defines a set of members by sending an expression to the cube	Identifies sets for use in other cube functions
CUBESETCOUNT	Returns the number of items in a set	Finds how many entries are in a set
CUBEVALUE	Returns an aggregated value from the cube	Displays values from the cube

The cube functions use a variety of arguments in their construction. Recall that an argument refers to any piece of information that the function needs in order to do its job. Arguments are placed in parentheses following the function name. Arguments are separated by commas. Table 10–3 lists some of the most common arguments used in the construction of cube functions.

For example, the following CUBEMEMBER function includes a reference to the connection or data model and then the name of the table followed by the name of the value. The function would return the calculated sum from the PivotTable.

=CUBEMEMBER("ThisWorkbookDataModel","[Measures].[Sum of Births]")

The reference to "ThisWorkbookDataModel" and the reference to Measures are standard references called constants; they should be entered exactly as written above. The reference to Sum of Births is a variable and would be changed to match the field name in the PivotTable.

Table 10–3: Cube Function Arguments

Argument	Definition
Caption or property	An alternate text to display in the cell that is perhaps more user-friendly than the database, field, or row name
Connection	Names the table, query, or data model
Key performance indicator (KPI)	A quantifiable measurement, such as net profit, used to monitor performance
Measures	A pivot calculation such as sum, average, minimum, or maximum
Member expression	Uses database field-like references to the data rather than cell references
Rank	An integer to represent which piece of data to return in an ordered list
Set	A string to represent a set of values that has been defined or returned by another cube function
Sort by	A field name to sort by when a function returns a set of values
Sort order	An integer to represent how the data should be ordered when a function returns a set of values
Tuple	A row of values in a relational database

To Display Cube Functions

The following steps use the 'Convert to Formulas' command. **Why?** The command converts the cells in a Power Pivot report or a PivotTable report to cube references, allowing you to access the functions behind the scenes.

- Click cell E3 in the Power Pivot PivotTable.
- Display the PivotTable Analyze tab.
- Click the OLAP Tools button (PivotTable Analyze tab | Calculations group) to display the menu (Figure 10–39).

Q&A What does OLAP stand for?
OLAP stands for Online Analytical Processing, which is an advanced analytic tool to assist users in data warehousing and data mining, especially with multidimensional data such as a PivotTable with two outside sources.

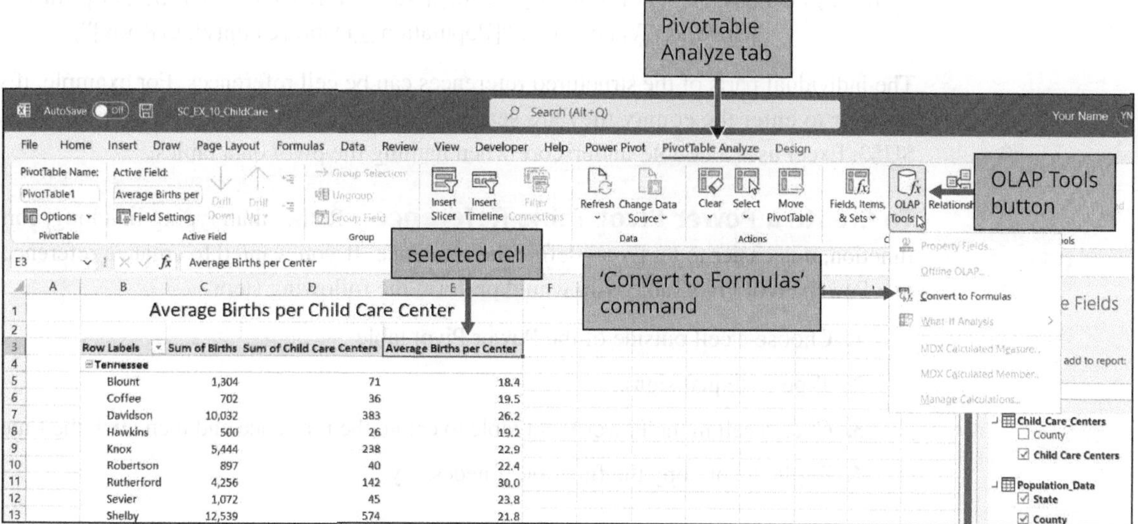

Figure 10–39

- Click 'Convert to Formulas' on the OLAP Tools menu to display the cube function in the formula bar (Figure 10–40).
- **Experiment:** Click various cells in the table, including the row and column headings, while paying attention to the formula bar. Note the various cube functions that make up the PivotTable.

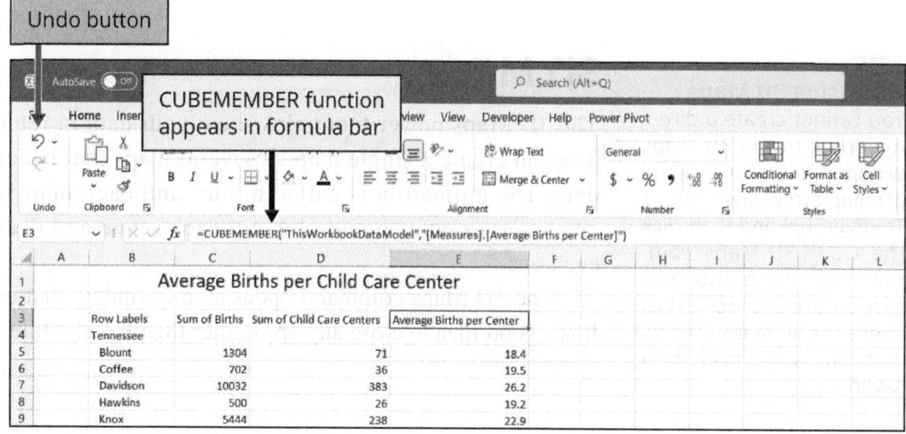

Figure 10–40

- Click the Undo button on the Quick Access Toolbar to undo the Convert to Formulas command.
- Save the file.

The GETPIVOTDATA function

Another way to access data in a PivotTable is to use the GETPIVOTDATA function. The function takes the following arguments:= GETPIVOTDATA (data field, location of pivot table, search field, search item)

In a regular PivotTable, an example might be:

= GETPIVOTDATA ("Population", $B$3, "County", "Knox")

The specific names of the fields are in quotation marks when not referencing a cell location.

However, because the PivotTable in this module is a Power Pivot PivotTable, based on two different imported files, the reference is more complex and must include structured references to the file, field, and data, as displayed in the following:

=GETPIVOTDATA("[Population__Data].[Sum of Births]", $B$3,"[Population_Data].[State].&[Tennessee]", "[Population__Data].[County].&[Knox]")

The individual parts of the structured references can be cell references. For example, if you want the user to enter the county they are searching for in cell H3, you could replace [Knox] with $H$3. Excel uses a double-underscore when naming the pivot data tables.

To Create a Power Pivot Table Reference Rather than typing in a long, complicated function, it is easier to let Excel define the reference. If you wanted to create a reference to a cell in a Power Pivot PivotTable, you would perform the following steps.

1. Choose a cell outside of the Power Pivot table.
2. Type = (equal sign).
3. Click a cell in the Power Pivot table to create the reference and then click the Enter button.
4. Replicate or copy the function if necessary.

Break Point: If you want to take a break, this is a good place to do so. You can exit Excel now. To resume later, start Excel, open the file called SC_EX_10_ChildCare.xlsx, and continue following the steps from this location forward.

3D Maps

The 3D Maps power tool helps show your data in relation to a geographical area on a map. You can create a single map or several maps that become an animation focusing in on your data. The animation is called a tour, and each map is called a scene. If you are going to create a tour, you should plan out each scene and decide what data you want to display in each one.

The 3D Maps command opens a new window that uses a lot of your computer's resources. It is a good idea to close any apps other than Excel while working with 3D Maps.

BTW
Accessing 3D Maps
You cannot create a direct hyperlink to the 3D Maps window. You must click the 3D Map arrow (Insert tab | Tours group) and then click the 'Open 3D Maps' command on the menu. You can create a macro that opens the 3D Maps window or create a hyperlink to a saved tour.

To Open the 3D Maps Window

The following steps open the 3D Maps window. **Why?** The 3D Maps windows has the tools to create a map or tour.

- Click the Child Care Centers sheet tab, and then click anywhere within the data if necessary to select the table.
- Display the Insert tab (Figure 10–41).

Q&A Do I have to be in a specific worksheet to access 3D Maps?
No. 3D Maps can be accessed from any worksheet or window. However, if you want tables to appear in the Field List, it is best to start from a worksheet associated with the data model.

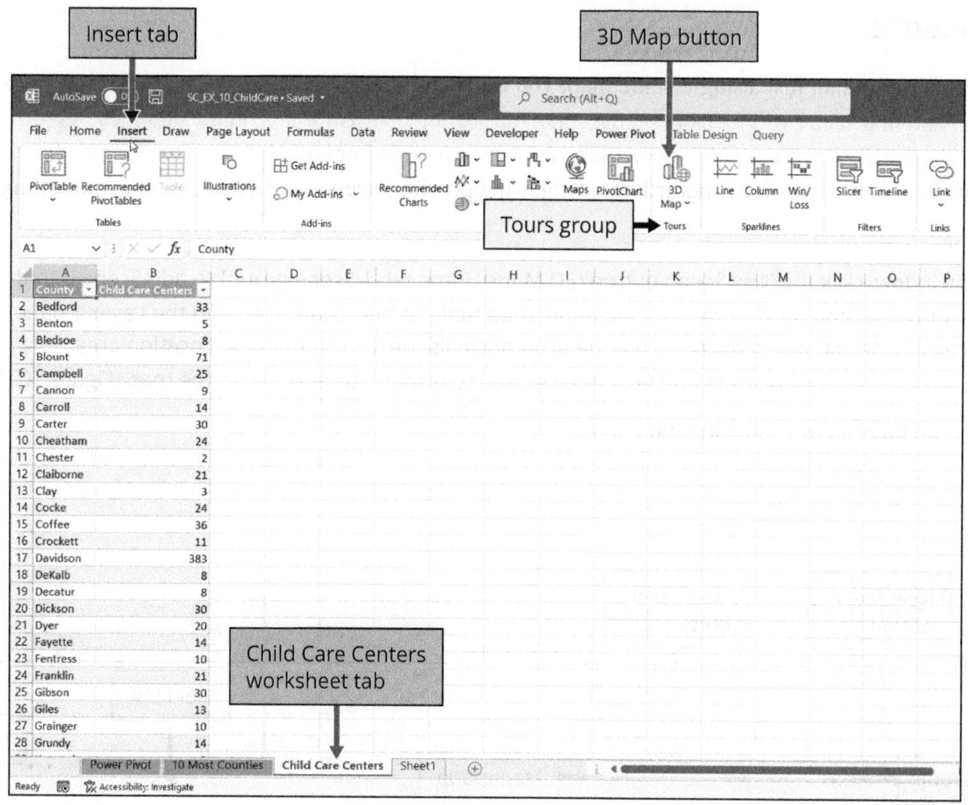

Figure 10–41

2

- Click the 3D Map button (Insert tab | Tours group) to open the 3D Maps window (Figure 10–42).

Q&A I do not have two tables in my field list. What should I do?

No. 3D Maps can be accessed from any worksheet or window. However, if you want tables to appear in the Field List, it is best to start from a worksheet associated with the data model.

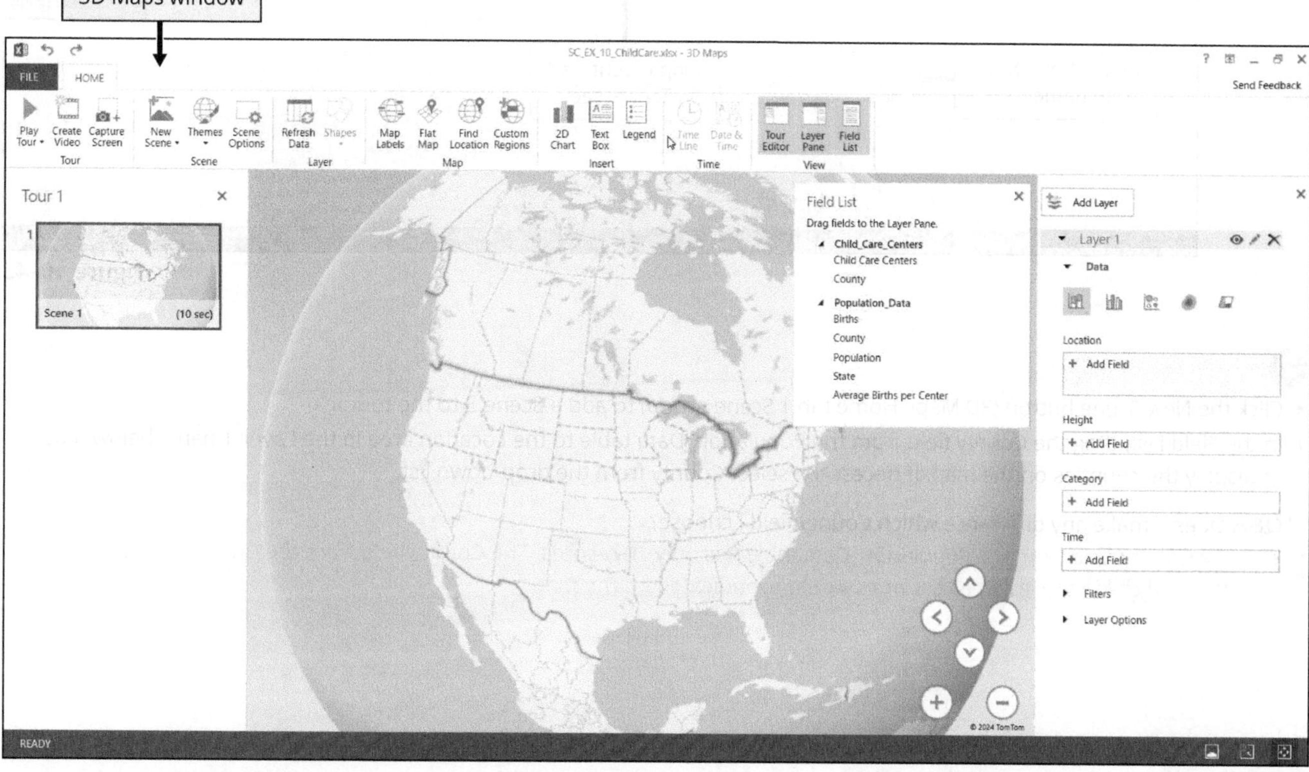

Figure 10–42

To Create Scenes

If you want to create more than just a single static map, you must add scenes to the tour. The following steps add four scenes to the tour. **Why?** The first scene will focus in on the state, the second one will focus on the counties, the third will display the population for each of the 10 most populous counties, and the fourth will annotate the chosen county for the new child care center. When you add a new scene, it temporarily duplicates the previous scene until you customize its settings.

- In the 3D Maps window, click the New Scene button (3D Maps Home tab | Scene group) to add Scene 2 to the tour.
- In the Field List, drag the State field from the Population_Data table to the Location area in the Layer 1 pane to focus in on the state. If necessary, select State/Province from the drop-down list next to State in the Location area.
- Click the Map Labels button (3D Maps Home tab | Map group) to display state labels on the map (Figure 10–43).

Q&A Does the map have its own worksheet tab in Excel?
3D Maps opens in a new window accessible only via the 3D Map button. If you close the window without saving, you will have to start over. To revisit a saved map, click the 3D Map button (Insert tab | Tours group). Excel will display a 3D Map dialog box from which you can choose the specific map you have created.

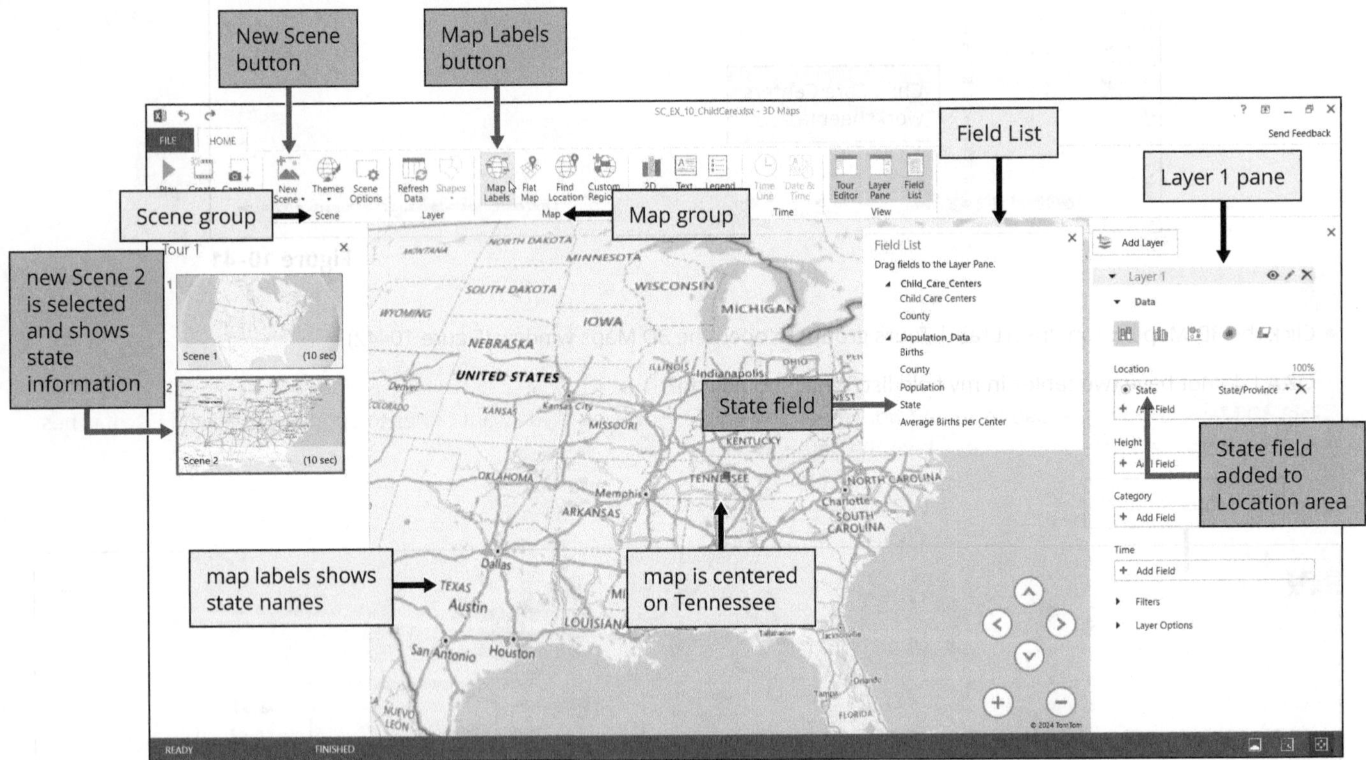

Figure 10–43

- Click the New Scene button (3D Maps Home tab | Scene group) to add a Scene 3 to the tour.
- In the Field List, drag the County field from the Population_Data table to the Location area in the Layer 1 pane, below State, to display the counties on the map. If necessary, select County from the drop-down list.

Q&A Does it make any difference which County field I choose?
Yes. The County field from the Population_Data table has only 10 records. The County field from the Child Care Centers table has 79. If you chose the latter, all counties would be indicated on the map.

- Click the Zoom in button on the map several times to zoom in on the state of Tennessee.
- If necessary, drag in the map and use the tilt buttons to better position the state so all 10 counties fit on the screen (Figure 10–44).

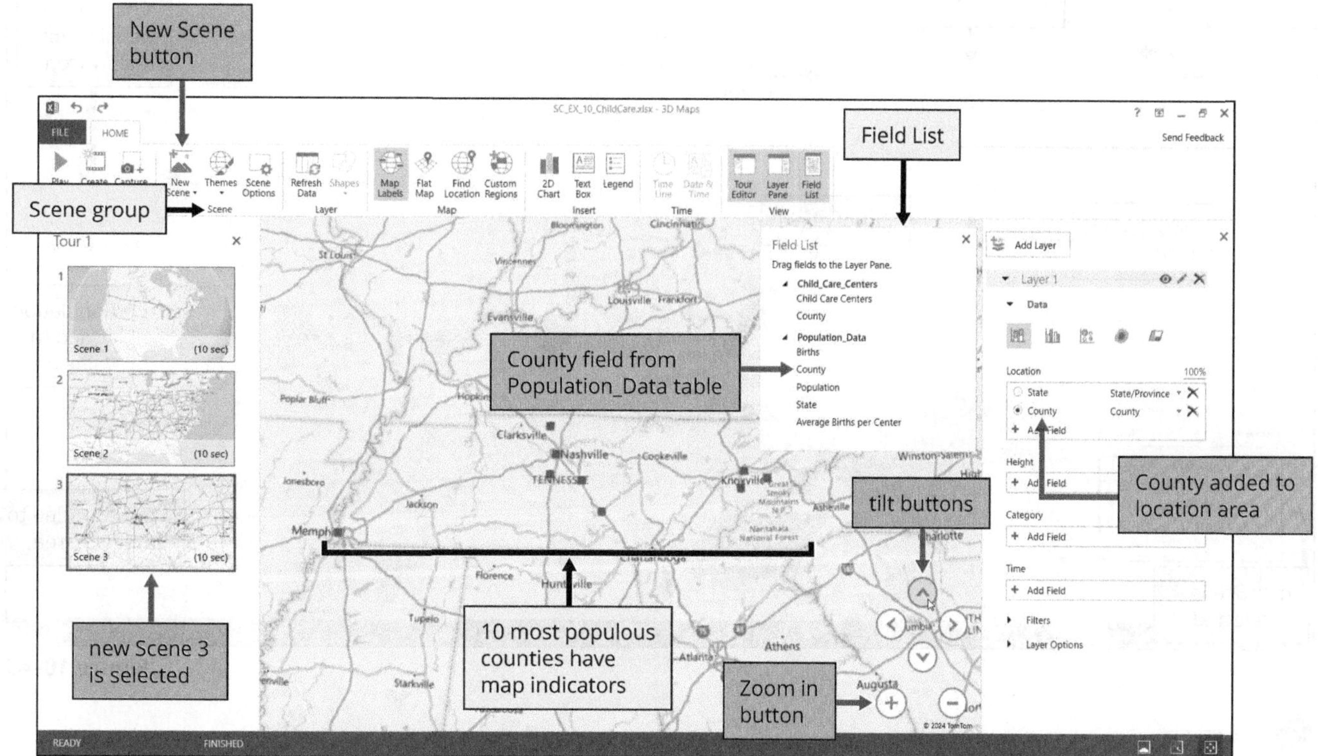

Figure 10–44

3

- Click the New Scene button (3D Maps Home tab | Scene group) to add a Scene 4 to the tour.
- Scroll as necessary in the Layer 1 pane to move to the Data icons above the Location area.
- Click the 'Change the visualization to Region' icon.
- Drag the field list to the left so it does not obscure the counties.
- **Experiment:** One at a time, click each of the icons in the Layer 1 pane and note how the map changes. When you are finished, click the 'Change the visualization to Region' icon again.

4

- In the Field List, drag the Population field from the Population_Data table to the Value area in the Layer 1 pane to change the map. If a legend appears, select the legend and then press DELETE. You may need to right-click and select Remove to delete the legend.
- In the Field List, drag the County field from the Population_Data table to the Category area in the Layer pane to change the map (Figure 10–45).
- **Experiment:** On the map itself, point to any of the colored county regions to display its data card, which lists the county name, state name, and population.

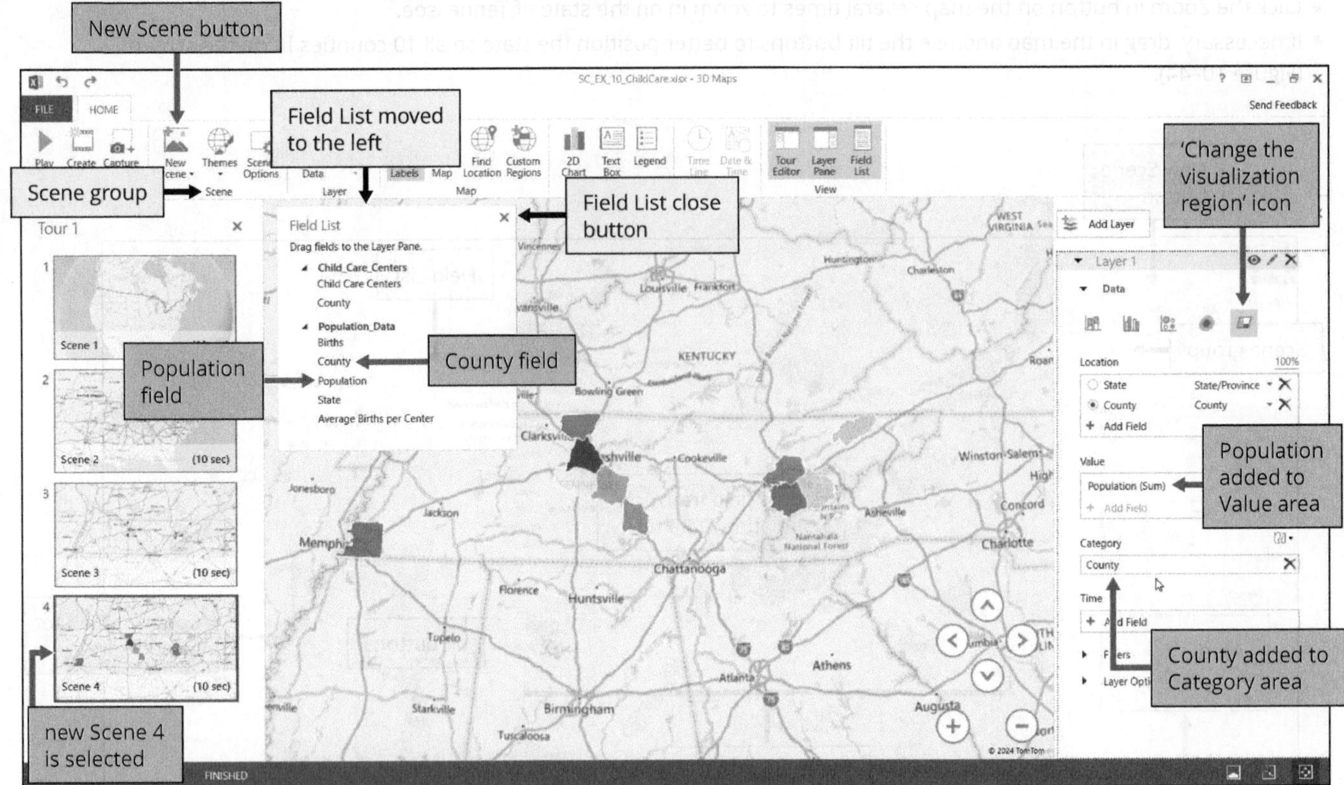

Figure 10–45

5

- Click the Field List button (3D Maps Home tab | View group) to close the Field List.
- Click the Layer Pane button (3D Maps Home tab | View group) to close the Layer 1 pane.
- Drag in the map to position the state slightly to the left of center. Make sure all the edges of the state outline are displayed.
- Click the Legend button (3D Maps Home tab | Insert group) to display the legend.
- Right-click the legend to display the shortcut menu (Figure 10–46).

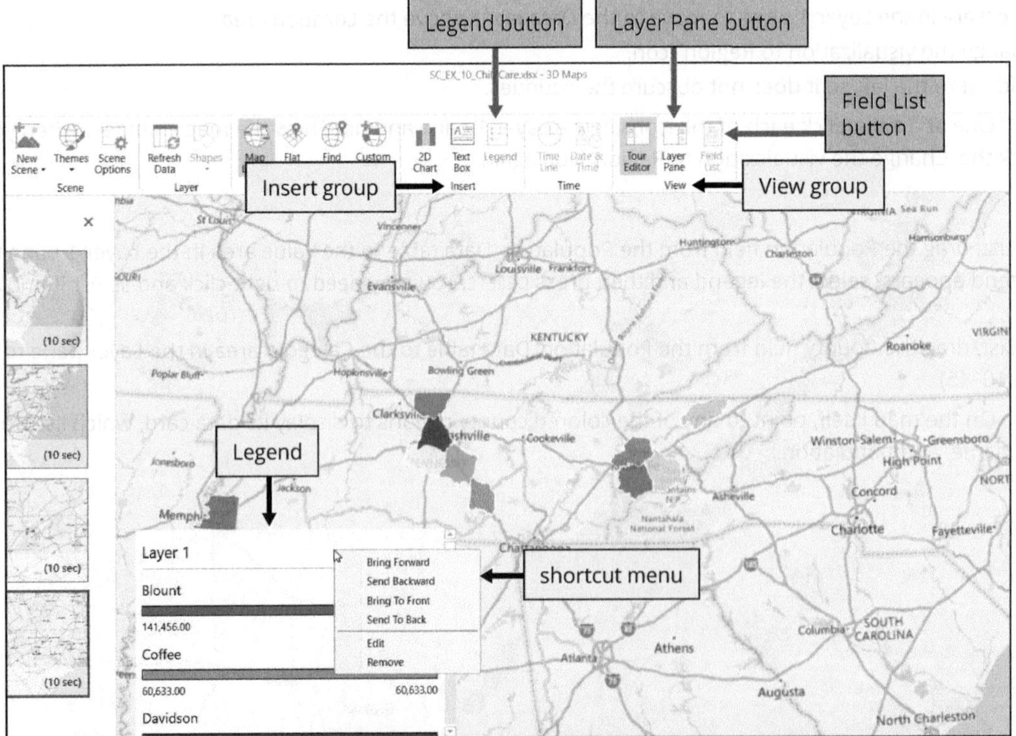

Figure 10–46

6

- Click Edit on the legend shortcut menu to display the Edit Legend dialog box.
- Click to remove the check mark in the Show Title check box.
- Change the font size of the Title to 10 and of the Categories to 8 (Figure 10–47).

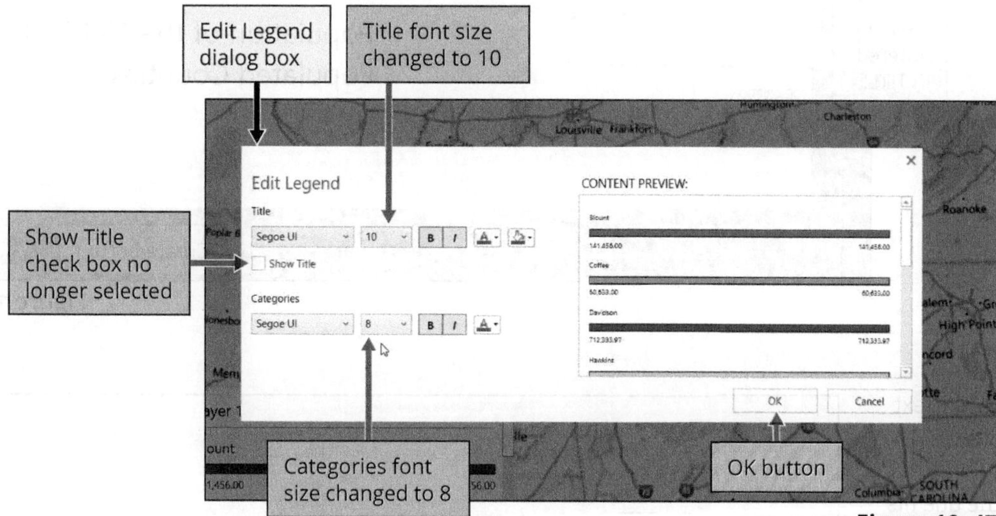

Figure 10–47

7

- Click OK (Edit Legend dialog box) to close the dialog box.
- Resize the legend to be as tall as the map itself.
- Resize the legend to make it very narrow, just wide enough to display the name of each county and population.
- Drag the legend to the far-right side of the map (Figure 10–48).

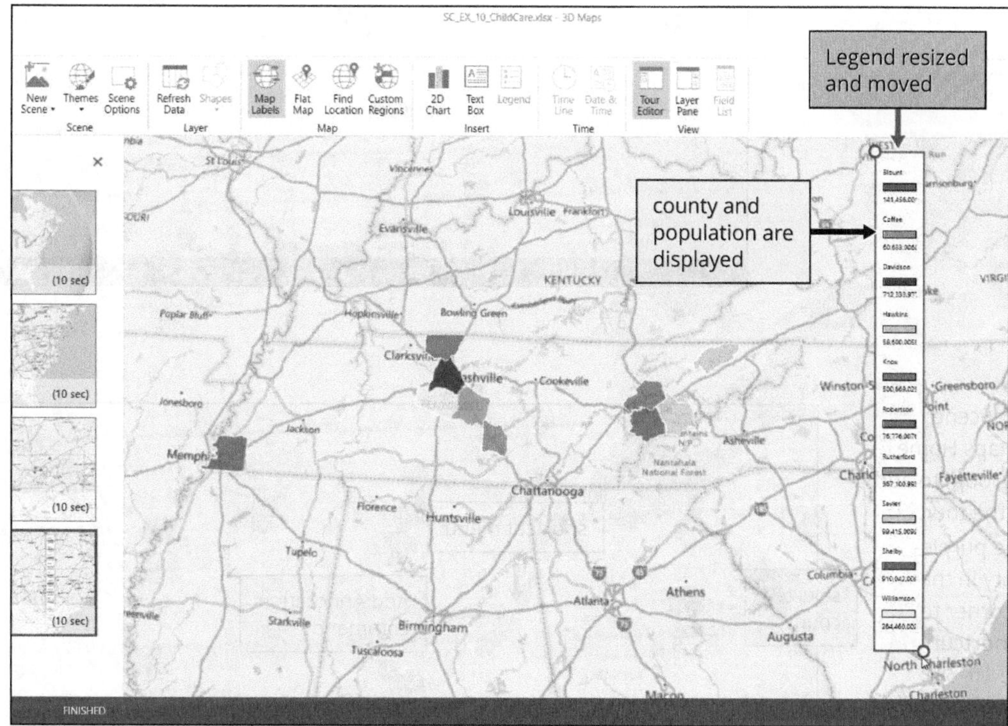

Figure 10–48

- Click the Text Box button (3D Maps Home tab | Insert group) to display the Add Text Box dialog box.
- In the TITLE box, type **Population of the 10 Most Populated Counties** to enter the title (Figure 10–49).

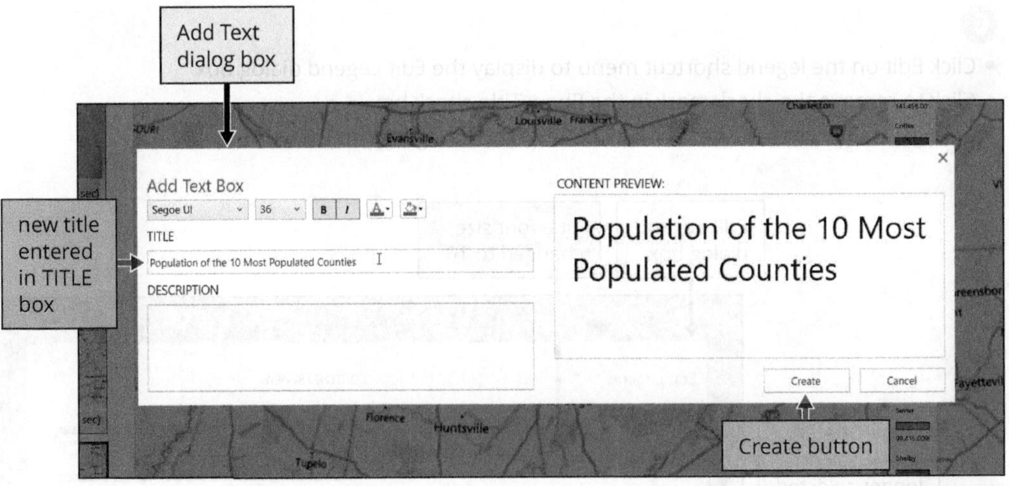

Figure 10–49

- Click the Create button (Add Text Box dialog box) to create a text box title for the map.
- Resize the text box so the title fits on one line.
- Drag the text box to the center of the map, above the state of Tennessee.
- Adjust the size of the map and center as necessary (Figure 10–50).

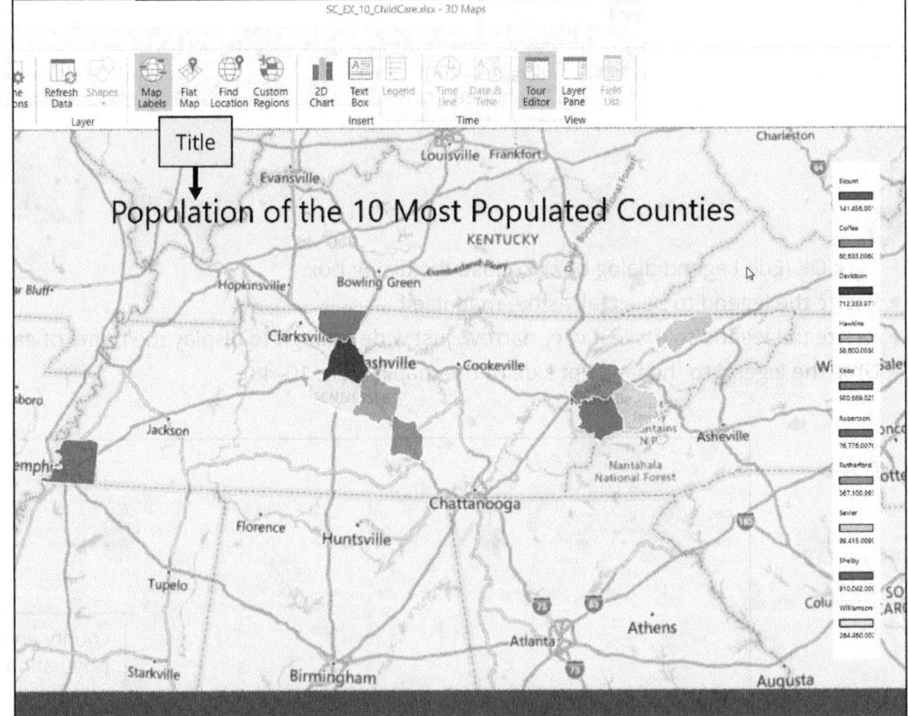

Figure 10–50

10

- Click the New Scene button (3D Maps Home tab | Scene group) to add a Scene 5 to the tour.
- Right-click the purple-colored county in the bottom-left corner to display the shortcut menu (Figure 10–51).

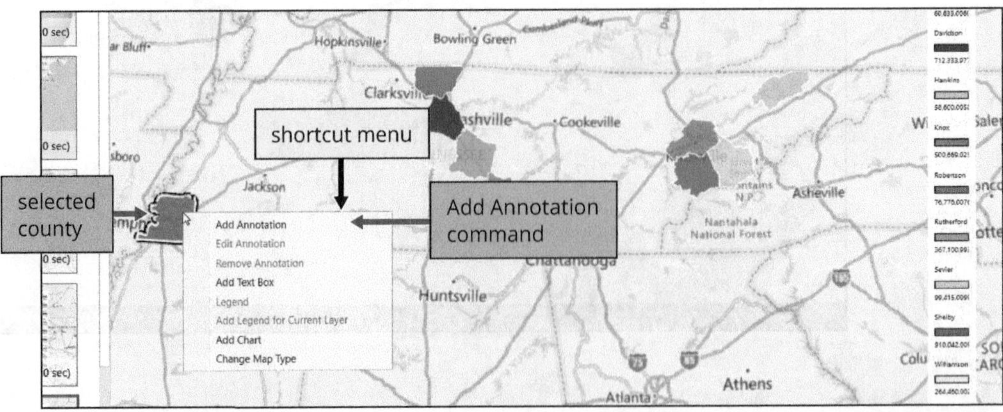

Figure 10–51

- Click Add Annotation to display the Add Annotation dialog box.
- Type **Most Populated** in the TITLE box.
- Type **SHELBY COUNTY** in the DESCRIPTION box (Figure 10–52).

Q&A What do the PLACEMENT option buttons do?
You can choose on which side of the selected item the annotation will appear.

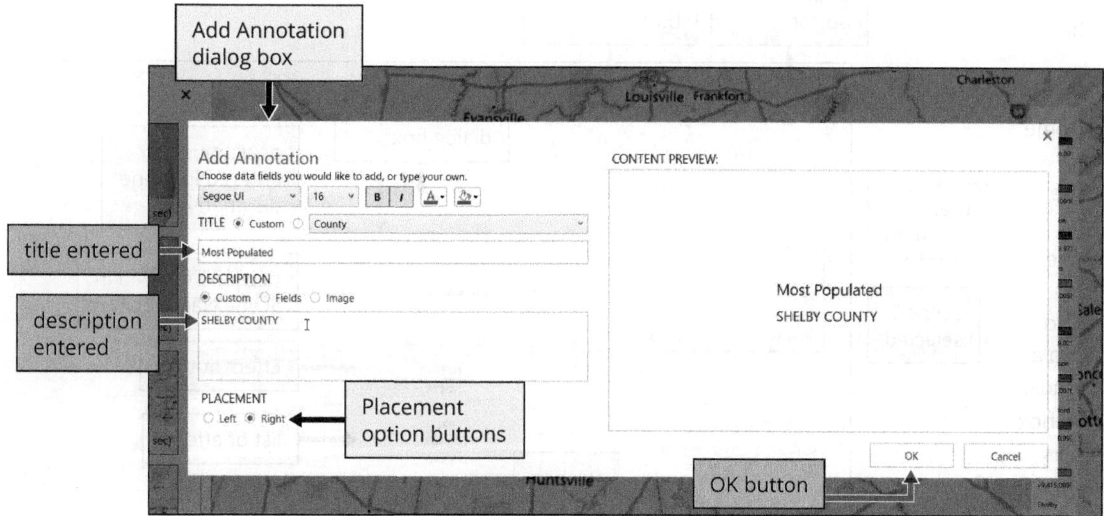

Figure 10–52

- Click OK (Add Annotation dialog box) to add the annotation to the map (Figure 10–53).

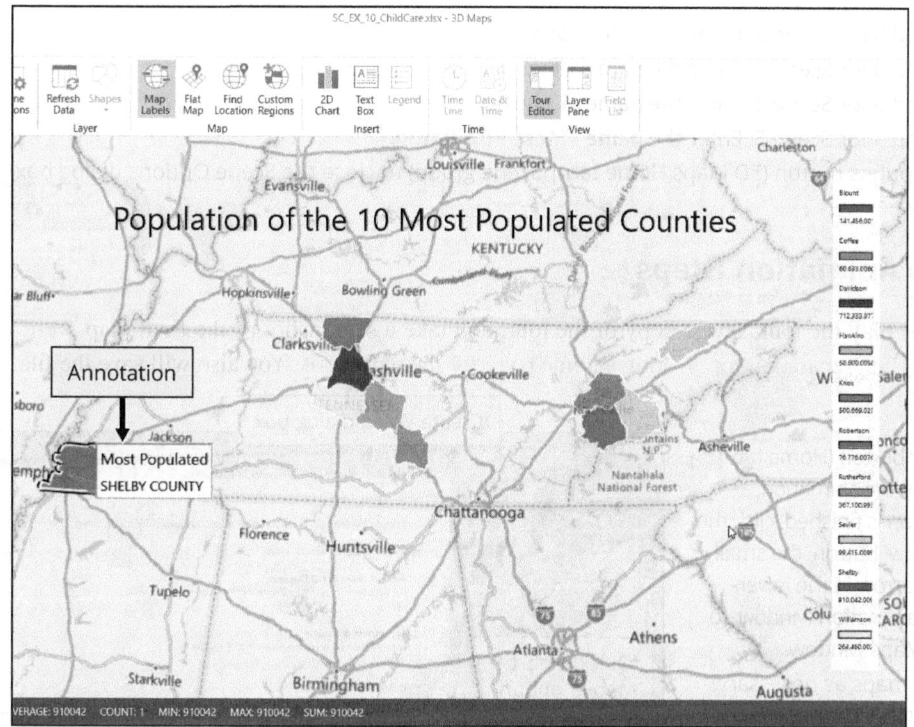

Figure 10–53

To Format Scene Options

The following steps format scene options. **Why?** To make the animation smoother, you will change the duration of each scene and then select a scene effect.

- Select the text, Tour 1, at the top of the Tour pane. Type **Most Populated** to replace the text.

- Click Scene 1 in the Tour pane.
- Click the Scene Options button (Home tab | Scene group) to display the Scene Options dialog box.
- Select the text in the Scene duration box and then type **2** to change the scene to a length of two seconds.
- In the Scene Name box type **United States** to change the name.
- Click the Effect button to display the list of effects (Figure 10–54).

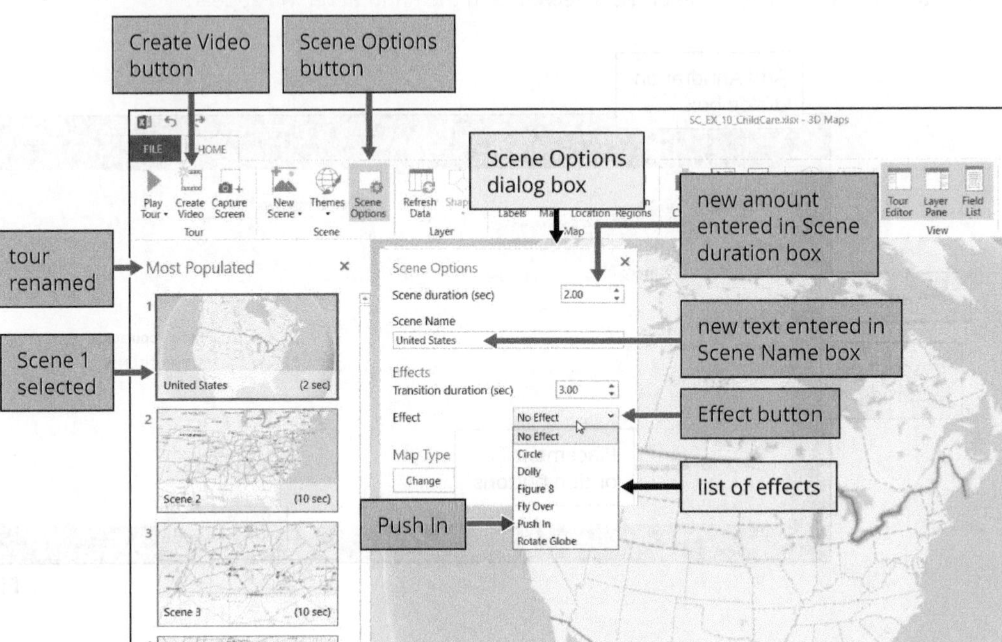

Figure 10–54

- Click Push In to select the effect.

- Repeat Steps 2 and 3 for Scene 2. Enter the name **State**.
- Repeat Steps 2 and 3 for Scene 3. Enter the name **Region**.
- Repeat Steps 2 and 3 for Scene 4. Enter the name **County**.
- Repeat Steps 2 and 3 for Scene 5. Enter the name **Most Populated**.
- Click the Scene Options button (3D Maps Home tab | Scene group) to close the Scene Options dialog box.

To Finish the Animation Steps

The following steps play the tour, save a copy of the tour, and take a screenshot of the final map. **Why?** You will paste the screenshot to Sheet1 in preparation for creating a home page for the workbook. You also will save the file.

1

- Click the Play Tour button (Home tab | Tour group) to play the animation. When the animation is finished, click the 'Go back to Edit view' button, the small leftward-pointing arrow in the lower-left corner of the animation window, to return to the 3D Maps window.
- Adjust any of the maps as necessary.
- Click the Create Video button (Home tab | Tour group) to display the Create Video dialog box.
- Click the 'Quick Export & Mobile' option button (Figure 10–55).

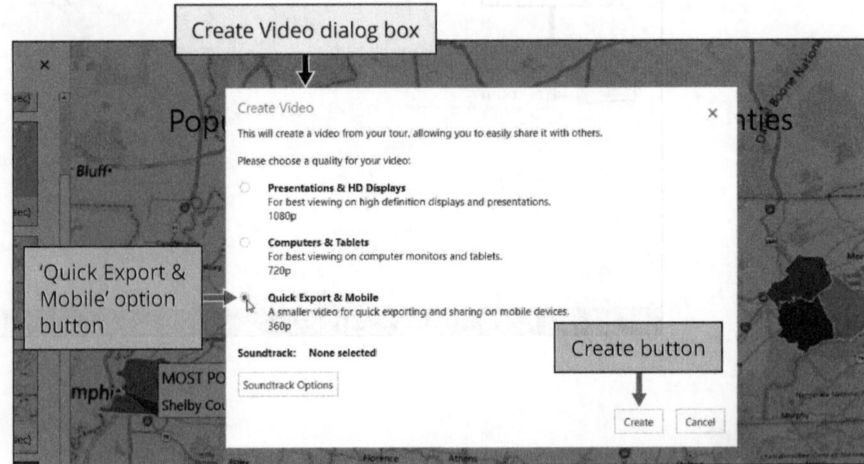

Figure 10–55

- Click the Create button (Create Video dialog box) to display the Save Movie dialog box.
- Type **SC_EX_10_MostPopulated** in the File name box and then navigate to your storage location (Figure 10–56).

- Click Save (Save Movie dialog box) to save the video. When Excel has finished saving the video, click the Close button, if necessary.

Q&A Can I play the video?
Yes, if you wish to access the video, open File Explorer, navigate to the storage location, right-click the file, and then click Open or Play on the shortcut menu. When the video is finished, click the Close button in the video window.

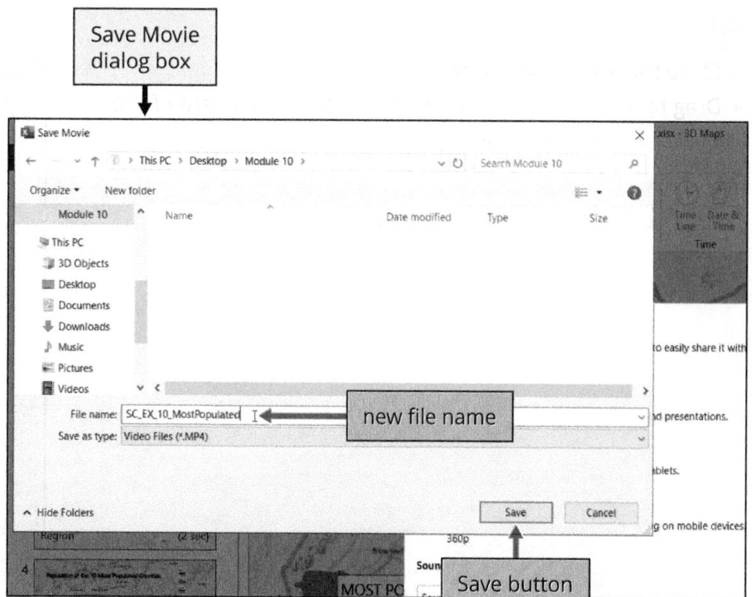

Figure 10–56

To Capture a Screen

The following steps capture a screen of the current scene. **Why?** You can then use the screen capture as a picture on a different sheet in the workbook. Capturing a screen stores it on the clipboard, and the resulting picture can be used easily in other locations.

1

- If necessary, click the Close button of any open dialog boxes. Close the Field List if necessary.
- If necessary, select Scene 5 and then click the Capture Screen button (Home tab | Tour group) to place a copy of this scene on the clipboard (Figure 10–57).

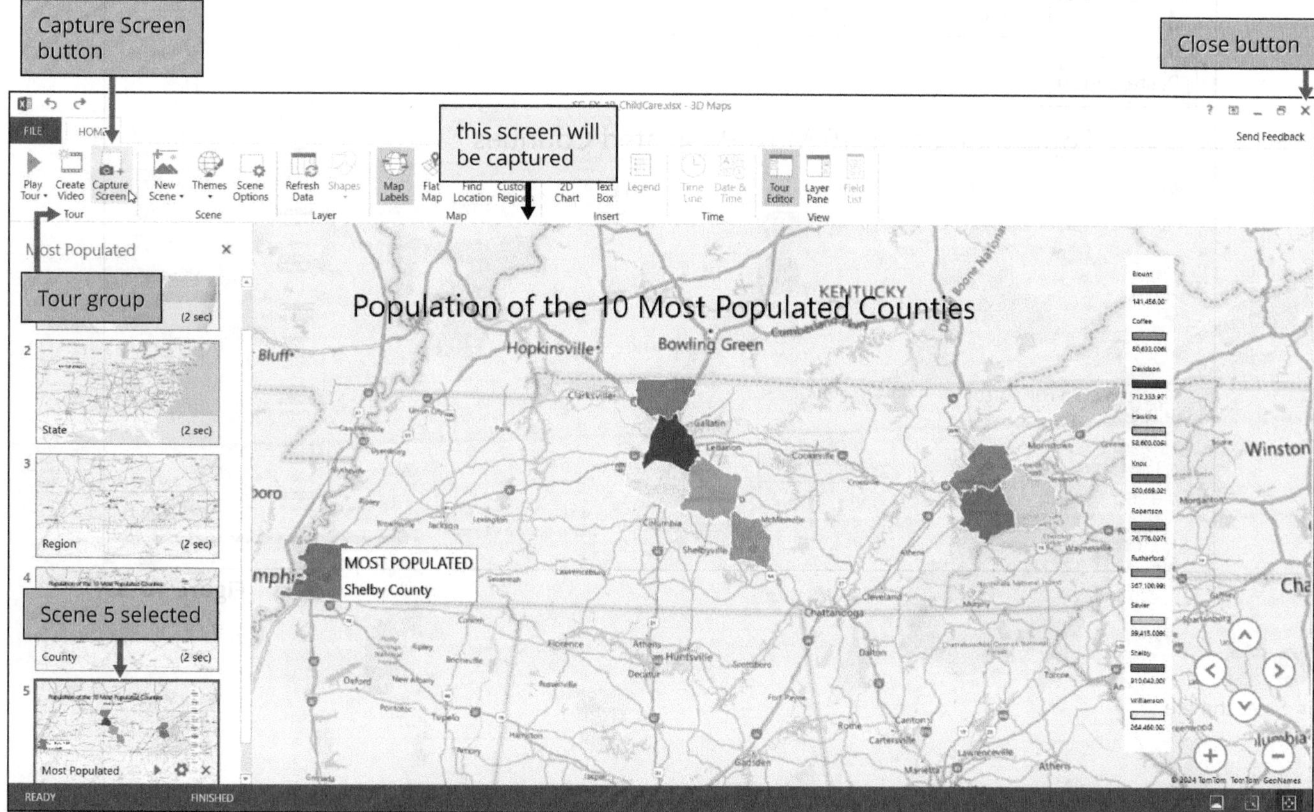

Figure 10–57

- Close the 3D Maps window.
- Drag to move the 3D Maps Tours text box to the right of the Child Care Centers table (Figure 10–58).

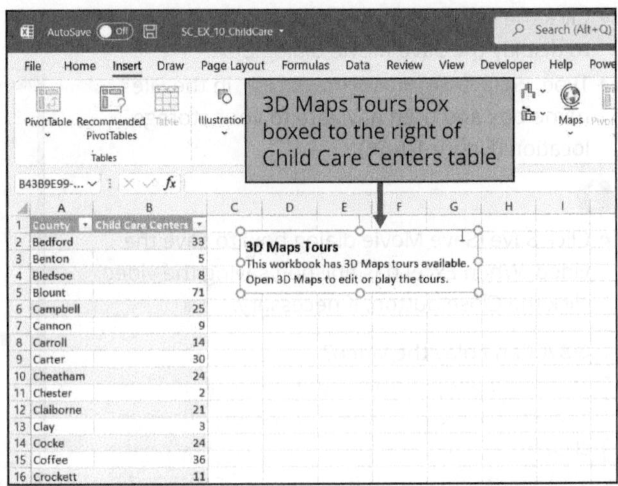

Figure 10–58

- Navigate to Sheet1 in the workbook.
- Click the Paste button (Home tab | Clipboard group) to paste the screenshot to Sheet1. If necessary, close the Queries & Connections pane, and drag the screenshot so the top left corner is in cell A1 and the screenshot extends to column T (Figure 10–59).

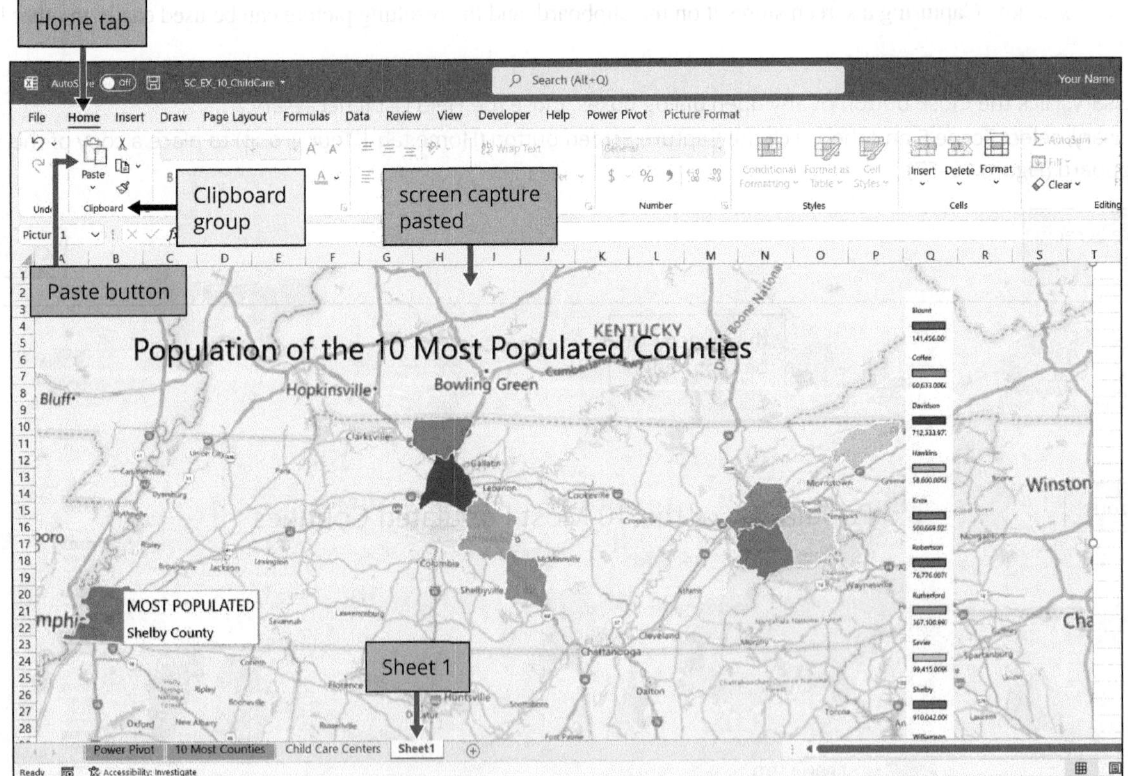

Figure 10–59

- Save the file.

Formatting a Home Page with Hyperlinks and Symbols

Some Excel users create a home page or introductory worksheet to help with navigation, especially when novice users of Excel may need to interact with complex workbooks. A home page should display a title, links to other worksheets or pertinent materials, and optionally a graphic.

A **hyperlink** is a specially formatted word, phrase, or graphic which, when clicked or tapped, lets you display a webpage on the Internet, another file, an email, or another location within the same file; also called hypertext or a link. Users click links to navigate or browse to the location. In Excel, hyperlinks can be created using cell data or linked to a graphic.

BTW
Email Hyperlinks
You can create a hyperlink that will open the user's default email app such as Outlook or Gmail, allowing them to send an email message to a specified email address. Click the Email Address button in the Insert Hyperlink dialog box (displayed in Figure 10–63) and enter an email address and subject.

To Insert a Hyperlink

To create a hyperlink in Excel, you select the cell or graphic and then decide from among four type of hyperlinks: links to places in the workbook, links to files or webpages, a link to create a new file, or links to email addresses. Table 10–4 displays the text and hyperlinks that you will enter on the home page of the SC_EX_10_ChildCare workbook.

The following steps create hyperlinks on the home page. **Why?** Creating links to other tabs, files, and websites will help users navigate through the workbook.

Table 10–4: Home Page Text and Hyperlinks

Cell	Text	Hyperlink location	Hyperlink
U6	Tennessee Demographics	<none>	<none>
U8	Links:	<none>	<none>
V9	Top Ten Counties by Population	Place in This Document	10 Most Counties
V10	Child Care Centers	Place in This Document	Child Care Centers
V11	Power Pivot	Place in This Document	Power Pivot
V12	Map Animation	Existing File or Web Page	SC_EX_10_MostPopulated.mp4
V13	Contact	Email Address	tennesseefamilyhealth@cengage.com

- Change the width of column V to 40.
- Zoom out to 85%, or any percentage where all of column V is included onscreen.
- Enter the text from the Text column in Table 10–4 into the appropriate cells. Change cell U6 to the Title Style.
- Change cells U8:V13 to be font size 14, and then change the font to Calibri if necessary.
- Bold the title in cell U6 and change the text color to black if necessary (Figure 10–60).

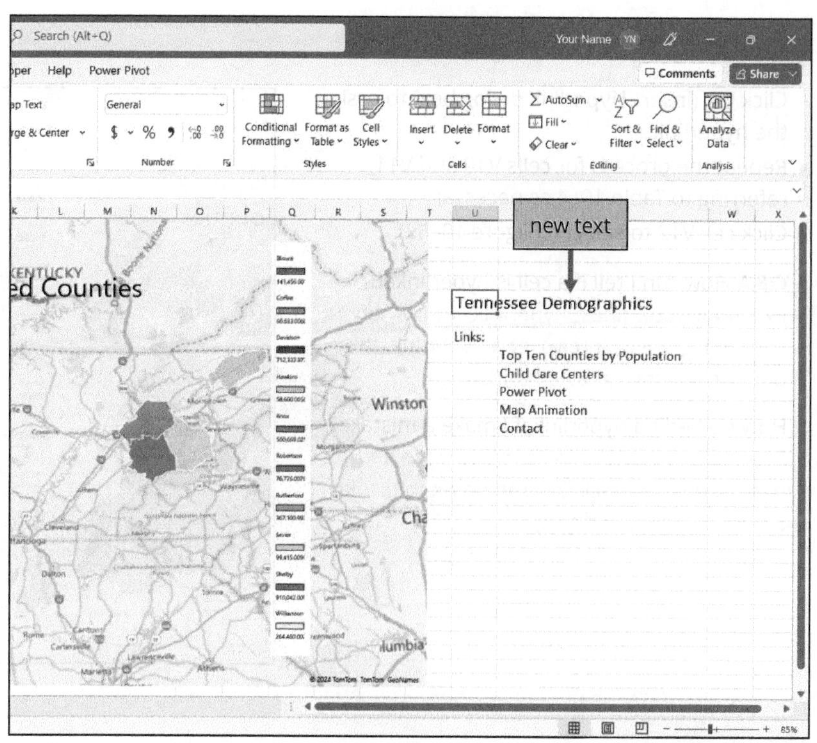

Figure 10–60

- Display the Insert tab.
- Select the cell you wish to make a hyperlink (in this case, cell V9) and then click the Link button (Insert tab | Links group) to display the Insert Hyperlink dialog box.
- In the Link to area, click the 'Place in This Document' button to identify the type of hyperlink.
- In the 'Or select a place in this document' area, click '10 Most Counties' (Figure 10–61).

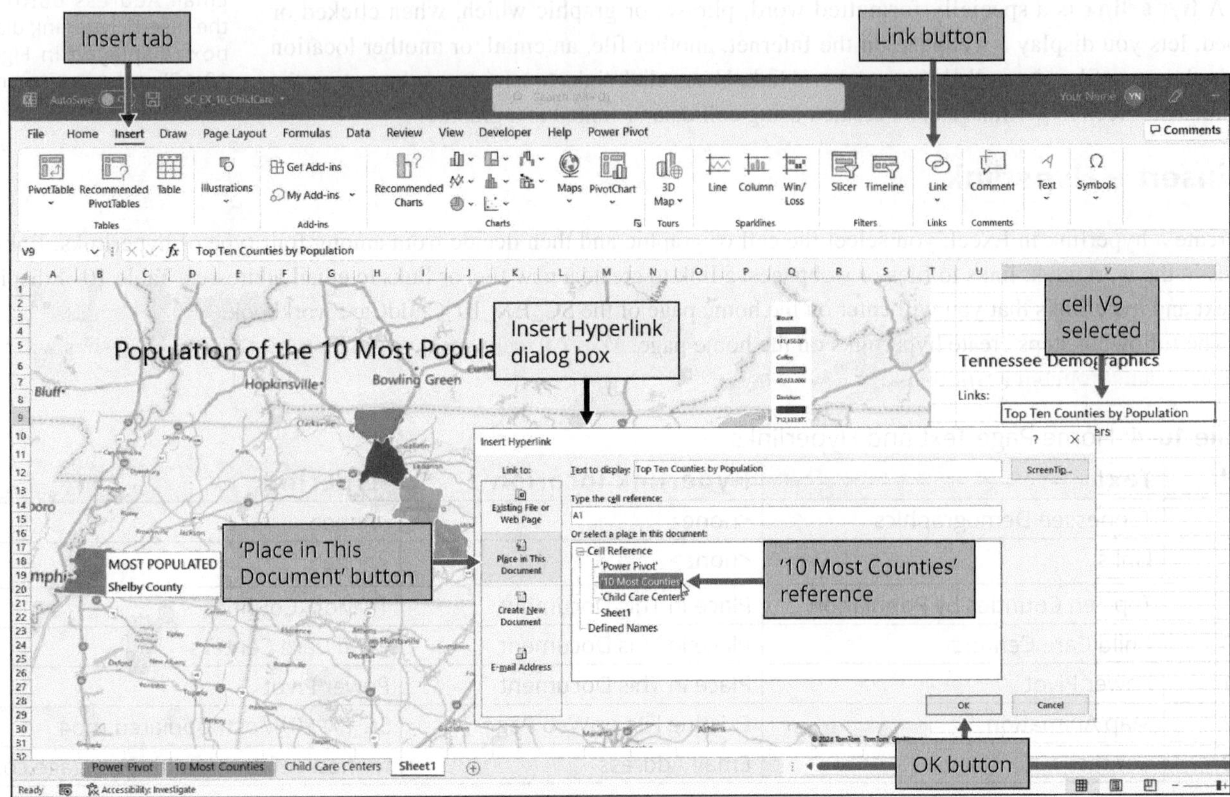

Figure 10–61

- Click OK (Insert Hyperlink dialog box) to assign the hyperlink.
- Repeat the process for cells V10 and V11, referring to Table 10–4 as necessary.
- Click cell V12 to select it (Figure 10–62).

Q&A How can I tell if a cell is hyperlinked?
Excel will underline a hyperlink, and, when a user holds the pointer over a hyperlink, the pointer will appear as a hand.

How do I edit a hyperlink if I make a mistake?
Right-click the hyperlink to display the shortcut menu and then click Edit Hyperlink to display the Edit Hyperlink dialog box.

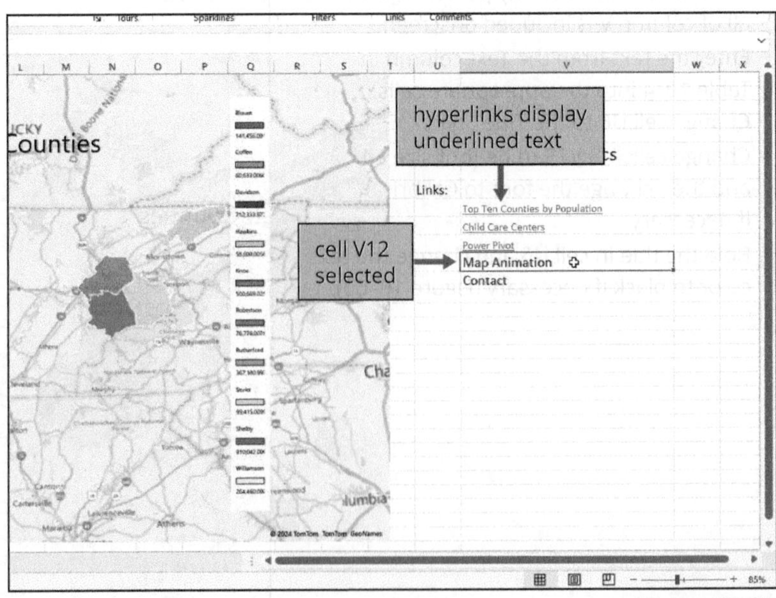

Figure 10–62

4

- Click the Link button (Insert tab | Links group) again and then click the 'Existing File or Web Page' button to identify the type of hyperlink.
- If necessary, click Current Folder in the Look in area.
- Click SC_EX_10_MostPopulated.mp4 to select the file (Figure 10–63).

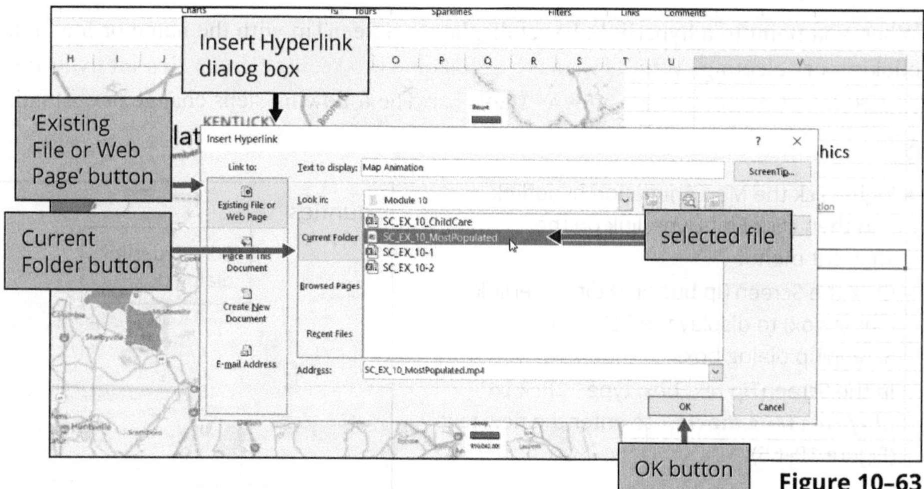

Figure 10–63

5

- Click OK (Insert Hyperlink dialog box) to apply the hyperlink.
- Click cell V13, click the Link button (Insert tab | Links group), and then click the E-mail Address button to identify the last hyperlink.
- In the E-mail address box, type **tennesseefamilyhealth@cengage.com** to enter the link to the email address.
- In the subject box, type **presentation link** to enter the email subject line (Figure 10–64).

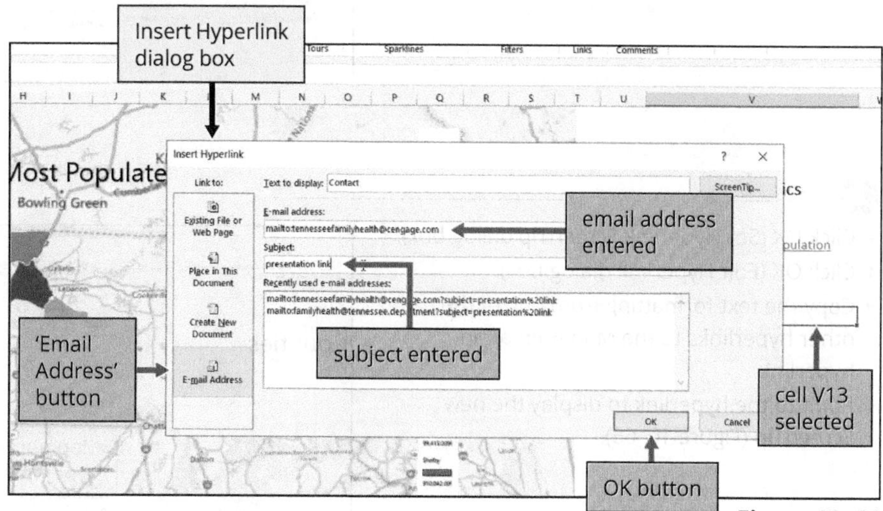

Figure 10–64

6

- Click OK (Insert Hyperlink dialog box) to apply the hyperlink.
- Select cells V8:V13. Change the font size to 14 and the font color to Blue in the Standard Colors.

Q&A Why am I selecting V8:V13 rather than just the hyperlink cells?
Excel will underline a hyperlink, and, when a user holds the pointer over a hyperlink, the pointer will appear as a hand.

- One at a time, point to each of the hyperlinks to display the ScreenTip and then click the hyperlink to verify its functionality.

Other Ways

1. Right-click cell, click Link, enter settings and hyperlink address (Insert Hyperlink dialog box), click OK
2. Press CTRL+k, enter settings and hyperlink address (Insert Hyperlink dialog box), click OK

To Customize a Hyperlink's Screen Tip

When you point to a hyperlink, Excel displays a ScreenTip with the name or location of the hyperlink and instructions for clicking or selecting. **Why?** Users are accustomed to seeing ScreenTips on hyperlinks in browsers, sometimes beside the hyperlink, other times on the browser status bar. The following steps change or customize the ScreenTip.

- Right-click the Map Animation hyperlink and then click Edit Hyperlink on the shortcut menu.
- Click the ScreenTip button (Edit Hyperlink dialog box) to display the Set Hyperlink ScreenTip dialog box.
- In the ScreenTip text box, type **Click to play this MP4 movie.** to enter the new text (Figure 10–65).

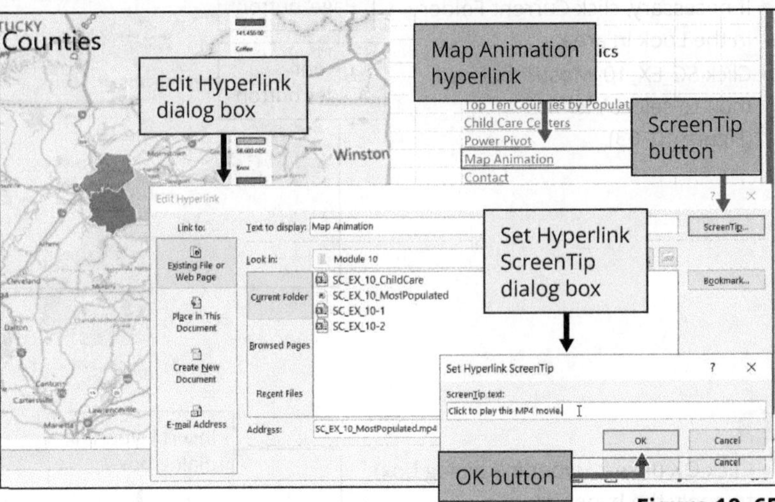

Figure 10–65

- Click OK (Set Hyperlink ScreenTip dialog box).
- Click OK (Edit Hyperlink dialog box).
- Copy the text formatting from one of the other hyperlinks to the Map Animation hyperlink.
- Point to the hyperlink to display the new ScreenTip (Figure 10–66).

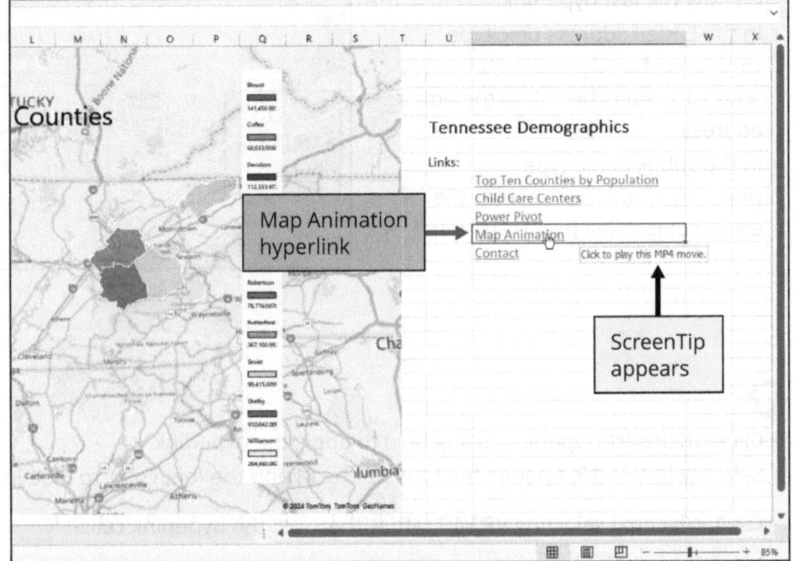

Figure 10–66

To Remove a Hyperlink If you wanted to delete a hyperlink, you would perform the following steps.

1. Right-click the hyperlink you wish to delete.
2. On the shortcut menu, click Remove Hyperlink.

To Create an External Link If you wanted to create an external link to the data, rather than a query or connection, you would perform the following steps. (If you have completed earlier modules, you already may have learned to create an external link.)

1. Open both the source and destination files.
2. In the destination file, select a cell to receive the data.
3. If it is a cell reference, type = and then click the cell in the source file. Excel will create an absolute reference to the source file. An example might be: **='[SC_EX_10-1.xlsx]Child Care Centers!$A$1**
4. If it is a range, such as those used in functions, type = followed by the function name and opening parenthesis; then, drag the range in the source file. Excel will create an absolute link to the range. An example might be: **=SUM('[SC_EX_10-1.xlsx]Child Care Centers!$A$1:$B$80)**
5. Save the destination file.

To Update Data Associated with External Links If you wanted to update the data associated with external links, you would perform the following steps.

1. Close all workbooks and then open only the destination workbook, such as SC_EX_10_ChildCare.xlsx.
2. Click the Edit Links button (Data tab | Queries & Connections group) to display the Edit Links dialog box.
3. Click the Update Values button (Edit Links dialog box).
4. Click Close (Edit Links dialog box).

BTW
Distributing a Workbook
Instead of printing and distributing a hard copy of a workbook, you can distribute the workbook electronically. Options include sending the workbook via email; posting it on cloud storage (such as OneDrive) and sharing the file with others; posting it on a social networking site, blog, or other website; and sharing a link associated with an online location of the workbook. You also can create and share a PDF or XPS image of the workbook, so that users can open the file in Acrobat Reader or XPS Viewer instead of in Excel.

To Insert a Symbol

A **symbol** is a character that is not on your keyboard, such as ½ and ©, or a **special character**, such as an em dash (—) or ellipsis (…). Some symbols use ASCII characters or Unicode characters. **ASCII** and **Unicode** are coding systems that represent text and symbols in computers, communications equipment, and other devices that use text. The following steps insert a link symbol on the homepage.

- Select cell V8. Click the Symbol button (Insert tab | Symbols group) to expand the Symbols group (Figure 10–67).

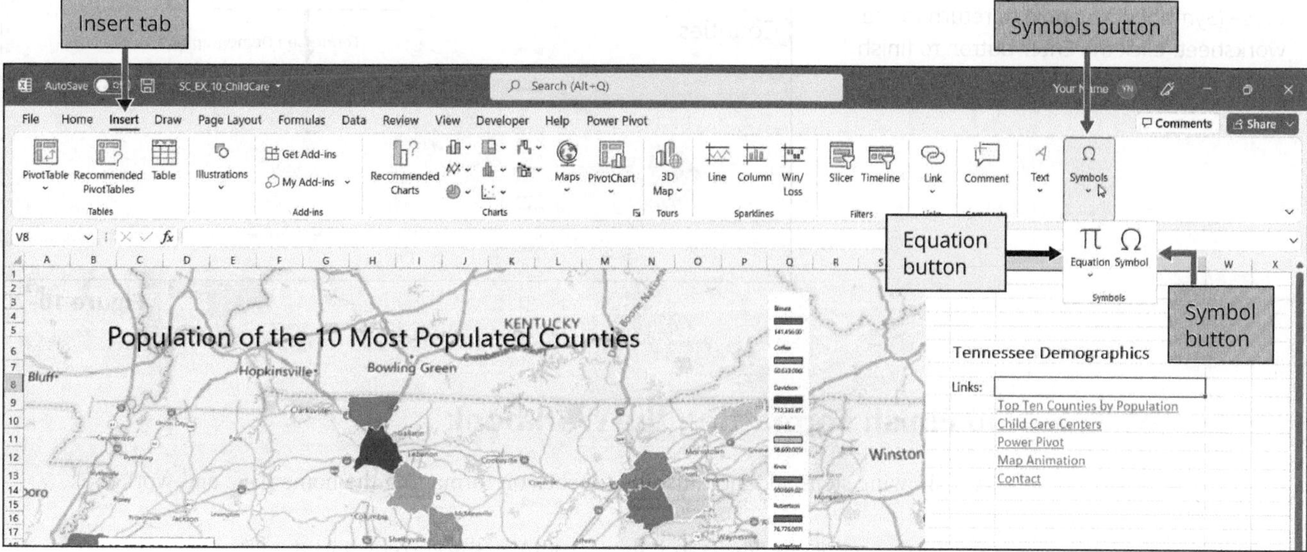

Figure 10–67

2

- Click the Symbol button in the expanded group to display the Symbol dialog box.
- Click the Font arrow (Symbol dialog box) to display the list (Figure 10–68).

Q&A What does the Equation button do?
The Equation button opens the Equation tab that displays mathematical, statistical, and other symbols to help you with formulas and scientific equations.

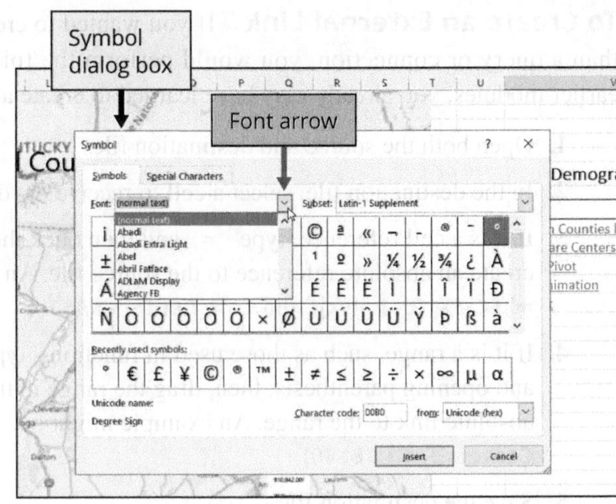

Figure 10–68

3

- Scroll as necessary and then click 'Segoe UI Emoji' in the list.
- Scroll down more than halfway and then click the Link Symbol, character code 1F517 (Figure 10–69). Your symbol may differ slightly, as symbols are printer dependent.

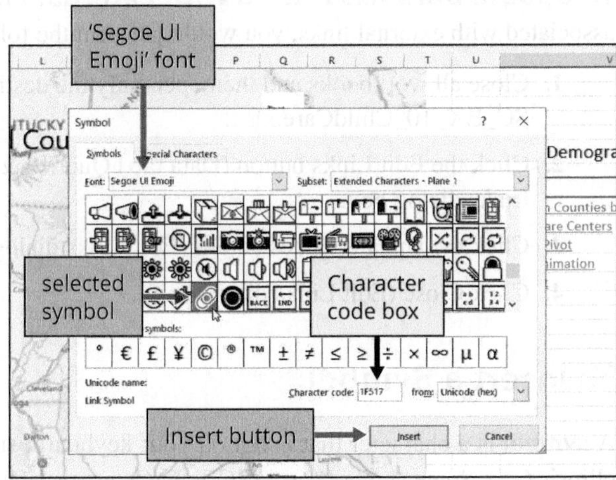

Figure 10–69

4

- Click the Insert button (Symbol dialog box) to insert the symbol and then click Close (Symbol dialog box) to return to the worksheet. Click the Enter button to finish inserting the symbol (Figure 10–70).

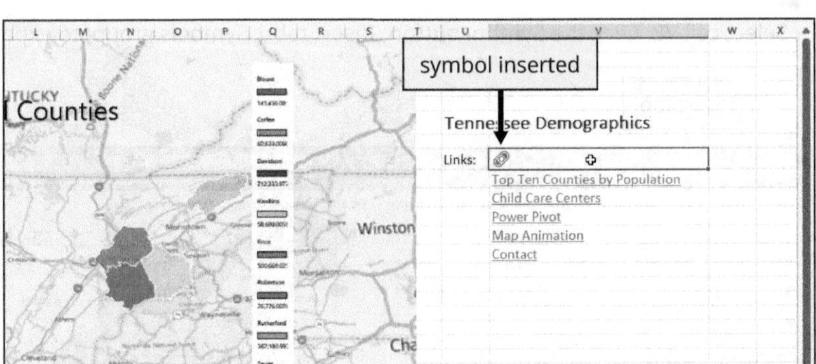

Figure 10–70

To Finish Formatting the Workbook

The following steps add the finishing touches on formatting the home page and workbook.

1. Turn off gridlines (View tab | Show group) on the current worksheet.
2. Change the tab color of the Child Care Centers sheet to Purple in the Standard Colors.

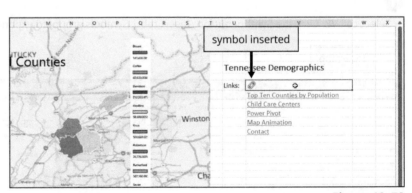

3 Rename the Sheet 1 worksheet tab, entering the one-word name **Homepage**. Change the tab color to Orange, in the Standard Colors. Drag the tab to the far left so it becomes the first page.

4 With the Homepage sheet selected, save the file.

Break Point: If you wish to take a break, this is a good place to do so. Exit Excel. To resume later, start Excel, open the file called SC_EX_10_ChildCare, and then continue following the steps from this location forward.

Macros

A **macro** is a named set of instructions, written in the Visual Basic programming language, that performs tasks automatically in a specified order. It is a set of commands and instructions grouped together to allow a user to accomplish a task automatically. Because Excel does not have a command or button for every possible worksheet task, you can create a macro to group together commonly used tasks, which then can be reused later. People also use macros to record commonly used text, to ensure consistency in calculations and formatting, or to manipulate non-numeric data. In this module, you will learn how to create a macro using the macro recorder. After recording a macro, you can play it back, or execute it, as often as you want to repeat the steps you recorded with the macro recorder. Three steps must be taken in preparation for working with macros in Excel. First, you must display the Developer tab (which you did earlier in the module). Second, a security setting in Excel must be modified to enable macros whenever you use Excel. Finally, Excel requires that a workbook which includes macros be saved as an Excel Macro-Enabled Workbook file type; the file extension is .xlsm.

BTW
Naming Macros
If you use an uppercase letter when naming a macro, the user will have to use the SHIFT key when executing the macro.

BTW
Enabling Macros
Excel remembers your decision about enabling macros. If you have enabled macros in a worksheet, Excel will not ask you about enabling them the next time you open the worksheet, but will open the worksheet with macros enabled.

Consider This

Should you customize applications with macros?

Casual Microsoft Office users do not know that customization is available. Creating special macros, events, or buttons on the ribbon can help a user to be more productive. Creating a macro for repeating tasks also saves time and reduces errors. If you understand how to do so, customization is an excellent productivity tool.

To Enable Macros

The following steps enable macros in the workbook. **Why?** Enabling macros allows the workbook to open with executable macros.

- Click the Developer tab to make it the active tab.
- Click the Macro Security button (Developer tab | Code group) to display the Trust Center dialog box.
- Click 'Enable VBA macros' to select the option button (Figure 10–71). Note that this option is not generally recommended but is safe for workbooks that you will be using or sharing with trusted collaborators.

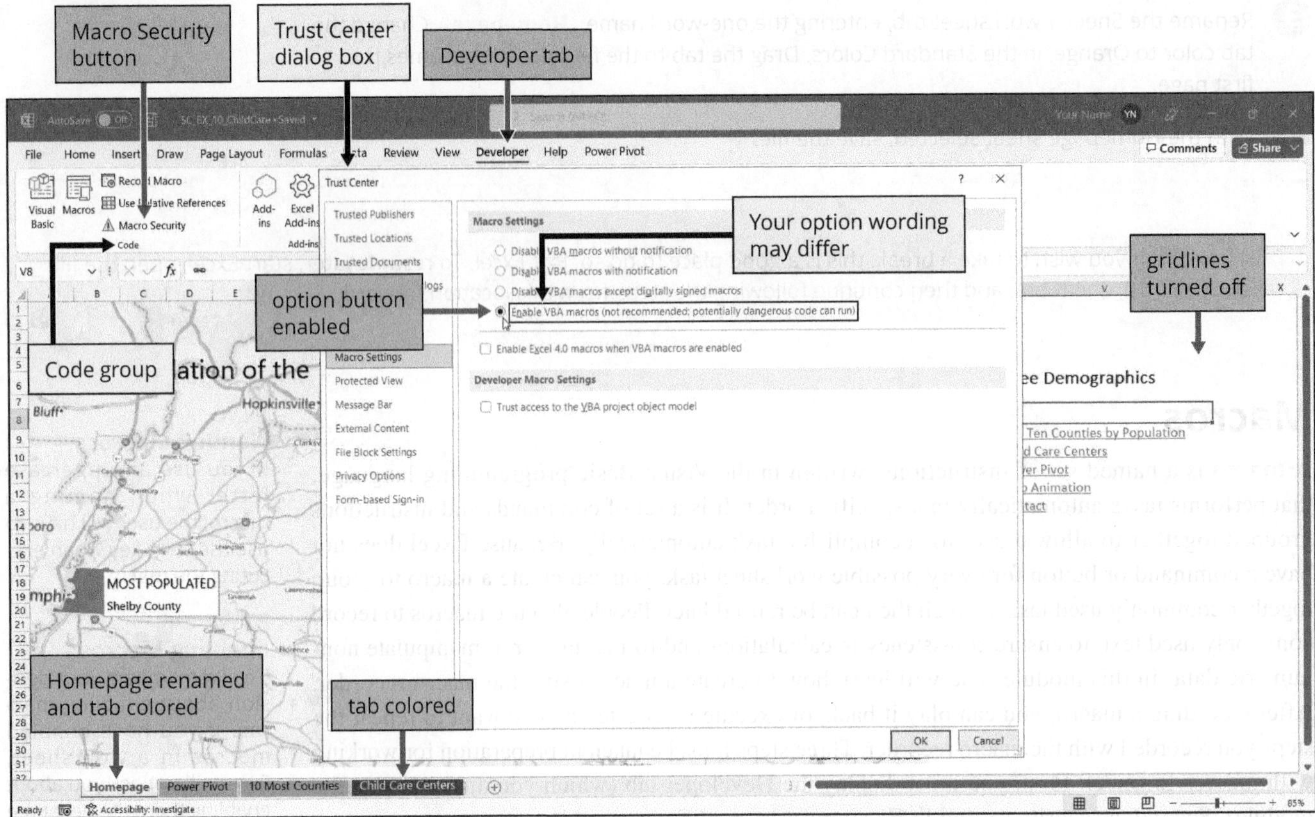

Figure 10–71

- Click OK (Trust Center dialog box) to close the dialog box and enable macros.

BTW
Starting Macros
Before recording a macro, you should select your starting cell. If you select it after you begin recording the macro, the macro always will start in that particular cell, which may limit the macro's usefulness.

BTW
Shortcut Keys
Macro shortcut keys take precedence over existing Excel shortcut keys. If you assign an existing shortcut key to a macro, it no longer will work for its original purpose. For instance, assigning CTRL+C to a macro means that you no longer will be able to use that keyboard shortcut to copy content, which is the default action assigned to this shortcut.

Recording Macros

A macro is created by recording a set of steps as they are performed. The steps and their order should be determined and rehearsed before creating the macro. When you create a macro, you assign a name to it. A macro name can be up to 255 characters long; it can contain numbers, letters, and underscores, but it cannot contain spaces or other punctuation. The name is used later to identify the macro when you want to execute it. Executing a macro causes Excel to perform each of the recorded steps in order.

Entering a cell reference always directs the macro to that specific cell. Navigating to a cell using keyboard navigation, however, requires the use of relative cell addressing. If you will be using keyboard navigation, you must ensure that the 'Use Relative References' button (Developer tab | Code group) is selected so that the macro works properly. For example, suppose you record a macro in cell C1 that moves the focus to cell C4 and then enters text. If the 'Use Relative References' button is not selected, the macro will always move focus to C4 and enter text; C4 would be considered an absolute reference. If the 'Use Relative References' button is selected while recording, the macro will instead move three cells to the right of the current position (which will not always be cell C4) and enter text.

As you record a macro, you do not have to hurry. The macro executes by keystroke, not the time between keystrokes during the creation process. You can copy macros to other workbooks by copying the macro code.

To Record a Macro

The following steps record a macro named Address_Block, with the shortcut key CTRL+M to execute the macro. **Why?** The Department of Family Health Services wants to be able to use the shortcut to display departmental information.

- In the Homepage worksheet, select cell V16.
- Click the 'Use Relative References' button (Developer tab | Code group) to select the option to record relative references.
- Click the Record Macro button (Developer tab | Code group) to display the Record Macro dialog box.
- In the Macro name box, type **Address_Block** to enter the macro name.
- Type **m** in the Shortcut key box to set the shortcut key for the macro to CTRL+M.
- In the Description box, type **This macro prints the name of the department and the address in a block of three cells.** to enter the text (Figure 10–72).

Q&A Where are macros stored?
In this module, the macro will be stored in the current workbook. If you want a macro to be available in any workbook, you would click the 'Store macro in' button and then select Personal Macro Workbook.

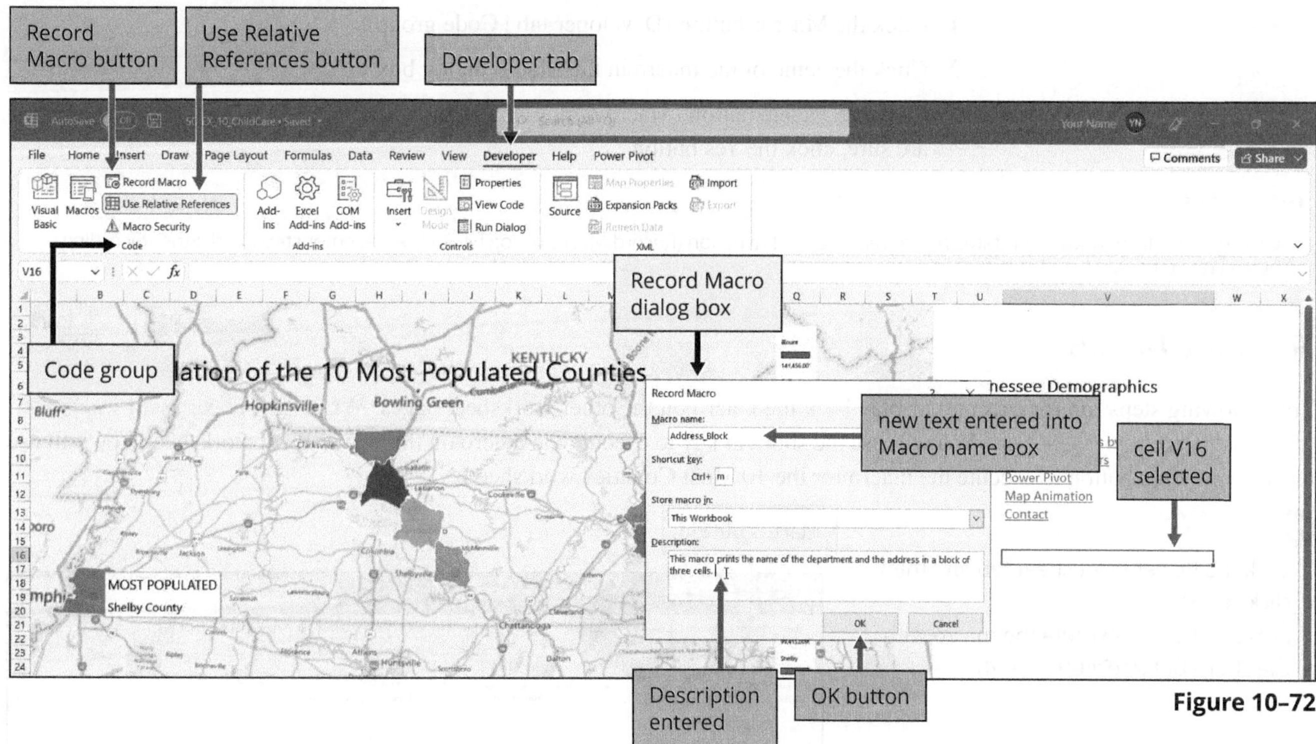

Figure 10–72

- Click OK (Record Macro dialog box) to begin recording the macro and to change the Record Macro button to the Stop Recording button.

Q&A What will be included in the macro?
Any task you perform in Excel will be part of the macro. When you are finished recording the macro, clicking the Stop Recording button on the ribbon or on the status bar ends the recording.

What is the purpose of the Record Macro button on the status bar?
You can use the Record Macro button on the status bar to start or stop recording a macro. When you are not recording a macro, this button is displayed as the Record Macro button. If you click it to begin recording a macro, the button changes to become the Stop Recording button.

- Type **Department of Family Health Services** and press the DOWN ARROW key.
- Type **387 Downtown Way** and press the DOWN ARROW key.
- Type **Nashville, TN 37201** and press the DOWN ARROW key to complete the text (Figure 10–73).

- Click the Stop Recording button (Developer tab | Code group) to stop recording the worksheet activities.

Q&A What if I make a mistake while recording?
If you make a mistake while recording a macro, delete the macro and record it again.

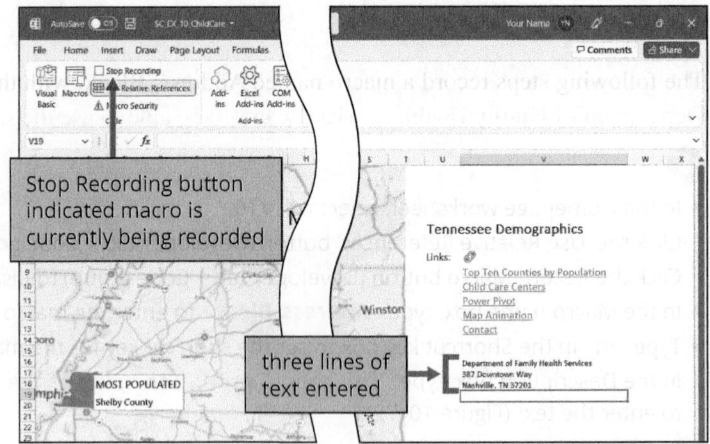

Figure 10–73

To Delete a Macro If you wanted to delete a macro, you would perform the following steps.

1. Click the Macros button (Developer tab | Code group).
2. Click the name of the macro in the Macro dialog box.
3. Click the Delete button (Macro dialog box). If Excel displays a dialog box asking if you are sure, click the Yes button.

Other Ways

1. Click Record Macro button on status bar, enter macro information (Record Macro dialog box), click OK, enter steps, click Stop Recording button on status bar

To Run a Macro

The following steps run (or execute) or play back the macro on the other worksheet pages. **Why?** The department wants their name and address on each sheet. You will use the shortcut key to execute the macro on the Power Pivot worksheet. You will use the View Macros button to execute the macro for the 10 Most Counties worksheet.

- Click the Power Pivot sheet tab and then click cell F19.
- Press CTRL+M to execute the macro with the shortcut key (Figure 10–74).

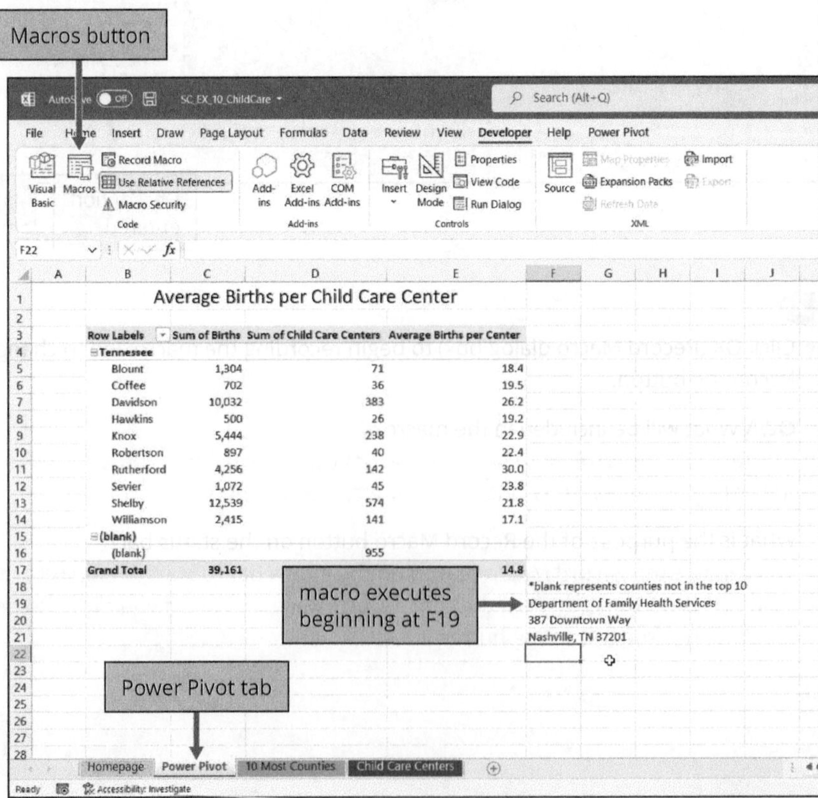

Figure 10–74

2

- Click the '10 Most Counties' sheet tab, and then click cell A14.
- Click the Macros button (Developer tab | Code group) to display the Macro dialog box (Figure 10–75).

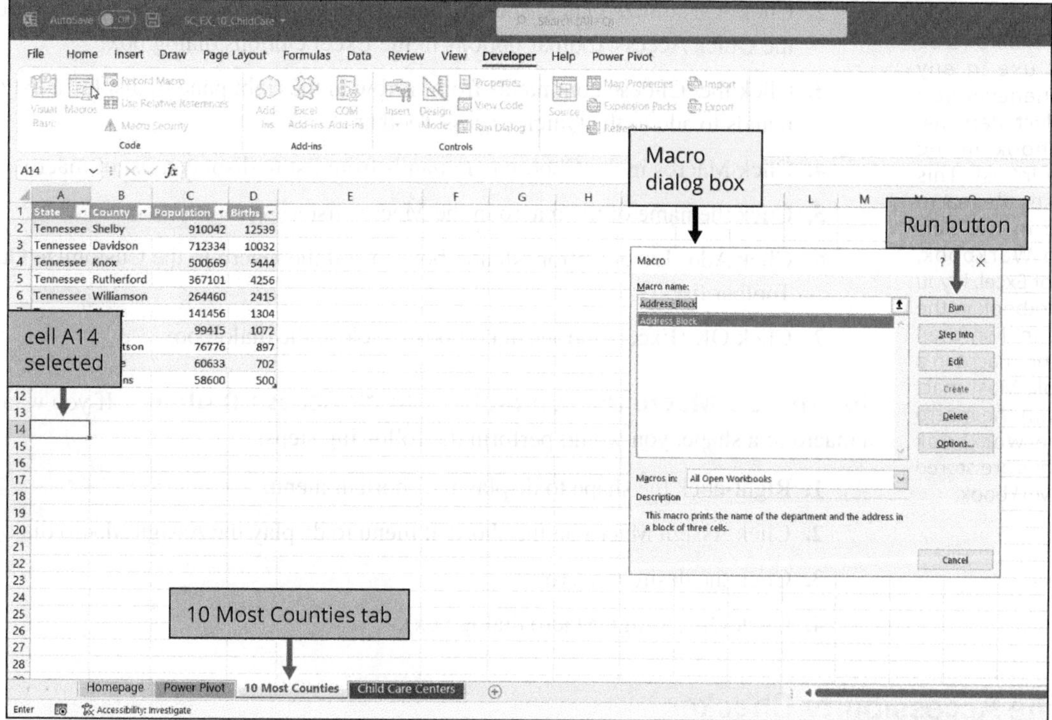

Figure 10–75

3

- Click Run (Macros dialog box) to execute the selected macro (Figure 10–76).

4

- Repeat the process for cell D7 on the Child Care Centers tab.

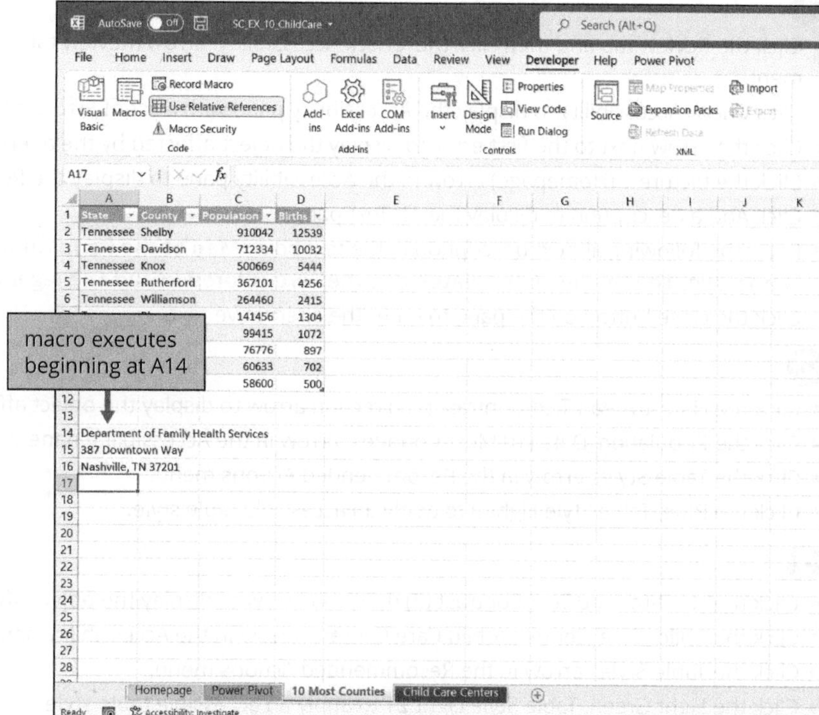

Figure 10–76

Other Ways

1. Press ALT+F8, select macro, click Run (Macro dialog box)

BTW
Storing Macros
In the Record Macro dialog box, you can select the location to store the macro in the 'Store macro in' box. If you want a macro to be available to use in any workbook whenever you use Excel, select 'Personal Macro Workbook' in the 'Store macro in' list. This selection causes the macro to be stored in the Personal Macro Workbook, which is part of Excel. If you click New Workbook in the 'Store macro in' list, then Excel stores the macro in a new workbook. Most macros created with the macro recorder are workbook specific and thus are stored in the active workbook.

To Create a Macro Button on the Quick Access Toolbar If you wanted to create a button on the Quick Access Toolbar to run the macro, you would perform the following steps.

1. Right-click anywhere on the Quick Access Toolbar to display the shortcut menu.
2. Click 'Customize Quick Access Toolbar' on the shortcut menu to display the Customize the Quick Access Toolbar options in the Excel Options dialog box.
3. Click the 'Choose commands from' arrow in the right pane to display a list of commands to add to the Quick Access Toolbar.
4. Click Macros in the Choose commands from list to display a list of macros.
5. Click the name of the macro in the Macros list to select it.
6. Click Add (Excel Options dialog box) to add the macro to the Customize Quick Access Toolbar list.
7. Click OK (Excel Options dialog box) to close the dialog box.

To Create a Macro Button on the Quick Access Toolbar If you wanted to assign a macro to a shape, you would perform the following steps.

1. Right-click the shape to display the shortcut menu.
2. Click Assign Macro on the shortcut menu to display the Assign Macro dialog box.
3. Click the desired macro.
4. Click OK (Assign Macro dialog box).

To Use the Accessibility Checker

The following steps use the Accessibility Checker to identity and fix an accessibility issue.

- Click the Review tab and then click the 'Check Accessibility' arrow (Review tab | Accessibility group) to display the Accessibility menu.
- Click Check Accessibility to display the Accessibility pane with a list of Errors or Warnings in the Inspection Results box.
- Click the arrow next to the first error to display the object affected by the alternative text issue.
- Click the Picture 1 (Homepage) arrow in the Accessibility pane to display the Recommended Actions list.
- Click Add a description to display the Alt Text pane.
- Enter the following alt text description in the text box: **Map of the Population of the 10 Most Populated Counties in Tennessee. The ten most populated counties are colored in and the legend shows the population numbers for each.**
- Click the close button on the pane to enter the alternative text.

2

- Click the Hard-to-read Text Contrast (2) direction arrow to display the object affected by the issue.
- Click the Population_Data (10 Most Counties) arrow in the Accessibility pane to display the Recommended Actions list.
- Click the Table Styles arrow in the Recommended Actions menu.
- Click the Blue, Table Style Light 9 to apply an accessible table style.

3

- Click the Hard-to-read Text Contrast (2) direction arrow to display the object affected by the issue.
- Click the Child_Care_Centers (Child Care Centers) arrow in the Accessibility pane to display the Recommended Actions list.
- Click the Table Styles arrow in the Recommended Actions menu.
- Click the Light Green, Table Style Light 21 to apply an accessible table style.
- The Accessibility pane is now updated to confirm there are no accessibility issues in the worksheet. Click the close button on the Accessibility pane.

To Save a Workbook as a Macro-Enabled Workbook

The following steps save the workbook as a macro-enabled workbook. **Why?** Workbooks with macros must be saved as macro-enabled.

- Navigate to the Homepage sheet. Click File to display Backstage view, click Save As, click Browse, and then navigate to your storage location if necessary.
- Click the 'Save as type' button (Save As dialog box) and then click 'Excel Macro-Enabled Workbook (*.xlsm)' to select the file format (Figure 10–77).

- sam Click the Save button (Save As dialog box) to save the workbook as an Excel Macro-Enabled Workbook file. Close the file.

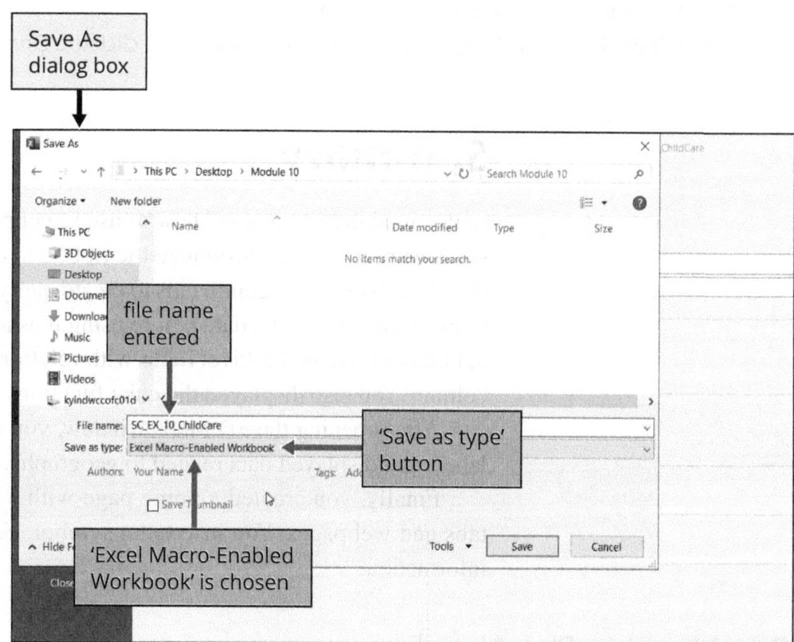

Figure 10–77

To Reset the Ribbon

It is a good idea to reset the ribbon when you are finished using the customized tools. **Why?** Other Excel users may not expect to have access to new tabs and new button groups, especially in lab situations. The following steps reset the ribbon, removing all customization, and then exit Excel.

- Right-click a blank area of the ribbon and then click 'Customize the Ribbon' on the shortcut menu to display the Excel Options dialog box.
- Click the Reset button to display its menu (Figure 10–78).

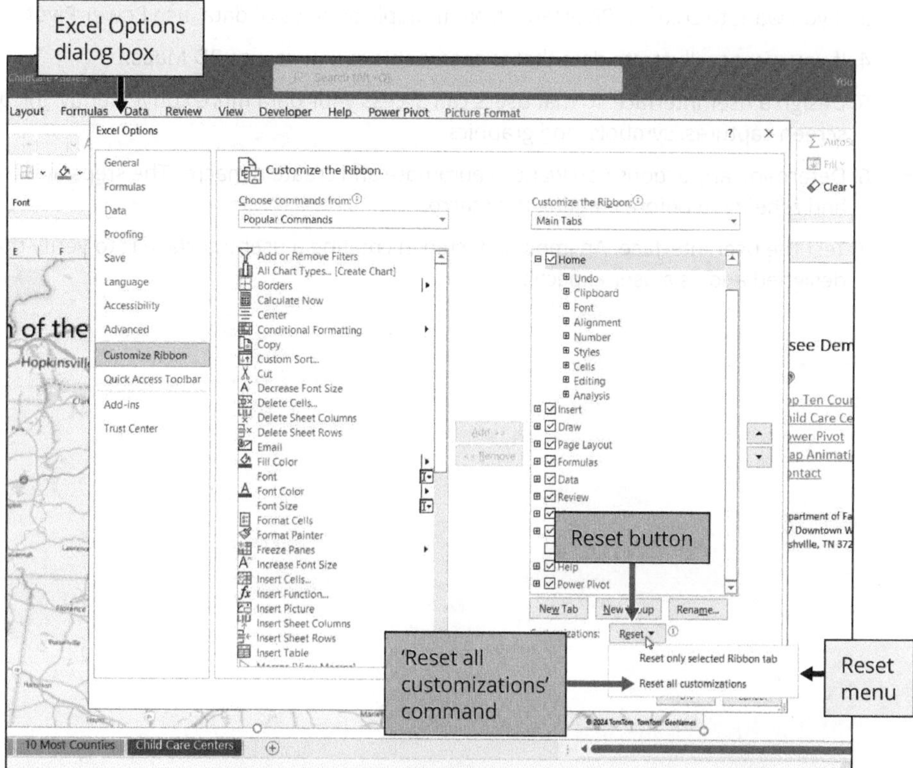

Figure 10–78

- Click 'Reset all customizations' in the Reset menu.
- When Excel displays a Microsoft Office dialog box asking if you want to delete all customizations, click the Yes button.
- Click OK to close the Excel Options dialog box.
- Exit Excel. If the Microsoft Office Excel dialog box is displayed, click the Don't Save button.

Summary

In this module, you learned how to use Excel power tools. You learned how to enable data analysis in workbooks and customize the ribbon to display different tabs. You imported data by using the Get & Transform commands to create query tables. You used the Power Query Editor window to make changes to the data before using it as a table. Using Power Pivot, you added tables to the data model, created a PivotTable with relationships, and used a measure to create a calculated column. You also displayed the cube functions in Power Pivot.

After opening the 3D Maps window, you created scenes with different map views and map labels and displayed data related to geography. You created a tour animation and saved it.

Finally, you created a home page with a captured screenshot and hyperlinks to the other tabs and webpages. You inserted a symbol. You recorded a reusable macro with the company information.

Consider This: Plan Ahead

What decisions will you need to make when using Power Tools, creating hyperlinks, inserting symbols, and recording macros?

Use these guidelines as you complete the assignments in this module and create your own worksheets for evaluating and analyzing data outside of this class.

1. Select your data carefully. Make sure it is in a tabular format. If the original data could possibly move, copy the data in a new folder and create your spreadsheet in that folder.
2. Choose the kind of visualization you wish to create.
3. If you want to create a PivotTable from multiple sources of data, use Power Pivot.
4. If you want to illustrate data that is geographic in nature, use 3D Maps.
5. Design a user interface so that users can access your data more conveniently. Include hyperlinks, macro instructions, screen captures, symbols, and graphics.
6. Determine any actions you want to automate and create a macro. The steps and their order should be determined and rehearsed before creating the macro.
7. Test the user interface. An important step in creating a user interface is to verify that the interface behaves as designed and as a user expects.

Student Assignments

Apply Your Knowledge

Reinforce the skills and apply the concepts you learned in this module.

Using Power Pivot

Note: To complete this assignment, you will be required to use the Data Files. Please contact your instructor for information about accessing the Data Files.

Instructions: Start Excel and open a blank workbook. You are to create a Power Pivot PivotTable from two data files related to university data for the Big Ten Conference.

Perform the following tasks:

1. If necessary, customize the ribbon as described in the module to include the Power Pivot tab. Save the file on your storage location with the file name, SC_EX_10_ConferencePivotTable.
2. Using File Explorer, copy the Data Files named Support_EX_10–3.xlsx and Support_EX_10–4.xlsx, and paste them to your storage location.
3. Use the Get Data button (Data tab |Get & Transform Data group) to import the workbook named Support_EX_10–3.xlsx and load the Institutions table.
4. Click Edit (Query tab | Edit group) to open the Power Query Editor window. Click the 'Use First Row as Headers' button (Power Query Editor Home tab | Transform group). Click the Close & Load button (Home tab | Close group).
5. If necessary, rename the sheet tab, Institutions.
6. Use the Get Data button (Data tab | Get & Transform Data group) to import the workbook named Support_EX_10–4.xlsx, and then load the Conference Data table. If necessary, rename the worksheet tab, Conference Data.
7. Click Edit (Query tab, Edit group) to open the Power Query Editor window. Click the 'Use First Row as Headers' button (Power Query Editor Home tab | Transform group). Close and load the query table.
8. Create a Power Pivot PivotTable as follows:
    a. Display the Power Pivot tab. Click the 'Add to Data Model' button (Power Pivot tab | Tables group) to add the Conference Data table to the data model. Minimize the Power Pivot for Excel window.
    b. Click the Institutions sheet tab, and then click the 'Add to Data Model' button (Power Pivot tab | Tables group) to add the Institutions table to the data model.
    c. Use the Power Pivot for Excel window to create a Power Pivot PivotTable on a new worksheet.
    d. In the Excel window, in the PivotTable Fields pane, place check marks in the University, City Population, and Acceptance Rate % check boxes from the Conference Data table. Drag the University field from the Institutions table to the Filters area. Create a relationship using the University field common to both tables.
    e. Drag the Type field from the Institutions table to the Filters area.
    f. Use the filter to display Public Universities in the Pivot Table. (**Hint:** Place a checkmark in the Select Multiple Items checkbox.)
    g. Click the down arrow of Sum of Acceptance Rate % field in the Values box and select Value Field Settings. Select Average from the Summarize value field by and then click OK.
    h. Format the City Population column with a comma and no decimal places.
    i. Format the Acceptance Rate % as a percentage with no decimal places.
    j. Format the PivotTable with the Dark Blue, Pivot Style Dark 2. Use the Value Field Settings dialog box to rename the columns to remove the words, 'Sum of' and the space after, from the 'Sum of City Population' column. Name the sheet tab Power Pivot (Figure 10–79).

Continued on next page

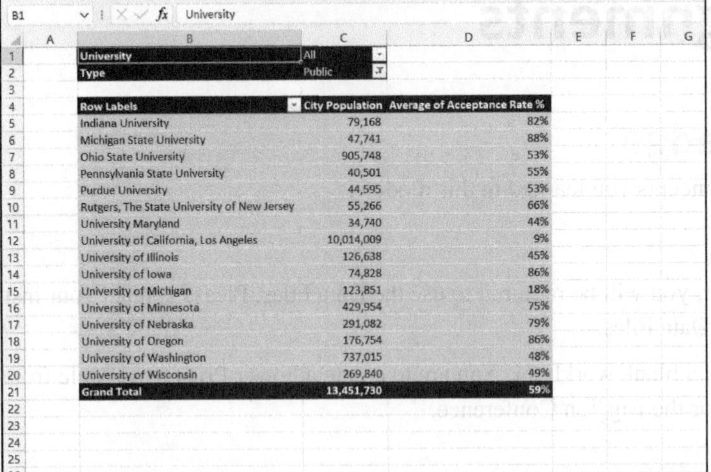

Figure 10–79

9. Rename the Sheet1 tab to, Homepage. Arrange all tabs from left to right as Homepage, Power Pivot, Conference Data, and Institutions.
10. On the Homepage sheet, in cell A1, insert the title, Big Ten Conference Pivot Table, apply the Title cell style to the new text, and then bold it. Merge and Center the title across the range A1:F1. Insert hyperlinks in the range C2:C4 to each of the other sheets in the following order; Power Pivot, Conference Data, and Institutions, and use the sheet name as the hyperlink text. Format the hyperlinks to be blue, and with a font size of 14, if necessary. Remove gridlines from the sheet.
11. Run the Accessibility checker and address the Hard-to-read Text contrast warnings by changing the Conference Data table style to Blue, Table Style Light 9 and the Institutions table style to Light Blue, Table Style Light 16. Close the Accessibility pane.
12. On the Homepage sheet, click cell A1. Save the workbook. Remove the ribbon customization. Submit the revised document in the format specified by your instructor.
13. **Consider This:** How would you use this data to make decisions about the colleges included in the PivotTable? What questions does it answer that might be useful if you were considering attending one of these universities? What other data would you add to the PivotTable to make it more useful when considering a university?

Extend Your Knowledge

Extend the skills you learned in this module and experiment with new skills. You may need to use Help to complete the assignment.

Creating a Macro, Editing a Macro, and Assigning It to a Button

Note: To complete this assignment, you will be required to use the Data Files. Please contact your instructor for information about accessing the Data Files.

Instructions: Start Excel. Open the workbook SC_EX_10–1.xlsx from the Data Files, and then save the workbook as an Excel Macro-Enabled Workbook file type using the file name, SC_EX_10_ GameDesign.xlsm.

In the following steps, you are to create a macro to add a column to a worksheet, assign the macro to a button on the Ribbon, and then execute the macro. Figure 10–80 shows the completed worksheet.

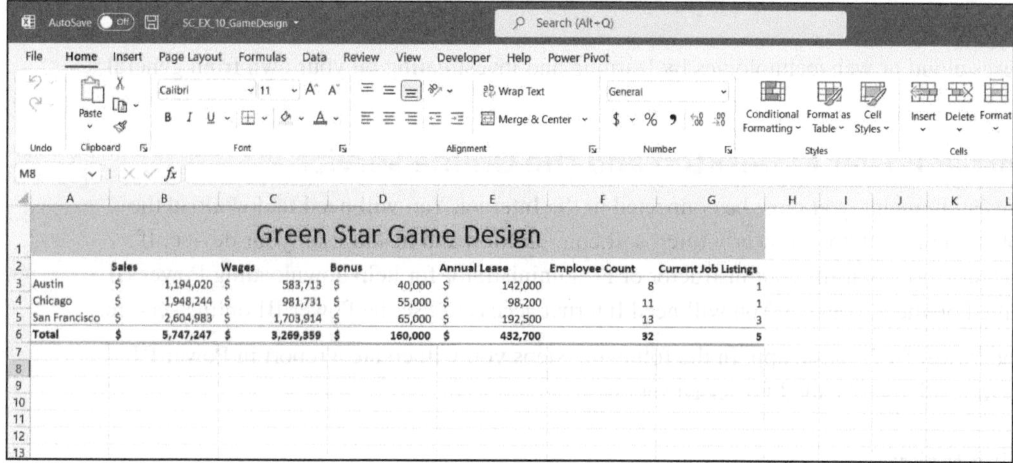

Figure 10–80

Perform the following tasks:

1. If the Developer tab is not displayed on the ribbon, display Backstage view, click Options in the left pane to display the Excel Options dialog box, click Customize Ribbon, click the Developer check box in the Customize the Ribbon area, and then click OK (Excel Options dialog box).
2. Create a macro that adds a column before the Employee Count column by doing the following:
   a. Click the Record Macro button (Developer tab | Code group).
   b. When the Record Macro dialog box appears, name the macro, AddColumn, and assign the keyboard shortcut CTRL+R. Store the macro in this workbook, enter your name in the Description box, and then click OK (Record Macro dialog box) to start the macro recording process.
   c. Select cell D3, click the Insert arrow (Home tab | Cells group), and then click the 'Insert Sheet Columns' command from the Insert Cells menu.
   d. Select cell D6, sum the cell range D3:D5, and then click the Stop Recording button (Developer tab | Code group).
3. In the newly added column, enter **Annual Lease** in cell D2, **142000** in cell D3, **98200** in cell D4, and **192500** in cell D5.
4. Right-click anywhere on the Quick Access Toolbar and then click 'Customize the Ribbon' on the shortcut menu. When the Excel Options dialog box is displayed, click the 'Choose commands from' arrow and click Macros. With Developer selected in the Main Tabs column, click the New Group button. Rename the New Group as Macros. With the Macros group selected, click AddColumn, click the Add button, and then click OK to add a Macro button to the Developer tab on the ribbon.
5. While still in column C, run the macro by clicking the AddColumn button. Enter the following data: **Bonus** as the column heading, **40000** in cell D3, **55000** in cell D4, and **65000** in cell D5. If requested by your instructor, add the following text to the end of the text in cell A1: **(EST. <year of birth>),** replacing <year of birth> with your year of birth.
6. Right-click the AddColumn button on the ribbon and then click 'Customize the Ribbon' on the shortcut menu, right-click the Macros (Custom) group and click remove. Click OK to remove the button from the ribbon.
7. Save the workbook. Submit the revised workbook as specified by your instructor.
8. **Consider This:** How would using the 'Use Relative References' button when recording your macro change how you insert columns using the AddColumn macro?

Expand Your World

Create a solution that uses cloud or web technologies by learning and investigating on your own from general guidance.

Creating a Report in Power BI Desktop and the Online Service

Note: To complete this assignment, you must be connected to the Internet. You will need to download the Power BI Desktop application from https://powerbi.microsoft.com/desktop and install it on your device. If you are working in a lab situation, consult your instructor or IT administrator for help downloading Power BI if it is not already installed on the lab device. You will need Internet access to use the Power BI online service.

Instructions: Start the Power BI Desktop app. In the following steps you will create a report in Power BI Desktop and publish to the online tool called Power BI service.

Perform the following tasks:

1. On the report canvas, select Learn with sample data, and then click Load sample data.
2. Load the sample data from the financials table.
3. Save the report using the file name, SC_EX_10_PowerBI.pbix.
4. Examine the table in Table view. Analyze the possible connections that can be made within the data.
5. Navigate to the Report canvas and perform the following analysis:
   a. Create a Clustered bar chart visualization using the fields Country, Product, and Gross Sales (Figure 10–81).
   b. Add a second page. On the new page, create a Donut chart visualization using the fields Month Name and Units Sold. Change the value of Sales from Sum to Count.
   c. Add a third page. On the new page, create a third visualization of your choice using three fields.
   d. Experiment by selecting different fields and highlighting various pieces of data.
   e. Deselect all visualizations and save your work.

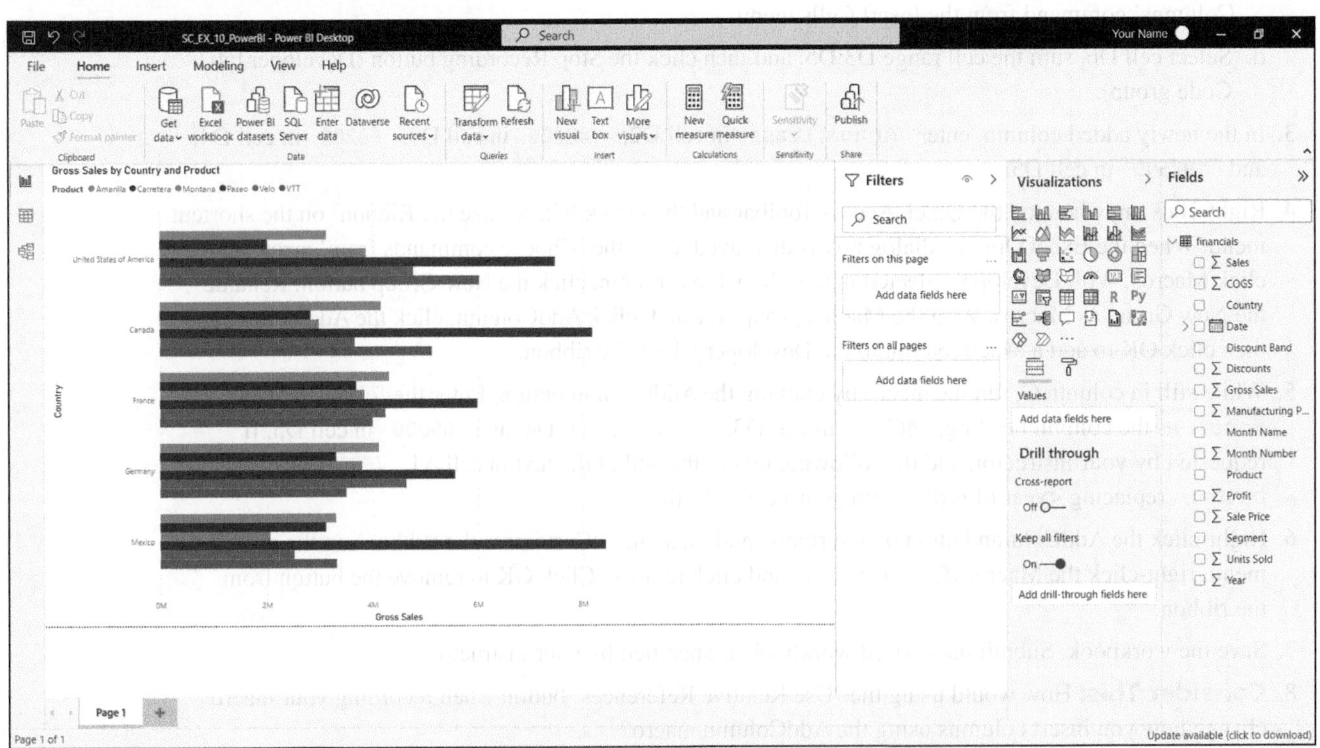

Figure 10–81

6. You will now publish your report to the Power BI service.
7. Select Publish (Home tab | Share group).
8. Save your changes, if prompted, and select My workspace in the Publish to Power BI window.
9. Click 'Open "SC_EX_PowerBI.pbix" in Power BI' in the Publishing to Power BI window to open the report in the Power BI online service. The application will open in your browser. (If you are unable to create a Microsoft Fabric free trial account, or unable to publish to the Power BI service for any other reason, skip to Step 14.)
10. Click Edit on the top ribbon. The online service will now show the Filters, Visualizations, and Fields panes and allow you to edit the report.
11. Note the different options presented on this page. You could elect to Visualize this data and create a new report from scratch using the financials data table, or you could Auto-create a report. You could also Share this data and collaborate with others.
12. Exit the Power BI online service and navigate back to Power BI Desktop.
13. Save the report and submit the document to your instructor.
14. If you were unable to access the Power BI service in the steps above, follow the alternative directions here:
    a. Search the web to research the Power BI service and Microsoft Fabric. Microsoft has many resources available.
    b. What differences can you find between Power BI Desktop and the Power BI service?
    c. What sharing capabilities are available with the Power BI service?
    d. What is Microsoft Fabric and how can you use it?
15. **Consider This:** In your SC_EX_10_PowerBI.pbix report, what visualization did you decide to create and what fields did you use? Did you use any data labels? How might you change your visualizations to improve their formatting or make them more informative?

In the Lab

Design and implement a solution using creative thinking and problem-solving skills.

Create a Visual Report and Video

Note: To complete this assignment, you will be required to use the Data Files. Please contact your instructor for information about accessing the Data Files.

Problem: The State of Washington wants a visual report displaying the number of visitors to its five large state parks in a recent year. They also would like to be able to access the Washington State Park website within the report. You decide to create a workbook with a home page and 3D Map.

Part 1: Using File Explorer, copy the Data File named Support_EX_10–5.xlsx and paste it to your storage location. Start Excel and open a blank workbook. Save the file on your storage location with the name, SC_EX_10_StateParks. Get the data from Support_EX_10–5.xlsx, using the State Parks table. Using the Power Query Editor window, make the first row the header row. Close and load the query. Rename the sheet tab to read, State Parks. Format the Visitors data with a comma style with no decimal places. Click the 3D Map button (Insert tab | Tours group) to open the 3D Maps window and create the three scenes described in Table 10–5. Rename the sheet tab with an appropriate name.

Continued on next page

Table 10-5: Washington State Parks

Scene	Scene Name	Layer Pane	Instructions	Zoom & Position	Scene Options
1	United States	Remove any locations		Zoom to entire continental United States	3 seconds duration, 1 second Fly Over effect
2	Washington	Add State field	Create a text box with the word WASHINGTON	Zoom to Washington	3 seconds duration, 1 second Fly Over effect
3	State Parks	Click the 'Change the visualization to Bubble' icon. Add the Zip Code field to the Location area. Add the Visitors field to the Size area. Add the State Park field to the Category area. Right-click the Legend and then click Remove.	Remove the Washington text box and turn on Map Labels. One at a time, right click each region on the map and then click Add Annotation. Click the Fields option button under Description (Add Annotation dialog box), select State Park, and then select Visitors. Adjust Placement as necessary so all Annotations are visible. Adjust the font size to 12 if necessary.	Zoom in as close as possible, while keeping all of the regions on the map.	3 seconds duration, 1 second Fly Over effect

Play the tour and then make any adjustments necessary. Capture a screenshot of scene 3. Save a video of the tour, using the 'Quick Export & Mobile' option, with the name, SC_EX_10_StateParksVideo. Change the tour name from Tour 1 to **State Parks.**

Add the screen capture to the Sheet1 worksheet, and rename the sheet, Homepage. If necessary, move the Homepage sheet to the left of the State Parks sheet. To the right of the screen capture, add a hyperlink to the State Parks sheet. Add a hyperlink to your saved video of the map animation. Below the State Parks hyperlink, add a hyperlink to the appropriate website on the Washington State Park Service website (https://parks .wa.gov/). Drag the 3D Map Tour graphic to the right of the State Parks table. Use the Accessibility checker to review the workbook for issues and resolve the issues using the skills you have learned. Navigate to the homepage and save the file. Submit the workbook to your Instructor.

Part 2: Consider This: Would you use Excel for a presentation? What are the advantages and disadvantages of using visualizations in Excel versus apps like PowerPoint or Prezi?

User Interfaces, Visual Basic for Applications (VBA), and Collaboration Features

Objectives

After completing this module, you will be able to:

- Create custom color and font schemes and save them as an Excel theme
- Create a new cell style
- Add and configure worksheet form controls
- Record user input to another location on the worksheet
- Define Visual Basic for Applications (VBA) code and explain event-driven programs
- Explain sharing and collaboration techniques
- Use passwords to assign protected and unprotected status to a worksheet
- Review a digital signature on a workbook
- Insert and edit comments in a workbook
- Format a worksheet background
- Enhance charts and sparklines
- Save a custom view of a worksheet

Introduction

This module introduces you to user interface design using form controls and ActiveX controls in a worksheet, the Visual Basic for Applications (VBA) programming environment, sharing and collaboration features of worksheets and workbooks, the use of comments in Excel, and the process of finalizing workbooks.

With Excel, you can design a user-friendly interface that permits users to enter information into the workbook easily, regardless of prior experience using the app. Form controls include interface elements such as option buttons, check boxes, and group boxes. ActiveX controls, including the label and command button controls used in this module, provide the same core functionality as the form controls but allow you, as the designer, greater power to customize the appearance of the control. The VBA programming environment is used to program the functionality of the ActiveX controls.

When you are working on a team, the sharing features of Excel make it easy to provide team members access to worksheet data and protect information as necessary. Distributing a workbook through OneDrive, Exchange, Office 365, or SharePoint maintains ownership of the file while providing all members of the team access to the most current version of the data at all times. Commenting features of Excel encourage feedback on specific content within the worksheet.

Additional collaboration tools permit users to display multiple versions of the same workbook side-by-side for comparison.

Project: Parks & Recreations Suppliers Sales Analysis

The project in this module follows proper design guidelines and uses Excel to create the workbooks shown in Figure 11–1. Parks & Recreation Suppliers (PRS) manufactures and markets metal products such as tables, benches, grills, and combination waste bins (trash and recycling) for the parks and recreation industry, focusing on small to medium-sized municipalities. Because PRS's reach is national, members of the sales team are located in offices throughout the United States. The head of sales wants to use advanced features of Excel to share information about PRS's prospective clients and projected revenue among the sales team. The PRS Sales Analysis workbook consists of three worksheets—Prospect Recorder, Sales Data Analysis, and a hidden Prospect List. The PRS Events workbook consists of two worksheets—Event Expenses and Prior Years.

The Prospect Recorder worksheet (Figure 11–1a) in the PRS Sales Analysis workbook provides a framework for recording information about sales prospects. You will add form controls and ActiveX controls to finish the interface development. You then will create VBA code to add functionality to the command button controls added to the worksheet. The functionality added through the VBA programming environment will present a series of dialog boxes instructing the salesperson to enter the prospect's contact information, and then will copy the prospect's information into the Prospect List worksheet (Figure 11–1b), which will be hidden from casual users.

The Sales Data Analysis worksheet (Figure 11–1c) in the PRS Sales Analysis workbook provides production details for 2028 and 2029 related to the three production lines (production facilities are located in California, Kansas, and Virginia) and four product types (tables, benches, grills, and bins). You will co-author the workbook and add comments.

The Event Expenses worksheet (Figure 11–1d) in the PRS Events workbook contains estimated costs for three sales events throughout the year 2029. You will add a watermark to this worksheet.

The Prior Years worksheet (Figure 11–1e) in the PRS Events workbook contains attendance figures for prior events (2022 through 2028) and a chart representing the data. You will add a background to this worksheet. You will add finishing touches to the existing chart and add sparklines for each event. You also will create a custom display for the worksheet and prepare the workbook for distribution to users of older versions of Excel.

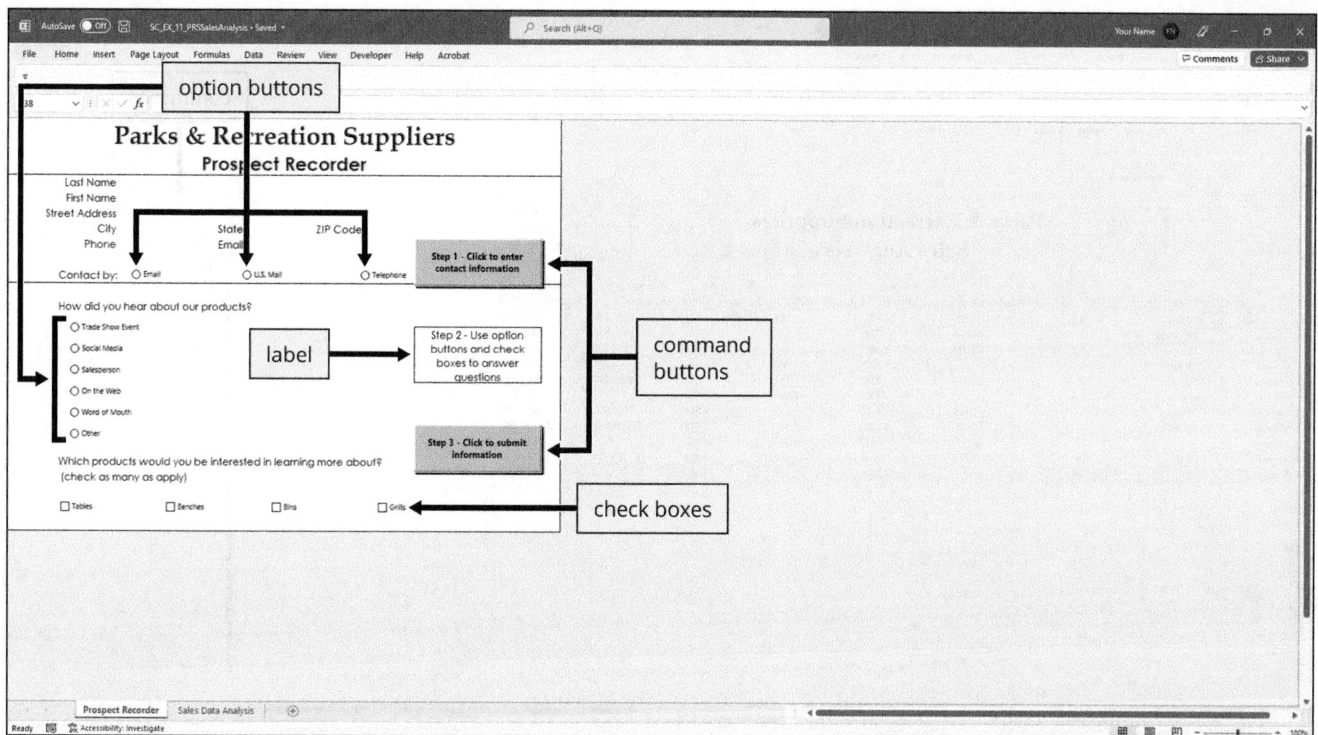

Figure 11–1(a): Prospect Recorder Form

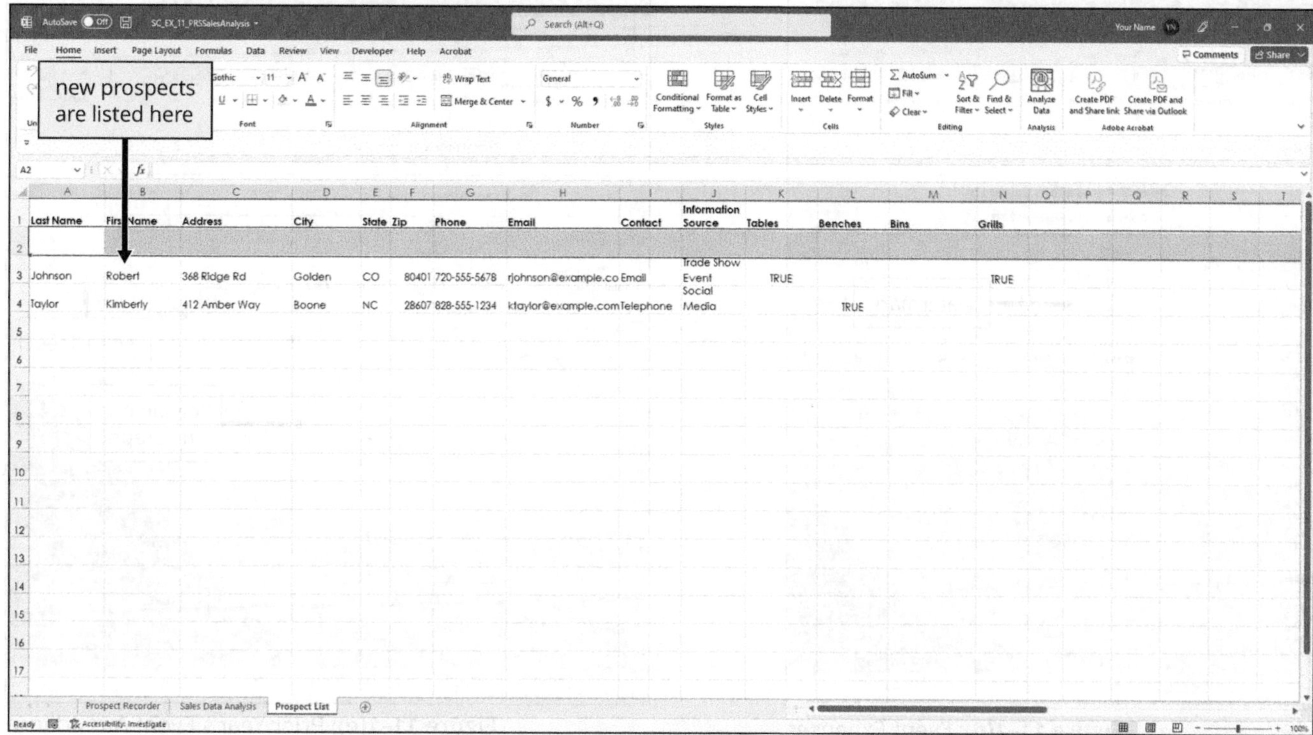

Figure 11–1(b): Hidden Prospect List

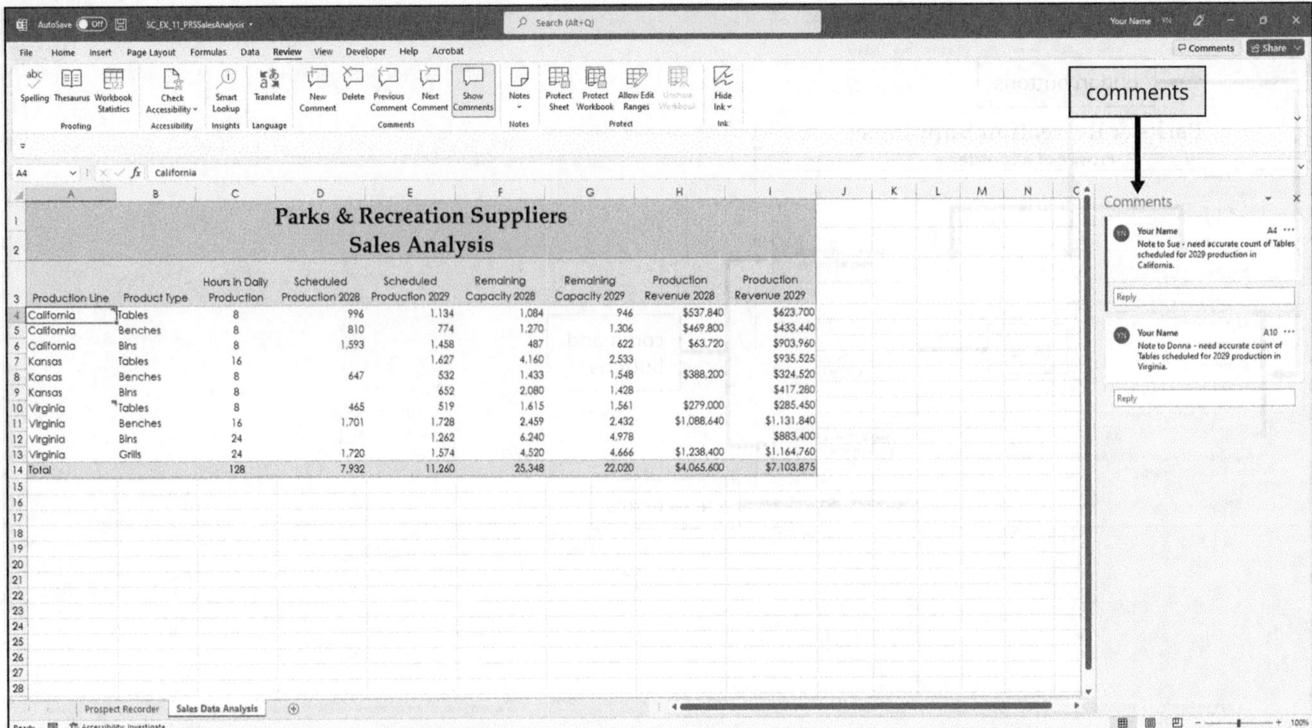

Figure 11–1(c): Sales Data Analysis

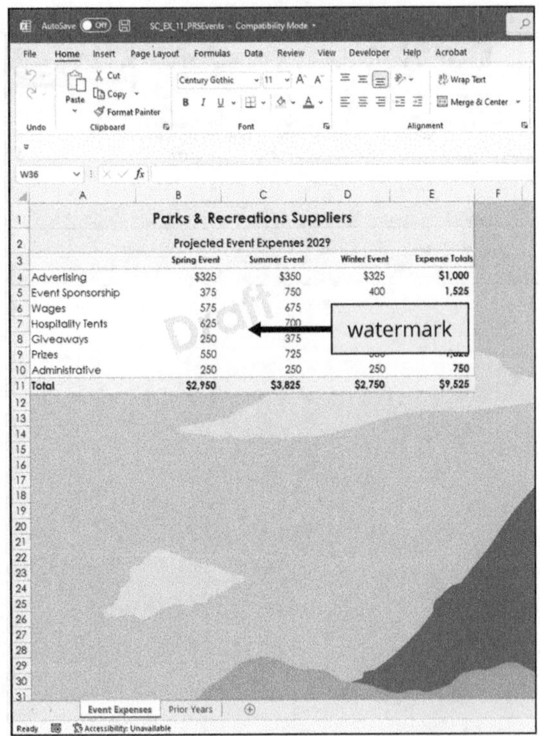

Figure 11–1(d): Event Expenses

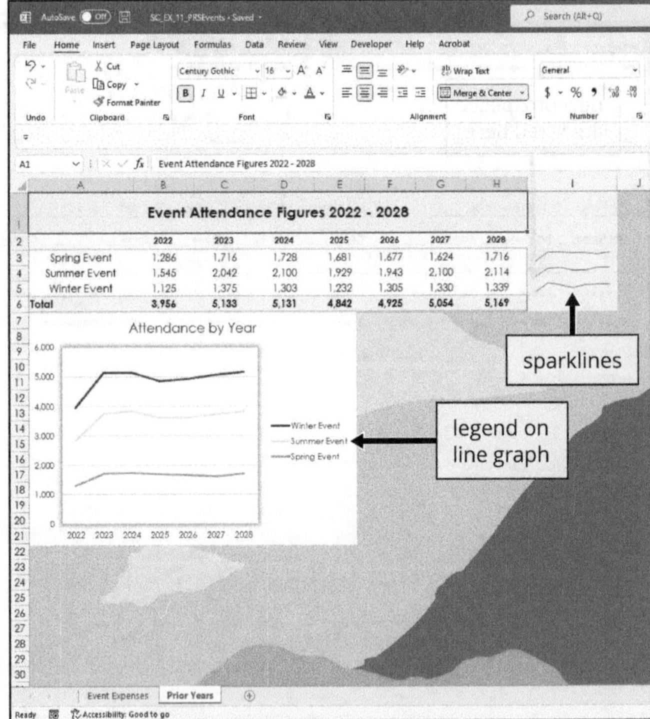

Figure 11–1(e): Prior Year's Event Attendance

The requirements document for the Parks & Recreation Suppliers Sales Analysis and Events workbooks is shown in Figure 11–2. It includes the needs, source of data, calculations, and other facts about the worksheets' development.

Worksheet Titles	Prospect Recorder, Sales Data Analysis, Event Expenses, and Prior Years
Needs	Parks & Recreation Suppliers (PRS) manufactures and markets four types of metal items (tables, benches, grills, and bins) to the parks and recreation industry nationwide. PRS has three production facilities in California, Kansas, and Virginia. The company would like a workbook to record information about sales prospects and maintain current information regarding scheduled production and sales. Additionally, a second workbook is needed to maintain current data on the upcoming 2029 sales events and consolidate historic attendance information on events held from 2022 through 2028. The information recorded from the prospects has been structured in a hidden Prospect List worksheet, but the sales manager wants a form created to make data entry easier. Changes need to be made to sales analysis data in a shared copy of the workbook. Finally, three copies of the shared events workbook exist with different cost values for the events. These values need to be merged into a single workbook, and visual enhancements to the worksheets are desired for presentation purposes.
Source of Data	A workbook has been developed with Sales Data Analysis and the start of a form. A master copy and two employee copies of the Events workbook exist.
Calculations	All formulas are set up in the workbooks. The worksheets in each workbook should be reviewed to familiarize yourself with the calculations.
Other Requirements	None.

Figure 11–2: Requirements Document

To Start Excel and Open a Workbook

The following steps start Excel and open a workbook named SC_EX_11-1.xlsx. To complete these steps, you will be required to use the Data Files. Please contact your instructor for information about accessing the Data Files.

1. **sam** Start Excel.
2. Open the file named SC_EX_11-1.xlsx from the Data Files.
3. If the Excel window is not maximized, click the Maximize button on its title bar to maximize the window.
4. Save the workbook on your hard drive, OneDrive, or other storage location as a macro-enabled workbook (.xlsm format), using **SC_EX_11_PRSSalesAnalysis** as the file name (Figure 11–3).

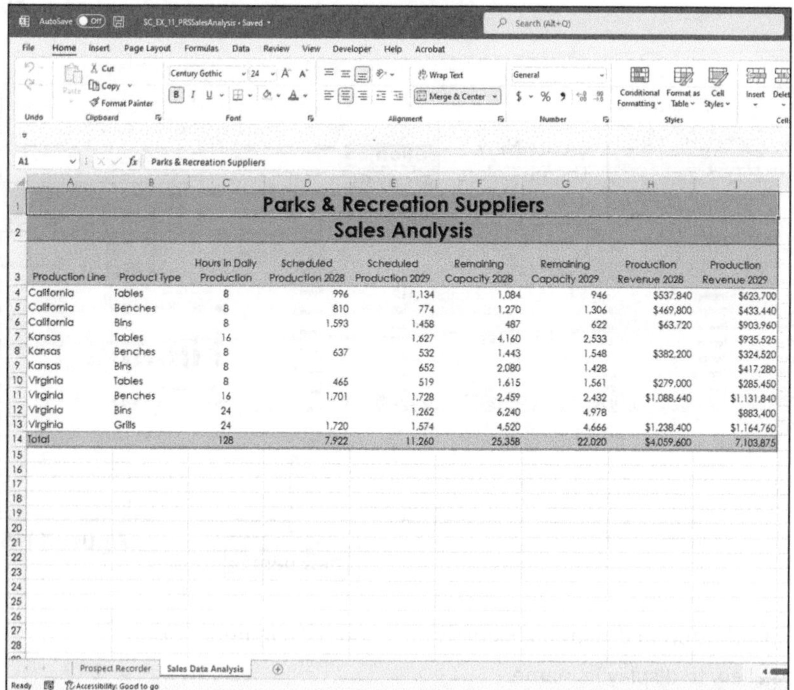

Parks & Recreation Suppliers
Sales Analysis

Production Line	Product Type	Hours in Daily Production	Scheduled Production 2028	Scheduled Production 2029	Remaining Capacity 2028	Remaining Capacity 2029	Production Revenue 2028	Production Revenue 2029
California	Tables	8	996	1,134	1,084	946	$537,840	$623,700
California	Benches	8	810	774	1,270	1,306	$469,800	$433,440
California	Bins	8	1,593	1,458	487	622	$63,720	$903,960
Kansas	Tables	16		1,627	4,160	2,533		$935,525
Kansas	Benches	8	637	532	1,443	1,548	$382,200	$324,520
Kansas	Bins	8		652	2,080	1,428		$417,280
Virginia	Tables	8	465	519	1,615	1,561	$279,000	$285,450
Virginia	Benches	16	1,701	1,728	2,459	2,432	$1,088,640	$1,131,840
Virginia	Bins	24		1,262	6,240	4,978		$883,400
Virginia	Grills	24	1,720	1,574	4,520	4,666	$1,238,400	$1,164,760
Total		128	7,922	11,260	25,358	22,020	$4,059,600	7,103,875

Figure 11–3

BTW

Create and Modify Custom Themes

Custom themes allow for personalization of workbooks with a custom set of colors, fonts, and effects. Use the Customize Colors option on the Colors menu (Page Layout tab | Themes group) or the Customize Fonts option on the Fonts menu (Page Layout tab | Themes group) to create custom options and select the desired effect setting from the Effects gallery. After selecting your desired options, click the Themes button and then click Save Current Theme to save your custom theme.

BTW
Touch Mode Differences
The Office and Windows interfaces may vary if you are using Touch Mode. For this reason, you might notice that the function or appearance of your touch screen differs slightly from this module's presentation.

Creating a Custom Theme

Excel provides an option for users to create color and font schemes rather than using one of the predefined sets. The chosen colors also will appear in the galleries related to formats, shapes, fills, and outlines. The chosen fonts will appear in the font box and in cell styles. Creating a **custom theme** means saving your own color and font schemes to a set.

To Create a New Color Scheme

The following steps create a custom color scheme. **Why?** Parks & Recreation Suppliers (PRS) wants to use the company colors of orange and brown.

- Click the Colors button (Page Layout tab | Themes group) to display the Color Scheme gallery (Figure 11–4).

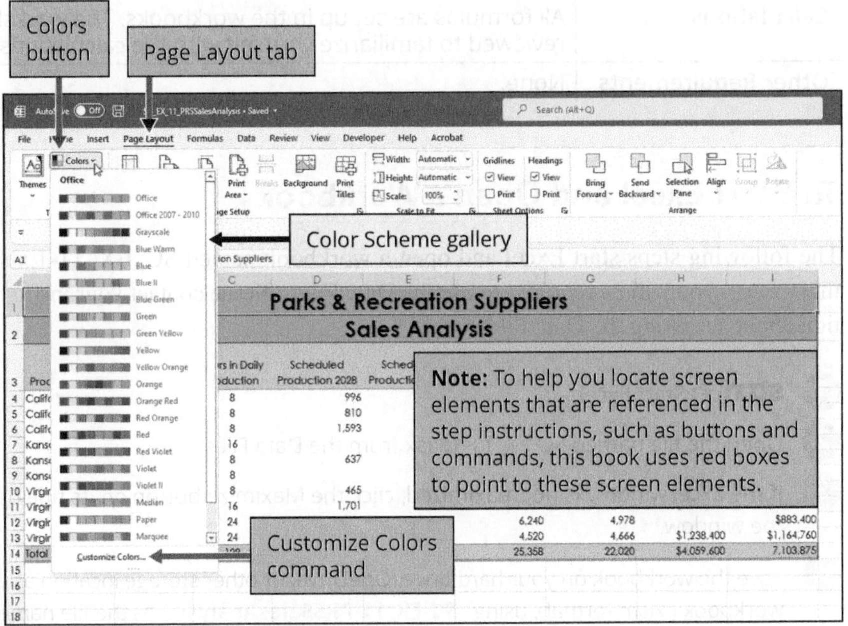

Figure 11–4

- Click Customize Colors to display the Create New Theme Colors dialog box.
- Type **PRS** in the Name box (Create New Theme Colors dialog box) to name the color scheme using the company's preferred acronym.

Q&A What if I do not enter a name for the modified color scheme?
Excel will save your color scheme with a default name that begins with the word, Custom, followed by a number (e.g., Custom 8).

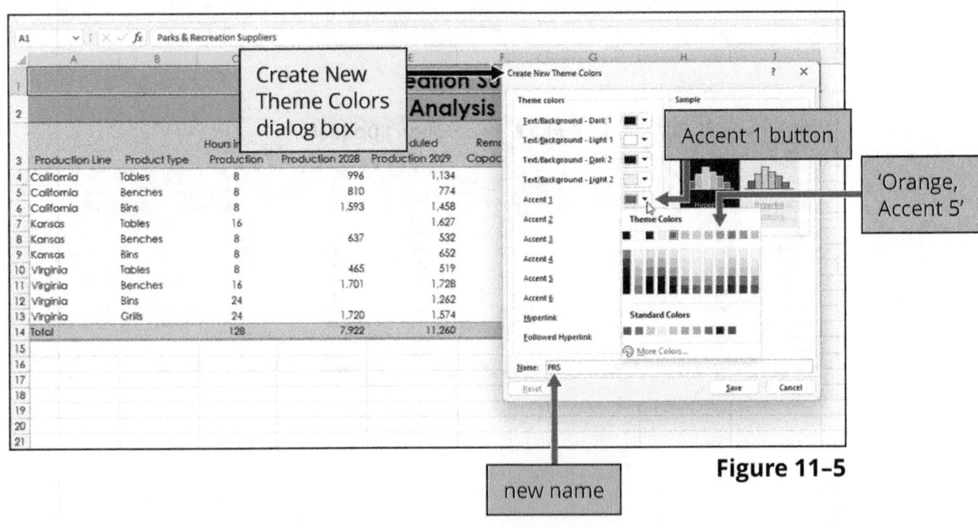

Figure 11–5

- In the Theme colors area, click the Accent 1 button to display a gallery of color choices (Figure 11–5).
- **Experiment:** Point to each color in the gallery to display its name.

- Click 'Orange, Accent 5' (in the first row of the Theme colors area, column 9) to select the Accent 1 color.
- Click the Accent 2 button, and then click 'Orange, Accent 5, Lighter 60%' (in the third row of the Theme colors area, column 9) to select the Accent 2 color.
- Click the Accent 3 button, and then click 'Orange, Accent 5, Darker 50%' (in the last row of the Theme colors area, column 9) to select the Accent 3 color (Figure 11-6).

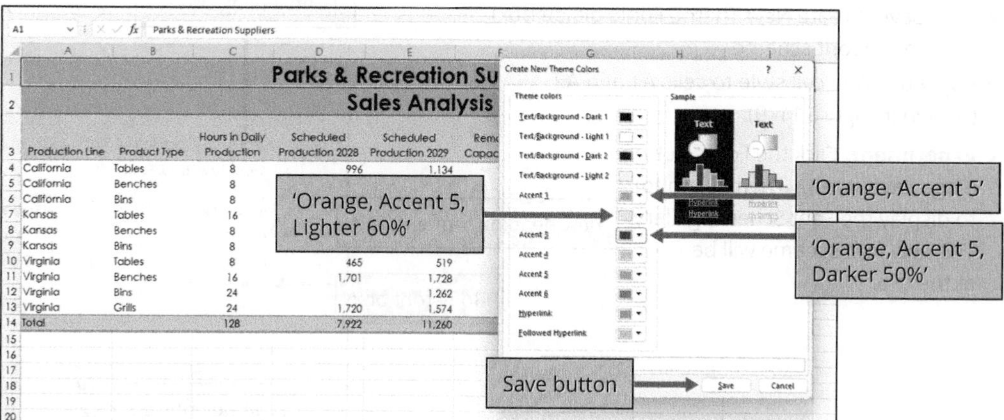

Figure 11-6

Q&A Can I delete a custom color scheme?
Yes. To delete a custom color scheme, first display the list of color schemes, right-click the custom color scheme, and then click Delete Scheme on the shortcut menu.

- Click Save (Create New Theme Colors dialog box) to save the color scheme.
- **Experiment:** Click the Colors button (Page Layout tab | Themes group) to display the Color Scheme gallery. The new color scheme will be in the Custom area at the top.

Q&A Why did the colors change immediately?
The cell styles were set previously to gray and dark gray. The new color scheme takes effect and changes all formatted cells.

To Create a Custom Font Scheme

The following steps create a custom font scheme. **Why?** Some companies associate certain fonts with branding; in this case, PRS wants to use the Book Antiqua font in 24 point bold for headings. Creating a custom font scheme affects only the the font, not the font size or attributes such as bold. You will make additional changes to the worksheet heading separately.

- Click the Fonts button (Page Layout tab | Themes group) to display the Font Scheme gallery, and then click Customize Fonts to display the Create New Theme Fonts dialog box (Figure 11-7).
- In the Name box, type **PRS** to name the font scheme.
- Click the Heading font arrow, and then scroll to and click Book Antiqua in the list to choose a heading font.
- If necessary, specify Century Gothic in the Body font box (Figure 11-8).

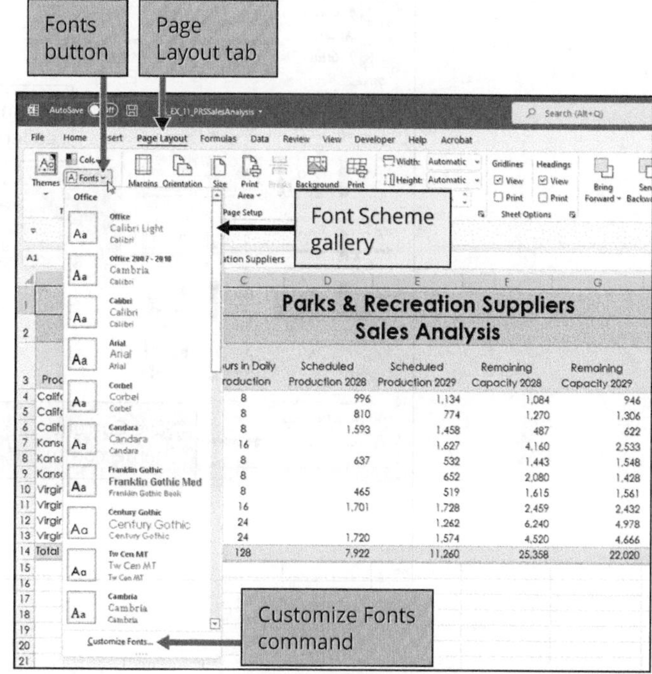

Figure 11-7

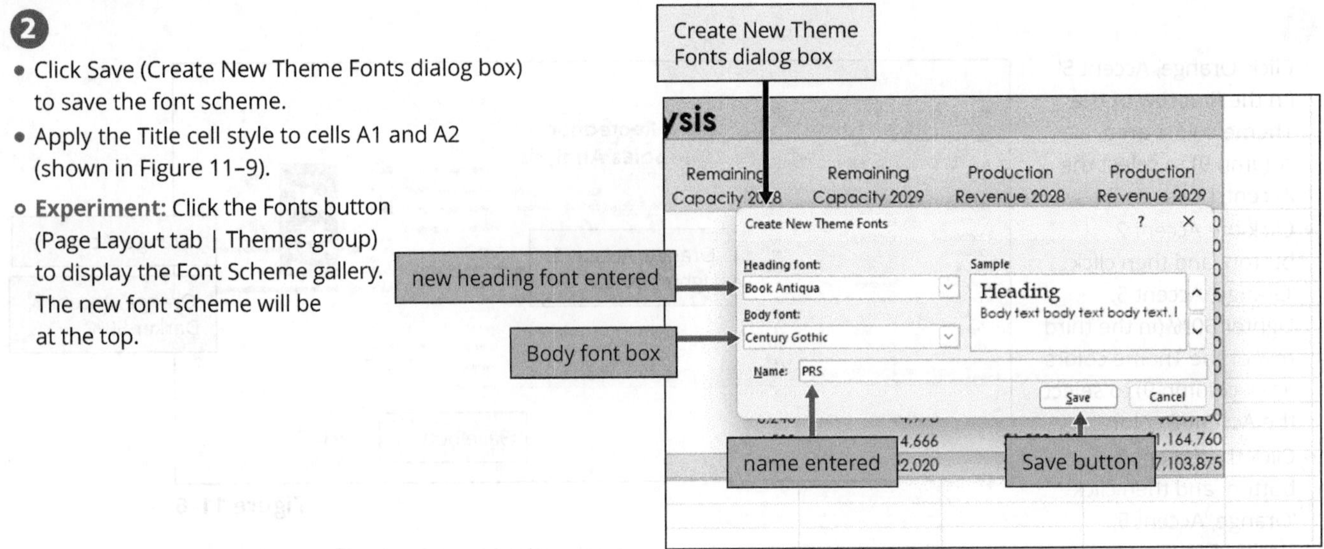

2

- Click Save (Create New Theme Fonts dialog box) to save the font scheme.
- Apply the Title cell style to cells A1 and A2 (shown in Figure 11–9).
- **Experiment:** Click the Fonts button (Page Layout tab | Themes group) to display the Font Scheme gallery. The new font scheme will be at the top.

Figure 11–8

To Save a Custom Theme

The following steps save the newly created color and font schemes as an Excel theme. **Why?** Saving them as a theme makes future use easier as you would not have to choose the color and font schemes individually. Excel saves themes with the extension, .thmx. If the theme is stored in the default storage location, Microsoft Themes, the new theme will appear in the list of themes. If you are working in a lab situation, you should save new themes on your storage device. You can browse for the theme when you need it and will not inconvenience other users of the shared device.

- Click the Themes button (Page Layout tab | Themes group) to display the Themes gallery (Figure 11–9).

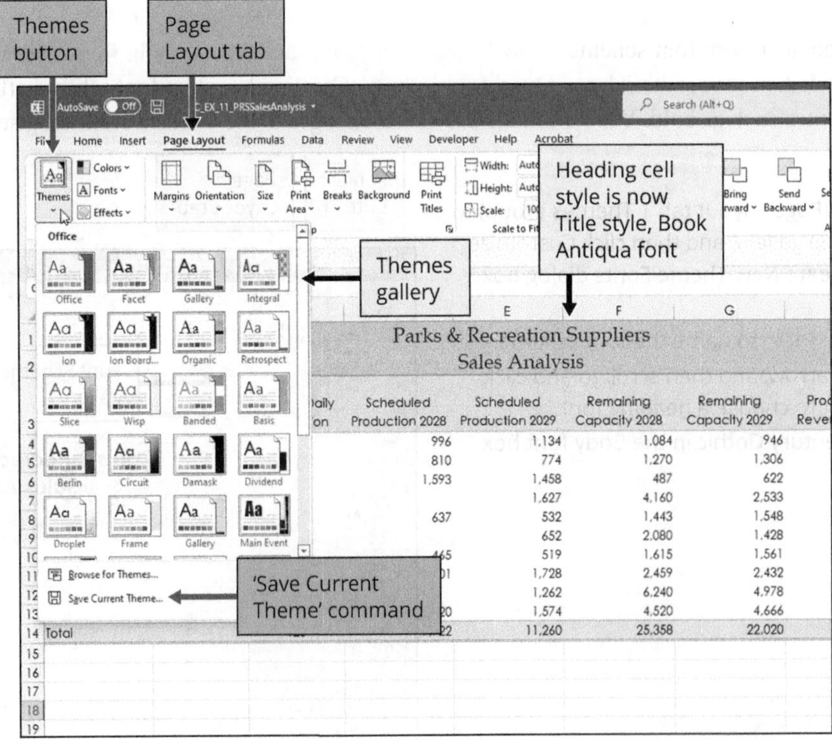

Figure 11–9

- Click Save Current Theme to display the Save Current Theme dialog box.
- In the File name box, type **PRS** and then browse to your Solution File storage location.

Q&A Where are themes usually stored?
By default, Microsoft themes are stored at C:\Users\Your Name\AppData\Roaming\Microsoft\Templates\Document Themes. You should save the PRS theme in your Solution File storage location.

3

- Click Save (Save Current Theme dialog box).

To Create a New Cell Style

The following steps create a new custom cell style. **Why?** Creating a cell style will enable you to quickly format cells in a consistent way and automate repetitive formatting.

1. Select cell H14, which contains the formatting you will use for the new cell style.
2. Click Cell Style (Home tab | Styles group).
3. Click New Cell Style to open the Style dialog box.
4. Review the check boxes to learn which elements will be included in the style. Do not make any changes.
5. Click Format to open the Format Cells dialog box.
6. In the Format Cells dialog box you would select the desired formatting for the cell(s). Do not make any changes.
7. Click OK to close the Format Cells dialog box and return to the Style dialog box.
8. Enter **Revenue** in the Style Name box as the name of the new style (Figure 11–10).
9. Click OK to close the Style dialog box and save the new Revenue cell style.

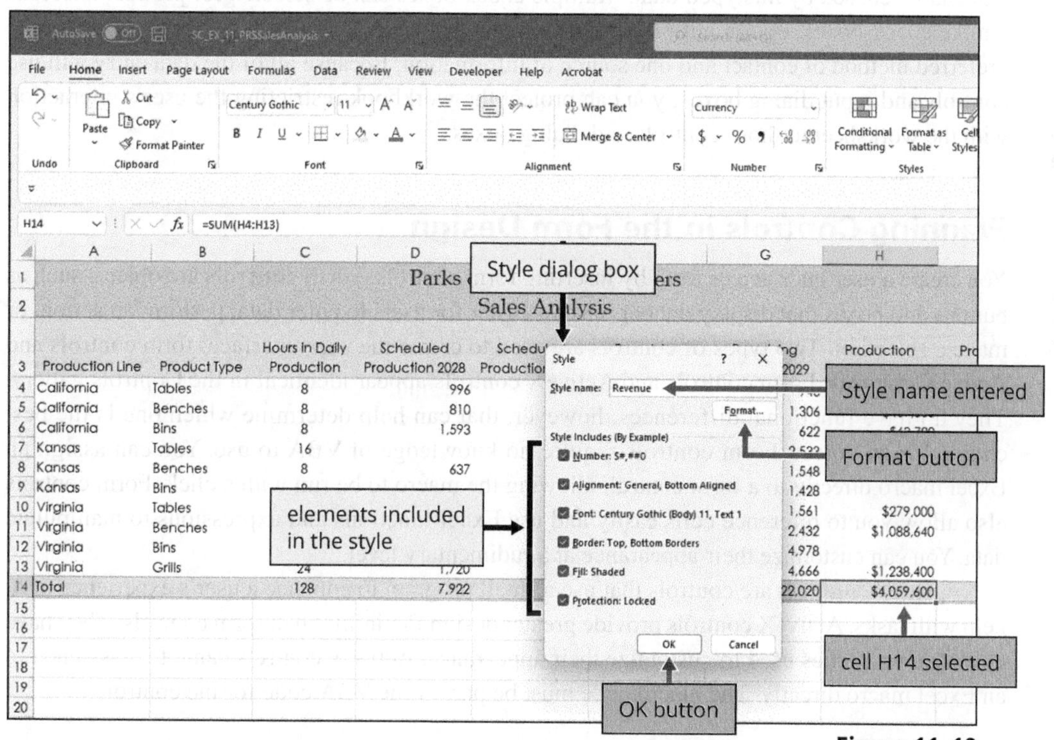

Figure 11–10

To Apply a Custom Cell Style

The following steps apply a custom cell style and complete the formatting of the worksheet heading. **Why?** You want to format another cell in the worksheet with the Revenue cell style. Applying the Revenue cell style to cell I14 is just like applying a cell style to any other cell. It is just convenient to create a unique cell style and apply it anywhere within your workbook without selecting all of the elements again.

1. Select cell I14. The new Revenue cell style will be applied to this cell.
2. Click Cell Style (Home tab | Styles group).
3. Click Revenue in the Custom cell style list. This will apply the Revenue cell style to cell I14.
4. Format cells A1 and A2 in bold, and increase the font size to 24.
5. Save the workbook again in the same storage location with the same file name.

BTW
Managing Theme Fonts
Each theme includes two font settings: one for body text and one for headings. To manage the fonts used for each, click the Fonts button (Page Layout tab | Themes group) and then click Customize Fonts to display the Create New Theme Fonts dialog box. Select the desired heading and body font options, enter a name for the theme, and then click Save to update and apply the font selections.

BTW
Ribbon and Screen Resolution
Excel may change how the groups and buttons within the groups appear on the ribbon, depending on the screen resolution of your computer. Thus, your ribbon may seem different from the ones in this book if you are using a screen resolution other than 1920 × 1080.

Designing the User Interface

The PRS sales team is using Excel to maintain information on prospective customers, known as prospects, and their product interests. The head of sales has requested a simple user interface that can be used by salespeople to record details about prospects in the workbook. A **user interface (UI)** is a collective term for all the ways you interact with a software program. Also called a **form** in Excel, it is a worksheet that provides an easy-to-use data entry screen. A form is convenient for people with little or no knowledge of Excel, who might not know which cells to select or how to navigate the worksheet. Figure 11–11 shows the approach you use to create the user interface and the design of the Prospect Recorder worksheet when complete.

When a user clicks the 'Step 1 - Click to Enter Contact Information' command button, code will trigger Excel to display a series of input dialog boxes to capture contact information. The remaining data (the prospect's preferred method of communication and how they heard about PRS's products) will be entered using check boxes and option buttons to help reduce input errors that can be caused by mistyped data. Multiple check boxes can be selected for product interests. Unlike check boxes, option buttons restrict users to one selection per group, in this case to one preferred method of contact and one source of information. Because all of the data entry will use controls and input dialog boxes, you can protect the workbook restricting the user's interaction with the worksheet to those controls and dialog boxes.

Planning Controls in the Form Design

You create a user interface or form by inserting form controls. **Form controls** are objects such as buttons and boxes that display data or make it easier for users to enter data, perform an action, or make a selection. Two types of controls are used to create the user interface: form controls and ActiveX controls. Form controls and ActiveX controls appear identical in the Controls gallery. They do have functional differences, however, that can help determine which one is the best choice for an object. Form controls require no knowledge of VBA to use. You can assign an Excel macro directly to a form control, allowing the macro to be run with a click. Form controls also allow you to reference cells easily and use Excel functions and expressions to manipulate data. You can customize their appearance at a rudimentary level.

ActiveX controls are controls that use a small program to enhance a user's experience or to help with tasks. ActiveX controls provide greater design flexibility than form controls. They have extensive properties used to customize their appearance. ActiveX controls cannot be assigned to an Excel macro directly. The macro code must be part of the VBA code for the control.

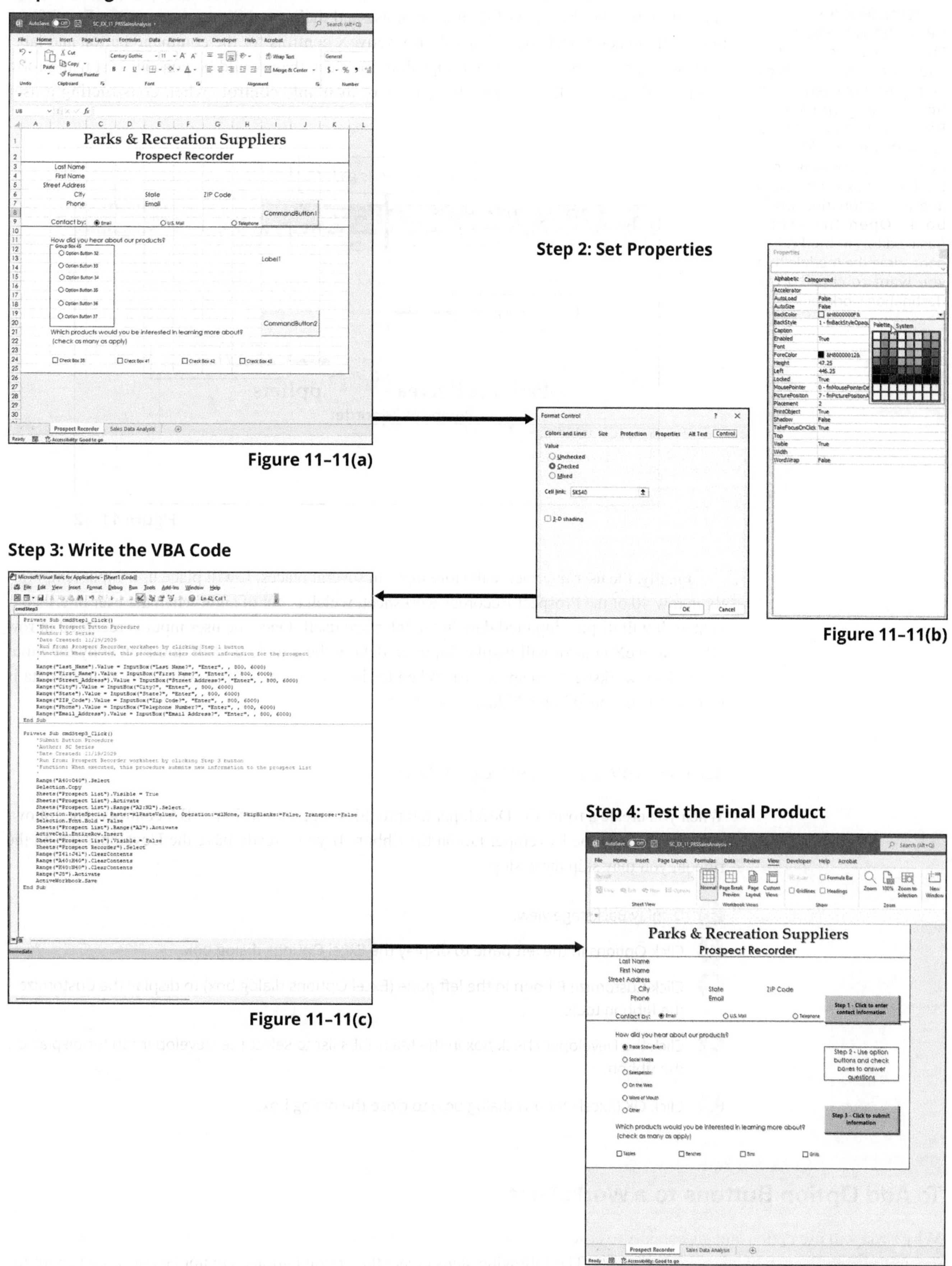

Figure 11–11(a)

Figure 11–11(b)

Figure 11–11(c)

Figure 11–11(d)

BTW

Copying Macros Between Workbooks

Macros consist of VBA code that can be edited or copied between workbooks using the Visual Basic Editor. To copy macros between workbooks, open the workbook containing the existing macro and the destination workbook. Open the Visual Basic Editor. In the Project pane, drag the module that you want to copy to the destination workbook.

To create the Prospect Recorder interface, you will use form controls for the check boxes and option buttons, because of their ease of use and their capability to incorporate Excel functions with no additional code. You will use ActiveX controls for the command button and label controls to provide a more visually appealing interface than would be possible just using form controls. Figure 11–12 displays the gallery of available controls when constructing a user interface.

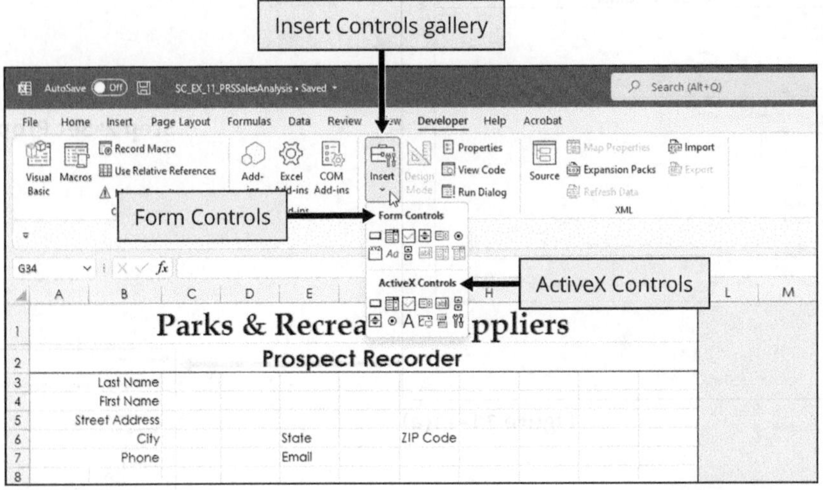

Figure 11–12

Finally, the user interface will store input in several places. It will place user input temporarily in row 40 of the Prospect Recorder worksheet, which is out of sight when the user interface is visible. It will display inputted data in the interface itself. Once the user input is recorded in row 40, an ActiveX control will display inputted data in the interface itself and then copy the input to a hidden worksheet, Prospect List. When testing the interface, you will verify that the data is recorded as intended in the hidden worksheet.

To Display the Developer Tab

When you create a form, the Developer tab provides access to various VBA controls. The following steps display the Developer tab on the ribbon. If you already have the Developer tab on the ribbon, you may skip these steps.

1. Display Backstage view.
2. Click Options in the left pane to display the Excel Options dialog box.
3. Click Customize Ribbon in the left pane (Excel Options dialog box) to display the Customize the Ribbon tools.
4. Click the Developer check box in the Main Tabs list to select the Developer tab for display on the ribbon.
5. Click OK (Excel Options dialog box) to close the dialog box.

To Add Option Buttons to a Worksheet

Why? You will use option buttons not only to ensure consistent data entry but also to make the final interface one that someone unfamiliar with Excel will be able to use easily. The following steps create the option buttons. Do not be concerned about the exact placement of controls on the form. The option buttons will be aligned later in the module.

1

- Display the Prospect Recorder worksheet.
- **Experiment:** Check out the worksheet to note what has been added already. Review the headings in row 39 and the data in column W, which displays stored text related to the option buttons and check boxes. You will use both later in the module. Click Cell A1 to return to the top of the spreadsheet.
- Display the Developer tab, and then click the Insert button (Developer tab | Controls group) to display the Controls gallery (Figure 11–13).

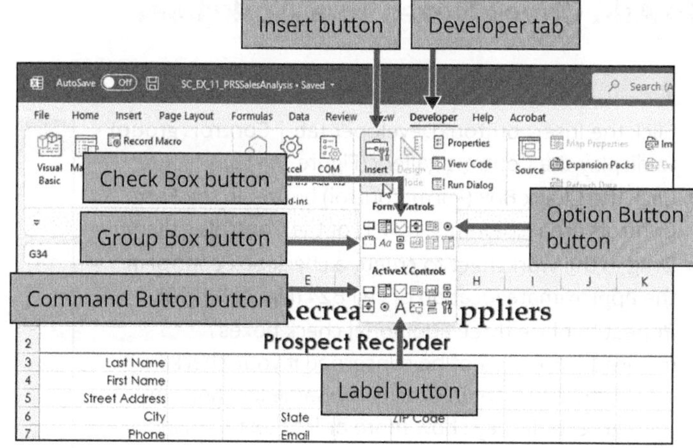

Figure 11–13

2

- Click the Option Button (Form Control) button in the Form Controls area (column 6, row 1) of the Controls gallery.
- Drag in the worksheet to create an option button control in the approximate location of cell C9 (Figure 11–14).
- Repeat to place eight additional option buttons (Figure 11–14). Do not be concerned if your option buttons are not in exactly the same locations in the figure, or if they show more or less text than in the figure.

Q&A Why does my option button display more or less label text than in the figure?
The amount of text displayed is determined by the size of the control. Dragging through a larger space on the worksheet will result in more label text being displayed. You can adjust the amount of visible label text by resizing the control.

My option buttons have numbers. Is that OK?
Yes, Excel may add a number in the caption or text beside the option button. You will change the caption later in the module.

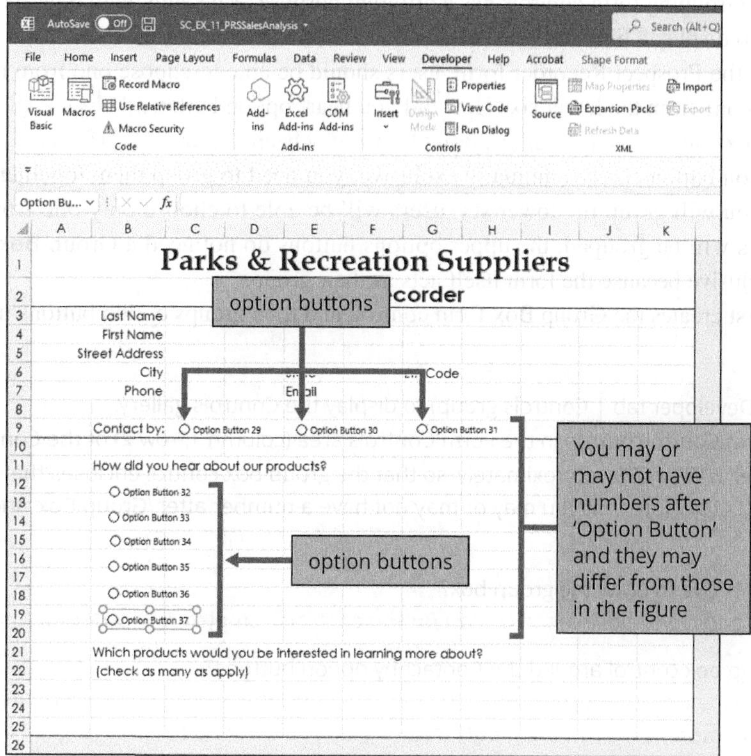

Figure 11–14

To Add Check Boxes to a Worksheet

- Click the Insert button (Developer tab | Controls group) to display the Controls gallery (Figure 11–13).
- Click the Check Box (Form Control) button in the Form Controls area (column 3, row 1) of the Controls gallery.
- Drag in the worksheet to create a check box control in the approximate location of cell B24 (Figure 11–15).
- Repeat to place three additional check boxes (Figure 11–15). Do not be concerned if your check box buttons are not in exactly the same locations in the figure, or if they show more or less text than in the figure.

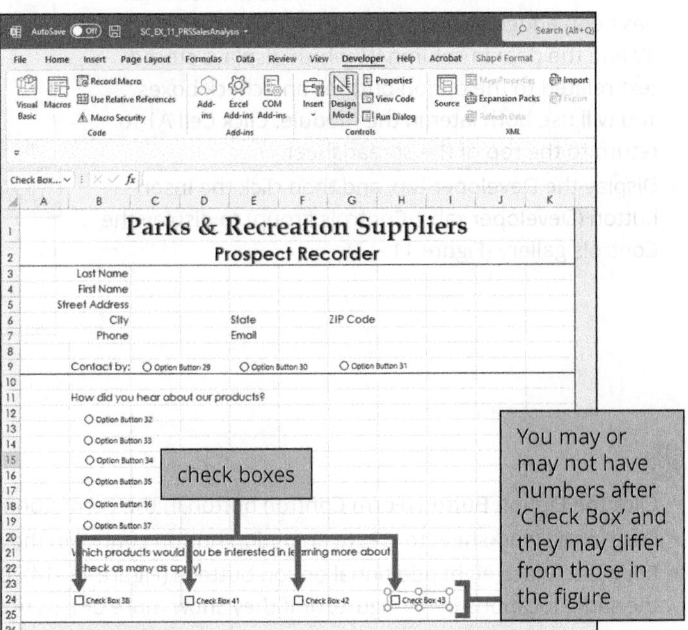

Figure 11–15

Q&A What if I placed a control incorrectly?
If you want to reposition a control, right-click the control to select it and then drag it to its new location. You can delete a control by right-clicking the control and selecting Cut on the shortcut menu.

The check box is not the size I need it to be. What can I do?
Check boxes are resized easily. The check boxes here will be resized after the captions are changed later in this module.

To Group Option Buttons Using a Group Box

You have grouped Excel objects, such as text boxes, pictures, and shapes for the purpose of keeping them together as they are moved, edited, or deleted. Grouping form controls has a different purpose, especially with regard to option buttons. An **option button** is a control used to display a limited list of mutually exclusive choices. In other words, a user can choose only one in a set of option buttons. In the Prospect Recorder form, users should be able to choose one from the upper three 'Contact by' options buttons, as well as one from the lower six 'How did you hear' option buttons. **Why?** PRS wants one indication of how customers would like to be contacted and one indication of how they heard about PRS products.

To make a set of option button choices mutually exclusive, you need to group them together using the Group Box form control. In this project, you will group the lower set; users will be able to choose only one from those six option buttons. Because the lower buttons will be grouped, the upper options buttons do not need a Group Box form control to keep them together and mutually exclusive because the form itself acts as their group.

The following step first creates the Group Box form control, and then groups option buttons inside it.

- Click the Insert button (Developer tab | Controls group) to display the Controls gallery.
- Click the Group Box (Form Control) button in the Form Controls area (column 1, row 2) of the Controls gallery (Figure 11–13).
- Drag the pointer from cell B12 to C20, approximately, so that the group box control encloses the six 'How did you hear' option buttons (Figure 11–16). Note that you may or may not have a number after 'Group Box' and it may differ from the one in the figure.

Q&A How accurately do I have to draw the group box?
The Group Box control needs to enclose in the Option Button controls completely in order for it to work correctly.

Why did I not add a group box control around the Contact by option buttons?
You could, but it is not necessary. Any option buttons not contained within a group box are treated as their own group contained by the form, so the Contact by option buttons are grouped by default. In this project, at least one group is necessary, however. Without the addition of at least one group box on the form, the user would only be able to select only one option button out of the nine option buttons.

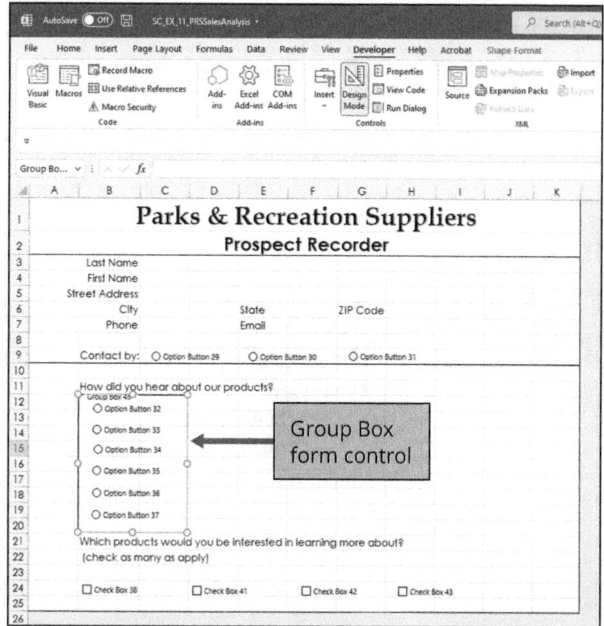

Figure 11–16

Labels and Text Boxes

Most forms contain text; option buttons usually need text labels that describe each option. In addition, users may need to enter text in response to a question. There are two types of text controls you can add to a form. A **Label ActiveX control** (also called a label) is a box with text used to display a message, such as identifying the purpose of a cell or text box. A label can also display descriptive text, such as titles, captions, or brief instructions on the form. A label can also display a descriptive picture.

A **Text Box ActiveX control** is a rectangular box in which the user can view, enter, or edit data. A Text Box ActiveX control is different from a regular text box that you would insert using the Text Box command (Insert tab | Text group). A Text Box ActiveX control is a special text box used for data entry, programmed with code to move the data from the text box to a specific location or into a formula on the worksheet. While you are creating a Text Box ActiveX control, Excel turns on Design Mode, allowing you to set properties and write code. After you are finished, you can turn off Design Mode, allowing users to enter text in the text box. You also can use a text box to display text that is independent of row and column boundaries, or free-floating, preserving the layout of a grid or table of data on the worksheet.

To Add a Label Control to the Worksheet

You have added many option buttons and check boxes to the form so far, and now you need to identify them. **Why?** Labels are an important part of a user interface because they guide users to select the correct controls as they enter their information. The following step adds a label control to the worksheet.

- Click cell G12 or another cell to deselect the group box.
- Click the Insert button (Developer tab | Controls group) to display the Controls gallery.
- Click the Label (ActiveX Control) button in the ActiveX Controls area (column 3, row 2) of the Controls gallery (refer to Figure 11–13).
- Drag in the worksheet from cell I13 through the lower-right corner of cell J15 to create a Label control (Figure 11–17). Note that you may or may not have a number after 'Label' and it may differ from the one in the figure.

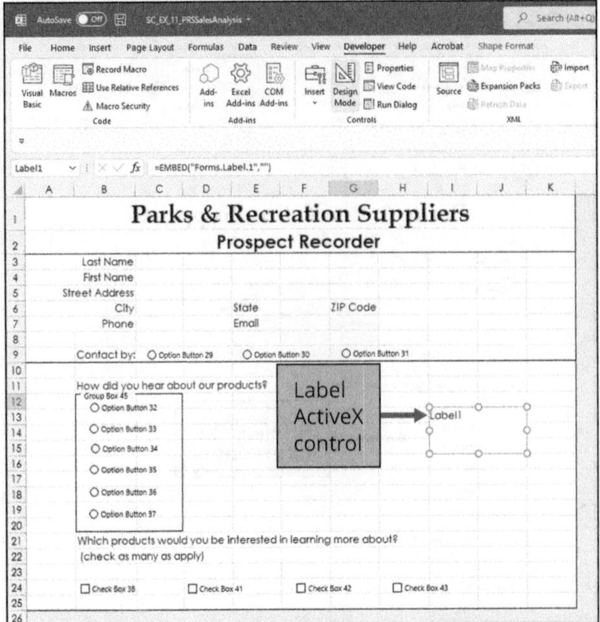

Figure 11–17

To Create a Text Box ActiveX Control In this project, you will not use a Text Box ActiveX control; the data entry will be supplied by a series of Input Boxes that you will learn about later. If you wanted to create a Text Box ActiveX control, you would do the following:

1. Click the Insert button (Developer tab | Controls group) to display the Controls gallery.
2. Click the Text Box (ActiveX Control) button in the ActiveX Controls area (column 5, row 1) of the Controls gallery.
3. Drag in the worksheet to create a text box.
4. Set properties and write code as necessary.
5. Before releasing the workbook to the public, click the Design Mode button (Developer tab | Controls group) to turn it off, making the text box active.

To Add Command Buttons to the Worksheet

The use of command buttons gives the user control over the execution of each step of the process when entering data into the form. There is a difference between a Command Button form control and a Command Button ActiveX control. Why? A Command Button ActiveX control can have Visual Basic code associated with it that accomplishes more complex actions than a macro or a Command Button form control can accommodate. The two buttons are created in a similar manner, however. The following steps add two Command Button ActiveX controls to the worksheet.

- Click the Insert button (Developer tab | Controls group) to display the Controls gallery.
- Click the Command Button (ActiveX Control) button in the ActiveX Controls area (column 1, row 1) of the Controls gallery.
- Drag in the worksheet from cell I7 through the lower-right corner of cell J9 to create a Command Button ActiveX control.

- Repeat Step 1 to add a second command button in the location shown in Figure 11–18. Note that you may or may not have a number after the 'CommandButton' text on your buttons and the numbers may differ from those shown in the figure.
- Save the workbook again in the same storage location with the same file name.

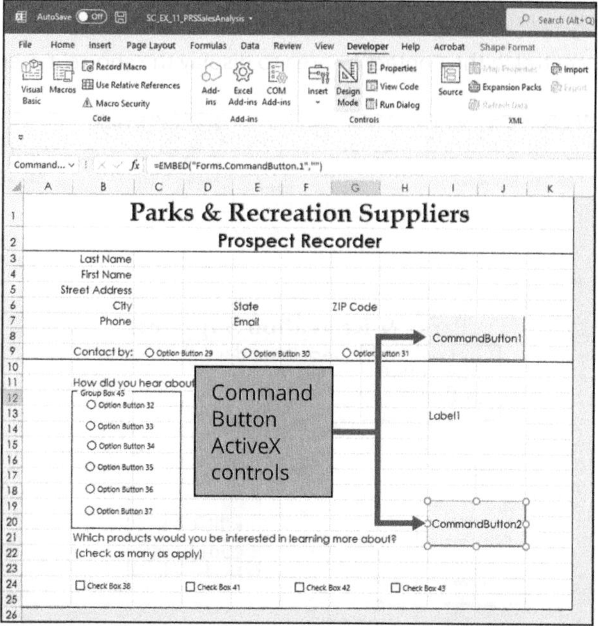

Figure 11–18

Break Point: If you want to take a break, this is a good place to do so. You can exit Excel now. To resume later, start Excel, open the file called SC_EX_11_PRSSalesAnalysis.xlsm, and continue following the steps from this location forward.

Setting Form Control Properties

Each form control in the Controls gallery has many properties, or characteristics, that can be set to determine the form control's appearance and behavior. You set these properties using the Format Control dialog box, which can be accessed by right-clicking the form control and selecting Format Control from the shortcut menu or by selecting the control and clicking the Control Properties button (Developer tab | Controls group) on the ribbon.

The next step is to set the properties for the 13 form controls (check boxes and option buttons) in the user interface. The group box, while technically a form control, will not be formatted here; it will be formatted using VBA later in the module. The three ActiveX controls also will be formatted later in the module.

To Format the Option Buttons

Why? The Option Button form controls must be formatted to identify their purpose for the user. Other formatting options can be used to make the controls and the worksheet itself easier to use. The following steps change the text associated with the option button controls and resize the controls.

- Right-click the first option button control in the Contact by area to display the shortcut menu (Figure 11–19).

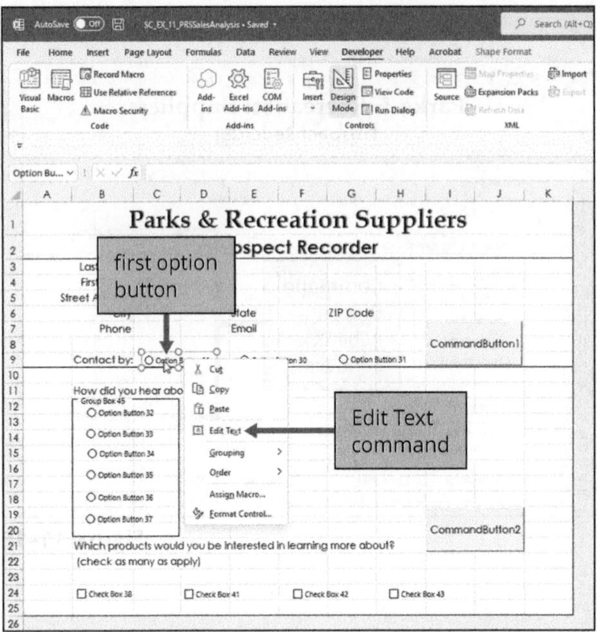

Figure 11–19

- Click Edit Text on the shortcut menu to edit the control text.
- Delete the text in the control and type **Email** to replace the text.
- Resize the control so that it just encloses the new text (Figure 11–20).

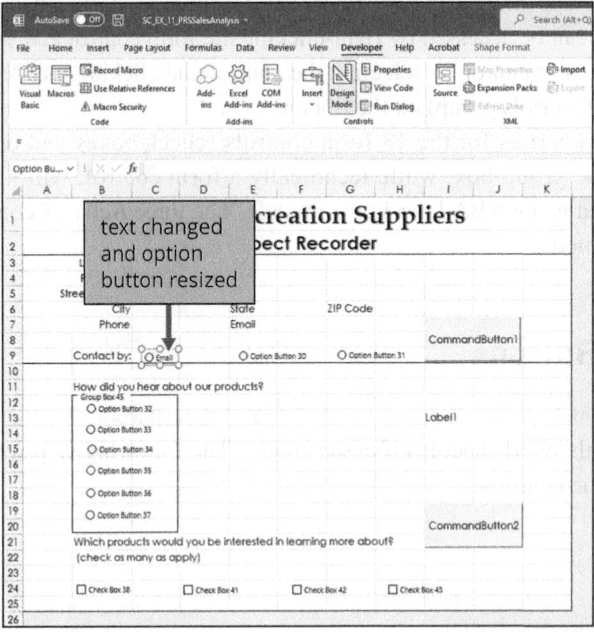

Figure 11–20

- Repeat Steps 1 and 2 to rename and resize the other two contact controls, entering the names **U.S. Mail** and **Telephone**, respectively.
- If necessary, right-click the Telephone control to select it.
- ALT+drag the control until the right edge is aligned with the right edge of column H (Figure 11–21).

Q&A Why did I hold down the ALT key while positioning the Telephone control?
Using the ALT key aligns the controls to the Excel gridlines, making it easier to place items on the form.

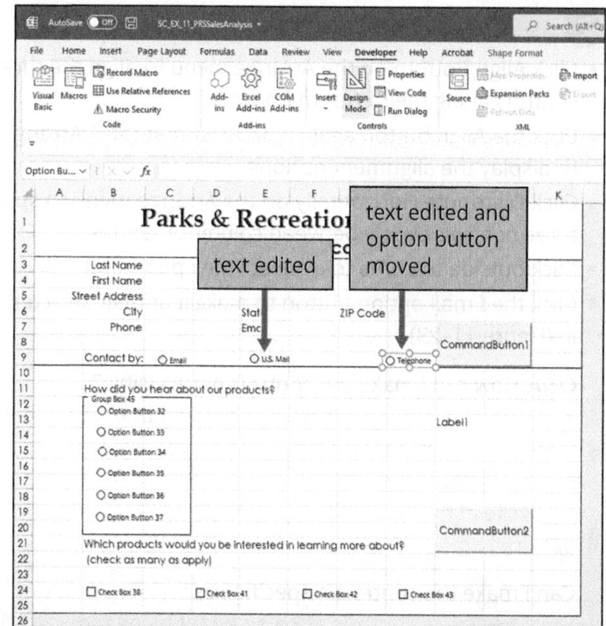

Figure 11–21

- With the Telephone control still selected, CTRL+click the other two controls to select all three option button controls.
- Display the Shape Format tab. In the Shape Height box (Shape Format tab | Size group), type **.2** and press ENTER to set the shape height.

Q&A Why did I need to hold down the CTRL key while clicking the other two controls?
The CTRL key adds additional controls to the selection so that formatting and alignment options can be adjusted on the set of controls rather than individually.

To Align and Distribute

You have previously aligned objects in Excel, which means you have made either an edge or center of an object line up with another object. You also can distribute objects. The **distribute** command evenly spaces multiple objects horizontally or vertically. The distribute command works on three or more objects.

1

- With the three option buttons still selected, click the Align button (Shape Format tab | Arrange group) to display the Align menu (Figure 11–22).

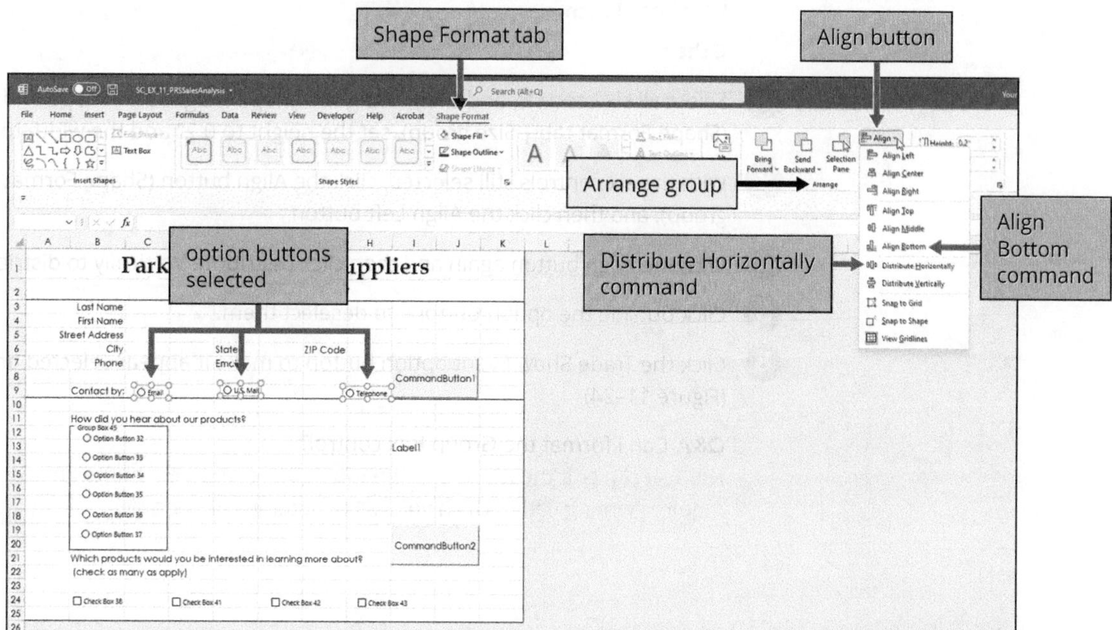

Figure 11–22

- Click Align Bottom on the Arrange menu to align the three controls along their bottom borders.
- Click the Align button again (Shape Format tab | Arrange group) to display the alignment options.
- Click Distribute Horizontally on the Arrange menu to space the three controls evenly between columns C and H.
- Click outside the area to deselect the option buttons.
- Click the Email option button to make it appear selected or filled in (Figure 11–23).

Q&A How can I make the controls more visible?
You can format the controls with borders and fill colors to make them stand out from the background. From the shortcut menu, you can select Format Control and then use the Colors and Lines tab in the Format Control dialog box to apply colors and patterns.

Can I make the controls a specific size?
Yes. The size of controls also can be set using the Size tab, which you display by selecting the Format Control command on the shortcut menu.

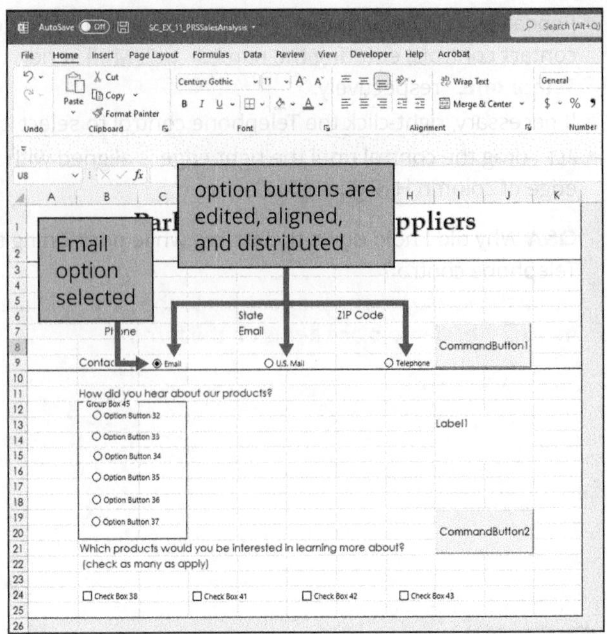

Figure 11–23

To Format the Option Buttons in the Group Box

The following steps format the option buttons in the group box control.

1. One at a time, right-click each of the six option buttons in the group box and edit the text to match the following:

   Trade Show Event

   Social Media

   Salesperson

   On the Web

   Word of Mouth

   Other

2. Select all six controls, and then, using the Shape Height and Shape Width boxes (Shape Format tab | Size group), set the height to 0.2" and the width to 1.1".
3. With the six controls still selected, click the Align button (Shape Format tab | Arrange group), and then click the Align Left button.
4. Click the Align button again and then click Distribute Vertically to distribute the objects.
5. Click outside the option buttons to deselect them.
6. Click the Trade Show Event option button to make it appear selected or filled in (Figure 11–24).

   Q&A Can I format the Group Box control?
   No. You can edit the text along the top of the group box, but to change it in any other way requires writing code, which you will do later in the module.

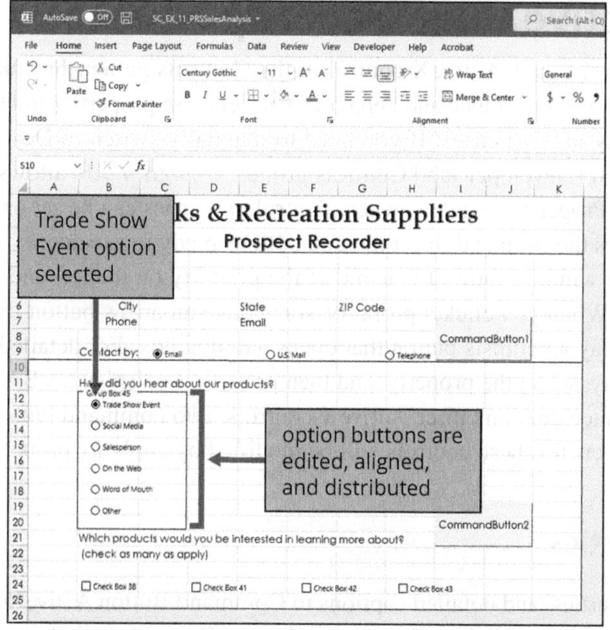

Figure 11–24

To Format the Check Box Controls

The check box controls are formatted in the same fashion as the option button controls. The following steps format and align the check box controls.

1. Select each of the four check box buttons, and in turn, type the following: **Tables**, **Benches**, **Bins**, and **Grills**.
2. Move the leftmost check box button so that its upper-left corner aligns with the upper-left corner of cell B24, and then move the rightmost check box button so that its upper-right corner aligns with the upper-right corner of cell H24.
3. Select all four controls and then, using the Shape Height and Shape Width boxes (Shape Format tab | Size group), set the height to 0.2" and the width to 1.2".
4. If necessary, select all four controls and then, using the Align button (Shape Format tab | Arrange group), apply the Align Top and Distribute Horizontally formats to the group. Deselect the check box controls (Figure 11–25).

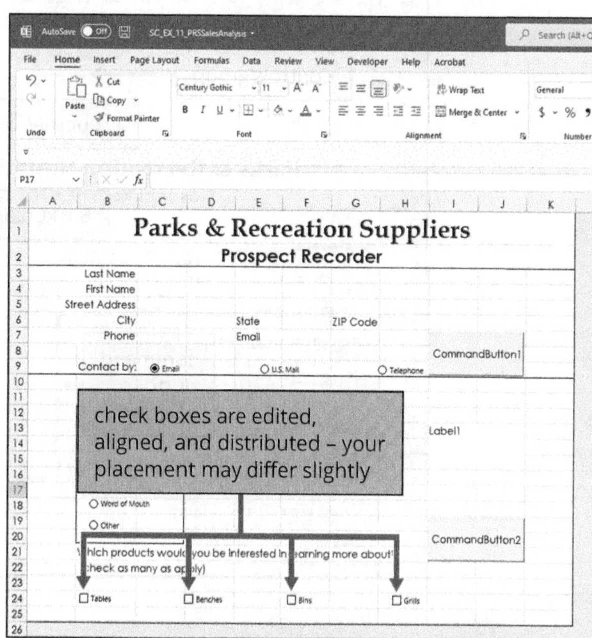

Figure 11–25

Setting ActiveX Control Properties

As with form controls, each ActiveX control in the Controls gallery has many properties that determine the control's appearance and behavior. You set these properties in Design Mode, which opens automatically in most cases. If you need to manually switch to Design Mode, click the Design Mode button (Developer tab | Controls group). **Design Mode** allows the use of various tools including the Properties window, where control properties can be set or edited. Turning off Design Mode makes the form and the command buttons ready to execute.

The Properties window shows the name of the property on the left and the setting, text, or value on the right. When you click a property, some have an arrow button that displays a list of choices; some display an ellipsis button that opens a dialog box. For detailed information about each format property, select the property, and then press F1 to display a VBA Help topic.

The user interface contains three ActiveX controls: two command buttons and a label. The color, font, and effects for these controls will be modified by applying property values.

To Set Command Button Properties

You can add color, font formatting, shadow properties, and detailed captions to Command Button ActiveX controls in order to draw a user's attention. You also can give both controls user-friendly names using the Properties window. The following steps set the command button properties, and add alternative text to improve accessibility. **Why?** Clearly formatted and customized command buttons will help users know what to do in the form.

- Select the two command button controls.
- Display the Developer tab and then click the Properties button (Developer tab | Controls group) to open the Properties window. If necessary, move the Properties window to the right of column K so it does not obscure the worksheet data.
- Click the BackColor property, and then click the BackColor arrow to display the BackColor options.
- Click the Palette tab to display the color options (Figure 11–26).

Q&A Why does the Properties window appear different from other dialog boxes in Excel?
The Properties window is part of the VBA interface and is used to manage ActiveX controls in Excel.

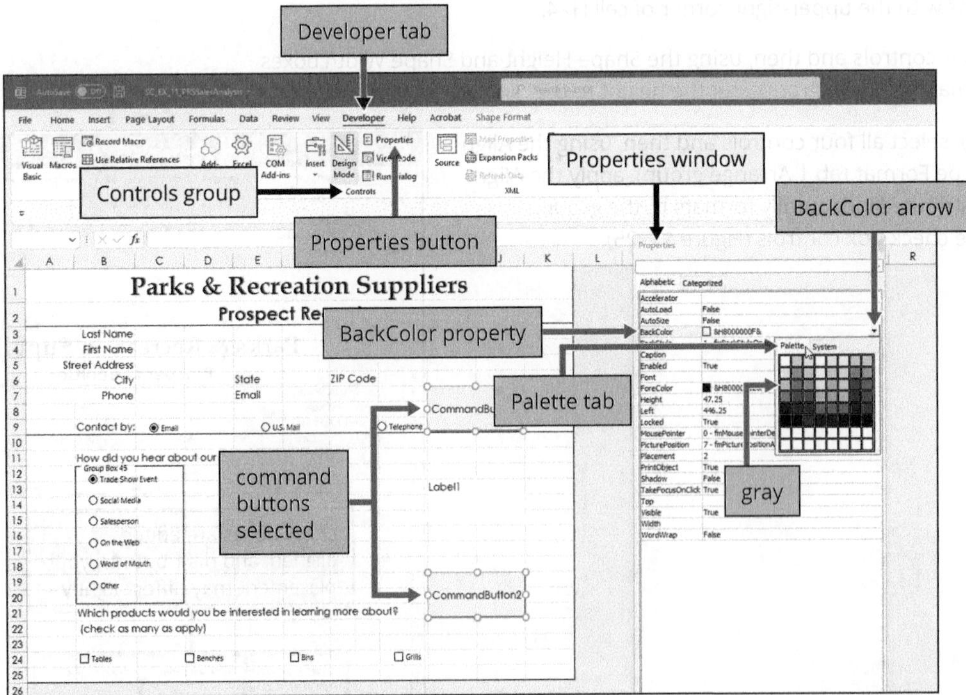

Figure 11–26

2

- Click gray (column 1, row 3) to add a gray background to the command buttons.
- Click the Font property to display the ellipsis button.
- Click the ellipsis button to display the Font dialog box.
- Select Segoe UI in the Font list, Bold in the Font style list, and 10 in the Size list to change the font on the command buttons (Figure 11–27).

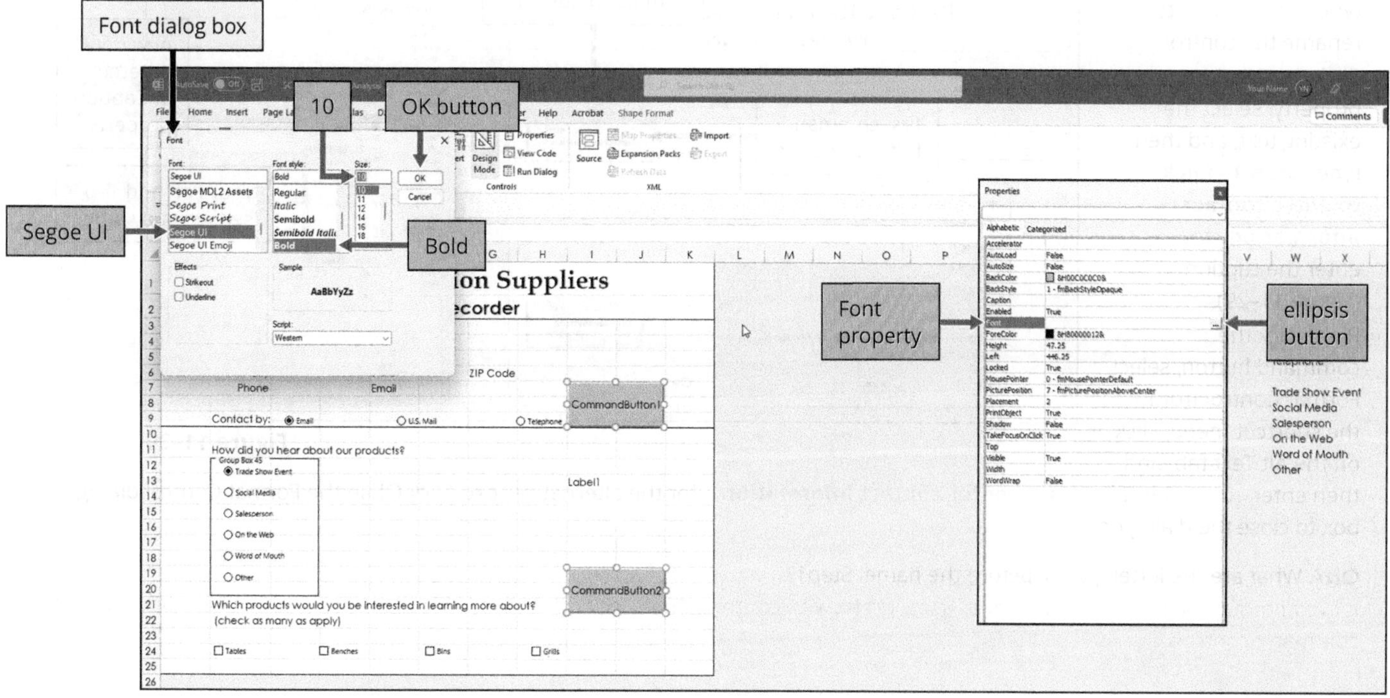

Figure 11–27

- Click OK (Font dialog box) to apply this font to the text in the controls.
- Set the Shadow property to True.
- Set the Height property to 50.25 and the Width property to 140.25.
- Set the WordWrap property to True (Figure 11–28).

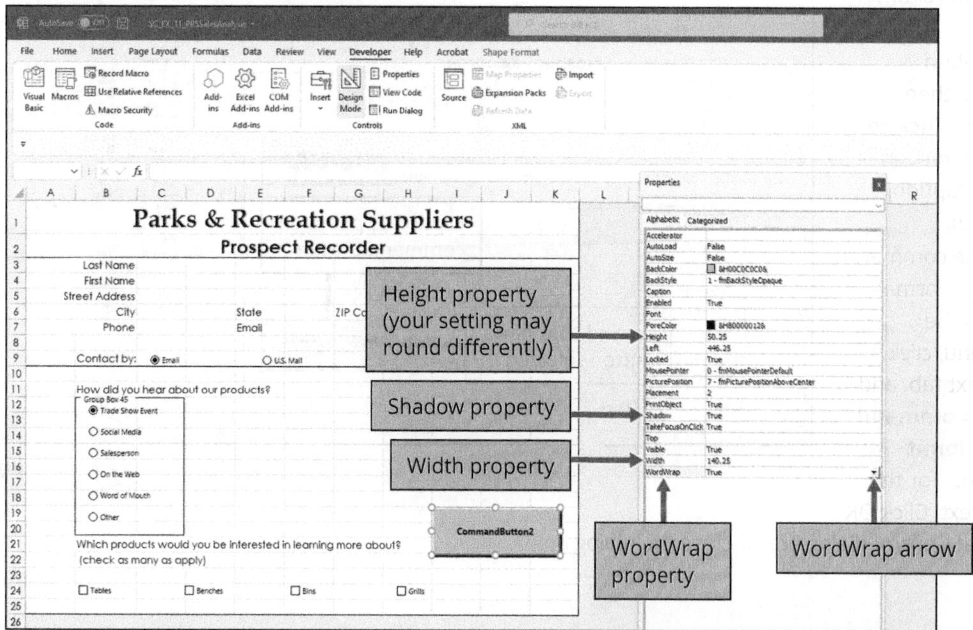

Figure 11–28

- Select the first command button only.
- In the Properties window, click the Name property, select the existing text, and then type **cmdStep1** to rename the control.
- Click the Caption property, select the existing text, and then type **Step 1 - Click to enter contact information** to enter the caption (Figure 11–29).
- Right-click the command button, select Format Control from the shortcut menu, click on the Alt Text tab, and then enter **Command button to enter contact information.** for the alternative text. Click OK in the Format Control dialog box to close the dialog box.

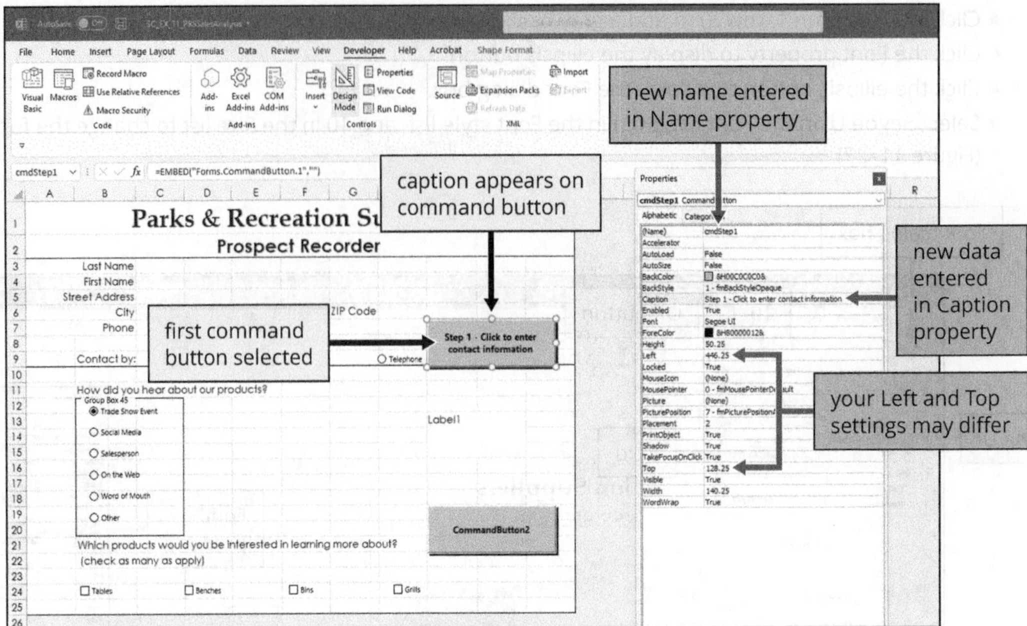

Figure 11–29

Q&A What are the letters, cmd, before the name, Step1?

It is common practice for developers to use a prefix with control names to indicate the type of control. In this case, it is a command control.

5

- Select the second command button only.
- In the Properties window, click the Name property, and then type **cmdStep3** to rename the control.
- Click the Caption property, and then type **Step 3 - Click to submit information** to enter the caption (Figure 11–30).
- Right-click the command button, select Format Control from the shortcut menu, click on the Alt Text tab, and then enter **Command button to submit information.** for the alternative text. Click OK in the Format Control dialog box to close the dialog box.

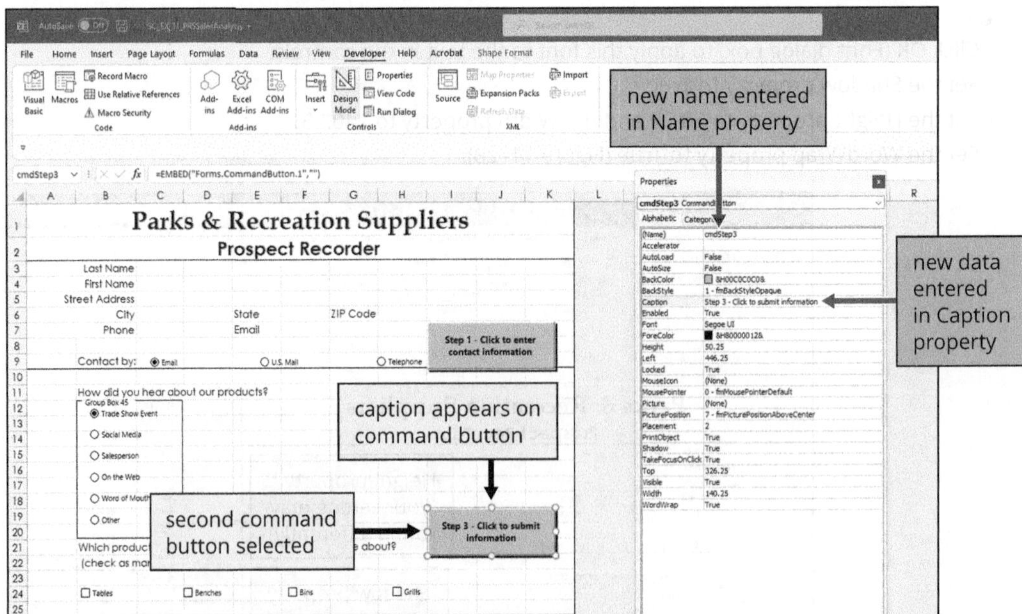

Figure 11–30

To Set Label Properties

The following steps set properties for the Label ActiveX Control.

1. Select the label control.
2. In the Properties window, click the Name property and then type **lblStep2** to rename the control.
3. In the Properties window, click the BorderColor property, and then click the BorderColor arrow to display the BorderColor options. Click the Palette tab to display the color options. Click black (column 1, row 6) to add a black border to the label.
4. Click the BorderStyle property, and then click the BorderStyle arrow. In the list, click '1 - fmBorderStyleSingle' to choose the setting for the border.
5. Click the Caption property, and then type **Step 2 - Use option buttons and check boxes to answer questions** to enter the caption.
6. Set the Height property to 60 and the Width property to 140.25.
7. Click the TextAlign property, click the list arrow, and then click 2 - fmTextAlignCenter (Figure 11–31).
8. Right-click the label control, select Format Control from the shortcut menu, click on the Alt Text tab, and then enter **Label giving directions to use option buttons and check boxes to answer questions.** for the alternative text. Click OK in the Format Control dialog box to close the dialog box.
9. Close the Properties window.

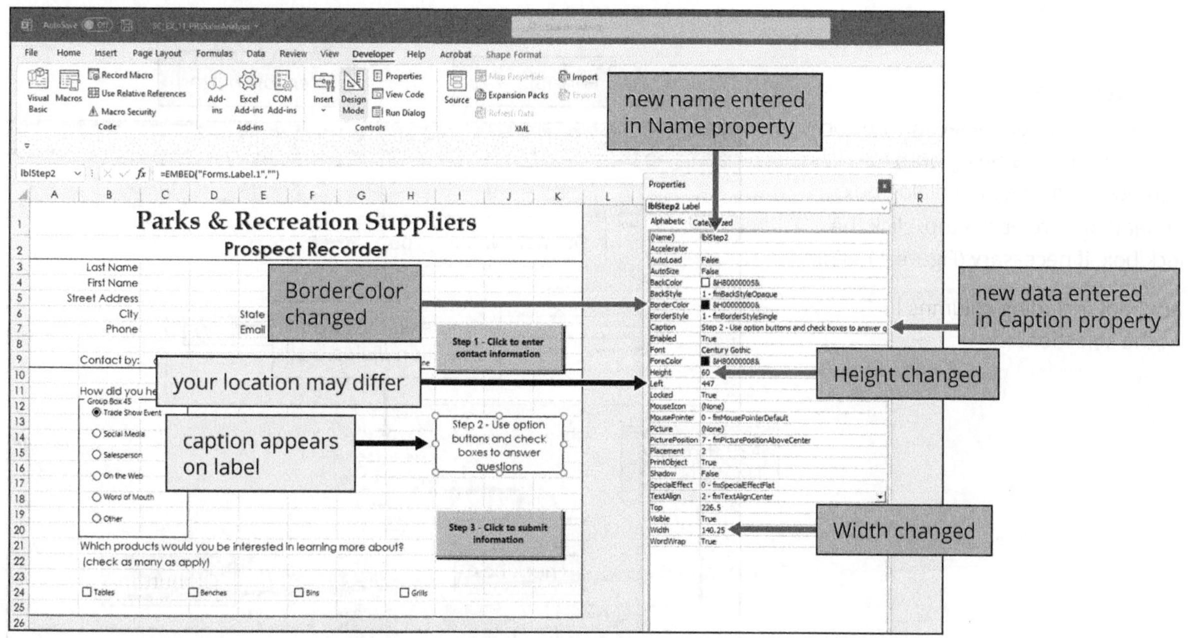

Figure 11–31

To Align and Distribute Controls

The following steps align and distribute the two command buttons and the label.

1. Select the command buttons and the label, and then use the Align button (Shape Format tab | Arrange group) to apply the Align Right and Distribute Vertically formats to the group.
2. Save the workbook again in the same storage location with the same file name.

Storing User Input

Once you have added the controls to the worksheet, consider where the inputted information will be stored or recorded. In most cases when you use an Excel form, you must store the information within the workbook, but it is a good idea to store it away from the form itself. You want the data to be accessible to experienced users but not distracting to users who are simply entering data in the form. For this project, you will store data input in row 40 of the worksheet. You then will copy that information into a hidden Prospect List worksheet for long-term retention.

Users will be entering their name, address, and other information into the form. In this module, entering and storing data will be a three-part process. Part 1: Rather than having the users try to move to specific cells and type in data, which may or may not fit in the cell, you will program a VBA function called INPUTBOX to collect their data. Users will click option buttons and check boxes to indicate their responses. Part 2: You will program Excel to transfer the data from the INPUTBOX collection to the temporary storage location in row 40 and display it on the form. Excel also will place the values for option buttons and check boxes in row 40. Part 3: When the user clicks the Submit button, Excel will transfer the data from the temporary location in row 40 to the hidden worksheet, Prospect List, and clear the form for the next entry.

To Create from Selection

In order to make the process more user-friendly, you will name specific cells and ranges. The 'Create from Selection' command names cells based on headings or adjacent cells. Excel uses the heading to name the cell, replacing any spaces with underscores. The following steps use the headings in row 39 to name the cells in row 40. **Why?** Row 40 will be the temporary storage location for inputted data.

- Select the range A39:H40.
- Click the 'Create Names from Selection' button (Formulas tab | Defined Names group) to display the Create from Selection dialog box.
- Because the headings are at the top, click the Top row check box, if necessary (Figure 11–32).

Q&A Why am I not including columns I through N in the selection?

I40:N40 will contain formulas or functions and do not need names.

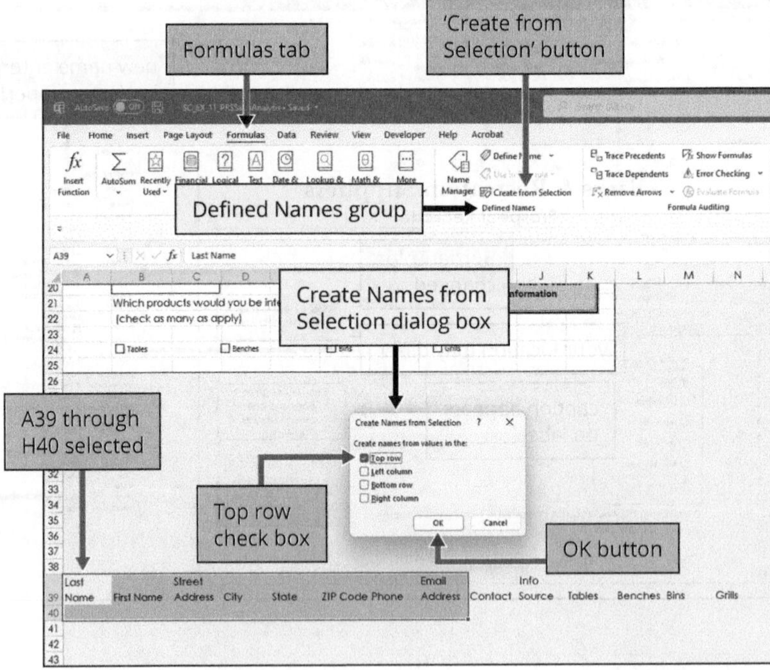

Figure 11–32

- Click OK (Create Names from Selection dialog box) to name the cells.
- **Experiment:** Click various cells in row 40 to verify their names in the Name Box on the formula bar.

To Assign Other Range Names

The following steps assign names to specific ranges in the form. The two ranges are in column W, which displays the captions of the option buttons.

1. Select the range W3:W5.
2. Click the Define Name button (Formulas tab | Defined Names group) to display the New Name dialog box.
3. Type **Contact_Options** in the Name text box.
4. Click OK (New Name dialog box).
5. Repeat steps 1 through 4 to name the range W7:W12 as **Source_Options**.

To Enter Cell References

The following steps enter cell references in the form. **Why?** These cell references will display user input from programming later in the module. The cells and references to enter are listed in Table 11–1.

Table 11–1: Cell References

Cell	Reference to Enter
C3	=A40
C4	=B40
C5	=C40
C6	=D40
C7	=G40
F6	=E40
H6	=F40
F7	=H40

1. One at a time, click each cell listed in the Cell column of Table 11–1 and enter the cell reference listed in the Reference to Enter column. No data will appear on the form yet, as the reference cells have not been filled by user input.
2. Verify your entries by clicking the cell and reviewing the formula bar.

Q&A My cells display an error icon triangle saying that the formula refers to empty cells. Is that OK?
The green triangles will not cause a problem, but you can turn them off if you find them distracting. To do so, click Options in Backstage view, click Formulas, and then clear the 'Formulas Referring to Empty Cells' check box in the Error checking rules area.

Evaluating Option Buttons

Recall that form users will click an option button in each group to select it. The first option button is already selected to be the default value in each group. Because those selections must be stored, you need to determine which option button of the group was clicked.

Excel maintains an index number behind the scenes for each option button; that index number is 1, 2, 3, and so on. To retrieve the option button index number, you use the Format Control dialog box to link to a cell reference that will display the index number. For example, if you link an option button to cell Z100, then during data input when the user clicks an option button, cell Z100 will display a 1, 2, or 3 to indicate which option button was selected. Excel only requires you to create a cell link for one option button per group; the cell link will work for all option buttons in the group.

Determining the caption of a selected option button is a separate process, however. Once you obtain the index number, you can search for the caption in column W, using the INDEX() function. Recall that the INDEX() function takes two arguments, a range and an index number. The function returns the cell value at that location in the range. For example, if your captions are located in cells A1, A2, and A3, you might type

=INDEX(A1:A3, $Z$100)

The INDEX() function would search in range A1:A3 for the specified index represented by Z100. It then would return, or display, the text at that location. Naming the range, A1:A3, would make it more user friendly.

=INDEX(My_Captions, $Z$100)

To Evaluate Option Button Selection

In this module, there are two option button groups: one for the prospect's preferred method of contact and one to indicate how the prospect heard about PRS's products. In the first group, by using the INDEX function, you will have Excel record the user's selection as one of the captions stored in W3:W5, Email, U.S. Mail, or Telephone, rather than the numerical values (1, 2, or 3). **Why?** User input should be changed from a numerical value to one that salespeople can quickly understand. Likewise, in the second option button group, Excel will return one of the captions stored in W7:W12 rather than a number 1 through 6.

The following steps store the user's option button selections. The cell link will be established using the Form at Control dialog box. The INDEX() function, entered in row 40, will use the previously named range and the index number. The function will return a caption from the range in column W.

- Right-click the Email option button control to display the shortcut menu.
- Click Format Control to display the Format Control dialog box.
- If necessary, click the Control tab (Format Control dialog box) to display the Control sheet.
- Type **$I$41** in the Cell link box (Format Control dialog box) to link the option button index number to cell I41 (Figure 11–33).

Q&A Why did I link only one of the option buttons to cell I41?

Option buttons work collectively as a group, with a single identity assigned to the set of options. The specific value of the selected option button will be assigned to an out-of-the-way cell, I41.

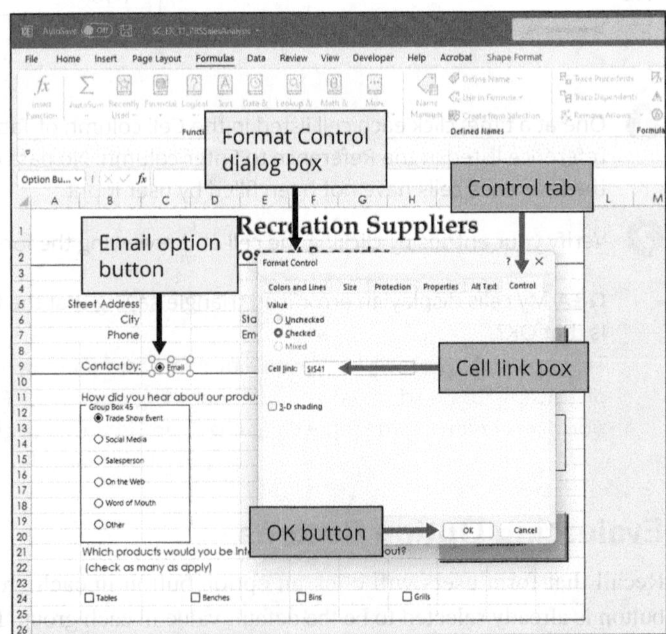

Figure 11–33

2

- Click OK (Format Control dialog box) to close the dialog box.
- If necessary, scroll down and then click cell I40 to make it the active cell.
- Type **=@INDEX(Contact_Options,$I$41)** to record text from the named range Contact_Options rather than numbers in cell I40 (Figure 11–34).
- Click the Enter button. Note that cell I40 currently shows an error icon because this value will be generated by the option buttons.

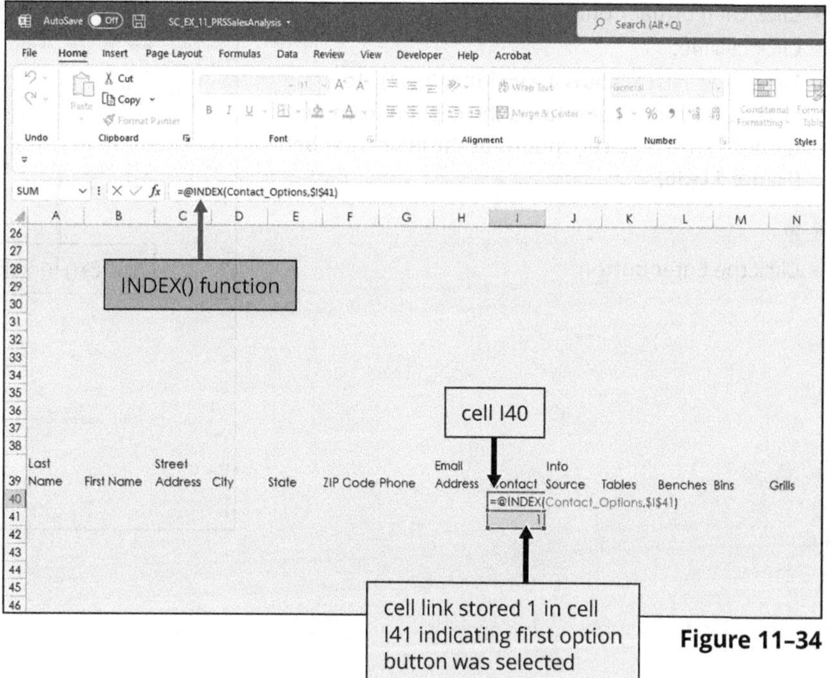

Figure 11–34

Q&A How does the INDEX function work here?

In this instance, the INDEX function notes the value in cell I41, which identifies which option button was selected, and returns the entry associated with that value from the named range, Contact_Method. The named range is found in column W in this worksheet. The @ symbol means to return a single value rather than all the values in the named range.

3

- Right-click the Trade Show Event option button control, and then click Format Control on the shortcut menu. If necessary, click the Control tab.
- Type **$J$41** in the Cell link box (Format Control dialog box) (Figure 11–35).

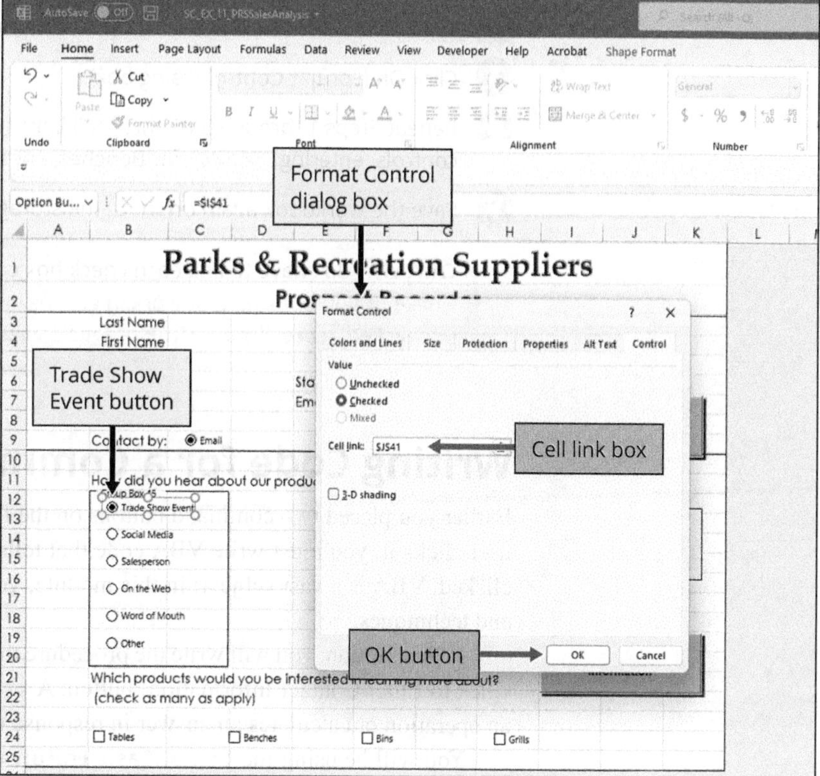

Figure 11–35

- Click OK (Format Control dialog box).
- Click cell J40.
- Type **=@INDEX(Source_Options,$J$41)** to enter a function that returns the caption from the named range Source_Options at the index number (Figure 11-36).

- Click the Enter button.

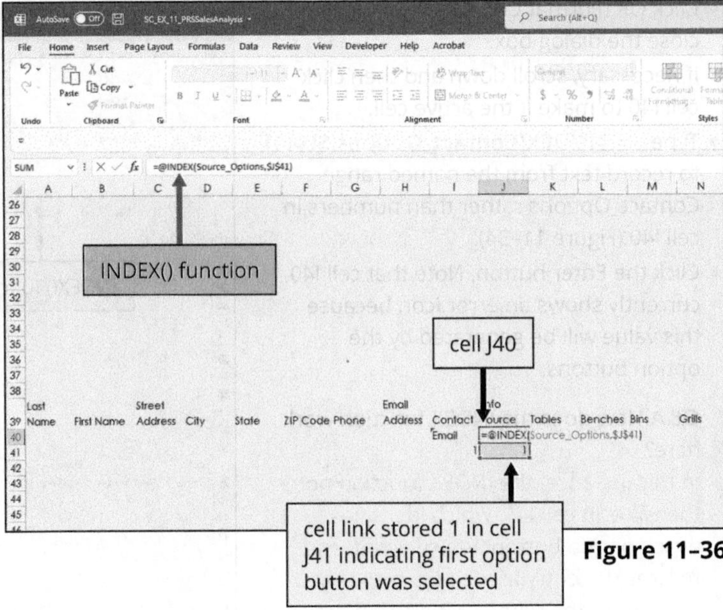

Figure 11-36

To Evaluate Check Box Control Selection

The following steps evaluate the check box selections by assigning each check box a cell link.

1. Right-click the Tables check box control. Use the shortcut menu to display the Format Control dialog box.
2. Type **$K$40** in the Cell link box (Format Control dialog box, Control tab).
3. Click OK (Format Control dialog box).
4. Repeat Steps 1 through 3 to enter cell links for each of the remaining three check box controls, entering **$L$40** for Benches, **$M$40** for Bins, and **$N$40** for Grills.
5. Save the workbook again on the same storage location with the same file name.

Q&A Why do I have to link each check box control to a specific cell?
Unlike option buttons that work in groups, check box controls can each be either checked or unchecked, representing TRUE or FALSE values. Each one needs to be evaluated.

Writing Code for a Command Button

Earlier you placed two command buttons on the form. To make a button trigger an action when a user clicks it, you must write VBA code that tells Excel what to do after the command button is clicked. VBA is a vast subject; in this module, you will learn only a few of its many commands and techniques.

In this section, you will write the procedure that will execute when the user clicks the 'Step 1 - Click to Enter Contact Information' button. A **procedure** is a series of statements that performs an operation or calculates an answer in response to a triggered event.

You will be using the **Visual Basic Editor**, which is a full-screen editor that lets you enter a procedure by typing lines of VBA code. Accessed from the Developer tab on the ribbon, the Visual Basic Editor is like an app within an app because it has its own ribbon, tabs, and groups and is navigated independently from Excel. You type lines of code, also called **statements**, in the Visual Basic Editor, using basic word processing techniques.

When the user triggers the event that executes a procedure, such as clicking a button, Excel steps through the Visual Basic statements one at a time, beginning at the top of the procedure. The statements should reflect the steps you want Excel to take, in the exact order in which they should occur.

After you determine what you want the procedure to do, write out the VBA, creating a table similar to Table 11–2. Test the code before you enter it in the Visual Basic Editor by stepping through the instructions one at a time yourself. As you do so, think about how the procedure affects the worksheet.

Consider This

Should you document your code?

Yes. Use comments to document each procedure. This will help you remember the purpose of the code or help somebody else understand it. In Table 11-2, the first six lines are comments. Comments begin with the word Rem (short for Remark) or an apostrophe ('). Comments have no effect on the execution of a procedure; they simply provide information about the procedure, such as name, creation date, and function. Comments can be placed at the beginning before the Private Sub statement, in between lines of code, or at the end of a line of code, as long as each comment begins with an apostrophe ('). It is good practice to place comments containing overall documentation and information at the beginning, before the Sub statement.

The Enter Prospect Button Procedure

Table 11–2 displays the VBA code executed when users click the first command button. Lines beginning with a single quote are called comments. In VBA, a **comment** is a statement in the code that documents it. Comments are not executed, nor are they visible to form users; they are seen only by programmers and other form developers.

Table 11-2: Enter Prospect Button Procedure

Line	Code
1	'Enter Prospect Button Procedure
2	'Author: SC Series
3	'Date Created: 11/19/2029
4	'Run from: Prospect Recorder worksheet by clicking Step 1 button
5	'Function: When executed, this procedure enters contact information for the prospect
6	'
7	Range("Last_Name").Value = InputBox("Last Name?", "Enter", , 800, 6000)
8	Range("First_Name").Value = InputBox("First Name?", "Enter", , 800, 6000)
9	Range("Street_Address").Value = InputBox("Street Address?", "Enter", , 800, 6000)
10	Range("City").Value = InputBox("City?", "Enter", , 800, 6000)
11	Range("State").Value = InputBox("State?", "Enter", , 800, 6000)
12	Range("ZIP_Code").Value = InputBox("Zip Code?", "Enter", , 800, 6000)
13	Range("Phone").Value = InputBox("Telephone Number?", "Enter", , 800, 6000)
14	Range("Email_Address").Value = InputBox("Email Address?", "Enter", , 800, 6000)

The rest of the procedure uses a VBA function named InputBox(). During Execution, the function displays a dialog box for user entry (Figure 11–37). The InputBox() function takes four arguments: a label or prompt, the title of the dialog box, the default value in the text box, the width, and the height. The dialog box automatically contains a text box, OK button, Cancel button, and Close button. The InputBox() function returns whatever the user enters in the text box.

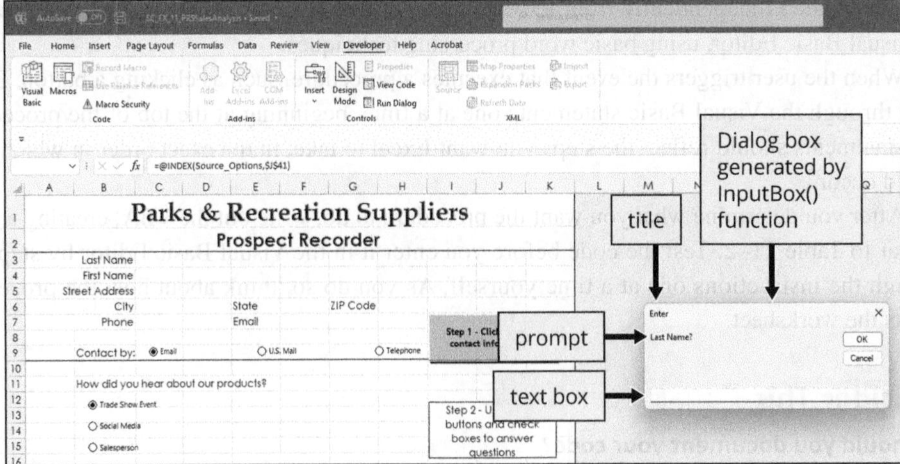

Figure 11–37

BTW

Printing VBA Code

Some people find it easier to review and edit code by working with a printout. To print out VBA code while using the Visual Basic Editor, click File on the menu bar and then click Print on the File menu.

In VBA, as in other programming languages, the function and its arguments are placed to the right of an equal sign; the return location is on the left. This kind of code, that sets or resets a value, object, or location, is called an **assignment statement**. In Table 11–2, the return location is the value in a named range, in this case the single cells that were named earlier in the module.

The Submit Button Procedure

Table 11–3 displays the VBA code executed when users click the first command button. This procedure copies the information to the hidden worksheet named Prospect List. A range is selected and copied; in this case, the range is row 40, where the user information was temporarily stored. The procedure then sets various properties of the Sheets object, short for worksheet. The code makes the worksheet visible, then active, then selects a range (lines 9–11).

Table 11–3: Submit Button Procedure

Line	Code
1	'Submit Button Procedure
2	'Author: SC Series
3	'Date Created: 11/19/2029
4	'Run from: Prospect Recorder worksheet by clicking Step 3 button
5	'Function: When executed, this procedure submits new information to the prospect list
6	'
7	Range(“A40:O40”).Select
8	Selection.Copy
9	Sheets(“Prospect List”).Visible = True
10	Sheets(“Prospect List”).Activate
11	Sheets(“Prospect List”).Range(“A2:N2”).Select
12	Selection.PasteSpecial Paste:=xlPasteValues, Operation:=xlNone, SkipBlanks:=False, Transpose:=False
13	Selection.Font.Bold = False
14	Sheets(“Prospect List”).Range(“A2”).Activate
15	ActiveCell.EntireRow.Insert
16	Sheets(“Prospect List”).Visible = False
17	Sheets(“Prospect Recorder”).Select
18	Range(“I41:J41”).ClearContents
19	Range(“A40:H40”).ClearContents
20	Range(“K40:N40”).ClearContents
21	Range(“J8”).Activate
22	ActiveWorkbook.Save

The Paste command in line 12 includes several assignment statements that Excel uses behind the scenes to complete a Paste Special. The code in lines 14 and 15 makes a specific cell active and inserts a row. In line 16, the worksheet is hidden again. The rest of the code clears the contents of rows 40 and 41 in the Prospect Recorder worksheet, making it ready for the next user entry. Finally, the workbook is saved in line 22.

The syntax of code statements is very important. As you enter the code, carefully type every comma, period, quotation mark, and parenthesis. For more information on any specific line of code, you can use the Help command on the Visual Basic Editor menu bar or press F1 while you are typing the code.

To Enter the Command Button Procedures

Why? To enter a procedure, you use the Visual Basic Editor. Each command button has a separate procedure. The following steps activate the Visual Basic Editor and create a procedure for each of the two command buttons.

- If necessary, display the Developer tab and then click the Design Mode button (Developer tab | Controls group) to make Design Mode active.
- Right-click the Step 1 button on the worksheet to display the shortcut menu (Figure 11–38).

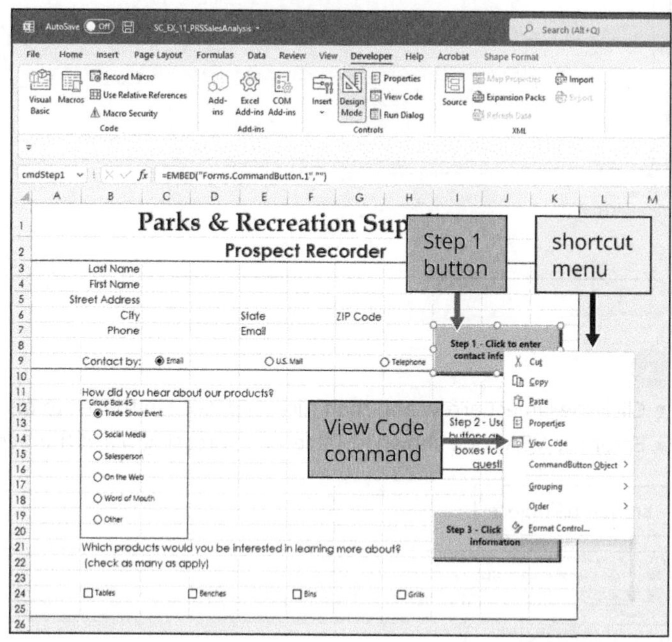

Figure 11–38

- Click View Code to display the Microsoft Visual Basic for Applications editor and then, if necessary, maximize the window.

Q&A What is displayed in the code window on the right?

The beginning and the end of the procedure is created for you already.

- If necessary, click the blank line between the beginning and end lines of code.
- Press TAB before you enter the first line of VBA code from Table 11–2. Enter each line as indicated in the table, but do not enter the line numbers from the table (Figure 11–39).

Q&A What is the purpose of the two commas in lines 9 through 15?

Commas must separate each argument in a function. In Lines 9 through 15, the third argument is the default text for the text box. Placing nothing between the commas indicates that nothing will appear in the text box.

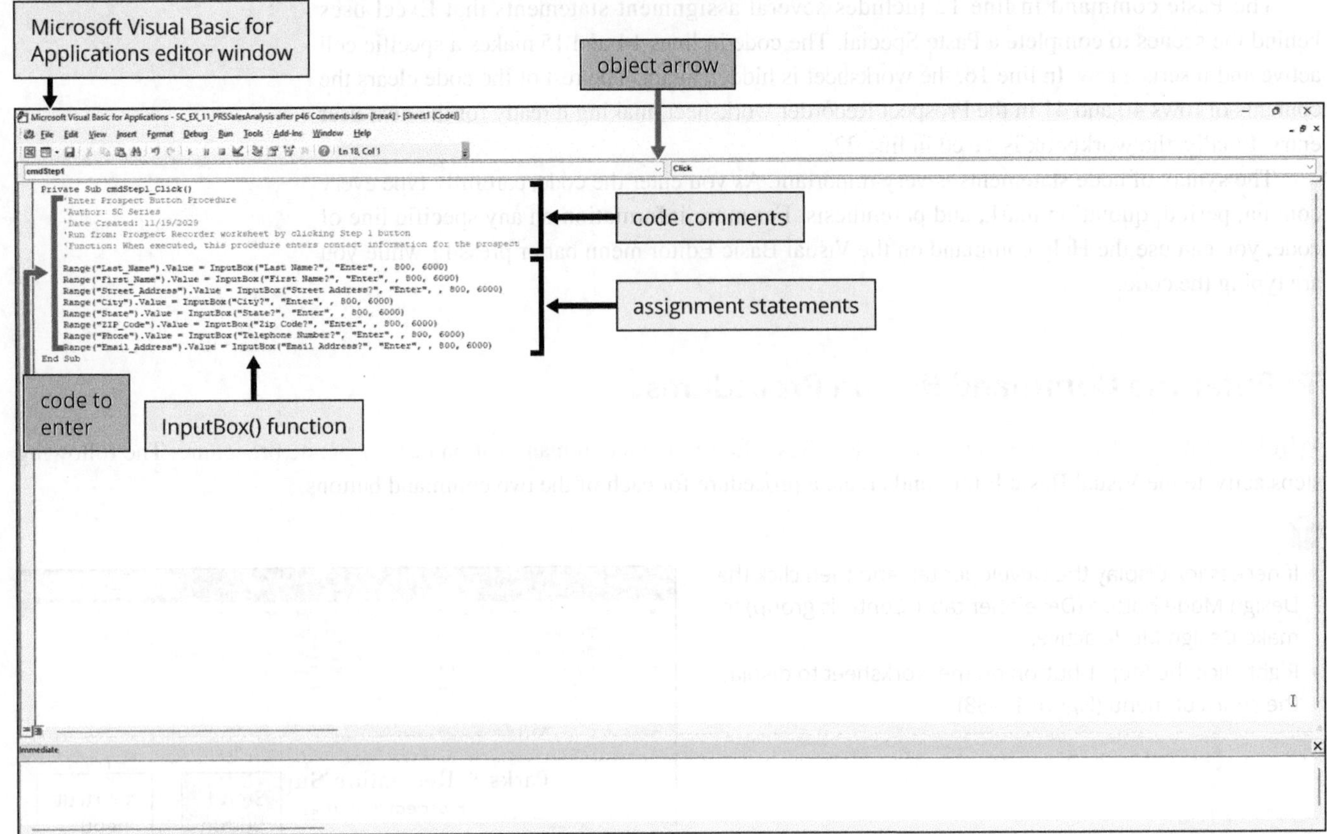

Figure 11–39

3

- Click the Object arrow and then click cmdStep3 in the list to display the beginning and ending code for the Submit button.
- Enter the VBA code shown in Table 11–3, pressing TAB at the beginning of the first line (Figure 11–40).

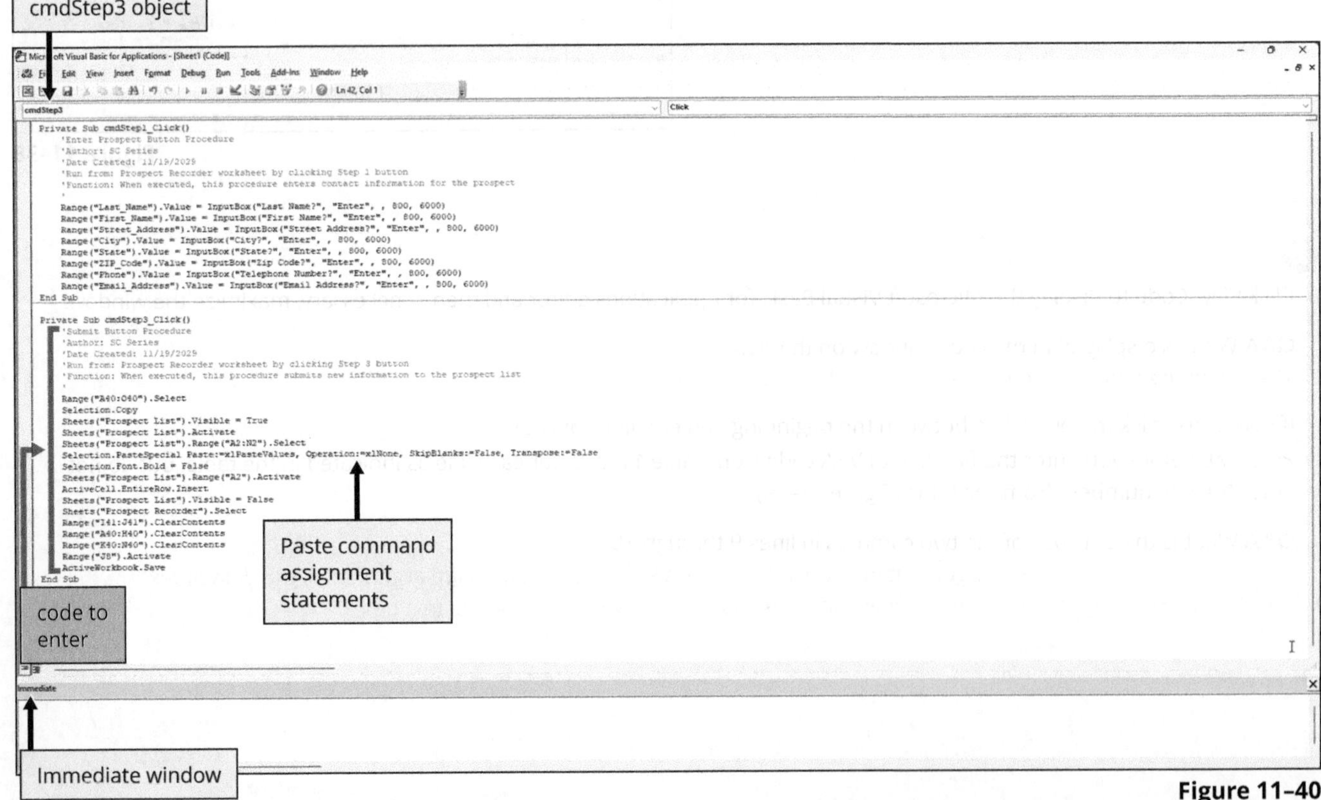

Figure 11–40

Q&A Do I have to press the TAB key?

No, but it is a common programming practice to do so because indenting the code improves readability.

- Verify your code by comparing it with the content of Tables 11-2 and 11-3.

Other Ways

1. Click View Code button (Excel Window | Developer tab | Controls group), enter code in Visual Basic Editor window

To Remove the Outline from the Group Box Control

Recall that the group box on the form displays a border and text. The following steps remove those from the group box control. **Why?** Removing the outline will result in a more visually pleasing user interface. Because the group box has no formatting options in the Excel window, you must set its visibility property with a line of VBA code. You will enter this in the Immediate window in the Visual Basic Editor. The **Immediate window** is a Visual Basic Editor window that lets you enter different values to test the procedures you create without changing any data in the database and often is used for debugging and executing statements during design. As its name suggests, code entered in this window is executed immediately upon exiting the Visual Basic Editor.

- If necessary, press CTRL+G to open the Immediate window at the bottom of the Visual Basic Editor.
- In the Immediate window, type **activesheet.groupboxes.visible = false** to enter the code.
- Press ENTER to execute the code, which hides the box around the group control (Figure 11-41).

Q&A What does the code mean?

The assignment statement code assigns the value false to the visible property of the group boxes on the active sheet, causing it not to be displayed.

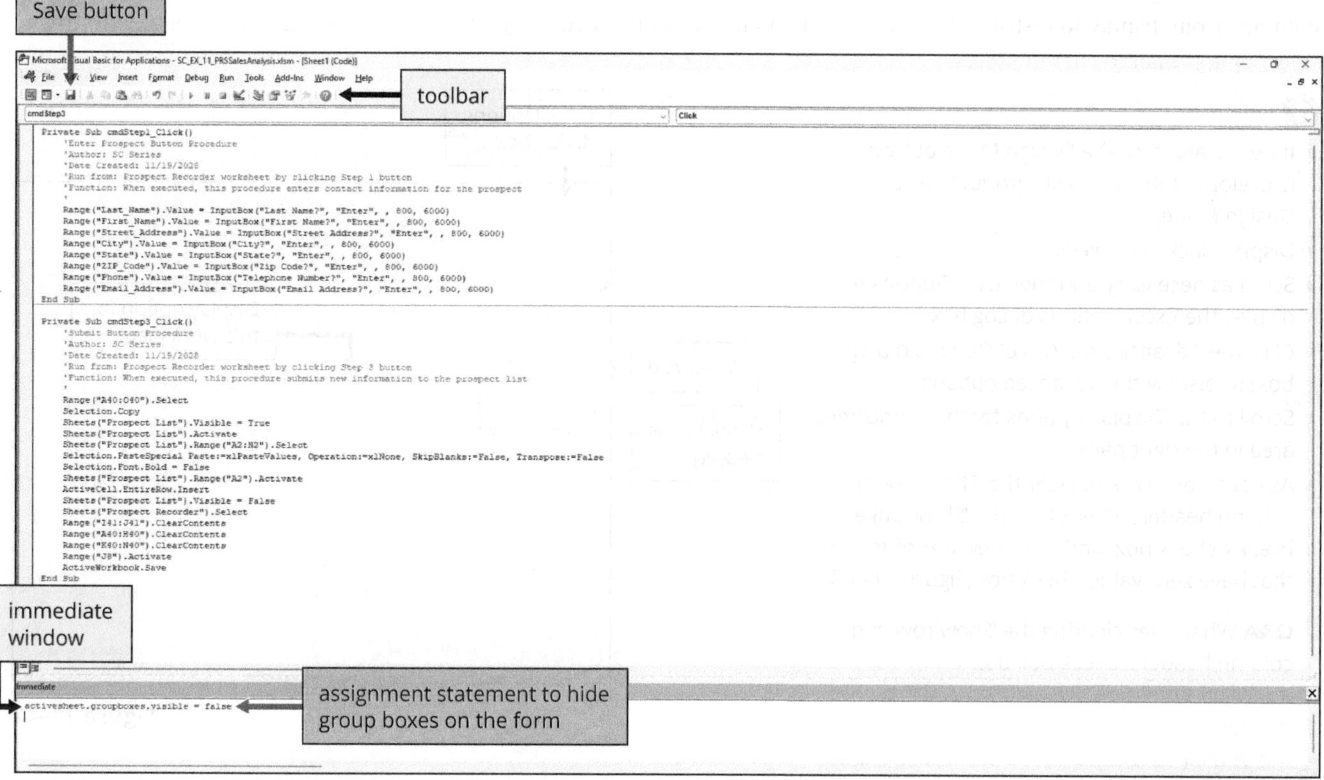

Figure 11-41

- Click the Save button (Visual Basic Editor toolbar).
- Close the Visual Basic Editor window.
- Save the workbook again in the same storage location with the same file name.

Other Ways

1. Click View on menu bar, click Immediate window, enter code

Break Point: If you wish to take a break, this is a good place to do so. You can now exit Excel. To resume at a later time, start Excel, open the file called SC_EX_11_PRSSalesAnalysis.xlsm, and continue following the steps from this location forward.

Preparing, Protecting, and Testing Worksheets

With any worksheet that you will distribute to others, you should consider how to prepare, protect, and test it. Excel provides several ways to prepare and protect worksheets. You can turn features on or off such as page breaks, zero values, gridlines, the formula bar, or headings. You also can limit distractions for the user by hiding the ribbon, hiding row and column headers, and hiding the active cell. It is a good idea to password protect worksheets that contain forms to prevent other users from accidentally or deliberately changing, moving, or deleting data. With worksheet protection, you can make only certain parts of the sheet editable so that users will not be able to modify data in any other region in the sheet or workbook. And, of course, before sharing a document, you must thoroughly test its functionality.

To Prepare Worksheet for Distribution

In the following steps, you prepare the worksheet for distribution to others. You will hide the ribbon, row numbers, and columns from display to restrict what the user can do in this worksheet. **Why?** You want users only to fill out the form and select options, not to alter the sheet.

- If necessary, click the Design Mode button (Developer tab | Controls group) to exit Design Mode.
- Display Backstage view.
- Scroll as necessary and then click Options to display the Excel Options dialog box.
- Click the Advanced tab (Excel Options dialog box) to display the advanced options.
- Scroll to the 'Display options for this worksheet' area in the right pane.
- As necessary, click to clear the 'Show row and column headers' check box, the 'Show page breaks' check box, and the 'Show a zero in cells that have zero value' check box (Figure 11-42).

Q&A What does clearing the 'Show row and column headers' check box do?
It turns that feature off, hiding the display of the row numbers and the column letters on this worksheet only. For users, only the edges of the form will be displayed.

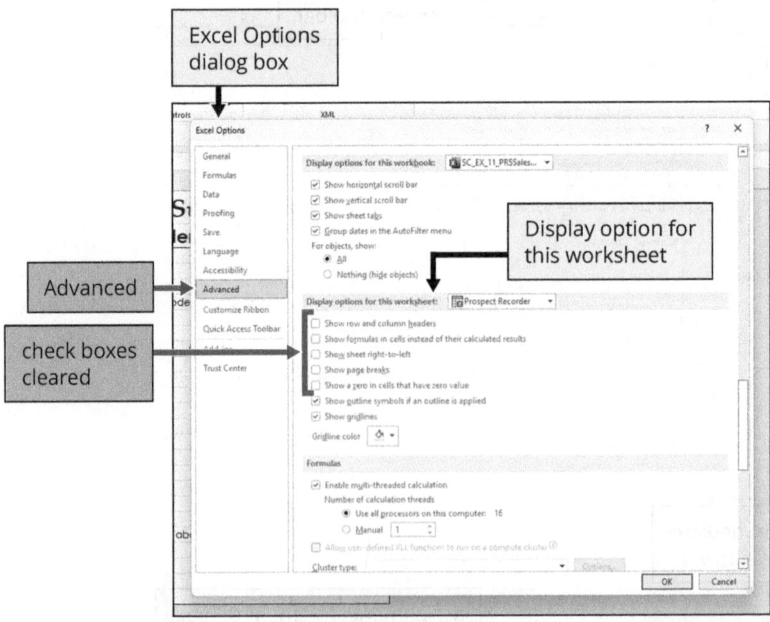

Figure 11-42

2

- Click OK to close the Excel Options dialog box.
- Display the View tab.
- As necessary, click to clear the Gridlines, Formula Bar, and Headings check boxes (View tab | Show group) to remove those features from the worksheet (Figure 11–43).

3

- Press CTRL+F1 to collapse the ribbon.

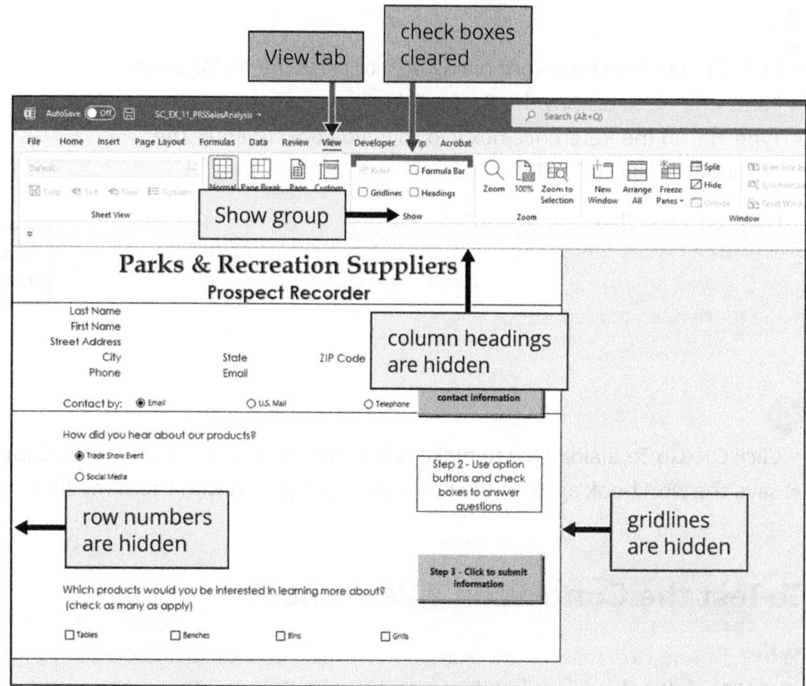

Figure 11–43

To Password Protect the Worksheet

The following steps password protect the worksheet. **Why?** A password prevents users from making changes to your VBA code and calculations. You also will choose to place the active cell in a hidden location so that it won't distract inexperienced spreadsheet users.

- Display the Review tab and then click the Protect Sheet button (Review tab | Protect group) to display the Protect Sheet dialog box.
- Type **Prospect19** in the 'Password to unprotect sheet' box (Figure 11–44).

Q&A Should I password protect the entire workbook?

No. You will edit other sheets later in the module.

What is the purpose of the check boxes?

You can click those check boxes to allow all users of the worksheet to edit, insert, and change various kinds of cells, even when the worksheet is password protected.

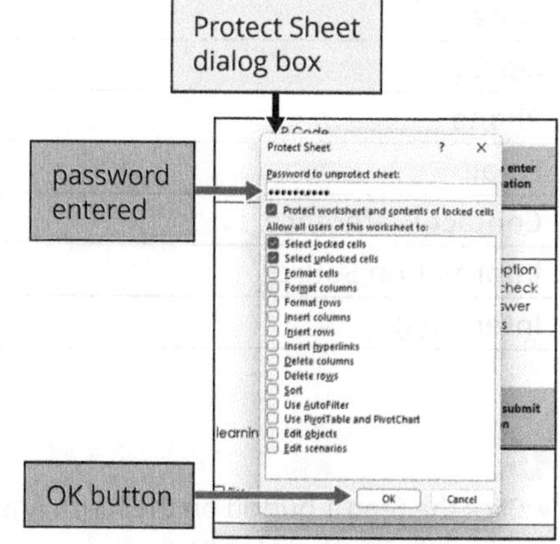

Figure 11–44

- Click OK (Protect Sheet dialog box) to display the Confirm Password dialog box.
- Type **Prospect19** in the 'Reenter password to proceed' box (Figure 11–45).

Q&A Do any rules apply to passwords?

Yes. Passwords in Excel can contain, in any combination, letters, numbers, spaces, and symbols, and can be up to 15 characters long. Passwords are case sensitive. If you decide to password-protect a worksheet, make sure you save the password in a secure place. If you lose the password, you will not be able to open or gain access to the password-protected worksheet.

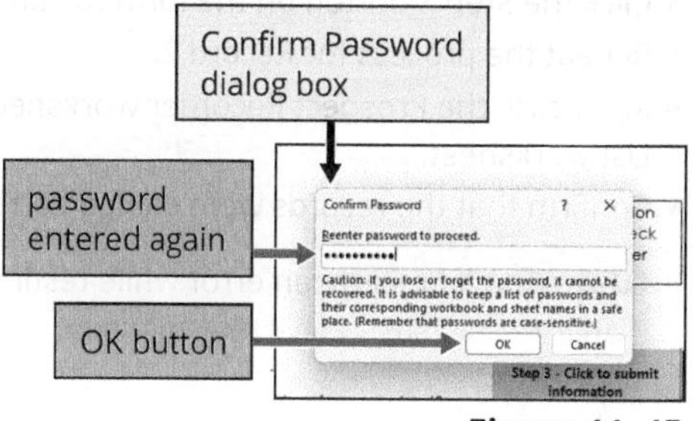

Figure 11–45

- Click OK (Confirm Password dialog box) to close the dialog boxes.
- Press CTRL+G to display the Go To dialog box.
- Type **J8** in the Reference box (Go To dialog box) to enter the destination (Figure 11–46).

Q&A Why use J8 as the new active cell?
The J8 cell is hidden behind the first command button, out of the way, so as not to elicit unintended data entry for inexperienced users.

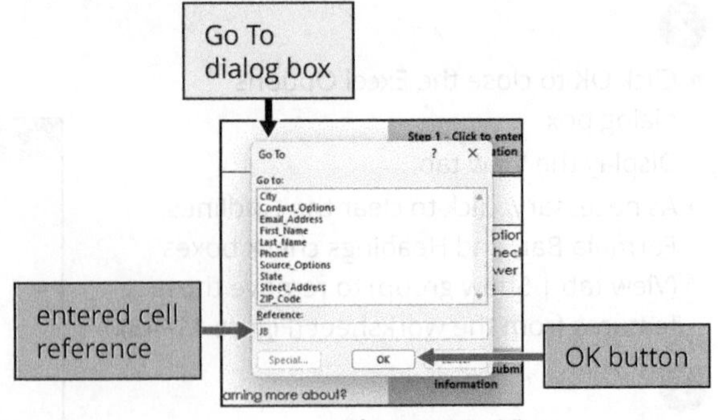

Figure 11–46

- Click OK (Go To dialog box) to make cell J8 the active cell and close the dialog box.
- Save the workbook again in the same storage location with the same file name.

To Test the Controls in a Worksheet

Why? Before distributing the workbook for use, you should test the controls and verify the proper functionality of the VBA code. The following steps test the controls in the Prospect Recorder worksheet using the data shown in Table 11–4.

Table 11–4: Prospect Records

Field	Record 1	Record 2
Last Name	Taylor	Johnson
First Name	Kimberly	Robert
Address	412 Amber Way	368 Ridge Rd
City	Boone	Golden
State	NC	CO
Zip Code	28607	80401
Phone	828-555-1234	720-555-5678
Email	ktaylor@example.com	rjohnson@example.com
Contact Preference	Telephone	Email
Information Source	Social Media	Trade Show Event
Interest(s)	Benches	Tables, Grills

- Click the Step 1 button on the form. Answer the prompts using the data from Record 1 in Table 11–4. Click OK when you have completed each dialog box.
- Check the option buttons and check boxes as indicated in the table, to complete this information for Record 1.
- Click the Step 3 button on the form to submit the data for Record 1.
- Repeat the process for Record 2.
- Right-click the Prospect Recorder worksheet tab, click Unhide, and then click OK (Unhide dialog box) to display the Prospect List worksheet.
- Confirm that the records were copied correctly. The order of your records may differ (Figure 11–47).

Q&A What if I receive an error while testing the controls?
If an error displays, Excel may highlight the code causing the error. Check your code for accuracy and make corrections as necessary.

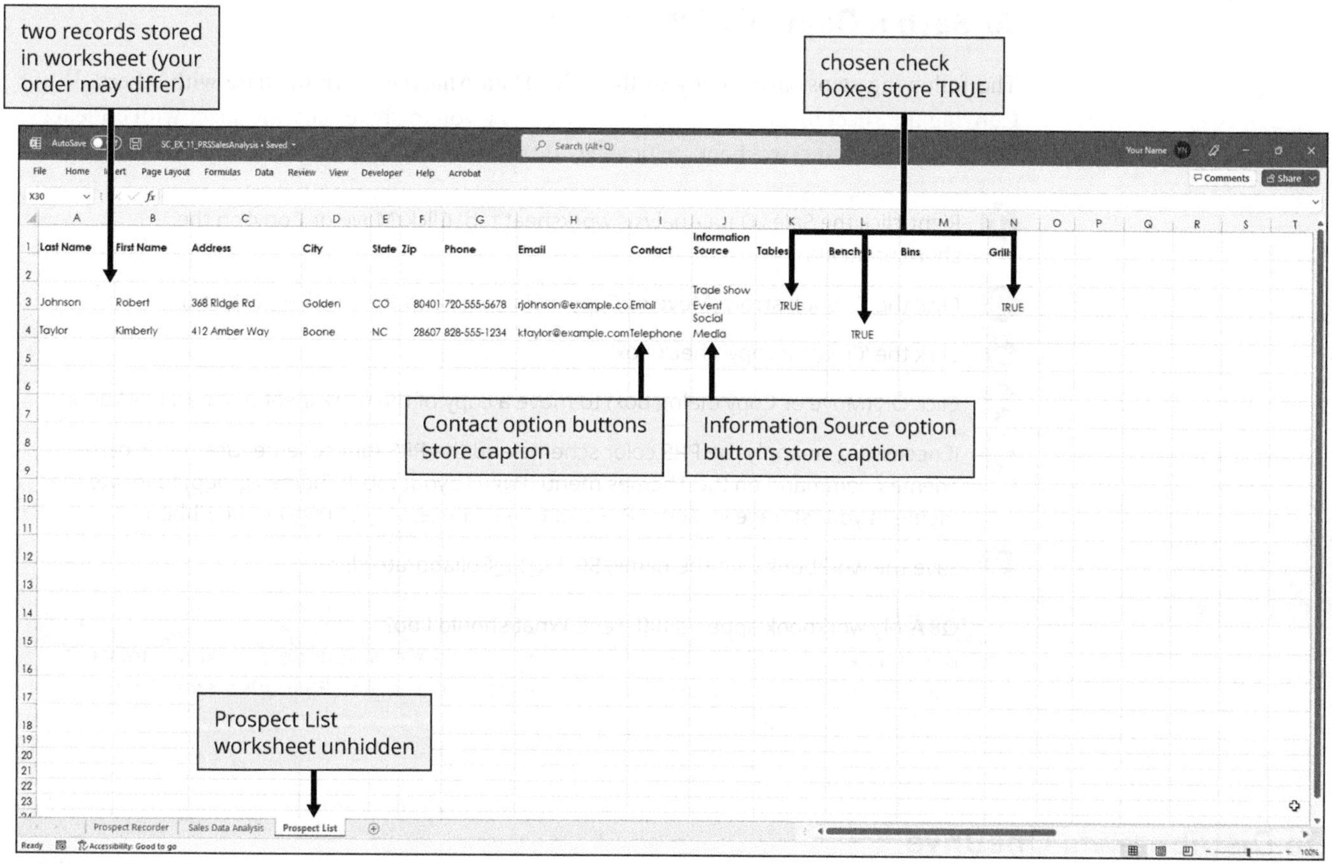

two records stored in worksheet (your order may differ)

chosen check boxes store TRUE

Last Name	First Name	Address	City	State	Zip	Phone	Email	Contact	Information Source	Tables	Benches	Bins	Grill
Johnson	Robert	368 Ridge Rd	Golden	CO	80401	720-555-5678	rjohnson@example.co	Email	Trade Show Event	TRUE			TRUE
Taylor	Kimberly	412 Amber Way	Boone	NC	28607	828-555-1234	ktaylor@example.com	Telephone	Social Media		TRUE		

Contact option buttons store caption

Information Source option buttons store caption

Prospect List worksheet unhidden

Figure 11–47

- Right-click the Prospect List worksheet tab and then click Hide on the shortcut menu.
- Make the Sales Data Analysis worksheet active.
- Save the workbook again in the same storage location with the same file name.

Sharing and Collaborating

Collaboration is the practice of sharing files with others, providing comments, and collecting feedback. Excel provides several ways to collaborate. As you have seen, you can physically distribute a workbook to others on storage media or through email using an attachment. In addition, you can save files in a variety of formats to a OneDrive, SharePoint, another networked site, or to a Power BI service. Available storage locations commonly are listed when you click Save As, Share, or Publish in Backstage view.

In Excel you also can **co-author** or collaborate on the same workbook at the same time. When you co-author, you can review each other's changes quickly—in a matter of seconds. And with certain versions of Excel, other people's selections are displayed in different colors. To co-author, rather than simply saving the file on OneDrive, you use the Share button on the Excel ribbon to distribute or save your file in a manner which allows others to access it.

BTW

Copying Comments

You can copy comments from one cell to other cells using the Paste Special command. Select the cell that contains the comment you need to copy, click the Copy button (Home tab | Clipboard group), select the cell or cells to which you want to apply the comment, click the Paste arrow, and then click Paste Special. In the Paste Special dialog box, in the Paste list, select Comments, and then click the OK button.

To Save a Copy of a Worksheet

The following steps save a copy of the Sales Data Analysis work to share with others. **Why?** Copying the sheet to another workbook will allow you to share only the sheet with colleagues rather than the entire workbook, which they do not require for their review.

1. Right-click the Sales Data Analysis worksheet tab. Click 'Move or Copy' on the shortcut menu.
2. Click the To book arrow (Move or Copy dialog box) and then click (new book).
3. Click the 'Create a copy' check box.
4. Click OK (Move or Copy dialog box) to move a copy of the worksheet to a new workbook.
5. If necessary, re-apply the PRS color scheme and the PRS font scheme. Use the 'Browse for Themes' command on the Themes menu (Page Layout tab | Themes group) to locate the theme in your storage location. Press CTRL+F1 if necessary to restore the ribbon.
6. Save the workbook with the name, SC_EX_11_Collaborate.xlsx.

Q&A My workbook appears different. What should I do?
Depending on how you saved the color and font schemes, your new workbook may not have those schemes. Choose the PRS color scheme and the PRS font scheme (Page Layout tab | Themes group) and save again.

To Distribute via OneDrive

You can use OneDrive to distribute workbooks. Colleagues can make changes and then save the workbook on OneDrive for review. Saving workbooks for distribution on OneDrive does not differ from using OneDrive to save your own files, although you do need to make the workbook available to others by saving it in an accessible location. **Why?** You may need to have a workbook reviewed by someone who does not share network access with you. The following steps distribute the workbook via OneDrive. If you cannot access OneDrive, simply review the steps.

- If necessary, press CTRL+F1 to restore the ribbon.
- In the upper-right corner of the ribbon, click Share button to open the Share menu. Choose Share from the menu to open the Share dialog box (Figure 11–48). Your sharing options may differ, based on your available networked locations.

Q&A What happened to the Protect and Share Workbook command?
That command, and the Changes group on the Review tab, have been replaced by co-authoring.

What are the buttons at the bottom of the Sharing dialog box?
Those commands are shortcuts to send the file as an attachment, both as an Excel file and as a PDF file. The same commands are available in Backstage view.

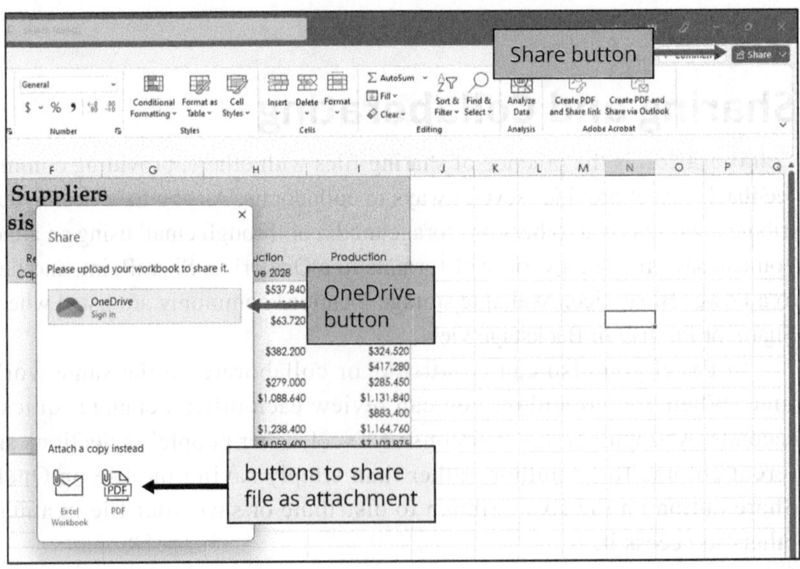

Figure 11–48

- Click the OneDrive button (Share dialog box) and sign in if necessary. Or, if you have access to another network, click its button and sign in.
- When Excel displays the Send Link dialog box, you can enter a name, group, or email associated with your OneDrive account (Figure 11–49).

Q&A Can I add a message?
Yes. Click in the Add a Message section and type a brief message.

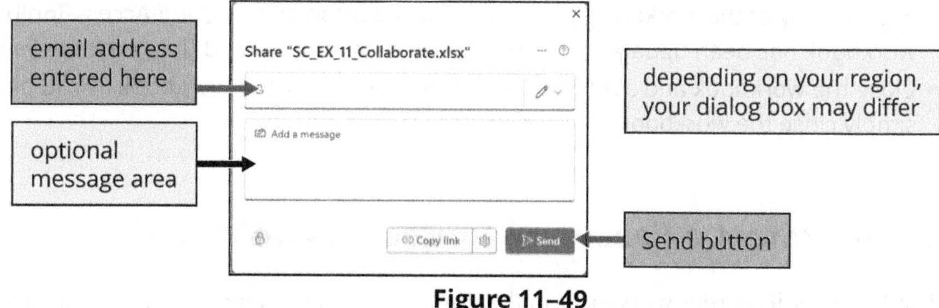

Figure 11–49

3

- If you entered an email address, click the Send button (Share dialog box).
- Close the Link Sent dialog box, if necessary.

Q&A How does the link work?
The recipient will receive an email message inviting them to open the file. They can click the link to open the workbook. A web browser will open, and the workbook will open in Excel Online.

Other Ways

1. Click Share in Backstage view, enter email address, click Send.

To Co-Author a Workbook

Working together in the same workbook at the same time can improve efficiency in networked team environments. **Why?** Co-authoring a workbook can provide you with a timely, interactive editing process with colleagues. The following steps assume you have distributed the workbook to a recipient connected to your OneDrive, and that the recipient, considered your co-author, has opened the file. If you did not share the workbook with another recipient, simply read the steps.

- Make sure that AutoSave is displayed in the upper-left corner of the title bar.
- Ask the co-author to click the link you sent.
- When the co-author comes online, click the Share button and choose Manage Access from the Share menu (Figure 11–50a). The Manage Access dialog box shows that both you and the second user have access. Close the Manage Access dialog box.
- Ask the user to click cell D8 and enter **647**. The new value is shown in your worksheet (Figure 11–50b).

Q&A Can I track the changes made by the co-author?
Excel no longer supports tracking changes; however, you can save a separate copy and compare workbooks, which you will do later in the module.

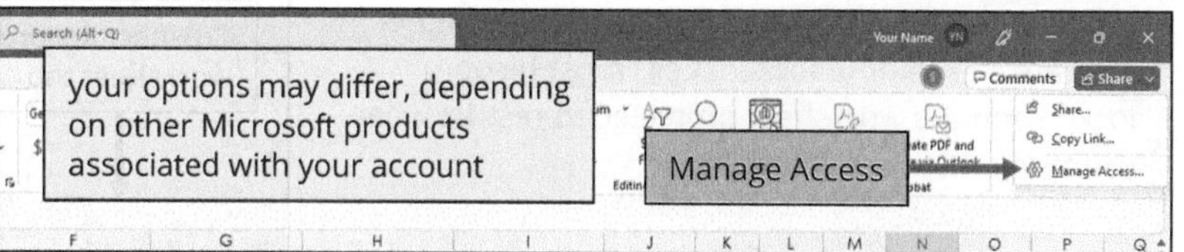

Figure 11–50(a)

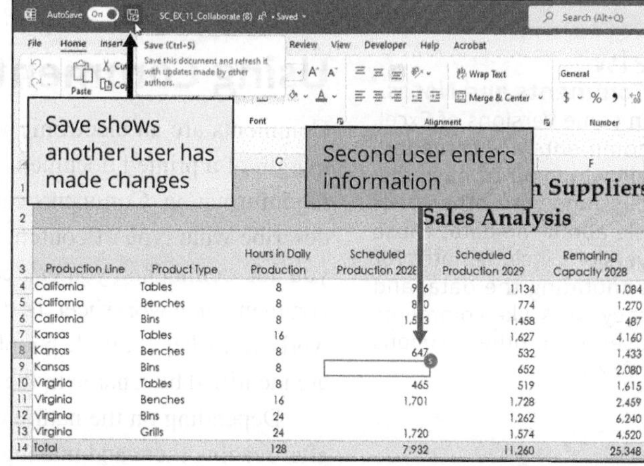

Figure 11–50(b)

- In your copy of the workbook, point to the Save button on the Quick Access Toolbar to display a ScreenTip indicating that the workbook has been updated with changes by another user, and then click the Save button to save your work.
- Close the workbook and ask the co-author to close his or her workbook. If you did not work with a co-author on these steps, simply close the workbook.

To Unprotect a Password-Protected Worksheet

The Prospect Recorder worksheet in the PRS Sales Analysis workbook is protected, which restricts the changes you can make to the worksheet to unlocked cells only. You cannot make changes to locked cells or modify the worksheet itself. You will unprotect the worksheet. **Why?** Unprotecting allows changes to locked cells and the worksheet itself. Recall that a password ensures that users cannot unprotect the worksheet simply by clicking the Unprotect button. Recall that the password for the worksheet is Prospect19. The following steps unprotect the password-protected Prospect Recorder worksheet.

- If necessary, open the file named SC_EX_11_PRSSalesAnalysis.xlsm. Re-display the ribbon if necessary.
- Display the Prospect Recorder worksheet.
- Click the Formula Bar check box (View tab | Show group) to redisplay the formula bar.
- Display the Review tab, and then click the Unprotect Sheet button (Review tab | Protect group) to display the Unprotect Sheet dialog box.
- In the Unprotect Sheet dialog box, type **Prospect19** in the Password box (Figure 11–51).

- Click OK (Unprotect Sheet dialog box) to unprotect the Prospect Recorder worksheet.
- Save and close the workbook.

Q&A Can I work with the entire worksheet now?

Yes. With the worksheet unprotected, you can modify the contents of cells, regardless of whether they are locked or unlocked. Cells must be both locked and the worksheet protected to restrict what users can do to cell contents.

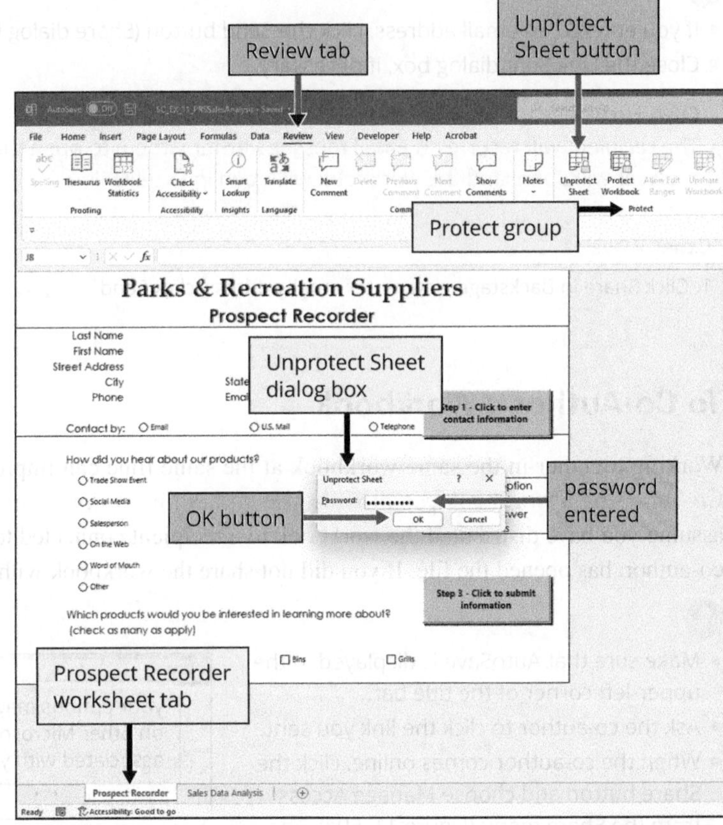

Figure 11–51

BTW
Comments and Notes
In some versions of Excel, comments are threaded, allowing you to have discussions with other people about the data. Those versions include notes for annotating the data, and they work like comments used from other versions of Excel.

Using Comments to Annotate a Worksheet

Comments are an electronic version of sticky notes or annotations you might jot down in the margin of a printed document. They can request additional information or clarification of existing information. Comments can provide direction to the reader about how to interpret content or describe what type of content to add. You can add a comment to any cell in a worksheet. Once you add comments, you can edit, format, move, copy, or resize them. You can choose to show comments in a worksheet, to display only a comment indicator, or to hide comments. Comments work well when multiple people are collaborating on a worksheet. Comments added by each user are identified by a name in the comment, set by the user.

Depending on the nature of the comments, you may decide to delete some or all comments after reading them and making edits to the worksheet, if appropriate.

To Add Comments to a Worksheet

Why? Comments in Excel can be used to remind the user of material that needs to be added or updated. The Sales Data Analysis worksheet in the PRS Sales Analysis workbook has some missing data. The following steps add comments to the worksheet in cells A9 and A12.

- Open the SC_EX_11_PRSSalesAnalysis.xlsm workbook and then, if necessary, click the Enable Content button in the yellow Security Warning bar below the ribbon.
- If necessary, display the Sales Data Analysis worksheet.
- If necessary, enter **647** in cell D8.
- Display the Review tab and, if necessary, click the Show Comments button (Review tab | Comments group) to toggle the option off and hide all comments in the workbook.
- Right-click cell A10 to display the shortcut menu (Figure 11–52).

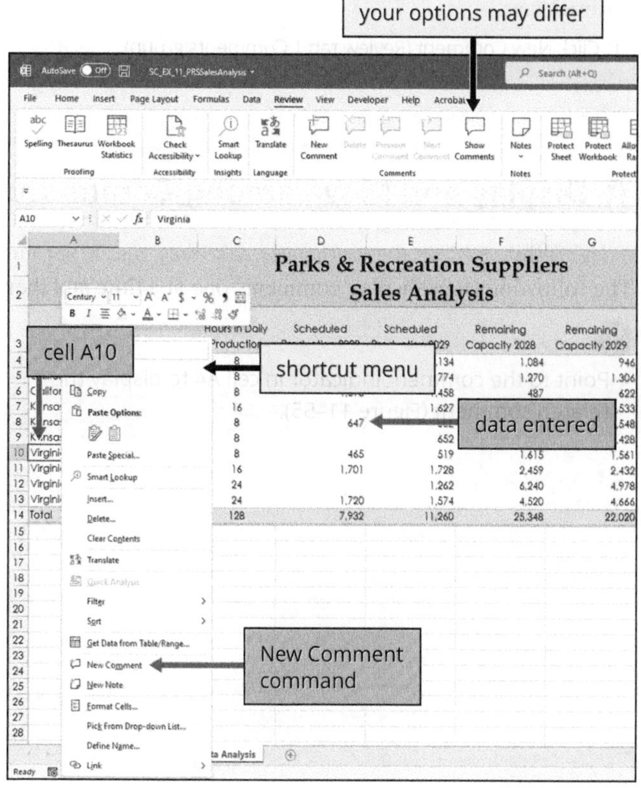

Figure 11–52

- Click New Comment on the shortcut menu to open a comment box next to the selected cell and display a comment indicator in the cell.
- Enter the text **Note to Donna - need accurate count of Tables scheduled for 2029 production in Virginia.** in the comment box (Figure 11–53).

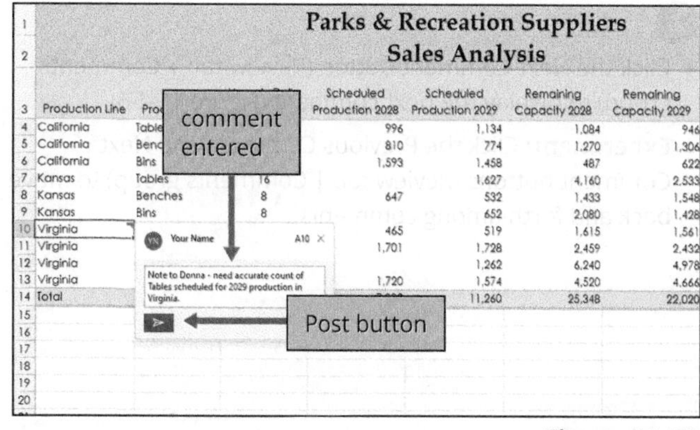

Figure 11–53

- Click the Post button, and then click outside the comment box to close the comment box and display only the purple comment indicator in cell A10.
- Enter a comment in cell A4 with the text **Note to Sue - need accurate count of Tables scheduled for 2029 production in California.** (Figure 11–54).

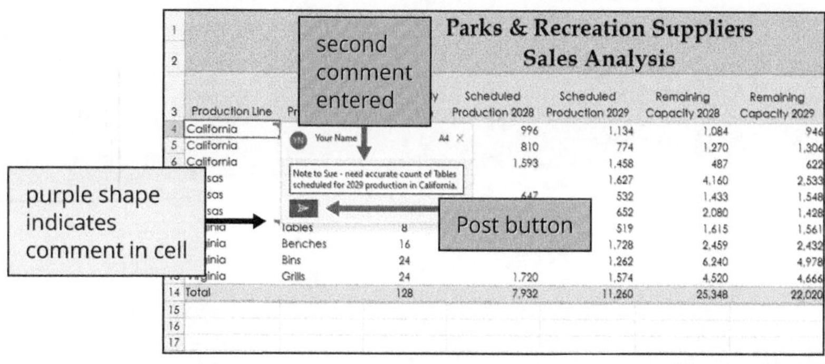

Figure 11–54

Q&A My comment boxes do not close when I click outside the comment box. Why?
Turn off the showing of comments by clicking the Show Comments button (Review tab | Comments group).

- Click the Post button, and then click outside the comment box to close the comment box and display only the purple comment indicator in cell A4.

Other Ways

1. Click New Comment (Review tab | Comments group)
2. Click Comments on title bar, click New

To Display and Move among Comments

Why? While editing the worksheet, you may find it helpful to have comments visible. The comments currently are hidden. The following steps display comments one at a time and then make all comments visible.

- Point to the comment indicator in cell A4 to display the related comment (Figure 11–55).

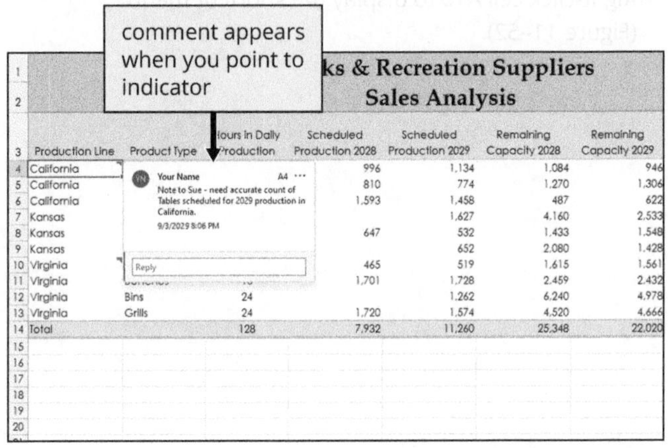

Figure 11–55

2

- Click the Next Comment button (Review tab | Comments group) to display the next comment (Figure 11–56).
- **Experiment:** Click the Previous Comment and Next Comment buttons (Review tab | Comments group) to move back and forth among comments.

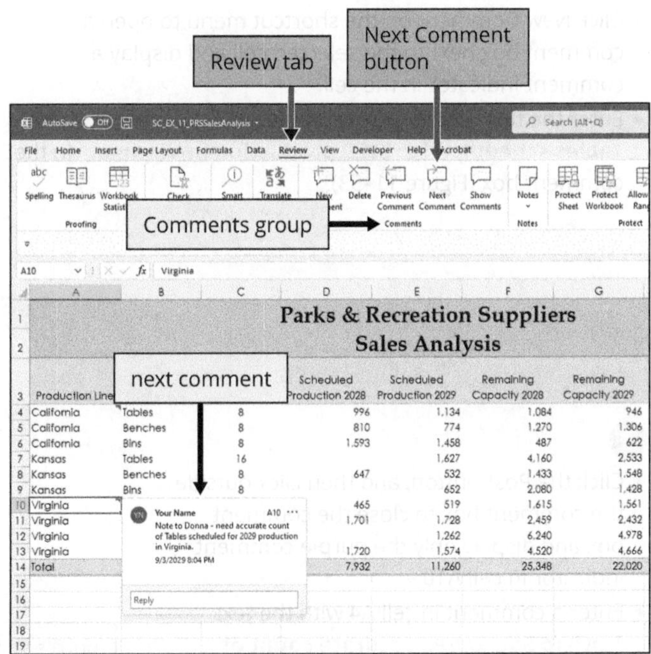

Figure 11–56

- Click the Show Comments button (Review tab | Comments group) to open the Comments pane and show all comments in the workbook (Figure 11-57).

Q&A Can I print comments?
Yes. You can print a list of comments separately using the Sheet tab in the Page Setup dialog box. To do so, click the Page Setup Dialog Box Launcher (Page Layout tab | Page Setup group), click the Sheet tab (Page Setup dialog box), click the 'Comments and notes' arrow, and then click 'At end of sheet' in the 'Comments and notes' list.

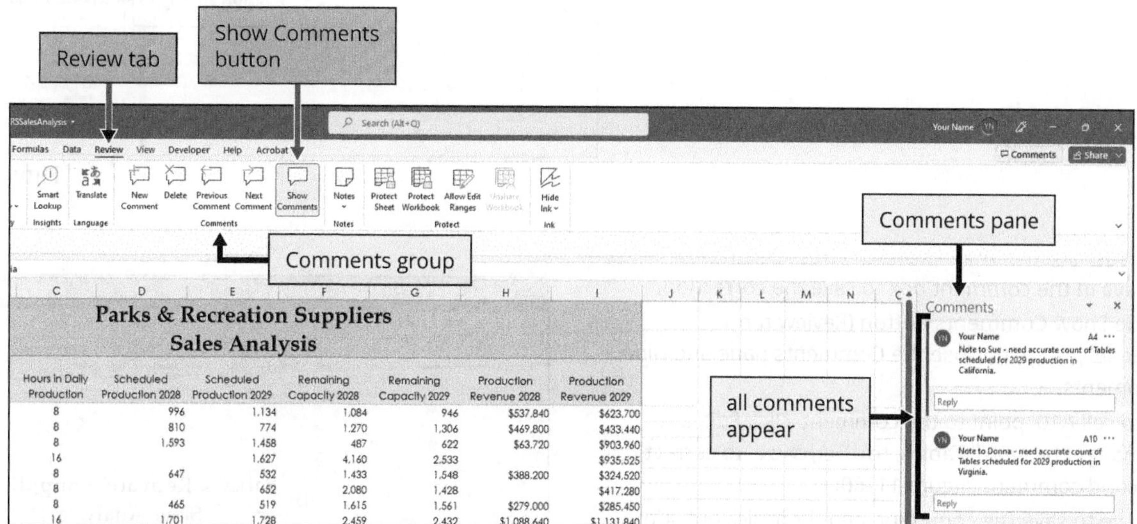

Figure 11–57

To Edit Comments on a Worksheet

You want to correct errors in the comments to Donna and Sue. **Why?** After adding comments to a worksheet, you may need to edit them to add or change information. The following steps edit the comments in cells A4 and A10.

- Click the comment for cell A4 to select the comment in the Comments pane.
- Click the Edit comment icon in the comment box to open the comment for editing.
- Select the word, Tables, in the comment (Figure 11-58).

Q&A Can I delete the text?
Yes, but if you want to delete the entire comment, click Cancel, click the More threaded actions button (...), and then click Delete thread.

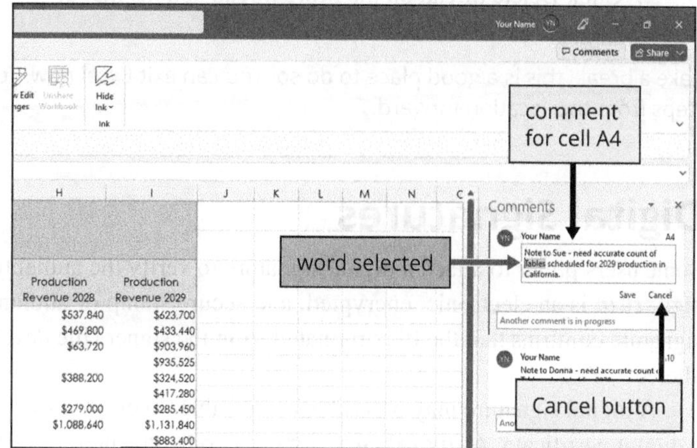

Figure 11–58

- Type **Benches** to replace the selected word and correct the comment text, adding a space if necessary (Figure 11–59).

Q&A Can I reply to a comment?
Yes. To reply, click in the Reply box for a comment, type the response, and then click the Post button.

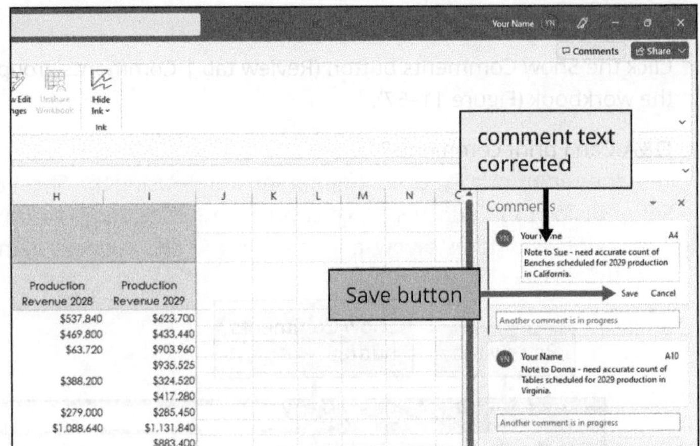

Figure 11–59

- Click Save in the comment box to save the correction.
- Click the Show Comments button (Review tab | Comments group) to close the Comments pane and hide all comments.
- Point to cell A10, point to the comment, click Edit, and then change the word, Tables, to **Benches** to correct the second comment (Figure 11–60).
- Click Save to save the comment, and then click outside the comment box to close the comment.
- Save the workbook again in the same storage location with the same file name and close it.

Q&A What if my box displays a Post Comment button instead of a Save button?
Depending on your version of Excel a Post button may be displayed instead of a Save button. In that case, click the Post Comment button to save the comment, and then proceed with the steps.

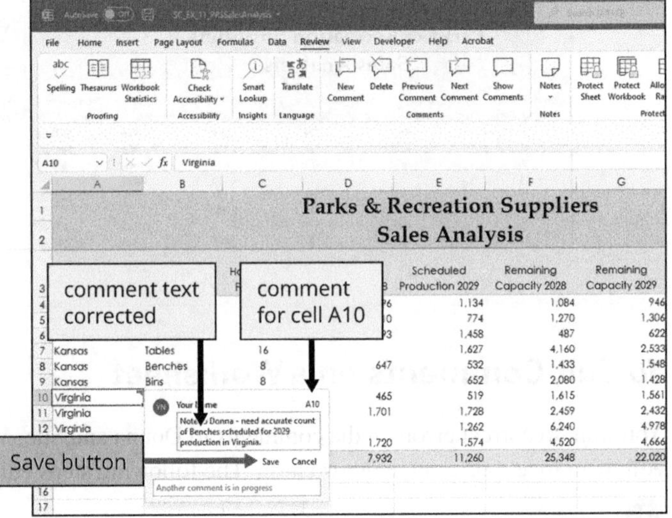

Figure 11–60

To Delete a Comment If you wanted to delete a comment, you would perform the following steps.

1. Click the More threaded actions button (...) in the comment.
2. Click Delete thread on the More thread actions menu.

Break Point: If you want to take a break, this is a good place to do so. You can exit Excel now. To resume later, start Excel and continue following the steps from this location forward.

Digital Signatures

Some users prefer to attach a digital signature to verify the authenticity of a document. A **digital signature** is an electronic, encrypted, and secure stamp of authentication on a document. This signature confirms that the file originated from the signer (file developer) and that it has not been altered.

A digital signature may be visible or invisible. In either case, the digital signature references a digital certificate. A **digital certificate** is code attached to a file that verifies the identity of the creator of the file. A digital certificate vouches for the file's authenticity, provides secure encryption, or supplies a verifiable signature. Many users who receive files containing macros enable the macros based on whether they are digitally signed by a developer on the user's list of trusted sources.

You can obtain a digital certificate from a commercial certificate authority (CA), from your network administrator, or you can create a digital signature yourself. A digital certificate you create yourself is not issued by a formal certification authority. Thus, signed macros using such a certificate are referred to as self-signed projects. Certificates you create yourself are considered unauthenticated and still will generate a warning when opened if the user's security level is set to very high, high, or medium. Many users, however, consider self-signed projects safer to open than those with no certificates at all.

To Add a Signature Box and Digital Signature to a Workbook After adding a digital signature, Excel will display the digital signature whenever the document is opened. If you wanted to add a digital signature to an Excel workbook, you would perform the following steps.

1. Open the SC_EX_11_PRSSalesAnalysis.xlsm workbook and, if necessary, unprotect the Prospect Recorder worksheet using the password, Prospect19.
2. Click the Insert tab and then click the Signature Line arrow in the Text group to display the list.
3. Click the 'Microsoft Office Signature Line' command.
4. Enter your name in the Suggested signer box (Signature Setup dialog box) and then click OK to add the signature box to the workbook.
5. Right-click the signature box and then click Sign on the shortcut menu to display the Sign dialog box. If necessary, you will be prompted to get a digital ID from a Microsoft Partner.
6. In the Sign dialog box, enter your name in the signature box or click the Select Image link to select a file that contains an image of your signature.
7. Click the Sign button (Sign dialog box) to digitally sign the document. If Excel displays a dialog box, click Yes.

BTW
Adding Alternative Text for Accessibility
Alternative text is essential for increasing accessibility in a workbook. To set alternative text on form controls, right-click the control, click Format Control on the shortcut menu, and then enter the desired alternative text on the Alt Text tab of the Format Control dialog box.

To Review a Digital Signature on a Workbook Excel will display the digital signature whenever the document is opened. When you open a digitally signed document, Excel displays a message announcing the signature on the status bar while the file opens. After the file is opened, Excel displays a certification icon on the status bar. You can click the icon to find out who digitally signed the document. The word, Signed, may also appear on the title bar in parentheses, indicating the document is signed digitally. If you wanted to review a digital signature on an Excel workbook, you would perform the following steps.

1. Display Backstage view. If necessary, click the Info tab and then click View Signatures to open the Signatures pane.
2. Select a name from the Valid signature list (Signature pane), click the arrow to display the shortcut menu, and then click Signature Details to display the certificate.
3. When you are finished reviewing the certificate, click the Close button (Signature Details dialog box) and then close the workbook.

Finalizing a Workbook

Once a workbook functions in the manner for which it was designed, final touches can be added to the worksheets to make them more attractive and easier to use. Excel provides several ways of finalizing a workbook that include enhancing existing objects and data, preparing custom views for multiple users, protecting your privacy, and saving the workbook in other formats. As you finalize the workbook, you should consider enhancements to charts and data that can make the information more visually appealing or easier to interpret.

BTW
Save a Chart as a Template
Chart objects can be saved as templates for reuse. To save a chart as a template, right-click the chart, click Save as Template on the shortcut menu, enter a file name for the template in the Save Chart Template dialog box, and then click Save.

For example, to improve the appearance of the Event Expenses worksheet, you will add a watermark identifying the content on the Event Expenses worksheet as a draft, to ensure that the salespeople understand that the details are subject to change. A watermark is semitransparent text overlaid on the worksheet that is used to convey something about the state of the worksheet, such as Draft or Confidential status. You will also add a background to the Prior Years worksheet. Worksheet backgrounds place an image behind the data in cells of a worksheet.

When preparing the workbook for distribution, consider establishing a custom display so that the content will display in your preferred way when you access the workbook after others have used it. In addition, regional settings in Excel allow for support of global users, so you might want to change the language settings (Excel Options dialog box), for example.

Before distributing your workbook to others, you should consider what hidden information might be in your workbook. As you learned in previous modules, rows and columns can be hidden from view, as can worksheets and workbooks. Cells also can be protected. You can use the Document Inspector to inspect and report such information, and then choose to remove the hidden information or leave the information in the workbook.

Furthermore, before distributing a workbook, you should consider whether the intended recipients have the most recent version of Excel. If this is not the case, Excel allows you to save a workbook for use in previous versions of Excel, such as Excel 97-2003. When you save a workbook in the Excel 97-2003 Workbook file format, Excel will enable the Compatibility Checker, which notifies you if any of the content of the workbook cannot be saved in that format. Additionally, the Compatibility Checker will inform you if any content will appear differently in the Excel 97-2003 Workbook format, such as cell or chart formatting.

To Add a Watermark to a Worksheet

Why? A watermark can be used to provide a reminder to the user. In this case, it will remind the users that the worksheet contains draft content. Excel does not have a watermark function, but you can use WordArt to mimic one. The following steps add a watermark to the Event Expenses worksheet.

1. Open the file named SC_EX_11-2.xlsx from the Data Files.

2. If the Excel window is not maximized, click the Maximize button on its title bar to maximize the window.

3. Save the workbook on your hard drive, OneDrive, or other storage location, entering **SC_EX_11_PRSEvents** as the file name.

4.
- With the SC_EX_11_PRSEvents.xlsx workbook open, make Event Expenses the active worksheet if necessary.
- Display the Insert tab, and then click the WordArt button (Insert tab | Text group) to display the Insert WordArt gallery (Figure 11-61).

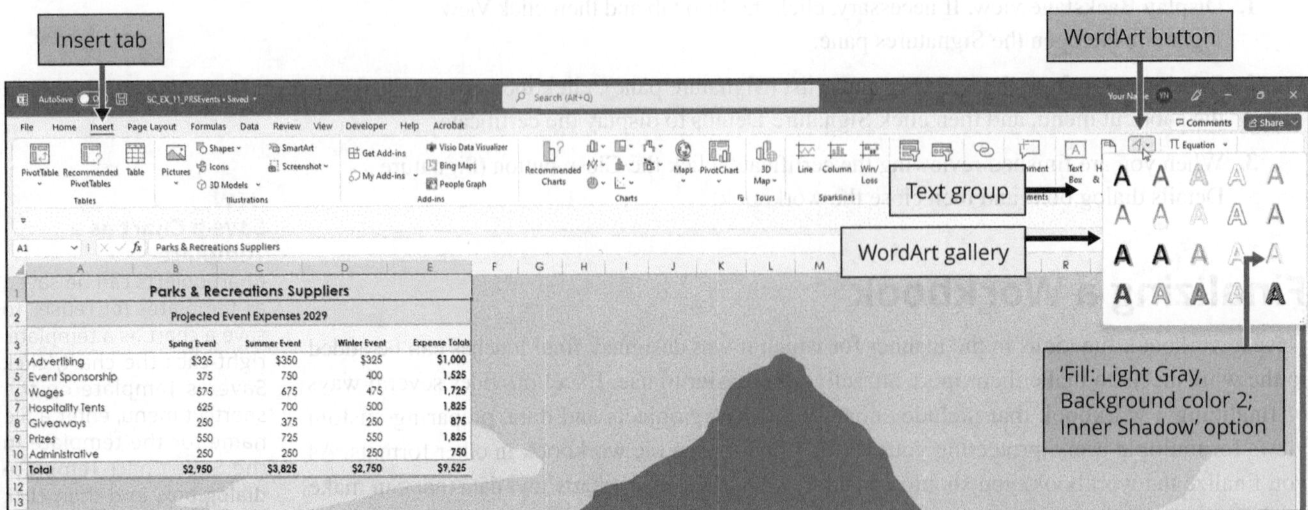

Figure 11-61

Q&A I don't have a WordArt button. What should I do?
Click the Text button to expand the Text group (Figure 11–61). The buttons in the Text group then should appear.

2

- Click 'Fill: Light Gray, Background color 2; Inner Shadow' (column 5, row 3 of the Insert WordArt gallery) to insert a new WordArt object.
- If necessary, select the text in the WordArt object, and then type **Draft** as the watermark text.
- Point to the border of the WordArt object, and when the pointer changes to a four-headed arrow, drag the WordArt object to the approximate center of the worksheet content, and then right-click the text to display a shortcut menu (Figure 11–62).

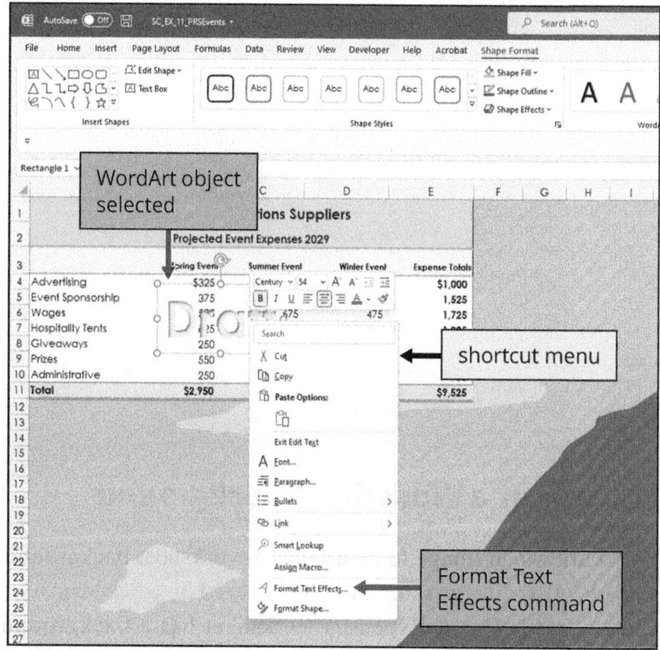

Figure 11–62

3

- Click 'Format Text Effects' on the shortcut menu to open the Format Shape pane.
- If necessary, click the Text Options tab (Format Shape pane) to display the text options.
- Click the 'Text Fill & Outline' option button (Format Shape pane) and then expand the Text Fill section.
- Set the Transparency slider to 80%, to change the transparency of the WordArt (Figure 11–63).

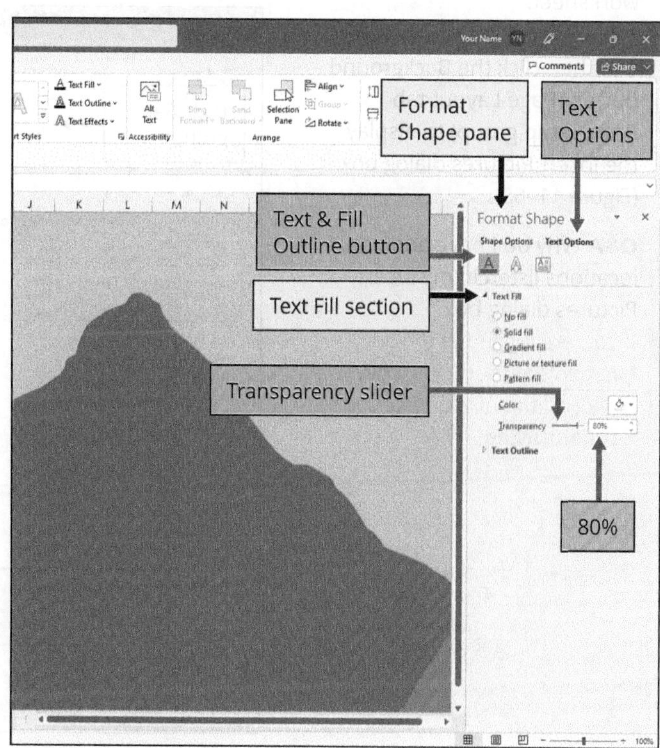

Figure 11–63

- Click the Close button in the Format Shape pane to close it.
- With the WordArt object still selected, drag the rotation handle until the orientation of the WordArt object is similar to Figure 11–64.

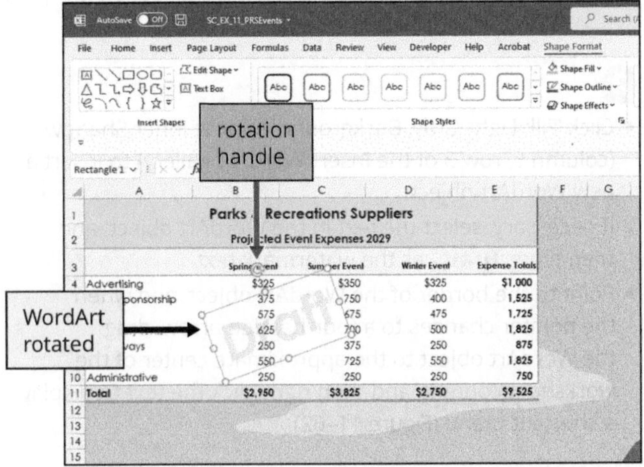

Figure 11–64

To Format a Worksheet Background

Excel allows an image to be used as a worksheet background. **Why?** Worksheet backgrounds can provide visual appeal to a worksheet, allowing for a corporate logo or other identifying image to serve as the background for an entire worksheet. Currently the Event Expenses worksheet has a background. The following steps add this same image as a worksheet background to the Prior Years worksheet.

- Display the Prior Years worksheet.
- Display the Page Layout tab and then click the Background button (Page Layout tab | Page Setup group) to display the Insert Pictures dialog box (Figure 11–65).

Q&A Why do I have additional locations listed in my Insert Pictures dialog box?

If you are logged in to your Microsoft account, you may have additional, cloud-based locations listed.

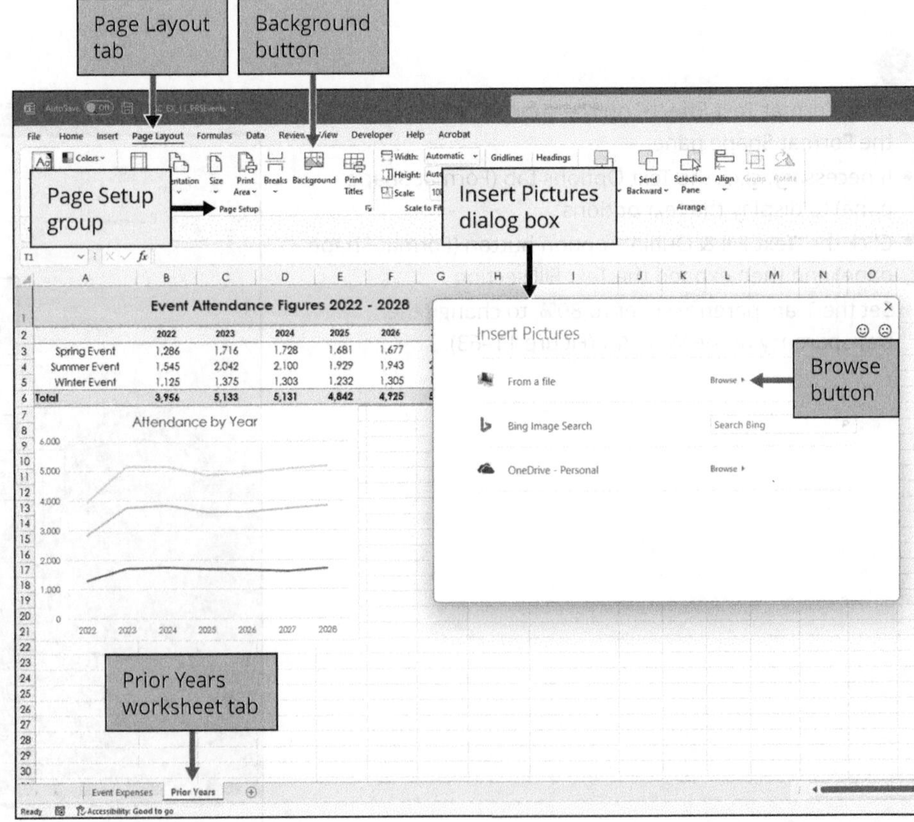

Figure 11–65

2

- Click the Browse button in the From a file area to display the Sheet Background dialog box.
- Navigate to the location of the Data Files, and then select the Support_EX_11_Mountains.jpg file (Figure 11–66).

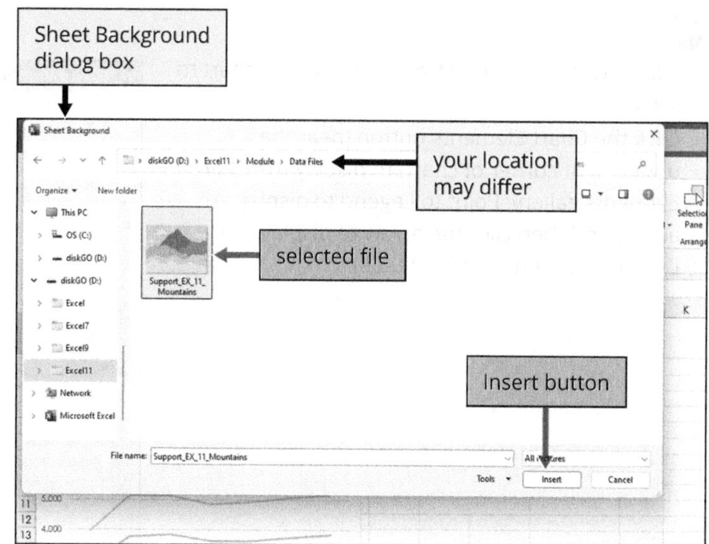

Figure 11–66

3

- Click the Insert button (Sheet Background dialog box) to display the image as the worksheet background.
- If gridlines are displayed, click the View Gridlines check box (Page Layout tab | Sheet Options group) to remove the checkmark and turn off gridlines (Figure 11–67).

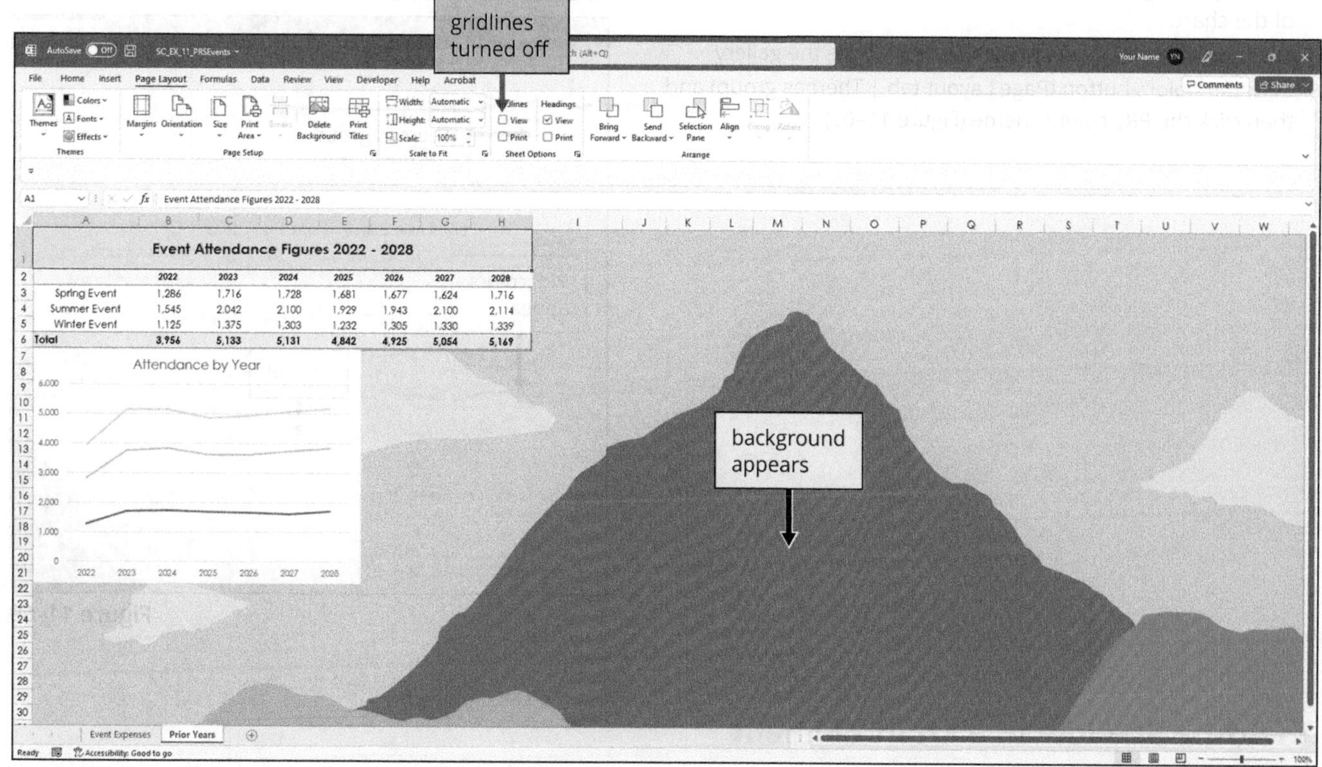

Figure 11–67

Add a Legend to a Chart

Adding a legend to the chart will improve the readability of the chart by identifying which event each line represents. **Why?** With line charts containing multiple lines, a legend is necessary for the reader to be able to understand the chart information. The following steps add a legend to the chart and apply a color scheme.

- Click anywhere in the Attendance by Year chart to select it.
- Click the Chart Elements button (near the upper-right corner of chart) to display the Chart Elements gallery. Point to Legend to display an arrow, and then click the arrow to display the Legend submenu (Figure 11–68).

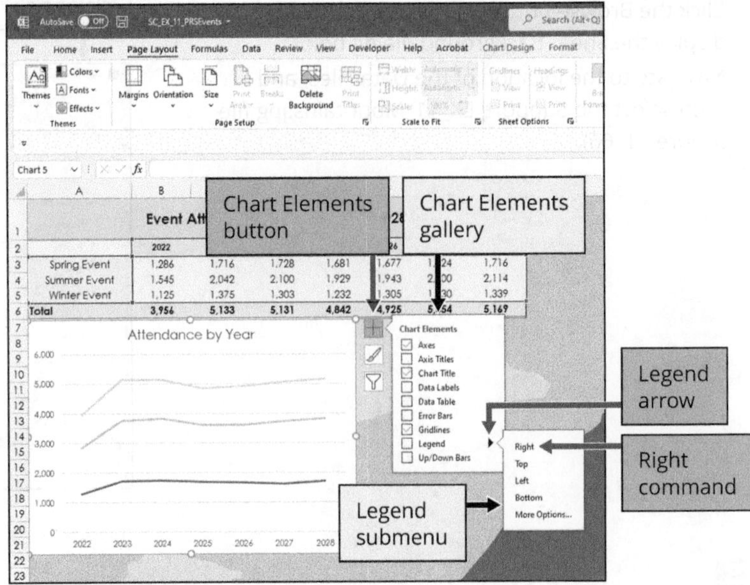

Figure 11–68

- Click Right (Legend submenu) to add a legend to the right side of the chart.
- Click the Chart Elements button again to close the gallery.
- Click the Colors button (Page Layout tab | Themes group) and then click the PRS color scheme (Figure 11–69).

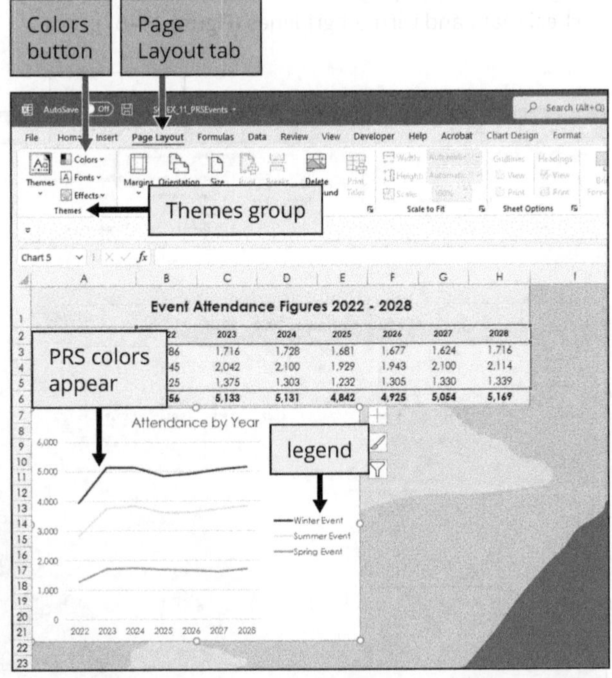

Figure 11–69

To Add a Shadow to a Chart Element

Adding a shadow to the plot area separates it from the other chart elements and improves the visual appeal of the chart. The following steps add a shadow to the plot area of the chart. **Why?** Shadows and other design features will add depth and a more professional appearance to the chart.

- Click anywhere in the plot area to select it. Do not click any of the plot lines.
- Right-click the plot area to display a shortcut menu (Figure 11–70).

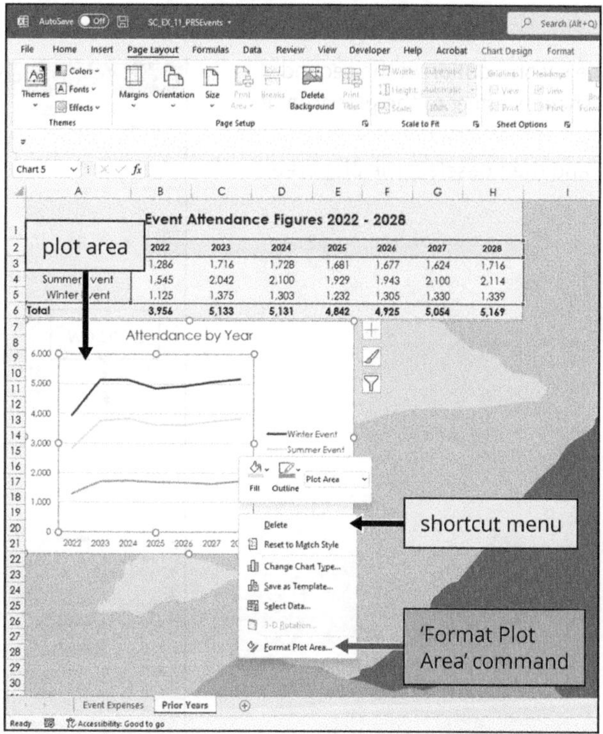

Figure 11–70

2

- Click 'Format Plot Area' on the shortcut menu to open the Format Plot Area pane.
- Click the Effects button (Format Plot Area pane), and then expand the Shadow settings.
- Click the Presets button to display the Shadow gallery (Figure 11–71).

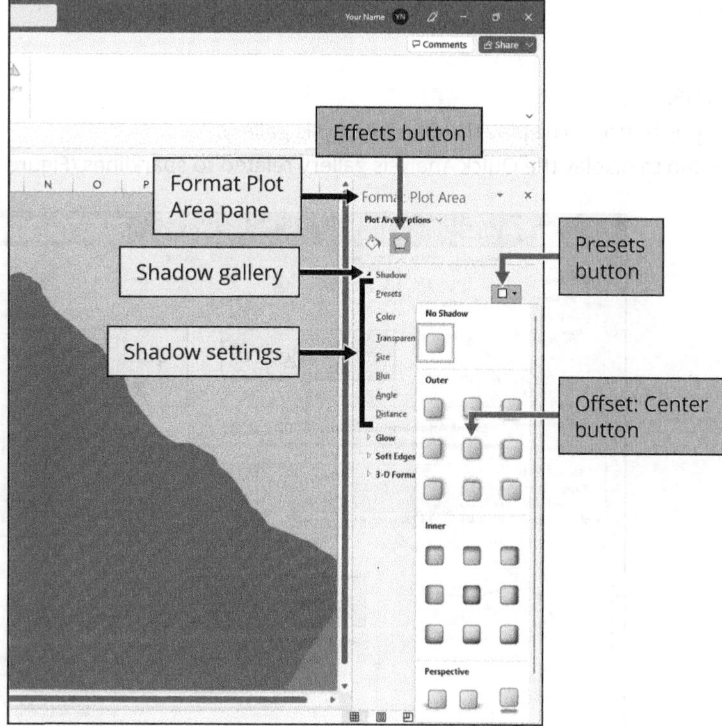

Figure 11–71

- Click the Offset: Center button (the second option in the second row of the Outer area) to apply a shadow effect to the plot area of the chart.
- Close the Format Plot Area pane, and then deselect the plot area (Figure 11–72).

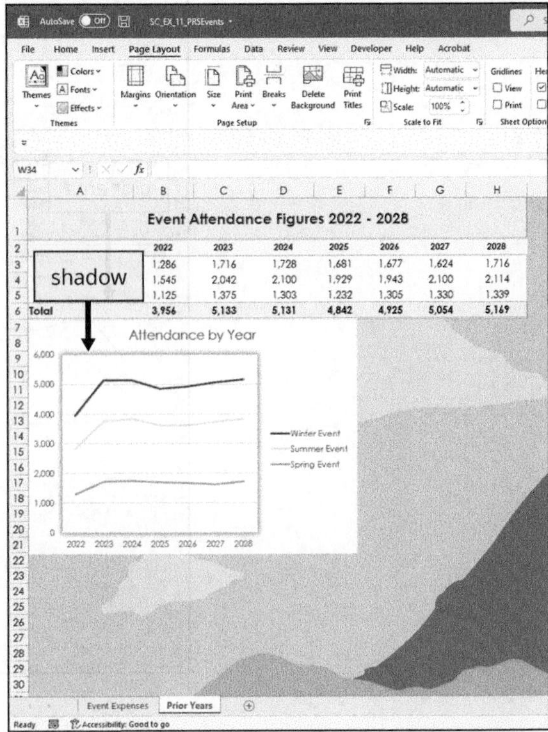

Figure 11–72

To Add Sparklines Using the Quick Analysis Gallery

Sparklines are charts that are inserted immediately beside the data that creates them, The following steps add sparkline charts for attendance figures. **Why?** Sparklines will allow for easy comparison of the numerical and graphical data.

- Select the range B3:H5.
- Click the Quick Analysis button to display the Quick Analysis gallery.
- Click the Sparklines tab to display the Quick Analysis gallery related to sparklines (Figure 11–73).

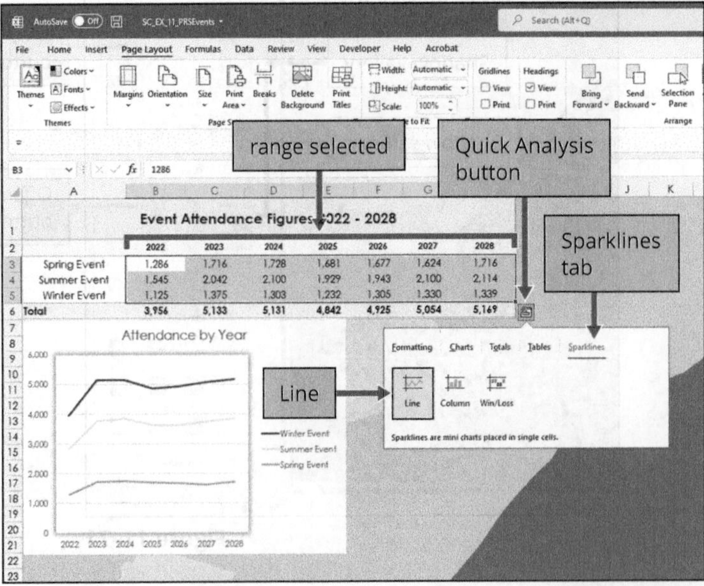

Figure 11–73

2

- Click the Line button (Quick Analysis gallery) to insert sparklines in cells I3:I5.
- Select the range I1:I6. Click the Fill Color arrow (Home tab | Font group) to display the Fill Color gallery. Click 'Orange, Accent 5, Lighter 80%' in the second row under Theme Colors to choose a fill color.
- Make cell A1 the active cell to deselect the range (Figure 11–74).
- Save the file.

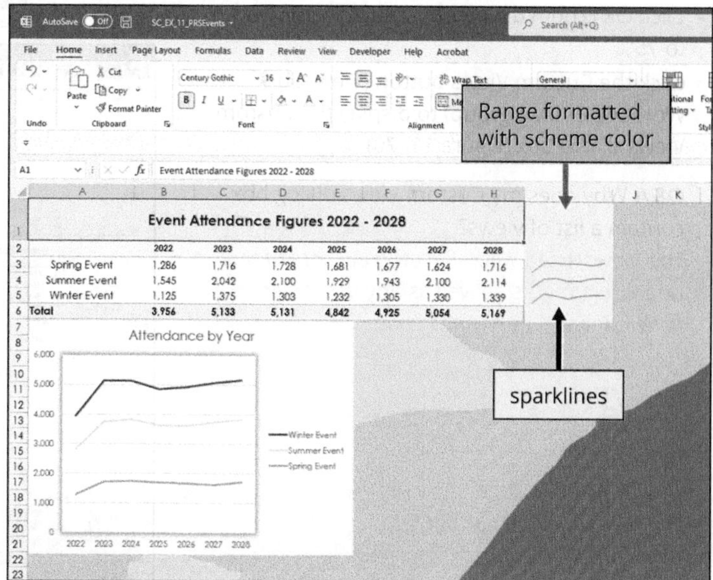

Figure 11–74

Saving Custom Views

A **custom view** allows certain layout and printing characteristics of a workbook to be saved and then used later. When a custom view of a workbook is saved, Excel stores information about the workbook's current window size and print settings. Before saving a custom view, make sure the workbook reflects the desired layout and print settings.

The Custom Views button on the View tab is used to save, delete, and display custom views. When a user saves a custom view, Excel also stores the name of the current worksheet. When a user displays a custom view by clicking the Show button in the Custom Views dialog box, Excel switches to the worksheet that was active in the workbook when the custom view was saved.

To Save a Custom View of a Workbook

Why? If a workbook requires that you customize certain layout and printing settings to use it effectively, using a custom view allows you to save those settings with the workbook. Whenever the workbook is opened, it will be opened with those settings active. The following steps create and save a custom view of the SC_EX_11_PRSEvents workbook.

- Click View on the ribbon to display the View tab.
- Click the Zoom button (View tab | Zoom group) to display the Zoom dialog box.
- Click the 75% option button (Zoom dialog box) to select 75% magnification (Figure 11–75).

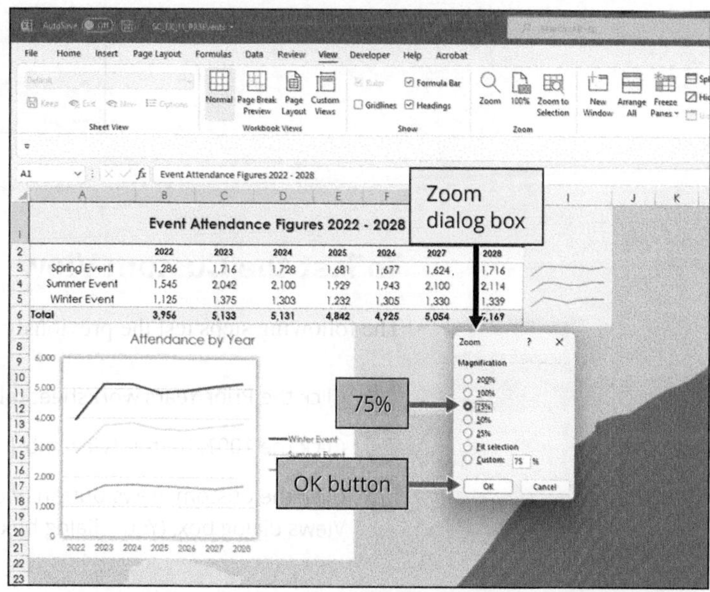

Figure 11–75

2

- Click OK (Zoom dialog box) to set the zoom to 75%.
- Click the Custom Views button (View tab | Workbook Views group) to display the Custom Views dialog box (Figure 11–76).

Q&A Why does my Custom Views dialog box contain a list of views?
The views listed will reflect the authors of any open documents as well as any users signed in to Windows.

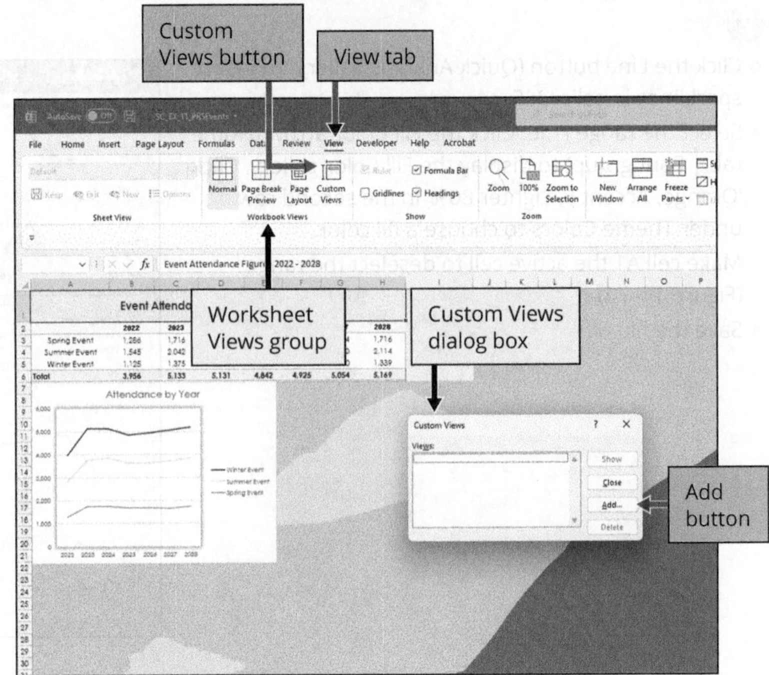

Figure 11–76

3

- Click the Add button (Custom Views dialog box) to display the Add View dialog box.
- Type **Event Attendance** in the Name box to provide a name for the custom view (Figure 11–77).

4

- Click OK (Add View dialog box) to close the dialog box.

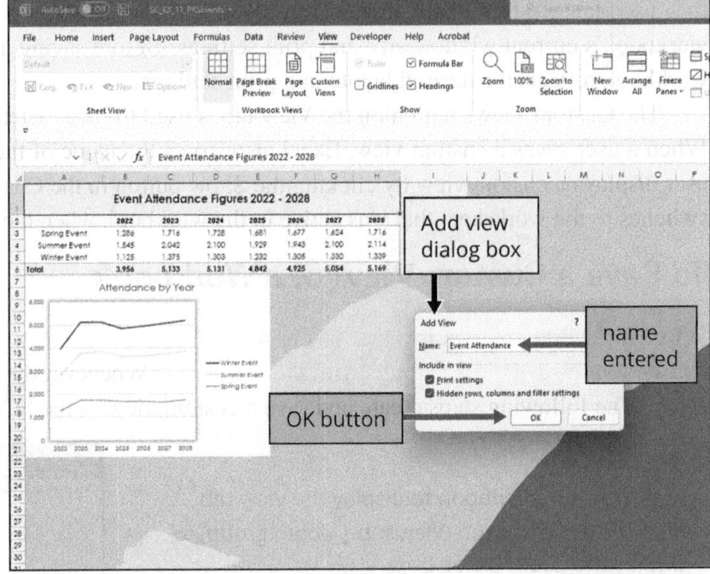

Figure 11–77

To Test the Custom View

The following steps test the previously created custom view named Event Attendance.

1. Click the Prior Years worksheet tab if necessary.
2. Click the 100% button (View tab | Zoom group) to set the zoom to 100%.
3. Click the Custom Views button (View tab | Workbook Views group) to display the Custom Views dialog box. (Your dialog box may contain additional views.)

4 Click Event Attendance in the Views list and then click the Show button (Custom Views dialog box) to display the Event Attendance view, which includes a zoom to 75%.

5 Click the 100% button (View tab | Zoom group) to set the zoom back to 100%.

6 Save the workbook again on the same storage location with the same file name.

Q&A Can I delete a custom view?
Yes. To delete custom views, select the view you want to delete, and then use the Delete button in the Custom Views dialog box shown in Figure 11–76.

To Customize Headers and Footers

If you decide to print the final version of your workbook, Excel offers many ways to customize the headers and footers. Not only can you include page numbers, but you can create custom headers and footers that include built-in elements such as text, graphics, and other spreadsheet data. To review the various built-in elements, click the Header & Footer button (Insert tab | Text Group) to display the Header & Footer tab. The elements are located in the Header & Footer Elements group. For a more exact and formatted customization, use the Header/Footer sheet in the Page Setup dialog box (Figure 11–78).

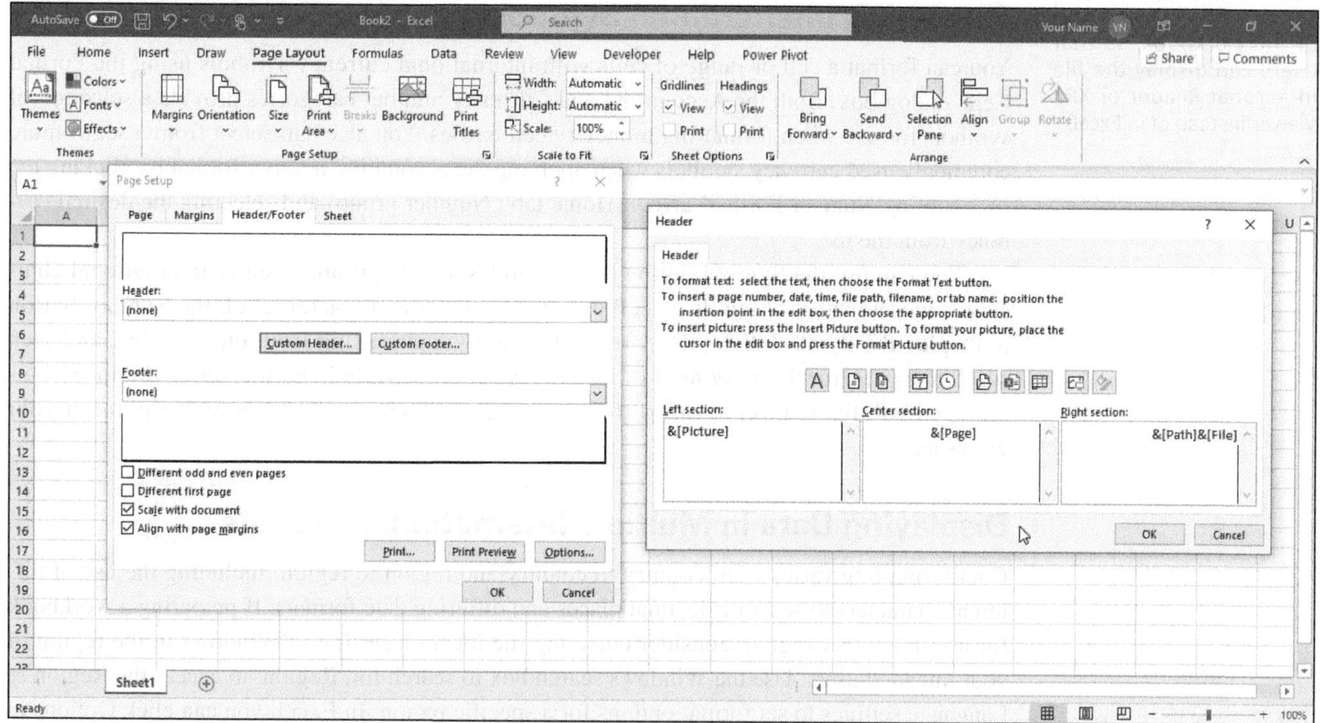

Figure 11–78

If you wanted to customize your header or footer, you would perform the following steps:

1. Click the Page Setup dialog box launcher (Page Layout tab | Page setup group).
2. On the Header/Footer tab, click the Custom Header button or Custom Footer button (Page Setup dialog box).
3. Click in the desired section box and then type text or click the appropriate button to insert a built-in element code.
4. Highlight the text or code and then click the Format Text button to display the Font dialog box. Select any format changes.

5. If you have inserted a picture, highlight the &[Picture] placeholder, and then click the Format Picture button to display the Format Picture dialog box. Select any format changes.
6. Click OK (Header dialog box or Footer dialog box), and then click OK again (Page Setup dialog box).

BTW
Distributing a Document
Instead of printing and distributing a hard copy of a workbook, you can distribute the workbook electronically. Options include sending the workbook via email; posting it on cloud storage (such as OneDrive) and sharing the file with others; posting it on social media, a blog, or other website; and sharing a link associated with an online location of the workbook. You also can create and share a PDF or XPS image of the workbook, so that users can display the file in Acrobat Reader or XPS Viewer instead of in Excel.

Setting Internationalization Features

Excel provides internationalization features you can use when creating workbooks, such as the language setting described earlier in this module. Use of these features should be determined based on the intended audience of the workbook. For instance, if you are creating a workbook that will be used in Asian countries where decimal notation differs from that used in North America, consider setting up the workbook to use the appropriate notation by creating custom number formats or changing the symbol used with the Currency or Accounting number formats.

By default, workbooks use formatting consistent with the country or region selected when installing Windows. Situations exist where a workbook will need to contain text or number formatting consistent with a different country or region. Several options are available for applying international formats to content.

Displaying International Symbols

You can format a cell or range of cells with international currency symbols using the Format Cells dialog box. Both the Accounting and Currency number categories provide a selection of symbols for use when formatting monetary cell entries. You also can select from a set of more commonly used currency symbols when applying the accounting number format by clicking the 'Accounting Number Format' arrow (Home tab | Number group) and selecting the desired currency from the list.

You can use the Symbol button (Insert tab | Symbols group) to enter international characters and monetary symbols as cell entries. To insert a character, click the Symbol button to display the Symbol dialog box, select the font you are using from the Font list, and then scroll until you reach the symbol of interest. Select the symbol and then click the Insert button (Symbol dialog box) to insert the symbol at the location of the insertion point in your worksheet.

Displaying Data in Multiple International Formats

Data formatting varies from country to country and region to region, including the use of different characters to separate decimal places and differing date formats. If preparing a workbook for use in another region, consider changing the location setting in Windows to the region of your intended users. Use the Windows search box to search for, Region, to access the Region & Language settings to set format options for a specific region. In Excel, you can click Options in Backstage view and then click Language in the left pane. In the 'Office authoring languages and proofing' area in the right pane, click the 'Add a language' button. Choose the language you are interested in. The Editing language is the language in which you type and edit your content. The lower part of the right pane offers ways to change the display language, which is used for all of the buttons, menus, and controls in Excel.

Excel has other language-specific features. For example, if you want to use a European style date, you can right-click a date and click Format Cells on the shortcut menu. In the Format Cells dialog box, click Date in the left pane. On the right, click the Locale button and then choose your language or region. You also can change the proofing language by clicking Options in Backstage view. Click Proofing in the Excel Options dialog box, click the Custom Dictionary button, and then choose your language.

Collaborating with Users Who Do Not Use the Same Version of Excel

It is not unusual to collaborate with others who are using different software versions, or different software entirely, to do their work. You even can find different versions of software being used within the same company. When collaborating with others, you should make decisions about how to save and distribute files after considering how your colleagues will be using the workbooks you create. In instances where people are working with earlier versions of software or different software, you need to provide workbooks in formats that they can use.

Before sharing a workbook with others, you can mark the workbook as being final. When another user of your workbook opens the workbook, he or she will be notified that you have marked the workbook as final. The workbook can still be edited, but only if the user clicks a button to indicate that he or she wants to edit the workbook.

To Save a Workbook in an Earlier Version of Excel

Why? You occasionally need to save a workbook for use in previous versions of Excel. Each version of Excel includes varying features, so you can use the Compatibility Checker to determine whether the features used in your workbook are compatible with earlier versions of Excel. The following steps check the compatibility of the workbook while saving the workbook in the Excel 97-2003 Workbook file format.

- Display Backstage view, click Save As, and then navigate to the location where you store your files.
- Click the 'Save as type' arrow (Save As dialog box) to display the list of file types (Figure 11–79).

Q&A Would saving the file using the same name overwrite the original version of the workbook?
No. It is not necessary to save the workbook with a new file name. The 'Excel 97-2003' version of the workbook will have a file extension of .xls, while the original has a file extension of .xlsx.

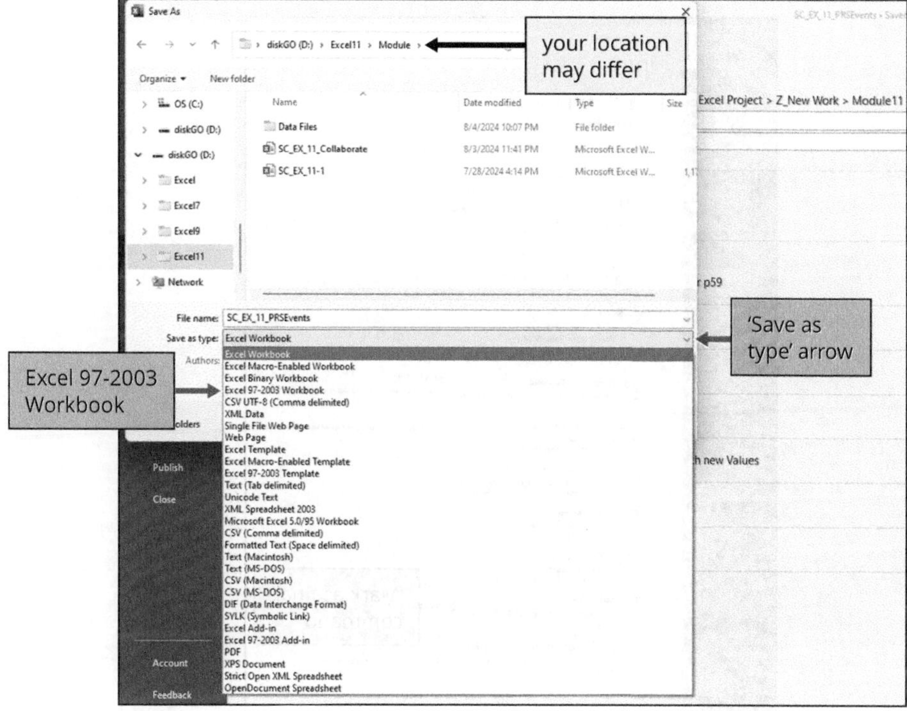

Figure 11–79

- Click 'Excel 97-2003 Workbook' to select the file format.
- Click the Save button (Save As dialog box) to display the Microsoft Excel - Compatibility Checker dialog box.
- Resize the dialog box so that it displays all the issues (Figure 11–80).

Q&A What is shown in the Microsoft Excel - Compatibility Checker dialog box?
The Summary states that some of the chart elements and the sparklines used on the Prior Years worksheet are not compatible with previous versions of Excel. While the workbook still can be saved in the Excel 97-2003 file format, the sparklines will not be saved. In addition, some cell formatting is unique to later releases. These formats will be converted to the nearest approximation in the earlier version of Excel.

- Click the Continue button (Microsoft Excel - Compatibility Checker dialog box) to save the workbook in the Excel 97-2003 Workbook file format. Note that the Accessibility message on the status bar reads "Unavailable" because you have saved the file in an earlier file format.

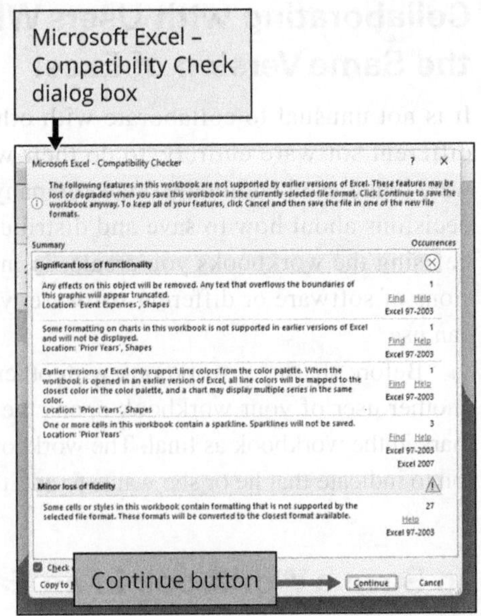

Figure 11–80

To Mark a Workbook as Final

The following steps mark the workbook as final. **Why?** The workbook is complete; marking it as final will prevent users from accidentally changing anything.

- Display Backstage view.
- Click Info in the navigation bar, and then click the Protect Workbook button in the Info gallery to display the Protect Workbook menu (Figure 11–81).

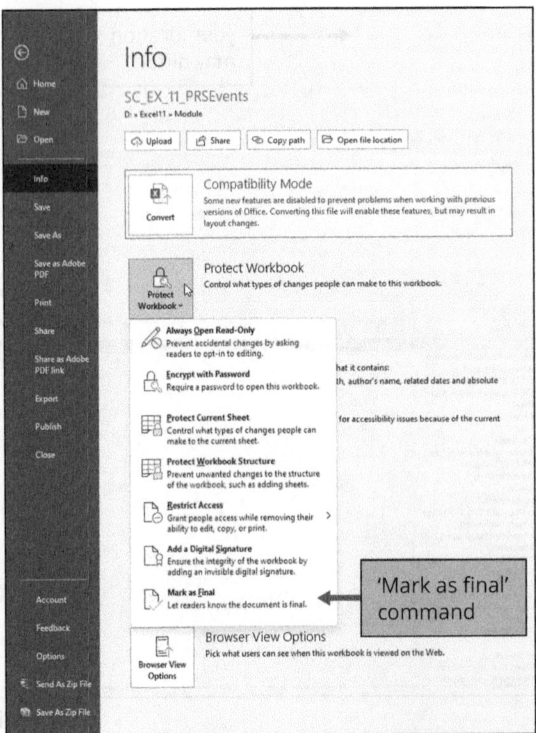

Figure 11–81

- Click 'Mark as Final' on the Protect Workbook menu to display the Microsoft Excel dialog box, and then click OK.
- If necessary, click the Continue button on the Microsoft Excel - Compatibility Checker dialog box.
- Click OK (Microsoft Excel dialog box) to indicate you want to mark the workbook as final (Figure 11–82).

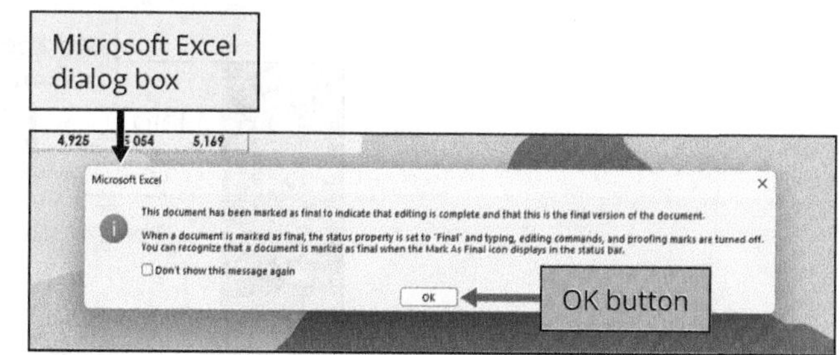

Figure 11–82

Q&A I have saved the workbook in .xls format, but the sparklines are still showing. Why?
Although the .xls format does not support newer features such as sparklines, more recent versions of Excel do. If you close the file and reopen the workbook saved in the older format, the sparklines will not be displayed.

- Click OK to close the Microsoft Excel dialog box and mark the workbook as final. Excel will display a MARKED AS FINAL yellow bar below the ribbon tabs.
- Close the workbook.

Information Rights Management

Information Rights Management (IRM) is a feature of Excel that allows you to restrict access to workbooks. With IRM, you can restrict who can view, modify, print, forward, and copy a workbook. The types of restrictions include a variety of options. For example, expiration dates for reading or modifying a workbook are available. Before using IRM, your computer first must be configured with IRM, as should the computers or mobile devices of anyone attempting to use a document that includes IRM features.

When IRM is installed properly, the Protect Workbook menu in the Info screen in Backstage view includes several commands for limiting access to the workbook. You can limit who can access the workbook and who can make changes to the workbook. For more information about IRM, search Excel Help using the search string, information rights management.

To Inspect a Document for Hidden and Personal Information

Why? The Document Inspector should be used before sharing a workbook publicly or when you suspect extraneous information remains in hidden rows and columns, hidden worksheets, document properties, headers and footers, or worksheet comments.

The following steps make a copy of the SC_EX_11_PRSSalesAnalysis.xlsm workbook and then inspect the copy for hidden and personal information.

- If necessary, open the file named SC_EX_11_PRSSalesAnalysis.xlsm and save the workbook with the file name **SC_EX_11_PRSSalesDistribute.**
- If necessary, turn off workbook sharing using the Unshare Workbook button (Review tab | Protect group). If the Unshare Workbook button is grayed out, this feature has already been turned off.
- If necessary, make Sales Data Analysis the active worksheet.
- Display Backstage view, and then click Info.
- Click the 'Check for Issues' button (Info gallery) to display the Check for Issues menu (Figure 11–83).

Q&A Why did I save this workbook with a different file name?
When preparing a workbook for distribution, you may decide to use the Document Inspector to make changes to the document. Saving the workbook with a different file name ensures that you will have a copy of the workbook with all of the original information intact for your records.

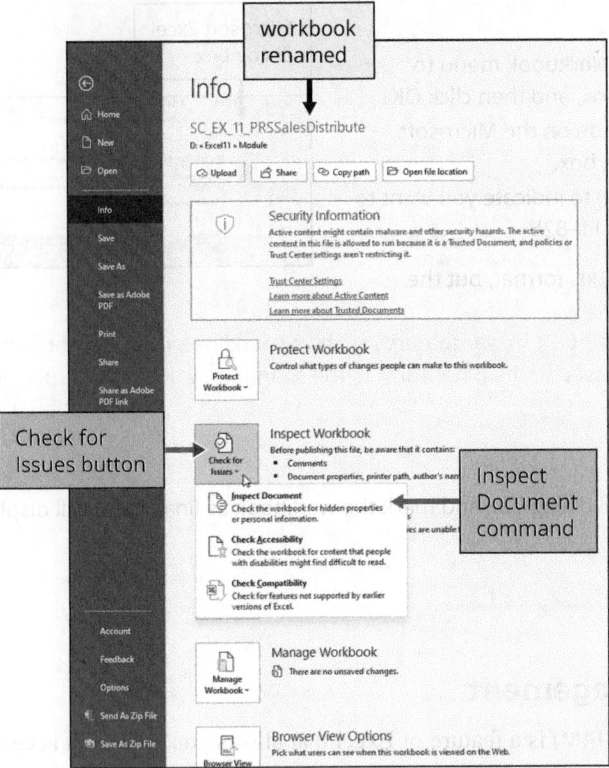

Figure 11–83

2

- Click Inspect Document (Check for Issues menu) to display the Document Inspector dialog box (Figure 11–84). If prompted, click the Yes button to first save the document.

Q&A What is shown in the Document Inspector dialog box?
The Document Inspector dialog box allows you to choose which types of content to inspect. Typically, you would leave all of the items selected, unless you are comfortable with some types of content not being inspected.

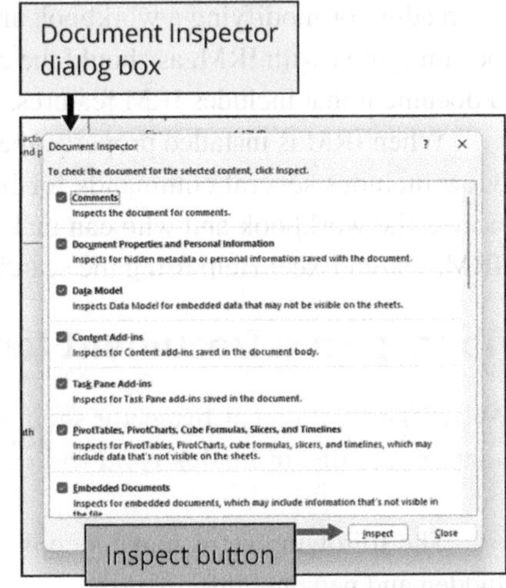

Figure 11–84

- Click the Inspect button (Document Inspector dialog box) to run the Document Inspector and display its results (Figure 11–85).
- **Experiment:** Scroll in the Document Inspector to review the issues.

Q&A What did the Document Inspector find?
The Document Inspector found the hidden Prospect List worksheet, comments, and personal information (Figure 11–85), including document properties, author information, related dates, absolute path to the workbook, and printer properties. The Remove All button in the dialog box allows you quickly to remove the items found if needed. In many instances, you may want to take notes of the results and then investigate and remedy each one separately. In this workbook, all of these items found by the Document Inspector are expected and do not need to be remedied.

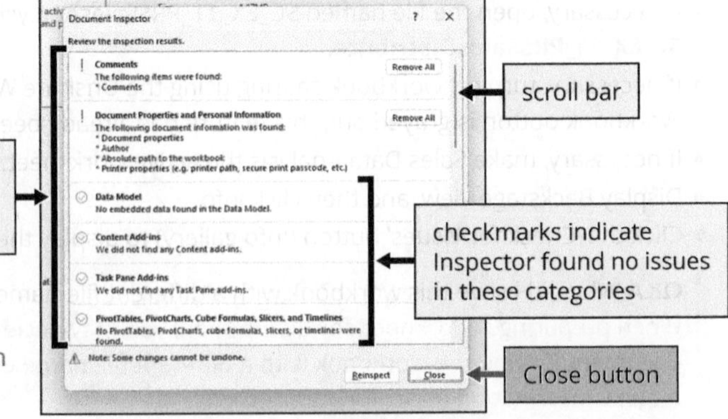

Figure 11–85

- Click the Close button (Document Inspector dialog box) to close the dialog box.
- Return to the worksheet.

To Delete Customization

The following steps delete the PRS color and font schemes. **Why?** Deleting custom color and font schemes serves as a courtesy to other users of a shared computer. Deleting the schemes does not change the workbook.

1. Click the Colors button (Page Layout tab | Themes group) and then right-click the PRS color scheme to display the shortcut menu. Click Delete. If Excel displays a dialog box confirming the deletion, click Yes.
2. Click the Fonts button (Page Layout tab | Themes group) and then right-click the PRS font scheme to display the shortcut menu. Click Delete. If Excel displays a dialog box confirming the deletion, click Yes.
3. If desired you can reset the ribbon. Click Options in Backstage view, click 'Quick Access Toolbar' in the left pane, and then click Reset button (Excel Options dialog box). Click 'Reset all customizations'.
4. sam Click OK to close the Excel Options dialog box. Save the file and then exit Excel.

Summary

In this module, you developed a custom form for accepting user input, using form controls, ActiveX controls, and VBA code. You shared workbooks on OneDrive and co-authored. You used comments to provide feedback and compared worksheet data from two workbooks. You added finishing touches to worksheets, learned about internationalization, and prepared workbooks for distribution.

Consider This: Plan Ahead

What decisions will you need to make when using Excel to collect information or collaborate with others?

Use these guidelines as you complete the assignments in this module and create your own worksheets for creating Excel forms and collaborating with others outside of this class.

1. Create custom fonts, schemes, and themes as necessary.
2. Determine the purpose and needs of the form data.
    a. Design a user interface with controls appropriate to the data being entered.
    b. Set control properties to give meaning and limitations to each control's use.
    c. Write the Visual Basic code associated with the user's actions, such as clicking a button.
    d. Test the user interface to prove that it behaves as expected.
3. Determine the audience, purpose, and options available for the collaboration.
4. Evaluate changes made by colleagues.
    a. With a single distributed workbook, use co-authoring.
    b. With multiple workbooks, compare workbooks side by side.
5. Add worksheet enhancements.
    a. Add watermarks and worksheet backgrounds as appropriate.
    b. Enhance charts if appropriate.
6. Prepare workbook(s) for distribution.

Student Assignments

Apply Your Knowledge

Reinforce the skills and apply the concepts you learned in this module.

Creating a Form

Note: To complete this assignment, you will be required to use the Data Files. Please contact your instructor for information about accessing the Data Files.

Instructions: Start Excel. Open the workbook SC_EX_11-3.xlsx, which is located in the Data Files. The spreadsheet you open contains the start of a form guardians will use to check out students at the local elementary school. Figure 11–86 shows the completed form.

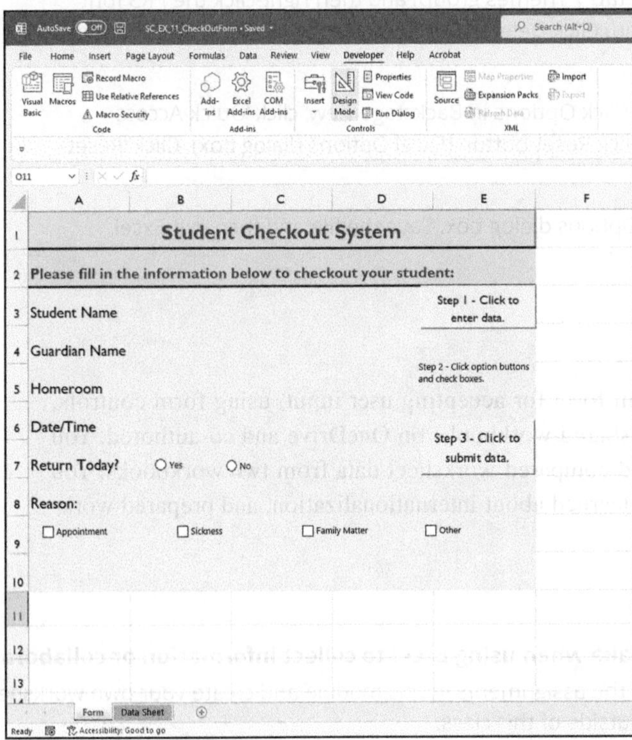

Figure 11–86

Perform the following tasks:

1. Save the workbook using the file name, SC_EX_11_CheckOutForm.xlsm (the macro enabled format). Examine row 39 and column W, then return to the top of the worksheet.
2. If necessary, add the Developer tab to the ribbon as described in the module.
3. Click the Insert button (Developer tab | Controls group) and then click the Option Button (Form Controls) button in the Form Controls area (column 6, row 1) in the Controls gallery. Drag in the worksheet to create an option button control in cell B7 (approximately). Right-click the option button and click Edit Text. Change the existing text to, Yes. Resize the control as necessary.
4. Repeat Step 3 to create an option button control in cell C7 (approximately) with the text, No. Select both option buttons and then click the Align button (Shape Format tab | Arrange group). Align the two option buttons on the top.
5. Right-click either option button control, and then click Format Control on the shortcut menu. If necessary, click the Control tab (Format Control dialog box) and then type **$E$41** in the Cell link box (Format Control dialog box) to link the option button index number to cell E41. Close the dialog box.

6. Click the Insert button (Developer tab | Controls group) and then click the Check Box (Form Control) button in the Form Controls area (column 3, row 1) in the Controls gallery. Drag in the worksheet to create a check box control in cell A9 (approximately). Change the existing text to Appointment. Resize so the check box is only slightly bigger than the text.
7. Repeat Step 6 to create a check box with the text, Sickness in cell B9. Repeat Step 6 to create a check box with the text, Family Matter in cell C9. Repeat Step 6 to create a check box with the text, Other in cell D9. Select all four check boxes, right-click, and then chose Format Object on the shortcut menu to open the Format Control dialog box. On the Size tab, set the height to .19. Align them on the top and distribute them horizontally.
8. One at a time, right-click each of the check boxes and click Format Control on the shortcut menu. Link the check boxes to cells $F$40, $G$40, $H$40, and $I$40, respectively.
9. Select the range A39:D40. Click the 'Create from Selection' button (Formulas tab | Defined Names group). Click the Top Row check box (Create from Selection dialog box). Click OK (Create from Selection dialog box) to name the cells.
10. Select cell E40. Type **=@INDEX(W2:W3,$E$41)** to enter the function that evaluates the option buttons.
11. Select cell B3 and type **=A40** to enter a cell reference that will display the name during execution of the code. Select cell B4 and type **=B40**. Select cell B5 and type **=C40**. Select cell B6 and type **=D40**.
12. Click the Insert button (Developer tab | Controls group), and then click the Command Button (ActiveX Control) button in the ActiveX Controls area (column 1, row 1) of the Controls gallery. Drag in the worksheet in cell E3 (approximately) create a Command Button ActiveX control.
13. If necessary, click the Design Mode button (Developer tab | Controls group) to turn it on. Click the Properties button (Developer tab | Controls group), and then change the name of the button to cmdStep1. In the Caption field, select the existing text and then type **Step 1 - Click to enter data**. Change the WordWrap property to True. Click the Font property and then click the ellipsis button to display the Font dialog box. Change the Font to size 12. Double-click the button and enter the code from Table 11–5, pressing TAB before typing each line if necessary.

Table 11–5: Code for cmdStep1 Button

'Author: SC Series
'Date Created: 11/19/2029
'Run from: Form Worksheet, cmdStep1 Button
'Function: When executed, this procedure enters contact information for the prospect.
Range("Student_Name").Value = InputBox("Student Name?", "Enter", , 800, 6000)
Range("Guardian_Name").Value = InputBox("Guardian Name?", "Enter", , 800, 6000)
Range("Homeroom").Value = InputBox("Homeroom?", "Enter", , 800, 6000)
Range("Date_Time").Value = InputBox("Date/Time?", "Enter", , 800, 6000)

14. Close the VBA window.
15. Click the Insert button (Developer tab | Controls group) and then click the Command Button (ActiveX Control) button in the ActiveX Controls area (column 1, row 1) of the Controls gallery. Drag in the worksheet in cell E6 create a Command Button ActiveX control.
16. If necessary, click the Design Mode button (Developer tab | Controls group) to turn it on. Click the Properties button (Developer tab | Controls group) and then change the name of the button to cmdStep3. In the Caption field, select the existing text and then type **Step 3 - Click to submit data**. Change the WordWrap property to True. Change the Font to size 12. Double-click the button, enter the code from Table 11–6, pressing TAB before typing each line, as necessary.

Continued on next page

Table 11-6: Code for cmdStep3 Button

'Author: SC Series
'Date Created: 11/19/2029
'Run from: Form Worksheet, cmdStep3 Button
'Function: When executed, this procedure submits new information to the prospect list
Range("A40:I40").Select
Selection.Copy
Sheets("Data Sheet").Visible = True
Sheets("Data Sheet").Activate
Sheets("Data Sheet").Range("A2:I2").Select
Selection.PasteSpecial Paste:=xlPasteValues, Operation:=xlNone, SkipBlanks:=False, Transpose:=False
Selection.Font.Bold = False
Sheets("Data Sheet").Range("A2").Activate
ActiveCell.EntireRow.Insert
Sheets("Data Sheet").Visible = False
Sheets("Form").Select
Range("E41").ClearContents
Range("A40:D40").ClearContents
Range("F40:I40").ClearContents
Range("E3").Activate
ActiveWorkbook.Save

17. Create a Label form control between the two command buttons, in approximately cell E5. Select the existing text, and enter **Step 2 - Click option buttons and check boxes.**
18. Enter the following alternative text for the first command button: **Command button to enter data**
19. Enter the following alternative text for the second command button: **Command button to submit data**
20. Turn off Design Mode and test the form. Unhide the Data Sheet and check to make sure the data was recorded. If there were errors, double-check the VBA code you entered.
21. When everything runs correctly, hide the Data Sheet. Password protect the Form sheet, enter **Checkout29** as the password. Save the workbook and then submit the revised workbook as specified by your instructor, along with the password. If you are working in a lab situation, delete all customization.
22. **Consider This:** What other things could you do to this workbook to make it appear more attractive or be more functional on a checkout form?

Extend Your Knowledge

Extend the skills you learned in this module and experiment with new skills. You may need to use Help to complete the assignment.

Writing VBA Code

Note: To complete this assignment, you will be required to use the Data Files. Please contact your instructor for information about accessing the Data Files.

Instructions: Start Excel. Open the workbook SC_EX_11-4.xlsm, which is located in the Data Files. The document contains the Sales Data Analysis worksheet. You are to create VBA code that will execute upon closing the file. It will include a message box shown in Figure 11–87.

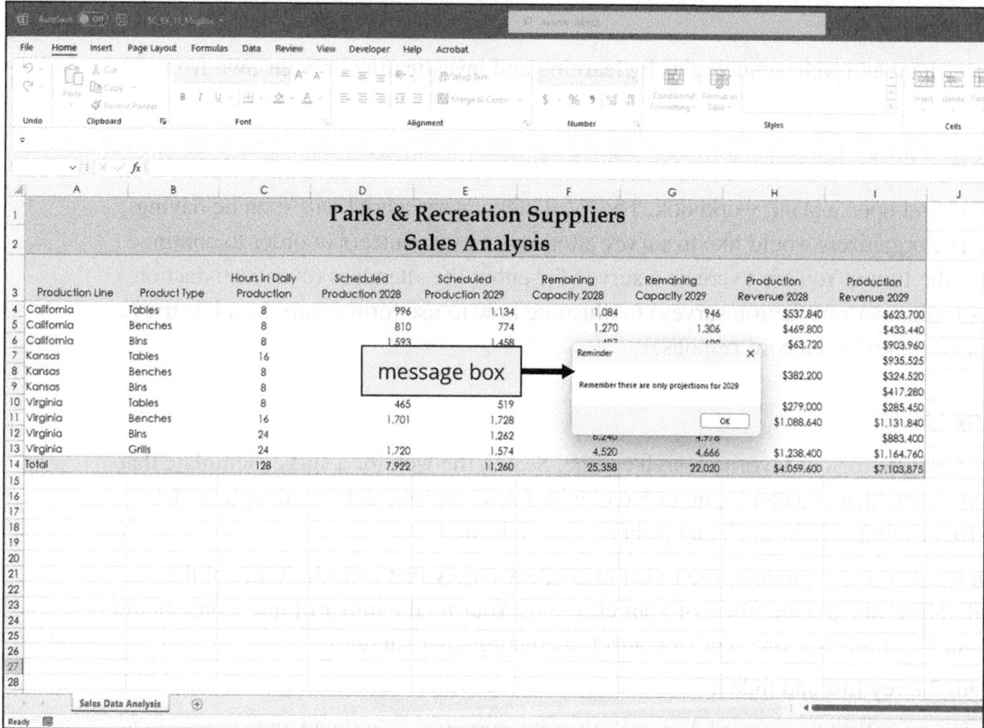

Figure 11–87

Perform the following tasks:

1. Save the file in the macro-enabled format with the name, SC_EX_11_MsgBox.xlsm.
2. With the Sales Data Analysis sheet displayed, click the Visual Basic button (Developer tab | Code group) to display the Microsoft Visual Basic for Applications editor.
3. On the menu bar, click Help, and then click Microsoft Visual Basic for Applications Help in the list. Click the link for Microsoft Visual Basic for Applications Help. In the Filter by Title box in the upper-left corner, search for information about MsgBox. Click MsgBox function (Visual Basic for Applications) in the list and learn more about the topic.
4. In the Project pane (the left pane of the VBA window), double-click ThisWorkbook, so the code will apply to the entire workbook. If the Project pane is not displayed, click on View and choose Project Explorer to display the Project pane.
5. In the main window, click the Object arrow and then click Workbook. Excel will create a procedure for when the Workbook Opens. Click within this procedure.
6. Press TAB and then type **'This procedure displays a message box when the user opens the workbook** to enter a code comment. Press ENTER to move to the next line. Enter two additional comments with your name and the date.
7. Create a message box by typing the code, **MsgBox "Remember these are only projections for 2029", vbOKOnly, "Reminder"** and then press ENTER.
8. Enter other comments explaining the purpose of the various parts of the MsgBox statement.
9. Save the workbook.
10. Test the workbook by clicking the Close button in the title bar. Reopen the workbook. When Excel displays the message box, click the OK button. If there are errors, review the VBA code and edit as necessary.
11. Submit the revised workbook in the format specified by your instructor.
12. **Consider This:** The MsgBox function can be displayed with multiple buttons, such as OK and Cancel. When used with an equal sign, MsgBox returns a value based on which button the user clicks in the message box (access the previous Help page and scroll down to the Return Values and Examples areas). What do you think VBA programmers do with that response value?

Expand Your World

Create a solution that uses cloud and web technologies by learning and investigating on your own from general guidance.

Preparing Surveys

Instructions: Start Excel and open a blank workbook. The local elementary school will soon be having their yearly fall festival. The organizers would like to survey attendees and volunteers in order to continue to improve the festival for the future. You are to create a survey for either the attendees (event satisfaction survey) or the volunteers (volunteer satisfaction survey) to illustrate how to use form controls and ActiveX controls in Excel to create a survey and record responses.

Perform the following tasks:

1. Open a browser and navigate to your favorite search engine. Search the web for a survey template that will meet your requirements that you can create in Excel with form controls. Select a template that contains at least 5–10 questions. Right-click and print a copy, if desired.
2. Using the skills you learned in this module, use Excel to create a survey that includes some of the questions you found online, along with others of your choosing. Your total number of questions should be at least 10. You should use more than one type of control in creating your survey.
3. Create a sheet named, Survey List and hide it.
4. Write a VBA procedure to collect the entered data each time the survey is completed and store it on a separate, hidden worksheet. (**Hint:** Use the code from Tables 11–6 and 11–7.)
5. Use worksheet protection and formatting to set up your survey so that a user can answer questions but not gain access to the hidden worksheet or areas on the current worksheet outside of the survey.
6. Save the file in the macro-enabled format as SC_EX_11_FestivalSurvey.xlsm and submit it in the format specified by your instructor, along with the password so the instructor can access the hidden worksheet.
7. **Consider This:** What was the hardest thing about this assignment? Why? Did you use Help at any time? If so, what search terms did you use?

In the Lab

Design and implement a solution using creative thinking and problem-solving skills.

Create Schemes and Themes

Problem: Recently, local youth organizations have joined forces to assist with various projects throughout the community. Whether it is reading to young children at the local library, assisting older people with basic yard work, or donating time at the community center, the youth feel they have a true purpose in serving their community. The youth would like to brand themselves and need your assistance. You have been asked to create a custom color scheme, font scheme, and workbook theme for them. The new title they have chosen for themselves is Youth Force.

Perform the following tasks:

Part 1: Start Excel and open a blank workbook. Click the Colors button (Page Layout tab | Themes group), and then click Customize Colors to open the Create New Theme Colors dialog box. Click the Accent 1 color button and then click More Colors. When Excel displays the Colors dialog box, click the Standard tab. Choose the color you feel will best represent Youth Force in their efforts. Repeat the process for Accent 2 and Accent 3 using different colors. If you do not have three colors, choose colors that complement the Accent 1 color. Before closing the dialog box, press ALT+PRT SC (print screen) to capture the dialog box in the clipboard. Enter a name for your color scheme. Click Save (Create New Theme Colors dialog box), and then paste the screen capture onto the worksheet.

Click the Fonts button (Page Layout tab | Themes group) and then click Customize Fonts to open the Create New Theme Fonts dialog box. Choose a heading font and body font that you feel will best represent Youth Force. Before closing the dialog box, press ALT+PRT SC (print screen) to capture the dialog box in the clipboard. Enter a name for your font scheme. Click Save (Create New Theme Fonts dialog box) and then paste the screen capture onto the worksheet.

Click the Themes button (Page Layout tab | Themes group) and then click Save Current Theme to open the Save Current Theme dialog box. Enter a name of your theme and then navigate to your Data File storage location. Before clicking Save, press ALT+PRT SC (print screen) to capture the dialog box in the clipboard. Click Save (Save Current Theme dialog box) to save the theme. Paste the screen capture onto the worksheet.

Arrange the three screen captures side by side and then save the workbook with the file name SC_EX_11_YouthForce. Submit the file along with your answers to the critical thinking questions in Part 2 as directed by your instructor.

Part 2: **Consider This:** How did you decide on the sources to use for the color and font schemes? How would Youth Force use these saved schemes and themes?

Macros, Navigation Forms, and Control Layouts

Objectives

After completing this module, you will be able to:

- Create a macro or a submacro
- Troubleshoot a macro
- Create a menu form containing command buttons
- Include an option group in a menu form
- Use an IF statement in a macro
- Set the value of a variable in a macro
- Create a datasheet form
- Create a UI (user interface) macro
- Create a navigation form
- Add a tab to a navigation form
- Create a data macro
- Describe options to manage cells in a form
- Explain how to modify a control layout in a form or report
- Explain how to modify Access application options

Introduction

Using built-in tools such as macros, you can design Access forms that provide an interactive user interface experience, complete with buttons and selection menus. In this module, you will learn how to create and test macros that open forms and that preview reports and export reports. You will create a menu form with command buttons as well as a menu form with an **option group**, which is an object that enables you to make a selection by choosing the option button corresponding to your choice. You will also create and use user interface (UI) macros in forms. You will learn about the use of data macros for ensuring that updates to the database are valid. Finally, you will learn how to use control layouts on forms and reports.

Project: Macros, Navigation Forms, and Control Layouts

Partners paralegals would like users to be able to access forms and reports simply by clicking tabs and buttons, rather than by using the Navigation Pane. A **navigation form**, like the one shown in Figure 8–1a, is a form that includes tabs that display other forms and reports. Partners paralegals plan to use the navigation form because they believe it will improve the user-friendliness of the database, thereby improving employee satisfaction and efficiency. This navigation form contains several useful features. With the Closings tab selected, you can click the Closing ID (or C-ID) in any row to view the data for the selected closing in a **pop-up form**, which is a form that stays on top of other open objects even when another object is active (Figure 8–1b).

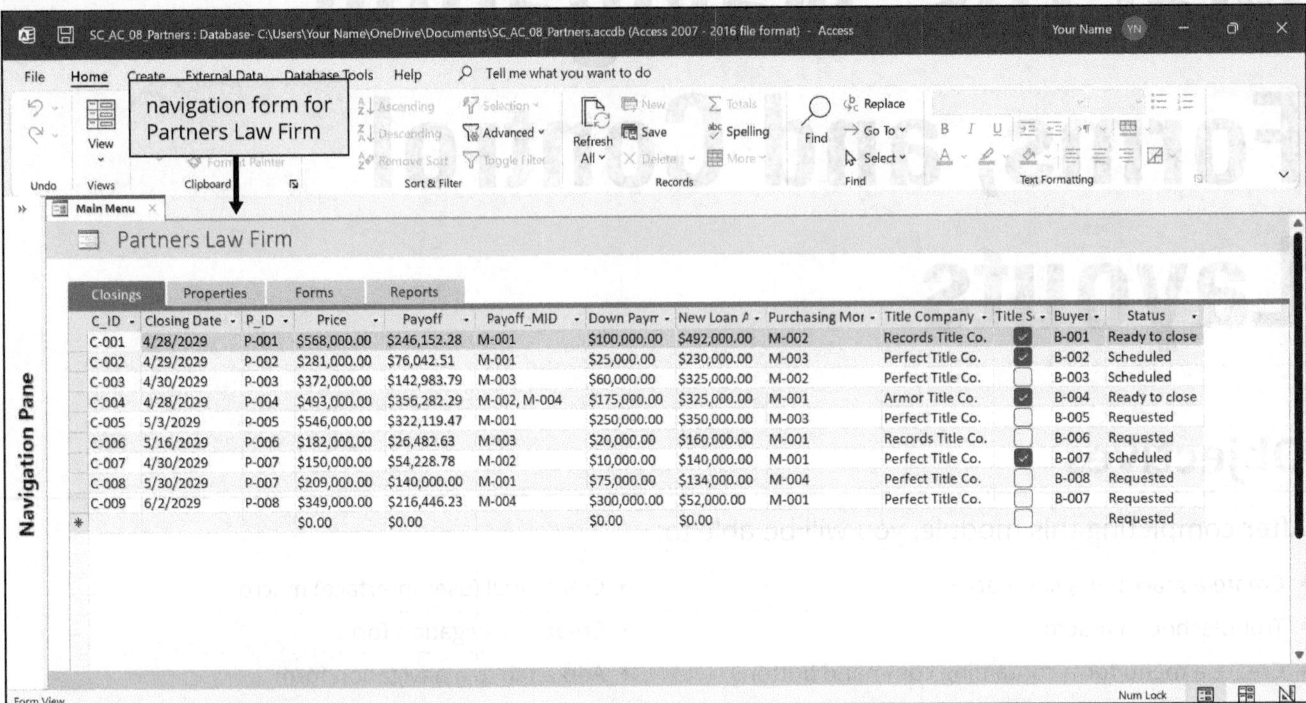

Figure 8–1a Navigation Form

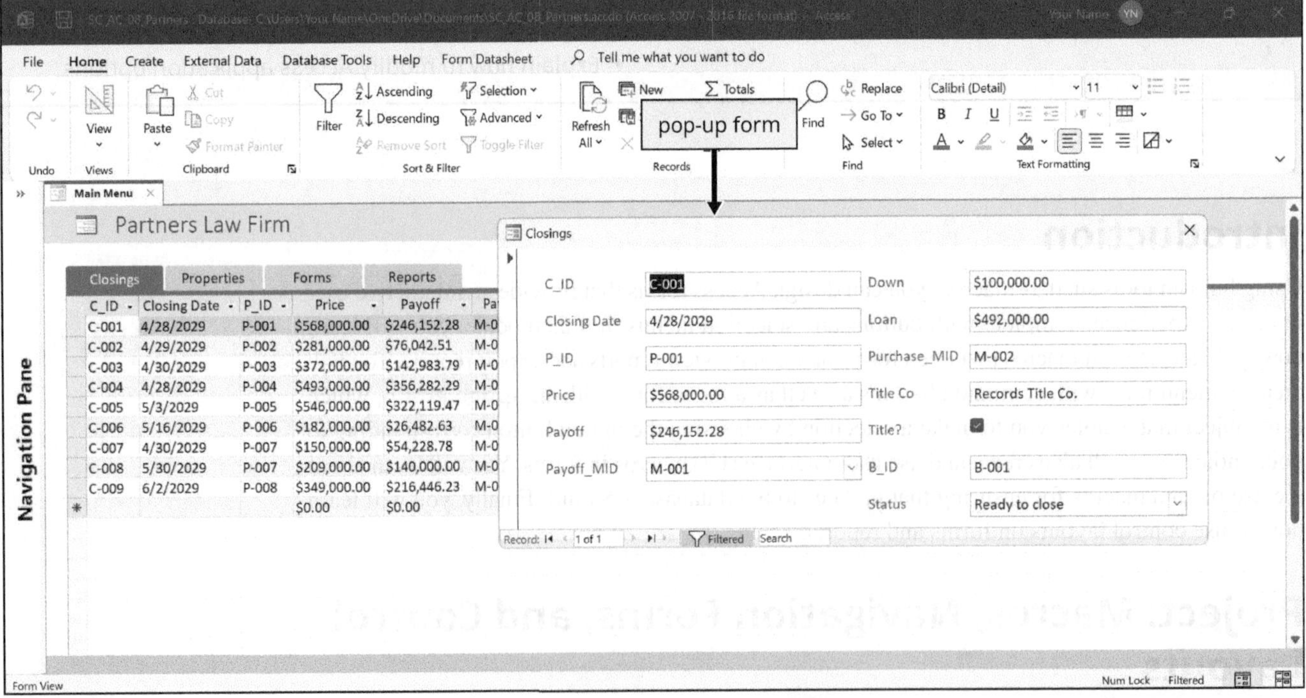

Figure 8–1b Pop-up Form Displaying Closing Data

Clicking the Properties tab of the navigation form displays a single property's data. As with closings, clicking the property number on any record displays data for that property in a pop-up form.

Clicking the Forms tab in the Partners navigation form displays a button for each of the available forms (Figure 8–1c). You can open the desired form by clicking the appropriate button.

Clicking the Reports tab displays an option group for previewing and exporting actions (Figure 8–1d). You can preview or export any of the reports one at a time by clicking the corresponding option button.

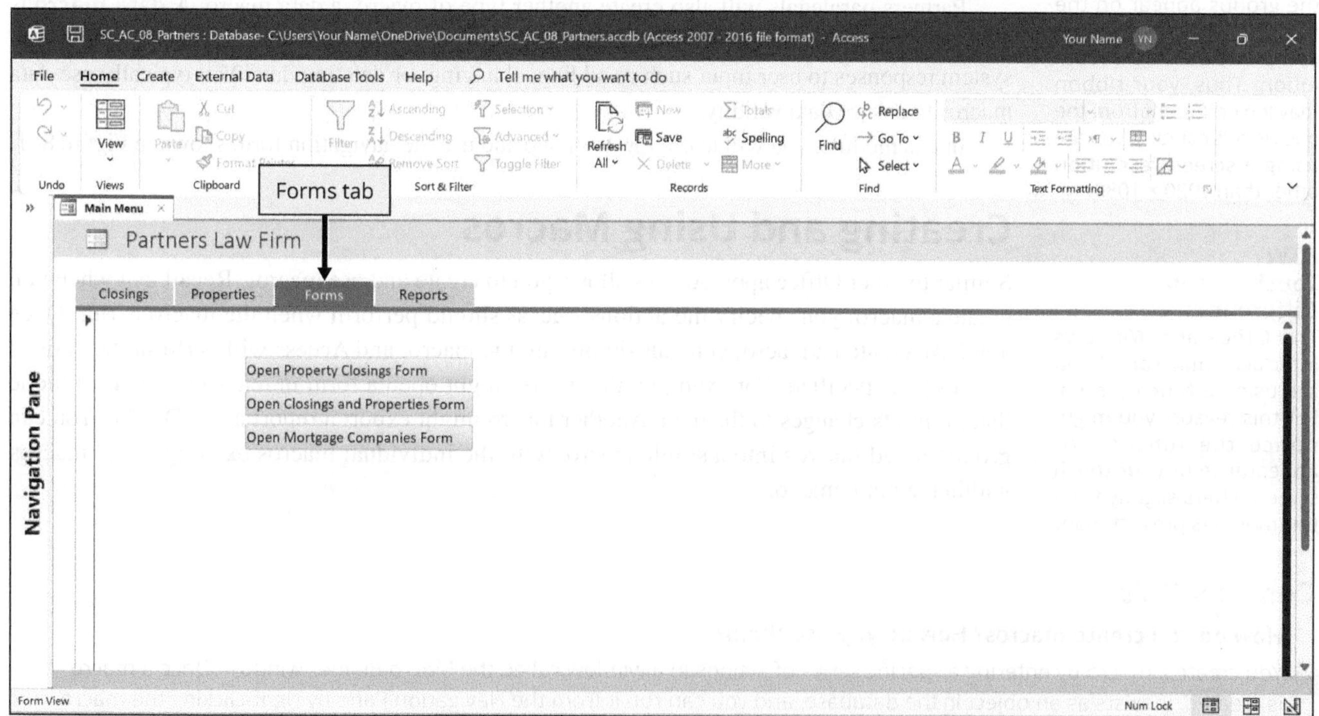

Figure 8–1c Buttons to Display Forms

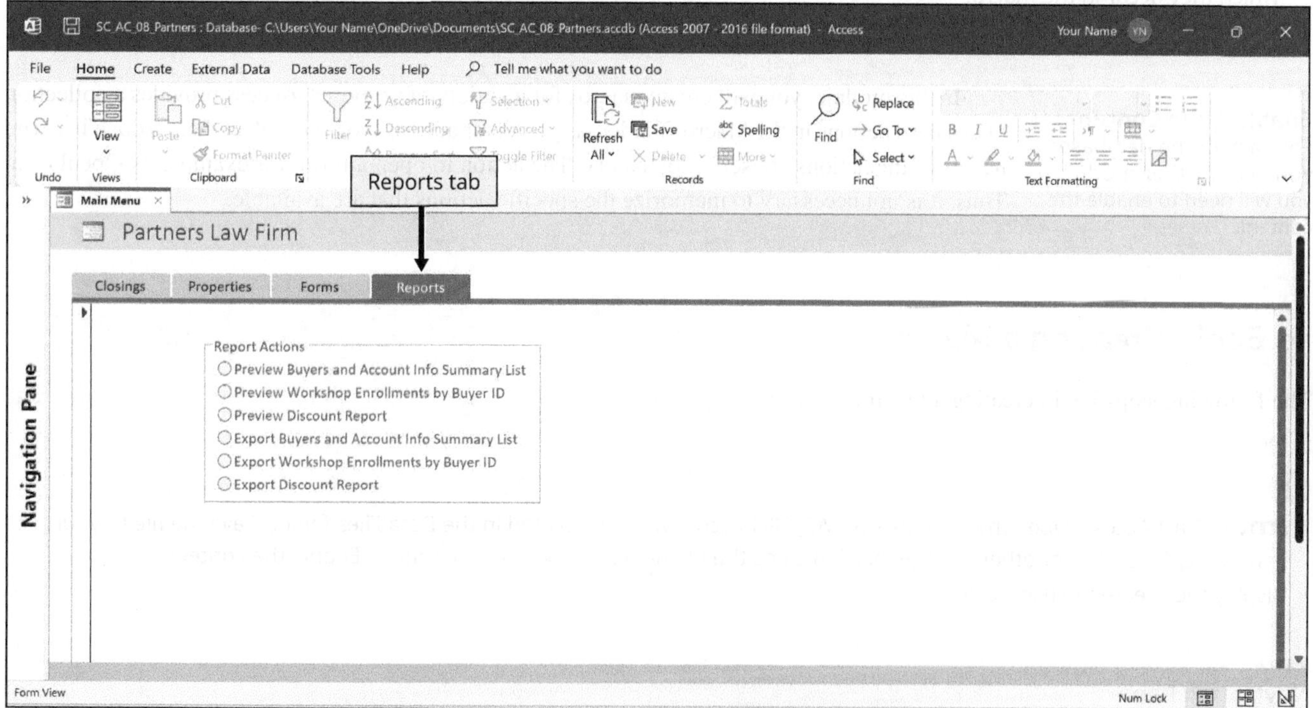

Figure 8–1d Option Group to Display or Export Reports

BTW
The Ribbon and Screen Resolution
Access may change how the groups and buttons within the groups appear on the ribbon, depending on the computer's screen resolution. Thus, your ribbon may look different from the ones in this course if you are using a screen resolution other than 1920 × 1080.

Before creating the navigation form, Partners paralegals will create macros, collections of actions designed to carry out specific tasks. Recall that to perform the actions in a macro, you run the macro. When you run a macro, Access will execute the various steps, called **actions**, in the order indicated by the macro. You run the navigation form macros by clicking certain buttons in the form.

Partners paralegals will also create another type of macro, a data macro. A **data macro** is a special type of macro that enables you to add coding logic to table events—that is, automated system responses to user input such as adding, changing, or deleting data. You typically use data macros to ensure data validity.

In this module, you will learn how to create and use the navigation form shown in Figure 8–1.

Creating and Using Macros

BTW
Touch Screen Differences
The Office and Windows interfaces may vary if you are using a touch screen. For this reason, you might notice the function or appearance of your touch screen differs slightly from this module's presentation.

Similar to other Office apps, Access allows you to create and use macros. Recall that when you create a macro, you specify the actions Access should perform when the macro is run. Once you have created a macro, you can simply run the macro, and Access will perform the various actions you specified. For example, the macro might open a form in read-only mode, a mode that prohibits changes to the data. Another macro might export a report as a PDF file. You can group related macros into a single macro, with the individual macros existing as submacros within the main macro.

Consider This

How do you create macros? How do you use them?

You create a macro by entering a specific series of actions in a window called the Macro Builder window. Once a macro is created, it exists as an object in the database, and you can run it from the Navigation Pane by right-clicking the macro and then clicking Run on the shortcut menu. Macros can also be associated with buttons on forms. When you click the corresponding button on the form, Access will run the macro and complete the corresponding action. Whether a macro is run from the Navigation Pane or from a form, the effect is the same: Access will execute the actions in the order in which they occur in the macro.

BTW
Enabling the Content
For each of the databases you use in this module, you will need to enable the content.

In this module, you will create macros for a variety of purposes. Access provides a collection of standard actions in the Macro Builder; as you enter actions, you will select them from a list. The names of the actions are self-explanatory. The action to open a form, for example, is OpenForm. Thus, it is not necessary to memorize the specific actions that are available.

To Begin Creating a Macro

The following steps begin creating a macro. **Why?** Once you have created the macro, you will be able to add the appropriate actions.

- **sam** Start Access. Open the database, SC_AC_08-1.accdb, which is located in the Data Files folder. Save the file to your hard drive, OneDrive, or other storage location using the file name, **SC_AC_08_Partners**. Enable the content.
- Display the Create tab (Figure 8–2).

BTW
Navigation Pane
As you work, you often need to open the Navigation Pane to view and select objects such as tables, forms, and reports. You may want to close the pane to make more room on the screen or to ensure your screen matches the figures in this course. Open the Navigation Pane as necessary to open an object when instructed, and then close or leave the pane open to suit your preferences.

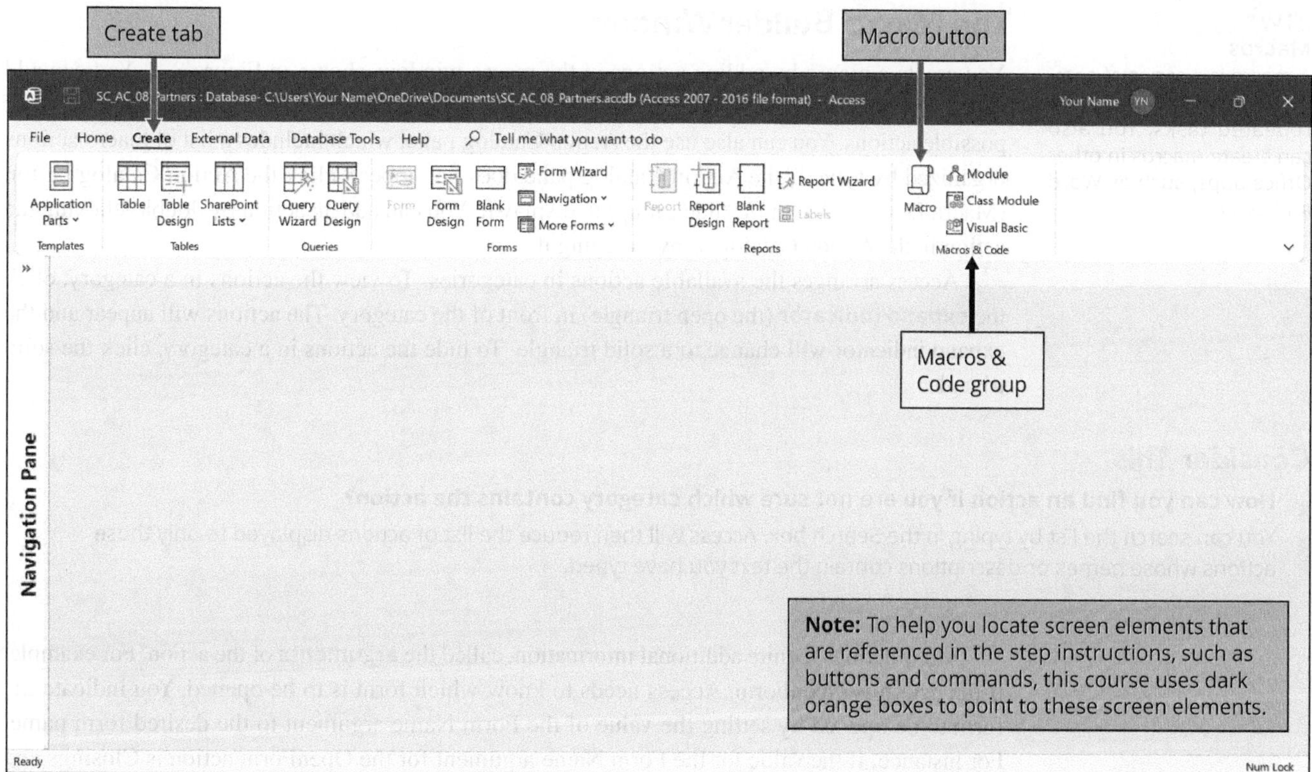

Figure 8–2

2

- Click the Macro button (Create tab | Macros & Code group) to create a new macro.
- If necessary, click the Action Catalog button (Macro Design tab | Show/Hide group) to display the Action Catalog pane (Figure 8–3).

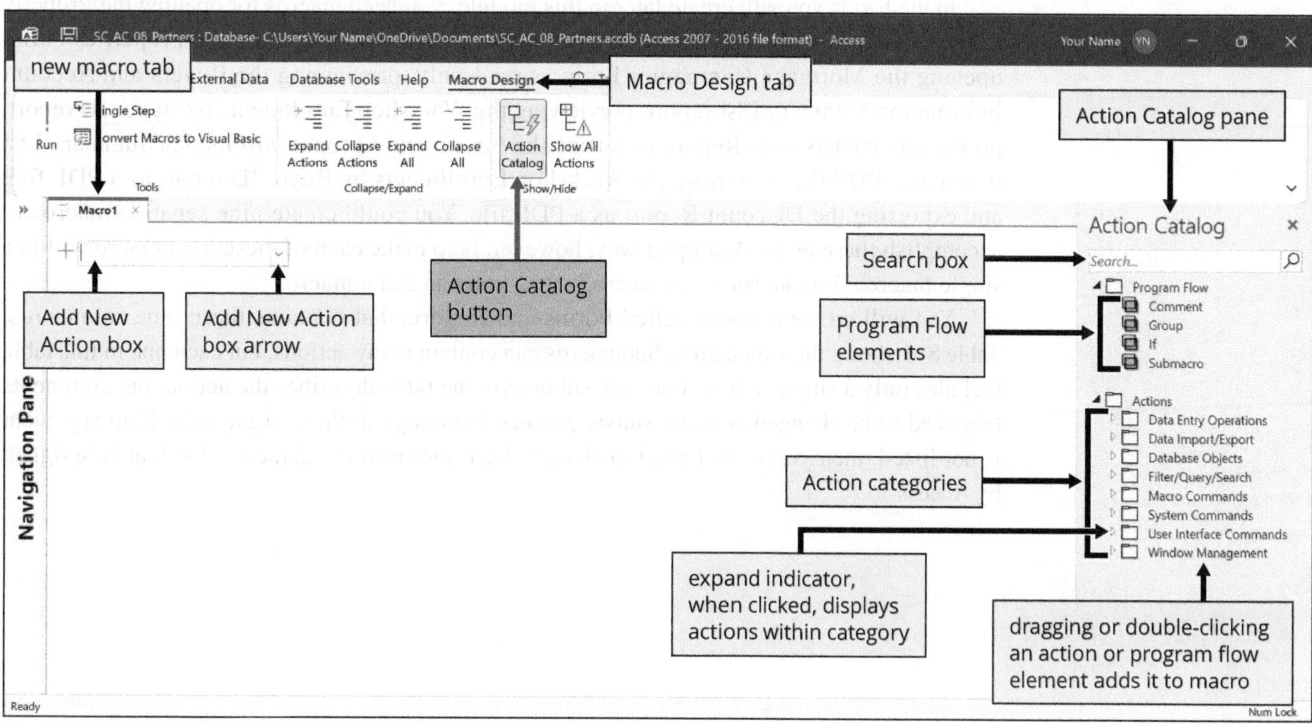

Figure 8–3

BTW
Macros
A macro is a series of commands used to automate repeated tasks. You also can create macros in other Office apps, such as Word and Excel.

The Macro Builder Window

You create a macro by adding actions in the macro window, shown in Figure 8–3. You can add actions by clicking the Add New Action box arrow and selecting the desired action from the list of possible actions. You can also use the Action Catalog pane, which includes a list of macro actions organized by type. If the Action Catalog pane does not appear, click the Action Catalog button (Macro Design tab | Show/Hide group) to display it. You can add an action by double-clicking the action in the Action Catalog or by dragging it.

Access arranges the available actions in categories. To view the actions in a category, click the **expand indicator** (the open triangle) in front of the category. The actions will appear and the expand indicator will change to a solid triangle. To hide the actions in a category, click the solid triangle.

Consider This

How can you find an action if you are not sure which category contains the action?

You can search the list by typing in the Search box. Access will then reduce the list of actions displayed to only those actions whose names or descriptions contain the text you have typed.

Many actions require additional information, called the **arguments** of the action. For example, if the action is OpenForm, Access needs to know which form is to be opened. You indicate the form to be opened by setting the value of the Form Name argument to the desired form name. For instance, if the value for the Form Name argument for the OpenForm action is Closings and Properties Form, then Access will open the Closings and Properties form when it executes this action.

Actions can have more than one argument. For example, in addition to the Form Name argument, the OpenForm action also has a Data Mode argument. If the value of the Data Mode argument is Read Only, then the form will be opened in read-only mode, which indicates users will be able to read, or view, data but not change it. When you select an action, the arguments will appear along with the action, and you can make any necessary changes to them.

In the forms you will create later in this module, you need macros for opening the Property Closings Form as read-only (to prevent updates), opening the Closings and Properties Form, opening the Mortgage Companies Form as read-only, previewing the Buyers and Account Information Summary List report, previewing the Workshop Enrollments by Buyer ID report, previewing the Discount Report, exporting the Buyers and Account Information Summary List report as a PDF file, exporting the Workshop Enrollments by Buyer ID report as a PDF file, and exporting the Discount Report as a PDF file. You could create nine separate macros to accomplish these tasks. A simpler way, however, is to make each of these a submacro within a single macro. You can run a submacro just as you can run a macro.

You will create a macro called Forms and Reports that contains these nine submacros. Table 8–1 shows the submacros. Submacros can contain many actions, but each one in this table includes only a single action. For each submacro, the table describes the action, the arguments that need to be changed, and the values you need to assign to those arguments. If an argument is not listed, then you do not need to change the value from the default value that is assigned by Access.

Table 8–1 Forms and Reports Macro

Submacro	Action	Arguments to Be Changed
Open Property Closings Form		
	OpenForm	Form Name: Property Closings Form Data Mode: Read Only
Open Closings and Properties Form		
	OpenForm	Form Name: Closings and Properties Form
Open Mortgage Companies Form		
	OpenForm	Form Name: Mortgage Companies Form Data Mode: Read Only
Preview Buyers and Account Information Summary List		
	OpenReport	Report Name: Buyers and Account Information Summary List View: Print Preview
Preview Workshop Enrollments by Buyer ID		
	OpenReport	Report Name: Workshop Enrollments by Buyer ID View: Print Preview
Preview Discount Report		
	OpenReport	Report Name: Discount Report View: Print Preview
Export Buyers and Account Information Summary List		
	ExportWithFormatting	Object Type: Report Object Name: Buyers and Account Information Summary List Output Format: PDF Format (*.pdf)
Export Workshop Enrollments by Buyer ID		
	ExportWithFormatting	Object Type: Report Object Name: Workshop Enrollments by Buyer ID Output Format: PDF Format (*.pdf)
Export Discount Report		
	ExportWithFormatting	Object Type: Report Object Name: Discount Report Output Format: PDF Format (*.pdf)

To Add an Action to a Macro

To continue creating the Forms and Reports macro, enter the actions on the Macro tab. In these steps, you will enter actions by double-clicking the action in the Action Catalog. **Why?** The actions in the Action Catalog are organized by function, making it easier to locate the action you want. Access will add the action to the Add New Action box. If more than one Add New Action box is displayed, you need to ensure the one where you want to add the action is selected before you double-click.

The following steps add the first action. They also make the necessary changes to any arguments. Finally, the steps save the macro.

- Double-click the Submacro element from the Program Flow section of the Action Catalog to add a submacro, and then type **Open Property Closings Form** as the name of the submacro (Figure 8–4).

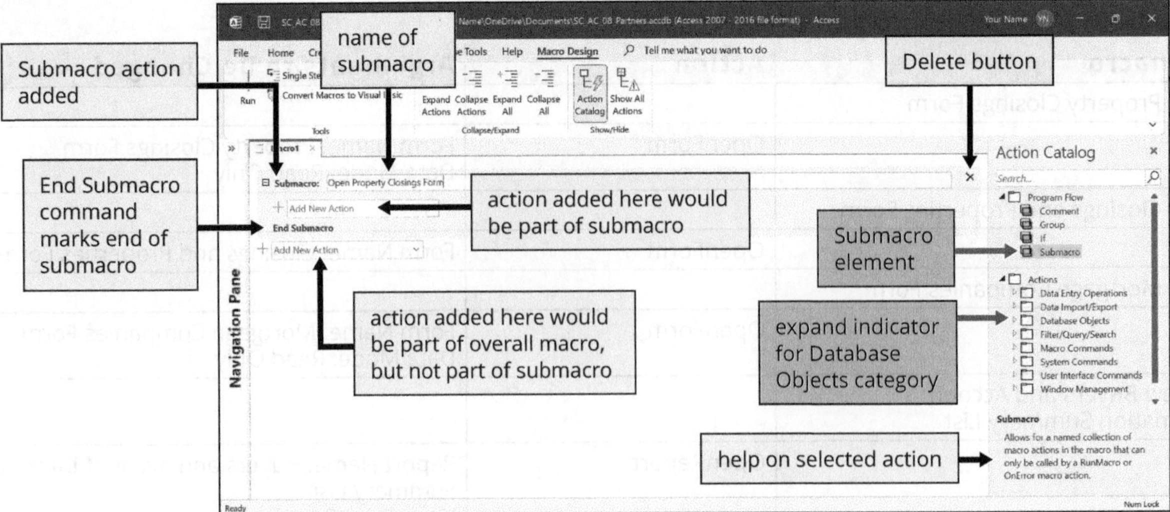

Figure 8–4

Q&A How can I tell the purpose of the various actions in the Action Catalog?
If necessary, expand the category containing the action so the action appears. Point to the action. An expanded ScreenTip will appear, giving you a description of the action.

- Click the expand indicator for the Database Objects category of actions to display the actions within the category.
- Double-click the OpenForm action to add it to the submacro (Figure 8–5).

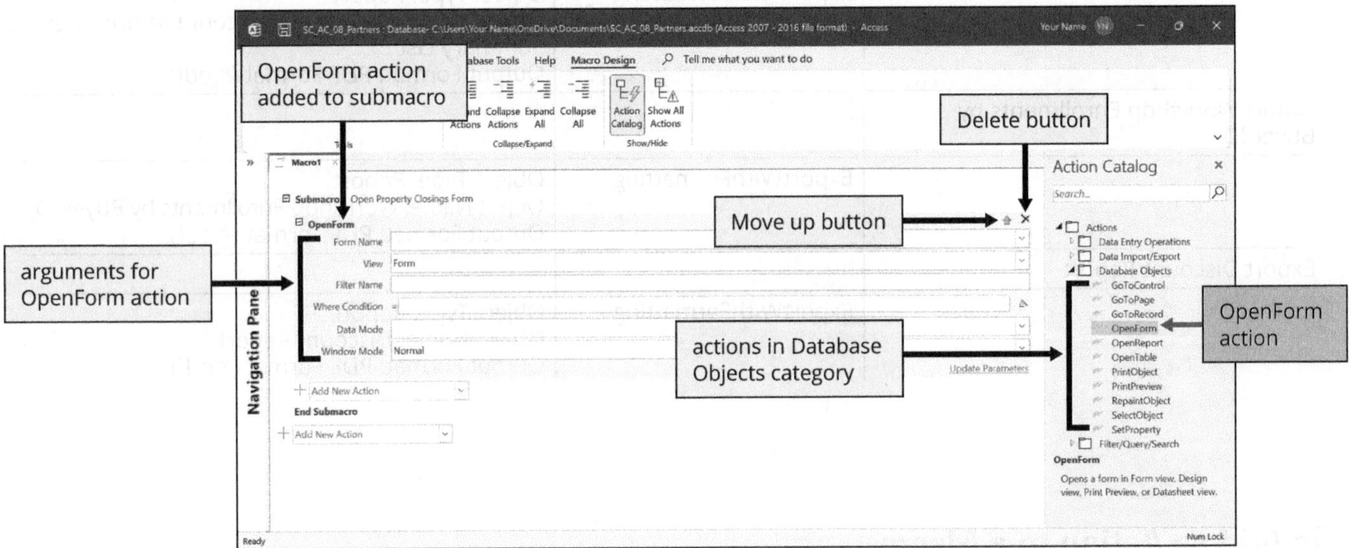

Figure 8–5

Q&A What should I do if I add an action in the wrong position? What should I do if I add the wrong action?
If you add an action in the wrong position, use the Move up or Move down buttons to move it to the correct position. If you add the wrong action, click the Delete button to delete the action, and then add the correct action.

BTW
Program Flow Actions
Actions in the Program Flow category can change the order in which macro actions are executed or help structure a macro.

BTW
Touch and Pointers
Remember that if you are using your finger on a touch screen, the pointer or ScreenTips will not appear.

- Click the drop-down arrow for the Form Name argument, and then select Property Closings Form as the name of the form to be opened.
- Click the drop-down arrow for the Data Mode argument, and then select Read Only to specify that users cannot change the data in the form (Figure 8–6).

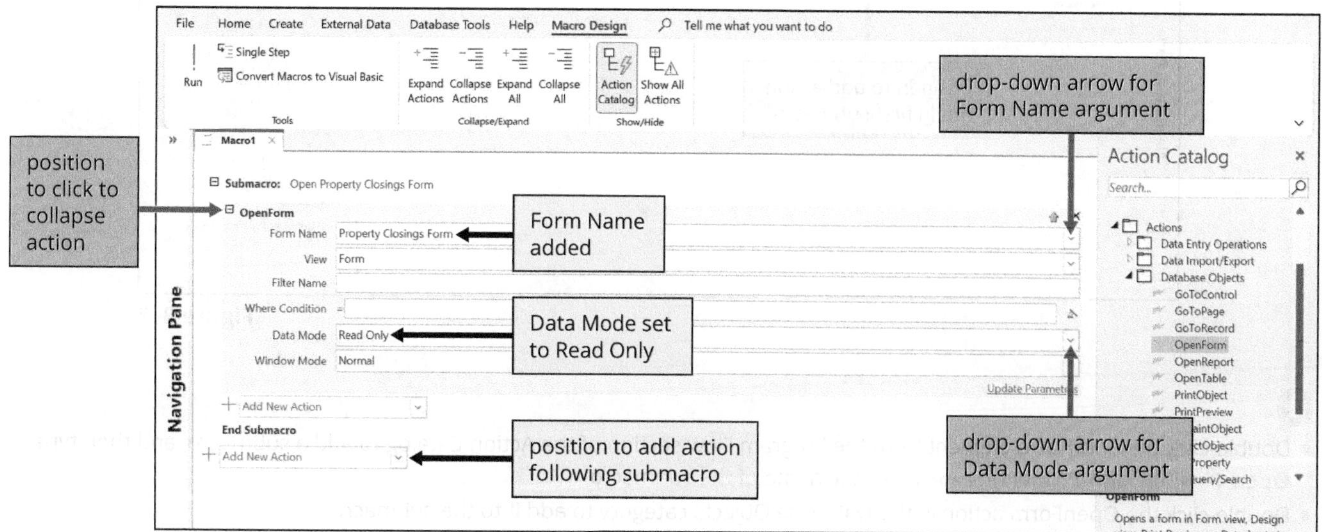

Figure 8–6

Q&A What is the effect of each of the other Data Mode options?
The Add option allows viewing records and adding new records, but not updating records. The Edit option allows viewing records, adding new records, and updating existing records.

- Click the Save button on the Quick Access Toolbar, type **Forms and Reports** as the name of the macro, and then click OK to save the macro.

To Add More Actions to a Macro

To complete the macro, you need to add the additional actions shown in Table 8–1. You add the additional actions just as you added the first action. Initially, Access displays all the actions you have added with their arguments clearly visible. After you have added several actions, you might want to collapse some or all of the actions. **Why?** Collapsing actions makes it easier to get an overall view of your macro. You can always expand any action later to view details concerning the arguments. The following steps add additional actions to a macro, collapsing existing actions when necessary to provide a better view of the overall macro structure.

- Click the minus sign (−) in front of the OpenForm action to collapse the action (Figure 8–7).

Q&A Could I also use the buttons on the ribbon?
Yes, you can use the buttons in the Collapse/Expand group on the Macro Design tab. Click the Expand Actions button to expand the selected action, or click the Collapse Actions button to collapse the selected action. You can expand all actions at once by clicking the Expand All button, or you can collapse all actions at once by clicking the Collapse All button.

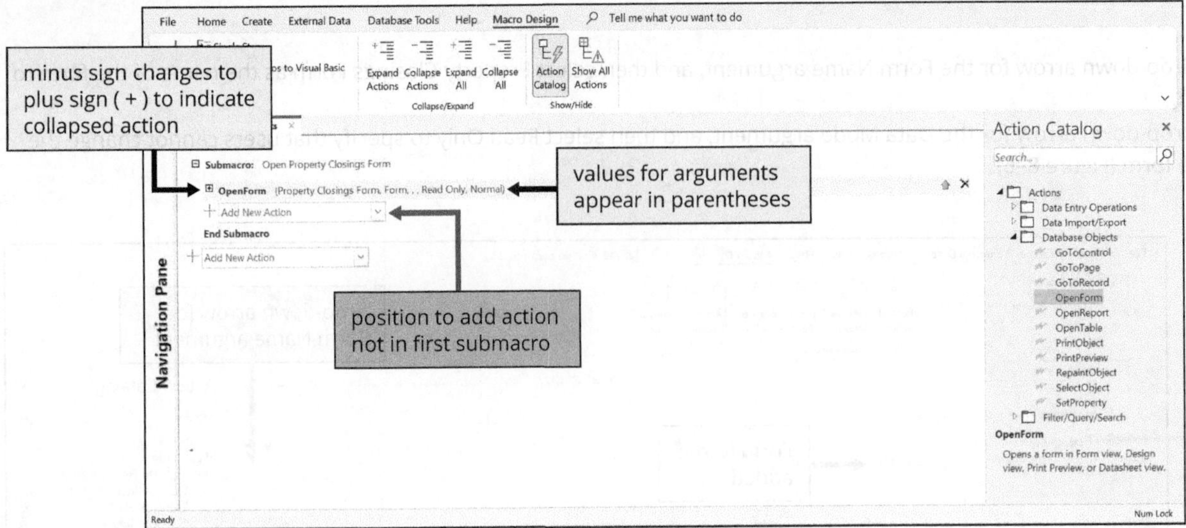

Figure 8–7

2

- Double-click the Submacro element from the Program Flow section of the Action Catalog to add a submacro, and then type **Open Closings and Properties Form** as the name of the submacro.
- Double-click the OpenForm action in the Database Objects category to add it to the submacro.
- Click the drop-down arrow for the Form Name argument, and then select Closings and Properties Form.
- Double-click the Submacro element again to create a third submacro, and then type **Open Mortgage Companies Form** as the name of the new submacro.
- Add the OpenForm action to the submacro.
- Select Mortgage Companies Form as the value for the Form Name argument.
- Set the Data Mode to Read Only and, if necessary, set Window Mode to Normal (Figure 8–8).

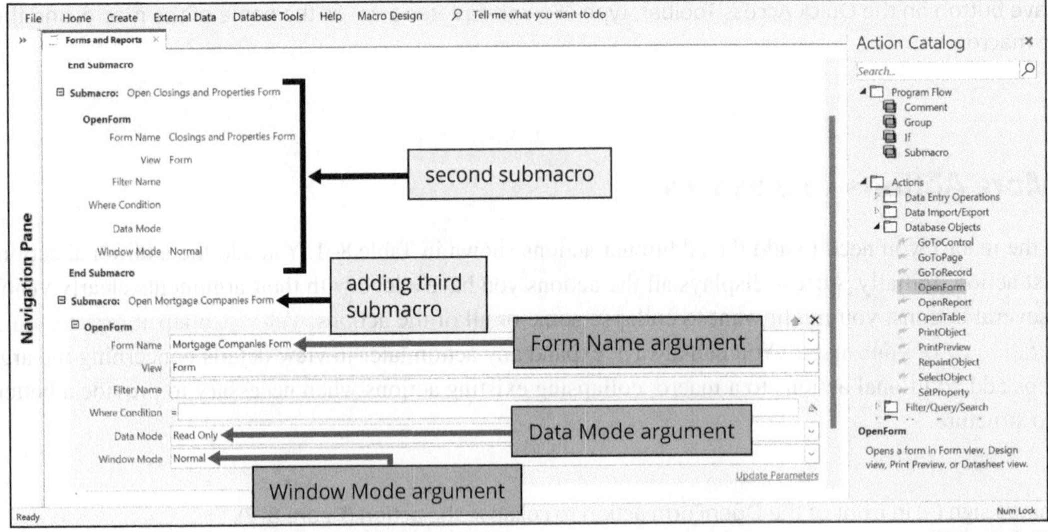

Figure 8–8

Q&A Do I have to change the values of any of the other arguments?

No. The default values that Access sets are appropriate.

3

- For each of the three new submacros, click the minus sign in front of it to collapse the submacro.
- Add a submacro named **Preview Buyers and Account Information Summary List**.

- Add the OpenReport action, which is located in the Database Objects category, to the submacro.
- Select Buyers and Account Information Summary List as the report name.
- Select Print Preview as the view (Figure 8–9).

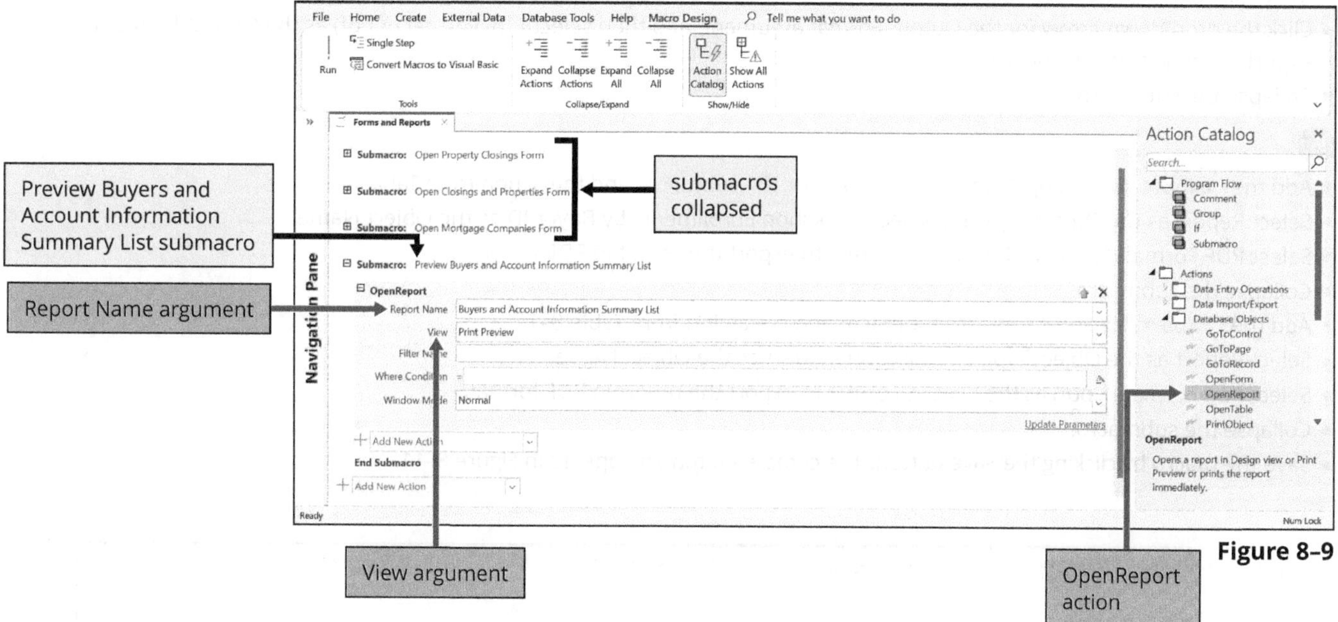

Figure 8–9

4

- Collapse the Preview Buyers and Account Information Summary List submacro.
- Add the **Preview Workshop Enrollments by Buyer ID** submacro. Include the action described in Table 8–1. The report name is Workshop Enrollments by Buyer ID and the view is Print Preview. Collapse the submacro.
- Add the **Preview Discount Report** submacro. Include the action described in Table 8–1. The report name is Discount Report and the view is Print Preview. Collapse the submacro.
- Click the triangle to the left of Database Objects in the Action Catalog to collapse the Database Objects category, and then click the expand indicator for the Data Import/Export category.
- Add a submacro called **Export Buyers and Account Information Summary List**.
- Add the ExportWithFormatting action, which will export and maintain any special formatting in the process.
- Click the drop-down arrow for the Object Type argument to display a list of possible object types (Figure 8–10).

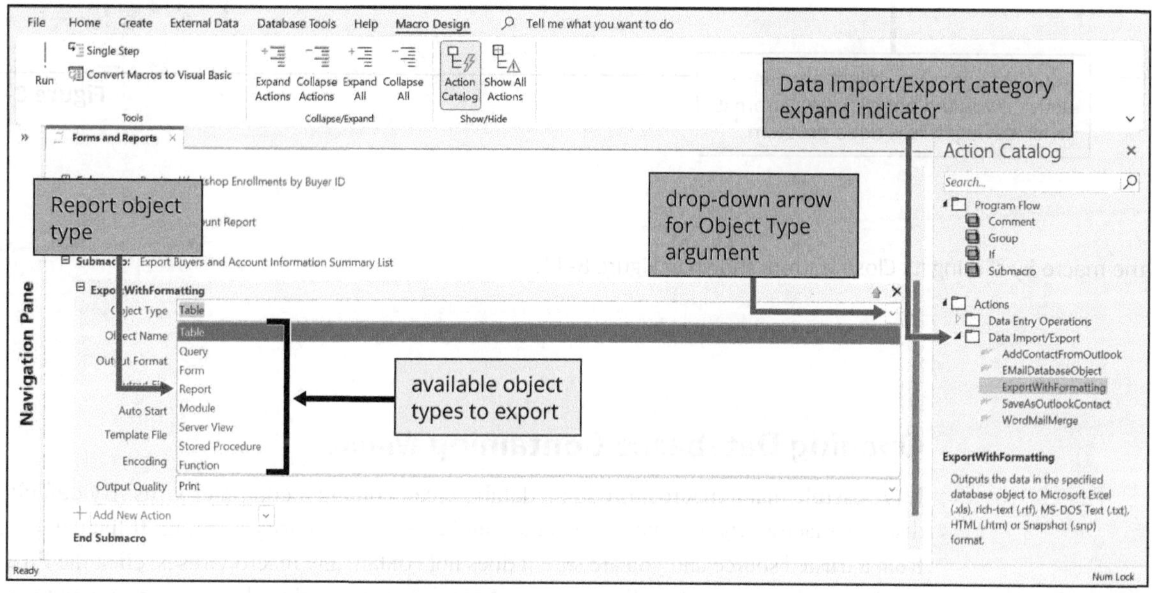

Figure 8–10

- Click Report in the list to indicate Access is to export a report.
- Click the drop-down arrow for the Object Name argument, and then select Buyers and Account Information Summary List as the object name.
- Click the drop-down arrow for the Output Format argument, and then select PDF Format (*.pdf) as the Output Format to export the report in PDF format.
- Collapse the submacro.

- Add the **Export Workshop Enrollments by Buyer ID** submacro and the action from Table 8–1.
- Select Report as the Object Type and select Workshop Enrollments by Buyer ID as the Object Name.
- Select PDF Format (*.pdf) as the Output Format to export the report in PDF format.
- Collapse the submacro.
- Add the **Export Discount Report** submacro and the action from Table 8–1.
- Select Report as the Object Type and Discount Report as the Object Name.
- Select PDF Format (*.pdf) as the Output Format to export the report in PDF format.
- Collapse the submacro.
- Save the macro by clicking the Save button. The completed macro appears in Figure 8–11.

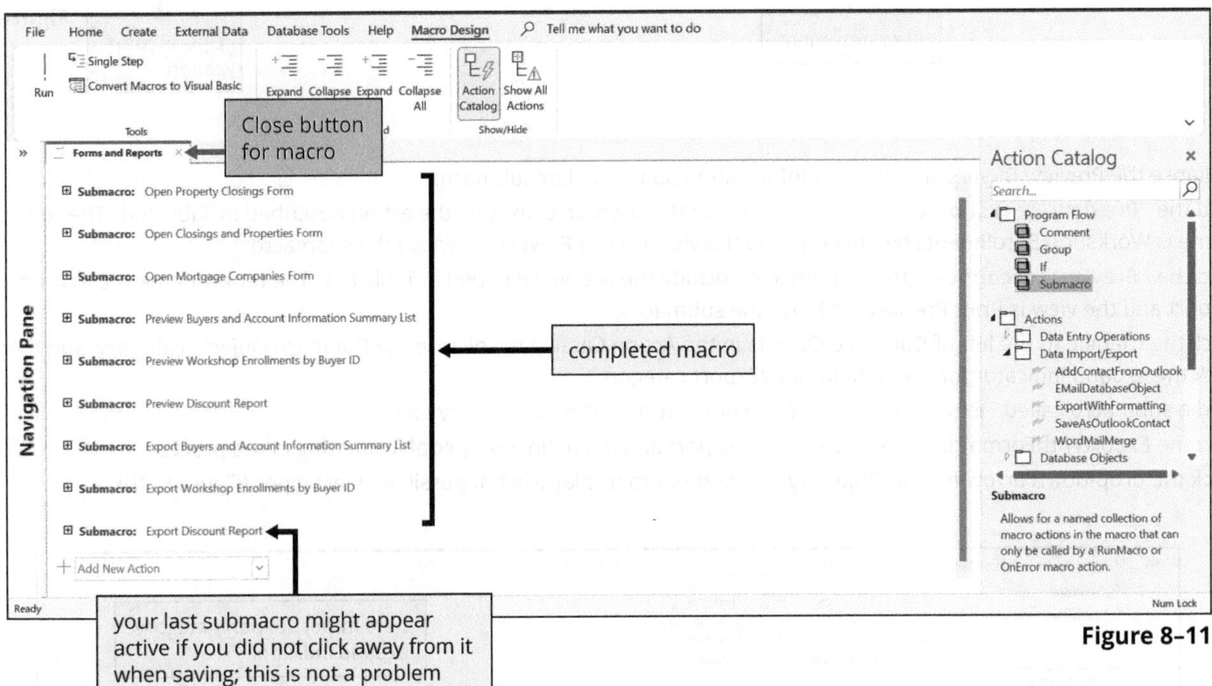

Figure 8–11

- Close the macro by clicking its Close button, shown in Figure 8–11.

Opening Databases Containing Macros

It is possible that a macro stored in a database can contain a computer virus. By default, Access disables macros when it opens a database and displays a security warning. If the database comes from a trusted source and you are sure it does not contain any macro viruses, click the Enable Content button. You can make adjustments to Access security settings by clicking File on the ribbon to open Backstage view, and then clicking Options to display the Access Options dialog box, clicking Trust Center, clicking Trust Center Settings, and then clicking Macro Settings.

Errors in Macros

Macros can contain errors. The macro might open the wrong table or produce a wrong message. If you have problems with a macro, you can **single-step the macro**, that is, proceed through a macro one step at a time in Design view.

Figure 8–12 shows a macro open in Design view. This macro first has an action to open the Closings table in Datasheet view in Read Only mode. It then changes the view to Print Preview. Next, it opens the Closings table in Datasheet view, this time in Edit mode. Finally, it opens the Properties Query in Datasheet view in Edit mode. The macro in the figure is a common type of macro that opens several objects at once. To open all these objects, the user only runs the macro. Unfortunately, this macro contains an error. The name of the Closings table is written as "Closing" in the second OpenTable action.

BTW
Converting a Macro to VBA Code
If you want to use many of the resources provided by Windows or communicate with another Windows app, you will need to convert any macros to VBA (Visual Basic for Applications) code. To convert a macro to VBA code, open the macro in Design view and click the 'Convert Macros to Visual Basic' button (Macro Design tab | Tools group). When the Convert Macro dialog box appears, select the appropriate options, and then click Convert.

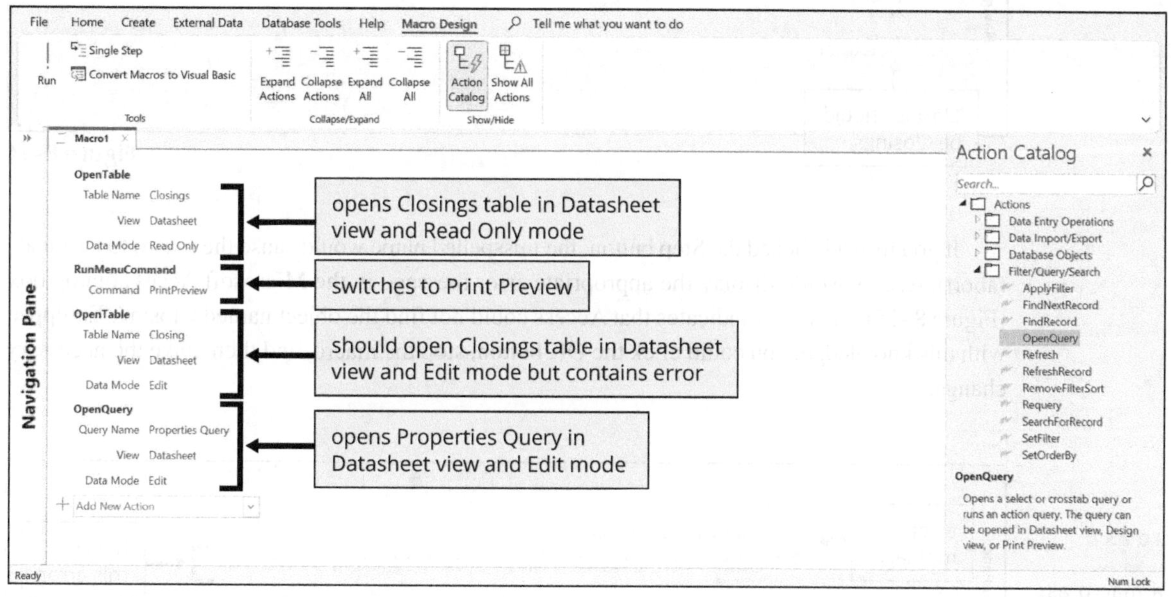

Figure 8–12

To run this macro in single-step mode, you would first save the macro and then click the Single Step button (Macro Design tab | Tools group). You would next click the Run button (Macro Design tab | Tools group) to run the macro. Because you clicked the Single Step button, Access would display the Macro Single Step dialog box (Figure 8–13). The dialog box shows the action

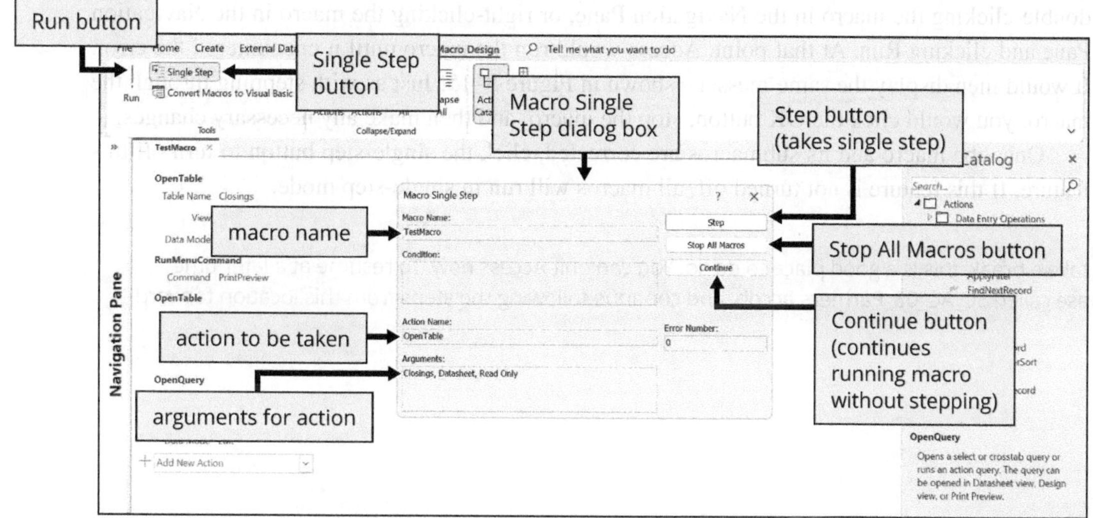

Figure 8–13

to be executed and the values of the various arguments. You can click the Step button to proceed to the next step.

With this macro, after you clicked the Step button twice, you would arrive at the screen shown in Figure 8–14. Access is about to execute the OpenTable command. The arguments are Closing, Datasheet, and Edit. At this point, you might spot the fact that "Closing" is misspelled. It should be "Closings" instead. If so, you could click the 'Stop All Macros' button and then correct the object name.

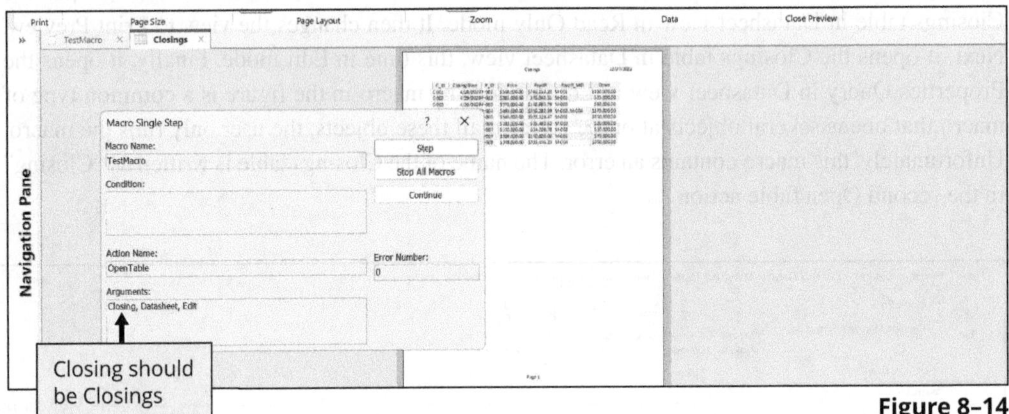

Figure 8–14

If you instead clicked the Step button, the misspelled name would cause the macro to terminate (abort). Access would display the appropriate error message in the Microsoft Access dialog box (Figure 8–15). This error indicates that Access could not find the object named Closing. Equipped with this knowledge, you could click the OK button, stop the macro, and then make the necessary change.

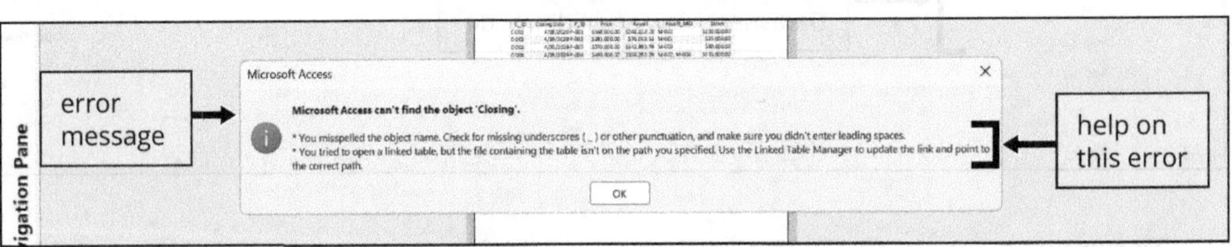

Figure 8–15

BTW

Saving a Macro as a VBA Module

You can save a macro as a VBA module using the Save Object As command in Backstage view. Open the macro in Design view, click File on the ribbon to open Backstage view, and then click Save As. When the Save As gallery appears, click 'Save Object As' in the File Types area, and then click the Save As button. When the Save As dialog box appears, click Module in the As text box, and then click the OK button.

You do not need to step through a macro to discover the error. You could simply run the macro, either by opening the macro and clicking the Run button (Macro Design tab | Tools group), double-clicking the macro in the Navigation Pane, or right-clicking the macro in the Navigation Pane and clicking Run. At that point, Access would run the macro until it encountered the error. It would then display the same message shown in Figure 8–15. Just as with stepping through the macro, you would click the OK button, stop the macro, and then make any necessary changes.

Once the macro and its submacros are corrected, click the single-step button to turn off this feature. If this feature is not turned off, all macros will run in single-step mode.

Break Point: If you wish to take a break, this is a good place to do so. You can quit Access now. To resume at a later time, start Access, open the database called SC_AC_08_Partners.accdb, and continue following the steps from this location forward.

Creating and Using a Navigation Form

Figure 8–1a showed a navigation form for Partners. A navigation form is a form that contains a **navigation control**, a control that can display a variety of forms and reports. Like the form in Figure 8–1, navigation controls contain tabs. Clicking a tab displays the corresponding form or report. The tabs can be arranged across the top and/or down the sides.

You can only include forms and reports on these tabs; you cannot include either tables or queries. The navigation form in Figure 8–1 appears to have a tab corresponding to the Closings table, but this is actually a datasheet form based on the Closings table, not the table itself. If you would find it desirable to display tables or queries on a navigation control tab, you can make it appear as though the navigation form contains these objects by creating a datasheet form based on the table or query.

Before creating the navigation form, you need to create some other forms. Partners Law Firm wants users to be able to click a tab in the navigation form and then choose from a list of forms or reports. Figure 8–16 shows a list of forms presented as buttons; these enable the user to simply click a button to open the desired form. Clicking the Open Property Closings Form button, for example, would display the Property Closings Form, as shown in Figure 8–17.

BTW
Navigation Forms
A navigation form often is used as a switchboard or main page for a database to reduce clutter and target the most commonly used database objects. A navigation form contains a navigation control and a subform control. After you create a navigation form, you can use the Navigation Where Clause property associated with a navigation control to automatically apply a filter.

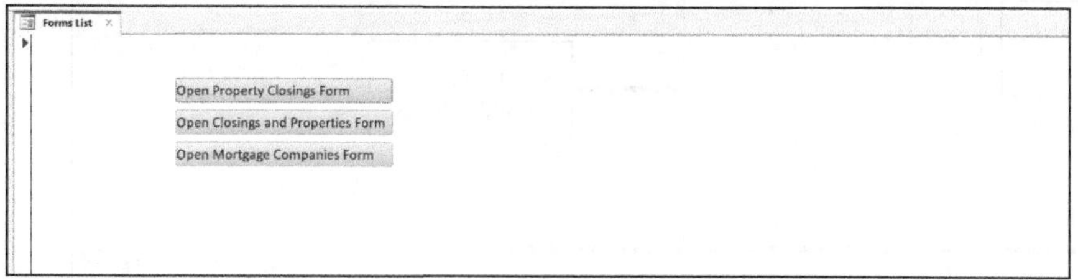

Figure 8–16

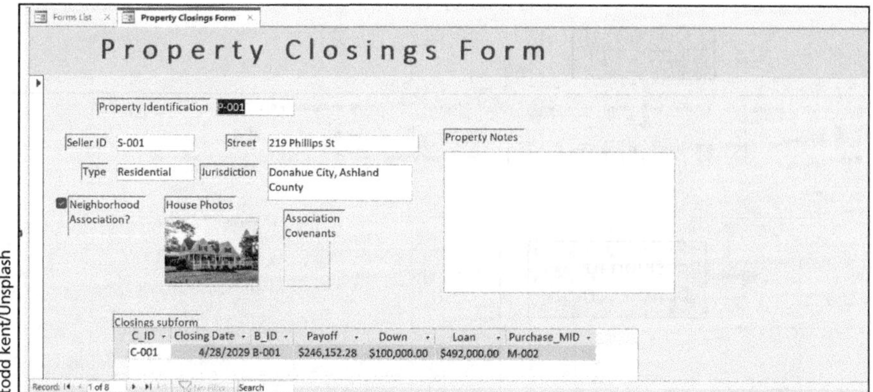

todd kent/Unsplash

Figure 8–17

To implement options like these, you create blank forms and add either command buttons or an option group. You then include the form you have created in the navigation form. When users click the corresponding tab, Access displays the form and users can then click the appropriate button.

To Create a Menu Form Containing Command Buttons

Why? A menu form in which you make a selection by clicking the appropriate command button provides a convenient way to select a desired option. You can create a menu form by adding command buttons to the form. The following steps use this technique to create a menu form with three buttons: Open Property Closings Form, Open Closings and Properties Form, and Open Mortgage Companies Form. The actions assigned to each button will run a macro that causes the desired action to occur. For example, the action for the Open Property Closings Form button will run the Open Property Closings Form submacro, which in turn will open the Property Closings Form.

The following steps create a form in Design view and then add the necessary buttons.

- Display the Create tab.
- Click the Form Design button (Create tab | Forms group) to create a blank form in Design view.
- If the Field List pane opens, click the 'Add Existing Fields' button (Form Design tab | Tools group) to close the Field List pane.
- If the Property Sheet pane opens, click the Property Sheet button (Form Design tab | Tools group) to close the Property Sheet pane.
- Confirm the 'Use Control Wizards' option is selected by clicking the More button located in the Controls group (Figure 8–18).

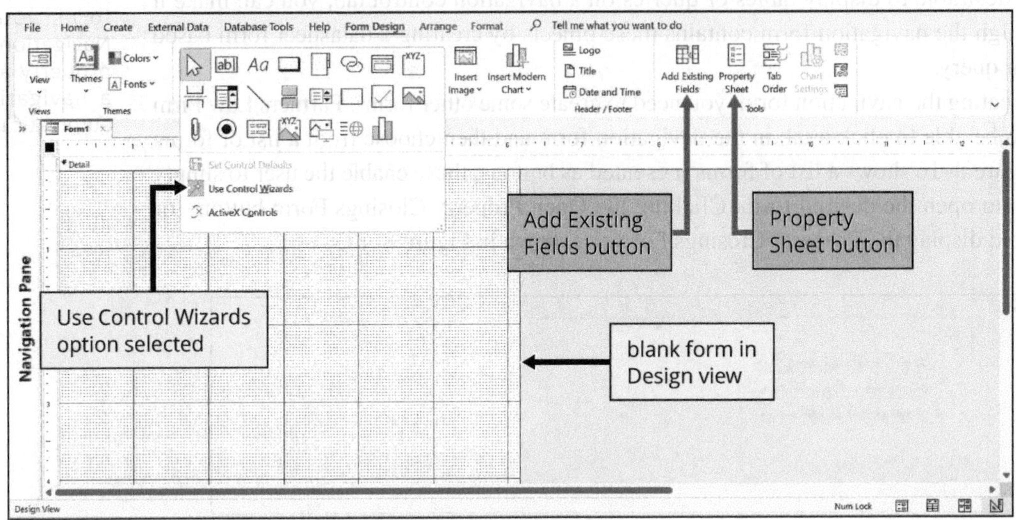

Figure 8–18

- Click the Button tool (Form Design tab | Controls group) and move the pointer to the approximate position shown in Figure 8–19.

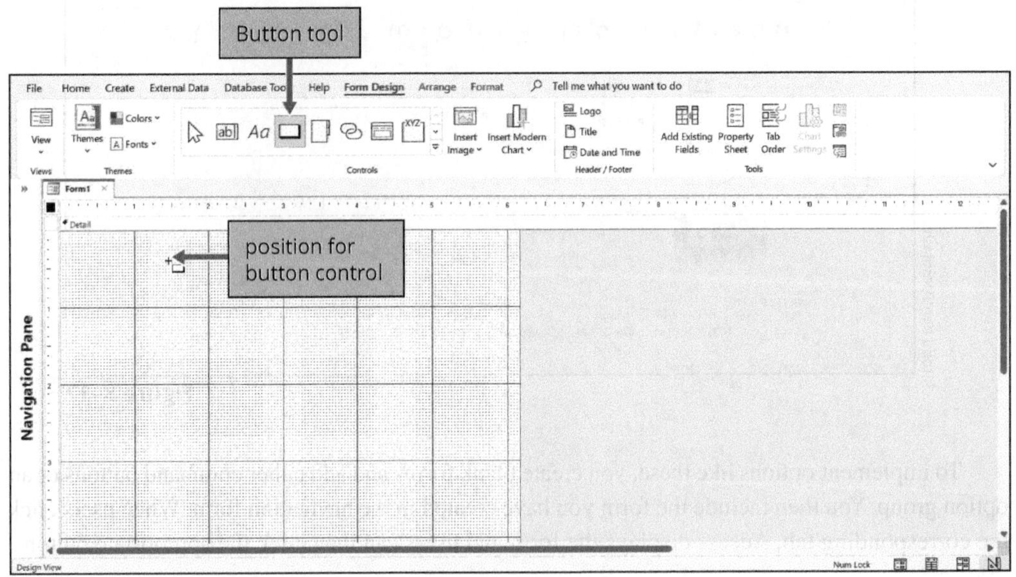

Figure 8–19

- Click the position shown in Figure 8–19 to display the Command Button Wizard dialog box.
- Click Miscellaneous in the Categories box, and then click Run Macro in the Actions box (Figure 8–20).

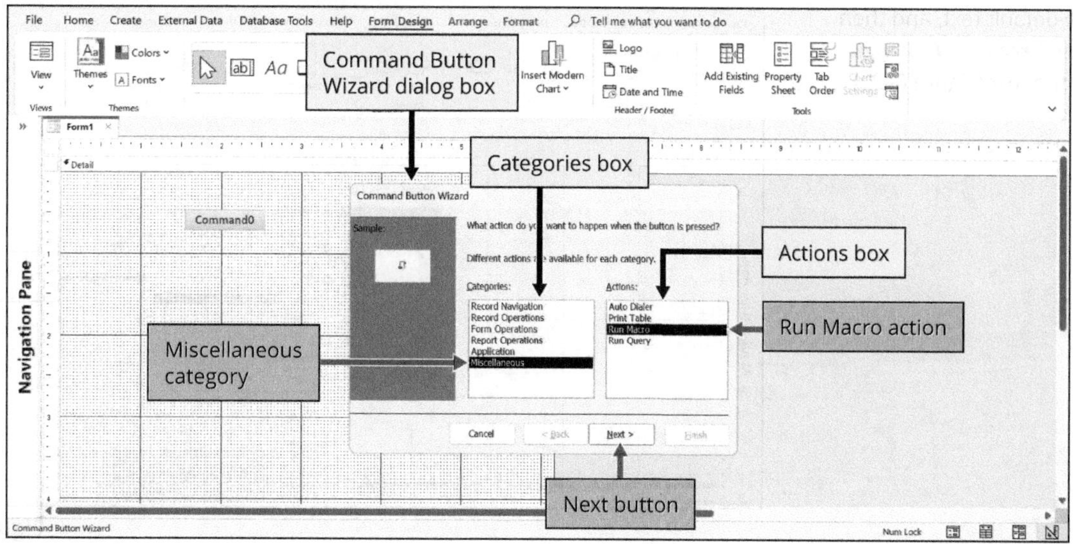

Figure 8–20

4

- Click Next to display the next Command Button Wizard screen.
- Click Forms and Reports. Open Property Closings Form to select the macro to be run (Figure 8–21).

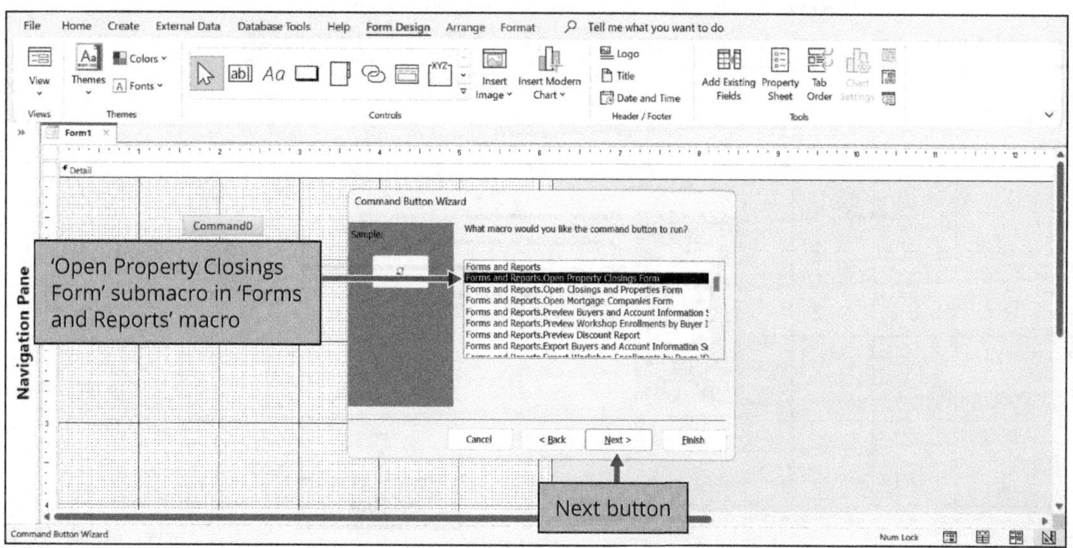

Figure 8–21

Q&A What does this notation mean?

The portion before the period is the macro and the portion after the period is the submacro. Thus, this notation refers to the Open Property Closings Form submacro within the Forms and Reports macro.

- Click Next to display the next Command Button Wizard screen.
- Click the Text option button to indicate the button should display explanatory text rather than an image.

Q&A What is the purpose of these option buttons?

Choose the first option button to place text on the button. You can then specify the text to be included or accept the default choice. Choose the second option button to place a picture on the button. You can then select a picture.

- Delete the default text, and then type **Open Property Closings Form** as the text (Figure 8–22).

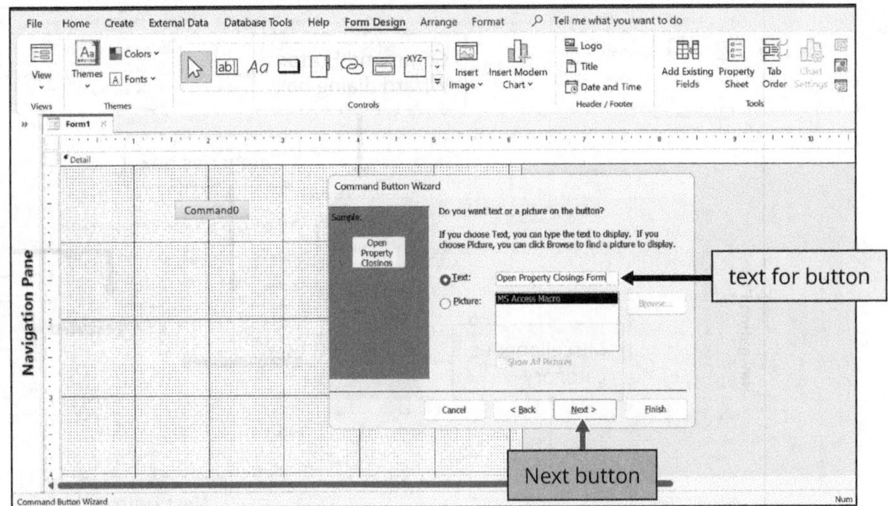

Figure 8–22

- Click Next.
- Type **Open_Property_Closings_Form** as the name of the button (Figure 8–23), and then click the Finish button to complete the button control's configuration.

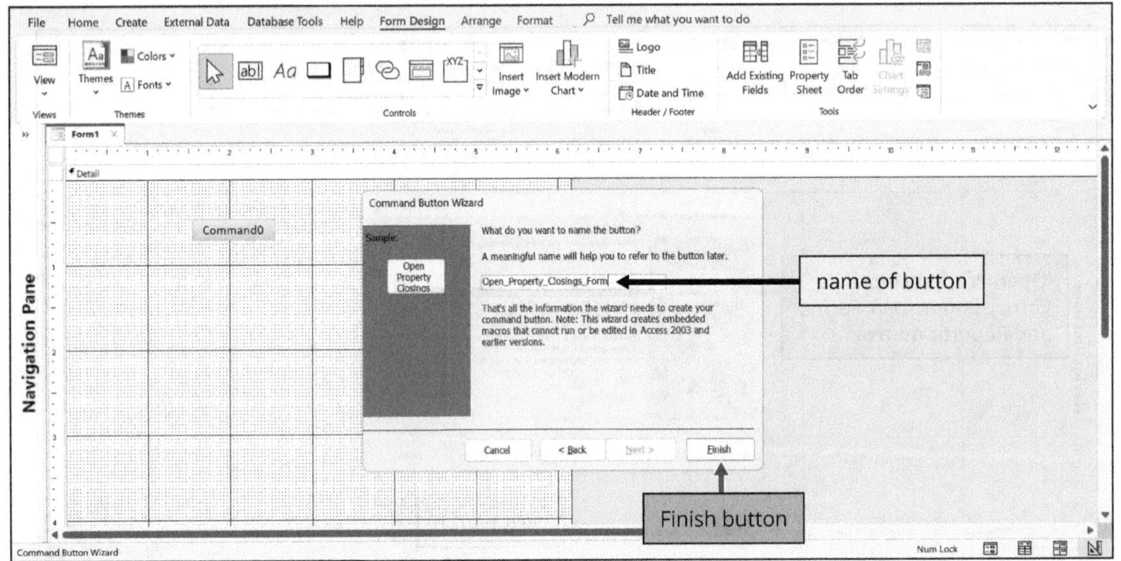

Figure 8–23

Q&A Why do I need to include the underscores in the name of the button?
If you are working with macros or VBA, you cannot have spaces in names. One way to avoid spaces and still make readable names is to include an underscore (_) where you would normally use a space. Thus, Open Property Closings Form becomes Open_Property_Closings_Form.

- Use the techniques in Steps 2 through 6 to place the Open Closings and Properties Form button below the Open Property Closings Form button. The only differences are that the macro to be run is the Open Closings and Properties Form submacro, the button text is **Open Closings and Properties Form**, and the name of the button is **Open_Closings_and_Properties_Form**.
- Use the techniques in Steps 2 through 6 to place the Open Mortgage Companies Form button below the Open Closings and Properties Form button. The only differences are that the macro to be run is the Open Mortgage Companies Form submacro, the text is **Open Mortgage Companies Form**, and the name of the button is **Open_Mortgage_Companies_Form**.

- Adjust the positions, sizing, and spacing of the buttons to approximately match those in Figure 8–24, using the tools on the Arrange tab. For equal spacing, select all the buttons, click the Size/Space button, and select the Equal Vertical option. To make the buttons the same width, select all the buttons, click the Size/Space button, and select the To Widest option.

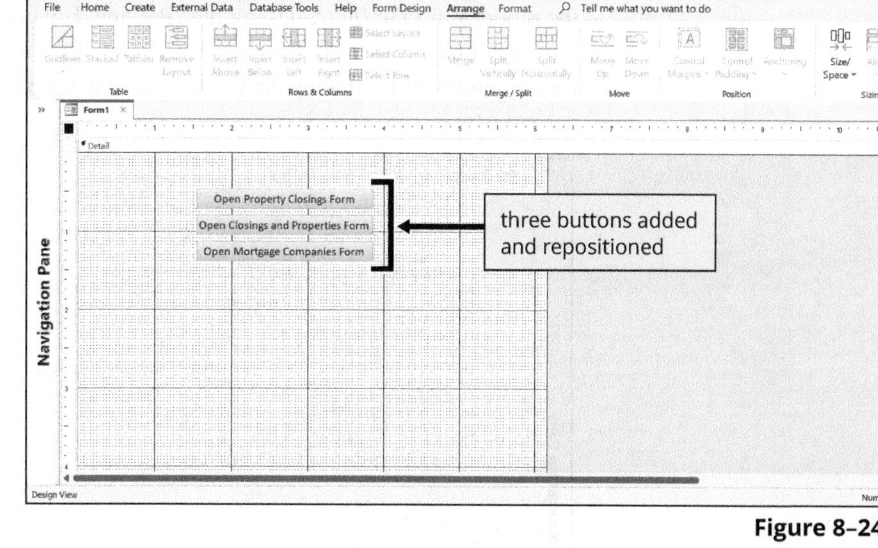

Figure 8–24

- Display the Form Design tab, click the Property Sheet button, and then, if necessary, click the Format tab.
- With all three buttons selected, click the Alignment property box (Property Sheet pane) to display an arrow, and then select Left from the list that appears.
- Close the Property Sheet pane.
- Save the form using the name, **Forms List**.
- **Experiment:** Use Form view to test each of the buttons on the form and ensure the correct form opens. If there are errors, correct the corresponding macro.

Q&A How can I test the buttons to make sure the macros work?
Switch to Form view. Click each of the buttons on the form. If there are errors in any of the macros, open the macro in Design view and correct the errors.

- Close the form.

Option Groups

You might find it useful to allow users to make a selection from some predefined options by including an option group, a rectangle containing a collection of option buttons. To perform an action, you simply click the corresponding option button. Figure 8–25 shows a list of reports presented

BTW
Viewing VBA Code
You can view VBA code that is attached to a form or report. To do so, open the form or report in Design view and click the View Code button (Report Design tab | Tools group) for reports or the View Code Button (Form Design tab | Tools group) for forms.

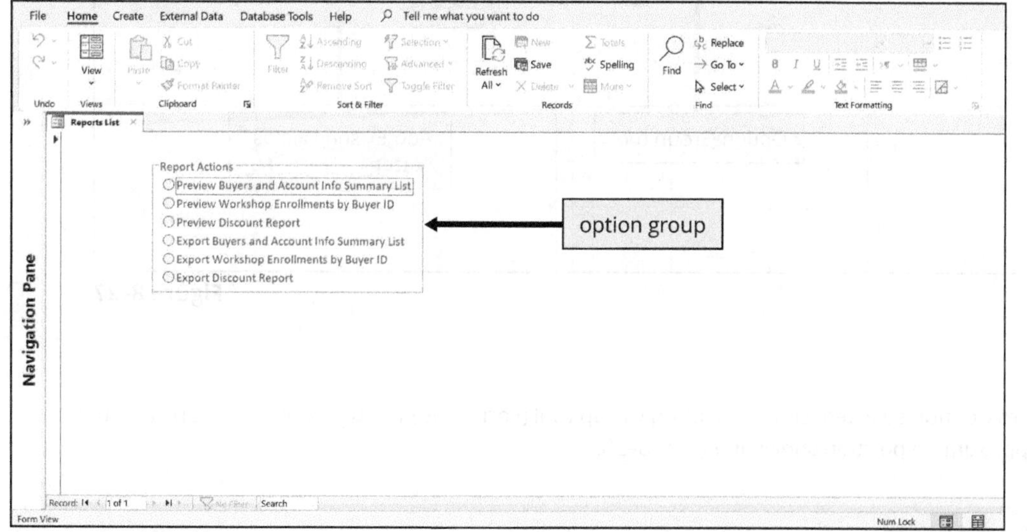

Figure 8–25

in an option group where the user would click the desired option button. Notice the user could click an option button to preview a report. The user could click a different option button to export the report as a PDF file. Clicking the 'Preview Buyers and Account Info Summary List' option button, for example, would display a preview of the Buyers and Account Information Summary List (Figure 8–26). Clicking the Close Print Preview button would return you to the option group.

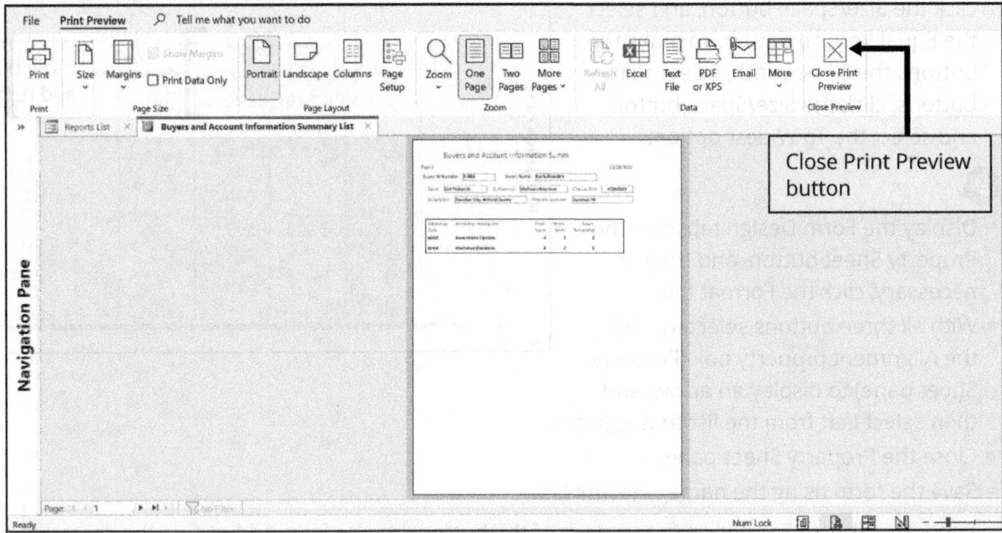

Figure 8–26

To Create a Menu Form Containing an Option Group

The form you are creating will contain an option group. **Why?** The option group allows users to select an option button to indicate either a report to preview or a report to export.

The following steps use the Option Group tool to create the option group named Report Actions.

- Display the Create tab.
- Click the Form Design button (Create tab | Forms group) to create a blank form in Design view.
- If a field list appears, click the 'Add Existing Fields' button (Form Design tab | Tools group) to remove the field list (Figure 8–27).

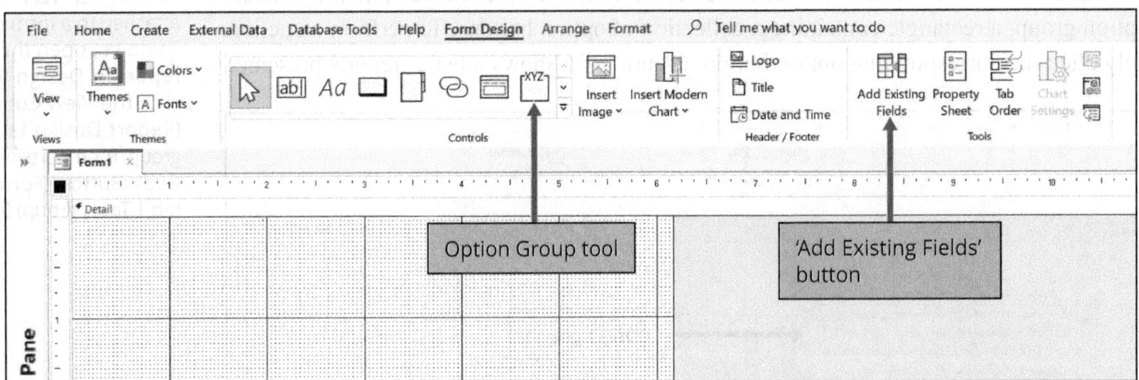

Figure 8–27

- With the 'Use Control Wizards' option selected, click the Option Group tool (Form Design tab | Controls group), and then move the pointer to the approximate position shown in Figure 8–28.

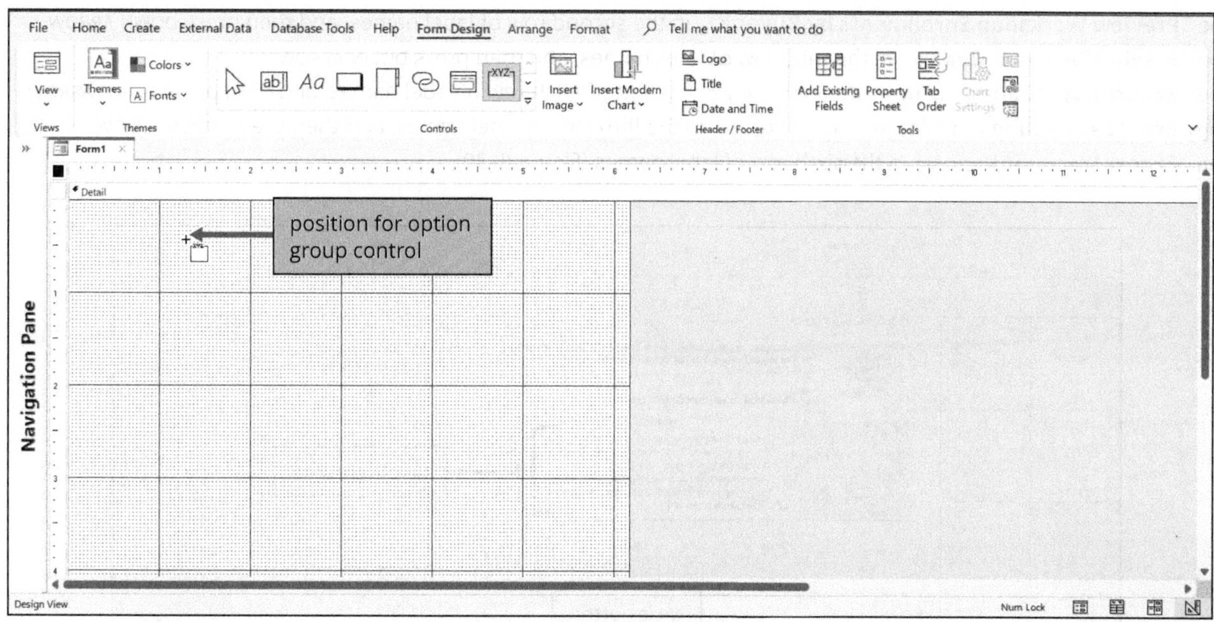

Figure 8–28

- Click the position shown in Figure 8–28 to place an option group and start the Option Group Wizard (Figure 8–29).

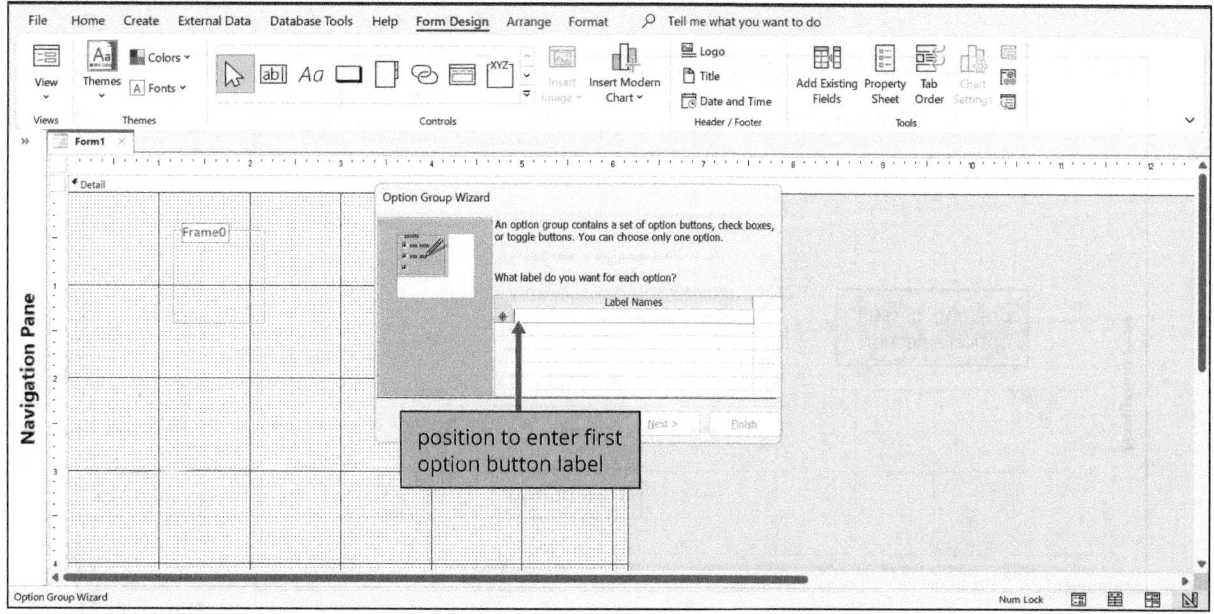

Figure 8–29

Q&A The Option Group Wizard did not start for me. What should I do?
You must not have had the 'Use Control Wizards' option selected. With the option group selected, press delete to delete the option group. Select the 'Use Control Wizards' button, and then add the option group a second time.

- Type **Preview Buyers and Account Info Summary List** in the first row of label names and press DOWN ARROW to specify the label for the first button in the group.

Q&A Why is the name of the form changed?
This form name is abbreviated from Information to Info here because there is not enough room for the entire name.

- Type **Preview Workshop Enrollments by Buyer ID** in the second row of label names, and then press DOWN ARROW.
- Type **Preview Discount Report** in the third row of label names, and then press DOWN ARROW.
- Type **Export Buyers and Account Info Summary List** in the fourth row of label names, and then press DOWN ARROW.
- Type **Export Workshop Enrollments by Buyer ID** in the fifth row of label names, and then press DOWN ARROW.
- Type **Export Discount Report** in the sixth row of label names (Figure 8–30).

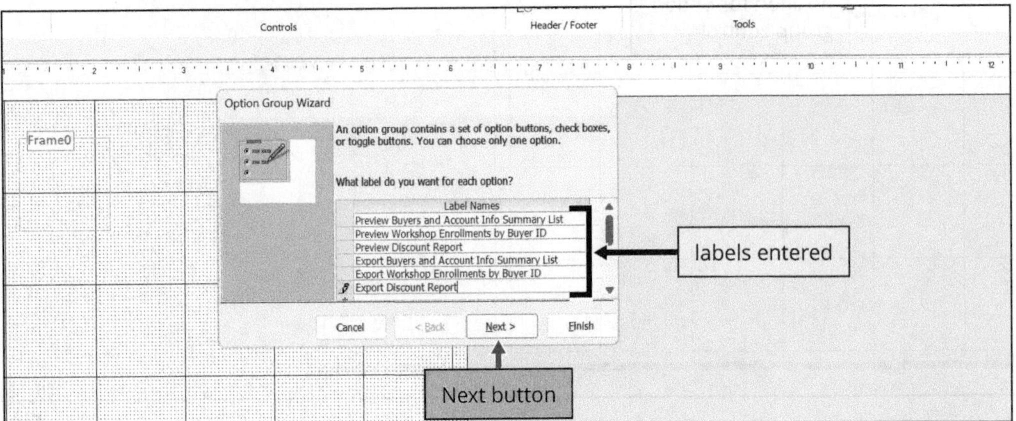

Figure 8–30

4

- Click the Next button to display the next Option Group Wizard screen.
- Click the 'No, I don't want a default.' option button to select it (Figure 8–31).

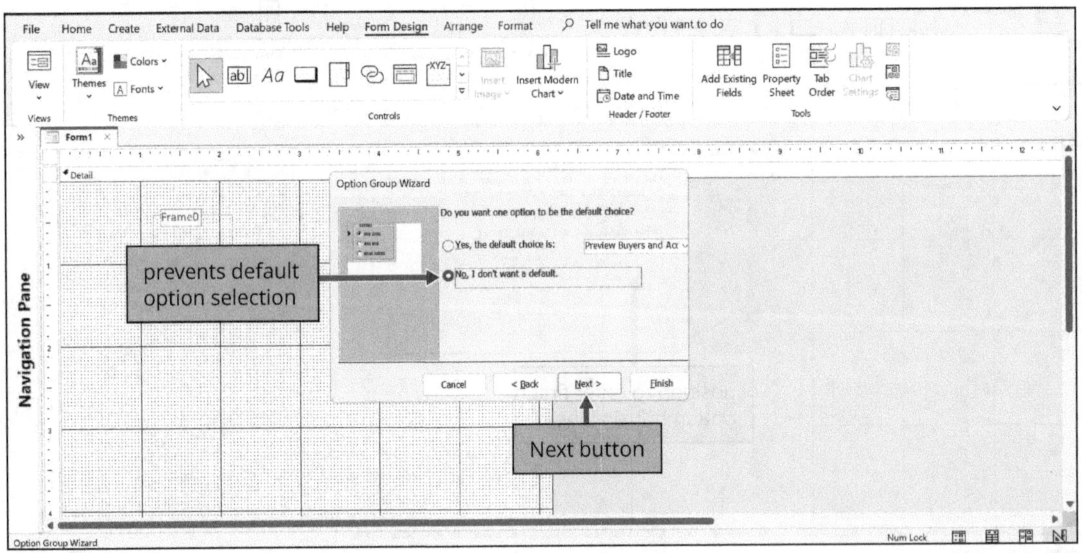

Figure 8–31

Q&A What is the effect of specifying one of the options as the default choice?
The default choice will initially be selected when you open the form. If there is no default choice, no option will be selected.

5

- Click Next to display the next Option Group Wizard screen, and then verify the values assigned to the labels match those shown in Figure 8–32.

Q&A What is the purpose of the values that appear for each option?

You can use the values in macros or VBA to refer to a specific option within the group. You will use them in a macro later in this module.

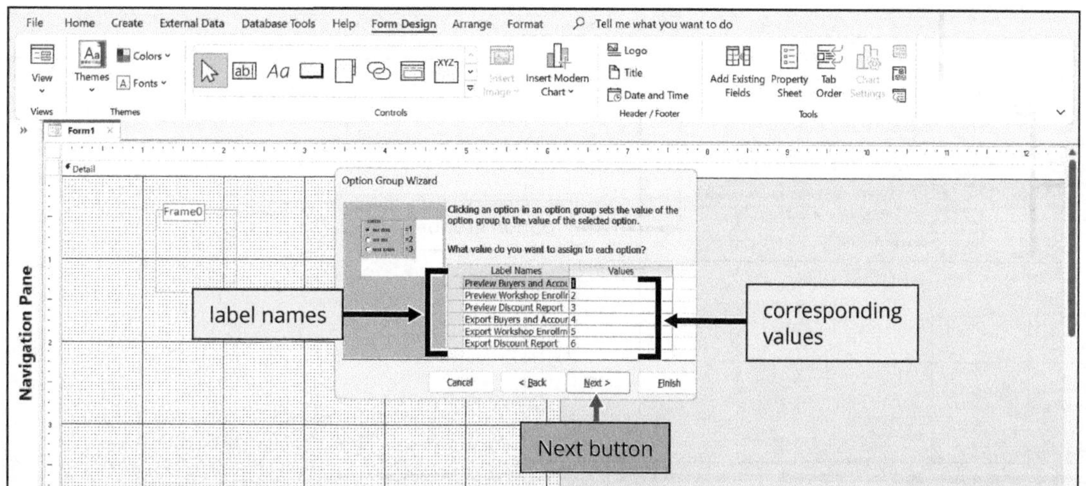

Figure 8–32

- Click Next to display the next Option Group Wizard screen, and then ensure Option buttons is selected as the type of control and Etched is selected as the style (Figure 8–33).
- **Experiment:** Click different combinations of types and styles to view the effects on the samples shown in the dialog box. When finished, select Option buttons as the type and Etched as the style.

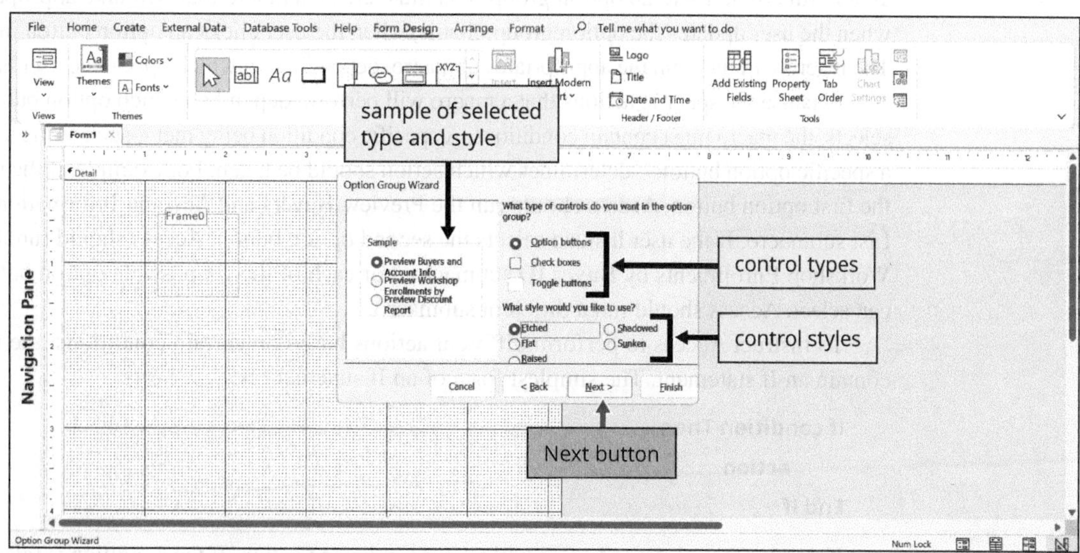

Figure 8–33

- Click Next to display the next Option Group Wizard screen, and then type **Report Actions** as the caption.
- Click Finish to complete the addition of the option group (Figure 8–34).

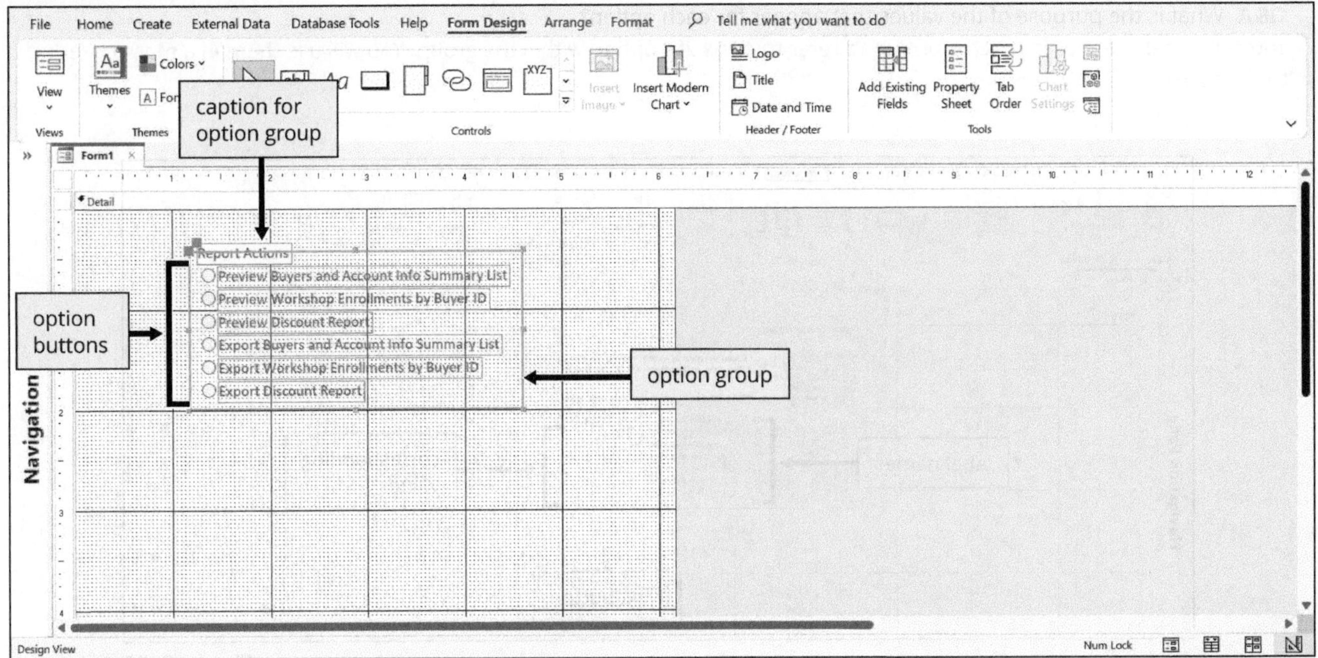

Figure 8–34

- Save the form using the name, **Reports List.**

Using an If Statement

To add functionality to an option group, you must create a macro that will take appropriate action when the user updates the option group, that is, when the user clicks an option button in the group. The macro will then run the appropriate submacro, depending on which option the user has selected.

Because the specific actions that a macro will perform depend on which option button the user selects, the macro must contain conditions. A specific condition being met—such as the user clicking a specific option button—determines which action should be taken. For example, if the user selects the first option button, Access should run the Preview Buyers and Account Information Summary List submacro. If the user instead selects the second option button, Access should run the Preview Workshop Enrollments by Buyer ID submacro. For each of the six possible option buttons a user can select, Access should run a different submacro.

To instruct Access to perform different actions based on certain conditions, the macro will contain an If statement. The simplest form of an If statement is:

If condition Then

action

End If

If the condition is true, Access will take the indicated action. If the condition is false, no action will be taken. For example, the condition could be that the user selects the first option button, and the action could be to run the Buyers and Account Information Summary List submacro. No action would be taken if the user selects any other button.

Another form of the If statement contains an Else clause. This form is:

If condition Then

first action

Else

second action

End If

If the condition is true, the first action is taken; if the condition is false, the second action is taken. For example, the condition could be the user selects option button 1; the first action could be to run the Preview Buyers and Account Information Summary List submacro, and the second action could be to run the Preview Workshop Enrollments by Buyer ID submacro. If the user selects option button 1, Access would run the Preview Buyers and Account Information Summary List submacro. If the user selects any other option button, Access would run the Preview Workshop Enrollments by Buyer ID submacro.

Because there are six option buttons, the macro needs to use an If statement with multiple Else Ifs to account for all the options. This type of If statement has the form:

```
If first condition Then
    first action
Else If second condition Then
    second action
Else If third condition Then
    third action
...
End If
```

The first condition could be the user selects the first option button; the second condition could be the user selects the second option button; the third condition could be the user selects the third option button, and so on. The first action could be that Access runs the first submacro, the second action could be that it runs the second submacro, and the third could be that it runs the third submacro. In this case, there are six option buttons and six submacros. For six conditions, as required in this macro, the If statement will contain five Else Ifs. The If statement along with the five Else Ifs will collectively contain six conditions: one to test if the user selected option 1, one for option 2, one for option 3, one for option 4, one for option 5, and one for option 6.

To Create a Macro with a Variable for the Option Group

The following steps begin creating the macro and add an action to set a variable to the desired value. The expression that contains the option number condition is [Forms]![Property Closings Form]![Form_Options]. The first portion of this expression, [Forms], refers to the Forms system object, which includes all the database's forms. A **system object** is a predefined object that contains a group of other objects. Referencing a system object helps Access choose the correct object even if multiple objects of different types have the same name (such as a form and a table both named Properties). If an object name has spaces, you must enclose it in square brackets. Thus, the name for the Property Closings Form is [Property Closings Form]. To reference a control that is part of any other form, the expression must include both the name of the form and the name of the control, separated by an exclamation point (!). Thus, the Form_Options control in the Property Closings Form would be [Forms]![Property Closings Form]![Form_Options].

Because this expression is fairly lengthy, the macro will begin by setting a temporary variable to this expression. A variable is a named location in computer memory. **Why?** You can use a variable to store a value that you can use later in the macro. You will assign the name Optno (short for option number) as the variable name for the expression. This location can contain a value, in this case, the option number on the form. In each of the conditions, you can then use Optno rather than the full expression.

- In Design view, select the option group if necessary.
- Click the Property Sheet button to display the Property Sheet pane. Ensure the selection type is Option Group.
- If necessary, click the All tab.
- Change the name of the option group to **Form_Options** (Figure 8–35).

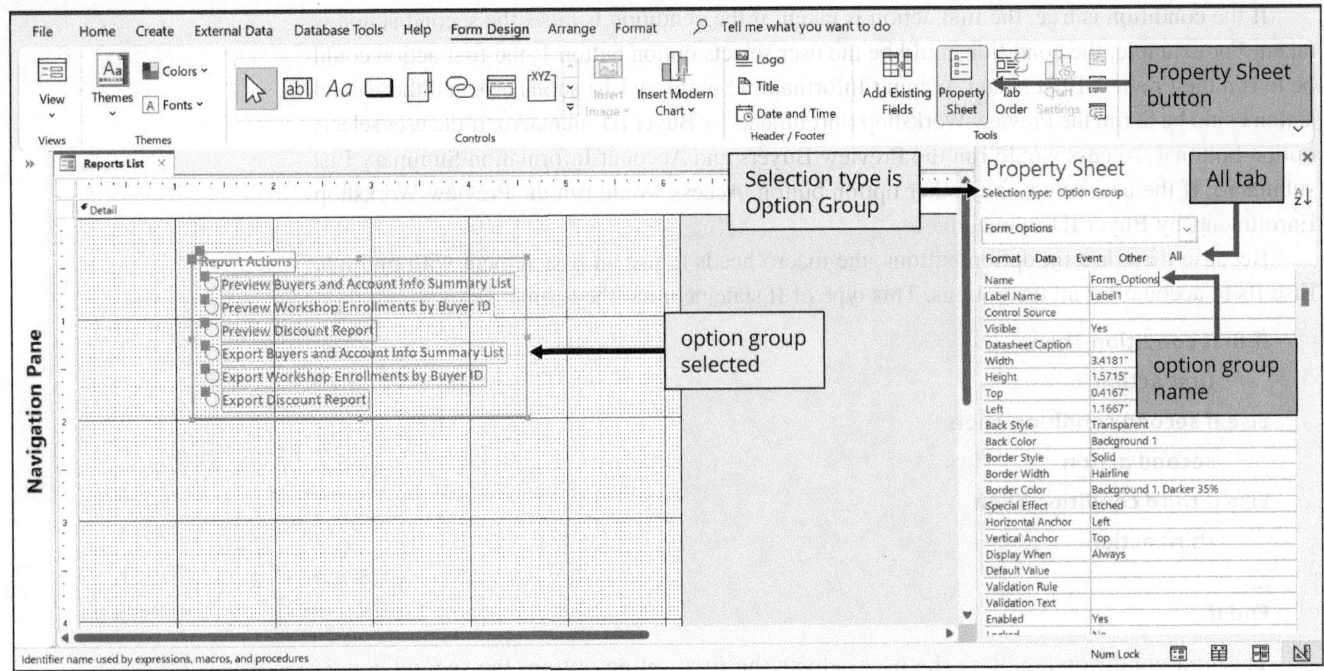

Figure 8–35

Q&A Why this name?

The name Form_Options reflects the fact that these options control the action that will be taken on this form. The underscore prevents the name from containing a space.

- Click the Event tab.
- Click the After Update property box.
- Click the Build button to display the Choose Builder dialog box (Figure 8–36).

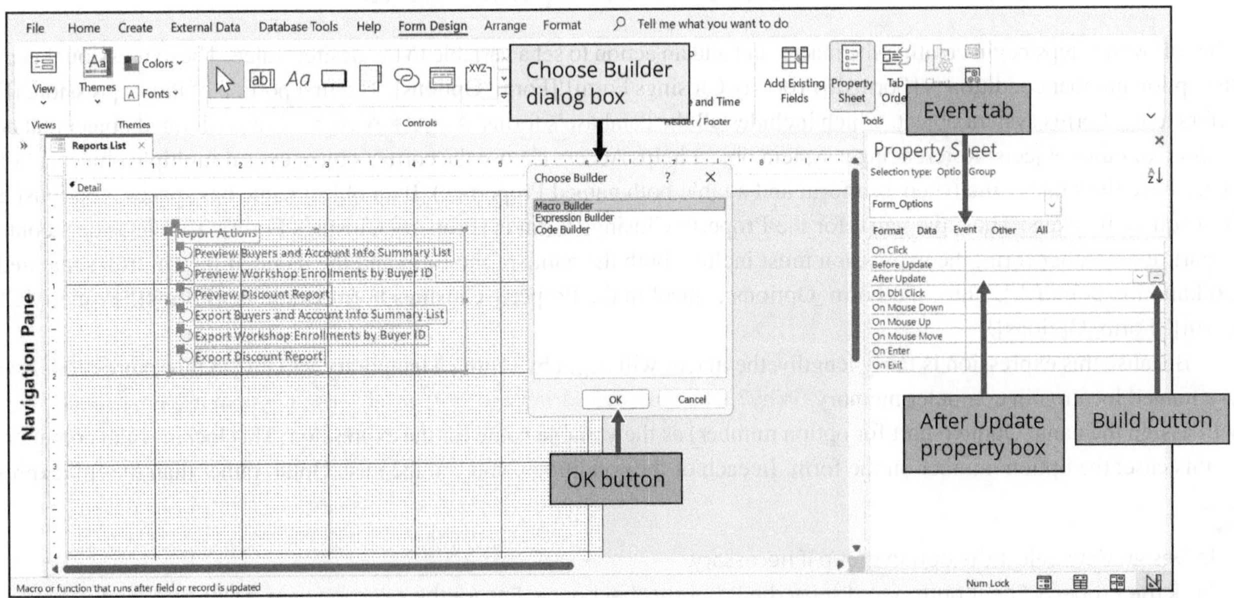

Figure 8–36

- With Macro Builder selected in the Choose Builder dialog box, click the OK button to create a macro.
- If necessary, click the Action Catalog button (Macro Design tab | Show/Hide group) to display the Action Catalog pane.

- If necessary, collapse any action category that is expanded.
- Expand the Macro Commands action category.
- Double-click the SetTempVar action in the Action Catalog to add the SetTempVar action to the macro.
- Type **Optno** as the value for the Name argument.
- Type **[Form_Options]** as the value for the Expression argument (Figure 8–37).

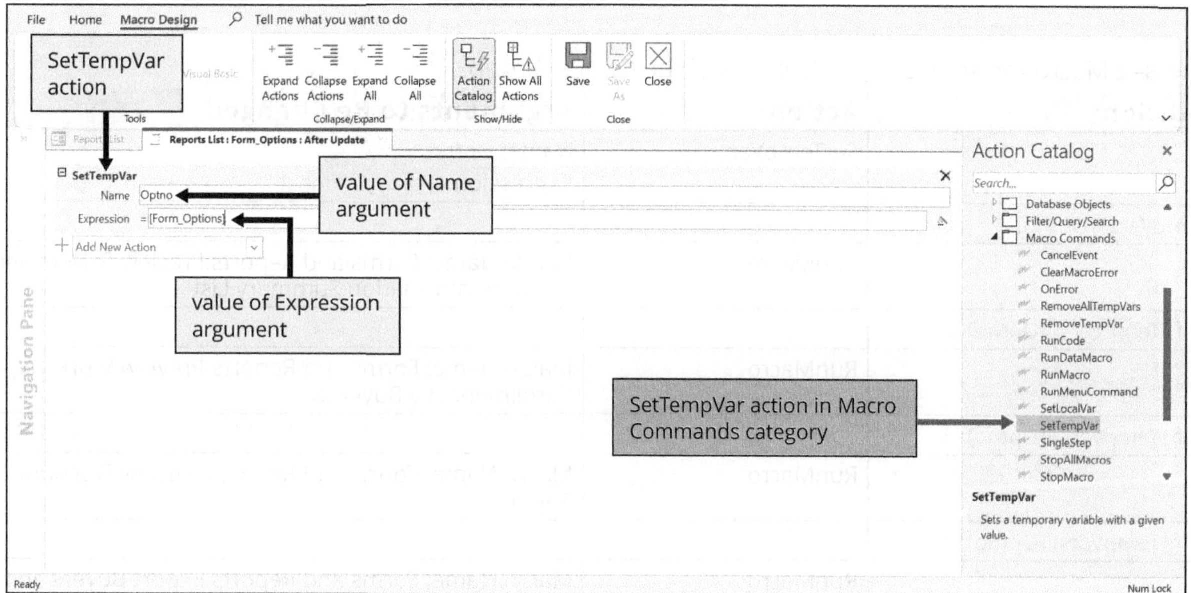

Figure 8–37

Consider This

How does Access make it easier to enter values for arguments?

Access helps you in three ways. First, if you point to the argument, Access displays a description of the argument. Second, many arguments feature a drop-down list, where you can display the list and then select the desired value. Finally, if you begin typing an expression, a feature called IntelliSense will suggest possible values that start with the letters you have already typed and that are appropriate in the context of what you are typing. If the value you want appears in the list, you can simply click it to select the value.

Macro Conditions for Option Group

As mentioned previously, the macro contains six conditions. The first is [TempVars]![Optno]=1, which simply means the value in the temporary variable Optno is equal to 1. In other words, this condition is met because the user selected the first option button. The action associated with this condition is RunMacro. The argument is the name of the macro. Because the macro to be run is a submacro, the name of the macro includes the name of the macro containing the submacro, a period, and then the name of the submacro. Because the submacro to be run is Preview Buyers and Account Information Summary List and is contained in the Forms and Reports macro, the value of the Macro Name argument is Forms and Reports.Preview Buyers and Account Info Summary List. (This name needs to be shortened to fit in the name space when creating the macro.)

The conditions and actions for options 2 through 6 are similar to the first submacro. The only difference is which submacro is associated with each option button. The conditions, actions, and arguments that you will change for the Form_Options macro are shown in Table 8–2. If the option number is 1, for example, the action is RunMacro. For the RunMacro action, you will change the Macro Name argument to Preview Buyers and Account Info Summary List submacro in the Forms and Reports macro. This name is shortened again to fit the space. On the other hand, if the option number is 2, for example, the action is again RunMacro. If the option number is 2, however, you will set the Macro Name argument to the Workshop Enrollments by Buyer ID submacro in the Forms and Reports macro. Similar actions take place for the other possible values for the Optno variable, that is, for option buttons 3 through 6. Because the temporary variable, Optno, is no longer needed at the end of the macro, the macro concludes with the RemoveTempVar command to remove this variable.

Table 8–2 Macro for After Update Property of the Option Group

Condition	Action	Arguments to Be Changed
	SetTempVar	Name: Optno Expression: [Form_Options]
If [TempVars]![Optno]=1		
	RunMacro	Macro Name: Forms and Reports.Preview Buyers and Account Information Summary List
Else If [TempVars]![Optno]=2		
	RunMacro	Macro Name: Forms and Reports.Preview Workshop Enrollments by Buyer ID
Else If [TempVars]![Optno]=3		
	RunMacro	Macro Name: Forms and Reports.Preview Discount Report
Else If [TempVars]![Optno]=4		
	RunMacro	Macro Name: Forms and Reports.Export Buyers and Account Information Summary List
Else If [TempVars]![Optno]=5		
	RunMacro	Macro Name: Forms and Reports.Export Workshop Enrollments by Buyer ID
Else If [TempVars]![Optno]=6		
	RunMacro	Macro Name: Forms and Reports.Export Discount Report
End If		
	RemoveTempVar	Name: Optno

To Add Actions to the Form_Options Macro

The following steps add the conditions and actions to the Form_Options macro. **Why?** Adding the conditions and actions will complete the macro.

- Double-click the If element from the Program Flow section of the Action Catalog to add an If statement to the submacro, and then type **[TempVars]![Optno]=1** as the condition in the If statement.
- With the Macro Commands category expanded, double-click RunMacro to add the RunMacro action.
- Click the drop-down arrow for the Macro Name argument and select the Preview Buyers and Account Information Summary List submacro within the Forms and Reports macro as the value for the argument (Figure 8–38).

Q&A What should I do if I add an action in the wrong position? What should I do if I add the wrong action?
If you add an action in the wrong position, use the Move up or Move down buttons to move it to the correct position. If you add the wrong action, click the Delete button to delete the action, and then add the correct action.

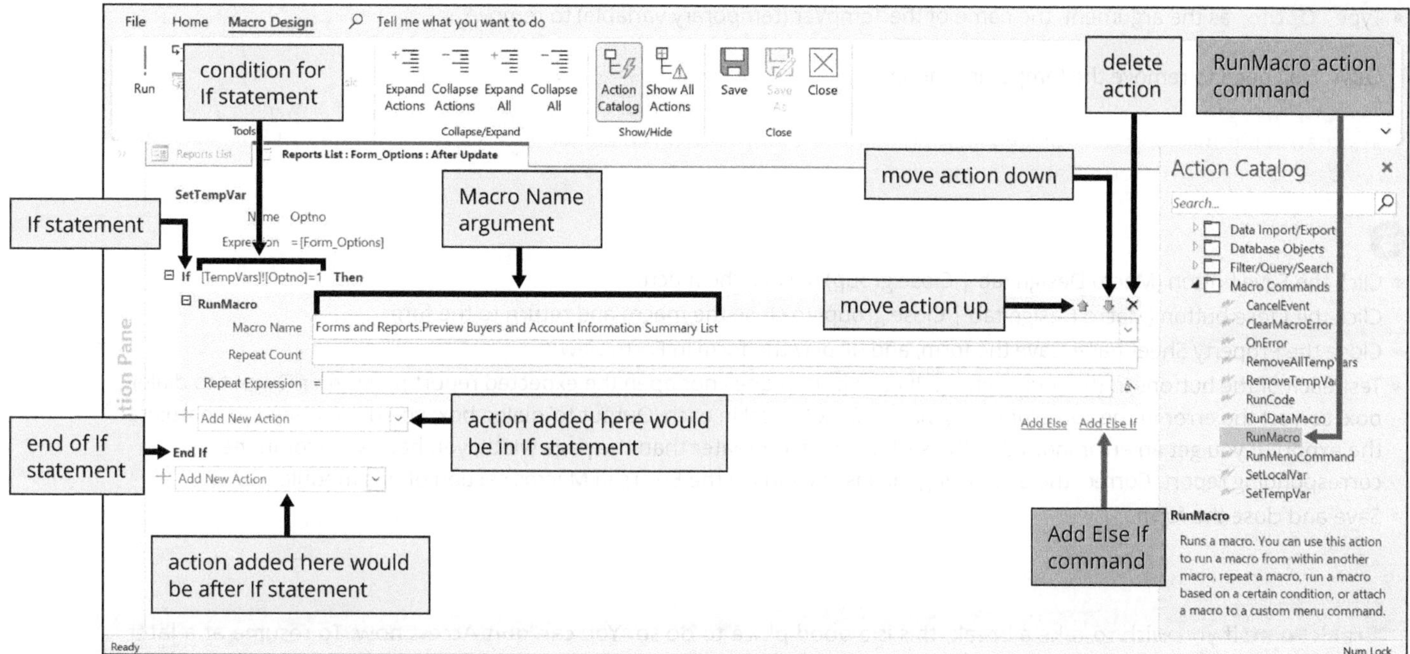

Figure 8–38

- Click 'Add Else If' to add an Else If clause to the If statement.
- Add the conditions and actions associated with options 2, 3, 4, 5, and 6 as described in Table 8–2, and specify the arguments for the actions. Click 'Add Else If' after adding each action except for the last one.

Q&A Do I have to enter all these actions? They seem to be very similar to the ones associated with option 1.
You can copy and paste the action for option 1. Right-click the action to select it and display a shortcut menu. Click Copy on the shortcut menu. Right-click the action just above where you want to insert the selected action and then click Paste. If the new action is not inserted in the correct position, select the new action and then click either the Move up or Move down buttons to move it to the correct location. Once the action is in the correct location, you can make any necessary changes to the arguments, such as changing the number 1 to the number 2.

- Click the Add New Action box below the End If statement, and then add the RemoveTempVar action and argument as shown in Figure 8–39.

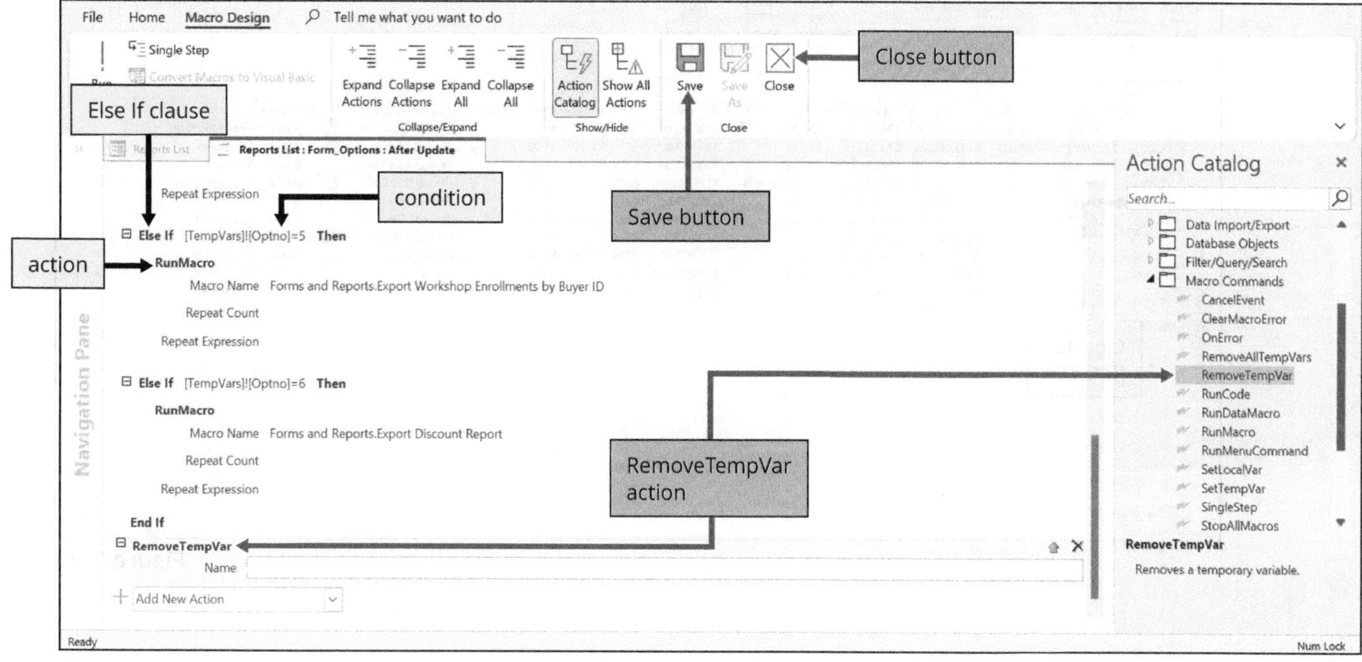

Figure 8–39

- Type **Optno** as the argument, the name of the TempVar (temporary variable) to remove.

Q&A Do I need to remove the temporary variable?
Technically, no. In fact, if you plan to use this temporary variable in another macro and want it to retain the value you assigned in this macro, you would definitely not remove it. However, if you do not plan to use it elsewhere, it is a good idea to remove it to maintain good database organization.

- Click the Save button (Macro Design tab | Close group) to save the macro.
- Click the Close button (Macro Design tab | Close group) to close the macro and return to the form.
- Close the Property Sheet pane, save the form, and display the form in Form view.
- Test each of the buttons in the option group. If each button does not open the expected report preview or Output to dialog box, correct the error in the corresponding macro. Click Cancel in each 'Output to' dialog box; you do not need to complete the export. If you get an error indicating the section width is greater than the page width, you have an error in the corresponding report. Correct the error using the instructions in the Errors in Macros section of this module.
- Save and close the form.

Break Point: If you wish to take a break, this is a good place to do so. You can quit Access now. To resume at a later time, start Access, open the database called SC_AC_08_Partners.accdb, and continue following the steps from this location forward.

User Interface (UI) Macros

A **user interface (UI) macro** is a macro that is attached to a user interface object, such as a command button, option group, or control on a form. The macro you just created for the option group is, therefore, a UI macro, as were the macros you attached to command buttons. A common use for UI macros is to associate actions with the clicking of a control on a form. In the Closings form shown in Figure 8–40, for example, if you click the Closing ID on the row in the datasheet where the Closing ID is C-005, Access displays the data for that account in a pop-up form (Figure 8–41), that is, a form that stays on top of other open objects, even when another object is active.

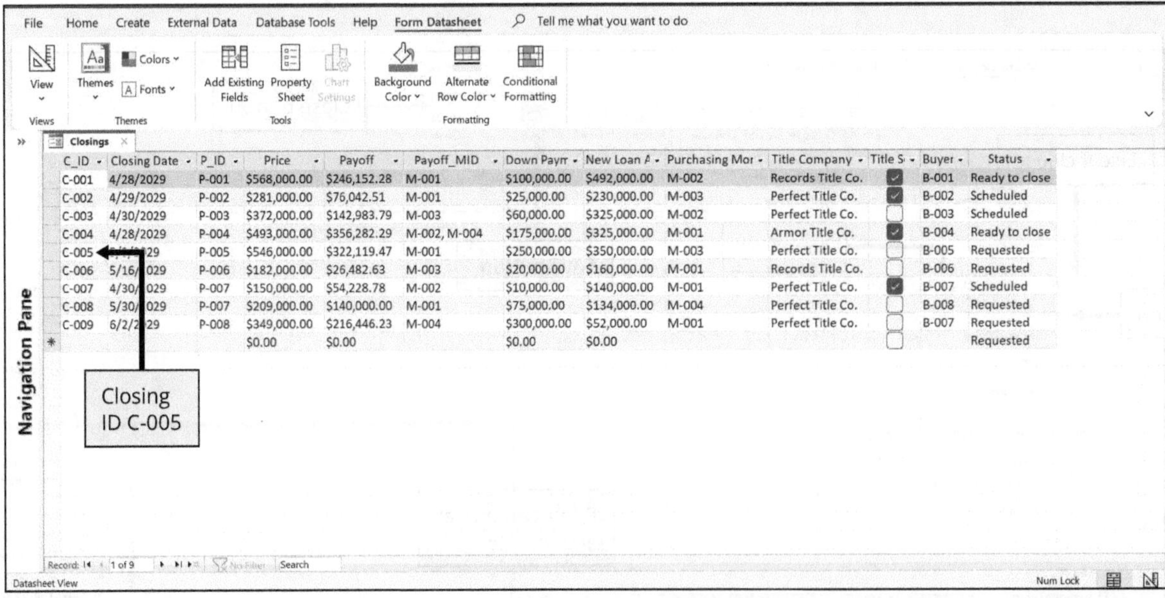

Figure 8–40

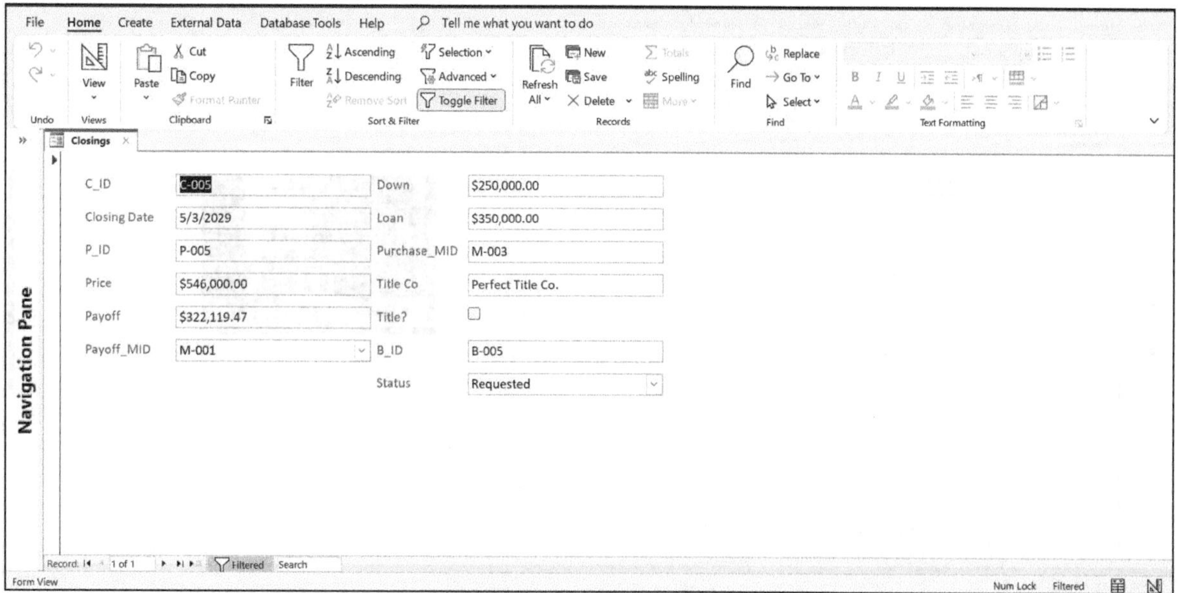

Figure 8–41

Similarly, in the Properties form shown in Figure 8–42, if you click the Property ID P-004, Access displays the data for that property in a pop-up form (Figure 8–43).

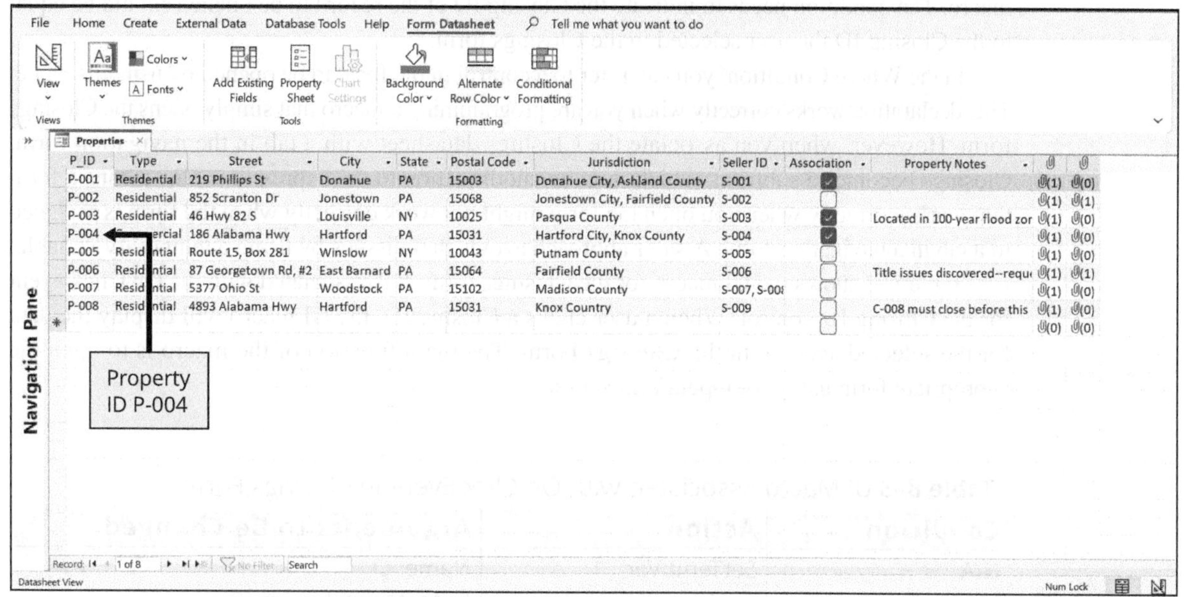

Figure 8–42

Recall that you can only use forms and reports for the tabs in a navigation form, yet the Closing ID tab appears to display the Closings table in Datasheet view. You can make it appear as though you are displaying the Closings table in Datasheet view by creating a datasheet form named Closings. You will create a UI macro in this Closings datasheet form. The UI macro that will be associated with clicking the Closing ID on some record in the Closings form will display the selected account in the Closings Form.

To display the Closings form, the UI macro will use the OpenForm action. You must set the Form Name argument of the OpenForm action to the actual name of the form to be opened, Closings. Partners wants to prevent the user from updating data using this form, so the Data Mode argument is set to Read Only. The form should appear as a pop-up, which you accomplish by setting the value of the Window Mode argument to Dialog.

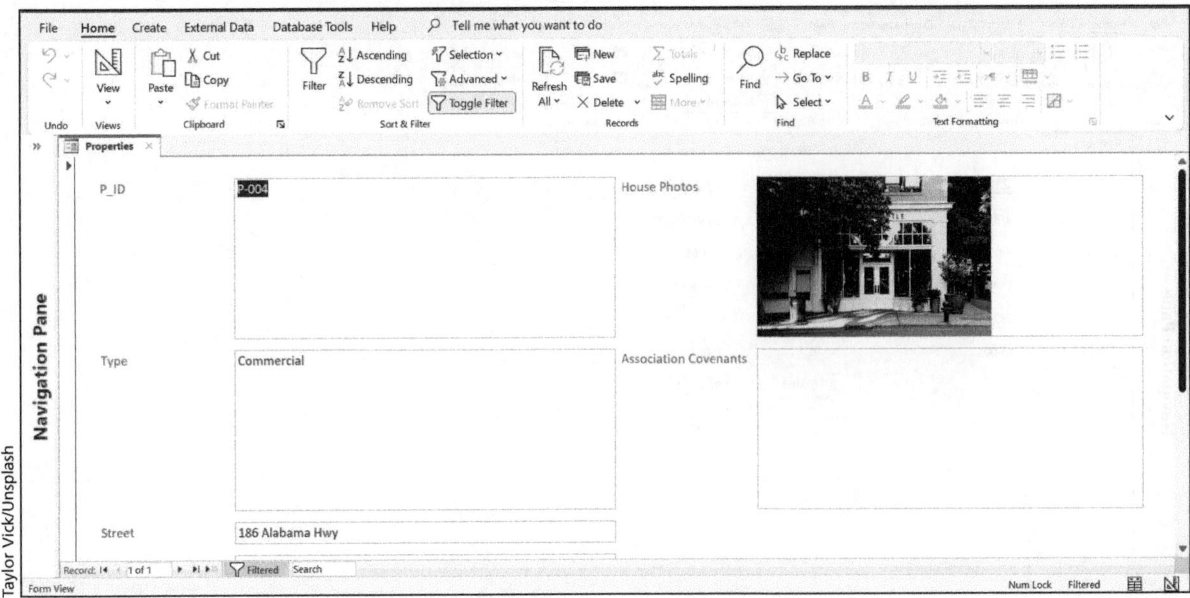

Figure 8–43

The form should display only the record the user selected. If the user clicks Closing ID C-005 in the Closings form, for example, the form should display only the data for record C-005. To restrict the record that appears in the form, you include the Where Condition argument in the UI macro. The condition needs to indicate the Closing ID of the record to be opened should be equal to the Closing ID the user selected in the Closings form.

In the Where Condition, you can refer to a control in the form to be opened by using its name. This declaration works correctly when you are programming a macro that simply opens the Closings form. However, when you associate the Closings datasheet with a tab in the navigation form, Closings becomes a subform, which requires modification to the expression. This means a form that works correctly when you open the form might not work correctly when the form is assigned to a tab in a navigation form. A safer approach avoids these issues by using a temporary variable.

Table 8–3 shows the UI macro for the Closings form. It is associated with the On Click event for the Closing ID control. When a user clicks a Closing ID, the UI macro will display the data for the selected account in the Closings Form. The main function of the macro is to open the appropriate form using the OpenForm action.

Table 8–3 UI Macro Associated with On Click Event in Closings Form

Condition	Action	Arguments to Be Changed
N/A	SetTempVar	Name: CI Expression: [Closing ID]
N/A	OpenForm	Form Name: Closings Where Condition: [Closing ID]=[TempVars]![CI] Data Mode: Read Only Window Mode: Dialog
N/A	RemoveTempVar	Name: CI

In the macro shown in Table 8–3, the first action, SetTempVar, assigns the temporary variable CI to the Closing ID. The two arguments are Name, which is set to CI, and Expression, which is set to [Closing ID]. The CI temporary variable refers to the Closing ID in the Closings form; recall that the completed macro will open the Closings form. You then can use this temporary variable in the Where Condition argument. The expression is thus [Closing ID]=[TempVars]![CI].

The [Closing ID] portion refers to the Closing ID in the Closings form. The [TempVars]![CI] portion is the temporary variable that has been set equal to the Closing ID in the Closings form. The macro ends by removing the temporary variable.

Table 8–4 shows the macro for the Properties form, which is very similar to the macro for the Closings form.

Table 8–4 UI Macro Associated with On Click Event in Properties Form

Condition	Action	Arguments to Be Changed
N/A	SetTempVar	Name: PI Expression: [Property ID]
N/A	OpenForm	Form Name: Properties Where Condition: [Property ID]=[TempVars]![PI] Data Mode: Read Only Window Mode: Dialog
N/A	RemoveTempVar	Name: PI

To Create Datasheet Forms

The following steps create two datasheet forms, one for the Closings table and one for the Properties table. **Why?** The datasheet forms enable the Closings and Properties tables to appear as if displayed in Datasheet view, despite the Access restriction that prevents tables from being used on tabs in a navigation form.

- In the Navigation Pane, select the Closings table.
- Display the Create tab, and then click the More Forms button (Create tab | Forms group) to display the More Forms gallery (Figure 8–44).

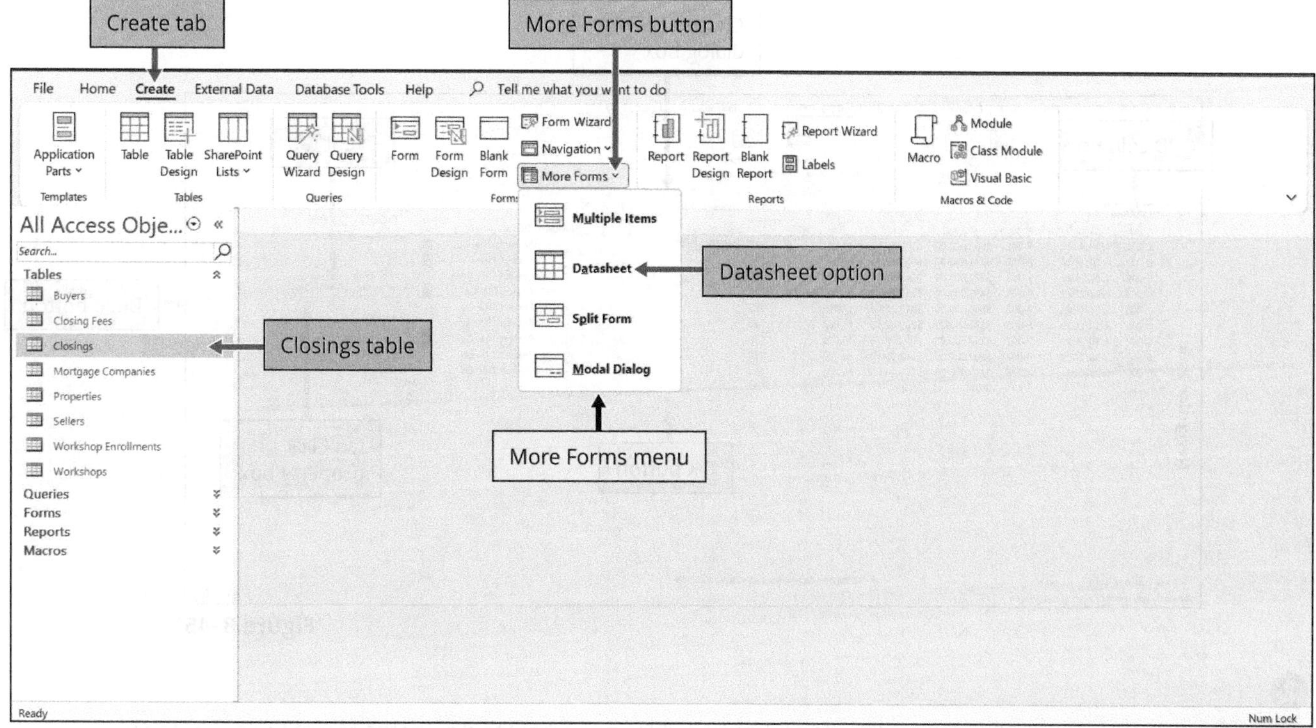

Figure 8–44

- Click Datasheet to create a datasheet form.
- Save the form using the name **Closings**.

Q&A Is it acceptable to use the same name for the form as for the table?
Yes. In this case, you want it to appear to the user that the Closings table is open in Datasheet view. One way to emphasize this fact is to use the same name as the table.

What is the difference between a datasheet form, such as this one, and a simple form, such as the Mortgage Companies Form?
The Mortgage Companies Form is a simple form that displays only one record at a time. The Closings form you just created displays all the closings records in a datasheet.

- Use the same technique to create a datasheet form named **Properties** for the Properties table.
- Close both forms.

To Create UI Macros for the Datasheet Forms

The following steps create the UI macro shown in Table 8–3 for the Closings datasheet form and the UI macro shown in Table 8–4 for the Properties datasheet form. **Why?** The UI macros will display the appropriate pop-up forms when a user clicks the appropriate position on the forms.

- Open the Closings form.
- Click the C_ID heading to select the C_ID column in the datasheet.
- If necessary, click the Property Sheet button (Form Datasheet tab | Tools group) to display the Property Sheet pane.
- If necessary, click the Event tab to display only event properties.
- Click the On Click property box, and then click the Build button (the three dots) to display the Choose Builder dialog box (Figure 8–45).

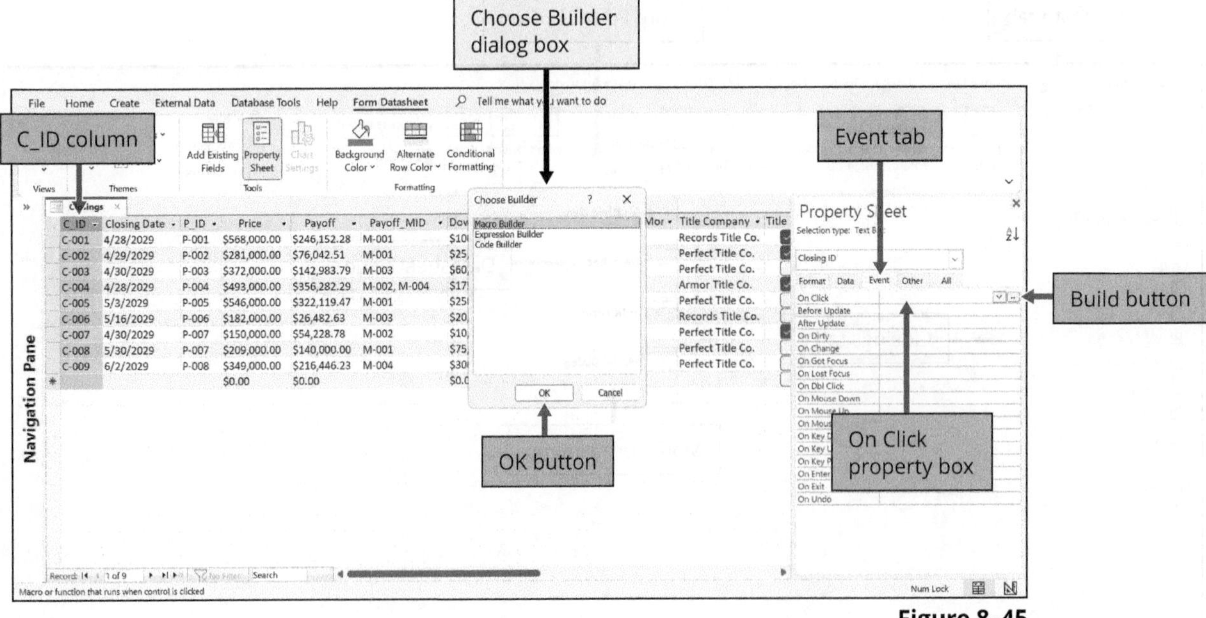

Figure 8–45

2

- With Macro Builder selected, click the OK button (Choose Builder dialog box) to display the Macro Builder window.
- Add the SetTempVar action to the macro, enter **CI** (be sure to use a capital i and not a number 1) as the value for the Name argument, and enter **[Closing ID]** as the value for the Expression argument.

- Expand the Database Objects category, add the OpenForm action to the macro, select Closings as the value for the Form Name argument, leave the value of the View argument set to Form, enter **[Closing ID]=[TempVars]![CI]** as the value for the Where Condition argument, select Read Only as the value for the Data Mode argument, and select Dialog as the value for the Window Mode argument.

Q&A Why am I setting a temporary value for the Closing ID field when the field in the datasheet form is called C_ID?
The Closing ID field has been given the caption, C_ID, to better fit the space in the table, and this caption also is what appears in the datasheet form. However, the actual name of the field is Closing ID.

What does the expression for the Where Condition value mean?
The portion before the equal sign, [Closing ID], refers to the Closing ID field in the form just opened, that is, in the Closings form. The portion to the right of the equal sign, [TempVars]![CI], is the temporary variable that was set equal to the Closing ID value on the selected record in the Closings form. This Where Condition guarantees the record displayed in the Closings form will be the record with the same Closing ID as the one selected in the Closings form.

- Add the RemoveTempVar action to the macro and enter **CI** as the value for the Name argument (Figure 8–46).

Q&A Why do I need to remove the temporary variable?
Technically, you do not. The temporary variable has fulfilled its function, however, so it makes sense to remove it at this point.

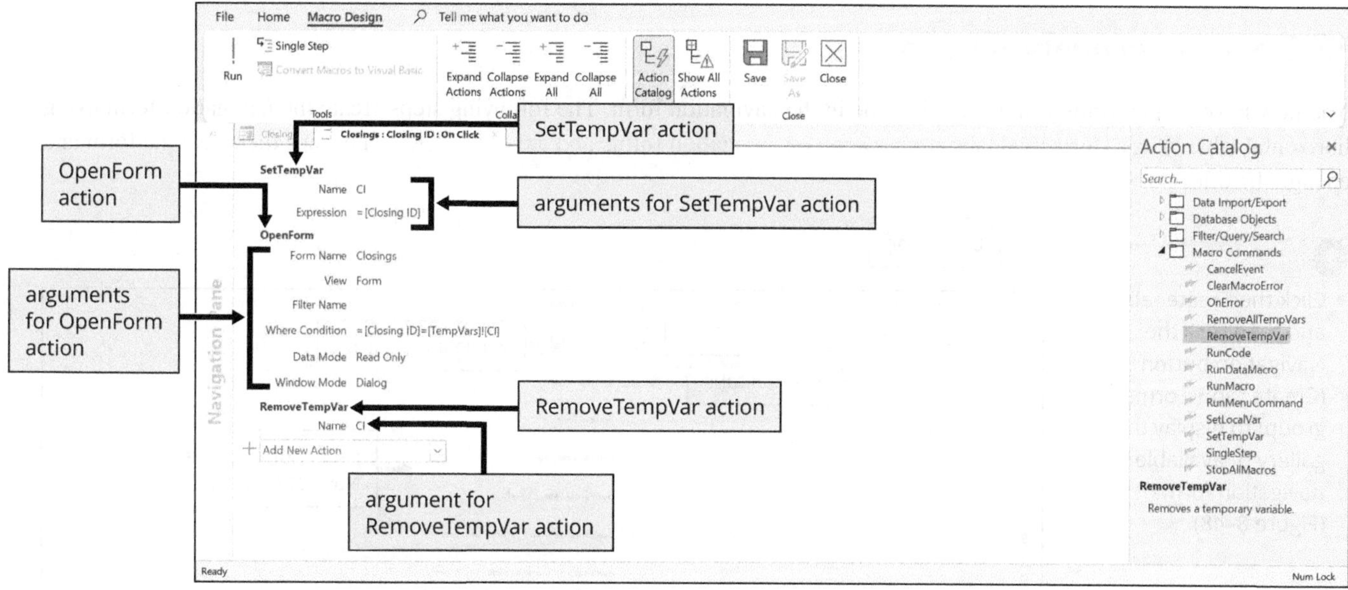

Figure 8–46

3

- Click the Save button (Macro Design tab | Close group) to save the macro.
- Click the Close button (Macro Design tab | Close group) to close the macro and return to the form.
- Close the Property Sheet pane.
- Save and close the form.

4

- Use the techniques in Steps 1 through 2 to create a UI macro for the Properties datasheet form called Properties, referring to Table 8–4 for the actions. Create the macro shown in Figure 8–47 associated with clicking the Property ID (P_ID) column.

5

- Click the Save button (Macro Design tab | Close group) to save the macro.
- Click the Close button (Macro Design tab | Close group) to close the macro and return to the datasheet form.
- Close the Property Sheet pane.
- Save and close the form.

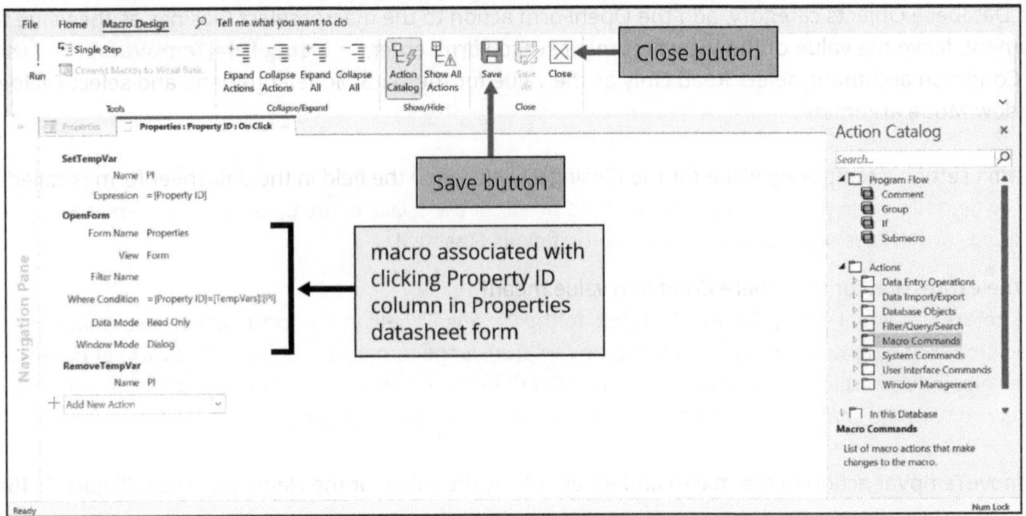

Figure 8–47

To Create a Navigation Form

You now have all the forms you need to include in the navigation form. The following steps create the navigation form using horizontal tabs. **Why?** Horizontal tabs are common on navigation forms and are easy to use. The steps then save the form and change the title.

- Click the Create tab, and then click the Navigation button (Create tab | Forms group) to display the gallery of available navigation forms (Figure 8–48).

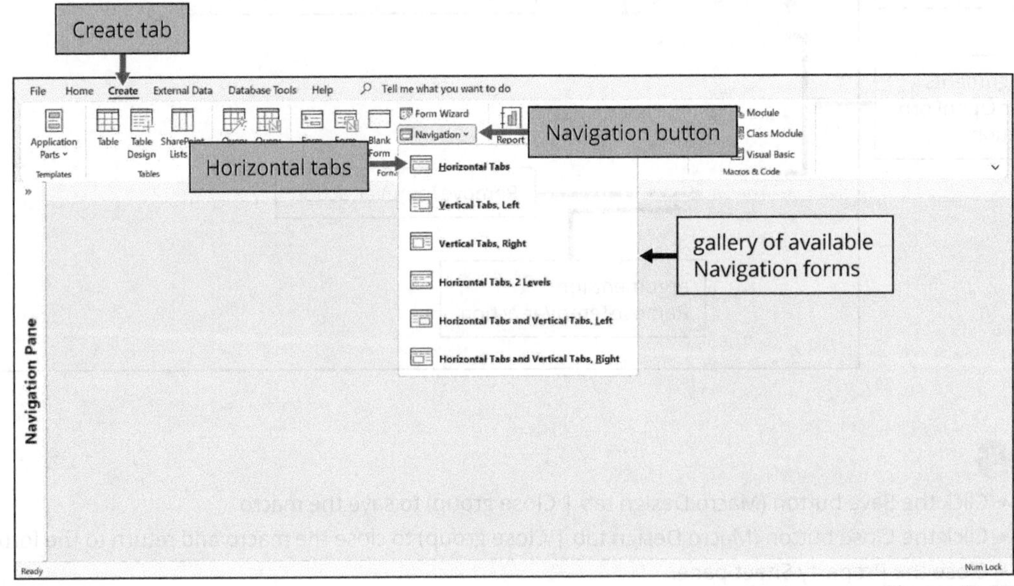

Figure 8–48

- Click Horizontal Tabs in the gallery to create a form with a navigation control in which the tabs are arranged horizontally in a single row.
- If necessary, click the 'Add Existing Fields' button (Form Layout Design tab | Tools group) to close the Field List pane (Figure 8–49).

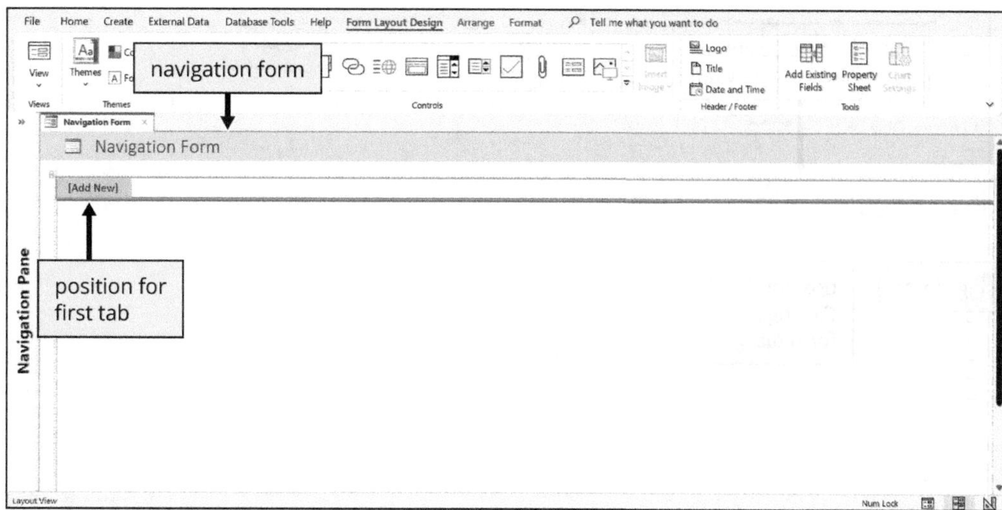

Figure 8–49

- Save the form using the name, **Main Menu.**
- Switch to Design view.
- Click the form title to produce an insertion point.
- Erase the current title, and then type **Partners Law Firm** as the new title (Figure 8–50).
- Save the form.

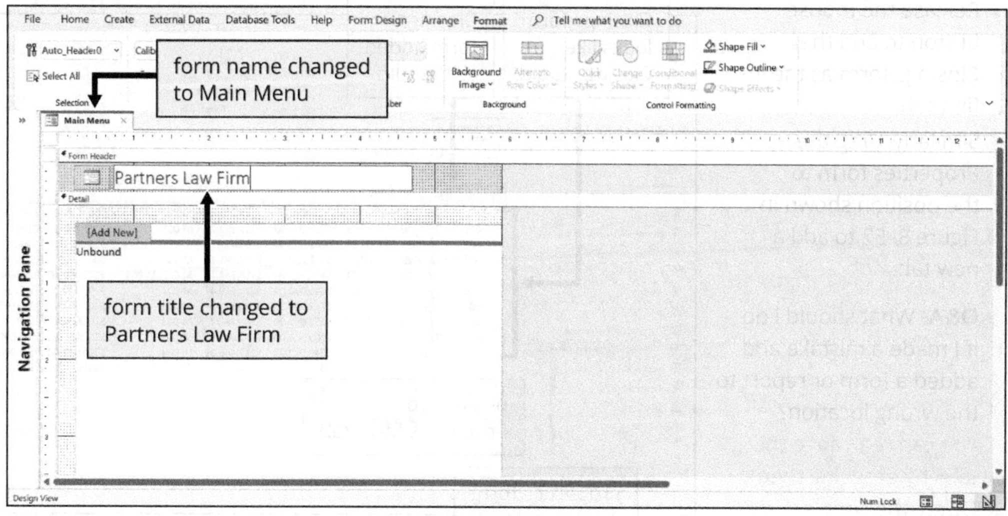

Figure 8–50

To Add Tabs to a Navigation Form

To add a form or report to a tab in a navigation form, be sure the Navigation Pane is open, and then drag the form or report to the desired tab. When using the navigation form, users can then display that form or report by clicking the tab. For the Partners Law Firm navigation form, you will drag four forms to the tabs. The first form is the Closings datasheet form that appears to display the Closings table open in Datasheet view. Similarly, the Properties form is a datasheet form that appears to display the Properties table open in Datasheet view. The Forms List form contains three buttons users can click to display the form of their choice. Finally, the Reports List form contains an option group where users can select a report to preview or export. The following steps add the tabs to the navigation form. They also change the name of the Forms List and Reports List tabs. **Why?** The names of the tabs do not have to be the same as the name of the corresponding forms. By changing them, you can often make tabs more readable.

- Return to Layout view (Home tab | Views group).
- In the Navigation Pane, scroll down so the form named Closings appears, and then drag the Closings form to the position shown in Figure 8–51 to add a new tab.

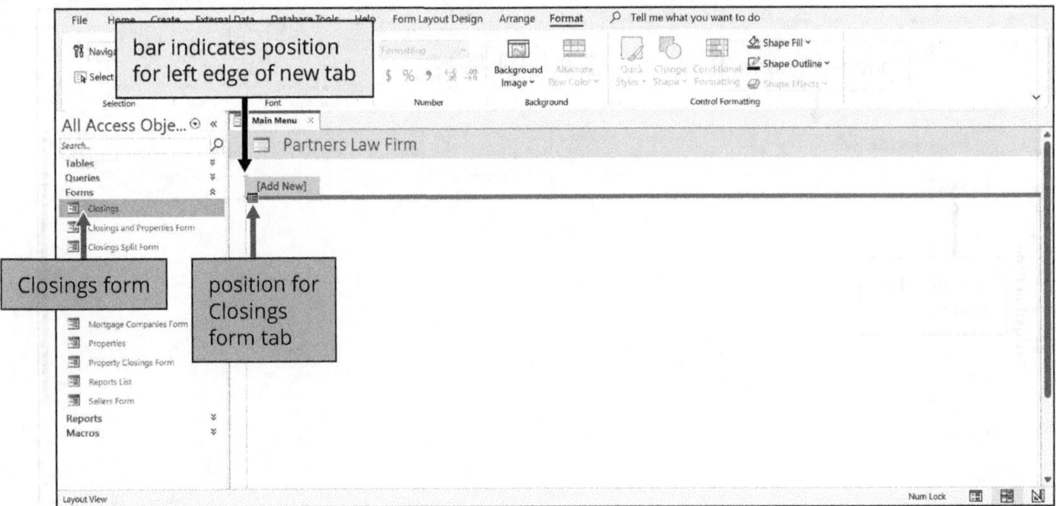

Figure 8–51

- Release the mouse button to add the Closings form as the first tab.
- Similarly, drag the Properties form to the position shown in Figure 8–52 to add a new tab.

Q&A What should I do if I made a mistake and added a form or report to the wrong location?
You can rearrange the tabs by dragging them. Often, the simplest way to correct a mistake is to click the Undo button to reverse your most recent action, however. You can also choose to simply close the form without saving it and then start over.

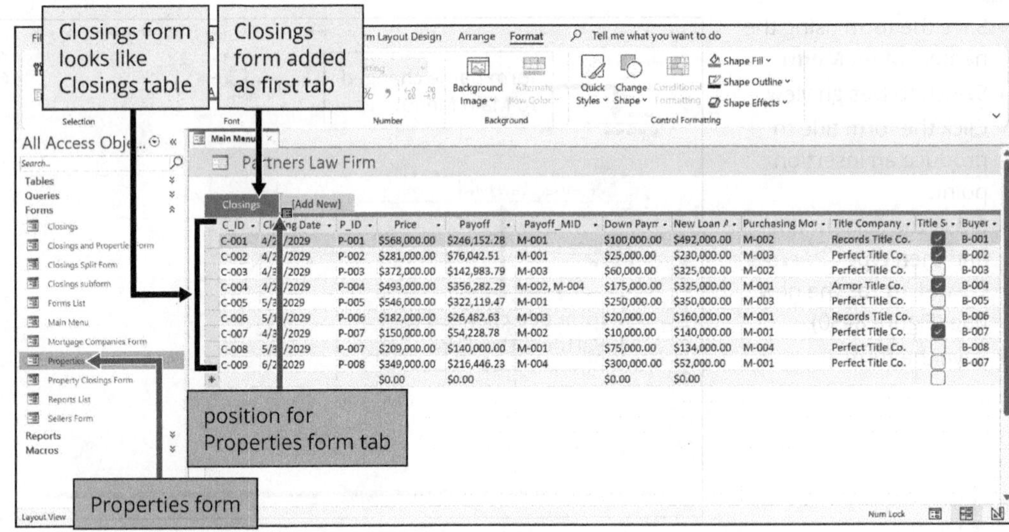

Figure 8–52

3

- Release the mouse button to add the Properties form as the second tab.
- Using the techniques described in Steps 1 and 2, add the Forms List form as the third tab and the Reports List form as the fourth tab (Figure 8–53).

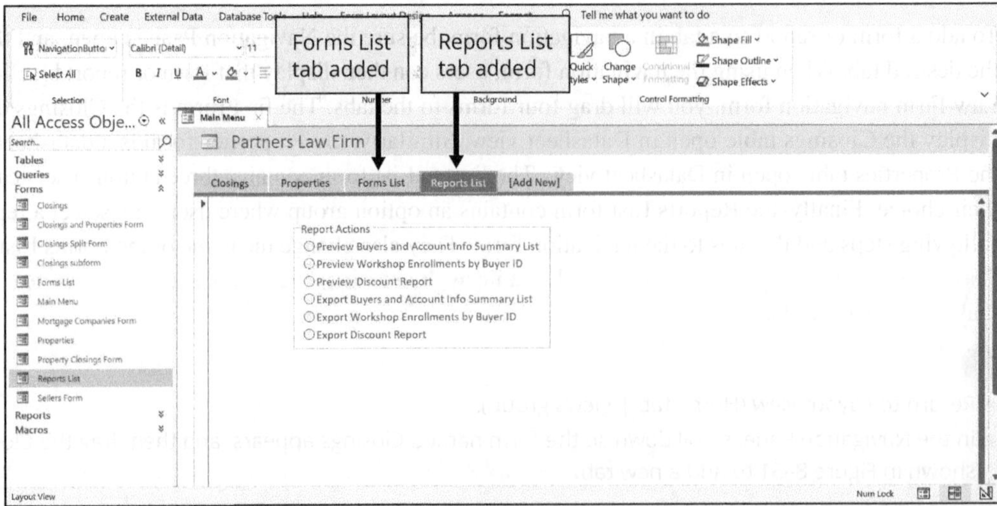

Figure 8–53

- Click the Forms List tab twice: once to select it and the second time to produce an insertion point.
- Change the name from Forms List to **Forms**.
- In a similar fashion, change the name of the Reports List tab from Reports List to **Reports** (Figure 8–54).

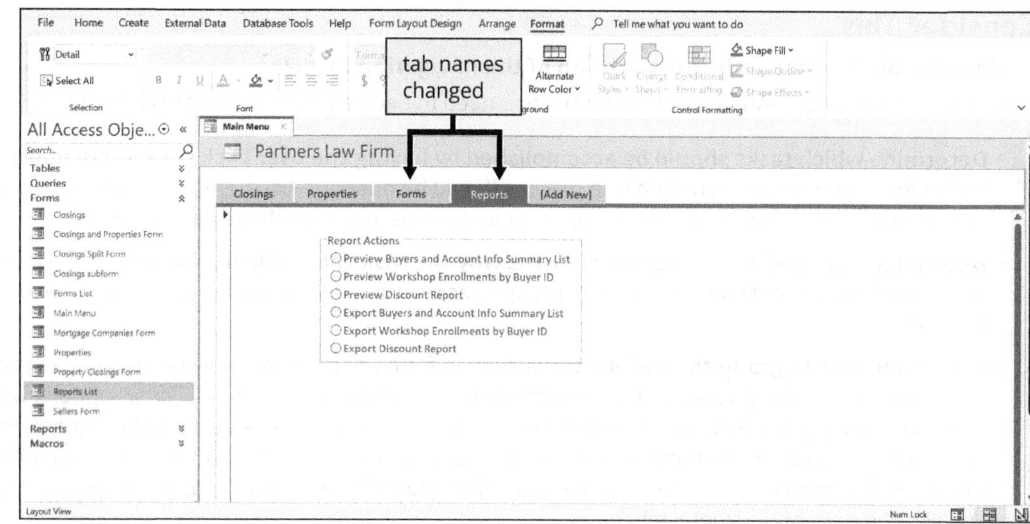

Figure 8–54

Q&A I created these two forms using the names Forms List and Reports List. Now I have changed the names to Forms and Reports. Why not call them Forms and Reports in the first place, so I would not have to rename the tabs?

Because the words, forms and reports, have specific meanings in Access, you cannot use these names when creating the forms. Thus, you needed to use other names, like Forms List and Reports List. Because tabs within forms are not database objects, you can rename them to be any name you want.

- Save the Main Menu form.
- Switch to Form view and click on each tab to test it for accuracy.
- If requested to do so by your instructor, rename the Main Menu form as LastName Main Menu where LastName is your last name.
- Close the form.

Using a Navigation Form

The Main Menu navigation form is complete and ready for use. To use the navigation form, double-click the form in the Navigation Pane. The Main Menu form then will appear with the first tabbed object (refer to Figure 8–1). To display the other forms, click the appropriate tab.

BTW
Quick Styles for Controls
To make a navigation form more visually appealing, you can change the style of command buttons or tabs. Quick styles change how the different colors, fonts, and effects are combined. To change the style of a command button or tab, open the navigation form in Layout view. Select the control(s) for which you want to change the style, and then click Quick Styles (Format tab | Control Formatting group). When the Quick Styles gallery appears, select the desired style. You also can change the style of a control in Design view.

BTW
Change the Shape of a Control
Command buttons and tabs have a default shape. For example, both command buttons and tabs have a rounded rectangle shape as the default shape. You can change the shape of a button or tab control on a navigation form. To do so, open the navigation form in Layout view. Select the control(s) for which you want to change the shape, and click Change Shape (Format tab | Control Formatting group). When the Change Shape gallery appears, select the desired shape. You also can change the shape of a command button or tab in Design view.

Consider This

How do you determine the organization of the navigation form?

Once you decide you want a navigation form, you need to decide how to organize the form.

- **Determine which tasks should be accomplished by having the user click tabs or buttons in the navigation form.** Which forms should be opened? Which reports should be opened? Are there any tables or queries that you need to be able to open in the navigation form? If so, you must create forms for the tables or queries.
- **Determine any special requirements for the way the tasks are to be performed.** When a form is opened, should a user be able to edit data, or should the form open as read-only? Should a report be exported or simply viewed on the screen?
- **Determine how to group the various tasks.** Should forms or reports simply be assigned to the tabs in the navigation form? Should they be grouped as buttons on a menu form? Should they be placed as options within an option group? (For consistency, you would usually decide on one of these approaches and use it throughout. In this module, one menu form uses command buttons, and the other uses an option group simply to illustrate both approaches.) As far as the navigation form is concerned, is a single set of horizontal tabs sufficient, or would you also like vertical tabs? Would you like two rows of horizontal tabs?

BTW
Distributing a Document
Instead of printing and distributing a hard copy of a document, you can distribute the document electronically. Options include sending the document via email; posting it on cloud storage (such as OneDrive) and sharing the file with others; posting it on a social networking site, blog, or other website; and sharing a link associated with an online location of the document. You also can create and share a PDF or XPS image of the document, so users can view the file in Acrobat Reader or XPS Viewer instead of in Access.

Data Macros

A data macro is a special type of macro that is associated with specific table-related events, such as updating a record in a table. The possible events are Before Change, Before Delete, After Insert, After Update, and After Delete. Data macros allow you to add logic to these events. For example, the data macro shown in Table 8–5 is associated with the Before Change event, an event that occurs after the user has changed the data but before the change is actually made in the database.

Table 8–5 Data Macro for Before Change Event

Condition	Action	Arguments to Be Changed
If [Hours Spent]>[Total Hours]		
	SetField	Name: [Hours Spent] Value: [Total Hours]
Else If [Hours Spent]<0		
	SetField	Name: [Hours Spent] Value: 0
End If		

BTW
Data Macros
Data macros are similar to SQL (Structured Query Language) triggers. You attach logic to record or table events, and any forms and code that update those events inherit the logic. Data macros are stored with the table.

This macro will examine the value in the Hours Spent field in the Workshop Enrollments table. If the user's update would cause the value in the Hours Spent field to be greater than the value in the Total Hours field, the macro will change the value in the Hours Spent field so it is equal to the value in the Total Hours field. Likewise, if the update would cause the value in the Hours Spent field to be less than zero, the macro will set the value in the Hours Spent field to 0. These changes take place after the user has made the change on the screen but before Access commits the change to the database, that is, before the data in the database is actually changed.

There are other events to which you can assign data macros. The actions in a data macro associated with the Before Delete event will take place after a user has given a delete command, but before the record is actually removed from the database. The actions in a macro associated with the After Insert event will take place immediately after a record physically is added to the database. The actions in a macro associated with the After Update event will take place immediately after a record is physically changed in the database. The actions in a macro associated with the After Delete event will take place immediately after a record is physically removed from the database.

To Create a Data Macro

The following steps create the data macro in Table 8–5, a macro that will be run after a user makes a change to a record in the Workshop Enrollments table, but before the record is updated in the database. **Why?** Partners paralegals want a way to prevent users from entering invalid data into the database.

- Open the Workshop Enrollments table in Datasheet view.
- Display the Table tab (Figure 8–55).

Q&A What is the meaning of the buttons in the Before Events and After Events groups?
Actions in macros associated with the Before Events group will occur after the user has taken action to change or delete a record, but before the change or deletion is made permanent in the database. Actions in macros associated with the After Events group will occur after the corresponding update has been made permanent in the database.

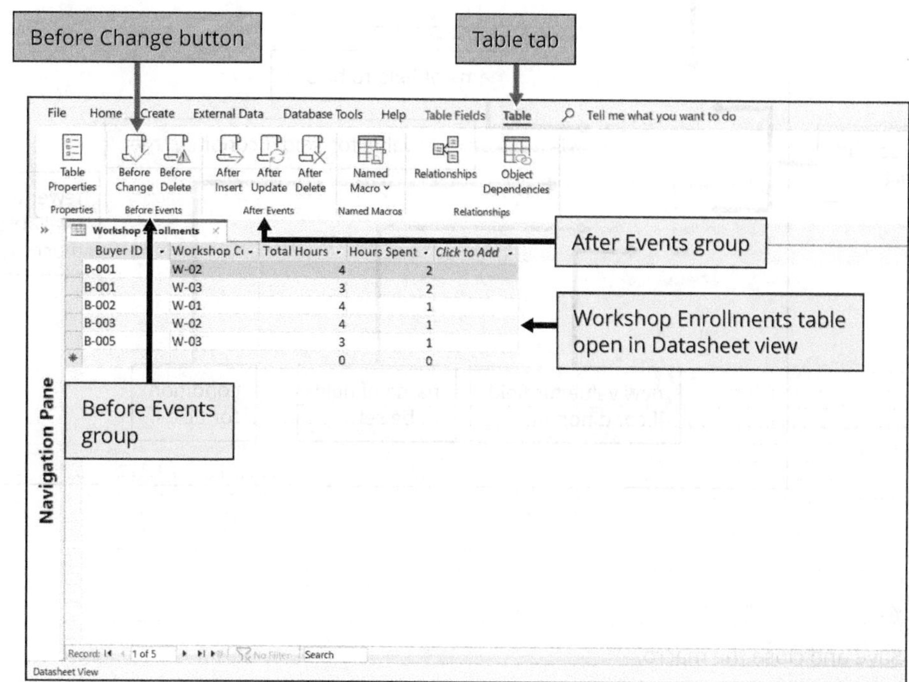

Figure 8–55

- Click the Before Change button (Table tab | Before Events group) to create a Before Change macro.
- Double-click the If element from the Program Flow section of the Action Catalog to add an If statement to the macro, and then type **[Hours Spent]>[Total Hours]** as the condition in the If statement.
- Add the SetField action to the macro.
- Enter **[Hours Spent]** in the Name field, and then enter **[Total Hours]** in the Value field.
- Add an Else If statement.
- Type **[Hours Spent]<0** for the Else If condition.
- Add the SetField action to the macro.
- Enter **[Hours Spent]** in the Name field, and then enter **0** (zero) in the Value field.
- Confirm that your macro looks like the one shown in Figure 8–56 and correct any errors if necessary.

Q&A What happened to all the actions that were in the list? In the previous macros I created, there were many more actions available.
There are only certain actions that make sense in data macros. Only those actions appear. Therefore, the list of actions that appears is much smaller in a data macro than in other macros.

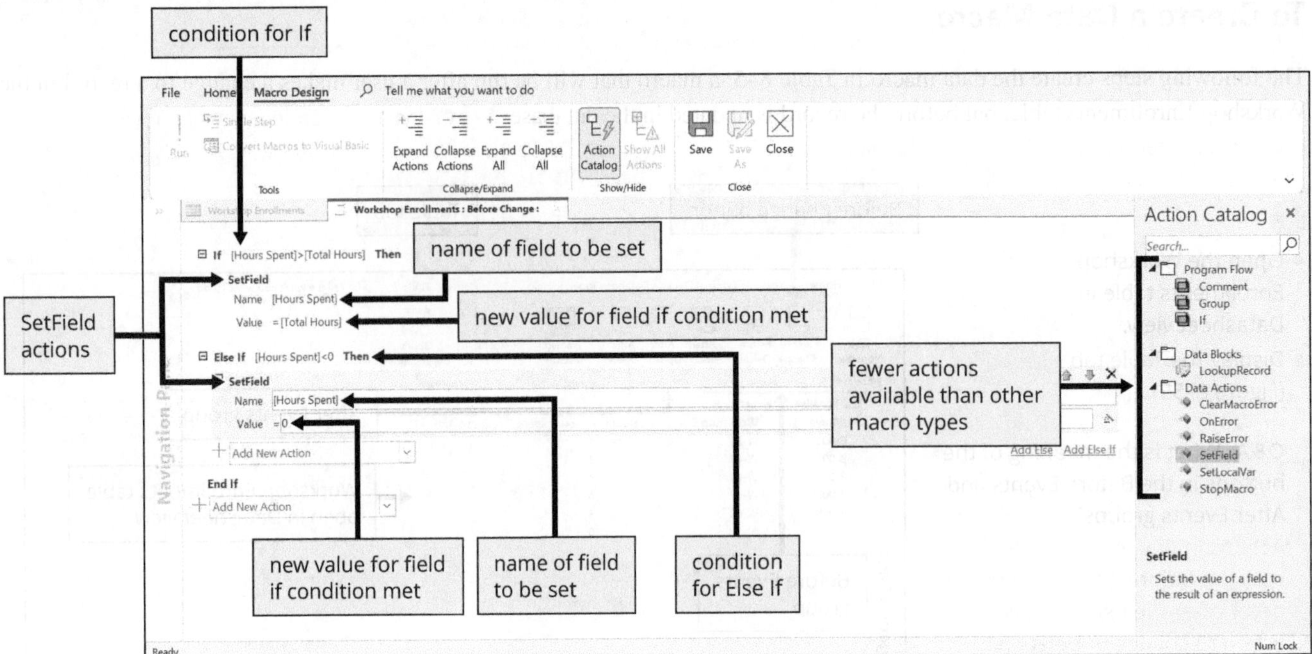

Figure 8–56

- Save and close the macro.
- Save and close the Workshop Enrollments table. The discussion in the following section will explore the effects of the new macro.
- If desired, sign out of your Microsoft account.
- **sam** Exit Access.

Note: Unless your instructor indicates otherwise, you are encouraged to simply read the material in this module from this point on for understanding without carrying out any operations.

Q&A What did I accomplish with these changes?
The preceding steps set parameters for data values in the Workshop Enrollments table. The following section will demonstrate the boundaries of these parameters and the actions the macro will take to prevent data from straying outside these limitations.

Using a Table That Contains a Data Macro

If you update a table that contains a data macro, the actions in the data macro will be executed whenever the corresponding event takes place. If the data macro corresponds to the Before Change event, the actions will be executed after the user has changed the data, but before the change is saved in the database. With the data macro you just created, for example, if a user attempts to change the data in such a way that the Hours Spent is greater than the Total Hours (Figure 8–57a), as soon as the user takes an action that would require saving the record, Access makes Hours Spent equal to Total Hours (Figure 8–57b). Likewise, if a user attempts to set Hours Spent to a negative number (Figure 8–58a), as soon as the user takes an action that would require saving the record, Access will set Hours Spent to 0 (Figure 8–58b). These changes will take place automatically, regardless of whether the user changes the values in Datasheet view, with a form, in an update query, or in any other fashion.

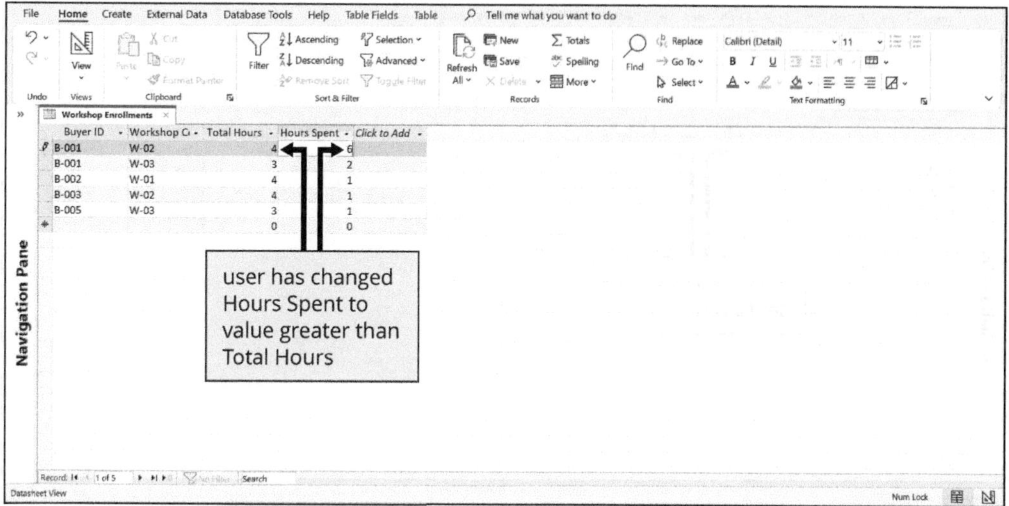

Figure 8–57a

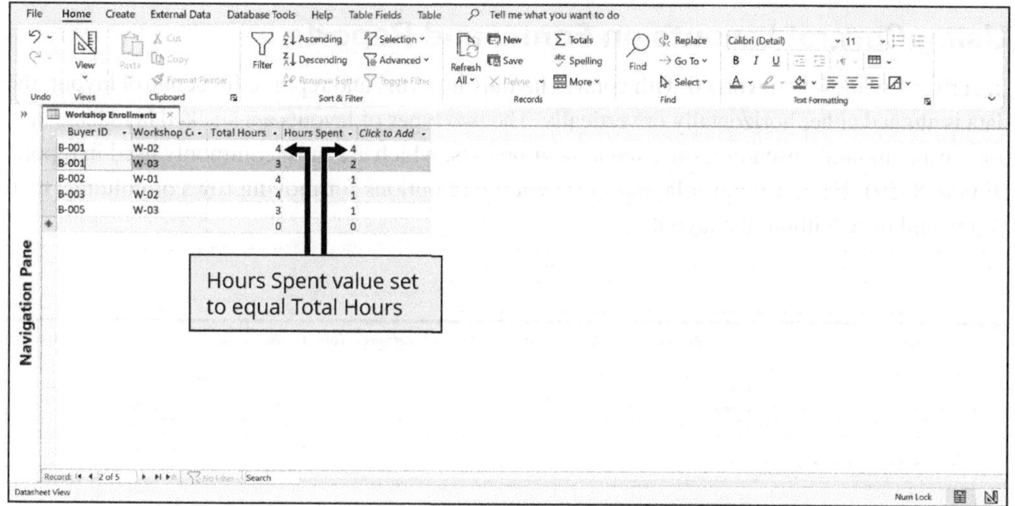

Figure 8–57b

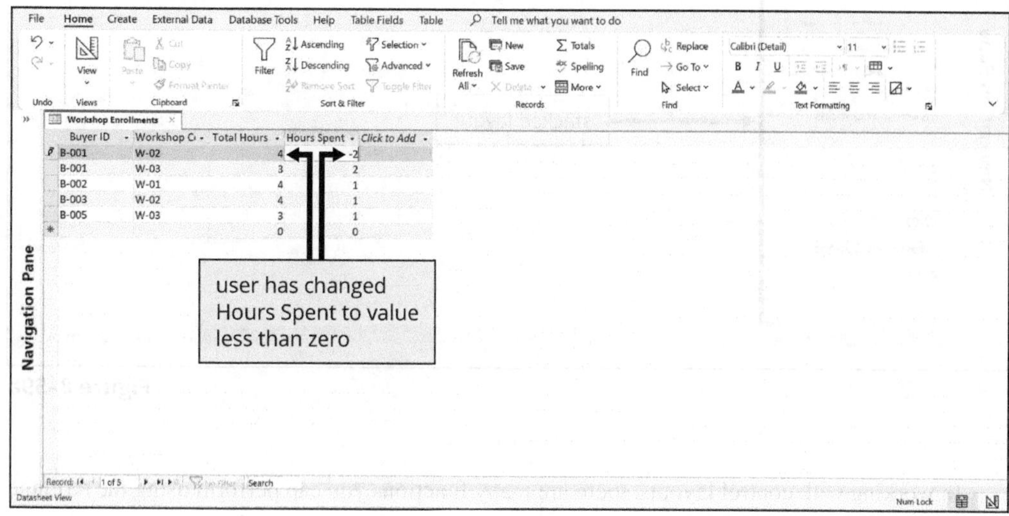

Figure 8–58a

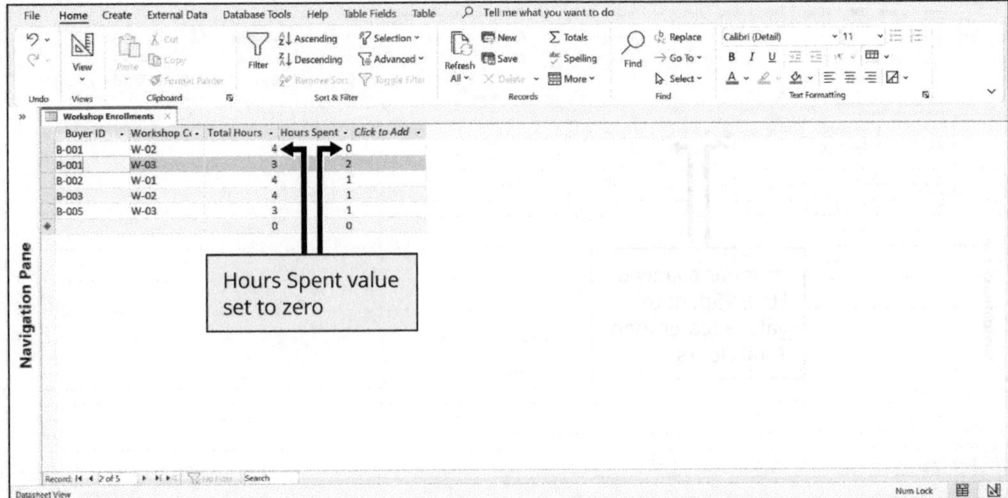

Figure 8–58b

Using Control Layouts on Forms and Reports

In earlier modules, you worked with control layouts in forms and reports. In a control layout, the data is aligned either horizontally or vertically. The two types of layouts are stacked layouts, which are most commonly used in forms, and tabular layouts, which are most commonly used in reports (Figure 8–59). Using a control layout gives you more options for moving rows or columns than you would have without the layout.

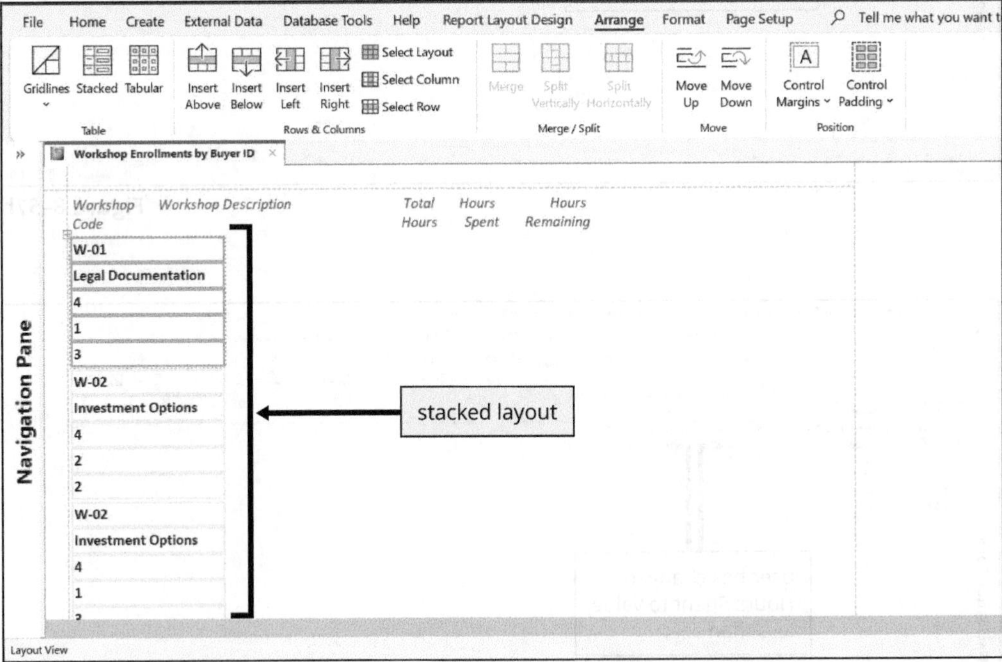

Figure 8–59a

In working with control layouts, there are many functions you can perform using the Arrange tab when the form is in Layout view. You can insert rows and columns, delete rows and columns, split and merge cells, and move rows. You can also change margins, which affects spacing within cells, and padding, which affects spacing between rows and columns. You can split a layout into

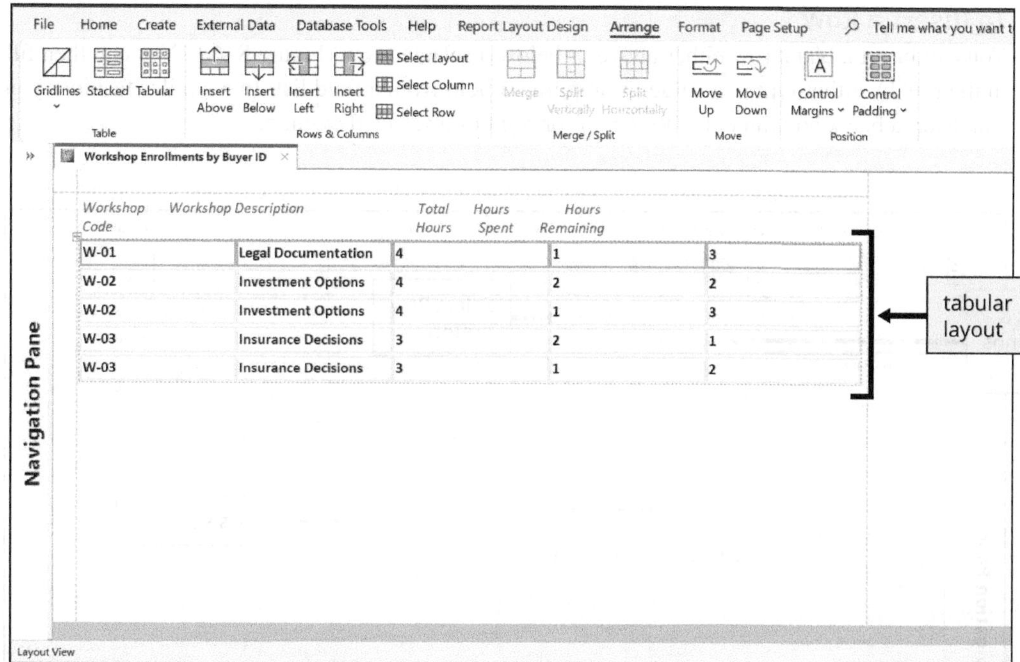

Figure 8–59b

two layouts and move layouts. Finally, you can anchor controls so they maintain the same distance between the control and the anchor position as the form or report is resized. Table 8–6 lists some of the functions available on the Arrange tab and the enhanced ScreenTip that explains their purpose.

Table 8–6 Arrange Tab

Button	Enhanced ScreenTip
Stacked	Create a layout similar to a paper form, with labels to the left of each field.
Tabular	Create a layout similar to a spreadsheet, with labels across the top and data in columns below the labels.
Split Vertically	Split the selected control into two rows.
Split Horizontally	Split the selected control into two columns.
Anchoring	Tie a control to a section or another control so that it moves or resizes in conjunction with movement or resizing of the parent.

To Create a Layout for a Form or Report

If you create a form using the Form button (Create tab | Forms group), Access automatically creates a stacked layout. If you create a report using the Report button (Create tab | Reports group), Access automatically creates a tabular layout. In other cases, you can create a layout using the Arrange tab. If you no longer want controls to be in a control layout, you can remove the layout.

To create a layout in either a form or report, you would use the following steps.

1. Select all the controls that you want to place in a layout.
2. Click the Stacked button (Arrange tab | Table group) to create a stacked layout or the Tabular button (Arrange tab | Table group) to create a tabular layout.

To Remove a Layout for a Form or Report

To remove a layout from either a form or report, you would use the following steps.

1. Right-click any control in the layout you want to remove to produce a shortcut menu.
2. Point to Layout on the shortcut menu, and then click Remove Layout on the submenu to remove the layout. Removing the layout does not reposition the controls.

To Insert a Row

You can insert a blank row either above or below a selected row (Figure 8–60). You can then fill in the row by either typing a value or dragging a field from a field list. In a similar fashion, you can insert a blank column either to the left or right of a selected column.

BTW
The Undo Button
When making changes with the Arrange tab buttons in Layout view, it is not uncommon to make a change that you did not intend, or one that you later change your mind about. Sometimes, taking appropriate action to reverse the change can prove difficult. If so, remember that you can undo the change by clicking the Undo button on the Quick Access Toolbar or on the Home tab. It is also a good idea to save your work frequently. That way, you can always close the form or report without saving. Then, when you reopen the form or report, it will not contain any of your most recent, unsaved, changes.

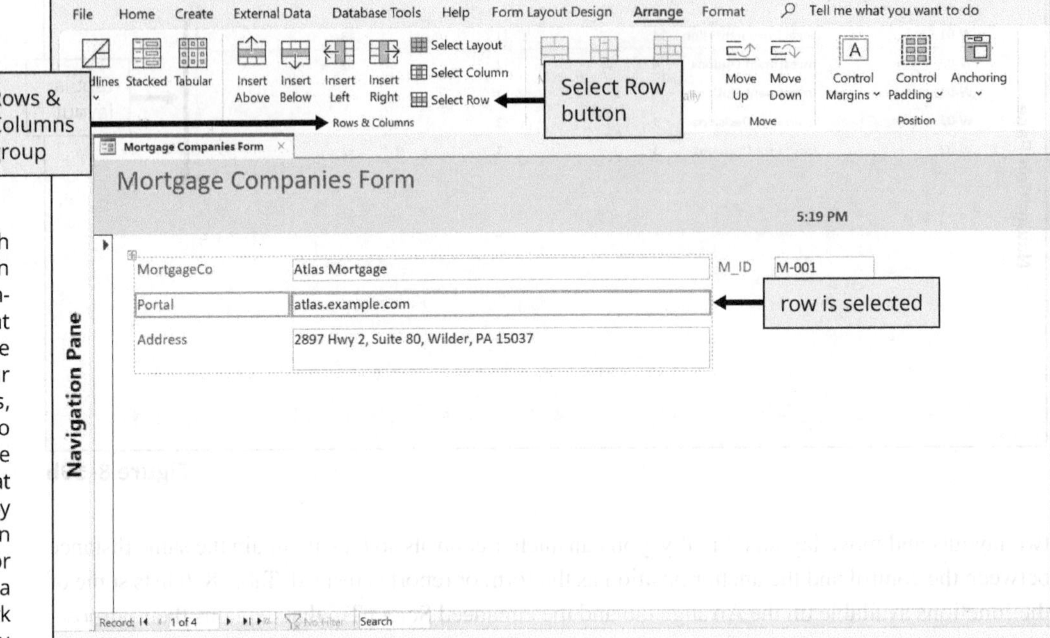

Figure 8–60a

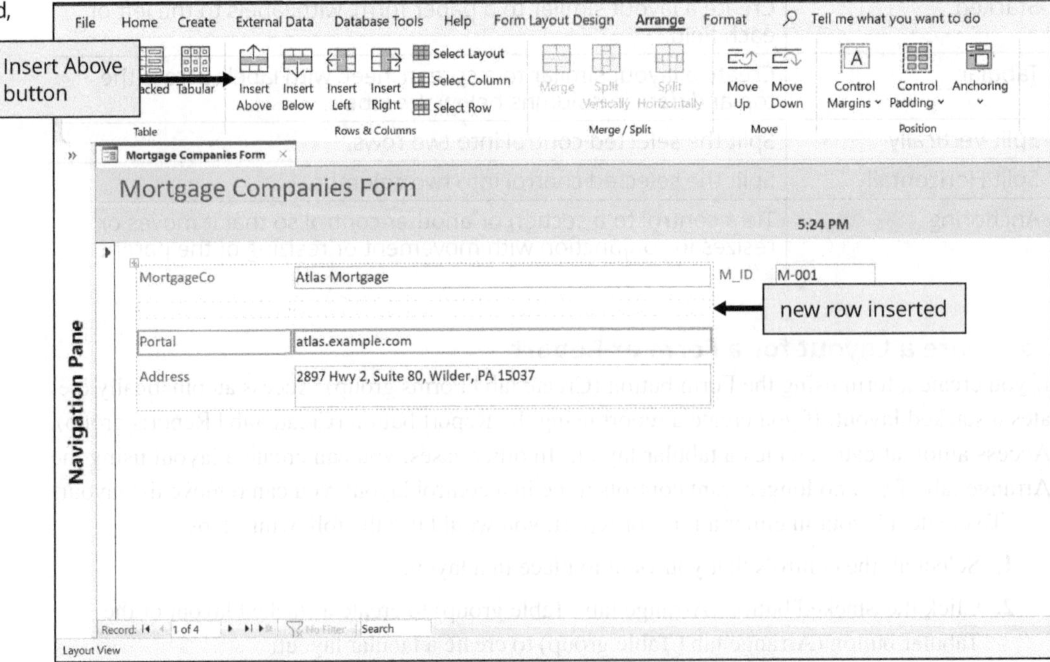

Figure 8–60b

You would use the following steps to insert a blank row.

1. Select any control in the row above or below where you want to insert a new row.
2. Click the Insert Above button (Arrange tab | Rows & Columns group) to insert a blank row above the selected row or the Insert Below button (Arrange tab | Rows & Columns group) to insert a blank row below the selected row.

As you learned earlier in the text, you also can insert a row containing a field by simply dragging the field from the field list to the desired location.

To Insert a Column

You would use the following steps to insert a new column.

1. Select any control in the column to the right or left of where you want to insert a new column.
2. Click the Insert Left button (Arrange tab | Rows & Columns group) to insert a blank column to the left of the selected column or the Insert Right button (Arrange tab | Rows & Columns group) to insert a blank column to the right of the selected column.

To Delete a Row

You can delete any unwanted row or column from a control layout. You would use the following steps to delete a row.

1. Click any control in the row you want to delete.
2. Click Select Row (Arrange tab | Rows & Columns group).
3. Press DEL to delete the row.

To Delete a Column

You would use the following steps to delete a column.

1. Click any control in the column you want to delete.
2. Click Select Column (Arrange tab | Rows & Columns group).
3. Press DEL to delete the column.

Splitting and Merging Cells

You can split a cell into two cells either horizontally, as shown in Figure 8–61, or vertically. You can then enter contents into the new cell. For example, in Figure 8–61, you could type text into the new cell that gives information about Property IDs or alternative contact information. You can also merge two cells into one.

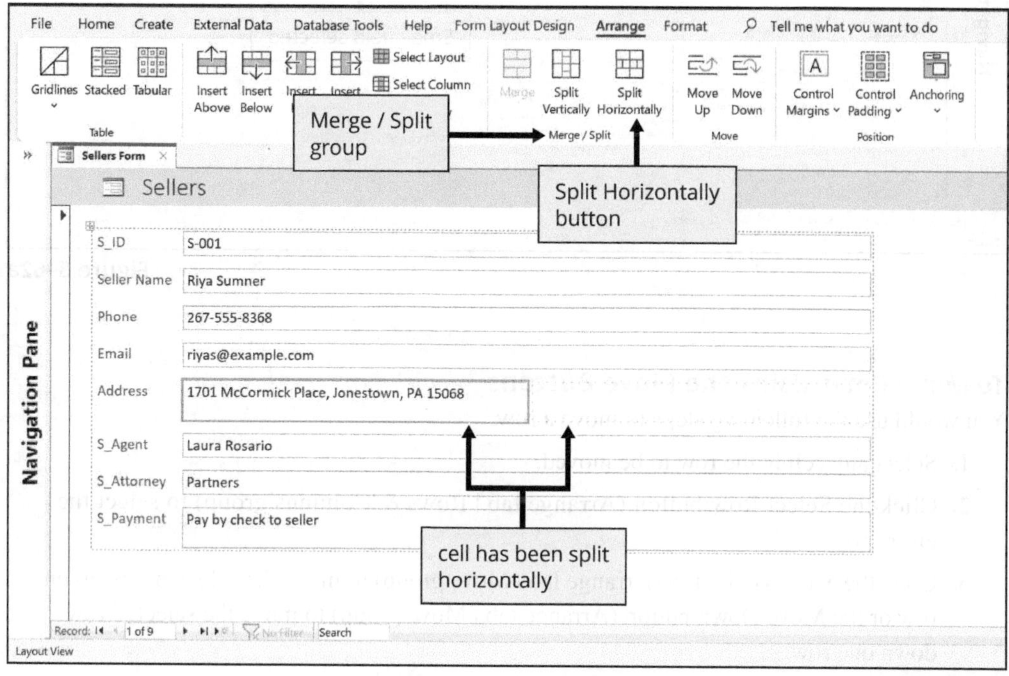

Figure 8–61

To Split a Cell

To split a cell, you would use the following steps.

1. Click the cell to be split.
2. Click the Split Vertically button (Arrange tab | Merge / Split group) to split the selected cell vertically or the Split Horizontally button (Arrange tab | Merge / Split group) to split the selected cell horizontally.

To Merge Cells

You would use the following steps to merge cells.

1. Select the first cell to be merged.
2. While holding down CTRL, click all the other cells to be merged.
3. Click the Merge button (Arrange tab | Merge / Split group) to merge the cells.

Moving Cells

You can move a cell in a layout by dragging it to its new position. Most often, however, you will not want to move individual cells, but rather whole rows (Figure 8–62). You can move a row by selecting the row and then dragging it to the new position, or you can use the Move buttons on the Arrange tab.

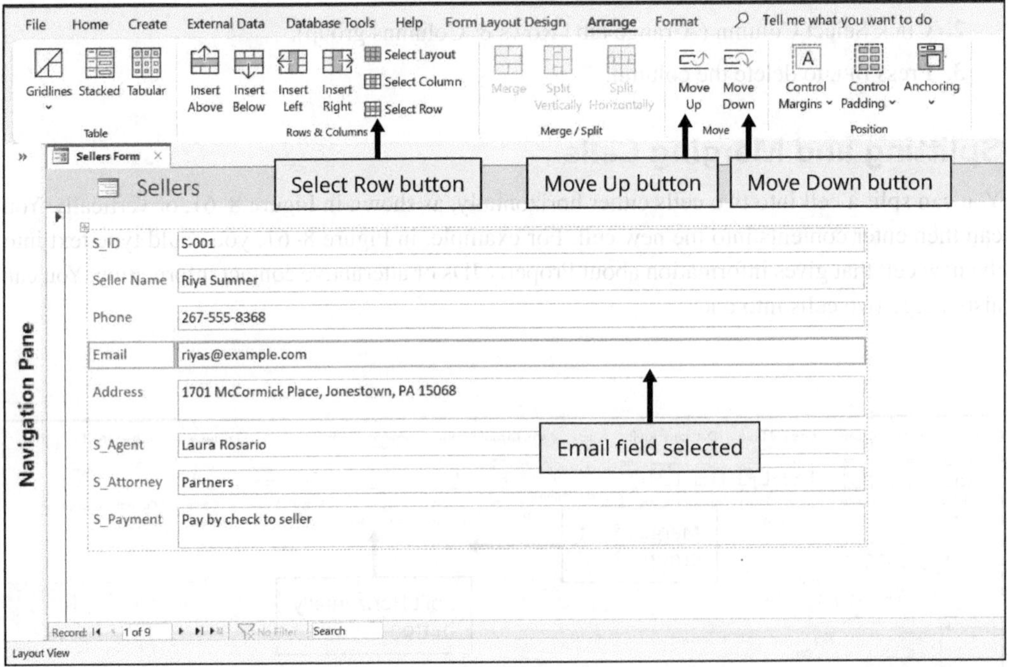

Figure 8–62a

To Move Rows Using the Move Buttons

You would use the following steps to move a row.

1. Select any cell in the row to be moved.
2. Click the Select Row button (Arrange tab | Rows & Columns group) to select the entire row.
3. Click the Move Up button (Arrange tab | Move group) to move the selected row up one row or the Move Down button (Arrange tab | Move group) to move the selected row down one row.

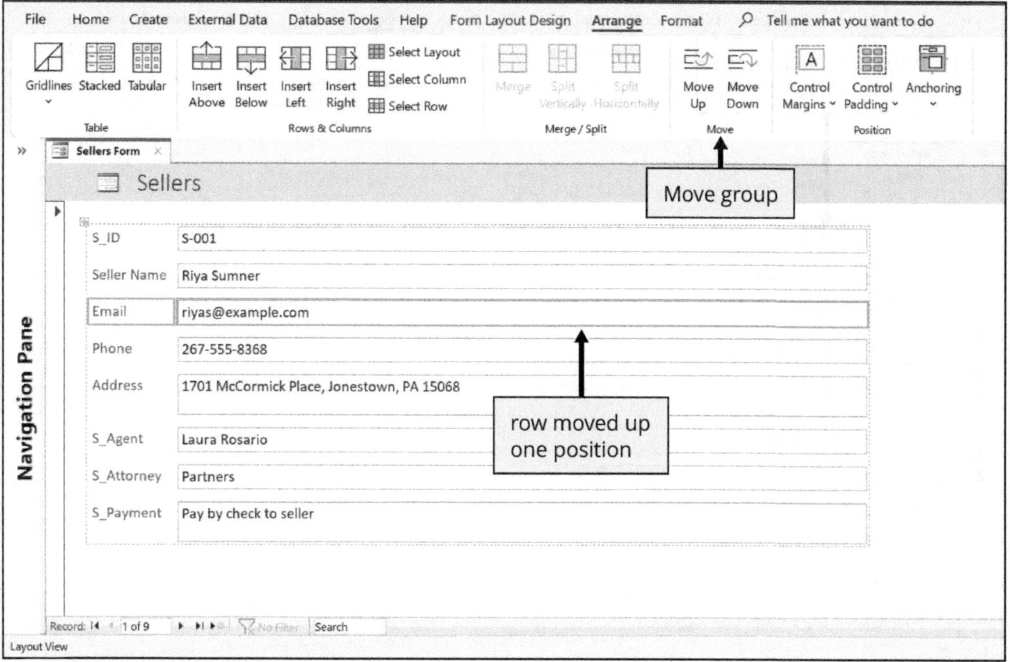

Figure 8–62b

Margins and Padding

You can change the spacing within a layout by changing the control margins and the control padding. The control margins, which you change with the Control Margins button, affect the spacing around the text inside a control. Figure 8–63 shows the various options as well as samples of two of the options.

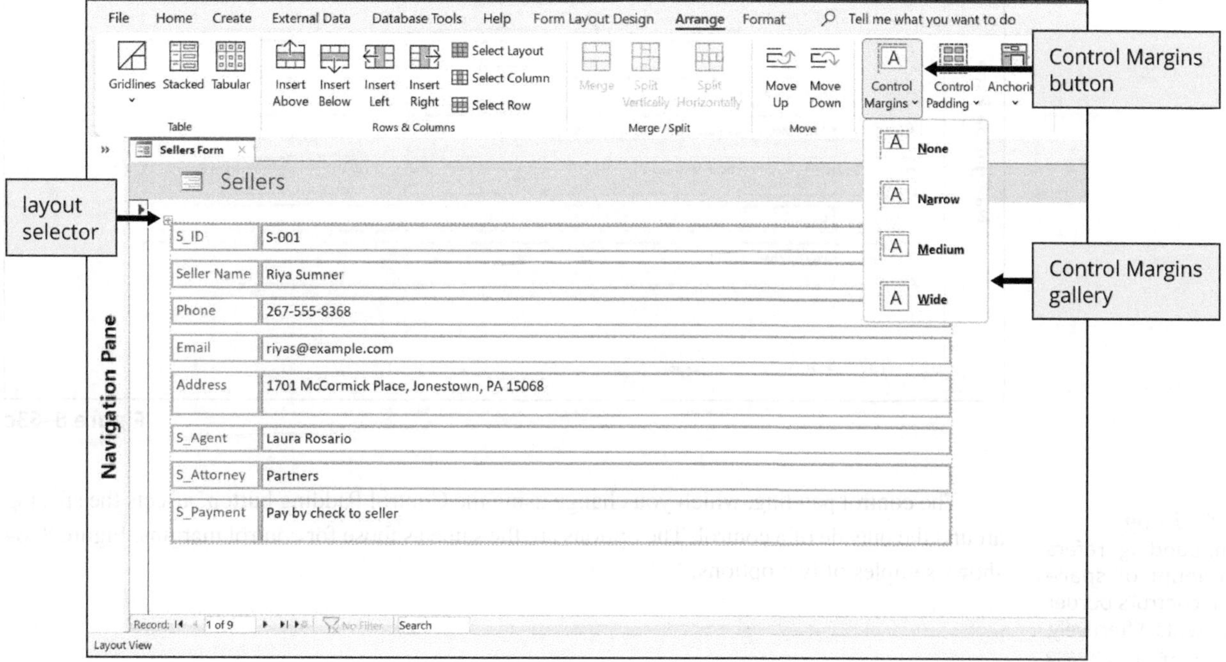

Figure 8–63a

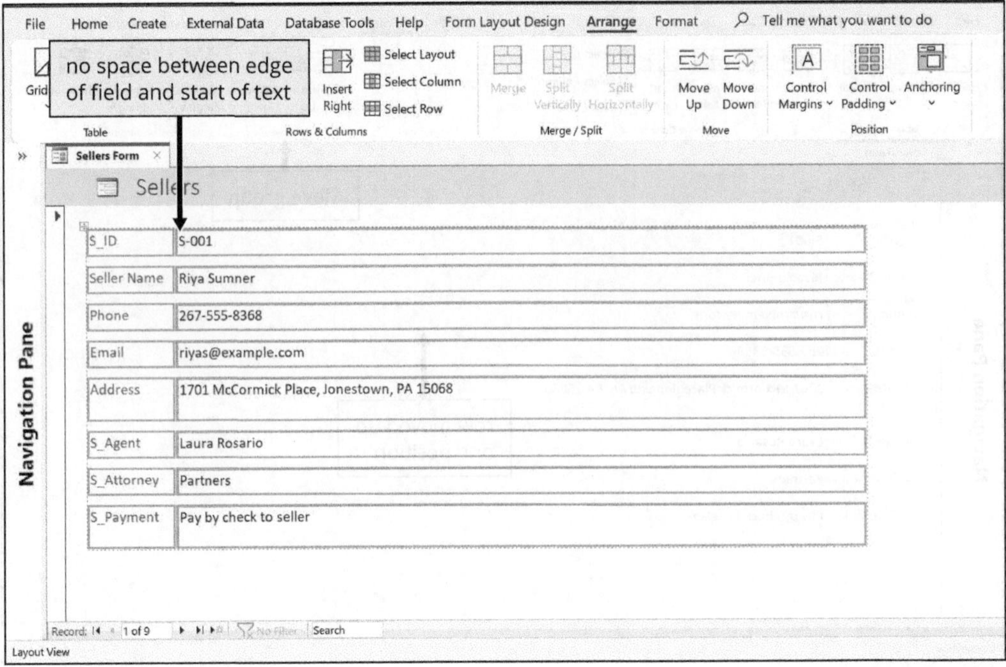

Figure 8–63b

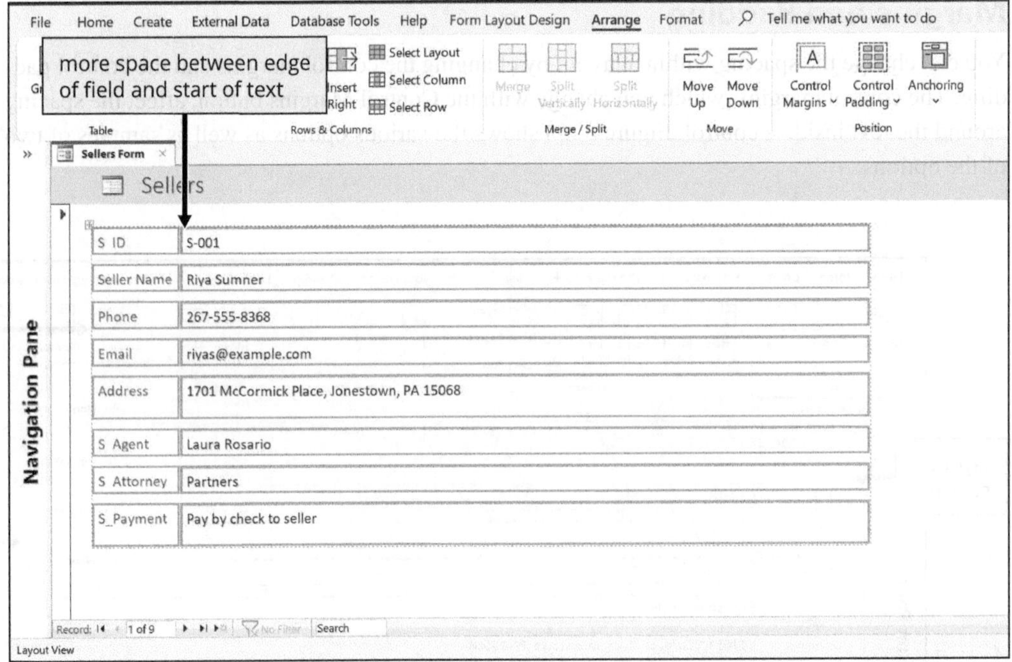

Figure 8–63c

BTW
Control Padding
The term, padding, refers to the amount of space between a control's border and its contents. Effectively, you can increase or decrease the amount of white space in a control.

The control padding, which you change using the Control Padding button, affects the spacing around the outside of a control. The options are the same as those for control margins. Figure 8–64 shows samples of two options.

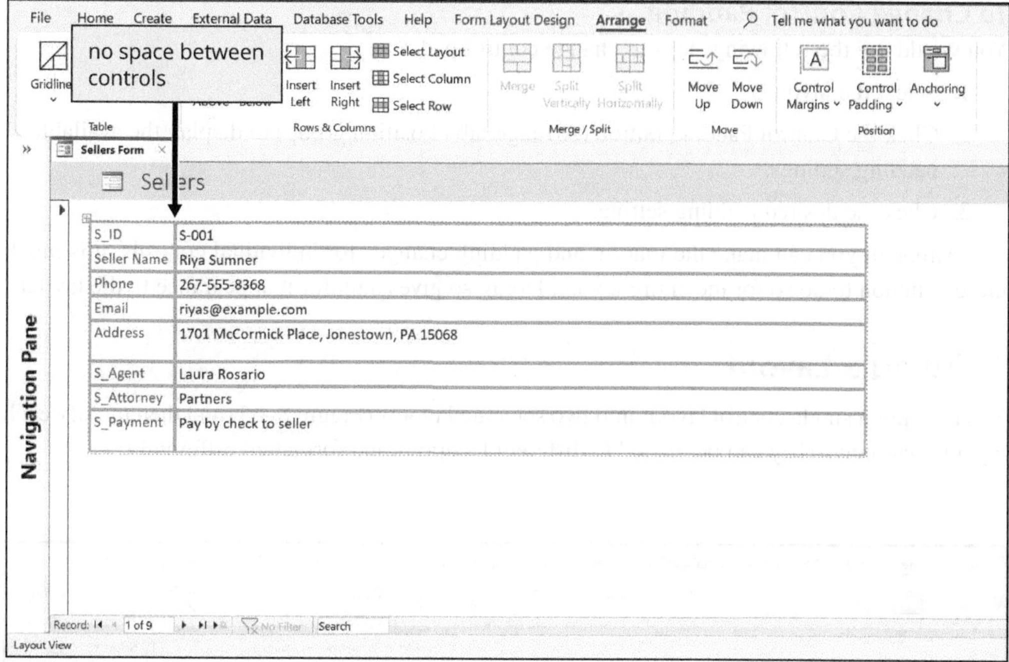

Figure 8–64a

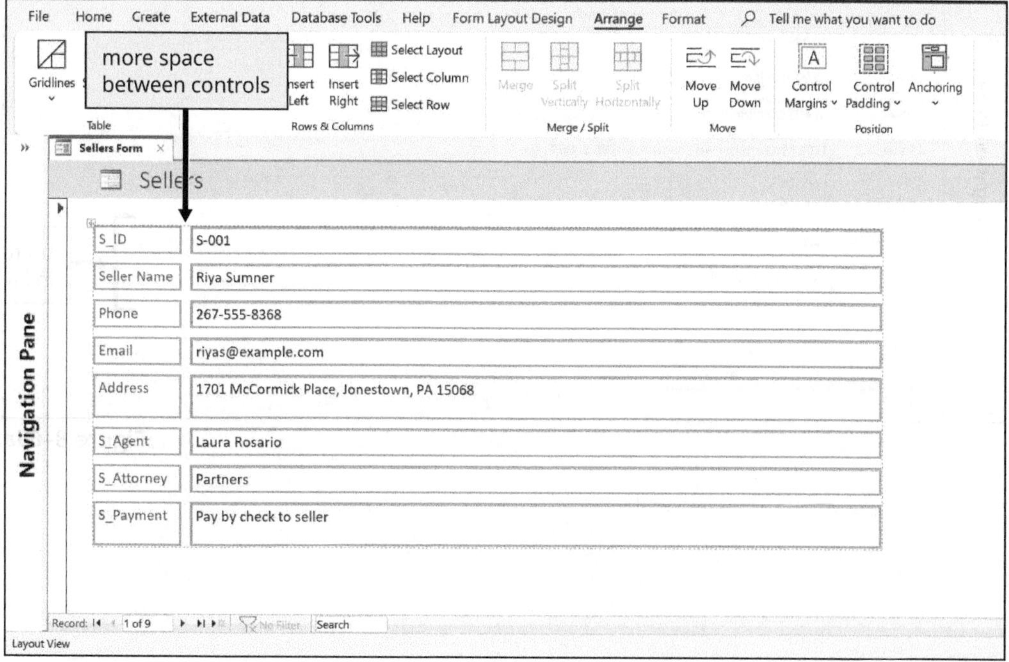

Figure 8–64b

To Change Control Margins

You would use the following steps to change a control's margins.

1. Select any cell in the layout.
2. Click the Select Layout button (Arrange tab | Rows & Columns group) to select the entire layout. (You also can select the layout by clicking the layout selector.)
3. Click the Control Margins button (Arrange tab | Position group) to display the available margin settings.
4. Click the desired margin setting.

To Change Control Padding

You would use the following steps to change control padding.

1. Select the layout.
2. Click the Control Padding button (Arrange tab | Position group) to display the available padding settings.
3. Click the desired padding setting.

Although you can make the margin and padding changes for individual controls, it is much more common to do so for the entire layout. Doing so gives a uniform appearance to the layout.

Splitting a Layout

You can split a single control layout into two separate layouts (Figure 8–65) and then modify each layout separately. They can be moved to different locations and formatted differently.

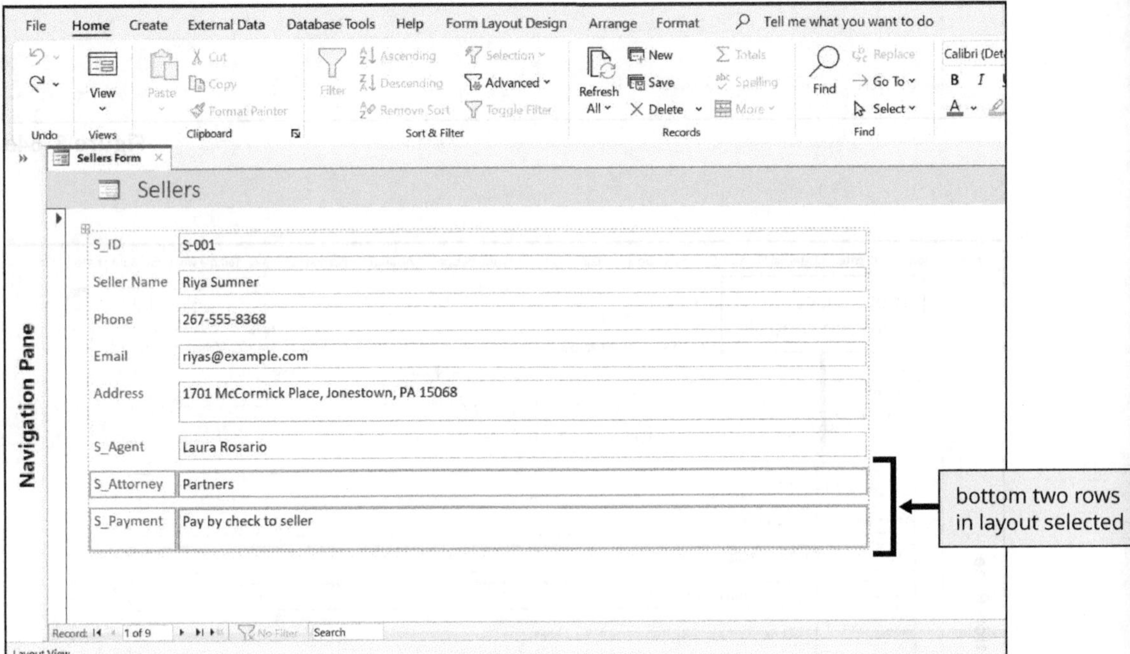

Figure 8–65a

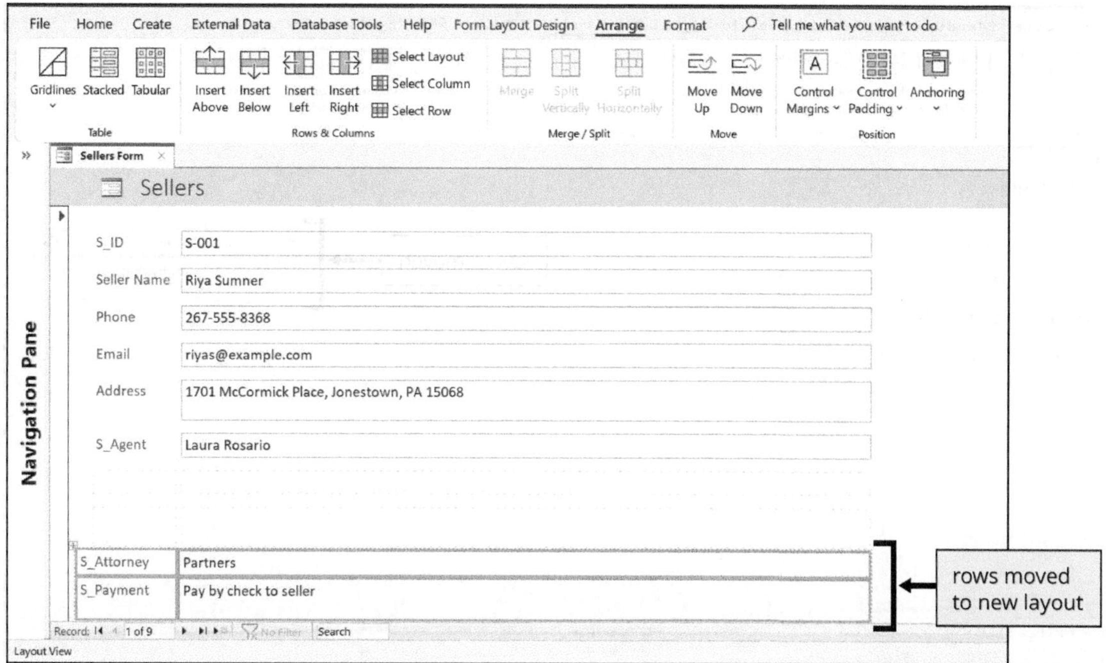

Figure 8–65b

To Split a Layout

To split a layout, you would use the following steps.

1. Select all the cells that you want to move to a new layout.
2. Click the Stacked button (Arrange tab | Table group) to place the cells in a stacked layout or the Tabular button (Arrange tab | Table group) to place the cells in a tabular layout.

BTW
Gridlines
You can add gridlines to a form. To do so, select the control(s) for which you want to add gridlines, then click the Gridlines button. When the Gridlines menu appears, select the desired option. You also can change the color, border, style, and width of gridlines using the Gridlines menu.

Moving a Layout

You can move a control layout to a different location on the form (Figure 8–66).

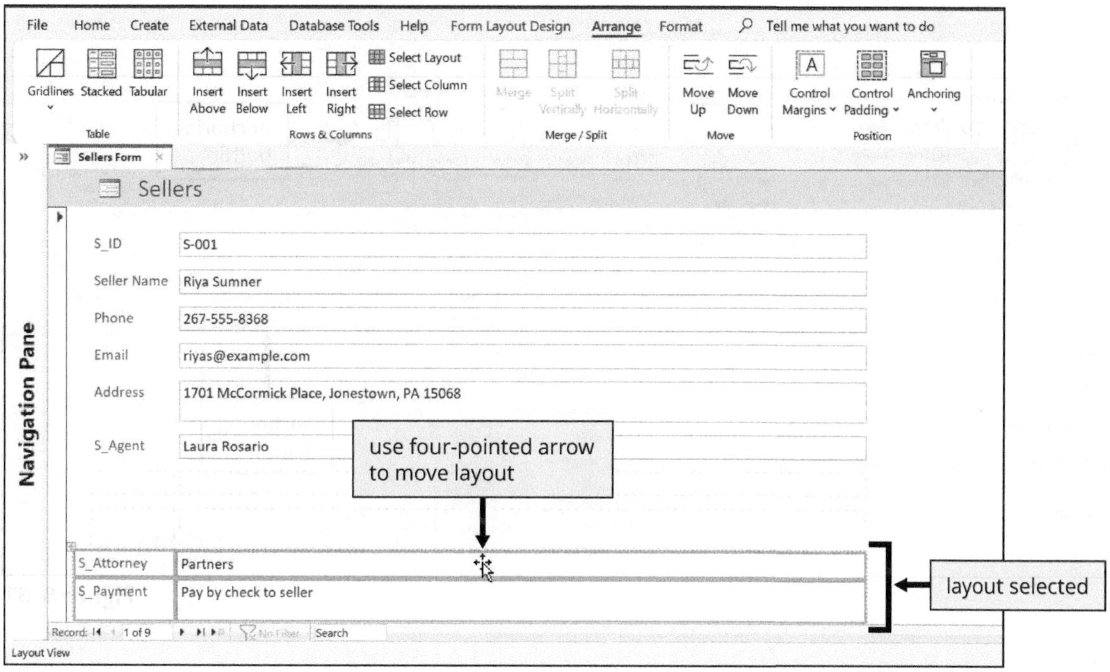

use four-pointed arrow to move layout

layout selected

Figure 8–66a

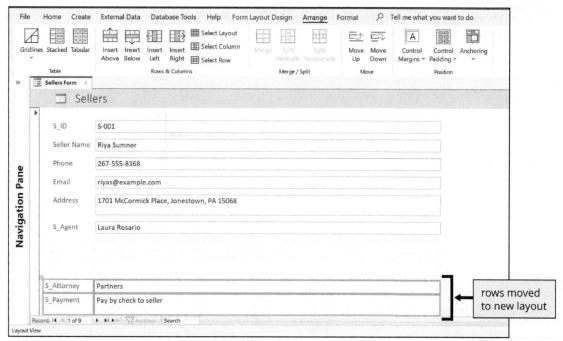

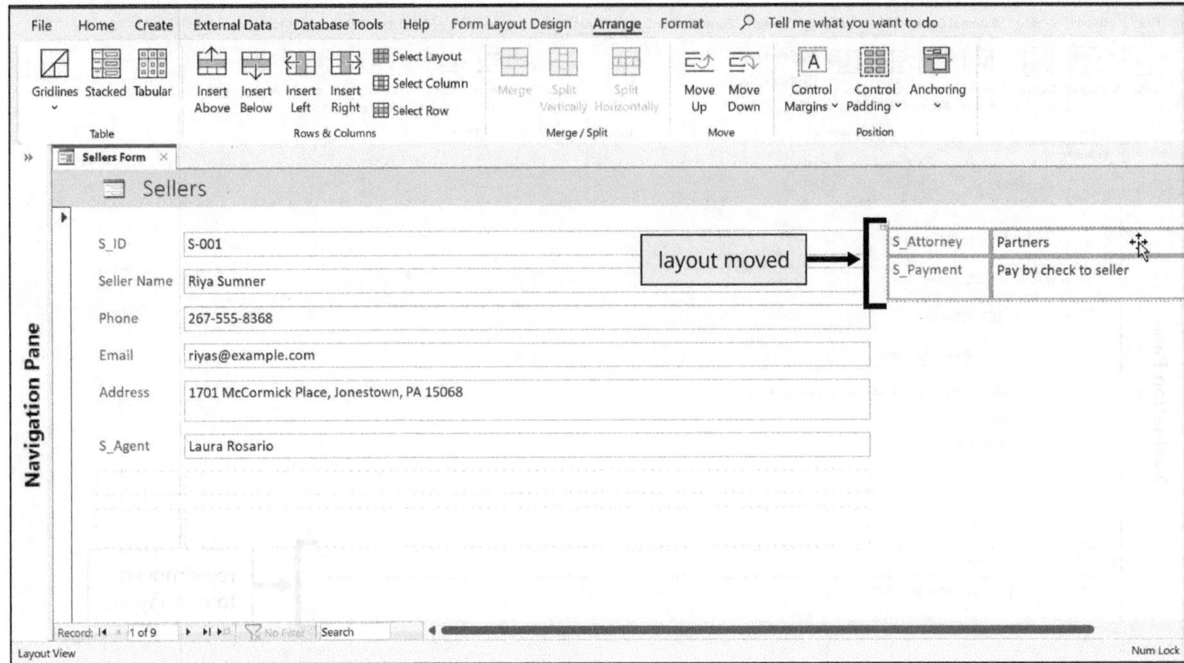

Figure 8–66b

To Move a Layout

You would use the following steps to move a layout.

1. Click any cell in the layout to be moved, and then click the Select Layout button (Arrange tab | Rows & Columns group) to select the layout.
2. Drag the layout to the new location.

Anchoring Controls

The Anchoring button allows you to tie (anchor) controls to a section or to other controls so they maintain the same distance between the control and the anchor position as the form is resized. To anchor the controls you have selected, you use the Anchoring gallery (Figure 8–67).

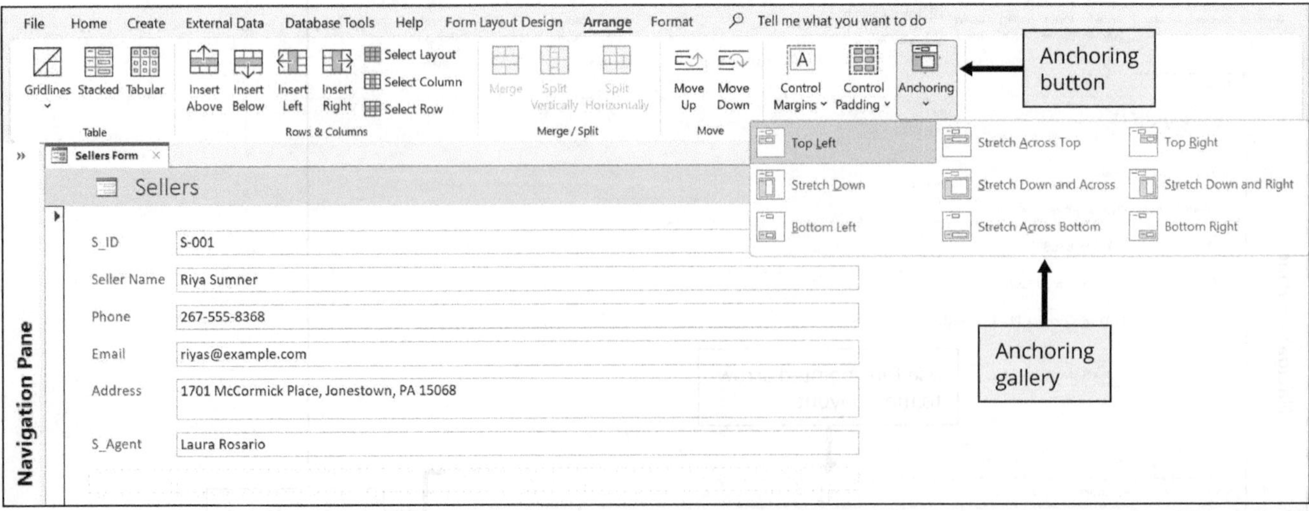

Figure 8–67

The Top Left, Top Right, Bottom Left, and Bottom Right options anchor the control in the indicated position on the form. The other five operations also stretch the controls in the indicated direction.

To Anchor Controls

You would use the following steps to anchor controls.

1. Select the control or controls to be anchored.
2. Click the Anchoring button (Arrange tab | Position group) to produce the Anchoring gallery.
3. Select the desired Anchoring option from the Anchoring gallery.

Overlapping Windows

To view the effect of anchoring, you need to display objects in overlapping windows rather than standard tabbed documents. With overlapping windows, you can resize the object by dragging the border of the object. Anchored objects keep their same relative position (Figure 8–68).

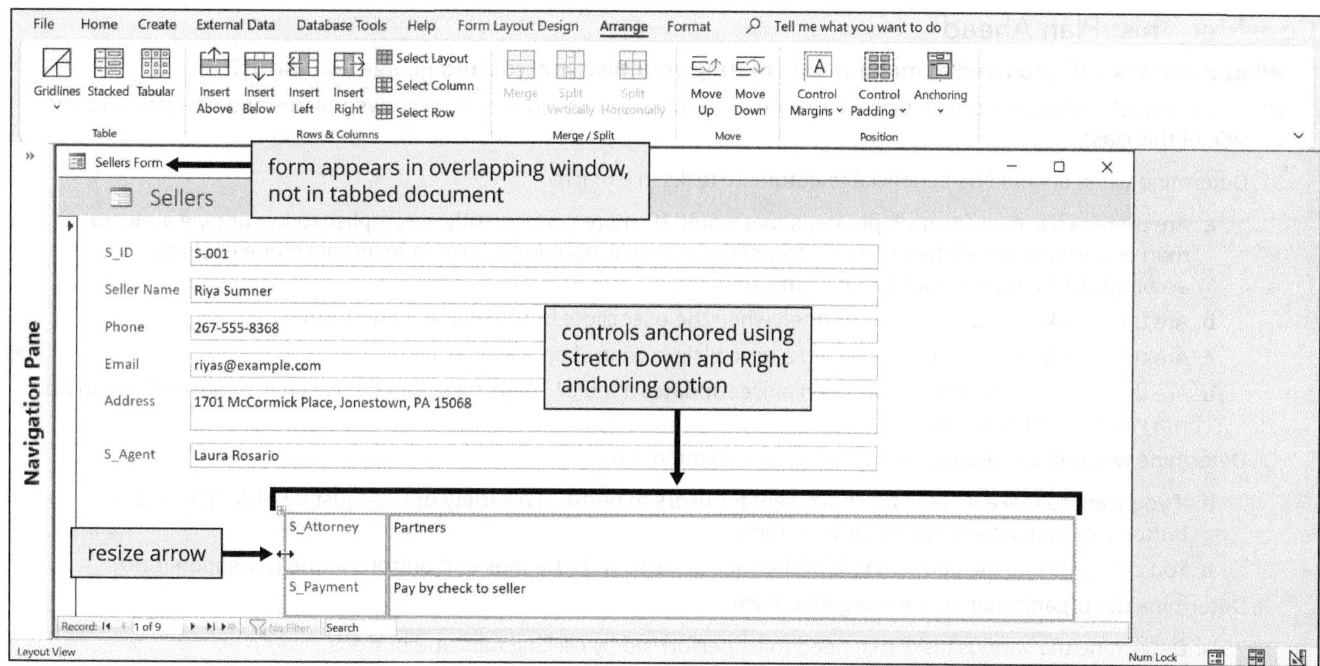

Figure 8–68

If you want to display objects in overlapping windows, you have to modify the appropriate Access option.

To Display Objects in Overlapping Windows

You would use the following steps to overlap windows.

1. Click File on the ribbon to open Backstage view.
2. Click Options to display the Access Options dialog box.
3. Click Current Database to display the Current Database options.
4. In the Application Options area, click the Overlapping Windows option button.
5. Click the OK button to close the Access Options dialog box.
6. For the changes to take effect, you will need to close and then reopen the database.

   You use a similar process to return to displaying objects in tabbed documents.

BTW
Overlapping Windows
When you display objects in overlapping windows, each database object appears in its own window. When multiple objects are open, these windows overlap each other. By default, Access displays database objects in a single pane separated by tabs.

To Display Objects in Tabbed Documents

You would use the following steps to display tabbed documents.

1. Click File on the ribbon to open Backstage view.
2. Click Options to display the Access Options dialog box.
3. Click Current Database to display the Current Database options.
4. In the Application Options area, click the Tabbed Documents option button.
5. Click the OK button to close the Access Options dialog box.
6. For the changes to take effect, you will need to close and then reopen the database.

Summary

In this module you have learned to create and use macros, create a menu form that uses command buttons for the choices, create a menu form that uses an option group for the choices, create a macro that implements the choices in the option group, create datasheet forms that utilize user interface macros, create a navigation form, add tabs to a navigation form, and create data macros. You also learned to modify control layouts.

Consider This: Plan Ahead

What decisions will you need to make when creating your own macros and navigation forms?

Use these guidelines as you complete the assignments in this module and create your own macros and navigation forms outside of this class.

1. Determine when it would be beneficial to automate tasks in a macro.
    a. Are there tasks involving multiple steps that would be more conveniently accomplished by running a macro than by carrying out all the individual steps? For example, opening a form in read-only mode could be accomplished conveniently through a macro.
    b. Are there tasks that are to be performed when the user clicks buttons on a menu form?
    c. Are there tasks to be performed when a user clicks a control on a form?
    d. Are there tasks to be performed when a user updates a table? These tasks can be placed in a macro that can be run when the button is clicked.
2. Determine whether it is appropriate to create a navigation form.
    a. If you want to make it easy and convenient for users to perform a variety of tasks just by clicking tabs and buttons, consider creating a navigation form.
    b. You can associate the performance of the various tasks with the tabs and buttons in the navigation form.
3. Determine the organization of the navigation form.
    a. Determine the various tasks that need to be performed by clicking tabs and buttons.
    b. Decide the logical grouping of the tabs and buttons.

Consider This

How should you submit solutions to critical thinking questions in the assignments?

Every assignment in this course contains one or more critical thinking questions. These questions require you to think beyond the assigned database. Present your responses to the questions in the format required by your instructor. Possible formats might include one or more of these options: write the answer; create a document that contains the answer; present your answer to the class; discuss your answer in a group; record the answer as audio or video using a webcam, smartphone, or portable media player; or post answers on a blog, wiki, or website.

Student Assignments

Apply Your Knowledge

Reinforce the skills and apply the concepts you learned in this module.

Creating UI Macros and a Navigation Form

Note: To complete this assignment, you will be required to use the Data Files. Please contact your instructor for information about accessing the Data Files.

Instructions: Start Access. Open the database, SC_AC_08-2.accdb, which is located in the Data Files folder. Enable the content.

Perform the following tasks:

1. Save the database using the file name, SC_AC_08_Construction. Enable the content.
2. Create a datasheet form for the Job Sites table and name the form Job Sites List.
3. Create a UI macro for the Job Sites List form. Use JS as the temporary variable name. When a user clicks a job site number on a row in the datasheet form, the Job Sites List form should appear in a dialog window in read-only mode. Remove the temporary variable.
4. Create a datasheet form for the Subcontractors table and save the form with the name Subcontractors. Create a UI macro for the Subcontractors form. Use SC as the temporary variable name. When a user clicks a subcontractor number on a row in the datasheet form, the Subcontractors form should appear in a dialog window in read-only mode. Remember to remove the temporary variable as part of good database management.
5. Create the navigation form shown in Figure 8–69. The purpose of the form is to display the two datasheet forms in the database as horizontal tabs. Name the form Main Menu and change the title to Build It Construction: Main Menu. Save and close the form.

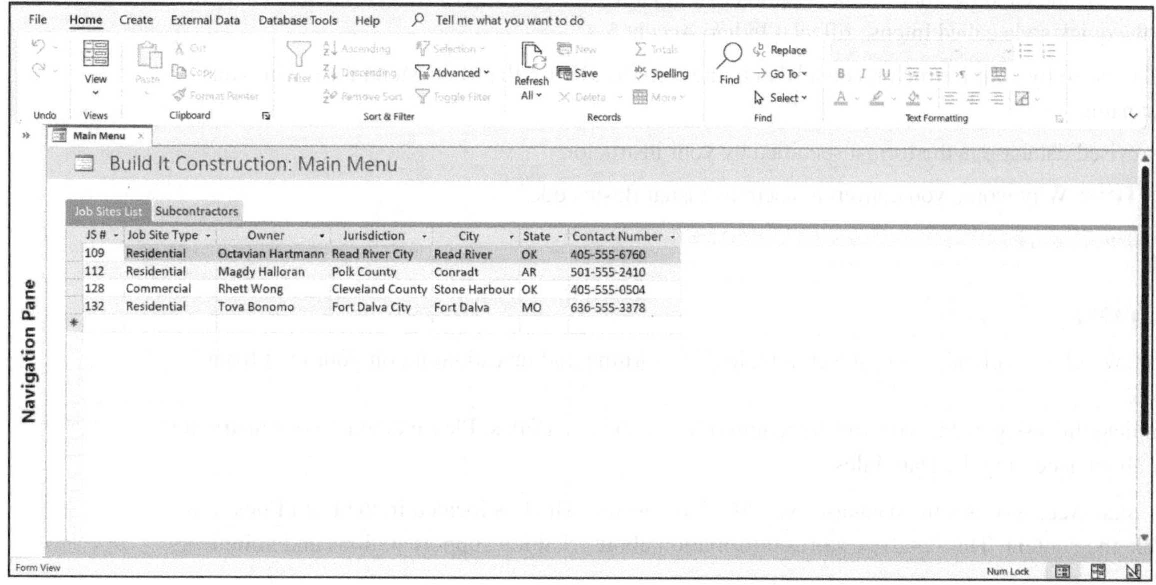

Figure 8–69

6. If requested to do so by your instructor, open the Subcontractors datasheet form and change the first and last names of subcontractor SC040 to your first and last name.
7. Submit the revised database in the format specified by your instructor.
8. **Consider This:** How could you add an Accounting datasheet form to the navigation form?

Extend Your Knowledge

Extend the skills you learned in this module and experiment with new skills. You may need to use Help to complete the assignment.

Creating and Modifying Navigation Forms

Note: To complete this assignment, you will be required to use the Data Files. Please contact your instructor for information about accessing the Data Files.

Instructions: Start Access. Open the database, SC_AC_08-3.accdb, which is located in the Data Files folder. PicsPlus is a photographers' cooperative that is applying for a grant. To complete the grant application, the PicsPlus database needs to be updated so it is compatible with the configurations required in the grant standards and so the files can be exported as required for grant consideration.

Perform the following tasks:

1. Save the database using the file name, SC_AC_08_PicsPlus. Enable the content.
2. Create a menu form named Forms List that contains command buttons that open the Clients by Photographer form and the Photographer Form in Edit mode.
3. Create a form named Reports List that contains a macro to open the Photographer Balances Summary Report.
4. Create a Main Menu form for forms and reports. The Forms List menu should include the command buttons for the Clients by Photographer form and the Photographer Form. The Reports List menu should include a command button for the summary report. Test the macros before closing the form.
5. Open the Forms List form in Design view. Select the button controls, and change the font weight to semi-bold. Use the Size/Space menu to adjust the controls to be the same width as the widest button. Change the buttons' back color and border color to colors of your choice. Change the buttons' hover color to Brown. Test the formatting changes in Form view.
6. Open the Reports List form in Design view and make the same changes that you made to the Forms List form.
7. Open the Main Menu navigation form in Layout view. Change the shape of the Forms List tab to Rectangle: Single Corner Rounded and the shape of the Reports List tab to Rectangle: Top Corners Rounded. On both tabs, apply the quick style called Intense Effect – Indigo Accent 5.
8. If requested to do so by your instructor, add a label to the form header for the Main Menu form with your first and last name.
9. Submit the revised database in the format specified by your instructor.
10. **Consider This:** Why would you convert a macro to Visual Basic code?

Expand Your World

Create a solution, which uses cloud and web technologies, by learning and investigating on your own from general guidance.

Note: To complete this assignment, you will be required to use the Data Files. Please contact your instructor for information about accessing the Data Files.

Instructions: Start Access. Open the database, SC_AC_08-4.accdb, which is located in the Data Files folder, and enable the content. This database stores information about triathlon support stations and volunteers at each station.

Perform the following tasks:

1. Save the database using the file name, SC_AC_08_Triathlon. Enable the content.
2. Open the Volunteer Station Form in Layout view. Split the existing control layout so the station information is listed to the right of the volunteer information, as shown in Figure 8–70. Be sure to remove any remaining blank rows.

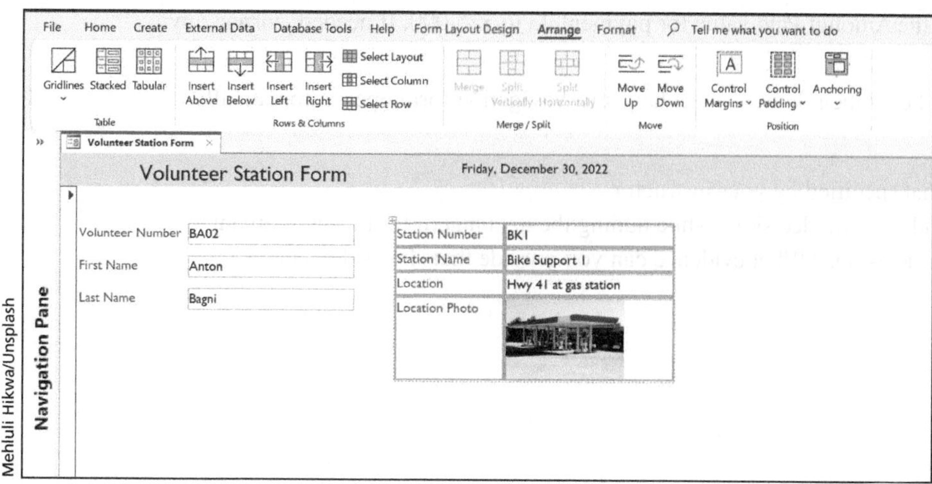

Figure 8–70

3. Insert a new row below the Last Name field. Name the new row Email.
4. Create a menu form named Reports List containing an option group with the caption Report Actions. Include options to preview or export to PDF each of the two reports, and configure no default choice.
5. **Consider This:** Research online to determine the differences between importing a database object between Access databases and exporting a database object between Access databases. What are two, significant limitations of the export operation compared to the import operation between Access databases?
6. Submit your research response and the revised database in the format specified by your instructor.
7. **Consider This:** What macros did you create for this project? Why did you make those choices?

In the Lab

Design and implement a solution using creative thinking and problem-solving skills.

Lab: Adding a Navigation Form to the Homegrown Nursing Staff Agency Database

Note: To complete this assignment, you will be required to use the Data Files. Please contact your instructor for information about accessing the Data Files.

Problem: Homegrown Nursing Staff Agency would like you to create a main menu that allows easy access to forms and reports. They also need a way to ensure traveler payments do not exceed the amount due.

Perform the following tasks:

Part 1: Open the SC_AC_08-5.accdb database from the Data Files folder. Save the file with the name, SC_AC_08_Travel-Nurses, and enable the content. Use the concepts and techniques presented in this module to perform each of the following tasks.

1. Create a form with macro command buttons that open the Facility Assignments Form and the Traveler Assignments Form in Read Only mode. Name the form List of Available Forms.
2. Create a form with macro buttons that opens the Assignment Bill Rates report and the Travelers and Payments Summary List report. Name the form List of Available Reports.
3. Create a Main Menu navigation form that includes the List of Available Forms form and the List of Available Reports form. Test the navigation form and correct any errors.
4. Add a data macro to the Traveler Payments table that replaces any value entered into the Amount Paid field that is greater than the value in the Current Due field with the value of the Current Due field.

Continued on next page

5. To test the data macro, change the Amount Paid value for payment 23 to $25,000. If needed, correct any errors in the data macro.
6. **Consider This:** Research and document how you can have the Navigation form open automatically when the database is opened.

Submit your assignment in the format specified by your instructor.

Part 2: **Consider This:** You made several decisions while adding the data macro for this assignment. What was the rationale behind your decisions? What evidence can you provide that shows the data macro works as intended?

Administering a Database System

Objectives

After completing this module, you will be able to:

- Explain how to convert a database between versions of Access
- Use the Table Analyzer, Performance Analyzer, and Database Documenter
- Create custom categories and groups in the Navigation Pane
- Modify table, database, and field properties
- Create an index
- Enable automatic error checking
- Create a custom data type
- Create a database template
- Select a startup form
- Create an application part
- Use a database template
- Explain how to encrypt a database with a password
- Explain how to lock a database
- Explain how to split a database

Introduction

Administering a database system is an important activity that has many facets. Administrative activities are an important aspect of database management because they improve the usability, accessibility, security, and efficiency of the database. In this module, you will learn how to perform a variety of database administration tasks.

Project: Administering a Database System

Clearnet realizes the importance of database administration, that is, the importance of administering its database system responsibly and with the user experience in mind. An important activity in administering databases is the creation of custom templates, application parts, and data type parts. A **custom template** is a customized database application that can be used as a basis for additional databases. The template contains tables, forms, queries, and other objects that can be used by others to create a database based on that template. Application parts and data type parts are templates included in Access that you can add to your database to extend its functionality. Clicking an application part adds to your database a predetermined collection of objects such as tables, queries, forms, reports, and macros. Clicking a data type part adds a predetermined collection of fields to a table. Creating an understandable startup form gives database users easy access to the forms when the database is opened.

Clearnet has decided to create a streamlined version of its database that drivers can use to track their own loads. As drivers are contacted with offers of additional loads, it's helpful for them to have all relevant information in one place to help them decide which loads will be cost effective for them to take. The Clearnet staff organizing the driver database realize that some drivers might not be familiar with operating a database, and a startup menu would be extremely helpful. Figure 9–1 shows a startup form that is automatically opened when the database is opened.

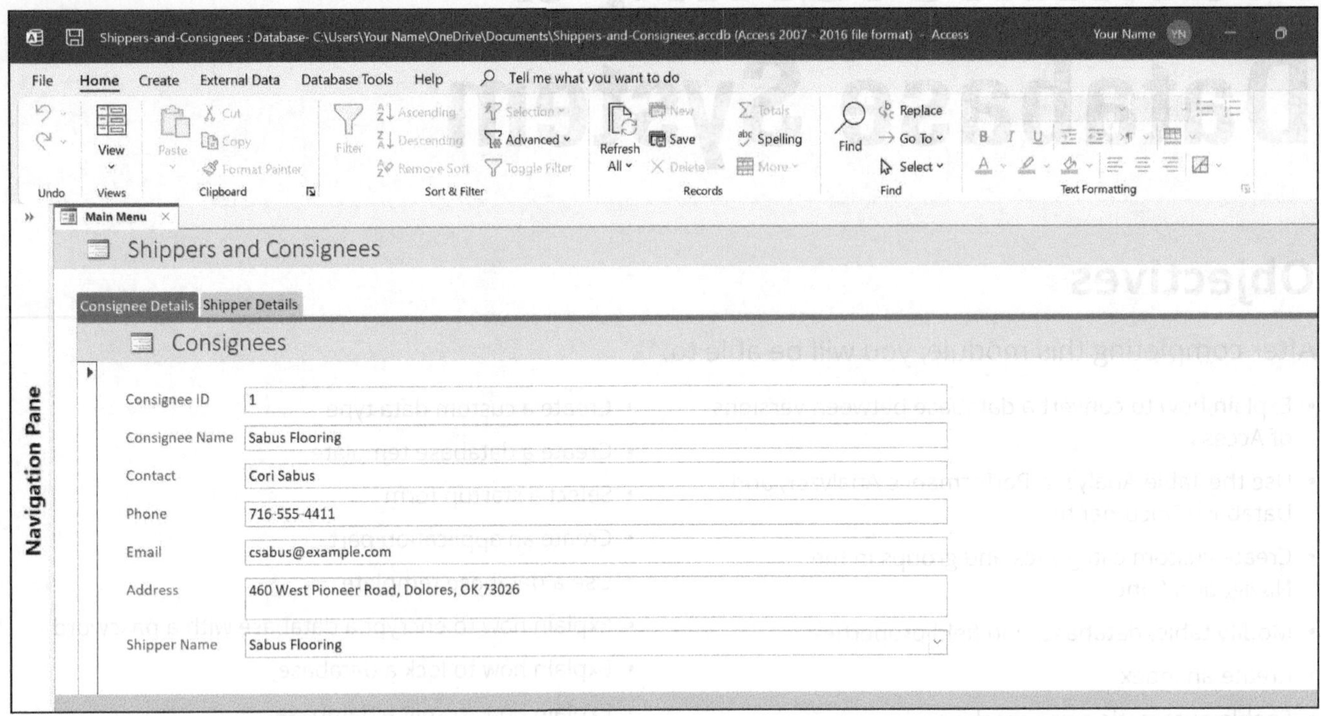

Figure 9–1

BTW
Enabling the Content
For each of the databases you use in this module, you will need to enable the content.

BTW
The Ribbon and Screen Resolution
Access may change how the groups and buttons within the groups appear on the ribbon, depending on the computer's screen resolution. Thus, your ribbon may look different from the ones in this book if you are using a screen resolution other than 1920 x 1080.

For Clearnet's own, internal database, performing administration tasks and reviewing database protection procedures will improve the Clearnet database system and enable all employees to use it more easily and securely. Figure 9–2 illustrates the range of activities involved in database administration, including the conversion of an Access database to an earlier version of Access. Database administration usually includes such activities as analyzing tables for potential problems, analyzing performance to see if changes could make the system perform more efficiently, and documenting the various objects in the database. It can include creating custom categories and groups in the Navigation Pane as well as changing table and database properties. It can also include the use of field properties in such tasks as creating a custom input mask and allowing zero-length strings. It can include the creation of indexes to speed up retrieval. The inclusion of automatic error checking is part of the administration of a database system. Understanding the purpose of the Trust Center is critical to the database administration function. Another important area of database administration is the protection of the database. This protection includes locking the database through the creation of an ACCDE file to prevent unauthorized changes from being made to the VBA source code or to the design of forms and reports. Splitting the database into a front-end and a back-end database is another way to protect the functionality and improve the efficiency of a database.

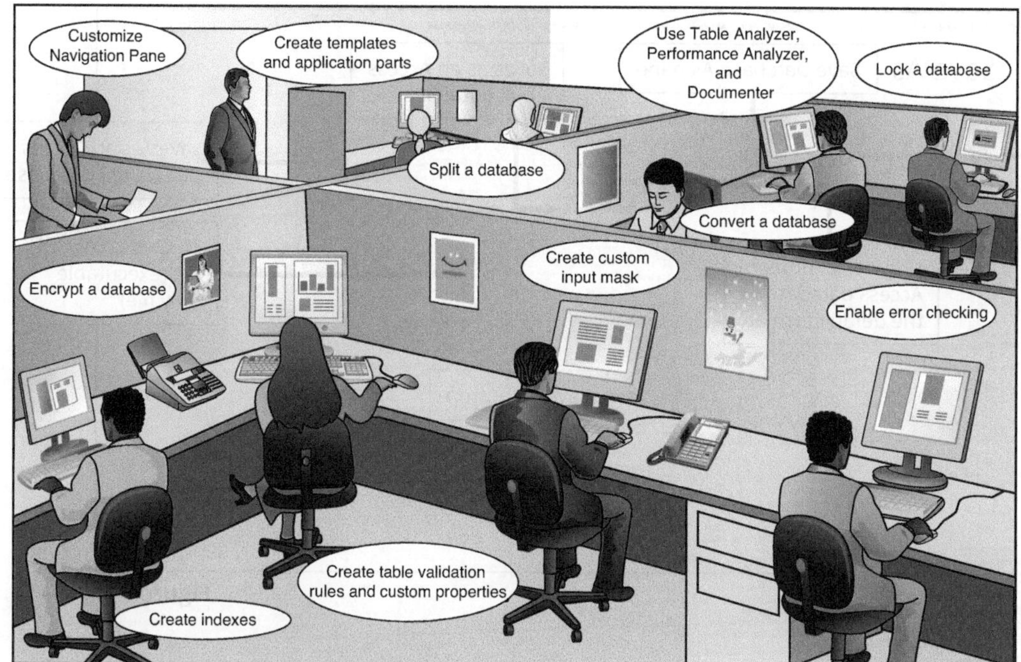

Figure 9–2

Converting Databases

Access 2007, Access 2010, Access 2013, Access 2016, Access 2019, Access 2021, and Access in Microsoft 365 all use the same file format, the .accdb format. The format is usually referred to as the Access 2007 file format due to that being the version of first use. Thus, in current versions of Access, you can use any database created with Access 2007 or beyond. You should be aware of the following changes in Access 2013 and later versions (including Access 2021 and Microsoft 365) from the earlier versions.

1. Unlike previous versions, these later versions do not support PivotTables or PivotCharts.
2. The Text data type is now Short Text, and the Memo data type is now Long Text.
3. Smart Tags are no longer supported.
4. Replication is no longer available.

To convert an Access 2007 database to an earlier version, the database cannot contain any features that are specific to Access 2007 or later. These include attachments, multivalued fields, large integers, offline data, data macros, calculated columns, links to unsupported external files, newer sort orders, newer encryption types, or navigation controls. Provided the database does not contain such features, you can convert the database by clicking the Save As tab in Backstage view (Figure 9–3). You can then choose the appropriate format.

BTW
Converting Databases
If you try to convert a database that contains features specific to a later version of Access, Access displays an error message alerting you that you cannot save the database as an earlier version because it contains features that require the current file format.

BTW
Maintaining Backward Compatibility
If you plan to share your database with users who may have an earlier version of Access, be sure to maintain backward compatibility. Do not include multivalued fields, attachment fields, or calculated fields in your database design. For example, if there is a calculation that is used frequently, create a query with the calculated field and use the query as the basis for forms and reports rather than adding the field to the table design.

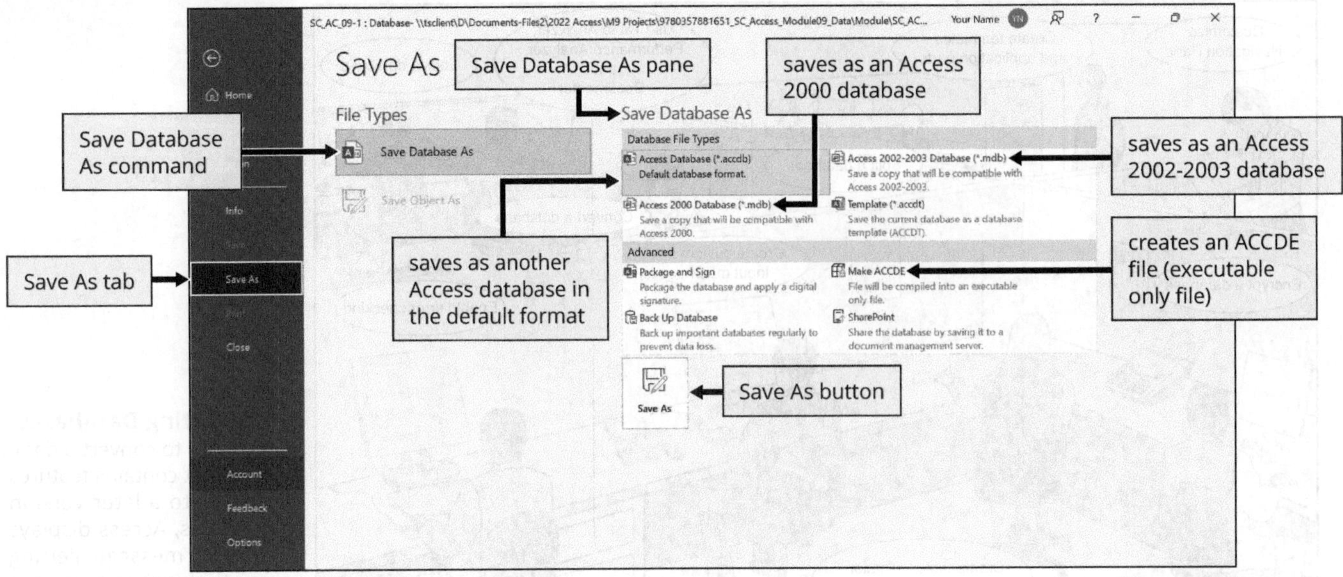

Figure 9–3

To Convert an Access 2007–2021 Database to an Earlier Version

Specifically, to convert an Access 2007–2021 database to an earlier version, you would use the following steps.

1. With the database to be converted open, click File on the ribbon to open Backstage view.
2. Click Save As.
3. With the 'Save Database As' command selected, click the desired format, and then click the Save As button.
4. Type the name you want for the converted database, select a location in which to save the converted database, and click the Save button.

> **BTW**
> **Saving Databases to External Locations**
> You also can save a database to an external location, such as OneDrive, and to any portable storage device, such as a USB flash drive. To do so, select the desired external location or portable storage device when you browse to specify a location for your database.

To Convert an Access 2000 or 2002–2003 Database to an Access 2021 Database

To convert an Access 2000 or Access 2002–2003 database to the default database format for Access 2021, you open the database in Access 2021. Initially, the database is open in compatibility mode, where features that are new to the current version of Access and that cannot easily be displayed or converted are disabled. In this mode, the database remains in its original format. If you want to convert it so you can use it in Access 2021, you use the Access Database command in Backstage view. Once the database is converted, the disabled features will be enabled. You will no longer be able to share the database with users of Access 2000 or Access 2002–2003, however.

Specifically, to convert an Access 2000 or 2002–2003 database to the default database format for Access 2021, you would use the following steps.

1. With the database to be converted open, click File on the ribbon to open Backstage view.
2. Click Save As.
3. With the Save Database As command selected, click Access Database (*.accdb), and then click the Save As button.
4. Type the name you want for the converted database, select a location, and click the Save button.

> **BTW**
> **Exporting XML Data**
> Database administration also might include responsibility for exchanging data between dissimilar systems or apps. Extensible Markup Language (XML) is a data interchange standard for describing and delivering data on the web. With XML, you can describe both the data and the structure (schema) of the data. You can export tables, queries, forms, or reports. To export a database object, select the object, click the More button (External Data tab | Export group), and then click XML File. Select the appropriate options in the Export - XML File dialog box.

Microsoft Access Analysis Tools

Microsoft Access has a variety of tools that are useful in analyzing databases. Analyzing a database gives information about how the database functions and identifies opportunities for improving functionality. You can use the Access analysis tools to analyze tables and database performance, and to create detailed documentation.

BTW
Creating Databases in Older Formats
To create a database in an older format, create a database and browse to select a location for creating the database, click the "Save as type" arrow in the File New Database dialog box, and select either the 2002–2003 format or the 2000 format.

To Use the Table Analyzer

Access contains a Table Analyzer tool that performs three separate functions. This tool can analyze tables while looking for potential redundancy (duplicated data). The Table Analyzer can also analyze performance and check for ways to make queries, reports, or forms more efficient. Then, the tool will make suggestions for possible changes. The final function of the analyzer is to produce detailed documentation describing the structure and content of the various tables, queries, forms, reports, and other objects in the database.

The following steps use the Table Analyzer to examine the Carriers table for **redundancy**, or duplicated data. Why? Redundancy is one of the biggest potential sources of problems in a database. If redundancy is found, the Table Analyzer will suggest ways to split the table to eliminate the redundancy.

- sam Start Access. Open the database, SC_AC_09-1.accdb, which is located in the Data Files folder. Save the file to your hard disk, OneDrive, or other storage location using the file name, **SC_AC_09_Clearnet**. Enable the content; or, if a message opens, stating that active content in the file is blocked, read the message and then click OK to close the dialog box. Then, enable the content.
- Display the Database Tools tab (Figure 9–4).

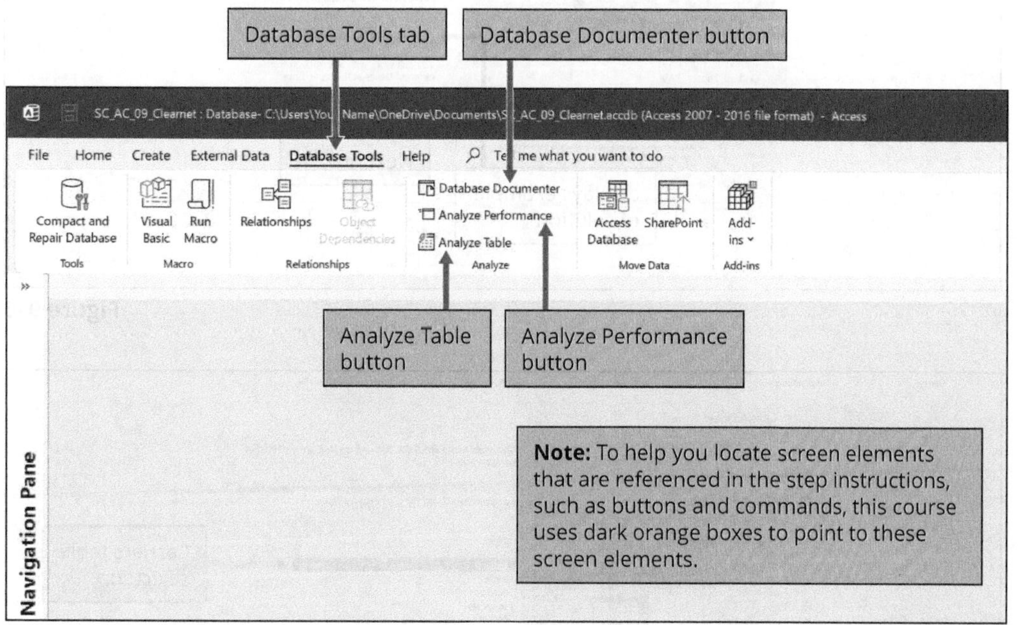

Figure 9–4

BTW
Navigation Pane
As you work, you often need to open the Navigation Pane to view and select objects such as tables, forms, and reports. You often need to close the pane to make more room on the screen or to ensure your screen matches the figures in this course. Open the Navigation Pane as necessary to open an object when instructed, and close the pane to suit your preferences.

BTW
Active Content
Depending on your Trust Settings, Access may initially block active content when it opens a database that contains macros. When you are opening content from a trusted source, such as databases included in this course, you can click OK in the dialog box and proceed with enabling the content.

2

- Click the Analyze Table button (Database Tools tab | Analyze group) to display the Table Analyzer Wizard dialog box (Figure 9–5).

Q&A Where did the data in the figure come from? It does not look like my data.
The data is fictitious. It is just intended to give you an idea of what the data might look like.

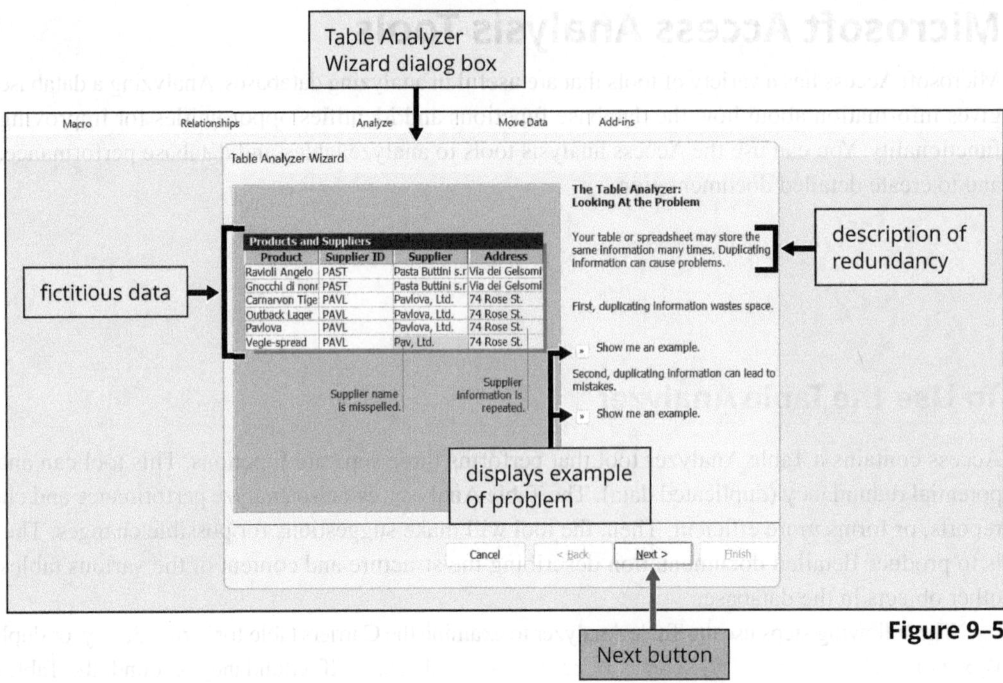

Figure 9–5

3

- Click Next to display the next Table Analyzer Wizard screen (Figure 9–6).

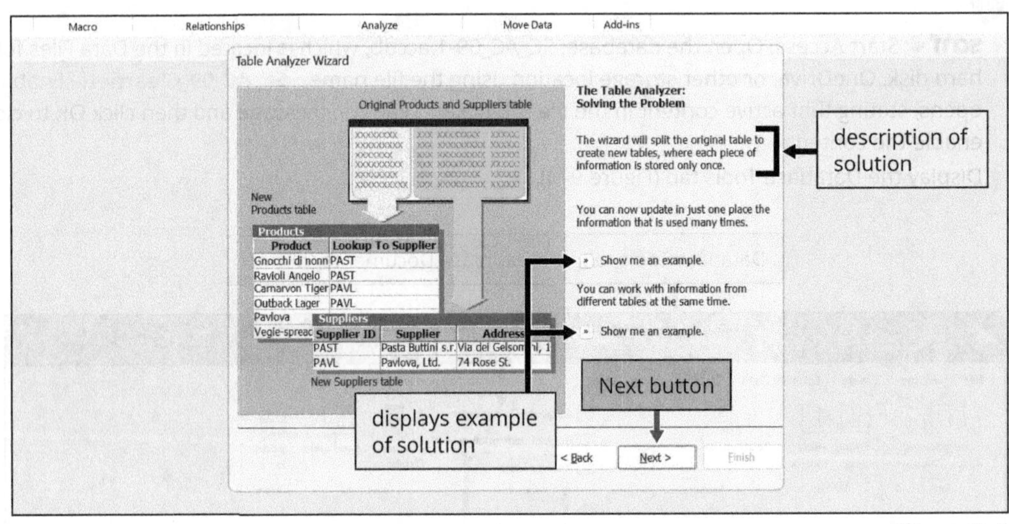

Figure 9–6

4

- Click Next to display the next Table Analyzer Wizard screen.
- If necessary, select the Carriers table (Figure 9–7).

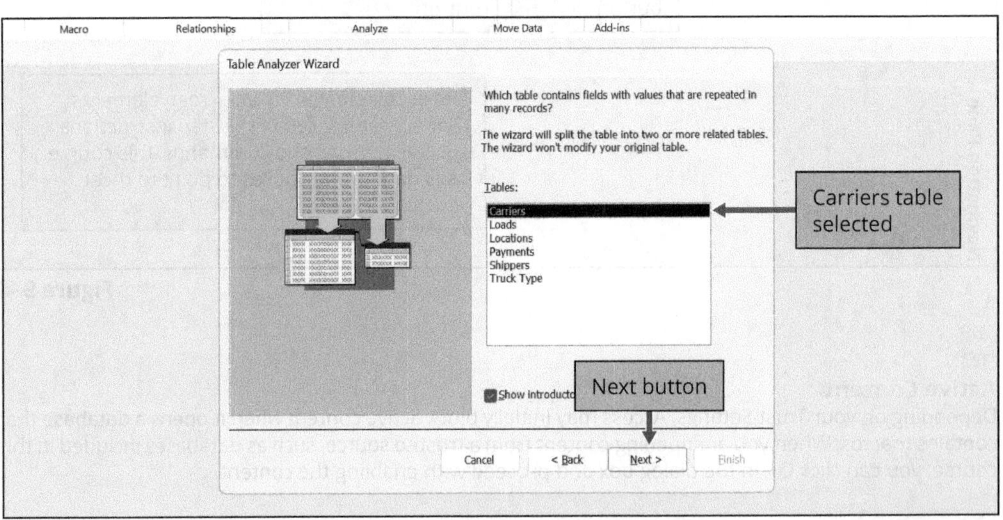

Figure 9–7

- Click Next.
- Be sure the 'Yes, let the wizard decide.' option button is selected (Figure 9–8) to let the wizard determine what action to take.

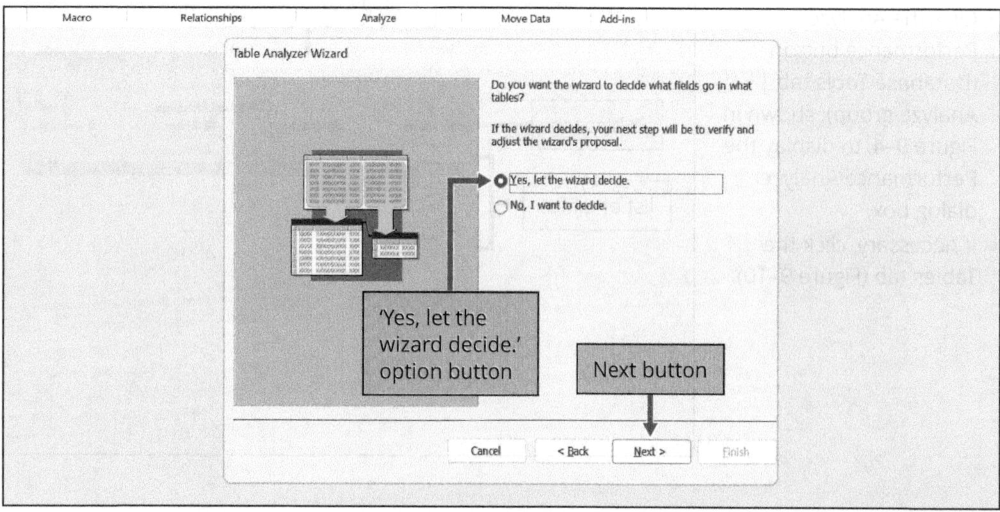

Figure 9–8

- Click Next to run the analysis, which indicates redundancy in the table.
- Reposition and resize the tables so you can see the field recommended to be split into a new table (Figure 9–9).

Q&A I do not really want to put the Carrier Payment Instructions field in a different table, even though I realize that this data does appear to be duplicated. Do I have to follow this advice? Certainly not. This is only a suggestion.

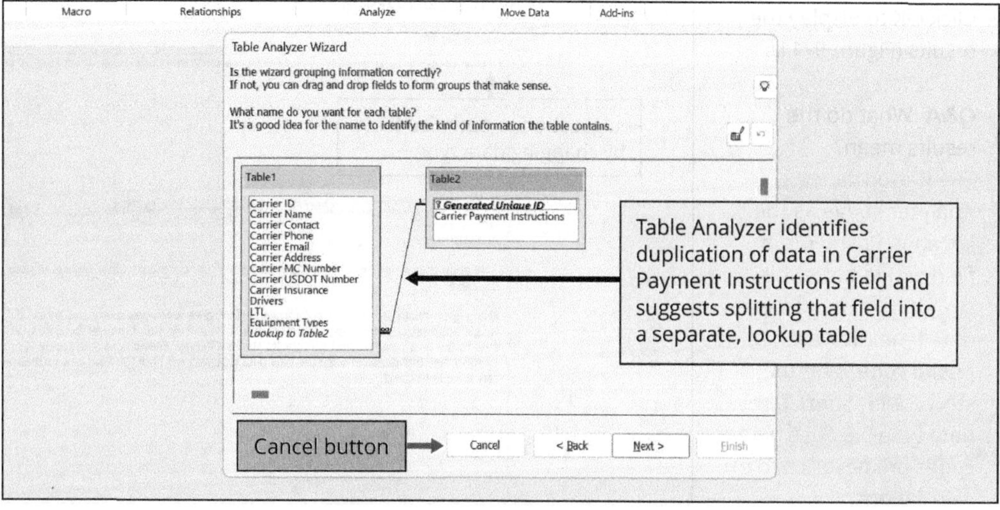

Figure 9–9

- Because the type of duplication identified by the analyzer does not pose a problem, click the Cancel button to close the analyzer.

To Use the Performance Analyzer

The Performance Analyzer examines the database's tables, queries, reports, forms, and other objects in your system, looking for ways to improve the efficiency of database operations. These improvements could include modifications to the way data is stored, as well as changes to the indexes created for the system. (You will learn about indexes later in this module.) The following steps use the Performance Analyzer. **Why?** The Performance Analyzer identifies possible areas for improvement in the Clearnet database. Users then can determine whether to implement the suggested changes.

- Click the Analyze Performance button (Database Tools tab | Analyze group), shown in Figure 9–4, to display the Performance Analyzer dialog box.
- If necessary, click the Tables tab (Figure 9–10).

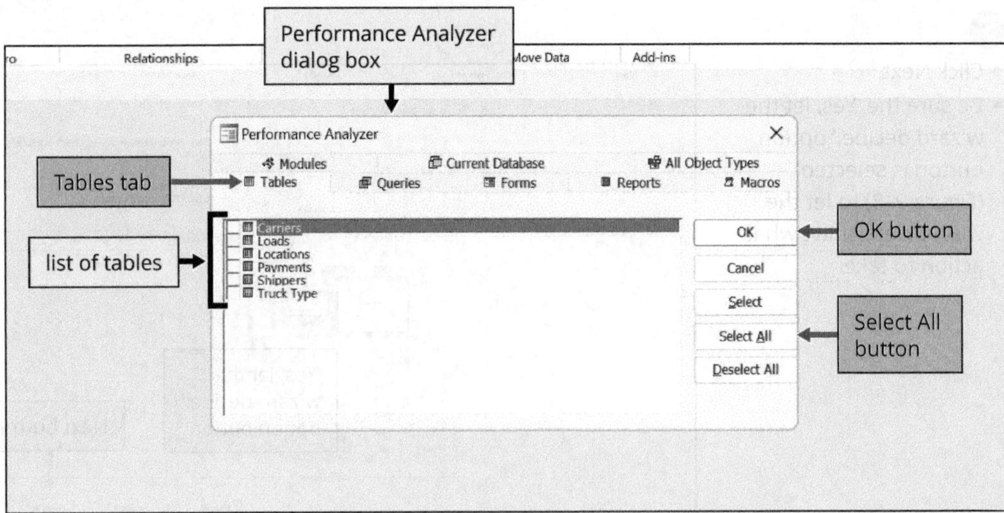

Figure 9–10

- Click the Select All button to select all tables.
- Click OK to display the results (Figure 9–11).

Q&A What do the results mean?
The Performance Analyzer suggests the Location Postal Code field would better be stored as a Long Integer data type. However, a postal code is better stored with Short Text data type because postal codes are never used in calculations.

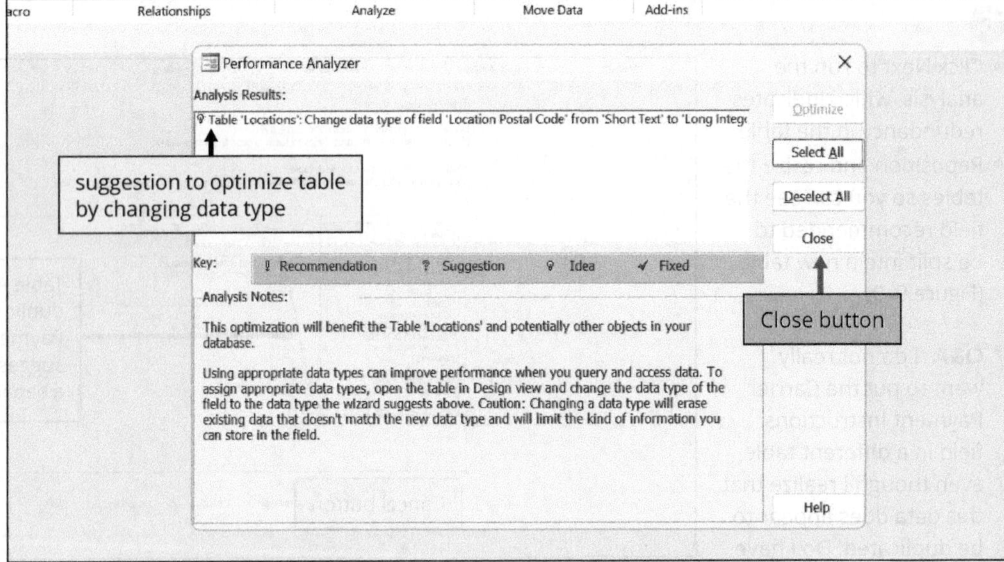

Figure 9–11

- Click Close to finish working with the Performance Analyzer.

To Use the Database Documenter

The Database Documenter allows you to produce detailed documentation of the various tables, queries, forms, reports, and other objects in your database. Documentation is required by many organizations. It is used for backup, disaster recovery, and planning for database enhancements. Figure 9–12 shows a portion of the documentation for the Loads table. The complete documentation is much lengthier than the one shown in the figure.

The following steps use the Database Documenter. **Why?** The Database Documenter is the easiest way to produce detailed documentation for the Loads table.

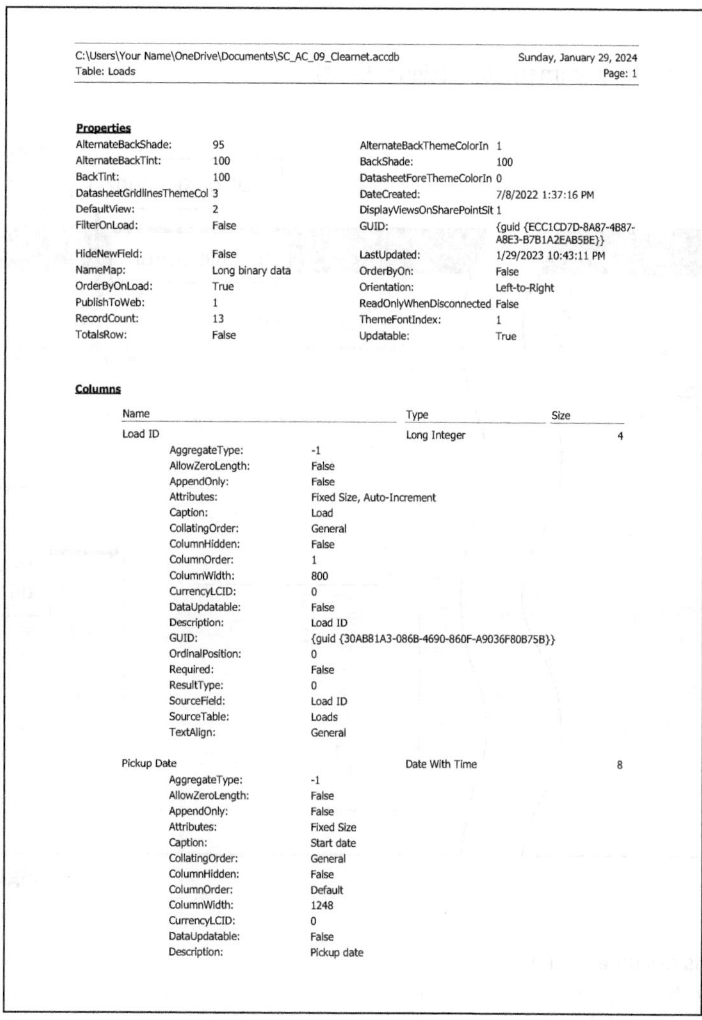

C:\Users\Your Name\OneDrive\Documents\SC_AC_09_Clearnet.accdb Sunday, January 29, 2024
Table: Loads Page: 1

Properties

AlternateBackShade:	95	AlternateBackThemeColorIn	1
AlternateBackTint:	100	BackShade:	100
BackTint:	100	DatasheetForeThemeColorIn	0
DatasheetGridlinesThemeCol	3	DateCreated:	7/8/2022 1:37:16 PM
DefaultView:	2	DisplayViewsOnSharePointSit	1
FilterOnLoad:	False	GUID:	{guid {ECC1CD7D-8A87-4B87-A8E3-B7B1A2EAB5BE}}
HideNewField:	False	LastUpdated:	1/29/2023 10:43:11 PM
NameMap:	Long binary data	OrderByOn:	False
OrderByOnLoad:	True	Orientation:	Left-to-Right
PublishToWeb:	1	ReadOnlyWhenDisconnected	False
RecordCount:	13	ThemeFontIndex:	1
TotalsRow:	False	Updatable:	True

Columns

Name		Type	Size
Load ID		Long Integer	4
AggregateType:	-1		
AllowZeroLength:	False		
AppendOnly:	False		
Attributes:	Fixed Size, Auto-Increment		
Caption:	Load		
CollatingOrder:	General		
ColumnHidden:	False		
ColumnOrder:	1		
ColumnWidth:	800		
CurrencyLCID:	0		
DataUpdatable:	False		
Description:	Load ID		
GUID:	{guid {30AB81A3-086B-4690-860F-A9036F80B75B}}		
OrdinalPosition:	0		
Required:	False		
ResultType:	0		
SourceField:	Load ID		
SourceTable:	Loads		
TextAlign:	General		
Pickup Date		Date With Time	8
AggregateType:	-1		
AllowZeroLength:	False		
AppendOnly:	False		
Attributes:	Fixed Size		
Caption:	Start date		
CollatingOrder:	General		
ColumnHidden:	False		
ColumnOrder:	Default		
ColumnWidth:	1248		
CurrencyLCID:	0		
DataUpdatable:	False		
Description:	Pickup date		

Figure 9–12

1

- Click the Database Documenter button, shown in Figure 9–4 (Database Tools tab | Analyze group), to display the Documenter dialog box.
- If necessary, click the Tables tab and then click the Loads check box to specify documentation for the Loads table (Figure 9–13).

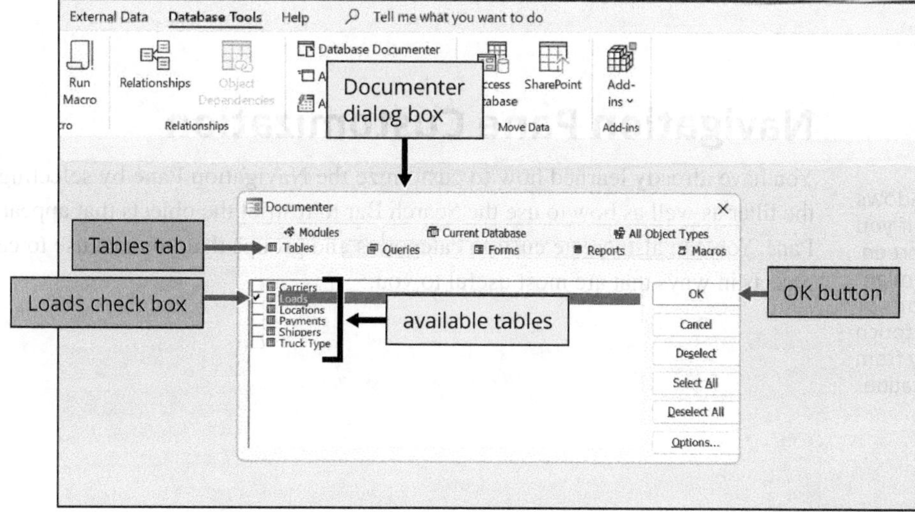

Figure 9–13

- Click OK to produce a preview of the documentation (Figure 9–14).

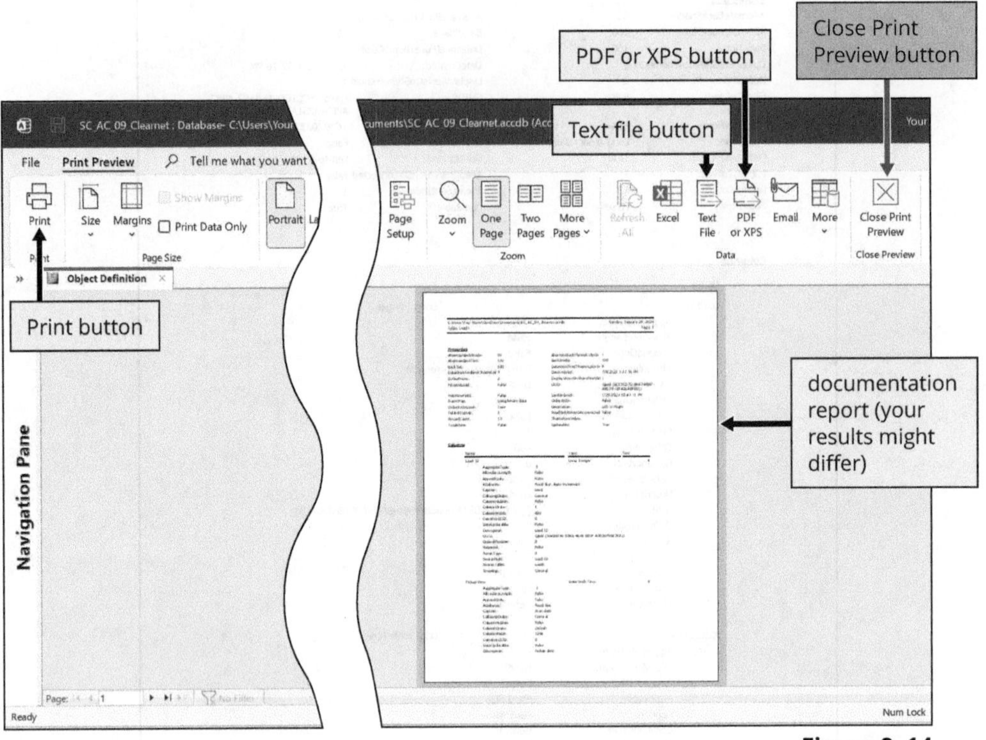

Figure 9–14

Q&A What can I do with this documentation?

You could print it by clicking the Print button (Print Preview tab | Print group). You could create a PDF or XPS file containing the documentation by clicking the PDF or XPS button (Print Preview tab | Data group) and following the directions. You could create a Word (RTF) file by clicking the More button (Print Preview tab | Data group), and then clicking Word and following the directions. Whatever option you choose, you might need to use this documentation later if you make changes to the database design.

- Click the 'Close Print Preview' button (Print Preview tab | Close Preview group) to close the preview of the documentation.
- **Experiment:** Try other options within the Database Documenter to see the effect of your choice on the documentation produced. Each time, close the preview of the documentation.

BTW
Touch Screen Differences
The Office and Windows interfaces may vary if you are using a touch screen. For this reason, you might notice the function or appearance of your touch screen differs slightly from this module's presentation.

Navigation Pane Customization

You have already learned how to customize the Navigation Pane by selecting the category and the filter as well as how to use the Search Bar to restrict the objects that appear in the Navigation Pane. You can also create custom categories and groups that you can use to categorize database objects in ways that are most useful to you.

To Create Custom Categories and Groups

You can create custom categories in the Navigation Pane. You can further refine the objects you place in a category by adding custom groups to the categories. **Why?** Custom categories and groups allow you to tailor the Navigation Pane for your specific needs. The following steps create a custom category called Loads Information. They then add two custom groups, Tracking and Accounting, to the Loads Information category.

- Display the Navigation Pane and resize it, if necessary, so you can read the full title of all listed objects.
- Right-click the Navigation Pane title bar to display a shortcut menu (Figure 9–15).

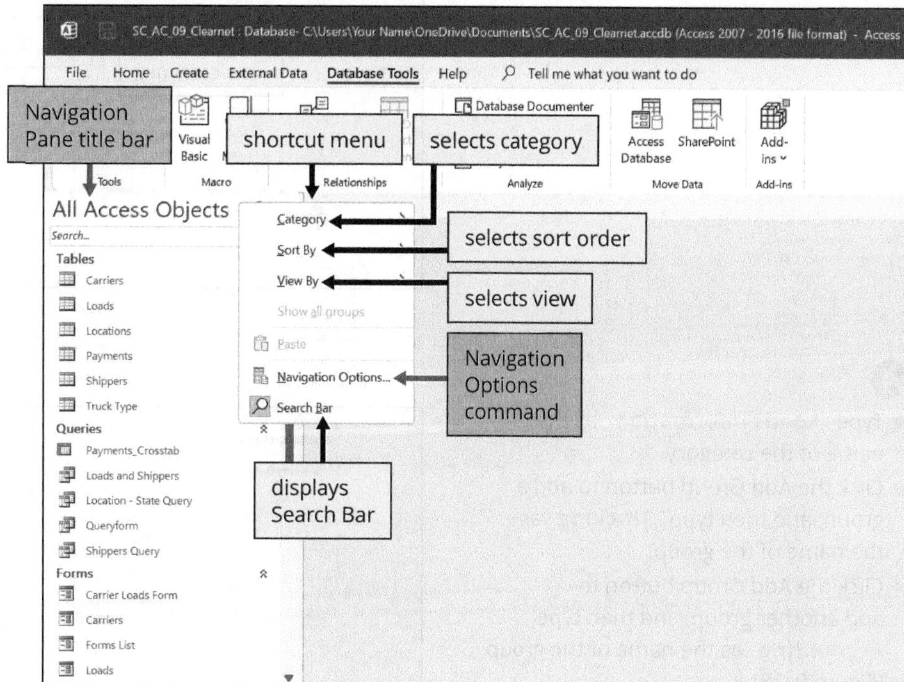

Figure 9–15

2

- Click the Navigation Options command on the shortcut menu to display the Navigation Options dialog box (Figure 9–16).

Q&A What else could I do with the shortcut menu?
You could select a category, select a sort order, or select how to view the items within the Navigation Pane.

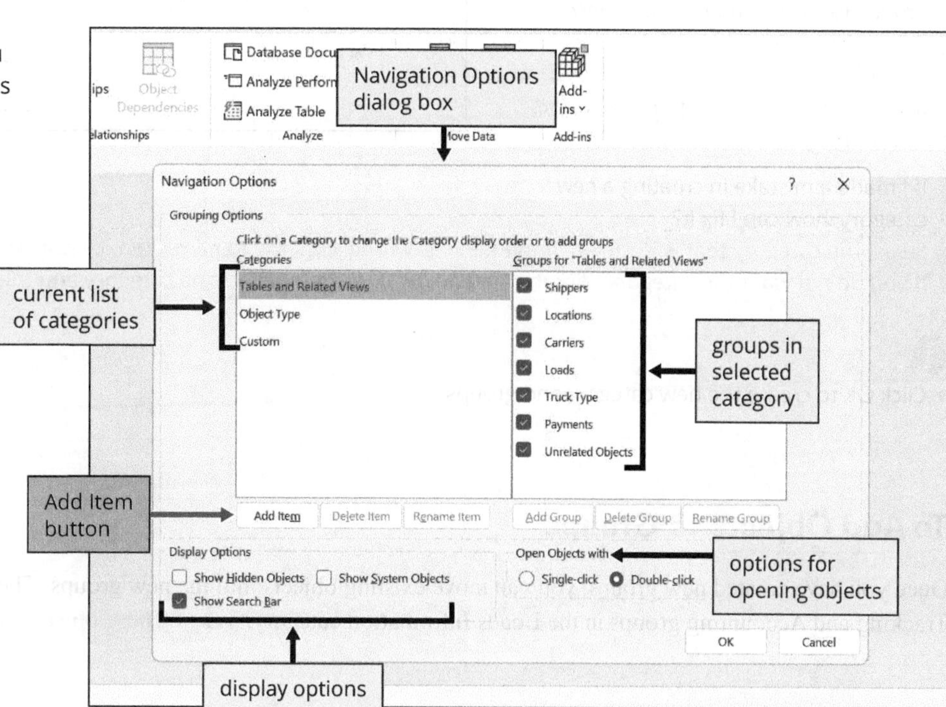

Figure 9–16

- Click the Add Item button to add a new category (Figure 9–17).

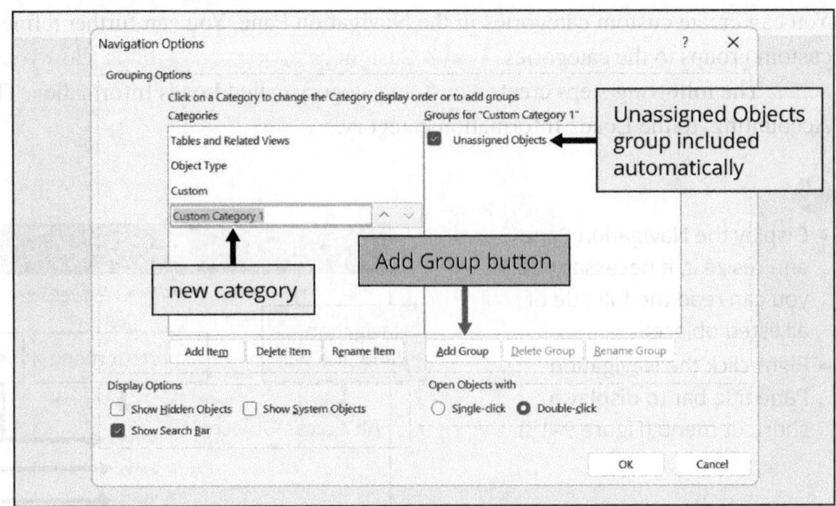

Figure 9–17

- Type **Loads Information** as the name of the category.
- Click the Add Group button to add a group, and then type **Tracking** as the name of the group.
- Click the Add Group button to add another group, and then type **Accounting** as the name of the group (Figure 9–18).

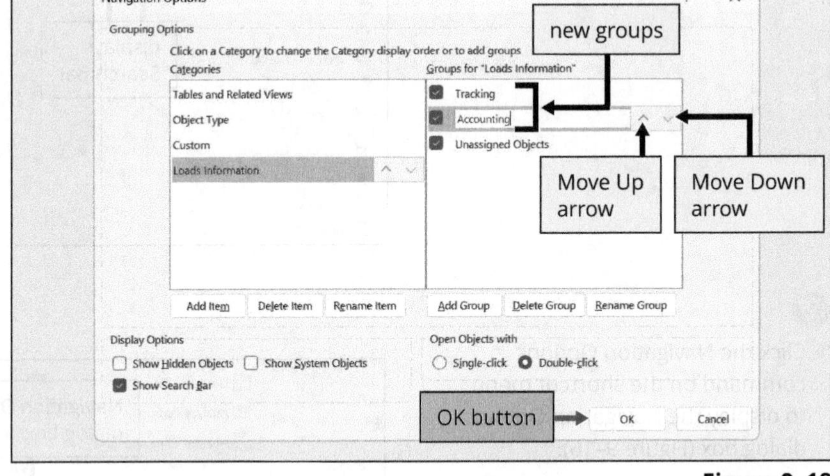

Figure 9–18

Q&A I added the groups in the wrong order. How can I change the order?
Select the group that is in the wrong position. Click the Move Up or Move Down arrow to move the group to the correct location.

If I made a mistake in creating a new category, how can I fix it?
Select the category that is incorrect. If the name is wrong, click the Rename Item button and change the name appropriately. If you do not want the category, click the Delete Item button to delete the category and then click OK.

- Click OK to create the new category and groups.

To Add Objects to Groups

Once you have created new groups, you can move existing objects into the new groups. The following steps add objects to the Tracking and Accounting groups in the Loads Information category. **Why?** These objects are all related to the loads.

1

- Click the Navigation Pane arrow to produce the Navigation Pane menu, and then scroll if necessary to display the Loads Information category (Figure 9–19).

Q&A Do I have to click the arrow?
No. If you prefer, you can click anywhere in the title bar for the Navigation Pane. Clicking arrows is a good habit, however, because there are many situations in which you must click the arrow.

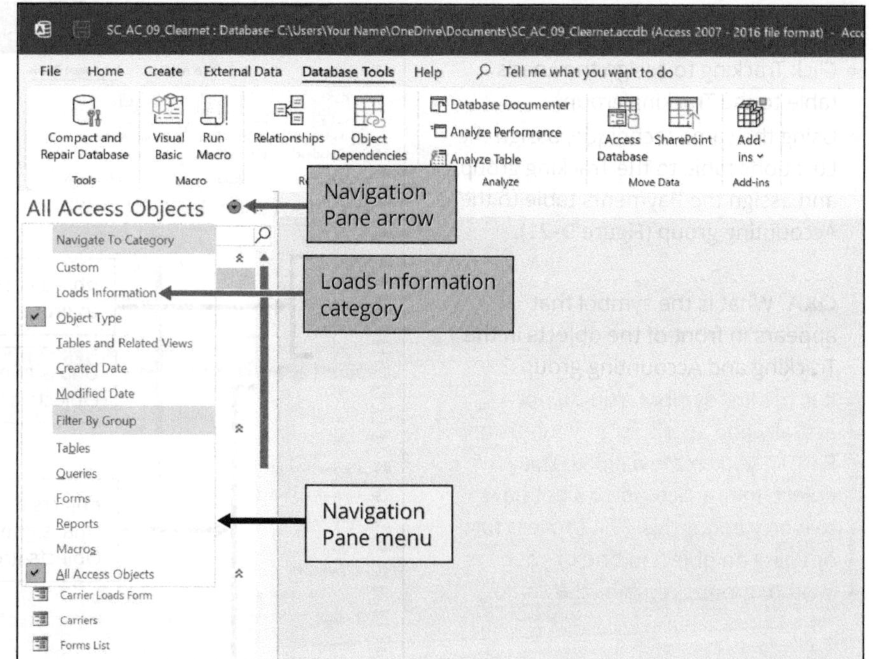

Figure 9–19

2

- Click the Loads Information category to display the groups within the category. Because you created the Tracking and Accounting groups but did not assign objects, the table objects all appear in the Unassigned Objects area of the Navigation Pane.
- Right-click the Loads table to display the shortcut menu.
- Point to the 'Add to group' command on the shortcut menu to display the list of available groups (Figure 9–20).

BTW
Touch and Pointers
Remember that if you are using your finger on a touch screen, you will not see the pointer.

Q&A I did not create an Unassigned Objects group. Where did it come from?
Access creates the Unassigned Objects group automatically. Until you add an object to one of the groups you created, it will be in the Unassigned Objects group.

What is the purpose of the New Group command on the submenu?
You can create a new group using this submenu. This is an alternative to using the Navigation Options dialog box. Use whichever approach you find most convenient.

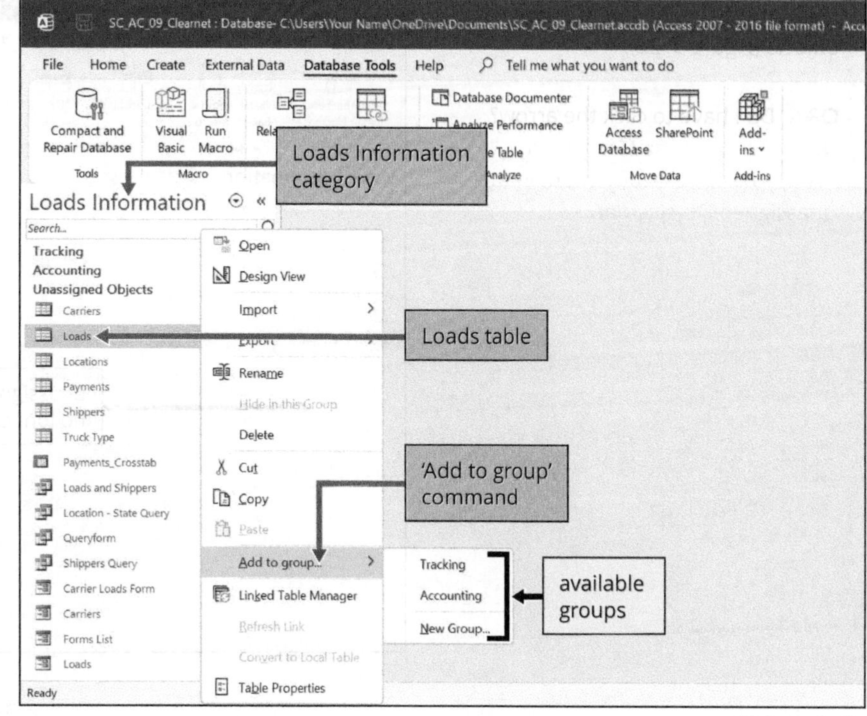

Figure 9–20

- Click Tracking to assign the Loads table to the Tracking group.
- Using the same technique, assign the Locations table to the Tracking group, and assign the Payments table to the Accounting group (Figure 9–21).

Q&A What is the symbol that appears in front of the objects in the Tracking and Accounting groups?
It is the link symbol. You do not actually add an object to your group. Rather, you create a link to the object. In practice, you do not have to worry about this. The process for opening an object in one of your custom groups remains the same.

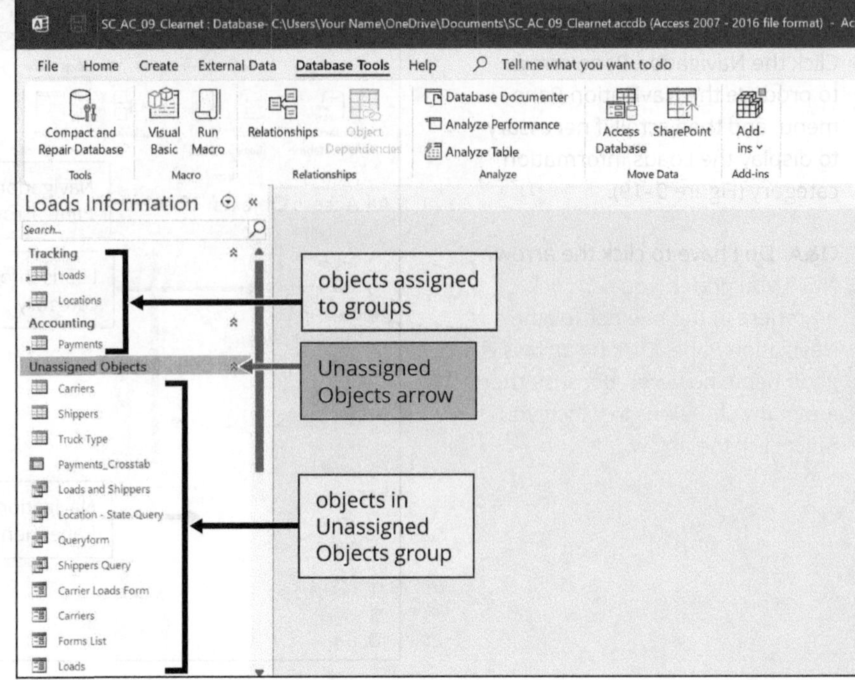

Figure 9–21

- Click the arrow in the Unassigned Objects bar to hide the unassigned objects (Figure 9–22).

Q&A Do I have to click the arrow?
No. Just as with the Navigation Pane, you can click anywhere in the Unassigned Objects bar.

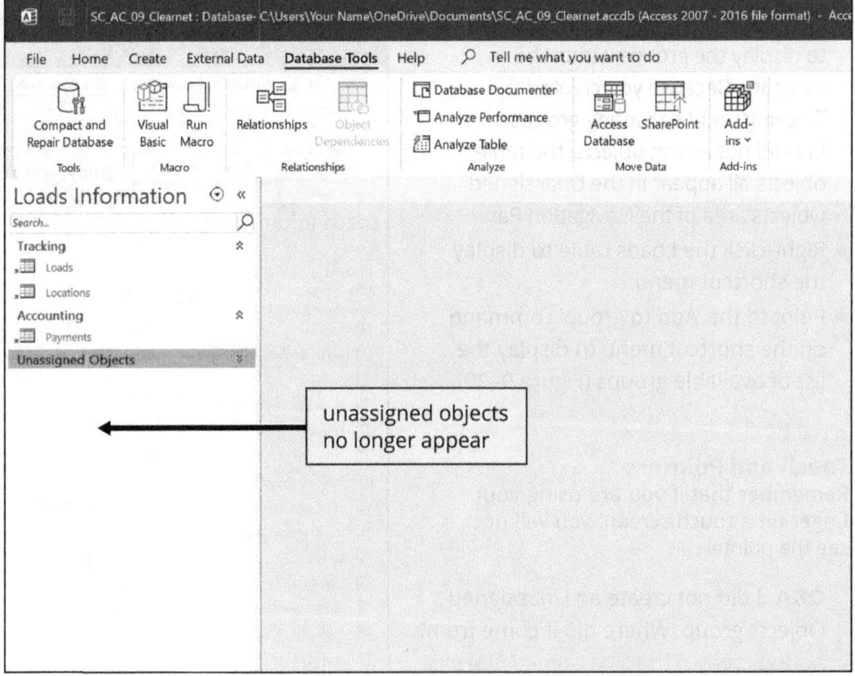

Figure 9–22

Consider This

What issues do you consider in determining the customization of the Navigation Pane?

The types of issues to consider include the following:

- Would a new category be useful?
- If so, are there new groups that would be useful to include in the new category?
- If you have created a new category and new groups, which objects should be included in the new groups, and which should be left uncategorized?

Break Point: If you wish to take a break, this is a good place to do so. You can quit Access now. To resume at a later time, start Access, open the database called SC_AC_09_Clearnet.accdb, and continue following the steps from this location forward.

Table and Database Properties

You can assign properties to tables. For example, you could assign a validation rule and validation text to an entire table. You can also assign properties to the database, typically for documentation purposes.

To Create a Validation Rule for a Table

Previously, you created validation rules that applied to individual fields within a table. Some, however, apply to more than one field. In the Workshop Enrollments table in the Partners database, you created a macro that would change the value of the Hours Spent field in such a way that it could never be greater than the Total Hours field. You can also create a validation rule that ensures this will never be the case; that is, the validation rule would require that the hours spent must be less than or equal to the total hours. In the Clearnet database's Payments table, you will create a validation rule that ensures, for every load, the agent commission value does not exceed four percent of the rate confirmation value. To create a validation rule that involves two or more fields, you need to create the rule for the table using the table's Validation Rule property. The following steps create a **table validation rule.** Why? This rule involves two fields: Agent Commission and Rate Confirmation.

- Open the Payments table in Design view.
- If necessary, click the Property Sheet button (Table Design tab | Show/Hide group) to display the table's property sheet.
- Click the Validation Rule property and type **[Agent Commission]<=[Rate Confirmation]*0.04** as the validation rule.
- Click the Validation Text property and type **Agent Commission cannot exceed 4% of Rate Con** as the validation text (Figure 9–23).

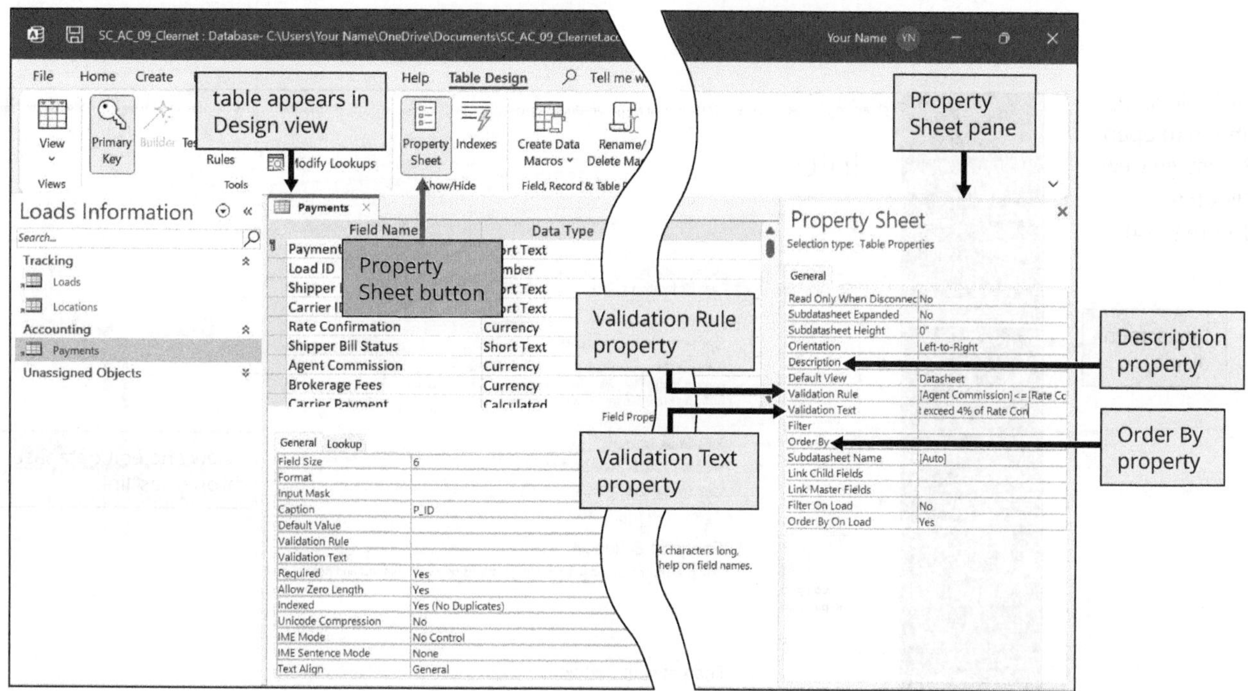

Figure 9–23

Q&A Why does the expression use 0.04 instead of 4%?
The value 4% needs to be converted to decimal form, which is 0.04.

Could I use the Expression Builder to create the validation rule?
Yes. Use whichever method you find most convenient.

- Close the Property Sheet pane.
- Click the Save button on the Quick Access Toolbar to save the validation rule and the validation text.
- When asked if you want to test existing data, click the No button.
- **Experiment:** Switch to Datasheet view and attempt to change the A_Comm value for P_ID 8 from $20.00 to $50.00 to confirm the validation rule and error message work correctly. When you attempt to move to a different record or close the datasheet, an error message appears. To fix the problem, reset P_ID 8's agent commission to $20.00.
- Close the Payments table.

BTW
Table Descriptions
To add a description for a table, right-click the table in the Navigation Pane and then click Table Properties on the shortcut menu. When the table's Properties dialog box appears, enter the description in the Description property and then click OK. To enter a description for a table in Design view, click the Property Sheet button, and then enter a description in the Description property on the Property Sheet pane (see Figure 9–23).

BTW
Changing Default Sort Order
To display the records in a table in an order other than the primary key (the default sort order), use the Order By property on the table's property sheet (see Figure 9–23).

To Create Custom Properties

In addition to the general database property categories, you can also use custom properties. **Why?** You can use custom properties to further document your database in a variety of ways. If you have needs that go beyond the custom properties, you can create your own original or unique properties. The following steps **populate** the Status custom property; that is, they set a value for the property. In this case, they set the Status property to Live Version, indicating this is the live version of the database. If the database were still in a test environment, the property would be set to Test Version. The steps also create and populate a new property, Production, which represents the date the database was placed into production.

1

- Click File on the ribbon to open Backstage view.
- Click Info (Figure 9–24).

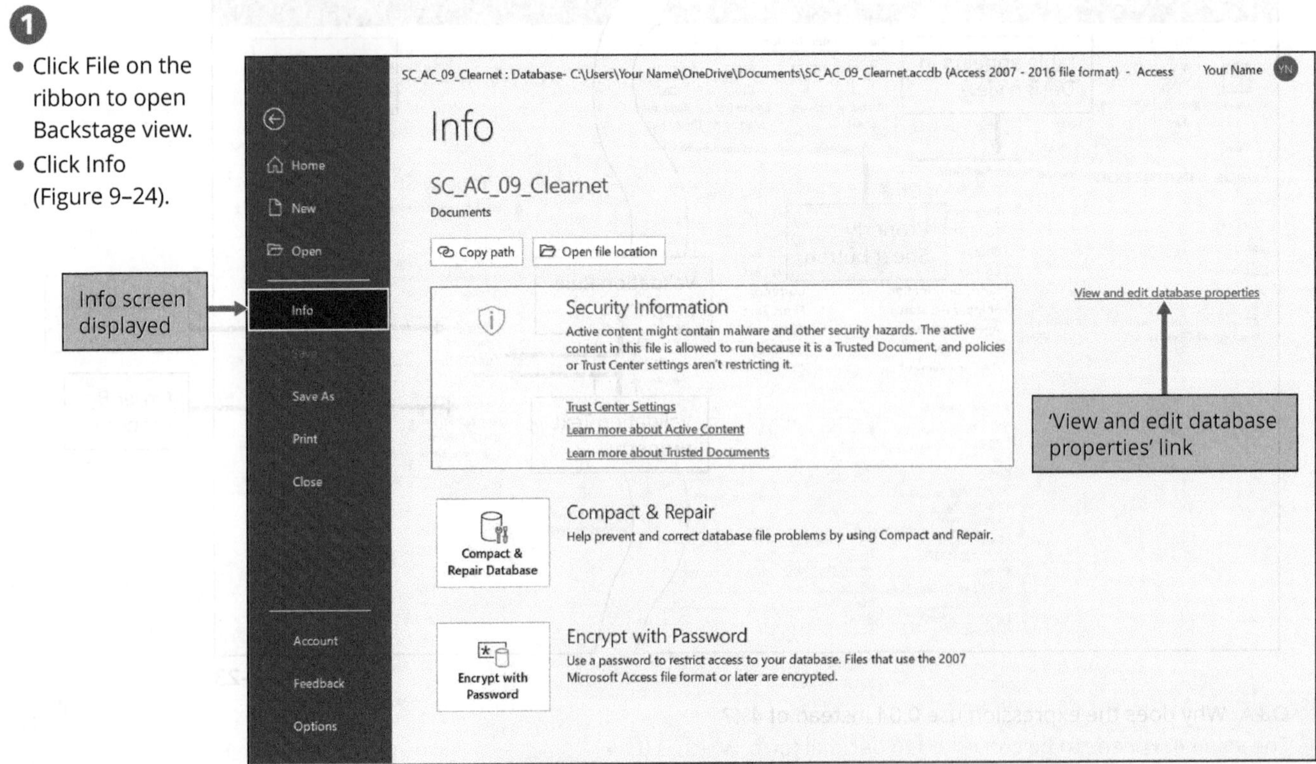

Figure 9–24

2

- Click the 'View and edit database properties' link to display the Clearnet database's Properties dialog box.
- Click the Custom tab.
- Scroll down in the Name list so Status appears, and then click Status.
- If necessary, click the Type arrow to set the data type to Text.
- Click the Value box, and type **Live Version** as the value to create the custom property (Figure 9–25).

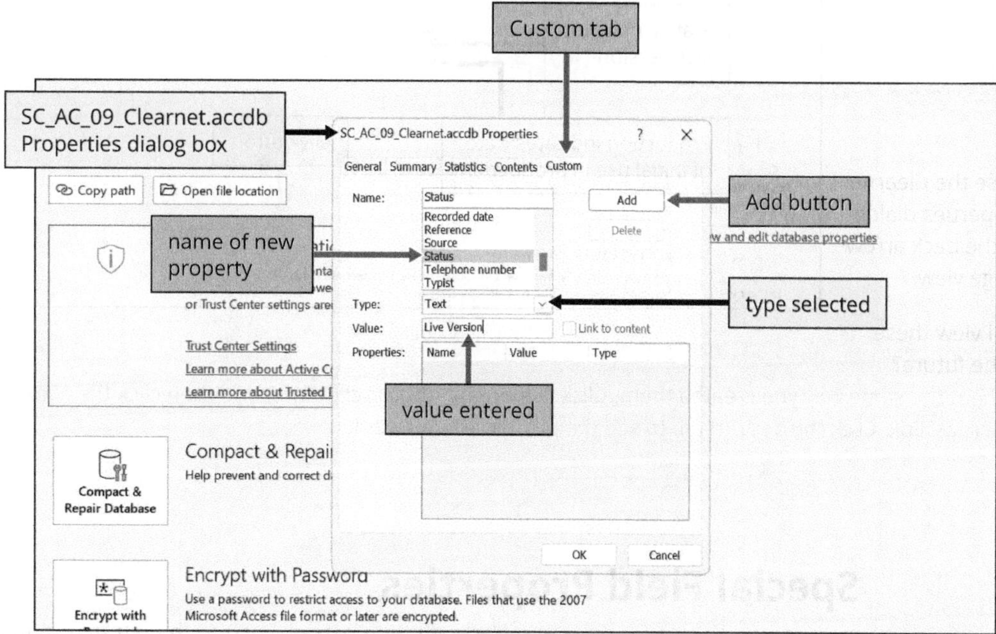

Figure 9–25

3

- Click the Add button to add the property.
- Type **Production** in the Name box to create a new property.
- If requested to do so by your instructor, type your first and last name in the Name box.
- Select Date as the Type.
- Type **6/25/2024** as the value (Figure 9–26) to indicate the database went into production on June 25, 2024.

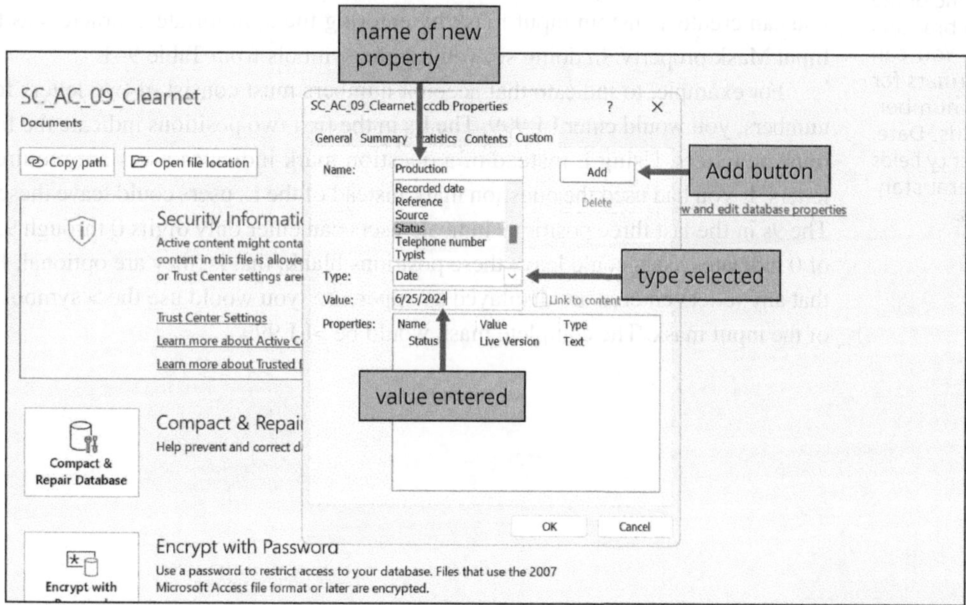

Figure 9–26

- Click the Add button to add the property (Figure 9–27).

Q&A What if I add a property that I decide I do not want?
You can delete it. To do so, click the property you no longer want and then click the Delete button.

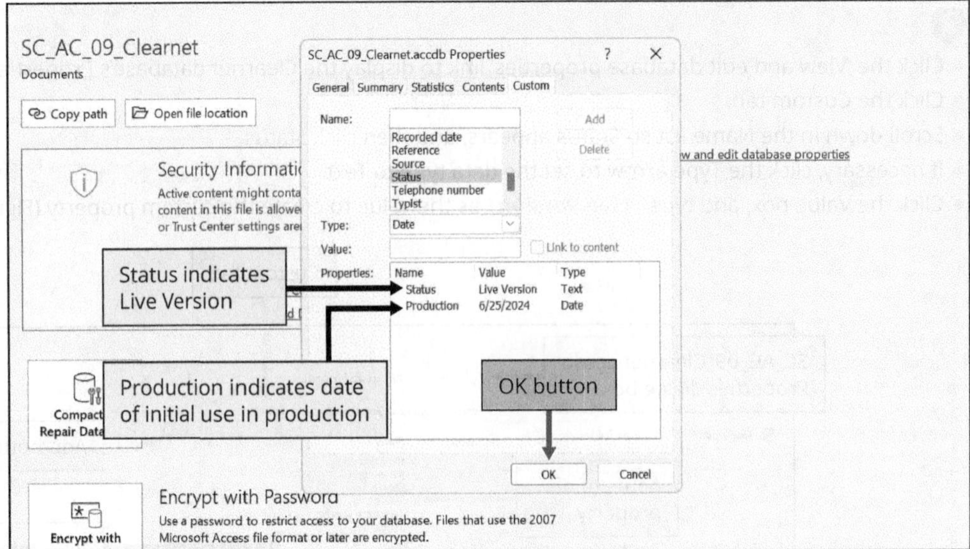

Figure 9–27

- Click OK to close the Clearnet database's Properties dialog box, and click the back arrow to exit Backstage view.

Q&A How do I view these properties in the future?
You can view them the same way you created them. Click File on the ribbon, click Info, and then click the 'View and edit database properties' link. Click the desired tab to see the properties you want.

BTW
Changing Data Formats
To create custom data formats, enter the necessary characters in the Format property of a table field. The characters can be placeholders (such as 0 and #), separators (such as periods and commas), literal text with the required text enclosed in double quotation marks (such as "literal text"), and colors with the name of the color enclosed in brackets (such as [blue]). You can create custom formats for short text, date, number, and currency fields. Date, number, and currency fields also include several standard data formats.

Special Field Properties

Each field in a table has a variety of field properties available. Recall that field properties are characteristics of a field. Two special field properties, the Custom Input Mask property and the Allow Zero Length property, are described in this section.

Custom Input Masks

One way to help users enter data using a certain format is to use an input mask. You have already used the Input Mask Wizard to create an input mask. Using the wizard, you can select the input mask that meets your needs. This is often the best way to create the input mask.

If the input mask you need to create is not similar to any in the list provided by the wizard, you can create a custom input mask by entering the appropriate characters as the value for the Input Mask property. In doing so, you use the symbols from Table 9–1.

For example, to indicate that account numbers must consist of two letters followed by three numbers, you would enter LL999. The Ls in the first two positions indicate the first two positions must be letters. Using L instead of a question mark indicates users are required to enter these letters. If you had used the question mark instead of the L, users could leave these positions blank. The 9s in the last three positions indicate users can enter only digits 0 through 9. Using 9 instead of 0 indicates users could leave these positions blank; that is, they are optional. Finally, to ensure that any letters entered are displayed as uppercase, you would use the > symbol at the beginning of the input mask. The complete mask would be >LL999.

Table 9–1 Input Mask Symbols

Symbol	Type of Data Accepted	Data Entry
0	Digits 0 through 9 without plus (+) or minus (−) sign are accepted. Positions left blank appear as zeros.	Required
9	Digits 0 through 9 without plus (+) or minus (−) sign are accepted. Positions left blank appear as spaces.	Optional
#	Digits 0 through 9 with plus (+) or minus (−) sign are accepted. Positions left blank appear as spaces.	Optional
L	Letters A through Z are accepted.	Required
?	Letters A through Z are accepted.	Optional
A	Letters A through Z or digits 0 through 9 are accepted.	Required
a	Letters A through Z or digits 0 through 9 are accepted.	Optional
&	Any character or a space is accepted.	Required
C	Any character or a space is accepted.	Optional
<	Symbol converts any letter entered to lowercase.	N/A
>	Symbol converts any letter entered to uppercase.	N/A
!	Characters typed in the input mask fill it from left to right.	N/A
\	Character following the slash is treated as a literal in the input mask.	N/A

To Create a Custom Input Mask

The following steps create a custom input mask for the Location ID field in the Locations table. **Why?** None of the input masks in the list meet the specific needs for the Location ID field.

- Open the Locations table in Design view.
- With the Location ID field selected, click the Input Mask property, and then type **>L-999** as the value (Figure 9–28). Access will add a backslash to your custom input mask, like this, >L\-999, when you click outside the property box.

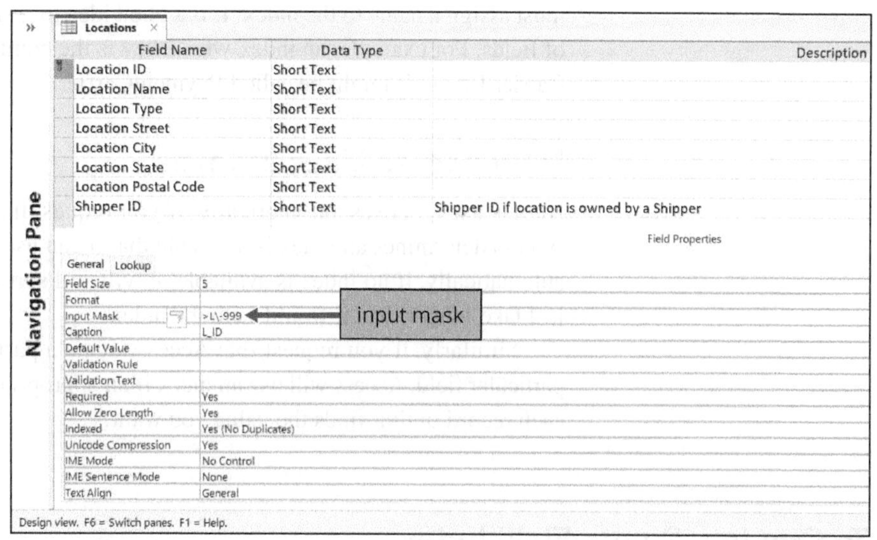

Figure 9–28

- Save the changes and close the table.

Q&A What is the difference between the Format property and the Input Mask property?
The Format property ensures that data is displayed consistently, for example, always in uppercase. The Input Mask property controls how data is entered by the user.

What is the effect of this input mask?
From this point on, anyone entering a location ID will be restricted to a letter in the first position, followed by a dash and numeric digits in the last three positions. Further, any letter entered in the first position will be displayed as uppercase.

Can you have a field that has both a custom input mask and a format requirement? Would this be a problem?
Technically, you do not need both. When the same field has both an input mask and a format, the format takes precedence. However, if the format specified for the field is the same as the input mask (uppercase), it will not affect the data.

Creating and Using Indexes

BTW
B-tree Indexes
The most common structure for high-performance indexes is called a B-tree. It is a highly efficient structure that supports very rapid access to records in the database as well as a rapid alternative to sorting records. Virtually all systems use some version of the B-tree structure.

You are already familiar with the concept of an index. The index in the back of a book contains important words or phrases along with a list of pages on which the given words or phrases can be found. An index for a table is similar. An **index** is a database object that is created based on a field or combination of fields. An index on the Carrier Name field, for example, would enable Access to rapidly locate a record that contains a particular carrier. In this case, the items of interest are carrier names instead of keywords or phrases, as is the case for the index in the back of most books. The field or fields on which the index is built is called the index key. Thus, in the index on account names, the Carrier Name field is the index key.

Each name occurs in the index along with the number of the record on which the corresponding account is located. Further, the names appear in the index in alphabetical order, so Access can use this index to rapidly produce a list of carriers alphabetized by account name.

Another benefit of indexes is that they provide an efficient way to order records. That is, if the records are to appear in a certain order in a database object, Access can use an index instead of physically having to rearrange the records in the database. Physically rearranging the records in a different order can be a very time-consuming process.

To gain the benefits of an index, you must first create one. Access automatically creates an index on some special fields. If, for example, a table contains a field called Postal Code, Access creates an index for this field automatically. You must create any other indexes you determine would improve database performance, indicating the field or fields on which the index is to be built.

Although the index key will usually be a single field, it can be a combination of fields. For example, you might want to sort records by carrier ID within payment status. In other words, the records are ordered by a combination of fields: Carrier Payment Status and Carrier ID. An index can be used for this purpose by using a combination of fields for the index key. In this case, you must assign a name to the index. It is a good idea to assign a name that represents the combination of fields. For example, an index whose key is the combination of the Carrier Payment Status and Carrier ID fields might be called PaymentCarrier.

How Access Uses Indexes

Access uses indexes automatically. If you request that data be sorted in a particular order and Access determines an index is available that it can use to make the process efficient, it will do so automatically. If no index is available, it will still sort the data in the order you requested; it will just take longer than it would with the index.

Similarly, if you request that Access locate a particular record that has a certain value in a particular field, Access will use an index if an appropriate one exists. If not, it will have to examine each record until it finds the value you want.

To Create a Single-Field Index

The following steps create a single-field index on the Carrier Name field in the Carriers table. **Why?** This index will make finding carriers based on their name more efficient than it would be without the index. It will also improve the efficiency of sorting by carrier name.

- Open the Carriers table in Design view. Note that you will need to unhide the unassigned objects in the Navigation Pane to do this. You can then hide the unassigned objects again if desired.
- Select the Carrier Name field.
- Click the Indexed property box in the Field Properties pane to select the property.
- Click the arrow that appears to display the Indexed list.

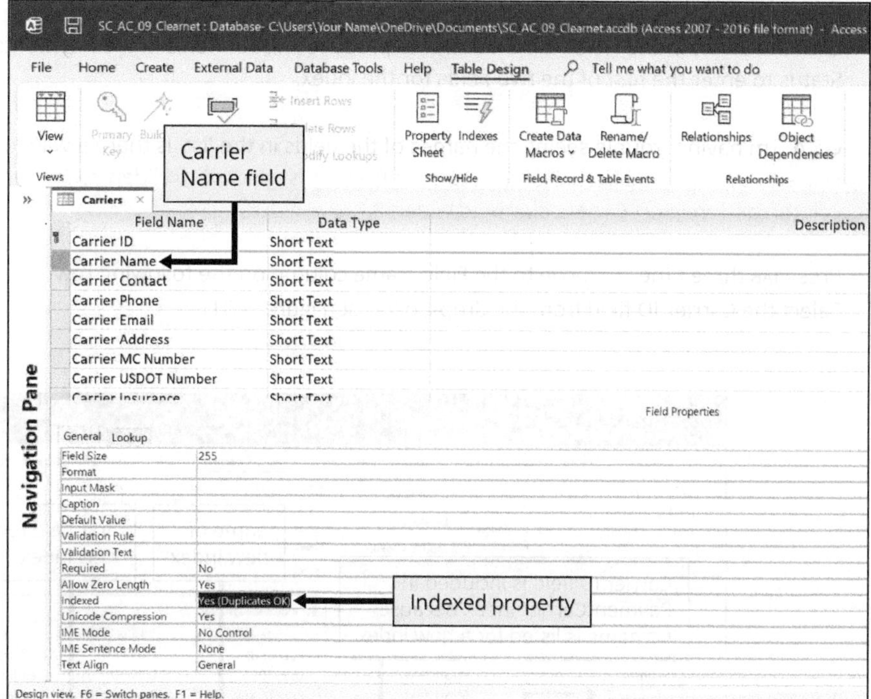

2

- Click Yes (Duplicates OK) in the list to specify that duplicates are to be allowed (Figure 9–29).

3

- Save your changes and close the table.

Figure 9–29

To Create a Multiple-Field Index

Creating a **multiple-field index** — that is, an index whose key is a combination of fields — involves a different process than creating a single-field index. To create a multiple-field index, you will use the Indexes button, enter a name for the index, and then enter the combination of fields that make up the index key. The following steps create a multiple-field index on the combination of Carrier Payment Status and Carrier ID. **Why?** Clearnet needs to sort records on the combination of Carrier Payment Status and Carrier ID and wants to improve the efficiency of this sort. The steps assign this index the name PaymentCarrier.

- Open the Payments table in Design view.
- Click the Indexes button (Table Design tab | Show/Hide group) to display the Indexes: Payments window, and then resize it as needed to see all the included data (Figure 9–30).

- Click in the blank row (the row below Shipper ID) in the Index Name column (Indexes: Payments window) to select the position to enter the name of the new index.

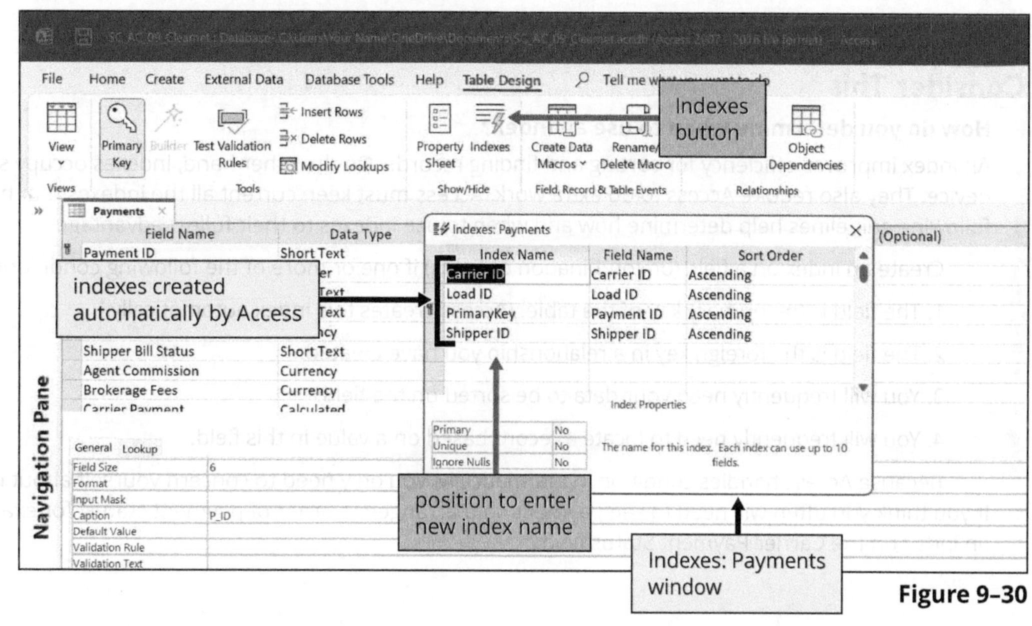

Figure 9–30

- Type **PaymentCarrier** as the index name, and then press TAB.
- Click the arrow in the Field Name column to produce a list of fields in the Payments table, and then click Carrier Payment Status to enter the first of the two fields for the index.

Q&A I'm having trouble seeing the names of the fields in the list. Is there a way to fix this?
Yes, you can drag the border of the Indexes: Payments window to widen it. Then, drag the border between the Field Name column and the Sort Order column to widen it.

- Press TAB three times to move to the Field Name column on the following row.
- Select the Carrier ID field from the drop-down list (Figure 9–31).

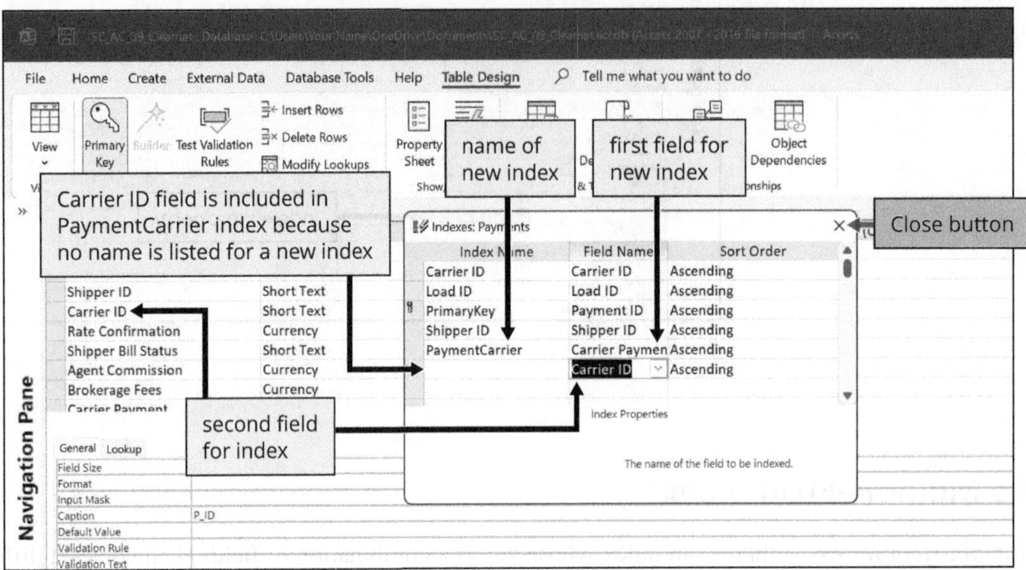

Figure 9–31

- Close the Indexes: Payments window by clicking its Close button.
- Save your changes and close the table.

Consider This

How do you determine when to use an index?

An index improves efficiency for sorting and finding records. On the other hand, indexes occupy space on your storage device. They also require Access to do extra work. Access must keep current all the indexes that have been created. The following guidelines help determine how and when to use indexes to their fullest advantage.

Create an index on a field (or combination of fields) if one or more of the following conditions are present:

1. The field is the primary key of the table. (Access creates this index automatically.)
2. The field is the foreign key in a relationship you have created.
3. You will frequently need your data to be sorted on the field.
4. You will frequently need to locate a record based on a value in this field.

Because Access handles condition 1 automatically, you only need to concern yourself about conditions 2, 3, and 4. If you think you often will need to see payment data arranged in order of payment status, for example, you should create an index on the Carrier Payment Status field.

Automatic Error Checking

Access can automatically check for several types of errors in forms and reports. When Access detects an error, it warns you about the existence of the error and provides you with options for correcting it. The types of errors that Access can detect and correct are shown in Table 9–2.

Table 9–2 Types of Errors

Error Type	Description
Unassociated label and control	A label and control are selected and are not associated with each other.
New unassociated labels	A newly added label is not associated with any other control.
Keyboard shortcut errors	A shortcut key is invalid. This can happen because an unassociated label has a shortcut key, there are duplicate shortcut keys assigned, or a blank space is assigned as a shortcut key.
Invalid control properties	A control property is invalid. For example, the property contains invalid characters.
Common report errors	The report has invalid sorting or grouping specifications, or the report is wider than the page size.

To Enable Error Checking

Why? For automatic error checking to take place, it must be enabled. The following steps ensure that error checking is enabled and that errors are found and reported.

- Click File on the ribbon and then click Options to display the Access Options dialog box.
- Click Object Designers to display the options for creating and modifying objects.
- Scroll down so the Error checking area appears.
- Ensure the 'Enable error checking' check box is checked (Figure 9–32).

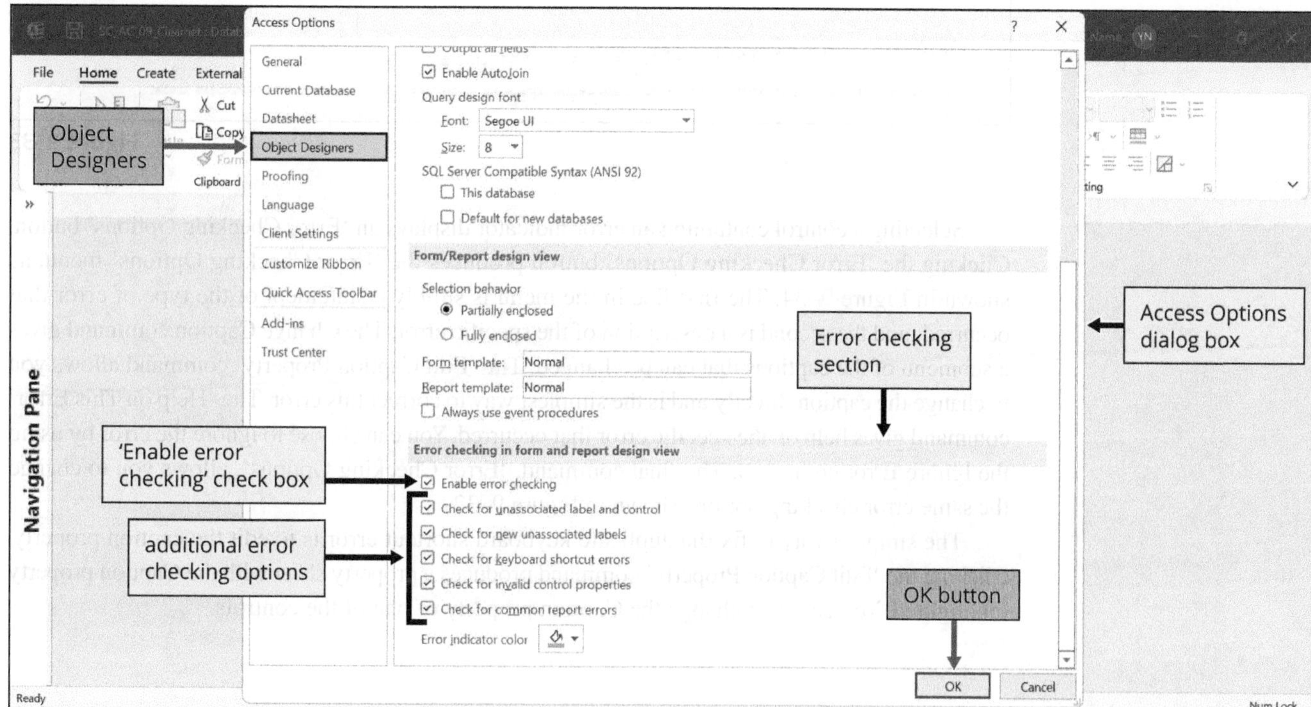

Figure 9–32

Q&A What is the purpose of the other check boxes in the section?
All the other check boxes are checked, indicating that Access will perform all the various types of automatic error checking that are possible. If there were a particular type of error checking that you would prefer to skip, you would remove its check mark before clicking OK.

- Click OK to close the Access Options dialog box.

Error Indication

With error checking enabled, if an error occurs, an error indicator appears in the appropriate field or control. For example, you could change the label for Load ID in the Loads Summary Form to include an ampersand (&) and the letter L, making it a keyboard shortcut for this control. This would be a problem because L is already a shortcut for Load to Find. If this happens, an error indicator appears in both controls in which L is the keyboard shortcut, as shown in Figure 9–33.

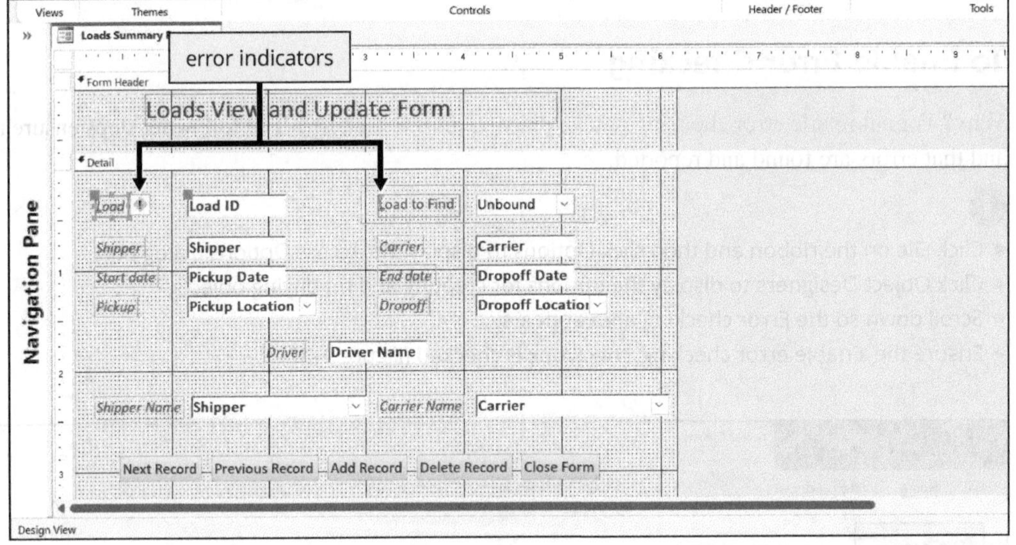

Figure 9–33

Selecting a control containing an error indicator displays an 'Error Checking Options' button. Clicking the 'Error Checking Options' button produces the 'Error Checking Options' menu, as shown in Figure 9–34. The first line in the menu is simply a statement of the type of error that occurred, and the second is a description of the specific error. The Change Caption command gives a submenu of the captions that can be changed. The 'Edit Caption Property' command allows you to change the caption directly and is the simplest way to correct this error. The 'Help on This Error' command gives help on the specific error that occurred. You can choose to ignore the error by using the Ignore Error command. The final command, 'Error Checking Options', allows you to change the same error checking options shown in Figure 9–32.

The simplest way to fix the duplicate keyboard shortcut error is to edit the caption property. Clicking the 'Edit Caption Property' command produces a property sheet with the Caption property highlighted. You can then change the Caption property of one of the controls.

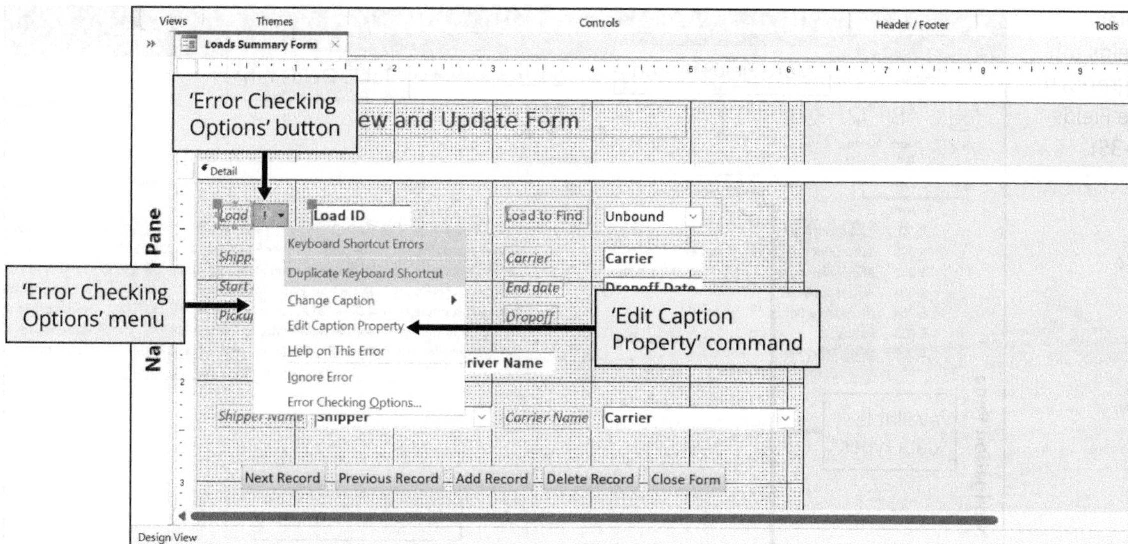

Figure 9–34

Data Type Parts

Access contains data type parts that are available on the More Fields gallery, which you might use when adding new fields to a table. Some data type parts, such as the Category part, consist of a single field. Others, such as the Address part, consist of multiple fields. In addition to the parts provided by Access, you can create your own parts. Quick Start fields act as a framework that lets you rapidly add several fields to a table in a single operation. For example, you could create a quick start field called Name-Address that consists of a Last Name field, a First Name field, a Street field, a City field, a State field, and a Postal Code field. Once you have created this quick start field, you can use it when creating tables in the future. Simply by selecting the Name-Address quick start field, you would immediately add the Last Name, First Name, Street, City, State, and Postal Code fields to a table.

To Create Custom Data Parts

Clearnet has decided that combining several address-related fields into a single data part would make future database updates easier. To create data parts in the Quick Start category from existing fields, you select the desired field or fields and then select the Save Selection as New Data Type command in the More Fields gallery. If you wish to select multiple fields, the fields must be adjacent.

The following steps create a Quick Start field consisting of the Shipper Name, Contact, Phone, Email, and Address fields from the Shippers table. **Why?** Once you have created this Quick Start field, users can add this collection of fields to a table by simply clicking the Quick Start field.

1

- Open the Shippers table in Datasheet view.
- Click the column heading for the Shipper Name field to select the field.
- Hold SHIFT and click the column heading for the Address field to select all the fields from the Shipper Name field to the Address field.
- Display the Table Fields tab.

- Click the More Fields button (Table Fields tab | Add & Delete group) to display the More Fields menu (Figure 9–35).

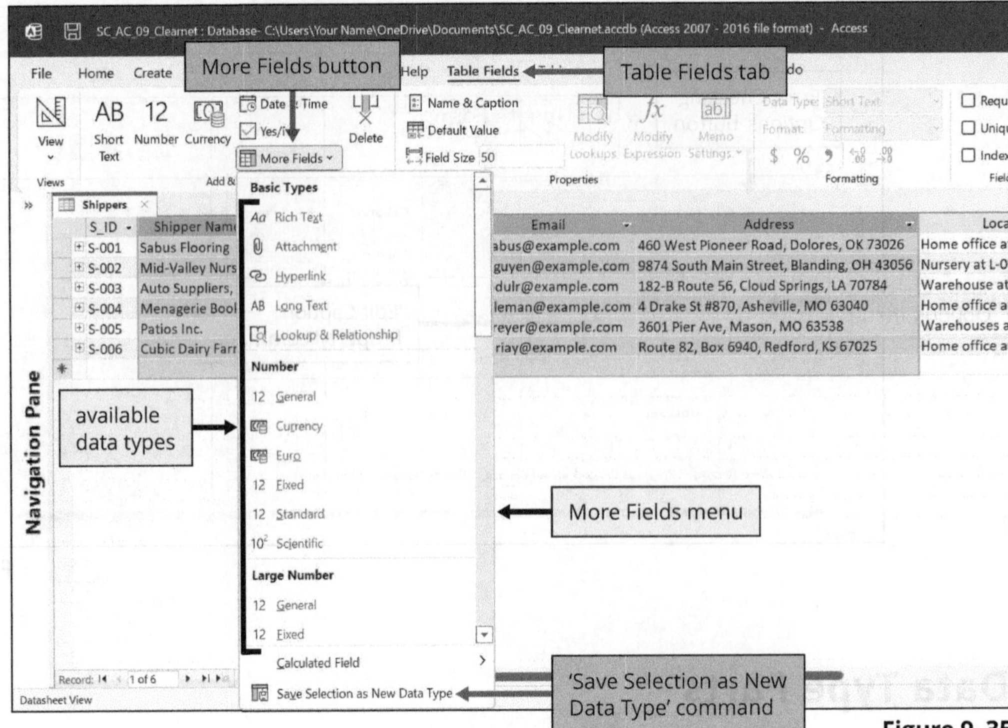

Figure 9–35

2

- Click 'Save Selection as New Data Type' to display the Create New Data Type from Fields dialog box.
- Enter **Name-Contact-Address** as the name.
- Enter **Name, Contact, Phone, Email, and Address fields** as the description.

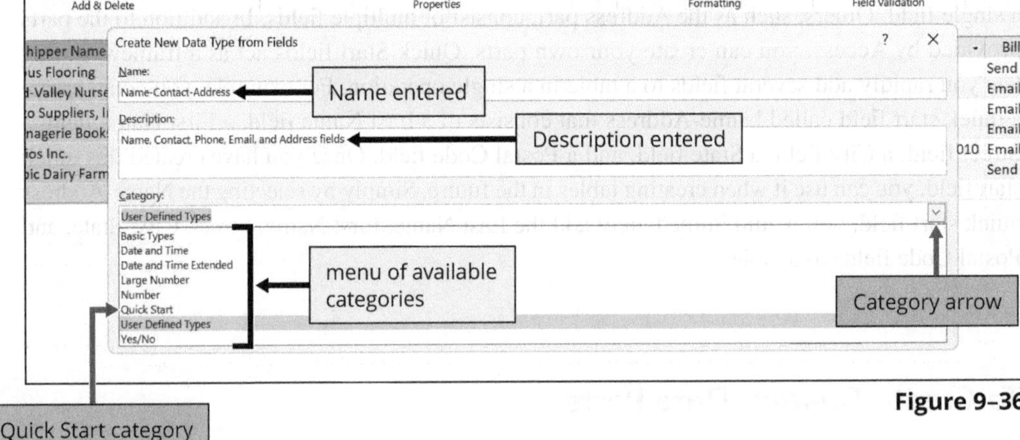

Figure 9–36

Q&A What is the purpose of the description?
When a user points to the Quick Start field you created, a ScreenTip will appear containing the description you entered.

- Click the Category arrow to display a list of available categories (Figure 9–36).

3

- Click Quick Start to indicate the new data type will be added to the Quick Start category.

Q&A What is the difference between the Quick Start and User Defined Types categories?
If you select the Quick Start category, the data type you create will be listed among the Quick Start data types that are part of Access. If you select the User Defined Types category, the data type you create will be in a separate category containing only those data types you create. In both cases, however, clicking the data type will produce the same result.

- Click OK (Create New Data Type from Fields dialog box) to save the data type.
- When Access indicates that your template (that is, your Quick Start field) has been saved, click OK (Microsoft Access dialog box).
- Close the table.
- If necessary, click No when asked if you want to save the changes to the layout of the table.
- sam Click File and then click Close to close the database without closing Access.

Consider This

How do you rearrange fields that are not adjacent?

When adding new data type fields, you can hide the fields that keep your fields from being adjacent. To hide a field, right-click the field to display a shortcut menu, and then click Hide Fields on the shortcut menu. To later unhide a field you have hidden, right-click any column heading and then click Unhide Fields on the shortcut menu. You will see a list of fields with a check box for each field. The hidden field will not have a check mark in the check box. To unhide the field, click the check box for the field.

Templates

Often, Access users find they create and use multiple databases containing the same objects. You can use a template to create a complete database application containing tables, forms, queries, and other objects. There are many templates available for Access.

You also can create your own template from an existing database. To do so, you must first ensure you have created a database with all the characteristics you want in your template. In this module, the database you create will have two tables, a query, two single-item forms, two datasheet forms that use macros, and a navigation form that will serve as the main menu. In addition, the navigation form will be set to appear automatically whenever you open the database. Once you have incorporated all these features, you will save the database as a template. From that point on, anyone can use your template to create a new database. The database that is created will incorporate all the same features as your original database.

BTW
Templates and Application Parts
By default, user-created templates and application parts are stored in the C:\Users*user name*\AppData\Roaming\Microsoft\Templates\Access folder using the .accft file type.

 **The following steps on pages 27–39 require completion in order to receive credit for this module's second SAM project.** Follow the instructions to create the desktop database you'll use to form the Shippers and Consignees template, and save it locally to your computer.

To Create a Desktop Database

The following steps create the Shippers and Consignees **desktop database**, that is, a database designed to run on a personal computer. **Why?** This database will become the basis for a template.

1

- With Access open, click File on the ribbon to open Backstage view.
- Click the 'Blank database' button.
- Type **Shippers-and-Consignees** as the name of the database file.
- Click the 'Browse for a location to put your database' button to display the File New Database dialog box, navigate to the desired save location (for example, the Access folder in the CIS 101 folder), and then click OK to return to Backstage view (Figure 9–37).

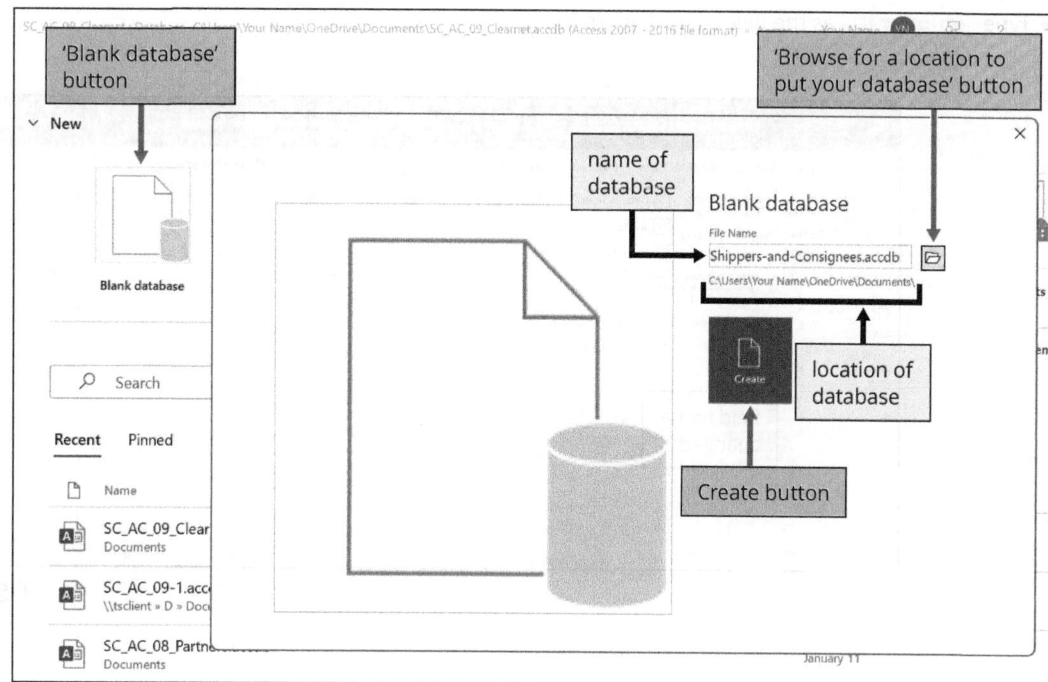

Figure 9–37

- Click the Create button to create the database (Figure 9–38).

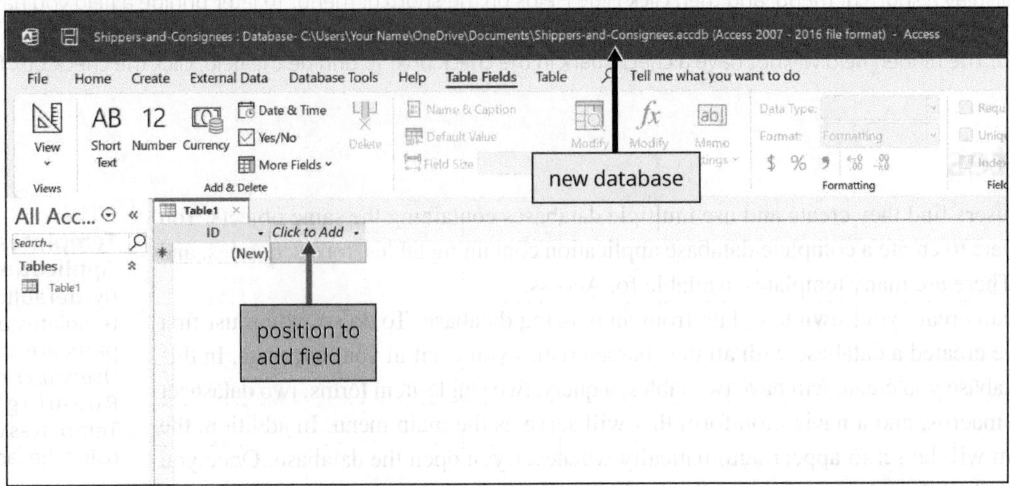

Figure 9–38

To Add Fields to the Table

The tables in the new database will each have an autonumber ID field as the primary key. The following steps add the Shipper ID, Shipper Name, Contact, Phone, Email, and Address fields to a table.

The steps rename the default ID field, which is the table's primary key and is an Autonumber data type, as the Shipper ID field. They add the Shipper Name, Contact, Phone, Email, and Address fields as a single operation by using the Quick Start field created earlier. After adding the fields, they save the table using the name, Shippers.

- Right-click the ID column heading and click Rename Field.
- Type **Shipper ID** as the field name (Figure 9–39).

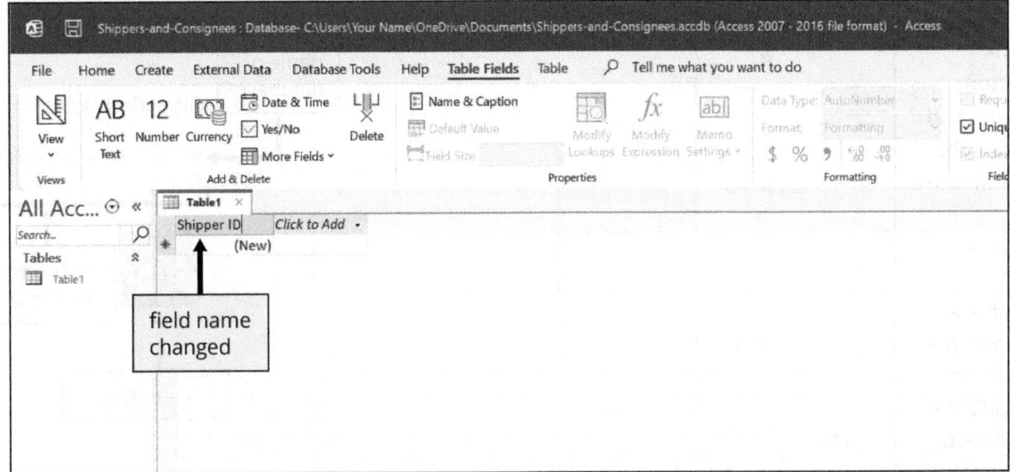

Figure 9–39

2

- Click under the 'Click to Add' column heading and then click it again to produce an insertion point in the next field.
- Click the More Fields button (Table Fields tab | Add & Delete group) to display the More Fields menu.
- Scroll as necessary to display the Name-Contact-Address Quick Start field you created earlier (Figure 9–40).

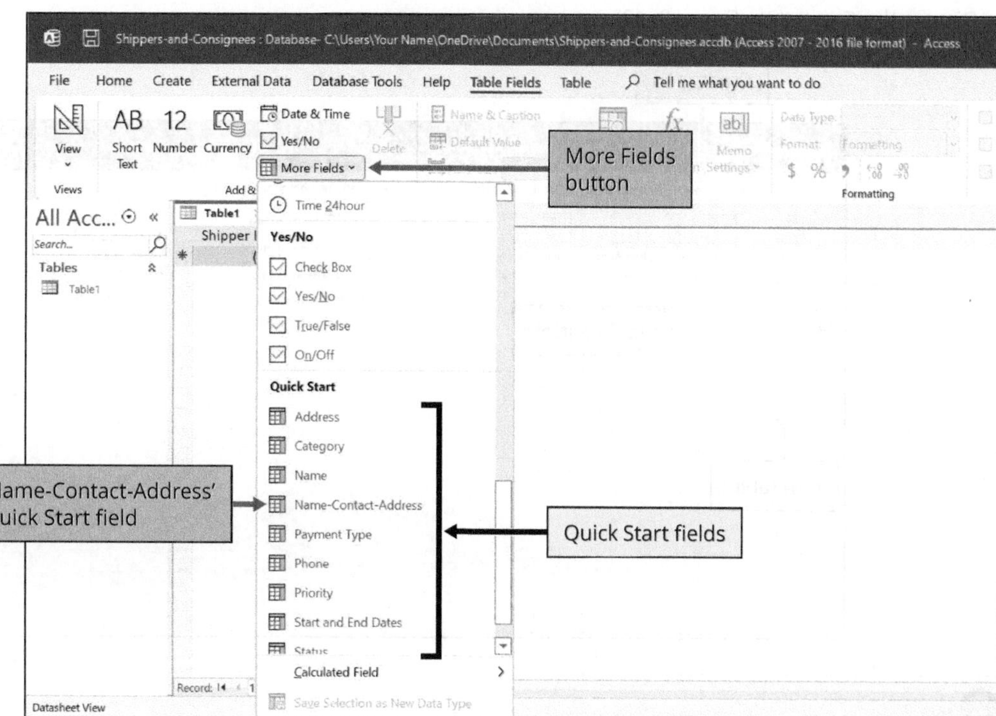

Figure 9–40

3

- Click the Name-Contact-Address Quick Start field to add the Shipper Name, Contact, Phone, Email, and Address fields (Figure 9–41).

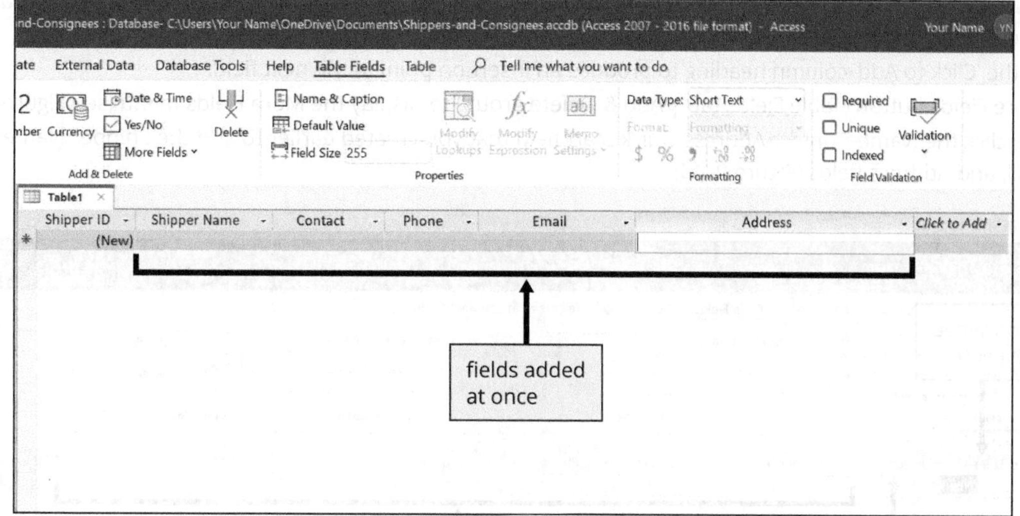

Figure 9–41

4

- Save the table, assigning **Shippers** as the table name.
- Close the table.

To Create a Second Table

The following steps create the Consignees table, which are companies that receive shipments transferred by carriers. The steps add a lookup field for Shipper Name to relate the two tables. **Why?** Because no existing field links the two tables, the relationship between the tables needs to be implemented using a lookup field.

- Display the Create tab (Figure 9–42).

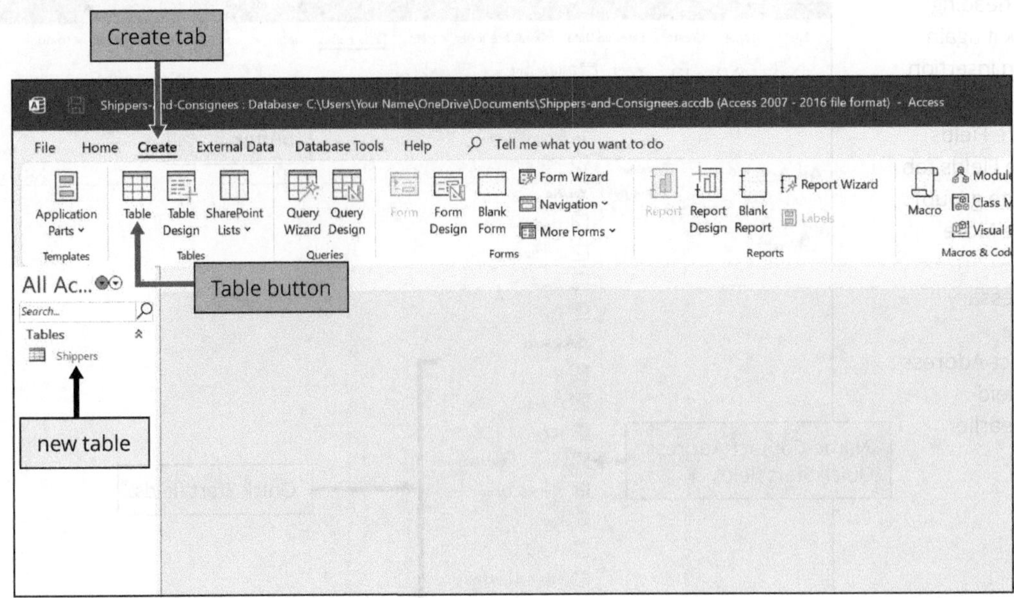

Figure 9–42

2

- Click the Table button (Create tab | Tables group) to create a new table.
- Right-click the ID column heading and click Rename Field.
- Type **Consignee ID** as the field name.
- Click the 'Click to Add' column heading and select Short Text as the data type.
- Type **Consignee Name** as the field name, change the field size to **50** (Table Fields tab | Properties group), and then click under the new field's heading to accept the changes.
- Click under the 'Click to Add' column heading to produce an insertion point in the next field.
- Click the More Fields button (Table Fields tab | Add & Delete group) to display the More Fields menu (see Figure 9–40).
- Scroll to and click the Name-Contact-Address Quick Start field that you created earlier to add the Shipper Name, Contact, Phone, Email, and Address fields (Figure 9–43).

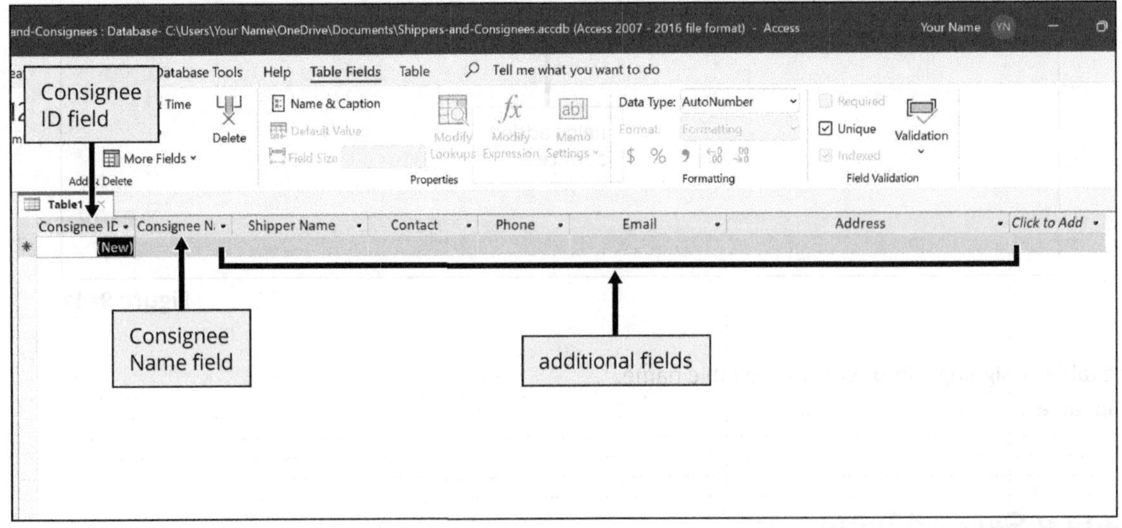

Figure 9–43

- Right-click the Shipper Name field to produce a shortcut menu, and then click Delete Field to delete the field.
- Save the table, assigning **Consignees** as the table name.

4

- Switch to Design view.
- Delete the word, Shipper, from the other fields (Figure 9–44).

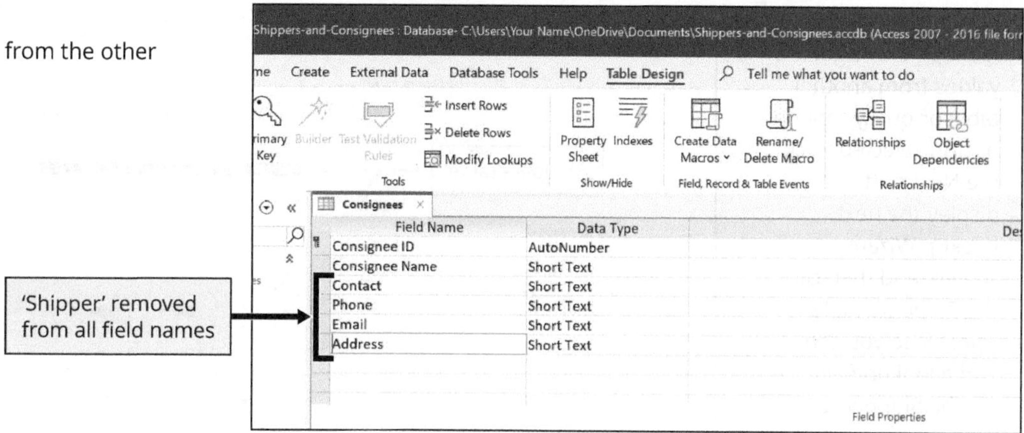

Figure 9–44

5

- Save the table, and switch to Datasheet view.
- Scroll if necessary so the 'Click to Add' column appears on your screen.
- Click the 'Click to Add' column heading to display a menu of available data types (Figure 9–45).

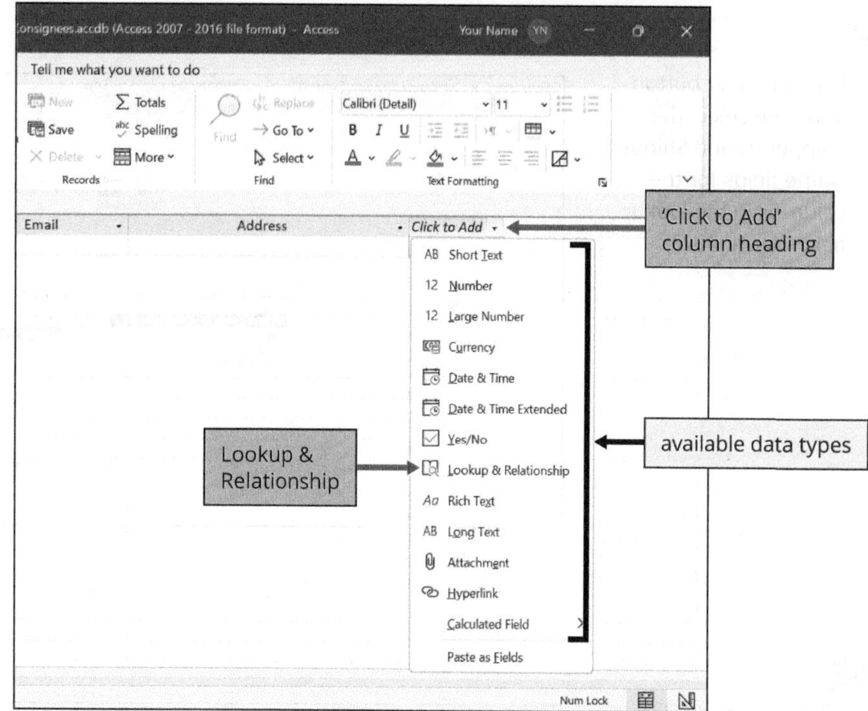

Figure 9–45

BTW
Freezing Fields
The Freeze Fields command allows you to place a column or columns in a table on the left side of the table. As you scroll to the right, the column or columns remain visible. To freeze a column or columns, select the column(s) in Datasheet view, right-click and click Freeze Fields on the shortcut menu. To unfreeze fields, click the `Unfreeze All Fields' command on the shortcut menu. When you freeze a column, Access considers it a change to the layout of the table. When you close the table, Access will ask you if you want to save the changes.

6

- Click Lookup & Relationship to display the Lookup Wizard dialog box (Figure 9–46).

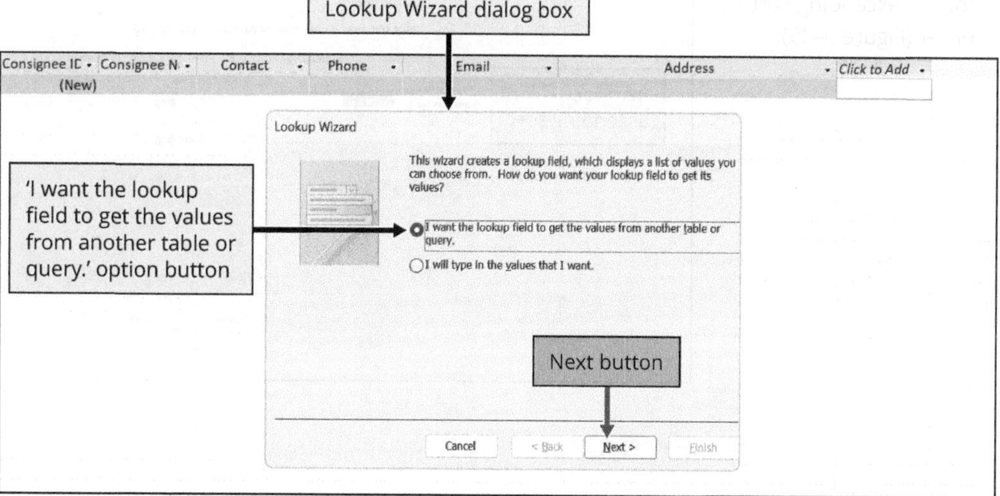

Figure 9–46

- With the 'I want the lookup field to get the values from another table or query.' option button selected, click the Next button to display the next Lookup Wizard screen, and then click the Shippers table to select it so you can add a lookup field for the Shipper ID to the Consignees table (Figure 9–47).

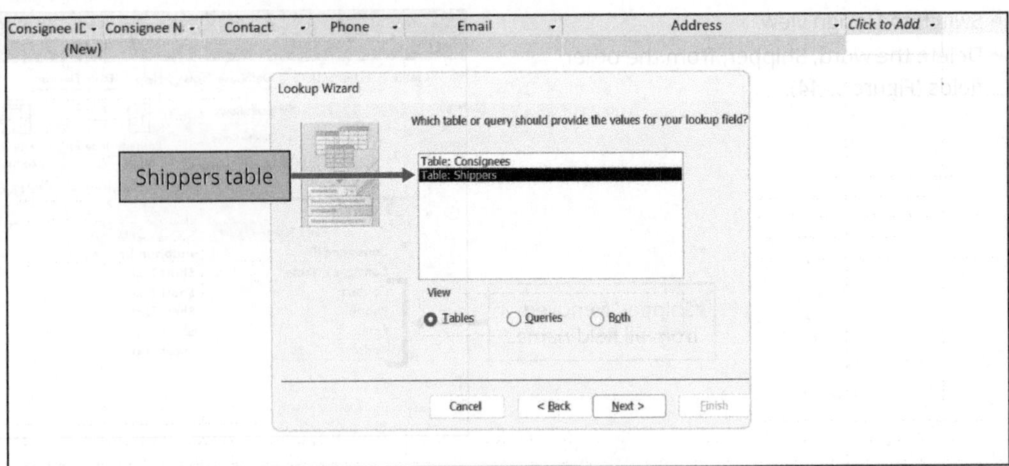

Figure 9–47

- Click the Next button, and then select the Shipper ID and Shipper Name fields for the columns in the lookup field (Figure 9–48).

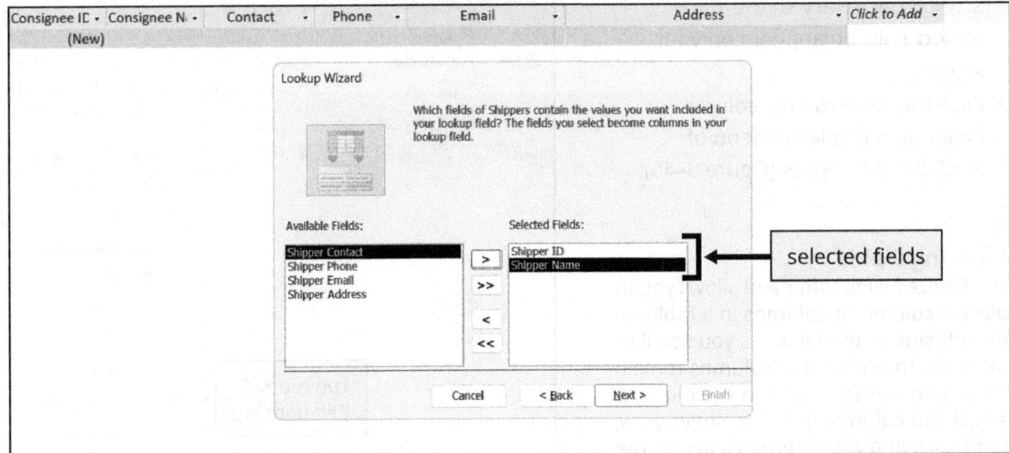

Figure 9–48

- Click Next and select the Shipper ID field for the ascending sort order (Figure 9–49).

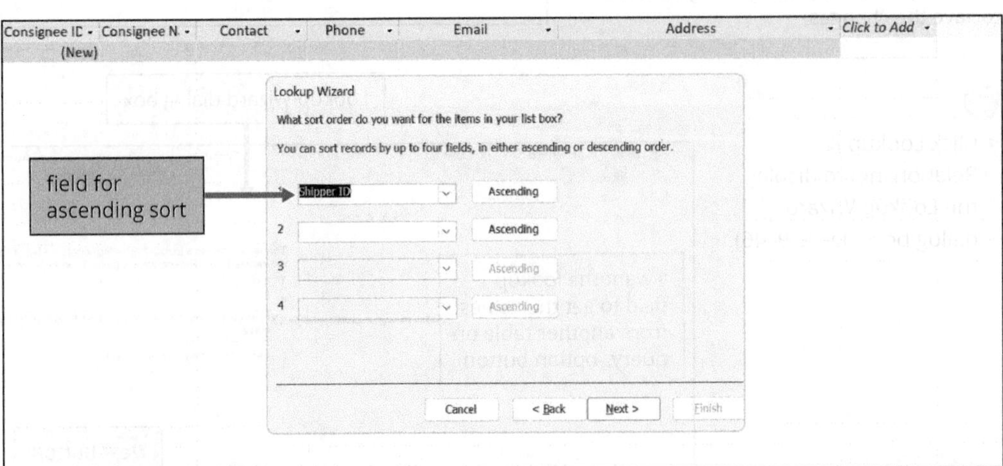

Figure 9–49

- Click Next.
- Ensure the 'Hide key column (recommended)' check box is selected, and then click Next.
- Type **Shipper ID** as the label for the lookup field.
- Click the 'Enable Data Integrity' check box to add a check mark (Figure 9–50).

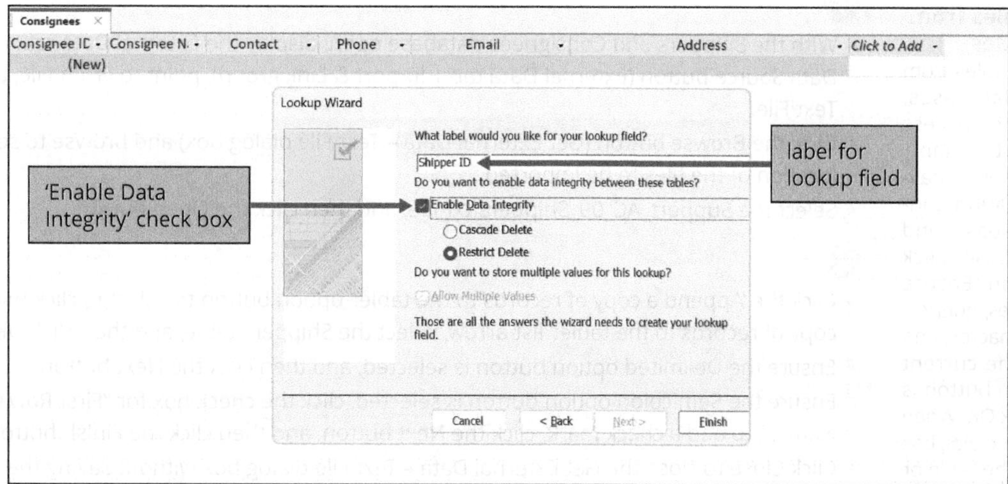

Figure 9–50

Q&A What is the effect of selecting Enable Data Integrity?
Access will enforce referential integrity for the Shipper ID field. That is, Access will not allow a Shipper ID in a consignee record that does not match a shipper in the Shippers table.

- Click Finish to add the lookup field.
- Switch to Design view.
- Select the Shipper ID field.
- Type **Shipper Name** in the Caption property box (Figure 9–51).

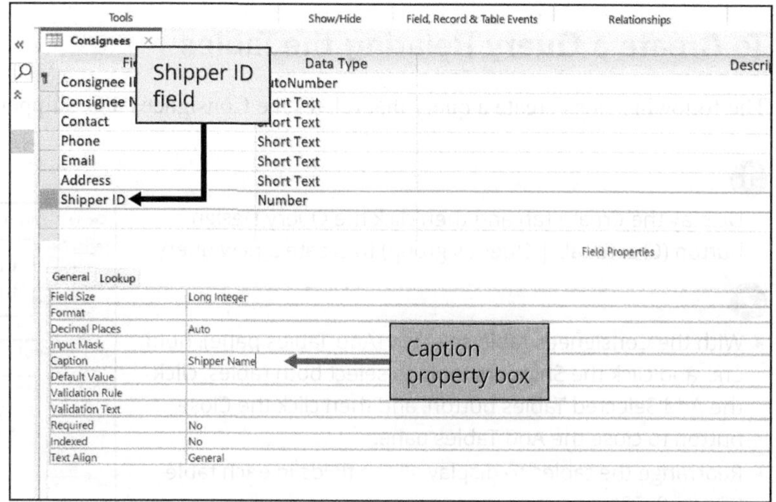

Figure 9–51

- Save the table and switch to Datasheet view.
- Resize the Consignee ID, Consignee Name, and Shipper Name fields for best fit.
- Save and close the table.

Q&A Why does the field's caption need to be Shipper Name if the field will look up the Shipper ID?
The lookup field will create a relationship in this table with the Shipper ID field in the Shippers table. However, you also added the Shipper Name field to the lookup, and the Shipper Name data is what will display in the Consignees table.

To Import the Data

Now that the tables have been created, you need to add data to them. You could enter the data, or if the data is already in electronic form, you could import the data. The data for the Shippers and Consignees tables is included in the Data Files as text files. The following steps import the data.

BTW
Importing Tables from Other Databases
You can import tables from other Access databases. To do so, click the Access button (External Data tab | Import & Link group), navigate to the location containing the database, and select the database. Click the Open button. Ensure the `Import tables, queries, forms, reports, macros, and modules into the current database' option button is selected and click OK. When the Import Object dialog box appears, select the table or tables you want to import and then click OK. You also can import other objects by clicking the appropriate object tabs.

- With the Shippers and Consignees database open, display the External Data tab, click the New Data Source button (External Data tab | Import & Link group), point to From File, and then click Text File.
- Click the Browse button (Get External Data – Text File dialog box) and browse to select the location of the files to be imported.
- Select the Support_AC_09_Shippers.txt file, and then click the Open button.

2

- Click the 'Append a copy of records to the table:' option button to select it, click the 'Append a copy of records to the table:' list arrow, select the Shippers table, and then click OK.
- Ensure the Delimited option button is selected, and then click the Next button.
- Ensure the Semicolon option button is selected, click the check box for "First Row Contains Field Names" to add a check mark, click the Next button, and then click the Finish button.
- Click Close to close the Get External Data – Text File dialog box without saving the import steps.
- Open the Shippers table to confirm the data imported correctly, troubleshoot any problems if necessary, resize all columns for best fit, and then save and close the table.

- Use the technique shown in Steps 1 and 2 to import the Support_AC_09_Consignees.txt file into the Consignees table.

To Create a Query Relating the Tables

The following steps create a query that relates the Consignees and Shippers tables.

- Display the Create tab and then click the Query Design button (Create tab | Queries group) to create a new query.

- With the Consignees table selected (Add Tables pane), hold CTRL and click the Shippers table to select both tables, click the Add Selected Tables button, and then click the Close button to close the Add Tables pane.
- Rearrange the tables to display all the fields in each table (Figure 9–52).

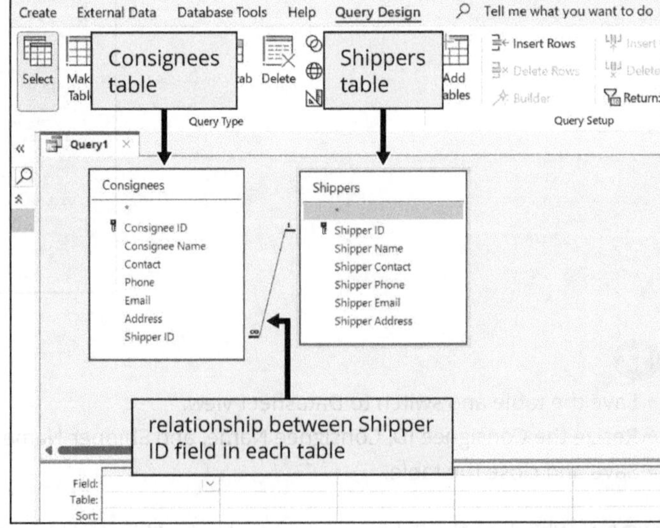

Figure 9–52

- Double-click the Consignee Name and Shipper ID fields from the Consignees table to add these fields to the design grid.
- Double-click the Shipper Contact field from the Shippers table to add this field to the design grid.

- Save the query with the name, **Consignee-Shipper Query**, and close the query.

Creating Forms

There are a few types of forms that need to be created for this database. The Consignee and Shipper detail forms each show a single record at a time. The Consignee, Shipper, and Consignee-Shipper Query forms are intended to look like the corresponding table or query in Datasheet view. Finally, the main menu is a navigation form.

BTW
Rearranging Fields in a Query
If you add fields to a query in the wrong order, you can select the field in the design grid, and drag it to the appropriate location.

To Create Single-Item Forms

The following steps create two single-item forms, that is, forms that display a single record at a time. The first form, called Consignee Details, is for the Consignees table. The second form is for the Shippers table and is called Shipper Details.

- Select the Consignees table in the Navigation Pane if necessary, and then display the Create tab.
- Click the Form button (Create tab | Forms group) to create a single-item form for the Consignees table.
- Save the form with the name, **Consignee Details**, and then close the form.

- Select the Shippers table in the Navigation Pane, display the Create tab, and then click the Form button (Create tab | Forms group) to create a form for the Shippers table that shows the consignees receiving loads from that particular shipper.

- Save the form with the name, **Shipper Details**, and then close the form.

To Create a Navigation Form

The following steps create a navigation form containing a single row of horizontal tabs. The steps save the form using the name, Main Menu. **Why?** This form is intended to function as a menu. The steps change the form title and add the appropriate tabs.

- Display the Create tab and then click the Navigation button (Create tab | Forms group) to display the menu of available navigation forms.
- Click Horizontal Tabs in the menu to create a form with a navigation control in which the tabs are arranged horizontally in a single row.
- If the Field List pane appears, click the 'Add Existing Fields' button (Form Layout Design tab | Tools group) to close the pane.
- Save the navigation form with the name, **Main Menu**, and do not close it yet.

- Click the form title twice, once to select it and the second time to produce an insertion point.
- Delete the current title and then type **Shippers and Consignees** as the new title (Figure 9–53).

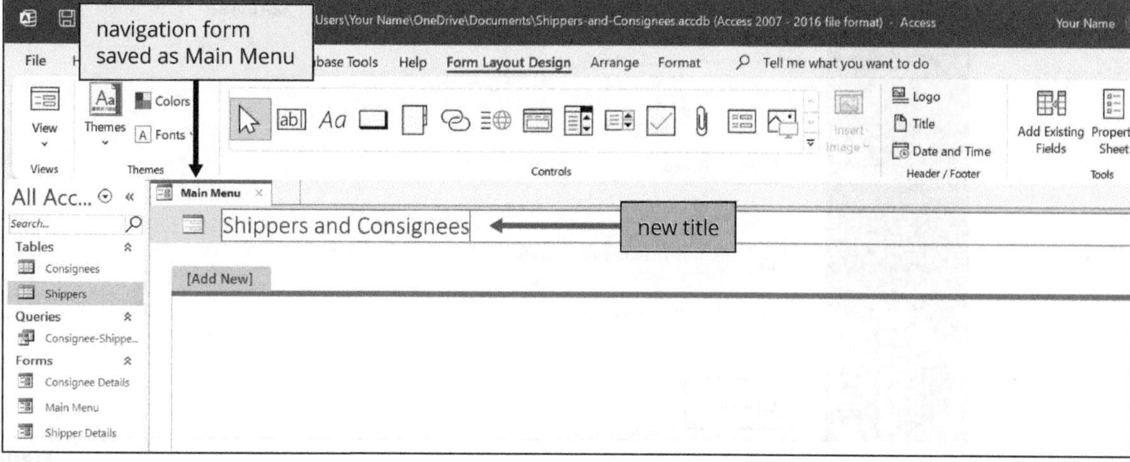

Figure 9–53

- One at a time, drag the Shipper Details form and the Consignee Details form to the positions shown in Figure 9–54.
- Save and close the form.

Q&A What should I do if I made a mistake and added a form to the wrong location?
You can rearrange the tabs by dragging. However, the simplest way to correct a mistake is to click the Undo button (Home tab | Undo group) to reverse your most recent action. You can also choose to simply close the form without saving it and then start over.

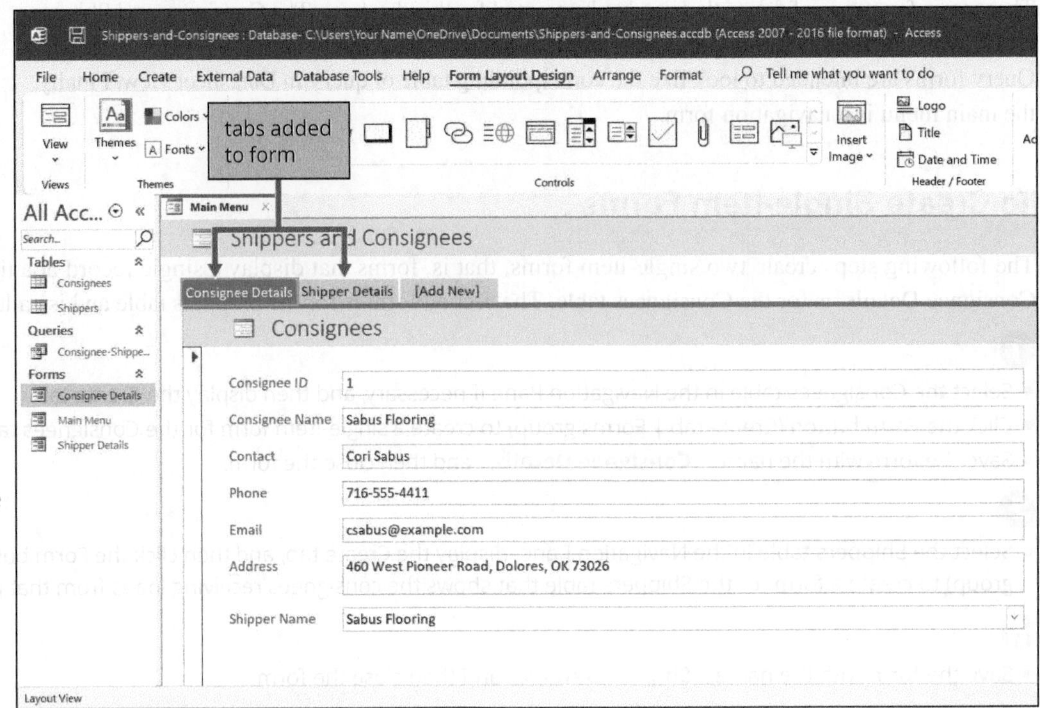

Figure 9–54

To Select a Startup Form

If the database includes a navigation form, it is common to select the navigation form as a **startup form**, which launches when the user opens the database. **Why?** Designating the navigation form as a startup form ensures the form will appear automatically when a user opens the database. The following steps designate the navigation form as a startup form.

- Click File on the ribbon to display Backstage view (Figure 9–55).

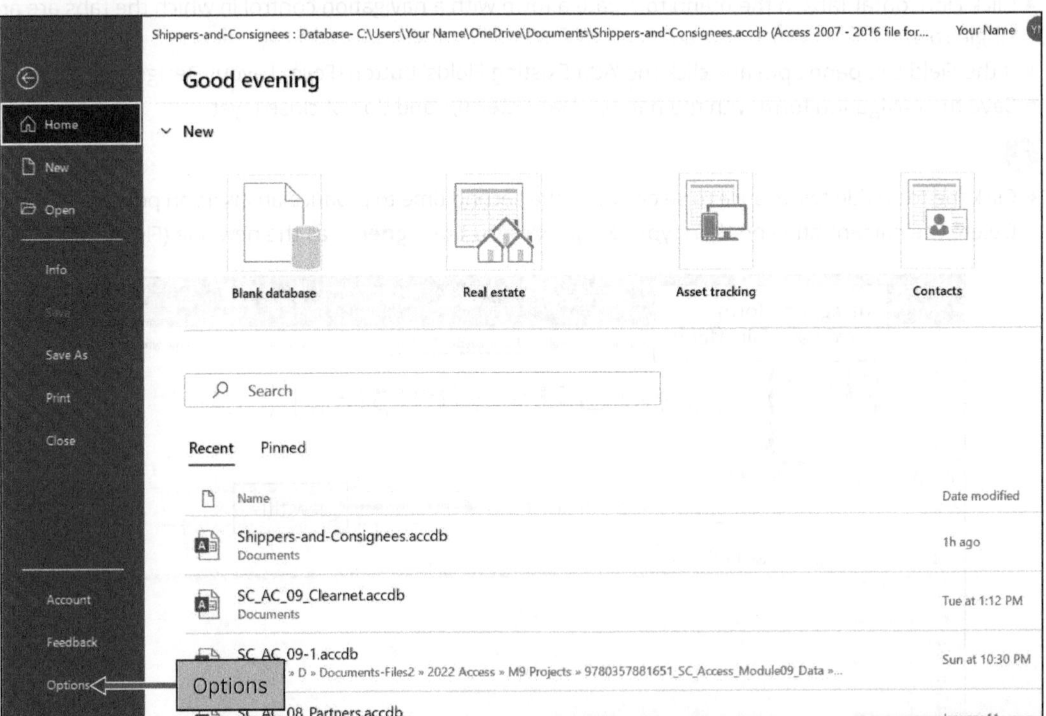

Figure 9–55

2

- Click Options to open the Access Options dialog box.
- Click Current Database (Access Options dialog box) to select the options for the current database.
- Click the Display Form arrow to display the list of available forms (Figure 9–56).

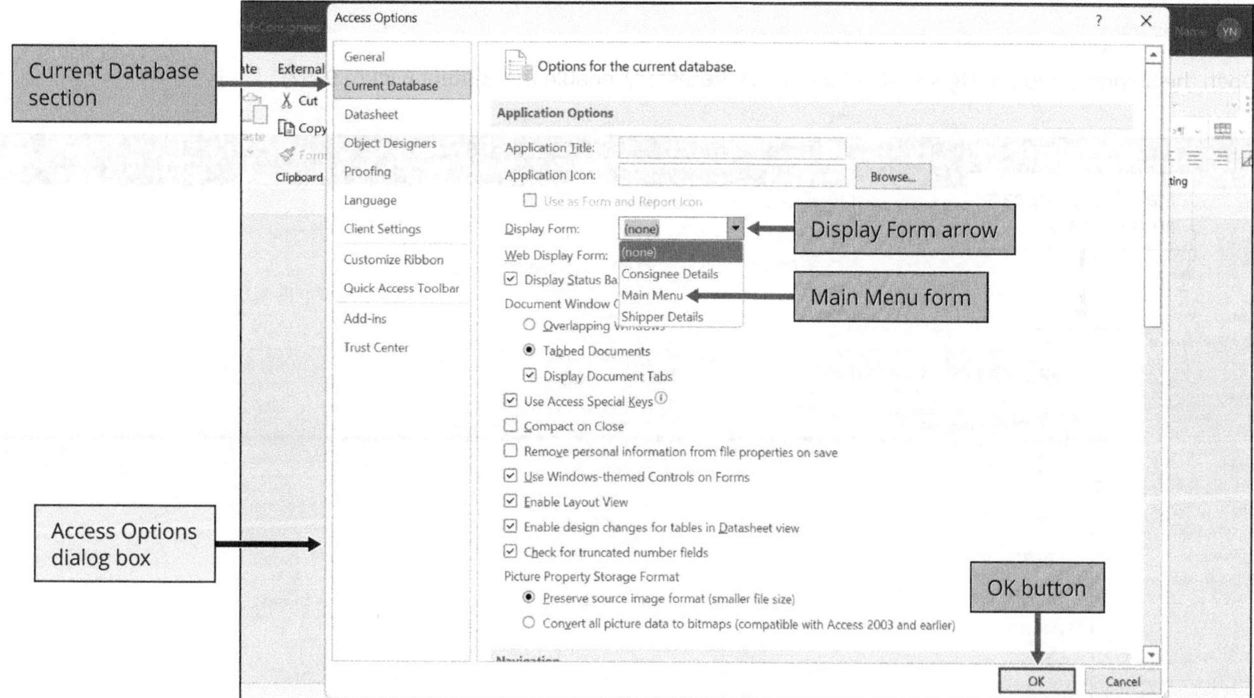

Figure 9–56

- Click Main Menu to select it as the form that will be automatically displayed whenever the database is opened.
- Click OK (Access Options dialog box) to save your changes.
- Click OK (Microsoft Access dialog box) when Access displays a message indicating that you must close and reopen the database for the change to take effect.
- Close the database without exiting Access.

Break Point: If you wish to take a break, this is a good place to do so. You can quit Access now. To resume at a later time, start Access and continue following the steps from this location forward.

Templates and Application Parts

An Access **template** is a file that contains the elements needed to produce a specific type of complete database. You can select a template when you create a database. The resulting database will contain all the tables, queries, forms, reports, and macros included in the template. In addition, with some templates, the resulting database might also contain data.

Some templates are also available as **application parts**. Application parts are a type of template, and selecting a single application part can also create tables, queries, forms, reports, and macros. Typically, application parts are used for adding one or a few objects, while larger templates are more often used to create a larger group of objects, even a complete database. Templates that are also saved as application parts can be accessed during database creation or after the database is created.

Access provides a number of templates representing a variety of types of databases. You can also create your own template from an existing database. When you create a template, you can choose to create an application part as well. When creating templates and application parts, you can also include data if desired.

To Create a Template and an Application Part

The following steps create a template from the Shippers and Consignees database. **Why?** The Shippers and Consignees database now contains all the tables, queries, and forms you want in the template. A template will create all the same objects when you want to create similar databases. The steps also create an application part from the database so you can reuse the parts in other databases.

- Open the Shippers and Consignees database and, if necessary, enable the content (Figure 9–57).

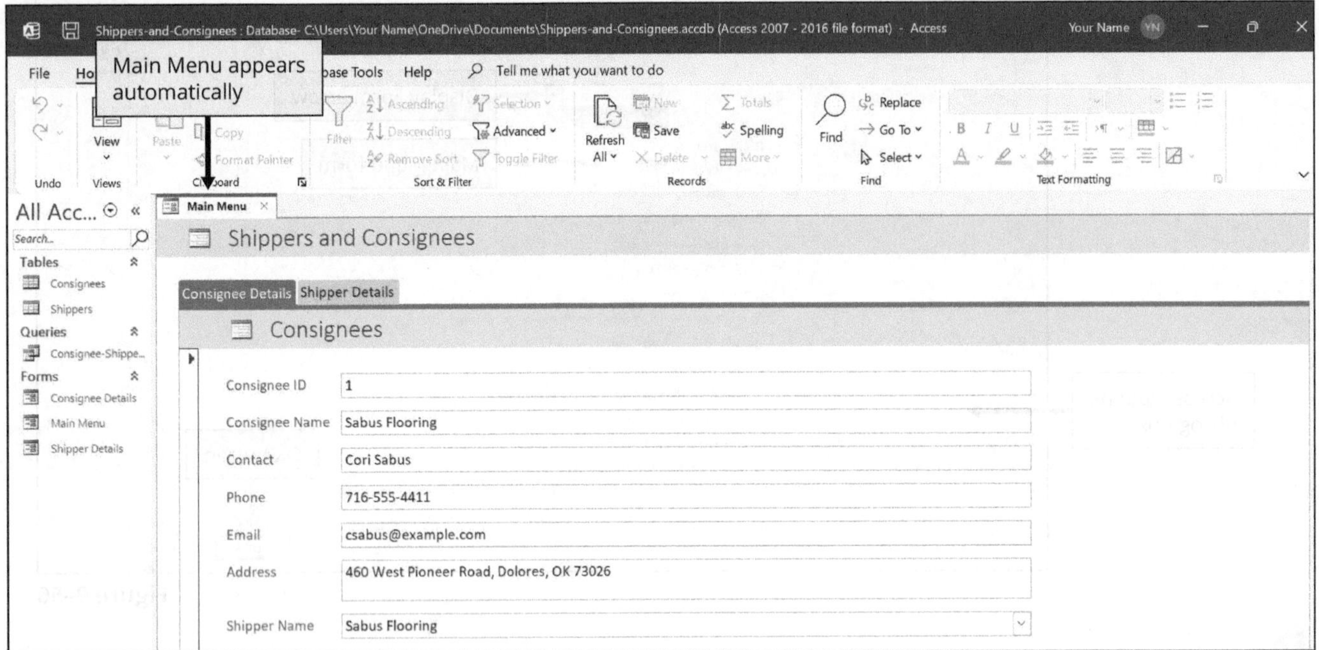

Figure 9–57

- Close the Main Menu form.
- Open Backstage view.
- Click Save As to open the Save As screen.
- Click the Template (*.accdt) button in the Save Database As area to indicate you are creating a template (Figure 9–58).

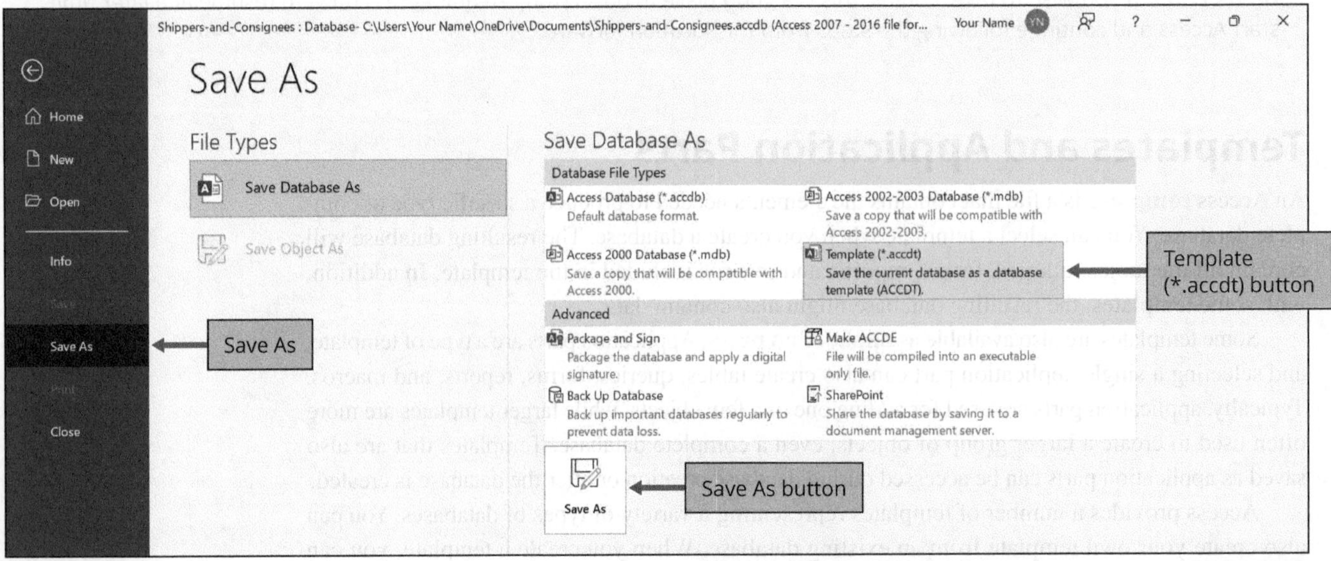

Figure 9–58

- Click the Save As button to display the Create New Template from This Database dialog box.
- Type **Shippers and Consignees** as the name for the new template.
- Type **Database of shippers and consignees with navigation form menu** as the description.
- Click the Application Part check box to indicate you also want to create an application part.
- Click the 'Include All Data in Package' check box to indicate you want to include the data in the database as part of the template (Figure 9–59).

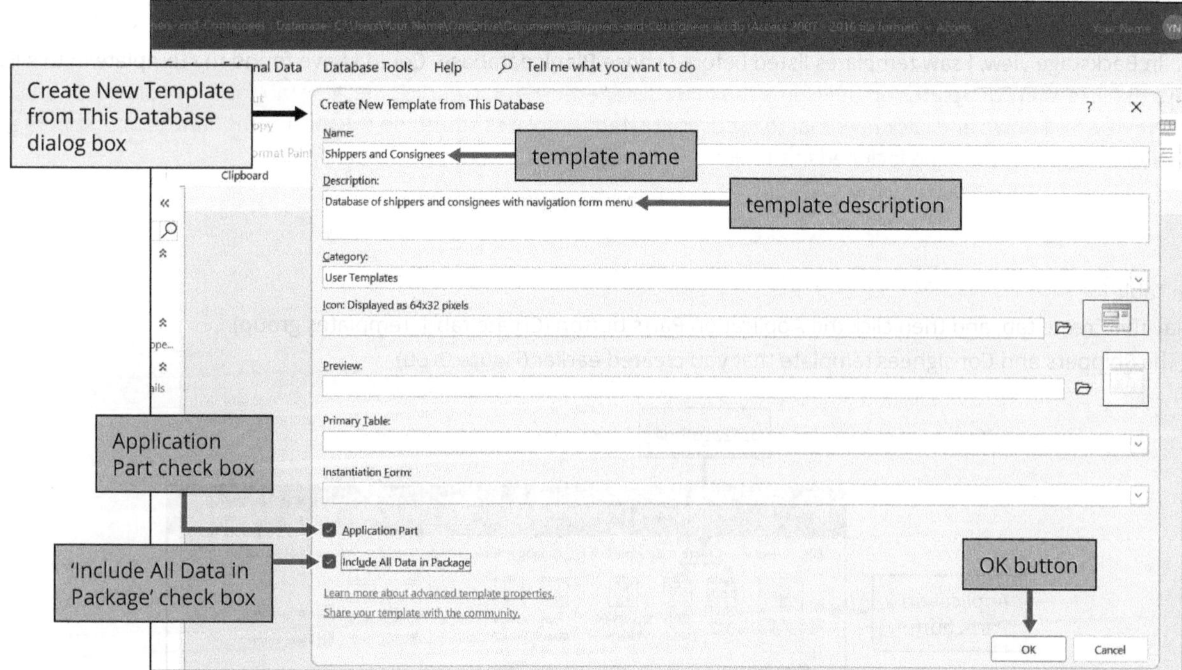

Figure 9–59

Q&A Why include data in the template?
Anytime a user creates a database using the template, the database will automatically include data. This enables the users to see what any reports, forms, or queries look like with data in them. Once the users have the reports, forms, and queries the way they want them, they can delete all this data. At that point, they can begin adding their own data to the database.

- Click OK (Create New Template from This Database dialog box) to create the template.
- When Access indicates the template has been successfully saved, click OK (Microsoft Access dialog box).

Q&A Access did not let me choose where to save my template. How can I find my template file?
By default, Access saves new templates to the following location:
C:\Users*user name*\AppData\Roaming\Microsoft\Templates\Access\
You can find your template at this location along with the quick start field you created earlier in this module. However, in the next section, you will access the template from within Access, which will know where your template is stored.

sam! The following steps on pages 40–41 require the Shippers and Consignees template created in the previous section. Credit will not be received unless the correct template is imported to the start file downloaded below. Please make sure you have completed the steps on pages 27–39 before starting the next section.

To Use a Template or Application Part

You can use the Shippers and Consignees template just as you would use any other template, such as the Blank database template you previously used. To do this, you click the Personal link in Backstage view to list any templates you have created and choose a template from that list. Alternatively, because you also created the template as an application part, you can apply the application part after creating a database. The only difference is that, after creating a blank database, you need to apply the template using the Application Parts button on the Create ribbon. **Why?** The application part contains the objects and data that should be created in the new database.

The following steps use the application part created earlier to create the Freightliners Customers database.

- sam With Access open, click File on the ribbon to open Backstage view.
- Click the 'Blank database' button.
- Type **SC_AC_09_Freightliners-Customers** as the name of the database, and then navigate to the location where you will store the new database.
- Click the Create button to create the database.

Q&A In Backstage view, I saw templates listed before I chose Blank database. Could I have found my template in this list?
Yes. Access lists a few templates on the Home tab in Backstage view. You can click the New tab for a longer list. On the New screen, scroll down and click Personal to list user-created templates stored on the local computer. Your Shippers and Consignees template would be included in this list.

- Close Table1.
- Display the Create tab, and then click the Application Parts button (Create tab | Templates group).
- Click the Shippers and Consignees template that you created earlier (Figure 9–60).

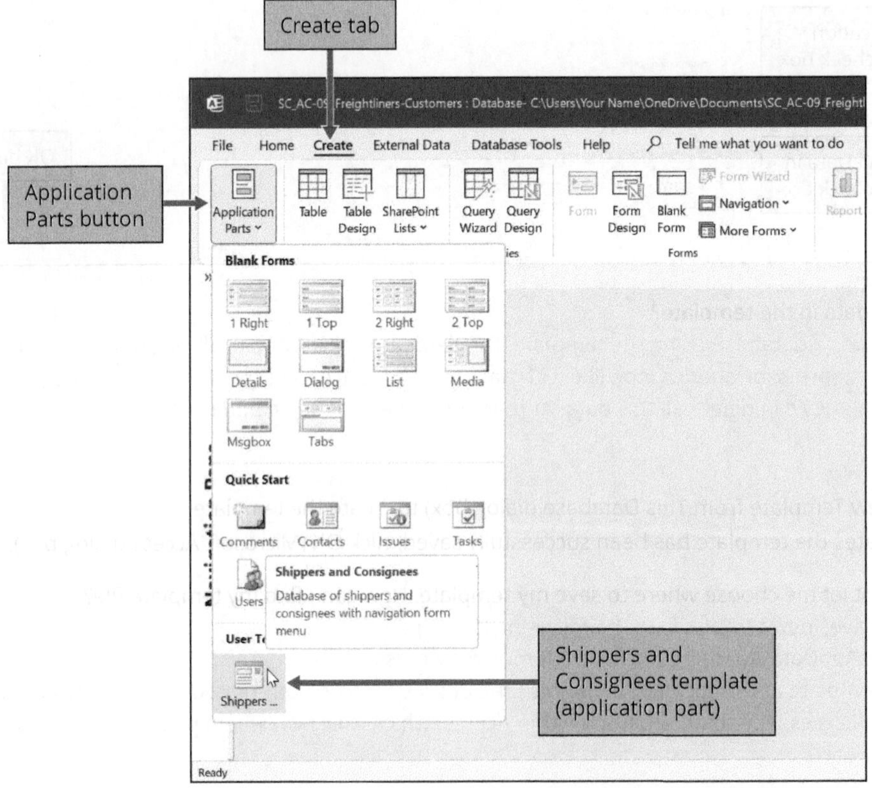

Figure 9–60

Q&A When I clicked my template, I got a message saying "All open objects must be closed before instantiating this application part." Is this a problem?
This is not a problem. You will receive this message if you did not first close the default Table1, and the message is offering to close all open objects. After you click the Yes button, Access will add all the objects in the application part to the database. If you had already created other objects in the database, they would still be included.

3

- Open the Navigation Pane and explore the database to confirm all the objects and data are included from the template (Figure 9–61). Make sure to open each table to confirm all data is included.
- Close the database.
- If desired, sign out of your Microsoft account.
- sam Exit Access.

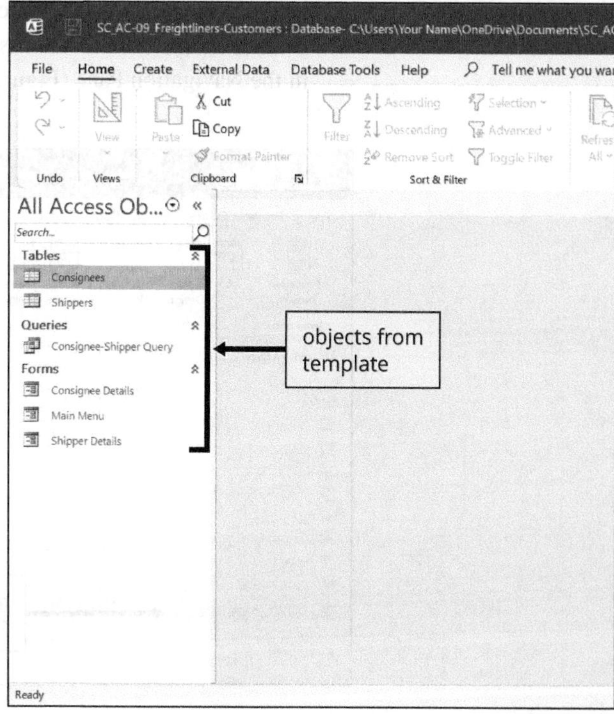

Figure 9–61

Note: Unless your instructor indicates otherwise, you are encouraged to simply read the material in this module from this point forward without carrying out any operations. If you decide to try these steps for yourself, it is important to make a backup copy of your database and store it in a secure location before performing the following operations. This way, if something damages your database or you can no longer access your database, you still can use the backup copy.

Blank Forms Application Parts

Blank Forms application parts (see Figure 9–62) represent a way to create certain types of forms. To do so, you click the Application Parts button to display the gallery of application part styles,

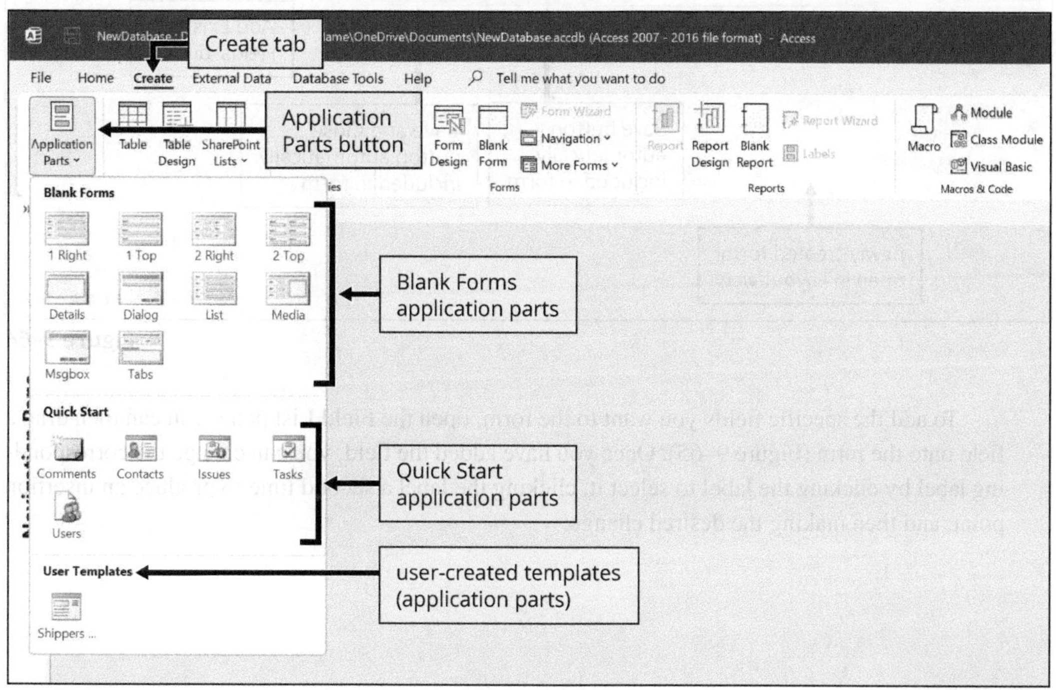

Figure 9–62

and then click the desired type of form, for example, 1 Right. Access then creates a form with the desired characteristics and assigns it a name. It does not open the form, but you can see the form in the Navigation Pane (Figure 9–63).

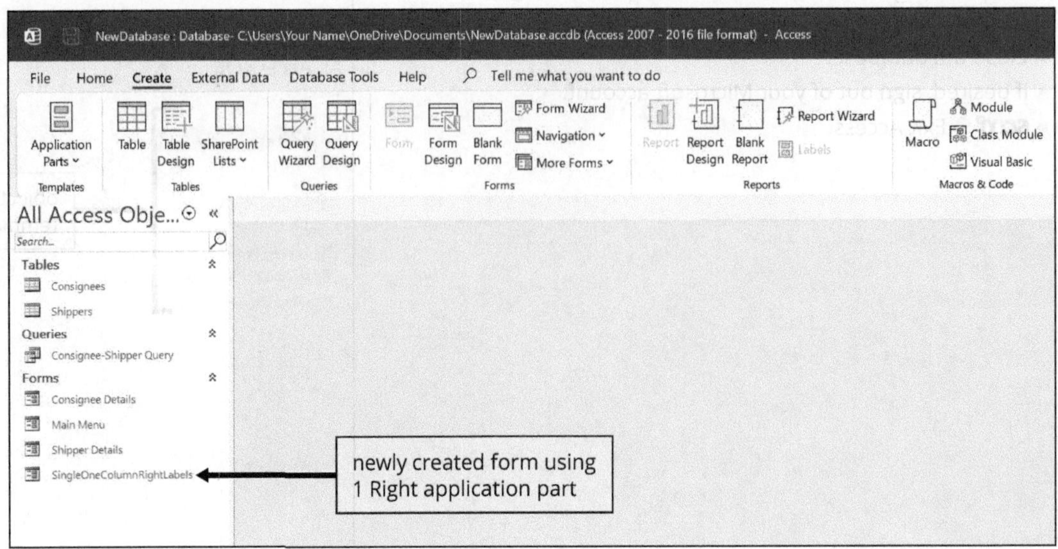

Figure 9–63

You can modify the form by opening the form in Layout or Design view (Figure 9–64). This particular form automatically creates a Save button. Clicking this button when you are using the form will save changes to the current record. The form also automatically includes a Save & Close button. Clicking this button will save changes to the current record and then close the form.

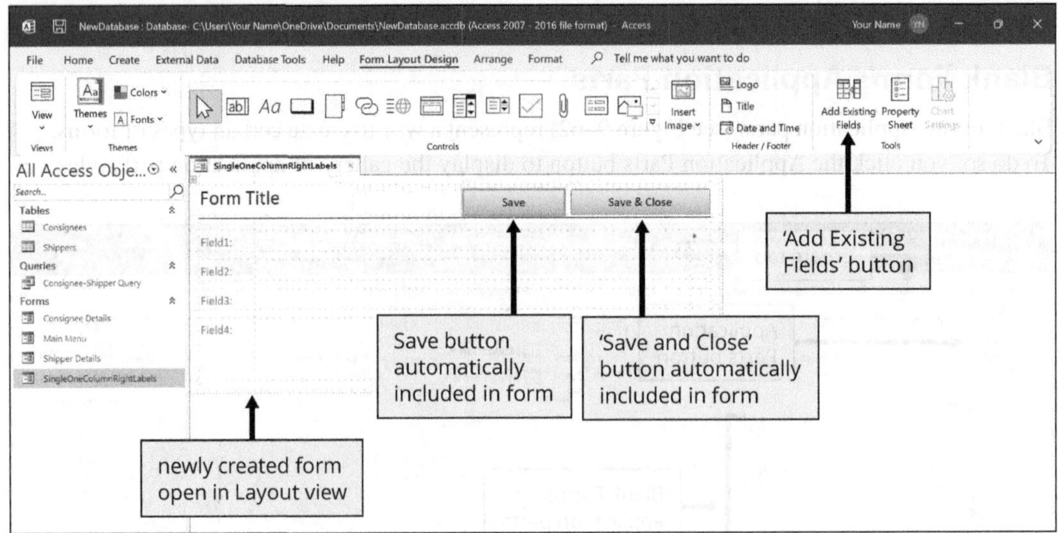

Figure 9–64

To add the specific fields you want to the form, open the Field List pane. You can then drag a field onto the form (Figure 9–65). Once you have added the field, you can change the corresponding label by clicking the label to select it, clicking the label a second time to produce an insertion point, and then making the desired change.

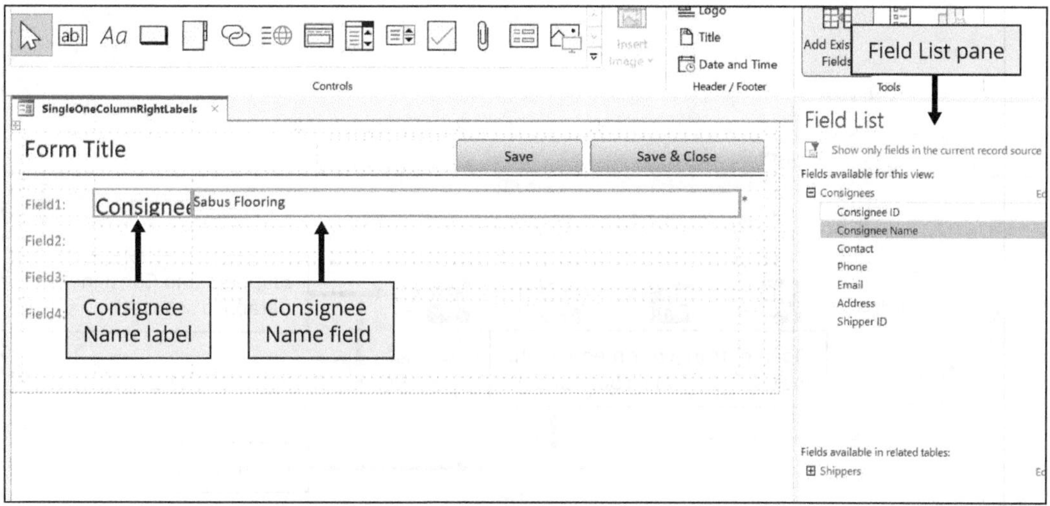

Figure 9–65

Q&A When adding fields to the form, can I add only the field itself and not the label?
Yes. If you want to add only the data within each field and not the label (such as "Consignee Name"), hold CTRL while dragging the field to the form from the Field List pane.

Database Encryption

Encryption refers to storing data in an encoded format that typically cannot be read without first decrypting it. Anytime a user stores or modifies data in the encrypted database, the database management system (DBMS) will encode the data before updating the database. When a legitimate user retrieves the data using the DBMS, the data is first decoded. The entire encryption process is transparent to legitimate users; that is, they are not even aware it is happening. If unauthorized users attempt to bypass all the controls of the DBMS and get to the database through a utility program or a word processor, however, they will only be able to see the encoded, and unreadable, version of the data. In Access, you encrypt a database and set a password as part of the same operation.

BTW
Encryption and Passwords
Encryption helps prevent unauthorized use of an Access database. Consider using encryption when the database contains sensitive data, such as medical records or employee records. Passwords should be 12 or more characters in length. The longer the length of the password and the more random the characters, the more difficult it is for someone to determine. Use a combination of uppercase and lowercase letters as well as numbers and special symbols when you create a password. Make sure that you remember your password. If you forget it, there is no method for retrieving it. You will be unable to open the encrypted database.

To Open a Database in Exclusive Mode

To encrypt a database and set a password, the database first must be open in exclusive mode, which prevents other users from accessing the database in any way. To open a database in exclusive mode, you use the Open arrow (Figure 9–66) rather than simply clicking the Open button.

To open a database in exclusive mode, you would use the following steps.

1. If necessary, close any open databases while keeping Access open.

   Q&A How can I close the database without closing Access?
   Click the File tab to open Backstage view, and then click Close.

2. Click Open to display the Open screen.
3. Click Browse on the Open screen to display the Open dialog box.
4. Navigate to the location of the database to be opened.
5. Click the name of the database to be opened.
6. Click the Open arrow to display the Open button menu.
7. Click Open Exclusive to open the database in exclusive mode.

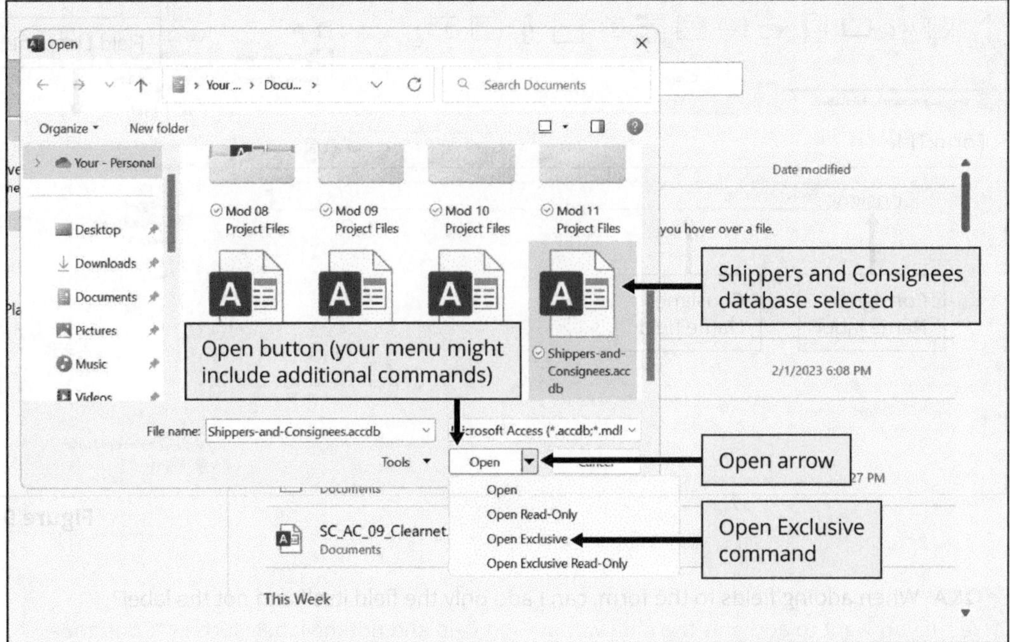

Figure 9–66

Consider This

What is the purpose of each of the other modes?

The Open option opens the database in a mode so it can be shared by other users. Open Read-Only allows you to read the data in the database, but not update the database.

Encrypting a Database with a Password

If you wanted to encrypt the database with a password, you first would open Backstage view and display the Info screen (Figure 9–67).

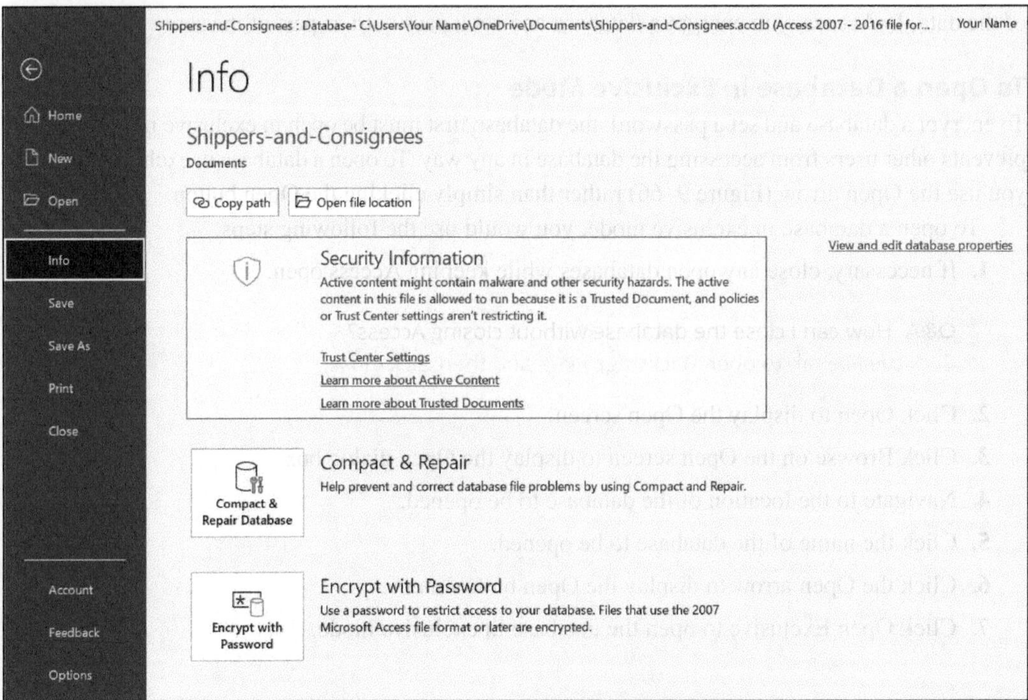

Figure 9–67

You would then click the 'Encrypt with Password' button to display the Set Database Password dialog box. Enter the password you have chosen in both the Password text box and the Verify text box (Figure 9–68).

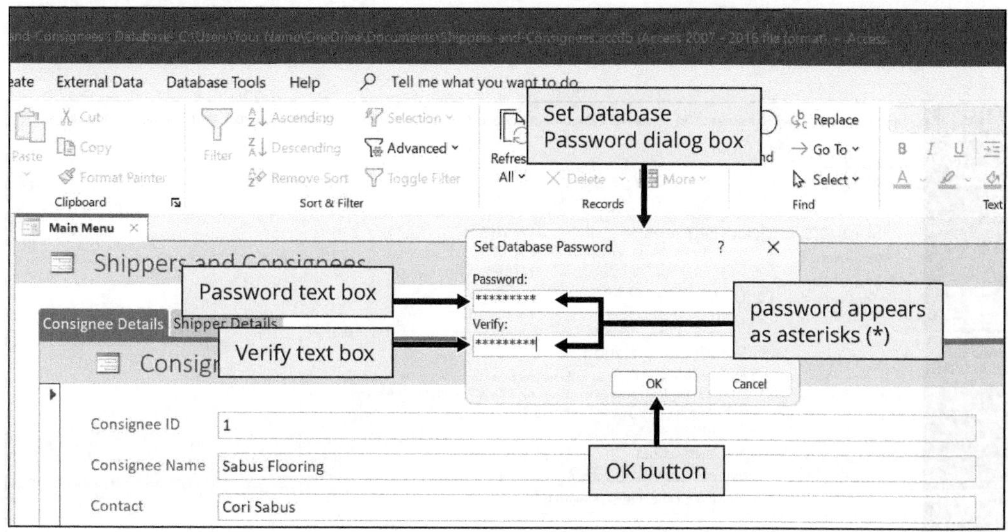

Figure 9–68

To Encrypt a Database with a Password

With the database open in exclusive mode, you would use the following steps to encrypt the database with a password.

1. Click File on the ribbon to open Backstage view and ensure that the Info screen is displayed.
2. Click the 'Encrypt with Password' button to display the Set Database Password dialog box.
3. Type the desired password in the Password text box (Set Database Password dialog box).
4. Press TAB and then type the password again in the Verify text box.
5. Click OK to encrypt the database and set the password.
6. If you get a message indicating that row level locking will be ignored, click OK.
7. Close the database.

Consider This

Is the password case sensitive?

Yes, you must enter the password using the same case you used when you created it.

Opening a Database with a Password

When you open a database that has a password, you will be prompted to enter your password in the Password Required dialog box. Once you have done so, click OK. Assuming you have entered your password correctly, Access will then open the database.

Decrypting a Database and Removing a Password

If the encryption and the password are no longer necessary, you can decrypt the database. The database will no longer have a password. If you later found you needed the database to be encrypted, you could repeat the steps to encrypt the database and add a password. On the Info screen in Backstage view, the button to encrypt a database with a password has changed to Decrypt Database (Figure 9–69).

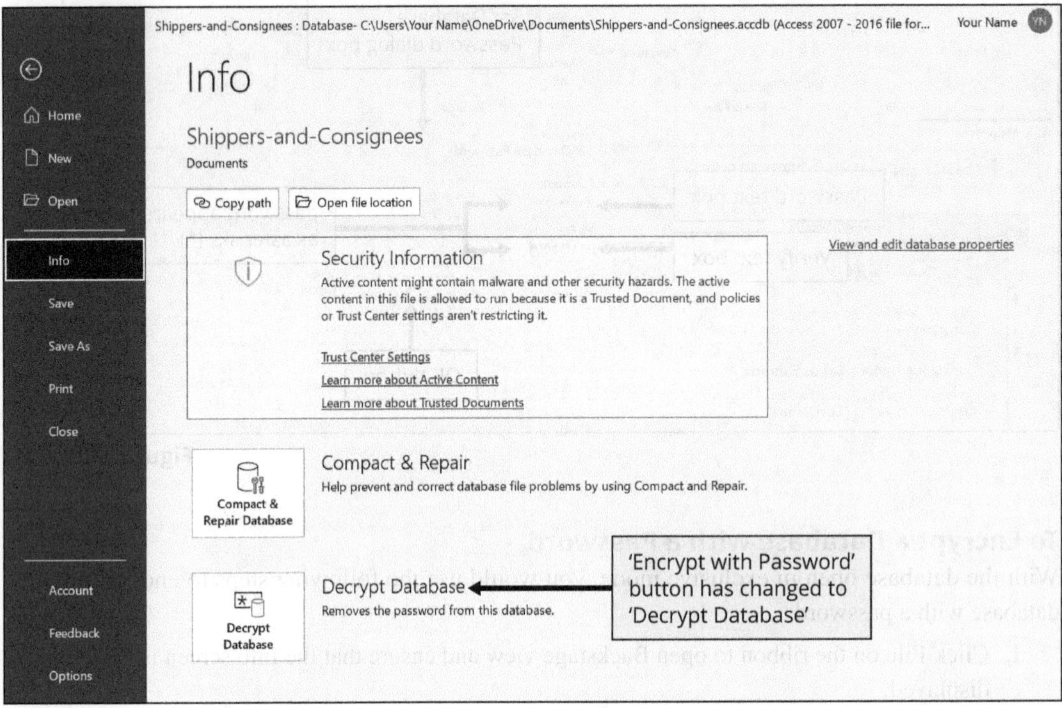

Figure 9–69

To Decrypt the Database and Remove the Password

To decrypt a database that you have previously encrypted and remove the password, you would use the following steps.

1. Open in exclusive mode the database to be decrypted, entering your password when requested.
2. Open Backstage view and then click Info.
3. Click the Decrypt Database button to display the Unset Database Password dialog box.
4. Type the password in the Password box.
5. Click OK to remove the password and decrypt the database.
6. Close the database.

BTW
Security
One part of database security is the prevention of unauthorized access to a database. Within an organization, the database administrator determines the types of access individual users can have to the database. Various government rules and regulations, such as the Sarbanes-Oxley Act (SOX) and the Health Insurance Portability and Accountability Act (HIPAA), require database administrators to have strict security procedures in place to protect data from unauthorized users.

The Trust Center

The Trust Center is a feature within Access where you can set security options and also find the latest information on technology related to privacy, safety, and security. To use the Trust Center, you click File on the ribbon and then click Options to display the Access Options dialog box. You then click Trust Center to display the Trust Center content (Figure 9–70). You then click the 'Trust Center Settings' button to display the Trust Center dialog box in which you can make changes in the following categories.

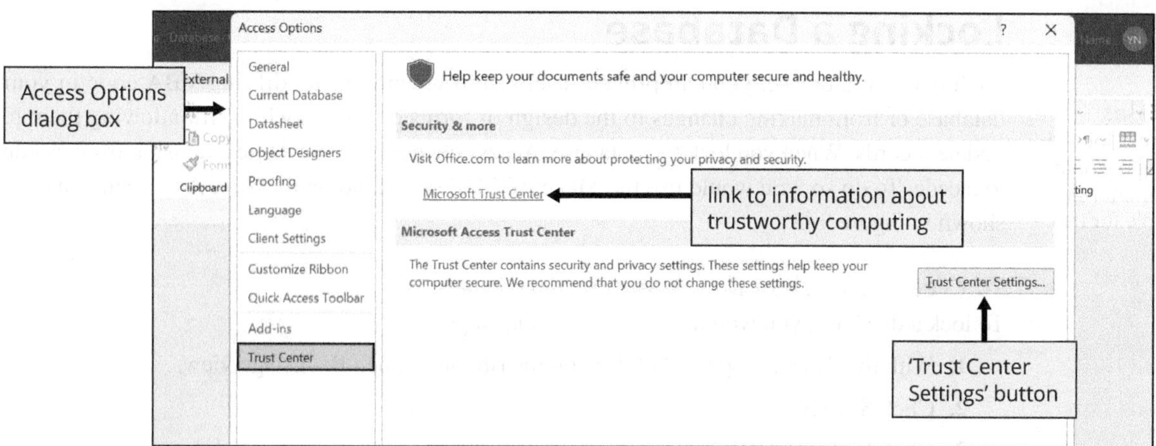

Figure 9–70

Trusted Publishers. Clicking Trusted Publishers in the Trust Center dialog box shows the list of trusted software publishers. To view details about a trusted publisher, click the publisher and then click the View button. To remove a trusted publisher from the list, click the publisher and then click the Remove button if it is available for that publisher. Users may also add trusted publishers.

Trusted Locations. Clicking Trusted Locations shows the list of trusted locations on the Internet or within a user's network. A trusted location is treated as a trusted source for opening a database stored in that location. To add a new location, click the 'Add new location…' button. To remove or modify an existing location, click the location and then click the Remove or Modify button.

Trusted Documents. You can designate certain documents, including database, Word, Excel, and other files, as trusted. When opening a trusted document, you will not be prompted to enable the content, even if the content of the document has changed. You should be very careful when designating a document as trusted and only do so when you are absolutely sure the document is from a trusted source.

Trusted Add-in Catalogs. Use this option to specify trusted catalogs of web add-ins. You can also indicate whether Access will allow web add-ins to start.

Add-ins. Add-ins are additional programs that you can install and use within Access. Some come with Access and are typically installed using the Access Setup program. Others can be purchased from other vendors. Clicking Add-ins gives you the opportunity to specify restrictions concerning Add-ins.

ActiveX Settings. When you use ActiveX controls within an Office app, Office prompts you to accept the controls. The ActiveX settings allow you to determine the level of prompting from Office.

Macro Settings. Macros written by other users have the potential to harm your computer; for example, a macro could spread a virus. The Trust Center uses special criteria, including valid digital signatures, reputable certificates, and trusted publishers, to determine whether a macro is safe. If the Trust Center discovers a macro that is potentially unsafe, it will take appropriate action. The action the Trust Center takes depends on the Macro Setting you have selected. Clicking Macro Settings enables you to select or change this setting.

Message Bar. Clicking Message Bar lets you choose whether the message bar should appear when content has been blocked.

Privacy Options. Clicking Privacy Options lets you set security settings to protect your personal privacy.

Form-based Sign-in. Clicking Form-based Sign-in lets you choose whether to allow sign-in prompts separate from an organizationally administered directory service (such as Active Directory). Because this setting introduces a security risk, the default setting blocks form-based authentication.

BTW
ActiveX controls
ActiveX controls are small programs that can run within an Office app. The calendar control is an example of an ActiveX control.

Locking a Database

BTW
Locked Databases
When you create a locked database, the original database remains unchanged and is still available for use.

By locking a database, you can prevent users from viewing or modifying VBA code in your database or from making changes to the design of forms or reports while still allowing them to update records. When you lock the database, Access changes the file name extension from .accdb to .accde. To do so, you would use the Make ACCDE command on the Save As screen, which is shown in Figure 9–3.

To Create a Locked Database (ACCDE File)

To lock a database, you would use the following steps.

1. With the database open, click File on the ribbon to open Backstage view.
2. Click Save As.
3. Click Make ACCDE in the Advanced area.
4. Click the Save As button.
5. In the Save As dialog box, indicate a location and name for the ACCDE file.
6. Click the Save button in the Save As dialog box to create the file.

Using a Locked Database

You would use an ACCDE file just as you use the databases with which you are now familiar, with two exceptions. First, you must select ACCDE files in the 'Files of type' box when opening the file. Second, be aware that you will not be able to modify any source code or change the design of any forms or reports. If you right-clicked the Consignee form, for example, you would find the Design View command on the shortcut menu is dimmed, as are many other commands (Figure 9–71).

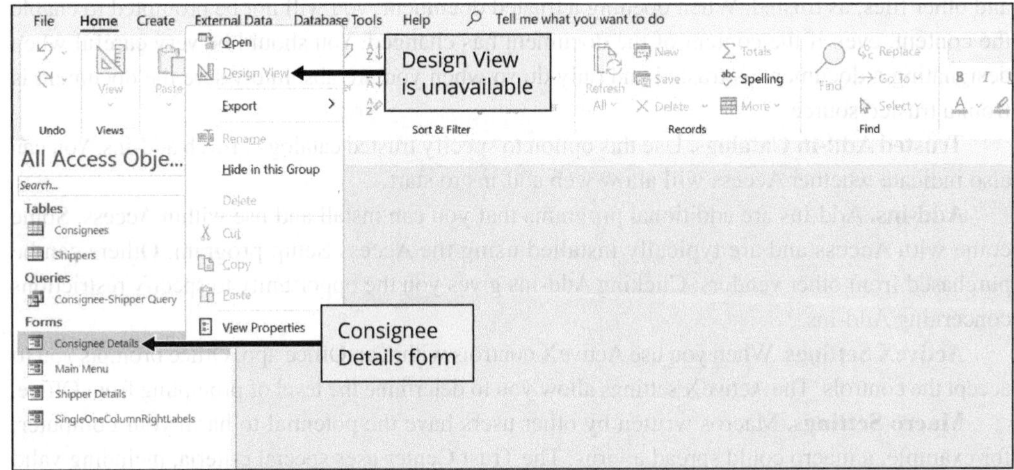

Figure 9–71

It is very important that you save your original database in case you ever need to make changes to VBA code or to the design of a form or report. You cannot use the ACCDE file to make such changes, nor can you convert the ACCDE file back to the ACCDB file format.

Record Locking

You can indicate how records are to be locked when multiple users are using a database at the same time. To do so, click File on the ribbon, click Options, and then click the Client Settings tab. Scroll down so the Advanced area appears on the screen (Figure 9–72).

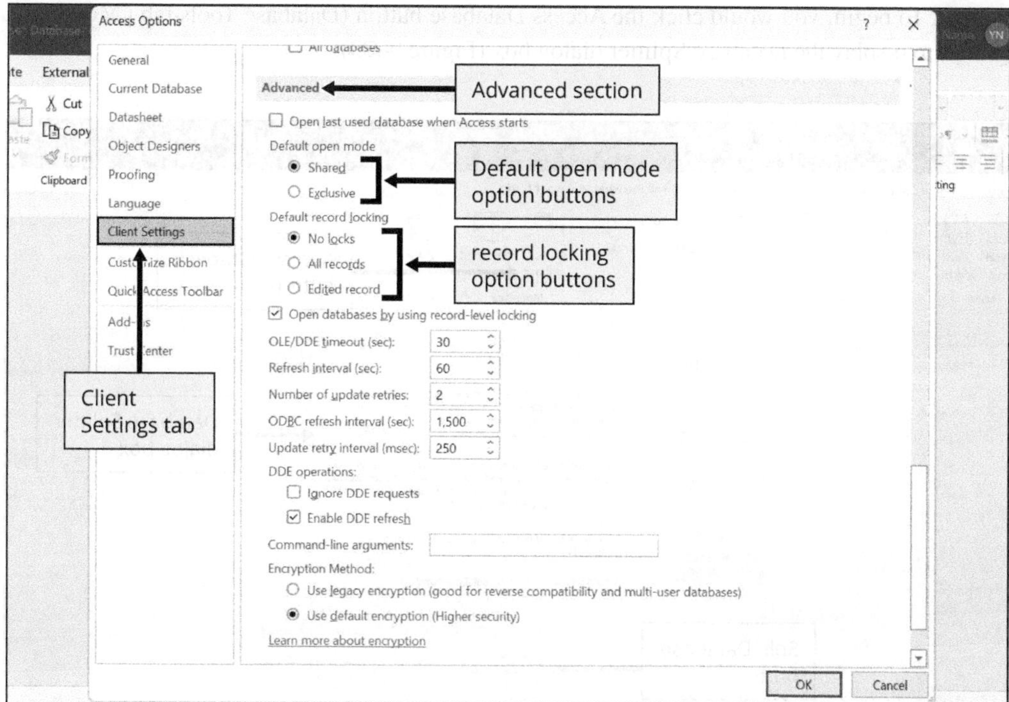

Figure 9–72

If you wanted the default open mode to be exclusive (only one user can use the database at a time) rather than shared (multiple users can simultaneously use the database), you could click the Exclusive option button. You can also select the approach you want for record locking by clicking the appropriate record locking option button. The possible approaches to record locking are shown in Table 9–3.

Table 9–3 Record Locking Approaches

Locking Type	Description
No locks	When you edit a record, Access will not lock the record. Thus, other users also could edit the same record at the same time. When you have finished your changes and attempt to save the record, Access will give you the option of overwriting the other user's changes (not recommended), copying your changes to the clipboard, or canceling your changes.
All records	All records will be locked as long as you have the database open. No other user can edit or lock the records during this time.
Edited record	When you edit a record, Access will lock the record. When other users attempt to edit the same record, they will not be able to do so. Instead, they will see the locked record indicator.

Database Splitting

You can split a database into two databases, one called the back-end database containing only table objects, and another database called the front-end database containing the other objects. Only a single copy of the back-end database can exist, but each user could have their own copy of the front-end database. Each user would create the desired custom reports, forms, and other objects in their own front-end database, thereby not interfering with any other user.

When splitting a database, the database to be split must be open. During the splitting process, you identify a name and location for the back-end database that will be created by the Access splitter. To begin, you would click the Access Database button (Database Tools tab | Move Data group) to display the Database Splitter dialog box (Figure 9–73).

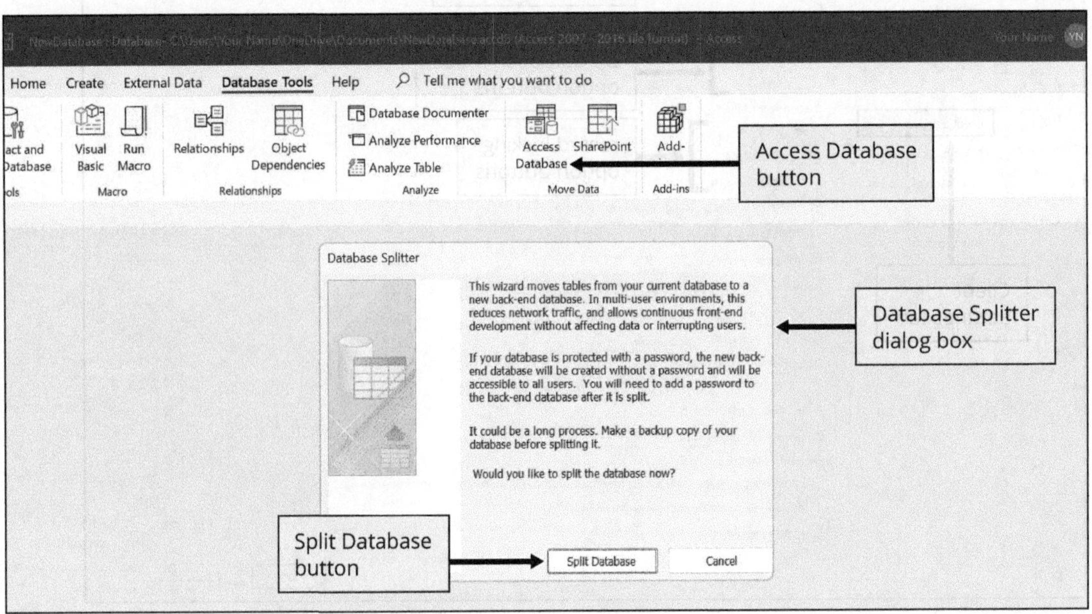

Figure 9–73

You would then select a location for the back-end database (Figure 9–74). Access assigns a name to the back-end database that ends with an underscore (_) and the letters, be. You can override this name if you prefer.

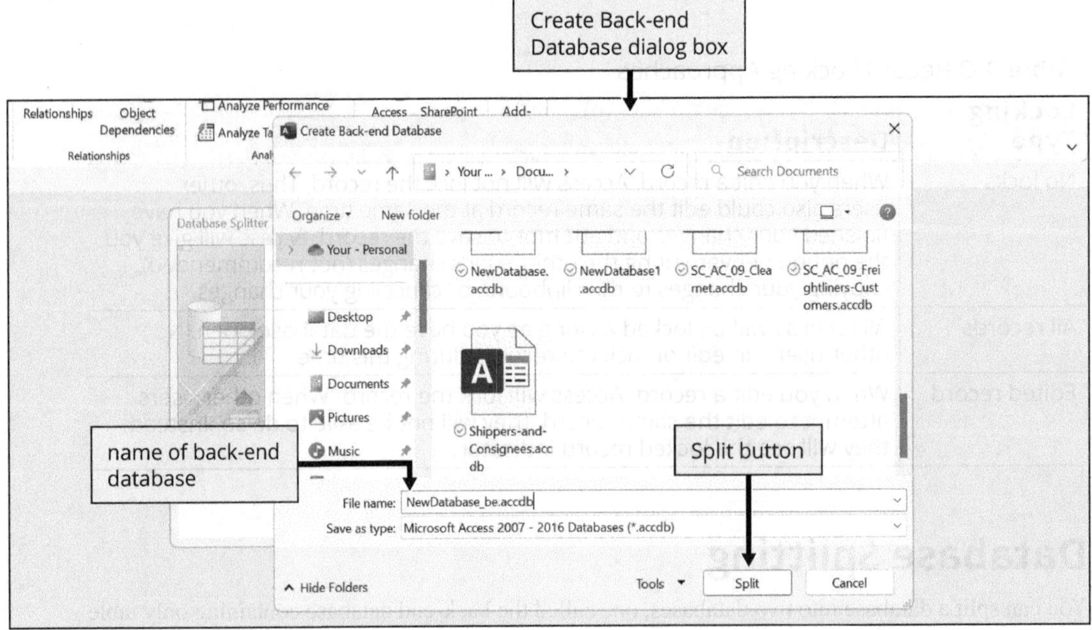

Figure 9–74

To Split a Database

To split a database, you would use the following steps.

1. Open the database to be split.
2. Display the Database Tools tab.

3. Click the Access Database button (Database Tools tab | Move Data group) to display the Database Splitter dialog box.
4. Click the Split Database button to display the Create Back-end Database dialog box.
5. Type a file name for the back-end database.
6. Select a location for the back-end database.
7. Click the Split button to split the database.
8. Click OK to close the dialog box reporting the split was successful.

The Front-End and Back-End Databases

The database has now been split into separate front-end and back-end databases. The front-end database is the one that you will use; it contains all the queries, reports, forms, and other components from the original database. The front-end database contains only links to the tables, however, instead of the tables themselves (Figure 9–75). The back-end database contains the actual tables but does not contain any other objects.

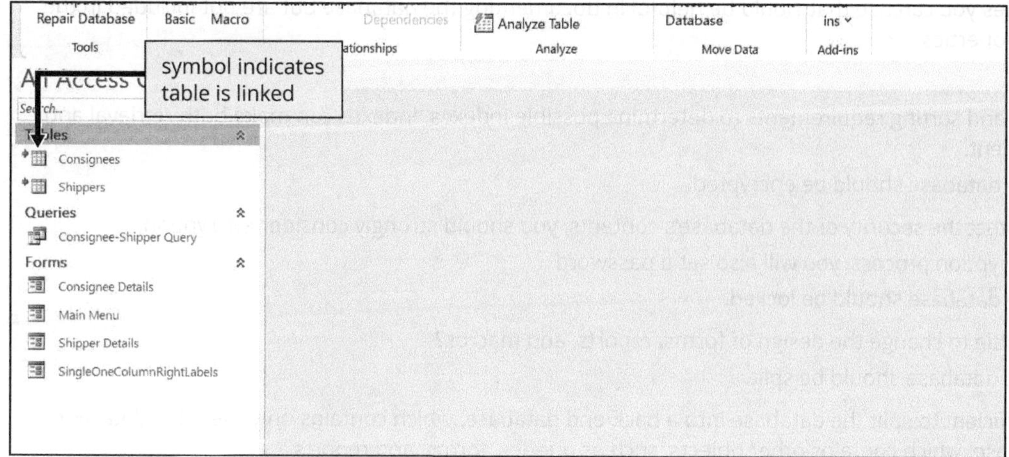

Figure 9–75

Summary

In this module you have learned to convert Access databases to and from earlier versions, use Microsoft Access tools to analyze and document an Access database, add custom categories and groups to the Navigation Pane, use table and database properties, use field properties to create a custom input mask, allow zero-length strings, create indexes, use automatic error checking, create custom data parts, create and use templates and application parts, encrypt a database and set a password, understand the Trust Center, lock a database, and split a database.

Consider This: Plan Ahead

What decisions will you need to make when administering your own databases?

Use these guidelines as you complete the assignments in this module and administer your own databases outside of this class.

1. Determine whether you should create any templates, application parts, or data type parts.
   a. Is there a particular combination of tables, queries, forms, reports, or macros you would like to enable users to easily include in their databases? If so, you could create a template and an application part containing the specific objects you want them to be able to include.
   b. Is there a particular collection of fields you would like to enable users to include in a table with a single click? If so, you could create a data type part containing those fields.

2. Determine whether a database needs to be converted to or from an earlier version.
    a. Do users of a previous version of Access need to be able to use the database? If so, you will need to be sure the database does not contain any features that would prevent it from being converted.
    b. Do you use a database that was created in an earlier version of Access that you would like to use in Access 2021 or Microsoft 365 Access? If so, you can convert the database for use in Access 2021 or Microsoft 365 Access.
3. Determine when to analyze or document the database.
    a. Once you create a database, you should use the table and performance analyzers to determine if any changes to the structure are warranted.
    b. You should also document the database.
4. Determine the most useful way to customize the Navigation Pane.
    a. Would it be helpful to have custom categories and groups?
    b. What objects should be in the groups?
    c. Would it be helpful to restrict the objects that appear to only those whose names contain certain characters?
5. Determine any table-wide validation rules.
    a. Are there any validation rules that involve more than a single field?
6. Determine any custom database properties.
    a. Are there properties you can use that would be helpful in documenting the database but are not included in the list of database properties?
7. Determine indexes.
    a. Examine retrieval and sorting requirements to determine possible indexes. Indexes can make both retrieval and sorting more efficient.
8. Determine whether the database should be encrypted.
    a. If you need to protect the security of the database's contents, you should strongly consider encryption.
    b. As part of the encryption process, you will also set a password.
9. Determine whether the database should be locked.
    a. Should users be able to change the design of forms, reports, and macros?
10. Determine whether the database should be split.
    a. It is often more efficient to split the database into a back-end database, which contains only the table data, and a front-end database, which contains other objects, such as queries, forms, and reports.

Consider This

How should you submit solutions to critical thinking questions in the assignments?

Every assignment in this course contains one or more critical thinking questions. These questions require you to think beyond the assigned database. Present your responses to the questions in the format required by your instructor. Possible formats might include one or more of these options: write the answer; create a document that contains the answer; present your answer to the class; discuss your answer in a group; record the answer as audio or video using a webcam, smartphone, or portable media player; or post answers on a blog, wiki, or website.

Student Assignments

Apply Your Knowledge

Reinforce the skills and apply the concepts you learned in this module.

Administering the City Tutoring Services Database

Note: To complete this assignment, you will be required to use the Data Files. Please contact your instructor for information about accessing the Data Files.

Instructions: Start Access. Open the database, SC_AC_09-2.accdb, which is located in the Data Files folder. Enable the content.

Perform the following tasks:

1. Save the database using the file name, SC_AC_09_City-Tutoring. Enable the content.
2. Open the Students table in Design view and create a custom input mask for the Student Number field. The first two characters of the student number must be uppercase letters and the last two characters must be numerical digits.
3. Create an index on the combination of Student Type and Counselor Number. Name the index TypeCnslr.
4. Save the changes to the Students table, and then close the table.
5. Use the Database Documenter to produce detailed documentation for the Accounting table. Export the documentation to a Word RTF file. Change the name of the file to LastName_Documentation where LastName is your last name.
6. Use the Table Analyzer to analyze the table structure of the Students table. Open the Word RTF file that you created in Step 5 and make a note at the end of the document describing the results of the table analysis.
7. Use the Performance Analyzer to analyze all the tables in the database. Describe the results of your analysis in your RTF file.
8. Populate the Status custom property for the database to Live Version.
9. Add a Production property with today's date.
10. Submit the revised database and the RTF file in the format specified by your instructor.
11. **Consider This:** Can you convert the City Tutoring database to an Access 2002–2003 database? Why or why not?

Extend Your Knowledge

Extend the skills you learned in this module and experiment with new skills. You may need to use Help to complete the assignment.

Administering the Physical Therapists Database

Note: To complete this assignment, you will be required to use the Data Files. Please contact your instructor for information about accessing the Data Files.

Instructions: Start Access. Open the database, SC_AC_09-3.accdb, which is located in the Data Files folder.

Perform the following tasks:

1. Save the database using the file name, SC_AC_09_Physical-Therapists. Enable the content.
2. Create a navigation form that is named and titled Clients and Technicians and that contains a single row with two horizontal tabs. Add two forms to the Navigation Form: Clients by Technician Form and Technician Form.

Continued on next page

3. Change the Current Database options to ensure the Main Menu opens automatically. Confirm your settings work as intended.
4. Currently, when you open the Potential Clients table in Datasheet view, the table is ordered by Client Number. Change the property for the table so the table is in order by Client Name.
5. Create an additional table called Potential Technicians. Add the Name-Contact-Address Quick Start fields to easily create the fields. For each field name, replace any instances of the word Shipper with the word Technician. Save the table and close it.
6. Customize the Navigation Pane by adding a custom category called Tracking. Then add two custom groups, Clients and Technicians, to the Tracking category.
7. Add the Client table, the Potential Clients table, and the Clients by Technician form to the Clients custom group under the Tracking category. Add the Technician table, the Technician Form, and the Technician Balances Summary Report to the Technicians custom group under the Tracking category.
8. Submit the revised database in the format specified by your instructor.
9. **Consider This:** What advantages are there to using a custom Navigation Pane as opposed to the standard Navigation Pane?

Expand Your World

Create a solution, which uses cloud and web technologies, by learning and investigating on your own from general guidance.

Instructions: There are many ways to share an Access database. Some ways require each user to have Microsoft Access installed on their computer, while others do not. The method you select depends on factors such as need and available resources.

Perform the following tasks:

1. Create a blog post, a Google document, or a Word document on OneDrive on which to store your findings for this project. Make sure the blog post or document is configured to share with other users when you provide them with a link.
2. Use the web to research different ways to share an Access database, such as Clearnet, with others. Be sure to note any specific resources needed, such as an Access database or a SharePoint server, explain any costs involved, and provide examples of different reasons for sharing a database such as Clearnet. Record your findings in your blog, Google document, or Word document, being sure to appropriately reference your sources.
3. Submit the blog or document's link in the format specified by your instructor.
4. **Consider This:** Based on your research, what method would you choose to share your Access databases?

In the Lab

Design and implement a solution using creative thinking and problem-solving skills.

Lab: Administering the Great Outdoors Campground Database

Note: To complete this assignment, you will be required to use the Data Files. Please contact your instructor for information about accessing the Data Files.

Problem: The staff at Great Outdoors Campground has asked you to perform a number of administrative tasks to help increase the functionality and efficiency of their database.

Perform the following tasks:

Part 1: Open the SC_AC_09-4.accdb database from the Data Files folder. Save the file with the name, SC_AC_09_Great-Outdoors, and enable the content. Use the concepts and techniques presented in this module to perform each of the following tasks.

1. Create a horizontal tabs navigation form that includes the Staff Activities Summary Form and the Filtered Staff WorkTeam form. Give the navigation form an appropriate form name and title that reflect its contents, such as Staff Forms. Whatever name you choose, make sure not to use a form name currently in use in the database.
2. Change the Current Database options to ensure that the Main Menu form opens automatically when the user opens the database.
3. Open the Counselors table in Design view and create an index for the LastName field that allows duplicates. Save the changes.
4. Open the Enrollments table in Design view and create an index named CamperIDEvent on the CamperID and the Event fields.
5. Open the Cabins table in Design view and create a validation rule to ensure the minimum campers value is always less than or equal to the maximum campers. Include validation text.
6. Create a new table called Vendors and add the Quick Start Name-Contact-Address field to the table. Replace the word Shipper with the word Vendor in all fields.
7. Create a template of the database as an application part and do not include the data. Name the template Campground-Template.
8. From that template, create a new database called SC_AC_09_YN-Campground, where YN is your own initials. Close the database.

Submit your assignment in the format specified by your instructor.

Part 2: **Consider This:** You made several decisions while completing this project, including creating a navigation form and a validation rule. What was the rationale behind your decisions? What other navigation forms or validation rules would you add to the Great Outdoors Campground database?

Using SQL

Objectives

After completing this module, you will be able to:

- Describe the background and purpose of SQL (Structured Query Language)
- Change the font or font size in a query
- Create a SQL query
- Include specific fields in a SQL query
- Apply criteria to a SQL query
- Include a computed field in a SQL query
- Sort the results of a SQL query
- Use a built-in, or aggregate, function in a SQL query
- Group the results of a SQL query
- Join tables in a SQL query
- Use a subquery
- Compare a SQL query with an Access query
- Use SQL commands to insert, update, and delete records
- Link external data to a table

Introduction

The language called **SQL (Structured Query Language)** is a very important language for querying and updating databases. It is the closest thing to a universal database language because the vast majority of database management systems, including Access, use it in some fashion. Although some users will be able to do all their queries through the query features of Access without ever using SQL, those in charge of administering and maintaining the database system should be familiar with this important language. You can also use Access as an interface to other database management systems, such as SQL Server. Using or interfacing with SQL Server requires knowledge of SQL. Nearly every relational DBMS supports SQL to some degree, as do many non-relational DBMSs.

Project: Using SQL

Partners Law Firm wants to be able to use the extended data management capabilities available through SQL. As part of becoming familiar with SQL, Partners would like to create a wide variety of SQL queries.

Similarly to creating queries in Design view, SQL provides a way of querying relational databases. In SQL, however, instead of making entries in the design grid, you type commands into SQL view to obtain the desired results, as shown in Figure 10–1a. You can then click the View button to view the results just as when you are creating queries in Design view. The results for the query in Figure 10–1a are shown in Figure 10–1b.

BTW
The Ribbon and Screen Resolution
Access may change how the groups and buttons within the groups appear on the ribbon, depending on the computer's screen resolution. Thus, your ribbon might look different from the ones in this course if you are using a screen resolution other than 1920 × 1080.

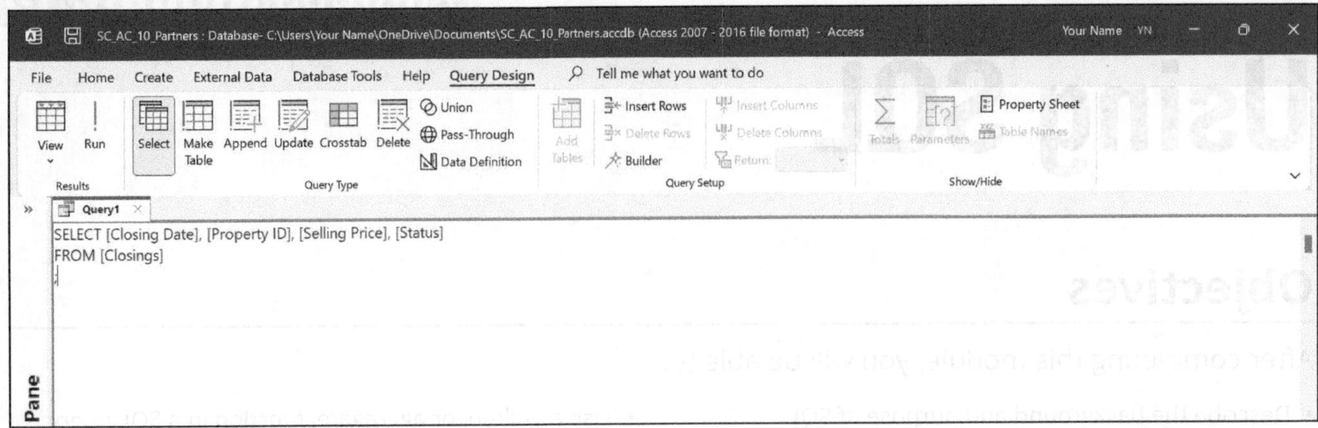

Figure 10–1(a): Query in SQL

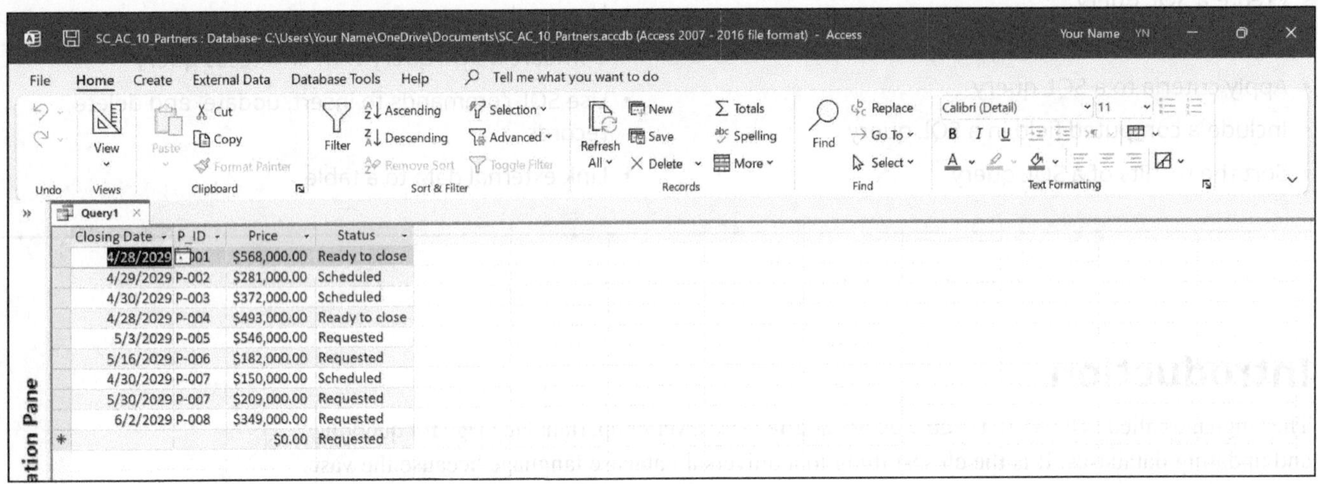

Figure 10–1(b): Query Results

In this module, you will learn how to create and use SQL queries like the one shown in Figure 10–1a.

BTW
Distributing a Document
Instead of printing and distributing a hard copy of a document, you can distribute the document electronically. Options include sending the document via email; posting it on cloud storage (such as OneDrive) and sharing the file with others; posting it on a social networking site, blog, or other website; and sharing a link associated with an online location of the document. You also can create and share a PDF or XPS image of the document, so that users can view the file in Acrobat Reader or XPS Viewer instead of in Access.

SQL Background

In this module, you query and update a database using the language called SQL (Structured Query Language). Similarly to using the design grid in the Access Query window, SQL provides users with the capability of querying a relational database. Because SQL is a language, however, you must enter **commands** to obtain the desired results, rather than completing entries in the design grid. SQL uses commands to update tables and to retrieve data from tables. The commands that are used to retrieve data are usually called queries.

SQL was developed under the name SEQUEL at the IBM San Jose research facilities as the data manipulation language for IBM's prototype relational model DBMS, System R, in the mid-1970s. In 1980, it was renamed SQL to avoid confusion with an unrelated hardware product called SEQUEL. Most relational DBMSs, including Microsoft Access and Microsoft SQL Server, use a version of SQL as a data manipulation language.

Some people pronounce SQL by pronouncing the three letters, that is, "ess-que-ell." It is very common, however, to pronounce it as the name under which it was developed originally, that is, "sequel." This course assumes the "sequel" pronunciation; for instance, it uses the wording "a SQL query" rather than "an SQL query."

To Change the Font Size

You can change the font and/or the font size for queries using the Options button in Backstage view and then the Object Designers section of the Access Options dialog box. There is not usually a compelling reason to change the font unless there is a strong preference for some other font. It often is worthwhile to change the font size, however. **Why?** Increasing the font size to 11 can make a big difference. The following steps change the font size for queries to 11.

- **sam** Start Access. Open the database, SC_AC_10-1.accdb, which is located in the Data Files folder. Save the file to your hard drive, OneDrive, or other storage location using the file name, **SC_AC_10_Partners.** Enable the content.
- Click File on the ribbon to open Backstage view.
- Click Options to display the Access Options dialog box.
- Click Object Designers to display the Object Designer section.
- In the Query design area, under Query design font, click the Size box arrow, and then click 11 in the list to change the size to 11 (Figure 10–2).

BTW
Active Content
Depending on your Trust Settings, Access may initially block active content when it opens a database that contains macros. When you are opening content from a trusted source, such as databases included in this course, you can click OK in the dialog box and proceed with enabling the content.

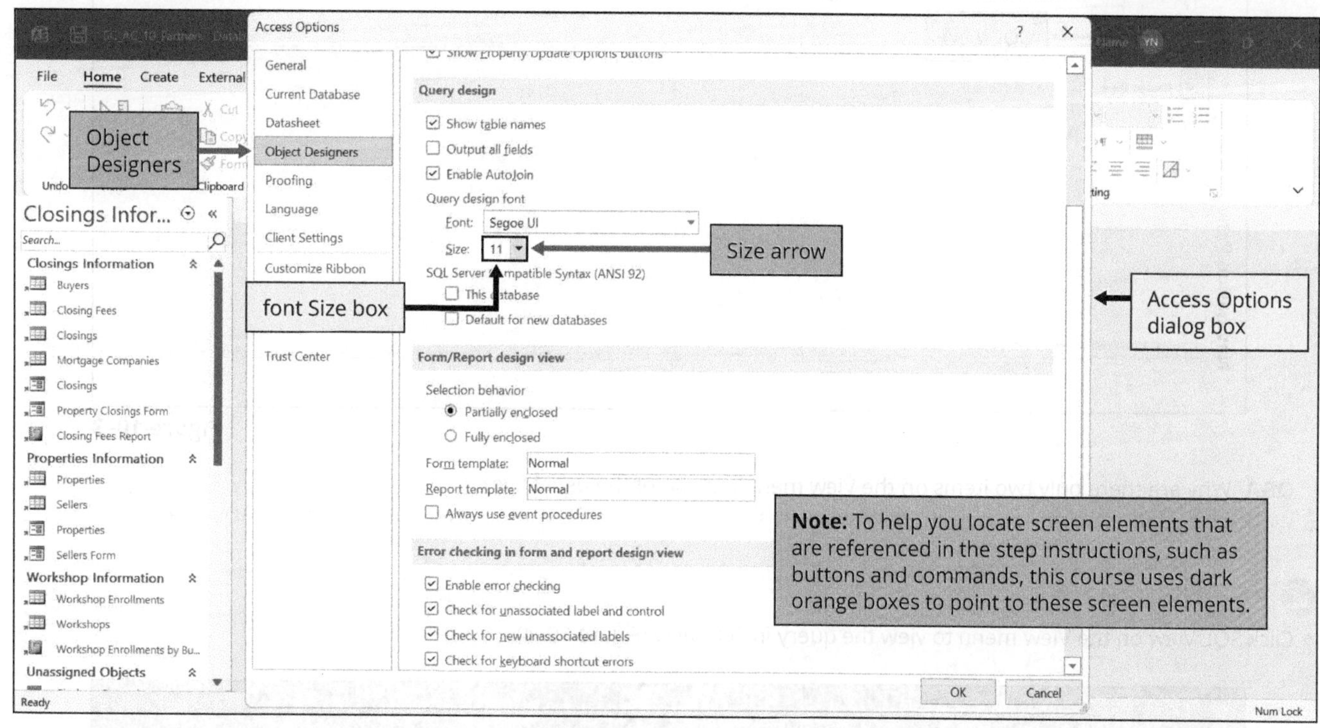

Figure 10–2

Q&A Can I choose a larger size if I need the font to be bigger?
Yes. Examples in this module will be given using the font size of 11. However, you can choose a larger size if that is helpful for you.

BTW
Enabling the Content
For each of the databases you use in this module, you will need to enable the content.

- Click OK to close the Access Options dialog box.

SQL Queries

When you query a database using SQL, you type commands in a blank window rather than filling in the design grid. When the command is complete, you can view your results just as you do with queries you create using the design grid.

BTW
Touch Screen Differences
The Office and Windows interfaces may vary if you are using a touch screen. For this reason, you might notice that the function or appearance of your touch screen differs slightly from this module's presentation.

To Create a New SQL Query

You begin the creation of a new **SQL query**, which is a query expressed using the SQL language, just as you begin the creation of any other query in Access. The only difference is that you will use SQL view instead of Design view. **Why?** SQL view enables you to type SQL commands rather than making entries in the design grid. The following steps create a new SQL query.

- Display the Create tab.
- Click the Query Design button (Create tab | Queries group) to create a query.
- Close the Add Tables pane without adding any tables.
- Click the View button arrow (Query Design tab | Results group) to display the View menu (Figure 10–3).

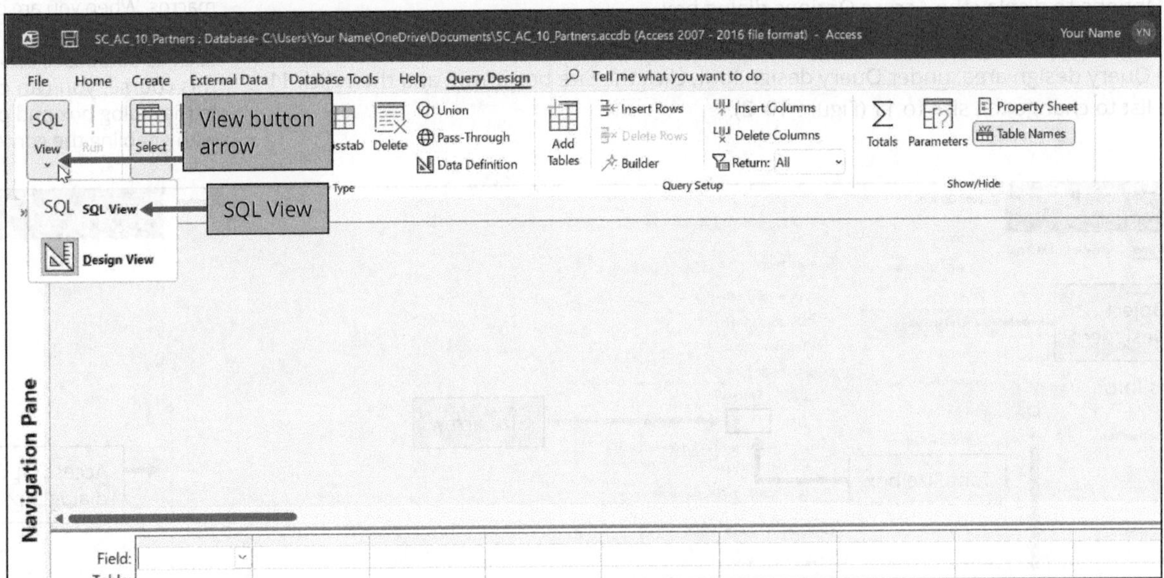

Figure 10–3

Q&A Why are there only two items on the View menu instead of the usual five?
Without any tables selected, you cannot view any results. You can only use the normal Design view or SQL view.

- Click SQL View on the View menu to view the query in SQL view (Figure 10–4).

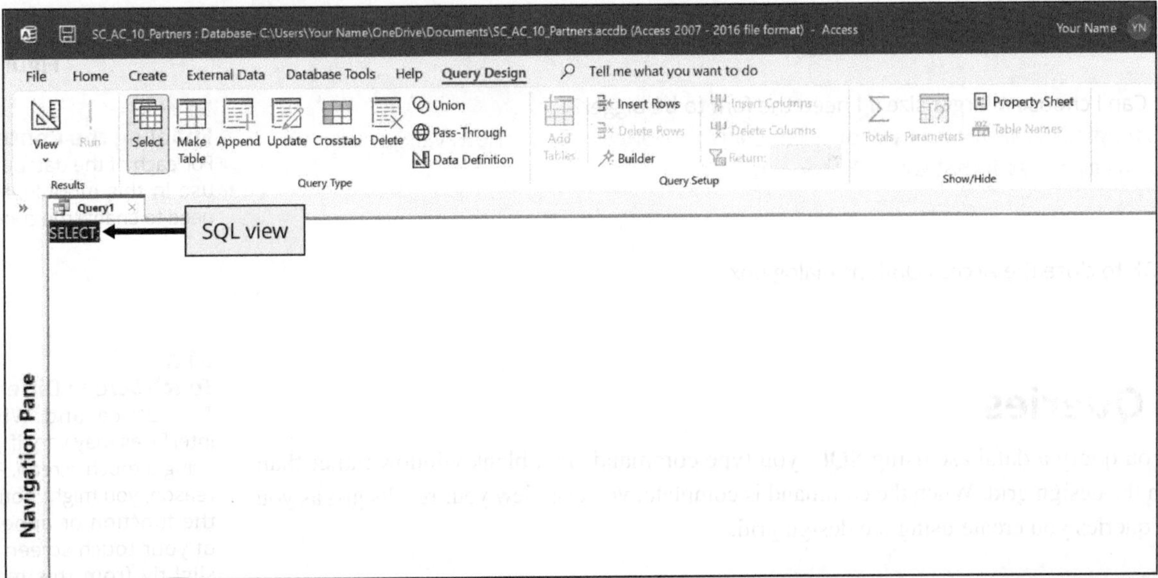

Figure 10–4

Q&A What happened to the design grid?
In SQL view, you specify the queries by typing SQL commands rather than making entries in the design grid.

BTW
Navigation Pane
As you work, you often need to open the Navigation Pane to view and select objects such as tables, forms, and reports. You often need to close the pane to make more room on the screen or to ensure your screen matches the figures in this course. Open the Navigation Pane as necessary to open an object when instructed, and close the pane to suit your preferences.

SQL Commands

The basic form of SQL expressions is quite simple: SELECT-FROM-WHERE. The command begins with a **SELECT clause**, which consists of the word, SELECT, followed by a list of those fields you want to include. The fields will appear in the results in the order in which they are listed in the expression. Next, the command contains a **FROM clause**, which consists of the word, FROM, followed by a list of the table or tables involved in the query. Finally, there is an optional **WHERE clause**, which consists of the word, WHERE, followed by any criteria that the data you want to retrieve must satisfy. The command ends with a semicolon (;), which in this text will appear on a separate line.

SQL has no special format rules for placement of terms, capitalization, and so on. One common style is to place the word, FROM, on a new line, and then place the word, WHERE (when it is used), on the next line. This style makes the commands easier to read. It is also common to show words that are part of the SQL language in uppercase and other words in a combination of uppercase and lowercase. This text formats SQL terms in uppercase letters. Because it is a common convention, and necessary in some versions of SQL, you will place a semicolon (;) at the end of each command.

Microsoft Access has its own version of SQL that, unlike some other versions of SQL, allows spaces within field names and table names. There is a restriction, however, to the way such names are used in SQL queries. When a name containing a space appears in SQL, it must be enclosed in square brackets. For example, a field named Closing Date must appear as [Closing Date] because the name includes a space. On the other hand, a field named Status does not need to be enclosed in square brackets because its name does not include a space. For consistency, all names in this text are enclosed in square brackets. Thus, the Status field would appear as [Status] even though the brackets are not technically required by SQL.

To Include Only Certain Fields

To include only certain fields in a query, list them after the word, SELECT. If you want to list all rows in the table, you do not include the word, WHERE. **Why?** If there is no WHERE clause, there is no criterion restricting which rows appear in the results. In that case, all rows will appear. The following steps create a query for Partners Law Firm that will list the closing date, property ID, selling price, and status for all closings.

- Click to the right of the word, SELECT, delete the semicolon (;), press SPACEBAR, type **[Closing Date], [Property ID], [Selling Price], [Status]** as the first line of the command, and then press ENTER.

Q&A What is the purpose of the SELECT clause?
The SELECT clause indicates the fields that are to be included in the query results. This SELECT clause, for example, indicates the Closing Date, Property ID, Selling Price, and Status fields are to be included.

- Type **FROM [Closings]** as the second line to specify the source table, press ENTER, and then type a semicolon (**;**) on the third line (Figure 10–5a).

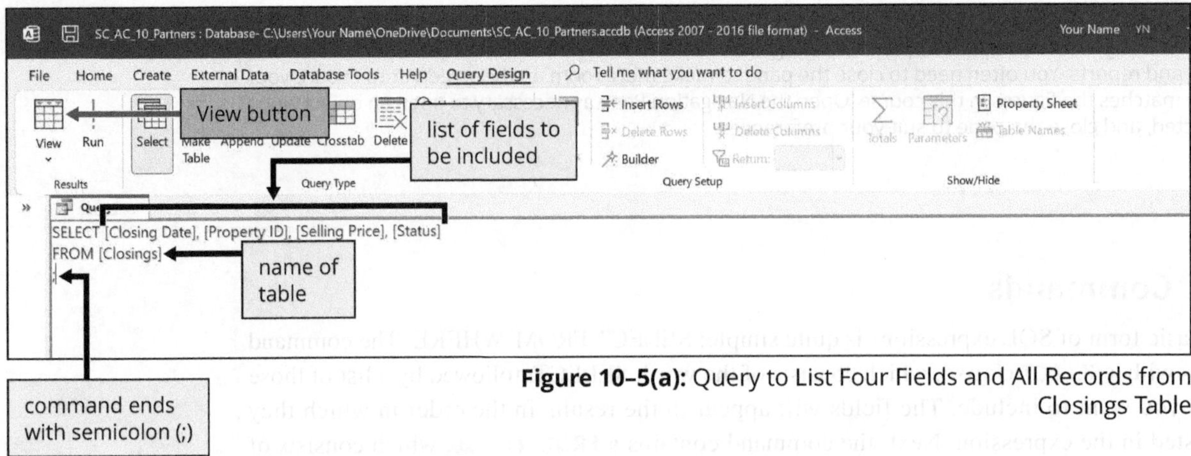

Figure 10–5(a): Query to List Four Fields and All Records from Closings Table

Q&A What is the purpose of the FROM clause?
The FROM clause indicates the table or tables that contain the fields used in the query. This FROM clause indicates that all the fields in this query come from the Closings table.

- Click the View button (Query Design tab | Results group) to view the results (Figure 10–5b).

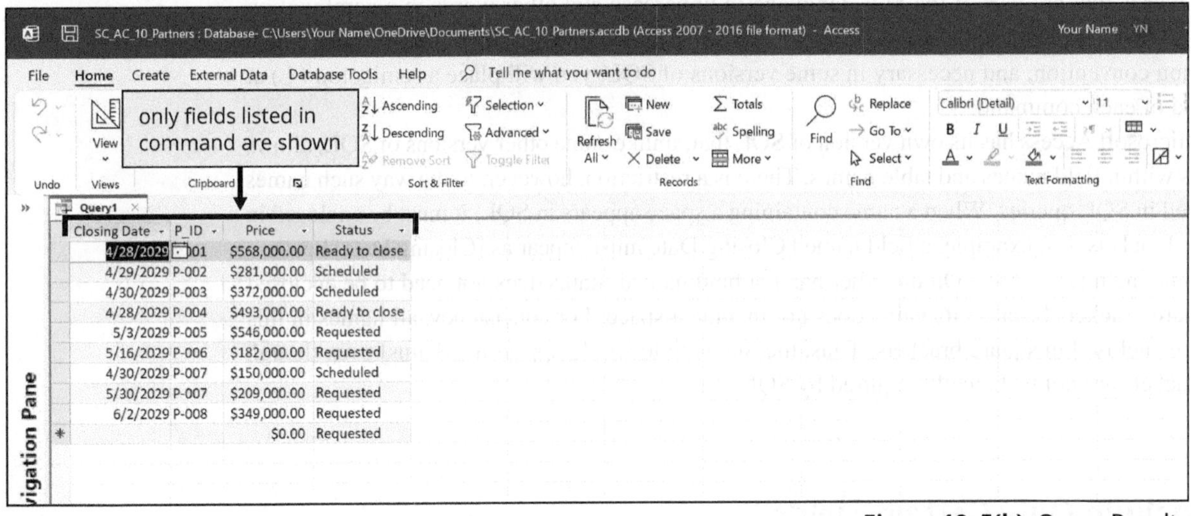

Figure 10–5(b): Query Results

Q&A My screen displays a dialog box that asks me to enter a parameter value. What did I do wrong?
You typed a field name incorrectly. Click Cancel to close the dialog box, and then correct your SQL statement.

- Click the Save button on the Quick Access Toolbar, type **m10q01** as the query name in the Save As dialog box, and then click OK to save the query.

BTW
SELECT Clause
When you enter field names in a SELECT clause, you do not need to enter a space after the comma. Access inserts a space after the comma when you save the query and close it. When you reopen the query in SQL view, a space will appear after each comma that separates fields in the SELECT clause, even if you did not enter spaces initially.

To Prepare to Enter a New SQL Query

To enter a new SQL query, you could close the window, click the No button when asked if you want to save your changes, and then begin the process again from scratch. A quicker alternative is to use the View menu and then select SQL View. **Why?** You will be returned to SQL view with the current command appearing. At that point, you could erase the current command and then enter a new one. If the next command is similar to the previous one, however, it often is simpler to modify the current command instead of erasing it and starting over. The following step shows how to prepare to enter a new SQL query.

- Click the View button arrow (Home tab | Views group) to display the View menu (Figure 10-6).
- Click SQL View to return to SQL view.

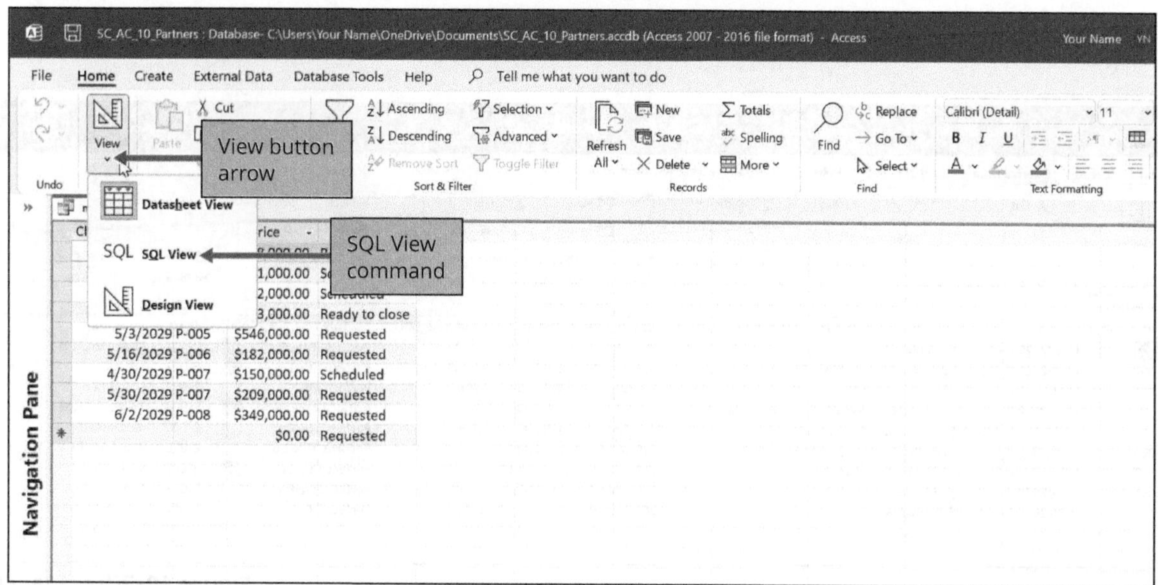

Figure 10-6

Q&A Could I just click the View button, or do I have to click the arrow?
Because the icon on the button is not the icon for SQL view, you must first click the arrow.

BTW
Editing or Replacing a Query
To ensure accuracy in the instructions, this module typically instructs you to delete an existing query's commands and type the new query's commands. However, you might find it more convenient instead to edit the previous query's commands to match a new query's commands. While either approach is acceptable, be careful to ensure you make all needed edits if you are changing existing text. It is easy to miss a small difference between the previous query and the new query that can have a significant effect on the query results.

To Include All Fields

To include all fields, you could use the same approach as in the previous steps, that is, list each field in the Closings table after the word SELECT. There is a shortcut, however. Instead of listing all the field names after SELECT, you can use the asterisk (*) symbol. **Why?** Just as when working in the design grid, the asterisk symbol represents all fields. This indicates that you want all fields listed in the order in which you described them to the system during data definition. The following steps list all fields and all records in the Closings table.

- Delete the current command, type **SELECT *** as the first line of the command, and then press ENTER.
- Type **FROM [Closings]** as the second line, press ENTER, and type a semicolon (;) on the third line (Figure 10-7a).

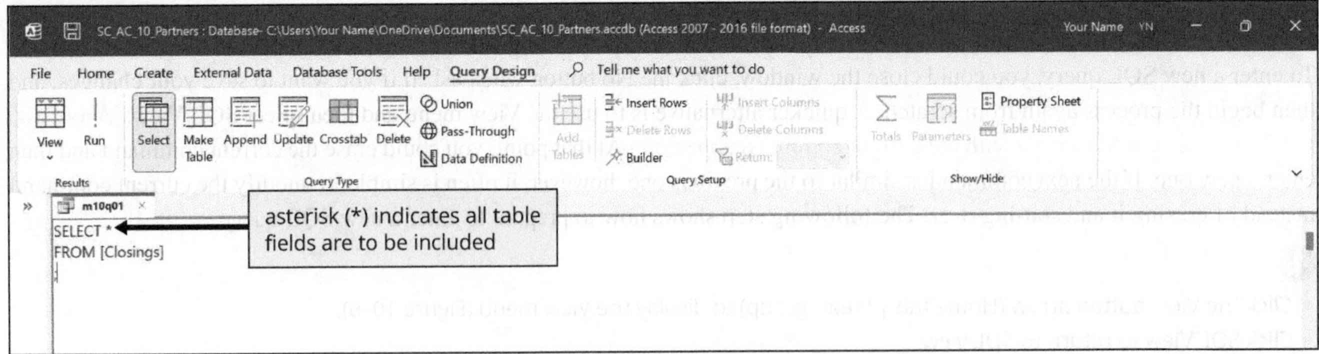

Figure 10–7(a): Query to List All Fields and All Records from Closings Table

- View the results (Figure 10–7b).

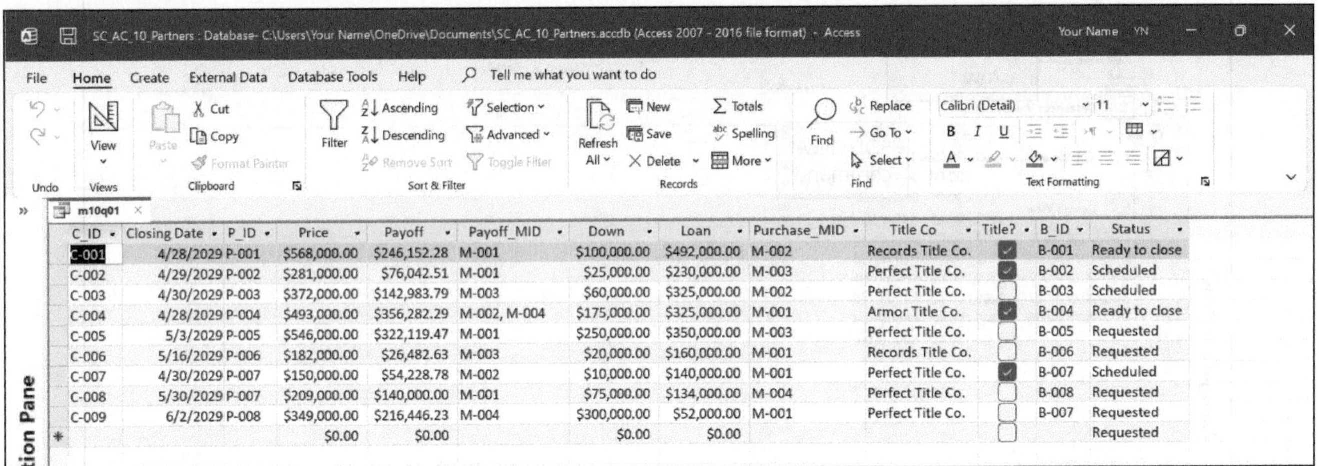

C_ID	Closing Date	P_ID	Price	Payoff	Payoff_MID	Down	Loan	Purchase_MID	Title Co	Title?	B_ID	Status
C-001	4/28/2029	P-001	$568,000.00	$246,152.28	M-001	$100,000.00	$492,000.00	M-002	Records Title Co.	☑	B-001	Ready to close
C-002	4/29/2029	P-002	$281,000.00	$76,042.51	M-001	$25,000.00	$230,000.00	M-003	Perfect Title Co.	☑	B-002	Scheduled
C-003	4/30/2029	P-003	$372,000.00	$142,983.79	M-003	$60,000.00	$325,000.00	M-002	Perfect Title Co.	☐	B-003	Scheduled
C-004	4/28/2029	P-004	$493,000.00	$356,282.29	M-002, M-004	$175,000.00	$325,000.00	M-001	Armor Title Co.	☑	B-004	Ready to close
C-005	5/3/2029	P-005	$546,000.00	$322,119.47	M-001	$250,000.00	$350,000.00	M-003	Perfect Title Co.	☐	B-005	Requested
C-006	5/16/2029	P-006	$182,000.00	$26,482.63	M-003	$20,000.00	$160,000.00	M-001	Records Title Co.	☐	B-006	Requested
C-007	4/30/2029	P-007	$150,000.00	$54,228.78	M-002	$10,000.00	$140,000.00	M-001	Perfect Title Co.	☑	B-007	Scheduled
C-008	5/30/2029	P-007	$209,000.00	$140,000.00	M-001	$75,000.00	$134,000.00	M-004	Perfect Title Co.	☐	B-008	Requested
C-009	6/2/2029	P-008	$349,000.00	$216,446.23	M-004	$300,000.00	$52,000.00	M-001	Perfect Title Co.	☐	B-007	Requested
*			$0.00	$0.00		$0.00	$0.00			☐		Requested

Figure 10–7(b): Query Results

Q&A Can I use copy and paste commands when I enter SQL commands?
Yes, you can use copy and paste as well as other editing techniques, such as replacing text. Throughout this module, directions are given to delete existing text from a SQL command and then type new text. However, you can keep text that will be reused and only replace text that is not needed for the new query. Be sure to check your new command carefully, as it is easy to miss minor changes in field names, punctuation, or clauses.

- Click File on the ribbon to open Backstage view, click Save As to display the Save As gallery, click Save Object As in the File Types area, click the Save As button to display the Save As dialog box, type **m10q02** as the name for the new query, and then click OK to save the new query and return to the query.

Q&A Can I just click the Save button on the Quick Access Toolbar as I did when I saved the previous query?
If you did, you would replace the previous query with the version you just created. Because you want to save both the previous query and the new one, you need to save the new version with a different name. To do so, you must use Save Object As, which is available through Backstage view.

To Use a Criterion Involving a Numeric Field

To restrict the records to be displayed, include the word, WHERE, followed by a criterion as part of the command. If the field involved is a numeric field, you simply type the value. In typing the number, you do not type commas or dollar signs. **Why?** If you enter a dollar sign, Access assumes you are entering text. If you enter a comma, Access considers the criterion invalid. The following steps create a query to list the property IDs of all closings where the selling price is equal to $150,000.

1

- Return to SQL view and delete the current command.
- Type **SELECT [Property ID], [Closing Date], [Selling Price]** as the first line of the command.
- Type **FROM [Closings]** as the second line.
- Type **WHERE [Selling Price]=150000** as the third line, and then type a semicolon (;) on the fourth line (Figure 10–8a).

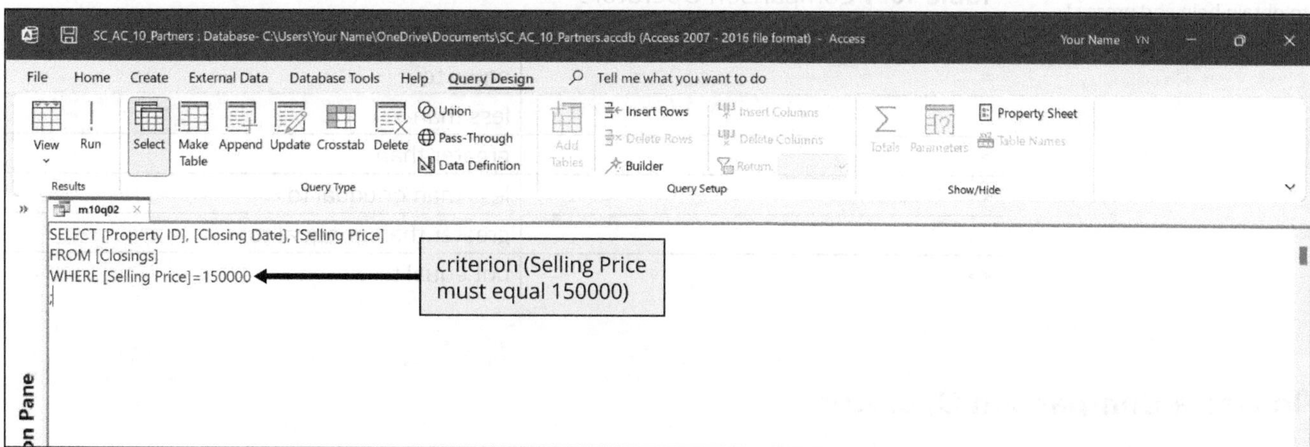

Figure 10–8(a): Query to List Property ID, Closing Date, and Selling Price for Closings Where Selling Price Is Equal to $150,000

Q&A What is the purpose of the WHERE clause?
The WHERE clause restricts the rows to be included in the results to only those that satisfy the criteria included in the clause. With this WHERE clause, for example, only those rows where the Selling Price is equal to $150,000 will be included.

- View the results (Figure 10–8b).

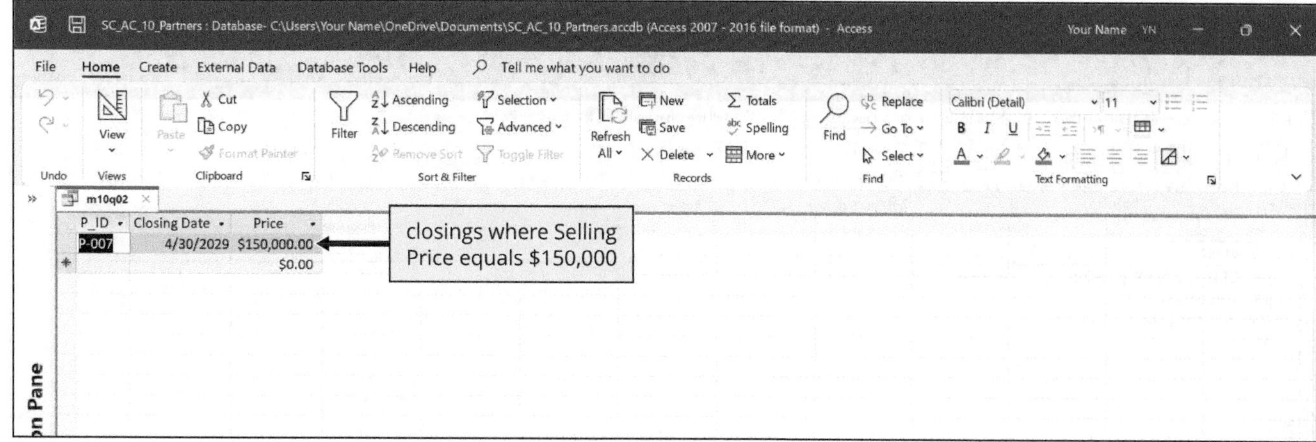

Figure 10–8(b): Query Results

2

- Save the query as **m10q03**.

BTW
Context-Sensitive Help in SQL
When you are working in SQL view, you can obtain context-sensitive help on any of the keywords in your query. To do so, click anywhere in the word about which you wish to obtain help and press F1.

Simple Criteria

The criterion following the word WHERE in the preceding query is called a simple criterion. A **simple criterion** has the form: field name, comparison operator, then either another field name or a value. The possible comparison operators are shown in Table 10–1.

Table 10–1 Comparison Operators

Comparison Operator	Meaning
=	equal to
<	less than
>	greater than
<=	less than or equal to
>=	greater than or equal to
<>	not equal to

To Use a Comparison Operator

In the following steps, you will use a comparison operator to list the property ID, closing date, and selling price for all vendors who have a selling price greater than $300,000. **Why?** A comparison operator allows you to compare the value in a field with a specific value or with the value in another field.

- Return to SQL view and delete the current command.
- Type **SELECT [Property ID], [Closing Date], [Selling Price]** as the first line of the command.
- Type **FROM [Closings]** as the second line.
- Type **WHERE [Selling Price]>300000** as the third line.
- Type a semicolon (;) on the fourth line (Figure 10–9a).

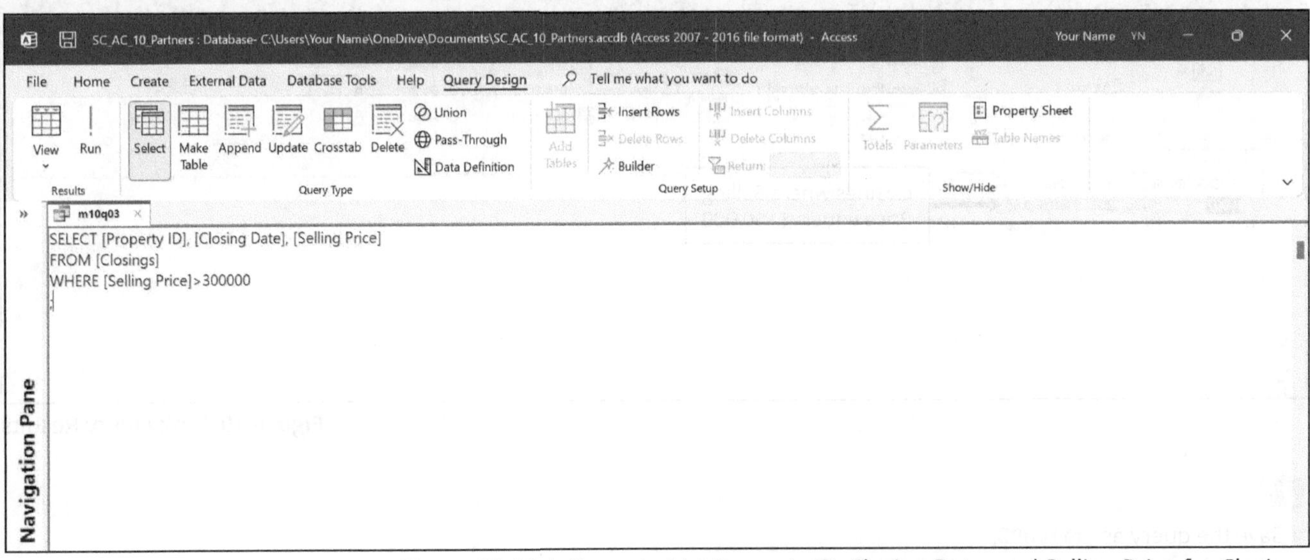

Figure 10–9(a): Query to List Property ID, Closing Date, and Selling Price for Closings Where Selling Price Is Greater Than $300,000

- View the results (Figure 10–9b).

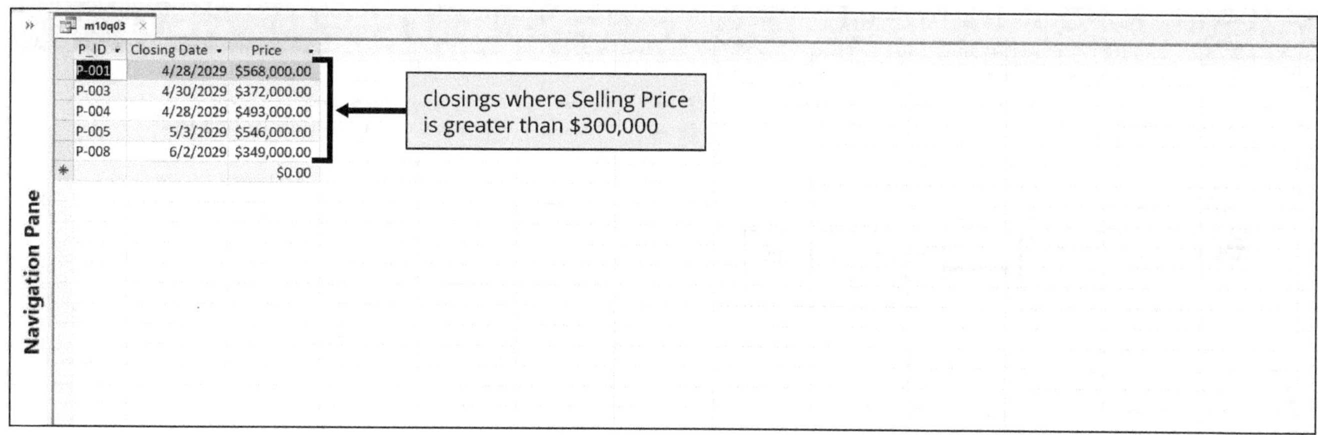

Figure 10–9(b): Query Results

- Save the query as **m10q04**.

To Use a Criterion Involving a Text Field

If the criterion involves a text field, the value must be enclosed in quotation marks. **Why?** Unlike when you work in the design grid, Access will not automatically insert in SQL view the quotation marks around text data. You need to include them yourself. The following steps create a query that lists the Property ID, Closing Date, and Status of all closings currently scheduled, that is, all closings where the value of the Status field is Scheduled.

- Return to SQL view, delete the current command, and then type **SELECT [Property ID], [Closing Date], [Status]** as the first line of the command.
- Type **FROM [Closings]** as the second line.
- Type **WHERE [Status]='Scheduled'** as the third line and type a semicolon (;) on the fourth line (Figure 10–10a).

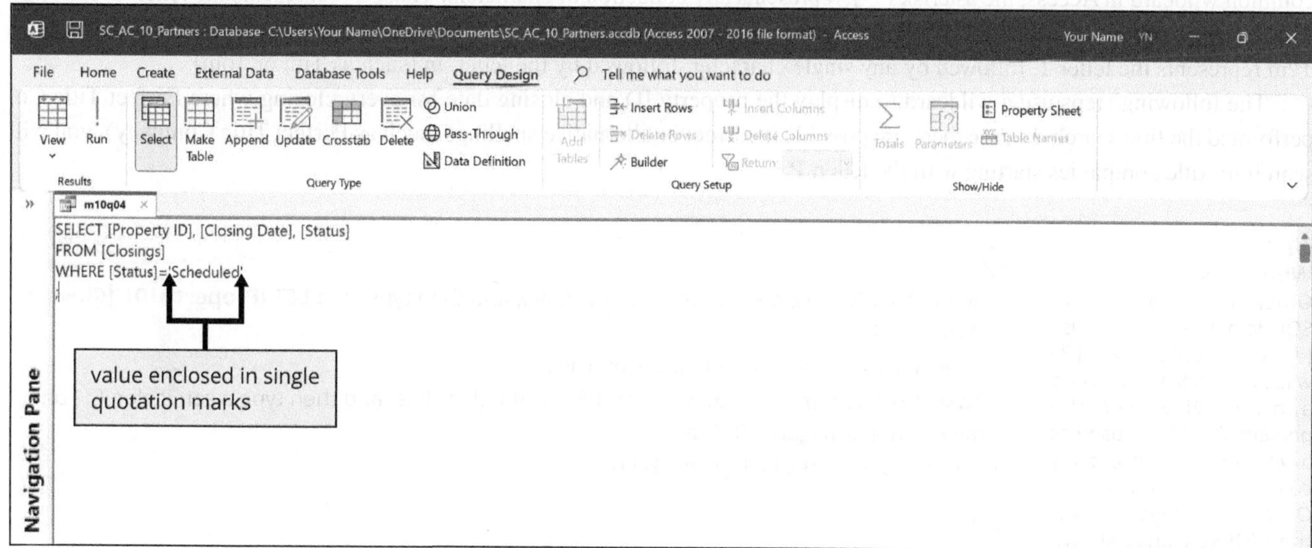

Figure 10–10(a): Query to List Currently Scheduled Closings

- View the results (Figure 10–10b).

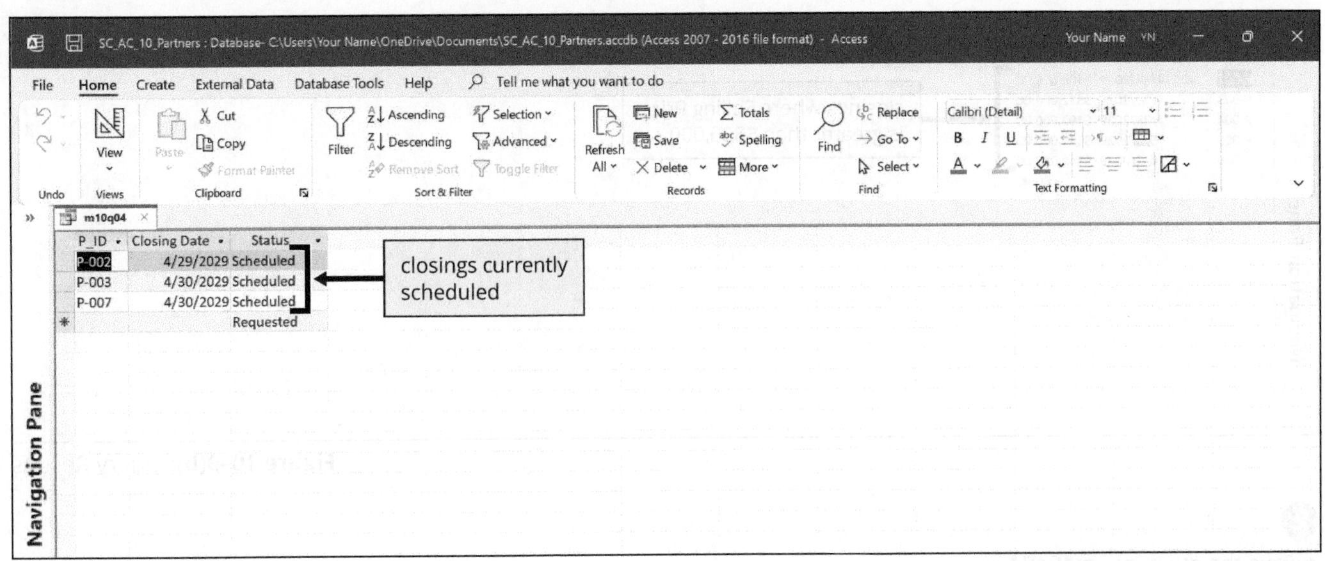

Figure 10–10(b): Query Results

Q&A Could I enclose the text field value in double quotation marks instead of single quotation marks?
Yes. It is usually easier, however, to use single quotes when entering SQL commands.

- Save the query as **m10q05**.

To Use a Wildcard

In most cases, the conditions in WHERE clauses involve exact matches, such as retrieving rows for each closing with a Scheduled status. In some cases, however, exact matches do not work. **Why?** You might only know that the desired value contains a certain collection of characters. In such cases, you use the LIKE operator with a wildcard symbol.

Rather than testing for equality, the LIKE operator uses one or more wildcard characters to test for a pattern match. One common wildcard in Access, the asterisk (*), represents any collection of characters. Thus, T* represents the letter, T, followed by any string of characters. Another wildcard symbol is the question mark (?), which represents any individual character. Thus, T?m represents the letter T, followed by any single character, followed by the letter, m (such as Tim or Tom).

The following steps use a wildcard to display the property ID and closing date for every closing where Perfect Title Co. performed the title search. In case there are possible incorrect or alternative spellings (such as Perfect Title Company), you will search for title companies starting with the letter, P.

BTW
Wildcards
Other implementations of SQL do not use the asterisk (*) and question mark (?) wildcards. In SQL for Oracle and for SQL Server, the percent sign (%) is used as a wildcard to represent any collection of characters. In Oracle and SQL Server, the WHERE clause shown in Figure 10–11a would be WHERE [Title Company] LIKE 'P%'.

- Return to SQL view, delete the previous query, and then type **SELECT [Property ID], [Closing Date], [Title Company].**
- Type **FROM [Closings]** as the second line.
- Type **WHERE [Title Company] LIKE 'P*'** as the third line, and then type a semicolon (;) on the fourth line (Figure 10–11a).
- View the query results (Figure 10–11b).

- Save the query as **m10q06**.

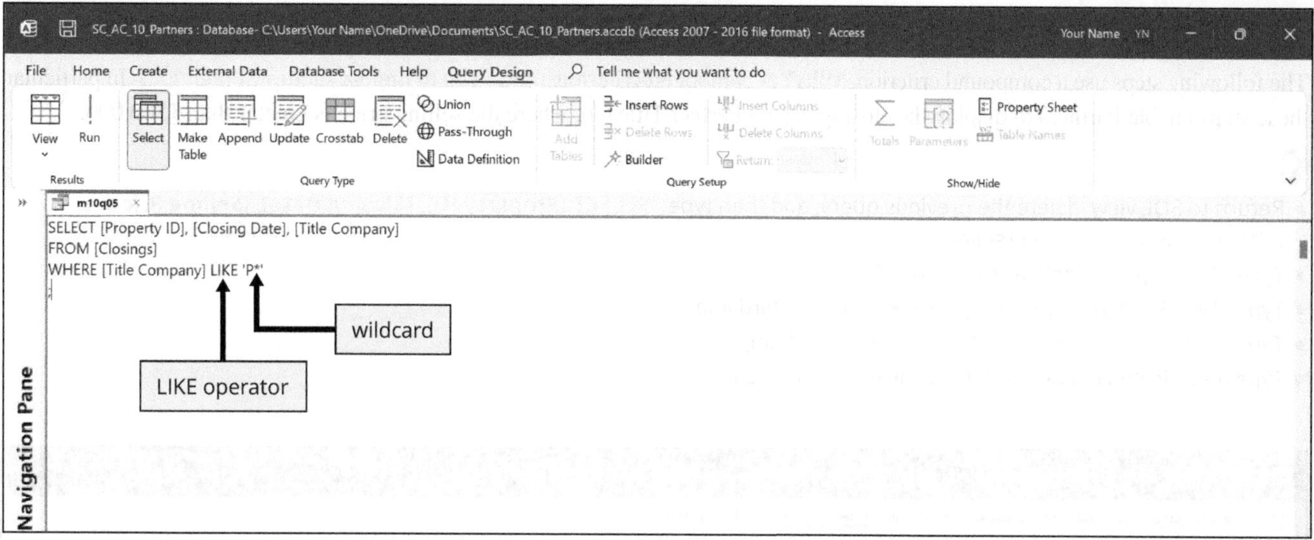

Figure 10–11(a): Query to List Property ID and Closing Date for Closings Where Title Company Starts with 'P'

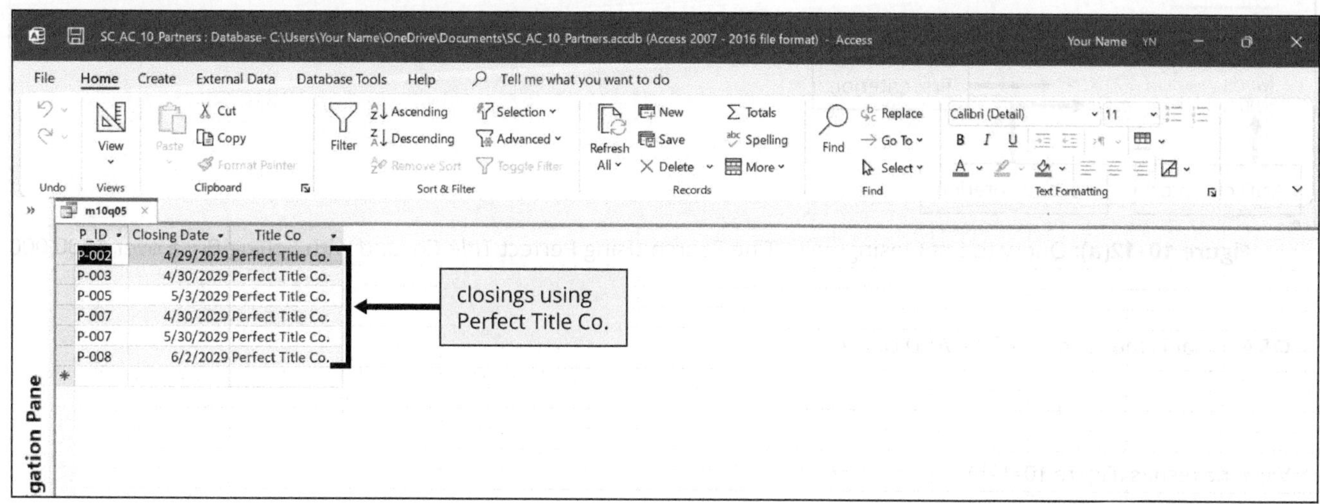

Figure 10–11(b): Query Results

Compound Criteria

You are not limited to simple criteria in SQL. You can also use compound criteria. Recall that compound criteria are formed by connecting two or more simple criteria using AND, OR, and NOT. When simple criteria are connected by the word, AND, all the simple criteria must be true for the compound criterion to be true. When simple criteria are connected by the word, OR, the compound criterion will be true when any one of the simple criteria is true. Preceding a criterion by the word, NOT, reverses the truth or falsity of the original criterion. That is, if the original criterion is true, the new criterion will be false; if the original criterion is false, the new one will be true.

BTW
SQL Standards
The International Organization for Standardization (ISO) and the American National Standards Institute (ANSI) recognize SQL as a standardized language. Different relational database management systems may support the entire set of standardized SQL commands or only a subset.

BTW
Entering Field Names
Be sure to enclose field names in square brackets. If you accidentally use parentheses or curly braces, Access will display a syntax error (missing operator) message.

To Use a Compound Criterion Involving AND

The following steps use a compound criterion. **Why?** A compound criterion allows you to impose multiple conditions. In particular, these steps enable Partners to display the closings using Perfect Title Co. where the selling price is greater than $300,000.

- Return to SQL view, delete the previous query, and then type **SELECT [Property ID], [Closing Date], [Selling Price], [Title Company]** as the first line.
- Type **FROM [Closings]** as the second line.
- Type **WHERE [Title Company] LIKE 'P*'** as the third line.
- Type **AND [Selling Price]>300000** as the fourth line.
- Type a semicolon (;) on the fourth line (Figure 10–12a).

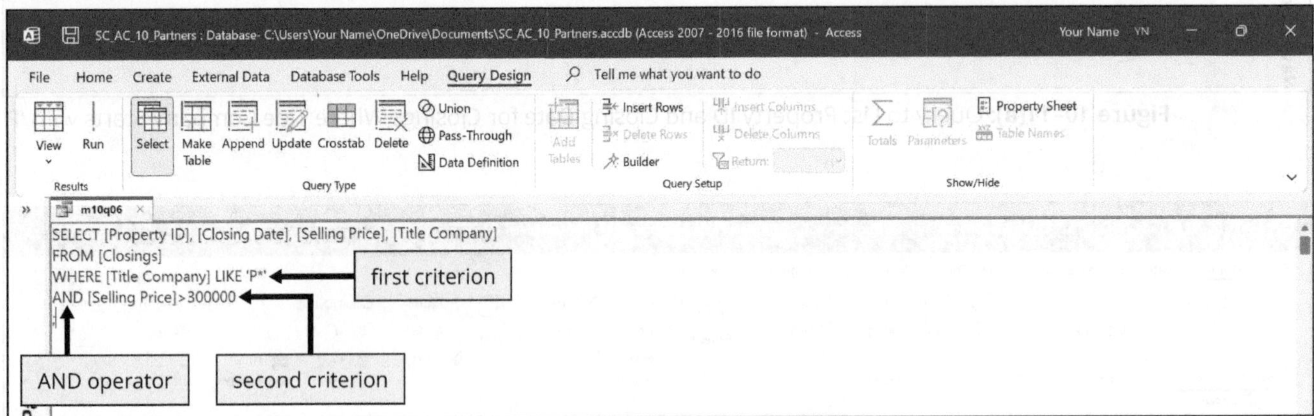

Figure 10–12(a): Query to List Closings with Title Search Using Perfect Title Co. and with Selling Price over $300,000

Q&A What is the purpose of the AND clause?
The AND clause indicates there are multiple criteria, all of which must be true. With this AND clause, only rows on which *both* Title Company starts with P (resulting in "Perfect Title Co.") *and* Selling Price is greater than $300,000 will be included.

- View the results (Figure 10–12b).

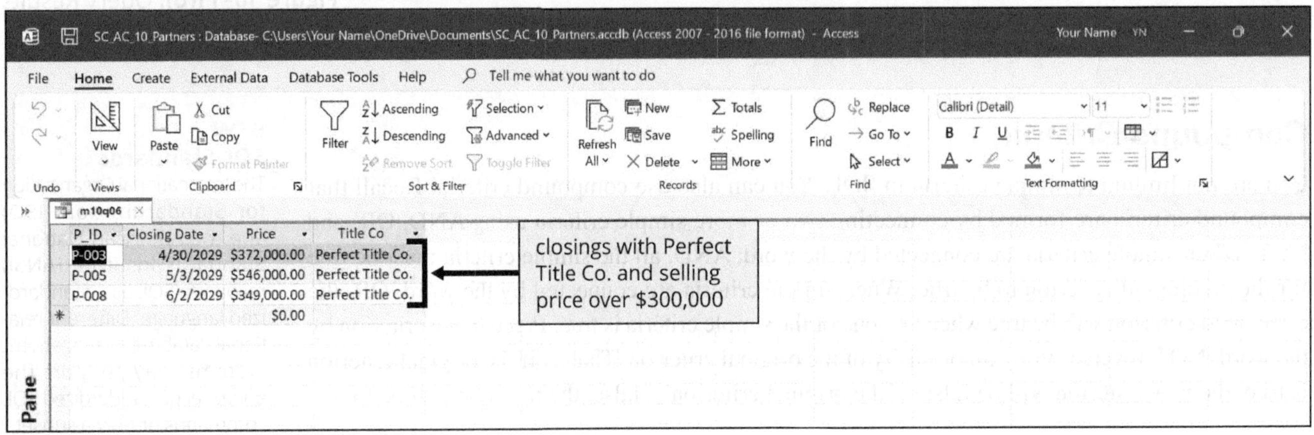

Figure 10–12(b): Query Results

- Save the query as **m10q07**.

To Use a Compound Criterion Involving OR

The following steps use a compound criterion involving OR to enable Partners to display closings with Perfect Title Co. *or* where the selling price is greater than $300,000. **Why?** In an OR criterion, only one of the individual criteria needs to be true for the record to be included in the results.

- Return to SQL view, delete the previous query, and type **SELECT [Property ID], [Closing Date], [Selling Price], [Title Company]** as the first line.
- Type **FROM [Closings]** as the second line.
- Type **WHERE [Title Company] LIKE 'P*'** as the third line.
- Type **OR [Selling Price]>300000** as the fourth line.
- Type a semicolon (;) on the fifth line (Figure 10–13a).

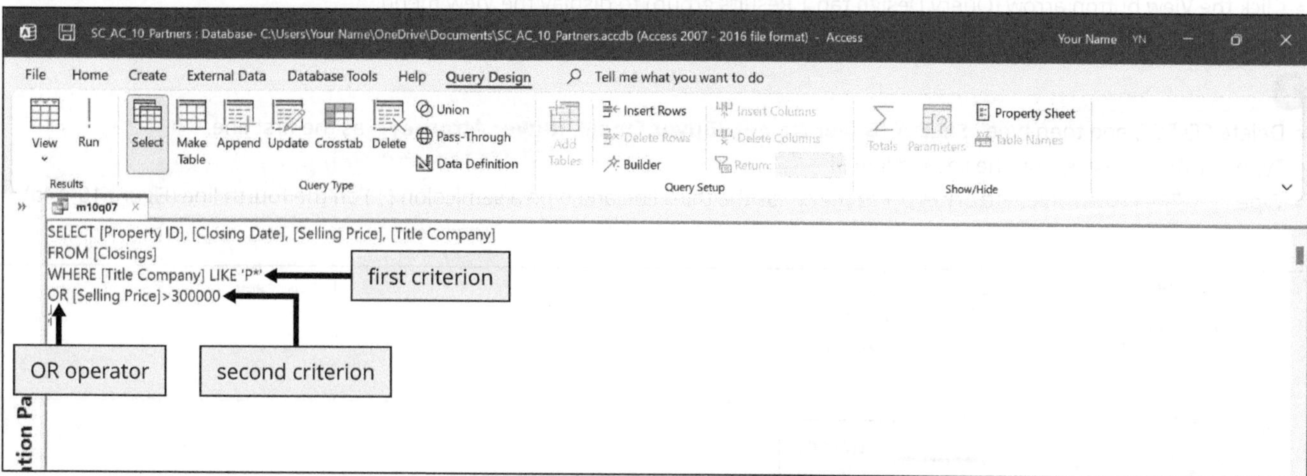

Figure 10–13(a): Query to List Closings Where Title Company Starts with 'P' or Selling Price Is over $300,000

Q&A What is the purpose of the OR clause?
The OR clause indicates there are multiple criteria, only one of which needs to be true. With this OR clause, those rows on which *either* Title Company is Perfect Title Co. *or* Selling Price is greater than $300,000 (or both) will be included.

- View the results (Figure 10–13b).

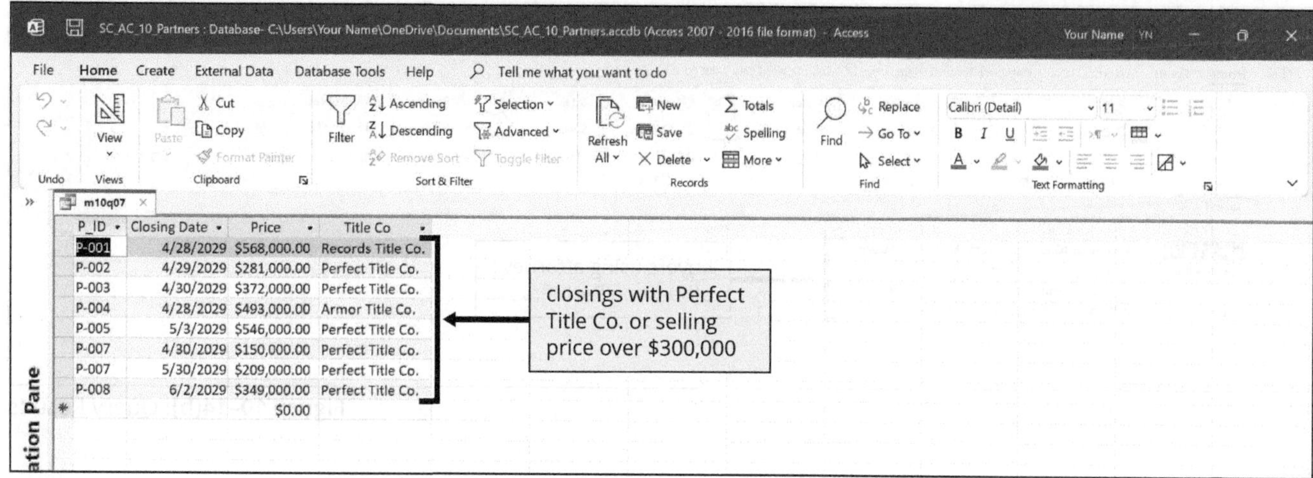

P_ID	Closing Date	Price	Title Co
P-001	4/28/2029	$568,000.00	Records Title Co.
P-002	4/29/2029	$281,000.00	Perfect Title Co.
P-003	4/30/2029	$372,000.00	Perfect Title Co.
P-004	4/28/2029	$493,000.00	Armor Title Co.
P-005	5/3/2029	$546,000.00	Perfect Title Co.
P-007	4/30/2029	$150,000.00	Perfect Title Co.
P-007	5/30/2029	$209,000.00	Perfect Title Co.
P-008	6/2/2029	$349,000.00	Perfect Title Co.
		$0.00	

Figure 10–13(b): Query Results

- Save the query as **m10q08**.
- Close the query.

Break Point: If you wish to take a break, this is a good place to do so. You can quit Access now. To resume at a later time, start Access, open the database called SC_AC_10_Partners.accdb, and continue following the steps from this location forward.

To Use NOT in a Criterion

Why? You can negate any criterion by preceding the criterion with the word NOT. The following steps use NOT in a criterion to list the name, email, and attorney of buyers who are not represented by Partners Law Firm for their closing.

- Click the Create tab, and then click the Query Design button (Create tab | Queries group) to create a query.
- Close the Add Tables pane without adding any tables.
- Click the View button arrow (Query Design tab | Results group) to display the View menu.
- Click SQL View on the View menu.

- Delete SELECT; and then type **SELECT [Buyer Name], [Buyer Email], [Buyer Attorney]** as the first line.
- Type **FROM [Buyers]** on the second line.
- Type **WHERE NOT [Buyer Attorney]='Partners'** as the third line and type a semicolon (;) on the fourth line (Figure 10–14a).

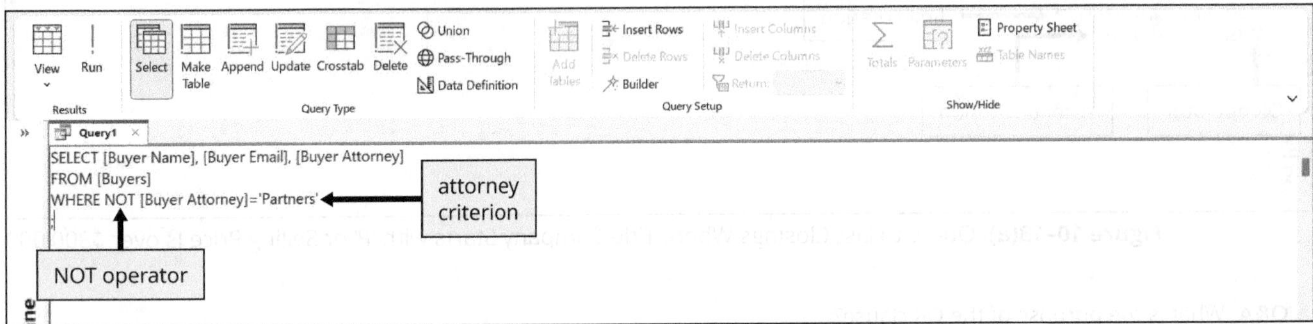

Figure 10-14(a): Query to List Buyer Name, Email, and Attorney for Buyers Not Represented by Partners Law Firm

- View the results (Figure 10–14b).

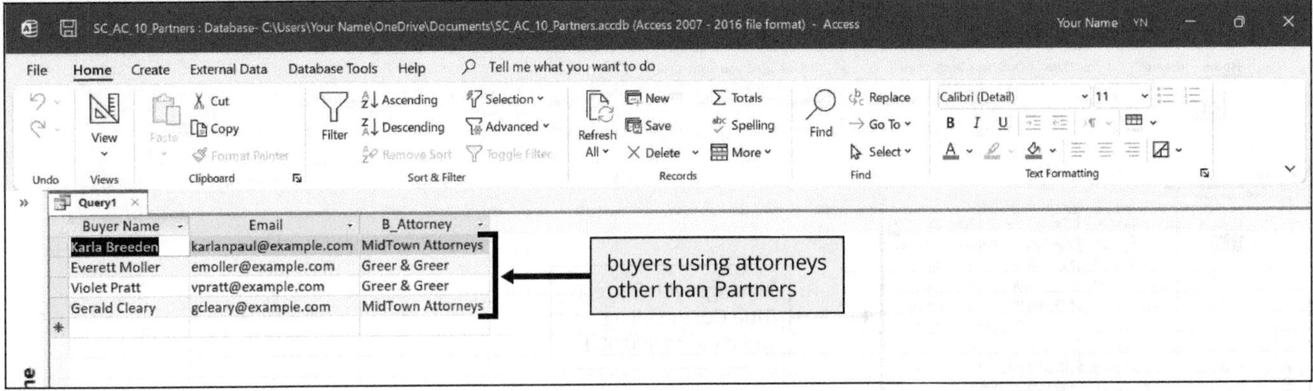

Figure 10-14(b): Query Results

- Save the query as **m10q09**.

To Use a Computed Field

Just as with queries created in Design view, you can include fields in queries that are not listed in the database but that can be computed from fields that are. Recall that such a field is called a computed or calculated field. Computations can involve addition (+), subtraction (–), multiplication (*), or division (/). The query in the following steps computes the workshop hours remaining, which is equal to the total hours minus the hours spent.

To indicate the contents of the new field (the computed field), you can name the field by following the computation with the word, AS, and then the name you want to assign the field. **Why?** Assigning the field a descriptive name makes the results much more readable. The following steps calculate the hours remaining for each workshop enrollment by subtracting the hours spent from the total hours and then assigning the name, Remaining, to the calculation. The steps also list the Buyer ID, Workshop Code, Total Hours, and Hours Spent for all workshop enrollments for which the number of hours spent is greater than 0.

- Return to SQL view and delete the previous query.
- Type **SELECT [Buyer ID], [Workshop Code], [Total Hours], [Hours Spent], [Total Hours]-[Hours Spent] AS Remaining** as the first line.
- Type **FROM [Workshop Enrollments]** as the second line.
- Type **WHERE [Hours Spent]>0** as the third line, and then type a semicolon (;) on the fourth line (Figure 10–15a).

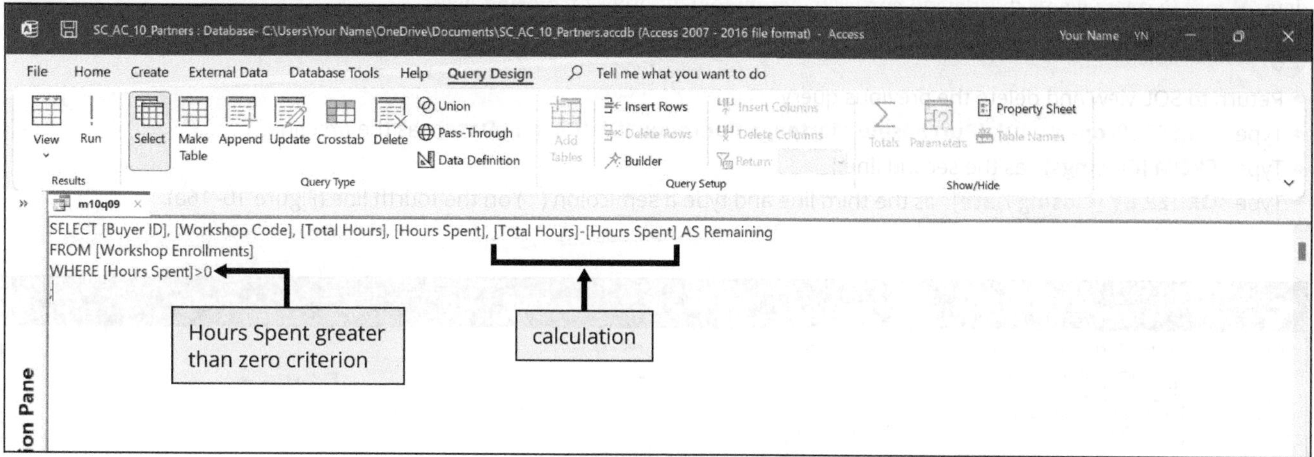

Figure 10–15(a): Query to List Total Hours and Remaining Hours for Each Workshop Enrollment Where Buyer Has Spent More Than 0 Hours

- View the results (Figure 10–15b).

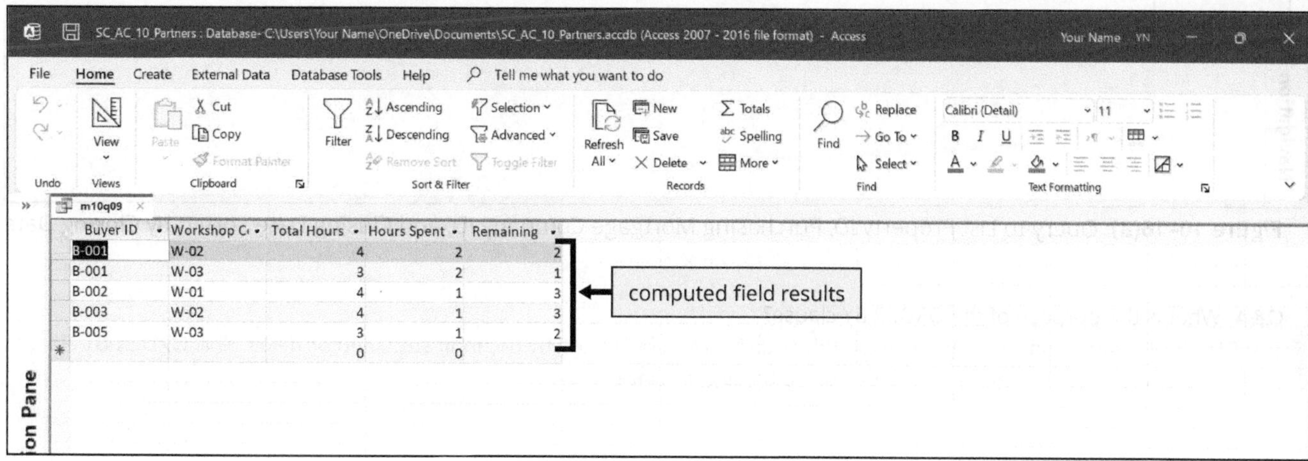

Figure 10–15(b): Query Results

- Save the query as **m10q10**.

Sorting

Sorting in SQL follows the same principles as when using Design view to specify sorted query results, employing a sort key as the field on which data is to be sorted. SQL uses major and minor sort keys when sorting on multiple fields. By following a sort key with the word, DESC, with no comma in between, you can specify descending sort order. If you do not specify DESC, the data will be sorted in ascending order.

To sort the output, you include an **ORDER BY clause**, which consists of the words, ORDER BY, followed by the sort key. If there are two sort keys, the major sort key is listed first. Queries that you construct in Design view require that the major sort key is positioned to the left of the minor sort key in the list of fields to be included. In SQL, there is no such restriction. The fields to be included in the query are listed in the SELECT clause, and the fields to be used for sorting are listed in the ORDER BY clause. The two clauses are independent of each other.

To Sort the Results on a Single Field

The following steps list the property ID, purchasing mortgage company ID, and closing date for all closings sorted by closing date. **Why?** Partners wants this data to appear in chronological order by closing date.

- Return to SQL view and delete the previous query.
- Type **SELECT [Property ID], [Purchasing Mortgage Company ID], [Closing Date]** as the first line.
- Type **FROM [Closings]** as the second line.
- Type **ORDER BY [Closing Date]** as the third line and type a semicolon (;) on the fourth line (Figure 10-16a).

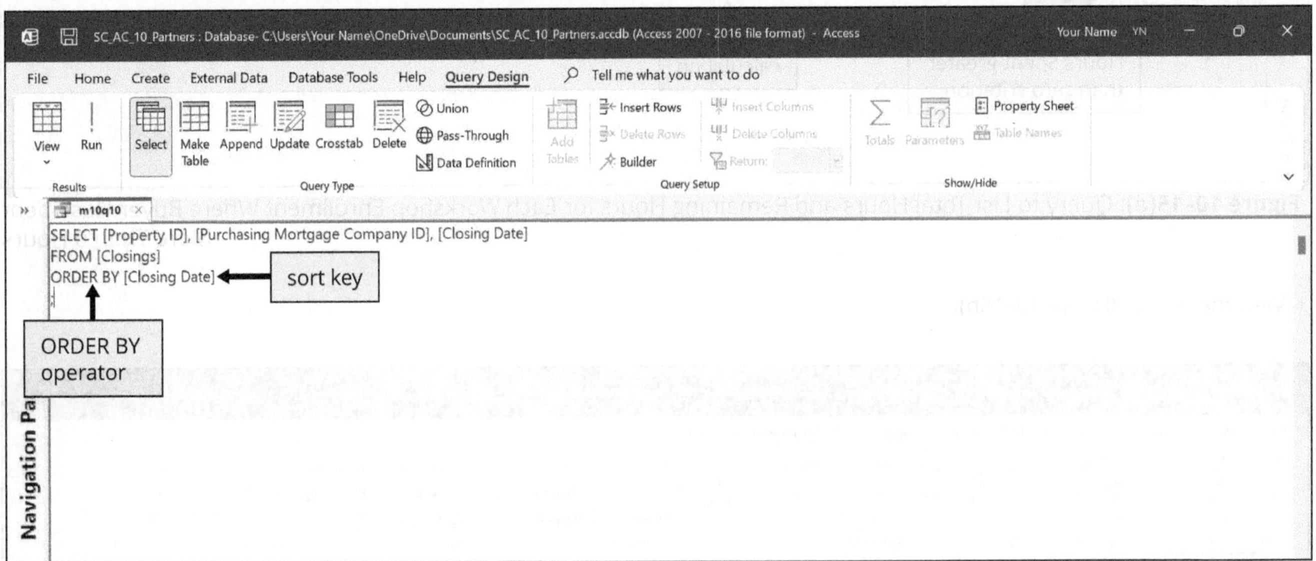

Figure 10-16(a): Query to List Property ID, Purchasing Mortgage Company ID, and Closing Date Sorted by Closing Date

Q&A What is the purpose of the ORDER BY clause?
The ORDER BY clause indicates the results of the query are to be sorted by the indicated field or fields. This ORDER BY clause, for example, would cause the results to be sorted by Closing Date.

- View the results (Figure 10-16b).

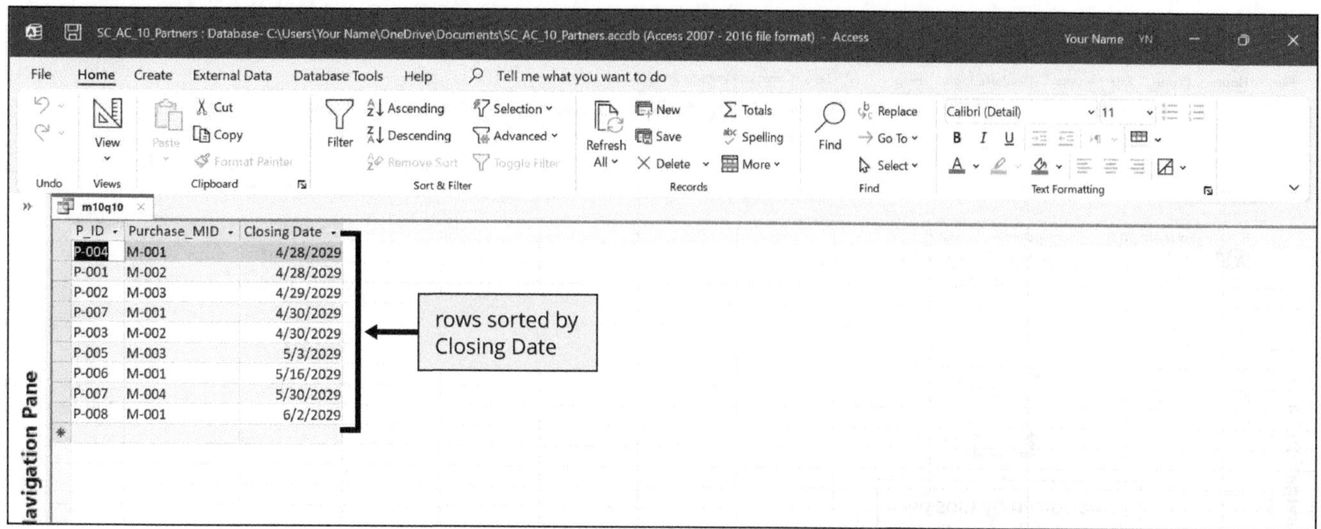

Figure 10-16(b): Query Results

- Save the query as **m10q11**.

To Sort the Results on Multiple Fields

The following steps list the property ID, purchasing mortgage company ID, closing date, and status for all closings. The data is to be sorted on multiple fields. **Why?** Partners wants the data to be sorted by status within closing date. That is, the data should be sorted by closing date. In addition, within the group of closings that have the same closing date, the data is to be sorted further by status. To accomplish this sort, the Closing Date field is the major (primary) sort key and the Status field is the minor (secondary) sort key. Remember that the major sort key must be listed first in the ORDER BY clause.

- Return to SQL view and delete the previous query.
- Type **SELECT [Property ID], [Purchasing Mortgage Company ID], [Closing Date], [Status]** as the first line.
- Type **FROM [Closings]** as the second line.
- Type **ORDER BY [Closing Date], [Status]** as the third line, and then type a semicolon (;) on the fourth line (Figure 10-17a).

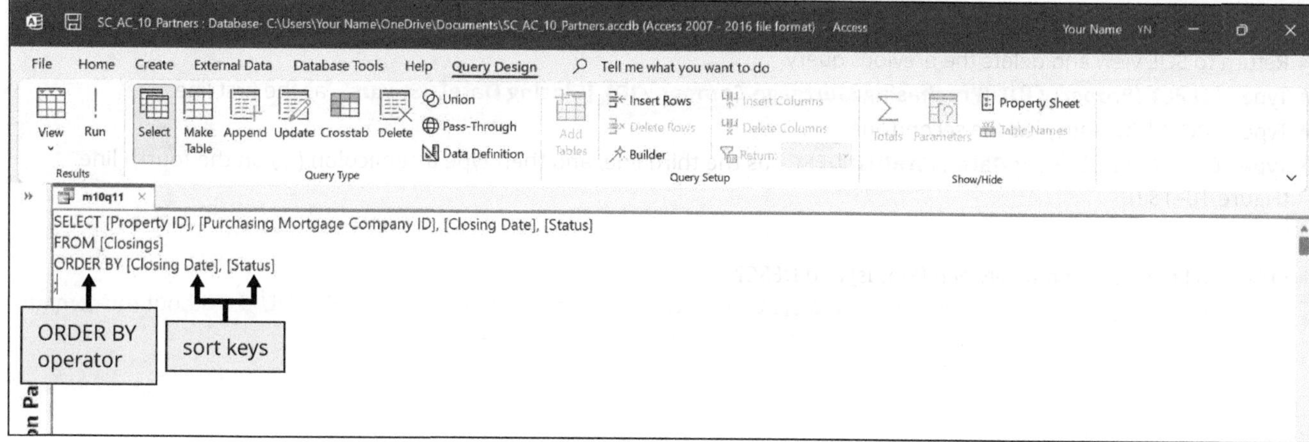

Figure 10-17(a): Query to List Property ID, Purchasing Mortgage Company ID, Closing Date, and Status Sorted by Closing Date and Status

- View the results (Figure 10–17b).

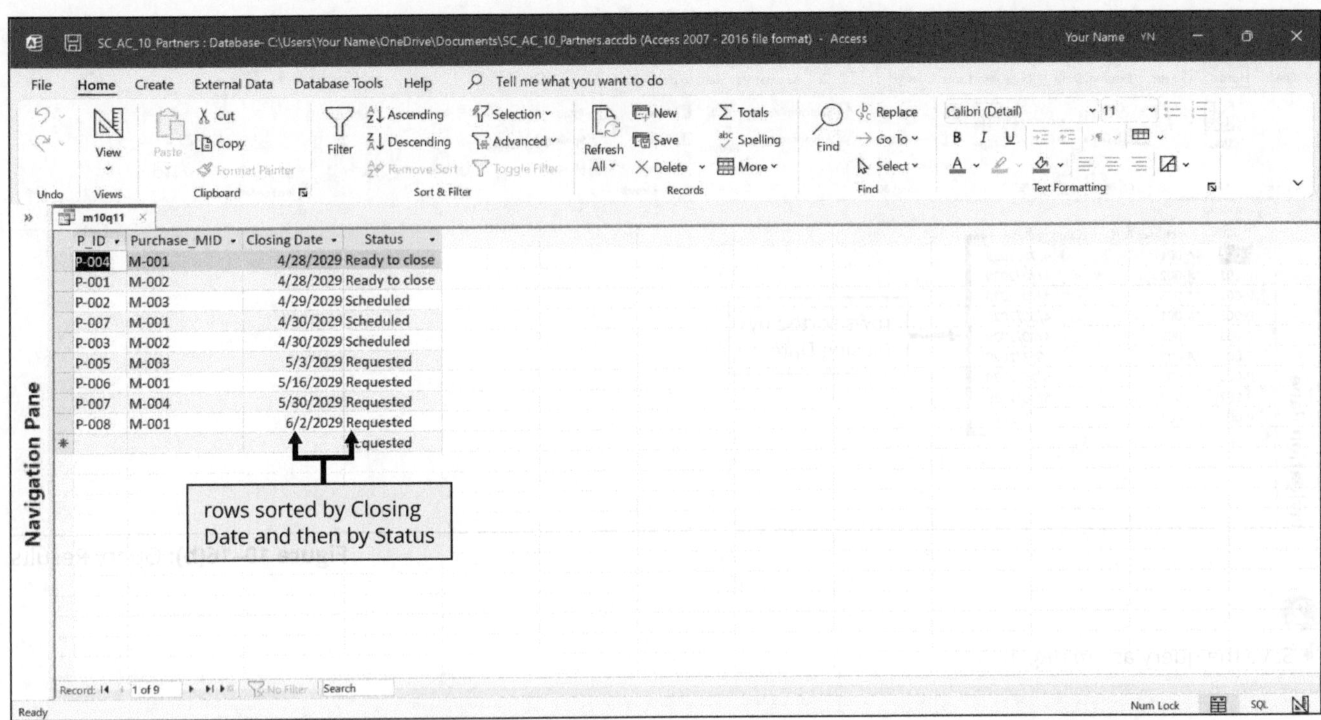

Figure 10–17(b): Query Results

- **Experiment:** Try reversing the order of the sort keys to see the effect. View the results to see the effect of your choice. When finished, return to the original sorting order for both fields.

- Save the query as **m10q12**.

To Sort the Results in Descending Order

Why? To show the results in high-to-low rather than low-to-high order, you sort in descending order. To sort in descending order, you follow the name of the sort key with the DESC operator. The following steps list the property ID, purchasing mortgage company ID, closing date, and status for all closings. Partners wants the data to be sorted by descending status within closing date. That is, within the closings having the same date, the data is to be sorted further by status in descending order.

- Return to SQL view and delete the previous query.
- Type **SELECT [Property ID], [Purchasing Mortgage Company ID], [Closing Date], [Status]** as the first line.
- Type **FROM [Closings]** as the second line.
- Type **ORDER BY [Closing Date], [Status] DESC** as the third line, and then type a semicolon (;) on the fourth line (Figure 10–18a).

Q&A Do I need a comma between [Status] and DESC?
No. In fact, you must not use a comma. If you did, SQL would assume that you want a field called DESC. Without the comma, SQL knows that the DESC operator indicates the sort on the Status field is to be in descending order.

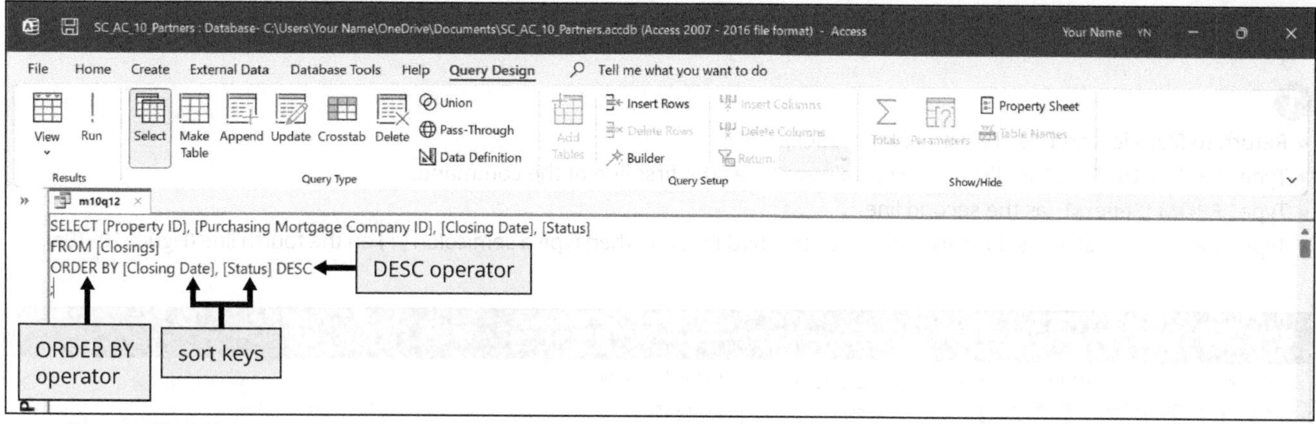

Figure 10–18(a): Query to List Property ID, Purchasing Mortgage Company ID, Closing Date, and Status with Results Sorted by Closing Date and Descending Status Order

- View the results (Figure 10–18b).

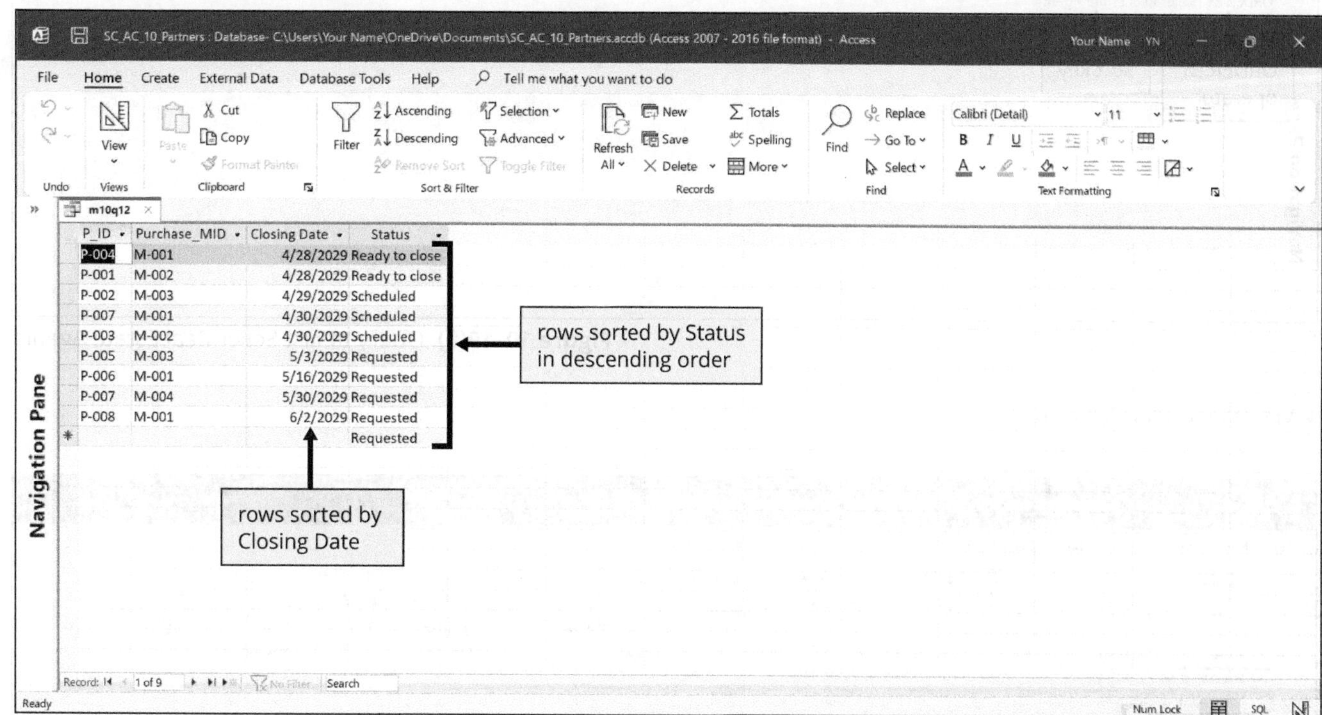

Figure 10–18(b): Query Results

2

- Save the query as **m10q13**.

To Omit Duplicates When Sorting

When you sort data, duplicates are normally included. For example, the query in Figure 10–19 sorts the Seller Real Estate Agents in the Sellers table. Because there are several real estate agents representing multiple sellers, Partners would like to eliminate duplicate agents in the list. To do so, use the DISTINCT operator in the query. **Why?** The DISTINCT operator eliminates duplicate values in the results of a query. To use the operator, you follow the word, DISTINCT, with the relevant field name in parentheses.

The following steps display the Seller Real Estate Agents from the Sellers table in alphabetical order, but with any duplicates removed.

1

- Return to SQL view and delete the previous query.
- Type **SELECT DISTINCT [Seller Real Estate Agent]** as the first line of the command.
- Type **FROM [Sellers]** as the second line.
- Type **ORDER BY [Seller Real Estate Agent]** as the third line, and then type a semicolon (;) on the fourth line (Figure 10–19a).

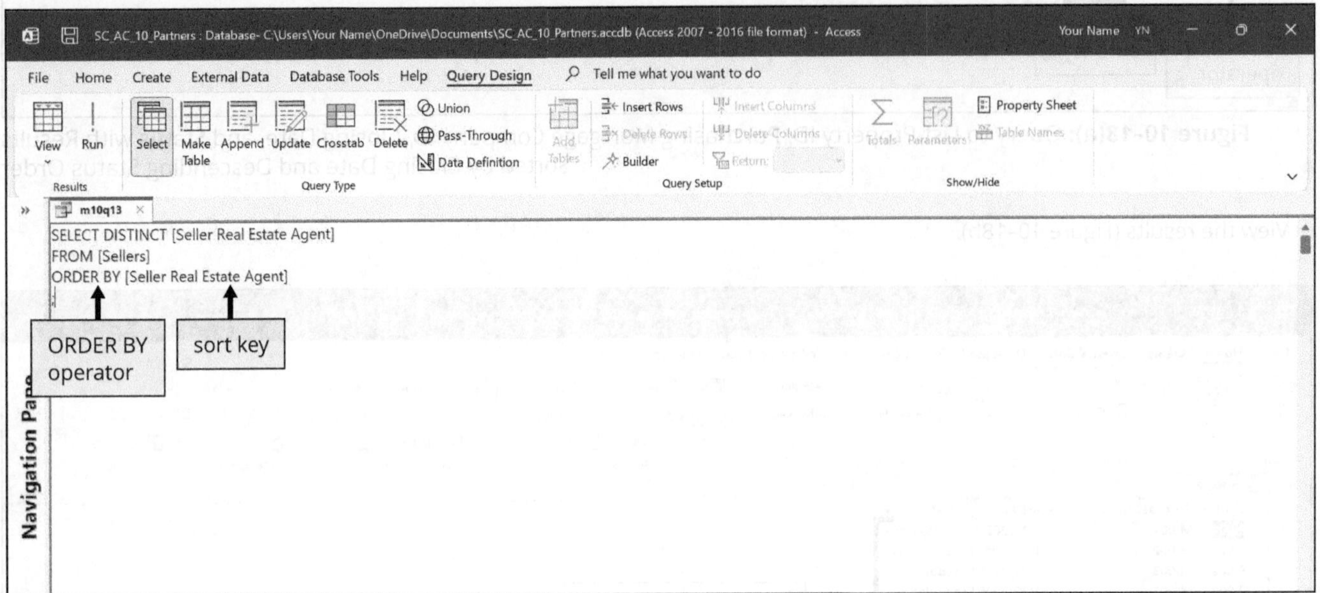

Figure 10–19(a): Query to List Seller Real Estate Agents

- View the results (Figure 10–19b).

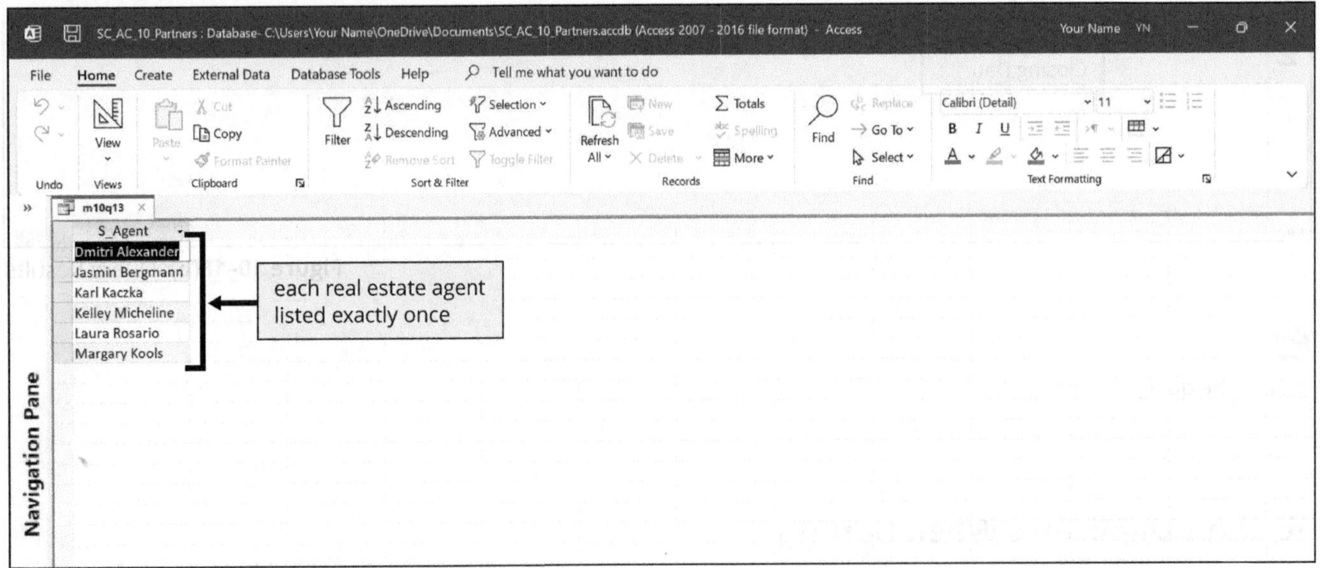

Figure 10–19(b): Query Results

2

- Save the query as **m10q14**.

Consider This

How do you determine sorting when creating a query?

Examine the query or request to see if it contains words such as *order* or *sort* that would imply the order of the query results is important. If so, you need to sort the query.

- **Determine whether data is to be sorted.** Examine the requirements for the query looking for words like *sorted by, ordered by, arranged by*, and so on.
- **Determine sort keys.** Look for the fields that follow sorted by, ordered by, or any other words that signify sorting. For example, if the requirements for the query include the phrase, ordered by real estate agent name, then real estate agent name is a sort key.
- **If there is more than one sort key, determine which one will be the major sort key and which will be the minor sort key.** Look for words that indicate which field is more important. For example, if the requirements indicate the results are to be ordered by status within closing date, then Closing Date is the more important sort key.

To Use a Built-In Function

SQL has built-in functions, also called aggregate functions, to perform various calculations. Similar to the functions you learned about in an earlier module, these functions in SQL are COUNT, SUM, AVG, MAX, and MIN, respectively. Partners uses the following steps to determine the number of property purchases closing with Atlas Mortgage (M-001) by using the COUNT function with an asterisk (*). **Why use an asterisk rather than a field name when using the COUNT function?** You could select a field name, but that would be cumbersome and imply that you were just counting that field. You are really counting records. It does not matter whether you are counting names or street addresses or anything else.

- Return to SQL view and delete the previous query.
- Type **SELECT COUNT(*)** as the first line of the command.
- Type **FROM [Closings]** as the second line.
- Type **WHERE [Purchasing Mortgage Company ID]='M-001'** as the third line, and then type a semicolon (;) on the fourth line (Figure 10–20a).

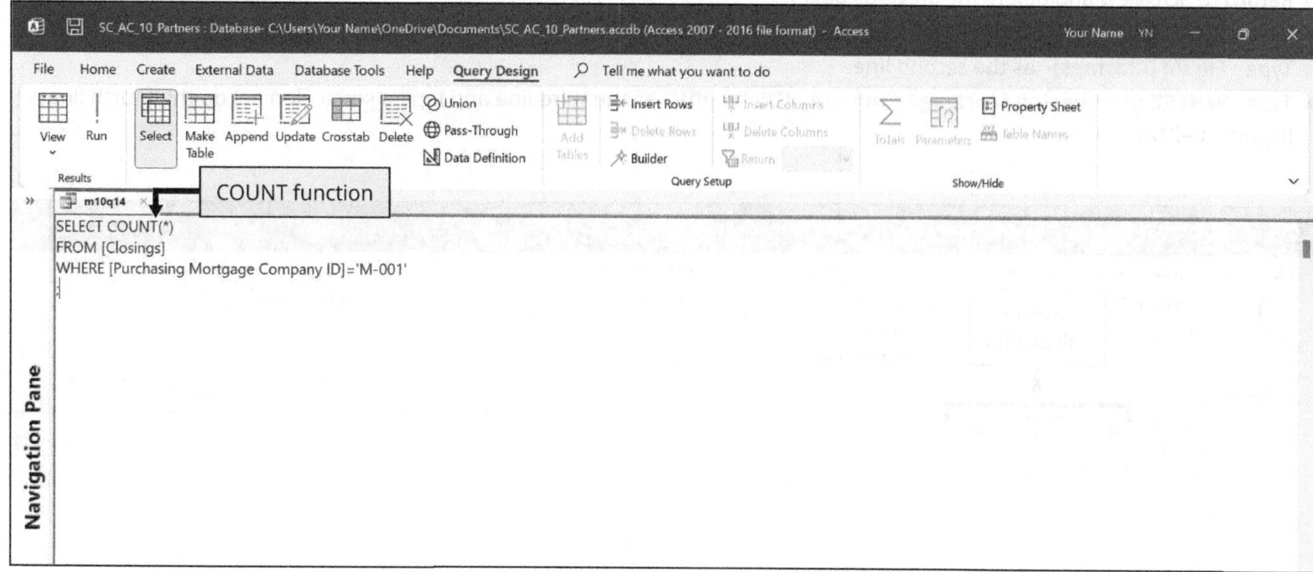

Figure 10–20(a): Query to Count Closings for Mortgage Company M-001

- View the results (Figure 10–20b).

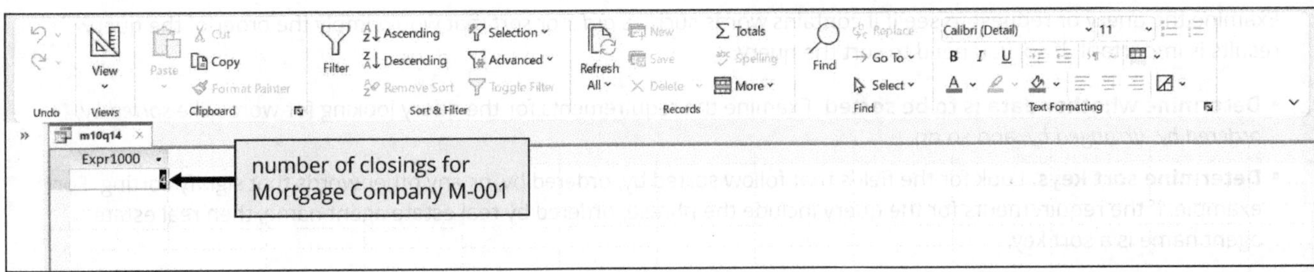

Figure 10–20(b): Query Results

Q&A Why does Expr1000 appear in the column heading of the results?
Because the field is a computed field, it does not have a name. Access assigns a generic expression name. You can assign a meaningful name for the field by including the AS clause in the query, and it is good practice to do so.

- Save the query as **m10q15**.

To Assign a Name to the Results of a Function

Partners would prefer to have a more meaningful name than Expr1000 for the results of counting closings. **Why?** The default name of Expr1000 does not describe the meaning of the calculation. Fortunately, just as you can assign a name to a calculation that includes two fields, you can assign a name to the results of a function. To do so, follow the expression for the function with the word, AS, and then the name to be assigned to the result. The following steps assign the name, Atlas Mortgage Purchases, to the expression in the previous query.

- Return to SQL view and delete the previous query.
- Type **SELECT COUNT(*) AS [Atlas Mortgage Purchases]** as the first line of the command.
- Type **FROM [Closings]** as the second line.
- Type **WHERE [Purchasing Mortgage Company ID]='M-001'** as the third line and type a semicolon (;) on the fourth line (Figure 10–21a).

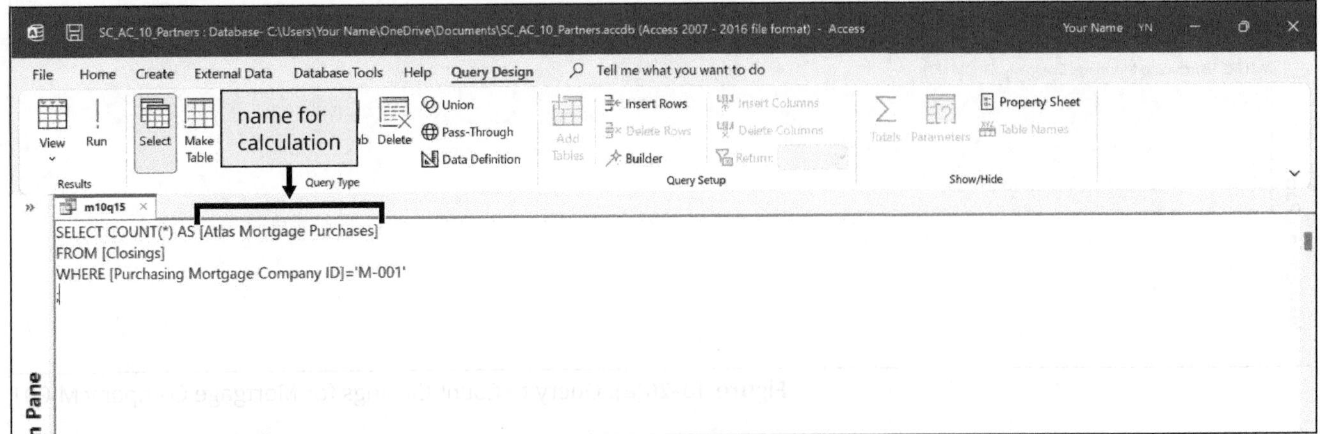

Figure 10–21(a): Query to Count Closings for Mortgage Company M-001 and to Name the Expression

- View the results. If necessary, increase the width of the Atlas Mortgage Purchases column to view the entire field name (Figure 10–21b).

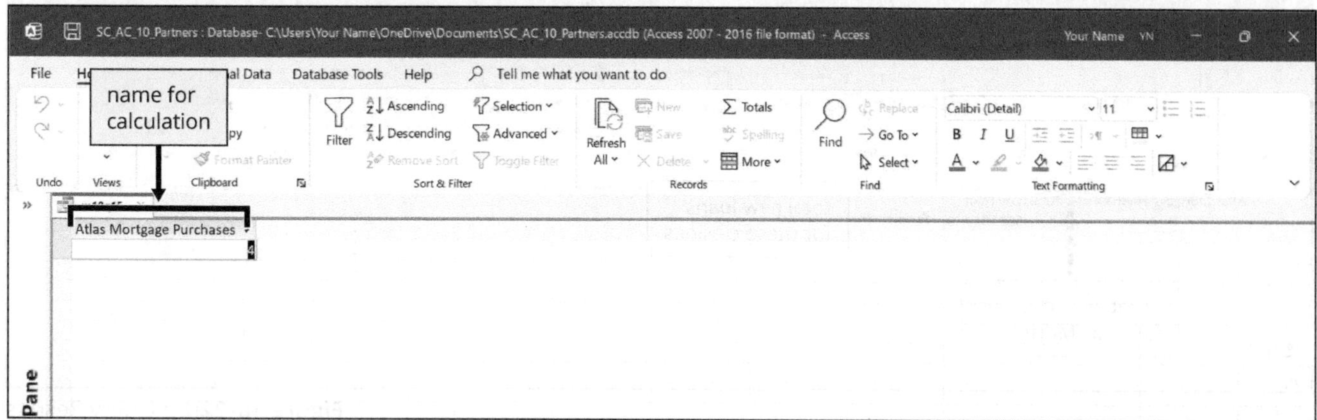

Figure 10–21(b): Query Results

- Save the query as **m10q16**.

To Use Multiple Functions in the Same Command

There are two differences between COUNT and SUM, other than the fact they are computing different statistics. First, in the case of SUM, you must specify the field for which you want a total, instead of using an asterisk (*); second, the field must be numeric. **Why?** If the field is not numeric, it does not make sense to calculate a sum. You could not calculate a sum of names or addresses, for example. The following steps use both the COUNT and SUM functions to count the number of closings whose purchasing mortgage company ID is M-001 and to calculate the sum (total) of the new loan amounts. The steps use the word, AS, to name COUNT(*) as Atlas Mortgage Purchases and to name SUM([New Loan Amount]) as Total New Loans.

- Return to SQL view and delete the previous query.
- Type **SELECT COUNT(*) AS [Atlas Mortgage Purchases], SUM([New Loan Amount]) AS [Total New Loans]** as the first line of the command.
- Type **FROM [Closings]** as the second line.
- Type **WHERE [Purchasing Mortgage Company ID]='M-001'** as the third line and type a semicolon (;) on the fourth line (Figure 10–22a).

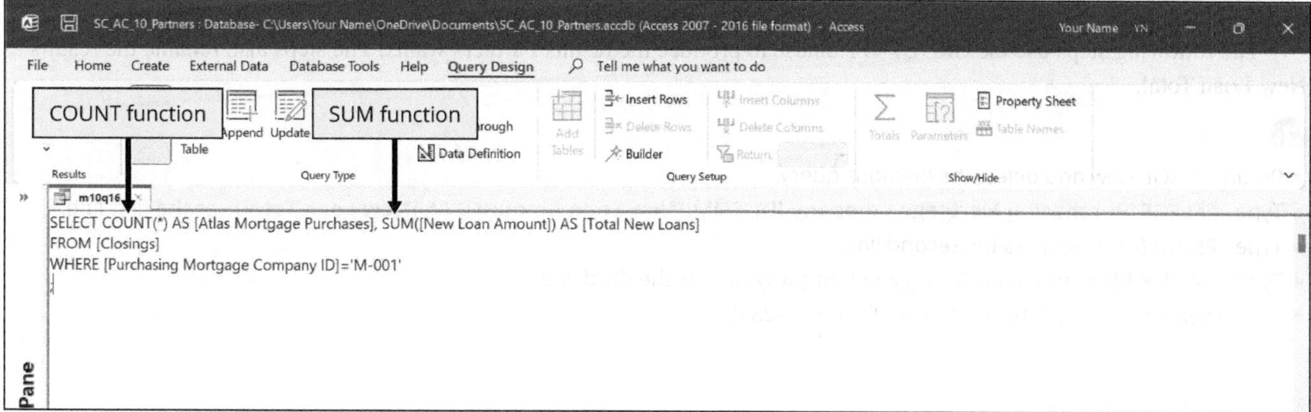

Figure 10–22(a): Query to Count Closings for Mortgage Company M-001 Using a Named Expression and to Calculate Sum of New Loan Amounts Using a Named Expression

- View the results. If necessary, increase the width of the Total New Loans column to view the entire field name (Figure 10–22b).

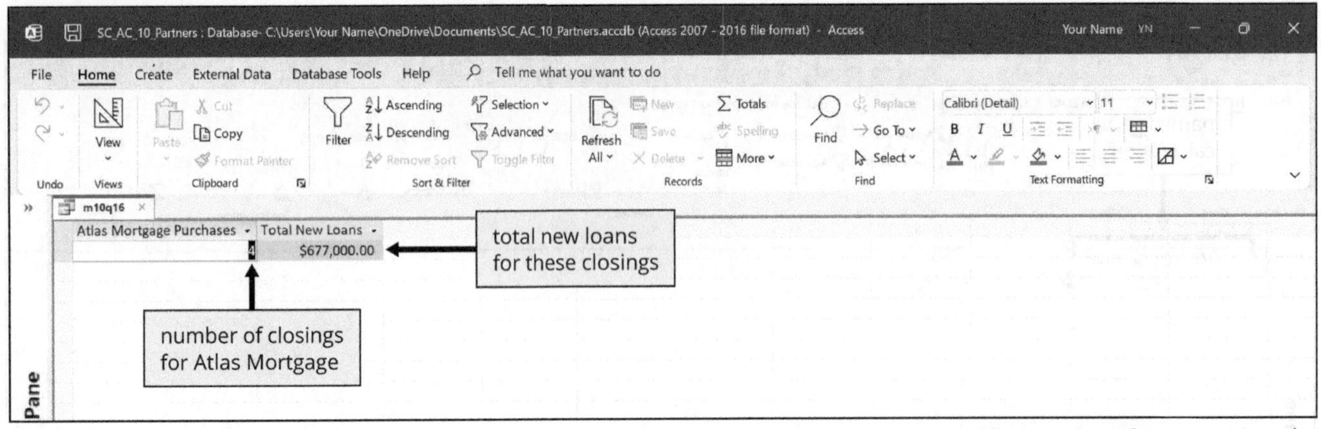

Figure 10–22(b): Query Results

- **Experiment:** Try using other functions in place of SUM. The use of AVG, MAX, and MIN is similar to SUM. The only difference is that a different statistic is calculated with each function. In each case, view the results to see the effect of your choice. When finished, once again select SUM.

- Save the query as **m10q17**.

Grouping

Recall that grouping means creating groups of records that share some common characteristic. When you group rows, any calculations indicated in the SELECT command are performed for the entire group.

To Use Grouping

Partners wants to calculate the totals of the New Loan Amount field for all Purchasing Mortgage Company IDs in the Closings table. To calculate the totals, the query will include the calculation, SUM([New Loan Amount]). To get totals for each mortgage company, the query will also include a **GROUP BY clause**, which consists of the words, GROUP BY, followed by the field used for grouping, in this case, Purchasing Mortgage Company ID. **Why?** Including GROUP BY Purchasing Mortgage Company ID will cause the new loan amounts for each mortgage company to be grouped together; that is, all new loan amounts with the same purchasing mortgage company will form a group. Any statistics, such as new loan totals, appearing after the word, SELECT, will be calculated for each of these groups. Using GROUP BY does not mean the information will be sorted.

The following steps use the GROUP BY clause to produce the results Partners wants. The steps also rename the results as New Loan Total.

- Return to SQL view and delete the previous query.
- Type **SELECT [Purchasing Mortgage Company ID], SUM([New Loan Amount]) AS [New Loan Total]** as the first line.
- Type **FROM [Closings]** as the second line.
- Type **GROUP BY [Purchasing Mortgage Company ID]** as the third line.
- Type a semicolon (;) as the fourth line (Figure 10–23a).

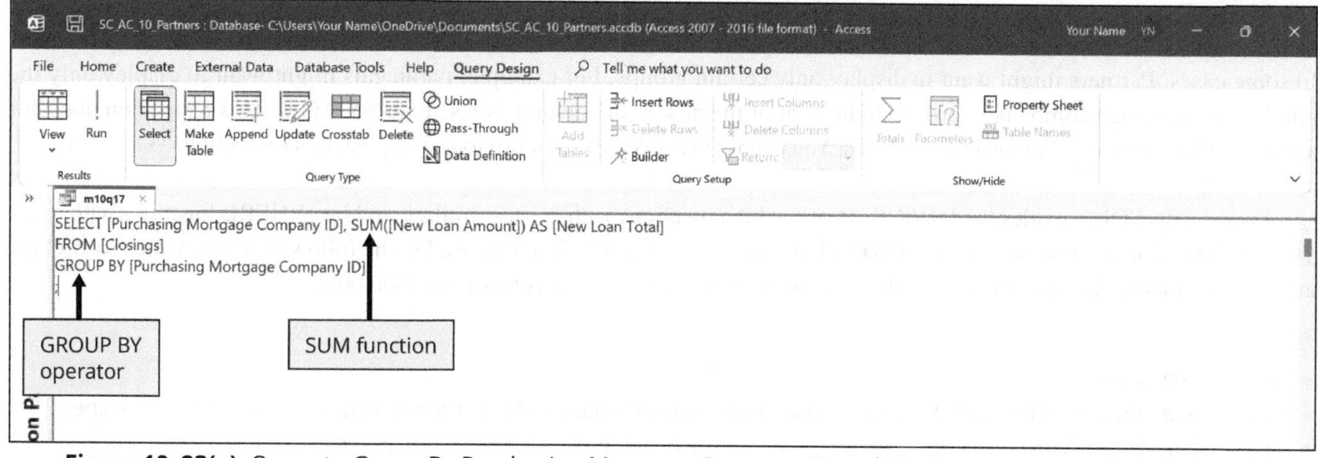

Figure 10–23(a): Query to Group By Purchasing Mortgage Company ID and Display New Loan Totals for Each Group

Q&A What is the purpose of the GROUP BY clause?
The GROUP BY clause causes the rows to be grouped by the indicated field. With this GROUP BY clause, the rows will be grouped by Purchasing Mortgage Company ID.

- View the results. If necessary, increase the widths of the columns to display their entire field names (Figure 10–23b).

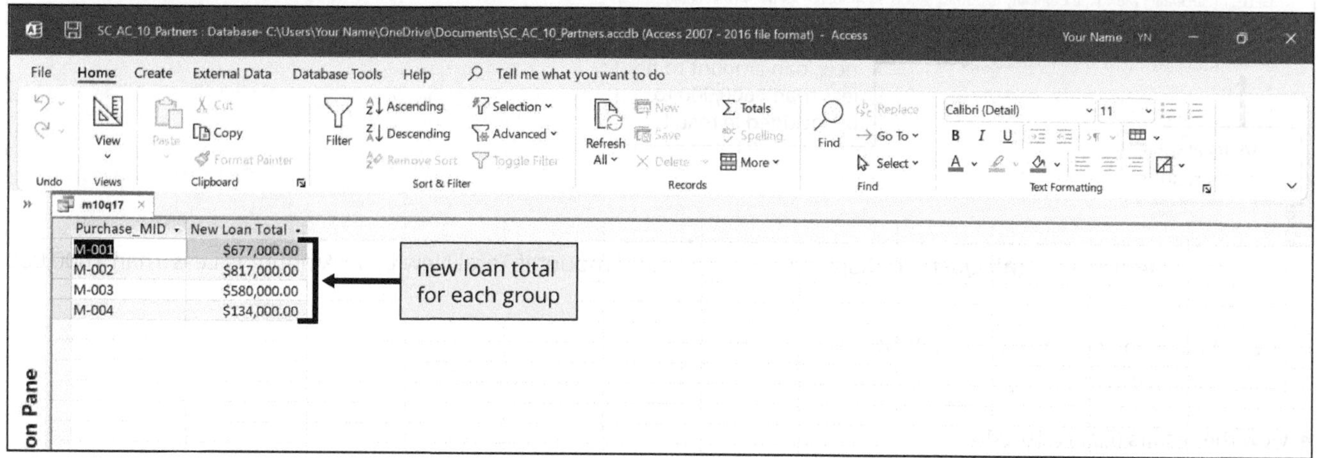

Figure 10–23(b): Query Results

- Save the query as **m10q18**.

Grouping Requirements

When rows are grouped, one line of output is produced for each group. The only output that SQL can display is statistics that are calculated for the group or fields whose values are the same for all rows in a group. For example, when grouping rows by purchasing mortgage company as in the previous query, it is appropriate to display the purchasing mortgage company ID, because the ID in one row in a group must be the same as the ID in any other row in the group. It is appropriate to display the sum of the new loan amounts because this is a statistic calculated for the group. It would not be appropriate to display a buyer ID, however, because the buyer varies on the rows in a group; the purchasing mortgage company ID is associated with many closings. SQL would not be able to determine which buyer ID to display for the group. SQL will display an error message if you attempt to display a field that is not appropriate for the query, such as the buyer ID.

To Restrict the Groups That Appear

In some cases, Partners might want to display only certain groups. For example, paralegals might want to display only the purchasing mortgage companies for which the sum of the new loan amounts is less than $600,000. This restriction does not apply to individual rows, but instead to groups. You cannot use a WHERE clause to accomplish this restriction. **Why?** WHERE applies only to rows, not groups.

Fortunately, SQL provides the **HAVING clause**, which functions with groups similarly to how WHERE functions with rows. The HAVING clause consists of the word, HAVING, followed by a criterion. It is used in the following steps, which restrict the groups to be included to those for which the sum of the new loan amounts is less than $600,000.

- Return to SQL view.
- Click the end of the third line (GROUP BY [Purchasing Mortgage Company ID]) and press ENTER to insert a new blank line.
- Type **HAVING SUM([New Loan Amount])<600000** as the new fourth line. See Figure 10–24a.

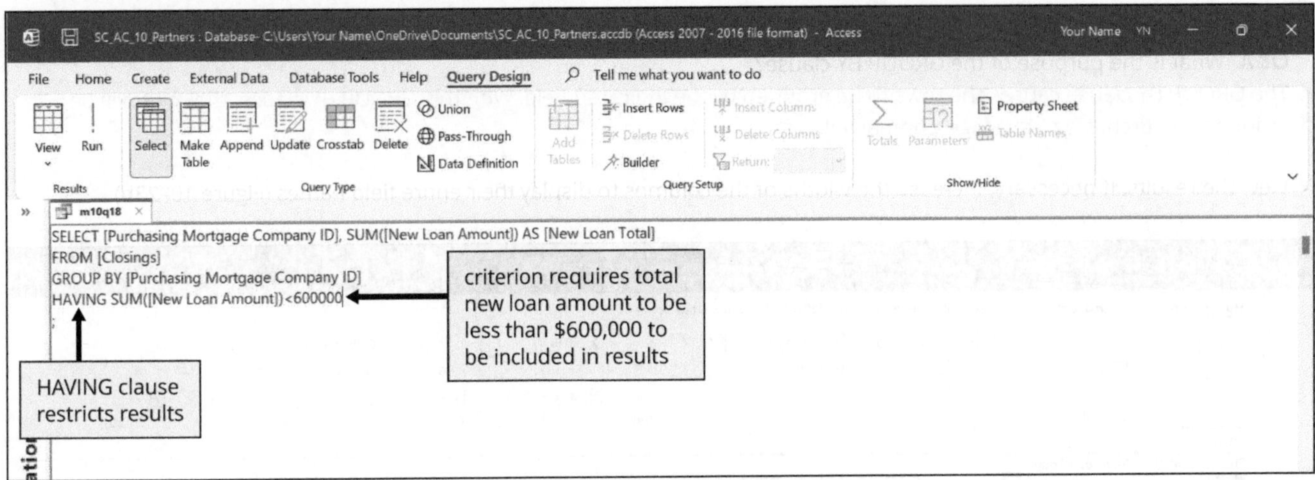

Figure 10–24(a): Query to Display Total New Loan Amount if Total New Loan Amount Is Less Than $600,000

Q&A What is the purpose of the HAVING clause?
The HAVING clause restricts the groups that will be included in the results to only those satisfying the indicated criteria.

- View the results (Figure 10–24b).

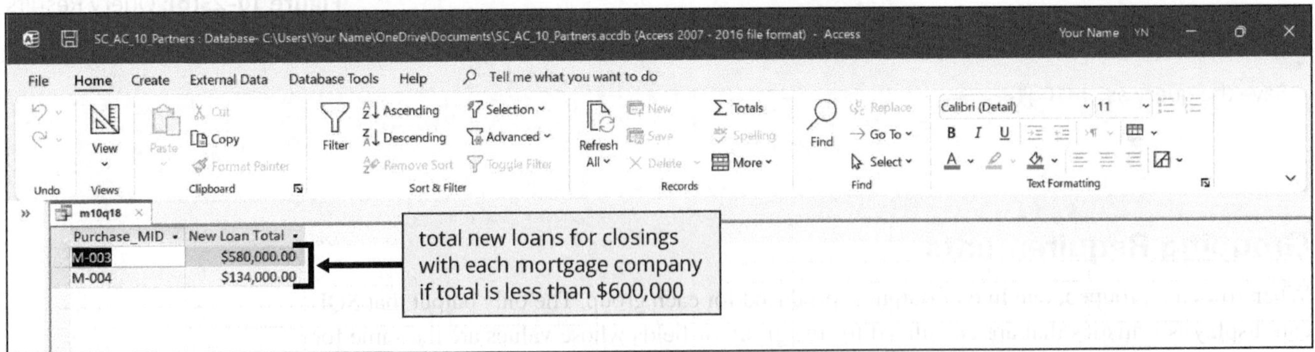

Figure 10–24(b): Query Results

- Save the query as **m10q19**.

BTW
BETWEEN Operator
The BETWEEN operator allows you to search for a range of values in one field. For example, to find all closings where the new loan amount is between $100,000 and $200,000, the WHERE clause would be WHERE [New Loan Amount] BETWEEN 100000 AND 200000.

Consider This

How do you determine grouping when creating a query?
Examine the question or request to determine whether records should be organized by some common characteristic.

- **Determine whether data is to be grouped in some fashion.** Examine the requirements for the query to see if they contain individual rows or information about groups of rows.
- **Determine the field or fields on which grouping is to take place.** By which field is the data to be grouped? Look to see if the requirements indicate a field along with several group calculations.
- **Determine which fields or calculations are appropriate to display.** When rows are grouped, one line of output is produced for each group. The only output that can appear are statistics that are calculated for the group or fields whose values are the same for all rows in a group. For example, it would make sense to display the mortgage company ID, because all the closings in the group have the same mortgage company ID. It would not make sense to display the Buyer ID, because the Buyer ID will vary from one row in a group to another. SQL could not determine which Buyer ID to display for the group.

Break Point: If you wish to take a break, this is a good place to do so. You can quit Access now. To resume at a later time, start Access, open the database called SC_AC_10_Partners.accdb, create a new query in SQL view, and continue following the steps from this location forward.

Joining Tables

Many queries require data from more than one table. Just as with creating queries in Design view, SQL should provide a way to join tables, that is, to find rows in two tables that have identical values in matching fields. In SQL, this is accomplished through appropriate criteria following the word, WHERE.

If you want to list the closing date, buyer ID, and name of the buyer for all closings, you need data from both the Closings and Buyers tables. The Buyer ID field is in both tables, the Closing Date field is only in the Closings table, and the Buyer Name field is only in the Buyers table. You need to access both tables in your SQL query, as follows:

1. In the SELECT clause, you indicate all fields you want to appear.
2. In the FROM clause, you list all tables involved in the query.
3. In the WHERE clause, you give the criterion that will restrict the data to be retrieved to only those rows included in both of the two tables, that is, to the rows that have common values in matching fields.

Qualifying Fields

If there is a problem with matching fields, such as a field named Buyer ID that exists in both tables, it is necessary to **qualify** Buyer ID, that is, to specify to which field in which table you are referring. You do this by preceding the name of the field with the name of the table, followed by a period. The Buyer ID field in the Buyers table, for example, is [Buyers].[Buyer ID]. The Buyer ID field in the Closings table would then be indicated as [Closings].[Buyer ID]. If the fields had slightly different names (such as Buyer ID and Buyer), it would not be necessary to qualify the fields; however, it is permissible to qualify fields even if there is no confusion. For example, instead of [Buyer Name], you could type [Buyers].[Buyer Name] to indicate the Buyer Name field in the Buyers table, even though no other table contains a field called Buyer Name. Some people prefer to qualify all fields, and this is not a bad approach. In this text, you will only qualify fields when it is necessary to do so and for learning purposes.

BTW
Qualifying Fields
There is no space on either side of the period that is used to separate the table name from the field name. Adding a space will result in an error message.

To Join Tables

Partners wants to list the closing date, buyer ID, and buyer name for all closings. The following steps create a query to join the tables using an INNER JOIN. **Why?** The data comes from two tables. The steps also order the results by closing date.

- If necessary, return to SQL view and delete the previous query.
- Type **SELECT [Closings].[Buyer ID], [Closings].[Closing Date], [Buyers].[Buyer ID], [Buyers].[Buyer Name]** as the first line of the command.
- Type **FROM [Closings] INNER JOIN [Buyers] ON [Closings].[Buyer ID] = [Buyers].[Buyer ID]** as the second line.

Q&A Why does the FROM clause contain more than one table?
The query involves fields from both tables.

- Type **ORDER BY [Closings].[Closing Date]** as the third line, and then type a semicolon (;) on the fourth line (Figure 10–25a).

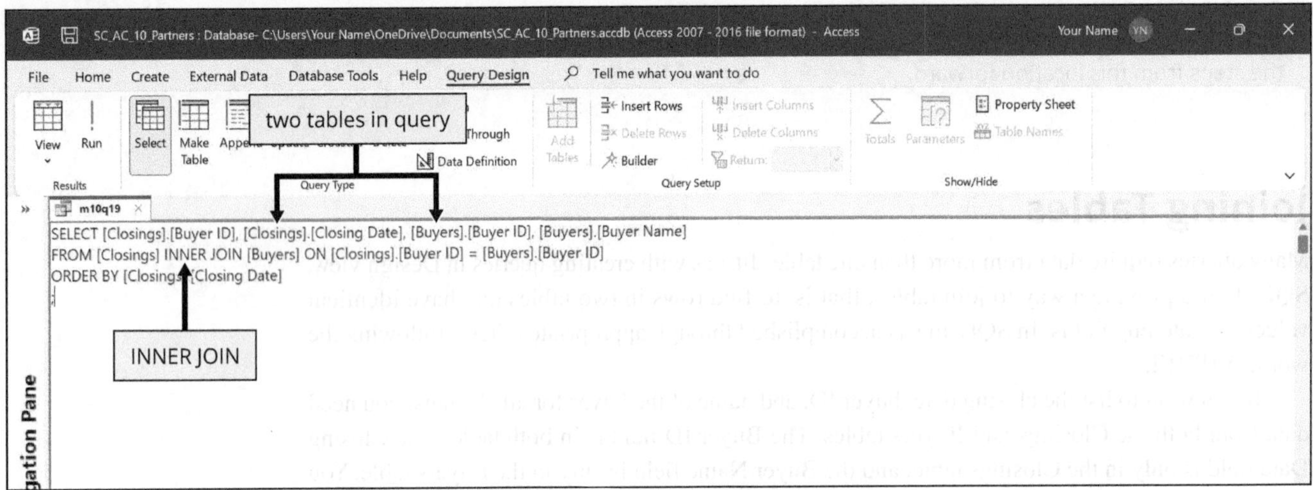

Figure 10–25(a): Query to Join Tables and Order by Closing Date

- View the results (Figure 10–25b).

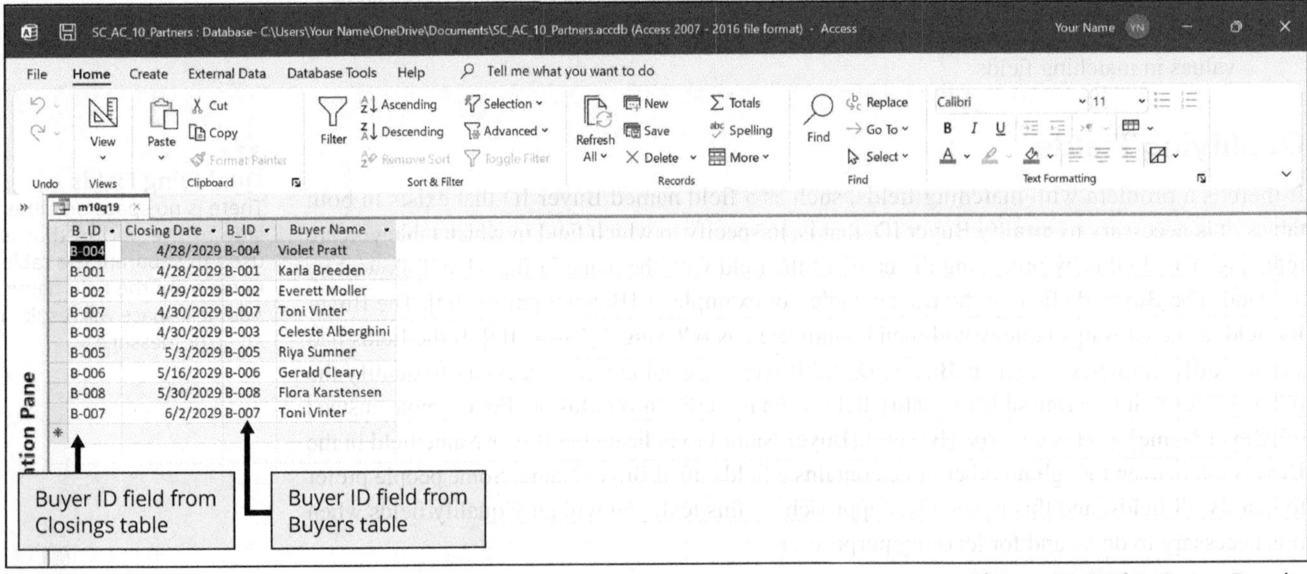

Figure 10–25(b): Query Results

- Save the query as **m10q20**.

To Restrict the Records in a Join

You can restrict the records to be included in a join by creating a compound criterion. The compound criterion will include the criterion necessary to join the tables along with a criterion to restrict the records. The criteria will be connected with AND. **Why?** Both the criterion that determines the records to be joined and the criterion to restrict the records must be true.

Partners would like to modify the previous query so that only closings whose start date is prior to May 1, 2029, are included. The following steps modify the previous query appropriately. The WHERE command is included as the join. The date is enclosed between hash signs (#), which is the date format used in the Access version of SQL.

- Return to SQL view and delete the previous query.
- Type **SELECT [Closings].[Buyer ID], [Closings].[Closing Date], [Buyers].[Buyer ID], [Buyers].[Buyer Name]** for the first line.
- Type **FROM [Closings], [Buyers]** for the second line.
- Type **WHERE [Closings].[Buyer ID] = [Buyers].[Buyer ID]** as the third line.
- Type **AND [Closing Date]<#5/1/2029#** for the fourth line.
- Type **ORDER BY [Closings].[Closing Date]** as the fifth line, and then type a semicolon (;) on the sixth line (Figure 10–26a).

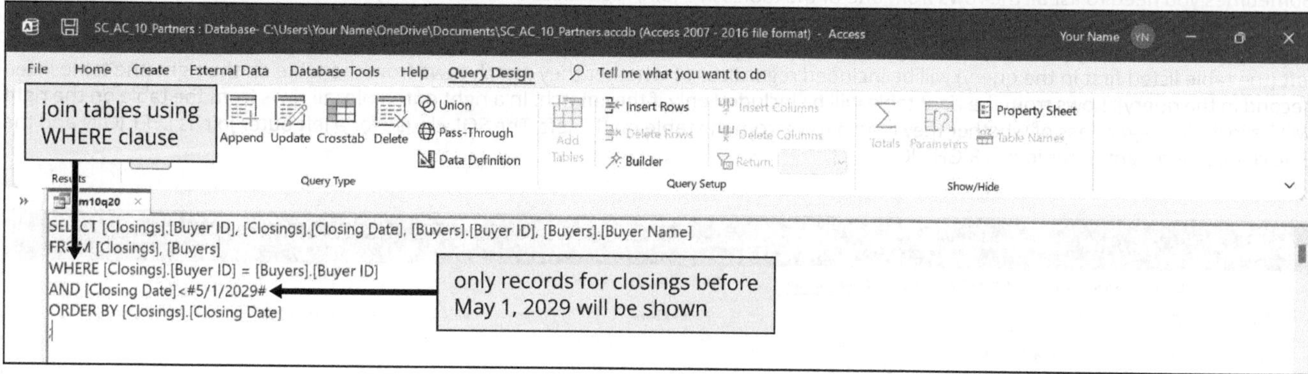

Figure 10–26(a): Query to Display Closings Before May 1, 2029

Q&A Could I use other formats for the date in the criterion?
Yes. You could type #May 1, 2029# or #1-May-2029#.

- View the results (Figure 10–26b).

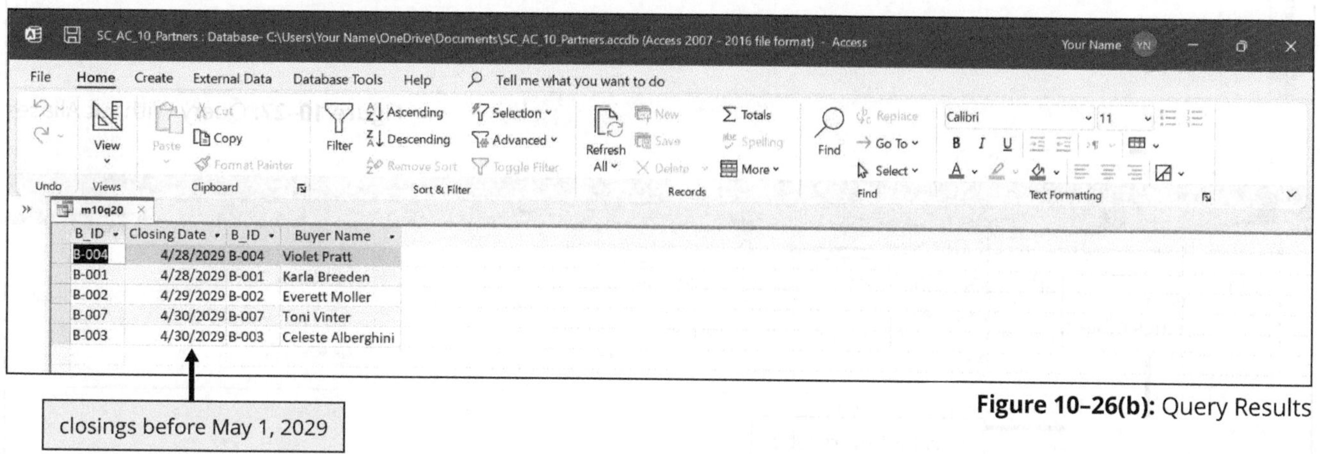

Figure 10–26(b): Query Results

- Save the query as **m10q21**.

BTW
Inner Joins
A join that compares the tables in the FROM clause and lists only those rows that satisfy the condition in the WHERE clause is called an inner join. As you saw earlier in this module, SQL has an INNER JOIN clause. You could replace the second line of the query shown in Figure 10–26a with FROM [Buyers] INNER JOIN [Closings] ON [Buyers].[Buyer ID] = [Closings].[Buyer ID] to get the same results as shown in Figure 10–26b.

Aliases

When tables appear in the FROM clause, you can give each table an **alias**, or an alternative name, that you can use in the rest of the statement. You create an alias by typing the name of the table, pressing SPACEBAR, and then typing the name of the alias. No commas or periods are necessary to separate the two names.

You can use an alias for two basic reasons: for simplicity or to join a table to itself. Figures 10–27 and 10–28 show the same query, but Figure 10–28 assigns the letter, C, as an alias for the Closings table and the letter, B, as an alias for the Buyers table. The query in Figure 10–28 is less complex. Whenever you need to qualify a field name, you can use the alias. Thus, you only need to type C.[Buyer ID] rather than [Closings].[Buyer ID].

BTW
Outer Joins
Sometimes you need to list all the rows from one of the tables in a join, regardless of whether they match any rows in the other table. For example, you can perform a join on the Buyers and Closings tables that displays all records in Closings—but displays only those records from Buyers where the joined fields are equal. This type of join is called an outer join. In a left outer join, all rows from the table on the left (the table listed first in the query) will be included regardless of whether they match rows from the table on the right (the table listed second in the query). Rows from the right table will be included only if they match. In a right outer join, all rows from the table on the right will be included regardless of whether they match rows from the table on the left. The SQL clause for a left outer join is LEFT JOIN and the SQL clause for a right outer join is RIGHT JOIN.

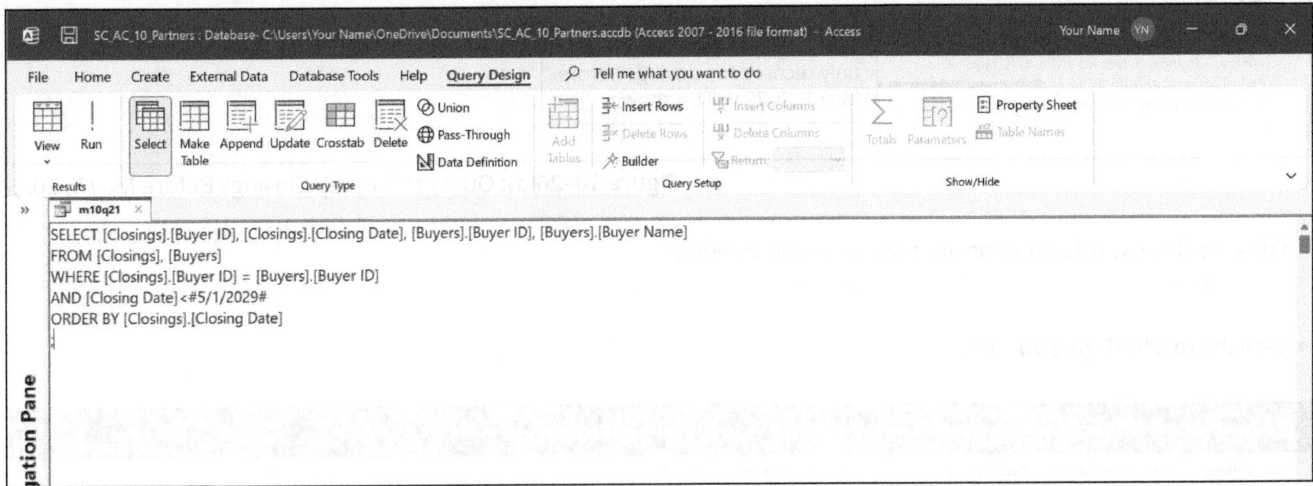

Figure 10–27: Query Without Aliases

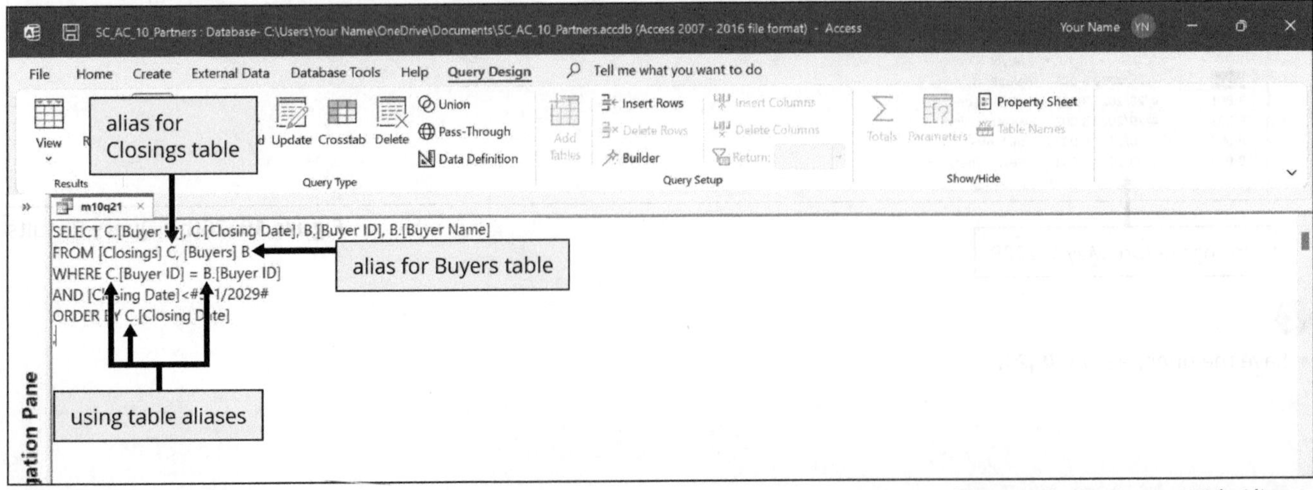

Figure 10–28: Query With Aliases

To Join a Table to Itself

The other use of aliases is in joining a table to itself. An example of this type of join would enable Partners to find buyer ID and names for every buyer using the same real estate agent. One such pair, for example, would be Buyer ID B-003 (Celeste Alberghini) and Buyer ID B-006 (Gerald Cleary) because both buyers are using the same real estate agent (Jeong-Ho Azzara). Because there are two buyers working with this agent, you will see the buyers for this agent appear on more than one line in the results.

If there were two Buyers tables in the database, Partners could obtain the results they want by simply joining the two Buyers tables and looking for rows where the buyer agent were the same. Even though there is only one Buyers table, you can actually treat the Buyers table as two tables in the query by creating two aliases. You would change the FROM clause to:

FROM [Buyers] A, [Buyers] B

SQL treats this clause as a query of two tables. The clause assigns the first Buyers table the letter, A, as an alias. It also assigns the letter, B, as an alias for the Buyers table. The fact that both tables are really the single Buyers table is not a problem. The following steps assign two aliases (A and B) to the Buyers table and list the Buyer ID and Buyer Name of both records using the same real estate agent. The steps also include a criterion to ensure A.[Buyer ID] < B.[Buyer ID]. **Why?** If you did not include this criterion, the query would contain four times as many results. On the first row in the results, for example, the first Buyer ID is B-003 and the second is B-006. Without this criterion, there would additionally be a row on which both the first and second Buyer IDs are B-003, a row on which both are B-006, and a row on which the first is B-006 and the second is B-003. This criterion only selects the one row on which the first Buyer ID (B-003) is less than the second Buyer ID (B-006).

- Return to SQL view and delete the previous query.
- Type **SELECT A.[Buyer ID], A.[Buyer Name], B.[Buyer ID], B.[Buyer Name], A.[Buyer Real Estate Agent]** as the first line of the command to select the fields to display in the query result.
- Type **FROM Buyers A, Buyers B** as the second line to create the aliases for the first and second Buyers tables.
- Type **WHERE A.[Buyer Real Estate Agent] = B.[Buyer Real Estate Agent]** as the third line to indicate that the agents in each table must match.
- Type **AND A.[Buyer ID] < B.[Buyer ID]** as the fourth line to indicate that the Buyer ID from the first table must be less than the Buyer ID from the second table.
- Type **ORDER BY A.[Buyer ID], B.[Buyer ID]** as the fifth line to ensure that the results are sorted by the Buyer ID from the first table and further sorted by the Buyer ID from the second table.
- Type a semicolon (;) on the sixth line (Figure 10–29a).

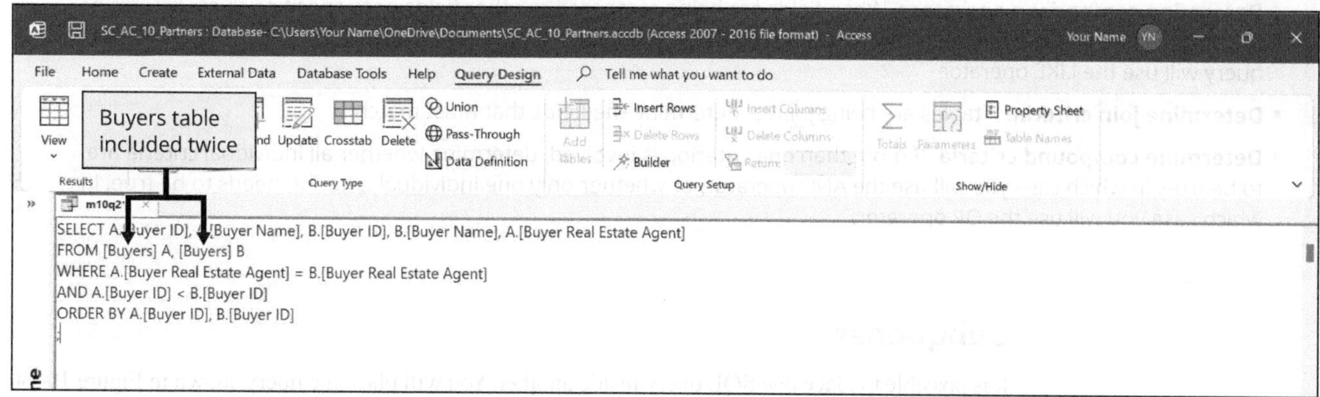

Figure 10–29(a): Query for Buyers Using the Same Agents

- View the results (Figure 10–29b).

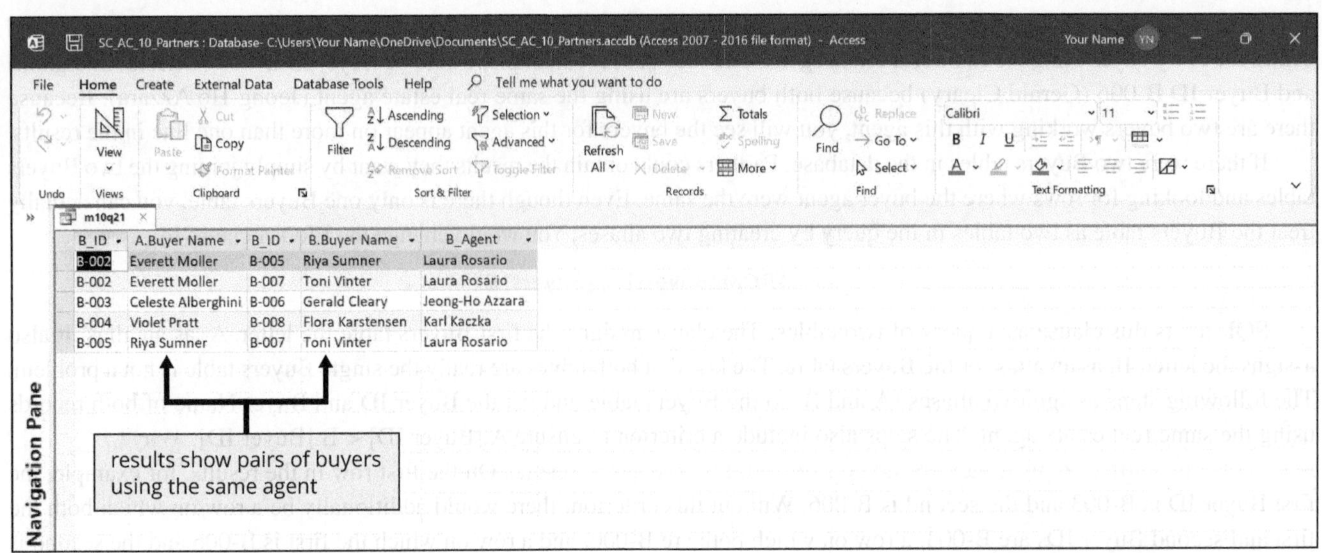

Figure 10–29(b): Query Results

- Save the query as **m10q22.**

Consider This

How do you determine criteria when creating a query?
Examine the query or request to determine any restrictions or conditions that records must satisfy to be included in the results.

- **Determine the fields involved in the criteria.** For any criterion, determine the fields that are included. Determine the data types for these fields. If the criterion uses a value that corresponds to a Text field, enclose the value in single quotation marks. If the criterion uses a date, enclose the value between hash signs (for example, #5/1/2029#).
- **Determine comparison operators.** When fields are being compared to other fields or to specific values, determine the appropriate comparison operator (equals, less than, greater than, and so on). If a wildcard is involved, then the query will use the LIKE operator.
- **Determine join criteria.** If tables are being joined, determine the fields that must match.
- **Determine compound criteria.** If more than one criterion is involved, determine whether all individual criteria are to be true, in which case you will use the AND operator, or whether only one individual criterion needs to be true, in which case you will use the OR operator.

Subqueries

It is possible to place one SQL query inside another. You will place the query shown in Figure 10–30 inside another query. When you have done so, it will be called a **subquery**, which is an inner query contained within parentheses that is evaluated first. Then the outer query can use the results of the subquery to find its results. In some cases, using a subquery can be the simplest way to produce the desired results.

To Use a Subquery

The following steps use the query shown in Figure 10–30 as a subquery. **Why?** Partners can use this query to select buyers who are being represented by Partners in their property purchases. After the subquery is evaluated, the outer query will select the buyer ID, closing date, purchasing mortgage company, and status for those closings where the Buyer ID is in the list produced by the subquery.

- Return to SQL view and delete the previous query.
- To first test the inner query, type **SELECT [Buyers].[Buyer ID]** as the first line of the command.
- Type **FROM [Buyers]** as the second line.
- Type **WHERE [Buyers].[Buyer Attorney] = 'Partners'** as the third line and type a semicolon (;) on the fourth line (Figure 10–30a).

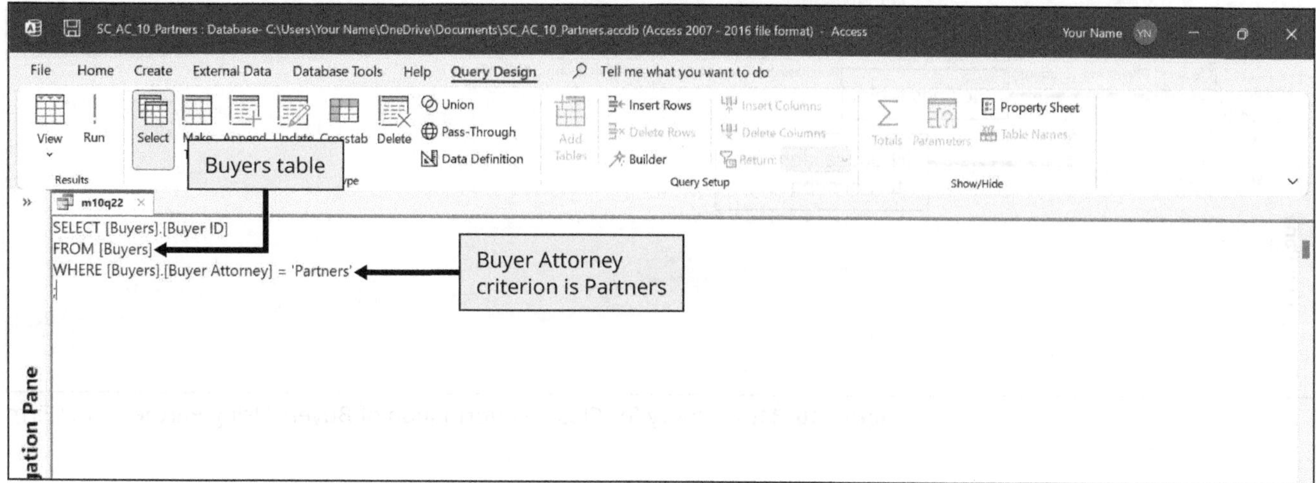

Figure 10–30(a): Test Query for Buyers Using Partners Law Firm

- View the results (Figure 10–30b). You will not save the current query. Now that you have confirmed that the subquery works, you will delete it and then place it in the correct location in the new query.

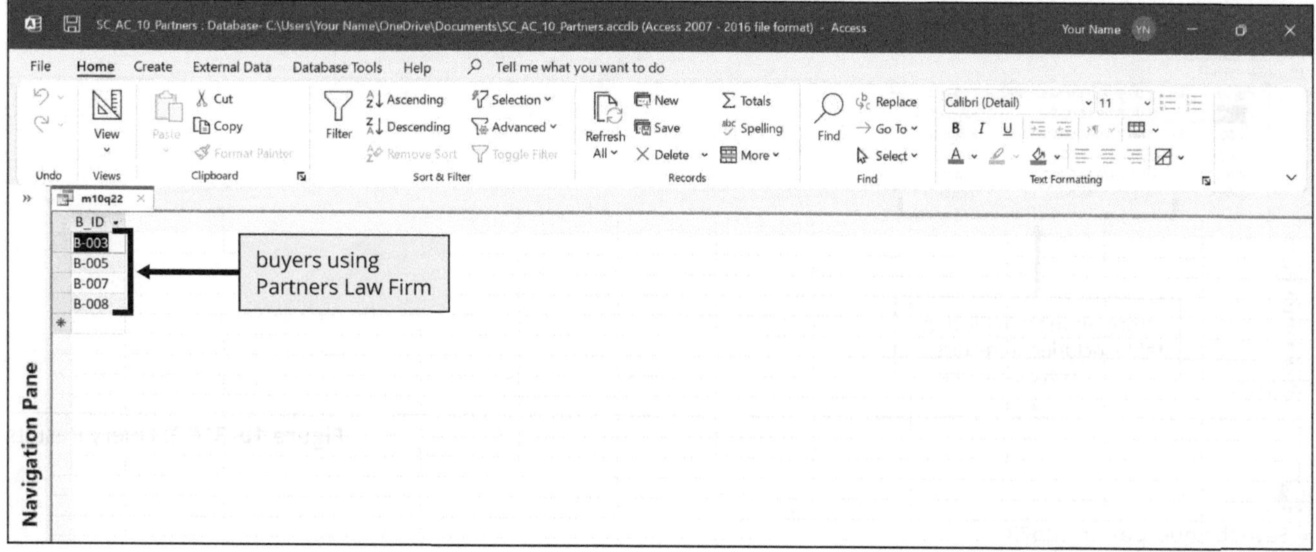

Figure 10–30(b): Test Query Results

- Return to SQL view and delete the previous query.
- To build the query and subquery, type **SELECT [Closings].[Buyer ID], [Closings].[Closing Date], [Closings].[Purchasing Mortgage Company ID], [Closings].[Status]** as the first line of the command.
- Type **FROM [Closings]** as the second line.
- Type **WHERE [Closings].[Buyer ID] IN** as the third line.

- Type **(SELECT [Buyers].[Buyer ID]** as the fourth line.
- Type **FROM [Buyers]** as the fifth line.
- Type **WHERE [Buyers].[Buyer Attorney] = 'Partners')** as the sixth line and type a semicolon (;) on the seventh line (Figure 10–31a).

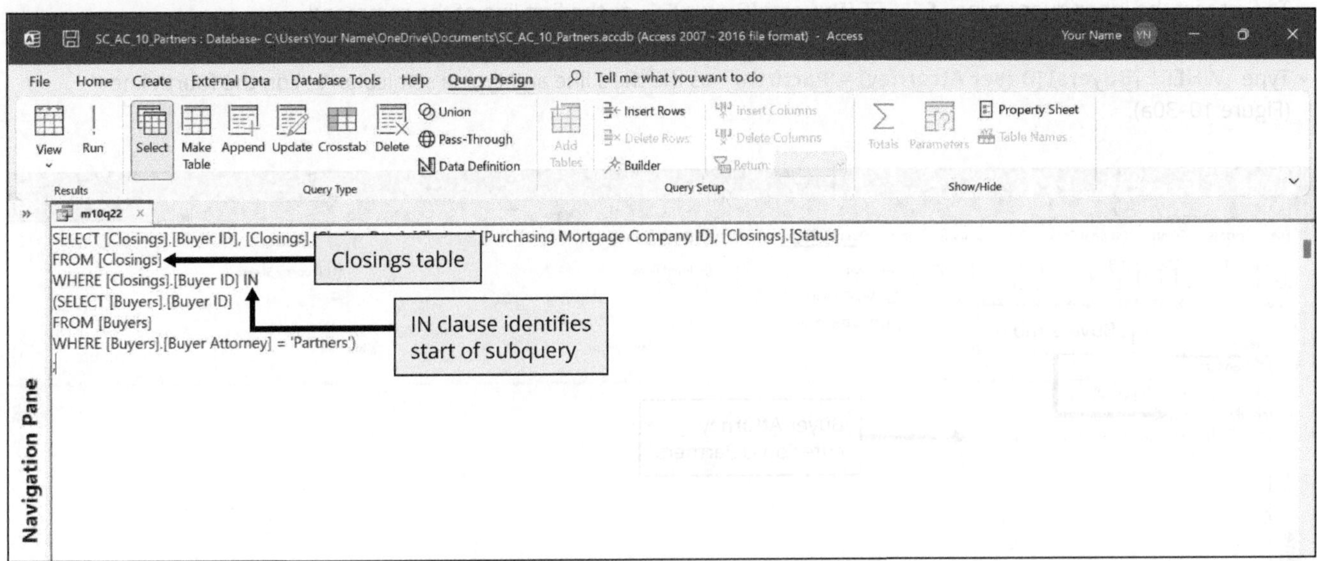

Figure 10–31(a): Query for Closing Information of Buyers Using Partners Law Firm

- View the results (Figure 10–31b).

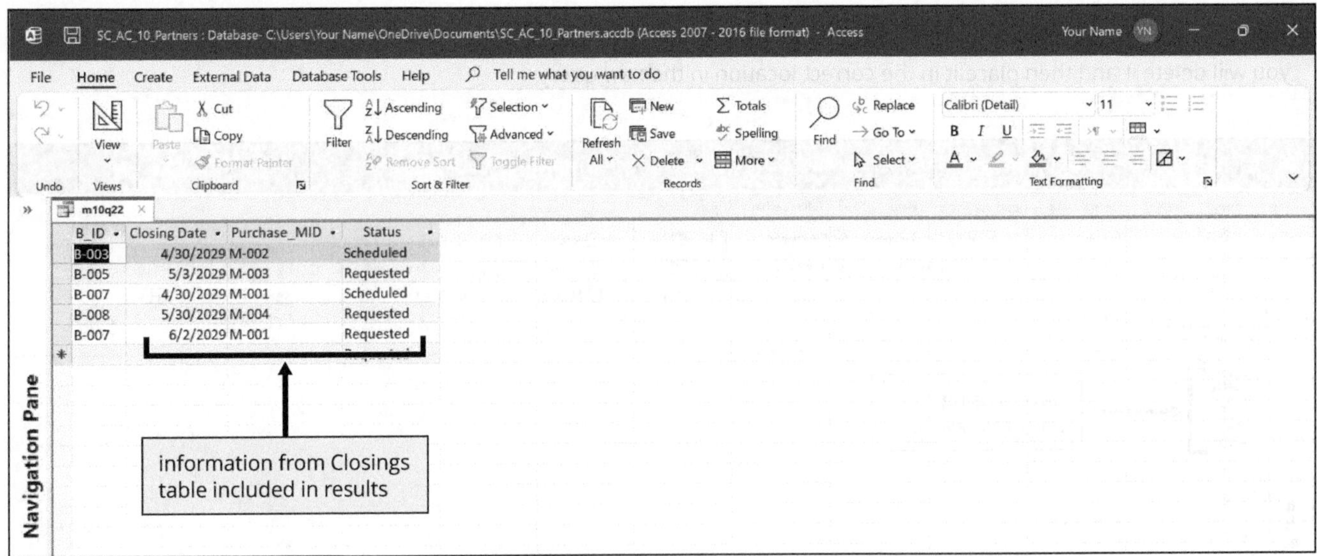

Figure 10–31(b): Query Results

- Save the query as **m10q23**.

Using an IN Clause

The query in Figure 10–31 uses an IN clause with a subquery. You can also use an IN clause with a list as an alternative to an OR criterion when the OR criterion involves a single field. For example, to find properties whose city is Donahue, Jonestown, Hartford, or Woodstock, the criterion using IN would be the following:

City IN ('Donahue', 'Jonestown', 'Hartford', 'Woodstock')

The corresponding OR criterion would be the following:

City='Donahue' OR City='Jonestown' OR City='Hartford' OR City='Woodstock'

The choice of whether to use an IN clause with a list or an OR criterion is a matter of personal preference.

You can also use this type of IN clause when creating queries in Design view. To use the criterion in the previous paragraph, for example, include the City field in the design grid and enter the criterion in the Criteria row.

Comparison with Access-Generated SQL

When you create a query in Design view, Access automatically creates a corresponding SQL query that is similar to the queries you have created in this module. The Access query shown in Figure 10–32, for example, was created in Design view and includes the Property ID, Association, Property Street, and Property City fields. The Property City field has a criterion (Hartford).

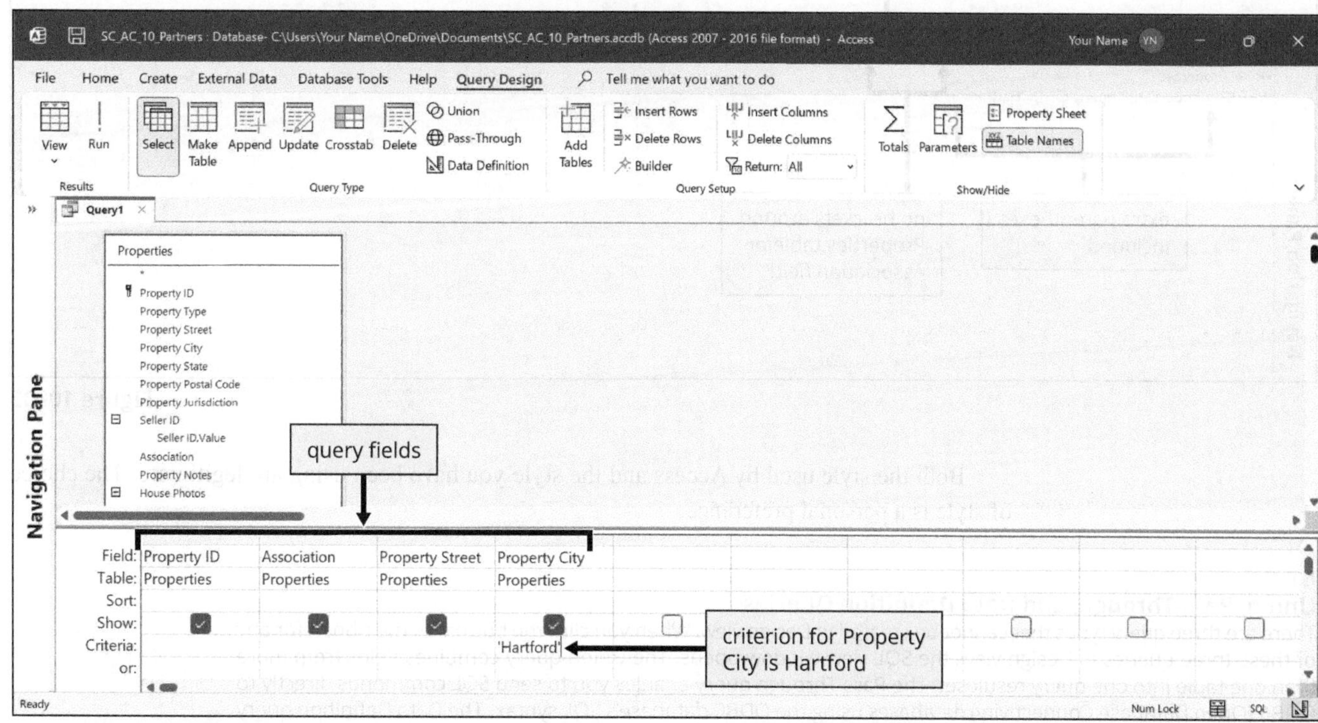

Figure 10–32(a): Query to List Property ID, Association, Property Street, and Property City for Properties in Hartford

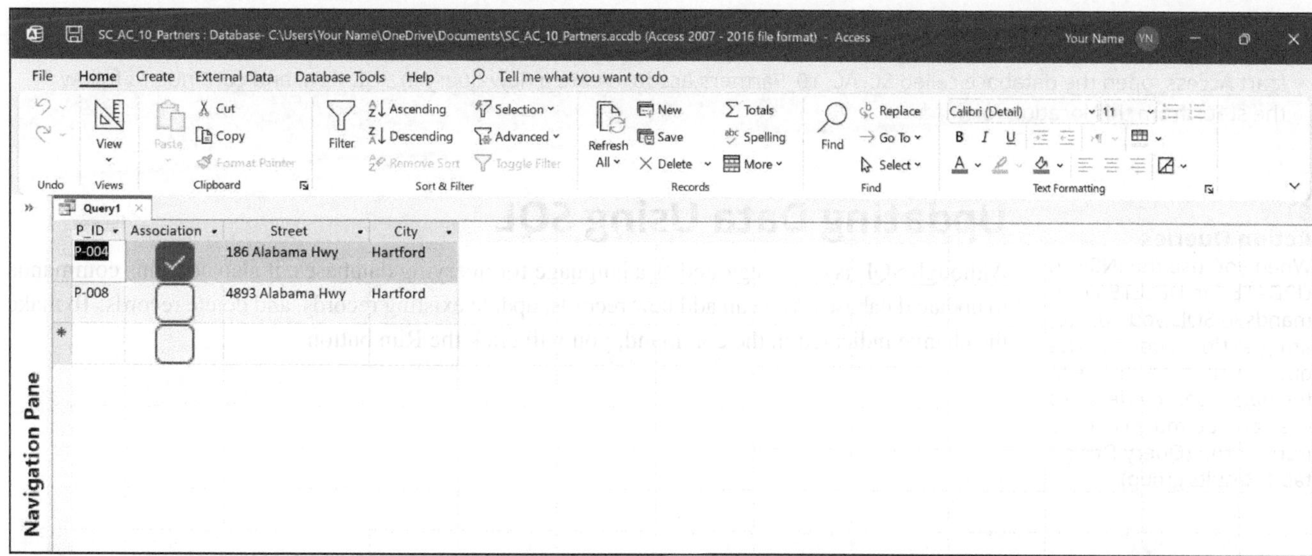

Figure 10–32(b): Query Results

The SQL query that Access generates in correspondence to the Design view query is shown in Figure 10–33. The query is very similar to the queries you have entered, but there are three slight differences. First, the Properties.[Property ID], Properties.[Association], Properties.[Property Street], and Properties.[Property City] fields are qualified, even though they do not need to be; only one table is involved in the query, so no qualification is necessary. Second, the Properties table and the Association field are not enclosed in square brackets. The table and field names are legitimately not enclosed in square brackets because there are no spaces or other special characters in each name. Finally, there are extra parentheses in the WHERE clause.

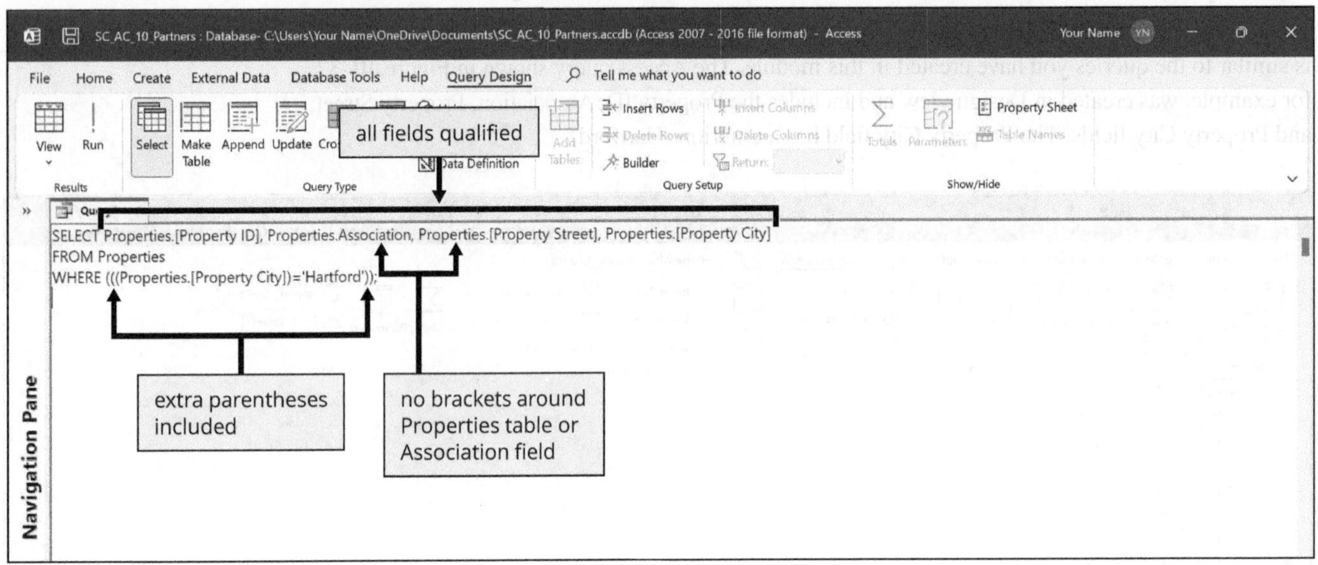

Figure 10–33

Both the style used by Access and the style you have been using are legitimate. The choice of style is a personal preference.

BTW
Union, Pass-Through, and Data Definition Queries
There are three query types that cannot be created in Design view. When you click the button on the ribbon for any of these three queries in Design view, the SQL view window opens. The Union query combines fields from more than one table into one query result set. The Pass-Through query enables you to send SQL commands directly to ODBC (Open Database Connectivity) databases using the ODBC database's SQL syntax. The Data Definition query allows you to create or alter database tables or create indexes in Access directly.

Break Point: If you wish to take a break, this is a good place to do so. You can quit Access now. To resume at a later time, start Access, open the database called SC_AC_10_Partners.accdb, create a new query in SQL view, and continue to follow the steps from this location forward.

BTW
Action Queries
When you use the INSERT, UPDATE, or DELETE commands in SQL, you are creating action queries. The query is making a change to the database. To effect this change, you must click the Run button (Query Design tab | Results group).

Updating Data Using SQL

Although SQL is often regarded as a language for querying databases, it also contains commands to update databases. You can add new records, update existing records, and delete records. To make the change indicated in the command, you will click the Run button.

To Use an INSERT Command

You can add records to a table using the SQL INSERT command. The command consists of the words, INSERT INTO, followed by the name of the table into which the record is to be inserted. Next is the word, VALUE, followed by the values for the fields in the record. Values for text fields must be enclosed within quotation marks. **Why?** Just as you needed to type the quotation marks when you used text data in a criterion, you need to do so when you use text values in an INSERT INTO command. The following steps add a record to the Workshop Enrollments table. The record is for Buyer ID B-007 and Workshop W-01, and it indicates the workshop will be offered for a total of 4 hours, of which 0 hours have already been spent.

- If necessary, return to SQL view and delete the existing query.
- Type **INSERT INTO [Workshop Enrollments]** as the first line of the command.
- Type **VALUES ('B-007', 'W-01', 4, 0)** as the second line.
- Type a semicolon (;) on the third line (Figure 10–34).

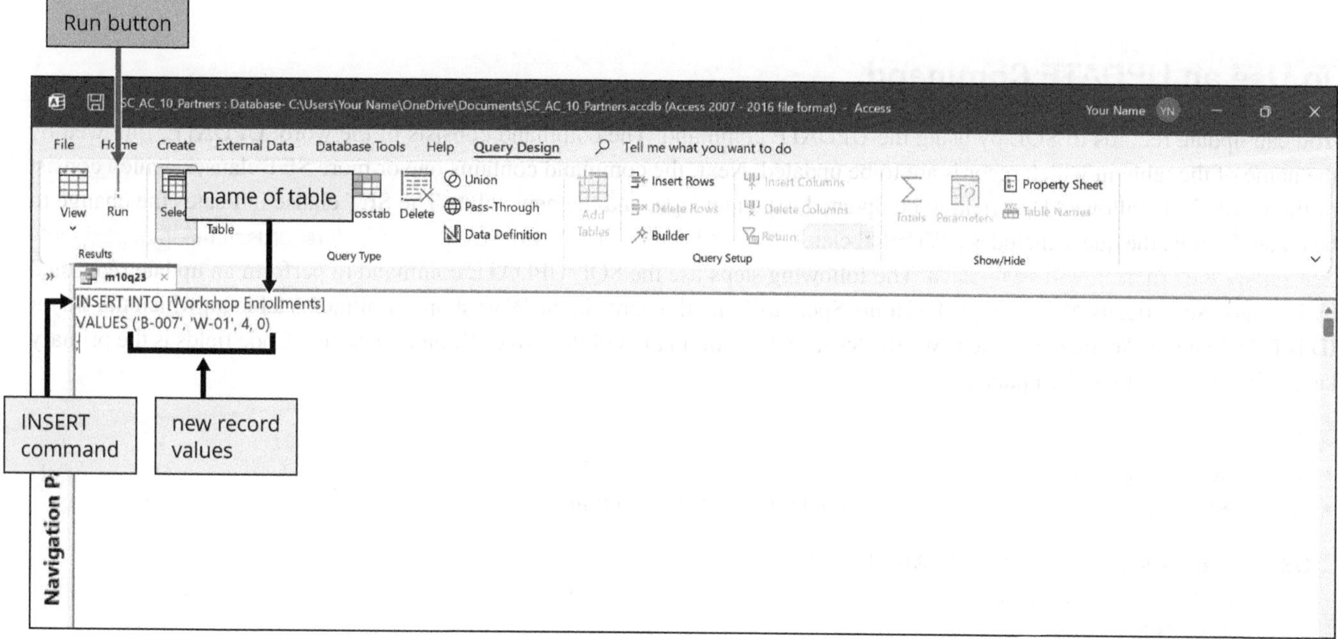

Figure 10–34

Q&A What is the purpose of the INSERT INTO clause?
The clause indicates the table into which data is to be inserted.

What is the purpose of the VALUES clause?
The VALUES clause, which typically extends over two lines, indicates the values that are to be inserted into a new record in the table. For readability, it is common to place the word, VALUES, on one line and the actual values on a separate line.

- Run the query by clicking the Run button (Query Design tab | Results group).
- When Access displays a message indicating one row is to be appended (inserted), click the Yes button to insert the row.

Q&A I clicked the View button and did not get the message. Do I need to click the Run button?
Yes. You are making a change to the database by adding a record to a table, so you must click the Run button, or the change will not be made.

How can I see if the record was actually inserted?
Use a SELECT query to view the records in the Workshop Enrollments table, or you can just open the table and view the records.

BTW
Touch and Pointers
Remember that if you are using your finger on a touch screen, you will not see the pointer.

- Save the query as **m10q24.**

Q&A Why does this query have a different icon in the Navigation Pane than the other queries do?
In the Navigation Pane, the query is saved in a separate location from the other queries and is marked with a different icon because this query is an append query, that is, it appends (or adds) data in a table when the query is run rather than simply displaying data gathered from one or more tables. If you point your cursor to the append query in the Navigation Pane, the ScreenTip shows not only the query name but also the table affected by the query. All this information helps users decide if or when to use a query that will make changes to data. Other query types with different icons include update queries and delete queries. Because all these queries make changes to data in one or more tables, you might choose to first open the query in Design view or SQL view to evaluate or edit the query before running it.

To Use an UPDATE Command

You can update records in SQL by using the UPDATE command. The command consists of the word, UPDATE, followed by the name of the table in which records are to be updated. Next, the command contains one or more SET clauses, which consist of the word, SET, followed by a field to be updated, an equal sign, and the new value. The SET clause indicates the change to be made. Finally, the query includes a WHERE clause. **Why?** When you execute the command, all records in the indicated table that satisfy the criterion will be updated. The following steps use the SQL UPDATE command to perform an update requested by Partners. Specifically, they change the Hours Spent to 4 on all records in the Workshop Enrollments table on which the Buyer ID is B-007 and the Workshop Code is W-01. Because the combination of the Buyer ID and Workshop Code fields is the primary key, only one record will be updated.

- Delete the existing query.
- Type **UPDATE [Workshop Enrollments]** as the first line of the command.

Q&A What is the purpose of the UPDATE clause?
The UPDATE clause indicates the table to be updated. This clause indicates that the update is to be applied to the Workshop Enrollments table.

- Type **SET [Hours Spent]=4** as the second line.

Q&A What is the purpose of the SET clause?
The SET clause indicates the field to be changed as well as the new value. This SET clause indicates the hours spent value is to be set to 4.

Why did I not have to type spaces on either side of the equals sign in the SET clause?
Spaces around comparative operators, such as equals (=) and greater than (>), are not required when typing statements in SQL. Whether or not you type the spaces around these operators is a matter of personal preference. In this course, spaces are included when they help improve readability of the statement in the instructions. For shorter statements such as this one, spaces do not contribute to readability.

- Type **WHERE [Buyer ID]='B-007'** as the third line.
- Type **AND [Workshop Code]='W-01'** as the fourth line, and then type a semicolon (;) on the fifth line (Figure 10–35).

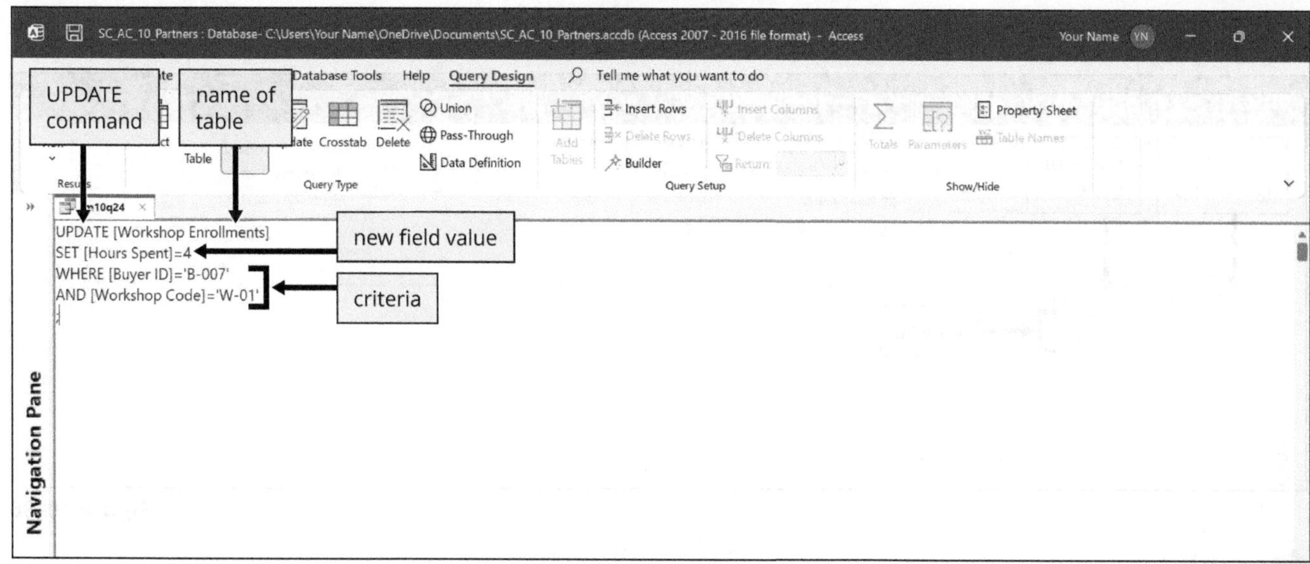

Figure 10–35

Q&A Do I need to change a field to a specific value such as 4?

No, you could use an expression. For example, to add $1,000 to the New Loan Amount in the Closings table, the SET clause would be SET [New Loan Amount] = [New Loan Amount]+100.

- Run the query.
- When Access displays a message indicating one row is to be updated, click the Yes button to update the row.

Q&A How can I see if the update actually occurred?

Use a SELECT query to view the records in the Workshop Enrollments table or open the table and view the results.

- Save the query as **m10q25**.

To Use a DELETE Command

You can delete records in SQL using the DELETE command. The command consists of DELETE FROM, followed by the name of the table from which records are to be deleted. Finally, you include a WHERE clause to specify the criteria. **Why?** When you execute the command, all records in the indicated table that satisfy the criteria will be deleted. The following steps use the SQL DELETE command to delete all records in the Workshop Enrollments table on which the Buyer ID is B-007, and the Workshop Code is W-01. Because the combination of the Buyer ID and Workshop Code fields is the primary key, only one record will be deleted.

- Delete the existing query.
- Type **DELETE FROM [Workshop Enrollments]** as the first line of the command.

Q&A What is the purpose of the DELETE clause?

The DELETE clause indicates the table from which records will be deleted. This DELETE clause indicates that records will be deleted from the Workshop Enrollments table.

- Type **WHERE [Buyer ID]='B-007'** as the second line.

- Type **AND [Workshop Code]='W-01'** as the third line and type a semicolon (;) on the fourth line (Figure 10–36).

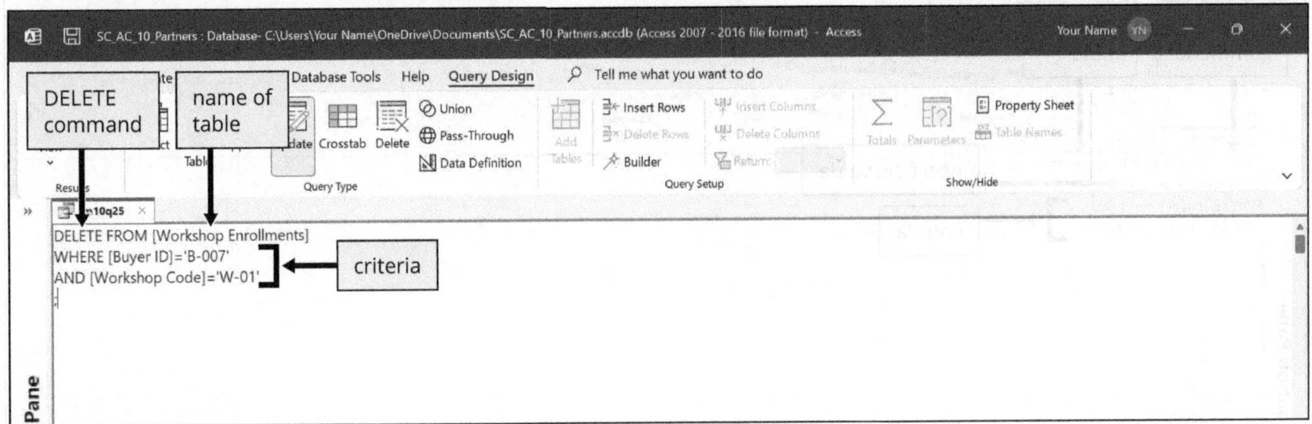

Figure 10–36

- Run the query.
- When Access displays a message indicating one row is to be deleted, click the Yes button to delete the row.

Q&A How can I see if the deletion actually occurred?
Use a SELECT query to view the records in the Workshop Enrollments table or open the table and view the results.

- Save the query as **m10q26**.
- Close the query.

Consider This

How do you determine any update operations to be performed?

Examine the database to determine if records must be added, updated, and/or deleted.

- **Determine INSERT operations.** Determine whether new records need to be added. Determine to which table they should be added.
- **Determine UPDATE operations.** Determine changes that need to be made to existing records. Which fields need to be changed? Which tables contain these fields? What criteria identify the rows that need to be changed?
- **Determine DELETE operations.** Determine which tables contain records that are to be deleted. What criteria identify the rows that need to be deleted?

Linking a Table to an Another File

Linking an Access database to data in other programs, such as an Excel worksheet, lets you work with this data in Access without having to maintain a copy of the Excel data in the database. When linking to an Excel workbook, or a named range in Excel, Access creates a new table in the database that is linked to the source cells. New records can be added, records edited, and records deleted in the Excel file, but only in Excel. You cannot make changes to the Excel data in the linked Access table.

To Link a Table to an Outside Data Source

Partners created a file containing information about real estate agents, allowing the practice to refer clients to agents who have worked well with Partners for past closings. You will link to the Excel file and then add a record to the file in Excel. **Why?** Linking to an external file allows you to store and access information in other file formats. When you link an Excel file in the database, an Excel icon appears next to the table name. The following steps first create a copy of the Partners Agents file so you can later make changes to it, and then create a link to the file in a database table.

- Open the spreadsheet, Support_AC_10_Agents.xlsx, which is located in the Data Files folder.
- Save the file to your hard drive, OneDrive, or other storage location using the file name, **SC_AC_10_Agents**. Saving the spreadsheet with a new name preserves the original support file in case you need to return to this project. Enable the content and then close the file.

2

- With the Partners database open, click the External Data tab.
- Click the New Data Source button arrow and point to From File (Figure 10-37), and then click Excel.

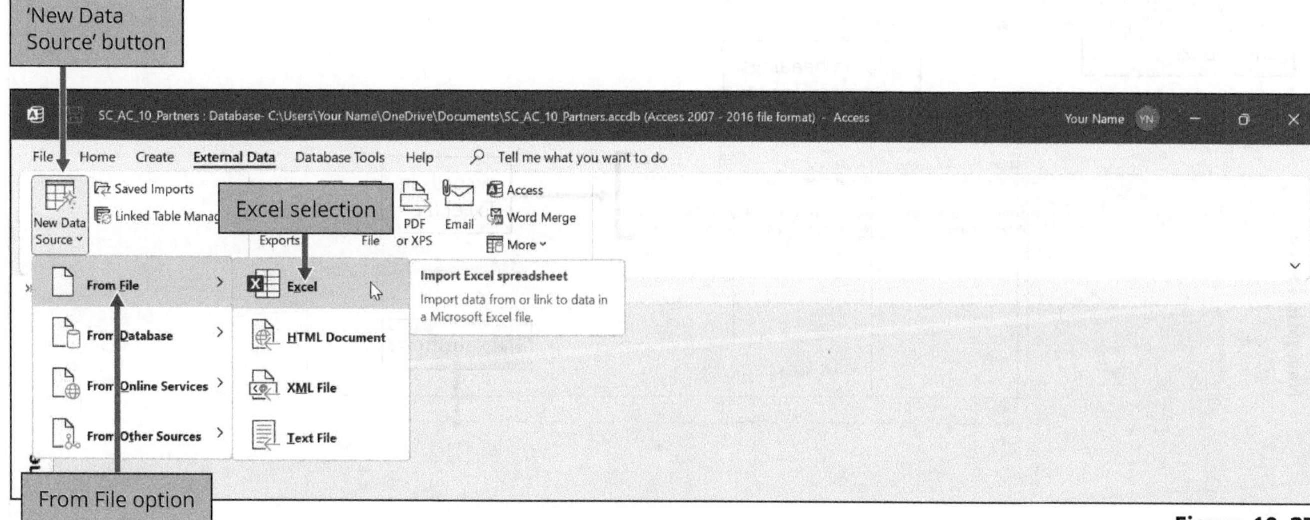

Figure 10-37

- Click the Browse button (Get External Data – Excel Spreadsheet dialog box), navigate to the file named SC_AC_10_Agents.xlsx, click to select it, and then click Open.
- Click the 'Link to the data source by creating a linked table.' option button (Figure 10-38).

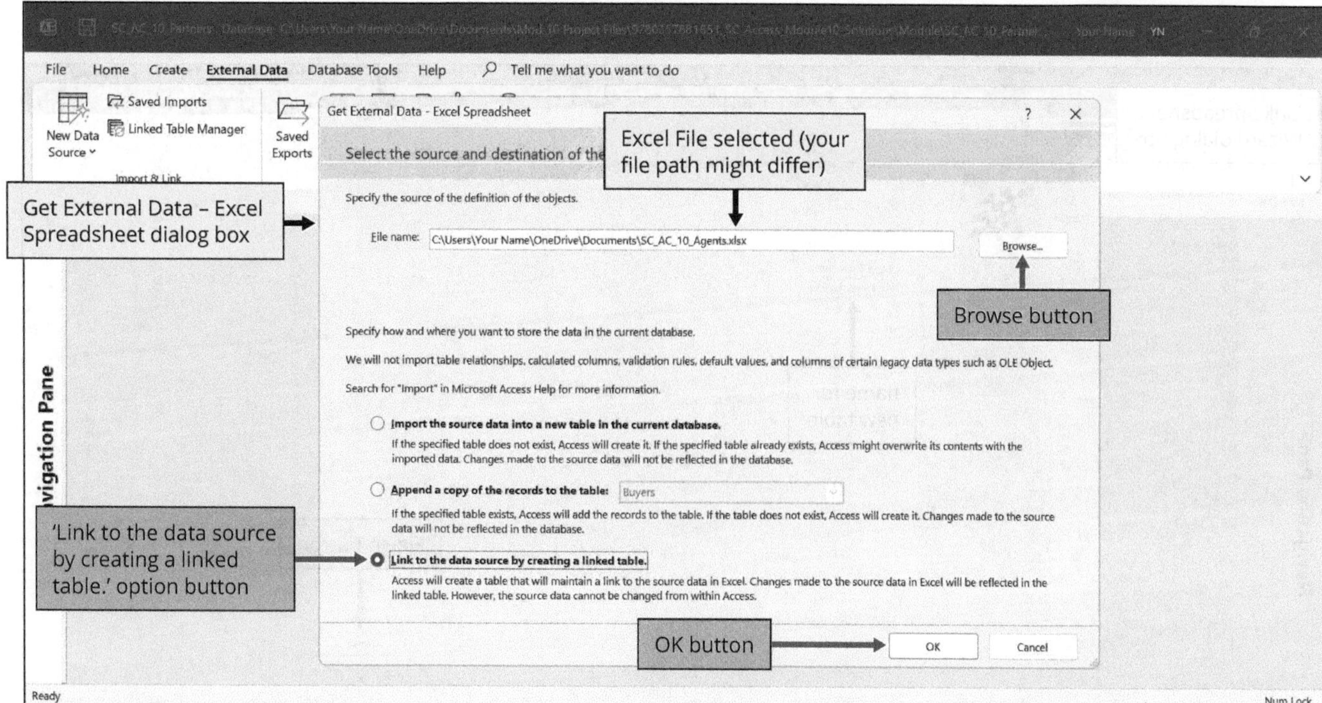

Figure 10-38

- Click OK.
- Check the First Row Contains Column Headings check box to select it (Figure 10–39), and then click Next.

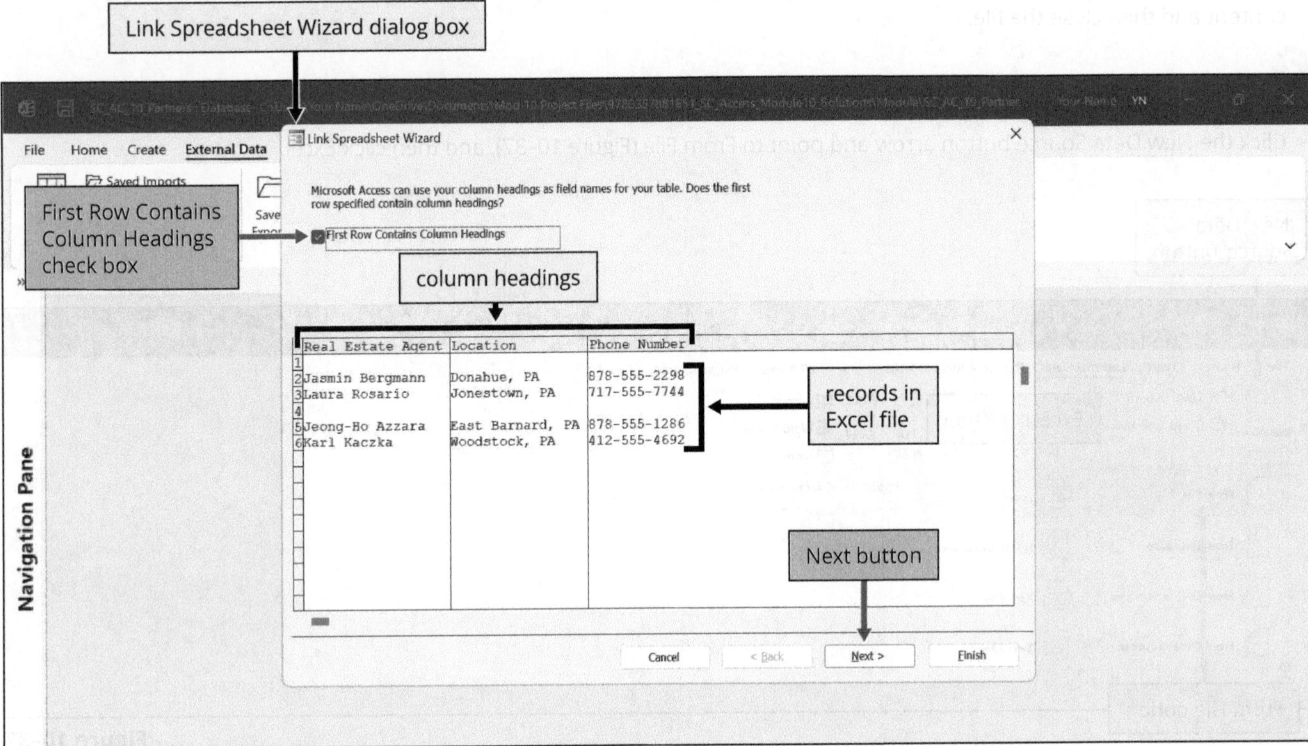

Figure 10–39

Q&A Why is there a blank row in the middle of the data being linked from Excel?
Later in these steps, you will add a new record to the Excel table in the blank line. Because this course is not designed to teach Excel, the data file already contains a blank row, and you will not have to insert a new row in the needed location.

- Type **Real Estate Agents** in the Linked Table Name box (Figure 10–40).

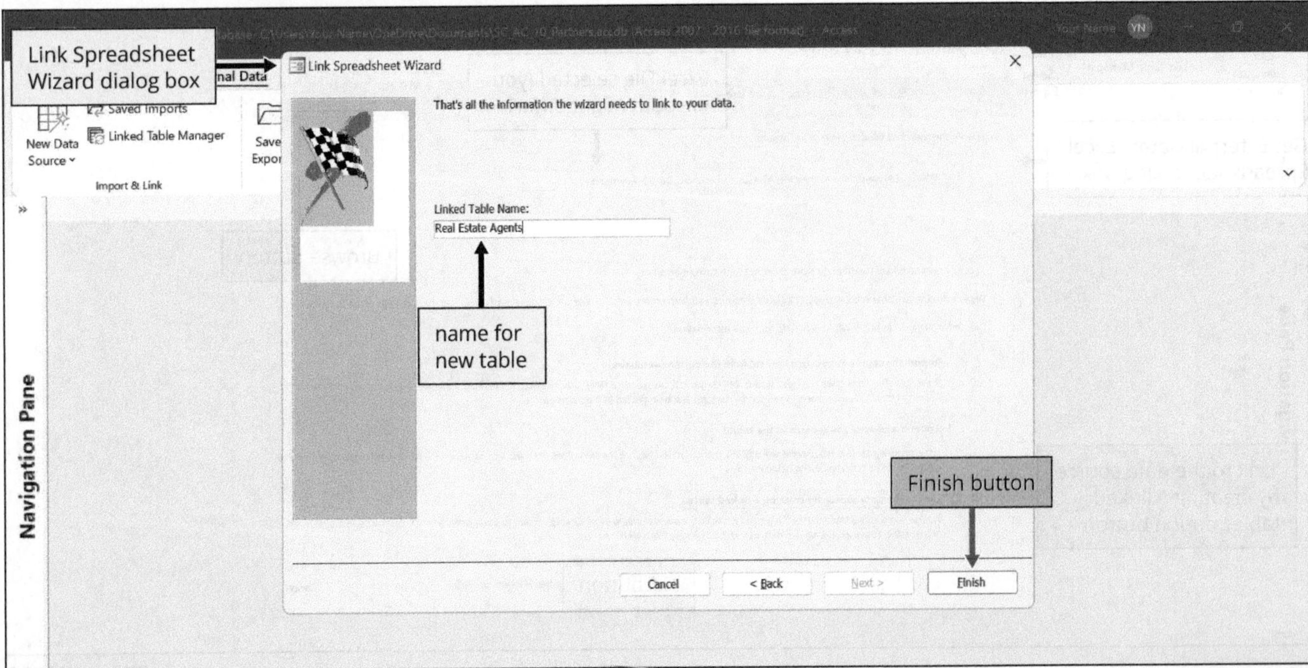

Figure 10–40

- Click Finish.
- Click OK in the Link Spreadsheet Wizard dialog box.
- Open the Navigation Pane, if necessary, to see the new linked Real Estate Agents table (Figure 10–41).

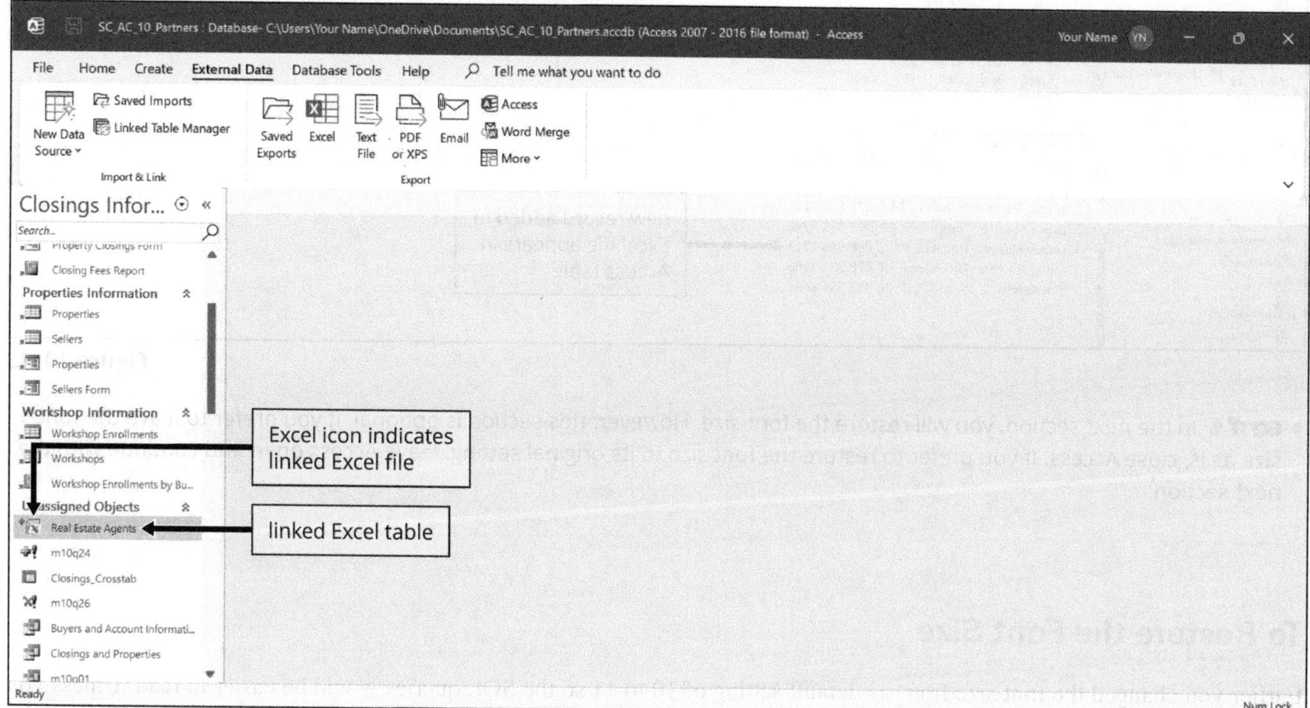

Figure 10–41

- Open the table to view the four records (Figure 10–42).

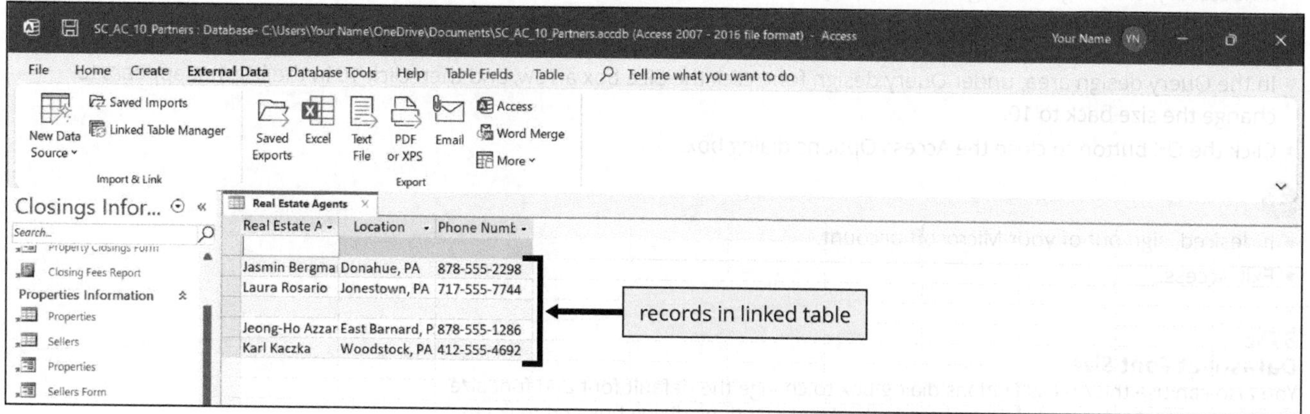

Figure 10–42

- Click in a cell with no data and try to add a record. Notice that Access prohibits you from entering data.
- Close the Real Estate Agents table.
- Open the SC_AC_10_Agents.xlsx spreadsheet in Excel, and add the following record to the worksheet as the fifth row:
  Dmitri Alexander **Hartford, PA** **888-555-2713**
- Save the Excel file and exit Excel.

- View the revised table in Access (Figure 10–43), and then close the table.

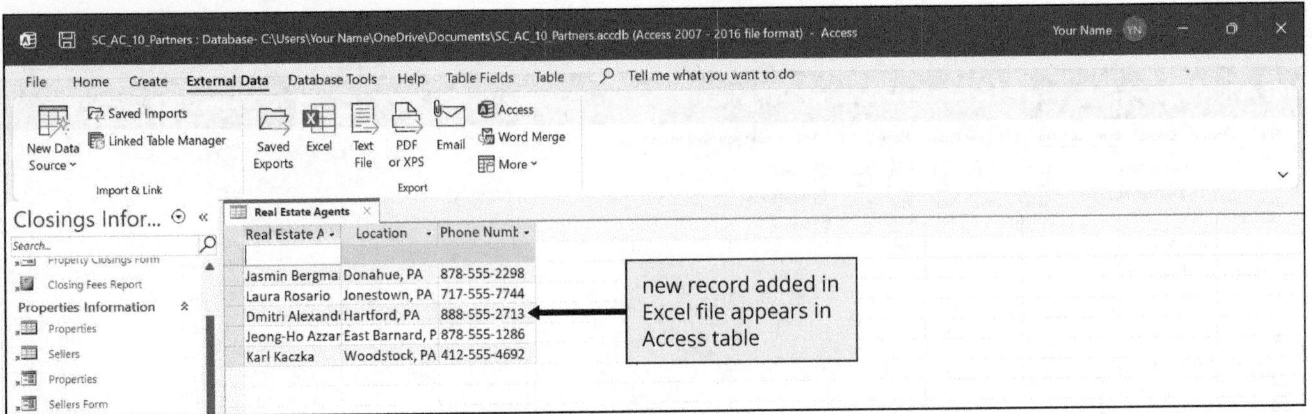

Figure 10–43

- **sam** In the next section, you will restore the font size. However, this section is optional. If you prefer to leave the font size as is, close Access. If you prefer to restore the font size to its original setting, leave Access open and continue with the next section.

To Restore the Font Size

Earlier you changed the font size from its default setting of 10 to 11 so the SQL queries would be easier to read. Unless you prefer to retain this new setting, you should change the setting back to the default. The following steps restore the font size to its default setting.

- Click File on the ribbon to open Backstage view.
- Click Options to display the Access Options dialog box.
- If necessary, click Object Designers to display the Object Designer section.

- In the Query design area, under Query design font, click the Size box arrow, and then click 10 in the list that appears to change the size back to 10.
- Click the OK button to close the Access Options dialog box.

- If desired, sign out of your Microsoft account.
- Exit Access.

BTW
Datasheet Font Size
You also can use the Access Options dialog box to change the default font and font size for datasheets. To do so, click Datasheet in the Access Options dialog box and make the desired changes in the Default font area.

Summary

In this module you have learned to create SQL queries, include fields in a query, use criteria involving both numeric and text fields as well as use compound criteria, use computed fields and rename the computation, sort the results of a query, use the built-in functions, group records in a query and also restrict the groups that appear in the results, join tables and restrict the records in a join, and use subqueries. You looked at a SQL query that was generated automatically by Access. Then, you used the INSERT, UPDATE, and DELETE commands to update data. Finally, you learned how to create a table in Access that is linked to an Excel spreadsheet.

Consider This: Plan Ahead

What decisions will you need to make when creating your own SQL queries?

Use these guidelines as you complete the assignments in this module and create your own queries outside of this class.

1. Select the fields for the query.
    a. Examine the requirements for the query you are constructing to determine which fields are to be included.
2. Determine which table or tables contain these fields.
    a. For each field, determine the table in which it is located.
3. Determine criteria.
    a. Determine any criteria that data must satisfy to be included in the results.
    b. If there are more than two tables in the query, determine the criteria to be used to ensure the data matches correctly.
4. Determine sort order.
    a. Is the data to be sorted in some way?
    b. If so, by what field or fields is it to be sorted?
5. Determine grouping.
    a. Is the data to be grouped in some way?
    b. If so, by what field is it to be grouped?
    c. Identify any calculations to be made for the group.
6. Determine any update operations to be performed.
    a. Determine whether rows need to be inserted, changed, or deleted.
    b. Determine the tables involved.

Consider This

How should you submit solutions to critical thinking questions in the assignments?

Every assignment in this course contains one or more critical thinking questions. These questions require you to think beyond the assigned database. Present your responses to the questions in the format required by your instructor. Possible formats might include one or more of these options: write the answer; create a document that contains the answer; present your answer to the class; discuss your answer in a group; record the answer as audio or video using a webcam, smartphone, or portable media player; or post answers on a blog, wiki, or website.

Student Assignments

Apply Your Knowledge

Reinforce the skills and apply the concepts you learned in this module.

Using Criteria, Joining Tables, and Sorting in SQL Queries in the Build It Construction Database

Note: To complete this assignment, you will be required to use the Data Files. Please contact your instructor for information about accessing the Data Files.

Instructions: Start Access. Open the database, SC_AC_10-2.accdb, which is located in the Data Files folder. Enable the content. Use SQL to query the Build It Construction database in the following steps. Note that for each new query, you can either edit the existing query and save a copy of it with the name indicated, or you can create a new query.

Perform the following tasks:

1. Save the database using the file name, SC_AC_10_Construction. Enable the content.
2. Find all subcontractors whose specialty is HVAC. Display all fields in the query results. Save the query as AYK Step 2 Query.
3. Find all subcontractors listed in the Accounting table whose current due is over $500.00. Display the fields SC #, Subcontractor Name, Amount Paid, and Current Due in the query results. Save this query as AYK Step 3 Query.
4. Find all job sites in the Job Sites table that are not located in OK. Display the fields Job Site Number, Owner, City, and State in the query results. Save the query as AYK Step 4 Query.
5. Display the fields Job Site Number, Subcontractor Number, Subcontractor Name, Mobile Phone, and Specialty for all subcontractors. Sort the records in ascending order by Job Site Number and Subcontractor Number. Save the query as AYK Step 5 Query.
6. Display the fields Subcontractor Number, Subcontractor Name, Specialty, and Employees for all subcontractors who are licensed. Save the query as AYK Step 6 Query.
7. If requested to do so by your instructor, rename the AYK Step 6 Query as Last Name Query where Last Name is your last name.
8. Submit the revised database in the format specified by your instructor.
9. **Consider This:** What WHERE clause would you use if you wanted to find all subcontractors whose specialty starts with the letter C? How might these query results be helpful in a real-world scenario?

Extend Your Knowledge

Extend the skills you learned in this module and experiment with new skills. You may need to use Help to complete the assignment.

Creating Queries to Find Specific Criteria

Note: To complete this assignment, you will be required to use the Data Files. Please contact your instructor for information about accessing the Data Files.

Instructions: Start Access. Open the database, SC_AC_10-3.accdb, which is located in the Data Files folder. The PicsPlus cooperative would like more information about some of the clients of its member photographers. Use SQL queries to find specific information.

Perform the following tasks:

1. Close the Main Menu, and then save the database using the file name, SC_AC_10_PicsPlus. Enable the content.
2. Find all clients where the Client Number begins with either R or S. Display the Client Number, Client Name, City, and State fields in the query results. Save the query as EYK Step 2 Query.
3. Find all clients who live in Kirkland or Medina. Use the IN operator. Display the Client Number, Client Name, City, and State fields in the query results. Save the query as EYK Step 3 Query.
4. Find all clients whose amount paid is greater than or equal to $500 and less than or equal to $1,000. Use the BETWEEN operator. Display the Client Number, Client Name, Photographer Number, and Amount Paid fields in the query results. Save the query as EYK Step 4 Query.
5. Use an INNER JOIN in a query to find all photographers who are located in Kirkland and whose clients are also located in Kirkland. Display the Client Name, Photographer Number, Photographer First Name, Photographer Last Name, and Photographer City fields in the query result. Save the query as EYK Step 5 Query.
6. If requested to do so by your instructor, rename the EYK Step 5 Query as First Name City Query where First Name is your first name and City is the city where you currently reside.
7. Submit the revised database in the format specified by your instructor.
8. **Consider This:** What WHERE clause would you use to find the answer to Step 3 without using the IN operator?

Expand Your World

Create a solution, which uses cloud and web technologies, by learning and investigating on your own from general guidance.

Instructions: Many SQL tutorials are available on the web. One site, www.w3schools.com/sql, has an online SQL editor that allows you to edit SQL commands and then run commands. You will use this editor to create and run queries in the following steps.

Perform the following tasks:

1. Create a blog, Google document, or Word document on OneDrive on which to store your SQL statements and the number of results obtained from the query. Include your name and the current date at the beginning of the blog or document.
2. Access the www.w3schools.com/sql website, and spend some time becoming familiar with the tutorial and how it works.
3. Using the website, explain how you would create a query to find records in a table where the CustomerName value begins with the letter P. Note the section of the website where you located the answer.
4. Submit the document containing your responses in the format specified by your instructor.
5. **Consider This:** In this module, you learned to use the asterisk (*) as a wildcard for an undetermined number of characters. However, in this exercise, you used a different symbol. Why is this different wildcard symbol required?

In the Lab

Design and implement a solution using creative thinking and problem-solving skills.

Lab: Using SQL in the Travel Nurses Database

Note: To complete this assignment, you will be required to use the Data Files. Please contact your instructor for information about accessing the Data Files.

Continued on next page

Problem: The administration at Homegrown Nurse Staffing Agency has asked you to perform a number of queries to collect information from their database.

Perform the following tasks:

Part 1: Open the SC_AC_10-4.accdb database from the Data Files folder. Close the Main Menu and save the file with the name, SC_AC_10_Travel-Nurses, and then enable the content. Use the concepts and techniques presented in this module to perform each of the following tasks. Create all queries using SQL view.

1. Find all the assignments where the bill rate is less than $25,000. Show all Assignments table fields in the results and save the query as ITL Step 1 Query.
2. Use the WHERE command to identify all hospital type facilities and showing all Facilities table fields. Save the query as ITL Step 2 Query.
3. Use the AND command to identify all travelers whose background check and drug screen have been completed. Show the Traveler ID field in the query. Save the query as ITL Step 3 Query.
4. Using the NOT command, find all facilities that are not a private practice. Show the Facility ID field in the query. Save the query as ITL Step 4 Query.
5. Using the ORDER BY command, sort the travelers by their license and then by their Traveler ID. Sort both fields in ascending order. Save the query as ITL Step 5 Query.
6. Use the AND command to find the housing ID for apartment type housing in location L-001, include contact name and phone number in the results, and sort the results in descending order by Housing ID. Save the query as ITL Step 6 Query.
7. Group the traveler payments by Traveler ID and count the number of payments with an amount paid greater than $1,000. Assign the name, Payments over $1,000, to the COUNT column, and autofit the column width in the query results to show the full column name. Save the query as ITL Step 7 Query.
8. Close the database.

Submit your assignment in the format specified by your instructor.

Part 2: **Consider This:** You made several decisions while creating these queries, including the decision of how to design the SELECT clause for the final query. What was the rationale behind your decisions for the last query's SELECT clause? What is another clause you could add to this query that you think would be relevant within the context of the Travel Nurses scenario?

Database Design

Objectives

After completing this module, you will be able to:

- Compare entities, attributes, and relationships
- Describe the characteristics of a relational database
- Identify functional dependence between fields
- Identify a table's primary key
- Explain the basic process of database design
- Explain how to convert an unnormalized relation to first normal form
- Explain how to convert a table from first normal form to second normal form
- Explain how to convert a table from second normal form to third normal form
- Describe information that can be obtained about a database from available documentation
- Describe how diagrams can represent a database's design

Introduction

This module presents a method for determining the tables and fields necessary to satisfy a set of requirements. **Database design** is the process of determining the particular tables and fields that will comprise a database. When designing a database, you must identify the tables that will be in the database, the fields in the tables, the primary keys of the tables, and the relationships between the tables.

This module begins by examining some important concepts concerning relational databases and then presents the design method. To illustrate the process, the module presents the requirements for the Clearnet Freight Brokers database. It then applies the design method to those requirements to produce the database design. The module applies the design method to a second set of requirements, which are requirements for a watersports company called Water Fun Rentals. It next examines normalization, which is a process that you can use to identify and fix potential problems in database designs. You will see normalization techniques applied to design requirements for the Partners Law Firm database. The module concludes by explaining how to use a company's policies and objectives—which are typically addressed in existing documentation—to plan and design a database. Finally, you will learn how to represent a database design with a diagram.

Project: Design a Database

BTW

Systems Analysis

The determination of database requirements is part of a process known as systems analysis. A systems analyst interviews users, examines existing and proposed documents, investigates current procedures, and reviews organizational policies to determine exactly the type of data needs the database must support.

This module expands on the database design guidelines presented earlier. Without a good understanding of database design, you cannot use a database management system such as Access effectively. In this module, you will learn database design principles by using the database design process shown in Figure 11–1.

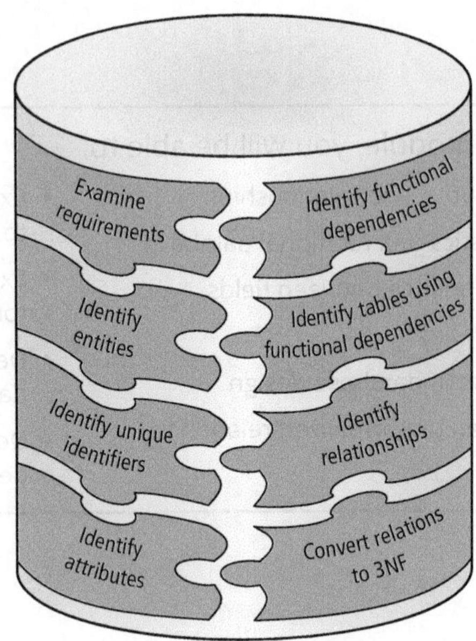

Database Design Process

Figure 11–1

You will design a database for Clearnet that is similar to the database you have used in previous modules. You will also design a new database for Water Fun Rentals, a watersport equipment rental company. You will then make normalization design improvements for the Partners database, based on the database you have used in previous modules, and for the Water Fun Rentals database.

Entities, Attributes, and Relationships

BTW

Entities

Clearnet could include many other entities in a database, such as entities for employees and hours the employees work. The decisions on which entities to include are part of the process of determining database requirements based on user needs.

Working in the database environment requires that you be familiar with some specific terms and concepts. The terms *entity*, *attribute*, and *relationship* are fundamental when discussing databases. An **entity** in a database is similar to a noun in grammar: it is a person, place, thing, or event. The entities of interest to Clearnet, for example, are such things as shippers, carriers, locations, and loads. The entities that are of interest to a college include students, faculty, and classes; a real estate agency is interested in buyers, sellers, properties, and agents; and a watersports company is interested in boats, rentals, customers, and boaters. When creating a database, an entity is represented as a table.

An **attribute** is a property of an entity. The term is used here exactly as it is used in everyday English. For the entity *company*, for example, the list of attributes might include such things as name and address. For Clearnet, the attributes of interest for the entity *carriers* are such things as name, contact person, address, insurance company, and so on. For the entity *faculty* at a school, the attributes would be such things as faculty number, name, office number, phone, department, and so on. For the entity *boat* at a watersports company, the attributes are such things as the hull identification number, brand, color, type of boat, and so on. In databases, attributes are represented as the fields in a table or tables.

A **relationship** is an association between entities. For example, there is an association between carriers and loads at Clearnet. A carrier is associated with all of its loads, and a load is associated with the one carrier to whom the load is assigned. Technically, you say that a carrier is *related* to all of its loads, and a load is *related* to a specific carrier.

The relationship between carriers and loads is an example of a one-to-many relationship because one carrier is associated with many loads, but each load is associated with only one carrier. Recall that in a one-to-many relationship, a table's record can be related to many records in another table. The other table's records are only related to one record in the first table. In this type of relationship, the word *many* is used in a way that is different from everyday English; it might not always mean a large number. In this context, for example, the term *many* means that a carrier might be associated with *any* number of loads. That is, one carrier can be associated with zero, one, or more loads.

There is also a relationship between shippers and carriers. Each shipper sends loads with many carriers, and each carrier can handle loads with many different shippers. This is an example of a **many-to-many relationship**.

How does a relational database handle entities, attributes of entities, and relationships between entities? Entities and attributes are fairly simple. Each entity has its own table; in the Clearnet database, there is one table for carriers, one table for loads, and so on. The attributes of an entity become the columns in the table. In the table for carriers, for example, there is a column for the carrier ID, a column for the carrier name, and so on.

What about relationships? Relationships are implemented through matching fields. One-to-many relationships, for example, are implemented by including matching fields in the related tables. Carriers and loads are related, for example, by including the Carrier ID field in both the Carriers table and the Loads table.

Many-to-many relationships are implemented through an additional table that contains matching fields for both related tables. Carriers and shippers are related, for example, through the Loads table. The Loads table contains the Shipper ID and the Carrier ID. This table links the two tables, Carriers and Shippers, together in the many-to-many relationship.

BTW
One-to-One Relationships
One-to-one relationships also can occur, but they are not common. To implement a one-to-one relationship, treat it as a one-to-many relationship. You must determine which table will be the "one" table and which table will be the "many" table. To do so, consider what may happen in the future. In the case of one project that has one employee assigned to it, more employees could possibly be added, even if that is not the current plan. Therefore, the project table would be the "one" table and the employee table would be the "many" table.

Relational Databases

A relational database is a collection of tables. Figure 11–2 shows portions of two of the tables from the Clearnet database. The Loads table contains information about the loads booked by Clearnet agents (Figure 11–2a).

Loads

Load ID	Pickup Date	Pickup Location	Rate	Mileage	Carrier	Shipper
1	6/30/2024	L-002	$500	159	C-001	S-002
2	7/1/2024	L-001	$1,900	687	C-003	S-001
3	7/1/2024	L-002	$715	218	C-001	S-002
4	7/2/2024	L-003	$2,000	694	C-002	S-001
5	7/3/2024	L-002	$700	159	C-002	S-002
6	7/5/2024	L-003	$675	243	C-001	S-003

Figure 11–2(a): Loads Table

Clearnet assigns each load to a specific carrier. The Carriers table contains information about the carriers to whom these loads are assigned (Figure 11–2b).

Carriers

Carrier ID	Carrier Name	Carrier Contact	Carrier Phone	Carrier Insurance
C-001	Williams Trucking	Marco Bailey	220-555-6682	Shipping Insurance, Inc.
C-002	Freightliners Inc.	Teresa Gomez	435-555-4545	Overland Insurers
C-003	Spotters Freight	Lata Gaspar	617-555-9888	US Motor Group
C-004	Freight Mobile	Doris Cracchiolo	816-555-4933	Shipping Insurance, Inc.
C-005	Truck-n-Go Inc.	Filipa Martinez	816-555-2442	Overland Insurers

Figure 11–2(b): Carriers Table

The formal term for a table is *relation*. If you study the tables shown in Figure 11–2, you might see that there are certain restrictions you should place on relations. Each column in a table should have a unique name, and entries in each column should match this column name. For example, in the Pickup Date column, all entries should in fact *be* dates. In addition, each row should be unique. After all, if two rows in a table contain identical data, the second row does not provide any information that you do not already have. In addition, for maximum flexibility, the order in which columns and rows appear in a table should be immaterial. Finally, a table's design is less complex if you restrict each position in the table to a single entry, that is, you do not permit multiple entries, often called **repeating groups**, in the table. These restrictions lead to the following definition.

A **relation** is a two-dimensional table in which:

1. The entries in the table are single-valued; that is, each location in the table contains a single entry.
2. Each column has a distinct name, technically called the *attribute name*.
3. All values in a column are values of the same attribute; that is, all entries correspond to the column name.
4. Each row is distinct; that is, no two rows are identical.

Figure 11–3a shows a table with repeating groups, which violates Rule 1. Figure 11–3b shows a table in which two columns have the same name, which violates Rule 2. Figure 11–3c shows a table in which one of the entries in the Pickup Date column is not a date, which violates Rule 3. Figure 11–3d shows a table with two identical rows, which violates Rule 4.

repeating group (more than one entry in a single table row)

Loads

Load ID	Pickup Date	Pickup Location	Rate	Mileage	Carrier	Shipper
1	6/30/2024	L-002 L-004 L-005	$500 $715 $675	159 218 243	C-001	S-002 S-004 S-001
2	7/1/2024	L-001	$1,900	687	C-003	S-001
3	7/1/2024	L-002	$715	218	C-001	S-002
4	7/2/2024	L-003	$2,000	694	C-002	S-001
5	7/3/2024	L-002	$700	159	C-002	S-002
6	7/5/2024	L-003	$675	243	C-001	S-003

Figure 11–3(a): Loads Table Violation of Rule 1—Table Contains Repeating Groups

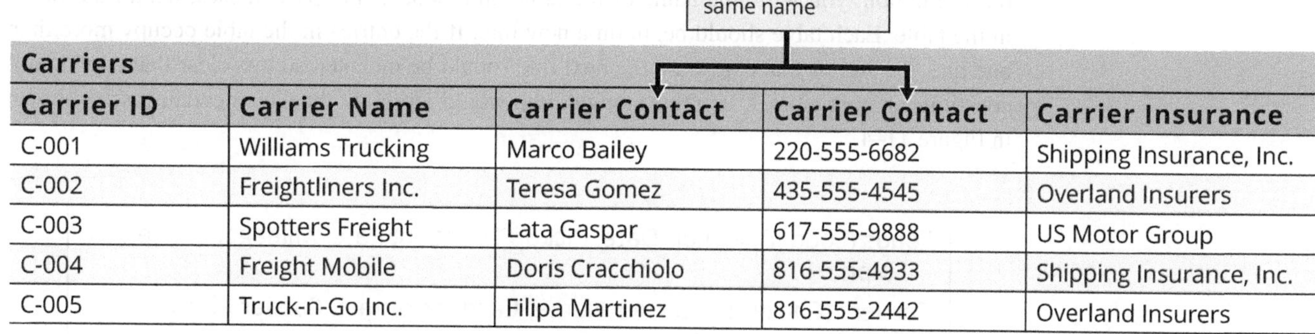

Carriers				
Carrier ID	**Carrier Name**	**Carrier Contact**	**Carrier Contact**	**Carrier Insurance**
C-001	Williams Trucking	Marco Bailey	220-555-6682	Shipping Insurance, Inc.
C-002	Freightliners Inc.	Teresa Gomez	435-555-4545	Overland Insurers
C-003	Spotters Freight	Lata Gaspar	617-555-9888	US Motor Group
C-004	Freight Mobile	Doris Cracchiolo	816-555-4933	Shipping Insurance, Inc.
C-005	Truck-n-Go Inc.	Filipa Martinez	816-555-2442	Overland Insurers

Figure 11–3(b): Carriers Table Violation of Rule 2—Each Column Should Have a Distinct Name

Loads						
Load ID	**Pickup Date**	**Pickup Location**	**Rate**	**Mileage**	**Carrier**	**Shipper**
1	6/30/2024	L-002	$500	159	C-001	S-002
2	Monday AM	L-001	$1,900	687	C-003	S-001
3	7/1/2024	L-002	$715	218	C-001	S-002
4	7/2/2024	L-003	$2,000	694	C-002	S-001
5	7/3/2024	L-002	$700	159	C-002	S-002
6	7/5/2024	L-003	$675	243	C-001	S-003

value does not correspond to column name; that is, it is not a Pickup Date

Figure 11–3(c): Loads Table Violation of Rule 3—All Entries in a Column Must Correspond to the Column Name

Carriers				
Carrier ID	**Carrier Name**	**Carrier Contact**	**Carrier Phone**	**Carrier Insurance**
C-001	Williams Trucking	Marco Bailey	220-555-6682	Shipping Insurance, Inc.
C-002	Freightliners Inc.	Teresa Gomez	435-555-4545	Overland Insurers
C-002	Freightliners Inc.	Teresa Gomez	435-555-4545	Overland Insurers
C-003	Spotters Freight	Lata Gaspar	617-555-9888	US Motor Group
C-004	Freight Mobile	Doris Cracchiolo	816-555-4933	Shipping Insurance, Inc.
C-005	Truck-n-Go Inc.	Filipa Martinez	816-555-2442	Overland Insurers

identical rows

Figure 11–3(d): Carriers Table Violation of Rule 4—Each Row Should Contain Distinct Data

In a relation, the order of columns is immaterial. The order of rows is also immaterial. You can view the columns or rows in any order you want. Rows in a table (relation) are often called records or **tuples**. Columns in a table (relation) are often called fields or attributes. Typically, the terms *record* and *field* are used in Access. A relational database is a collection of relations.

To depict the structure of a relational database, you can use a commonly accepted shorthand representation: you write the name of the table and then, within parentheses, list all the fields in the table. Each table should begin on a new line. If the entries in the table occupy more than one line, the entries that appear on the next line should be indented so it is clear that they do not constitute another table. Using this method, you would represent the Clearnet database as shown in Figure 11–4.

Loads (Load ID, Pickup Date, Pickup Location, Rate, Mileage, Carrier,
  Shipper)
Carriers (Carrier ID, Carrier Name, Carrier Contact, Carrier Phone,
  Carrier Insurance)

Figure 11–4

Duplicate field names in different tables can also cause problems. This is why the modules in this course often had you name a field with additional information referencing the table the field belonged to. For example, the Contact field in the Carriers table is named Carrier Contact. In the Shippers table, the Contact field is named Shipper Contact. Consider if the Clearnet database named the Contact field simply the word, Contact, in *both* the Carriers table *and* the Shippers table. This duplication of names can lead to possible confusion. If you write Contact, it is not clear to which Contact field you are referring.

When duplicate field names exist in different tables in a database, you need to indicate the field to which you are referring. You do so by writing both the table name and the field name, separated by a period. You would write the Contact field in the Carriers table as Carriers.Contact and the Contact field in the Shippers table as Shippers.Contact. As you learned previously, when you combine a field name with a table name, you say that you qualify the field names. It is *always* acceptable to qualify field names, even if there is no possibility of confusion. If confusion might arise, however, it is *essential* to qualify field names.

Functional Dependence

In the Clearnet database (Figure 11–2), a given carrier ID in the database will correspond to a single carrier because carrier ID numbers are unique. Thus, if you are given a carrier ID in the database, you could find a carrier name that corresponds to it. No ambiguity exists. The database terminology for this relationship between carrier ID numbers and carrier names is that Carrier ID determines Carrier Name, or, equivalently, that Carrier Name is functionally dependent on Carrier ID. Specifically, if you know that whenever you are given a value for one field, you will be able to determine a single value for a second field, the first field is said to **determine** the second field. In addition, the second field is said to be **functionally dependent** on the first.

There is a shorthand notation that represents functional dependencies using an arrow. To indicate that Carrier ID determines Carrier Name, or, equivalently, that Carrier Name is functionally dependent on Carrier ID, you would write Carrier ID → Carrier Name. The field that precedes the arrow determines the field that follows the arrow.

If you were given an insurance company name and asked to find a single carrier's name, you could not do it. Given Overland Insurers, for example, you would find two carrier names, Freightliners Inc. and Truck-n-Go Inc. (Figure 11–5). Formally, you would say the insurance company does *not* determine Carrier Name, or that Carrier Name is *not* functionally dependent on Carrier Insurance.

BTW
Functional Dependence
To help identify functional dependencies, ask yourself the following question. If you know a unique value for an attribute, do you know the specific values for other attributes? For example, when you have three attributes—Carrier ID, Carrier Name, and Carrier Insurance—and you know a unique value for Carrier ID, do you also know a specific value for Carrier Name and Carrier Insurance? If so, then Carrier Name and Carrier Insurance are functionally dependent on Carrier ID.

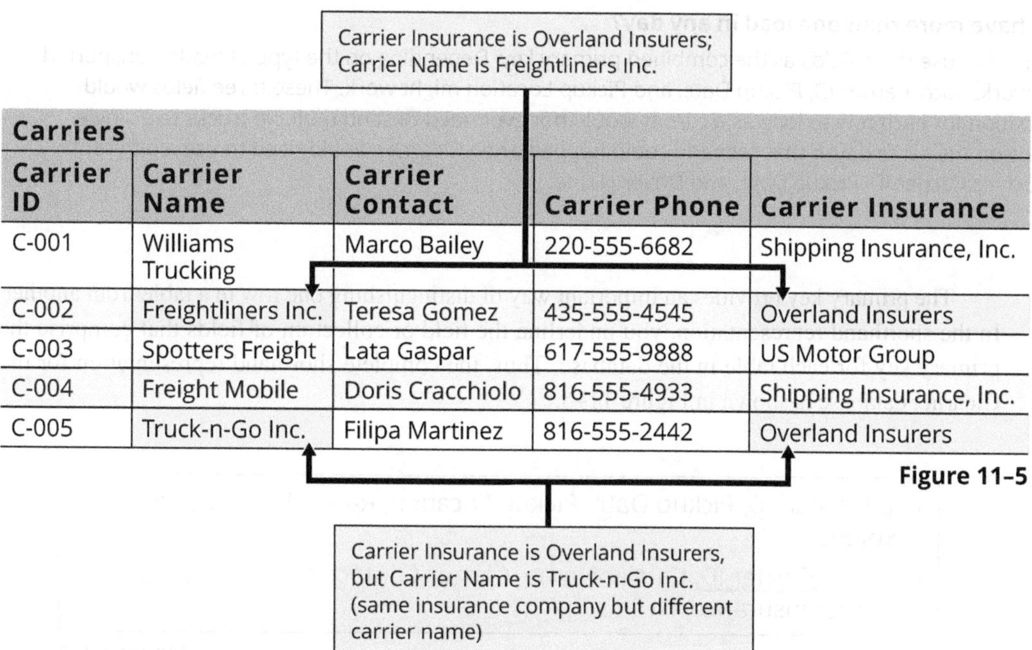
Carrier Insurance is Overland Insurers; Carrier Name is Freightliners Inc.

Carriers				
Carrier ID	Carrier Name	Carrier Contact	Carrier Phone	Carrier Insurance
C-001	Williams Trucking	Marco Bailey	220-555-6682	Shipping Insurance, Inc.
C-002	Freightliners Inc.	Teresa Gomez	435-555-4545	Overland Insurers
C-003	Spotters Freight	Lata Gaspar	617-555-9888	US Motor Group
C-004	Freight Mobile	Doris Cracchiolo	816-555-4933	Shipping Insurance, Inc.
C-005	Truck-n-Go Inc.	Filipa Martinez	816-555-2442	Overland Insurers

Carrier Insurance is Overland Insurers, but Carrier Name is Truck-n-Go Inc. (same insurance company but different carrier name)

Figure 11–5

Consider This

In the Loads table, is Shipper ID functionally dependent on Load ID?

Yes. If you are given a value for Load ID, for example 4, you will always find a *single* Shipper ID, in this case S-001, associated with it.

In the Loads table in the Clearnet database, is Shipper ID functionally dependent on Carrier ID?

No. There is a row, for example, in which the Carrier ID is C-003 and the Shipper ID is S-001. There is another row in which the Carrier ID is C-002 and the Shipper ID is again S-001. A carrier can transport loads from multiple shippers. Thus, carriers are associated with more than one shipper.

On which fields is the Contents field functionally dependent?

To determine the Contents value, you need the Load ID.

Primary Key

The primary key of a table is the field or minimum collection of fields—the fewest number of fields possible—that uniquely identifies a given row in that table. In the Loads table, the Load ID uniquely identifies a given row. Any Load ID appears on only one row of the table. Thus, Load ID is the primary key. Similarly, Carrier ID is the primary key of the Carriers table.

Consider This

Is the Carrier Name another possibility for the key field in the Carriers table?

No. While unlikely in a list of businesses, it is possible there may be two carriers with the same name. This is even more likely in a list of people where multiple people can have the same name. A key field must be unique for each row.

Could the combination of the Carrier Name and the Carrier Phone fields be the primary key for the Carriers table?

Yes, the combination of the two fields, Carrier Name and Carrier Phone, make each row unique. This would be an alternative to using the current key field, Carrier ID.

Could the combination of the Carrier Name and the Pickup Date fields be the primary key for the Loads table?

The combination of the two fields, Carrier Name and Pickup Date, does make each row unique, assuming that each carrier has only one load each day. This could be an alternative to using the current key field, Load ID. However, many loads are entered in the database before a carrier is assigned. In these cases, you would either have to wait to enter the load until a carrier is assigned, or you would have to temporarily assign a placeholder carrier value (such as Unassigned) until a carrier is selected. Further, you could only have one unassigned load for each day at a time, which is unreasonable in this scenario.

What if some carriers have more than one load in any day?

In this case, you would need to use three fields as the combined primary key. Depending on the type of loads transported by the carriers Clearnet works with, Carrier ID, Pickup Date, and Pickup Location might work. These three fields would provide a unique combination for each row as long as a carrier would not ever need to send multiple trucks to a single location for multiple loads on the same day. If that scenario could happen, then Clearnet would need to use a different combination of fields, such as Carrier ID, Pickup Date, and Driver Name.

The primary key provides an important way of distinguishing one row in a table from another. In the shorthand representation, you underline the field or collection of fields that comprise the primary key for each table in the database. Thus, the complete shorthand representation for the Clearnet database is shown in Figure 11–6.

Loads (Load ID, Pickup Date, Pickup Location, Rate, Mileage, Carrier, Shipper)
Carriers (Carrier ID, Carrier Name, Carrier Contact, Carrier Phone, Carrier Insurance)

Figure 11–6

BTW
Candidate Keys
According to the definition of a candidate key, a Social Security number is a legitimate primary key. Many databases use a person's Social Security number as a primary key. However, many institutions and organizations are moving away from using Social Security numbers because of privacy issues. Instead, many institutions and organizations use unique student numbers or employee numbers as primary keys.

Occasionally, but not often, there might be more than one possibility for the primary key. For example, if the Clearnet database included an Employees table with employees' Social Security numbers, either the Employee ID or the Social Security number could serve as the primary key. In this case, both fields are referred to as candidate keys. Similar to a primary key, a **candidate key** is a field or combination of fields on which all fields in the table are functionally dependent. Thus, the definition for primary key really defines candidate key as well. There can be many candidate keys, although having more than one is very rare. By contrast, there is only one primary key. The remaining candidate keys are called **alternate keys**.

Database Design

This section presents a specific database design method, based on a set of requirements that the database must support. The section then presents a sample of such requirements and illustrates the design method by designing a database to satisfy these requirements.

Design Process

The following is a method for designing a database for a set of requirements.

1. Examine the requirements and identify the entities, or objects, involved. Assign names to the entities. The entities will become tables. If, for example, the design involves the entities departments and employees, you could assign the names, Departments and Employees. If the design involves the entities accounts, orders, and parts, you could assign the names, Accounts, Orders, and Parts.

BTW
Singular Vs. Plural Table Names
A common debate in database design is whether to use singular or plural table names when designing a database. Most experts agree this decision is a matter of personal opinion. However, the important thing is to be consistent—if you start with singular names, then continue to use singular names throughout, and vice versa. However, some singular names you might want to use are not allowed by Access. For example, the word, Order, has special meaning in SQL. If you use it for the name of a table, you will not be able to use SQL to query that table. A common approach to avoid this problem is to make the name plural. That is one reason for choosing Orders rather than Order as the name of the table. If you will need to use a name for a table that must be plural, such as Orders, you might prefer to use plural names for all your tables in the interest of consistency. Still, there are many other valid reasons why singular names might be preferred, such as lending more intuitive sense when a field is qualified by its table name in a SQL query, such as [Customer].[Customer Name]. Again, the important thing is to choose one approach, either singular or plural, and be consistent as much as possible.

2. Assign a unique identifier to each entity. For example, if one of the entities were "item," you would determine what it takes to uniquely identify each individual item. In other words, what enables the organization to distinguish one item from another? For an item entity, it might be Item Number. For an account entity, it might be Account Number. If there is no such unique identifier, it is a good idea to add one. Perhaps the previous system was a manual one where accounts were not assigned numbers, in which case this would be a good time to add Account Numbers to the system. If there is no natural candidate for a primary key, you can add an AutoNumber field, which is similar to the ID field that Access adds automatically when you create a new table.

3. Identify the attributes for all the entities. These attributes will become the fields in the tables. It is possible that more than one entity has the same attribute. At Clearnet, for example, carriers and shippers both have the attributes of contact, phone, email, and address. To handle this duplication, you can follow the name of the attribute with the corresponding entity in parentheses. Thus, Contact (Shippers) would be the contact person for a shipper, whereas Contact (Carriers) would be the contact person for a carrier.

4. Identify the functional dependencies that exist among the attributes.

5. Use the functional dependencies to identify the tables. You do this by placing each attribute with the attribute or minimum combination of attributes on which it is functionally dependent. The attribute or attributes on which all other attributes in the table are dependent will be the primary key of the table. The remaining attributes will be the other fields in the table. Once you have determined all the fields in the table, you can assign an appropriate name to the table.

6. Determine and implement relationships among the entities. The basic relationships are one-to-many and many-to-many.
   - **One-to-many.** You implement a one-to-many relationship by including the primary key of the "one" table as a foreign key in the "many" table. A foreign key is a field in one table whose values are required to match the primary key of another table. In the one-to-many relationship between loads and carriers, for example, you include the *primary key* of the Carriers table, which is Carrier ID, as a foreign key in the Loads table. You might have already included this field in the earlier steps. If so, you would simply designate it as a foreign key. If you had not already added it, you would need to add it at this point, designating it as a foreign key.
   - **Many-to-many.** A many-to-many relationship is implemented by creating a new table whose primary key is the combination of the keys of the original tables.

BTW
Line Items
A line item is a unit of information that appears on its own line. For example, when you purchase groceries, each grocery item appears on its own line. Line items also can be referred to as order line items or item detail lines.

You may have already identified such a table in the earlier steps, in which case, all you need to do is be sure you have designated each portion of the primary key as a foreign key that is required to match the primary key of the appropriate table. If you have not, you would add the table at this point. The primary key will consist of the primary keys from each of the tables to be related. If there are any attributes that depend on the combination of fields that make up the primary key, you need to include them in this table. (*Note:* There might not be any other fields that are dependent on this combination. In that case, there will be no fields besides the fields that make up the primary key.)

The following sections illustrate the design process by designing the database for Clearnet. The first section gives the requirements the database must support, and then the following section creates a database design based on those requirements.

Requirements for the Clearnet Database

Systems analysts have examined the needs and organizational policies at Clearnet and have determined that the Clearnet database must support the following requirements:

1. For a shipper, Clearnet needs to maintain the shipper's name, contact person and their information, locations, and billing notes.

2. For a carrier, Clearnet needs the carrier's name, contact person and their information, MC Number, USDOT Number, insurance and payment information, and information on the drivers and trucks.
3. For locations, Clearnet needs the location name, type, address, and related shipper if applicable.
4. Each load must be recorded as well. Information for loads indicates when and where the load is scheduled for pickup and dropoff, rate confirmation, mileage, contents, required truck type, current status, assigned driver with their contact information, and identification of the related carrier, shipper, and agent.
5. Any given carrier can have many loads, and any shipper can also have many loads.

Design of the Clearnet Database

The following represents the application of the design method for the Clearnet requirements.

1. There appear to be four entities: shippers, carriers, locations, and loads. Reasonable names for the corresponding tables are Shippers, Carriers, Locations, and Loads.
2. The unique identifier for shippers is the shipper ID. The unique identifier for carriers is the carrier ID. The unique identifier for locations is the location ID. The unique identifier of loads is the load ID. Reasonable names for the unique identifiers are Shipper ID, Carrier ID, Location ID, and Load ID, respectively.
3. The attributes are:

   Shipper ID
   Shipper Name
   Shipper Contact
   Shipper Phone
   Shipper Email
   Shipper Address
   Shipper Locations
   Shipper Billing Notes
   Carrier ID
   Carrier Name
   Carrier Contact
   Carrier Phone
   Carrier Email
   Carrier Address
   Carrier MC Number
   Carrier USDOT Number
   Carrier Insurance
   Carrier Payment Instructions
   Drivers
   LTL
   Equipment Types
   Driver Photos
   Carrier Documentation

Location ID
Location Name
Location Type
Location Street
Location City
Location State
Location Postal Code
Shipper ID
Load ID
Pickup Date
Pickup Location
Dropoff Date
Dropoff Location
Rate Confirmation
Mileage
Contents
Truck Type
Status
Driver Name
Driver Phone
Carrier
Shipper
Load Notes
Agent

Remember that, if two entities contain attributes with the same name, parentheses after an attribute indicate the entity to which the attribute corresponds. Thus, Address (Shippers) represents the address of a shipper in a way that distinguishes it from Address (Carriers), which represents the address of a carrier. In this case, however, each attribute is named with a built-in reference to the entity, such as Shipper Address and Carrier Address.

4. The functional dependencies among the attributes are:

Shipper ID → Shipper Name, Shipper Contact, Shipper Phone, Shipper Email, Shipper Address, Shipper Locations, Shipper Billing Notes

Carrier ID → Carrier Name, Carrier Contact, Carrier Phone, Carrier Email, Carrier Address, Carrier MC Number, Carrier USDOT Number, Carrier Insurance, Carrier Payment Instructions, Drivers, LTL, Equipment Types, Driver Photos, Carrier Documentation

Location ID → Location Name, Location Type, Location Street, Location City, Location State, Location Postal Code, Shipper ID

Load ID → Pickup Date, Pickup Location, Dropoff Date, Dropoff Location, Rate Confirmation, Mileage, Contents, Truck Type, Status, Driver Name, Driver Phone, Carrier, Shipper, Load Notes, Agent

The pickup and dropoff dates and locations are dependent only on load ID. Because a load has a single shipper and a single carrier, the shipper and carrier are dependent on load ID as well. The carrier's name, contact information, and documentation information are dependent only on the carrier ID. The shipper's name, contact information, locations, and billing notes are dependent only on the shipper ID. Similarly, the location name, type, and address are dependent only on the location ID. The shorthand representation for the tables is shown in Figure 11–7.

Loads (Load ID, Pickup Date, Pickup Location, Dropoff Date, Dropoff Location, Rate Confirmation, Mileage, Contents, Truck Type, Status, Driver Name, Driver Phone, Carrier, Shipper, Load Notes, Agent)

Carriers (Carrier ID, Carrier Name, Carrier Contact, Carrier Phone, Carrier Email, Carrier Address, Carrier MC Number, Carrier USDOT Number, Carrier Insurance, Carrier Payment Instructions, Drivers, LTL, Equipment Types, Driver Photos, Carrier Documentation)

Shippers (Shipper ID, Shipper Name, Shipper Contact, Shipper Phone, Shipper Email, Shipper Address, Shipper Locations, Shipper Billing Notes)

Locations (Location ID, Location Name, Location Type, Location Street, Location City, Location State, Location Postal Code, Shipper ID)

Figure 11–7

5. The following are the relationships between the tables:
   a. The Loads and Carriers tables are related using the Carrier ID fields, which is the primary key of the Carriers table. The Carrier field in the Loads table is a foreign key.
   b. The Loads and Shippers tables are related using the Shipper ID fields, which is the primary key of the Shippers table. The Shipper field in the Loads table is a foreign key.
   c. The Loads and Locations tables are related using either the Pickup Location field or the Dropoff Location field in the Loads table and the Location ID field, which is the primary key of the Locations table. This creates two relationships between the Loads table and the Locations table, one on each Location field in the Loads table. The Pickup Location and Dropoff Location fields in the Loads table are both foreign keys.

Note: In the shorthand representation for a table containing a foreign key, you would represent the foreign key by using the letters, FK, followed by an arrow, followed by the name of the table in which that field is the primary key. For example, to indicate that the Carrier ID in the Loads table is a foreign key that must match the primary key of the Carriers table, you would write FK Carrier ID → Carriers.

The shorthand representation for the tables and foreign keys is shown in Figure 11–8. It is common to list a table containing a foreign key after the table that contains the corresponding

Shippers (Shipper ID, Shipper Name, Shipper Contact, Shipper Phone, Shipper Email, Shipper Address, Shipper Locations, Shipper Billing Notes)

Carriers (Carrier ID, Carrier Name, Carrier Contact, Carrier Phone, Carrier Email, Carrier Address, Carrier MC Number, Carrier USDOT Number, Carrier Insurance, Carrier Payment Instructions, Drivers, LTL, Equipment Types, Driver Photos, Carrier Documentation)

FK Shipper ID → Shippers

Locations (Location ID, Location Name, Location Type, Location Street, Location City, Location State, Location Postal Code, Shipper ID)

Loads (Load ID, Pickup Date, Pickup Location, Dropoff Date, Dropoff Location, Rate Confirmation, Mileage, Contents, Truck Type, Status, Driver Name, Driver Phone, Carrier, Shipper, Load Notes, Agent)

FK Carrier ID → Carriers

FK Location ID → Locations

Figure 11–8

primary key, when possible. Thus, in the figure, the Loads table comes after the other tables because it contains foreign keys from the tables listed above it.

Water Fun Rentals

The management of Water Fun Rentals, a watersport equipment rental company, has determined that the company's rapid growth requires a database to maintain information about rentals, customers, and boating equipment such as kayaks and canoes. With the data stored in a database, management will be able to ensure that the data is current and more accurate. In addition, managers will be able to obtain answers to their questions concerning the data in the database quickly and easily, with the option of producing a variety of reports. Note that the cost of the rentals and the payments to the Water Fun Rentals company are handled by a third party and are not requirements of this database design.

Requirements for the Water Fun Rentals Database

A system analyst has interviewed users and examined documents at Water Fun Rentals and has determined that the company needs a database that will support the following requirements:

1. For a customer, store the customer's first name, last name, street address, city, state, postal code, telephone number, and email address.
2. For a paddler, store the paddler's first name, last name, street address, city, state, postal code, telephone number, and email address. (Note that there might be many paddlers under one customer. For example, a business customer could pay for all the rentals of a group of paddlers on a company outing.)
3. For rented boats, store the hull identification number, type, brand, and color. The database also should store the rental agreement number under which each boat is rented.
4. The paddler and boat must be associated; the database must include a table that links these two entities.
5. The analyst also obtained the following information concerning boat rentals:
   a. A customer could rent more than one boat.
   b. There could be multiple paddlers associated with one rental agreement.
   c. A customer can rent boats many times.
   d. Each rental is effective on a single day for a certain number of hours.

Design of the Water Fun Rentals Database

The following steps apply the design process to the requirements for Water Fun Rentals to produce the appropriate database design:

1. Assign entity names. There appear to be four entities: customers, paddlers, rentals, and boats. The names assigned to these entities are Customers, Paddlers, Rentals, and Boats, respectively.
2. Determine unique identifiers. From the collection of entities, review the data and determine the unique identifier for each entity. For the Customers, Paddlers, and Rentals entities, the unique identifiers are the customer ID, paddler ID, and rental number, respectively. These unique identifiers are named Customer ID, Paddler ID, and Rental Number, respectively. For the Boats, the unique identifier is the hull identification number, known as HIN, which is a unique number assigned to each boat by its manufacturer.
3. Assign attribute names. The attributes mentioned in the first requirement all refer to customers. The specific attributes mentioned in the requirement are the customer ID,

first name, last name, street address, city, state, postal code, telephone number, and email address. Assigning appropriate names to these attributes produces the following list:

Customer ID

First Name

Last Name

Street

City

State

Postal Code

Telephone

Email Address

Consider This

Do you need to include the rental associated with the customer in the list of attributes for the first requirement?

There is no need to include rental information in this list because that information will be determined with a relationship between tables later on.

The attributes mentioned in the second requirement refer to paddlers. The specific attributes are the paddler ID, first name, last name, street address, city, state, postal code, telephone number, and email address. Assigning appropriate names to these attributes produces the following list:

Paddler ID

First Name

Last Name

Street

City

State

Postal Code

Telephone

Email Address

There are attributes named Street, City, State, and Postal Code for customers as well as attributes identically named Street, City, State, and Postal Code for paddlers. To distinguish these attributes in the final collection, the name of the attribute is followed by the name of the corresponding entity. For example, the street address for a customer is Street (Customers) and the street address for a paddler is Street (Paddlers).

The attributes mentioned in the third requirement refer to rental agreements. The specific attributes are the rental number, effective date, expire time, and customer, who is the rental holder. Assigning appropriate names to these attributes produces the following list:

Rental Number

Effective Date

Expire Time

Customer ID

The attributes mentioned in the fourth requirement refer to rental boats. The specific attributes include the hull identification number, type, brand, color, and rental number associated with the boat. Assigning appropriate names to these attributes produces the following list:

HIN

Type

Brand

Color

Rental Number

The statement concerning the linkage of paddler to boat indicates there are specific attributes to be stored for each boat when it is rented. These attributes are the boat and paddler. Assigning appropriate names to these attributes produces the following list:

HIN

Paddler ID

The complete list grouped by entity is as follows:

Customers

- **Customer ID**
- **First Name**
- **Last Name**
- **Street**
- **City**
- **State**
- **Postal Code**
- **Telephone**
- **Email Address**

Paddlers

- **Paddler ID**
- **First Name**
- **Last Name**
- **Street**
- **City**
- **State**
- **Postal Code**
- **Telephone**
- **Email Address**

Rentals

- **Rental Number**
- **Effective Date**
- **Expire Time**
- **Customer ID**

Boats

- **HIN**
- **Type**
- **Brand**
- **Color**
- **Rental Number**

For paddlers of boats:

HIN

Paddler ID

4. Identify functional dependencies. The fact that the unique identifier for customers is Customer ID gives the following functional dependencies:

   Customer ID → First Name (Customers), Last Name (Customers), Street (Customers), City (Customers), State (Customers), Postal Code (Customers), Telephone (Customers), Email Address (Customers)

   The fact that the unique identifier for paddlers is Paddler ID gives the following preliminary list of functional dependencies:

   Paddler ID → First Name (Paddlers), Last Name (Paddlers), Street (Paddlers), City (Paddlers), State (Paddlers), Postal Code (Paddlers), Telephone (Paddlers), Email Address (Paddlers)

   The fact that the unique identifier for rentals is Rental Number gives the following functional dependencies:

   Rental Number → Effective Date, Expire Time, Customer ID

   The fact that the unique identifier for boats is HIN gives the following functional dependencies:

   HIN → Type, Brand, Color, Rental Number

Consider This

Do you need to include the name of a customer in the list of attributes determined by the rental number?

There is no need to include the customer name in this list because you can determine that information from the customer ID, and names are already included in the list of attributes determined by customer ID.

The final attributes to be examined are those associated with the paddlers and boats: HIN, Paddler ID.

Consider This

Why is Paddler ID not included in the Boats table?

There could be multiple paddlers for each boat, so this requires an additional table.

The following shorthand representation indicates the combination of HIN and Paddler ID. There are no functionally dependent fields in this table.

HIN, Paddler ID →

The complete list of functional dependencies with appropriate revisions is as follows:

Customer ID → First Name (Customers), Last Name (Customers), Street (Customers), City (Customers), State (Customers), Postal Code (Customers), Telephone (Customers), Email Address (Customers)

Paddler ID → First Name (Paddlers), Last Name (Paddlers), Street (Paddlers), City (Paddlers), State (Paddlers), Postal Code (Paddlers), Telephone (Paddlers), Email Address (Paddlers)

Rental Number → Effective Date, Expire Time, Customer ID

HIN → Type, Brand, Color, Rental Number

HIN, Paddler ID →

5. Create the tables. Using the functional dependencies, you can create tables with the attribute(s) to the left of the arrow being the primary key and the items to the right of the arrow being the other fields. For tables corresponding to those entities identified in Step 1, you can simply use the name you already determined. Because you did not identify any entity that had a unique identifier that was the combination of HIN and Paddler ID, you need to assign a name to the table whose primary key consists of these two fields.

Because this table represents the individual paddlers for one boat, the name Boat Paddlers is a good choice. The final collection of tables for Water Fun Rentals is shown in Figure 11–9.

Customers (<u>Customer ID</u>, First Name, Last Name, Address, City, State, Postal Code, Telephone, Email Address)
Paddlers (<u>Paddler ID</u>, First Name, Last Name, Address, City, State, Postal Code, Telephone, Email Address)
Rentals (<u>Rental Number</u>, Effective Date, Expire Time, Customer ID)
Boats (<u>HIN</u>, Type, Brand, Color, Rental Number)
Boat Paddlers (<u>HIN</u>, <u>Paddler ID</u>)

Figure 11–9

6. Identify relationships.
   a. The Customers and Rentals tables are related using the Customer ID fields. The Customer ID field in the Customers table is the primary key. The Customer ID field in the Rentals table is a foreign key.
   b. The Rentals and Boats tables are related using the Rental Number fields. The Rental Number field in the Rentals table is the primary key. The Rental Number field in the Boats table is a foreign key.
   c. The Boats and Paddlers tables are related using the HIN and Paddler ID fields. Both the HIN and the Paddler ID are key fields together.

Consider This

Does a many-to-many relationship exist between boats and paddlers?

Yes. The Boat Paddlers table will implement a many-to-many relationship between boats and paddlers. You identified this table as Boat Paddlers in the database design process.

In the Boat Paddlers table, the primary key consists of two fields, HIN and Paddler ID. Do you need both fields to be key fields?

Yes, because this table implements the many-to-many relationship between boats and paddlers. It is perfectly legitimate for the table that implements a many-to-many relationship to contain only the two columns that constitute the primary key.

The shorthand representation for the tables and foreign keys is shown in Figure 11–10.

Customers (<u>Customer ID</u>, First Name, Last Name, Address, City, State, Postal Code, Telephone, Email Address)
Paddlers (<u>Paddler ID</u>, First Name, Last Name, Address, City, State, Postal Code, Telephone, Email Address)
Rentals (<u>Rental Number</u>, Effective Date, Expire Time, Customer ID)
FK Customer ID → Customers
Boats (<u>HIN</u>, Type, Brand, Color, Rental Number)
FK Rental Number → Rentals
Boat Paddlers (<u>HIN</u>, <u>Paddler ID</u>)
FK HIN → Boats
FK Paddler ID → Paddlers

Figure 11–10

Sample data for the Water Fun Rentals database is shown in Figure 11–11.

Customers

Customer ID	Customer First Name	Customer Last Name	Customer Street Address	Customer City	Customer State	Customer Postal Code	Customer Phone	Customer Email Address
C398	Tricia	Morris	460 West Longberg Rd	Gainesville	SC	29101	854-555-4411	tmorris@example.com
C416	Shinju	Niack	9874 South Main St	Gainesville	SC	29103	854-555-5670	sniack@example.com

Paddlers

Paddler ID	Paddler First Name	Paddler Last Name	Paddler Street Address	Paddler City	Paddler State	Paddler Postal Code	Paddler Phone	Paddler Email Address
P410	Steve	Chen	3 Hanover Park	Newberry	NC	27237	828-555-4234	schen@example.com
P434	Tiffanie	D'Vivo	14435 Keller Way	Gainesville	SC	29101	854-555-9135	tdvivo@example.com
P552	Cyrus	Killigan	784 Hilltop Cir	Gainesville	SC	29101	854-555-6547	ckilligan@example.com

Rentals

Rental Number	Effective Date	Expire Time	Customer ID
R-123	2/13/2029	14:00	C398
R-142	4/1/2029	19:30	C416

Boats

HIN	Type	Brand	Color	Rental Number
ALL7HA470011	1-person kayak	Water Systems	Green	R-123
ALS7DA761712	2-person kayak	SeaCruise	Blue	R-142
JMB4A1138112	Canoe	Water Systems	Yellow	R-142

Boat Paddlers

HIN	Paddler ID
ALL7HA470011	P410
ALS7DA761712	P552
ALS7DA761712	P434

Figure 11–11

Break Point: If you wish to take a break, this is a good place to do so. To resume at a later time, continue reading from this location forward.

Normalization

After you create your database design, you should analyze it using a process called **normalization** to make sure the design is free of potential update, redundancy, and consistency problems. This process also supplies methods for correcting these problems.

The normalization process involves converting tables into various types of **normal forms**. A table in a particular normal form possesses a certain desirable set of properties. Several normal forms exist, the most common being first normal form (1NF), second normal form (2NF), and third normal form (3NF). The forms create a progression in which a table that is in 1NF is better than a table that is not in 1NF, a table that is in 2NF is better than one that is in 1NF, and so on. The goal of normalization is to take a table or collection of tables and produce a new collection of tables that represents the same information but is free of problems.

First Normal Form

A table that contains a repeating group, or multiple entries for a single row, is called an **unnormalized table** and is, therefore, in **unnormalized form (UNF)**. An unnormalized table is one that does not meet the definition of a relation. Recall from earlier in this module that a relation is a two-dimensional table in which the entries in the table are single valued, each column has a distinct name, all values in a column are values of the same attribute (that is, all entries must correspond to the column name), and each row is distinct.

BTW
UNF
Some databases are intentionally designed to support unnormalized form. These databases are called nonrelational databases or NoSQL (Not-only SQL) databases.

The normalization process consists of multiple tests of the database's tables to ensure they meet certain rules. Removal of repeating groups is the starting point in the goal of having tables that are as free of problems as possible. In fact, in most database management systems, tables cannot contain repeating groups. A table (relation) is in **first normal form (1NF)** if it does not contain repeating groups.

In designing a database, you might have created a table with a repeating group. For example, you might have created a Closings Worked table in which the primary key is the Attorney ID and there is a repeating group consisting of Property ID and Attorney Fees. In the example, each attorney appears on a single row, and Property ID and Attorney Fees are repeated as many times as necessary for each attorney (Figure 11–12).

Closings Worked

Attorney ID	Property ID	Attorney Fees
A-001	P-003	350
A-002	P-008 P-005 P-006	350 350 250
A-003	P-002	1
A-004	P-001 P-007	250 250
A-005	P-004	250

repeating group (more than one entry in a single table location) indicates each of these attorneys is performing more than one closing

Figure 11–12

In the shorthand representation, you represent a repeating group by enclosing the repeating group within parentheses. The shorthand representation for the Closings Worked table from Figure 11–12 is shown in Figure 11–13.

Closings Worked (<u>Attorney ID</u>, Property ID, Attorney Fees)

Figure 11–13

Conversion to First Normal Form

Figure 11–14 shows the normalized version of the table. Note that the second row of the unnormalized table (Figure 11–12) indicates that attorney A-002 has closed properties P-008, P-005, and P-006. In the normalized table, this information is represented by *three* rows: the second, third, and fourth. The primary key for the unnormalized Closings Worked table was the Attorney ID only. The primary key for the normalized table is now the combination of Attorney ID and Property ID.

Closings Worked		
Attorney ID	**Property ID**	**Attorney Fees**
A-001	P-003	350
A-002	P-008	350
A-002	P-005	350
A-002	P-006	250
A-003	P-002	1
A-004	P-001	250
A-004	P-007	250
A-005	P-004	250

Figure 11–14

In general, when converting a non-1NF table to 1NF, the primary key will typically include the original primary key concatenated with the key of the repeating group, that is, the field that distinguishes one occurrence of the repeating group from another within a given row in the table. In this case, Property ID is the key to the repeating group and thus becomes part of the primary key of the 1NF table.

To convert the table to 1NF, remove the parentheses enclosing the repeating group and expand the primary key to include the key to the repeating group. The shorthand representation for the resulting table is shown in Figure 11–15. Notice that the primary key is now the combination of the Attorney ID field and the Property ID field.

Closings Worked (<u>Attorney ID</u>, <u>Property ID</u>, Attorney Fees)

Figure 11–15

BTW

Primary Key for 1NF

Creating a compound primary key consisting of two fields is not the only way to convert an unnormalized table to 1NF. You could instead create a completely new field for the primary key. For example, for the Closings Worked table, you could add a new field called something like Assignment ID and make that field the table's primary key. Each assignment would then list the attorney ID, property ID, and attorney fees as functional dependencies.

Second Normal Form

Even though the following table is in 1NF, problems may exist that will cause you to want to restructure the table. In the database design process, for example, you might have created the Closings Worked table shown in Figure 11–16.

Closings Worked (<u>Attorney ID</u>, Attorney Last Name, <u>Property ID</u>, Property Street Address, Attorney Fees)

Figure 11–16

This table contains the following functional dependencies:

Attorney ID → Attorney Last Name

Property ID → Property Street Address

Attorney ID, Property ID → Attorney Fees

This notation indicates that Attorney ID alone determines Attorney Last Name, and Property ID alone determines Property Street Address, but it requires *both* an Attorney ID *and* a Property ID to determine Attorney Fees. Figure 11–17 shows a sample of this table.

same Attorney Last Name appears more than once

Closings Worked				
Attorney ID	Attorney Last Name	Property ID	Property Street Address	Attorney Fees
A-001	Hastings	P-003	46 Hwy 82 S	350
A-002	Black	P-008	4893 Alabama Hwy	350
A-002	Black	P-005	Route 15, Box 281	350
A-002	Black	P-006	87 Georgetown Rd, #2	250
A-003	Edwards	P-002	852 Scranton Dr	1
A-004	Konig	P-001	219 Phillips St	250
A-004	Konig	P-007	5377 Ohio St	250
A-005	Gomez	P-004	186 Alabama Hwy	250

Figure 11–17

The name of a specific attorney, A-002 for example, occurs multiple times in the table. This redundancy causes several problems. It is certainly wasteful of space, but that is not nearly as serious as some of the other problems. These other problems are called **update anomalies**, and they fall into four categories:

1. **Update.** A change to the name of attorney A-002 requires not one change to the table, but several: you must change each row in which A-002 appears. This certainly makes the update process much more cumbersome; it is logically more complicated and takes longer to update.
2. **Inconsistent data.** There is nothing about the design that would prohibit attorney A-002 from having two or more different names in the database. The first row, for example, might have Black as the name, whereas the second row might have Blacks, a typo.
3. **Additions.** There is a real problem when you try to add a new property ID and its address to the database. Because the primary key for the table consists of both Attorney ID and Property ID, you need values for both these fields to add a new row. If you have a new property to add (that is, a purchase contract has been received by the office), but there is so far no attorney assigned to it, what do you use for an Attorney ID? The only solution would be to make up a placeholder Attorney ID and then replace it with a real Attorney ID once the attorney is assigned. This is certainly not an acceptable solution.
4. **Deletions.** In Figure 11–17, if you deleted Attorney A-003 from the database, you would need to delete all rows on which the Attorney is A-003. In the process, you would delete the only row on which property P-002 appears, so you would also lose all the information about property P-002. You would no longer know that the street address of property P-002 is 852 Scranton Dr.

These problems occur because there is a field, Attorney Last Name, that is dependent only on Attorney ID, which is just a portion of the primary key. There is a similar problem with Property Street Address, which depends only on the Property ID, not the complete primary key. This leads to the definition of second normal form. Second normal form represents an improvement over first normal form because it eliminates update anomalies in these situations. To understand second normal form, you need to understand the term, nonkey field.

A field is a **nonkey field**, also called a **nonkey attribute**, if it is not a part of the primary key. A table (that is, a relation) is in **second normal form (2NF)** if it is in first normal form and no nonkey field is dependent on only a portion of the primary key.

Note that if the primary key of a table contains only a single field, the table is automatically in second normal form. In that case, there could not be any field dependent on only a portion of the primary key.

Conversion to Second Normal Form

To correct the problems, convert the table to a collection of tables in second normal form, and then name the new tables. The following is a method for performing this conversion.

1. Take each subset of the set of fields that make up the primary key, and begin a new table with this subset as its primary key. The result of applying this step to the Closings Worked table is shown in Figure 11–18.

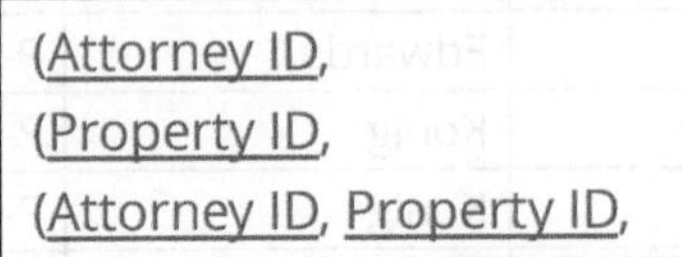

Figure 11–18

2. Place each of the other fields with the appropriate primary key; that is, place each one with the minimal collection of fields on which it depends. The result of applying this step to the Closings Worked table is shown in Figure 11–19.

(Attorney ID, Attorney Last Name
(Property ID, Property Street Address
(Attorney ID, Property ID, Attorney Fees

Figure 11–19

3. Give each of these new tables a name that is descriptive of the meaning of the table, such as Attorneys, Properties, and Closings Worked.

Attorneys

Attorney ID	Attorney Last Name
A-001	Hastings
A-002	Black
A-003	Edwards
A-004	Konig
A-005	Gomez

each attorney name appears only once

Properties

Property ID	Property Street Address
P-003	46 Hwy 82 S
P-008	4893 Alabama Hwy
P-005	Route 15, Box 281
P-006	87 Georgetown Rd, #2
P-002	852 Scranton Dr
P-001	219 Phillips St
P-007	5377 Ohio St
P-004	186 Alabama Hwy

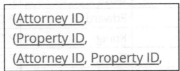

Closings Worked		
Attorney ID	**Property ID**	**Attorney Fees**
A-001	P-003	350
A-002	P-008	350
A-002	P-005	350
A-002	P-006	250
A-003	P-002	1
A-004	P-001	250
A-004	P-007	250
A-005	P-004	250

Figure 11–20

The new design eliminates the update anomalies. An attorney's last name occurs only once for each attorney ID, so you do not have the redundancy that occurred in the earlier design. Changing an attorney's name is now a simple process involving a single change. Because the attorney's name occurs in a single place, it is not possible to have multiple versions of a name for the same attorney.

To add a new property, you create a new row in the Properties table, and thus there is no need to have an attorney already assigned to that property. In addition, deleting attorney A-003 has nothing to do with the Properties table and, consequently, does not cause property P-002 to be deleted. Thus, you still have the property's street address, 852 Scranton Dr, in the database. Finally, you have not lost any information in the normalization process.

Third Normal Form

Problems can still exist with tables that are in 2NF, as illustrated in the Closings table whose shorthand representation is shown in Figure 11–21.

Closings (<u>Closing ID</u>, Closing Date, Property ID, Purchase Price, Buyer ID, Buyer First Name, Buyer Last Name)

Figure 11–21

The functional dependencies in this table are:

Closing ID → Closing Date, Property ID, Purchase Price, Buyer ID, Buyer First Name, Buyer Last Name

Buyer ID → Buyer First Name, Buyer Last Name

As these dependencies indicate, Closing ID determines all the other fields. In addition, Buyer ID determines Buyer First Name and Buyer Last Name.

Because the primary key of the table is a single field, the table is automatically in second normal form. As the sample of the table shown in Figure 11–22 demonstrates, however, this table has problems similar to those encountered earlier, even though it is in 2NF. In this case, it is the first name and last name of a buyer that can occur many times in the table; see buyer B-007, Toni Vinter, for example.

Closings						
Closing ID	Closing Date	Property ID	Purchase Price	Buyer ID	Buyer First Name	Buyer Last Name
C-001	4/28/2029	P-001	568,000	B-001	Karla	Breeden
C-002	4/29/2029	P-002	281,000	B-002	Everett	Moller
C-003	4/30/2029	P-003	372,000	B-003	Celeste	Alberghini
C-004	4/28/2029	P-004	493,000	B-004	Violet	Pratt
C-005	5/3/2029	P-005	546,000	B-005	Riya	Sumner
C-006	5/16/2029	P-006	182,000	B-006	Gerald	Cleary
C-007	4/30/2029	P-007	150,000	B-007	Toni	Vinter
C-008	5/30/2029	P-007	209,000	B-008	Flora	Karstensen
C-009	6/2/2029	P-008	349,000	B-007	Toni	Vinter

buyer name appears more than once

Figure 11–22

This redundancy results in the same set of problems described previously with the Closings Worked table. In addition to the problem of wasted space, you have similar update anomalies, as follows:

1. **Updates.** A change to the name of a buyer requires not one change to the table but possibly several changes. Again, the update process becomes very cumbersome.
2. **Inconsistent data.** There is nothing about the design that would prohibit a buyer from having two different names in the database. Closing C-007, for example, shows the name of buyer B-007 as Toni Vinter, whereas in Closing C-009 (another closing with the same buyer B-007), the name might appear as Toni Winter (which contains a typo).
3. **Additions.** To add a new buyer to the database, they must have at least one closing (which most likely would be the case, but not always). For example, consider the situation in which Maryanne Webb, who has made an offer on a property, does not yet have a finalized purchase contract. She would like to register with Partners Law Firm now in order to schedule the closing soon, but you could not input her buyer information and schedule the closing without the property and closing information from the purchase contract. Perhaps you could create a fictitious property and closing for her while she waits for the sellers to sign the contract. Again, this is not a desirable solution to the problem.
4. **Deletions.** If a buyer, such as B-006, dies, you might delete or archive all the accounts of buyer B-006 from the database, and then you would also lose all information concerning each closing for that buyer. This could be problematic if your law firm needs to review information about that closing in the future.

These update anomalies are due to the fact that Buyer ID determines Buyer First Name and Buyer Last Name, but Buyer ID is not the primary key. As a result, the same Buyer ID, and consequently the same Buyer First Name and Buyer Last Name, can appear on many different rows.

You have seen that 2NF is an improvement over 1NF, but to eliminate 2NF problems, you need an even better strategy for creating tables in the database. Third normal form (3NF) provides that strategy.

Before looking at third normal form, you need to become familiar with the special name that is given to any field that determines another field, like Buyer ID in the Closings table. Any field or collection of fields that determines another field is called a **determinant**. Certainly the primary key in a table is a determinant. Any candidate key is a determinant as well. (Remember that a candidate key is a field or collection of fields that could function as the primary key.) In this case, Buyer ID is a determinant, but because several rows in the Closings table could have the same Buyer ID, that field is not a candidate key for the Closings table shown in Figure 11–22, and that is the problem.

A table is in **third normal form (3NF)** if it is in second normal form and if the only determinants it contains are candidate keys.

BTW
3NF
The definition given for third normal form is not the original definition. This more recent definition, which is preferable to the original, is often referred to as Boyce-Codd normal form (BCNF) when it is important to make a distinction between this definition and the original definition. This text does not make such a distinction but will take this to be the definition of third normal form.

Conversion to Third Normal Form

You have now identified the problem with the Closings table: it is not in 3NF. You need a way to correct the deficiency in the Closings table and in all tables having similar deficiencies. Such a method follows.

First, for each determinant that is not a candidate key, remove from the table the fields that depend on this determinant, but do not remove the determinant. Next, create a new table containing all the fields from the original table that depend on this determinant. Finally, make the determinant the primary key of this new table.

In the Closings table, for example, Buyer First Name and Buyer Last Name are removed because they depend on the determinant Buyer ID, which is not a candidate key. A new table is formed, consisting of Buyer ID as the primary key, Buyer First Name, and Buyer Last Name. Specifically, you would replace the Closings table in Figure 11–22 with the two tables shown in Figure 11–23.

Closings (Closing ID, Closing Date, Property ID, Purchase Price, Buyer ID)
Buyers (Buyer ID, Buyer First Name, Buyer Last Name)

Figure 11–23

Figure 11–24 shows samples of the tables.

Closings

Closing ID	Closing Date	Property ID	Purchase Price	Buyer ID
C-001	4/28/2029	P-001	568,000	B-001
C-002	4/29/2029	P-002	281,000	B-002
C-003	4/30/2029	P-003	372,000	B-003
C-004	4/28/2029	P-004	493,000	B-004
C-005	5/3/2029	P-005	546,000	B-005
C-006	5/16/2029	P-006	182,000	B-006
C-007	4/30/2029	P-007	150,000	B-007
C-008	5/30/2029	P-007	209,000	B-008
C-009	6/2/2029	P-008	349,000	B-007

Buyers

Buyer ID	Buyer First Name	Buyer Last Name
B-001	Karla	Breeden
B-002	Everett	Moller
B-003	Celeste	Alberghini
B-004	Violet	Pratt
B-005	Riya	Sumner
B-006	Gerald	Cleary
B-007	Toni	Vinter
B-008	Flora	Karstensen

buyer Toni Vinter appears only once

Figure 11–24

This design corrects the previously identified problems. Each buyer's name appears only once, thus avoiding redundancy and making the process of changing a buyer's name a very simple one. With this design, it is not possible for a buyer to have two different versions of their name in the database. To add a new buyer to the database, you add a row in the Buyers table; it is not necessary to have a preexisting property or closing for the buyer. Finally, deleting or archiving a buyer will not remove the closing records from the Closings table, so you will retain the closing and property information; all the data in the original table can be reconstructed from the data in the new collection of tables. All previously mentioned problems have indeed been solved.

Special Topics

BTW
Existing Documents
Other examples of existing documents could include purchase orders, procedure manuals, organizational policy manuals, inventory lists, insurance policies, and so on.

In addition to knowing how to design a database and how to normalize tables, there are two other topics with which you should be familiar. First, you may be given a requirement for a database in the form of a document that contains data and business requirements for the database; for example, a rental agreement. In addition, you should know how to represent your design with a diagram.

Obtaining Information from Existing Documents

Existing documents can often furnish helpful information concerning the database design. You need to know how to obtain information from a document that you will then use in the design process. An existing document, like the rental agreement for Water Fun Rentals shown in Figure 11–25, will often provide the details that determine the tables and fields required to produce the database.

Rental Agreement

Water Fun Rentals, Inc
5000 Hwy 64 S
Blue Peaks, SC 29470

Water Fun Rentals

1. Name: Tricia (First Name) Morris (Last Name) (Date of Birth (if Under 18))
2. Address: 460 West Longberg Rd (Street Address) Gainesville (City) SC (State) 29101 (Postal Code)

I understand that using kayaks and other boat types incurs risk. I release Water Fun Rentals from all responsibilities of liability, injury, or property damage.

3 Boat Rentals for Rental Number: R-123

	HIN	Type, Brand, Color
Boat	1ALLDVAF7HA470011	1-person kayak, Water Systems, green
Boat		
Boat		
Boat		

Rental Date: 2/13/2029

Expiration Time
ATTN: This is the time your rentals are due to be returned to the dock. Missing this time will result in additional charges.
14:00

5. Signature　　Date of Signature

Figure 11–25

The first step in obtaining information from an existing document is to identify and list all fields and give them appropriate names. You also need to understand the business needs and policies of the organization. For example, in the rental agreement shown in Figure 11–25, the information on Water Fun Rentals is preprinted on the form, and it is not necessary to describe the company. The following is a list of the fields you can determine from the document shown in Figure 11–25.

Rental Number

Rental Effective Date

Rental Expire Time

Customer First Name

Customer Last Name

Address (Customers)

City (Customers)

State (Customers)

Postal Code (Customers)

Boat HIN

Boat Type

Boat Brand

Boat Color

Next, you need to identify functional dependencies. If the document you are examining is unfamiliar to you, you might have difficulty determining the dependencies and might need to get all the information directly from the user. On the other hand, you can often make intelligent guesses based on your general knowledge of the type of document you are studying. You might make mistakes, of course, and these should be corrected when you interact with the user. After initially determining the functional dependencies, you might discover additional information. The following are possible initial functional dependencies:

Customer ID → First Name (Customers), Last Name (Customers), Address (Customers), City (Customers), State (Customers), Postal Code (Customers)

Rental Number → Effective Date, Expire Time, Customer ID

HIN → Type, Brand, Color, Rental Number

You might realize that other attributes of the customer are required. For example, you might want to include the customer's telephone number and email address. If that is the case, then telephone number and email address are functionally dependent on the customer.

You might also realize that the rental agreement does not include any information about approved paddlers. For example, the customer shown in Figure 11–25 could be paying for a group of three friends who will be paddling together in their rented boats. In that case, you will need to add all information about the paddler entity and then also have an entity that combines the boat (HIN) with the paddlers who will operate each boat.

Given these corrections, a revised list of functional dependencies might look like the following:

Customer ID → First Name (Customers), Last Name (Customers), Address (Customers), City (Customers), State (Customers), Postal Code (Customers), Telephone (Customers), Email Address (Customers)

Paddler ID → First Name (Paddlers), Last Name (Paddlers), Address (Paddlers), City (Paddlers), State (Paddlers), Postal Code (Paddlers), Telephone (Paddlers), Email Address (Paddlers)

Rental Number → Effective Date, Expire Time, Customer ID

HIN → Type, Brand, Color, Rental Number

HIN, Paddler ID →

After you have determined the preliminary functional dependencies, you can begin determining the tables and assigning fields. You could create tables with the determinant—the field or fields to the left of the arrow—as the primary key and with the fields to the right of the arrow as the remaining fields. This would lead to the initial collection of tables shown in Figure 11–26.

Customers (<u>Customer ID</u>, First Name, Last Name, Address, City, State, Postal Code, Telephone, Email Address)
Paddlers (<u>Paddler ID</u>, First Name, Last Name, Address, City, State, Postal Code, Telephone, Email Address)
Rentals (<u>Rental Number</u>, Effective Date, Expire Time, Customer ID)
Boats (<u>HIN</u>, Type, Brand, Color, Rental Number)
Boat Paddlers (<u>HIN</u>, <u>Paddler ID</u>)

Figure 11–26

Adding the foreign key information produces the shorthand representation shown in Figure 11–27.

Customers (<u>Customer ID</u>, First Name, Last Name, Address, City, State, Postal Code, Telephone, Email Address)
Paddlers (<u>Paddler ID</u>, First Name, Last Name, Address, City, State, Postal Code, Telephone, Email Address)
Rentals (<u>Rental Number</u>, Effective Date, Expire Time, Customer ID)
FK Customer ID → Customers
Boats (<u>HIN</u>, Type, Brand, Color, Rental Number)
FK Rental Number → Rentals
Boat Paddlers (<u>HIN</u>, <u>Paddler ID</u>)
FK HIN → Boats
FK Paddler ID → Paddlers

Figure 11–27

At this point, you would need to verify that all the tables are in third normal form. If any are not in 3NF, you need to convert them. For example, if you had not determined the functional dependency of Effective Date and Expire Time on Rental Number earlier, you would have had Effective Date and Expire Time as fields in the Customers table. These fields are dependent on Rental Number, making Rental Number a determinant that is not a primary key, which would violate third normal form. Once you converted that table to 3NF, you would have the tables shown in Figure 11–27.

You might have already created some tables in your database design. For example, you might have obtained financial data on customers from the company's sales records following a recent social media campaign selling special event t-shirts. If so, you would need to merge the tables in Figure 11–27 with those tables you already created.

To merge tables, you combine tables that have the same primary key. The new table contains all the fields in either individual table and does not repeat fields that are present in both tables. Figure 11–28, for example, illustrates the merging of two tables that both have the Customer ID field as the primary key. In addition to the primary key, the result contains the City, State, and Postal Code fields, which are included in both the original tables; the Address, Telephone, and Email Address fields, which are only in the first table; and the Credit Card Number, Expiration Date, and CVV (Card Verification Value) fields, which are only in the second table. The order in which you decide to list the fields is immaterial.

BTW
Merging Entities
When you merge entities, do not assume that the merged entities will be in 3NF. Apply normalization techniques to convert all entities to 3NF.

Merging

Customers (<u>Customer ID</u>, First Name, Last Name, Address, City, State, Postal Code, Telephone, Email Address)

And

Customers (<u>Customer ID</u>, City, State, Postal Code, Credit Card Number, Expiration Date, CVV Code)

Gives

Customers (<u>Customer ID</u>, First Name, Last Name, Address, City, State, Postal Code, Telephone, Email Address, Credit Card Number, Expiration Date, CVV Code)

Figure 11–28

BTW

Storing Private Customer Data

Many types of data collected and stored about customers—such as customer names, addresses, and credit card numbers—are called personally identifiable information (PII). Most country and state governments require special protections for this data. Furthermore, some data requires additional layers of protection due to industry standards. For example, credit card information is protected by rules defined by the Payment Card Industry Data Security Standard (PCI DSS). Medical information in the United States is protected by the Health Insurance Portability and Accountability Act (HIPAA).

If you work with any of this protected information, you must understand the laws and regulations that apply, and be diligent to comply with these requirements. When hired by a company that handles this data, you should receive appropriate training relevant to the data you will encounter. If you start your own business, make sure to research the requirements for any data you will store. Many small business owners do not have the expertise on staff to establish secure payment systems and instead will contract with payment services to handle customer financial transactions. This arrangement provides small businesses with some protection from the liability of having access to legally protected customer data.

Diagrams for Database Design

You have now seen how to represent a database design as a list of tables, fields, primary keys, and foreign keys. It is often helpful to also be able to represent a database design with a diagram. If you have already created the database and relationships in Access, the Relationships window and Relationships report provide a helpful diagram of the design. Figure 11–29 shows the Access Relationship diagram and report for the Clearnet database. In these diagrams, rectangles represent tables. The fields in the table are listed in the corresponding rectangle with a key symbol appearing in front of the primary key. Relationships are represented by lines with the "one" end of the relationship represented by the number, 1, and the "many" end represented by the infinity symbol (∞).

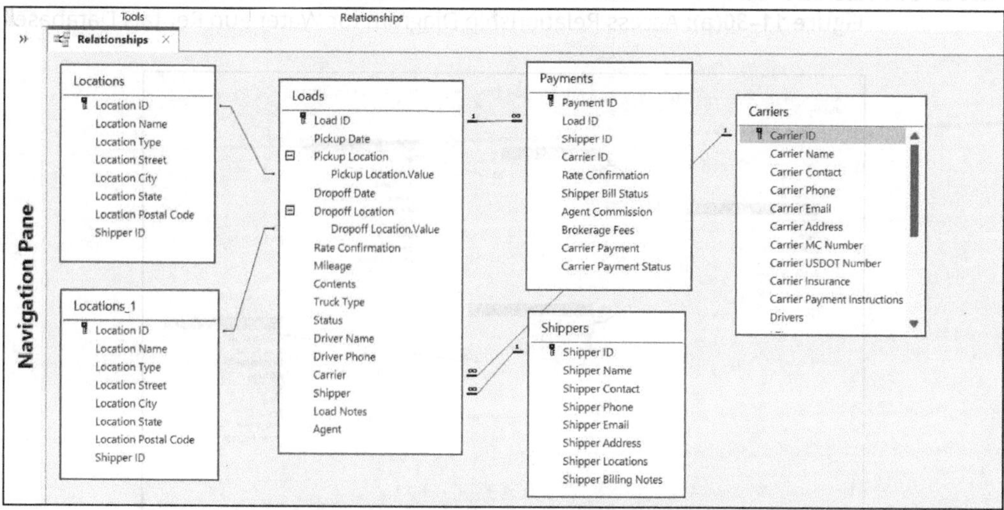

Figure 11–29(a): Access Relationship Diagram for Clearnet Database

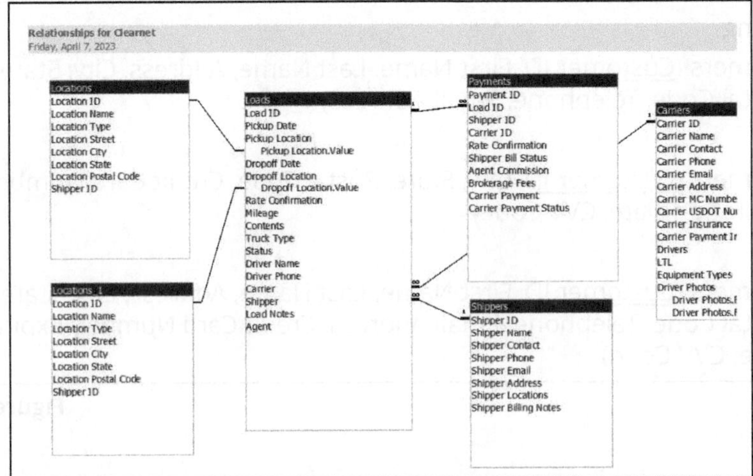

Figure 11–29(b): Access Relationship Report for Clearnet Database

Figure 11–30 shows the Access Relationship diagram and report for the Water Fun Rentals database.

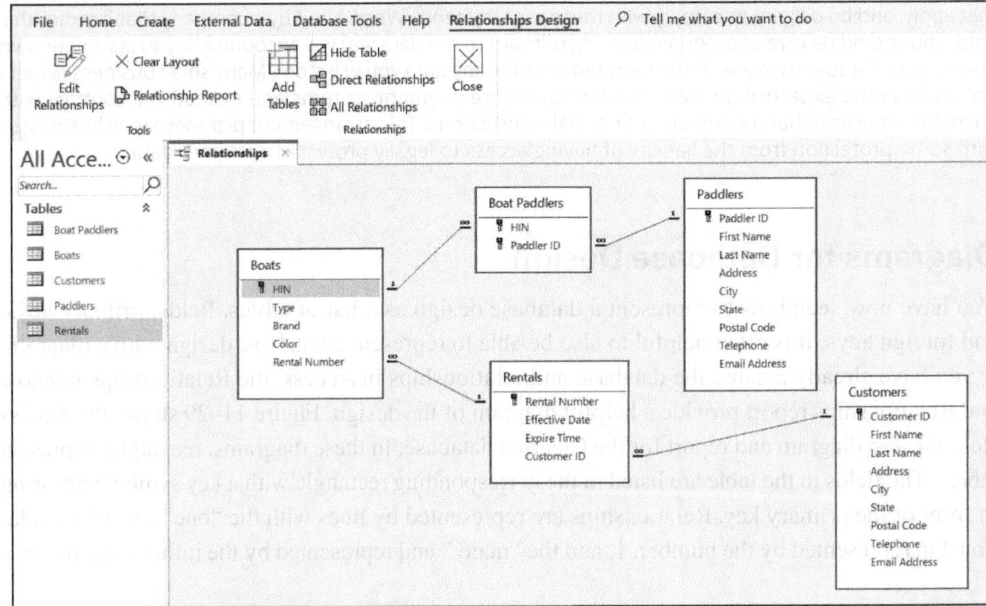

Figure 11–30(a): Access Relationship Diagram for Water Fun Rentals Database

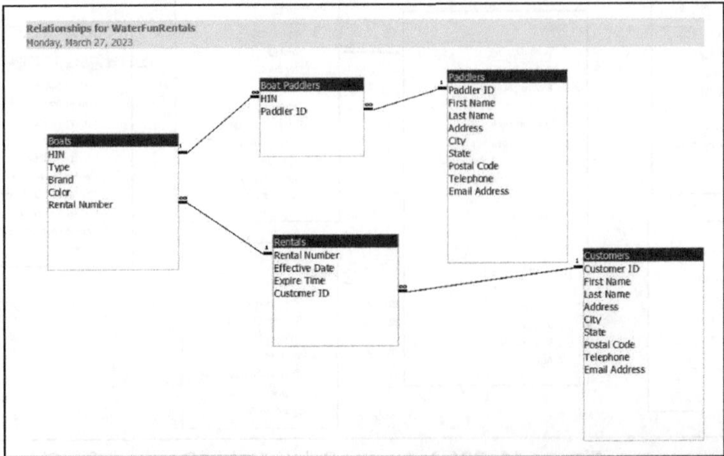

Figure 11–30(b): Access Relationship Report for Water Fun Rentals Database

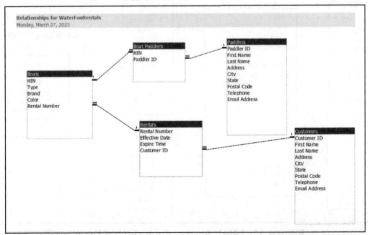

Another popular option for diagramming a database design is the **entity-relationship diagram (ERD)**. Figure 11–31 shows a sample ERD for a portion of the Clearnet database. In this type of diagram, rectangles represent the tables. The primary key is listed within the table above a line. Below the line are the other fields in the table. The arrow goes from the rectangle that represents the "many" part of the relationship to the "one" part of the relationship.

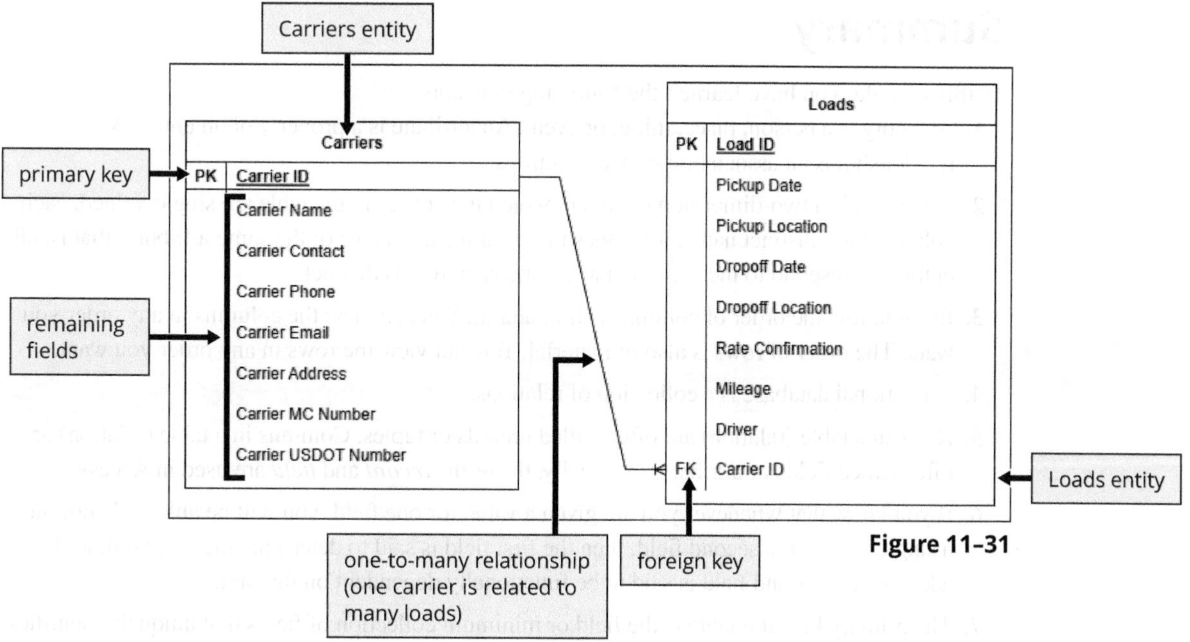

Figure 11–31

Figure 11–32 shows a similar diagram for the full Water Fun Rentals database.

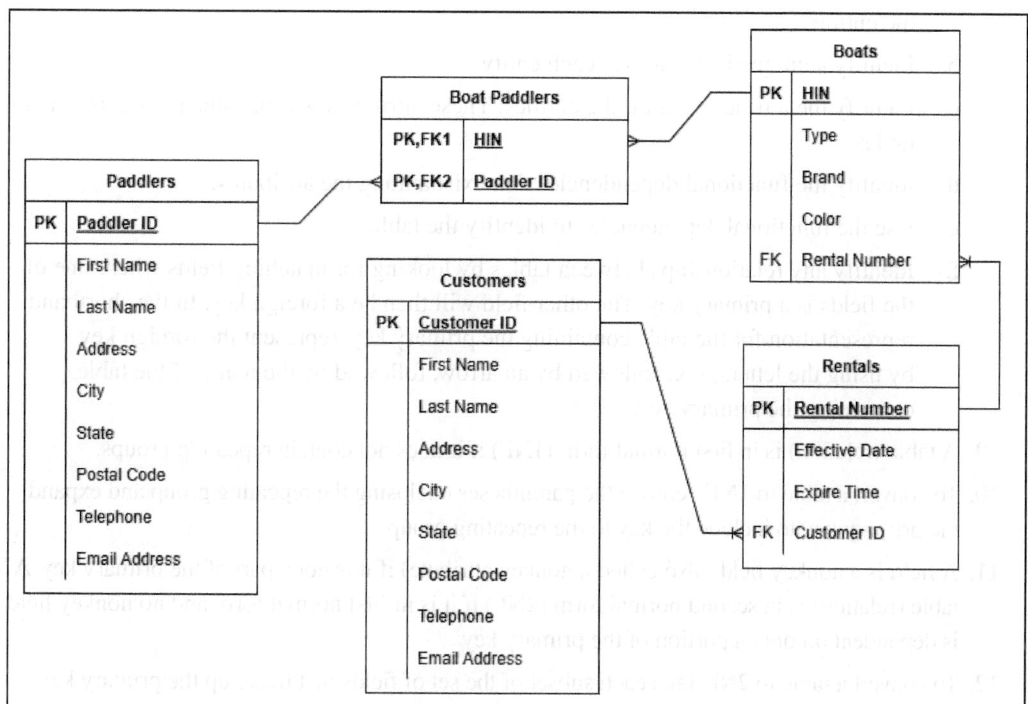

Figure 11–32

There are many options for such diagrams. Some options include more detail than shown in the figure. You can include, for example, such details as data types and indexes. Other options have less detail, showing only the name of the table in the rectangle, for example. There are also other options for the appearance of the lines representing relationships.

Summary

In this module, you have learned the following concepts.

1. An entity is a person, place, thing, or event. An attribute is a property of an entity. A relationship is an association between entities.
2. A relation is a two-dimensional table in which the entries in the table are single-valued, each column has a distinct name, all values in a column are values of the same attribute (that is, all entries correspond to the column name), and each row is distinct.
3. In a relation, the order of columns is immaterial. You can view the columns in any order you want. The order of rows is also immaterial. You can view the rows in any order you want.
4. A relational database is a collection of relations.
5. Rows in a table (relation) are often called records or tuples. Columns in a table (relation) are often called fields or attributes. Typically, the terms *record* and *field* are used in Access.
6. If you know that whenever you are given a value for one field, you will be able to determine a single value for a second field, then the first field is said to determine the second field. In addition, the second field is said to be functionally dependent on the first.
7. The primary key of a table is the field or minimum collection of fields that uniquely identifies a given row in that table.
8. The following is a method for designing a database for a set of requirements.
    a. Examine the requirements and identify the entities (objects) involved. Assign names to the entities.
    b. Identify a unique identifier for each entity.
    c. Identify the attributes for all the entities. These attributes will become the fields in the tables.
    d. Identify the functional dependencies that exist among the attributes.
    e. Use the functional dependencies to identify the tables.
    f. Identify any relationships between tables by looking for matching fields where one of the fields is a primary key. The other field will then be a foreign key. In the shorthand representation for the table containing the primary key, represent the foreign key by using the letters, FK, followed by an arrow, followed by the name of the table containing the primary key.
9. A table (relation) is in first normal form (1NF) if it does not contain repeating groups.
10. To convert a table to 1NF, remove the parentheses enclosing the repeating group and expand the primary key to include the key to the repeating group.
11. A field is a nonkey field (also called a nonkey attribute) if it is not a part of the primary key. A table (relation) is in second normal form (2NF) if it is in first normal form and no nonkey field is dependent on only a portion of the primary key.
12. To convert a table to 2NF, take each subset of the set of fields that make up the primary key and begin a new table with this subset as its primary key. Place each of the other fields with the appropriate primary key; that is, place each one with the minimal collection of fields on which it depends. Give each of these new tables a name that is descriptive of the meaning of the table.

13. Any field (or collection of fields) that determines another field is called a determinant. A table is in third normal form (3NF) if it is in second normal form and if the only determinants it contains are candidate keys.
14. To convert a table to 3NF, for each determinant that is not a candidate key, remove from the table the fields that depend on this determinant, but do not remove the determinant. Create a new table containing all the fields from the original table that depend on this determinant and make the determinant the primary key of this new table.
15. An entity-relationship diagram (ERD) is a diagram used to represent database designs. In ERDs, rectangles represent tables and lines between rectangles represent one-to-many relationships between the corresponding tables. You can also diagram a database design by using the Access relationship window.

Consider This: Plan Ahead

How should you submit solutions to critical thinking questions in the assignments?

Every assignment in this course contains one or more critical thinking questions. These questions require you to think beyond the assigned database. Present your responses to the questions in the format required by your instructor. Possible formats might include one or more of these options: write the answer; create a document that contains the answer; present your answer to the class; discuss your answer in a group; record the answer as audio or video using a webcam, smartphone, or portable media player; or post answers on a blog, wiki, or website.

Student Assignments

Apply Your Knowledge

Reinforce the skills and apply the concepts you learned in this module.

Understanding Keys and Normalization

Instructions: Answer the following questions in the format specified by your instructor.

1. Figure 11–33 contains sample data for a Competitors table in an art competition database. Use this figure to answer the following:
   a. Is the table in first normal form (1NF)? Why or why not?
   b. Is the table in second normal form (2NF)? Why or why not?
   c. Is the table in third normal form (3NF)? Why or why not?
   d. Identify candidate keys for the table.

Competitors				
CID	**FirstName**	**LastName**	**ContestID**	**ContestName**
23483	Nadra	Como	SA-1	Street Art
23423	Samuel	Oliver	PH-1	Photography
23480	Paulinha	Davies	DA-1	Digital Art
23468	Braden	Draper	SA-1	Street Art

Figure 11–33

2. Figure 11–34 contains sample data for tutors and clients who hire those tutors. In discussing the data with users, you find that tutor IDs—but not tutor names—uniquely identify tutors and their offered pay rate, and that client IDs uniquely identify clients. Multiple clients can use the same tutor and clients can use more than one tutor. For example, client Lizzy Haywood uses tutors Gena Romano and Sofie Roberts.
   a. Convert the data in Figure 11–34 into a relation in first normal form (1NF) using the shorthand representation used in this module. Recommend additional fields as needed to design a 1NF structure.
   b. Identify all functional dependencies using the notation demonstrated in the module.

Clients				
ClientID	**FirstName**	**LastName**	**TutorName**	**HourlyRate**
21	Felix	Coy	Sofie Roberts	$20
			Gena Romano	$25
			Stefan Tomczak	$20
24	Lizzy	Haywood	Gena Romano	$25
			Sofie Roberts	$20
27	Karoline	Janson	Karel Gott	$20
34	Conway	Ottosen	Stefan Tomczak	$20

Figure 11–34

3. **Consider This:** Using only the data in Figure 11–33, how could you identify the entities and attributes that would be the starting point for a database design? Include indications of the primary key for each table and any foreign keys.

Extend Your Knowledge

Extend the skills you learned in this module and experiment with new skills. You may need to use Help to complete the assignment.

Modifying a Database Design and Understanding Diagrams

Instructions: Answer the following questions in the format specified by your instructor.

1. Using the shorthand representation illustrated in this module, indicate the changes you would need to make to the Clearnet database design shown in Figure 11–8 so that a given load may be assigned to more than one carrier.
2. Using the shorthand representation illustrated in this module, indicate the changes you would need to make to the Water Fun Rentals database design shown in Figure 11–10 so that it supports the following requirements:
   a. Water Fun Rentals is expanding its business to rent rafts and large canoes for customers with children or others who will ride along as passengers but not as paddlers.
   b. Due to data security concerns related to minors, the company does not want to include data on individual children, only the number of passengers in each boat.
   c. In this expansion, the number of passengers must be recorded for each boat.
3. Use the Access Relationships Report for the Build It Construction database shown in Figure 11–35 to answer the following:
   a. What is the foreign key in the Subcontractors table?
   b. What is the primary key of the Job Sites table?
   c. What is the purpose of the Accounting table?

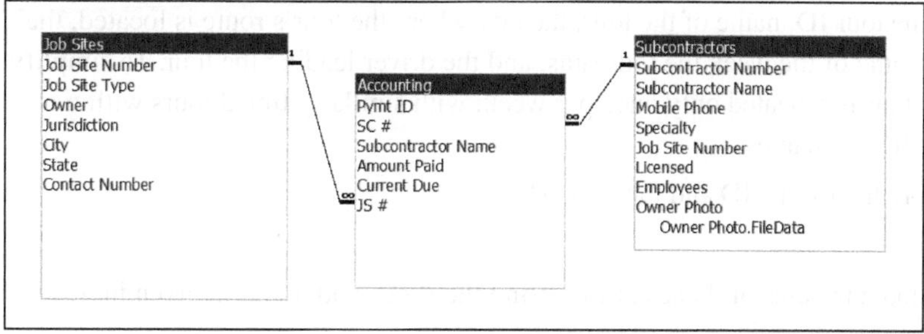

Figure 11–35

4. **Consider This:** Build It Construction has decided to add project managers to the database. One project manager can service many job sites, and job sites might use different project managers, depending on their needs. What changes would you need to make to the database design for Build It Construction?

Expand Your World

Create a solution, which uses cloud and web technologies, by learning and investigating on your own from general guidance.

Instructions: There are several websites that provide descriptions of various types of databases, including both relational and nonrelational databases. Comparing these database types helps clarify the purpose of each type and provides a good starting point for creating your own database design.

1. Create a blog, a Google document, or a Word document on OneDrive on which to store your assignment. Include your name and the current date at the beginning of the blog or document.
2. **Consider This:** Find a website of your choice that lists and describes different types of databases. For example, the MongoDB website provides a list and concise descriptions at mongodb.com/databases/types. What website did you choose and why?

Continued on next page

3. **Consider This:** Compare relational and nonrelational (also called NoSQL) databases in your own words. Other than Access for relational databases, give an example of each type.
4. Browse the different database types and select one (other than Access) in which you have an interest.
5. **Consider This:** In your own words, describe a scenario for which the database type would provide appropriate data storage and management. Why is the database type you chose better for this scenario than another database type would be?
6. **Consider This:** Why did you select the database type that you did? How easy was it to understand the elements of this database type? What design standards are required for this database type?

In the Lab

Design and implement a solution using creative thinking and problem-solving skills.

Lab: Designing a Database for Sunrise Bus Tours

Instructions: Sunrise Bus Tours is a downtown tour service with routes along area beaches and overlooks in three cities. You have been asked to create a database to keep track of the tourists, drivers, tours, and tour reservations. Use the concepts and techniques presented in this module to design a database to meet the following requirements, and record it using this module's shorthand notation style.

Part 1: The Sunrise Bus Tours database must support the following requirements:

1. For each bus driver, store their commercial driver's license (CDL) number, last name, first name, street address, city, state, postal code, telephone number, and date hired.
2. For each tourist, store their tourist ID, last name, first name, street address, city, state, postal code, telephone number, and email address.
3. For each tour offered, store the tour ID, name of the tour, the city where the tour's route is located, the price of the tour, the day and time of the week the tour runs, and the driver leading the tour. To simplify the design, assume that each tour is repeated only once per week, with similarly timed tours within a week being given a different ID and name.
4. For each tour reservation, store the tourist ID and the tour ID.

Based on these requirements:

5. Identify and list the entities and attributes of those entities using the shorthand notation given in this module.
6. Identify and list the functional dependencies using the shorthand notation given in this module.
7. Ensure that in both lists, the database is in third normal form (3NF). Identify all primary keys and foreign keys appropriately.

Submit your database design in the format specified by your instructor.

Part 2: **Consider This:** You made several decisions while designing this database. What was the rationale behind these decisions? Are there other requirements, such as specific business practices, that would have been helpful to you in the design process?

Index

Note: **Bold** page numbers indicate key terms.

B

C

D

E

J

K

L

P

Q

R

S

T

U

V

W

Z